THE OXFORD HAN

ARISTOTLE

THE OXFORD HANDBOOK OF

ARISTOTLE

Edited by
CHRISTOPHER SHIELDS

OXFORD
UNIVERSITY PRESS

OXFORD
UNIVERSITY PRESS

Oxford University Press is a department of the University of Oxford.
It furthers the University's objective of excellence in research, scholarship,
and education by publishing worldwide.

Oxford   New York
Auckland   Cape Town   Dar es Salaam   Hong Kong   Karachi
Kuala Lumpur   Madrid   Melbourne   Mexico City   Nairobi
New Delhi   Shanghai   Taipei   Toronto

With offices in
Argentina   Austria   Brazil   Chile   Czech Republic   France   Greece
Guatemala   Hungary   Italy   Japan   Poland   Portugal   Singapore
South Korea   Switzerland   Thailand   Turkey   Ukraine   Vietnam

Oxford is a registered trade mark of Oxford University Press
in the UK and certain other countries.

Published in the United States of America by
Oxford University Press
198 Madison Avenue, New York, NY 10016

© Oxford University Press 2012

First issued as an Oxford University Press paperback, 2015.

Library of Congress Cataloging-in-Publication Data
The Oxford handbook of Aristotle / edited by Christopher Shields.
p. cm.
Includes bibliographical references and index.
ISBN 978-0-19-518748-9 (hardcover: alk. paper); 978-0-19-024484-2 (paperback : alk. paper)
1. Aristotle.   I. Shields, Christopher John.
B485.O94 2012
185—dc23
2011030064

Acknowledgements

THIS Handbook has been long in gestation, and its editor has incurred an unrecoverable number of debts during its protracted pre-birth. I thank first Peter Ohlin of Oxford University Press for recommending the project and for his persistence and welcome guidance in helping to bring it to fruition. I thank also the University of Oxford for research leave during which the serious editing could be undertaken, and both the John Fell Fund and the Alexander von Humboldt-Stiftung for generous financial support which freed me from other obligations inimical to its completion, especially as the final stages of preparation were underway.

During these final stages, I was fortunate to rely on the good offices of Colin Shields, who kindly assisted with the proofing, and Ana Laura Edelhoff, who not only offered judicious advice when it was most needed but also worked through the text with a remarkable and assiduous sharp-eyed intelligence, effecting more corrections than I can comfortably count. Any remaining errors or infelicities are the responsibility of the editor alone.

My deepest thanks are due, however, to the twenty-four contributors to this volume. Some have been asked to wait an unconscionably long time between their original submissions and their eventual publications; they did so with welcome good grace and with encouraging support, for which I remain grateful. Above all, however, I thank them for what they have taught me about Aristotle: their breadth and depth of knowledge is truly astonishing, and I have been honoured to serve as a conduit to its expression. Interacting with them as they wrote and revised their chapters has left me with the highest esteem for their collective learning. My hopeful expectation as editor is that the work's eventual audience—scholars, students, the broader educated public—will come to learn from them as I have learned, and will find themselves inspired, as I have been inspired, to carry their Aristotelian explorations forward.

Contents

PART III   EXPLANATION AND NATURE

PART IV   BEING AND BEINGS

PART V   ETHICS AND POLITICS

PART VI   RHETORIC AND THE ARTS

PART VII   AFTER ARISTOTLE

PREFACE

HAD it hoped to represent the full range of Aristotelian studies as they are pursued throughout the world today, *The Oxford Handbook of Aristotle* could aspire to no more than lamentable failure. It would be a happy sort of failure, perhaps, but a failure all the same: research into matters broadly Aristotelian thrives worldwide today in many different guises, beginning with the narrowest and most exacting kinds of paleographical and philological scholarship and extending through careful textual exegesis to the loosest forms of philosophical, political, and artistic appropriation, this last as often as not at the hands of those generally inspired by Aristotle's thought, even if they evince at most a passing concern for fidelity to the texts he has actually handed down to us.

This broad compass of activity moves forward under the banners of a variety of philosophical orientations, some beholden to a particular movement or method, others more open-textured, some avowedly religious, others avowedly not, and still others avowing nothing at all in matters of religion or philosophical tradition but seeking instead to understand Aristotle afresh through the cautious eyes of patient textual exegesis. Those preferring to relate Aristotle to recent trends in philosophy often find grounds for identifying in his writings the original seeds of various positions promulgated by philosophers of the present day; others decry such efforts as faddish foistings and grotesque anachronisms, bound only to distort Aristotle's actual views by ignoring their authentic intellectual context and social milieu.

Conferences adopting these and other postures dedicated to interpreting and assessing Aristotle's philosophy are now a fixture of the academic landscape across Europe, North and South America, Asia, Africa, and the Middle East. Indeed, Aristotelian studies flourish wherever higher education has a hold. Some conferences take up questions of narrowly defined textual matters; others pursue themes within Aristotle's philosophy or science; others investigate matters of reception and appropriation, ranging from late Antiquity down to the present day, some seeking to bring Aristotle into dialogue with non-Aristotelian traditions and some investigating his reception by earlier generations of Aristotelian scholars, often with an eye on shedding corrective light on our own scholarly preoccupations and predilections; and still others, doxographical in orientation, try to understand the sources and influences of Aristotle's predecessors on his philosophy and philosophical development. The list goes on, in an impressive array of distinct directions.

Of course, all of this activity generates new scholarship, and in its wake there follow new controversies and so also ever more publications on Aristotle and Aristotelian themes. A new online bibliography, cited in the bibliography of the present volume, boasts 50,000 entries and grows with each passing academic year.

It is worth appreciating that a print version of that bibliography would dwarf the present, already stout volume many times over.

Consequently, any attempt to reproduce the full variety of voices heard clattering under the big tent of 'Aristotelianism' would yield only cacophony. For these reasons, *The Oxford Handbook of Aristotle* does not seek to be a general compendium of Aristotelian thought nor even a full and complete reflection of the many forms of Aristotelian study carried out throughout the world today. Instead, it seeks to represent a core activity of this variegated patchwork of international Aristotelian study by drawing contributors from various parts of the world, all of whom share a broadly common orientation and methodology, all equipped with a developed facility for reading Aristotle's often demanding Greek, and all prepared to engage in critical exegesis and interpretation.

The contributors in their various ways investigate the primary areas of inquiry as Aristotle himself divided them: into sciences (*epistêmai*) which are either theoretical, practical, or productive. Each Aristotelian science is a branch of learning, where the branches are divided by Aristotle into broad categories individuated by their ends or goals: theoretical science seeks knowledge for its own sake; practical science investigates and recommends the optimal forms of goodness in action, whether individual or societal; and productive science aims at the creation of beautiful or useful objects (*Top.* 145a15–16; *Phys.* 192b8–12; *DC* 298a27–32, *DA* 403a27–b2; *Met.* 1025b25, 1026a18–19, 1064a16–19, b1–3; *EN* 1139a26–28, 1141b29–32).

The current volume represents work in each of these branches, in some cases, in less well-trammeled areas of scholarly inquiry, through the presentation of a discursive overview given by a scholarly authority, and in others by the exploration of some crucial, often determinative issue within a broader area of study. The volume begins, however, looking backward from Aristotle to his predecessors, because he himself emphasized as requisite for philosophical progress the careful consideration of one's intellectual forebears, and ends looking forward to the philosophical traditions whose foundations Aristotle indisputably laid and so whose lineaments we could not begin to understand without first understanding their relation to him.

Together these forms of inquiry and assessment provide a partial picture of Aristotelian studies as they proceed throughout the world today, always with a view to inviting new participants drawn from the broadest variety of perspectives, by demonstrating the liveliness of current Aristotelian philosophy in as many guises as is practicable within the confines of a single, even modestly coherent volume.

Notes on the Contributors

Peter Adamson is Professor of Ancient and Medieval Philosophy at King's College London and as of summer 2012 Professor of Philosophy in Late Antiquity and the Arabic Tradition, at the Ludwig-Maximilians-Universität in Munich. He is the author of *The Arabic Plotinus* (Duckworth: 2002) and *Al-Kindi* (Oxford University Press: 2007), and has edited numerous volumes on philosophy in the Islamic world, including most recently *In the Age of Averroes* (Warburg Institute: 2011). With Peter E. Pormann he has translated *The Philosophical Works of al-Kindi* (Oxford University Press: 2012).

Robert Bolton is Professor of Philosophy at Rutgers University. He is author, recently, of *Science, Dialectique et Ethique chez Aristote* (Louvain: 2010), and author or editor of numerous books and articles on Aristotle's methodology, epistemology and psychology, and on other aspects of ancient philosophy. He is a former Rhodes Scholar and research fellow of the Centre National de la Recherche Scientifique (Paris).

David Bostock is a Fellow of Merton College, Oxford. He has written quite extensively on Aristotle; his most recent publication in this area is a collection of essays on Aristotle's *Physics* entitled *Space, Time, Matter, and Form* (Oxford, Clarendon Press: 2006). He has also written quite extensively on logic and the philosophy of mathematics; in this area he recently published *Philosophy of Mathematics: An Introduction* (Wiley-Blackwell: 2009). His next book will be on *Bertrand Russell's Philosophy of Logical Atomism* (Oxford University Press, forthcoming).

David Charles is Research Professor of Philosophy at Oriel College, Oxford. He is the author of *Aristotle on Meaning and Essence* (2000), *Aristotle's Philosophy of Action* (London: 1984), and has recently edited *Definition in Greek Philosophy* (Oxford: 2010).

Kei Chiba is Professor of Philosophy in the Graduate School of Letters Hokkaido University. He is the author of 'Aristotle on the Possibility of Metaphysics: Complementary Development between Dialectic and Natural Philosophy' (Tokyo: 2002). His central contribution to Aristotelian studies is 'Aristotle on Essence and Defining-Phrase in his Dialectic' in *Definition in Greek Philosophy*, ed. D. Charles (Oxford University Press: 2010).

S. Marc Cohen is Professor Emeritus of Philosophy at the University of Washington, where he taught courses in the history of ancient Greek philosophy, logic, and the philosophy of language. He has also taught at Minnesota, Rutgers, Berkeley, and Indiana. His publications have mainly concerned the metaphysics and epistemology of Plato and Aristotle. He is co-editor of *Readings in Ancient Greek Philosophy* (Hackett: 2011) and co-author of *Ammonius: On Aristotle's Categories* (Duckworth: 1991).

Ursula Coope is Tutor and Fellow of Corpus Christi College and Professor of Ancient Philosophy in the University of Oxford. She is the author of *Time for Aristotle: Physics V.10–14* (Oxford: 2005).

Paolo Crivelli is Associate Professor of Ancient Philosophy in the University of Geneva. He is author of *Aristotle on Truth* (Cambridge University Press: 2004) and of several articles on Plato's logic and epistemology, Aristotle's philosophical logic, and Stoic logic. Forthcoming is *Plato's Account of Falsehood: A Study of the Sophist* (Cambridge University Press).

Edward Hussey is an Emeritus Fellow of All Souls College, Oxford, and was formerly University Lecturer in Ancient Philosophy at the University of Oxford. He is the author of *The Presocratics* (London: 1972), *Aristotle: Physics III and IV* (1983), and of many contributions to collaborative volumes on early Greek philosophy and on Aristotle.

T. H. Irwin is Professor of Ancient Philosophy in the University of Oxford and a Fellow of Keble College. From 1975 to 2006 he taught at Cornell University. He is the author of: *Plato's Gorgias, translation and notes,* (Oxford University Press: 1979), in the Clarendon Plato Series, *Aristotle's Nicomachean Ethics, translation and notes* (Hackett Publishing Co., 2nd ed.: 1999), *Aristotle's First Principles,* (Oxford University Press: 1988), *Classical Thought* (Oxford University Press: 1989), *Plato's Ethics* (Oxford University Press: 1995), and *The Development of Ethics,* 3 vols. (Oxford University Press: 2007–9).

Richard Kraut is Charles and Emma Morrison Professor in the Humanities at Northwestern University. He is the author of *Socrates and the State* (Princeton University Press: 1984), *Aristotle on the Human Good* (Princeton University Press: 1989), *Aristotle's Politics VII and VIII,* translation with commentary (Clarendon Press: 1997), *Aristotle: Political Philosophy* (Oxford University Press: 2002), and *What is Good and Why: The Ethics of Well-Being* (Harvard University Press: 2007). He also edited *The Cambridge Companion to Plato* (Cambridge University Press: 2002).

James G. Lennox is Professor of History and Philosophy of Science at the University of Pittsburgh. He is author of *Aristotle, On the Parts of Animals* (Oxford: 2001), *Aristotle's Philosophy of Biology* (Cambridge: 2001); and co-editor of *Philosophical Issues in Aristotle's Biology* (Cambridge: 1987), *Self-motion from Aristotle to Newton* (Princeton: 1994), and *Concepts, Theories and Rationality in the Biological Sciences* (Konstanz and Pittsburgh: 1995). He has held fellowships at the Center for Hellenic Studies (1983–4), Clare Hall, Cambridge (1986–7), and the Istituto di Studi Avanzati, University of Bologna (2006).

Michael J. Loux is Shuster Professor emeritus in the Department of Philosophy at the University of Notre Dame. He is the author of *Substance and Attribute* (Reidel: 1979), *Ockham's Theory of Terms* (Notre Dame: 1974), *Primary Ousia* (Cornell: 1991), *Metaphysics, third edition* (Routledge: 2006), *Nature, Norm, and Psyche* (Scuola Normale Superiore: 2007); editor of *Universals and Particulars* (Anchor

Doubleday: 1971), *The Possible and the Actual* (Cornell: 1979), *The Oxford Handbook of Metaphysics* (Oxford: 2003), *Metaphysics: Readings*, second edition (Routledge: 2008); and the author of numerous articles on topics in metaphysics, the philosophy of language, medieval philosophy, and Aristotle.

Stephen Makin is Reader in Ancient Philosophy at the University of Sheffield. He is the author of *Indifference Arguments* (Blackwell: 1993) and the Clarendon Aristotle Series volume *Aristotle Metaphysics Book* Θ (Oxford University Press: 2006). He has also published papers on philosophy of religion, Democritean atomism, Zeno, Melissus, method in ancient philosophy, the metaphysics of Aristotle, and Aquinas' philosophy of nature.

Stephen Menn is Associate Professor of Philosophy, McGill University, and Professor für Philosophie der Antike und Gegenwart, Humboldt-Universität Berlin. He is the author of *Plato on God as Nous* (Southern Illinois University Press: 1995, reissued by St. Augustine's Press: 2002), of *Descartes and Augustine* (Cambridge University Press: 1998, revised paperback edition: 2002), and of *The Aim and the Argument of Aristotle's Metaphysics* (forthcoming from Oxford University Press). He also has a book in draft entitled *Feuerbach's Theorem: an Essay on Euclidean and Algebraic Geometry*, and is working on a book entitled *Fârâbî's Kitâb al-Ḥurûf and the History of the Many Senses of Being*. With Rachel Barney of the University of Toronto he has translated Simplicius' commentary on Aristotle's *Physics I.1–2*, for the series *Ancient Commentators on Aristotle*, edited by Richard Sorabji (Bloomsbury and Cornell University Press), and with Calvin Normore of McGill and UCLA he is working on a book entitled *Nominalism and Realism, from Boethius to Hobbes*.

Fred D. Miller, Jr. is Professor of Philosophy and Executive Director of the Social Philosophy and Policy Center at Bowling Green State University. He is the author of *Nature, Justice, and Rights in Aristotle's Politics* (Oxford University Press: 1995). He is editor, with David Keyt, of *A Companion to Aristotle's Politics* (Blackwell: 1991) and *Freedom, Reason, and the Polis: Essays in Ancient Greek Political Philosophy* (Cambridge University Press: 2007), and editor, with Carrie-Ann Biondi, of *A History of Philosophy of Law from the Ancient Greeks to the Scholastics* (Springer: 2007). He is also co-editor of *Social Philosophy and Policy* and a related book series published by Cambridge University Press. Forthcoming is *Aristotle's De Anima and Parva Naturalia: Complete Psychological Works*, translation with introduction and notes (Oxford University Press).

Robert Pasnau is Professor of Philosophy at the University of Colorado. He is the author of many articles and books on the history of philosophy, most recently *Metaphysical Themes 1271–1674* (Oxford University Press: 2011) and the *Cambridge History of Medieval Philosophy* (Cambridge University Press: 2010).

Pierre Pellegrin, Directeur de Recherche au Centre National de la Recherche Scientifique (Paris) a principalement travaillé sur la biologie d'Aristote (*Aristotle's Classification of Animals: Biology and the conceptual Unity of the*

Aristotelian corpus, Berkeley, University of California Press: 1986) et la philosophie politique aristotélicienne. Il a traduit *Les Politiques, la Physique, Les
Seconds Analytiques, le De Caelo, Les Parties des Animaux* en français. Il a aussi
publié nombre d'articles sur le Scepticisme antique et la médecine grecque et
romaine. Il a coédité avec Mary-Louise Gill *A Companion to Ancient Philosophy*,
(Oxford: Blackwell 2006).

Christof Rapp is Professor of Philosophy at the Ludwig-Maximilians-Universität
in Munich, where he is the Academic Director of the LMS-Center for Advanced
Studies. In addition to many articles in Ancient and Contemporary Philosophy,
he is the author of *Identität, Persistenz und Substantialität* (Karl Alber: 1995),
Vorsokratiker (C.H. Beck Verlag: 1997; 2nd Edition 2007), *Aristoteles zur Einführung*
(Junius-Verlag: 2001, 2nd Edition 2004, 3rd Edition 2008), *Aristoteles, Rhetorik;
Übersetzung und Kommentar* (Akademie Verlag: 2002), and *Epikur, Ausgewählte
Schriften, Übersetzung und Einleitung* (Alfred Kröner: 2010). He has also edited or
co-edited an additional nine volumes covering themes across a broad spectrum of
topics in Ancient Philosophy.

C. D. C. Reeve is Delta Kappa Epsilon Distinguished Professor of Philosophy at
the University of North Carolina at Chapel Hill. He works primarily on Plato and
Aristotle, but is interested in philosophy generally and has published on film and on
the philosophy of sex and love. His books include *Philosopher-Kings* (1988, reissued
2006), *Socrates in the Apology* (1989), *Practices of Reason* (1995), *Aristotle: Politics*
(1998), *Plato: Cratylus* (1998), *The Trials of Socrates* (2002), *Substantial Knowledge:
Aristotle's Metaphysics* (2003), *Plato: Republic* (2005), *Love's Confusions* (2005), and
Plato on Love (2006). His *Immortal Life: Action, Contemplation, and Happiness in
Aristotle* is forthcoming from Harvard University Press.

Annamaria Schiaparelli is 'Professeure Suppléante' at the Department of Philosophy,
University of Geneva. She took her Doctorate at Padua University (Italy). From 2003
to 2011 she was Lecturer at the Queen's College, Oxford. Her area of research is
Ancient Philosophy. She is the author of *Galen and the Linguistic Fallacies* (Venice:
2002) and has published several articles on Aristotle and Plotinus including 'Aristotle
on the Fallacy of Combination and Division in *Sophistici Elenchi* 4,' 'Epistemological
Problems in Aristotle's Concept of Definition (*Top*. VI.4),' 'Essence and Cause in
Plotinus: An Outline of Some Problems,' and 'Plotinus on Dialectic.'

Christopher Shields is a Fellow of Lady Margaret Hall and Professor of Classical
Philosophy in the University of Oxford. He is the author of *Order in Multiplicity:
Homonymy in the Philosophy of Aristotle* (Oxford University Press: 1999), *Classical
Philosophy: A Contemporary Introduction* (Routledge: 2003), *Aristotle* (Routledge:
2007), *Ancient Philosophy: A Contemporary Introduction* (Routledge: 2011), and,
with Robert Pasnau, *The Philosophy of Thomas Aquinas* (Westview: 2003). He is the
editor of *The Blackwell Guide to Ancient Philosophy* (Blackwell: 2002). Forthcoming
is *Aristotle's De Anima, Translated with Introduction and Commentary* (Oxford
University Press).

Richard Sorabji is Honorary Fellow of Wolfson College, Oxford. He is the author of 12 volumes and editor of 110. The 12 volumes authored include *Aristotle on Memory*; *Necessity Cause and Blame*; *Time, Creation and the Continuum*; *Matter, Space and Motion*; *Animal Minds and Human Morals*; *Emotion and Peace of Mind*; *Self: Ancient and Modern Insights about Individuality, Life and Death*; 3 volumes of *The Philosophy of the Commentators 200–600 AD, A Sourcebook*; *Opening Doors: The Untold Story of Cornelia Sorabji*, and (forthcoming) *Gandhi and the Stoics: Modern Experiments on Ancient Values*. He is currently writing a history of the idea of Moral Conscience. He is the General Editor of the series Ancient Commentators on Aristotle, which celebrates its 100th volume in 2012, and he is editor or co-editor of 10 further volumes, including *The Ethics of War: Shared Problems in Different Traditions*.

Paul Studtmann is an Associate Professor of Philosophy at Davidson College. He is the author *of Hylomorphism and Aristotle's Categorial Scheme* (Marquette: 2008), and *Empiricism and the Problem of Metap*hysics (Lexington: 2010), as well as numerous articles on Aristotle and in contemporary metaphysics.

Hermann Weidemann is retired Professor of Philosophy. He is the author of Aristoteles, *Peri hermeneias, übersetzt und erläutert* [translation and commentary] (Akademie Verlag: 1994; second edition, revised 2002) and of numerous articles on Ancient Philosophy, Medieval Philosophy, Philosophy of Language, and Logic. Forthcoming is a new critical edition of Aristotle's *De Interpretatione*, based on a collation of the seven oldest surviving manuscripts (including the fragmentary *Codex Sinaiticus* M 138 discovered in 1975), to appear in the series *Bibliotheca Teubneriana*.

ABBREVIATIONS OF ARISTOTLE'S WORKS

- *Categories (Cat.)*
- *De Anima (DA) [On the Soul]*
- *De Caelo (DC) [On the Heavens]*
- *De Interpretatione (DI) [On Interpretation]*
- *Eudemian Ethics (EE)*
- *Generation and Corruption (Gen. et Corr.)*
- *Generation of Animals (GA)*
- *History of Animals (HA)*
- *Magna Moralia (MM) [Great Ethics]*
- *Metaphysics (Met.)*
- *Meteorology (Meteor.)*
- *Movement of Animals (MA)*
- *Nicomachean Ethics (EN)*
- *Parva Naturalia (PN) [Brief Natural Treatises]*
  - *De Insomniis (Insomn) [On Dreams]*
  - *De Memoria (Mem) [On Memory]*
  - *De Sensu et Sensibilibus (Sens) [Sense and Sensibilia]*
- *Parts of Animals (PA)*
- *Physics (Phys.)*
- *Prior Analytics (APr)*
- *Posterior Analytics (APo)*
- *Problems (Prob)**
- *Progression of Animals (IA)*
- *Poetics (Poet.)*
- *Politics (Pol.)*

- *Rhetoric (Rhet.)*

- *Sophistical Refutations (SE)*

- *Topics (Top.)*

The titles provided are those in most common use today in English language scholarship, followed by standard abbreviations in parentheses. For no discernible reason, in some cases scholars prefer Latin titles over English. Where Latin titles are generally preferred, English equivalents are given in square brackets. (* = Questions of authenticity remain viable.)

PART I

ARISTOTLE'S PHILOSOPHICAL MILIEU

CHAPTER 1

ARISTOTLE'S PHILOSOPHICAL LIFE AND WRITINGS

CHRISTOPHER SHIELDS

IF restricted in its appeal to widely attested facts only, Aristotle's biography would be pleasingly brief: he was born in Stagira, in Macedon, in 384 BC; at some point as a young man he came to Athens and associated himself with Plato's Academy; around the time that Plato died in 347 BC, he left Athens for Assos, in Asia Minor, settling there for three years, followed by another two in nearby Lesbos; he returned to Macedon in 343 BC, perhaps at the behest of Philip, the father of Alexander the Great; thereafter he returned to Athens in 335 BC to head his own school, the Lyceum; and finally he left Athens for a second time in 323 BC, upon the death of Alexander, a year or so before his death, which befell him of natural causes in Chalcis in 322 BC at the age of 62. Beyond that, speculation creeps in, some grounded and plausible, some flighty and fanciful. Indeed, even prior to the onset of speculation, what is 'widely attested' is not universally affirmed: several of the contentions even in this skeletal summary are strenuously denied by credible sources.[1]

Despite a paucity of contemporary information about Aristotle's life and affairs, our ancient sources are only too happy to supply missing details and additional colour, much of it centred on his relationship with his teacher, Plato.[2] Aristotle left Athens when Plato died. Why? As we have them, the probable facts are that Plato died, Plato's nephew Speusippus became the head of the school he had founded, the Academy, and Aristotle left Athens for Assos, on the coast of Asia Minor. Later historians connected these events by contending that the second happened after the first with the result that the third happened because of the second. With a bit of added colour, this becomes: Aristotle left Athens after Plato's death in a snit brought on by his having been passed over for the headship of the Academy in favour of Plato's nepotistically selected nephew. Maybe this is so. Or maybe Aristotle was lured away by a handsome invitation to engage in marine biological research, since animal studies were never far from his heart. These he might have conducted in Assos even as a continuing member of the Academy, since a letter ascribed to Plato treats the researchers in Assos as forming a sort of satellite campus of the Academy.[3] This suggestion gains further credence from the authoritative source who reports that Aristotle left Athens even before Plato's death.[4] So, maybe he was pulled to Assos rather than pushed from Athens. Maybe, but, again, we do not know. Still less do we know what Aristotle held in his heart when he left Athens, not even to the point of informed conjecture. Neither Aristotle himself nor any acquaintance of his, friend or foe, reports anything at all about his motives pertaining to this move. In the end, then, such conjectures mainly tell us something about the explanatory practices of those who offer them.

Of similar worth are the reports of Aristotle's appearance and manner. Writing a half millennium after his death, Diogenes Laertius retails a second-hand portrait of him this way:

> He had a lisping voice, as is asserted by Timotheus the Athenian, in his *Lives*. He had also very thin legs, they say, and small eyes; but he used to indulge in very conspicuous garments and rings, and he used to dress his hair carefully.[5]

So, Aristotle was a dapper chap—if, that is, Timotheus of Athens is to be our guide. He seems to have written in the second or third century AD and is preserved only in Diogenes Laertius; we do not know his sources. So, it is unclear what to make of his characterisation.

Still less is it clear what value it should be accorded if true. Many of the speculations about Aristotle's character and motives, however rooted in a natural curiosity to come to know the man and his ways, stem from an understandable but misplaced motive: to understand his thought more fully. In fact, though, many of the speculations we have tend to run in the wrong direction. Finding something significant on display in Aristotle's voluminous output, something distinctive or oddly brilliant, biographers project back onto the man those features they suppose will help explain the genius on display in his writings. A remarkable instance of this tendency owes to Werner Jaeger, easily one of the greatest Aristotelian scholars of the last two centuries. Jaeger discerns in Aristotle's will, which was preserved by Diogenes Laertius,[6] a deeply humane but sadly alienated man. Pulsing below the surface of the formulaic language of the will, Jaeger detects 'the warm tone of true humanity, and at the same time an almost terrifying gulf between him and the persons by whom he was surrounded. These words were written by a lonely man.'[7] While it is true that Jaeger had an impressively intimate familiarity with Aristotle's writings—their tone, their nuance, their idiosyncrasies—it is hard to escape the conclusion that when he travels beneath the words of Aristotle's will he spies lurking there only the man whose character he projects into that space.

This is not to say that biographical speculation about Aristotle is as a matter of course jejune, but rather that we will learn more about Aristotle from reading

Aristotle than from studying the conjectures of those who wrote about his dress or demeanour in late antiquity and beyond. So, after a brief recapitulation of the main facts of his life as they pertain to his intellectual endeavours, we will characterize Aristotle's writings briefly as an aid to their study, primarily by illustrating the delicate difficulties involved in contemporary Aristotelian scholarship.

Aristotle's philosophical life began in Athens, when he came to be associated with Plato's Academy. In all likelihood, he went to Athens as a young man of about 18 in 367 BC, having been raised in Macedon, in what is now northeastern Greece. He was born to Nicomachus, a physician in the court of King Amyntas II, and Phaistis, a woman with family origins in Euboia, an island in the Aegean Sea, where Aristotle's own life was to end in 332. Because his parents died when he was still a boy, Aristotle was raised by a family relation, perhaps his uncle, Proxenus, who came from Atarneus, near Assos, the town to which Aristotle travelled after the death of Plato.

Not much is known of Aristotle's childhood, though two features of his birth likely proved consequential. First, his lifelong interest in biology presumably found its formative influences in the practices of the medical guild to which his father belonged, the Asclepiadae, who carried out detailed anatomical inquiries, including dissections, and who reportedly trained their sons in these same practices.[8] Second, his connections to the Macedonian court, which he would have visited at Pella as a boy, followed him throughout his life. They explain his being recalled there to tutor Alexander the Great, and they may be responsible for his decision, taken a year before the end of his life, to leave Athens, which was just then experiencing one of its periodic surges of anti-Macedonian sentiment, this one brought on by the death of Alexander in 323.

In any event, at the end of his childhood, Plato's Academy brought Aristotle to Athens. In all likelihood he was sent there, since he was only about 17 or 18 when he arrived in 367, at a time when Plato himself would have been absent (he was in Sicily until 365). He remained in the Academy for nineteen years, until around the time of Plato's death in 347 BC, by which time, of course, Aristotle had grown into a fully mature man. Aristotle's relationship to Plato is the source of endless debate and controversy. Plainly Aristotle found much of value in the Academy and in Plato's headship of it, else he would not have remained there for nearly two decades. Many of his works must have been written there, including some early, lost dialogues, which were described by Cicero, who was certainly in a position to judge, as beautifully composed and executed: he called them 'flowing rivers of gold.'[9] These dialogues stand in stark contrast to other works written at the same period and beyond, which read more like crabbed, terse sets of lecture notes and records of ongoing investigations, written, re-worked, unpolished, and not produced for general consumption. These are the works we possess today.

Aristotle's relationship to Plato during this period and beyond is at least obliquely on display in some of these writings. Sometimes Aristotle describes himself as a member of Plato's circle, even when criticizing Plato's views; other times, in equally critical veins, he disassociates himself from Plato and his teachings, writing as if from an opposing camp. Although the views of those working in Plato's Academy were hardly monolithic, Aristotle's varying attitudes seem at times presented as from a member of the Academy and at other times as someone writing from the outside. These different attitudes may be the result of editorial interpolations, or they may derive from different periods of Aristotle's life. Perhaps, though, Aristotle simply maintained a deep respect for the teachings of Plato and other Academicians even while seeking to undermine them. Indeed, that he regards Plato's views as worthy of discussion already reflects some indication of his attitude towards their worth. Probably the single best passage capturing Aristotle's bi-modal attitude towards Plato occurs in a digression in the first book of his *Nicomachean Ethics*:

> We had perhaps better consider the universal good and run through the puzzles concerning what is meant by it, even though this sort of investigation is unwelcome to us, because those who introduced the Forms are friends of ours. Yet presumably it would be the better course to destroy even what is close to us, as something necessary for preserving the truth—and all the more so, given that we are philosophers. For although we love them both, piety bids us to honour the truth before our friends (*EN* 1096a11–16).

Aristotle evinces both genuine affection and critical distance, presumably because he reveres and respects Plato, even while concluding that one of his signature theses is unsustainable. We do not, then, need to regard Aristotle as 'the foal who kicked its mother,' an ingrate too ill mannered and truculent to revere his magnanimous teacher.[10] It is true that he can be at times rather caustic, as once when he mocks Plato's theory of Forms,[11] but in the main his time in the Academy left him honouring Plato as 'a man whom the wicked have no place to praise: he alone, unsurpassed among mortals, has shown clearly by his own life and by the pursuits of his writings that a man becomes happy and good simultaneously.'[12]

Whatever his relationship to Plato, which was doubtless rich and variegated, Aristotle, whether pushed or pulled, left Athens at around the time of Plato's death for Assos, on the northwest coast of present-day Turkey. There he carried on his philosophical activity augmented by intensive marine biological research.[13] He had been invited to Assos by Hermias, reportedly a friend from the Academy who had subsequently become the ruler of the region incorporating Assos and Atarneus, the birthplace of Aristotle's guardian, Proxenus. When Hermias died, Aristotle relocated to Lesbos, an island off the coast and sufficiently close to Assos that one acropolis could be seen from the other. He remained working in Lesbos for an additional two years. There, again by at least some reports, he was joined by his long-term colleague and fellow ex-Academician Theophrastus. During his two years in Lesbos, Aristotle married Pythias, the niece of Hermias, with whom he had a daughter, also named Pythias.

The period of Aristotle's life following his time in Asia Minor has been a source of rich speculation for historians, though, again, we have little determinate or reliable data upon which we may rely. Aristotle was called or invited by Philip, king of Macedon, in 342, to return to Pella, the seat of Macedonian power where he had presumably visited as a boy. Almost all historians accept that during this period Aristotle offered tuition to Philip's son Alexander, later the Great. There was a private school at Mieza, the royal estate near Pella, and Aristotle might well have taught Alexander there. The tuition began when Alexander was 13, and probably lasted only two or three years. It is possible that it carried on for a longer period, though this seems unlikely since Alexander was already serving as a deputy military commander for his father by the age of 15. Aristotle did, however, remain in Macedon for another five or so years, perhaps back in Stagira, the city of his birth, until the death of Philip by assassination in 336.

Again, while the exact motives for his relocation are unclear, Aristotle returned to Athens for his second and final stay in 335. Once there, he established his own school in the Lyceum, a location outside of the centre of Athens in an area dedicated to the god Apollo Lykeios. This second period of residency in Athens was an astonishingly productive one for Aristotle. Together with his associates, who included Theophrastus, Eudemus, and Aristoxenus, Aristotle built a great library and pursued a very wide range of research programmes, leading well beyond philosophy as we conceive of that discipline today but in keeping with the more comprehensive courses of study in Aristotle's intellectual orientation. That allowed, many of the philosophical works of Aristotle that we possess today probably derive from this period. It seems that research in the Lyceum carried forward at a feverish pace into a variety of distinct areas, up to the time of Aristotle's final departure from Athens in the year prior to his death.

During his second sojourn in Athens, Aristotle's wife Pythias died, and he formed a new relationship, whether into formal marriage or not remains unclear, with Herpyllis, who was also a native of Stagira. They had a child, Nicomachus, after whom his *Nicomachean Ethics* is named.

Aristotle withdrew to Chalcis on the island of Euboia, in 323, likely because of a resurgence of anti-Macedonian feeling in Athens, always present in an undercurrent there and flooding forth after the death of Alexander the Great. Aristotle's real and perceived associations with Macedon would have made life in Athens just then unpleasant if not precarious for him.[14] As a metic, or resident alien, Aristotle would have been extended fewer protections than citizens of Athens received and would also have been more likely to be regarded with suspicion than a native Athenian. Diogenes Laertius reports that Aristotle was charged with actionable impiety by Eurymedon,[15] which charge, like the similar accusation laid against Socrates before him, was no doubt spurious. No matter: a spurious charge against a man in Aristotle's marginal position could well have proven deleterious to his well-being.

A year after his departure from Athens, Aristotle died in Chalcis on the island of Euboia, presumably of natural causes. That presumption notwithstanding, a charming aetiology of Aristotle's death helps bring into sharp relief the credibility of many of the sources relied upon in constructing even this minimal biography. According to a story preferred by the Church Fathers,[16] Aristotle died in a revealing sort of way: maniacally devoted to the pursuit of explaining natural phenomena and deeply frustrated by his inability to explain the tidal currents he observed in the straight of Euripus, the channel separating Euboia from mainland Greece, he grew morose and moribund. Aristotle died of terminal curiosity.

Stories such as this capture something authentically Aristotelian: his writings are broadly cast, arrestingly deep, and coursing with curiosity. The works we possess today range widely across an astonishing number of fields, including aesthetic theory, argumentation theory, astronomy, botany, biology, category theory, cosmology, epistemology, ethics, government, history of thought, literary theory, logic, mathematics, metaphysics, music, medicine, meteorology, pedagogy, philosophy of science, political theory, psychology, physics, rhetoric, semantic theory, political history, theology, and zoology. All these areas Aristotle pursued with genuine, unselfconscious zeal, under a general rubric of his own invention. He distinguishes three broad categories of inquiry. The first class is *theoretical*, comprising disciplines pursuing knowledge for its own sake; the second is *practical*, including ethics, politics, and all study concerned with conduct and goodness in action, whether individual or societal; and the third is *productive*, covering those sciences and crafts which aim at the creation of beautiful or useful objects, broadly conceived so as to include drama and dance (on Aristotle's characterisations of the sciences, see *Top.* 145a15–16; *Phys.* 192b8–12; *DC* 298a27–32, *DA* 403a27–b2; *Met.* 1025b25, 1026a18–19, 1064a16–19, b1–3; *EN* 1139a26–28, 1141b29–32).

With one glaring exception, Aristotle's extant works slot reasonably well into this classificatory schema. Thus, among the theoretical works are the *Metaphysics*, the *Physics*, and *De Anima*; among the practical works are the *Nicomachean Ethics*, the *Eudemian Ethics*, and the *Politics*; and among the productive works are the *Rhetoric* and *Poetics*. The glaring exception is the family of works which came to be known as Aristotle's *Organon*, roughly the tools for study rather than the objects of study (*organon* = tool, in Greek): logic, dialectic, argument theory, philosophy of science, and the doctrines of propositions and terms. These include *The Categories, De Interpretatione, Prior* and *Posterior Analytics, Topics,* and *Sophistical Refutations*. The relation of these works to the rest of Aristotle's writings gave rise to a series of lively controversies in later Aristotelianism, though Aristotle himself shows no reflexive awareness of the wellsprings of these controversies. Instead, he simply treats the subjects pursued in his *Organan* as matters worthy of concern in their own right and then puts his tools to work in his practical, productive, and theoretical sciences.

As these controversies about the relation between the *Organon* and the discipline-specific treatises attest, later Aristotelian philosophers and scholars have investigated Aristotle's works minutely from a number of complementary angles. There remain in the first instance unsettled questions about transmissions of Aristotle's texts from antiquity to the present day,[17] as well as related questions about the internal constitutions of the works as we now possess them. Some of our works, including notably the *Metaphysics* and the *Politics*, show signs of being editorial compilations rather than continuous treatises conceived and executed as such by Aristotle. Other questions pertain to the relation between the works we possess and the three main lists of Aristotle's works from late antiquity, owing to Diogenes Laertius (third century AD, who lists 143 titles), Ptolemy (fourth century AD, who catalogues 99 titles),[18] and Hesychius (sixth century AD, who reports 187 titles). Although these lists do not cohere completely, the numbers of titles reported in them are not as nearly as disparate as they first appear, because the different lists report the titles differently, so that, for instance, Hesychius mentions as separate titles works treated as books or chapters by Ptolemy.[19] Still, many of the works included in the ancient lists are not, by current scholarly consensus, by Aristotle at all, while other works which we accept as genuine make no appearance in the ancient catalogues of Aristotle's works. Today, although the matter is not without lingering controversy, scholars accept thirty-one surviving works, those contained in the *Corpus Aristotelicum* of our medieval manuscripts judged to be authentic.

That said, as we read Aristotle today, it is salutary to bear in mind that judgements about the authenticity of his works have varied with the times.[20] Some works today accepted as canonical were as recently as the nineteenth century regarded as spurious. Thus, in the nineteenth century, even so centrally canonical a work as the *Categories* was able to be regarded as spurious by no less eminent an authority than Jaeger, who was convinced that it was the work of a later compiler.[21] Several of Aristotle's works would benefit from new critical editions, and all of them should be read with an awareness that the texts constituted and translated in our modern editions bear the marks of editorial judgement in a host of different ways: decisions about the relative priority of our existing manuscripts relative to one another; appraisals concerning the authenticity of individual words and sentences in our texts, many of which show signs of being interpolations by scribes and scholars seeking to explicate or amplify Aristotle's own words rather than merely to reproduce them; arrangements of individual sentences and paragraphs, which sometimes, from the standpoint of sense or argumentative progression, seem to have been transposed; and the status of doublets, or passages which are repeated, or largely repeated, in different parts of the corpus as we have it.

To take just one especially useful illustration: a doublet in *Metaphysics* I and XIII repeats a series of criticisms of Platonic Forms in virtually identical language, though in one case putting the case against Plato using the first person (*Met.* I 990b8: 'of the ways in which *we prove* that the Forms exist, none is convincing') and in the other using an impersonal third person (*Met.* XIII 1079a4: 'of the ways in which *it is proven* that the Forms exist, none is convincing'). These passages intertwine a series of editorial difficulties, all consequential for our thinking about the proper constitution of the text of the *Metaphysics*. Should we say that one is authentic and the other corrected? Was the original passage written by Aristotle when he was still a member of the Academy—hence the use of the first person? If so, was it later revised by him after leaving the Academy, or by some later scholar seeking to 'correct' the impression that Aristotle was once a critical Platonist? The matter is further complicated by the fact that some of these divergent readings come down to us under two different branches in the family of manuscripts of the *Metaphysics*.[22] If one family shows a tendency of offering late editorial corrections and interpolations in passages where direct comparisons are possible because of the existence of doublets, then that result might be cautiously generalized, so that other editorial decisions about the relative strengths and weaknesses of the manuscript families can be favourably exploited in the constitution of our texts.

This is but one small, if significant example of the sort of work that needs to be undertaken before we come to the point where we can read and appraise the philosophical content of a text of Aristotle. We possess no manuscript of Aristotle's works written by him or even in his own time. Our earliest useable manuscripts date to the ninth century, and the vast majority of them come from the centuries following. So, there is a long line of transmission between the words composed by Aristotle and a translation of Aristotle read today—if his works were composed by him rather than by a compiler or by members of his school charged with keeping notes.

Standing behind each modern publication is thus a series of decisions, most proximately by the translator, determining how to wrestle Aristotle's often wiry Greek into some suitably faithful but still readable modern language syntax, and before the translator, by an editor constituting the text from the various manuscripts available to us, and often enough, before the editor, by a paleographer determining the readings of the manuscripts, and then also, even before the paleographer, by a scribe, or series of scribes, who also needed to determine what a manuscript being copied had written on it, since styles of writing altered through the centuries. (Sometimes, but rarely, the paleographer, the editor, and the translator may be one and the same person, discharging different roles in the constitution of the text in a co-ordinated way.) Many of these intersecting editorial decisions are delicate and mutually implicating, with the result that by the time we pick up a translation of a given text of Aristotle, we have already benefited from the critical acumen of a full range of philosophical and philological scholars—but then we also to some extent remain hostage to the critical judgements and determinations of those scholars. Accordingly, when contemporary philosophers go to work on a text of Aristotle, they should be mindful that what they are reading bears some resemblance to a committee report composed incrementally, in slow motion over two millennia. Happily, this awareness can also be liberating: Aristotle's philosophically suggestive texts bear repeated study not least because they remain open to surprising developments, both interpretative and philosophical.

Of special interest to philosophical scholarship over the last century has been the question of the relative dates of the treatises now mainly accepted as genuine.[23] Because we do not have secure information concerning the dates of composition for Aristotle's works, scholars, assuming that such knowledge will assist in the twin projects of interpretation and assessment, rely on a series of mutually reinforcing considerations to determine their relative order. These include stylometric data, involving features of Aristotle's diction and syntax;[24] doctrinal matters, including some permanently disputed issues regarding Aristotle's philosophical development, especially as regards his relationship to Plato; some less tendentious matters involving his use of place names and historical allusions; and finally, intertextual references, which provide *prima facie* support for the thesis that the referring work is later than the work to which it refers.

Each of these criteria introduces controversies and small surprises of various sorts. Thus, to take just one example, intertextual references often enough have the feel of editorial interpolations; this, then, tends to undercut the *prima facie* plausible judgement that a referring text is later than the text to which it refers. In the same vein, as previously suggested, many of Aristotle's works bear the marks of being revisited and revised, each occasion of which provides the opportunity for cross-referencing by Aristotle himself, rather than by an editor. One especially stark instance of this sort of worry concerning internal cross-referencing occurs in *De Interpretatione*, regarded almost universally as an early work from the *Organon*, and presumably composed during Aristotle's first period in Athens when he was a member of the Academy. In this work, Aristotle—or some editor on his behalf—refers to his *De Anima*, almost certainly, judged in terms of doctrine and diction, one of his very last productions (*DI* 16a9). Another is the simple observation of Jaeger pertinent to his attitude towards the authorship of the *Categories*, which is also thought by most scholars to be a production of Aristotle's time in the Academy. As Jaeger observes, Aristotle illustrates the category of place with the example of 'being in the Lyceum' (*Cat.* 2a1).[25] To Jaeger this suggests a date of composition much later than Aristotle's time in the Academy, relying as it does on a place name which is associated with Aristotle's second stay in Athens rather than his first. Other scholars respond that if the *Categories* is in fact early, the example might merely have been interpolated later, by Aristotle or by someone else, so that the presumed early date of its composition is not threatened. That is certainly fair enough, but Jaeger's simple observation serves to introduce some instability into our easy preconceptions about the relative sophistication of Aristotle's works and their relation to one another. In general, scholars must tread lightly when making arguments about the dating of Aristotle's works. No one criterion seems terribly decisive on its own. Still, to the degree that the different sorts of criteria coalesce, a reasonably clear picture regarding the order of composition begins to emerge.

One might wonder, of course, whether the composition order of Aristotle's works is of any significance to our understanding his philosophy. In one way, it is not. After all, some of the greatest and most incisive philosophical commentaries on Aristotle were written in Late Antiquity and in the Arabic and Latin Middle Ages, long before techniques of stylometry were even invented. Thus, for instance, using a characteristically medieval hermeneutic technique of the sort practiced by biblical exegetes bent on reconciling apparently inconsistent verses of the bible, various Aristotelians of these earlier periods were able to prise out striking forms of intertextual consistency which would likely have eluded later scholars altogether, especially if those scholars were attacking their texts secure in the knowledge that, for example, the *Politics* was written later than the *Nicomachean Ethics*, or that the theory of substance developed in the *Metaphysics* revises and replaces the coarser theory of the *Categories*. On this latter point, it is striking that many sophisticated medieval commentators actually attempt to derive the doctrine of *Categories* from the hylomorphic principles of the *Metaphysics*, completely reversing the almost universal judgement of present-day scholars that the *Metaphysics* post-dates the *Categories*. According to the currently received view, far from grounding Aristotle's categorialism, the *Metaphysics* in fact proves positively incompatible with some of the central contentions of the *Categories*.[26] So, one might reasonably observe that something of value is lost in the modern drive to read Aristotle's works in the supposed order of their composition.

Still, heading in the other direction, a great deal turns on questions of relative dating. We may consider as one illustration the question of whether we should think of Aristotle's *De Anima* as early or late. The hylomorphic theory of body and soul adumbrated in this work seems plainly incompatible with Platonism, and, more to the point, with the Platonic doctrine of soul embraced in Aristotle's early, lost dialogues (sufficient numbers of quotations and fragments exist that reasonably secure ascriptions can be made to the lost works).[27] If the appearance of conflict is genuine, then some philosophically fecund questions come to the fore. What in Aristotle's subsequent development led him to abandon his earlier views? Is, for example, the hylomorphism of his *Physics* and *Metaphysics* genuinely inconsistent with Platonism? What—in fact or in Aristotle's eyes—commends hylomorphism over Platonism? When we pursue these sorts of questions, we move swiftly into the style of philosophical scholarship engaged by nearly all the papers in the current volume: all agree that simple, non-critical exegesis of Aristotle's works is hardly possible. Rather, exegesis is inevitably also a critical enterprise, just as any critical assessment of a philosopher's thought (of any era) presupposes some form of fair-minded exegesis. Thus, the cross-fertilizing intersection of exegesis and critical assessment emerges in developmentally driven scholarship no less—if in a different guise—than in the unitarian frameworks assumed in the Middle Ages and Late Antiquity. We may let each approach be judged by its fruits and adapt our own hermeneutical methodologies accordingly.

However one is disposed to approach the corpus in terms of Aristotle's development, the canonical list of generally accepted works can be informed by his own division of the sciences to yield a list as follows (an asterisk indicates a continuing controversy about authenticity):

- Organon
  - *Categories (Cat.)*
  - *De Interpretatione (DI) [On Interpretation]*
  - *Prior Analytics (APr)*
  - *Posterior Analytics (APo)*
  - *Sophistical Refutations (SE)*
  - *Topics (Top.)*
- Theoretical Sciences
  - *De Anima (DA) [On the Soul]*
  - *De Caelo (DC) [On the Heavens]*
  - *Generation and Corruption (Gen. et Corr.)*
  - *Generation of Animals (GA)*

- *History of Animals (HA)*
- *Metaphysics (Met.)*
- *Parva Naturalia (PN) [Brief Natural Treatises]*
- *Meteorology (Meteor.)*
- *Movement of Animals (MA)*
- *Parts of Animals (PA)*
- *Physics (Phys.)*
- **Problems (Prob)*
- *Progression of Animals (IA)*
- Practical Sciences
  - *Eudemian Ethics (EE)*
  - *Nicomachean Ethics (EN)*
  - **Magna Moralia (MM) [Great Ethics]*
  - *Politics (Pol.)*
- Productive Science
  - *Poetics (Poet.)*
  - *Rhetoric (Rhet.)*

One may reasonably doubt whether any system of classifying Aristotle's works supersedes his own.[28]

NOTES

1. Düring (1957) collects the ancient sources concerning Aristotle's life. We have twelve surviving *Lives of Aristotle,* the earliest of which is the *Epistola ad Ammaeum* by Dionysius of Halicarnassus, who lived in Rome three centuries after Aristotle's death (c. 60 BC to after 7 AD). The remaining *Lives* range from that date to several Arabic *Lives* from the period AD 950–1270. Especially important is a work written three centuries after Dionysius, by Diogenes Laertius, who has an entry on Aristotle in his *Lives of the Philosophers.* Many of Diogenes' contentions are suspect, but he does seem to have relied on some very ancient sources, including Hermippus, who was possibly even a member of Aristotle's own school. Diogenes also reproduces Aristotle's will, an important document for his life, though also one open to interpretive controversy. Later lives are mainly of Neoplatonic or Byzantine pedigree, including the *Vita Marciana,* the *Vulgata,* and the *Latina.* A still useful overview and assessment of the biographical traditions surrounding Aristotle is Grote (1880, 1–26). A more recent set of papers pertaining to Aristotle's life and political activities is Chroust (1973, vols. 1 and 2). These are informed but also energetically conjectural. For a fuller presentation of the two main ancient traditions surrounding Aristotle's life, see Shields (2007), Chapter One.
2. Jaeger's (1934, 15) attitude is apposite: 'He had accepted Plato's doctrines with his whole soul, and the effort to discover his own relation to them occupied all his life, and is the clue to his development. It is possible to discern a gradual progress, in the various stages of which we can clearly recognize the unfolding of his own essential nature...Just as tragedy attains its own special nature..."out of the dithyramb" by

leading the latter through various forms, so Aristotle made himself out of the Platonic philosophy.' Compare Owen (1966, 150): 'It seems now possible to trace [Aristotle's] progress from sharp and rather schematic criticism of Plato to an avowed sympathy with Plato's general metaphysical programme.'

3. This is the Sixth Letter, putatively written from Plato to Hermias of Atarneus, an Academic who ruled over the region from Atarneus to Assos. This letter is, however, very probably spurious. Aristotle also had an independent family connection to Atarneus, since Proxenus, perhaps Aristotle's uncle and his guardian after the death of Aristotle's father, had been born there. See Bury (1949, 454–5).

4. Diogenes Laertius, *Lives of the Philosophers* v 2.

5. Diogenes Laertius, *Lives of the Philosophers* v 2.

6. Diogenes Laertius v 11–16, translated in the *Revised Oxford Aristotle*, pp. 264–5.

7. Jaeger (1962, 321).

8. Galen, *On Anatomical Procedures* ii 1.

9. Cicero, *Ac. Pr.* 38.119, cf. *Top.* 1 3, *De or.* 1.2.49.

10. Diogenes Laertius, *Lives of the Philosophers* v 2.

11. 'Farewell to the Forms: they are but ding-a-lings and even if they do exist they are wholly irrelevant' (*APo.* 83a32–34).

12. Frag. 650 R3; Olympiodorus, *Commentarius in Gorgiam* 41.9.

13. Detailed study of Aristotle's biological treatises, including especially the *Historia Animalium*, certify that much of his research in marine biology was conducted in this region. See Thompson (1913) and Lee (1948).

14. The anti-Macedonian sentiment in Athens had an understandable basis. In 335 Alexander had repressed a revolt by the Thebans and then handed them a vicious reprisal, effectively obliterating the city. He then demanded that Athens, in view of its pro-Theban sympathies, surrender its anti-Macedonian politicians for execution. The implicit suggestion was that any refusal would earn the Athenians the fate of the Thebans. Although he eventually relented, permitting Athens to signify its fealty by exiling two of its citizens, Alexander's entirely credible threat remained hanging over the city. The result was galling: hostile sentiment directed against Alexander and Macedon ran deep and broad in Athens.

15. Diogenes Laertius v 7. Diogenes also reports a conflicting account, which he says owes to Favorinus, who reports Aristotle's prosecutor as Demophilus. The pretext offered in Aristotle's case was his composition of a paean or hymn praising the character of Hermias, his sponsor in Assos. Aristotle had also erected a statue in his honour at Delphi, along with an inscription praising his virtue. The inscriptions compare Hermias, reportedly a eunuch and former slave, to several Greek heroes, a coupling likely to rankle Athenians of a better class. See Ford (2011) for a discussion of the character of Aristotle's inscription at Delphi and some of the controversies surrounding it.

16. Collected in Düring (1957, 347).

17. Somewhat outdated, but still engaging is Shute (1888). For more up-to-date discussions, see Moraux (1951), Barnes (1997), Primavesi (2007).

18. Ptolemy's text has been printed in Arabic, and translated into German, by Hein (1985).

19. Düring (1957) discusses the evidence thoroughly.

20. The Victorian translator of Plato, Benjamin Jowett (1964, 27), characterizes Aristotle's works in this way: 'There is of course no doubt of the great influence exercised upon Greece and upon the world by Aristotle and his philosophy. But on the other hand almost everyone who is capable of understanding the subject acknowledges that his

writings have not come down to us in an authentic form like most of the dialogues of Plato. How much of them is to be ascribed to Aristotle's own hand, how much is due to his successors in the Peripatetic School, is a question which has never been determined and probably never can be, because the solution depends upon internal evidence only.' Although unduly pessimistic due to the sorts of techniques for authenticating and dating mentioned in the text, Jowett's cautionary note is none the less worth recalling.

21. See Jaeger (1962, 46 n. 3).

22. This small example, which could easily be multiplied, derives from Primavesi (forthcoming), who, continuing the work of Harlfinger (1979), has assembled an impressive set of considerations, no less philosophically than philologically adroit, for the compelling conclusion that the *Metaphysics* stands in need of an entirely new edition. His work provides an exciting illustration of the ways in which Aristotelian textual criticism continues unabated down to the present day: as unlikely as it sounds, we are probably now closer to the texts that Aristotle actually wrote than we have been at any time in the history of their transmission.

23. Graham (1990) offers an incisive overview of the controversy. See also the papers collected in Wians (1996) for a variety of approaches and perspectives.

24. Kenny (2001) provides several unusually rich and sophisticated instances of this approach to the dating of Aristotle's works, with a special emphasis on his ethical writings.

25. Jaeger (1962, 39).

26. For a preliminary account of this supposed incompatibility, see Shields (2007, §§4.5 and 5.1). One well-developed dissenter is Wedin (2000).

27. Fragments of Aristotle's lost dialogues are translated in the *Revised Oxford Aristotle* (Barnes, 1984: 2389–2426). See Hutchinson and Johnson (2005) on the status of one early work, the *Protrepticus*. They also attempt a provisional reconstruction of the *Protrepticus*, accessible here: http://www.protreptic.info/.

28. I am grateful to Stephen Menn for his helpful and astute comments and corrections.

Bibliography

Barnes, J. ed. (1984) *The Complete Works of Aristotle: The Revised Oxford Translation vols.* I and II (Princeton: Princeton Univ. Press).

——— (1997) 'Roman Aristotle', in *Philosophia Togata* II, ed. J. Barnes and M. Griffith (Oxford: Oxford Univ. Press), 1–69.

Bury, R.G. (1949) 'Introduction to the Epistles', in *Plato: Timaeus. Critias. Cleitophon. Menexenus. Epistles* (Cambridge: Harvard Univ. Press).

Chroust, A.-H. (1973) *Aristotle: new light on his life and on some of his lost works*, 2 vols. (London: Routledge).

Düring, I. (1957) *Aristotle in the Ancient Biographical Tradition* (Göteborg: Amqvist & Wiksell).

Düring, I. and Owen, G.E.L, eds. (1960) *Aristotle and Plato in the Mid-Fourth Century* (Göteborg: Almqvist & Wiksell).

Ford, A. (2011) *Aristotle as Poet: The Song for Hermias and its Context* (Oxford: Oxford Univ. Press).

Graham, D. (1990) *Aristotle's Two Systems* (Oxford: Oxford Univ. Press).

Grote, G. (1880) *Aristotle* (London: Thoemmes Continuum).

Harlfinger, D. (1979) 'Zur Überlieferungsgeschichte der Metaphysik', in *Études sur la Métaphysique d'Aristote. Actes du VIe Symposium Aristotelicum*, P. Aubenque, ed. (Paris: J. Vrin), 7–33.

Hein, C. (1985) *Definition und Einteilung der Philosophie. Von der spätantiken Einleitungsliteratur zur arabischen Enzyklopädie* (New York: Peter Lang).

Hutchinson, D.S. and M.R. Johnston (2005) 'Authenticating Aristotle's *Protrepticus*', *Oxford Studies in Ancient Philosophy*, 193–294.

Jaeger, W. (1934) *Aristotle: Fundamentals of the History of his Development*, trans. R. Robinson (Oxford: Oxford Univ. Press).

Jowett, B., trans. and ed. (1964) *The Dialogues of Plato*, 4th ed., corr. (Oxford: Oxford Univ. Press).

Kenny, A. (2001) *Essays on the Aristotelian Tradition* (Oxford: Oxford Univ. Press).

Lee, H.D.P. (1948) 'Place-names and the Dates of Aristotle's Biological Works', *Classical Quarterly* 42, 61–67.

Moraux, P. (1951) *Les listes anciennes des ouvrages d'Aristote* (Louvain: Éditions universitaires).

Owen, G.E.L. (1966) 'The Platonism of Aristotle', *Proceedings of the British Academy* 51, 125–50; reprinted in *Logic, Science, and Dialectic*, M. Nussbaum, ed. (Ithaca, N.Y.: Cornell Univ. Press, 1986), 200–21.

Primavesi, O. (2007) 'Ein Blick in den Stollen von Skepsis: Vier Kapitel zur frühen Überlieferung des Corpus Aristotelicum', *Philologus* 151, 51–77.

——— (forthcoming) 'A Revised Text of *Metaphysics* I'.

Ross, W.D. (1960) 'The Development of Aristotle's Thought', in *Aristotle and Plato in the Mid-Fourth Century*, I. Düring and G.E.L. Owen, eds. (Göteborg: Almqvist & Wiksell), 1–18.

Shields, C. (2008) 'Plato and Aristotle in the Academy: an Aristotelian Criticism of Platonic Forms', in *The Oxford Handbook on Plato*, G. Fine, ed. (Oxford: Oxford Univ. Press), 504–26.

——— (2007) *Aristotle* (London: Routledge).

Shute, R. (1888) *On the History of the Process by which the Aristotelian Writings Arrived at Their Present Form* (Oxford: Clarendon Press).

Thompson, D'A. (1913) *On Aristotle as a Biologist* (Oxford: Oxford Univ. Press).

Wedin, M. (2000) *Aristotle's Theory of Substance* (Oxford: Oxford Univ. Press).

Wians, W., ed. (1996) *Aristotle's Philosophical Development* (Lanham, MD: Rowman & Littlefield).

CHAPTER 2

ARISTOTLE ON EARLIER NATURAL SCIENCE

EDWARD HUSSEY

A. Introduction

1. In the field of natural science, Aristotle recognizes as his forerunners a select group of theorists; he names, individually, barely a dozen. Thales, Anaximander and Anaximenes of Miletus; Heraclitus of Ephesus; Empedocles of Acragas; Anaxagoras of Clazomenae; and Leucippus and Democritus of Abdera: these are the leading lights, though others are occasionally referred to, by name or anonymously. Beside these, he mentions in the same contexts some whose claims to be 'natural philosophers' are doubtful, yet who deserve notice in the same context: either because their theories questioned the very foundations of natural science (notably Parmenides of Elea and Melissus of Samos), or because their accounts of the natural world, though containing elements alien to natural science, also produced ideas worth considering: notably 'the people called Pythagoreans' (or 'the Italians'), and Plato as the author of the *Timaeus*.

Aristotle takes seriously almost all of these people, treating them as exemplary pioneers and valuable partners in the enterprise of 'natural philosophy'. Without qualification or irony, he gives them the honourable titles of *phusiologos*, *sophos*, *philosophos*; their activity is *sophia*, *theôria*, *philosophia*, *phusiologia* (or the corresponding verbs are used: *philosophein*, *theôrein*, *phusiologein*, *peri phuseôs skopein*). The object of their study was 'the truth concerning the things that are' (*peri tôn ontôn tên alêtheian eskopoun*). They are distinguished from, and preferred to, the makers of mythical cosmogonies and theogonies.[1] These are no empty compliments: their implication is borne out by the amount of space devoted, in Aristotle's extant writings, to the exposition and critical discussion of the earlier theories. These are part of the material from which the student of natural science can and indeed must learn, regardless of whether he ultimately accepts or rejects it: the foundations of the existing theoretical heritage.

2. The prescriptions of the *Topics* for dialectical reasoning are clearly relevant to many aspects of Aristotle's practice in the discussion of foundations. Among the 'reputable materials' (*endoxa*) to which dialectical arguments must appeal, the *Topics* lists 'the things held by all or by most people or by the experts (*sophois*), and, among the experts, by all or most or the most well-known and well-reputed'. The theories of earlier experts on natural science must therefore either be accepted, or shown to be mistaken. If they conflict among themselves, this conflict will constitute one of the initial problems to be resolved, which can be done better once we have taken into account the arguments on both sides. In such cases Aristotle sometimes presents himself as not so much an interested party as an arbitrator, sifting through the inherited mass of conflicting opinion and argument.[2]

3. In these programmatic remarks, as in all or much of his actual practice, Aristotle treats his predecessors as contemporary partners in debate. But this indisputable fact immediately raises the general question: how usable, for the modern historian of earlier theorising, are these reports and discussions of sixth- and fifth-century theorists which, as a matter of deliberate purpose, transfer them into a fourth-century context?

The question is unavoidable, and for its answer demands a close examination of the entire range of Aristotle's reports and discussions about earlier natural science. These two points were rightly and forcibly made by Harold Cherniss, whose book *Aristotle's Criticism of Presocratic Philosophy* (first published in 1935) attempted just such a comprehensive examination. Unfortunately, Cherniss' pertinacious scholarship was not matched by any willingness to explore patiently and flexibly the variety of assumptions and aims present in the different parts of Aristotle's works; and he reached too hastily conclusions which, like his accompanying rhetoric, were unfailingly hostile to Aristotle. His questions were much better than his answers; yet, since Cherniss, there seems to have been no systematic attempt to re-examine the problems he raised.[3]

The present chapter aims to consider a central case: that of earlier opinions on certain fundamental questions about the natural world, as treated in the first three books of the *Physics*, and in the first book of the *Metaphysics*.[4]

B. BEGINNINGS: THE IDEA OF A SCIENCE OF NATURE

1. In the *Physics* Aristotle expounds and argues for the foundations of his natural science, in doing which he has his predecessors constantly on his mind. The first three books of the *Physics*, in particular, show that he sees himself as continuing

their work. The foundations of natural science are to be identified as such by the application of pre-scientific general reasoning to truths of experience.

2. 'It is ridiculous to try to demonstrate that there is such a thing as nature', remarks Aristotle (*Phys.* II 1 193a3), 'for it is obvious that there are many such things'. That is, there are many recognizable *kinds* of thing in the world, and the members of each kind *regularly* (in the absence of supervening hindrances), and *of themselves*, originate changes (in themselves and/or in other adjacent things), and/or bring these changes to an end; the changes themselves being classifiable into kinds, and each kind of thing being capable of so originating a certain set of kinds of change. And those kinds of thing that themselves come into being and cease to be, do so as the result of a process originated in this way. These are 'the things that are by nature', and that themselves have 'natures'; while 'nature' in the larger sense is constituted by all the various natures of 'the things that are by nature', and by their interactions. Aristotle's ways of using the word *phusis* ('nature') are all dependent on the use that applies it to an individual thing falling into a recognizable kind.

This much Aristotle takes to be obvious to all who look at the world, unlike the less obvious entities and relationships that underlie mathematics or 'first philosophy'.[5] It is no surprise, then, that the first attempts at science in Greece were directed at a 'science of nature'. For Aristotle, serious theoretical effort starts in Greece with Thales of Miletus, the 'pioneer' of natural science.[6]

3. How much of his own fully-developed conception of a science does Aristotle ascribe to the early scientists? *Metaphysics* I 1 relies on distinctions made at *Nicomachean Ethics* VI 2–7, in stating that 'all suppose that what is called "wisdom" is concerned with the first causes and the principles' (981b25–29, referring to *EN* 1141a9-20). In I 2, the question is then: with what sort of causes and principles? The answer turns out to be: those which are truly primary, i.e., most general and fundamental (982b7–10). For Aristotle these early seekers after wisdom are recognisably scientists. This implies, as *Metaphysics* I and other texts confirm, that he saw them as, at least, setting up what he recognized as intended to be fundamental principles for a science of everything ('principles and causes of all things'), and as deducing from those principles, in a way intended to be demonstrative, what he recognized as intended to be scientific explanations of the phenomena of the cosmos.[7]

Aristotle does not suppose that any of his predecessors carried out both of these tasks with entire competence; nor, even, that they had a wholly clear conception of what they were about—least of all the earliest ones. They were moved by the natural desire for knowledge (*Met.* I 1 980a21), and 'compelled by the truth itself' (*Met.* I 3 984b8–11), but without at that stage being fully able to account for their procedures. Even in the original demarcation of the subject of their inquiry, Aristotle considers that most of his predecessors never achieved clarity, for a simple reason. They made the primitive assumption that 'all substances' (i.e., all those things that for them were ontologically basic) were sense-perceptible, place-occupying, and movable bodies.[8] Hence their general aim, to 'seek the truth about things that are', or to 'seek the principles, elements and causes of substance', was reduced, for them, to the study of sense-perceptible, place-occupying and movable bodies, which is one of Aristotle's ways of defining the study of nature. In his terminology, they thought that natural science embraced the whole of science or philosophy.[9]

C. Foundations: The Principles of Natural Things (*Physics* I)

1. At the beginning of *Physics* I, Aristotle puts himself, for expository purposes, into the position of a would-be natural scientist seeking the principles appropriate for his subject. To *begin* the search for principles, all that is needed is common human experience of the sense-perceptible objects in our world, and the ill-defined general notions which ordinary people apply to that experience. Then (184a21-b14), as our general notions become better-defined by critical reflection, eventually to qualify as principles, we can get a better grip on the particular cases that fall under them, and then proceed to consider those. Aristotle proposes to show us how that should be done. This is to repeat the journey of his predecessors, but with better initial equipment: a knowledge of the previous history, greater methodological awareness, and sharper analytical tools (including, for instance, the notion of 'categories', and the distinction between being potentially and being actually).

2. The meaning of the word *phusis* itself does not get discussed in *Physics* I, in fact not until *Physics* II 1. This implies that a sufficient first conception of natural science may be formed in advance of any clear account of *phusis*. The principles that are being looked for are specified in *Physics* I simply as 'the principles of natural things', with a stress on their role in the coming-to-be (*genesis*) of those things.[10] The natural world is grasped as a subject of study, even in advance of a definition of 'nature', as something characterized by the interdependence of natural kinds and natural changes. Sense-perceptible substances are characterized generally by being subject to change (*Met.* XII 1 1069b3); hence Aristotle says: 'Let us take it as a basic assumption that things that are by nature are, all or some of them, changing' (*Phys.* I 2 185a12-13). Moreover, there is as yet no reason to make any essential distinction between the parts of the natural world, and the whole observable cosmos as a natural system. In the absence of any overriding reason to the contrary (and there can be none at this stage of the inquiry), the nature and behaviour of the cosmos as a whole must be assumed to be determined by the same principles as apply to its parts. So the principles of natural things will be expected to be, above all, principles of the genesis of the cosmos as a whole, if the cosmos is taken as something that comes into being.

This also explains why, when Aristotle comes to summarize the principles of the earlier natural scientists in *Physics* I 4 187a12-23, his account is phrased in terms of their theories of the *genesis* of the observable cosmos. For these, in his view, are what is central to and characteristic of their thinking.[11] Two groups are recognized: those who start with only one 'underlying body', using the mechanism of condensation and rarefaction to derive the variety of observable stuffs in the world; and those who start out with a 'mixture', from which everything else 'emerges', having been 'in' the mixture all along in the form of 'contrarieties'.[12] At I 5 188a19–27, this first classification is slightly refined to take account of Parmenides, in his dualistic aspect, and Democritus, also apparently taken here as a dualist, neither of whom fits easily into the previous dichotomy.[13] But Aristotle is not here concerned to waterproof the classification, nor to inquire closely into any details of the earlier systems (except in the case of Anaxagoras, whose use of an infinity of principles is disturbing to him, and whom he takes some time to explore and refute (187a26–188a18) on that particular point). His declared overriding purpose is to extract from all of these theories a simple structural message: the principles of natural genesis necessarily include at least one pair of contraries (188a26–30). This was rightly accepted in one way or another, by all the predecessors mentioned, though they had no reasoned explanation for it (*kaiper aneu logou tithentes*, 188b28–29). It was as though they were 'compelled by the truth itself' (188b29–30). As a result, all of their theories, in spite of superficial differences, show significant structural analogies with one another, and with the truth (188b35–189a9). But the 'one underlying body' theorists are closer to the truth, since they provide the substrate as well; and, of those, those in whose theories this underlying body is seen as, in itself, not determined by any of the contraries. So the essential truth seems to have been foreshadowed by an 'ancient opinion' (189a34–b16).

3. The discussion in *Physics* I 4–6 is an insightful and sympathetic attempt to reconstruct the ways of thinking of Aristotle's predecessors. Naturally, it is condescending; Aristotle is conscious of being much better equipped than those predecessors were to navigate the logical and philosophical mazes that troubled them.

It might also be claimed that it is anti-historical. Certainly, Aristotle imposes upon the theories discussed a schematism determined by his own thinking on the questions at issue. (There is no question of subterfuge here: he does not claim or pretend that he is doing otherwise.) For him, the real significance of the apparently universal use of opposites as principles lies in the tripartite schema: substrate-privation-form; and the significance of the tripartite schema derives, not from its use by any theorist, but from its success in giving a coherent account of what is common to all cases of 'becoming', as shown in I 7. Since the phenomena of 'becoming' (including every kind of natural alteration of existing states) are accessible to all, Aristotle expects the earlier theorists, if not consciously and explicitly, at least by following the grain of the material, to have been led towards theories that exhibit just that schema. He therefore reads earlier theories as necessarily tending towards this structure. To read them in this light is, for him, the way to understand, better than the theorists themselves, what they were about. Its success in illuminating the historical development is a secondary proof of his principal thesis.

This is one among many indications that Aristotle never makes or wishes to make a clean separation of 'the history' from 'the science' or 'the philosophy'. It is probable that on the contrary he would have rejected any such attempted separation as both impossible and undesirable. For it is clear that he holds that the history of the science in question, read aright, must broadly support, in the way indicated, the conclusions of the science, assuming these are correct. There is a 'teleology of truth' at work, as he sometimes insists; theorists are guided or impelled towards the correct view by 'the thing itself' or 'the truth itself' (*auto to pragma, autê hê alêtheia*). Correspondingly, where any particularly striking errors occur, some special explanation of that should be available; and to understand and demonstrate why earlier theorists went wrong requires an understanding of their place in the historical development.[14]

4. Aristotle's reading of the predecessors in *Physics* I 4–6 sees their theories as exhibiting significant analogies, or (in modern terms) sharing a common structure. It is the shared structure that is the really valuable part, which is restated in Aristotle's own terms as the essential truth about the principles of natural change. Then, in *Physics* I 7, it is deduced by a *logos*, consisting of a logical analysis of change in general, plus an inductive survey of the kinds of substrate observable in various particular cases.

This progression, from particular kinds of body (as in earlier theories) to an abstractly specified 'substrate', is for Aristotle a decisive advance in understanding, and only achievable by the general logical analysis such as earlier theorists could not give. Guided by some inarticulate awareness, rather than by *logos*,—and, it seems, looking only for principles of the generation of the cosmos rather than for principles of natural change in general,—they grasped only particular instances of the underlying structure, and hence could give no general account of it, and no rational justification for their use of it.[15] In addition, as *Physics* I 8–9 explains, they were left without satisfactory defence against the logical problems raised by *genesis* and change generally; which led some of them into further errors.

D. The Misunderstanding of Nature: (1) False Explanations (*Physics* II 8–9)

1. The second book of the *Physics* is equally central to Aristotle's understanding of earlier natural science. Here, with the initial official definition of 'nature' finally given, and the distinction between 'nature as matter' and 'nature as form' (II 1–2), the focus of interest shifts from 'principles' to 'causes' in natural science. Having set out his list of four types of 'cause' (II 3 and II 7), Aristotle turns to the connected questions of 'luck and chance' (II 4–6) and 'necessity' (II 8–9).

In the discussion of luck and chance, for the first time in the *Physics*, Aristotle confronts his predecessors with a demand, not just for 'principles' of the genesis of the observed cosmos, but for 'causes', that is, for things that may be invoked to furnish some sort of explanation of it. We learn that while the earlier theorists never invoked chance in their explanations of genesis, and apparently thought that nothing occurred by chance (II 4 195b36–196a24), some other, presumably later, theorists attributed to chance the genesis of the cosmos (II 4 196a24-b5).[16]

2. Even more instructive is *Physics* II 8–9. The programme for these chapters reads thus: 'We must say first why nature is among the causes for the sake of something; then we must speak about the necessary, for it is to that cause that everyone reduces [their explanations]: for example, since the hot is of such a nature and the cold and each of such things, these particular things necessarily are and come about. And, even if they do speak of some other cause, they merely touch on it and then let it drop: one [speaks] of Love and Strife, another of Mind [in this way]' (198b10–16). This marks a decisive break in the treatment of the predecessors within the *Physics*. No longer do they appear, as in *Physics* 1, as worthy forerunners in natural science, whose understandable errors are outweighed by their insights and the value of their example. Here one and all, without exception, are judged to have gone down a hopelessly wrong road. For, as Aristotle proceeds to argue, it is radically mistaken to try to explain natural things and changes (even partially) by 'the necessary', in the sense in which these predecessors did.[17]

The primary aim of *Physics* II 8 is to show that 'nature is among the causes that are for the sake of something': that whenever something happens or comes to be 'by nature', or through or because of the nature of something, a 'final cause' (a cause 'as the end') is always present. The natural scientist, therefore, has always to invoke final causes along with the other kinds.

3. Once the need for final cause explanations has been established, it follows that the earlier natural scientists made a fundamental error: not only was this need not seen by any of them; Aristotle claims that without exception they all in effect denied it, by their invocation of 'the necessary' as a supposed kind of explanation. We are given in II 8 the example of Empedocles, distinguished among the earlier thinkers for the quantity and breadth of his biological theorizing; according to Aristotle, even he misconceived the *modus operandi* of nature, as revealed in natural changes. Nature was envisaged by Empedocles, not as a cunning craftsman, but as a piece of mere machinery operating simply 'from necessity'.

For Aristotle, the false kind of explanation that he labels 'the (absolutely) necessary' (*to haplôs anagkaion*) has two fatal defects. One is simply that it is false. There is a room for necessity of a kind in nature, but not for 'the absolutely necessary' as conceived of by the earlier theorists. Another, as *Physics* II 8–9 shows, is that, if used, it leaves no room for a final cause. For both reasons, it is evidently not to be identified with, or subsumed under, any of Aristotle's other kinds of cause. (The question of how he thought his predecessors combined it with, or substituted it for, those other kinds of explanation, will return when we consider *Metaphysics* I.) It is clear that 'absolute necessity' here is meant to be understood as a blind necessity, one having no inherent reference to any intelligible goal or aim. This gives the required contrast with the 'conditional necessity' of *Physics* II 9, which we may understand as being equally necessitating, *when* it operates in nature; the crucial difference is that it operates only as and when it can serve as an instrument in the service of the final cause.[18]

4. To understand what happens in *Physics* II 8, we must briefly go back to the account of the meanings of 'nature' in *Physics* II 1, which may be taken as established doctrine by the time we reach *Physics* II 8–9.

The 'nature' of a thing is defined as 'a principle of change and of rest', and the question is then: is the nature of a thing to be identified with its matter or its form? At this point the four causes have not yet been officially introduced; but Aristotle evidently takes the matter-form dichotomy to be already intelligible, just as in *Physics* I he takes the notion of 'nature' itself to be, and presumably for much the same reasons (see B 1 above). As between 'nature as matter' and 'nature as form', Aristotle opts for an inclusive answer: nature is both matter and form; but its 'nature as form', he argues, is more truly the nature of any natural thing. So a natural change is one that originates in the nature of an individual natural substance; and rather in the 'nature as form' than in the 'nature as matter'. We are already on notice that to ignore the 'form'-aspect of the natural world is to leave out something essential. Aristotle does not stop to underline the point, but notes in passing a serious failure here on the part of earlier theorists: they were apparently almost completely unaware of 'nature as form' in their natural science.[19] This prepares us for the related but additional errors unfolded in *Physics* II 8.

5. If, as *Physics* II 1 implies, we must always explain natural changes only by reference to the natures of things, then it follows that they must not be ascribed to 'the necessary', if 'necessity' acting on anything is conceived of as something that is superimposed *from outside* upon the thing's own nature. If necessity pushes the thing along the path it would naturally take anyway, then necessity is explanatorily redundant; if it pushes it along a different path, then the ensuing change is by definition not natural; but it is only natural changes that are here to be explained. So, at the beginning of *Physics* II 8, we already know that any kind of absolute necessity imposed on natural things from outside must be rejected in explaining natural changes, unless some further sufficient reason can be invoked for bringing it in.[20] Moreover, it is taken as a fact of common observation (199a20–29) that most if not all natural changes are goal-directed: appeal being made here to biology above all. (The account of 'nature as form' in *Physics* II 1, even in advance of the introduction of the final cause, includes a reference to the goal-directedness, 'the for-the-sake-of-which' of the things which have natures (194a28–36).) There is then the question: what sort of explanation is possible for this prevalent goal-directedness, and for the almost invariable success with which the goals are reached?

Aristotle's answer has two claims; they are presented together. First, the only adequate kind of explanation is one that is itself irreducibly in terms of the goal itself. Secondly, such an explanation must be anchored in the natures of those natural things for which the goal is a goal. In short, the natures of things must themselves be intrinsically and irreducibly goal-directed.[21] To support these claims,

Aristotle sketches an argument in two parts (or possibly two separate but parallel arguments; 198b34–199a8, 199a8–12), against his predecessors' alleged view. Their kind of explanation, he claims, would involve coincidences on a fantastic scale: the 'necessity' they postulated is blind to its own end-results, so that it would have to be just by chance, repeated over and over again, that it happened to push things in the right direction and not in a quite different one. So we need something that is guaranteed always to *direct* the course of events towards the goal; and that something must be located in the natures of the things themselves, since these types of events are by hypothesis natural.

6. Much effort has been made to uncover the presuppositions that may underlie each step of this two-step reasoning; for, taken on its own, it seems to be open to certain rather obvious objections. We are not here directly concerned with filling in the gaps in Aristotle's train of reasoning, but we must spell out what exactly he is attributing to his predecessors. (1) They invoked a 'necessity' that (a) arose simply from the basic material constitutions or circumstances of the things involved ('since the hot is of such a kind, and the cold, and all of those kind of things, such-and-such things necessarily are and come to be', 198b12–14), and that (b) operated automatically in the given circumstances, independently of anything else, and in particular not as the instrument of any 'higher' directive force. Only the conjunction of (a) and (b) guarantees that this necessity will be blind to its supposed end-results. (2) This type of necessity was essentially the only or the dominant type of explanation in their theories. (3) Consequently, they had no room at all for explanations making essential reference to the 'end', for teleology.

There is some reason to doubt whether this can be correct as an interpretation of the earlier theorists; for there is some evidence that, for some of them at least, natural events were guided from outside what Aristotle regards as the realm of nature. This question must be held in suspense for the present.

E. The Misunderstanding of Nature: (2) The Infinitely Extended Universe (*Physics* III 4–5 and *De Caelo* I 5–9)

1. *Physics* II shows that for Aristotle earlier natural science had failed almost completely to arrive at in practice, let alone formulate theoretically, a correct notion of explanation by causes 'for the sake of which'. An associated, and worse, failure was that it had espoused a false kind of 'cause', one that excluded the possibility of explanations by true final causes. *Physics* III, in its discussion of the infinite, reveals an equally serious error, and one that, equally, presupposes a

misunderstanding of what nature and natural science have to be like. Aristotle gives no detailed doxography here, since according to him most of his predecessors made exactly the same mistake: they took it that their original principle or principles, in so far as they were bodies, were also infinitely extended (*Phys.* III 4 cf. *DC.* I 5 271b2–3).[22] In *De Caelo* I 5, he underlines in unusually strong terms the seriousness of the error, and the crucial importance of getting the right answer: 'whether the matter is thus or otherwise makes no small difference, but is wholly and totally decisive for scientific truth. In fact, it is pretty much the case that this has been, and may in future be, the origin of all disagreements among those who give their views on nature as a whole. After all, even a small departure from truth, when one sets out, results in thousandfold greater error when one is further away' (271b4–9).

2. The arguments against this second great error (*Phys.* III 5 204b1–206a8) are divided into those that occur when we inquire *logikôs* ('with regard to definitions/ accounts' or 'with regard to words') and when we inquire *phusikôs* ('with regard to nature').[23]

The *logikôs* argument (204b4–10) is simply that the notion of 'body' cannot be defined without reference to a boundary or surface, which an infinite body would lack. The *phusikôs* arguments (204b10–206a8) are essentially confined to two points. It is taken as a given in the conception of nature that it must include the observed regularities of our cosmos. Two of these that Aristotle takes to be unquestionable and structurally fundamental are the perpetual transmutation of 'elemental' bodies among themselves, and the existence of particular regions of cosmos ('natural places') that are the places naturally occupied by the different kinds of body. These, he claims, are incompatible with an infinite extent of any one kind of body, or even with an infinite extent of many kinds.

Given the crucial importance of what is at stake, it is natural to be puzzled and disappointed by this chapter at a first reading. Aristotle does not seem to have met the requirement of answering the obvious possible objections on behalf of some of his predecessors. In particular it is reasonable to think that he has not produced anything that would count as an answer to the Atomists. Their vision of an infinite void populated by infinitely many atoms, and interspersed with *kosmoi* like our own, required that 'nature' in its essentials was exhibited *outside* the *kosmoi*, not inside; the working of nature *inside* any cosmos was for them necessarily a special case. Hence, the Atomists could have insisted, it is a begging of the question to assume from the outset that we should take our cosmos as exhibiting to observation, straightforwardly, the fundamentals of nature.

3. Aristotle does not meet such objections in the *Physics*. Later, as though to stifle any doubts, he returns to the question at greater length in *De Caelo* I 5–9. Here, with even less in the way of doxography, there is fuller and more systematic argumentation, explicitly presented (274a19–24) as supplementary to the *Physics*. Some of these arguments seem intended to be immune even to possible Atomist objections of the kind just suggested. This confirms other signs that Aristotle in his later

writings had a keener appreciation of the strength and robustness of the Atomist theory.[24]

F. The Misunderstanding of Nature: (3) Two Questions and a Hypothesis

1. In *Physics* II and III, Aristotle represents most if not all of his predecessors as disastrously misunderstanding, in more than one way, the nature underlying the natural world. Here, then, Aristotle's own natural science parts company, clearly and irrevocably, with the earlier Ionian tradition. The questions at issue are therefore just as central to the understanding of Aristotle's own natural science as they are to his account of his predecessors.

As noted, the arguments of *Physics* III, taken on their own, look simply inadequate as a critique of the thesis of an infinite body. Setting aside the presumably later arguments of *De Caelo* I (in any case *De Caelo* represents a more advanced level of study), we must ask whether, in the first three books of the *Physics*, Aristotle is not taking far too much for granted. In order to demolish other theorists' conception of what is natural, he has assumed the truth of substantial parts of his own conception. That is all very well for a teacher teaching dogmatically and explicitly from within his own already established system. But what reasons have we been given, in the apparently open inquiry instituted by the *Physics*, for accepting that natural places and elemental interchange must be universal phenomena, rather than just local features of this cosmos or of cosmoi in general?

The parallel problem which was earlier left in suspense must now be raised again: that of the alleged failure of the predecessors to use final causes. Why should final causes, even if one accepts the arguments of *Physics* II 8 that they are *ultimately* determinative, necessarily be operative in a way detectable within the observable cosmos? There is evidence, even in the *Physics* itself, that many of these predecessors attributed purposeful intelligence to the infinitely extended bodies that they took as their 'principles'. He tells us, though only in passing, that they thought that these infinite bodies 'encompass everything and govern everything (*panta kubernan*), as say all those who do not make other principles beside the infinite, such as Mind or Love; and that, they say, is the divine; for (as Anaximander and most of the natural philosophers say) it is deathless and imperishable' (*Phys.* III 4 203b11–15). As for Anaxagoras, he is elsewhere praised for introducing Mind even into the *natural* world: 'he who said that Mind is present in nature, as it is in animals, as the cause of the cosmos and of all order, was like a sober man in comparison with those before him, with their random talk' (*Met.* I 4 994b10–13).

But if that is so, then must not Aristotle be wrong about their overall explanations? Perhaps 'the necessary' was not intended to be an explanation on its own,
but merely represents the ineluctable expression, within our cosmos, of a guiding
intention imposed from outside, so that a kind of final cause was after all rein-
stated? (After all *Metaphysics* I, at 993a13–15 and elsewhere, recognizes that some
of the predecessors did in some sense use the notion of a 'cause for the sake of
which'.) If so, then any particular cosmos will offer to observation only a restricted
cross-section of 'nature', and is not after all to be taken as a pattern for the whole
universe, if that is infinite in extent. Our two questions, and their corresponding
doubts about Aristotle, here merge into one.

2. We are thus naturally led to question both the fairness (even on Aristotle's own
terms) of Aristotle's criticisms, and the accuracy of his reporting. No progress is
possible in understanding, unless the reality of the problem, and its fundamental
significance, is fully recognized and acknowledged.

The next step is to formulate and test some general hypothesis that offers some
kind of explanation. The explanation both of Aristotle's apparently unfair criticisms, and of his extensive and (to us) misleading silences, must first be looked for
in Aristotle's own conception of natural science.

In Aristotle's conception of natural science, one point that is both clearly fundamental and possibly relevant is that natural science is, as a science, wholly autonomous.[25] It has its own principles, which are to be discovered, independently of any
metaphysics, from ordinary unspecialized experience of the natural world, and
inductions from that; hence, necessarily from this cosmos alone, since that is the
only one of which we have direct knowledge. That does not preclude the existence
of a realm of nature outside the cosmos too, provided that *within* the cosmos there
is sufficient evidence for such a thing. Unless and until such evidence appears,
though, natural science is bound to try to explain everything in this cosmos in
terms of this cosmos alone.

3. All this suggests a preliminary hypothesis about how Aristotle's reporting and
criticism of his predecessors in the *Physics*, and other works on natural science,
may be made intelligible, as follows.

First, any mistakes that affect the very foundations of natural science, such as
the theory of the infinite universe, must of course be reported and intensively criticized; for it is absolutely necessary to establish that the universe is finite. Likewise
with the systematic use of false kinds of explanations, such as 'the necessary'. But
the argumentation on these points is entitled to assume as indisputable the uniformity and autonomy of the realm of nature. For that is essential to the possibility
of an autonomous natural science. And that means that what we observe to be
part of nature's workings in *this* cosmos (such as natural movements and elemental
changes) must obtain *everywhere*, even if the universe is supposed infinite.

Next, this uniformity and autonomy of the natural realm (once the foundations of natural science are securely in place) serve as unspoken reasons for
rejecting, without even reporting them, all mistaken views which are based on a

misunderstanding of the notion of nature. So everything in the earlier theories that depends on the supposition of an infinite extra-cosmic realm, in which nature if it exists at all is radically different, and which supposedly determines the workings of nature in this cosmos (such as supposed divine beings and their purposeful 'steering') not merely may, but perhaps should, be ignored in reporting those theories: for motives of charity, if not simply for economy of effort. And such criticisms as are made of earlier theories, in so far as they deal with this cosmos, may reasonably ignore any appeal that their authors might have made to anything supposedly outside this cosmos: for example, to some sort of divine purposefulness, as a kind of 'final cause', if 'the divine' was taken to be something pre-cosmic and/or extra-cosmic.[26]

G. The Misunderstanding of Nature:
(4) Further Examples from the *Physics*

1. The hypothesis put forward in the previous section may be compared with several further places in the *Physics*, in which there are fundamental criticisms of some of the earlier theorists, and these make explicit appeal to what Aristotle takes to be fundamental features of nature. Here it is particularly the later natural philosophers that are in his sights.

2. At *Physics* VIII 1–2, the question at issue is: 'has there always been, and will there always be, change?' With most of his predecessors, including for once the Atomists, Aristotle here has no quarrel on this point; since most agreed, for their own reasons (250b15–21), that there always had been and always would be change. (Where he deeply disagrees with them is on the question of *why* there is always change, a question here touched on only briefly.) Aristotle's targets here are only and specifically Empedocles and Anaxagoras, whose theories (respectively, of alternating periods of change and rest, and of an infinite period of rest followed by an infinite period of change) are reported at 250b23–251a5, and attacked at 252a3–32. Against Anaxagoras first, Aristotle puts the fundamental demand that nature should not be 'disorderly' (*ataktos*). Part of what this implies then emerges. First, an 'order' (*taxis*) consists in a 'ratio' or 'rational account' (*logos*), but there can be no ratio (or 'rational relation') between two infinites. Next, there should be some stated difference, sufficient to explain why the period of change begins just when it does (but none such, it is implied, is or could be given). In sum, Nature is either always simply uniform in its operation, or if not at least there is a *logos* to make comprehensible its non-simplicity. Empedocles at least provides an order in making alternating finite and equal periods of change and rest; but he fails to explain why his active cosmic

forces, Love and Strife, should behave so as to produce them. What is required is an explanation grounded in induction from experience or in deductive reasoning from necessary truths.

More generally (252a32–b5), it is never good enough, where an explanation or a principle is needed, merely to say that 'something always is or comes to be so'. This structural demand on explanations in natural science is directed particularly against a certain principle of the Atomists (see on *Metaphysics* I 4 985b19–20 in Section H.8 below).

3. At *Physics* I 4 187a26–188a18, Aristotle digresses from his survey of earlier views on 'the principles' to examine more closely, and to give reasons for reject-ing, Anaxagoras' theory of the infinitely many ultimate material constituents here and elsewhere labelled 'homoeomeries'. He uses a variety of arguments; suitably to the position of this critique, early on in the *Physics*, he does not appeal to devel-oped Aristotelian natural science. This reveals all the more clearly what he sees as two absolutely fundamental features of the natural world, to be postulated even in advance of scientific knowledge. In advance of the examination of the infinite in *Physics* III, he here argues (187b7–13) that infinite totalities of any kind are at the least undesirable, because they are unknowable. The assumption is that the natu-ral world must be in all essentials knowable, with the implication that an infinite universe is excluded. Further, he claims (187b13–21), as something equally beyond doubt, that animals and plants, and hence their components, have fixed sizes, from which they cannot much diverge either by being smaller or larger. That every kind of natural substance has its naturally determined size, within a cosmos of fixed size, is characteristic of Aristotelian thinking; here it is taken by Aristotle as axi-omatic even before the relevant science has been constructed.

4. At least three other parts of the *Physics* contain argumentation on fundamental matters, directed against theses characteristic of the Atomists, though they are not named. Much of *Physics* VI, notably, is devoted to the assertion and exploration of the infinite divisibility and the continuity of natural magnitudes, natural changes, and the time-stretches in which they occur. (A recognition of the importance of their counter-arguments is found in *Gen. et Corr.* I 2.) Likewise at *Physics* VIII 256a4–257a27, on the structure of 'chains of changes': Aristotle's thesis, that these cannot extend backwards without ending, is directly opposed to the Atomist con-ception, according to which all such chains were indeed infinite in the sense of having no beginning.

Most instructive of all is *Physics* IV 8 214b12–216a26, an extended critique of a theory of void (the Atomists must be the prime target). To the first part of this (214b13–28), as to the attack on the infinite universe in *Physics* III, a natural first reaction is that it is hopelessly unfair to the Atomists. For it appeals to theses that would never have been accepted by them: that everywhere in the universe, all nat-ural bodies will have natural motions, and that consequently there will be 'up' and 'down' directions uniquely defined by the natural motions of simple bodies. There follows a second part (214b28–216a21), which, like the *De Caelo* I arguments against infinite bodies, appeal not to general requirements about nature, but rather to supposed truths of observation, and to supposed absurdities in the mathematical understanding of motion, when a void is postulated. There are also general arguments in *De Caelo* III 2, appealing only to a division of motion and rest into 'natural' and 'forced', for the thesis that all the simple bodies must have some natural motion. These are used to construct (300b8–16, 300b31–301a11) challenges to the Atomists. Here again it seems that these are reinforcements added when Aristotle came to take the Atomist challenge more seriously. In any case, the first part of *Physics* IV 8 follows the pattern that has already been seen: it assumes that nature's ways are confined to what we can observe within this cosmos. To postulate, without a proven necessity, exotic regions where things behave radically otherwise than in our cosmos, is bad method.

H. The Development of Scientific Explanation: *Metaphysics* I on Earlier Uses of 'Causes'

1. So far we have seen how Aristotle's setting-up of his natural science in the *Physics* is shaped by certain assumptions, not all made explicitly, about the realm of nature as we observe it within our cosmos, and about how one should proceed to make it a subject of science. These assumptions determine his selective reporting of his predecessor's theories, and underlie his critique of them. On this reading, it is not necessary to resort, as has sometimes been done, to hypotheses of negligent misunderstanding, failure of historical sense, or wilful dishonesty on Aristotle's part. Such hypotheses, difficult to establish directly and in themselves implausible, should in any case be entertained only as a last resort.[27]

2. The failure, as Aristotle sees it, of the early scientists to interpret nature overall in the right way does not mean that he thinks it acceptable to reject their opinions en bloc. Any opinion of any acknowledged expert on a given topic has the right to be considered, whatever view is taken about that expert's overall theory. Nor is it helpful to the cause of instructing and persuading, if one leaves well-known contrary opinions unmentioned and unrefuted. Consequently, in other works on natural science, as well as in the *Physics*, there is a further significant amount of reportage and critique of earlier opinions that is integrated with Aristotle's substantive treatments. Outstanding in respect of their bulk, strategic importance, and difficulty are (a) the long survey of earlier theories of the soul, in *De Anima* I 2–5 403b25–411b30, as a preliminary to Aristotle's own theorising; and (b) the series of reports, scattered around in various places in *Physics*, *De Caelo*, and *Generation*

and Corruption, on the earlier theories about the existence and nature of 'substantial change' (*genesis* and *phthora,* 'coming-to-be' and 'ceasing-to-be'); and, related to that, the nature of the elements, and the question of whether or not the elements change into one another.[28]

3. *Metaphysics* I is different again. It is the introduction to a work which discusses problems relating to all possible sciences, on the way to establishing a demarcation of them and establishing the foundations of 'first philosophy'. The general doctrine of the 'causes', taken to be applicable in any possible science, is assumed, at least provisionally; but, apparently, nothing else from the *Physics,* or from Aristotelian natural science. Chapters 3 to 7 report, in approximately chronological order, on the use of 'causes' by all earlier theorists, down to and including Plato; chapters 8 and 9 contain Aristotle's criticisms.

Aristotle states and refutes at some length the ontological innovations of the Pythagoreans and Plato, which make the most formidable challenges to his own ontology. The many 'natural philosophers' are given proportionately less space in the critical chapters; yet they too are included, and in the expository section they figure at great length. As in *Physics* I, it is underlined that they had a very general ambition (to discover the truth about things that are), which was first manifested in inquiries about 'the most obvious of the strange phenomena' (*ta prokheira tôn atopôn,* 982b13–14) and then systematically pursued in the study of natural science. At 982b11–17, a reconstruction of the mental situation of the earliest natural philosophers points, as in the *Physics,* to the inquiry into the genesis of the cosmos as the starting-point of their science.

The professed aim of the survey is to take predecessors for consultation as colleagues, not for refutation as opponents. 'Though we have given a sufficient account [of the four causes] in the *Physics,* nevertheless let us consult in addition [the earlier theorists].... For it is clear that they too speak of 'principles' and 'causes' of some sort. So for us, to make a survey [of them] will be a contribution to our present inquiry: either we shall find some other kind of cause or we shall be more confident in the ones we have just mentioned' (983a33-b6). The four causes, it is clear, are to be the foundation; what the survey aims to achieve is greater confidence, not in the correctness but in the completeness of the list of four. Aristotle examines the ways in which, and the extent to which, each of these came to be recognized. This necessarily involves some departure from strict chronological order, but what Aristotle sees as the determining thoughts of earlier theorising are revealed and to some extent explained. As in *Physics* I, the approach is historically informed and perceptive; and mostly sympathetic to the ambitions, at least, if not the achievements, of all earlier theorists (except possibly the Atomists). It concentrates on the steps by which the predecessors could be seen to have approached the *correct* understanding of the nature and use of 'the causes'. The overall impression given is that, while all earlier theorizing was a mixture of success and failure, there was a slow but persistent and roughly cumulative process, in which errors were one by one removed and perceptions of the truth preserved and refined.

4. Aristotle seems to be concerned with two kinds of question, though he does not distinguish them: what sorts of explanations his predecessors gave; and how far they recognized these explanations as falling into functionally distinct types, such as the 'four causes' (and, with that, how far they rightly envisaged the functions of such types in natural science).

At the lower level, it seems that all Aristotle requires, for the recognition of something as a 'cause' by one of his predecessors, is that it should be something that is essential to, or the ultimate term in, some explanation, the scientific answer to some question beginning with 'why'. Aristotle sometimes ascribes to his predecessors recognition of something as 'a cause', without any suggestion that it was recognized by them as belonging to any particular type. Thus in *Metaphysics* I 2 he notes that '(a) god is thought by everyone to be among the causes' (983a8–9). To recognize something as 'a cause', then, is not yet to recognize it as being a cause of a certain type, or as being a cause in the kind of way in which it really is a cause.

So the survey is, primarily, a survey of the predominant explanatory devices of the earliest theorists. And yet explanation by invocation of 'the necessary' is not once mentioned. That was, as has been seen, the earlier type of explanation which Aristotle in *Physics* II rejected as radically unsatisfactory. In *Metaphysics* I, it must be that it is taken as established that the use of 'the necessary' as a kind of cause was a grave error. Otherwise, it would be inexplicable why there is no mention of it. There can be no question of its being a candidate for recognition as a new type of cause, nor even as a variant of one of the four Aristotelian types. The survey, then, is tailored to its purpose: it does not aim at historical completeness for its own sake, but selects its material, just as the *Physics* does, in the light of that purpose.

Correspondingly, in the relatively short section of criticism (I 8), Aristotle's complaint against the earlier natural scientists (the Pythagoreans and Plato's *Timaeus* excepted) is not that their explanations were wrong, so far as they went, or misconceived as explanations; but that they left prominent phenomena totally unexplained: notably, the origin of change generally, and the coming-into-being and perishing of material bodies.

5. The second level of the story, corresponding to the second kind of question distinguished earlier, is the slowly increasing awareness of the four 'causes' as types of explanation, and of the theoretical need for them and of their theoretical implications in turn. In one case, at least, the earlier theorists went all or most of the way. *Metaphysics* I shows them as successful in recognizing the need for causes of the 'material' kind; it further implies that they had a clear conception of this type of explanation as such, and of its implications and systematic function. What exactly this entailed, in terms of their theories, is explained at 983b6–18. The function of this type of cause was to provide the materials out of which everything else could be constructed. These materials, though, were quite capable of existing in a separated state on their own, before and after being incorporated into something more complex.

Caveats are needed here. There is no implication that what they took to be the 'cause as matter' was something held by the early theorists to be purely passive, or even lifeless. Apart from the evidence of other sources, *Physics* III 4 and *De Anima* I 2 show that in fact the material cause, for many of these theorists, was something endowed with life, perception, intelligence, and intelligent action. Nor, in ascribing to earlier theorists a certain view as to the 'material cause(s)' of things, is Aristotle necessarily suggesting that they held any kind of reductionist view, in which everything was to be explained in terms of the material constitution of things.

6. The discovery of the need for the 'cause as matter', and the clarification of its nature and implications, is for Aristotle the one great and unambiguous success of the early natural scientists in this field.[29] As to the other three causes, the story is far less impressive. In brief, though the need for them was increasingly felt, if not formulated, by the theorists, yet neither the 'formal' nor the 'final' cause were recognized as such by any predecessor. We are told often enough about the failure in regard to the 'formal' cause, and the few partial and ineffective approaches to it;[30] it is presumably also related to the failure 'through lack of experience' to perceive the abstract analysis of change given in *Physics* I (191a23–31, 191b30–34). The failure in regard to the final cause comes as no surprise after *Physics* II 8.[31] In *Metaphysics* I, the situation is put thus: 'as for that for the sake of which actions and alterations and changes occur, this they do, in a way, state as a cause, but not in *that* way [i.e., not as *that* kind of cause], and not as it is a cause in nature' (988b6–8). Aristotle's examples of this failure among earlier natural scientists are Anaxagoras and Empedocles: they obviously intend Mind and Love, respectively, to be 'a good thing', but instead of explaining other things as being or coming into being *for the sake of* Mind or Love, they make Mind or Love the *motors* of the changes involved. *Physics* II 8 has told us that the changes themselves then come about by 'the necessary'; we now see, conversely, that it was the failure to reach true final causes that made 'the necessary' necessary for these theorists.

The need for something like the moving cause was more immediately recognizable, and therefore influenced theorizing from early on. Even here, the candidates put forward to fulfil the function of a moving cause were at first doubling as material causes, and later were loaded with the burden of functioning as a substitute for the final cause as well. The theoretical implications of the notion were simply not grasped. 'In one way all the causes were earlier spoken of', remarks Aristotle retrospectively, 'but in another way not at all'; they were at best seen 'dimly', or 'glimpsed' (*Met.* I 10 993a11–15).

7. At this point a further instructive problem arises out of the comparison of *Metaphysics* I with *Physics* II.

In *Physics* II 8, part of the complaint against all of the predecessors is that 'the necessary' is practically the *only* kind of cause they use to explain things; just one or two of them 'touch on' some other kind of cause such as Love and Strife (Empedocles) or Mind (Anaxagoras). How is this to be reconciled with the elaborate parade of evidence in *Metaphysics* I 3 for the earlier use of a true material cause? It might seem at first that either Aristotle takes two substantially different views of the interpretation of earlier natural science in the two books, or there is an implied identification of 'the necessary' with the material cause. Yet neither of these propositions is attractive. The hypothesis of a change of opinion, though it can hardly be completely excluded, is a last resort, and would need to be buttressed by evidence for other systematically related changes in Aristotle's views or interpretations. Nor can the material cause, being a type of explanation approved by Aristotle himself, be identical with 'the necessary', one he flatly rejects.

Part of the solution to this apparent discord must clearly be that the mistaken use of 'the necessary' to give the *ultimate* explanations of natural changes ('it is to this cause that they all reduce [their explanations]', *Phys.* II 8 198b12) need not exclude the correct recognition of Aristotelian kinds of cause in a subsidiary role. But this point is not made clearly anywhere; and this because it is in different ways irrelevant to the different purposes of *Metaphysics* I and *Physics* II 8, which determine the difference of their approach and selection of material. *Physics* II 8 is expressly polemical, intent on demolishing a position that is hostile to an essential ingredient of Aristotle's own philosophy. *Metaphysics* I, on the contrary, is as inclusive and charitable as possible in its approach to the predecessors. It makes no mention of 'the necessary', nor gives any example of the kind of explanation that Aristotle rejects in *Physics* II 8. Its use by his predecessors was a terrible mistake, which in *Metaphysics* I is charitably not mentioned, and in fact strictly does not need to be mentioned, under the terms of the inquiry as set out in *Metaphysics* I 3.

8. We have given most space to the earlier books of the *Physics*, whose importance, relative to *Metaphysics* I, for the understanding of Aristotle's treatment of his predecessors has often been underestimated. We cannot enter into much further detail on the story told in *Metaphysics* I, but there is one more point of some importance.

In the gradual discovery of the moving cause, the first question to exert theoretical pressure on the early natural scientists was: what is it that causes the material cause to change (984a18–27)? Aristotle finds the early response inadequate. As in *Physics* II 8, he brings out what he sees as a grave failure of the earlier theorists, and of the Atomists too: either they did not try to meet the need at all, or if they did, they did so in an inadequate way, by identifying the 'moving cause' with one of their material causes.[32] Once again, we have to ask whether Aristotle's reports and adverse judgements are correct and fair; once again, to answer justly we have to take into account Aristotle's unspoken assumptions.

The worst failure, allegedly, was that some theorists took no notice of the problem at all: 'those who were right at the beginning in this inquiry, and said that there was one substrate, did not trouble themselves [about the question]' (*ouden eduskheranan heautois*: 984a27–29); so too the early Atomists (985b19–20): 'but as for change, from where and how it can come to occur to things, they too, similarly to the others, lazily dropped [the question]' (*rhaithumôs apheisan*).

These remarks must not be taken at face value. We cannot suppose that the earliest theorists offered no sort of explanation at all (other than one in material-cause terms) for the changes that constituted the genesis and the regular running of the cosmos. In fact, we know better, since the sort of explanation they had to offer may be gathered from other evidence, including that of Aristotle himself. It was, no doubt, a vague one, in general terms, which invoked the general planning and 'steering' activity of the extra-cosmic infinite. We can, by now, understand why he does not report that here: that kind of 'cause', as already explained, simply did not count for Aristotle as part of legitimate natural science. What he is looking for here is causes active wholly *within* the cosmos, indeed within 'nature' (in the sense of the realm of natural things and processes *in* the cosmos) and forming part of that nature.

It may be objected that, even so, his charge of laziness against his predecessors is unjustified. Yet he clearly holds that further and better reflection would have pushed them along the right path; the evidence of that is that their immediate successors moved in the right direction (984a18–27, 984b8–15).

With the Atomists, the complaint is similar, but the case is significantly different. Democritus at least had a systematic treatment of motion, a key part of which was a 'principle of inertia': an atom keeps moving at the same speed in the same straight line direction, unless and until it strikes another atom. This was but a special case of a more general 'principal of causal inertia': whatever had always been so, always would be so (in the absence of interference from outside), and did not admit further explanation. Aristotle elsewhere protests against the use of such a principle; here again, he sees its use as evidence of a misunderstanding of what a science of nature requires. Yet the deliberate and systematic use of such a principle, even if mistaken, is not exactly evidence of 'laziness'. Here, if anywhere, Aristotle goes beyond the bounds of legitimate criticism.[33] It is one indication among others that, in the period when *Physics* I–III and *Metaphysics* I were written, Aristotle underrated the early Atomists. They appear as marginal figures, not mentioned in their due place in *Metaphysics* I; though an account of their views does appear, at 985b4–20, it is not well-placed, nor is it properly integrated with the rest of the story. It appears that they are seen as throwbacks to primitive material monism, who made the additional dire mistake of introducing a void; and that they are therefore considered as almost beneath criticism. By contrast, both in *De Caelo* and in *Generation and Corruption* I (2 316a14–317a17; 8 325b34–326b6) there are elaborate and respectful refutations of Atomist arguments and theses. It is, moreover, striking that Aristotle twice in *Generation and Corruption* I 2 (315a34-b1; 316a6–14) goes out of his way to give (contrary to his usual practice) outspoken tribute precisely to the professionalism and hard work of Democritus in the field of natural science. It is hard not to see this as a palinode.

I. Conclusion

1. The survey in *Metaphysics* I agrees in sum with the assessment implied by *Physics* I-III: the earlier natural scientists, after an impressive start, failed to grasp fully

the implications of their own enterprise. It was a failure to understand the presuppositions inherent in the notions of *science* and of *nature*. The consequent errors in their positive theorising are shown in the *Physics*. In *Metaphysics* I, the negative side is revealed: a fumbling approach to the moving cause, and no proper and systematic use of it; effectively no grasp at all of the formal and final causes and of their centrality in the natural world.

This looks like a paradox: how can these forerunners deserve the name of 'natural scientists' or 'naturalists' (*phusiologoi*) at all, if, as he puts it in one place, 'they have (so to speak) nothing to say about nature' (*PA* 642a16–18)? And why, on the other hand, if they have 'nothing to say about nature', does Aristotle frequently discuss their opinions, not just on the question of foundations and methods, but on substantive questions as well? One must not press an isolated comment too hard, especially one containing the escape-phrase 'so to speak'. But it is supported by the whole series of 'misunderstandings of nature' we have examined, and it sums up clearly the negative side in Aristotle's final judgement.

2. Aristotle's criticisms of his predecessors can all too easily leave the impression, even after several readings, that he holds them in some contempt. Two principal causes for this, one negative and one positive, are as follows. The negative one: in line with what seems to have been general practice in early Ionian scientific writings, Aristotle rarely if ever acknowledges expressly a particular intellectual debt to a predecessor.[34] That is not to say that he tries, or even wishes, to deny or conceal his indebtedness in general. In fact it is clear that he regards himself as the fortunate heir to all that is worthwhile in the heritage of earlier theorising. The positive reason is that in the discussions of predecessors Aristotle's primary aim is always to establish what he himself takes to be the truth. He criticizes his predecessors if he takes their views to be a serious obstacle to the grasping of the truth. He is then determined to show in what respects they were wrong, and to uncover if possible the reasons for their failure to reach what he takes to be the truth. The refutation must be the more thorough and convincing, the higher the standing of the opponent and the greater the initial attractions of his theory.

Further, in looking back at the earlier theorists Aristotle is also self-consciously looking down on them from what he believes to be a more advanced stage of theoretical activity. He sees his own theories, with their advantage of being later in the process of development, as more intellectually advanced in every way, as well as closer to the truth, than the earlier ones. Hence, in so far as he notices the existence of a tradition and of a developmental process within it, his comments underline both his acute sense of the history of the subject, and his belief in the natural superiority of later (especially his own) theorizing over earlier. Such observations are not acts of gratuitous insult or self-congratulation. (When Aristotle uses harsh terms about particular theorists, there is an implication that they were below the level of the best of their contemporaries.[35])

3. Aristotle is clear in general terms about what fuels the movement towards greater understanding: it is the natural 'desire to know' proclaimed in the first sentence of

the *Metaphysics*. What makes it possible for this desire to be fulfilled is the inherent knowability of the truth (since 'God is not jealous', *Met.* I 2 983a2–4). When the attention of those with sufficient leisure is concentrated strongly enough on the problems of science, progress will be made. The subject matter itself will often point inquirers in the right direction.[36]

Why then is progress often slow and difficult? Even given the required level of material wealth and leisure, there are natural retarding forces. There has to be progress, both in the individual and in the collective mind, from what is more well-known by ordinary experience, to what is more intrinsically knowable because it is in reality and theory more basic; this is a process of sorting out what is at first confused, of advancing from an approximate grasp of generalities to a precise grasp of details (*Phys.* I 1 184a16-b14). This progress inevitably takes time, since it calls for the making of distinctions and the development of techniques of argument and approach to a subject matter which is in obvious ways remote from ordinary life. Aristotle recognizes that earlier theorists were not at the same stage as himself, and that that fact is often part of the explanation of their errors.[37] Thus, the reason for their ignorance of the formal cause was that 'there was no such thing as the essence and the defining of the *ousia*' (*to ti ên einai kai to horisasthai tên ousian ouk ên*, 642a24–26). It was Socrates who, though interested not in natural science but in ethics, first saw the importance of proper definitions and first applied his mind to the question of what exactly was required for them. There had been attempts at definitions before, by the early Pythagoreans, but these are regarded by Aristotle as failures since they do not remotely meet the requirements worked out by Socrates, as enshrined in the early Platonic dialogues.[38]

Here Socrates appears as a kind of natural boundary-stone, marking the definitive end (in the logical, not necessarily the chronological, sense) of the early style of natural philosophy. The modern term 'pre-Socratic' has not been used in this chapter, and Aristotle himself used no such term. Yet it is worth pointing out that he might well have done so, given his perception that the earlier natural philosophers, including some contemporary with or younger than Socrates, were made 'archaic' by two by-products of Socrates' ethical inquiries: the increased attention to definitions, and the development of 'dialectic' as a technique of argument.[39] In fact, Aristotle's elastic term 'the ancients' (*hoi arkhaioi*) seems in some places (e.g., *Physics* I 2, 185b26; I 8 191a23) to have much the same extension as 'pre-Socratic' in its present use.

4. Aristotle recognizes too that the chronological sequence is never quite the same as the logical or epistemological one. There are theorists who are 'ahead of their time' in recognizing types of causes or substances, or adopting methods, not yet generally recognized; and there are those who are 'behind their time', in sticking to a more limited repertoire than others of their contemporaries. Thus the mistake of some Platonists was to pose a problem 'in an old-fashioned way' (*arkhaikôs: Met.* XIV 2 1089a1–2); whereas Anaxagoras, on a certain charitable interpretation, turns out to 'speak in a rather modern way' (*kainoprepesterôs legein: Met.* I 8 989b4–6), and some

unnamed theorists 'though older temporally, had a more modern conception' (*kaiper ontes arkhaioteroi tais hêlikiais kainoterôs enoêsan*: *De Caelo* IV 2 308b30–32).

The gradual formation of a science is a developmental process. But it does not look much like one of Aristotle's natural processes. Aristotelian Nature goes to her goal like a skilled craftsman who knows exactly what he is doing, by the simplest possible route, with a minimum of waste and error. By contrast, the development of natural science contains a great amount of error and wasted effort: wrong assumptions, mistaken lines of inquiry, false reasonings. It is far more like the linguistic, cognitive, social and moral development of a child, or the erratic path of a beginner or an uneducated person, in acquiring some skill, art or learning. It is comparisons drawn from this area, which depreciate while they exculpate, that Aristotle applies to the natural philosophers: 'like [a child] who speaks with a lisp', 'they are like those untrained in boxing who sometimes land good blows but by chance', 'talking at random [like people full of wine]'.[40] Typically, in all these developmental processes, progress is erratic and discontinuous, marked by occasional moments of sudden and decisive advance in insight, a 'catching sight of' (*sunidein*: 984b2) something new[41].

5. Aristotle's sensitivity and insight, in regard to the historical aspect, is unusual among philosophers. Even accepting that, one may still question the adequacy of Aristotle's understanding and reporting of his predecessors, and the fairness of his criticisms. One may argue on the basis of other, non-Aristotelian evidence that Aristotle, in good faith or not, misunderstood and misrepresented them; this line of attack, which calls for close scrutiny of that evidence, lies outside the scope of this chapter. Here it has here been argued that the Aristotelian reports and criticisms may be vindicated from objections brought against them on internal grounds, if we accept the presence of certain unexpressed assumptions behind Aristotle's treatments of earlier natural science in the *Physics* and in *Metaphysics* I. If this is correct, then only when such unexpressed assumptions are taken into account can one set about using Aristotle's testimony in the reconstruction of earlier theorising. In particular, any argument from the *silence* of Aristotle will be of extremely uncertain value, unless we can show clearly that it is a kind of silence that would be inconsistent with the rest of his practice as we have reconstructed it. In short, one should not cite and use Aristotle's testimony or lack of testimony, unless one has first stated and justified a general position about the principles on which he selects the information he gives, in the various works.

The hypothesized assumptions themselves should be judged on how well they allow us make sense of the texts overall; and how they fit in with what else we know of Aristotle's own conception of natural science. If confirmed, they may even help to delineate more precisely Aristotle's own vision of nature. But that is another story.

Notes

1. The terms listed are frequent in *Metaphysics* I but occur in other places as well. Thales as the pioneer of natural philosophy, *Met.* I 3 983b20–21. 'Human wisdom' (i.e., science)

preferable to mythical stories, *Met.* III 4 1000a5–22. Aristotle's reports probably draw on previous doxographic reports (by, e.g., Hippias, Plato, or even by his own pupil Theophrastus: so Gigon); on these matters see particularly Mansfeld 1990, 22–83; and on the relation between Aristotle's and Theophrastus' work on the history of natural science, Mansfeld 1996.

2. *Topics* on use of expert opinion: *Top.* I 1 100b21–23; I 2 101a36-b4; I 10 104a8–15; I 14 105a34-b18; arbitration between conflicting opinions: *Met.* III 1 995a24-b4; *DC* I 10 279b7–12; *Phys.* III 6 206a12–14. On Aristotle's procedures for establishing the foundations of a science, particularly natural science, and how far they are to be seen as dialectical, there are classic statements by Wieland and Owen, while Bolton is a valuable further contribution; but the points of disagreement are not crucial for the purposes of this chapter.

3. The views of Cherniss are repeated, sometimes in rather more extreme form, by McDiarmid. Guthrie, against Cherniss, makes some commonsense general observations but (as pointed out by Stevenson) does not attempt any substantive reply. There seems to be now a general consensus that Cherniss 'goes too far'; but this view in itself is of no value unless one can show in a number of particular but central cases how and where Cherniss was mistaken.

4. I am much indebted to Hywel Clifford for his kindness in reading an early draft of this chapter and for his acute and helpful comments.

5. 'The existence of number is not as clear as that of hot and cold' (*APo* I 10 76b18–19).

6. *Met.* I 1 981b20–25 implies that in Egypt mathematics existed as a genuine science before the time of Thales; the earliest Greek mathematical activity mentioned is that of Pythagoras and his early followers (*Met.* I 5 985b23–26). Two lost and presumably early works, *De Philosophia* and *Protrepticus*, may have given a slightly different account of the earliest stages of science; see *De Philosophia* 13 Rose³ = 8 Ross; *Protrepticus* 53 Rose³ = 8 Ross = C55:2 Düring.

   On the detail of the theories of Thales himself, Aristotle is cautious; but the fact that he has no hesitation in classing him with the 'natural philosophers' indicates that he has positive evidence to that effect.

7. On how the 'principles' (*arkhai*) of a science are discovered and identified as principles, the principal sources of information are *APo* II 19 and *EN* VI 3 and VI 6. Discovery of principles needs induction applied to data supplied by perception; this can include *endoxa*, which are the result of past attempts to do this, the inherited stock of accepted inductions.

8. The earlier natural scientists were concerned with everything, investigated the truth about all that is, sought the principles of 'substance' (*ousias*) generally: *Met.* I 3 983b1–3; VII 988a24–27; 8, 989b21–27, 989b33–990a5 (Pythagoreans); XII 1 1069a25–26. But they thought that all that is (substance), is sense-perceptible: *Met.* I 8 990a3–5; III 5 1002a8–11; IV 3 1005a29–33; IV 5 1010a1–3; XII 1 1069a28–30, XII 10 1075b24–27, cf. *DC* III 1 298b21–22 (even the Pythagoreans are hardly an exception: *Met.* I 8 989b29–990a5). It is important to note that this assumption is not treated as a mistake in *Metaphysics* I; understandably so, since the question of its truth is still open, as one of the fundamental problems of metaphysics, in *Metaphysics* III (997a34–998a19). Likewise, their consequential reducing of all sciences to one is not taken as a mistake in *Metaphysics* I, and in *Metaphysics* III it is still an open question (996a22-b1) whether there is one science or more than one. What *Metaphysics* I does see as error (I 8 998b23–25) is the specifying of 'elements' of bodies only (not of non-bodily entities as well).

9. Except possibly mathematics; but Aristotle does not state this exception, and he mentions mathematics only in connection with the Pythagoreans. He recognizes in any case that this restricted conception did not at all preclude an interest in matters that (for him) fall outside the scope of natural science: e.g., general truths of logic: *Met.* IV 3 1005a29-b2.

10. *Phys.* I 7 190b17-20 ('causes and principles of things that are by nature, from which first they are and have come to be ...') and 191a3-4 ('the principles of natural things [or possibly: 'of natural scientists'?] concerned with *genesis*': *tôn peri genesin phusikôn*). Mostly I shall just use '*genesis*' for Aristotle's *genesis*, except when it is coupled with *phthora* (when I use 'coming-to-be' and 'ceasing-to-be').

    The principles so described are presumably also included among 'the principles of natural science' (as perhaps indicated by 184a10-16); but they concern Aristotle here as principles of natural change.

11. *Phys.* VIII 1 250b15-18: 'all those who say anything about nature say that there is change because they create *cosmoi* and their entire science is concerned with coming-to-be and ceasing-to-be'; also *Met.* I 8 988b26-28, *PA* I 1 640b4-11, *EE* VII 1 1235a10-13.

12. It is here notably left open whether, in these theories, 'being in the mixture' was actual or merely potential; perhaps because, as Aristotle elsewhere in this book claims (*Phys.* I 8 191b27-34), the actual-potential distinction was not known to the earlier theorists. At *Met.* XII 2 1069b15-32, the distinction is used in this connection to offer clarifying reformulations of the theories of Empedocles, Anaxagoras, and Democritus (there are unfortunately uncertainties about both text and translation; see Charles, 97-103 and 106-110).

13. At *Met.* XII 2 1069b22-23 Democritus is simply put among the 'mixture' theorists.

14. For a different kind of reading of *Phys.* I, which sees Aristotle as engaged in 'violent' manipulation and distortion of historical truth in order to establish a 'precedent' for his own views, see Cherniss, 46-57.

15. As he elsewhere remarks: '[Platonists] posit universal things as substances; for genera are universal, and it is these that they rather say are principles and substances, because they inquire in a way that has regard to the general account of a thing (*logikôs*); but the ancients [posited] particular things, e.g., fire and earth, and not that which is common, body' (*Met.* XII 1 1069a26-30).

16. Perhaps the early Atomists, but for present purposes it does not matter exactly who. Cf. *PA* I 1 641b15-23.

17. Likewise, at *Parts of Animals* I 1 639b22-23, we are told that 'more or less all' of the natural scientists 'try to bring back their accounts to' necessity, but did not distinguish between different senses of 'necessity': namely Aristotle's conditional necessity (as in *Phys.* II 9) and absolute necessity. The implication is that the natural scientists wrongly try to explain natural things and processes by invoking a supposed absolute necessity. On the argumentation in *Phys.* II 8, which has been endlessly discussed, I have found helpful the discussions of Judson and Waterlow; Judson's bibliography lists some other useful contributions.

18. This reading of the contrast between 'absolute' and 'conditional' necessity avoids any conflict with Aristotle's insistence elsewhere on necessitation in natural processes. On necessity in Aristotle's natural science generally, another much-discussed topic, see, e.g., Sorabji, 143-54.

19. Only Empedocles and Democritus touched on it 'to a small extent', but then 'said goodbye' to it; the implication is that they made practically no use of it. This is the same failure that is reported in *Metaphysics* I as the failure to arrive at any proper

conception of the formal cause, in which connection Empedocles is again mentioned (*Met.* I 10 993a15–24) as a partial though imperfect exception. On the assumptions and implications of the discussion in *Physics* II 1, see Waterlow, 55–68.

20. As seems to be the case for the absolute necessity involved in unending cyclic processes, such as the transformations of the elements: see *Gen. et Corr.* II 11.

21. At *Generation of Animals* V 1 778b7–10, the crucial step is put thus. The earlier natural scientists thought that 'the substance is determined by the process of genesis', whereas the truth is the opposite: 'the process of genesis is determined by the substance'. They made this mistake because 'they did not see that there are several kinds of cause: they only saw the material cause and that of [the source of] the change, and that without distinguishing them clearly; but the cause of the *logos*, and of that of the end, they did not consider'. On 'the necessary' as a false substitute for the final cause, see also *GA* V 8 789a2–15.

22. Those who 'made the elements finitely many [but more than one]', which must include Empedocles, are excepted from the generalisation. For what follows, it is important to note that the critique of 'infinitely extended body' is explicitly intended to apply to the Atomists too, even though their infinitely many atoms did not form a single continuous body: see 203a19–23, 203a33-b2.

23. There is no good short English equivalent for *logikôs* in such contexts; it implies that one relies on the senses and/or definitions of key terms; and on verbal distinctions and such matters. At *Gen. et Corr.* I 2 316a10–14, Aristotle casts doubt on the use of '*logikôs*' arguments in natural science, but there is no such suggestion here.

24. The *De Caelo* arguments are divided into 'special' (*kata meros*) and 'general' (*katholou*). The 'general' arguments (274a30–276a17) are of the same sort as those of *Physics* III; they do not appeal to Aristotelian natural science but claim that the notion of an infinite body cannot fit into any comprehensible conception of nature. They make use of mathematical paradoxes that seem to arise when one attributes physical properties to an infinite body; and they go over into parallel arguments against an infinite universe and for the uniqueness of this cosmos. The 'special' arguments (271b17–274a18) appeal to the results of *De Caelo* I 1–4, especially the mathematical analysis of the possible types of 'simple motion' and hence of 'simple bodies'. (In general, it is on mathematical argumentation that Aristotle mostly relies when confronting the Atomists in his later writings.) The arguments of *Physics* IV 8 against Atomist void are in many ways comparable. On Aristotle's later appreciation of the Atomists, see below Section H.8.

25. On some points of detail, it has to use mathematics in an auxiliary role; this does not affect the general point. It is a mistake (which the Eleatics committed) to import metaphysical arguments into natural science: *DC* 298b14–24. On the autonomy of natural science and its exclusion of 'metaphysical possibilities', compare Berti, and Waterlow, 3.

26. This would apply even to the theories of Empedocles and Anaxagoras; Anaxagoras as noted is specifically praised for saying that there was Mind *in* nature (*Met.* I 3 984b15–20), yet he apparently also supposed that Mind *preceded* any cosmos. Plato's *Timaeus* is founded on a radically different metaphysics, but one that also intrudes into the realm of 'natural science'; Aristotle's treatment of it unfortunately cannot be examined here. About Plato's later views on natural science as expressed in *Laws* X 891b8–899d3, with its sombre denunciation of earlier natural science as the root of disastrous impiety, Aristotle is totally silent; perhaps he considers them as a mere extension of the point of view underlying the *Timaeus*.

    The hypothesis outlined in the text is not incompatible with the fact that Aristotle, in at least one place, constructs arguments on the assumption of an infinite universe, without appeal to general theses about nature or the infinite: this is *DA* I 5 411a7–23, which contains a refutation of certain earlier theories of soul as a fundamental ingredient of the (supposedly infinite) universe.

27. The prime example of the use of such hypotheses is Cherniss (see Section A.3 above, and note 12 above).

28. The principal texts are: *Phys.* I 8 191a23–34, I 9 191b35–192a12 (the problem of the logic of genesis; cf. *Phys.* I 4 187a26–35); *DC* III 1 298b12- 299a1 (summary of opinions about genesis); *DC* III 8 306b3–307b24 (critique of Platonic and Atomist theories of elements); *Gen. et Corr.* I 1 314a6–315a15 (critical review of earlier opinions; in *Gen. et Corr.* I 2, there follow critiques of the Atomist view and of Plato's *Timaeus* theory); *Gen. et Corr.* II 6 333a16–334b7 (critique of Empedocles' theory of elements and related ones). There are also criticisms of earlier theories of genesis in *Met.* XII 6 1071b26–1072a18, though here the context and the assumptions are not those of natural science. There was also some treatment of earlier pre-Platonic theorists in some of the lost works of Aristotle, in particular the work *On Philosophy* and the reported monographs on individual thinkers or groups of thinkers, but their content is not recoverable in detail.

29. Noted also at *Met.* XII 2, 1069b20–24.

30. For the general claim: *Phys.* II 2 194a18–21 (cf. II 1 193a21–28); *PA* I 1 640b4–641a17, 642a14–31; *GA* V 1 778b7–10; *Met.* I 7 988a34-b1; for the partial exceptions: *Phys.* II 2 194a20–21 (Empedocles and Democritus), *PA* I 1 642a18–24 (Empedocles), *Met.* I 5 987a20–27 (Pythagoreans), I 10 993a15–24 (Empedocles); for Empedocles' 'formula for bone' and general recognition of the determining of properties by ratios in compounds, see also *DA* I 4 408a18–24, I 5 409b32–410a10; *GA* V 1 779b15–20.

31. Omission of final cause: besides *Physics* II 8–9 and the parallel treatment in *PA* I 1 639b21–640a9, see: *Resp.* III 471b23–25, 472a1–3; *PA* I 1 641a7–15; *GA* V 1 778b7–10, V 8 789b2–15 (Democritus).

32. Note also *Gen. et Corr.* II 9 335b7–12: earlier faint inklings of need for moving cause; failure of theories omitting it.

33. Though there is piquancy and polemical bite in the thought, apparently suggested here, that to postulate such a principle is evidence of one's own mental inertia. The Atomists' principle is stated and attacked in full generality at *Phys.* VIII 1 252a32-b5, *GA* II 6 742b17–35; elsewhere it is just stated that the Atomists held that there was always motion or that the atoms were always in motion: *DC* III 2 300b8–16, *Met.* XII 6 1071b31–34. (*Phys.* VIII 9 265b23–26 does not say, as some have claimed, that the Atomists made the void a cause of motion.) It is clear, though the evidence is miserably sparse, that there was more to Democritus' thinking about motion than this.
    At *GA* IV 1 764a12–23, it is Empedocles who is accused of laziness on a particular point, while Democritus by contrast is rated 'better'; another instance of later upgrading of the Atomists?

34. For Ionian science, the observation goes back at least to Tannery.

35. As notably with Hippon (*DA* 405b1–2, *Met.* I 3 984a3–5). The derogatory terms *phortikos* and *agroikos* are also applied to the work of Zeno and of two theorists associated with the Eleatics (Xenophanes and Melissus), on matters that do not fall within the scope of natural science (*Phys.* I 2 185a5–12, I 3 186a4–7; *Met.* I 5 986b25–27, 1001b13–14). Forthright speaking about rival theories was also part of the Ionian scientific tradition (see, e.g., Lloyd, 56–70).

36. *Met.* I 1 980a21; I 2 982b28–983a4; I 3 984a18–19, 984b8–11. The rapidity of progress in recent times was stressed (perhaps for protreptic or polemical reasons) in the *Protrepticus* and/or the *De Philosophia*: frr. 52, 53 Rose³ = *Protrepticus* frr. 5, 8 Ross = Düring B 55, C 55:2; but see the comments of Düring 227–31.

37. For example: *Phys.* I 3 186a29–32 (Parmenides not aware of a certain distinction); *Phys.* I 8 191b27–34 (earlier unawareness of potentially-actually distinction).

38. Early development of definitions: *PA* I 1 642a24–31; *Met.* I 5 987a20–27, I 6 987b1–4; XIII 4 1078b17–30; a contribution by Democritus too is hinted at.

39. Dialectic: invented by Zeno, fr. 65 Rose³ = *Sophistês* fr. 1 Ross; not much developed before Socrates: *Met.* I 6 987b32–33; XIII 4 1078b25–27.

40. *Met.* I 3 984b15–18; I 4 985a10–17; I 10 993a15–16.

41. *Sunoran/sunidein* is used of an insight which marks a decisive advance in understanding, also at *Phys.* 186a32, *Gen. et Corr.* 316a5, *GA* 721a14–17, 755b27–29, 764a36–b2, *Met.* 1048a37, *EN* 1127a17, 1181b21.

BIBLIOGRAPHY

Berti, Enrico (1969) 'Physique et métaphysique selon Aristote: *Phys.* I 2, 184b25–185a5', in I. Düring, ed., *Naturphilosophie bei Aristoteles und Theophrast* (Heidelberg: Lothar Stiehm Verlag), 18–31.

Bolton, Robert (1991) 'Aristotle's Method in Natural Science: *Physics* 1', in L. Judson, ed., *Aristotle's Physics: A Collection of Essays* (Oxford: Clarendon Press), 1–29.

Charles, David (2000) '*Metaphysics* Λ 2', in M. Frede and D. Charles, eds., *Aristotle's* Metaphysics *Lambda: Symposium Aristotelicum* (Oxford: Clarendon Press), 81–110.

Cherniss, Harold (1935) *Aristotle's Criticism of Presocratic Philosophy* (Baltimore: Johns Hopkins Press), (reprinted, New York: Octagon Books, 1964).

Düring, Ingemar (1961) *Aristotle's Protrepticus: An Attempt at Reconstruction* (Göteborg: Institute of Classical Studies of the University of Göteborg).

Gigon, Olof (1969) 'Die ἀρχαί der Vorsokratiker bei Theophrast and Aristoteles', in I. Düring, ed., *Naturphilosophie bei Aristoteles und Theophrast* (Heidelberg: Lothar Stiehm Verlag), 114–23.

Guthrie, W.K.C. (1957) 'Aristotle as Historian of Philosophy: Some Preliminaries', *Journal of Hellenic Studies* 77, Part 1, 35–41, [reprinted in D.J. Furley and R.E. Allen, eds., *Studies in Presocratic Philosophy, vol. I: The Beginnings of Philosophy* (London: Routledge & Kegan Paul, 1970), 239–54].

Judson, Lindsay (2005) 'Aristotelian Teleology', *Oxford Studies in Ancient Philosophy* 29, 341–66.

Lloyd, G.E.R. (1987) *The Revolutions of Wisdom* (Berkeley/Los Angeles/London: University of California Press).

McDiarmid, J.B. (1953) 'Theophrastus on the Presocratic Causes', *Harvard Studies in Classical Philosophy* 61, 85–156.

Mansfeld, Jaap (1990) *Studies in the Historiography of Greek Philosophy* (Assen/Maastricht: Van Gorcum).

—— (1996) 'Aristote et la structure du De Sensibus de Théophrast', *Phronesis* 41, 158–88.

Owen, G.E.L. (1961) 'τιθέναι τὰ φαινόμενα [*Tithenai ta phainomena*]', in S. Mansion, ed., *Aristote et les Problèmes de Méthode* (Louvain : Publications Universitaires de Louvain and Paris : Éditions Béatrice-Nauwelaerts).

Sorabji, Richard (1980) *Necessity Cause and Blame: Perspectives on Aristotle's Theory* (London: Duckworth).

Stevenson, J.G. (1974) 'Aristotle as Historian of Philosophy', *Journal of Hellenic Studies* 94, 138–43.

Tannery, Paul (1887) *Pour L'Histoire de la Science Hellène* (Paris: Félix Alcan).

Waterlow, Sarah (1982) *Nature, Change and Agency in Aristotle's Physics* (Oxford: Clarendon Press).

Wieland, Wolfgang (1975) 'Aristotle's Physics and the Problem of Enquiry into Principles', in J. Barnes, M. Schofield, R. Sorabji, eds., *Articles on Aristotle: I. Science* (London: Duckworth), 127–40 [a translation into English of W. Wieland, 'Das Problem der Prinzipienforschung und die Aristotelische Physik', *Kant-Studien* 52 (1960–1), 206–19].

CHAPTER 3

SCIENCE AND SCIENTIFIC INQUIRY IN ARISTOTLE: A PLATONIC PROVENANCE

ROBERT BOLTON

1. The Platonic Background

Aristotle's word for science is *epistêmê*. It is important, however, to keep in mind, as writers sometimes do not, that this term *epistêmê* has at least a dual use in the Greek of Aristotle's day. It is standardly used, in one way, as a count noun, to mean 'a science.' Thus, in this usage, one can say that geometry, or *phusikê* (natural science), or metaphysics is (an) *epistêmê*, is a science. Here the term *epistêmê* designates a special sort of systematic body of truth or fact which may or may not have yet been discovered, or fully discovered. But the term is also used very commonly to designate not a body, or an item, of fact or of truth, but rather a cognitive state of someone who has appropriately grasped an *epistêmê*, in the sense of a science, or of one who has grasped a suitable part of it.[1]

In this second use, to designate a certain type of cognitive state, the term *epistêmê* is applied in the ordinary Greek of Aristotle's day to more or less anything that we would now commonly call *knowledge*, from the expert knowledge one might have by demonstration of some mathematical or scientific theorem, to knowledge from experience of, say, the way from Princeton to New Brunswick, or to eyewitness knowledge of who robbed the bank. In the *Meno* for instance (97b), Plato uses the term *epistêmê* in this ordinary sense for knowledge from experience of the way from Athens to Larissa, and in the *Theaetetus* (201b-c) he uses the term *epistêmê* for eyewitness knowledge of who did or did not commit some crime. In Plato's *Protagoras* (352cff.) Socrates uses the term *epistêmê* for knowledge of the particular right moral action to perform on some specific occasion and he is followed in this use of the term by Aristotle in *Nicomachean Ethics* VII.2 (1145b21ff.). These examples all follow ordinary usage, even though the *epistêmê* or knowledge in question here is not at all theoretical scientific knowledge. However, despite this ordinary usage, in a famous passage in *Republic* V (476dff.), Plato introduces, and also argues for, a severely restricted range of application for the term *epistêmê* in the use in which it designates a cognitive state of a knower. The interpretation of this passage in *Republic* V is very controversial on numerous points, and we cannot enter into all of the complexities here.[2] But it is at least relatively uncontroversial that one basic idea that Plato presents there is that *epistêmê*, which we may think of initially in accord with common Greek usage as *knowledge*, is a cognitive state which has or is about an object which is able to be and is *accurately represented* by that state or its content (477b, 478a). This idea, clearly, has a good deal of plausibility as regards knowledge, as we understand it. Further, Plato claims, the object of *epistêmê*, or knowledge, must be able to be and must be accurately represented by that cognitive state *in every way* (477a, 479a-e). That is, the cognitive representation cannot be partly accurate and partly inaccurate of a genuine object of *epistêmê*. This also has a certain plausibility as concerns knowledge as we, or ordinary Greeks, would standardly think of it. It is important, and Plato clearly indicates in *Republic* V (476d-e), that he expects his argument there to have force with ordinary intelligent Greeks, even those who do not share and may well oppose his special philosophical views. So he ought to be relying in his argument on premises with some general plausibility.

What Plato means, however, by this complete and unqualified accuracy of representation by *epistêmê* of its object is more fully spelled out in other middle dialogues, especially the *Symposium* and *Timaeus*. In *Symposium* 210cff. Plato characterizes the object of *epistêmê* somewhat negatively, as an object that cannot be accurately represented by that state: (1) only in one part but not in another, or (2) only at one time but not at another, or (3) only in one relation but not in another or (4) only in one location but not in another. This helps to spell out for us what Plato has in mind by that complete and unqualified accuracy of representation by genuine *epistêmê* of its object on which he insists in *Republic* V. Of these various dimensions of accuracy, or of avoidance of inaccuracy, by *epistêmê* in the representation of its object, the most important perhaps for our purposes here is the temporal one. The proper object of *epistêmê*, Plato claims, cannot be only accurately represented by that cognitive state at one time but not at another.

From certain passages in the *Timaeus* in particular (27dff., 37c-38c, 51dff.), it is reasonably clear that Plato means by this that an item of *epistêmê*—at least if that item is propositional in form—is not simply in fact always true, i.e., true at every time. Rather, it is true in an atemporal way so that it is unable to change its truth value over time. That is, it is a necessary truth. In the *Timaeus* (37c-38c) Plato contrasts what is capable of being different in the past, present, and/or future with what simply *is* something or other in a way such that it is *incapable* of change over or in time. We should not even say, Plato tells us, of what *has* changed that it *is* something that has changed. So, for Plato, what *is* in this special unqualified sense is not what *is now* or *is at the present* since he could hardly deny that what has changed (and still exists) *is now* something that has changed. He must mean, then, that what *is* something or other, in the special sense he has in mind, is so timelessly.[3] Plato also seems here to hold, further, that what is 'in time' will inevitably change in such a way that any representation of how it is in particular at a given time can at best accurately represent it only at one time but not at another. Thus, since *epistêmê* must avoid this restriction, there can only be genuine *epistêmê* of what is something or other timelessly and, thus, necessarily.

Plato himself largely avoids the use of the term *necessity* (*anagkê*) in describing items of *epistêmê*, presumably because of his tendency to reserve the application of this term in theory construction to what is *forced* by factors outside of the scope of ideal rational order.[4] This leads Plato to devise a special use of the term *is* to characterize proper items of *epistêmê* in a way that guarantees that they are timeless necessary truths.[5] But this, as we have already seen from examples, does not easily fit the ordinary use in Greek of the term *epistêmê*, nor, of course, does it fit our ordinary use of the term *knowledge*. In the *Republic* itself Plato does not do much to defend this idea directly—that the content of an item of *epistêmê* is always a necessary truth—but from other early and middle dialogues we can see, I think, how he would want to defend it even to an ordinary intelligent Greek, if not to us. So let us see if we can piece that story together. This will turn out to be very important for understanding Aristotle.

To begin with, then, the term *epistêmê*, or the verb *epistasthai* (= to have *epistêmê*), derives, etymologists tell us, from the verb *ephistasthai* (= to stop or stand [oneself] on). Aristotle himself, at least, seems to accept this derivation as we can see from *Physics* VII 3 247b11ff.[6] Thus *epistêmê*, on this derivation, is something one makes a stop or a stand on or, as we might say, something one relies on. This root idea is quite prominent already in Plato's early dialogue *Protagoras* (352aff.) where *epistêmê* is regarded, at least by Socrates and Protagoras, as the sort of cognitive state that is sufficiently powerful so that it will not ever abandon you or lead you astray or let you down. This is by contrast with desires, emotions, and other affections (including perceptions) which can and regularly do subject you to error, Plato thinks. (Cf. *Phd.* 65c, *Tim.* 51d-e) This point in the *Protagoras* is directly echoed in *Republic* V. 477d-e where *epistêmê* is called 'the most powerful (*erromenestatê*) of all capacities (*dunameis*).' This view, moreover, that *epistêmê* has this strongly reliable accuracy is treated not as just some philosopher's arcane idea but as a generally credible and acceptable one in Aristotle's presentation of that view in *Nicomachean Ethics* VII 2 1145b21ff., where he is reporting on this view as found in the *Protagoras*.

Plato does not say much directly in the *Protagoras* itself about what he thinks the basis or grounding is for this strong reliability of *epistêmê*, for the one who has it. But in a somewhat later dialogue, *Meno* (97bff.), he argues explicitly that unlike even *true* opinion or belief *epistêmê* is not the sort of thing that will ever let you down or lead you astray because genuine *epistêmê* always comes with a certain kind of guarantee or backing which ties it down and makes it reliably firm and stable as well as true and accurate. This backing, Plato says in the *Meno*, involves and requires the grasp of an account (*logismos* or *logos*) of the cause or reason (*aitia*) which accounts for why the item in question is so. This is anticipated already perhaps in the *Protagoras* (356eff.) where *epistêmê* of what is best on some particular occasion is properly to be reached by use of an art or science of measurement of goods and evils. This idea, then, that given its strong reliability, *epistêmê* must involve and must always be reached through a grasp of the cause or account (*logos*) of why the item is so, is then very prominent indeed throughout Plato's middle dialogues (e.g., at *Rep.* VII 531eff.).[7] In the *Timaeus* in particular, it is especially clear that it is just this backing provided by the grasp of its cause or account that gives an item of *epistêmê* its stability and its rational unshakability. Plato says there (*Tim.* 51d-e with 29b-c) that *epistêmê* (or *nous*) comes by teaching (*didachê*) via a true *logos* or account and, as such, it is unshakable (*akinêton*) and irreversible by persuasion or argument (*ametapeiston*).[8]

The natural question that arises at this point is this: What sort of thing must the grasp of the cause (*aitia*) or account (*logos*) of some item of *epistêmê* be, such that the derivation of that item of *epistêmê* from that cause or account would guarantee its total cognitive reliability in an atemporal way and, as such, would guarantee its necessity. Here again Plato is perhaps not as explicit as we might like. But in the *Meno* for instance, and very often elsewhere, he puts forward the idea that to properly know, or to have *epistêmê* of, anything else about something, one must first come to know the essence of that thing, or *what it is*, (it's *ousia* or *ti esti*) and then base one's knowledge of other matters about the thing on the explicit knowledge of its essence. (*Meno* 71b, 86d-e, 100b. Cf. *Euthyph.* 6d-e, *Prot.* 360eff., *Laches* 189e-190b, *Lysis* 223b, *Rep.* I 354b-c, Xen. *Mem.* IV vi.1. Cf. Arist. *Met.* M 4 1078b 17–29). It is evident enough that for Plato, as for us I take it, the essence of a thing is a fundamental unchangeable feature of it. (See, e.g., *Rep.* VI 511b-e with VII 531d-535a.) So any truth that could be derived directly *from* an account of the essence of something would be equally necessary, just as a statement of the essence is.

In sum then so far, I am suggesting, Plato seems to take as his starting point the generally accepted idea that *epistêmê*, or knowledge even, must be completely reliable and trustworthy in its accuracy. He then argues that the only proper guarantee of that *complete* trustworthiness is through grasp of the cause or account of one's item of *epistêmê* where the grasp of that cause or account is or involves grasp of the essence of what one has *epistêmê* of. One's item of *epistêmê* is then guaranteed to be, and is grasped as, a necessary truth since it is seen to derive from the essence of the thing. It has been common for recent philosophers to object rather strongly to Plato's requirement, in his early and middle dialogues, that knowledge or *epistêmê* of any other features of, say, virtue, or courage or justice must be based on a grasp of the essence (or definition) of that object—and this doctrine can seem to us quite implausible.[9] But if we see that Plato starts from the plausible assumption, at least for the Greeks, that knowledge, or *epistêmê*, must be completely trustworthy in its accuracy, we can at least see the coherence of his proposal that the way that this gets fully guaranteed is the way he suggests, namely by basing that *epistêmê* on an account of the essence of the thing.

Let me now briefly contrast this story, this account of the rationale for Plato's requirement that true *epistêmê* must be based on a grasp of the essence of the item in question, with two other influential accounts. On the first, the rationale for Plato's requirement, at least in certain passages, is that basing *epistêmê* on a grasp of essence promotes or gives one *systematic understanding* of what one has *epistêmê* of.[10] While this is not the place to consider this view, or arguments for it, in any detail, in the passages that we have been considering, Plato's starting point, his root idea if you will, is not that *epistêmê* involves systematic understanding, but rather that it involves completely trustworthy and reliable multidimensional accuracy of representation of its object. Basing *epistêmê* on grasp of essence serves to guarantee, or to help guarantee, that. Of course, this is not to deny that systematic understanding of its object may also be achieved on Plato's requirements for *epistêmê*. One might also argue that this systematic understanding itself promotes reliable accuracy for *epistêmê*. Nevertheless, the root idea remains reliability.[11]

Another alternative account of the rationale for Plato's requirement that *epistêmê* must be based on a grasp of the essence of the item in question was offered by Gregory Vlastos. He took it, contrary to many scholars, that this requirement is not in fact to be found in Plato's earliest Socratic dialogues and was first introduced in 'transitional dialogues' such as the *Meno* after Plato came under the influence of the methods of 'advanced mathematics' where, according to Vlastos, such a doctrine was generally accepted.[12] Vlastos' approach here involves, first of all, a largely undefended historical thesis, namely that in mathematical practice in Plato's day, say in geometry or arithmetic, it was agreed that definitions must be known first, independent of any prior certain knowledge of any truths these definitions were then used in the proof of. This assumption can easily be questioned. Did ancient mathematicians not suppose that they knew, and knew with certainty, that 2+2 = 4, and many other such truths, before they were able to axiomatize arithmetic and settle on the proper ultimate definitions of its basic terms? But even if Vlastos were right on this historical point, his account would still leave the question we have been addressing here in the main unanswered, namely, what is it about *epistêmê*, as generally understood, that would make the requirement that it be based on knowledge of essence appropriate and defensible, in mathematics or elsewhere.

The final question now to ask in our sketch of Plato's view of *epistêmê* is this: How does one reach that knowledge of *essence* on the basis of which one is able to ground and guarantee the complete and trustworthy accuracy, including especially the atemporal accuracy and thus the necessity, of an item of *epistêmê*? Here Plato's answer is, at least verbally, very clear, for instance in *Republic* VII 533a-534e. The method for reaching knowledge of essence, Plato says there, is nothing other than dialectic. In the *Republic* Plato is not as explicit as one might like on what precisely this involves—this reaching of knowledge of essence through dialectic. But there are strong indications at least in somewhat later dialogues that he regarded, or came to regard, the method of definition by division—through genus and differ-entiae—as the proper procedure to use dialectically to reach knowledge of essence. This doctrine is first found explicitly, perhaps, in *Phaedrus* 265dff. But the best and most well-known examples of how this method of division works dialectically for Plato are found in his late dialogues *Sophist* and *Statesman*.[13]

2. ARISTOTLE'S DEBT TO PLATO

With this Platonic background in view, the question for us now to ask is this: How much of this conception of *epistêmê* and of how it is reached does Aristotle accept and take over from Plato? The answer, as it turns out, is a very great deal and, some would likely argue, all of it. This is clear already in the early chapters of the *Posterior Analytics* where Aristotle offers us a detailed account of *epistêmê* as he understands it. Consider first the opening lines of *APo* I 2.

> We consider ourselves to have *epistêmê* without qualification, and not accidentally in the sophistical manner, when we think we know the cause (*aitia*) on account of which the thing is so—that it is the cause—and that it is not possible for this to be otherwise (71a9–12).

Here Aristotle directly carries over *three* basic requirements for *epistêmê* from Plato. It must be (1) based on a grasp of the *cause* (*aitia*) of the item in question as such; (2) it must be a *necessary truth* and grasped as such; and (3) it cannot be known to hold only accidentally. By this last requirement Aristotle means, in effect, that the item of *epistêmê* in question, the proposition in question, cannot be such that the predicate is known to belong to the subject only accidentally as opposed to belonging to it *in itself* (*kath' hauto*) as the *kind* of thing it is. That is, the predicate must be known to belong to the subject in virtue of the nature or essence of the subject. This carries over a third Platonic requirement for *epistêmê*, namely that *epistêmê* must be based on a grasp of the essence of the item in question. That this is what Aristotle intends here is clear, for instance, in *APo* I 5 where he equates knowing that some predicate belongs to some subject non-accidentally or in itself (*kath' hauto*) with knowing that it belongs to the subject as the kind of thing it is (*kat' eidos*). He equates the latter with knowing that it belongs in virtue of the essence and definition of the thing in question. (74a25ff., cf. I 4 73b10ff.).[14]

Aristotle also says in *APo* I 2 that 'we' understand *epistêmê* as meeting these three requirements. (71a9) As we have seen, the 'we' in question here cannot be ordinary people in general since these requirements do not simply reflect the ordinary usage of the term *epistêmê*, even if Plato tries to argue for these requirements starting from and on the basis of important features of the ordinary conception. Nor is the 'we' here the royal 'we'. That is, Aristotle is not simply stipulating that he intends to use the term *epistêmê* in this way. (see 71b13–16) Rather the 'we' here, as we have seen, is 'we philosophers', i.e., those in Aristotle's Academic circle, especially Plato. We should notice also that Aristotle himself does here distinguish what he calls unqualified *epistêmê* from other actual if only accidental *epistêmê*. So he does not insist, as Plato seems to do in *Republic* V, that any cognitive state that fails to meet the requirements here (i.e., Plato's own requirements) for strict *epistêmê* is at best mere opinion (*doxa*) and not knowledge (*epistêmê*) at all. Here, then, Aristotle is somewhat closer to ordinary usage than is Plato in *Republic* V. However, there is a Platonic precedent for this distinction, too. In the *Phaedrus* at least (247c-e), Plato distinguishes what he there calls *true epistêmê* from 'that *epistêmê* which concerns what changes, which varies [in its accuracy] with the [changing] things we commonly [but mistakenly] say *are*'. It is only the former *epistêmê*, Plato says, which 'really is *epistêmê* of what really *is*'. Having given this philosopher's characterisation, if you will, of *epistêmê*, Aristotle then goes on in *APo* I 2 to describe how *epistêmê*, so understood, is to be reached. He argues that it must be reached by what he calls, now perhaps stipulatively, a demonstration (*apodeixis* 71b15ff., 71b17). We will come back to the question of exactly what a demonstration is, noting for now only that Aristotle says here that this must be a proof from what he calls 'first principles' (*archai*). This involves crucially, as we have already seen, proof ultimately based on the essence or definition of the entity or entities in question. (72a7ff.) This point enables us to appreciate the force of the final lines of *APo* I 2 (72a37ff.) where Aristotle says:

> Anyone who is going to have that *epistêmê* which comes through a demonstration must not only know better, and have as more credible, the first principles [on which the demonstration is based] than he does of what is proved, but there can be nothing more credible for him nor better known, among things that are opposed to these principles, from which there would be proof of any error that is contrary [to what is demonstrated], since anyone who has unqualified *epistêmê* must be incapable of being persuaded otherwise (*ametapeiston*) (72a37ff).

Here, quite explicitly, the ultimate basis or rationale for the idea that *epistêmê* must be reached by derivation from first principles of a special sort, particularly as it turns out from an account of essence, is that this is needed to guarantee the reliability and rational unshakability of *epistêmê*. It is for this reason that Aristotle supposes that a demonstration, from proper principles, must provide a *more credible proof* of its conclusion than any purported counter proof or demonstration could provide of any incompatible conclusion. So, Aristotle repeats here Plato's root idea and his basic line of argument concerning *epistêmê* in the passages in the *Protagoras, Meno,* and *Timaeus* that we have considered. In fact, he uses the same language that Plato uses in the *Timaeus* when he says that the one who has *epistêmê* must be *ametapeiston* (incapable of being persuaded otherwise), with a special expansion on what that entails. One commentator in his note on this passage says: 'The unpersuadability [otherwise] of knowers was an Academic commonplace...; [but] it is hard to think of any satisfactory argument for it.'[15] This reaction, we can now see, is uncharitable to Plato. It fails to take account of the intuitive appeal, for the Greeks at least, of the idea that Plato draws on, that knowledge (*epistêmê*) should have a certain strong reliability and not ever rationally let you down. In any case, the repetition here by Aristotle of this basic Platonic idea does help to confirm again that the primary interest or value of *epistêmê* for both Plato and Aristotle lies more in the stable and reliable multidimensional accuracy of conviction which it provides than it does in any systematic understanding which it may also provide or in any simple deference to mathematical practice.

There are two further occurrences worth noting of this basic thought in Aristotle, first in *EN* VI 3 where he gives a short summary treatment of *epistêmê*. He begins as follows:

> We all believe that what we have *epistêmê* of cannot be otherwise; of things which can be otherwise, when they fall outside our observation, we are unaware whether they are the case or not. Therefore, the object of *epistêmê* must be the case of necessity (1139b19–23).

Here the thesis that *epistêmê* is of necessary truths is defended on the ground that *epistêmê* is something you should be able to reliably count on even apart from continued observation of the state of affairs in question to see that it does not change. Also, it should be noted that here in *EN* VI 3 *epistêmê* is being investigated as one of the so-called intellectual virtues. (see VI 2) But a virtue (*aretê*) for Aristotle is not only an achievement or excellence but also a relatively permanent state, one difficult if not impossible to dislodge under normal circumstances. In *Cat.* 8 Aristotle says, in a recent translation:

> A state (*hexis*) differs from a condition (*diathesis*) in being more stable and lasting longer. Such are the branches of knowledge (*epistêmai*) and the virtues. For knowledge (*epistêmê*) seems to be (*dokei*) something permanent and hard to change if one has even a moderate grasp of a branch of knowledge (*epistêmê*), unless a great change is brought about by illness or some other such thing (8b27–32, revised Oxford tr.).

Here the translator[16] is guilty of the confusion mentioned at the beginning. The term *epistêmai* (the plural of *epistêmê*) is translated here 'branches of knowledge'. But it is not the branches of knowledge, or the sciences, that Aristotle takes to be stable or permanent and hard to change. The branches of knowledge are not states (*hexeis*). It is the cognitive state of *epistêmê* of the one who has it that is of this sort. So *epistêmai* here refers to instances of that cognitive state, not to the branches of knowledge or the sciences. We should note also that Aristotle says here that this view of *epistêmê* 'is held to be' (*dokei*) the case (not 'seems to be' the case as the above translation has it). This thesis is described later in the passage as what people in general *say*. (9a5ff.) This is further indication that Plato himself was already drawing on a widely accepted assumption about *epistêmê*, namely that it has a certain unshakability and reliability of accuracy for its possessor.

All of this shows us, then, that Aristotle's conception of *epistêmê* owes a very great deal to Plato but also, as with Plato, that it owes a great deal to common views or common intuitions about *epistêmê*. That is, even if it is not a common intuition, as we might put it, for the Greeks, that *epistêmê* is only of necessary truths, it *is* a basic common intuition for them (according to Plato and Aristotle at least) that *epistêmê* has a certain strong reliability and permanence of accuracy, on the basis of which one can argue, as both Plato and Aristotle do, that strict *epistêmê*, at least, is only of necessary truths grasped in a certain manner. This procedure of argument, moreover, follows a familiar pattern. Often philosophers, when they are investigating some topic, will find that commonly accepted, or commonly credible, ideas on that topic conflict, or are in some sort of tension with each other; and they will move to refine if they can, or reject if necessary, some of those ideas in the interest of preserving others that are taken as more basic. This type of procedure has been called the method of 'reflective equilibrium.'[17] This point leads directly to the next item we need to consider.

3. WHERE DOES ARISTOTLE DIFFER FROM PLATO?

There is a celebrated methodological passage in Aristotle's preface to his discussion of incontinence in *EN* VII 1 in which he seems, or has been thought, to generally recommend the procedure of inquiry we have just outlined, at least in moral philosophy. He says there:

> It is necessary, as in the other cases, after (1) setting out the things that appear to be so (*ta phainomena*), then (2) having first raised the difficulties, (3) to go on to establish, if possible, all of the noted opinions (*endoxa*) about these affections, or, if not all, most of them, and especially the most authoritative (*kuriotata*). For if the troubles are resolved and the noted opinions (*endoxa*) are left standing that will be sufficient proof.... Some of the points [that give rise to the difficulties] must be undermined and the others left in place. For the resolution of the difficulty [in this manner] is the discovery [of the truth] (1145b2–7, 1146b6–8).

One can easily see both Plato and Aristotle as doing something like this in their treatment of *epistêmê*. They want most of all to preserve what they take to be the basic or most authoritative standing opinion (*endoxon*) that *epistêmê* has a certain strong reliability and accuracy for its possessor, and they are willing to restrict the scope of *epistêmê*, or of strict *epistêmê*, more narrowly than is usual in the interest of this. This point is of further relevance for our purposes since it leads us directly into the final topic we need to investigate. Aristotle's description of philosophical method in *EN* VII 1 has been commonly regarded by scholars as a description of his dialectical method, or at least of one use of that method.[18] This leads naturally to the question whether, in addition to the other points on which Aristotle follows Plato in his conception of *epistêmê*, he also accepts Plato's view on how you get the knowledge of essence, or of what something is, on which *epistêmê* is based and on which its necessity is grounded, namely that this knowledge of essence is reached by dialectic. There was a time, not so long ago, when it was nearly universally accepted that Aristotle agrees, or came to agree, with Plato on this point, too. Though there are defectors now, this view is still maintained in various versions by many scholars. It will be useful to consider here whether this is correct by looking at just two passages in Aristotle. The first is one which has been widely thought to commit Aristotle to the Platonic view. It is found in *Topics* I 2.

> [Dialectic has a use] in relation to the primary things (*ta prota*) in each science (*epistêmê*). For it is impossible to discuss them at all on the basis of the principles (*archai*) that are proper to a given science, since the principles are primary in relation to everything, and it is necessary to deal with them, in each case, through use of the noted opinions (*endoxa*). This task is unique, or most proper, to dialectic since as a technique for examination (*exetastikê*) dialectic offers a path [for discussion] concerning the principles of absolutely all inquiries (101a36-b4).

Here Aristotle has been thought to say that since you clearly cannot establish the principles of a discipline by a demonstrative proof starting from those very principles (such a purported proof would, of course, beg the question) you should use dialectic to establish those principles, including the definitional principles which give the essences of things. One difficulty with this reading of this passage is that Aristotle is not talking here about how to *establish* principles as such, but rather about how to *discuss* principles or purported principles, i.e., about how to proceed in case you have a disagreement or a question about some proposition which is a principle or a purported principle. Dialectic permits this discussion, Aristotle says, because it is a procedure or technique you can use to examine or test even some principle or purported principle. Aristotle has already said at the beginning of the *Topics* (I 1 100a20ff.) that dialectic enables one to reason (*sullogizesthai*) about 'any subject [at all] presented to us', on the basis of 'noted opinions' (*endoxa*). This would, of course, include reasoning about propositions which are principles or purported principles. But why does dialectic have this capacity? Aristotle's reference to the critical or examinational capacity of dialectic here in *Top.* I 2 is very important for understanding this. (101b3) Aristotle is alluding to the fact that dialectic standardly proceeds by the examination or testing of, and the attempt to refute, some position taken by an answerer in a two-party question and answer encounter, and to refute that position on the basis of concessions granted by that answerer in response to questions posed by a questioner. The so-called noted opinions (*endoxa*) that Aristotle mentions here are, roughly, the things which would *prima facie* be granted by an interlocutor or an answerer in such a discussion in response to questions. (See *Top.* I 1–11, VIII.) A Platonic dialogue such as the *Euthyphro* or *Meno* gives us a good sense of how this goes, where Socrates typically argues against and refutes various proposals of his interlocutors on the basis of what those interlocutors (and his audience too, including us readers for Plato) are liable to and do readily grant. Such a procedure can be used to examine any thesis at all, including one that may be a principle.

If such a dialectical interchange reaches a reasoned conclusion in a proper fashion, then the position of the answerer is dialectically refuted, even if that position has to do with some purported first principle in some science. If the interchange does not reach a reasoned conclusion then the answerer's position is *not* refuted. But in either case nothing in this process can have the result that any actual principle gets established *as a principle* by this procedure of examination, even though some purported principle could be refuted. To be established as a principle, a thesis must be shown to have certain demonstrative consequences, and a dialectical examination cannot show that. (See *APo* I 2.) Given this possibility of refutation, however, the dialectical examination of principles or of purported principles could easily be of use for scientific inquiry concerning principles, as Aristotle says it is, without it being the case that dialectic is able to discover or establish or confirm any principle as such, that is, for instance, as an account of the essence of something. We should notice also that Aristotle does not in the text speak of 'the path' offered by dialectic to the principles, as translators sometimes render it, but only of 'a path'. That is, as the context indicates, he is referring to a way to have a reasoned discussion of what are or may be principles. So he means here that dialectic is a technique of examination which offers a procedure for testing and thus for useful discussion in relation to purported principles. On this reading, Aristotle does not say that dialectic can or does enable us to discover or establish any principles as such.

This conception of the role of dialectic in regard to possible principles, and in regard to everything else—as a technique for criticism or examination—is more fully developed in a very closely related passage later in *Sophistical Refutations* 11 (*SE* 172a15–36). Aristotle says in this later passage that no discipline that has to do with establishing things that concern a particular nature (*phusis*) or genus (*genos*) proceeds by asking questions, that is, by asking for concessions (172a15–21, a36–b1). Since a science for Aristotle is just such a discipline (*APo* I 10 76b11–16), it follows that no science employs as its method any such interrogative procedure. In addition, since, as Aristotle also says here, dialectic does use such an interrogative procedure (*SE* 172a17–18), it follows that, for him, no science establishes anything using dialectic for its method. Further, there is no hint in this passage in *SE* 11 that dialectic can discover or establish any principles as such. What it *can* do, Aristotle repeats again, is to test or examine and, if successful, refute claims about purported principles or about anything else. Now, of course, in refuting one claim dialectic may be able to establish another, namely the negation of the claim refuted. But even if this negation of the claim refuted turned out in fact to be a principle it would, again, not be established by this means *as a principle*. For something to be established as a principle, as we have noted, it has to be shown or revealed to have a certain primitive place in a certain systematic body of truth; and dialectic, as we can see, has no means to show or reveal this even if it might, on occasion, establish some proposition which in fact is a principle. In *APo* I 2, as we have seen, Aristotle says that to have *epistêmê* you have to grasp the cause of your item of *epistêmê, as the cause*. By the grasp of *the cause*, as we earlier noted, Aristotle turns out to mean the grasp of the essence. (*APo* II 2) So to have *epistêmê*, you must grasp the cause and essence, or the principle that gives the cause and essence, *as such*. Dialectic, as a procedure of examination, cannot give you that.

This point is closely connected with another which comes out at the end of our passage in *SE* 11. Dialectic is described there as an 'art of deduction' (*technê sullogistikê* 172a35). This repeats Aristotle's characterisation of dialectic in the opening lines of the *Topics* as a procedure for deductive syllogistic reasoning and argument (I 1 101a2off.). Given this, a successful full dialectical argument is always a deductive argument.[19] To see the relevance of this for our current purposes consider again Aristotle's account of *epistêmê* in *EN* VI 3:

> Every science is held to be capable of being taught, and its object capable of being learned. But all teaching is based on things that are previously known, as we say also in the *Analytics*. For the teaching [of a science] is either by use of induction (*epagogê*) or by use of deductive proof (*sullogismos*). Induction is [used for the teaching] of a principle and universal, deductive proof [for teaching starting] from universals. Therefore, there are principles from which there is deductive proof of which there is no deductive proof. Therefore, it is induction [by which *principles* are learned] (1139b25–31).

Here it is clear that principles in science, including of course definitional principles or accounts of essence, are for Aristotle properly learned and taught by induction (*epagogê*) not deduction (*sullogismos*). Since, as we have just seen, a full dialectical argument or proof is always a deductive argument, this shows that one cannot learn or establish scientific principles, as such, by dialectical argument. This is closely connected with the point mentioned earlier, that to establish a principle *as such* one would have to show or reveal somehow that it has a certain primitive place in an appropriately structured systematic body of truth. A deductive proof of a proposition that happened to be a principle could not show that. In *APo* II 6 Aristotle argues further that a purported deductive proof of a proposition of the form 'E is the essence of X' would always turn out to beg the question. (92a6ff.) But, Aristotle must believe, an inductive proof of a principle of the sort that he has in mind in *EN* VI 3, could show or reveal not only that something which is in fact a principle and a statement of essence is true but also that it is a principle and a statement of essence. This is one main reason, perhaps the main reason, why Aristotle wants to hold, and perhaps must hold, that principles as such are reached by induction. In any case, the fact that principles are established and learned by induction shows us that, contrary to Plato, they cannot be established or learned by dialectic, since a full dialectical argument is always deductive.

4. Aristotle on the Learning of Principles by Induction

To understand this point in more detail, it is necessary for us now to investigate further what Aristotle means by his crucial claim in *EN* VI 3 that scientific principles are reached by induction (*epagogê*). The exploration of this matter leads us naturally to Book II of *APo*. In the famous final chapter of that book, II 19, Aristotle again makes, and there argues in detail for, the claim that principles in science are reached by and only by induction. The summary argument which leads to this conclusion comes at 100b 3–5 where Aristotle says:

> Thus it is clear that it is necessary to come to know the primary things by induction. For perception, in fact, implants the universal in this way.

Commentators have struggled with this. Their main suggestion follows the line taken by Ross:

> Just as the perception of one man, while we still remember perceiving another, leads to the grasping of the universal 'man', so perceiving that this thing, that thing and the other thing, are never white and black in the same part of themselves, we come to grasp the law of contradiction and so with the other *prota* [i.e., the other principles] of science.[20]

So understood, however, this procedure, at best, might, once again, lead one to learn something that happens to be a principle, not to come to know that principle as a principle. In *APo* II 19 Aristotle calls the state one is in when one has learned principles as such *nous*. (100b15) Earlier in *APo* I 34 he has already introduced a special talent or disposition that he calls 'quickness of *nous*' (*agchinoia*, 89b10). This he describes there not as a flair for grasping things that merely happen to be principles (could there even be such a flair?) but rather as a flair for grasping principles as principles, that is, he says, for grasping as such the things that explain and give the causes of the demonstrable truths of a science. In *APo* I 2, remember, Aristotle requires, for *epistêmê*, coming to know the principle which gives the cause (and essence) *as* the principle that gives the cause (and essence). It is the operation of this talent then that Aristotle has in mind when he speaks of induction in *Apo* I 19.

At this point we can clearly see what Aristotle means by the learning of principles by induction and why that can be the learning of principles *as principles* while the learning of any truths that happen to be principles by deduction, say by dialectical argument, is not. This shows us in more detail now, finally, why Aristotle wants to reject Plato's view that principles in science, especially those that give the essences of things, are reached by dialectic, even though in most other important respects Aristotle's conception of *epistêmê* is modeled very closely indeed on that of Plato.

NOTES

1. In a famous passage in *De Anima* II 5, Aristotle argues that the term *epistêmê* in this use, for a cognitive state, can designate each of three different types of such states. But these extra distinctions will not be particularly important for us here.
2. See recently, for some of these, G. Fine 1990 and L. Brown 1994.
3. See G.E.L. Owen 1986. Contrast U. Coope 2005, p. 146. For discussion of the issue, see R. Sorabji 1983, pp. 108ff.
4. See *Tim.* 42a, 47e-48a, Cf. *Laws* V 741a and Aristotle, *Met.* V 5 1015a26ff.
5. Here I speak, for convenience, of an item of *epistêmê* as propositional. One could equally well speak of any non-propositional state of *epistêmê*, should there be such, as necessarily accurately representative of its object.
6. See Ross 1936 *ad loc.* and cf. *DA* I 3 407a32–33 and Plato, *Cratylus* 437a.
7. Plato's dialogues can be, and should be, read individually and interpreted each in its own terms. But at least when we are interested in Plato's influence on Aristotle and other later thinkers this principle requires qualification since later thinkers tended to think of the dialogues, or of groups of them, as presenting a unified perspective.
8. The *Timaeus* uses the term *nous*, i.e., comprehension or intelligence, to draw the contrast with opinion (*doxa*) where the *Meno* and *Rep.* V use *epistêmê*. But cf. *Rep.* VI 511d-e.
9. This doctrine is now typically labelled the 'Socratic fallacy.' See P. Geach 1966. For recent literature see H. Benson 1990, M. Forster 2006.
10. See, e.g., M. Burnyeat 1990, pp. 4 n. 7, 131, 216f. with references there. Cf. Burnyeat 1979.
11. I thank Alan Code for discussion of this point.
12. See G. Vlastos 1988, 1994 and, *contra*, Benson 1990.
13. It should be noted, *pace* Vlastos, that it is unlikely that this particular dialectical approach on Plato's part to knowledge of essence was based on the practices of mathematicians.
14. Aristotle in fact supposes that basing *epistêmê* on knowledge of the true cause itself guarantees that this *epistêmê* is non-accidental and based on knowledge of the essence since, as later becomes clear in *APo* II 1–2, 8, he equates knowledge of the true cause with knowledge of the essence. See, further, on this matter, below.
15. J. Barnes 1993, p. 103.
16. J. Ackrill.
17. See J. Rawls 1971.
18. See G.E.L. Owen 1961, R. Bolton 1991 for a defence of this.
19. In *Top.* I 12 Aristotle does say that there are two kinds of reasoning used in dialectic: syllogistic and inductive. This would seem to conflict with what we find in I 1 and *SE* 11, as J. Brunschwig 1984/5 argues, until we see from *Top.* VIII 1 155b29ff. that the role of

induction in dialectic is to secure the concession of the necessary *premises* needed for a full dialectical deduction or *sullogismos*. This is granted in Brunschwig 1990.

20. Ross 1949, p. 85. Ross has in view here all of the different types of principles that Aristotle recognizes. See *APo* I 2, 10.

BIBLIOGRAPHY

Ackrill, J. (1963) *Aristotle's Categories and De Interpretatione* (Oxford: Clarendon Press).

Barnes, J. (1993) *Aristotle: Posterior Analytics* (Oxford: Clarendon Press).

Benson, H. (1990) 'The Priority of Definition and The Socratic Elenchus', *Oxford Studies in Ancient Philosophy* 8, 19–65.

Bolton, R. (1991) 'Aristotle on the Objectivity of Ethics', in J. Anton and A. Preus, eds., *Essays in Ancient Greek Philosophy IV* (Albany: State Univ. of New York Press), 59–72.

Brown, L. (1994) 'The Verb "to be" in Greek Philosophy: Some Remarks', in S. Everson, ed., *Companions to Ancient Thought 3: Language* (Cambridge: Cambridge Univ. Press), 212–236.

Brunschwig, J. (1984/5) 'Aristotle on Arguments Without Winners or Losers', *Wissenschaftskolleg Berlin Jahrbuch*, 31–40.

—— (1990) 'Remarques sur la Communication de Robert Bolton', in D. Devereux and P. Pellegrin, eds., *Biologie, Logique et Métaphysique chez Aristote* (Paris: Éditions du CNRS), 237–262.

Burnyeat, M. (1977) 'Examples in Epistemology: Socrates, Theaetetus and G.E. Moore', *Philosophy* 52, 381–398.

—— (1981) 'Aristotle on Understanding Knowledge', in E. Berti, ed., *Aristotle on Science: The Posterior Analytics* (Padova: Antenore), 97–139.

—— (1990) *The Theaetetus of Plato* (Indianapolis/Cambridge: Hackett).

Coope, U. (2005) *Time for Aristotle* (Oxford: Clarendon Press).

Fine, G. (1990) 'Knowledge and Belief in *Republic* V-VII', in S. Everson, ed., *Companions to Ancient Thought 1: Epistemology* (Cambridge: Cambridge Univ. Press), 85–115.

Forster, M. (2006) 'Socrates' Demand for Definitions', in *Oxford Studies in Ancient Philosophy* 3, 1–47.

Geach, P.T. (1966) 'Plato's *Euthyphro*: An Analysis and Commentary', in P.T. Geach, ed., *Logic Matters* (Oxford: Basil Blackwell), 1972.

Owen, G.E.L. (1961) '*Tithenai ta phainomena*', in G.E.L. Owen and M. Nussbaum, eds., *Logic, Science and Dialectic* (London: Duckworth), 1986.

—— (1966) 'Plato and Parmenides on the Timeless Present', in G.E.L. Owen and M. Nussbaum, eds., *Logic, Science and Dialectic* (London: Duckworth, 1986).

Rawls, J. (1971) *A Theory of Justice* (Cambridge, Mass: Belknap Press of Harvard Univ. Press).

Ross, W.D. (1936) *Aristotle's Physics* (Oxford: Clarendon Press).

—— (1949) *Aristotle's Prior and Posterior Analytics* (Oxford: Clarendon Press).

Sorabji, R. (1983) *Time, Creation and the Continuum* (London: Duckworth).

Vlastos, G. (1988) 'Elenchus and Mathematics', *American Journal of Philology* 109 (3), 362–396.

—— (1994), 'Is the 'Socratic Fallacy' Socratic?', *Ancient Philosophy* 10, 1–16.

PART II

THE FRAMEWORK OF PHILOSOPHY: TOOLS AND METHODS

CHAPTER 4

ARISTOTLE'S CATEGORIAL SCHEME

PAUL STUDTMANN

ARISTOTLE's categorial scheme had an unparalleled effect not only on his own philosophical system but also on the systems of many of the greatest philosophers in the Western tradition. The set of doctrines in the *Categories*, what I will henceforth call *categorialism*, play, for instance, a central role in Aristotle's discussion of change in the *Physics*, in the science of being *qua* being in the *Metaphysics,* and in the rejection of Platonic ethics in the *Nicomachean Ethics*. And commentators and philosophers ranging from Plotinus, Porphyry, Aquinas, Descartes, Spinoza, Leibniz, Locke, Berkeley, Hume, Kant, Hegel, Brentano, and Heidegger (to mention just a few) have explicitly defended, criticized, modified, rejected, or in some other way commented on some aspect if not the whole of Aristotle's categorial scheme.

Plainly, the enterprise of categorialism inaugurated by Aristotle runs deep in the philosophical psyche. Even so, despite its wide-reaching influence—and, indeed owing to that influence—any attempt to describe categorialism faces a significant difficulty: experts disagree on many of its most important and fundamental aspects. Each of the following questions has received markedly different answers from highly respected scholars and philosophers. What do the categories classify? What theory of predication underlies Aristotle's scheme? What is the relationship between categorialism and hylomorphism, Aristotle's other major ontological theory? Where does matter fit, if at all, in the categorial scheme? When did Aristotle write the *Categories*? *Did* Aristotle write the *Categories*? Is the list of kinds in the *Categories* Aristotle's considered list, or does he modify his views elsewhere? Is Aristotle's view of substance in the *Categories* consistent with his view of substance in the *Metaphysics*? Is there some method that Aristotle used in order to generate his list of categories? Is Aristotle's categorialism philosophically defensible in whole or in part? If only in part, which part of categorialism is philosophically defensible?

Perhaps even more prone to cause disagreement among scholars than these questions is the importance of various aspects of Aristotle's categorial scheme. Some scholars, for instance find Aristotle's list of highest kinds in the *Categories* to be of central importance; others find it at best a sloppy and unjustified bit of speculation. Some find Aristotle's views about substance in the *Categories* and the extent to which they differ from his views about substance in the *Metaphysics* to be critical; others find such apparent differences in his views to be minor and easily explained. As the flurry of papers inspired by G.E.L. Owen's 'Inherence' would suggest, some find Aristotle's views about non-substantial particulars in the *Categories* to be worth great scrutiny; others find such intense interest in that issue to be a case of sociology run amok. Some find Aristotle's theory of predication in the *Categories* to be of the utmost importance; others disagree. And so on. Indeed, it is safe to say that there is hardly any discussion of the *Categories* that either in substance or in emphasis will not appear to some scholar or other as seriously wrongheaded.

Why have I dwelt on the range of scholarly disagreement about the *Categories*? Well, I have done so in part to show what an endlessly fascinating work Aristotle's *Categories* is. One would be hard-pressed to find in the Western philosophical tradition a greater combination of brevity and provocative metaphysical speculation. And as is inevitable and fitting for such a work, philosophers and scholars will approach it with their own philosophical prejudices and predilections. I have, in addition, a second and more self-serving reason for dwelling on such disagreement. In this chapter, I shall discuss a tradition of interpretation that has for the most part been abandoned and shall do so by way of discussing two questions concerning Aristotle's categorialism that are not often treated together. By pointing out just how controversial any approach to Aristotle's *Categories* is bound to be, I hope to forestall any initial strong objections to the admittedly non-standard approach I shall take. And even if I fail to convince the reader of the cogency of the approach by the end of the chapter, I hope that the reader will have benefitted from seeing Aristotle's categorial scheme treated from a heterodoxical perspective. For what it is worth, it is my contention that Aristotle's categorial scheme, as is the case with many works in the history of philosophy, is best illuminated by opposing beams of interpretive light.

The following discussion is framed by two questions concerning Aristotle's categorialism: (1) How did Aristotle arrive at his list of categories? and (2) What is the connection between Aristotle's categories and his hylomorphic ontology. These questions are not often treated together, which is not altogether surprising, since each question is extremely difficult to answer in its own right. Hence, treating them together piles difficulty upon difficulty. Moreover, owing to their difficulty scholars have given wildly different answers to each of the questions. So the amount of scholarly disagreement about the issues involved is rather daunting. Nonetheless, there is an interpretively and philosophically interesting reason for discussing both questions in a single paper, namely the possibility of interestingly co-ordinated answers to the questions. The possibility stems from a tradition of interpretation that finds its origin in the Middle Ages. Because of its medieval origin, the interpretation is out of step with recent scholarly trends. Nonetheless, I hope at least to show the interest in the interpretation. My goal in this chapter is not to present anything like a definitive case for an interpretation of Aristotle's *Categories* but rather to discuss what I take to be a provocative and interesting interpretation that has the resources to provide systematic and co-ordinated answers to two very large questions concerning Aristotle's categorial scheme. In short, according to the interpretation, Aristotle's list of highest kinds can be derived a priori from his hylomorphic ontology. To understand the import of such a claim, however, first requires a discussion of the two questions I have just mentioned.

SECTION I—WHENCE THE CATEGORIES? (THE QUESTION)

At *Categories* 1b25–2a4, Aristotle provides a tenfold division 'of things that are said', *tôn legomenôn*, which are naturally interpreted as words. (*DI* 16a1–10). According to Aristotle, words signify the following basic types: (1) a substance, like a man; (2) a quantity, like a line two cubits long; (3) a quality, like the white; (4) a relation, like the double; (5) somewhere, like in the Lyceum; (6) at some time, like yesterday; (7) being in a position, like lies; (8) having, like is shod; (9) acting, like cuts; or (10) being acted upon, like is cut. (*Cat.* 1b25–2a4)

Although impressive for its philosophical insight, Aristotle's list raises the following very natural question: why think that it contains all and only the highest kinds in the world? Indeed, Aristotle gives some reason to suspect the correctness of his list, for even he seems unsettled about it. Only in one other place, at *Topics* 103b22, does he list ten categories, though in that list he replaces substance, *ousia* with what it is, *ti esti*. In *Posterior Analytics* I 22, on the other hand, Aristotle only lists eight categories: substance, quantity, quality, relatives, action, passion, where, and when. (*APo* 83b15). In *Metaphysics* V 7, he repeats the list from the *Posterior Analytics*, though he again replaces substance with what it is. And less directly, one might interpret Aristotle at *Metaphysics* 1089b18–25 as claiming that there are only four categories: substance, quality, relatives, and being acted upon.

The lack of any justification for his list of highest kinds has not gone unnoticed by critics and in fact has been the source of some famous criticisms. Kant, for instance, just prior to the articulation of his own categorial scheme, says:

> It was an enterprise worthy of an acute thinker like Aristotle to try to discover these fundamental concepts; but as he had no guiding principle he merely picked them up as they occurred to him, and at first gathered up ten of them, which he called categories or predicaments. Afterwards he thought he had discovered five

more of them, which he added under the name of post-predicaments. But his table remained imperfect for all that....[1]

According to Kant, Aristotle's list of categories was the result of an unsystematic, albeit brilliant, bit of philosophical brainstorming. Hence, it cannot stand firm as a correct set of categories.

Moreover, the troubles for Aristotle's scheme do not end with this list of highest kinds—Kant's criticism extends to Aristotle's intra-categorial divisions of quantity and quality as well. Aristotle divides each of these categories into several distinct species: quantity divides into continuous and discrete quantities, the former of which divides into body, line, surface, time, and place, the latter of which divides into speech and number; and quality divides into habits and dispositions, natural capacities, affective qualities and affections, and shape. Aristotle, however, never gives any justification for these divisions and as a result they appear just as arbitrary as his list of highest kinds. J.L. Ackrill, for instance, says about the category of quality:

> When Aristotle says that quality is 'spoken of in a number of ways' he does not mean that the word 'quality' is ambiguous but only that there are different kinds of quality. He proceeds to list and discuss four kinds. *He does not 'deduce' them or connect them on any principle....*[2]

And no doubt the lack of such a deduction lies behind Ackrill's criticisms of Aristotle a little later in his commentaries:

> He [Aristotle] gives no special argument to show that [habits and dispositions] are qualities. Nor does he give any criterion for deciding that a given quality is or is not a [habit-or-disposition]; why, for example, should affective qualities be treated as a class quite distinct from [habits and dispositions]?[3]

Ackrill finds Aristotle's division of the genus, quality, at best unjustified. Montgomery Furth, however, goes further. Furth has gone so far as to call the species in the category of quality a monstrous motley horde: 'I shall largely dispense with questions like...the rationale (if there be one) for comprehending into a single category the monstrous motley horde yclept Quality....'[4]

A first great question concerning Aristotle's categorial scheme, then, is this: is there some philosophically cogent way to justify both the highest kinds and the intra-categorial kinds in Aristotle's categorical scheme.

SECTION II—WHENCE THE CATEGORIES? (SOME ANSWERS)

The issue concerning the origin of the categories can be raised by asking the most difficult question there is about any philosophical position: why think that it is correct? Why, in other words, should we think that Aristotle's list of highest kinds contains all and only the highest kinds there are? One way of approaching this question is to ask whether there is some principled procedure by which Aristotle generated his list of categories. For, if there is, then one could presumably assess his list of highest kinds by assessing the procedure by which he generated it. Unfortunately, with the exception of some suggestive remarks in the *Topics*, Aristotle does not indicate how he generated his scheme. Without some procedure by which one can generate his list, however, Aristotle's categories arguably lack any justification. The issue is, of course, complicated by the fact that his list might be justified without some procedure to generate it—perhaps we can use a combination of metaphysical intuition and philosophical argumentation to convince ourselves that Aristotle's list is complete. Nonetheless, without some procedure of generation Aristotle's categories at least appear in an uneasy light.

As it turns out, scholars have offered at least four proposals as to ways Aristotle's scheme may have been generated, which I shall call: (1) *The Question Approach*; (2) *The Grammatical Approach*; (3) *The Modal Approach*; (4) *The Medieval Derivational Approach*.

J.L. Ackrill (1963) is the most prominent defender of the Question Approach. He takes as evidence for his interpretation Aristotle's remarks in *Topics* I 9. Ackrill claims that there are two different ways to generate the categories, each of which involves asking questions. According to the first method, we are to ask a single question—what is it?—of as many things as we can. So, for instance, we can ask of Socrates, what is Socrates? And we can answer—Socrates is a human. We can then direct the same question at the answer we have given: what is a human? And we can answer: a human is an animal. Eventually, this process of question asking will lead us to some highest kind, in this case Substance. If, on the other hand, we had begun asking that same question of Socrates' colour, say his whiteness, we would eventually have ended at the highest kind, quality. When carried out completely, Ackrill claims, this procedure will yield the ten distinct and irreducible kinds that are Aristotle's categories. According to the second method of questioning, we are to ask as many different questions as we can about a single primary substance. So, for instance, we might ask—how tall is Socrates? Where is Socrates? What is Socrates? And in answering these questions, we will respond: five feet; in the Agora; Human. We will then realize that our answers to our various questions group into ten irreducible kinds.

Of all the proposals that scholars have given, Ackrill's is the most supported by Aristotle's texts, though the evidence he cites is far from conclusive. But from a philosophical point of view, the question method suffers from some serious problems. First, it is far from clear that either method actually produces Aristotle's list. Suppose, for instance, I employ the second method and ask: does Socrates like Plato? The answer, let us grant, is 'yes'. But where does that answer belong in the categorical scheme? Ackrill might respond by forcing the question to be one that is not answered with 'yes' or 'no'. But we can still ask the question: is Socrates present-in or not present-in something else? The answer, of course, is: not present-in; but where in Aristotle's list of categories does not present-in belong? It is indeed hard to see. Similar problems face the first method. Suppose I were to ask: what is Socrates' whiteness? I might respond by saying 'a particular'. Again, where does being a particular belong in Aristotle's list of categories? Ackrill's method, as intuitive as it is, does not provide any principled way of filtering such questions from those which more readily generate Aristotle's preferred categories of being.

Further, even if Ackrill can find some plausible route from questions to Aristotle's categories, the methods he proposes still seem unsatisfactory for the simple reason that they depend far too much on our question-asking inclinations. It may be that the questions that we in fact ask will yield Aristotle's categories, but what we should want to know is whether we are asking the right questions. Unless we can be confident that our questions are tracking the metaphysical structures of the world, we should be unimpressed by the fact that they yield any set of categories. But to know whether our questions are tracking the metaphysical structures of the world requires us to have some way of establishing the correctness of the categorial scheme. Clearly, at this point we are in a circle that is too small to be of much help. Maybe all metaphysical theorizing is at some level laden with circularity; but circles this small are generally unacceptable to a metaphysician.

According to the grammatical approach, which traces to Trendelenburg (1846) and has most recently been defended by Michael Baumer (1993), Aristotle generated his list by paying attention to the structures inherent in language. On the assumption that the metaphysical structure of the world mirrors the structures in language, we should be able to find the basic metaphysical structures by examining our language. This approach is quite involved but for our purposes can be illustrated with a few examples. The distinction between substance and the rest of the categories, for instance, is built into the subject-predicate structure of our language. Consider, for instance, the two sentences: (1) Socrates is a human; and (2) Socrates is white. First, we see that each sentence has a subject, namely 'Socrates'. Corresponding to that subject, one might think, is an entity of some kind, namely a primary substance. Moreover, the first sentence contains what might be called an individuating predicate—it is a predicate of the form, *a* such and such, rather than of the form, such and such. So, one might think, there are predicates that attribute to primary substances properties the having of which suffices for that substance to be an individual of some kind. On the other hand, the second sentence contains a non-individuating predicate. So by examining the details of the predicates in our language, we have some grounds for distinguishing between the category of substance and the accidental categories.

The grammatical approach certainly does have some virtues. First, we have ample evidence that Aristotle was sensitive to language and the structures inherent in it. So it would not be all that surprising were he led by his sensitivity to linguistic structures to his list of categories. Moreover, some of the peculiarities of his list are nicely explained in this way. Two of the highest kinds are action and passion. In *Physics* III 3, however, Aristotle argues that in the world there is only motion and that the distinction between action and passion lies in the way in which one is considering the motion. So why should there be two distinct categories, namely action and passion, rather than just one, namely motion? Well, the grammatical approach offers an explanation: in language we differentiate between active and passive verbs. Hence, there are two distinct categories, not just one.

Despite these virtues, the grammatical approach faces a difficult question: why think that the structures we find in language reflect the metaphysical structures of the world? For instance, it may simply be a historical accident that our language contains individuating and non-individuating predicates. Likewise, it may be a historical accident that there are active and passive verbs in our language. Of course, this type of objection, when pushed to its limits, leads to one of the more difficult philosophical questions, namely how can we be sure that the structures of our representations are in any way related to what some might call the basic metaphysical structures and to what others might call the things in themselves? But one might hold out hope that some justification for a categorial scheme could be given that did not rest entirely on the unjustified assertion of some deep correspondence between linguistic and metaphysical structures.

The Modal Approach, which traces back to Bonitz (1853) and has most recently been defended by Julius Moravscik (1967), avoids the defects of both the previous two approaches. As Moravscik formulates this view, the categories are those types of entity to which any sensible particular *must* be related. He says:

> According to this interpretation the constitutive principle of the list of categories is that they constitute those classes of items to each of which any sensible particular—substantial or otherwise—must be related. Any sensible particular, substance, event, sound, etc. must be related to some substance; it must have some quality and quantity; it must have relational properties, it must be related to times and places; and it is placed within a network of causal chains and laws, thus being related to the categories of affecting and being affected.

By virtue of its explicitly modal nature, the Modal Approach avoids the defects of the previous two approaches. Whereas the first two approaches ultimately rely on some connection between metaphysical structures and what appear to be merely contingent features of either our question-asking proclivities or the structures inherent in our language, the Modal Approach eliminates contingency altogether.

Despite its explicitly modal character, the Modal Approach does face a difficulty similar to the one faced by the Question Approach. It might turn out that employing the approach yields exactly the list of Aristotle's categories, but then again it might not. So, for instance, every material particular must be related to a particular. But there is no category of particulars. There are, of course, beings that are not said-of other beings. But not being said-of is not one of Aristotle's categories. Moreover, must not every material particular be related to matter? But matter is not a highest kind. Indeed, it is far from clear where matter belongs in the categories. So, even if the Modal Approach is a good one for generating some list of kinds, it is not obvious that it is a good approach for generating Aristotle's list of kinds. This problem could of course be alleviated somewhat if instead of merely appealing to modal structures as such, one could appeal to modal structures that arguably Aristotle would have thought are part of the very fabric of the world. Then one would at least have an explanation as to why Aristotle derived the list he in fact derived, even if one is inclined to reject Aristotle's list.

The last approach to the categories, namely the Medieval Derivational Approach, goes some way in the direction suggested but not taken by Moravscik's Modal Approach. There is a rich tradition of commentators including Radulphus Brito, Albert the Great, Thomas Aquinas, and most recently their modern heir Franz Brentano, who provide precisely the kind of derivation for Aristotle's categorical scheme found wanting by Kant. According to the commentators in this tradition, Aristotle's highest kinds are capable of a systematic and arguably entirely a priori derivation. The following quotation from Brentano captures nicely the philosophical import of such derivations.

> On the contrary, it seems to me that there is no doubt that Aristotle could have arrived at a certain a priori proof, a deductive argument for the completeness of the distinction of categories.... (Brentano 1975)

Brentano's enthusiasm about the possibility of deriving Aristotle's categories is perhaps unjustified; but the idea that an a priori proof of the completeness of Aristotle's categories is certainly an intriguing one.

Perhaps the best representative of this type of interpretation occurs in Aquinas's commentaries on Aristotle's *Metaphysics*. All of Aquinas's derivation deserves considerable attention; but for our purposes it will suffice to quote just a portion of it so as to bring out its general character as well as one of its more interesting aspects.

> A predicate is referred to a subject in a second way when the predicate is taken as being in the subject, and this predicate is in the subject either essentially and absolutely and as something flowing from its matter, and then it is quantity; or as something flowing from its form, and then it is quality; or it is not present in the subject absolutely but with reference to something else, and then it is relation (Aquinas 1961).

This passage illustrates the tenor of the Medieval Derivational Approach. Aquinas articulates what appear to be principled metaphysical principles concerning the way in which a predicate can be, in his words, 'taken as being in a subject'. There are two such ways: (1) essentially and absolutely; or (2) essentially and not absolutely but with reference to something else. The latter way corresponds to the category of relatives; the former, to the categories of quality and quantity. Aquinas then divides the former way of being in a subject in terms of form and matter. He claims, strikingly, that the category of quality *flows from* form and that the category of quantity *flows from* matter.

Inspecting all of Aquinas's derivation to determine its cogency is far too large a project to undertake here. I have quoted the portion above to show the way in which the Medieval Derivational Approach augments in an interesting way Moravscik's Modal Approach. The Modal Approach would gain some plausibility if there were some way of seeing Aristotle's own attitudes about the modal structures in the material world somehow determining the generation of the categories. By invoking a combination of a priori–sounding semantic principles and theses about the relationship between form and quality and matter and quantity, Aquinas has gone some way toward doing this. For Aristotle is certainly committed to the claim that form and matter are two of the absolutely fundamental aspects of the material world. Indeed, he argues in the *Physics* that form and matter are necessary for the existence of motion, which, he thinks, essentially characterizes bodies.

If the Medieval Derivational Approach is correct, then Aristotle's categories ultimately trace to the ways in which form, matter, and perhaps motion relate to substances and the predicates that apply to them.

Section III—The Categories and Hylomorphism (The Question)

Unlike the first question, the second concerns the way in which categorialism relates to doctrines Aristotle articulates in other works. The question arises as a result of a rather common story that is told about the categories and its apparent deep tensions with hylomorphism.[5] According to the story, Aristotle wrote the *Categories* during a phase of his thought characterized by logical concerns. The *Organon*, the collection of works to which the *Categories* is generally thought to belong, contains an articulation of Aristotle's logic along with the semantic and ontological foundations of a philosophy motivated by logical inquiry. The *Categories* presents this ontological foundation; and one of its central tenets is that the metaphysically basic entities are primary substances,[6] which, if we are to judge by Aristotle's examples in the *Categories*, include living members of natural kinds as well as parts of substances, e.g., heads and hands (*Cat.* 3a29–32, 8a13–28), bodies (2b1–2), bits of matter, e.g., logs (8a23), and stuffs, e.g., honey (9a33). All other entities bear some sort of asymmetric ontological relation to primary substances. For example, all accidents inhere in primary substances while primary substances do not inhere in anything (*Cat.* 1a20–1b8). Furthermore, within the categorial scheme primary substances appear to be ontological primitives and hence do not appear to admit of ontological analysis into further constituents.[7]

Aristotle's attention, according to this common interpretation, eventually turned to the physical world. And though Aristotle never lost sight of the categorial scheme, his attempts at physical explanation forced him to a different view about the metaphysically basic entities. In his physical and metaphysical treatises, Aristotle claims that physical entities are composites of form and matter. According to this view, called *hylomorphism*, not only are physical entities ontologically complex but they depend for their existence on form. (*Met.* 1041b29) Thus, while categorialism treats physical entities as ontological bedrock, explaining the existence of all other entities in terms of them, hylomorphism finds a layer of reality below this bedrock. Form, not the composite of form and matter, is ontologically basic.

This apparent disparity between categorialism and hylomorphism is all the more striking in view of Aristotle's development of the categorial scheme without the central concepts he employs in his development of hylomorphism. The Greek word for matter (*hulê*) does not appear in the *Categories* or anywhere else in the *Organon*. Furthermore, although Aristotle uses the concept of form (*eidos*) in the *Categories*, his use of it in his physical/metaphysical treatises is far more varied and extensive and is not obviously commensurate with his use of it in the *Categories*.[8] Thus, categorialism and hylomorphism, far from representing two obviously complementary ontologies that permit an easy synthesis into a single coherent system, instead seem to manifest deep tensions both with respect to their fundamental presuppositions and the very terminology used in their construction.

SECTION IV—THE CATEGORIES AND HYLOMORPHISM (SOME ANSWERS)

Not surprisingly, the discrepancies between categorialism and hylomorphism have been the source of considerable scholarly speculation about the relationship between the two systems. The resolution of these discrepancies and the articulation of the relationship between the two systems have promised to provide acute insights into the contours of Aristotle's thought. Yet the difference of scholarly opinion about the relation between the two systems, as a brief examination of three prominent scholars' views will reveal, is almost as drastic as the difference between the two systems themselves.

Michael Frede argues that the later Aristotle developed hylomorphism in response to perceived inadequacies of categorialism.

> While Aristotle has spoken in the *Categories* as if the claim that substances underlie properties is totally unproblematic, in the *Metaphysics* he begins to draw consequences from this claim as to what really is the object of substance. As one can see in *Met Z* 3 he considers whether to say that substance, that which underlies everything else, is matter or form; by contrast in the *Categories* he had still spoken as if substances were the concrete things of our experience —tables, horses, trees, men—just as we are acquainted with them. How does it come about, we must ask, that Aristotle is no longer satisfied with the answer of the *Categories*?[9]

According to Frede, Aristotle's theory of substance underwent a transformation from the *Categories* to the *Metaphysics*. In the *Categories*, Aristotle thought it unproblematic to view the concrete things of our experience as substances; while in

the *Metaphysics*, Aristotle carefully considers whether the form and matter of concrete things are substances. Thus, Frede sees Aristotle addressing the same problems in the *Categories* and *Metaphysics* but developing different and incompatible
theories. According to Frede, the discrepancies between categorialism and hylomorphism point to Aristotle's dissatisfaction with the former ontology: Aristotle
developed hylomorphism as a response to his own criticisms of categorialism.

In *Aristotle's Two Systems*, Daniel Graham proposes an interpretation that, like
Frede's, finds a deep tension between categorialism and hylomorphism. In fact,
Graham argues for the radical conclusion that categorialism and hylomorphism
contradict each other. Unlike Frede, however, Graham thinks that Aristotle was
never critical of categorialism; indeed, Graham thinks that Aristotle, unaware of
the contradiction in his own thought, attempted an ill-fated synthesis of the two
systems:

> What emerges is an Aristotle that is bifurcated into a young philosopher with
> brilliant logical insights and the energy and organization to work out their
> implications while astutely applying them to design a priori a programme of
> scientific research; and a mature philosopher with a powerful and flexible theory
> which better adapts itself to the more practicable scientific projects which he
> engages in carrying out. Aristotle's early system [categorialism] was elaborated
> on a linguistic model that rendered it particularly suitable for generating a
> logical system of discrete terms in which strict connections could be established.
> Dependent from the start on the craft model, the later system [hylomorphism] was
> less rigorous in its articulation but more flexible in application, pluralistic in its
> outlook but more powerful in scope, less perspicuous in dealing with phenomena
> but more penetrating in analysis ... The late Aristotle wished to integrate his
> early principles with his later ones ... [but] he never succeeded, and he could not
> have, for the gulf between the two systems was a logical one. But in the process
> of developing his theories he gave us two of the greatest philosophies the world
> has known.[10]

Graham thus agrees with Frede that Aristotle's hylomorphism is in tension with
categorialism. Unlike Frede, however, Graham does not think Aristotle was ever
dissatisfied with categorialism. Instead, the mature Aristotle tried to synthesize his
two systems, an attempt that was in vain since, unbeknownst to Aristotle, the two
systems contradict each other.

Although both Graham and Frede find a tension between Aristotle's two systems, not all scholars think an irreconcilable tension exists. Montgomery Furth
advances an interpretation according to which Aristotle's two systems, despite
appearances, do not conflict; instead, the *Categories* is a work of limited scope—it
does not address the problems hylomorphism does. Hence, it is a self-consciously
simpler ontology than hylomorphism, yet one that properly and consistently supplies the basis for a richer hylomorphic ontology.

> ...the *Categories* is a carefully limited work—possibly an introductory one—
> which seems determined to contain the discussion at a metaphysical level that
> is, though in some ways sophisticated, still simple, and especially to block any
> descent from its own curtailed universe into the much deeper as well as wider

universe of the *Metaphysics*. There is also evidence of a notable concern not to get involved in 'causes'—to set out some ontological phenomena...without delving—here—into the underlying structure of the nature of things from which these phenomena eventuate. And a critical factor in maintaining that simplicity is the designation of the substantial individuals as ultimate objects, as the 'floor of the world'....[11]

Furth thus agrees with Graham as against Frede that Aristotle did not see any tension between categorialism and hylomorphism. Unlike Graham, however, Furth thinks that the discrepancies between the two systems are due to a difference in subject matter. Aristotle developed hylomorphism in response to 'deeper' and 'wider' questions than those that were the source of the categorial scheme. Thus, hylomorphism, though more sophisticated than categorialism, is not in tension with it. The difference between the two systems is one of degree, not kind: hylomorphism was not an abandonment or even an implicit criticism of categorialism; rather it was a natural extension of categorialism.[12]

There is one final interpretation about the relationship between hylomorphism and categorialism worth discussing, an interpretation that has already been discussed, namely the Medieval Derivational interpretation. Recall that many Medieval philosophers thought that Aristotle's categorial scheme was capable of a systematic derivation. Moreover, an inspection of their derivations shows that they invoke the concepts of form, matter, and motion, which are the central concepts in Aristotle's hylomorphism. Hence, if the Medieval approach is correct, the categories and hylomorphism are not at odds with each other. Moreover, the categories are not somehow surpassed by Aristotle's hylomorphism. Rather, Aristotle's categorial scheme is derived from hylomorphism. So viewed, Aristotle's metaphysical system displays a deep and fascinating coherence.

Section V—The Derivational Interpretation

We are now in a position to see the primary interest of the Medieval Derivational Approach to Aristotle's categorial scheme. If some version of such an interpretation is correct, then two very significant and difficult questions concerning Aristotle's categories admit of a unified answer. Not only would there be some systematic method by which Aristotle derived his set of highest kinds but there would be deep structural relations between hylomorphism and those kinds. It must be admitted, I think, that the possibility of co-ordinated answers to these two questions should at the very least spark some interest in the Medieval Derivational Approach. That being said, however, it must also be admitted that such an approach faces some significant challenges. I will finish this chapter by briefly discussing some of the more salient difficulties such an interpretation faces.

One initial challenge concerns the precise connection between hylomorphism and the categories. Consider again Aquinas's derivation.

> A predicate is referred to a subject in a second way when the predicate is taken as being in the subject, and this predicate is in the subject either essentially and absolutely and as something flowing from its matter, and then it is quantity; or as something flowing from its form, and then it is quality....

According to Aquinas, the category of quantity flows from matter and the category of quality flows from form. But what exactly does it mean for a category to 'flow from' matter or form. If this interpretation is to be made more precise, some non-metaphorical sense must be made of such claims.

The need for such precision in explicating the relationship between the categories and hylomorphism is related to a second difficulty that a derivational interpretation faces: what exactly is meant by 'form' and 'matter'? This question is of course not uniquely faced by a derivational interpretation. Any interpretation of Aristotle's metaphysical system must answer these questions. Nonetheless, if a derivational thesis is to be made precise, it must not only specify precisely the relation between hylomorphism and the categories, but it must also specify what is related. In this regard, a derivational interpretation would be made significantly more plausible if it were possible to see the intra-categorial derivations in quantity and quality as being systematically related to form and matter. For, the criticism that Aristotle's categorial scheme does not exhibit principled onotological divisions extends not just to his list of highest kinds but also to his divisions within the categories of quantity and quality. In addition to a detailed treatment of the categories of quantity and quality, a derivational approach must also contend with the most important category, namely substance as well as the categories that are often ignored: relatives, action, passion, where, when, having, and position.

It should be clear from these brief remarks that the plausibility of a derivational approach depends at least in part on its details. Stated in the abstract, the possibility of an a priori derivation of the categories from hylomorphism is an intriguing suggestion. But unless that suggestion can be filled in with substantive and plausible accounts of form, matter, substance, quantity, quality, and the other main concepts involved, a derivational interpretation will remain too underdeveloped to be of significant interest. Interestingly, however, such a fact points to what may be one of the most interesting aspects of such an interpretation: it acts as a kind of interpretive paradigm. Not only does it place constraints on some of the other fundamental concepts in Aristotle's system but does so in a way that has a satisfying interpretive and philosophical payoff. Supposing, for the moment, that Aristotle's categorial scheme admits of a systematic derivation from hylomorphism, one can ask: what would Aristotle's metaphysical views end up looking like? For instance, what view of form and its relation to the category of quality would be needed in order to carry out such a derivation? Likewise, what view of matter and its relation to the category of quantity would be needed?[13]

There is one final large issue that a Medieval Derivational interpretation faces. Any such interpretation faces the charge that it is an overinterpretation of Aristotle. Aristotle simply does not provide in his surviving writings the sort of conceptual connections that underlie the Medieval derivations. So perhaps the Medievals have succumbed to the temptation to read into Aristotle's system connections that Aristotle did not accept. Indeed, from a contemporary perspective, the Medieval derivations look very strange. It is commonplace in contemporary Aristotle scholarship to view the *Categories* as an early work and to think that Aristotle had not developed his theory of form and matter until later in his career.

Whether a Medieval Derivational interpretation can provide answers to these many questions is an open question. Despite the challenges, however, such a project is certainly worth pursuing. Aristotle thought that first philosophy must study being *qua* being. (*Met.* 1003a24–30) Because categorial being is one type of being, first philosophy must study the categories. But because substance is the primary category, first philosophy must study substance. (*Met.* 1028a10–15) And because substance has three aspects—form, matter, and the composite of the two—first philosophy must study each. (*Met.* 1029a3) Understanding Aristotle's first philosophy thus requires understanding his theory of substance, which inevitably runs into the question as to the relationship between his categorial scheme and hylomorphism. But of course, Aristotle thought that what is posterior depends on what is prior and hence that in some sense all other philosophy depends on first philosophy. At the risk of linguistic impropriety, therefore, one might very well consider the interpretive issues about the relationship between Aristotle's categorial scheme and his hylomorphic ontology as comprising first interpretation. That the Medieval Derivational approach would provide a unified first interpretation at the very least makes it worth pursuing.

NOTES

1. Immanuel Kant, *Critique of Pure Reason*, trans. N. Kemp Smith (London: St. Martin's Press, 1965), 114.
2. Aristotle, *Categories and De Interpretatione*, trans. J.L. Ackrill (Oxford: Clarendon Press, 1963), 104.
3. *Ibid.* p. 104. Ackrill translates the words *hexis* and *diathesis* as 'states' and 'conditions' respectively. I have interpolated 'habits' and 'dispositions' to provide continuity with my translations.
4. Montgomery Furth, *Substance, Form and Psyche: An Aristotelian Metaphysics* (Cambridge: Cambridge University Press, 1988), 14.
5. I should say that the view I am presenting is only one among several views about Aristotle's development that were proposed in the twentieth century. Starting with Jaeger, *Aristotle: Fundamentals of the History of his Development,* trans. Richard Robinson (Oxford: Clarendon Press, 1925), scholars have proposed theories of

Aristotle's development in terms of his gradual acceptance or rejection of Plato's philosophical positions. Jaeger argued that Aristotle originally accepted a Platonic framework and broke from the framework later in his career. David Ross, 'The Development of Aristotle's Thought,' in *Aristotle and Plato*, ed. I. Düring (Göteborg, 1960): 1–17, accepted a modified version of such a theory. Ingemar Düring, 'Aristotle on Ultimate Principles From 'Nature and Reality", in *Aristotle and Plato*, ed. Düring (Göteborg, 1960): 35–55, strongly disagreed with Jaeger's view, arguing that Aristotle was too strong a spirit ever to be so taken with Plato's theories. Cf. also, C. J. De Vogel, 'The Legend of the Platonizing Aristotle', in *Aristotle and Plato*, ed. I. Düring (Göteborg, 1960): 248–256. G. E. L. Owen, 'Logic and Metaphysics in some early works of Aristotle,' in *Aristotle and Plato*, ed. Düring (Göteborg, 1960): 163–190, 'The Platonism of Aristotle,' in *Logic, Science and Dialectic*, ed. Düring (London, 1960): 200–220, reversed Jaeger's position, arguing that Aristotle started out rejecting Plato's views and gradually came to accept them. Daniel Graham, *op. cit.*, on the other hand, argues that Aristotle's development should be viewed in reference to the internal dynamics of his own view rather than in reference to his attitudes towards Plato's view. Graham then argues that an inconsistency can be found between hylomorphism and the categorial scheme. On the basis of such an inconsistency, Graham argues that Aristotle wrote the *Organon* early and then developed hylomorphism, an ontology designed to accommodate the possibility of change. As opposed to these developmentalist views, cf. Mary Louise Gill, *Aristotle on Substance* (Princeton: Princeton University Press, 1989): 3–12.

6. That Aristotle's categorial scheme is a classification of entities is a controversial claim. Evangeliou, *Aristotle's Categories and Porphyry* (Leiden: Brill 1988), pp. 17–33 presents an excellent discussion of the historically prominent interpretations of the subject matter of the categorial scheme.

7. The ontological simplicity of primary substances in the *Categories* is a controversial claim. In support of such a claim, one can point to the fact that Aristotle says of primary substances that they are indivisible (*atomon*), unitary *(hen arithmô(i))* and hence a this (*tode ti*) (3b10–13). Cf. Daniel Graham *Aristotle's Two Systems* (Oxford: Oxford University Press, 1987), pp. 25–27, for a defence of this view.

8. The extent to which form and matter and the closely related concepts of actuality and potentiality are present in the *Organon* is debatable. Although matter is not mentioned in the *Organon*, there is evidence at *Posterior Analytics* 94a20–95a10 that Aristotle had developed his four-cause scheme of explanation by the time he wrote the *Posterior Analytics*. Such a scheme obviously includes both form and matter. Scholars have questioned the extent to which Aristotle's use of four causes in the *Posterior Analytics* is evidence that he had a fully developed four-cause scheme of explanation when he wrote the *Organon*. Some interpret the discussion of the four causes in the *Posterior Analytics* as a later interpolation; some, as a rudimentary and unsatisfactory account of the four-cause scheme that Aristotle uses in his physical-metaphysical treatises. Cf. David Ross *Aristotle* (London: Methuen & Co. LTD 1947), pp. 51–2; Jonathan Barnes, trans. and ed., *Aristotle: Posterior Analytics* (Oxford: Oxford University Press 1975), p. 215, Graham, *op. cit.*, p. 157. The distinction between actuality and potentiality is clearly in the *Organon* though it seems restricted to contexts in which Aristotle discusses necessity and contingency; cf., for example, *De Intepretatione* (19a30–19b4, 22b30–23a25) and *Prior Analytics* (25a37).

9. Michael Frede, 'Individuals in Aristotle', *Antike und Abendland* 24, (1978), p. 24.

10. Daniel Graham, *op.cit.* p. 332.

11. Montgomery Furth, 'Trans-temporal Stability in Aristotelian Substances', *Journal of Philosophy* 75 (1978), 627–32.
12. A notable exception to the dominant trend in contemporary scholarship is Michael Wedin, *Aristotle's Theory of Substance* (New York: Oxford University Press, 2000). Much of what I say in this chapter is compatible with Wedin's general line of interpretation, though I will not try to be explicit about specific points of agreement or disagreement.
13. I provide answers to these questions in *The Foundations of Aristotle's Categorial Scheme* (Marquette: Marquette University Press, 2008). Part of the present article derives from my entry on Aristotle's Categories in the *Stanford Encyclopedia of Philosophy*. I thank the editors for permission for the use of that material.

BIBLIOGRAPHY

Ackrill, J.L. (1963) *Aristotle: Categories and De Interpretatione* (Oxford: Clarendon Press).

Allen, R.E. (1969) 'Individual Properties in Aristotle's *Categories*', *Phronesis* 14, 31–39.

Ammonius (1991) *On Aristotle Categories*, S.M. Cohen and G.B. Matthews, trans. (Ithaca: Cornell Univ. Press).

Annas, J. (1974) 'Individuals in Aristotle's *Categories*: Two Queries', *Phronesis* 19, 146–152.

Aquinas, T. (1948) *Summa Theologica*, translated by the Fathers of the English Dominican Republic (New York: Benzinger Bros).

——— (1961) *Commentary on Aristotle's* Metaphysics, J.P. Rowan, (trans.), (Notre Dame: Dumb Ox Press).

——— (1984) *Treatise on the Virtues*, John A. Oesterle (trans.), (Notre Dame: Univ. of Notre Dame Press).

Brentano, F. (1975) *On the Several Senses of Being in Aristotle*, R. George (trans. and ed.), (Berkeley: Univ. of California Press).

Baumer, M. (1993) 'Chasing Aristotle's Categories Down the Tree of Grammar', *Journal of Philosophical Research* 18, 341–449.

Bonitz, H. (1853) 'Über die Kategorien des Aristoteles', *Sitzungsberichte der Wiener Akademie* 10, 591–645.

Code, A. (1985) 'On the Origins of Some Aristotelian Theses About Predication', in J. Bogen and J.E. McGuire, eds., *How Things Are: Studies in Predication and the History of Philosophy* (Dordrecht: Reidel), 101–131.

Cresswell, M.J. (1975) 'What Is Aristotle's Theory of Universals?', *Australasian Journal of Philosophy* 53, 238–247.

Dancy, R. (1975) 'On Some of Aristotle's First Thoughts about Substances', *Philosophical Review* 84, 338–373.

——— (1978) 'On some of Aristotle's Second Thoughts about Substances: Matter', *Philosophical Review* 87, 372–413.

——— (1983) 'Aristotle on Existence', *Synthèse* 54, 409–442.

Devereux, D.T. (1992) 'Inherence and Primary Substance in Aristotle's *Categories*', *Ancient Philosophy* 12, 113–131.

De Vogel, C.J. (1960) 'The Legend of the Platonizing Aristotle', in I. Düring, ed., *Aristotle and Plato in the Mid-Fourth Century* (Göteborg: Almqvist & Wiksell), 248–256.

Dexippus (1990) *On Aristotle Categories*, John Dillon (trans.) (London: Duckworth).

Driscoll, J. (1981) 'Eidê in Aristotle's Earlier and Later Theories of Substance', in
    D.J. O'Meara (ed.), *Studies in Aristotle* (Washington: Catholic Univ. Press), 129–159.
Düring, I. (1960) 'Aristotle on Ultimate Principles From "Nature and Reality"', in *Aristotle
    and Plato in the Mid-Fourth Century*. I. Düring, ed., (Göteborg: Almqvist & Wiksell),
    35–55.
Duerlinger, J. (1970) 'Predication and Inherence in Aristotle's *Categories*', *Phronesis* 15,
    179–203.
Engmann, J. (1973) 'Aristotle's Distinction Between Substance and Universal', *Phronesis* 18,
    139–55.
Ferejohn, M.T. (1980) 'Aristotle on Focal Meaning and the Unity of Science', *Phronesis* 25,
    117–28.
Furth, M. (1978) 'Trans-temporal Stability in Aristotelian Substances', *Journal of Philosophy*
    75, 627–32.
——— (1988) *Substance, Form and Psyche: an Aristotelian Metaphysics* (Cambridge:
    Cambridge Univ. Press).
Graham, D.W. (1987) *Aristotle's Two Systems* (Oxford: Oxford Univ. Press).
Granger, H. (1980) 'A Defense of the Traditional Position concerning Aristotle's non-
    substantial Particulars', *Canadian Journal of Philosophy* 10, 593–606.
——— (1984) 'Aristotle on Genus and Differentia', *Journal of the History of Philosophy* 22,
    1–24.
——— (1989) 'Aristotle's Natural Kinds', *Philosophy* 64, 245–247.
Heinaman, R. (1981) 'Non-substantial Individuals in the *Categories*', *Phronesis* 26, 295–307.
Irwin, T.H. (1988) *Aristotle's First Principles* (Oxford: Clarendon Press).
Jones, B. (1972) 'Individuals in Aristotle's *Categories*', *Phronesis* 17, 107–123.
——— (1975) 'An Introduction to the first five chapters of Aristotle's *Categories*', *Phronesis*
    20, 146–172.
Kant, I. (1965) *Critique of Pure Reason*, N. Kemp Smith (trans.), (London: St. Martin's
    Press).
Matthews, G.B. (1989) 'The Enigma of *Categories* 1a20ff and Why It Matters' *Apeiron* 22,
    91–104.
McMahon, W. (1987a) 'Radulphus Brito on the Sufficiency of the Categories', *Cahiers de
    l'Institut du Moyen-Age Grec et Latin* 39, 81–96.
——— (1987b) 'Aristotelian Categorial Theory Viewed as a Theory of Componential
    Semantics', in Hans Aarsleff, Louis G. Kelly, and Hans Josef Niederhe, eds., *Studies in
    the History of the Language Sciences* vol. XXXVIII, 53–64.
Moravcsik, J.M.E. (1967a) 'Aristotle on Predication', *Philosophical Review* 76, 80–96.
——— 1967b. 'Aristotle's Theory of Categories', in *Aristotle: A Collection of Critical Essays*
    (Garden City, NY: Doubleday & Co.), 125–148.
Owen, G.E.L. (1960) 'Logic and Metaphysics in some early works of Aristotle', in *Aristotle
    and Plato in the Mid-Fourth Century*. I. Düring, ed., (Göteborg: Almqvist & Wiksell),
    163–190.
——— (1965a) 'Inherence', *Phronesis* 10, 97–105.
——— (1965b) 'Aristotle on the Snares of Ontology', in R. Bambrough, ed., *New Essays on
    Plato and Aristotle* (London: Routledge and Kegan Paul), 69–95.
——— (1965c) 'The Platonism of Aristotle', *Proceedings of the British Academy* 50, 125–150.
——— (1978) 'Particular and General', *Proceedings of the Aristotelian Society* 79, 1–21.
Owens, J. (1978) *The Doctrine of Being in the Aristotelian Metaphysics*. 3d ed., rev. (Toronto:
    Pontifical Institute of Mediaeval Studies).

Porphyry (1992) *On Aristotle's Categories*, Steven K. Strange (trans.), (Ithaca: Cornell Univ. Press).

Porphyry (1994) *Isagoge*, in P.V. Spade (trans. and ed.), *Five Texts on the Medieval Problem of Universals* (Indianapolis, IN: Hackett).

Ross, W.D. (1960) 'The Development of Aristotle's Thought', in *Aristotle and Plato in the Mid-Fourth Century*, I. Düring, ed., (Göteborg: Almqvist & Wiksell), 1–17.

Schofield, M., and R.R.K. Sorabji, eds. (1975), *Articles on Aristotle, Vol 1. Science* (London: Duckworth), 14–34.

Simplicius (2000) *On Aristotle's Categories 9–15*. R. Gaskin (trans.), (London: Duckworth).

——— (2001) *On Aristotle's Categories 5–6*, F. De Haas and B. Fleet (trans.), (London: Duckworth).

——— *On Aristotle's Categories 7–8*, B. Fleet (trans.), (Ithaca, NY: Cornell Univ. Press).

——— *On Aristotle's Categories 1–4*, M. Chase (trans.), (London: Duckworth).

Stough, C.L. (1972) 'Language and Ontology in Aristotle's *Categories*', *Journal of the History of Philosophy* 10, 261–272.

Studtmann, P. (2008) *The Foundations of Aristotle's Categorial Scheme* (Marquette: Marquette Univ. Press).

Thorp, J.W. (1974) 'Aristotle's Use of *Categories*', *Phronesis* 19, 238–256.

Trendelenburg, A. (1846) *Geschichte der Kategorienlehre* (Berlin: Verlag von G. Bethge).

Wedin, M.V. (1993) 'Nonsubstantial Individuals', *Phronesis* 38, 137–165.

CHAPTER 5

DE INTERPRETATIONE

HERMANN WEIDEMANN

BOTH the title of this treatise (in Greek: *Peri Hermêneias*, in Latin: *De Interpretatione*), which I shall abbreviate to '*DI*', and its traditional placement as the second of Aristotle's logical writings, neither of which is due to Aristotle himself, are highly misleading. What, on the one hand, *DI* deals with is not, as its title suggests, a theory of interpretation, but rather a theory of statement-making sentences of different sorts and the logical relations that obtain between them; and what, on the other hand, this theory aims at is not, as suggested by the place which *De Interpretatione* traditionally occupies in the *Organon* between the *Categories* and the *Prior Analytics*, providing preliminaries to the study of syllogistic by examining statement-making sentences as possible parts of syllogisms, but rather underpinning the study of dialectical debates[1] by examining such sentences as possible members of contradictory pairs.[2]

A dialectical debate is carried on by a questioner and an answerer in such a way that the latter answers the questions he is asked by the former, which are questions of the form 'Is it the case that *p*?', either in the affirmative or in the negative, thus selecting one of the two members of a contradictory pair of sentences as true and rejecting the other as false, whereas the former tries to deduce from the answers he receives from the latter the contradictory opposite of the thesis which the latter tries to defend. Hence, it is essential for the participants in such a debate to know two things: They must know, on the one hand, by which sentence a given statement-making sentence is contradicted, and, on the other hand, the members of which contradictory pairs of sentences are disqualified for being used in a dialectical debate because the pairs they are members of are exceptions to the rule, called '*RCP*' (i.e., 'Rule of Contradictory Pairs') by C. W. A. Whitaker,[3] that of every contradictory pair of statement-making sentences one member must be true and the other false. To provide his students with this knowledge is Aristotle's foremost aim in *DI*.[4]

Having explained in chapter 6 what it is for the members of a contradictory pair of statement-making sentences to contradict each other, Aristotle examines in chapter 7 three types of contradictory pairs: those whose members are both singular sentences (e.g., 'Socrates is white'/'Socrates is not white'), those one of whose members is a universal sentence and the other a particular one (e.g., 'Every man is white'/'Not every man is white', 'No man is white'/'Some man is white'), and those whose members are both indefinite sentences, i.e., sentences which have a general term as subject without a quantifying expression, like 'every' or 'some', being attached to it (e.g., 'A man is white'/'A man is not white'[5]). Contradictory pairs of the third of these three types are regarded by Aristotle as exceptions to RCP because their members can both be true.

Other exceptions to this rule are examined in chapters 8 and 9. The exceptions dealt with in chapter 8 are contradictory pairs whose members fail to make a simple statement on the ground that either their subject term or their predicate term 'is adopted to stand for two separate things misleadingly taken together as if they were a single unit'.[6] Whether it is the possibility that their members are both false which, in Aristotle's view, makes such contradictory pairs exceptions to RCP or rather, as the *Sophistical Refutations* suggest (cf. *SE* 17, 175b39–176a18; 30, 181a36–b8), the possibility that their members are neither true nor false, is a question that is left open by the text. At any rate, it is in the case of the contradictory pairs dealt with in chapter 9 that, according to Aristotle, the latter possibility accounts for the violation of RCP. Being singular sentences about future events, the members of these pairs are, to Aristotle's mind, neither true nor false if the events they are about are contingent in the sense that their occurrence is neither necessary nor impossible.

In chapters 10 and 12 the examination of contradictory pairs of statement-making sentences is continued. It is extended to pairs the subject or the predicate of whose members is a negated term in chapter 10, and to pairs whose members are sentences that make modal statements (i.e., statements of possibility or necessity) in chapter 12. Chapters 11 and 13, on the other hand, deal with the validity of certain inferences. The topic of chapter 11 is inferences of the form 'x is a B and x is A; therefore x is an AB' as well as inferences of the converse form 'x is an AB; therefore x is a B and x is A', whereas in chapter 13, which is closely linked to chapter 12, inferences of modal statements from other modal statements are discussed. In chapter 14, which is the last chapter of *DI*, contrary pairs of beliefs and the sentences expressing them are examined. Since 'the chapter contains some astounding confusions',[7] its authenticity, which was questioned already in Antiquity, is dubious.

The first six chapters of *DI* are introductory in character. Their topics are the relationship between linguistic expressions, the thoughts they express, and the things that are meant by them (ch. 1), nouns (ch. 2), and verbs (ch. 3) as the constituents of simple statement-making sentences, phrases and sentences in general and statement-making sentences in particular (ch. 4), the difference between simple statement-making sentences and composite ones (ch. 5), and the notion of a contradictory pair of statement-making sentences (ch. 6). (Instead of the expression 'statement-making sentence' I shall henceforward simply use the word 'statement'.)

Obviously it was the semantic theory sketched out in the first half of chapter 1 which gave rise to bestowing on *DI* the title *Peri Hermêneias*, whose sense is: 'On interpreting thoughts by means of words'.[8] In what follows I shall first outline this semantic theory and then expound the doctrine concerning the truth and falsity of singular statements about future events which Aristotle develops in chapter 9. Of the two passages in question the former is considered as 'the most influential text in the history of semantics',[9] whereas the latter can fairly be said to be not only one of the most difficult, but also one of the most interesting and most often discussed texts in the work of Aristotle that has survived. Especially interesting and worth studying in detail are also chapters 11–13, which I shall finally scrutinize.

DI 1: Words as Signs of Thoughts and Things

The semantic theory that Aristotle designs in the first chapter of *DI* is contained in the passage 16a3–8. This passage, which constitutes the bulk of the first half of the chapter, can be summarized as follows: The expressions of spoken language are symbolized by the expressions of written language and are themselves symbols, or signs, of certain 'affections in the soul' (16a3–4, cf. 6–7),[10] which, for their part, are likenesses of things. While these mental affections, of which linguistic expressions are signs in the first instance, as well as the things they are likenesses of are the same for all men, linguistic expressions are not.

According to the traditional interpretation of the text in question,[11] by saying that mental affections are what linguistic expressions are 'in the first place signs of' (16a6),[12] Aristotle implies that linguistic expressions are in the second place signs of the things of which the mental affections they primarily signify are likenesses. Interpreted in this way, our text indeed sketches out a semantic theory.

At first sight this theory might remind a modern reader of the sort of 'uncritical semantics' described by Quine as 'the myth of a museum in which the exhibits are meanings and the words are labels'.[13] That Aristotle is not committed to this 'mentalistic myth of the meaning museum',[14] however, is shown by the way in which he explains what it is for spoken words to signify something. A spoken word, he points out in *DI* 3 (16b20–21), signifies something in virtue of the fact that 'the speaker arrests his thought and the hearer pauses'.[15] As the passage in Plato's *Cratylus* to which Aristotle is alluding here (*Cra.* 437a4–5) makes clear, it is the thing referred to by a word at which, according to Aristotle, 'the speaker arrests his thought' and upon which 'the hearer pauses'. This answers the question in what sense the mental affections mentioned in the first half of *DI* 1, which in the second half of this chapter are called thoughts (cf. 16a10, 14), are likenesses of things, on the one hand, and, on the other, that which is primarily signified—or symbolized—by linguistic expressions. The words we utter, Aristotle wants to say, refer to the things meant by them by expressing thoughts, which represent these things in our mind to the effect that to think these thoughts is nothing but to mean the things they represent.[16]

The semantic theory according to which words have a meaning in so far as thoughts are expressed and things are referred to by them in such a way that to think the thoughts they express is to mean the things they refer to may be illustrated, following H.-H. Lieb[17], by means of two interrelated semiotic triangles:[18]

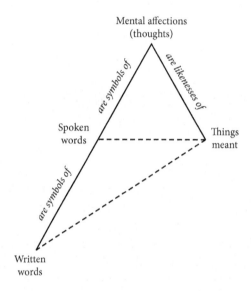

As for Aristotle's claim that, unlike things and mental affections, 'spoken sounds' and 'written marks are not the same for all men' (*DI* 1, 16a5–6),[19] it has to be understood as underpinning his claim, made in *DI* 2 (cf. 16a26–29), that linguistic expressions are symbols—i.e., conventional signs as opposed to natural ones—of what they signify. Being symbols, the expressions of spoken language can be written down, whereas non-linguistic sounds are 'inarticulate'[20]—*agrammatoi* (16a28–29)—in the sense of being 'unwritable'[21] and 'unspellable'.[22] Aristotle's insistence on the identity of things and thoughts for all men must not be misunderstood. Far from taking the strange view 'that all men meet the same things or have the same thoughts',[23] he simply stresses the fact that the members of different linguistic communities can, using their different vocabularies, express the same thoughts and mean the same things.

In at least one respect Aristotle's theory is unsatisfactory. For his notion of thought is ambiguous in that on the one hand, being mental affections, thoughts are individually distinct acts of thinking, whereas on the other hand, being the same for all men, they are the objective contents of such acts of thinking. It is to the credit of the Stoics that they consciously avoided such an ambiguity by introducing into their semantic theory what they called—using as a technical term a word whose literal translation is 'sayable'[24]—a *lekton*. A *lekton* is the meaning of a linguistic expression in the sense of being the objective content of the respective acts of thinking performed by a speaker who utters the expression in question with the intention to say something, and a hearer who understands what the speaker intends to say. In relation to Aristotle, who lacks the notion of *lekton*, 'the Stoics can be interpreted as filling a gap in his most celebrated doctrine of meaning',[25] thereby making an outstanding contribution to the development of the theory of language.

DI 9: Truth, Bivalence, and Determinism

What Aristotle seeks to establish in this chapter[26] is a negative answer to the question whether it holds good of all sorts of singular statements about future events that they have already at present (and have had already in the past) a truth-value. His reason for answering this question in the negative is his belief that, unless those singular statements which are meant to be about contingent future events were at present neither true nor false, there would be no such thing as a contingent future event and, hence, determinism would hold. Thus, it is Aristotle's considered opinion that in order not to be committed to the thesis of determinism that whatever will happen will happen of necessity we must restrict, with respect to singular statements about contingent future events, the validity of the principle of bivalence, according to which every statement is either true or false. Aristotle argues, in other words, as follows: If all sorts of singular statements about future events were already at present true or false, no future event would be contingent; but it is not the case that no future event is contingent; therefore not all sorts of singular statements about future events are already at present true or false (but only those which are about non-contingent events).

It is to this argument that Aristotle's line of thought in *DI* 9 can be condensed. Being an argument whose conclusion is inferred from its premises by means of the valid rule of inference called *modus (tollendo) tollens*, i.e., an argument of the valid form 'If *p* then *q*; but not-*q*; therefore not-*p*', this argument is undoubtedly valid itself. Whether it is not only valid, but also sound, depends on whether its premises are both true. As for its second premise, which states that it is not the case that no future event is contingent, its truth is regarded by Aristotle as a matter of experience. As he says in so many words, 'we see that what will be has an origin both in deliberation and in action, and that, in general, in things that are not always actual there is the possibility of being and of not being' (19a7–10).[27] Since it is not the question whether determinism is tenable or not which is at issue in *DI* 9, but rather the question by what sorts of assumptions determinism is implied, we should not bother with the second premise of Aristotle's argument and simply grant him that there are, as this premise states, future events that are contingent, i.e., future events for which it is both possible to occur and possible not to occur.

With the argument's first premise, however, it is quite different. For according to this premise the non-existence of contingent future events and, hence, determinism is implied by an assumption which at first sight does not appear to be such as to imply determinism at all, namely by the assumption that the principle of bivalence—in short: *PB*—is unrestrictedly valid. In view of the fact that the truth of the premise in question is far from obvious, one would have expected Aristotle to be at some pains to argue for its truth. But this is not the case. Before trying to explain why Aristotle takes the truth of the premise in question for granted, I shall summarize the moves he makes in the various sections of *DI* 9.

Having put forward, albeit in a manner which is not as clear as one may wish, the thesis he wants to prove, namely the thesis that, unlike statements concerning the present or the past, singular statements about the future are not subject to PB without exception (18a28–34), Aristotle points out a series of consequences which, in his view, would follow one after the other if this thesis failed to be true. He attempts to show, firstly, that if all singular statements about the future were subject to PB, all contradictory pairs of such statements would be subject to RCP (18a34–b4); secondly, that if this were the case, nothing at all would happen contingently, but whatever happens would happen of necessity (18b5–16), and, finally, after having rejected as futile the suggestion that the members of a contradictory pair of singular statements about the future might both be false (18b17–25), that from the last mentioned consequence the further consequence would follow that human deliberation and deliberate action would be pointless (18b26–19a6). In view of what we experience in life as deliberately acting persons, Aristotle goes on to argue (19a7–22), the consequences that would follow, if all contradictory pairs of singular statements about the future were subject to RCP, prove to be absurd. Since, as Aristotle has shown in 18a34–b4, singular statements about the future cannot be subject to PB without the contradictory pairs they are members of being subject to RCP, it is not only the conclusion that certain contradictory pairs of statements, namely those whose members are singular statements about contingent future events, are exceptions to RCP which can be drawn from the fact that the consequences in question are absurd, but also the conclusion that the members of these pairs are exceptions to PB. Only the former conclusion, however, is explicitly drawn in the final section of the chapter (19a23–b4; cf. in particular 19a39–b4), whereas the task to draw the latter, which actually is the thesis to be proved, is left to the reader.

It is remarkable that in the chapter's final section Aristotle does not confine himself to drawing the said conclusion, but endeavours to explain why things really are as this conclusion asserts them to be. His explanation, which, due to its occasional lack of clarity, is not always easy to understand, can be paraphrased as follows (cf. 19a28–39): It holds good of every state of affairs that before any given point of time it has always been necessary that at this point of time it will either obtain or not obtain; but it does not hold good of every state of affairs that before any given point of time it has either always been necessary that at this point of time it will obtain or always been necessary that at this point of time it will not obtain. Consequently, since it is according to how the states of affairs they express obtain or fail to obtain that statements are true or false, in the case of statements which express states of affairs for which it is both possible to obtain and possible not to obtain at some given future point of time one of the two members of a contradictory pair *will come out true* and the other *will come out false* in due course, namely at this future point of time at the latest, without one of them *being true* and the other *being false* already at present.

In the light of this explanation the reason why Aristotle takes the truth of the problematic first premise of his argument for granted appears to be the following: To be true or false according to how the states of affairs they express obtain or fail to obtain (cf. 19a33) is, in his view, for singular statements about future events to be, on the one hand, at present either true or false just in case the states of affairs they express will or will not obtain in such a way that it is already settled whether they will obtain or not, and to be, on the other hand, at present neither true nor false just in case the states of affairs they express will or will not obtain in such a way that it is not yet settled, but still open, whether they will obtain or not. Aristotle 'seems to hold', as Ackrill aptly puts it, 'a rather crude realistic correspondence theory of truth, and we might well expect him to think that if the state of affairs now is such that it is not settled whether X will or will not occur, then "X will occur" is not now either true or false: there is not yet anything in the facts for it to correspond or fail to correspond with'.[28]

In order to render Aristotle's position more perspicuous it is advisable to reconstruct it within the framework of a modal-cum-tense logic the semantic theory of which is what might be called a possible routes semantics, i.e., a possible worlds semantics in which the role of possible worlds is played by the different routes along which the actual world can develop at the different moments of its history.[29] A small portion of the so-called tree structure which these possible routes of the development of the world form is shown by the following diagram:

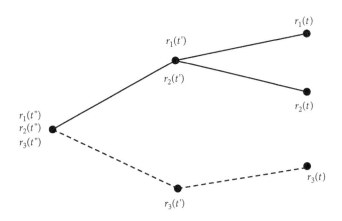

In mathematical terms the possible routes that form the sort of tree structure here devised can be described as functions which map points of time onto states of the world possibly subsisting at them. Since possible routes can branch only to the right, on the left-hand side of each node all routes that pass through it run an identical course.

The above diagram, in which, for the sake of simplicity, only three points of time t, t' and t'' and particular stages of three possible routes r_1, r_2 and r_3 are taken into consideration, is meant to represent the following situation: At the past moment t'' of its history the world was in the state $r_1(t'')$, which is identical with the states $r_2(t'')$ and $r_3(t'')$; at the present moment t' of its history it is in fact in the state $r_1(t')$, which is identical with the state $r_2(t')$, but could be in the state $r_3(t')$ instead, if its previous development had taken another route; and, depending on which route its further development will take, it will at the future moment t of its history either be in the state $r_1(t)$ or in the state $r_2(t)$, whereas the possibility to be at this moment in the state $r_3(t)$, which it still had at t'', is at t' no longer open to it. In order to indicate that r_3 is a route along which the world could have developed, but in fact did not and never will develop, it has been represented by a broken line.

In a modal-cum-tense logic whose semantics is based on the sort of tree structure here devised, each possible route of such a structure is at each point that it passes through what a possible world is in classical modal logic. That is to say that in such a logic the counterpart of a possible world is not a possible route of the development of the actual world *tout court*, but a possible route of its development, insofar as it has developed along this route up to a particular point, or, in other words, a possible route of its development, insofar as its development has on this route a particular past and a particular future. Hence, the relation of accessibility is defined not over the set of the possible routes of a tree structure alone, but over the set of the points of time which each of these routes maps onto the points that it passes through as well: A possible route r_j is accessible from a possible route r_i at a point of time t if and only if at least up to t r_i and r_j run an identical course, i.e., if and only if $r_i(t)$ and $r_j(t)$ are one and the same possible state of the world. Since a relation of accessibility thus defined is an equivalence relation, the modal-cum-tense logic at issue is as strong as the system S5 of classical modal logic.

The basic statements which the semantics of the modal-cum-tense logic at issue can be used to interpret are atomic present-tense statements and, provided that such statements are what the letter 'p' stands for, complex statements of one of the following four forms:

(1a) 'It is (now) possible that it is/was/will be the case at t that p',
(1b) 'It is (now) necessary that it is/was/will be the case at t that p',
(2a) 'It was the case at t that p',
(2b) 'It will be the case at t that p'.

The interpretation of these sorts of statements, i.e., the assignment of truth-values to them relative to a given point of a given tree structure and an arbitrarily selected route that passes through this point, is governed by the following rules:

Each atomic present-tense statement is arbitrarily assigned some truth-value or other at each point of each route of the tree structure at issue. Depending on whether it is of the form (1a) or the form (1b), a statement of one of these two forms is assigned truth relative to a given point $r_i(t')$ and the arbitrarily selected route r_i, which passes through this point, (a) if p is true at t on some route or other that passes through this point, i.e., on some route or other that at t' is accessible from r_i, or (b) if p is true at t on every such route; otherwise it is assigned falsehood relative to $r_i(t')$ and r_i. A statement of the form (2a) is assigned truth relative to a given point $r_i(t')$ whose temporal component t' is later than t and the arbitrarily selected route r_i, which passes through this point, if p is true at t on the common section of all routes that pass through this point; otherwise it is assigned falsehood relative to this point and the route r_i.

In the case of statements of the form (2b) it is convenient to distinguish, following Arthur Norman Prior, between *prima facie* assignments of truth-values and actual ones.[30] A *prima facie* assignment of a truth-value to a statement of the form (2b) is made if a truth-value is assigned to such a statement, relative to a given point $r_i(t')$ whose temporal component t' is earlier than t and a given route that passes through this point, irrespective of the other routes that pass through this point. If, for example, in the tree structure shown above the statement p is assigned truth at the point $r_1(t)$ and falsehood at the point $r_2(t)$, the statement "It will be the case at t that p" has two different *prima facie* assignments at the point $r_1(t')$, which is identical with the point $r_2(t')$, namely a *prima facie* assignment of truth relative to the route r_1 and a *prima facie* assignment of falsehood relative to the route r_2.

Faced with the question according to what sort of rule an actual assignment of a truth-value to a statement of the form (2b) is made we have to choose between the following two answers:[31]

(i) As its actual truth-value that *prima facie* value is assigned, relative to a given point $r_i(t')$ whose temporal component t' is earlier than t and the arbitrarily selected route r_i, to a statement of the form (2b) which it has at the point $r_i(t')$ relative to that one of the routes that pass through this point (provided that it is in fact one of these routes) which in the course of time will prove to be not only a possible route of the development of the world, but the actual route of its development. The *prima facie* value it has at the point $r_i(t')$ relative to this route is at this point its actual truth-value relative to each route that passes through this point.

(ii) An actual truth-value is assigned, relative to a given point and an arbitrarily selected route that passes through this point, to a statement of the form (2b) only if at this point it has one and the same *prima facie* value relative to all the routes that pass through this point, which is then its actual truth-value at this point relative to each of these routes. If at this point it has different *prima facie* values relative to these routes, it does not have an actual truth-value at this point relative to any of them.

It is obvious that if they are interpreted according to rule (i), singular statements about future events are actually either true or false even in case the events they are about are contingent, whereas, if their interpretation is governed by rule (ii), they are actually neither true nor false in this case. It is equally obvious that on the basis of an interpretation of such statements according to rule (i) the problematic first premise of the argument brought forward in *DI* 9 is false, whereas, if such statements are interpreted according to rule (ii), this premise is true. Ackrill calls the inference which is valid if this premise is true, namely the inference by which from the unrestricted validity of PB the non-contingency of all events is inferred, a 'highly dubious inference'.[32] Whether this inference is in fact 'dubious' and whether in the 'argument from truth to necessity' by means of which Aristotle tries to support it in 18b5–16 there is in fact a 'flaw', as Ackrill presumes,[33] can now be seen to depend on what sort of interpretation of singular statements about future events underlies Aristotle's reasoning.

That the interpretation of such statements which Aristotle tacitly presupposes is of a sort that is in accordance not with rule (i), but with rule (ii) is evidenced by the way in which he applies to such statements the above-cited principle that statements are true or false according to how the states of affairs they express obtain or fail to obtain (cf. 19a28–39). If it is entirely open, Aristotle seems to think, which of the different routes that are possible for the future development of the world will turn out to be the actual one, the mere fact that a sea battle, e.g., is taking place on a certain day cannot be a sufficient condition for the statement 'A sea battle will take place tomorrow' (cf. 19a30) to have been true the day before.[34] In other words: If the route the future development of the world will actually take is not fixed in advance, but comes into being step by step in such a way that at every point of time only that part of it exists which it then shares with all possible routes whose course has thus far been identical with its own, it is not by future facts that statements about future events can be made true or false, but only by present facts which necessitate the occurrence or the non-occurrence of the events in question; and if this is the case, a statement about a future event neither the occurrence nor the non-occurrence of which is necessitated by a present fact is at present neither true nor false.

The opinion that it is nothing but a future fact that makes a statement about a future event true or false, on which the first of the two rules of interpretation at issue is based, would certainly have struck Aristotle as unnatural. For to hold this opinion would have seemed to him 'to treat what is still future in a way in which it would only be proper to treat what *has been* future',[35] i.e., to view it 'as it would be proper to view it from the end of time'.[36] However foreign it was to Aristotle, the rather sophisticated option to anticipate in this manner as already present or even past what is still future and, hence, to single out from the possible routes of the future development of the world that one which eventually its future development will actually have taken[37] was enthusiastically embraced by Cicero, who seems to have borrowed it from the New-Academic philosopher Carneades, and, later on in the Middle Ages, by William of Ockham. As Cicero, who in his treatise *On Fate* resolutely defends this option against the Epicureans and the Stoics, does not tire of impressing on his readers, it is 'because it *did* so happen' that whatever has happened 'was certainly going to happen just as it did happen' ('quod ita cecidit certe casurum, sicut cecidit, fuit': *De fato*, § 19), in other words: 'that it was going to be should be understood from the fact that it did indeed happen' ('futurum autem fuisse ex eo, quia factum est, intellegi debet': *De fato*, § 18).[38]

It is remarkable that the Epicureans are credited by Cicero with a thesis which gives the impression of being a clarification of the position adopted by Aristotle in *DI* 9, namely with the thesis that in the case of statements like 'Philoctetes will be wounded', i.e., in the case of singular statements about contingent future events, disjunctions whose components are contradictory opposites of one another are true without any of their components being either true or false (cf. *De fato*, § 37). Cicero is indignant at this thesis to such an extent that he exclaims: 'What amazing presumption and pitiful ignorance of logical discourse!' (*De fato*, § 38).[39] As far as Aristotle is concerned, Cicero's indignation has a modern counterpart in W. V. Quine's derisive talk about 'Aristotle's fantasy that "It is true that p or q" is an insufficient condition for "It is true that p or it is true that q"',[40] which carelessly passes over the fact, however, that it is only in the case of certain disjunctions of the form 'p or not-p' that, according to Aristotle's view, their truth is an insufficient condition for the truth of one or other of their components. Hintikka, who correctly describes the view in question, but denies that it was held by Aristotle, joins its critics by denouncing 'the intrinsic absurdity of this alleged doctrine of Aristotle's, which has provoked the deserved ridicule of Cicero [...] and W. V. Quine [...]'.[41]

From the viewpoint of classical propositional logic Ciceros's and Quine's ridicule is indeed deserved. If, however, a system of logic is adopted which results from extending the framework of classical logic in such a way that truth-value gaps are admitted and dealt with by applying the so-called method of supervaluations, Aristotle and the Epicureans no longer deserve to be derided. The method of supervaluations, which has been developed by Bas C. van Fraassen, is tailor-made for cases in which a complex statement contains one or more atomic statements to which, due to the fact that they lack a fixed truth-value, truth-values can arbitrarily be assigned in different ways. In such a case for the complex statement in question and the atomic statement or statements it contains several classical valuations, i.e., arbitrary assignments of truth-values to the latter and, dependent on them, assignments of truth-values to the former according to the semantic rules of classical logic, are available. To apply the method of supervaluations to a complex statement of the sort just described is to assign to it, in case it is assigned one and the same truth-value by all classical valuations that are available, that very same truth-value, and otherwise no truth-value at all.[42]

It is obvious that if this method is used, not every disjunction of the form 'p or q', but every disjunction of the form 'p or not-p' comes out true even in cases where its components are neither true nor false. Thus, within a logical system in which this method is at one's disposal it is perfectly legitimate to do 'what Aristotle appears to be doing'[43] in *DI* 9 and what to do is in Martha Kneale's view 'a mistake',[44] namely 'to question the Principle of Bivalence while accepting the Law of

Excluded Middle',[45] i.e., the law which says that the disjunction of any statement and its negation is logically true.[46]

As R. H. Thomason has shown, it is not only the thesis, regarded as 'very odd and puzzling'[47] by Martha Kneale, that this law can unrestrictedly be valid without PB so being too which can be vindicated by appealing to the method of supervaluations, but also the thesis that PB is subject to restrictions in the case of singular statements about future events, i.e., if the events in question are dated, in the case of statements of the above-mentioned form (2b), 'It will be the case at t that p', in short: '$F/t(p)$'. For the second of the two above-mentioned rules between which a choice has to be made, if truth-values are to be assigned to statements of this form, can be regarded as 'a special case of van Fraassen's theory':[48] If this rule is applied, the *arbitrary assignment* of a truth-value to p at the point $r_i(t)$ of any route r_i that passes through a given point $r_j(t')$ whose temporal component t' is earlier than t, on the one hand, and the *prima facie assignments* of truth-values to $F/t(p)$ at the point $r_j(t')$ relative to the different routes that pass through this point, on the other hand, are the *classical* (i.e., bivalent) *valuations* with respect to which the *actual assignment* to $F/t(p)$, at the point $r_j(t')$ relative to the arbitrarily selected route r_j, of either the truth-value assigned to it by all its *prima facie* assignments at this point, if there is such a single truth-value, or no truth-value at all is the corresponding *supervaluation*.[49] Thus it is at two stages that a modern reconstruction of Aristotle's line of thought can benefit by the method of supervaluations: With the help of this method it can be made understandable, first, that with respect to singular statements about contingent future events Aristotle restricts PB and, second, that in his view this restriction of PB does not affect at all the law of excluded middle.

In addition to that, the method of supervaluations can help to clarify the strange-seeming doctrine of the ancient commentators on *DI* that in the case of singular statements about contingent future events the members of a contradictory pair 'always divide the true and false, not in a definite, however, but in an indefinite manner'.[50] In the light of the method of supervaluations, this doctrine can be restated as saying that in the case of such statements the members of a contradictory pair are assigned different truth-values at any point of a given tree structure by every classical valuation which is available at this point, i.e., by every *prima facie* assignment which can be made at this point, but not in such a way that one and the same truth-value is assigned to either of them by all these classical valuations, so that neither of them is assigned a truth-value at the point in question by the corresponding supervaluation.

A modern philosopher who, for whatever reason, is dissatisfied with both the position adopted by Aristotle in *DI* 9 and the rival view taken by Cicero and Ockham can resort to one or the other of two alternative positions, one of which is a modification of the Aristotelian point of view that has been suggested by Prior and the other a modification of what Prior calls 'the Ockhamist position'.[51] According to Prior's suggestion[52] we can avoid accepting truth-value gaps without committing ourselves to giving one of the possible routes of a tree structure the privileged status of the actual route by using the future tense not in the *weak* sense in which 'will be' just means 'will *in fact* be', but in the *strong* sense in which 'will be' means '*definitely* will be', i e., '*necessarily* will be'. If the future tense is used in this sense, two possible readings of statements of the form 'It will not be the case at t that p', one of which is the contradictory opposite of

(A) $F/t(p)$,

i.e., 'It (definitely) will be the case at t that p', and the other the contradictory opposite of

(B) $\sim F/t(\sim p)$,

i.e., 'It is not the case that it (definitely) will be the case at t that not-p', must carefully be distinguished, namely

(A') $\sim F/t(p)$,

i.e., 'It is not the case that it (definitely) will be the case at t that p', on the one hand, and

(B') $F/t(\sim p)$,

i.e., 'It (definitely) will be the case at t that not-p', on the other hand. Depending on whether the state of affairs described by p is such that it is necessary or such that it is impossible or such that it is neither necessary nor impossible for it to obtain at t, (A) and (B) are true and (A') and (B') false, or (A') and (B') are true and (A) and (B) false, or (A') and (B) are true and (A) and (B') false.[53]

The position that results from modifying the Aristotelian standpoint in the way just described has been christened 'Peircean' by Prior.[54] What is characteristic of this position is the fact that by replacing Aristotle's use of the future tense in the weak sense by its use in the strong sense it makes dispensable Aristotle's strong conception of truth and, along with it, Aristotle's restriction of the validity of PB. Those who are unwilling to dispense with the weak future tense are by no means forced back to either the Aristotelian or the Ockhamist position, however. For in view of the fact that, due to its weak conception of truth, the latter position, unlike the former, adheres to 'a tensed use of the phrase "it is true that"' which is 'spurious',[55] within its framework this 'tensed' (or 'temporalized') use of the phrase in question can be replaced by an 'atemporal' one.[56] The Ockhamist position can, in other words, be modified in such a way that the ancient and medieval conception of truth as 'truth-at-a-time'[57] is replaced by the modern conception of truth and falsity as properties which timelessly (or atemporally) belong to their bearers. To this sort of modification the Aristotelian position does not lend itself unless as compensation for weakening its strong conception of truth its weak future tense is strengthened.

DI 11: Logically Attributive Adjectives

The topic of this chapter[58] is, if its introductory section (20b12–30) is left out of consideration, the conditions on which it is permissible to draw an inference of the form

(1) *x* is a *B* and *x* is *A*; therefore *x* is an *AB*,

on the one hand, and the conditions on which it is permissible to draw an inference of the converse form

(2) *x* is an *AB*; therefore *x* is a *B* and *x* is *A*,

on the other hand, the letters '*A*' and '*B*' standing for two predicate-expressions the former of which is, as a rule, an adjective and the latter a noun. In the case of each of these two sorts of inferences whether it is valid or not depends, according to Aristotle, on the fulfilment of two conditions. The two conditions on whose fulfilment the validity of inferences of form (1) depends and the two conditions which must be fulfilled for inferences of form (2) to be valid—let us call the former (1a) and (1b) and the latter (2a) and (2b)—correspond to each other in that condition (2a) is a counterpart of condition (1a) and condition (2b) a counterpart of condition (1b).

Let us first consider conditions (1a) and (2a). Condition (1a) is the condition that of the two predicates '*A*' and '*B*' the former is not contained, whether as part of its wording or as part of its meaning, in the latter (cf. 21a16). This condition is not fulfilled, for instance, in the case of the inference 'Socrates is a white man, and Socrates is white; therefore he is a white white man' or in the case of the inference 'Socrates is a man, and Socrates is two-footed; therefore he is a two-footed man' (cf. 20b37–40; 21a4, 16–18). For the predicate 'white' is contained in the predicate 'white man' as part of its wording, and the predicate 'two-footed' is contained in the predicate 'man' as part of its meaning.

Condition (2a) is the condition that of the two predicates '*A*' and '*B*' the former does not contain anything which is opposite to the latter in such a way that in virtue of what it is by definition to be a *B*, on the one hand, and to be *A*, on the other hand, to be a *B* and to be *A* implies a contradiction (cf. 21a21–22, 29–30).[59] As an example of an inference which is invalid because this condition is not fulfilled Aristotle adduces, albeit in an elliptical manner, the inference 'He is a dead man; therefore he is a man, and he is dead' (cf. 21a23). In the case of this inference condition (2a) is not fulfilled on the ground that to be a man is by definition to be a certain kind of living thing, whereas to be dead is by definition to be no longer a living thing, so that to be a man and to be dead implies a contradiction.

It should be noticed that, according to Aristotle, it is not as elements of the composite predicate 'dead man' that the predicates 'dead' and 'man' implicitly contradict each other, but only as two separate predicates. Obviously it is for the following reason that this opinion is held by Aristotle: The concept which is signified by the composite predicate 'dead man' is not simply composed of what the predicates 'dead' and 'man' signify in their own right, but contains the concept which is signified by the predicate 'man' as a concept which is modified in a certain way by what the predicate 'dead' signifies. By combining it with the predicate 'dead' we alter the meaning of the predicate 'man' in such a way that in combination with the predicate 'dead' it is not true of anyone of whom it is true in separation from this predicate. A dead man is not a man in the ordinary and strict sense of the word and cannot, therefore, be called a man without qualification (cf. *Meteor.* IV 12 389b31; *PA* I 1 640b34–35).

Let us now turn to conditions (1b) and (2b). Condition (1b) is the condition that it is not the case that the two predicates 'A' and 'B' are predicated (or, as Aristotle puts it, that the things signified by them 'are said') 'accidentally, either of the same thing or of one another' (*legetai kata sumbebêkos ê kata tou autou ê thateron kata thaterou:* 21a8–9).[60] As Ackrill convincingly argues in his commentary, it is in two different senses that Aristotle speaks of accidental predication in stating this condition.[61] If two predicates are said to be predicated accidentally 'of the same thing' (*kata tou autou:* 21 a 9), their predication is said to be accidental in the sense that each of them ascribes a property to the thing in question which is *not essential* to it; if, however, two predicates are said to be predicated accidentally 'of one another' (*thateron kata thaterou: ibid.*) their predication is said to be accidental in the sense that one of them ascribes a property to a thing which, being referred to under a description furnished by the other, is referred to under that description not as the sort of thing as which it is meant to have the property ascribed to it, but in a manner which is irrelevant to its having that property, so that the predicate which ascribes that property to it is predicated of it not directly, but *indirectly.*

In the sentence 'This man is white and musical', for instance, the predicates 'white' and 'musical' are predicated accidentally of the same thing in that each of them ascribes an inessential property to the man in question, whereas in the sentence 'This white thing is musical' one of them is predicated accidentally of the other in that anybody who is both white and musical is musical not as something white, but as a man.

Contrary to what I have maintained, following the ancient commentator Ammonius,[62] in my own commentary on *DI*,[63] the two parts of the disjunctive phrase 'are said accidentally, either of the same thing or of one another' (21a8–9) are by no means equivalent. For there are cases in which a thing to which an adjective 'A' and a noun 'B' both ascribe a property which is not essential to it can, as something referred to as a B, be said to be A not only indirectly, but also directly. This kind of case can be exemplified by substituting for 'A' the adjective 'good' and for 'B' the noun 'cobbler'. For a cobbler can be good not only in his capacity as a man, but also in his capacity as a cobbler, so that he can be said to be good, as someone referred to as a cobbler, not only indirectly as a man, but also directly as a cobbler.

As this example shows, what matters in the present context is not accidental predication in the sense of *inessential* predication, but accidental predication in the sense of *indirect* predication only. The appeal to inessential predication in Aristotle's statement of condition (1b) is just a red herring. Yet it would not do simply to drop the phrase 'are said accidentally of the same thing' and to restate condition (1b) merely in terms of indirect predication. For there are cases in which an object *x*, as an object referred to as a *B*, is said to be *A* indirectly without there being any good cause for rejecting as invalid the inference from '*x* is a *B* and *x* is *A*' to '*x* is an *AB*'. After all, to borrow a telling example from Ackrill,[64] why should a man who is a cobbler and six foot tall not deserve to be called a six-foot-tall cobbler? Thus condition (1b), even if restated as a condition to the effect that it is not the case that *x*, as an object referred to as a *B*, is said to be *A* indirectly, proves to be inadequate.

As for condition (2b), it is stated by Aristotle as the condition that 'predicates [...] are predicated in their own right and not accidentally' (21a29–31).[65] This rather brief statement of the condition in question has to be understood in the light of the example that Aristotle adduces, which is, however, 'not a happy one',[66] as Ackrill rightly protests. 'For example', Aristotle explains,

> Homer is something (say, a poet). Does it follow that he is? No, for the 'is' is predicated accidentally of Homer; for it is because he is a poet, not in its own right, that the 'is' is predicated of Homer (21a25–28).[67]

It would have been better and more to the point if Aristotle had adduced this example in a different form, namely by saying:

> For example, Homer is something good (say, a good poet). Does it follow that he is good? No, for 'good' is predicated accidentally of Homer; for it is because he is a poet, not in its own right, that 'good' is predicated of Homer.

Since it is clearly in the sense of indirect predication that accidental predication is spoken of here,[68] Aristotle's statement of condition (2b) can be paraphrased as saying that a predicate '*A*' which is predicable of an object *x* in combination with a predicate '*B*' is predicable of *x* also in separation from '*B*' only if it is not the case that '*A*', as an element of the composite predicate '*AB*', is predicated indirectly of *x*.

The question under what sort of description in the sentence '*x* is an *AB*' *x* is said to be *A* indirectly if condition (2b) is not fulfilled is left open by Aristotle. In any case it must be a description different from that which is furnished by the predicate '*B*'. For in its capacity as a *B*, *x* is said to be *A* directly in this sentence if condition (2b) is not fulfilled. Evidently it is under the same description under which it is said to be a *B* directly that in the sentence '*x* is an *AB*' *x* is said to be *A* indirectly if condition (2b) is not fulfilled, namely under the description describing it as the sort of thing which it is essentially. In the sentence '*x* is a *B* and *x* is *A*', however, it is just the other way round. For in this sentence, *x* is said to be *A* directly under the same description under which it is said to be a *B* directly, whereas under the description which is furnished by the predicate '*B*', i.e., in its capacity as a *B*, it is said to be *A* indirectly.

In the sentence 'Homer is a good poet', for instance, Homer is said to be good directly in his capacity as a poet and indirectly in his capacity as a man; in the sentence 'Homer is a poet and Homer is good', however, Homer is said to be good directly in his capacity as a man and indirectly in his capacity as a poet. In other words, if Homer is said to be a good poet, he is said to be good not as what he is meant to be a good poet as, namely as a man, but as a poet, whereas, if he is said to be a poet and to be good, he is said to be good not as a poet, but as what he is meant to be a poet and to be good as, namely as a man. Since it is in two different respects that the adjective 'good' is predicated of Homer in the two sentences at issue, neither the inference from the first to the second is valid nor the inference from the second to the first.

According to Aristotle both condition (1b) in the case of inferences of form (1) and condition (2b) in the case of inferences of form (2) is only one of two conditions which are separately necessary and jointly sufficient for an inference of the form in question to be valid. As the modified Homer example shows, it is one and the same condition, however, namely condition (2b), on whose fulfilment both the validity of inferences of form (1) and the validity of inferences of form (2) depends if the respective supplementary conditions (1a) and (2a) are fulfilled, i.e., if the predicate 'A' is neither contained in nor incompatible with the predicate 'B'. Thus, condition (2b) plays not only the role which Aristotle has assigned to it, but also the role erroneously assigned by him to condition (1b).

Borrowing the grammatical terminology according to which the attributive use of an adjective has to be distinguished from its predicative use, Peter Geach has drawn a logical distinction between attributive adjectives and predicative ones which he explains as follows: 'I shall say that in a phrase "an A B" ("A" being an adjective and "B" being a noun) "A" is a (logically) predicative adjective if the predication "is an A B" splits up logically into a pair of predications "is a B" and "is A"; otherwise I shall say that "A" is a (logically) attributive adjective.'[69] According to this distinction, an adjective 'A' is logically predicative if together with a noun 'B' to which it can meaningfully be attached it licences both an inference of form (1) and an inference of form (2), and logically attributive otherwise. We can say, therefore, that in stating the conditions on which inferences of form (1) are valid Aristotle misses this distinction, whereas in stating the conditions of the validity of inferences of form (2) he adequately takes account of it.

As Aristotle seems to have seen more or less clearly, it is characteristic of logically attributive adjectives that they cannot stand by themselves as predicates without a noun to which they belong being understood from the context.[70] A sentence of the form 'x is A' is, if the letter 'A' stands for a logically attributive adjective, always short for 'x is an AB' or 'x is A as a B', the letter 'B' standing for an appropriate noun. Thus, what the predicate of such a sentence signifies is a relation which is of different levels in regard to the arguments of which it is a function, namely the relation of being A as …, which is a function one of whose arguments is an object, namely the object which is said to be A, and the other a concept, namely the concept falling under which this object is meant to be A as.[71]

DI 12 AND 13: MODAL STATEMENTS

Apart from the fact that they 'contain important first steps in modal logic',[72] chapters 12 and 13 of *DI* reflect in an especially impressive manner the circumstances to which Aristotle's scholarly writings owe their origin. They clearly show that, in expounding his doctrine, Aristotle follows a strategy which is motivated by the didactic purposes of someone engaged in oral teaching. What he wants to teach his audience is, on the one hand, how an affirmative modal statement is turned into its contradictory opposite (chapter 12) and, on the other hand, how the different sorts of modal statements are logically related to one another (chapter 13).[73]

For reasons which will become obvious later on, Aristotle does not write out the modal statements he is dealing with in full, but abbreviates them to the following expressions: *(ou) dunaton (mê) einai, (ouk) endechomenon (mê) einai, (ouk) adunaton (mê) einai, (ouk) anagkaion (mê) einai* (22a24–31), which may be rendered as follows: '(not) possible (not) to be', '(not) admissible (not) to be', '(not) impossible (not) to be', '(not) necessary (not) to be'.[74] As the use to which these expressions are put makes clear, the modal statements they are meant to abbreviate are not statements of the form 'It is (not) possible/admissible/impossible/necessary that (not-)*p*', where '*p*' stands for an assertoric (i.e., non-modal) statement, but statements of the form 'It is (not) possible/admissible/impossible/necessary for *x* (not) to be *P*', where '*P*' stands for a predicate noun.

I

Chapter 12 opens with the exposition of a difficulty. Faced with the question how the negation of an affirmative modal statement has to be formed, we are asked to consider non-modal statements first. What sort of non-modal statements Aristotle has in mind is at first sight unclear. For in formulating the three examples he adduces he resorts to expressions only one of which, namely *anthrôpos badizei* ('a man walks': 21b7), has the form of a statement, whereas the other two are infinitival phrases the first of which (*einai anthrôpon*: 21b1) can mean either 'that a man exists' or 'to be a man' and the second (*einai leukon anthrôpon*: 21b2) either 'that a man is white' or 'to be a white man'. In order to make it evident that the negation of the two last-mentioned expressions is formed by negating the word *einai* ('to be') and not by negating the word that follows *einai*, Aristotle produces an argument which shows, as Ackrill rightly points out,[75] that he wants these expressions to be understood in the sense 'to be a man' and 'to be a white man', respectively. If the negation of *einai leukon anthrôpon* ('to be a white man') were not *mê einai leukon anthrôpon* ('not to be a white man'), but *einai mê leukon anthrôpon* ('to be a not-white man'), he argues, we would be committed by the principle of excluded middle to regarding a log, which cannot truly be said to be a white man, of course, as something that can truly be said to be a not-white man (cf. 21b2–5).

As is obvious from this argument, the expressions *einai anthrôpon* and *einai leukon anthrôpon* are meant to be nominalizations of (the Greek equivalents of) the predicates '… is a man' and '… is a white man', respectively. When Aristotle adduces these predicates, by means of which he evidently wants to exemplify non-modal statements of the form '*x* is *P*', in the shape of infinitival phrases of the form 'to be *P*', his motive for doing so is the same as his motive for abbreviating modal statements of the form 'It is possible for *x* to be *P*', for example, to 'possible to be'. By contrasting 'possible to be' with 'to be a man' and 'to be a white man', Aristotle deliberately seduces his audience into regarding modal and non-modal statements as sufficiently similar in structure to be subject to the same rule of forming contradictory pairs. He further strengthens this intended appearance of similarity by adducing in addition to the two expressions 'to be a man' and 'to be a white man' the statement 'a man walks', whose nominalization 'a man to walk' (*anthrôpon badizein*: 21b9) he expands into 'a man to be walking' (*anthrôpon badizonta einai*: 21b9–10), thus ending up with a non-modal expression which in Greek has the same word order as the modal expression 'possible to be' (*dunaton einai*: 21b10). So the illusion he has created is perfect. The rule according to which 'of combined expressions those are the contradictory opposites of one another which are ordered by reference to "to be" and "not to be"' (21a38–39)[76] seems to apply not only to non-modal expressions, but to modal expressions as well. Just as the negation of 'to be a man' is not 'to be a not-man', but 'not to be a man' (cf. 21b1–2), the negation of 'possible to be' seems to be not 'not possible to be', but 'possible not to be' (cf. 21b10–12).

So far Aristotle has delineated one of the two conflicting aspects of an aporetic situation the other aspect of which he expounds by reminding us of the fact that there are things for which it is both possible to be and possible not to be such and such, for instance both possible to be seen and possible not to be seen. This being so, there would be things of which two contradictorily opposed expressions would be both true if 'possible not to be' were in fact the negation of 'possible to be'. Faced with the choice of rejecting the principle of non-contradiction or of conceding that 'it is not on account of "to be" and "not to be" being added that affirmations and negations are produced' (21b21–22),[77] we must no doubt opt for the latter horn of this dilemma: 'So if the former is impossible we must choose the latter' (21b22–23).[78]

Having arrived at the conclusion that in order to negate a modal expression like 'possible to be' we have to negate not the infinitive 'to be', but the word which signifies the modality in question, Aristotle tries to explain why this is so. The rather tortuous sentence by means of which he formulates his explanation is the key sentence of the chapter. It extends over the passage 21b26–32, the last lines of which it is indeed, as Ackrill remarks, 'hard to know how to translate'.[79] I propose to translate the whole passage as follows:

For as in the case of the previous examples 'to be' and 'not to be' are additions, while what is subject (to them) are 'white (man)' on the one hand and 'man' on the other, so here 'to be' and 'not to be' become what is subject, while 'to be possible' and 'to be admissible' are additions that separate, just as in the previous cases 'to be' and 'not to be' do, in the case of (say) 'possible to be' and 'not possible to be' the true and the false.[80]

In this text, Aristotle contrasts those contradictory pairs of expressions for which he had previously adduced as examples the two pairs 'to be a man'—'not to be a man' and 'to be a white man'—'not to be a white man' with those for which the pair 'possible to be'—'not possible to be' serves him as an example. What makes both sorts of pairs contradictory is the fact that, by some affirmative expression and its negation being added to another expression which is subject to—i.e., serving as the basis for— the additions in question, two predicates are formed which 'separate the true and the false' in the sense that of each object exactly one of them is true and the other false. Whereas in the case of contradictory pairs of the sort mentioned first the copula 'is', referring to which Aristotle uses the infinitive 'to be', and its negation are added to a predicate noun 'P' to form the predicates '... is P' and '... is not P', in the case of contradictory pairs of the last-mentioned sort the copula 'is' and its negation are subjected to having additions made to them in the sense that both to the predicate '... is P', in its nominalized form 'to be P', and to the predicate '... is not P', in its nominalized form 'not to be P', a modal expression like 'It is possible for ...' and its negation are added to form, for instance, the predicates 'It is possible for ... to be P' and 'It is not possible for ... to be P', on the one hand, and the predicates 'It is possible for ... not to be P' and 'It is not possible for ... not to be P', on the other hand.

According to the position adopted by Aristotle in 21b26–32 modal statements are formed out of assertoric statements neither by attaching the modal expressions 'possible', 'necessary', etc. as *semantic* (or *metalinguistic*) *predicates* to the names of assertoric statements, nor[81] by attaching them as *statement-forming operators on statements* to assertoric statements themselves, but rather by attaching them as *predicate-forming operators on predicates* to the predicates of assertoric statements. Thus, in *DI* 12 Aristotle is committed neither to the first of the 'three grades of modal involvement' distinguished by Quine,[82] according to which a modal statement is a statement of the form '"p" is possible/necessary (etc.)', nor to the second, according to which a modal statement is a statement of the form 'It is possible/necessary (etc.) that p'. By regarding modal statements as having the form 'It is possible/ necessary (etc.) for x (not) to be P' he comes rather close instead to Quine's third grade of modal involvement.[83]

Since in contrasting predicates of the form '... is P' with those of the form 'It is possible for ... to be P' Aristotle puts the former into the infinitive 'to be P' and abbreviates the latter to 'possible to be', he consciously conceals the fact that not only in the case of the former but also in the case of the latter it is by negating the copula 'is' that we form their negations.[84] His reason for doing so is his endeavour to teach his audience that it is not the addition of some predetermined sort of affirmative and negative expressions to some other expression that accounts for the formation of contradictory pairs of predicates and statements, but rather the addition to some other expression of those affirmative and negative expressions which 'separate the true and the false'. The lesson he wants his pupils to learn is, in other words, this: In order to decide whether a given pair of predicates or statements is contradictory or not we have to apply not the *syntactical* criterion of 'to be' and 'not to be' (or 'is' and 'is not') being added to something, but the *semantic* criterion of truth and falsity being (necessarily) distributed among the members of the pair in question.

After having applied, in 22a3–8, the rule which governs the formation of contradictory modal expressions to expressions of necessity and impossibility Aristotle recalls this rule to his hearers' minds. Depending on whether the participle *poiounta* in 22a10 is taken to mean 'facientia' or 'facientem'[85] the sense of the sentence 22a8–10 is caught either by the first or by the second of the following two possible translations:

(1) Generally speaking, as has been said, one must treat 'to be' and 'not to be' as what is subject, and, since it is these (other expressions, i.e. the modal ones) which make affirmations and negations, one must join them on to 'to be' and 'not to be'.

(2) Generally speaking, as has been said, one must treat 'to be' and 'not to be' as what is subject, and in making these (other expressions, i.e. the modal ones) into affirmations and negations one must join them on to 'to be' and 'not to be'.

Presumably Aristotle wants the sentence in question to be understood in the sense of the second translation; for it brings out more clearly that, in order to form the contradictory opposite of a modal statement of the form 'It is (not) possible/admissible/impossible/necessary for x (not) to be P', what we have to add the word 'not' to or what we have to remove it from are not 'to be P' and 'not to be P', respectively, but rather 'possible', 'admissible', etc. and 'not possible', 'not admissible', etc., respectively.

At the end of the chapter the following five pairs of contradictorily opposed expressions are listed: 'possible'—'not possible', 'admissible'—'not admissible', 'impossible'—'not impossible', 'necessary'—'not necessary', 'true'—'not true' (22a11–13). Since the expressions 'true' and 'not true' do not belong to the modal expressions dealt with in chapters 12 and 13, their presence in the text is probably due to a later addition, which may have been caused by a misunderstanding of what is said in 21b30–32.

II

In chapter 13 Aristotle examines the implications (*akolouthêseis*: 22 a 14) holding between the different sorts of modal statements that expressions like 'possible to be' or 'not necessary not to be' are meant to abbreviate. After having described these implications in 22a15–22, he illustrates them, in 22a24–31, by means of a table. If we symbolize the expressions 'possible', 'admissible', 'impossible', and 'necessary' by 'M',

'A', 'I', and 'N', respectively, and the expressions 'to be' and 'not to be', which are subordinate to them, by 'P' and '~P', respectively, we can represent this table as follows:[86]

Ia	1	$M(P)$	Ib	1	$\sim M(P)$
	2	$A(P)$		2	$\sim A(P)$
	3	$\sim I(P)$		3	$I(P)$
	4	$\sim N(P)$		4	$N(\sim P)$
IIa	1	$M(\sim P)$	IIb	1	$\sim M(\sim P)$
	2	$A(\sim P)$		2	$\sim A(\sim P)$
	3	$\sim I(\sim P)$		3	$I(\sim P)$
	4	$\sim N(\sim P)$		4	$N(P)$

As is obvious from the three passages 22a15–22, 22b3–10, and 22b14–16, the implications the table is meant to illustrate are such that in each quadrant each entry implies every entry below it and is implied by every entry above it. Although it is only the first two entries of Ia and the last two entries of Ib and IIb which are expressly characterized as following from one another (22a15–16) or as having the same meaning (22b4–5, 8–10), Aristotle can safely be assumed to have regarded as equivalent all four entries of each quadrant[87]—at least after the table has been corrected in 22b10–28.

Having drawn up the table Aristotle comments on what might strike anyone who is looking at it closely as peculiar to it. The first peculiarity of the table he comments on is the fact that both in its upper and in its lower half the expressions of the third line 'follow' from those of the second and the first line 'contradictorily but conversely' (*akolouthei men antiphatikôs, antestrammenôs de*: 22a33–34). As Ackrill correctly explains, this means that 'from the contradictories "possible" and "not possible" there follow the contradictories "impossible" and "not impossible"— but *not* respectively: the negative "not impossible" follows from the affirmative "possible", the affirmative from the negative.'[88]

In 22a38–b3 Aristotle points out a second peculiarity of his table, which is even more striking. 'But what about the necessary?', he asks and continues:

> Evidently things are different here: it is contraries which follow, and the contradictories are separated. For the negation of 'necessary not to be' is not 'not necessary to be'. For both may be true of the same thing, since the necessary not to be is not necessary to be.[89]

What causes difficulties in this text is the extremely condensed sentence 'it is contraries which follow, and the contradictories are separated' (*hai enantiai hepontai, hai d' antiphaseis chôris*: 22a39). Ackrill takes the contraries mentioned in this sentence to be the two expressions placed in 'the adjacent fourth lines in the upper half of the table',[90] i.e., '~N(P)' and 'N(~P)'. These expressions 'are called contraries', he suggests, 'presumably because they display the maximum difference from one another; they differ both in quality of mode ("not necessary"—"necessary") and in quality of *dictum* ("to be"—"not to be")'.[91] In making this suggestion Ackrill evidently follows Julius Pacius, who in his *Commentarius Analyticus* refers to the definition of contrariety, mentioned in the *Categories*, according to which contraries are 'those things in the same genus which are most distant from one another' (*Cat.* 6, 6a17–18).[92] Pacius concedes that the pair '~$N(P)$'—'$N(\sim P)$' is not really ('reipsa') a pair of contraries, it is true, but he thinks that the definition just quoted applies to it nevertheless as far as its verbal form is concerned ('voce tenus').[93]

Pace Seel,[94] this interpretation is far from plausible. For notwithstanding his distinction between real opposites and merely verbal ones, made in *APr* II 15 (63b23–28), Aristotle would surely have refused to regard the expressions '~$N(P)$' and '$N(\sim P)$' as contraries, even with respect to their verbal form only, in the sense defined in the *Categories*. If he had granted them the status of contraries, he could rightly be expected to have granted this status, by parity of reasoning, also to, for example, the statements 'Not every man is wise' and 'Every man is not-wise'. It is his considered opinion, however, put forward in *DI* 10 (20a27–30), that it is not the former statement itself, but its contradictory opposite 'Every man is wise' to which the latter is contrarily opposed. The same relationship which holds between the three statements 'Not every man is wise', 'Every man is not-wise', and 'Every man is wise' in that the first is the *contradictory* opposite and the second the *contrary* opposite of the third also holds between the three modal expressions '~$N(P)$', '$N(\sim P)$', and '$N(P)$'. It is the last two, not the first two of them which are contraries.

Is there a plausible interpretation of the sentence 'it is contraries which follow, and the contradictories are separated' (22a39) which makes Aristotle refer by the word 'contraries' to the expressions in lines Ib 4 and IIb 4 of his table, i.e., to the expressions '$N(\sim P)$' and '$N(P)$'? Indeed, there is such an interpretation, and it is due to Boethius.[95] As Boethius has clearly seen, what Aristotle intends to point out by saying that in the case of the necessary 'evidently things are different' (22a38)— different, that is to say, from how they are in the case of the impossible—is the fact that on the right-hand side of his table its symmetry is upset in the fourth line of both the upper and the lower quadrant. Whereas in the case of the impossible both '$I(P)$' and '$I(\sim P)$' are adjacent to their respective contradictories '~$I(P)$' and '~$I(\sim P)$', in the case of the necessary it is on the one hand not '$N(P)$' itself, but rather its contrary opposite '$N(\sim P)$', which is adjacent to its contradictory opposite '~$N(P)$', and on the other hand not '$N(\sim P)$' itself, but rather its contrary opposite '$N(P)$', which is adjacent to its contradictory opposite '~$N(\sim P)$'. In contrast to what considerations of symmetry might lead an unprejudiced viewer of the table to expect, in the case of the necessary, to put it briefly, instead of '$N(P)$' and '$N(\sim P)$' themselves their respective contraries '$N(\sim P)$' and '$N(P)$' are adjacent to their respective contradictories '~$N(P)$' and '~$N(\sim P)$', and in just this sense 'it is contraries which follow' (on the right-hand side of the table), while 'the contradictories are separated' (on the table's left-hand side).

With this interpretation the passage 22b3–10, which Ackrill suspects of being 'misplaced',[96] makes good sense as it stands. For its function is to explain why on the right-hand side of the table it is '$N(\sim P)$', instead of '$N(P)$', which is quite properly placed beneath 'I(P)', and 'N(P)', instead of 'N(~P)', which is no less properly placed beneath 'I(~P)'. The reason why this arrangement is correct is 'that it is in a contrary way (*enantiôs*) that an expression of impossibility is rendered by an equivalent expression of necessity' (22b4–5).[97] That is to say that 'I(P)' and 'I(~P)', which are themselves contraries, are equivalent to the respective contraries of 'N(P)' and 'N(~P)' (cf. 22b5–7). Thus, both the adverb *enantiôs* in 22b4, which is replaced by the adverb *antestrammenôs* in 22b9–10, and the adverbial phrase *ex enantias* in 22b8 take up the *enantiai* of 22a39, which refers to the expressions 'N(P)' and 'N(~P)'.

What the passage 22b3–10 explains is not, then, 'why in any quadrant the infinitive (*dictum*) must have a different quality in the last line from that which it has in the first three', as Ackrill maintains,[98] but only why in the two right-hand quadrants Ib and IIb this must be so. Since, *pace* Ackrill,[99] it is not 'a feature of the correct revised table', but 'a feature of the incorrect original table' which is explained in 22b3–10, this passage does not need to be and indeed, given its function within the context it is embedded in, must not be transported to where Ackrill thinks it 'properly belongs', namely '*after* the amendment of the original table'.[100] When Aristotle confines himself, in 22b3–10, to justifying the manner in which 'N(P)' and 'N(~P)' are arranged on the right-hand side of the table, this is due to the fact that it is these two expressions rather than their respective contradictories on the left-hand side of the table whose arrangement anybody who is not trained in modal logic is likely to be suspicious about at first sight.

Having dispelled the suspicion that 'N(P)' and 'N(~P)' might not be in their proper places Aristotle tries to show, in 22b10–28, that contrary to expectation it is the seemingly innocuous placements of 'the contradictories in the case of the necessary' (22b10–11),[101] i.e., the respective placements of '~N(P)' and '~N(~P)', which are in need of correction. He proceeds as follows: First, in 22b11–17, he argues that '~N(P)' is misplaced in Ia 4, since from the assumption that it is implied by 'M(P)', which is placed in Ia 1, the absurdity follows that it is also implied by 'N(P)', which implies 'M(P)'. Then, in 22b17–22, he shows that '~N(P)' can be replaced neither by 'N(P)' nor by 'N(~P)', because neither expression is true of anything of which both 'M(P)' and 'M(~P)' are true. And finally, in 22b22–28, he points out that the remaining expression '~N(~P)' is the right candidate for Ia 4 in that it is adjacent there—as well as the expression '~N(P)', which it has to change places with, in IIa 4—to the expression of which it is the contradictory opposite.

In 22b29–37, where Aristotle reverts to the question whether 'possible to be' follows from 'necessary to be', the argument put forward in 22b11–14 in favour of an affirmative answer to this question is confronted with an argument to the contrary, which runs as follows:

> On the other hand, the same thing seems to be capable of being cut and of not being cut, of being and of not being, so that the necessary to be will be admissible not to be; but this is false (22b33–36).[102]

Aristotle refutes this argument by pointing out that not for everything for which something is possible is the opposite possible, too. 'Well now', he says according to what we read in the manuscripts, 'it is evident that not everything capable either of being or of walking is capable of the opposites also. There are cases of which this is not true' (22b36–37).[103] In view of the fact, expressly acknowledged by Aristotle, that there is no such thing as a walker who cannot but walk all along (cf. *DI* 12, 21b16: 'what can walk is capable also of not walking'[104]), the manuscripts' reading *ê einai ê badizein* ('either of being or of walking') looks rather strange. What Aristotle probably wrote instead is *ê einai ê mê einai* ('either of being or of not being'). If this is the authentic reading, the origin of what is presented to us in the manuscripts can easily be explained as follows: First, due to homoeoteleuton, the words *ê mê einai* were omitted, and then the resulting gap, to which the remaining words *ê einai* drew the reader's attention, was filled by someone who was inattentive to the context by adding after these words the words *ê badizein*.

As for the rest of the chapter, the details of which this is not the place to enter into, it is metaphysical topics rather than logical ones that are discussed in it. This is especially true of the concluding paragraph 23a21–26, on which Ackrill rightly comments as follows: 'This paragraph reeks of notions central to the *Metaphysics* but out of place in the present work and only tenuously connected with what preceded. It is safe to regard it as a later addition, whether by Aristotle or by another.'[105] Ackrill also justly complains of Aristotle's failure plainly to point out that ' "possible" (one-sided) does follow from "necessary" and does not imply "possible not ...", while "possible" (two-sided) does not follow from (but is inconsistent with) "necessary" and does imply "possible not ..." '.[106] In fact, the distinction between one-sided and two-sided possibility is crucial for a proper understanding of what is at issue in *DI* 13. For in the incorrect original table, as it is shown in 22a24–31, the word *dunaton* is equivocal in that it means two-sided possibility in the two left-hand quadrants and one-sided possiblity in the two right-hand ones.[107] What Aristotle's amendment of the table, effected in 22b10–28, amounts to is nothing but an elimination of this equivocation in favour of one-sided possibility. This is not to say, however, that before making up his mind to revise his table Aristotle himself was confused about the two different concepts of possibility underlying it. What chapter 13 as well as chapter 12 presents Aristotle to us as doing is not disentangling himself from a bewilderment that besets him, but simply teaching his pupils philosophy.

NOTES

1. Cf. the introductory section of chapter 11, where this sort of debate is expressly referred to (20b22–30). Implicit references are to be found in chapters 5 and 10, where the speech acts of asking and answering a question are mentioned (cf. 17a19–20, 20a23–30).—References to the lines of the Greek text of *DI* are made following Minio-Paluello's edition even in those cases in which the line numbering of this edition does not exactly fit that of the Royal Prussian Academy edition of Aristotle's works

(*Aristoteles Graece ex recensione Immanuelis Bekkeri*, Berlin 1831), from which it in principle derives.

2. This has convincingly been shown by Whitaker, who rightly stresses the 'dialectical motivation of Aristotle's study of assertions in the *De Interpretatione*' (1996: 102; cf. 131). For an evaluation of both the merits and the shortcomings of his book see my review (Weidemann 1998).

3. Cf. Whitaker 1996: 79.

4. Cf. Whitaker 1996: 1–4, 180–182.

5. Literally: 'Man is white'/'Man is not white'.

6. Whitaker 1996: 97.

7. Dancy 1975: 143.

8. Cf. Kapp 1942, 47: 'The title *De interpretatione* means "on the expression of thoughts in speech"'.

9. Kretzmann 1974: 3.

10. Ackrill's translation (1963: 43).

11. Cf. for this interpretation Weidemann 2002: 134–151. The present exposition is borrowed from Weidemann 2006. For other texts relevant to Aristotle's theory of language, cf. Ax 1992 and Weidemann 1996.

12. Ackrill's translation (1963: 43).

13. Quine 1969: 27.

14. Quine 1969: 30.

15. Ackrill's translation (1963: 45).

16. Cf. Weidemann 2001.

17. Cf. Lieb 1981: 148.

18. Cf. Weidemann 2002: 149.

19. Ackrill's translation (1963: 43).

20. Ackrill's translation (1963: 44).

21. Kretzmann 1974: 17.

22. Arens 1984: 40, 87.

23. Ackrill 1963: 113.

24. Cf. Long/Sedley I 1987: 195–202.

25. Long/Sedley I 1987: 201.

26. For a more detailed analysis of *DI* 9 see Weidemann 2002: 223–328. My interpretation of the chapter is essentially the traditional one, which is also called the standard interpretation. As for the 'ever new efforts to read the text in non-standard ways' (Frede 1985: 32), suffice it here to say that 'they don't do justice to the text as a whole' (*ibid.*).

27. Ackrill's translation (1963: 52).

28. Ackrill 1963: 140–141.

29. For what follows cf. Weidemann 2002: 251–260, where further relevant literature is cited. See also Belnap/Perloff/Xu 2001: 29–32, 177–189, 194–196.

30. Cf. Prior 1967: 126–127, 132.

31. The first of these two answers, neither of which is explicitly given by Prior, is (*pace* Gaskin; cf. 1995: 189) implied by his account (cf. 1967: 121–127, 130–131, and 133, where he mentions, obviously with the intention to contrast them with the tense-logical system of which this answer is characteristic, 'time-systems with a branching future—in which no possible future is singled out as the actual one [. . .]'), whereas the second is due to Thomason (cf. 1970: 271–274, 1984: 144–146).

32. Ackrill 1963: 137. Similarly Quine reckons among certain 'confusions' which he characterizes as 'popular and in part Aristotelian' the view 'that sentences about the

future are as yet neither true nor false, and that otherwise fatalism would reign and striving would be useless' (1981: 95).

33. *Ibid.*

34. In order to exemplify a *singular* statement about the future, this statement must be supposed to be an elliptical way of making the assertion that, say, *off the coast of Salamis* a sea battle will take place tomorrow. That it is the battle of Salamis (480 BC), expressly mentioned elsewhere by him (cf. *Pol.* V 4 1304a22–23; *Rhet.* II 22 1396a12–13; *Poet.* 23 1459a25–26), which Aristotle has in mind when he adduces his famous example of tomorrow's sea battle is not unlikely.

35. Prior 1967: 131; Prior's emphasis.

36. *Ibid.* This assessment of 'the Ockhamist position', as he calls the opinion in question (1967: 128), is ascribed by Prior to 'the Peircean' (1967: 130), i.e., the adherent of the Aristotelian position which C. S. Peirce, by whom it is emphatically endorsed, describes as follows: '[...] everything in the Future is either *destined*, i.e., necessitated already, or is *undecided*, the contingent future of Aristotle. In other words, it is not Actual [...]; but is either Necessary or Possible' (*CP* 5. 459; cf. Prior 1967: 132).

37. For a thorough criticism of 'the beguiling but harmful doctrine of "the actual future," which says that among the many courses of events that *might* come to pass, there now exists a privileged such course that *will* actually do so', cf. Belnap/Perloff/Xu 2001: 135–136, 160–170 (quotation: viii).

38. Text and translation: Sharples 1991: 68–71.

39. Sharples' translation (1991: 85).

40. Quine 1976: 19.

41. Hintikka 1973: 163.

42. Cf. Van Fraassen 1966: 486–487, Thomason 1970: 272.

43. Kneale 1978: 47.

44. Kneale 1978: 48.

45. Kneale 1978: 47.

46. Cf. Van Fraassen 1966: 493–494.

47. Kneale 1978: 46.

48. Thomason 1970: 273.

49. Cf. Thomason 1970: 273–274. The future-tense statements to which the method of supervaluations is applied by Thomason are not temporally *definite* statements of the form (2b), but temporally *indefinite* statements of the form 'It will be the case (at some time or other) that *p*'.

50. Ammonius 1897: 138, 16–17; translation: Blank/Schneider/Seel 2001: 93. See also Ammonius 1897: 139, 14–15; Boethius II 1880: 13, 14–16; 245, 9–10.

51. Prior 1967: 128.

52. Cf. Prior 1967: 128–129, 136.

53. The same account holds for statements of the form 'It is/is not the case that it (definitely) will be the case the interval *n* hence that *p*/not-*p*', with respect to which Prior has modified Aristotle's position in the way described above.

54. Cf. Prior 1967: 130, 132. For the reason why Prior has chosen this label see note 36 above.

55. Von Wright 1979: 241.

56. Cf. von Wright 1979: 241–242.

57. Kneale 1978: 122.

58. In the present exposition I have corrected some errors which my interpretation of *DI* 11 presented in Weidemann 2002 (370–393) is affected with.
59. It is from Boethius' Latin translation of and his commentary on the passage 21a21–22 that the familiar phrase 'contradictio in adiecto' derives (cf. *Arist. Lat.* II 1–2: 25, 9–10; Boethius II 1880: 373, 24–25; 374, 13–14).
60. Ackrill's translation (1963: 58).
61. Cf. Ackrill 1963: 147–148.
62. Cf. Ammonius 1897: 207, 2–27.
63. Cf. Weidemann 2002: 382–383.
64. Cf. Ackrill 1963: 147.
65. Ackrill's translation (1963: 59).
66. Ackrill 1963: 148.
67. Ackrill's translation (1963: 59).
68. Cf. Ackrill 1963: 148.
69. Geach 1967: 64.
70. Cf. Geach 1967: 65–66.
71. Functions of two arguments which are of different levels in regard to them are called 'unequal-levelled functions' by Gottlob Frege (Geach/Black 1980: 40). Thus, as far as their meaning is concerned, logically attributive adjectives can be taken to be unequal-levelled two-place predicates (cf. Weidemann 2008: 133). A different view is held by Brekle with respect to adjectives like 'good' or 'bad', which he takes to be second-level one-place predicates (cf. Brekle 1970: 170–172).
72. Ackrill 1963: 149.
73. For a more detailed interpretation of the two chapters see my commentary (Weidemann 2002: 394–457), on which cf. the critical comments, referring to the first edition, by Gaskin (1996: 58–59). I am grateful to David Sedley for stylistic improvements to an earlier draft of the present exposition and to the editor of the journal *Dianoia*, in which an expanded Italian version of it appeared (Weidemann 2005), for permission to reproduce it here in English.
74. Ackrill's translation (1963: 62).
75. Cf. Ackrill 1963: 150.
76. Ackrill's translation (1963: 59).
77. Ackrill's translation (1963: 60) modified.
78. Ackrill's translation (1963: 60).
79. Ackrill 1963: 150.
80. My translation, which differs considerably from Ackrill's, is based on the following reading of the Greek text: *gignetai gar, hôsper ep' ekeinôn to einai kai to mê einai prostheseis, ta d' hupokeimena pragmata to men leukos to de anthrôpos, houtôs entautha to men einai kai mê einai hôs hupokeimenon gignetai, to de dunasthai kai to endechesthai prostheseis diorizousai, hôsper ep' ekeinôn to einai kai mê einai to alêthes kai to pseudos, homoiôs hautai epi tou einai dunaton kai einai ou dunaton* (21b26–32).
    Contrary to Minio-Paluello I have adopted *to* before *mê einai* in line 27, *leukos* instead of *leukon* in line 28, *kai mê einai* in line 29, *to* before *endechesthai* in line 30, and *kai to pseudos* in line 31.
81. *Pace* W. and M. Kneale (cf. 1978: 82–84), who are followed by Seel (cf. 1982: 135, 144–145).
82. Cf. Quine 1976: 158–159.

83. Wiggins correctly rates the passage 21b26–32 among the 'historic sources' of the idea of treating a modal expression 'as a modifier of predicates, or [...] of the copula' (2001: 112, note 8; cf. 1980: 107, note 8).

84. It should be noticed that in *DI* 12 Aristotle carefully avoids mentioning the copula that combines with a modal word like 'possible' to form a modal expression like 'It is possible for ...' (which in Greek, by the way, is construed personally like the English '... is capable of'; cf. Ackrill 1963: 149). What is meant by *einai dunaton* and *einai ou dunaton* in 21b32 is not 'to be possible' and 'to be not-possible', but 'possible to be' and 'not possible to be'; and what I have translated, following Ackrill (1963: 60), 'to be possible' and 'to be admissible' in 21b30 are the verbs *dunasthai* and *endechesthai*.

85. It is rendered as 'facientem' by Boethius and as 'facientia' by William of Moerbeke; cf. *Arist. Lat.* II 1–2: 29, 3 and 56, 14.

86. Both the numeration of the four quadrants of the table and the numeration of the lines of each quadrant have been added.—It should be noticed that the order in which the different modal expressions and their negations are listed in the table is the same as the order in which they are enumerated in the list drawn up at the end of chapter 12 (22a11–13). The first sentence of chapter 13 (*kai hai akolouthêseis de kata logon gignontai houtô tithemenois*: 22a14–15), which does not mean 'With this treatment the implications work out in a reasonable way' (Ackrill 1963: 61), but 'In accordance with their being arranged in this order their implications work out as well', takes account of this.

87. This is not to say, of course, that he intends their equivalence to be expressed by the verb *akolouthein*, which—*pace* Hintikka (cf. 1973: 45–47)—he never uses in *DI* 12 and 13 to express logical equivalence, but simply to express logical consequence. In order to state the fact that two expressions are equivalent he either adds *allêlais* to *akolouthein* (*DI* 12 21b35) or resorts to the verb *antistrephein* (*DI* 13 22a16).

88. Ackrill 1963: 151.

89. Ackrill's translation (1963: 62).

90. Ackrill 1963: 151.

91. Ackrill 1963: 152.

92. Ackrill's translation (1963: 16).

93. Cf. Pacius 1597: 100 a. According to Pacius the same holds for the pair '~N(~P)'—'N(P)'.

94. Cf. Seel 1982: 152.

95. Cf. Boethius I 1877: 184–189, II 1880: 426–429.

96. Ackrill 1963: 152.

97. Translation: H. W.

98. Ackrill 1963: 152.

99. Cf. *ibid.*

100. *Ibid.*

101. Ackrill's translation (1963: 63).

102. Ackrill's translation (*ibid.*).

103. Ackrill's translation (1963: 63–64).

104. Ackrill's translation (1963: 60).

105. Ackrill 1963: 153.

106. Ackrill 1963: 152.

107. This equivocation entails, of course, a corresponding equivocation on the part of the words *endechomenon* and *adunaton*.

BIBLIOGRAPHY

Ackrill, J.L. (1963) *Aristotle's* Categories *and* De Interpretatione. Translated with notes (Oxford: Clarendon Press).

Ammonius. *Ammonius, In Aristotelis* De interpretatione *commentarius*, edidit A. Busse (*CAG* IV-5) (Berlin: G. Reimer, 1897).

Arens, H. (1984) *Aristotle's theory of language and its tradition. Texts from 500 to 1750* (Amsterdam/Philadelphia: Benjamins).

Aristoteles Graece ex recensione Immanuelis Bekkeri, edidit Academia Regia Borussica. Aristotelis Opera, vol. I-II (Berlin: G. Reimer, 1831).

[*Arist. Lat.* II 1–2:] *Aristoteles Latinus* II 1–2. De Interpretatione vel Periermenias. Translatio Boethii, Specimina Translationum Recentiorum, edidit L. Minio-Paluello. Translatio Guillelmi de Moerbeka, edidit G. Verbeke, revisit L. Minio-Paluello (Bruges/Paris: Desclée de Brouwer, 1965).

Ax, W. (1992) 'Aristoteles (384–322),' in M. Dascal, D. Gerhardus, K. Lorenz, G. Meggle, eds., *Sprachphilosophie. Ein internationales Handbuch zeitgenössischer Forschung*, vol. 1 (Berlin/New York: W. de Gruyter), 244–59.

Belnap, Nuel, Perloff, Michael, Xu, Ming (2001) *Facing the Future. Agents and Choices in Our Indeterminist World* (Oxford: Univ. Press).

Blank, Schneider, Seel (2001) *Ammonius and the Seabattle. Texts, Commentary, and Essays,* edited by G. Seel in collaboration with J.-P. Schneider and D. Schulthess (Berlin/New York: W. de Gruyter); part III: Ammonius on Aristotle: *De Interpretatione* 9 (and 7, 1–17), Greek text established by A. Busse, reprint from *CAG* (IV/v), English translation by D. Blank, revised by J.-P. Schneider and G. Seel.

Boethius, I 1877/II 1880. *A. M. S. Boetii commentarii in librum Aristotelis Peri hermêneias,* recensuit C. Meiser. Pars prior, versionem continuam et primam editionem continens; pars posterior, secundam editionem et indices continens (Leipzig: B.G. Teubner).

Brekle, H.E. (1970) 'A Note on Aristotle's *De interpretatione* 20b–21a', *Folia Linguistica* 4, 167–73.

Dancy, R.M. (1975) *Sense and Contradiction. A Study in Aristotle* (Dordrecht/Boston: D. Reidel).

Fraassen, B.C. van (1966) 'Singular Terms, Truth-value Gaps, and Free Logic', *Journal of Philosophy* 63, 481–95.

Frede, D. (1985) 'The Sea-Battle Reconsidered. A Defence of the Traditional Interpretation', *Oxford Studies in Ancient Philosophy* 3, 31–87.

Gaskin, R. (1995) *The Sea Battle and the Master Argument. Aristotle and Diodorus Cronus on the Metaphysics of the Future* (Berlin/New York: W. de Gruyter).

—— (1996) 'Sea Battles, Worn-out Cloaks, and other matters of interpretation: Weidemann on Aristotle's *Peri Hermeneias*', *Archiv für Geschichte der Philosophie* 78, 48–59.

Geach, P.T. (1967) 'Good and Evil', *Analysis* 17 (1956), 33–42; reprinted in Ph. Foot, ed., *Theories of Ethics* (Oxford: Univ. Press, 1967), 64–73.

Geach, P., and Max Black, eds. (1980) *Translations from the Philosophical Writings of Gottlob Frege*, 3rd ed. (Oxford: Blackwell).

Hintikka, J. (1973) *Time and Necessity. Studies in Aristotle's Theory of Modality* (Oxford: Clarendon Press).

Kapp, E. (1942) *Greek Foundations of Traditional Logic* (New York: Columbia Univ. Press).

Kneale, W., and M. Kneale (1978) *The Development of Logic* (Oxford: Clarendon Press, 1962; reprinted 1978).

Kretzmann, N. (1974) 'Aristotle on Spoken Sound Significant by Convention', in J. Corcoran, ed., *Ancient Logic and Its Modern Interpretations* (Dordrecht: D. Reidel), 3–21.

Lieb, H.H. (1981) 'Das "semiotische Dreieck" bei Ogden und Richards: eine Neuformulierung des Zeichenmodells von Aristoteles', in H. Geckeler, B. Schlieben-Lange, J. Trabant, H. Weydt, eds., *Logos Semantikos. Studia Linguistica in Honorem Eugenio Coseriu (1921–1981)*, vol. I (Berlin/New York: W. de Gruyter/Madrid: Editorial Gredos), 137–56.

Long, A.A. and D.N. Sedley, eds., I/II (1987). *The Hellenistic philosophers*, vol. 1: *Translations of the principal sources with philosophical commentary*, vol. 2: *Greek and Latin texts with notes and bibliography* (Cambridge: Cambridge Univ. Press).

Minio-Paluello, L. (1956) *Aristotelis* Categoriae *et liber* De Interpretatione. Recognovit brevique adnotatione critica instruxit L. Minio-Paluello. (Oxford: Clarendon Press, 1949; 2nd edition).

Pacius, J., Iul. Pacii a Beriga *In Porphyrii Isagogen, et Aristotelis Organum, Commentarius Analyticus* [...]. Frankfurt a. M. 1597 (reprinted Hildesheim: G. Olms, 1966).

Peirce, C.S. (1965) *Collected Papers of Charles Sanders Peirce*, vol. V and vol. VI, edited by C. Hartshorne and P. Weiss (Cambridge, Mass.: The Belknap Press of Harvard Univ. Press).

Prior, A.N. (1967) *Past, Present, and Future* (Oxford: Clarendon Press).

Quine, W.V. (1969) *Ontological relativity and other essays* (New York/London: Columbia Univ. Press).

—— (1976) *The Ways of Paradox and Other Essays*. Revised and enlarged edition (Cambridge, Mass./London: Harvard Univ. Press).

—— (1981) *Theories and Things* (Cambridge, Mass./London: The Belknap Press of Harvard Univ. Press).

Seel, G. (1982) *Die Aristotelische Modaltheorie* (Berlin/New York: W. de Gruyter).

Sharples, R.W. (1991) *Cicero:* On Fate (De Fato)/*Boethius:* The Consolation of Philosophy (Philosophiae Consolationis) IV.5–7, V; edited with an introduction, translations and commentaries by R.W. Sharples (Warminster: Aris & Phillips).

Thomason, R.H. (1970) 'Indeterminist time and truth-value gaps', *Theoria* 36, 264–81.

—— (1984) 'Combinations of Tense and Modality', in D. Gabbay, F. Guenthner, eds., *Handbook of Philosophical Logic*, vol. II: *Extensions of Classical Logic* (Dordrecht/ Boston/Lancaster: D. Reidel), 135–65.

Weidemann, H. (1996) 'Grundzüge der Aristotelischen Sprachtheorie', in P. Schmitter, ed., *Sprachtheorien der abendländischen Antike (Geschichte der Sprachtheorie*, vol. 2). (Tübingen: G. Narr, 1991; 2nd, revised edition), 170–92.

—— (1998) [Review of Whitaker 1996], *History and Philosophy of Logic* 19, 161–65.

—— (2001) 'War Aristoteles ein Repräsentationalist?', in D. Perler, ed., *Ancient and medieval theories of intentionality* (Leiden/Boston/Köln: Brill), 97–104.

—— (2002) *Aristoteles*, Peri hermeneias. Übersetzt und erläutert von H. Weidemann (*Aristoteles, Werke in deutscher Übersetzung*, ed. H. Flashar, vol. 1, part II) (Berlin: Akademie Verlag, 1994; 2nd, revised edition).

—— (2005) 'Le proposizioni modali in Aristotele, *De interpretatione* 12 e 13', *Dianoia* 10, 27–41.

—— (2006) 'Aristotle and the Stoics on Language', in K. Brown (ed.), *Encyclopedia of Language and Linguistics*, 2nd ed., vol. 1. (Oxford: Elsevier), 471–73.

—— (2008) 'Die Variabilität von Wortbedeutungen im Satzkontext bei Aristoteles', *Incontri Linguistici* 31, 121–35.

Whitaker, C.W.A. (1996) *Aristotle's* De Interpretatione. *Contradiction and Dialectic* (Oxford: Clarendon Press).

Wiggins, D. (1980/2001) *Sameness and Substance* (Oxford: Blackwell, 1980), *Sameness and Substance Renewed* (Cambridge: Cambridge Univ. Press, 2001).

Wright, G.H. von (1979) 'Time, Truth and Necessity', in C. Diamond and J. Teichman, eds., *Intention and Intentionality. Essays in Honour of G. E. M. Anscombe* (Brighton, Sussex: Harvester Press), 237–50.

CHAPTER 6

ARISTOTLE'S LOGIC

PAOLO CRIVELLI

ARISTOTLE created logic and developed it to a level of great sophistication. There was nothing there before; and it took more than two millennia for something better to come around. The astonishment experienced by readers of the *Prior Analytics*, the most important of Aristotle's works that present the discipline, is comparable to that of an explorer discovering a cathedral in a desert.[1]

Since Aristotle discusses many themes in logical theory, my presentation is selective. I attempt to explain and evaluate some of Aristotle's views about propositions and syllogisms. The most important omission is the difficult subject of syllogisms involving modalities.[2]

1. PROPOSITIONS

Propositions in syllogisms. Aristotle deals with logic in six works: *Categories*, *De Interpretatione*, *Prior Analytics*, *Posterior Analytics*, *Topics*, and *Sophistical Refutations*. The *Prior Analytics* have the lion's share. Aristotle's logic, as it is presented in the *Prior Analytics*, is mainly about syllogisms. A syllogism is an inference and consists of propositions: one is its conclusion, the others are its premises.

In *Prior Analytics* 1.1 Aristotle offers the following definition of proposition:

T1   A proposition is a sentence affirming or denying something about something. (*APr* I 1 24a16–17)[3]

In *De Interpretatione* 4 he gives the following definition of sentence:

T2   A sentence is a significant utterance one of the parts of which is significant in separation—as a saying, not as an affirmation. (*DI* 4 16b26–8)[4]

Since T1 commits Aristotle to the view that all propositions are sentences and T2 to the view that all sentences are significant utterances, the two passages jointly commit him to the view that all propositions are significant utterances, i.e., linguistic expressions endowed with signification. T1 also makes it clear that propositions are predicative declarative sentences and distinguishes between affirmative and negative propositions: an affirmative proposition affirms something about something, a negative one denies something about something.

Although T1's characterisation allows him to apply 'proposition' to the conclusion as well as to the premises of any syllogism,[5] Aristotle tends to use it to refer exclusively to the premises and to contrast it with 'conclusion'.[6] Consider the following instruction: 'Every patrol will consist of two or three individuals and report to an officer. The individuals will not be officers and will wear camouflage whereas the officer will remain in the base wearing his normal uniform.' In this instruction, the plural description 'the individuals' refers exclusively to the members of each patrol: this reference is fixed by the context (specifically, by the occurrence of 'individuals' in the preceding sentence). Although 'individual' is contrasted with 'officer', there is no implication that the officer should not be an individual (on the contrary, the occurrence of 'his' in penultimate position presupposes that the officer should be an individual man). Moreover, there is no reason to think that 'individual' is used here with a special meaning.[7] Something similar happens with the use of 'proposition' in the *Prior Analytics*. When 'proposition' is used to refer exclusively to the premises of a syllogism and is contrasted with 'conclusion', this reference is fixed by the context; but there is no implication that the syllogism's conclusion should not be a proposition nor is there any reason to think that 'proposition' is used with a special meaning.[8]

Kinds of propositions. Aristotle offers a three-tiered classification of propositions.[9] On the first tier, he distinguishes between assertoric, apodictic, and problematic propositions; on the second, between affirmative and negative propositions; on the third, between universal, particular, and indeterminate propositions.[10] The distinction drawn on a later tier cuts across each of the kinds in the preceding one. Thus, assertoric propositions are divided into affirmative and negative, and similarly with apodictic and problematic propositions; assertoric affirmative propositions are divided into universal, particular, and indeterminate; assertoric negative propositions are analogously divided into universal, particular, and indeterminate; and parallel cuts occur within apodictic affirmative, apodictic negative, problematic affirmative, and problematic negative propositions.

The distinction between assertoric, apodictic, and problematic propositions concerns modality: an assertoric proposition states that something holds, or fails to hold, of something; an apodictic proposition states that something necessarily holds, or fails to hold, of something; and a problematic proposition states that something possibly holds, or fails to hold, of something. I shall focus on assertoric propositions. Following Aristotle's lead, I shall often use 'proposition' to mean 'assertoric proposition'.

A universal affirmative proposition states that something holds of all of something (e.g., 'Every pleasure is good'); a particular affirmative proposition states that something holds of some of something (e.g., 'Some pleasure is good'); an indeterminate affirmative proposition states that something holds of something, without specifying whether of all or some of it (e.g., 'Pleasure is good'); a universal negative proposition states that something holds of none of something (e.g., 'No pleasure is good'); a particular negative proposition states that something does not hold of some of something (e.g., 'Some pleasure is not good'); an indeterminate negative proposition states that something does not hold of something, without specifying whether of none or not of some of it (e.g., 'Pleasure is not good').[11] I shall ignore indeterminate propositions because they are rarely mentioned in Aristotle's syllogistic. In traditional logic, which developed from Aristotle's syllogistic and dominated until the end of the 19th century, the status of a proposition as affirmative or negative is called its *quality*; its status as universal or particular is called its *quantity*.[12]

Terms. Terms play a fundamental role in the syllogistic. Here is Aristotle's definition of term:

> T3   I call 'term' that into which a proposition is dissolved, namely what is predicated and that of which it is predicated, 'to be' or 'not to be' being added (*APr* I 1 24b16–18).

One exegesis (call it 'the ontological interpretation') takes terms to be items signified by significant utterances, i.e., the item signified by the predicate-expression of a proposition and the item signified by its subject-expression; another (call it 'the linguistic interpretation') maintains that terms are significant utterances, i.e., the predicate-expression and the subject-expression of a proposition.[13]

Some considerations favor the ontological interpretation, others the linguistic. A proper evaluation of the competitors would require too long a discussion for this study.[14] Two facts induce me to support the linguistic interpretation. First, a term is defined as 'that into which a proposition is dissolved' (24b16 < T3). Since, as we have seen, a proposition is a significant utterance, it is more likely to be dissolved into constituent significant utterances than into items signified by constituent significant utterances. Secondly, in the course of the *Prior Analytics* Aristotle mentions propositions and terms almost in the same breath.[15] This would be awkward if propositions and terms were items of radically different kinds. But propositions are significant utterances.

Aristotle's 'reversed' formulation of propositions. Aristotle often adopts a 'reversed' formulation of propositions, with the predicate-expression before the subject-expression. Thus, Aristotle prefers '"White" is predicated of all of "horse"' to 'Every horse is white', '"White" is predicated of none of "horse"' to 'No horse is white', etc. He often uses '…holds of…' or '…follows…' or '…is said of…' in place of

'...is predicated of...'.[16] In these 'reversed' formulations the verbs 'to be predicated of' and 'to be said of' do not indicate the speech-act of predicating, which can be carried out falsely as well as truly. Rather, in these 'reversed' formulations 'to be predicated of' and 'to be said of' are equivalent to 'to be true of'.[17] They therefore indicate a relation which entails the truth (and excludes the falsehood) of certain speech-acts.

Consider the following passages:

> T4   Whenever three terms [*horoi*] are so related to one another that the last one [*ton eschaton*] is in the middle one [*tô(i) mesô(i)*] as a whole and the middle one [*ton meson*] either is in or is not in the first one [*tô(i) prôtô(i)*] as a whole, it is necessary for there to be a perfect syllogism of the extreme ones (*APr* I 4 25b32–5).

> T5   If the first [*to prôton*] follows all of the middle [*tô(i) mesô(i)*] and the middle [*to meson*] holds of none of the last [*tô(i) eschatô(i)*] there will not be a syllogism of the extremes (*APr* I 4 26a2–4).[18]

Passages T4 and T5 are separated by a short portion of text (7 lines, 25b35–26a2). In T4, 'the last one', 'the middle one', and 'the first one' (which translate masculine Greek expressions, cf. '*ton eschaton*' and '*ton meson*') call for the integration of 'term', and are therefore strictly equivalent to 'the last term', 'the middle term', and 'the first term'. In T5, 'the first', 'the middle', and 'the last' do not call for the integration of 'term' (they translate neuter Greek expressions, cf. '*to prôton*' and '*to meson*'), and therefore are not strictly equivalent to 'the first term', 'the middle term', and 'the last term'. Nevertheless, 'the first', 'the middle', and 'the last' in T5 surely have the same reference as 'the first one', 'the middle one', and 'the last one' in T4 (this is dictated by the closeness of the passages). Since 'the first one', 'the middle one', and 'the last one' in T4 refer to terms, 'the first', 'the middle', and 'the last' in T5 must also refer to terms. This requires that Aristotle's 'reversed' formulations, which occur in T5, refer to terms.

Further evidence corroborates this result. In T4 Aristotle speaks of terms being in terms as in wholes. This strongly suggests that Aristotle's view is that the relation of parthood obtains between terms, i.e., that terms are parts of terms.[19] Aristotle's talk of terms as parts of terms must not be taken literally, as indicating syntactic parthood: Aristotle does *not* have in mind the containment of 'cat' in 'catamountain' or 'caterpillar'. His talk of terms as parts of terms alludes to a containment that concerns the semantic values of terms. Now, Aristotle claims that 'for one item to be in another as a whole is the same as for the one to be predicated of all of the other' (*APr* I 1 24b26–8).[20] By claiming this he commits himself to granting that the items linked by the relation of parthood are the same as those linked by the relation expressed by 'to be predicated of all of'. This again requires Aristotle's 'reversed' formulations to refer to terms.

Given that Aristotle's 'reversed' formulations refer to terms, and given that terms are subject- and predicate-expressions of propositions, it follows that Aristotle's 'reversed' formulations refer to subject- and predicate-expressions of propositions (recall that the subject- and predicate-expressions of propositions are significant utterances). This result is in fact presupposed by my rendering of Aristotle's 'reversed' formulations (e.g., the sentence '"White" is predicated of all of "horse"' refers to the significant utterances 'white' and 'horse').[21]

Aristotle does not explain why he adopts these 'reversed' formulations. His main reason is probably that he is interested in formulations that display the truth-conditions of different but reciprocally equivalent propositions with the same sub- ject- and predicate-expressions, truth-conditions which mention the terms that are the shared subject- and predicate-expressions of those propositions. For instance, it does not matter whether one uses the proposition 'Every horse is white', or 'All horses are white', or 'Each horse is white', or 'Any horse is white'. All these propo- sitions have the same truth-conditions and have the terms 'white' and 'horse' as their predicate- and subject-expression. Their common truth-conditions may be specified by saying that each one of them is true just if 'white' (the term that is their shared predicate-expression) is predicated of all of 'horse' (the term that is their shared subject-expression)[22] (in a later subsection I shall explain what it is for a term to be predicated of all of a term). In this sense, all the propositions mentioned are propositions to the effect that 'white' is predicated of all of 'horse'.[23]

The letters adopted by traditional logic. In the later logical tradition, some abbre- viations were introduced to allow a compact presentation. The letters '*a*', '*e*', '*i*', and '*o*' were used to indicate universal affirmative, universal negative, particular affir- mative, and particular negative propositions ('*a*' and '*i*' are the first two vowels in '*affirmo*', '*e*' and '*o*' are the first two in '*nego*').

I shall adopt these abbreviations, with the further stipulation that they stand for Aristotle's 'reversed' formulations. Thus, every instance of every schema in the following left-hand column will have the same meaning as the corresponding instance of the schema on the same line in the following right-hand column:

'ΠaΣ'	'Π is predicated of all of Σ'
'ΠeΣ'	'Π is predicated of none of Σ'
'ΠiΣ'	'Π is predicated of some of Σ'
'ΠoΣ'	'Π is not predicated of some of Σ'

Contrariety and contradiction. Aristotle distinguishes two relations of opposition which can obtain between propositions with the same subject- and predicate-ex- pressions: contrariety and contradiction.[24]

A universal affirmative and a universal negative proposition with the same subject- and predicate-expressions are contrary: for every term P, for every term S, any proposition to the effect that PaS is contrary to any proposition to the effect that PeS. For instance, 'Every horse is white' and 'No horse is white' are contrary. Contrary propositions are not true together.[25]

The relation of contradiction obtains in two cases. First, a universal affirma- tive and a particular negative proposition with the same subject- and predicate- expressions are contradictory: for every term P, for every term S, any proposition to the effect that PaS contradicts any proposition to the effect that PoS. For instance, 'Every horse is white' and 'Some horse is not white' are contradictory. Secondly, a universal negative and a particular affirmative proposition with the same subject- and predicate-expressions are contradictory: for every term P, for every term S, any proposition to the effect that PeS contradicts any proposition to the effect that PiS. For example, 'No horse is white' and 'Some horse is white' are contradictory. Contradictory propositions are neither true together nor false together.[26]

In the later logical tradition, the relations of opposition between propositions with the same subject- and predicate-expressions were illustrated by means of a drawn square where the upper corners are taken by universal propositions and the left-hand corners by affirmative propositions. The diagonals would represent contradiction, the upper side contrariety.[27]

'To be predicated of all' and 'to be predicated of none'. At the end of *Prior Analytics* I 1 Aristotle discusses the relations of being-predicated-of-all-of and being-predicated-of-none-of, which play fundamental roles in his syllogistic:

> T6   We use 'to be predicated of all' whenever none of the subject can be taken of which the other will not be said.[28] Likewise with 'to be predicated of none'. (*A Pr* I 1 24b28–30)

Passage T6 records how we ordinarily use the expressions 'to be predicated of all' and 'to be predicated of none'.[29] This record yields characterisations of the relations of being-predicated-of-all-of and being-predicated-of-none-of (in the later logical tradition, these characterisations came to be called '*dictum de omni et de nullo*'). Here are two anodyne paraphrases:

> [1] For every term P, for every term S, PaS just if it is not the case that for some z, both S is said of z and it is not the case that P is said of z.
>
> [2] For every term P, for every term S, PeS just if it is not the case that for some z, both S is said of z and P is said of z.

For example, 'animal' is predicated of all of 'vertebrate' just if it is not the case that there is something such that both 'vertebrate' is said of it and 'animal' is not said of it; and 'bee' is predicated of none of 'vertebrate' just if it is not the case that there is something such that both 'vertebrate' and 'bee' are said of it. The reason why [1] and [2] are anodyne is that nothing is said about the meaning of 'to be said of', the verb that does some of the heavy work in them. Later I shall come back to the question of the meaning of 'to be said of' in these and other principles.

Principles [1] and [2] foster simple proofs of the validity of certain syllogisms. For example, consider a syllogism in *Barbara* (see Table 6.1 on page 128), where one premise is a proposition to the effect that one term is predicated of all of a second term, the other premise is a proposition to the effect that the second term is predicated of all of a third one, and the conclusion is a proposition to the effect that the first term is predicated of all of the third. Let A, B, and C be terms such that AaB and BaC. Since AaB, it is not the case that for some z, both B is said of z and it is not the case that A is said of z (by [1]). Since BaC, it is not the case that for some z, both C is said of z and it is not the case that B is said of z (again by [1]). Suppose that for some z, both C is said of z and it is not the case that A is said of z. Let then *d* be such that both *C* is said of *d* and it is not the case that *A* is said of *d*. Then *B* is said of *d*: otherwise it would be the case that both *C* is said of *d* and it is not the case that *B* is said of *d*, whence it would follow that for some *z*, both *C* is said of *z* and it is not the case that *B* is said of *z*, contrary to an earlier result. Then *B* is said of *d* and it is not the case that *A* is said of *d*, so that for some *z*, both *B* is said of *z* and it is not the case that *A* is said of *z*, contrary to an earlier result. Therefore it is not the case that for some *z*, both *C* is said of *z* and it is not the case that *A* is said of *z*, so that *AaC* (by [1]).[30]

Again, consider a syllogism in *Celarent* (see Table 6.1 on page 128), where one premise is a proposition to the effect that one term is predicated of none of a second term, the other premise is a proposition to the effect that the second term is predicated of all of a third one, and the conclusion is a proposition to the effect that the first term is predicated of none of the third. Let *A*, *B*, and *C* be terms such that *AeB* and *BaC*. Since *AeB*, it is not the case that for some *z*, both *B* is said of *z* and *A* is said of *z* (by [2]). Since *BaC*, it is not the case that for some *z*, both *C* is said of *z* and it is not the case that *B* is said of *z* (by [1]). Suppose that for some *z*, both *C* is said of *z* and *A* is said of *z*. Let then *d* be such that both *C* is said of *d* and *A* is said of *d*. Then *B* is said of *d*: otherwise it would be the case that both *C* is said of *d* and it is not the case that *B* is said of *d*, whence it would follow that for some *z*, both *C* is said of *z* and it is not the case that *B* is said of *z*, contrary to an earlier result. Then *B* is said of *d* and *A* is said of *d*, so that for some *z*, both *B* is said of *z* and *A* is said of *z*, contrary to an earlier result. Therefore it is not the case that for some *z*, both *C* is said of *z* and *A* is said of *z*, so that *AeC* (by [2]).[31]

Characterisations of being-predicated-of-some-of and not-being-predicated-of-some-of. Aristotle never formulates characterisations of being-predicated-of-some-of and not-being-predicated-of-some-of; but some results he claims to be able to establish require them. On the model of [1] and [2], I propose:

[3] For every term *P*, for every term *S*, *PiS* just if for some *z*, both *S* is said of *z* and *P* is said of *z*.

[4] For every term *P*, for every term *S*, *PoS* just if for some *z*, both *S* is said of *z* and it is not the case that *P* is said of *z*.

Why does Aristotle never formulate principles [3] and [4]? Principles [1] and [2] are rather surprising because they characterize universal quantifications by negated existential quantifications.[32] There is nothing comparably surprising about [3] and [4]. Aristotle perhaps regards [3] and [4] as too obvious to be mentioned.

Once more, Aristotle's apparatus allows simple proofs of the validity of certain syllogisms. Consider a syllogism in *Darii* (see Table 6.1 on page 128), where one premise is a proposition to the effect that one term is predicated of all of a second term, the other premise is a proposition to the effect that the second term is predicated of some of a third one, and the conclusion is a proposition to the effect that the first term is predicated of some of the third. Let *A*, *B*, and *C* be terms such that *AaB* and *BiC*. Since *AaB*, it is not the case that for some *z*, both *B* is said of *z* and it is not the case that *A* is said of *z* (by [1]). Since *BiC*, it follows that for some *z*, both

C is said of z and B is said of z (by [3]). Let then d be such that both C is said of d and B is said of d. Then A is said of d: otherwise it would be the case that both B is said of d and it is not the case that A is said of d, whence it would follow that for some z, both B is said of z and it is not the case that A is said of z, contrary to an earlier result. Then C is said of d and A is said of d, so that for some z, both C is said of z and A is said of z, whence AiC (by [3]). A similarly simple proof is available for the validity of syllogisms in *Ferio*, where one premise is a proposition to the effect that one term is predicated of none of a second term, the other premise is a proposition to the effect that the second term is predicated of some of a third one, and the conclusion is a proposition to the effect that the first term is not predicated of some of the third (this proof will appeal also to [4]).[33]

Contradiction and contrariety.[34] Principles [1]–[4] entail that contradictory propositions are neither true together nor false together. This follows from:

> [5] For every term P, for every term S, PaS just if it is not the case that PoS.
> For every term P, for every term S, PeS just if it is not the case that PiS.

The proof is an immediate consequence of the fact that the right-hand member of the biconditional embedded in [1] (or, respectively, [2]) is the negation of the right-hand member of the biconditional embedded in [4] (or, respectively, [3]).

Let the following thesis be available:

> [6] Every term is said of something.[35]

Whether thesis [6] can be made available by a proof based on principles [1]–[4] depends on the meaning of the verb 'to be said of': as we shall see in the next subsection, there is a way of understanding 'to be said of' that makes [6] provable from [1]–[4]. If 'to be said of' is understood in a way that does not make [6] provable from [1]–[4], then [6] must be made available as an additional principle (on a par with [1]–[4]).

With thesis [6] in place, it can be proved that contrary propositions are not true together. In other words, the following can be proved:

> [7] For every term P, for every term S, it is not the case that both PaS
> and PeS.

Let A and B be terms. Suppose that both AaB and AeB. Since AaB, it is not the case that for some z, both B is said of z and it is not the case that A is said of z (by [1]). Since AeB, it is not the case that for some z, both B is said of z and A is said of z (by [2]). By [6], B is said of something. Let then c be such that B is said of c. Then it is not the case that A is said of c: otherwise it would be the case that both B is said of c and A is said of c, from which it would follow that for some z, both B is said of z and A is said of z, contrary to an earlier result. Then B is said of c and it is not the case that A is said of c, so that for some z, both B is said of z and it is not the case that A is said of z, contrary to an earlier result. Therefore it is not the case that both AaB and AeB. Since A and B were arbitrarily chosen, we may generalize and deduce [7].[36]

Theses [5] and [7] are fundamental for Aristotle's logical theory. In particular, they are used in simple proofs of the validity of conversions. First, consider the conversion of universal negative propositions, where the starting point is a proposition to the effect that one term is predicated of none of a second term and the conclusion is a proposition to the effect that the second term is predicated of none of the first. Let A and B be terms such that AeB. Suppose it is not the case that BeA. Then BiA (by [5]), so that for some z, both A is said of z and B is said of z (by [3]). Let then c be such that both A is said of c and B is said of c. Then B is said of c and A is said of c, so that for some z, both B is said of z and A is said of z. Then AiB (by [3]), so that it is not the case that AeB (by [5]), contrary to the hypothesis. Therefore BeA. Secondly, consider the conversion of universal affirmative propositions, where the starting point is a proposition to the effect that one term is predicated of all of a second term and the conclusion is a proposition to the effect that the second term is predicated of some of the first. Let A and B be terms such that AaB. Suppose it is not the case that BiA. Then BeA (by [5]), so that AeB (by the conversion of universal negative propositions). Hence AaB and AeB, contrary to [7]. Therefore BiA. Thirdly, consider the conversion of particular affirmative propositions, where the starting point is a proposition to the effect that one term is predicated of some of a second term and the conclusion is a proposition to the effect that the second term is predicated of some of the first. Let A and B be terms such that AiB. Suppose it is not the case that BiA. Then BeA (by [5]), so that AeB (by the conversion of universal negative propositions). Then it is not the case that AiB (by [5]), contrary to the hypothesis. Therefore BiA.[37]

On several occasions, I have pointed out that [1]–[4] and [6] allow *simple* proofs of the validity of certain inferences. This *simplicity* amounts to the fact that a minimal logical apparatus is involved: the main moves are existential instantiation (the passage from an existentially quantified sentence to an instance of it containing a new name of an arbitrarily chosen item, a passage Aristotle calls 'exposition'),[38] existential generalization, and reduction to the impossible. What is conspicuously absent is universal generalization (the passage from an instance containing a name of an arbitrarily chosen item to a universally quantified sentence). I suspect that the main reason for Aristotle's surprising choice of characterising universal quantifications by negated existential quantifications[39] is that it allows proofs involving such a minimal logical apparatus.

Two interpretations of Aristotle's semantic principles. An important question remains: what is the meaning of the verb 'to be said of' in [1]–[4] and [6]? There are two main options: on the 'orthodox interpretation', 'to be said of' means 'to be true of';[40] on the 'heterodox interpretation', it means 'to be predicated of all of'.[41] I shall not take sides in the dispute between these two exegeses, but I shall examine their logical implications and their credentials vis-à-vis Aristotle's text.

The heterodox interpretation makes thesis [6] provable from principles [1]–[4]. For principle [1] entails that every term is predicated of all of itself (because for every term T, it is not the case that for some z, both T is said of z and it is not the case that T is said of z).[42] Since, according to the heterodox interpretation, 'to be said of' means 'to be predicated of all of', it follows that every term is said of itself, so that every term is said of something. Since the heterodox interpretation can prove [6] from [1]–[4], it can also prove [7] from those principles. By contrast, on the orthodox interpretation, thesis [6] cannot be proved from principles [1]–[4]. Thus, the orthodox interpretation must assume [6] as an additional principle (on a par with [1]–[4]). Since the orthodox interpretation takes 'to be said of' to mean 'to be true of', by assuming [6] as an additional principle the orthodox interpretation is in effect requiring every term to be true of something.

The situation just described seems to give a logical advantage to the heterodox interpretation. But care is needed because the heterodox interpretation must also make additional assumptions to avoid wrong results. In the first place, suppose there were a term of all of which all terms are predicated. Then, by [3] and [2], the heterodox interpretation would be committed to the view that for every term P, for every term S, PiS and it is not the case that PeS. In other words, all particular affirmative propositions would be true and all universal negative propositions would be false. To be sure, this consequence is not logically impossible. But it is surely wrong, and it would be rejected by Aristotle (who at *APr* I 4 26a9 commits himself to the truth of the universal negative proposition 'No stone is an animal'). To avoid this wrong consequence (to which, let it be noted, the orthodox interpretation is not committed), the heterodox interpretation must assume that there is no term of all of which all terms are predicated. Secondly, consider 'Every round square is round, every round square is a square, therefore some square is round'. On the orthodox interpretation, this is not a valid argument because it involves an empty term ('round square'). Suppose the heterodox interpretation were not to make any additional assumptions about empty terms. Then the heterodox interpretation should regard the above as a valid argument. It is also unclear whether the heterodox interpretation could reject the premises: on what grounds could it do so? However, if the heterodox interpretation were to treat the above as a valid argument and accept the premises then it ought also to swallow the conclusion. And a similar situation arises for every pair of terms. Thus, while the orthodox interpretation must make additional assumptions to yield the results Aristotle accepts with respect to validity and invalidity, the heterodox interpretation must make additional assumptions to yield the results Aristotle accepts (and we also accept) with respect to truth and falsehood.[43]

The textual evidence relevant to the two interpretations. Some passages tell in favor of the heterodox interpretation. First, in the course of his discussion of modal syllogisms with one apodictic and one assertoric premise, Aristotle says:

> T7 Since A necessarily holds, or does not hold, of all of B, and C is one of the Bs, it is evident that either of these [*sc.* being A or not being A] will belong necessarily to C (*APr* I 9 30a21–3).

The expression 'one of the Bs' in T7's sentence 'C is one of the Bs' recalls the expression 'none of the subject' in T6. Since letters stand for terms, T7's sentence 'C is one of the *Bs*' is probably saying that the term which the letter '*C*' stands for bears a certain relation to the term which the letter '*B*' stands for. Given the types of syllogism examined in T7, the claim made by the sentence '*C* is one of the *Bs*' could also have been made by using the sentence '*B* is predicated of all of *C*'. This suggests that in T6 the phrase 'none of the subject' means something like 'nothing of all of which the subject term is predicated'.[44]

Secondly, in *Prior Analytics* I 41 (49b14–32) Aristotle distinguishes '*A* holds of all of that of which *B* holds' from '*A* holds of all of that of all of which *B* holds' and examines their reciprocal entailment. One would expect Aristotle to address such an issue if the heterodox interpretation is right; it is not clear why he should address it if the orthodox interpretation is right.[45]

On the other hand, other textual considerations speak for the orthodox interpretation. First, if the heterodox interpretation is right, then in T6 Aristotle is characterising the relation of being-predicated-of-all-of by saying that one term is predicated of all of one term just if it is not the case that there is something such that the second term is predicated of all of it while the first term is not predicated of all of it. This is an awkward characterisation. Surely it cannot be a definition because it would be guilty of circularity.[46] To meet this charge, the heterodox interpretation must deny that T6's characterisation of the relation of being-predicated-of-all-of is a definition.[47] In other words, it must insist that in T6 Aristotle does not define the relation of being-predicated-of-all-of but only indicates an important characteristic of it. Even if this may pass, the characterisation of the relation of being-predicated-of-all-of attributed to Aristotle by the heterodox interpretation is somewhat surprising (and unparalleled in Aristotle).

Secondly, in *Posterior Analytics* 1.4 Aristotle says:

> T8   I call 'of every' what is not about one thing but not about another, nor at
> one time but not another. For instance, if animal of every man, then if it is true
> to call this one a man, it is true to call him an animal too [*ei alêthes tond'eipein
> anthrôpon, alêthes kai zôon*], and if now the one then the other, and similarly if in
> every line there is a point (*APo* I 4 73a28–32).

In passage T8 Aristotle explains his use of 'of every' by bringing in the concept of truth: 'If animal of every man, then if it is *true* to call this one a man, it is *true* to call him an animal too' (73a30–1). Such an appeal to truth chimes with the orthodox interpretation, whose hallmark is the view that the verb 'to be said of' in [1]–[4] and [6] means 'to be true of'.[48]

Non-empty terms. If the orthodox interpretation is correct, Aristotle is committed to assuming that every term is true of something, or that no terms are empty. Such an assumption might be, and has been, regarded as crippling, especially because syllogistic must serve not only science but also dialectical debates, which are prone to involve propositions with empty subject- or predicate-expressions. What could motivate Aristotle to hold that no terms are empty? What could he say about declarative sentences that look like propositions whose subject- or predicate-expressions are empty?

I address the first question first. The linguistic theory of *De Interpretatione*[49] posits that primary declarative sentences, i.e., declarative sentences of the most fundamental kind, state that something holds, or does not hold, either of a universal or of an individual. Propositions, the sentential units studied by the *Prior Analytics*, seem to coincide with those significant utterances which, according to *De Interpretatione*, are primary declarative sentences which state that something holds, or does not hold, of a universal. If this is right, then the term that constitutes the subject-expression of any proposition signifies some universal. Since the predicate-expression of any proposition is the subject-expression of some other proposition (this is required by conversion), every term occurring as subject- or predicate-expression in any proposition signifies some universal. But, for Aristotle, every universal is instantiated by at least one individual.[50] Hence every term occurring as subject- or predicate-expression in any proposition is true of at least one individual. This might provide some motivation for endorsing the (possibly stronger) claim that all terms are non-empty.[51]

Now the second question: what could Aristotle say about declarative sentences that look like propositions whose subject- or predicate-expressions are empty? According to the linguistic theory of *De Interpretatione*, declarative sentences that look like primary declarative sentences whose subject- or predicate-expressions are empty are not primary declarative sentences, but have a hidden complexity: disguised 'molecular' declarative sentences composed of primary ones. If, as I suggested in the last paragraph, we assume that propositions, the sentential units studied by the *Prior Analytics*, are included in the significant utterances which, according to *De Interpretatione*, are primary declarative sentences, the strategy of *De Interpretatione* can be deployed to explain declarative sentences that look like propositions whose subject- or predicate-expressions are empty. Aristotle never works out the details of how this hidden complexity of disguised 'molecular' declarative sentences works. Had he tried, he would have faced a hard job.

The position we are exploring does not deprive empty nouns or adjectives (like 'goatstag') of signification.[52] It merely bars them from being subject- or predicate-expressions of propositions. Empty nouns and adjectives still make a semantic contribution, and therefore are significant, within declarative sentences that look like propositions whose subject- or predicate-expressions are empty: they fix the propositions of which the disguised 'molecular' declarative sentences are composed.

Singular propositions. Singular propositions, which include propositions whose subject-expression is a proper name (e.g., 'Socrates is a man'), do not play a prominent role in the *Prior Analytics*. But they are mentioned.[53] Their status is unclear. One passage (*APr* II 27 70a24–30) suggests that they should be treated as universal propositions; another (*APr* I 33 47b21–29) that they should not.[54] Perhaps they fall outside the remit of syllogistic because 'arguments and inquiries are mostly concerned with' species between individuals and highest genera (*APr* I 27 43a42–3). If so, the rare references to singular propositions should be regarded as slips of the pen.

II. SYLLOGISMS

Syllogism defined. In *Prior Analytics* I 1 Aristotle offers the following definition of syllogism:

> T9   A syllogism is a discourse in which, certain things having been posited, something different from the things laid down results of necessity due to these things being. By 'due to these things being' I mean 'to result because of these things', and by 'to result because of these things' I mean 'needing no further term from outside for the necessity to come about' (*A Pr* I 1 24b18–22).[55]

Some commentators[56] hold that syllogisms are true universally quantified conditionals. For example, the following true universally quantified conditional would be a syllogism: 'For all A, B, and C, if AaB and BaC then AaC'. This is wrong: syllogisms are not true universally quantified conditionals, but inferences of a certain type. For, proofs are syllogisms of a special sort,[57] and proofs are inferences (not universally quantified conditionals).

   Passage T9 requires that every syllogism be an inference whose conclusion follows necessarily from the premises, i.e., a valid inference ('invalid syllogism' is an oxymoron). The plural clause 'certain things having been posited' indicates that only inferences with two or more premises are syllogisms.[58] The requirement that the syllogism's conclusion be 'different from the things laid down' intends to banish *petitio principii*: a syllogism must not assume what it sets out to establish.[59] Aristotle therefore applies 'syllogism' to some (but not all) of the inferences that modern logicians usually regard as valid.

The three figures. Aristotle concentrates on syllogisms of a particular kind. These 'canonical syllogisms', as I shall call them, involve exactly three propositions: two premises and one conclusion. These propositions involve at most three terms. Not all syllogisms that consist of three propositions involving at most three terms are canonical syllogisms. By focusing on canonical syllogisms, Aristotle does not tacitly restrict the meaning of 'syllogism'. In fact, in *Prior Analytics* I 23 he argues that all syllogisms can be brought back to canonical syllogisms.

   Canonical syllogisms come in three 'figures'. It is not clear on what grounds Aristotle singles out these three figures. I shall describe a procedure which could have been the one he adopted.

   Aristotle often[60] refers to canonical syllogisms by mentioning triples of terms, which must then be organized in such a way as to constitute canonical syllogisms. Take three terms in a row:

   A, B, C

There are exactly three left-to-right pairs (without repetition): AB, AC, and BC. Now generate three sequences of these pairs. Let each of these sequences be generated by taking one of the terms in the original row and placing the two pairs that share it first (giving precedence to the pair whose non-shared term comes first in the original row). Specifically, begin by taking the central term (B) of the original row (A, B, C) and setting the two pairs that share it (AB, BC) first:

AB, BC, AC

(here AB precedes BC because A, the non-shared term of AB, comes before C, the non-shared term of BC, in the original row). Then take the first term (A) of the original row (A, B, C) and set the two pairs that share it (AB, AC) first:

AB, AC, BC

(here AB precedes AC because B comes before C in the original row). Finally, take the last term (C) of the original row (A, B, C) and set the two pairs that share it (AC, BC) first:

AC, BC, AB

(here AC precedes BC because A comes before B in the original row). Finally, take the first two pairs to represent premises and the last pair to represent a conclusion; and let the left-to-right direction within each pair indicate predication (predicate-before subject-expression). Thus:

A predicated of B, B predicated of C, therefore A predicated of C
A predicated of B, A predicated of C, therefore B predicated of C
A predicated of C, B predicated of C, therefore A predicated of B

The first arrangement corresponds to Aristotle's 'first figure', the second to his 'second figure', and the third to his 'third figure'.

The process described does not generate a fourth figure:

B predicated of C, A predicated of B, therefore C predicated of A

For, such a figure should correspond to the sequence of pairs BC, AB, CA, whose last member is not among the original left-to-right pairs. Later logicians within the Aristotelian tradition introduced a fourth figure. Their reasoning was different from Aristotle's. For Aristotle, the inferences which were later regarded as fourth-figure syllogisms are syllogisms, but not canonical syllogisms (not 'syllogisms in the figures').[61]

Middle and extremes. In every canonical syllogism, one term is common to the two premises: it is called 'middle term', or simply 'middle'.[62] The remaining two terms of the premises are the only ones occurring in the conclusion: they are called 'extreme terms', or simply 'extremes'.[63] In the first figure, the middle is the subject-expression of one premise and the predicate-expression of the other; in the second figure, the middle is the predicate-expression of both premises; in the third figure, it is the subject-expression of both premises.[64]

Consider the three figures as they were presented in the last subsection. In the first the middle is B, which in the original series A, B, C occupied the middle position: to this Aristotle is probably alluding when he says that in the first figure the middle term 'comes to be middle also in position' (APr I 4 25b36).[65] In the second figure the middle is *A*, which in the original series *A*, *B*, *C* came first: for this reason Aristotle says that in the second figure the middle is 'first in position' (I 5 26b39). Finally, in the third figure the middle is *C*, which in the original series *A*, *B*, *C* came last: this is why Aristotle says that in the third figure the middle is 'last in position' (I 6 28a15).

Of the extremes, one is called 'major extreme'[66] (or, occasionally, 'major term'),[67] the other 'minor extreme'[68] (or, occasionally, 'minor term').[69] Aristotle gives different definitions of the major and the minor extreme for each figure.

In the case of the first figure, he says:

> T10   I call 'major extreme' that in which the middle is, and 'minor' that which is under the middle. (*APr* I 4 26a21–3)

He probably means that in first-figure syllogisms the major extreme is predicated of the middle whereas the minor extreme is a subject for it.[70]

With respect to the second figure, Aristotle says:

> T11   I call ... 'major extreme' the one situated next to the middle, 'minor' the one further away from the middle. (*APr* I 5 26b36–8)

This characterisation alludes to the position of the terms within the original series *A*, *B*, *C* which generates the three figures: in the case of the second figure, the major extreme is *B* (which in the series *A*, *B*, *C* is 'situated next to the middle', which is *A*), and the minor extreme is *C* (which in the series *A*, *B*, *C* is 'further away from the middle'). The characterisation of the major and the minor extreme for the second figure is radically different from that for the first: in the case of the first figure, the distinction relies on the different predicative relations the extremes entertain with the middle; in the case of the second figure, it is based on the position of the extremes within the original series *A*, *B*, *C*. This must be because in the second figure the extremes cannot be distinguished by their predicative relations to the middle, which is predicated of both.

In the case of the third figure, Aristotle says:

> T12   I call ... 'major extreme' the one further away from the middle, 'minor' the closer one. (*APr* I 6 28a12–14)

This characterisation also alludes to the position of the terms within the original series *A*, *B*, *C*: in the case of the third figure, the major and the minor extreme are *A* and *B* (which in the series *A*, *B*, *C* are 'further away from' and 'closer' to the middle, which is *C*). This characterisation recalls that of the second figure, and shares with it the trait of being radically different from the characterisation of the first figure. Note that in the third figure also the extremes cannot be distinguished by their predicative relations to the middle, of which they are both predicated.

In the later logical tradition, the major extreme came to be defined as the term that is the predicate-expression of the conclusion, the minor extreme as the term that is the subject-expression of the conclusion. In Aristotle there is no trace of these definitions.[71] Moreover, in this logical tradition the premises containing the major and the minor extreme were called (respectively) 'major premise' and 'minor premise'. Aristotle never uses these labels.[72]

Kinds of canonical syllogisms. Aristotle identifies 14 kinds of canonical syllogisms. They are described by the following tables (which include their traditional names).

The first four kinds are in the first figure:

Table 6.1 The First Figure

For some term A, for some term B, for some term C			
One premiss is a proposition to the effect that	One premiss is a proposition to the effect that	The conclusion is a proposition to the effect that	*Prior Analytics* I 4
Barbara AaB	BaC	AaC	25^b37–40
Celarent AeB	BaC	AeC	25^b40–26^a2
Darii AaB	BiC	AiC	26^a23–5
Ferio AeB	BiC	AoC	26^a25–8

The next four kinds are in the second figure:

Table 6.2 The Second Figure

For some term M, for some term N, for some term X			
One premiss is a proposition to the effect that	One premiss is a proposition to the effect that	The conclusion is a proposition to the effect that	*Prior Analytics* I 5
Cesare MeN	MaX	NeX	27^a5–9
Camestres MaN	MeX	NeX	27^a9–14
Festino MeN	MiX	NoX	27^a32–6
Baroco MaN	MoX	NoX	27^a36–27^b1

The last six kinds are in the third figure:

Table 6.3 The Third Figure

For some term P, for some term R, for some term S			
One premiss is a proposition to the effect that	One premiss is a proposition to the effect that	The conclusion is a proposition to the effect that	*Prior Analytics* I 6
Darapti PaS	RaS	PiR	28^a17–26
Felapton PeS	RaS	PoR	28^a26–30
Disamis PiS	RaS	PiR	28^b7–11
Datisi PaS	RiS	PiR	28^b11–14
Bocardo PoS	RaS	PoR	28^b17–21
Ferison PeS	RiS	PoR	28^b31–5

In the above tabular presentation, the letters 'A', 'B', and 'C' stand for (respectively) the major, middle, and minor terms of first-figure syllogisms; 'M', 'N', and 'X' stand for the middle, major, and minor terms of second-figure syllogisms; and 'P', 'R', and 'S' for the major, minor, and middle terms of third-figure syllogisms. Aristotle himself employs these letters in *Prior Analytics* I 4–6, when he discusses syllogisms in the corresponding figures.[73]

The traditional names of the kinds of canonical syllogisms encode useful information. The three vowels indicate the predicative relations of the syllogism's major premise, minor premise, and conclusion. For instance, in every syllogism in *Ferison*, the major premise is an *e*-type proposition (universal negative), the minor premise is an *i*-type proposition (particular affirmative), and the conclusion is an *o*-type proposition (particular negative).[74]

Perfect and imperfect syllogisms. Aristotle distinguishes 'perfect' from 'imperfect' syllogisms:

> T13   I call 'perfect' a syllogism which needs nothing else apart from the assumptions for the necessity [*sc.* of something following from these assumptions] to be apparent, whereas I call 'imperfect' that which needs one or more things which are necessary because of the underlying terms, but have not been assumed by means of premises (*APr* I 1 24b22–6).[75]

A syllogism is 'perfect' just if it is evident that its conclusion follows necessarily from its premises, i.e., it is evidently valid. A syllogism is 'imperfect' just if it is not perfect, i.e., it is not evidently valid.[76]

It is important that a syllogism's validity be evident. A syllogism whose validity is not evident is of no use. For we employ inferences to persuade ourselves or others that a certain conclusion follows necessarily from certain premises; but if a syllogism's validity is not evident, then the syllogism will not persuade anyone. Hence, if a syllogism is imperfect, i.e., fails to be evidently valid, we need ways of transforming it so that its validity becomes evident. Aristotle has a theory of how to achieve this. He uses the verb 'to perfect' to describe such a transformation.[77] The perfecting of an imperfect syllogism involves interlarding it with intermediate steps which render its validity evident. In many (though not all) cases, the inserted steps evidently follow from what precedes and have the desired conclusion evidently following from them, so that the procedure may be viewed as a breaking down of the originally imperfect syllogism into shorter evidently valid inferences. The result obtained by adding intermediate steps is the same syllogism as the original one (because it has the same premises and conclusion and a syllogism is identified by its premises and conclusion). The difference is a matter of presentation: once perfected, the syllogism is so presented that its validity is evident.[78]

Which canonical syllogisms are perfect? All first-figure syllogisms (i.e., syllogisms in *Barbara, Celarent, Darii,* or *Ferio,* which are represented in Table 6.1) are perfect; all second-figure syllogisms (i.e., syllogisms in *Cesare, Camestres, Festino,* or *Baroco,* which are represented in Table 6.2) and third-figure syllogisms (i.e., syllogisms in *Darapti, Felapton, Disamis, Datisi, Bocardo,* or *Ferison,* represented in

Table 6.3) are imperfect.[79] Since a syllogism is perfect just if it is evidently valid, and imperfect just if it is not perfect, two consequences follow:

[8] Every first-figure syllogism is evidently valid.
[9] No second- or third-figure syllogism is evidently valid.

On three occasions Aristotle appeals to T6's characterisations of being-predicated-of-all-of and being-predicated-of-none-of to justify a first-figure syllogism's validity.[80] This suggests that T6's characterisations are supposed to support a syllogism's claim to perfection.[81] This, in turn, suggests justifications of propositions [8] and [9].

The suggested justification of [8] is that the validity of a first-figure syllogism can be easily proved on the basis of T6's characterisations of being-predicated-of-all-of and being-predicated-of-none-of by elementary logical operations. I already showed that T6's characterisations of being-predicated-of-all-of and being-predicated-of-none-of allow simple proofs of the validity of syllogisms in *Barbara*, *Celarent*, *Darii*, and *Ferio*.[82] Thus, the suggested justification of [8] works.

The suggested justification of [9] is that the validity of second- or third-figure syllogisms cannot be easily proved on the basis of T6's characterisations of being-predicated-of-all-of and being-predicated-of-none-of by elementary logical operations. However, simple proofs are available for second- and third-figure syllogisms: for example, the proof of the validity of syllogisms in *Datisi* is not harder than that of syllogisms in *Barbara*. This is a stumbling block for the suggested justification of [9] as it implies that second- and third-figure syllogisms are evidently valid.[83]

In such circumstances, there are two alternatives: either Aristotle made a mistake, or we must abandon the suggested justification of [9], and therefore also that of [8] (the two hold or fail together). I do not rule the first alternative out, but I explore the second. Specifically, I explore a different approach to justifying propositions [8] and [9]. These propositions, which jointly amount to the claim that first-figure syllogisms are all and only the evidently valid canonical syllogisms, have perhaps nothing to do with provability on the basis of T6's characterisations of being-predicated-of-all-of and being-predicated-of-none-of. Perhaps they concern different aspects of syllogisms. The most likely candidate is the pattern of occurrence of terms: for only in first-figure syllogisms is the middle repeated shortly after its first occurrence, so that once the second premise is stated there is no need to make the effort of looking back to see what had been said about the middle term in the first premise; and only in first-figure syllogisms do both extremes occur in the premises with the same roles (of predicate- and subject-expression) as in the conclusion.[84]

One problem remains. Given that first-figure syllogisms are evidently valid, what is the purpose of proving their validity on the basis of T6's characterisations of being-predicated-of-all-of and being-predicated-of-none-of? Why prove something evident?[85] Consider an analogous phenomenon in modern logic. Some of the rules of inference of certain logical systems are chosen, at least in part, because they are evidently valid (for instance, the validity of MP, one of the rules of inference of most axiomatic systems, is as evident as one might wish for). Despite the evidence of their validity, logic textbooks normally proceed to prove that these rules of inference are valid (they do this within a metalogical semantic theory). These proofs of validity are parts of a larger proof of the soundness of the whole logical system, whereby it is shown that every result established by the logical system is logically acceptable (in the case of an axiomatic system, what is shown is that every result established by it is logically true). Why do modern logicians prove the validity of evidently valid rules of inference? At least part of the reason is probably that they want to explain why these rules of inference are valid, i.e., provide some foundation for the evident fact that they are valid.[86] I suspect that something analogous is going on in Aristotle's case. Aristotle is groping for a proof of the soundness of syllogistic, and in the process he proves the validity of evidently valid inferences (e.g., first-figure syllogisms) so as to explain why they are valid.[87] This account is corroborated by two facts. First, first-figure syllogisms are the only canonical syllogisms for which Aristotle alludes to proofs of validity based on T6's characterisations of being-predicated-of-all-of and being-predicated-of-none-of; in the case of conversions (whose role in perfecting syllogisms requires them to be as evidently valid as perfect syllogisms), he offers proofs of validity.[88] This is precisely what Aristotle should do if he were pursuing the larger project of proving the soundness of syllogistic (he would be assigning to the proofs involved in perfecting the imperfect syllogisms the double role of showing not only that but also why these other syllogisms are valid). Secondly, Aristotle distinguishes two kinds of search: 'searching whether' so-and-so and 'searching why' so-and-so.[89] These two kinds of search are answered by two kinds of proof: 'proofs of the fact' and 'proofs of why'. 'Proofs of the fact' establish that so-and-so and bring to an end our 'searching whether' so-and-so; 'proofs of why' explain why so-and-so and bring to an end our 'searching why' so-and-so.[90] If we already know that so-and-so, we do not 'search whether' so-and-so,[91] and we do not embark on a 'proof of the fact' that so-and-so. However, even when we know that so-and-so, we can go on to 'search why' so-and-so;[92] in this case we attempt to offer a 'proof of why' so-and-so. Since perfect syllogisms are evidently valid, there is no need of a 'proof of the fact' that they are valid; but a 'proof of why' they are valid is still desirable.[93]

Conversion. Let me now explain how syllogisms are perfected. In a syllogism, the initial steps are premises. Aristotle allows various procedures to introduce intermediate steps leading to the desired conclusion. One such procedure is conversion, whereby a proposition's predicate- and subject-expressions are interchanged. Conversion can be of three types:

> C1   For all terms *S* and *P*, if from certain premises a proposition to the effect that *SeP* is inferred, then from those premises any proposition to the effect that *PeS* may be inferred.

> C2   For all terms *S* and *P*, if from certain premises a proposition to the effect that *SiP* is inferred, then from those premises any proposition to the effect that *PiS* may be inferred.

C3   For all terms S and P, if from certain premises a proposition to the effect that SaP is inferred, then from those premises any proposition to the effect that PiS may be inferred.

Aristotle proves the validity of conversions.[94] He also shows that particular negative propositions cannot be converted by pointing out that 'although "man" does not hold of all of "animal", "animal" holds of all of "man"' (*APr* I 4 25a25–6).

In the later logical tradition, the Latin '*conversio simplex*' ('simple conversion') was used for conversions of the first two types: for in these cases conversion is merely a swap of the subject- and predicate-expressions. '*Conversio per accidens*' ('accidental conversion') was reserved for conversions of the third type, where a change from universal to particular also occurs.

Perfect syllogisms. Another procedure allowed by Aristotle in perfecting imperfect syllogisms is the application of perfect syllogisms, namely first-figure syllogisms. Specifically:

PS1   For all terms A, B, and C, if from certain premises a proposition to the effect that AaB is inferred, and if from certain premises a proposition to the effect that BaC is inferred, then from all premises involved any proposition to the effect that AaC may be inferred.

PS2   For all terms A, B, and C, if from certain premises a proposition to the effect that AeB is inferred, and if from certain premises a proposition to the effect that BaC is inferred, then from all premises involved any proposition to the effect that AeC may be inferred.

PS3   For all terms A, B, and C, if from certain premises a proposition to the effect that AaB is inferred, and if from certain premises a proposition to the effect that BiC is inferred, then from all premises involved any proposition to the effect that AiC may be inferred.

PS4   For all terms A, B, and C, if from certain premises a proposition to the effect that AeB is inferred, and if from certain premises a proposition to the effect that BiC is inferred, then from all premises involved any proposition to the effect that AoC may be inferred.

For example, consider how syllogisms in *Cesare* are perfected:

T14   Let M be predicated of none of N, but of all of X. Since, then, the privative converts, N will hold of none of M. But M was posited to hold of all of X, so that N will hold of none of X (for this was shown earlier). (*APr* I 5 27a5–9)

The syllogism to be perfected is in *Cesare* (Table 6.2): for some terms M, N, and X, the premises are propositions to the effect that MeN and MaX, the conclusion one to the effect that NeX. Begin by assuming the syllogism's premises, namely propositions to the effect that MeN and MaX. By C1, the rule of conversion for universal negative propositions, go from the proposition to the effect that MeN to one to the effect that *NeM*. The propositions to the effect that *NeM* and *MaX*, which you have now reached, enable you to apply a syllogism in *Celarent* (Table 6.1), so you can employ PS2 and draw the corresponding conclusion, namely a proposition to the effect that *NeX*.

Reduction to the impossible. All syllogisms of twelve of Aristotle's fourteen kinds can be perfected by the procedures contemplated so far. These procedures are how-ever ineffective for syllogisms of two kinds, namely *Baroco* (Table 6.2) and *Bocardo* (Table 6.3). For these something else is needed:

> PI   If from certain premises a certain conclusion is inferred, then any contra-dictory of any of those premises may be inferred from the result of replacing that premise with any contradictory or contrary of that conclusion.

Syllogisms perfected by PI 'are brought to a conclusion through the impossi-ble' (otherwise they 'are brought to a conclusion ostensively').[95] 'PI' abbreviates the Latin *'per impossibile'*.

Consider how syllogisms in *Baroco* are perfected by reduction to the impossible:

> T15   Again, if *M* holds of all of *N*, but not of some of *X*, it is necessary for *N* not to hold of some of *X*; for if it holds of all, and *M* is also predicated of all of *N*, then it is necessary for *M* to hold of all of *X*; but it was assumed not to hold of some. (*APr* I 5 27a36–27b1)

The syllogism to be perfected is in *Baroco*: for some terms *M*, *N*, and *X*, the prem-ises are propositions to the effect that *MaN* and *MoX*, the conclusion one to the effect that *NoX*. Since the conclusion of the syllogism to be perfected is a propo-sition to the effect that *NoX*, assume a contradictory of it as a hypothesis: a prop-osition to the effect that *NaX*. Focus on the first premise of the syllogism to be perfected: the proposition to the effect that *MaN*. A syllogism in *Barbara* (Table 6.1) may be deployed: its premises are the propositions to the effect that *MaN* and *NaX*, its conclusion one to the effect that *MaX*. Now use this syllogism in *Barbara* as the starting point of an application of PI: any contradictory of the second pre-mise may be inferred from the result of replacing that premise with any contradic-tory or contrary of the conclusion. This yields the inference where the premises are the propositions to the effect that *MaN* and *MoX*, the conclusion that to the effect that *NoX*: the desired syllogism in *Baroco*.[96]

Rejection by counter-examples. When he discusses syllogisms in a given figure, Aristotle proves two things. First, he proves that for certain ways of arranging terms in an inference's premises (ways that fit the figure in question), there is a way of arranging these terms in the inference's conclusion (a way that also fits the figure in question) whereby all inferences where terms are thus arranged are valid. When he proves this, Aristotle mentions (when it is possible) only the 'logi-cally strongest' way of arranging terms in the conclusion: for instance, when, in his discussion of syllogisms in the first figure, he examines the first-figure way of arranging terms in an inference's premises whereby for some terms *A*, *B*, and

C, the premises are propositions to the effect that AaB and BaC, Aristotle mentions the first-figure way of arranging terms in the inference's conclusion whereby the conclusion is a proposition to the effect that AaC; but he does not mention the first-figure way of arranging terms in the inference's conclusion whereby the conclusion is a proposition to the effect that AiC (note that any proposition to the effect that AaC entails any proposition to the effect that AiC).[97] Secondly, Aristotle proves that for all the remaining ways of arranging terms in an inference's premises (ways that fit the figure in question), it is not the case that there is a way of arranging these terms in the inference's conclusion (a way that also fits the figure in question) whereby all inferences where terms are thus arranged are valid. This second task he carries out by means of a compact 'method of rejection' based on counter-examples.

Aristotle's most extensive discussion of his method of rejection occurs in connection with its first application:

> T16   However, if the first follows all of the middle and the middle holds of none of the last, there will not be a syllogism of the extremes: for nothing necessary results due to these things being. For it is possible for the first to hold of all as well as of none of the last, so that neither the particular nor the universal becomes necessary. And, since nothing is necessary through these things, there will not be a syllogism. Terms for holding of all are 'animal', 'man', 'horse'; for holding of none, 'animal', 'man', 'stone' (*APr* I 4 26a2–9).

Passage T16 belongs to Aristotle's treatment of first-figure syllogisms. Aristotle proves that in the case of the first-figure way of arranging terms in the premises whereby for some terms A, B, and C, the premises are propositions to the effect that AaB and BeC, there is no first-figure way of arranging these terms in the conclusion, i.e., no way of arranging terms in the conclusion such that the conclusion is a proposition to the effect that A is predicated of C (in any of the four ways in which predication can occur), whereby all inferences where terms are thus arranged are valid.

Since four styles of predication can be involved in the conclusion, Aristotle is in fact considering, in one go, four ways of arranging an inference's terms. In all four cases, the inferences involve terms A, B, and C arranged in such a way that one premise is a proposition to the effect that AaB and the other premise is a proposition to the effect that BeC. In the first case, the conclusion is a proposition to the effect that AaC; in the second, it is a proposition to the effect that AiC; in the third, a proposition to the effect that AeC; in the fourth, one to the effect that AoC. For each of these four ways of arranging an inference's terms, Aristotle provides a trio of terms from which an inference can be constructed where terms are thus arranged, the premises are true, and the conclusion is false. Let us consider in turn each of these four ways of arranging terms.

The first way of arranging an inference's terms is that whereby one premise is a proposition to the effect that AaB, the other premise is a proposition to the effect that BeC, and the conclusion is a proposition to the effect that AaC. Consider the trio of terms 'animal', 'man', 'stone'. From these terms, construct an inference satisfying the following conditions:

[a] one premise is a proposition to the effect that 'animal' is predicated of all of 'man'

the other premise is a proposition to the effect that 'man' is predicated of none of 'stone'

the conclusion is a proposition to the effect that 'animal' is predicated of all of 'stone'

Any such inference has the terms arranged in the way under examination and has true premises and a false conclusion. Hence this way of arranging terms does not guarantee that inferences where terms are thus arranged are valid.

The second way of arranging an inference's terms differs from the first only in that the conclusion is a proposition to the effect that AiC. Consider again the trio of terms 'animal', 'man', 'stone'. Construct an inference satisfying the following conditions:

[i] one premise is a proposition to the effect that 'animal' is predicated of all of 'man'

the other premise is a proposition to the effect that 'man' is predicated of none of 'stone'

the conclusion is a proposition to the effect that 'animal' is predicated of some of 'stone'

Any such inference has the terms arranged in the way under examination and has true premises and a false conclusion. Hence this second way of arranging terms also fails to guarantee validity.

The third way of arranging an inference's terms differs from the first two only in that the conclusion is a proposition to the effect that AeC. Consider the trio of terms 'animal', 'man', 'horse'. Construct an inference satisfying the following conditions:

[e] one premise is a proposition to the effect that 'animal' is predicated of all of 'man'

the other premise is a proposition to the effect that 'man' is predicated of none of 'horse'

the conclusion is a proposition to the effect that 'animal' is predicated of none of 'horse'

Any such inference has the terms arranged in the way under examination and has true premises and a false conclusion. Hence the third way of arranging terms also fails to guarantee validity.

The fourth way of arranging an inference's terms differs from the others only in that the conclusion is a proposition to the effect that AoC. Take again the trio of terms 'animal', 'man', 'horse'. Construct an inference satisfying the following conditions:

> [o] one premise is a proposition to the effect that 'animal' is predicated of all of 'man'
> the other premise is a proposition to the effect that 'man' is predicated of none of 'horse'
> the conclusion is a proposition to the effect that 'animal' is not predicated of some of 'horse'

Any such inference has the terms arranged in the way under examination and has true premises and a false conclusion. Hence the fourth way of arranging terms also fails to guarantee validity.

The first two ways of arranging an inference's terms are ruled out by the fact that 'animal' is predicated of none of 'stone': this entails the falsehood both of propositions to the effect that 'animal' is predicated of all of 'stone' and of propositions to the effect that 'animal' is predicated of some of 'stone'. Similarly, the last two ways of arranging an inference's terms are ruled out by the fact that 'animal' is predicated of all of 'horse': this entails the falsehood both of propositions to the effect that 'animal' is predicated of none of 'horse' and of propositions to the effect that 'animal' is not predicated of some of 'horse'. This enables Aristotle to economize on terms. Two trios of terms are enough: one trio must generate a pair of true propositions that fit the pattern originally given and moreover a *true universal negative* proposition that fits the figure in question; the other trio must instead generate a pair of true propositions that fit the pattern originally given and moreover a *true universal affirmative* proposition that fits the figure in question.[98] In fact, Aristotle economizes even further by providing two trios of terms that differ in only one member.

Note that the way of arranging an inference's terms whereby one premise is a proposition to the effect that AaB, the other premise is a proposition to the effect that BeC, and the conclusion is a proposition to the effect that CoA *does* guarantee that inferences where terms are thus arranged are valid. Moreover, Aristotle is aware of this fact.[99] This however neither refutes Aristotle's earlier points nor shows an inconsistency. For the way of arranging an inference's terms just described does not fit the first figure: in the arrangement just described the conclusion is a proposition to the effect that C is predicated of A, whereas in a first-figure arrangement the conclusion must be a proposition to the effect that A is predicated of C.

In general, Aristotle's method of rejection can be characterized as follows. The question is: does a certain way of arranging an inference's terms guarantee that inferences where terms are thus arranged are valid? One may answer this question negatively if one finds terms which by being arranged in the way under consideration give rise to an inference with true premises and a false conclusion: for if an inference has true premises and a false conclusion, then surely it is not valid.

The following tables summarize the arrangements of terms in premises considered by Aristotle with his counterexamples (where applicable):

Table 6.4 The First Figure

Arrangement of terms in premises	Traditional name of syllogism (if applicable)	Trio of terms for a-counterexample (if applicable)	Trio of terms for e-counterexample (if applicable)	*Prior Analytics* I 4
aa	*Barbara*			25^{b}37–40
ea	*Celarent*			25^{b}40–26a2
ae		'animal', 'man', 'horse'	'animal', 'man', 'stone'	26^{a}2–9
ee		'knowledge', 'line', 'medicine'	'knowledge', 'line', 'unit'	26^{a}9–13
ai	*Darii*			26^{a}23–5
ei	*Ferio*			26^{a}25–8
ia, oa		'good', 'state', 'wisdom'	'good', 'state', 'ignorance'	26^{a}33–6
ie, oe		'white', 'horse', 'swan'	'white', 'horse', 'raven'	26^{a}36–9
ao		'animal', 'man', 'swan'	'animal', 'man', 'snow'	26^{b}3–10
eo		'inanimate', 'man', 'snow'	'inanimate', 'man', 'swan'	26^{b}10–14
ii, io, oi, oo		'animal', 'white', 'horse'	'animal', 'white', 'stone'	26^{b}21–5

The ways of arranging an inference's terms considered by Aristotle are not a purely syntactical matter. Rather, they concern the truth-conditions of an inference's premises and conclusion given with respect to the terms they involve. Let me explain with an example. In the inference 'All ravens are birds, all birds are bipeds, therefore all ravens are bipeds', one premise is a proposition to the effect that the term 'biped' is predicated of all of the term 'bird', the other is a proposition to the effect that 'bird' is predicated of all of the term 'raven', and the conclusion is a proposition to the effect that 'biped' is predicated of all of 'raven'. Again, in the inference 'Every horse is a vertebrate, every vertebrate is an animal, therefore every horse is an animal', one premise is a proposition to the effect that the term 'animal' is predicated of all of the term 'vertebrate', the other is a proposition to the effect that 'vertebrate' is predicated of all of the term 'horse', and the conclusion is a proposition to the effect that 'animal' is predicated of all of 'horse'. Hence in both inferences terms are so arranged that one premise is a proposition to the effect that a term *A* is predicated of all of a term *B*, the other premise is a proposition to the effect that *B* is predicated of all of a term *C*, and the conclusion is a proposition to the effect that *A* is predicated of all of *C*. In the two inferences terms are therefore arranged

Table 6.5 The Second Figure

Arrangement of terms in premises	Traditional name of syllogism (if applicable)	Trio of terms for a-counterexample (if applicable)	Trio of terms for e-counterexample (if applicable)	*Prior Analytics* I 5
ea	Cesare[100]			27^a5–9
ae	Camestres			27^a9–14
aa		'substance', 'animal', 'man'[101]	'substance', 'animal', 'number'	27^a18–20
ee		'line', 'animal', 'man'	'line', 'animal', 'stone'	27^a20–3
ei	Festino			27^a32–6
ao	Baroco			27^a36–27b1
oa		'animal', 'substance', 'raven'	'animal', 'white', 'raven'	27^b4–6
ie		'animal', 'substance', 'unit'	'animal', 'substance', 'knowledge'	27^b6–8
eo		'line', 'animal', 'man'	'black', 'snow', 'animal'	27^b12–23
ai		'substance', 'animal', 'man'	'white', 'swan', 'stone'	27^b23–8
oe		'white', 'animal', 'raven'	'white', 'stone', 'raven'	27^b28–32
ia		'white', 'animal', 'swan'	'white', 'animal', 'snow'	27^b32–4
ii, io, oi, oo		'white', 'animal', 'man'	'white', 'animal', 'inanimate'	27^b36–9

in the same way. The two inferences, however, are not instances of the same valid inference-schema. To be sure, the first inference is an instance of the valid inference-schema 'All Σs are Ms, all Ms are Πs, therefore all Σs are Πs'; and the second inference is an instance of the valid inference-schema 'Every Σ is a(n) M, every M is a(n) Π, therefore every Σ is a(n) Π'. But these are different inference-schemata, and there is no single valid inference-schema of which both inferences are instances (they are both instances of the inference-schema 'A, B, therefore Γ', which however is invalid). In this sense, the ways of arranging an inference's terms considered by Aristotle are not a syntactical matter, but concern the truth-conditions of an inference's premises and conclusion given with respect to the terms they involve.

We can now cash in some dividends of adopting the linguistic interpretation of terms, according to which terms are significant utterances.[103] For suppose that the

Table 6.6 The Third Figure

Arrangement of terms in premises	Traditional name of syllogism (if applicable)	Trio of terms for a-counterexample (if applicable)	Trio of terms for e-counterexample (if applicable)	*Prior Analytics* I 6
aa	*Darapti*			28^a17-26
ea	*Felapton*			28^a26-30
ae		'animal', 'horse', 'man'[102]	'animal', 'inanimate', 'man'	28^a30-3
ee		'animal', 'horse', 'inanimate'	'man', 'horse', 'inanimate'	28^a33-6
ia	*Disamis*			28^b7-11
ai	*Datisi*			28^b11-14
oa	*Bocardo*			28^b17-21
ao		'animate', 'man', 'animal'	'animal', 'inanimate', 'man'	28^b22-31
ei	*Ferison*			28^b31-5
ie, oe		'animal', 'man', 'wild'	'animal', 'knowledge', 'wild'	$28^b36-29a2$
eo		'animal', 'horse', 'inanimate'	'raven', 'snow', 'white'	29^a2-6
ii, io, oi, oo		'animal', 'man', 'white'	'animal', 'inanimate', 'white'	29^a6-10

alternative ontological interpretation had been right, according to which terms are items signified by significant utterances. Aristotle surely maintains that the way of arranging an inference's terms whereby for some term *A*, for some term *B*, for some term *C*, the premises are propositions to the effect that *AaB* and *BaC* and the conclusion is a proposition to the effect that *AaC*, guarantees the validity of inferences where terms are thus arranged. But now, if for Aristotle terms are items signified by significant utterances, i.e., the items signified by a proposition's predicate- and subject-expressions, he must concede that

> [c] Every cloak is a garment. Every garment is an artifact. Therefore every robe is an artifact

is a valid inference where for some term *A*, for some term *B*, for some term *C*, the premises are propositions to the effect that *AaB* and *BaC* and the conclusion is a proposition to the effect that *AaC* (for 'cloak' and 'robe' signify the same item).[104] But Aristotle would resist making such a concession.[105]

The clause 'due to these things being'. In T16 Aristotle remarks that a successful application of the method of rejection by counter-examples shows that 'nothing necessary results due to these things being [*ouden gar anagkaion sumbainei tô(i) tauta einai*]' (26a4–5). This remark recalls T9's definition of syllogism, according to which in a syllogism 'something...results of necessity due to these things being [*ti...ex anangkês sumbainei tô(i) tauta einai*]' (24b19–20).[106] Note that in the *Analytics* the formula 'due to these things being' occurs nowhere outside T9 and T16. Note also that near the end of T16 Aristotle replaces the formula 'due to these things being' with the formula 'through these things': for he says that 'since nothing is necessary through these things [*dia toutôn*], there will not be a syllogism' (26a7–8). In the *Topics* Aristotle offers the following definition of syllogism: 'A syllogism is a discourse in which, certain things having been posited, something different from the things laid down results of necessity through the things laid down [*dia tôn keimenôn*]' (*Top.* I 1 100a25–7). This definition matches that of the *Prior Analytics* except that the formula 'through the things laid down' replaces the formula 'due to these things being'. This suggests that the two formulae are equivalent (at least in the context of syllogistic theory). So when, near the end of T16, he replaces the formula 'due to these things being' with the formula 'through these things', Aristotle is probably helping himself to a stylistic variant.

It may then be plausibly deduced that when in T9's definition of syllogism he says that in a syllogism 'something...results of necessity due to these things being' (24b19–20), Aristotle means that a syllogism must not only be valid but also have its validity guaranteed by its structure, so that no inference with the same structure has true premises and a false conclusion. The requirement that no inference with the same structure have true premises and a false conclusion is close to the Tarski-style characterisation of a valid inference as one in which no interpretation of the non-logical language makes the premises true but not the conclusion. Therefore there is some plausibility in assuming that in his characterisation of syllogisms by means of the formula 'due to these things being', Aristotle is imposing a condition that is close to Tarski-style validity.

Aristotle's position presupposes a clear conception of what is to count as an inference with the same structure. For, suppose one were to grant that every inference with two premises and one conclusion has the same structure as any canonical syllogism (they would both be instances of the schema 'A, B, therefore Γ'). Then in no canonical syllogism would it be the case that 'something...results of necessity due to these things being' (24b19–20), so that no canonical syllogism would be a syllogism. Clearly, this is not something Aristotle wants. Aristotle would probably maintain that the structure shared by the inference to be rejected and the one with true premises and false conclusion must be as 'specific' as possible and comprise only the pattern of reoccurrence of terms and what is expressed by the logical expressions '... is predicated of all of...', '... is predicated of none of...', '... is predicated of some of...', and '... is not predicated of some of...'. None of this surfaces in the *Analytics*. However, since the method of rejection by counter-examples is always properly applied, we may credit Aristotle with an implicit grasp of this point.

Independence from external conditions. In T9, his definition of syllogism, Aristotle offers a gloss on the formula 'due to these things being' in terms of independence from external conditions: 'By "due to these things being" I mean "to result because of these things", and by "to result because of these things" I mean "needing no further term from outside for the necessity to come about"' (*APr* I 1 24b20–2). I argued that the formula 'due to these things being' expresses a condition which requires that no inference with the same structure have true premises and a false conclusion. What connection is there between the explanation of the formula 'due to these things being' in terms of independence from external conditions and its expressing a condition which requires that no inference with the same structure have true premises and a false conclusion?

Passage T9 makes it clear that what must be independent of external conditions is the conclusion's following necessarily from the premises. Let me explain with a rough example. Suppose that the test tube contains nitroglycerine: then the conclusion 'There will soon be an explosion' follows necessarily from the premise 'The test tube is violently shaken' (plus 'ordinary' ambience conditions). In this case the conclusion's following necessarily from the premise obviously depends on external circumstances. By contrast, the conclusion 'Felix is a vertebrate' follows necessarily from 'Felix is a cat' independently of external circumstances.

My rough example suggests that the point made by the formula 'due to these things being' in T9's definition of syllogism is that the conclusion's following necessarily from the premises must be independent of circumstances external to what is stated by the premises themselves. But this cannot do: for, on such a showing, we should grant that the conclusion 'Every Siamese is a vertebrate' follows necessarily from the premises 'Every cat is a mammal' and 'Every Siamese is a cat' 'due to these things being', something which Aristotle would surely deny (the method of rejection by counter-examples could be easily applied to show this). But perhaps the point made by the formula 'due to these things being' is that the conclusion's following necessarily from the premises must be independent of circumstances external to the structure of the premises. If this is the point Aristotle intends to make with the formula 'due to these things being', one can easily see why the method of rejection by counter-examples can establish that an inference's conclusion does not follow necessarily from the premises 'due to these things being'. If this is correct, perhaps the literal meaning of the formula 'due to these things being' is something like 'due to just *these* premises being present', i.e., 'due to the premises being of this sort'.[107] However far-fetched, this is, as far as I can see, the only reading of the formula that gives Aristotle a coherent position.[108]

NOTES

1. This study is based on material I used in seminars at the University of Saõ Paulo in March and April 2006. A draft was presented at a conference in the Scuola Normale

Superiore of Pisa in March 2009. I am grateful to the audiences, and in particular to Marco Zingano, for many helpful remarks. I would also like to thank Walter Cavini, David Keyt, Marko Malink, and Tim Williamson for their comments on earlier versions. The responsibility for the remaining deficiencies is of course only mine.

2. Accounts of modal syllogisms in harmony with the approach taken in this study may be found in Malink (2006) and Johnson (2004).

3. Cf. *DI* 24a28–9; *DI* 11 20b23–4; *APo* I 2 72a8–9; *SE* 6 169a7–8; 169a10–1; 169a14.

4. Cf. *DI* 14 23a27–35.

5. Cf. *APr* I 23 40b23–5; II 1 53a8–9.

6. Cf. *APr* I 10 30b7–9; 11 31a18–21; 15 34a22–4. On one occasion, Aristotle does use 'proposition' to refer to the conclusion of a syllogism: *APr* I 29 45b7 (cf. Phlp. *in APr* 300, 14–15; Smith (1989), 155).

7. Small variations generate numerous parallel examples (e.g., substitute 'soldier' for 'individual').

8. Cf. Charles (2009), 67–9; Crivelli and Charles (2011), 200.

9. *APr* I 2 25a1–5.

10. Cf. *Top.* II 1 108b37–109a1.

11. *APr* I 1 24a18–22. For the examples of propositions with 'pleasure' and 'good' as subject- and predicate-expressions, cf. *APr* I 2 25a6–7; 25a9; 25a11; *Top.* II 1 109a1; III 6 120a7–8.

12. The earliest occurrence of this terminology is in Apuleius (*DI* 3 190, 17–191, 5 Moreschini) and Alexander of Aphrodisias (*in APr* 11 29–12, 2).

13. Ontological interpretation: Prantl (1855–70), I 212, 271. Linguistic interpretation: Alex. Aphr. *in APr* 14 27–15, 4; Ammon. *in APr* 14 24–5; Łukasiewicz (1957), 6; Barnes (1996), 176–7; Drechsler (2005), 257–8. Bocheński (1956), 54 regards 'term' (as well as 'proposition' and 'syllogism') as covering linguistic, mental, and objective items in one go.

14. Cf. Barnes (2007), 113–28.

15. I 5 27b32–4; 42a32–5; 42b1–4.

16. '... holds of...': *APr* I 1 24a18–22; 2 25a14–26. '... follows...': I 4 26b5–6; 28 44a21. '... is said of...': I 41 49b22–32. '... is predicated of...': I 1 24a14–15; 4 25b37–9.

17. At *APr* I 37 49a6–7 (cf. 36 48b2–4) Aristotle treats 'to be true of' as equivalent to 'to hold of', which in turn is a variant of 'to be predicated of' and 'to be said of'.

18. Cf. 26a9–11; 26b5–6.

19. Also in other passages of the *Prior Analytics* Aristotle speaks of terms as parts of terms: I 25 42a9–12; 42a15–16; II 15 64b12–13.

20. Cf. *EN* V 2 1130b10–16.

21. Cf. Ebert and Nortmann (2007), 214.

22. Note however that Aristotle never formulates truth-conditions in this way.

23. Cf. Barnes (1996), 186–7; Striker (2009), 75–6. Many commentators maintain that Aristotle's 'reversed' formulations aim at a clear distinction between the logical predicate (in the nominative) and the logical subject (in an oblique case): Alex. Aphr. *in APr* 54, 21–2 and 23–4; Łukasiewicz (1957), 17; Kneale and Kneale (1962), 62; Patzig (1968), 11; Striker (2009), 76. Different explanations of Aristotle's 'reversed' formulations are offered by Ebert and Nortmann (2007), 214–17.

24. *APr* I 5 27a29–31; II 8 59b8–11; 15 63b23–30; *DI* 7 17b16–37.

25. *APr* I 2 25a19; II 15 63b28–30; *DI* 7 17b20–25; 10 20a16–20; 14 24b6–7; *Top.* II 2 109b23–25.

26. *APr* II 11 62a11–19; *DI* 7 17b26–27; 9 18a28–33.

27. The earliest occurrence of this illustration is in Apuleius (*DI* 5 195 Moreschini). Modern commentators and logicians still speak of 'the square of logical opposition'.

28. At 24b29–30, I follow the reading of most main MSS: *labein tou hupkeimenou kath' hou.*

29. Cf. *APr* I 4 26a27.

30. The proof of the validity of syllogisms in *Barbara* in the main text above is not explicitly offered by Aristotle. It accounts for Aristotle's remark (I 4 25b39–40) that the validity of syllogisms in *Barbara* follows from the characterisation of being-predicated-of-all-of. Occasionally (I 9 30b2; 14, 33a27; 15, 35a35), Aristotle uses 'proof' (*apodeixis*) to describe arguments for the validity of perfect syllogisms (cf. I 5 27a8–9).

31. Aristotle never mentions a proof of the validity of syllogisms in *Celarent*.

32. Cf. below, text to n. 39.

33. Aristotle (I 4 26a24–5, 26a27) says that the validity of syllogisms in *Darii* and *Ferio* follows from the characterisations of being-predicated-of-all-of and being-predicated-of-none-of.

34. Cf. above, subsection to n. 24.

35. Thesis [6] is never stated in Aristotle's logical works.

36. Cf. Malink (2008), 526.

37. The proofs of the validity of conversions in the main text above mimic Aristotle's proofs at *APr* I 2 25a14–22.

38. *APr* I 6 28a23; 28b14; 8 30a9–13.

39. Cf. above, text to n. 32.

40. Mignucci (2000), 13; Barnes (2007), 141–2, 406–12; Ebert and Nortmann (2007), 229–30, 292–3.

41. Alex. Aphr. *in APr* 375, 19–22; Maier (1896/1936), II.II 150; Mignucci (1997a), 138–9; Malink (2006), 106–8. Barnes (2007), 406–12 explores a different version of the heterodox interpretation (cf. below, n. 43).

42. Aristotle never says that every term is predicated of all of itself. But in one passage (*APr* II 22 68a16–21) he infers a conclusion by appealing to the claim that a certain term is predicated of all of itself (interestingly enough, he does not rank this claim among the inference's initial premises).

43. Matters hardly improve with the alternative version of the heterodox interpretation considered by Barnes (2007), 406–12 (cf. above, n. 41). The hallmark of this alternative version is the replacement of [2] with:

[2*] For every term P, for every term S, PeS just if it is not the case that for some z, both S is predicated of all of z and it is not the case that P is predicated of none of z.

The problem now is that [1] and [2*] do not suffice to prove [7] (there is a countermodel in the domain of all subsets of a given set, with inclusion and disjointedness interpreting being-predicated-of-all-of and being-predicated-of-none-of).

44. Cf. Malink (2006), 107; Malink (2008), 530–1.

45. Cf. Malink (2006), 106–7.

46. Cf. Barnes (2007), 412.

47. Cf. Morison (2008), 214–15. The second sentence of *Prior Analytics* I 1 outlines the chapter's task: 'to determine [*diorisai*] what a proposition is [*ti esti*], what a term is, and what a syllogism is (and which is perfect and which imperfect); and, after this, what

it is for this to be or not to be in this as a whole and what we call [*ti legomen*] to be predicated of all or of no' (24a11–15). In the case of proposition, term, syllogism, being-in-something-as-a-whole, and not-being-in-something-as-a-whole, Aristotle promises to determine *what each of them is*: this probably amounts to a commitment to offer definitions. In the case of being-predicated-of-all-of and being-predicated-of-none-of, Aristotle promises to determine *what we call each of them*. This different formulation might indicate that Aristotle is not committing himself to offer definitions (in *DC* I 3 269b20–3 he distinguishes specifying 'what we call' something from giving its essence). Later in the *Prior Analytics* Aristotle refers back to his determinations of 'how we speak of [*pôs legomen*] "of all"', (I 4 25b39–40) and 'how we speak of [*pôs legomen*] "of no"', (I 4 26a27). Perhaps, when he promises 'to determine…what we call to be predicated of all or of no', Aristotle is merely committing himself to specifying certain characteristics of being-predicated-of-all-of and being-predicated-of-none-of that can be gleaned from our ordinary ways of speaking.

48. Cf. Crivelli (2004), 264–5.

49. *DI* 5 17a8–22; 7 17a38–17b12; 8 18a12–27; 11 20b12–26 (cf. Crivelli (2004), 152–80).

50. On Aristotle's views about universals, cf. *Cat.* 11 14a7–10; *DI* 7 17a38–17b1; *APr* I 27 43a25–43; *APo* I 11 77a5–9; 24 85a31–5; *SE* 22 178b37–9; 179a8–10; *PA* I 4 644a27–8; *Met.* III 4 999b33–1000a1; V 26 1023b29–32; VII 13 1038b11–12; 1038b15–16; 16 1040b25–7; XI 2 1060b20–2; XII 3 1070a22–4; XIII 9 1086a31–1086b11; Mignucci (1993), 355–60, 369–73; Crivelli (2004), 78–82; Loux (2009), 189–93.

51. In some passages Aristotle seems to allow syllogisms with propositions whose subject- or predicate-expressions are empty: *APr* I 38 49a11–26; II 15 64b17–21.

52. Cf. *DI* 1 16a16–17; *APo* II 7 92b5–8.

53. *APr* I 33 47b21–37; II 27 70a16–20; 70a24–34.

54. Cf. *Met.* V 9 1018a3–4.

55. Cf. *Top.* I 1 100a25–7; *SE* 1 164b27–165a2; *Rhet.* I 2 1356b16–18.

56. E.g., Łukasiewicz (1957), 1–3, 20–3; Patzig (1968), 3–4, 26–7.

57. *APr* I 4 25b26–31; *APo* I 2 71b17–18; 4 73a24 (cf. *APr* I 23 40b23).

58. Cf. *APr* I 14 34a16–19; 23 40b33–7; II 2 53b16–24; *APo* I 3 73a7–11; II 11 94a21–2; 94a24–7; Alex. Aphr. *in APr* 17, 10–18, 7; Mignucci (1997b), 71–3; Mignucci (2008), 257–8; Striker (2009), 79–80.

59. Cf. *APr* I 23 40b31–3; II 16 65a7–9; *APo* I 3 73a4–6; Alex. Aphr. *in APr* 18, 8–19, 3; Mignucci (1997b), 71–2; Mignucci (2008), 257–8; Striker (2009), 80.

60. E.g., at *APr* I 4 26a8–9.

61. The above reconstruction of the three figures is based on Rose (1968), 16–26 and Smiley (1994), 37. Its most important traits are due to Walter Cavini (private communication).

62. *APr* I 32 47a39–40. 'Middle term': I 4 25b32–4. 'Middle': I 4 26a3.

63. *APr* I 4 25b32–4; 25b36.

64. *APr* I 23 41a13–16; 32 47a40–47b7.

65. Aristotle also says: 'I call that "middle" which both is itself in another and has another in it' (I 4 25b35–6). He probably means that *in the most important* first-figure syllogisms (i.e., syllogisms in *Barbara*) the middle is *claimed* to be a part of a term and is *claimed* to contain one as a part (cf. Ebert and Nortmann (2007), 296–7).

66. *APr* I 4 26a18; 26a21–2; I 5 26b37–8; I 6 28a13–14.

67. *APr* I 6 28b32.

68. *APr* I 4 26a18–19; 26a21–3; I 5 26b37–8; I 6 28a13–14.

69. *APr* I 6 28b32.

70. Literally: *in the most important* first-figure syllogisms (i.e., syllogisms in *Barbara*) the middle is *claimed* to be a part of the major extreme and the minor extreme is *claimed* to be a part of the middle (cf. n. 65 above). For 'under' expressing containment, cf. *APr* II 1 53a17–24; *Top.* VII 1 152a16 with 152a29–30.

71. Cf. Patzig (1968), 120. The earliest occurrence of these later definitions seems to be in Philoponus (*in APr* 67, 27–9).

72. The earliest occurrence of 'major premise' and 'minor premise' is perhaps in Alexander of Aphrodisias (*in APr* 48, 7–10, cf. Phlp. *in APr* 67, 29–30).

73. An important contribution made by Aristotle to logic is the introduction of letters ('*A*', '*B*', '*C*', etc.) standing for terms. According to some commentators, Aristotle treats the letters as *variables* (cf. Łukasiewicz (1957), 7–8; Thom (1981), 19). Aristotle, however, seems to employ the letters as *names* of arbitrarily chosen terms connected with (existential or universal) quantifications over terms. He appears not to treat the letters as *variables* ranging over terms and he never attaches them to quantifiers (cf. Frede (1974), 113; Mignucci (1997*b*), 80; Ierodiakonou (2002), 130–7; Keyt (2009), 39). In my presentation, I sometimes treat letters as variables, and I sometimes attach them to quantifiers. In this respect, my use of letters differs from Aristotle's.

74. The traditional names were introduced in a brief medieval poem, which may be found in Patzig (1968), 13.

75. Cf. *APr* I 5 28a5–7; 6 29a15–16; 15 35a40–35b1; 25 42a33–5.

76. Cf. Alex. Aphr. *in APr.* 24, 7–11; Ross (1949), 291–2; Lear (1980), 2–3; Smith (1989), 110; Mignucci (1996), 369; Keyt (2009), 38; Striker (2009), 82–3.

77. Cf. Corcoran (1974), 91–2.

78. Cf. Corcoran (1974), 91–2; Striker (1996), 205–8.

79. *APr* I 4 26b28–9; 5 28a4–5; 6 29a14–15.

80. *APr* I 4 25b39–40; 26a24; 26a27.

81. Cf. Maier (1896/1936), II.II 151; Smith (1989), 111; Mignucci (1996), 369; Striker (1996), 216–17; Mignucci (1997*b*), 85–6; Ebert and Nortmann (2007), 230, 292–5. Some commentators deny that any justification or proof is ever offered of the validity of perfect syllogisms: cf. Lear (1980), 2–3; Boger (2004), 183.

82. Cf. above, paragraphs to nn. 30, 31, 33, and 39.

83. Cf. Striker (2009), 83. Several ancient logicians claimed against Aristotle that first-figure syllogisms are not the only ones to be perfect. The evidence is discussed in Barnes (2007), 373–8.

84. Cf. Ross (1949), 34; Patzig (1968), 50–1; Keyt (2009), 44.

85. Cf. Smith (1989), 111.

86. Some rules of inference (e.g., universal generalization in axiomatic systems) are not evidently valid. Accordingly, logicians prove not only *why* but also *that* they are valid.

87. Cf. Keyt (2009), 43–4. Aristotle is probably concerned not only with the soundness but also with the completeness of syllogistic: cf. *APr* I 23 40b17–41b5 (especially 40b30–41a20); Smiley (1994), 25–34; Keyt (2009), 44–50. For a proof of the completeness of syllogistic based on modern techniques, see Corcoran (1972).

88. Cf. above, n. 37 and text thereto.

89. *APo* II 1 89b23–31.

90. *APo* I 13 78a22–79a16 (cf. *APr* II 2 53b7–10; *APo* I 9 76a10–13; 27 87a31–3; II 1 89b24–31).

91. *APo* II 1 89b28–9.

92. *APo* II 1 89b29–31.

93. Objection: 'After alluding to a proof of the validity of inferences where terms are arranged according to the *Ferio* pattern, a proof based on T6's characterisation of being-predicated-of-none-of (*APr* I 4 26a25–7), Aristotle remarks: "Hence there will be a perfect syllogism" (26a28). This surely shows that Aristotle uses T6's characterisations to prove that first-figure syllogisms are perfect, i.e., evidently valid?' This objection can be blocked by offering an alternative account of what goes on in the passage (cf. Barnes (2007), 392–3). The proof of the validity of inferences where terms are arranged according to the *Ferio* pattern to which lines 26a25–7 allude belongs to the project of proving the soundness of syllogistic, i.e. explaining why all canonical syllogisms are valid. The subsequent remark that 'there will be a perfect syllogism' (26a28) has two components: the first is that inferences where terms are arranged according to the *Ferio* pattern are syllogisms, the second that such inferences are perfect, i.e., evidently valid. Both components go beyond the result that was established and explained by the preceding proof: there is more than validity to being a syllogism (cf. *APr* I 32 47a31–5), and the evidence of validity is independent of proofs explaining why there is validity (it has to do with the pattern of occurrence of terms).

94. *APr* I 2 25a14–22. Cf. above, paragraph to n. 37.

95. *APr* I 7 29a30–9.

96. In *Prior Analytics* I 5–6 Aristotle perfects all second- and third-figure syllogisms through one or other of the first-figure syllogisms; but in chapter 7 (29b1–25), he argues that all other canonical syllogisms can be 'reduced' to 'the universal syllogisms in the first figure', i.e., syllogisms in *Barbara* and *Celarent* (cf. I 23 40b17–20; 41b3–5). On the metalogical outlook thereby taken cf. Corcoran (1974), 113–15; Smith (1995), 42; Keyt (2009), 41–3.

97. Some of the 'logically weaker' ways of arranging terms in the inference's conclusion are covered at *APr* II 1 53a3–14. Some, but not all: the conversions mentioned in this passage do not enable one to go from a universal negative to a corresponding particular negative conclusion. Another limit of Aristotle's procedure is indicated by Keyt (2009), 45: when Aristotle shows that for a given nth-figure way of arranging terms in the premises there is an nth-figure way of arranging terms in the conclusion whereby all inferences where terms are thus arranged are valid, and when the arrangement of terms in the conclusion is *particular*, namely in the *i* (or *o*) style, he does not prove that the arrangement of terms in the conclusion that is either *universal and of the same quality*, namely in the *a* (or *e*) style, or *particular but of the opposite quality*, namely in the *o* (or *i*) style, fails to guarantee that all inferences where terms are thus arranged are valid. For instance, Aristotle never proves that the first-figure way of arranging terms in an inference whereby for some terms A, B, and C, the premises are propositions to the effect that AaB and BiC and the conclusion is a proposition to the effect that AoC fails to guarantee that all inferences where terms are thus arranged are valid. This omission bears on later claims. For instance, the claim that in every canonical syllogism the conclusion must be of the same quality as at least one of the premises (cf. *APr* I 24 41b27–31) turns out to lack adequate justification.

98. Cf. *APr* I 14 33b11–13.

99. *APr* I 7 29a19–26.

100. The traditional names allow one to reconstruct how syllogisms in the second and third figure are perfected (cf. above, paragraph to n. 74). The first letter indicates which first-figure syllogism must be used: thus, the 'B' of 'Baroco' and

'Bocardo' indicates the use of Barbara, the 'C' of 'Cesare' and 'Camestres' the use of Celarent, the 'D' of 'Darapti', 'Disamis', and 'Datisi' the use of Darii, and the 'F' of 'Festino', 'Felapton', and 'Ferison' the use of Ferio. An 's' (as in 'Cesare', 'Camestres', 'Festino', 'Disamis', 'Datisi', and 'Ferison') signals that the proposition corresponding to the preceding vowel undergoes conversio simplex (cf. above, subsection to n. 94). A 'p' (as in 'Darapti' and 'Felapton') reveals instead that the proposition corresponding to the preceding vowel undergoes conversio per accidens. Finally, a 'c' (as in 'Baroco' and 'Bocardo') indicates that the proposition corresponding to the preceding vowel is the result of a transformation per contradictionem: it is a contradictory of the conclusion of a syllogism whose premisses are the other premiss of the syllogism to be perfected and a contradictory of its conclusion. I forgo perfecting each second- or third-figure syllogism because the traditional names enable one to do this on the basis of the examples discussed in the paragraphs encompassing T14 and T15.

101. In the second figure the order of terms is: middle, major, minor (cf. above, the paragraph encompassing T11).
102. In the third figure the order of terms is: major, minor, middle (cf. above, the paragraph encompassing T12).
103. Cf. above, paragraph to n. 13.
104. *Top.* VI 11 149a3–4; *SE* 6 168a28–33; *Phys.* I 2 185b19–20; III 3 202b12–13; *Met.* IV 4 1006b25–8.
105. *SE* 6 168a28–33.
106. Cf. Striker (2009), 95–6.
107. This interpretation of the formula 'due to these things being' (*tô(i) tauta einai*) is confirmed by a later application of the method of rejection by counter-examples, where it is replaced with 'due to the terms being in this condition' (*tô(i) houtôs echein tous horous*, *APr* I 4 26b19).
108. At *Top.* VIII 1 161b28–30 and *SE* 6 168b22–5 the clause 'due to these things being' banishes redundant premisses (cf. Ebert and Nortmann (2007), 227–8; Mignucci (2008), 255–6; Striker (2009), 81).

BIBLIOGRAPHY

Barnes, J. (1996) 'Grammar on Aristotle's Terms', in M. Frede and G. Striker, eds., *Rationality in Greek Thought* (Oxford), 175–202.
———— (2007), *Truth, etc.* (Oxford).
Bocheński, I.M. (1956) *Formale Logik* (Munchen).
Boger, G. (2004) 'Aristotle's Underlying Logic', in D.M. Gabbay and J. Woods, eds., *Handbook of the History of Logic*, I (Amsterdam), 101–46.
Charles, D. (2009) '*Nicomachean Ethics* VII. 3: Varieties of *Akrasia*', in C. Natali, ed., *Aristotle's* Nicomachean Ethics, *Book vii* (Oxford), 41–71.
Corcoran, J. (1972) 'Completeness of an Ancient Logic', *Journal of Symbolic Logic* 37, 696–702.
———— (1974) 'Aristotle's Natural Deduction System', in J. Corcoran, ed., *Ancient Logic and Its Modern Interpretations: Proceedings of the Buffalo Symposium on*

Modernist Interpretations of Ancient Logic, 21 and 22 April (1972) (Dordrecht/Boston), 85–131.

Crivelli, P. (2004) *Aristotle on Truth* (Cambridge).

Crivelli, P. and D. Charles (2011), ' "ΠΡΟΤΑΣΙΣ" in Aristotle's *Prior Analytics*', *Phronesis* 56, 193–203.

Drechsler, M. (2005) *Interpretationen der Beweismethoden in der Syllogistik des Aristoteles* (Frankfurt am Main).

Ebert, T. and U. Nortmann, trans. and comm., (2007) *Aristoteles: Analytica Priora, Buch i* (Berlin).

Frede, M. (1974) 'Stoic vs. Aristotelian Syllogistic', in M. Frede, *Essays in Ancient Philosophy* (Oxford, 1987), 99–124.

Ierodiakonou, K. (2002) 'Aristotle's Use of Examples in the *Prior Analytics*', *Phronesis* 47, 127–72.

Johnson, F. (2004) 'Aristotle's Modal Syllogisms' in D.M. Gabbay and J. Woods, eds., *Handbook of the History of Logic* I (Amsterdam), 247–307.

Keyt, D. (2009) 'Deductive Logic', in G. Anagnostopoulos, ed., *A Companion to Aristotle* (Chichester), 31–50.

Kneale, W. and M. Kneale (1962) *The Development of Logic* (Oxford).

Lear, J. (1980) *Aristotle and Logical Theory* (Cambridge).

Loux, M. (2009) 'Aristotle on Universals', in G. Anagnostopoulos, ed., *A Companion to Aristotle* (Chichester), 186–96.

Łukasiewicz, J. (1957) *Aristotle's Syllogistic from the Standpoint of Modern Formal Logic*, 2nd edition (Oxford).

Maier, H. (1896/1936) *Die Syllogistik des Aristoteles*, 2nd edition, repr. (Hildesheim, 1969).

Malink, M. (2006) 'A Reconstruction of Aristotle's Modal Syllogistic', *History and Philosophy of Logic* 27, 95–141.

———— (2008) 'ΤΩΙ vs ΤΩΝ in *Prior Analytics* 1.1–22', *Classical Quarterly* 58, 519–36.

Mignucci, M. (1993) 'La sémantique des termes généraux chez Aristote', *Revue philosophique de la France et de l'étranger* 118, 355–73.

———— (1996) 'Logic', in J. Brunschwig and G.E.R. Lloyd, eds., *Greek Thought: A Guide to Classical Knowledge* (Cambridge, Mass. and London, 2000), 355–85.

———— (1997a) 'Remarks on Aristotle's Theory of Predication', in H.C. Günther and A. Rengakos, eds., *Beiträge zur Antiken Philosophie: Festschrift für Wolfgang Kullman* (Stuttgart), 135–51.

———— (1997b) 'Logica', in E. Berti, ed., *Aristotele* (Rome/Bari), 47–101.

———— (2000) 'Parts, Quantification and Aristotelian Predication', *The Monist* 83, 3–21.

———— (2008) 'Il sillogismo aristotelico', in M. Migliori and A. Fermani, eds., *Platone e Aristotele: Dialettica e logica* (Brescia), 243–64.

Morison, B. (2008) 'Aristotle, etc.', *Phronesis* 53, 209–22.

Patzig, G. (1968) *Aristotle's Theory of the Syllogism*, trans. by J. Barnes (Dordrecht).

Prantl, C. (1855–70) *Geschichte der Logik im Abendlande* (Leipzig).

Rose, L.E. (1968) *Aristotle's Syllogistic* (Springfield, Ill.).

Ross, W.D., ed. and comm. (1949) *Aristotle's Prior and Posterior Analytics* (Oxford).

Smiley, T. (1994) 'Aristotle's Completeness Proof', *Ancient Philosophy* 14 (Special Issue), 25–38.

Smith, R. (1995) 'Logic', in J. Barnes, ed., *The Cambridge Companion to Aristotle* (Cambridge), 27–65.

Smith, R., trans. and comm. (1989) *Aristotle: Prior Analytics* (Indianapolis, Ind./
    Cambridge).

Striker, G. (1996) 'Perfection and Reduction in Aristotle's *Prior Analytics*', in M. Frede and
    G. Striker, eds., *Rationality in Greek Thought* (Oxford), 203–19.

Striker, G., trans. and comm. (2009) *Aristotle: Prior Analytics, Book i* (Oxford).

Thom, P. (1981) *The Syllogism* (München).

....

CHAPTER 7

ARISTOTLE'S PHILOSOPHICAL METHOD

C. D. C. REEVE

A problem (*problêma*) is posed: Is pleasure choiceworthy, or not? The answerer claims that yes it is (or, alternatively, that no it isn't). The questioner must refute him by asking questions—by offering him premises (*protaseis*) to accept or reject. The questioner succeeds if he forces the answerer to accept a proposition contrary to the one he undertook to defend (*SE* 2 165b3–4). The questioner fails if the answerer always accepts or rejects premises in a way consistent with that proposition. To a first approximation, *dialectic* is the art or craft (*technê*) enabling someone to play the role of questioner or answerer successfully (*Top.* I 1 100a18–21, VIII 14 164b2–4). Also to a first approximation, it is the distinctive method of Aristotelian philosophy.

At the heart of dialectic is the dialectical deduction (*dialektikos sullogismos*). This is the argument lying behind the questioner's questions, partly dictating their order and content, and partly determining the strategy of his attack. Understanding dialectic is primarily a matter of grasping the nature of dialectical deductions and the type of premises they employ.

In *Topics* I 1, such deductions are contrasted with three other types of arguments: scientific, eristic, and paralogistic. In *Sophistical Refutations* I 2, they are distinguished from didactic, peirastic, and eristic arguments. Our task in sections 1–4 is to explore and co-ordinate these two sets of contrasts. When it is completed, we shall turn in sections 5–7 to a discussion of dialectical premises, *endoxa* (reputable beliefs), and *aporiai* (puzzles). Section 8 deals with the uses of dialectic in intellectual training (*gumnasia*), ordinary discussion (*enteuxeis*), and the philosophical sciences; section 9, with its use in regard to scientific starting-points or first principles (*archai*). Section 10 returns to dialectic and philosophy and an important difference between them.

1. Dialectic, Eristic, and Sophistry

Dialectical deductions differ from scientific ones only in their premises: the latter are deductions from starting-points and hence are demonstrations (*apodeixeis*); the former are deductions from *endoxa* (*Top.* I 1 100a1-b23; *Met.* III 1 995b23–4). In the case of eristic arguments the differences are potentially twofold: they are either genuine deductions from apparent *endoxa* or apparent deductions from genuine or apparent *endoxa* (*Top.* I 1 100b23–5). Paralogistic arguments differ from all these: unlike dialectical or eristic arguments, their premises are not *endoxa*, but 'premises proper to a specialized science' (*Top.* I 1 101a5–7); unlike scientific demonstrations, their premises are false (*Top.* I 1 101a14).

'In dialectic,' Aristotle tells us, 'a sophist is so called on the basis of his deliberate choice (*prohairesis*), and a dialectician is so called not on the basis of his deliberate choice, but on the basis of the ability he has' (*Rhet.* I 1 1355b20–1). If dialectic is understood in this way, it is a neutral craft, and a dialectician who decides to employ eristic arguments is a sophist (*Rhet.* I 1 1335a24-b7). A contender (*eristikos*) also employs such arguments, but differs from a sophist in his purposes: 'Sophistry…is a way of making money out of apparent wisdom….Contenders and sophists use the same arguments, but not to achieve the same goal….If the goal is apparent victory, the argument is eristic or contentious; if it is apparent wisdom, sophistic' (*SE* 11 171b27–9).

In the *Topics* and *Sophistical Refutations*, by contrast, the person who decides to use only genuine and never eristic arguments is a dialectician, since in both treatises dialectic differs from eristic precisely in employing genuine *endoxa* and genuine deductions rather than merely apparent ones (*Top.* I 1 100a29-b25, *SE* 2 165b3–8, 11 171b34–172a2). For clarity's sake, let us say that *plain* dialectic is the neutral craft contenders, sophists, and *honest* dialecticians use for different purposes, imposing different restrictions on which of its resources may be legitimately employed.

2. Peirastic Deductions and Sophistical Refutations

Peirastic (*peirastikê*) is 'a type of dialectic which has in view not the person who knows (*eidota*), but the one who pretends to know but does not' (*SE* 11 171b4–6). It is the type particularly useful in arguments with sophists, since they are the archetypal pretenders to knowledge and wisdom (*SE* 1 165a21). Though Aristotle usually uses the term *peirastikê* to refer to honest peirastic rather than to the plain craft (*SE* 2 165b4–6), he courts confusion, as we shall see, by using it to refer to the plain craft too.

The best way to distinguish honest peirastic from honest dialectic pure and simple is by exploring sophistical refutations, which are the dishonest twins of honest peirastic arguments. Honest peirastic arguments expose the genuine ignorance of a sophist answerer, who has only apparent knowledge and wisdom (*SE* 11 171b3–6); sophistical refutations give the appearance of exposing the ignorance of someone who really does have scientific knowledge (*SE* 6 168b4–10). Such refutations are of two sorts. An *a-type* sophistical refutation is 'an apparent deduction or refutation rather than a real one'; a *b-type* is 'a real deduction that is only apparently proper to the subject in question' (*SE* 8 169b20–3). A-type sophistical refutations are eristic arguments, therefore, whereas b-types are like paralogisms (*SE* 11 171b34–7).

The paralogisms *proper to a craft or science* are those based on the starting-points and theorems belonging to it (*SE* 11 171b38–172a1). Thus Hippocrates' argument for squaring the circle by means of lunes is a geometrical paralogism, because it 'proceeds from starting-points proper to geometry' and 'cannot be adapted to any subject except geometry' (*SE* 11 172a4–5).[1] Someone who uses Zeno's argument that motion is impossible in order to refute a doctor's claim that it is better to take a walk after dinner, however, has produced a b-type sophistical refutation, since Zeno's arguments are not proper to geometry or medicine but '*koinos* (common)' (*SE* 11 172a8–9). Such an argument is paralogistic, indeed, even when sound: 'Bryson's method of squaring the circle,[2] even if the circle is thereby squared, is still sophistical because it is not in accord with the relevant subject matter' (*SE* 11 171b16–18). The only difference between paralogisms and b-type sophistical refutations is that the former have premises proper to the answerer's science but false, while the latter have premises not proper to it but true.

Because paralogisms depend on premises proper to a science, it is the job of the scientist himself to diagnose and refute them. It is not his job to deal with b-type sophistical refutations (*Phys.* I 2 185a16–17, *SE* 9 170a36–8), however, but that of a dialectician: 'It is *dialecticians* who study a refutation that depends on *koina*, that is to say, that do not belong to any [specialized] craft' (*SE* 9 170a38–9). Dialecticians must also deal with Antiphon's argument for squaring the circle, which is an a-type sophistical refutation, since by assuming that a circle is a polygon with a large but finite number of sides, it 'does away with the starting-points of geometry' (*Phys.* II 185a1–2)—in particular, with the principle that magnitudes are divisible without limit.[3] It cannot be discussed in a way that presupposes those starting-points, therefore, and so must be discussed on the basis of *koina* (*Top.* II 101a35-b4).

One view about *koina* is that they are axioms (*axiômata*)—starting-points common to all or many sciences (*APo* I 2 72a15–17, I 9 76b14–15). The laws of logic, such as the principle of noncontradiction, which hold at least analogically of all beings, are examples, as are other somewhat less general laws, such as the axioms of equality, which are not universally applicable, but are also not proper to a single science or single genus of beings (*APo* I 10 76a38-b2). On one manuscript reading, indeed, *SE* 11 172a36-7 actually identifies *koina* with *axiômata*, with 'identical (τ' αὐτα) starting-points which hold true of everything.' On another reading, it says only that there are 'many of these (ταῦτα) [common] things in each area.' Though most editors favour the first reading, the second is preferable.[4] Axioms, as common to many sciences, cannot by themselves entail a proposition contrary to a conclusion proper to a specific science. Hence it is impossible to construct b-type sophistical refutations using axioms alone. Yet that is precisely what b-type sophistical refutations must use *koina* to do.

As we saw in section 1, the only propositions that can figure as premises in dialectical arguments are *endoxa*. Since *koina*, too, can figure as such premises, they must be *endoxa*: 'It is plain that it is the dialectician's job to be able to grasp the various ways in which a real or apparent refutation—that is to say, one that is an example of dialectic or apparent dialectic or peirastic—can be achieved on the basis of *koina*' (*SE* 9 170b8–11; compare *Rhet.* I 1 1354a1–3). The following two passages—the first referring to the second—settle the matter: 'Even if one had the most rigorous sort of scientific knowledge, it would not be easy to persuade some people by arguments based on it…rather, it is necessary to construct our persuasions and arguments on the basis of *koina*, as we said in the *Topics* about ordinary discussions with the many' (*Rhet.* I 1 1355a24–9); '(Plain) dialectic is useful in ordinary discussions because once we have catalogued the beliefs of the many, our approach to them will begin from their own views, not from other people's, and we will redirect them whenever they appear to us to be wrong' (*Top.* I 2 101a30–4). It follows that axioms that are *endoxa* will also be *koina*. Since the noncontradoxical[5] views of philosophers are *endoxa* (section 5), it is a status that most if not all of them will have.

Honest peirastic deductions 'deduce from premises that are accepted by the answerer, and that must be known (*eidenai*) by anyone who claims to have the relevant scientific knowledge (*epistêmê*)' (*SE* 2 165b4–6). Premises of this sort are said to be taken 'not from the things from which one knows or even from those proper to the subject in question, but from the consequences that a man can know (*eidota*) without knowing the craft in question, but which if he does not know (*eidota*), he is necessarily ignorant of the craft' (*SE* 11 172a21–34). In other words, such premises are not starting-points of the answerer's science—not 'things from which one knows'—or other starting-points proper to it, but consequences of them. Peirastic premises, unlike those of b-type sophistical refutations, must be proper to the answerer's science, since they are syllogistic consequences of its starting-points. Later in the same passage these consequences are identified as *koina* (*endoxa*):

> Everybody, including those who do not possess a craft, makes use of dialectic as peirastic; for everyone tries to use peirastic to some extent in order to test those who claim to know things. And this is where the *koina* come in; for the testers

know (*isasin*) these things for themselves just as well as those who do possess the craft—even if they seem to say quite inaccurate things (*SE* 11 172a30–34).

Hence the premises of honest peirastic deductions must be true *endoxa* proper to the answerer's science—the one the sophist undergoing honest peirastic examination is pretending to know.

A person who in other respects does have scientific knowledge may yet be the victim of a sophistical refutation, since he may find himself caught in a contradiction when interrogated by a clever sophist. The mere fact that someone can be bested in a dialectical argument is not enough to show that he lacks scientific knowledge. What is further required is: first, that this argument not be a sophistical refutation (its premises must be true and proper to the science in question); second, those premises must be such that anyone who knows the science would have to know them (otherwise, the answerer could reject them and still know the science); finally, they must be propositions it is possible to know without knowing the science (otherwise, they could not figure in arguments available to nonscientists). Thus the various features that the premises of an honest peirastic argument must have are entailed by the fact that their purpose is to enable nonscientists to unmask pretenders to scientific knowledge.

In *Topics* VIII 5, Aristotle discusses 'dialectical explorations that are not competitive, but are conducted for the sake of examination (*peiras*) and inquiry' (159a32–33). From the account he provides of these, it is clear that they do not fit our characterisation of honest peirastic. For example, the questioner is not restricted to using true premises; he can and sometimes must use false ones:

> Since arguments of this kind are conducted for the sake of practice and examination (*peiras*), it is clear that the questioner must deduce not only true conclusions but also false ones, and not always from true premises but sometimes from false ones as well. For often, when a true proposition is put forward [by the answerer], the dialectician is compelled to demolish it, and so he has to offer [the answerer] false premises (*Top.* VIII 11 161a24–29).

Moreover, the answerer may defend a position he himself does not hold (*Top.* VIII 5 159b27–35), and accept premises that are not proper to the topic of the argument (*Top.* VIII 6 160a1–2). Yet the very fact that Aristotle discusses how the answerer should deal with *improper* premises (*Top.* VIII 6) in connection with dialectical explorations that examine and *inquire* suggests that such explorations are at least closely related to b-type sophistical refutations and honest peirastic deductions. Indeed, it suggests that these dialectical explorations are simply exercises in plain peirastic.

When Aristotle tells us in *Sophistical Refutations* I 2 that he has already discussed peirastic arguments, there is good reason to take him to be referring to the discussion of dialectical explorations that examine and investigate in *Topics* VIII 5–11. But to secure that reference, in the face of the manifest differences between what the two treatises say about peirastic, we must recognize that *Sophistical Refutations* mostly deals with honest peirastic, *Topics* with plain peirastic.[6]

3. DIDACTIC DEDUCTIONS

Didactic deductions (*didaskalikoi*) are 'those that deduce from the starting-points proper to each subject matter and not from the opinions held by the answerer, since learners have to take things on trust' (*SE* 2 165b1–3). This identifies them as scientific demonstrations of some sort—'arguments based on scientific knowledge' (*Rhet.* I 1 1355a26). But if they are scientific demonstrations, why are they included with honest dialectic, peirastic, and eristic arguments as one of the four types of argument used 'in question and answer discussions' (*SE* 2 165a38)?

Didactic deductions are not deductions 'from the opinions held by the answerer' (*SE* 2 165b2). Yet 'the student should always grant [only] what seems to him to be the case' (*Top.* VIII 5 159a28–9), suggesting that didactic arguments must indeed be deductions from the student's opinions. In *Topics* VIII, teaching sometimes takes the form of question and answer discussions. Yet teaching is also contrasted with asking questions: 'the teacher should not ask questions but make things clear himself, whereas the dialectician should ask questions' (*SE* 10 171b1–2).

To grasp the coherence of Aristotle's thought about didactic in the face of these apparent inconsistencies of doctrine, we need to appreciate the relevance to them of the distinction between an argument 'taken by itself' and one 'presented in the form of questions' (*Top.* VIII 11 161a16–17). Suppose a student has acquired the starting-points of a science, and his teacher wants to test his knowledge of it. The natural thing for him to do is to examine the student by offering him propositions to accept or reject. And, of course, 'the student should always grant [only] what seems to him to be the case' (*Top.* VIII 5 159a28–9), since otherwise the teacher will not be able to discover what he really knows. Here the teacher's didactic argument is 'presented in the form of questions.' But the admissions made by the student are not premises in the didactic argument (the scientific demonstration taken by itself) that underlies these questions and partly dictates their order and content. *It* is not a deduction 'from the opinions held by the answerer' (*SE* 2 165b2).

Suppose a phrase occurring in a scientific proposition has a double meaning, but that the student 'neither has considered nor knows nor conceives that a second meaning is possible' (*SE* 10 171a32–4). Then 'the teacher should not ask questions but make things clear himself' (*SE* 10 171b1–2). Here, unlike in the previous case, the teacher is not trying to find out what the student knows by asking him questions. He already knows that the student is ignorant and is providing him with information. So he uses a didactic argument 'taken by itself' to make things clear. Once we see that teaching may involve question and answer discussion as well as straightforward demonstration, so that didactic arguments can be understood in two different ways, we can see that these arguments do have a place in question and answer discussions and that Aristotle's account of them is consistent.[7]

4. THE CLASSIFICATION OF DEDUCTIONS

In *Topics* I 1, deductions are divided into four classes:
   (T1) scientific
   (T2) paralogistic
   (T3) honest dialectic
   (T4) eristic.
In *Sophistical Refutations* I 2 they are also initially divided into four:
   (S1) didactic
   (S2) peirastic
   (S3) honest dialectic
   (S4) eristic.
Then two more are added:
   (S5) a-type sophistical refutations
   (S6) b-type sophistical refutations.
Though apparently discordant, the two classifications fit together to constitute a single systematic classification of dialectical deductions.

   Deductions are generally of two kinds:
   (D1) genuine (valid)
   (D2) apparent (invalid).
The premises of each may be:
   (P1) true and proper starting-points of a science
   (P2) untrue but proper starting-points of a science
   (P3) true *endoxa* proper to a science
   (P4) true *endoxa* only apparently proper to a science
   (P5) *endoxa*
   (P6) apparent *endoxa*.
(D1–2) and (P1–6) together determine the various kinds of dialectical deductions:
   (D1)-(P1) scientific demonstrations (T1); presupposed in didactic arguments (S1)
   (D1)-(P2) paralogisms (T2)
   (D1)-(P3) peirastic deductions (S2)
   (D1)-(P4) b-type sophistical refutations (S6)
   (D1)-(P5) honest dialectic arguments (T3), (S3)
   (D1)-(P6) eristic arguments or a-type sophistical refutations (T4), (S4), (S5)
   (D2)-(P5) eristic arguments or a-type sophistical refutations (T4), (S4), (S5).

A striking feature of this classification is that it includes only one type of invalid deduction, namely, (D2)-(P5). This is so for a reason. The various kinds of formally valid and invalid deductions have already been studied in the *Prior Analytics*. *Topics* and *Sophistical Refutations* are primarily concerned not with them, therefore, but with sound or unsound ones—with the choice of premises rather than with the logical form of arguments (*APr* I 30 46a29–30). Hence the classification is both complete and systematic.

5. DIALECTICAL PREMISES

A dialectical premise consists in [a] making a question out of something that is *endoxos* to everyone or to the majority or to the wise—either to all of them, or to most, or to the most notable of them, provided it is not contradoxical; for a person would accept the opinion of the wise, provided it is not contrary to general opinion (*doxa*). Dialectical premises also include [b] things that are like *endoxa*, and [c] propositions that contradict the contraries of what seem to be *endoxa*, and also [d] all opinions that accord with [the starting-points of] the recognized crafts,...since a person would accept the opinions of those who have investigated the subjects in question—for example, on a question of medicine he will agree with the doctor, and on a question of geometry with the geometer (*Top.* I 10 104a8–37).

Later, in a reprise of this passage, Aristotle adds what seem to be two new cases to the account:

[e] Furthermore, statements that seem to hold in all or in most cases, should be taken as starting-points, that is to say, as accepted theses; for such statements are accepted by those who do not notice that there is a case in which they do not hold. [f] We ought also to select [premises] from written accounts and draw up lists of them on each type of subject, putting them under separate headings— for example, 'Dealing with good', 'Dealing with life'. And the one dealing with good, should deal with every kind of good, beginning with the essence (*Top.* I 14 105b10–15).

The fact that (b) describes propositions that are 'like *endoxa*,' that (c) speaks of the contraries of what 'seem to be *endoxa*,' and that (e) includes as *endoxa* statements that merely seem to be true to those 'who do not notice that there is a case in which they do not hold' strongly suggest that these clauses refer to apparent *endoxa*. Aristotle's illustrative examples bear this out: (i) 'If it is an *endoxon* that the science of contraries is the same, it might appear to be an *endoxon* that the perception of contraries is also the same' (*Top.* I 11 104a15–17); (ii) 'Propositions contradicting the contraries of *endoxa* will appear to be *endoxa*' (*Top.* I 10 104a20–3); (iii) 'If it is an *endoxon* that there is a single craft of grammar, it might also seem to be an *endoxon* that there is a single craft of flute-playing' (*Top.* I 10 104a17–20). (i) and (ii) explicitly refer to apparent *endoxa*, while (iii) makes sense only if it too has them in view, since if a proposition is a genuine *endoxon*, its contrary cannot be (*Top.* VIII 5 159b4–6). Since both *endoxa* and apparent *endoxa* can serve as premises in plain dialectical deductions, we cannot identify genuine *endoxa* with such premises, or infer that everything said about the latter applies willy-nilly to them.

The propositions referred to in (d) are in accord with the starting-points of the recognized crafts, so they must be genuine. But because they only *would be* accepted by anyone, they do not have to be already accepted so to count. Since written accounts are likely to have wise people or practitioners of the recognized crafts as authors, (f) is probably a new source of something already listed rather than a wholly new addition to the list. Aristotle himself suggests as much when he writes that we should note in the margins of the lists we distil from these writings the identity of the thinkers, such as Empedocles, who hold them, since 'anyone might assent to the saying of some *endoxos* (reputable) thinker' (*Top.* I 14 105b17–18).

Because medicine is itself an acknowledged craft or recognized area of expertise, the opinions of a doctor known to have studied medicine carry weight with everyone, whether or not the doctor himself has already acquired a good reputation. Hence if a person can show that he has been trained as a doctor, that is enough, everything else being equal, to guarantee that the answerer would accept his opinion on medical matters. Of course, someone can be wise without being a practitioner of a recognized craft, but his epistemic authority cannot then flow from his training. Nor is it enough that he *be* wise. If his opinions are to have any standing, the answerer must recognize him as a wise person. In other words, like Solon or Thales, he must be *notable* for his wisdom or have a *reputation* as a wise man. Hence the reference to notability and reputation in the relevant clause of the definition of *endoxa* (*Top.* I 1 100b23).

(a) corresponds closely to the official definition of genuine *endoxa* as 'things that are held by everyone, by the majority, or by the wise—either by all of them, or by most, or by the most notable and most *endoxos* (reputable)' (*Top.* I 1 100b21–3; repeated 101a11–13). But it also adds something new, namely, that views held by all, most, or the most reputable wise people have to meet a negative condition if they are to count as *endoxa*—they cannot be contradoxical or 'contrary to general opinion' (*Top.* I 10 104a11–12).

Some of the *endoxa* characterized in (a) are accepted by all or most answerers, because they are accepted by someone whose epistemic authority stems from his reputation for wisdom. Those characterized in (d) are accepted because they are accepted by someone whose epistemic authority stems not from his reputation but from his having been trained in an acknowledged area of expertise.[8] Some of the *endoxa* characterized in (a) and all of those characterized in (d) are thus *indirect*: they are (or would be) accepted by all or most answerers, because they are accepted by someone whose authority they recognize. The other *endoxa* characterized in (a) are *direct*: they are accepted on other grounds.

6. *ENDOXA* AND *PHAINOMENA*

From our discussion in section 5, we see that genuine *endoxa* fall into three classes: (1) propositions that all or most ordinary people would accept; (2) noncontradoxical propositions—propositions not contrary to what is already in (1)—that all, or most, or the most notable of the wise accept; (3) propositions in accord with—that follow from—the starting-points of the recognized crafts, since everyone, ordinary people included, would accept them. It seems, then, that (1) is acting as a sort of gatekeeper class. If p is in (2), it cannot be an *endoxon* unless it can be consistently added to (1). If p is a proposition in (3), it could, apparently, conflict with those in (1) while retaining its status as an *endoxon*, but only by joining (1) and depriving any conflicting propositions of membership in it.

The fact that all or most people believe something, Aristotle claims, leads us 'to trust it as something based on experience' (*Div. Somn.* 1 462b14–16). For 'human beings are naturally adequate as regards the truth and for the most part happen upon it' (*Rhet.* I 1 1355a15–17), so that each person 'has something of his own to contribute' to it (*EE* I 6 1216b30–1). Thus experience—whether in the form of perception or correct habituation (*Top.* I 11 105a3–7, *EN* I 4 1095b4–8, *EE* I 3 1214b28–1215a3)—must surely be what provides the evidence for direct *endoxa* in class (1). Direct *endoxa* are thus beliefs that seem true to us on the basis of experience. Presumably, that is why Aristotle occasionally refers to them as *phainomena*—as things that seem to be so (*Top.* I 10 104a12 with 14 105a37–b1, *EE* VII 2 1235b13–18 with *EN* VII 1 1145b2–7).

Phainomena include, in the first instance, basic perceptual observations: 'This [that the earth is spherical] is also shown by the sensory *phainomena*. For how else would lunar eclipses exhibit segments shaped as we see them to be?' (*DC* II 14 297b23–5; also 297a2–6). But though *phainomena* are for this reason typically contrasted with things that are supported by proof or evidence (*EE* I 6 1216b26–8), there seems to be no a priori limit on the degree of conceptualization or theory-ladenness manifest in them. They need not be, and in Aristotle rarely are, devoid of interpretative content. It is a *phainomenon*, for example, that the incontinent person 'knows that his actions are base, but does them because of his feelings, while the continent one knows that his appetites are base, but because of reason does not follow them' (*EN* VII 1 1145b12–14).

Since all the crafts and sciences—indeed, all types of knowledge, however humble or exalted—rest ultimately on experience (*APr* I 30 46a17–18, *Gen. et Corr.* I 2 316a5–6), what is true of direct *endoxa* also seems true of indirect ones. They are propositions that seem true on the basis of experience not to the untutored eyes of people in general, but to the relatively more trained ones of craftsmen and scientists, or the relatively more reflective ones of reputable philosophers. It follows, once we make proper allowance for the division of epistemic labor, that the entire class of *endoxa*—direct and indirect—is epistemically homogeneous: it consists of propositions that seem true on the basis of experience.

It is important to be clear, however, that Aristotle does not presuppose that *endoxa* are all guaranteed to be true. To be sure, an *endoxon* has epistemic credentials that are from the point of view of dialectic *nonpareil*. But that is because dialectic deals with things only 'in relation to opinion' not, as philosophy does, 'in relation to truth' (*Top.* I 14 105b30–1). If a proposition is an *endoxon*, if it would be accepted by all or most people, it is everything an honest dialectician could ask for in a premise. But that does not mean that it will retain its credibility when the philosopher has done his *aporematic* or *aporia*-related work.

7. Problems, Theses, and *Aporiai*

A dialectical problem

> is a subject of inquiry…about which [a] people hold no opinion either way, or
> [b] on which the many hold an opinion contrary to that of the wise, or [c] the
> wise contrary to that of the many, or [d] about which the members of either
> of these classes disagree among themselves.…Problems also occur [e] where
> deductions conflict, since there is an *aporia* about whether the thing holds or
> not, because there are strong arguments on both sides. They occur, too, [f] where
> we have no argument because they are so vast, and we find it difficult to give
> an explanation—for example, is the universe eternal or not? For one may also
> inquire into problems of that sort (*Top.* I 11 104b1–17).

If there is disagreement over some proposition, p, whether (b) between the many
and the wise or (c, d) within either party, p—or more accurately the corresponding question, p?—is a problem. However, not all problems result from conflicts in
opinion, or from the existence of contradoxical opinions, some exist (a) because we
have no opinions about them, or (f) no arguments for or against them.

If p is contradoxical, but is held by even one notable philosopher, or if there is
an argument for not-p, p (or p?) is a dialectical problem of a distinctive sort:

> A thesis is a contradoxical belief of some notable philosopher.…For it would
> be silly to pay any attention when an ordinary person expresses views that are
> contrary to general opinion. Or it may be a view contrary to general opinion that
> is supported by an argument.…For even if this view is unacceptable to someone,
> it might well be accepted [by the answerer] because it is supported by argument.
> A thesis is also a problem; but not every problem is a thesis, since some problems
> are such that we hold no opinion about them either way (*Top.* I 11 104b19–28).

Whenever there is some reason, however slight, in favour of a contradoxical proposition, a problem exists. But this means that the *endoxa* to which such a proposition
are contrary become problematic—especially as dialectical premises. The class of
endoxa, as we might put it, has a built-in tendency towards consistency—a tendency that dialectical practice itself helps further.

An *aporia*, (e) suggests, is a problem of a second particular sort. There is an
aporia about whether p just in case there are strong arguments for p and strong
arguments against it:

> The sophistical argument [against incontinence] is an *aporia*. For because they
> want to refute people in contradoxical ways, so that they will be clever in ordinary
> discussions, the deduction they construct gives rise to an *aporia*; for thought
> is tied up in a knot, since it does not want to stand still because it dislikes the
> conclusion, but it cannot move forward because it cannot undo the argument
> (*EN* VII 2 1146a21–7).

Philosophy, in its aporematic capacity, is particularly concerned with problems of
this sort: 'If we want to move forward [in philosophy], our first task is to explore

the *aporiai* well; for we will be in a position to do so later only if we free ourselves of earlier *aporiai* by undoing them; but we cannot undo them if we do not know that we are tied up' (*Met.* III 1 995a27–30).

8. USES OF DIALECTIC

Dialectic has four apparently distinct uses, three of which are the focus of the present section: (a) intellectual training, (b) ordinary discussions, and (c) in relation to the philosophical sciences (*Top.* I 2 101a26–7). Dialectic's usefulness for (a) training is 'immediately evident,' because 'if we have a line of inquiry, we can more easily take on a question proposed to us' (*Top.* I 2 101a28–30). Since all other uses provide intellectual training too, just as all sports provide physical training, this use is presumably the broadest one. If we are *dialektikos*—if we are dialectically proficient (*Top.* VIII 14 164b1–4)—we will be better able to deal with any question put to us by any sort of questioner. Contrariwise, dealing with all sorts of questioners will tend to make or keep us more dialectically proficient.

Dialectic is useful in (b) 'ordinary discussions,' because, as we saw, 'once we have catalogued the beliefs of the many, our approach to them will begin from their own views, not from other people's, and we will redirect them whenever they appear to us to be wrong' (*Top.* I 2 101a31–4). Here, it is dialectic's systematic collecting and categorizing of *endoxa* (*Top.* I 14 105b12–18) that proves particularly helpful. For by knowing what people will accept as premises, we will be better able to argue effectively and persuasively against them when they seem to be mistaken— even if their own lack of dialectical training means that the argument is sometimes 'bound to degenerate' (*Top.* VIII 14 164b9–10).

Aristotle sometimes applies the term 'philosophy' to any of the sciences that aim, in particular, at theoretical truth: 'It is also right that philosophy should be called scientific knowledge of the truth. For the end of theoretical knowledge is truth, while that of practical knowledge is action' (*Met.* II 1 993b19–20). In this sense, any non-practical science will count as philosophy. At the same time, Aristotle occasionally recognizes some non-theoretical philosophies, such as 'the philosophy of human affairs' (*EN* X 9 1180b15) or 'political philosophy,' classifying some of his own writings as 'those philosophical works of ours dealing with ethical issues' (*Pol.* III 12 1282b19–23). Finally, to make matters yet more complex, 'philosophy' also has a narrower, more specialized sense, in which it applies exclusively to sciences that provide theoretical knowledge of scientific starting-points (*Met.* XI 1 1059a18). It is in this sense of the term that there are 'three theoretical philosophies, mathematical, natural, and theological' (*Met.* VI (Epsilon) 1 1026a18–19).[9]

It is hard to know which sense of 'philosophical sciences' is pertinent in (c), so fortunately not much hangs on settling the matter. For what makes dialectic useful to these sciences, however we identify them, is that its 'ability to go through the *aporiai* on both sides of a subject makes it easier to see what is true and false' (*Top.* I 1 101a24–6). What this means is explained more fully as follows:

> Where knowledge (*gnôsin*) and philosophical wisdom are concerned, the ability to discern and hold in one view the consequences of either hypothesis is no insignificant tool, since then it only remains to make a correct choice of one of them. But a task of this sort requires *euphuia*. And true *euphuia* consists in just this—the ability to choose the true and avoid the false. For people with *euphuia* are the very ones who can do this well, since they judge correctly what is best by a correct love or hatred for what is set before them (*Top.* VIII 14 163b9–16).

Suppose that the problem a philosopher faces is, as before, to determine whether or not pleasure is always choiceworthy. If he is a competent dialectician, he will be able to follow out the consequences of supposing that it is, as well as those of supposing that it is not. He will be able to see what *aporiai* these consequences in turn face, and he will be able to go through these and determine which can be solved and which cannot.[10] For this is just what a dialectician has to be able to do in order successfully to play the role of questioner or answerer in a dialectical argument about the choiceworthiness of pleasure. But this ability alone will not tell the philosopher where the truth lies. For that he also needs *euphuia* (explained in section 10).

In the end, the philosopher will have concluded, we may suppose, that some sorts of pleasure are sometimes choiceworthy, while others are never choiceworthy. But in the process of reaching that conclusion, some of the *endoxa* on both sides will almost certainly have been modified or clarified, partly accepted and partly rejected (*Top.* VIII 14 164b6–7). Others will have been decisively rejected as false. But these the philosopher will need to explain away: 'We must not only state the true view, however, but also give the explanation for the false one, since that promotes confidence. For when we have a clear and good account of why a false view appears true, that makes us more confident of the true view' (*EN* VII 14 1154a24–5). In other words, some beliefs that seemed to be genuine *endoxa* will have been revealed to be merely apparent. But if 'most of them and the most compelling' are still in place, that will be 'an adequate proof' (*EN* VII 1 1145b5–7) of the philosopher's conclusion.

It might seem that philosophy, at least in this aporematic role, has now simply collapsed into honest dialectic, but this is not so. In an honest dialectical argument, the answerer may refuse to accept a proposition that a philosopher would accept:

> The premises of the philosopher's deductions or those of the man who is investigating by himself, though true and familiar, may be refused by the answerer because they lie too near to the original proposition, and so he sees what will happen if he grants them. But the philosopher is unconcerned about this. Indeed, he will presumably be eager that his axioms should be as familiar and as near to the question at hand as possible, since it is from premises of this sort that scientific deductions proceed (*Top.* VIII 1 155b10–16; also *APr* I 30 46a3–10).

Since the truth may well hinge on propositions whose status is just like the premises referred to here, there is no guarantee that honest dialectic and aporematic philosophy will reach the same conclusion on a given problem.

Perhaps enough has been said about this particular philosophical use of dialectic to show that it is relatively uncontroversial from the methodological and epistemological points of view. Dialectical ability helps an aporematic philosopher reach the truth in a way that is readily intelligible, but does not guarantee that he will reach it. For that he needs *euphuia* as well. The philosopher employs *endoxa* as premises of his arguments, but he does not employ all and only those available to a dialectician. And he does not simply accept them. They are presumptively true, but this presumption can be cancelled.

9. DIALECTIC AND STARTING-POINTS

In addition to its uses in training, ordinary discussions, and the philosophical sciences, dialectic is also

> [d] useful with regard to the starting-points in each science. For [e] it is impossible to discuss them at all from the starting-points proper to the science proposed for discussion, since the starting-points are primary among all [the truths contained in the science]; instead they must be discussed through the *endoxa* about them. This is distinctive of dialectic, or more appropriate to it than to anything else; for [f] since it examines (*exetastikê*), it provides a way towards the starting-points of all lines of inquiry (*Top.* I 2 101a36-b4).

According to (e), a certain kind of discussion of starting-points is impossible. Whether it is a dialectical discussion, in which starting-points appear as the contents of dialectical problems, or a philosophical investigation into starting-points, the premises involved cannot be the starting-points themselves, since they are the very things at issue. Instead, they must be *endoxa*. But, as we saw in the previous section, the class of *endoxa* the aporematic philosopher considers is typically broader than the class available to the honest dialectician, who is limited to employing *endoxa* that an answerer, eager not to be refuted, can reasonably be expected to accept. By the same token, when (f) tells us that dialectic provides a way towards starting-points because it examines (*exetastikê*), it could be referring to dialectical examination of some sort or to philosophical examination. The verb *exetazein* is used to refer to both sorts of activities. In the opening sentence of the *Rhetoric*, for example, it refers to dialectical questioning or examining in general: 'everyone attempts either to examine propositions or maintain them' (I 1 1354a4–5). At *EN* I 4 1095a28 and *EE* I 3 1215a6, it refers to an aporematic philosopher's examination of various views, popular as well as expert, on the nature of happiness.

Suppose that the discussion envisaged in (e) is dialectical. In that case, there are a set number of forms it can take. If *p* is a starting-point of geometry, the problem under discussion will be: p? If the answerer claims that p (as he may if he is a geometrician), the questioner's argument must be either an a-type or b-type sophistical refutation. If it is a b-type, the answerer's responses (provided he is honest) must be based on an honest peirastic argument. If it is an a-type, his answers must be based on an honest dialectical argument of some other sort. If the answerer claims that not-p (as he may if he is a sophist pretender to scientific knowledge of geometry), his underlying argument must be either an a-type or a b-type sophistical refutation (or what would be such a refutation if it were being used to refute rather than to defend), while questioner's argument (provided he is honest) must be either an honest peirastic argument or an honest dialectical argument of some other sort. In a dialectical discussion of starting-points, therefore, various types of honest dialectical argument will be involved, depending on what position the answerer takes and what sort of argument he employs in support of his position. Hence, if the way towards starting-points (f) envisages, is one that begins in such discussions, there is no reason to think that it has to be a peirastic one.[11]

It is useful to focus on honest peirastic arguments, nonetheless, in order to see the epistemic limitations of honest dialectic generally. Honest peirastic arguments have premises that are *endoxa* of a very special kind, namely, known (*eidenai*) truths—though not truths scientifically known (*epistasthai*) to the participants in these arguments (section 2). So even if these *endoxa* get refined through philosophical examination, they cannot be rejected or explained away. Thus honest peirastic arguments offer an epistemically better way towards starting-points than any other kind of dialectical argument. If what they offer has limitations, shifting our allegiance to some other type will simply make things worse.

The epistemic weakness of honest peirastic arguments emerges most clearly if we first presuppose that the science involved in them is in fact possessed by someone other than questioner or answerer. The situation we have to imagine is something like this. The science of geometry exists in finished form as a structure of demonstrations from starting-points. q is a conclusion of one of these demonstrations that is known—although not scientifically known—to both questioner and answerer. Indeed, if the answerer did not know q, his pretense to be a geometrician would be immediately revealed as just that, since q must be known to anyone who claims to know geometry. q can then function as a premise in an honest peirastic argument: it can be used to deduce the negation of the false geometrical claim (not-p) made by the sophist answerer. Since this deduction must be sound, it establishes that p is true. Since p is a starting-point of geometry, it establishes that some starting-point of geometry is true. Since its premises are known, it leads the sophist answerer, at least, to know p. Yet, because p is a starting-point of geometry, the operating presupposition is that it is already scientifically known. Consequently, our peirastic argument does nothing to increase anyone's store of scientific knowledge. For one cannot get scientific knowledge from premises that are not themselves known scientifically (*APo* I 3 72b18–23). Thus the peirastic way towards scientific starting-points is unimpressive. All it does is lead pretenders to scientific knowledge to a less profound kind of knowledge of starting-points than genuine scientists already possess.

If we now drop the presupposition that scientific knowledge of geometry is possessed by anyone, a different defect in peirastic arguments is revealed. If we do not have scientific knowledge of p as a starting-point of geometry, the peirastic deduction of p from q, will not even lead us to know that it *is* a starting-point, since this involves knowing its place in the demonstrative structure of completed geometry. Given this second failing of peirastic, it is hard to see it as giving us any kind of knowledge of starting-points *as such*.

We may conclude that if the way referred to in (f) is one that begins in dialectical discussions—if the examination it refers to is peirastic examination or some other sort of honest dialectical examination—it is not a way any scientist should bother to take. Aristotle himself acknowledges as much in the following text:

> What causes our inability to take a comprehensive view of the agreed-upon facts is lack of experience. That is why those who dwell in more intimate association with the facts of nature are better able to lay down starting-points which can bring together a good many of these, whereas those whom many arguments have made unobservant of the facts come too readily to their conclusions after looking at only a few facts. One can see, too, from this the great difference that exists between those whose researches are based on the facts of nature and those who inquire [merely] dialectically (*logikôs*) (*Gen. et Corr.* I 2 316a6–11).[12]

Experience based on intimate association with the natural facts is the scientific way to starting-points, not dialectical argument.

We turn now to the other alternative, where (f) is referring not to dialectical, but to philosophical examination. Experience has provided starting-points to the scientist and he has developed a finished science—a structure of demonstrations—from them. The philosopher is aware of this science and its status as such, and so accepts that its starting-points must—as inductively justified and explanatorily adequate—be true. Yet he also sees that the way towards those starting-points is blocked by *aporiai*, since arguments based on *endoxa* entail that they cannot be true. His goal is to solve these *aporiai*, by undoing the arguments that seem to support them—something he can only do if he is aware of the *aporiai* themselves:

> Those who wish to be free of *aporiai* must first go through the *aporiai* well; for the subsequent *aporia*-free condition is reached by untying the knots produced by the *aporiai* raised in advance, and it is not possible for someone who is unaware of a knot to untie it. An *aporia* in thought, however, reveals a knot in its subject matter.[13] For thought caught in an *aporia* is like people who are tied up, since in either case it is impossible to make progress. That is why one must have studied all the difficulties in advance, both for these reasons and because those who inquire without first going through the *aporiai* are like people who don't know where they have to go, and, in addition, don't even know whether they have found what they were inquiring about, since the end is not clear to them. But to someone who has first gone through the puzzles it is clear. Besides, one is necessarily in a better position to discern things when one has heard all the competing arguments, like opposing parties in a courtroom (*Met.* III 1 995a27-b4).

If he is successful in cataloguing and solving these *aporiai*, his way toward the starting-points will be cleared. And it is only when it is cleared that the starting-points themselves are grasped in the way requisite for scientific knowledge that is genuinely *unconditional*:

> If we are to have scientific knowledge through demonstration, ... we must know the starting-points better and be better convinced of them than of what is being proved, but we must also not find anything more convincing or better known among things opposed to the starting-points, from which a contrary mistaken conclusion may be deduced, since someone who has unconditional scientific knowledge must be incapable of being convinced [out of it] (*APo* I 2 72a37-b4).

Aporematic philosophy thus completes science by defending scientific starting-points in a way that science itself cannot. That is why theoretical wisdom (*sophia*), as the most rigorous (*akribês*) form of scientific knowledge, must be 'understanding plus scientific knowledge; scientific knowledge, having a head as it were' (*EN* VI 7 1141a16-20).

In defending some starting-points against dialectical objection, moreover, we provide a sort of demonstration of them, namely, a 'demonstration by refutation' (*Met.* IV 4 1006a11-12). Included among these are very secure or fundamental starting-points such as the principle of non-contradiction, which we must know in order to know anything. But it may also hold more generally: 'a disputant's refutation of what is opposed to his accounts is a demonstration of them' (*EE* I 3 1215a6-7). Even when philosophy doesn't offer us this sort of demonstration of starting-points, however, what it does offer is no puzzling knots—no impediments to clear and strict understanding (*EN* VII 2 1146a24-27).

10. PHILOSOPHY AND DIALECTIC

'Dialecticians practice dialectic about all things ... because all things are proper to philosophy. For ... dialectic treats the same genus as philosophy, but philosophy differs from dialectic in the type of power it has. ... Dialectic tests in the area where philosophy achieves knowledge (*esti de hê dialektikê peirastikê peri hôn hê philosophia gnôristikê*)[14] (*Met.* IV 2 1004b19-26). Because it can draw out the consequences of each of the hypotheses (p, not-p) in a problem and go through the *aporiai* they face, dialectic can test those hypotheses. But it cannot achieve knowledge, because it lacks a type of power that philosophy possesses. Our task now is to explain what this power is.

When dialectic has done its testing of p and of not-p, as we saw, it 'only remains to make a correct choice of one of them' (*Top.* VIII 14 163b9-12). Since *euphuia* is what enables people to 'discern correctly what is best by a correct love or hatred of what is set before them' (*Top.* VIII 14 163b15–16), it seems to be the power we are seeking. The reference to 'what is best' suggests too that the *euphuia* in question may be the sort referred to in the following passage:

> A person doesn't aim at the end [the good] through his own choice; rather, he must by nature have a sort of natural eye to make him discern well and choose what is really good. And the person who by nature has this eye in good condition is *euphuês*. For it is the greatest and noblest thing…and when it is naturally good and noble, it is true and complete *euphuia* (*EN* III 5 1114b5–12).

And that, in fact, is what the distinction between philosophy and sophistry, which uses all of plain dialectic's resources, might lead us to expect, since 'philosophy…differs from sophistic in its deliberate choice about how to live' (*Met.* IV 2 1004b23–5).

A deliberate choice of how to live is *au fond* a choice of an ultimate end or target for one's life: 'everyone who can live in accord with his own deliberate choice should adopt some target for the noble life, whether honour, reputation, wealth, or education, which he will look to in all his actions' (*EE* I 2 1214b6–9). And what 'teaches *correct* belief' about this end or target, thereby insuring that the deliberate choice of it is itself correct, is 'natural or habituated virtue of character' (*EN* VII 8 1151a18–19). It is this, we may infer, in which *euphuia* consists. Hence if we possess it, when we hear from political science that the starting-point it posits as the correct target for a human life is 'activity of the soul in accord with virtue, and if there are more virtues than one, in accord with the best and most complete' (*EN* I 7 1098a16–18), we will accept it as true, and so strive to clear away the *aporiai* that block our road to it. If we do not possess such *euphuia*, we will reject this starting-point and strive to sustain the *aporiai* that block our path to it, so that in our choice between p and not-p, we will go for the wrong one: 'the truth in practical matters must be discerned from the things we do and from our life, since these are what have the controlling vote. Hence when we examine everything that has been previously said, it must be by bringing it to bear on the things we do and on our life, and if it is in harmony with what we do, we should accept it, but if it conflicts, we should suppose it mere words.' (*EN* X 8 1179a17–22)

In the *Rhetoric*, we learn of an apparently different sort of *euphuia*, which seems from the company it keeps to be an exclusively intellectual trait: '*euphuia*, good memory, readiness to learn, quick-wittedness…are all productive of good things' (I 6 1362b24–5). When it comes to solving dialectical problems bearing on 'truth and knowledge,' we might conclude, such apparently intellectual *euphuia* is all a philosopher needs, even if, when it comes to those bearing on 'pursuit and avoidance' (*Top.* I 11 104b1–2; compare *EN* VI 2 1139a21–2), he also needs its apparently more ethical namesake. Whatever we decide about this, our account of intellectual *euphuia* can nonetheless take the account of ethical *euphuia* as a useful guide.

Aristotle sometimes refers to what he calls 'a well-educated person (*pepaideumenos*)'—someone who studies a subject, not to acquire scientific knowledge of it, but to become a discerning judge:

> Regarding every branch of theoretical knowledge and every line of inquiry, the more humble and more estimable alike, there appear to be two ways for the state to be, one which may be well described as scientific knowledge of the subject matter, the other a certain sort of educatedness. For it is characteristic of a person well educated in that way to be able accurately to discern what is well said and what is not. We think of someone who is well educated about the whole of things as a person of that sort, and we think that being well educated is being capable of doing such discerning. Except that, in the one case, we consider a single individual to be capable of being discerning in practically all subjects, in the other, in one of a delimited nature—for there might be another person disposed in the same way as the person we have been discussing, but about a part. So it is clear in the case of inquiry into nature, too, that there should be certain defining-marks by referring to which one can appraise the manner of its demonstrations, apart from the question of what the truth is, whether thus or otherwise (*PA* I 1 639a1–15).

A person well educated in medicine, for example, is capable of discerning whether someone has treated a disease correctly (*Pol.* III 11 1282a3–7), and the 'unconditionally well-educated person,' who is well educated in every subject or area, 'seeks rigor in each area to the extent that the nature of its subject matter allows' (*EN* I 3 1094b23–1095a2). Whether identical to intellectual *euphuia*, or a state developed from it by intellectual training in the way that habituated virtue is developed from natural virtue by adequate upbringing, it is surely this sort of educatedness the aporematic philosopher needs to perform the task Aristotle assigns to intellectual *euphuia*. For if he is well-educated he will be discerning in the realm of knowledge, able to distinguish genuine sciences from specious or sophistic look-alikes, and so be able to determine which starting-points he should be trying to find an *aporia*-free way toward.

Aporematic philosophy is not the only sort of philosophy Aristotle recognizes, of course. As we saw in section 8, he also recognizes a number of philosophies or philosophical sciences, some theoretical (mathematical, natural, theological), and some practical (ethics, politics). The way to the starting-points of these, as to those of all sciences, is aporematic. But the philosophies themselves—at any rate, insofar as they are or are like genuine Aristotelian sciences—are presumably structures of demonstrations from starting-points. But that means that their methodology, when it isn't dialectical, is simply that of such sciences. Dialectic, in other words, is not just the method of aporematic philosophy, but has a claim to being regarded as the distinctive method of Aristotelian philosophy generally.

NOTES

1. Hippocrates' argument is described in Thomas Heath, *A History of Greek Mathematics* Vol. I (Oxford: Clarendon Press, 1921), 183–201.
2. It is unclear just what Bryson's method is. See Heath, *A History of Greek Mathematics*, 223–25.
3. See Heath, *A History of Greek Mathematics*, 221–22, citing Simplicius.

4. As Robert Bolton, 'The Epistemological Basis of Aristotelian Dialectic,' in *Biologie, Logique et Métaphysique Chez Aristote*, Daniel Devereux and Pierre Pellegrin, eds. (Paris: Éditions du Centre National de la Recherche Scientifique, 1990), 215–17, convincingly argues.

5. I have translated *paradoxos* using the neologism 'contradoxical' to make clear that what is *paradoxos* in the relevant sense is not what we mean by 'paradoxical'.

6. Compare Daniel Devereux, 'Comments on Robert Bolton's "The Epistemological Basis of Aristotelian Dialectic'", in *Biologie, Logique et Métaphysique Chez Aristote*, 272 n. 18.

7. Compare Jonathan Barnes, 'Aristotle's Theory of Demonstration,' in *Articles on Aristotle*. Vol. 1, Jonathan Barnes, Malcolm Schofield, and Richard Sorabji, eds. (London: Duckworth, 1975), 80–1, and Devereux, 'Comments on Robert Bolton's "The Epistemological Basis of Aristotelian Dialectic'", 272–73 n. 19.

8. Robert Bolton, 'Definition and Scientific Method in Aristotle's *Posterior Analytics* and *Generation of Animals*,' in *Philosophical Issues in Aristotle's Biology*, Allan Gotthelf and James Lennox, eds. (Cambridge: Cambridge University Press, 1987), 122–23, conflates (a) and (d) when he claims that if an 'expert biologist with new empirical data were not yet so lucky as to stand among the most acclaimed biologists neither he nor anyone else would be entitled to use his new results in *dialectical* argument no matter how empirically well-grounded they might be.'

9. I discuss these sciences in *Substantial Knowledge: Aristotle's Metaphysics* (Indianapolis: Hackett, 2000), 258–60.

10. In *Soph.* fr. 1 (Ross), Aristotle says that Zeno invented dialectic. Zeno, too, saw the importance of examining 'the consequences that follow from the hypothesis, not only if each thing is hypothesized to be, but also if that same thing is hypothesized not to be' (Plato, *Prm.* 135d-136a).

11. Contrast Bolton, 'The Epistemological Basis of Aristotelian Dialectic'.

12. Also *APr* I 30 46a17–22, *DC* II 12 291b31–292a3, III 7 306a14–17, *DA* I 1 402b21–403a2, *GA* II 8 747b27–748a14, III 10 760b27–33.

13. In many texts, as here, Aristotle characterizes *aporiai* as knots aporematic philosophy enables us to untie (*Phys.* VIII 3 253a31–3, 8 263a15–18, *Met.* VII 6 1032a6–11, *EN* VII 2 1146a24–7). In others, he characterizes such philosophy as enabling us to make things—including starting-points—clear (*APr* I 30 46a17–30, *DA* II 2 413a11–13).

14. Robert Bolton, 'Aristotle's Conception of Metaphysics As a Science,' in *Unity, Identity and Explanation in Aristotle's Metaphysics*, T. Scaltsas, D. Charles, and M. L. Gill, eds. (Oxford: Clarendon Press, 1994), 327–28, argues that the final clause should instead be translated: 'When it comes to those matters which (first) philosophy deals with, dialectic should use its special peirastic form or capacity'. Translated in this way, he continues, it 'does not in the least require that when it deals with philosophical subjects dialectic merely probes or tests or criticizes but does not establish or lead one to know anything'. True. But it collapses the distinction Aristotle is trying to draw between philosophy and dialectic, and conflicts with *Top.* VIII 14 163b9–16, which tells us unequivocally that dialectic alone cannot reach the truth.

Bibliography

Barnes, J. (1975) 'Aristotle's Theory of Demonstration', in J. Barnes, M. Schofield, and R. Sorabji, eds. (London: Duckworth), 65–87.

Barnes, J., M. Schofield, and R. Sorabji, eds. (1975) *Articles on Aristotle*. Vol. 1. (London: Duckworth).

Bolton, R. (1987) 'Definition and Scientific Method in Aristotle's *Posterior Analytics* and *Generation of Animals*', in A. Gotthelf and J. Lennox, eds., *Philosophical Issues in Aristotle's Biology* (Cambridge: Cambridge Univ. Press), 120–66.

—— (1990) 'The Epistemological Basis of Aristotelian Dialectic', in D. Devereux and P. Pellegrin, eds., *Biologie, Logique et Métaphysique Chez Aristote* (Paris: Éditions du Centre National de la Recherche Scientifique), 185–236.

—— (1994) 'Aristotle's Conception of Metaphysics As a Science', in T. Scaltsas, D. Charles, and M.L. Gill, eds.,*Unity, Identity and Explanation in Aristotle's Metaphysics* (Oxford: Clarendon Press), 321–54.

—— (2009) 'Two Standards for Inquiry in Aristotle's *De Caelo*', in A.C. Bowen and C. Wildberg, eds., *New Perspectives on Aristotle's De Caelo* (Leiden: Brill), 51–82.

—— (2010) *Science, Dialectique et Ethique chez Aristote: Essais D'Épistémologie Aristotélicienne* (Louvain-La-Neuve: Éditions Peeters).

Bowen, A.C., and C. Wildberg, (2009) *New Perspectives on Aristotle's De Caelo* (Leiden: Brill).

Brunschwig, J. (1967) *Aristote: Topiques* I-IV (Paris: Les Belles Lettres).

—— (1984–5) 'Aristotle on Arguments Without Winners or Losers', *Wissenschaftskolleg Jahrbuch*, 31–40.

—— (1990) 'Remarques sur la Communication de Robert Bolton', in D. Devereux and P. Pellegrin, eds., *Biologie, Logique et Métaphysique Chez Aristote*, 237–62.

—— (2007) *Aristote: Topiques* I-IV (Paris: Les Belles Lettres).

Canto-Sperber, M. and P. Pellegrin, eds. (2002) *Le Style de La Pensée: Receueil de Texts en Homage à Jacques Brunschwig* (Paris: Les Belles Lettres).

Devereux, D. (1990) 'Comments on Robert Bolton's "The Epistemological Basis of Aristotelian Dialectic"', in D. Devereux and P. Pellegrin, eds., 263–86.

Deveraux, D., and P. Pellegrin, eds. (1990) *Biologie, Logique et Métaphysique Chez Aristote* (Paris: Éditions du Centre National de la Recherche Scientifique).

Dorion, L.A. (1995) *Les Réfutations Sophistiques d'Aristote* (Paris: Vrin).

—— (2002) 'Aristote et L'Invention de la Dialectique', in M. Canto-Sperber and P. Pellegrin, eds., *Le Style de la Pensée: Receueil de Texts en Homage à Jacques Brunschwig* (Paris: Les Belles Lettres), 182–220.

Gotthelf, A., and J. Lennox, eds. (1987) *Philosophical Issues in Aristotle's Biology* (Cambridge: Cambridge Univ. Press).

Heath, T. (1921) *A History of Greek Mathematics*. Vol. I. (Oxford: Clarendon Press).

Irwin, T.H. (1988) *Aristotle's First Principles* (Oxford: Clarendon Press).

Nussbaum, M.C. (1986) *The Fragility of Goodness* (Cambridge: Cambridge Univ. Press).

Owen, G.E.L. (1986) *Logic, Science, and Dialectic: Collected Papers in Greek Philosophy* (Ithaca, N.Y.: Cornell Univ. Press).

—— ed. (1968) *Aristotle on Dialectic: The Topics* (Oxford: Clarendon Press).

Reeve, C.D C. (2000) *Substantial Knowledge: Aristotle's Metaphysics* (Indianapolis, Ind.: Hackett).

—— (2012) *Action, Contemplation, and Happiness: An Essay on Aristotle* (Cambridge, Mass.: Harvard Univ. Press).

Scaltsas, T., D. Charles, and M.L. Gill, eds. (1994) *Unity, Identity and Explanation in Aristotle's Metaphysics* (Oxford: Clarendon Press).

Sim, M., ed. (1999) *From Puzzles to Principles?* (Lanham, Md.: Lexington Books).

Smith, R. (1997) *Aristotle Topics Books I and VII* (Oxford: Clarendon Press).

CHAPTER 8

....

ARISTOTLE ON HEURISTIC INQUIRY AND DEMONSTRATION OF *WHAT IT IS*

....

KEI CHIBA

1. INTRODUCTION

....

IN the *Posterior Analytics*, Aristotle develops a theory of demonstration as a way of gaining causal knowledge of things or events (*pragmata*) under the general plan of constructing both an ideal structure for demonstrative science and a unified, comprehensive theory of heuristic inquiry. His theory of demonstration emerged in the Academy, where Plato's theory of division was the official method of scientific knowledge, understood to comprise both inquiry and exposition. His intellectual controversies with his worthy rival theorists in this school induced Aristotle to develop a subtle and attractive theory of demonstration, on the basis of which he set a high standard for all subsequent treatments of a series of connected issues in this area, including, generally speaking, knowledge, causality, necessity, science, signification, essence, definition, inquiry, and discovery.

The Aristotelian idea of 'demonstrative science' (*hê apodeiktikê epistêmê*) is derived from his attempt to characterize the conditions for 'knowledge *simpliciter* (*epistêmê haplôs*)', that is causal and necessary knowledge (*APo* I 2 71b15, I 3

73a21, I 8 75b24 [hereafter only the Bekker page and line from this treatise will be indicated]).[1] A basic characteristic of demonstration (*apodeixis*) is what Aristotle calls a 'knowledge-producing (*epistêmonikon*) syllogism', through possession of which a scientist or an inquirer gains a piece of scientific knowledge within the system of demonstrative science (71b18f). Demonstration conveys the necessity of some immediate premises *via* a relevant middle term to a conclusion under the general logical constraints of syllogistic developed in the *Prior Analytics*. This wide-ranging theory, which is at root a theory of causal explanation, draws on elements in Aristotle's philosophy of science, logic, language, knowledge, and ontology.

While Aristotle pursues the ideal structure of demonstrative science as an axiomatic deductive system in *Posterior Analytics* I, taking as its paradigm the mathematics which led to Euclid's *Elements*, he also attempts to construct a theory of heuristic inquiry in *Posterior Analytics* II, by using demonstration as a means of *gaining* scientific knowledge as well, including knowledge of objects falling under the auspices of empirical science. The main task for Aristotle in Book II is thus to assign an effective role to demonstration as a viable tool for actual scientific investigation.

There is, however, a tension between these two enterprises: each assigns demonstration a distinctive role, but these roles seem divergent, perhaps even to the point of incompatibility. In particular, while the method of demonstration may seem suitable for a non-empirical science such as geometry and also well suited for presenting the results of inquiry within an axiomatic deductive science, it seems insufficiently flexible to cope with the various empirical sciences, especially if it is to play a useful role as a tool to be wielded in the process of scientific inquiry. Whereas the presentation of an axiomatic science requires precision to the point of rigidity, due especially to constraints peculiar to logic and mathematics, the process of empirical investigation is by its nature fluid and must be responsive to changing data. It is thus difficult to see how demonstration, the vehicle for presenting the results of inquiry in axiomatic form, might also play a role in the process of empirical inquiry. In fact, unsurprisingly, Aristotle makes full use of the mathematical sciences when elucidating the paradigmatic structure of demonstration within demonstrative science in Book I. This then leaves little room for the same notion of demonstration to find a role in the process of inquiry, especially in the empirical sciences. Yet any inquiry theory which ignored the realm of empirical sciences would be wholly unacceptable. Hence, while the theory of demonstrative science is rigorously built, it may prove unable to meet the shifting conditions and constraints within the various scientific roles assigned to it by Aristotle.[2]

In setting this concern, we should, however, distinguish distinct, but related forms of investigation. One might undertake to inquire into the character of a knowledge-producing system *simpliciter*; but one might also wish to ask how some one individual knows some particular thing. One Aristotelian answer to the first sort of question will be given by referring to the ideal structure of science, in which knowledge is characterized as propositional in character, once it has been produced by some demonstrative science. An Aristotelian answer to the latter will be given by referring to an inquirer's cognitive state, something which comes about in him by his using a single demonstration. It is natural to expect that these two enterprises complement one another. In marking both this division and the interaction between these complementary activities, Aristotle may offer a reservation to the effect that his idea of demonstrative science as the ideal structure for gaining knowledge *simpliciter* may not be *fully* met by any scientific activity. Insofar as there is no internal contradiction, however, Aristotle is entitled to hope that pieces of information gained in an ongoing inquiry within the constraints of a demonstrative science may contribute to the task of establishing a particular demonstrative science and may also offer information relevant to the task of examining even general features of relevant demonstrative systems.

If Aristotle's theory of demonstration is to play a genuine role in actual philosophical and scientific inquiry, it must be embedded into actual programmes of inquiry as they are conducted in the real world. Aristotle must show, in effect, that his method of demonstration is useful in inquiry and not only in exposition as a systematic way of presenting a body of knowledge already acquired.

Against these background conditions and objectives, Aristotle endeavors to develop his theory of demonstration within the context of a comprehensive and unified theory of inquiry, which he thinks of as governed by four basic questions relevant to every form of inquiry, whether empirical or otherwise (II1). Where 'S' and 'P' stand for a grammatical subject and a predicate:

- Whether S is P or not? (*poteron SP ê ou;*) (Scholars often speak in this connexion of inquiring into *the fact*; so, e.g.: 'Is man rational or not?' Or, more generally, 'Is it or is it not a fact that man is rational?')
- Why is S P? (*diati SP;*) (Here scholars speak of *the reason why*, e.g.: 'Why is man rational?')
- Whether S is *simpliciter* or not? (*ei esti S ê mê haplôs;*) [indirect question]) (Here scholars speak of existence, e.g.: 'Does man exist or not?')
- What is S? (*ti esti S;*) (Here, following Aristotle's Greek, scholars speak of *the what it is*, e.g.: What is man?)

These four items are supposed to exhaust any instance of knowledge-seeking activity, whether the physiologists' inquiry into nature or Socrates' inquiry into moral matters. Indeed, since any successful theory of inquiry must be as comprehensive as possible, all manner of potential objects of inquiry must be considered. In fact, the objects of inquiry mentioned in Book II include fictitious entities such as 'goatstag', natural events such as 'thunder', ethical entities such as 'pride', and mathematical entities such as 'triangle', biological things/events such as 'shedding leaves', and also a theological entity 'God' (cf. II 1, 7, 8,13,16). It is clear from these examples that Aristotle understands his project very broadly indeed. He thus undertakes a project of constructing a comprehensive inquiry theory intended to encompass all entities whatever they are. It will be doubted, however, whether there can be such a comprehensive inquiry. After all, we have no immediate reason for believing that every kind of inquiry will proceed along the same pathways of discovery. Perhaps different types of objects are known in irreducibly different ways; if so, all forms of inquiry cannot be subordinated to a single overarching cognitive system.

Hence Aristotle's dilemma: if one maintains strict conditions for demonstration, the scope of inquiry is threatened. If one pursues a comprehensive theory of inquiry, the demand for demonstration may constitute an excessive burden in view of its uniformity and generality. Aristotle's overarching theory of inquiry and demonstration must be both comprehensive and unified, yet capable of generating scientific knowledge in the widest range of areas possible. I shall call this dilemma 'the comprehensiveness strictness dilemma' (CSD). The most pressing question is whether Aristotle can simultaneously meet both objectives. If he is successful, his two projects will enhance one another in both scope and function. He pursues this ambitious plan, I argue, by advancing what I shall call a 'heuristic demonstrative inquiry' theory (HDI).

It is necessary for anyone attempting to meet these two objectives to make clear how demonstration can be used in inquiry theory, even while showing how heuristic inquiry can validate the claims of the method of demonstration to be a genuine method of inquiry. Further, as he progresses, Aristotle must proceed with an eye on various difficulties concerning the search for knowledge inherited from his predecessors, including most notably those encapsulated in *Meno*'s paradox of inquiry.

Aristotle's inquiry theory is, no doubt, to be located within the traditional framework he inherited from his predecessors. In a fundamental way, Socratic inquiry into the thing itself or, more generally, into the identity of a thing, largely determines the nature and course of inquiry theory in the Academy. In this sense, Socrates sets *strict identity* as the goal of inquiry. He wants to know what things are in themselves, taken by themselves, and not in relation to other things. Thus, Socratic inquiry into *what it is (ti esti)* provides a touchstone for the success (or failure) of any general theory of inquiry. This extends to Aristotle's own theory of inquiry. If its employment is limited in scope and fails to lead to knowledge of such objects or items, Aristotle's theory of demonstration will not constitute an attractive method of inquiry in terms of scope and function.

Aristotle is fully aware of the broader Academic framework of his theory of demonstration. One of 'the current methods' (*kata tous nun tropous*) of definitional practice he characterizes is precisely Plato's theory of division, as practiced in the Academy, which claims 'to make possible a demonstration of substance and the what it is' (*dunatou peri ousias apodeiksin genesthai kai tou ti estin*) (*APr* I 3146a36f., *APo* II 5 92b19). According to Aristotle's criticism, the theory of division is based on induction and plays only a limited role in elucidating the causal structures of things. Indeed, even if division happens to grasp a cause which is prior to its effect in the order of being, it cannot grasp it *as* the cause. For instance, suppose 'man' is properly defined by division as 'mortal, footed, two-footed, wingless animal' (92a1). Although division may hit on the cause in this case, it cannot determine which is causally prior: *two-footed* or *wingless*. In division-based defining-phrases, the question 'why is it so?' can always be asked (91b39). Such definitions cannot explain the unity of the components of the *definiens*, even if all the relevant components are, *in fact*, present (cf. 92a29–34, 92b19–25). According to Aristotle, this is an insurmountable shortcoming to the method of division, since a theory of demonstration must outline the explanatory conditions which establish what is prior. Aristotle intends his own theory to overcome the limitations in the theory of division so as to meet the unity condition of thing itself by specifying for each object of inquiry into *what it is*. To succeed in this endeavour, Aristotle must show the superior efficacy of his method of demonstration by indicating how demonstration of *what it is* and of substance is possible and how it overcomes the shortcomings inherent in the theory of division as well as all other rival theories. The shortcomings of these rival theories, he contends, are made clear when they are syllogized according to his underlying logic.

   In this chapter, I shall first confirm that Aristotle's inquiry theory is a heuristic theory and as such yields scientific knowledge within the scope of his theory of demonstration. Next I shall examine the difficulties which arise concerning the relation between demonstration and definition. In particular, if demonstrations and definitions turn out to be unrelated in terms of their objects, predications, or methods, Aristotle's general plan will be a failure. Then I shall investigate how Aristotle attempts to construct a demonstration of *what it is*. Finally by analysing his new theory of definition, I shall examine how far he has succeeded in developing his HDI.

2. Heuristic Inquiry Theory

Aristotle seeks to construct a comprehensive inquiry theory into all actual things/events in the world. He identifies four items as things to be learned and known (89b24):

- [Ia] the fact (*to hoti*) and [Ib] the reason why (*to dioti*)
- [IIa] the existence (*ei esti*) and [IIb] the *what it is* (*ti esti*).

Crucially, a process of inquiry may proceed along either track, along [I] from [Ia] to [Ib], or along [II] from [IIa] to [IIb]. Inquiry proceeds by pursuing questions corresponding to these items and ceases when one discovers one or more of the four states of things/events in the world. He says that 'by finding out that the moon suffers eclipse, we cease' (89b27). This is evidence that there is an inquiry relative already to [Ia], the fact, which in turn shows that the notion of discovery is key to his inquiry theory. Accordingly, it follows that this theory is the one of heuristic inquiry.

   Aristotle holds that these four items are exhaustive and comprehensive in terms of the items and scope of inquiry and exudes confidence concerning the comprehensiveness of his theory. He says that 'what we seek and what, on finding (*heurontes*), we know are these and thus many' (89b36f.). In other words, anything which can be discovered can be distributed into one of these four items of inquiry. His four basic questions are thus intended to cover any inquiry we can raise.

It is not initially clear why we should regard questions [Ia] and [IIa], concerning facticity and existence, as distinct. The first concerns *the fact* of something's being the case, while the second concerns its *existence*. Aristotle distinguishes these questions *syntactically* by introducing two adverbial constraints, respectively 'simpliciter' and 'in part'. Aristotle says that 'I mean by the fact or if it is *in part* and* simpliciter: (i) By *in part* I mean, e.g., does the moon suffer eclipse or wax? For in such cases we seek whether it is something or is not something. But (ii) by *simpliciter* I mean, e.g., if the moon or night is or is not' (90a2–5: Bekker [* 'or': Waitz]). He thus qualifies each question so as to make its focus clear. I shall call this qualification [Q1].

Aristotle explains that the question of 'if S is *simpliciter* or not' (where 'S' stands for a grammatical subject) is to be contrasted with 'if S is white or not' (89b34). This distinction is made from a linguistic perspective to establish that there is a question of existence as well as a question of fact. 'Night', for example, which might be reformulated as 'does darkness belong to air?' is qualified by '*simpliciter*' by Aristotle (90a5). This is because he adheres to the linguistic phenomena, noting that one ordinarily asks of existence using a single term as 'night' or 'eclipse' (90a26). In this context, the content of S does not matter. The relevant demarcation, as D. Charles notes, 'depends on the form of the question'.[3] Insofar as any entity/event can be referred to by a single term, one can ask 'if S is' in the sense of existence. This is simply to ask whether or not S exists.

This linguistic distinction shows that [Ia] and [IIa] are in fact different questions. The denial of the claim that 'the moon does not suffer eclipse' does not lead to the denial of the existence of the underlying subject, the moon, nor to the denial of the existence of the relevant state/property itself, an eclipse. The moon may exist without being eclipsed and an eclipse may belong to other planets. What is denied in this case is the connection designated by 'in part', which holds between two items signified respectively by the subject and the predicate. By contrast, in the case of the simple use of a term, what is denied when a single subject term such as *moon* or *night* is used, is the existence of the thing itself. Thus, one can deny the fact of something's being the case without thereby denying the existence of the entity implicated in the (putative) fact. *That it is* pertains to facticity; *if it is* pertains to existence.

An inquirer must not confuse either of these issues with the other. The introduction of these qualifications is made to show that route [I] should be distinguished from route [II] so as to separate different types of heuristic knowledge. It is evident that the knowledge of [Ia] the *fact* prompts an inquirer to ask [Ib], the *reason why* this fact obtains. One cannot ask [IIb] on the basis of knowledge of [Ia] because the latter is an articulated item with parts. It is also natural to ask [IIb], *what something is*, on the basis of knowledge of [IIa], that *it exists*. In these cases, however, nothing hinders one from discovering both [a] and [b] in these two routes simultaneously (e.g., 93a17, 35). In general, any thing/event to which the word 'discovery' is addressed is the object of inquiry at issue. All told, then, the number of the items of discovery is four. This is accordingly the range of cases for which the theory of heuristic inquiry is to be constructed.

Within this framework, Aristotle seeks to establish the connection between the language of heuristic inquiry and the language of demonstration. In executing his heuristic theory of inquiry, Aristotle seeks causal connections underlying the objects of inquiry and so, relying on his general form of demonstration, identifies the cause as the middle term in a syllogism. By doing this he unifies the two routes [I] and [II] such that:

> We seek, whenever we seek [Ia] the fact or [IIa] if it is *simpliciter*, [I & IIa] whether there is or is not a middle term for it. But whenever we become aware of either the fact or if it is—[Q1] either in part or *simpliciter*—and again seek [Ib] the reason why or [IIb] *what it is*, then we seek [I & IIb] what the middle term is (89b37–90a1).

In this passage, the syllogism or demonstration expressed by the middle term is built into the language of heuristic inquiry. Aristotle does not reduce one route to the other, but takes it that these two routes point to the pathways of authentic and genuine inquiries. This is because they are secured by the background process of inquiry, from [I & IIa] to [I & IIb] respectively. He tries to offer a comprehensive treatment of [I] and [II] and thus put them into order from the perspective of a unified process of inquiry.

By introducing [I & IIa] and [I & IIb], Aristotle takes [a] and [b] of [I] and [II] to constitute the same stages of one unified inquiry. This identification of routes exhibits Aristotle's understanding of what the items 'the fact (*to hoti*)', 'the existence (*to ei esti*)', 'the reason why (*to dioti*)' and 'the what it is (*to ti esti*)' signify. Without knowing the existence of a middle term, i.e., a cause, one is not entitled to claim the knowledge of the *fact* or the knowledge of the *existence*. Without knowing the concrete item signified by the middle term *M*, one is not entitled to claim the knowledge of the *reason why* or the knowledge of the *what it is*. This constraint on understanding the four items of inquiry derives from his idea of satisfying two objectives in his inquiry into demonstrative knowledge. His interest is not only in 'how inquiries of the type envisaged fit into his proof theory',[4] but also in how his inquiry theory makes use of his proof theory with strict scientific knowledge to construct a comprehensive and unified theory of inquiry. Unless demonstration has some role in scientific investigation, it would be simply a transmitter of the necessity from the premises to the conclusion within a demonstrative science understood as an axiomatic deductive system. A demonstration has a more positive role: A successful demonstration reflects the explanatory structure embedded in the world, whose discovery is the object of heuristic demonstrative inquiry (HDI).

The discovery of a relevant demonstration aims at introducing a comprehensive route [I & II]. Having found that there is *a* middle term (*meson*), an inquirer seeks *the* middle term (*to meson*), i.e., what the concrete middle term is. Aristotle makes this approach clear in the case of an eclipse. He says that 'When it is clear

that A [the eclipse] belongs to C [the moon], then to seek *why it belongs* is to seek
what B [=M] *is*, whether screening or rotation of the moon or extinction' (93b3–6).
That is, in the question of 'what is the middle term [M]?', he determines what M is
by asking 'what is S?'. While the question [IIb] is now made into a causal one and is
identified with a question seeking the cause which makes S *what it is*, the question
[I & IIb] is taken as a proper cause of the existence of S or a proper cause of the fact
of *SP*. Its proper answer explains the reason why *SP* obtains as well as determining
what S is. Because of this identification of [I & IIb], we are entitled to say that the
what it is and the *reason why* are the same. In questions [Ib] and [IIb], an inquirer
in fact asks [I & IIb]. This is the basis of Aristotle's demonstrative or causal interpretation of heuristic inquiry.

Aristotle next argues for the identity of the 'what?' and 'why?' questions by
appealing to examples such as harmony, and he proposes an ontological qualification: '*simpliciter vs.* something', which I shall call '[Q2]' to distinguish between the
three kinds of objects of inquiry to which the relevant causes respectively belong.
I shall label each of three objects (So), (Po), and (Ao)—that is, a substantial object
(So), a *per se* object (Po), and an accidental object (Ao):

> For the middle term [M] is the cause, and in all inquiries it is the cause which is
> sought. 'Does it suffer eclipse?' 'Is there any cause or not?' After that, having come
> to know that there is a cause, we then seek what it [M] is. Because the cause of being
> [Q2] not *this* or *that*, but (So) *simpliciter* the substance or of not *simpliciter* but of
> being (Po) *something* of its *per se* attributes or of being (Ao) accidental attributes
> is the middle term [M]. I mean by 'the one *simpliciter*' the underlying thing, e.g.,
> moon or earth or sun or triangle, but by 'the one *something*', e.g., eclipse, equality,
> or inequality, if it [earth] is in the middle or not. For in all these inquiries it is
> clear that the *what it is* and the *why it is* are the same. [IIb] 'What is an eclipse?',
> 'Loss of moon's light by earth's screening'. [Ib] 'Why is there an eclipse?' or rather
> (*ē*) 'Why does *the* moon suffer eclipse?' 'Because of '*the* to lose' '*the* light' 'by *the*
> earth's screening'. [IIb] 'What is harmony?', 'A numerical ratio in high and low'.
> [Ib] 'Why does *the* high harmonize with *the* low?' 'Because of '*the* high' and '*the*
> low' 'having *the* numerical ratio''. [I&IIa] 'Is there 'to harmonize between *the* high
> and *the* low'?' [IIa] 'Is there '*the* numerical ratio of these'?' Grasping that there is
> one, [I&IIb] 'What then is '*the* ratio'?' (90a6–23).

Although his language is technical, it is clear that Aristotle is here offering an
inductive argument for the identity of the 'why?' and 'what?' questions. In a sense,
what we have at this point is a case of a traditional Socratic 'what is S?'—a question seeking an essential definition—being subjected to a causal regimentation. In
effect, the causal interpretation is made possible by identity of [IIb] *what* and [Ib]
why questions, as based upon [I & IIb]. The middle term in syllogistic terminology
is employed to constitute a definition. I shall call this 'the causal turn (or regimentation) of *what it is*'. There remains an important contrast between different ways
of answering 'what?' and 'why?' questions, however. This is reflected in Aristotle's
linguistic precision, which does, though, result in the initially awkward sounding
locutions upon which Aristotle relies. When a 'why?' question is answered, the
terms chosen are preceded by the definite article '*the* (*to*)' as indicated by italics in

the above quotation (cf. 90a7–21, 93a37–39, 93b10–11, 94a4). The selection of terms in the formation of a knowledge-producing syllogism reflects the on-going process of HDI in reality. In fact, as Aristotle presents this process, without forming a syllogism, one cannot find the relevant middle term. The presence of the definite article in demonstration and its absence in definition suggest that while a knowledge-producing syllogism remains a linguistic activity, the definition based on the selection of syllogistic terms is directly of thing/event in the world. We shall see examples of inquiries of precisely this type in *Posterior Analytics* II 8.

Aristotle argues for an understanding of inquiries [I] and [II] by [I & II] from the ontological characteristics of things/events. The world which we claim to know is constituted of three kinds of object: (So) substance, (Po) its *per se*, i.e., necessary attributes, and (Ao) its accidental attributes. These are said to have their own causes of being. While the qualifications [Q1]: '*simpliciter*' and 'in part' function at the linguistic level, the newly introduced qualifications [Q2]: 'not this or that but *simpliciter*' and 'not *simpliciter* but of something' apply as ontological constraints at the level of reality. This ontological qualification [Q2] should be distinguished from [Q1] the linguistic qualification. While [Q1] is concerned with the ways in which an inquirer delivers questions, [Q2] is concerned with the ways in which the objects found differ from one another.

Since 'being (*to on*)' and 'substance (*hê ousia*)' are said in different ways, the phrase 'to be not *this* or *that* but (So) *simpliciter* the substance' is qualified by '*simpliciter*' so that it signifies the independent underlying object *simpliciter*. Thus 'substance' is here taken to be 'what underlies'. [Q2] offers three kinds of objects of inquiry, whose four items are supposed to be known. While two items of inquiry are syntactically distinguished, two kinds of objects of inquiry are ontologically distinguished. Some things can only exist by depending for their being on some 'underlying' subject. While the examples of underlying substance are moon, sun, and triangle, examples of *per se* attributes are eclipse (of the moon), equality or inequality (of the lines of a triangle), and the mid place or not (of the earth). These things/events have causes which can occupy the place of a middle term. In this way, Aristotle opens the possibility of having a knowledge-producing syllogism for all these types of things/events, including a substance in the sense of an independent underlying thing. Since syllogistic terms are built into the objects of discovery, the theory of demonstration is able to play an actual role in unified scientific investigation. Even so, commentators, however, have regularly failed to distinguish [Q1] from [Q2].[5] Consequently, in view of this failure, many have reduced route [II] to route [I] and have thus restricted and diminished the scope of inquiry. In particular, many have failed to appreciate how heuristic inquiry into substance might progress. Indeed, a question does arise as to how an independent entity such as substance can be analysed into syllogistic terms. Route [II], based on the simple use of being, appears unable to be accommodated within the framework of demonstration. Consequently, one might eventually expect a different method for substance in [II]. Otherwise, substance is in danger of being excluded from Aristotle's inquiry theory.[6]

To see how Aristotle addresses this worry, we should first appreciate that a failure to distinguish [Q1] from [Q2] is in fact a way of falling prey to one horn of the original dilemma: CSD. The four *items* of inquiry must be investigated in each of three *objects* of inquiry, where the field of inquiry remains heuristic rather than expositional. In this frame of inquiry, one should seek strict knowledge concerning four items of inquiry based on the relevant linguistic demarcations. Yet this form of inquiry should not exclude substance, the unified independent entity, from its scope. Furthermore it should not reduce [II] to [I], nor both [I] and [II] to [I & II].[7]

Aristotle finds a way out of this worry by adhering strictly to his plan of heuristic inquiry. When discovering that some entity is a substance or an attribute, one does not discover the mere existence of the relevant entity but always accompanies with either its 'accidental' attributes or 'something of thing itself' (93a22). He says that 'to the degree that we grasp [IIa] that *it exists* (*hoti esti*), to that extent we are also in a position to find out [IIb] the *what it is*' (93a28f.). Aristotle does not see any problem with these alleged difficulties because he constructs his inquiry theory on the basis of a wealth of heuristic information. Any object can be inquired into by route [II], insofar as the relevant question is asked by way of a single term placed as a grammatical subject. One can take either route because discovery of [Ia] and [IIa] is always accompanied by other pieces of information which lead to the discovery of [Ib] and [IIb]. Further [Ib] and [IIb] are understood on the basis of [I & IIb]. We now see that the claim of one horn of CSD can be dismissed. The wealth of information contained in discovery allows Aristotle to develop demonstrations in the realm of discovery.

Taking all that together, we can devise the following diagram concerning the scope, processes, and objects of heuristic inquiry, where the terms S, P, M are under the linguistic qualifications [Q1] '*simpliciter*' – 'in part' and these are chosen among the three kinds of objects (So), (Po), and (Ao) in the world under the ontological qualifications [Q2] '*simpliciter*' – 'something'. Each term of S, P, M which signifies some one of (So), (Po), (Ao) must be understood as a variable so that the object of inquiry signified by P in [I] SP can be expressed by S in [II]. It is possible insofar as these are syntactically distinguished:

[a]	[b]
[I] Whether is SP *in part* or not?	→ Why is SP?
=	=
[II] If S is *simpliciter* or not(?)	→ What is S?
=	=
[I & II] Whether is there M or not?	→ What is the M?

There is, however, another aspect of the dilemma of CSD which we have so far set aside. If discovery is carried out only by means of sense perception, one cannot achieve *strict* knowledge through inquiry. If sense perception is the only cognitive faculty available in inquiry, we fall prey to the other horn of the dilemma. In Aristotle's general plan of inquiry, all inquiries essentially involve a middle term. He says that 'Cases whose middle term is perceptible make clear that the search is for the middle term' (90a24). He argues for this claim by taking a perceptible example of a lunar eclipse as seen by a person standing on the moon. This shows the importance of actual location of his HDI, indicating its real-world orientation, even though his striking example was in his day, of course, only a thought experiment. He is suggesting that if an observer were on the moon, it would be simultaneously evident as a matter of perception that both the loss of light and the screening of earth were taking place. For both of these occurrences would, from that vantage point, prove to be perceptible facts. Even so, and importantly, grasping the screening *in fact* is not the same as grasping it *as* the cause of loss of light. The observed fact requires something more to be grasped *as* a cause.

The latter involves the thought, an activity of the noetic faculty rather than of the perceptual faculty (*noêsai, theôrein*), which, in effect, produces a universal proposition and so gains the status of a proper demonstration (cf. 71a1, 79a24, 81b2, 86a29, 88a3, 16, 89b12). 'By perceiving we would come to know the universal' (90a28), just as Newton grasped the law of universal gravitation by seeing an apple fall from a tree. As Aristotle says, 'Acumen (*ankinoia*) is a talent for hitting upon the middle term in an imperceptible time; e.g., if someone sees that the moon always holds its bright side toward the sun and quickly grasps why this is' (89b10f.). By being mediated by sense perception, 'the universal which is the object of thought (*noêtê*)' may be grasped by another faculty of mind (86a29). The reason why he mentions the simultaneous discovery so often is that two different cognitive faculties can be involved at once (90a27, 93a17, 35, 88a16, 89b12). Nothing hinders one from grasping the demonstration with these characteristics simultaneously. Only by introducing another faculty of mind, can Aristotle overcome the other horn of CSD.

Aristotle talks about discovery of a demonstration in a context where 'once the phenomena were adequately apprehended, the astronomical demonstrations were discovered (*heurethêsan*)' (46a20f). This is not surprising, because finding a middle term makes clear the entire demonstration. So understood, our inquiry always focuses on the middle term as the basis of the formation of a knowledge-producing syllogism. This is why we will not complete our inquiry only by perception: we need also some thought of the universal.

Although the context is novel, what Aristotle maintains here is in fact a standard feature of demonstration. Demonstrations must be constituted by two necessary premises which satisfy a condition of universality. Aristotle says that 'I call "universal" whatever belongs to its subject (U1) in every case and (U2) *per se* and (U3) *qua* itself' (73b25–27). Any ideal demonstrative premise must satisfy these three conditions. There are four kinds of *per se* predications all of which are ingredients of a demonstrative science.[8] The first, *per se* 1 predication, is such that a *per se* element *A* is an element of what *B* is in such a way that *A* belongs to *B* and '*A*' belongs to (or is predicated of) what '*B*' is. For example, in this sense, line belongs to triangle *per se*, and point belongs to line *per se*. The second kind of *per se* predication, *per se* 2, is such that an element *A* belongs to *B* and '*B*' belongs to (or is predicated of) what '*A*' is. For example, a straight and a curve belong to line *per se*, and odd and even belong to number *per se* (73a34–39). More fully, a proposition 'two right angles belongs to all isosceles' is true and necessary and thus qualifies as (U1) a universal quantification but does not satisfy (U2) or (U3). The necessity of a proposition is partly transferred from its premise that 'the two right angles belongs to all triangles *per se* and *qua* triangle'. Two right angles belongs to isosceles not *qua* isosceles but *qua* triangle which is commensurate with two right angles and is predicated of what two right angles is (*per se* 2). The (U3), or *qua* itself, condition endorses the commensurate universal among the terms being reciprocally predicable. Likewise, an inquirer on the moon may immediately discover the universal demonstration:

> Major premise: An eclipse belongs to all things being screened by the earth ((U1),(U2) *per se* 2, (U3)).
> Minor premise: Being screened by the earth belongs to the moon (all moons of kind K) ((U1), (U2) *per se* 2 (in the account of what the being screened by the earth is, the moon of kind K necessarily belongs, where 'K' stands for satellites in such and such orbit and so on)).
> Conclusion: An eclipse belongs to the moon (all moons of the kind K) ((U1) and necessity because of the necessity in the major and minor premises) (cf. 93a30–37).

This establishes that Aristotle's heuristic inquiry theory aims at *grasping* a demonstration. In other words, the demonstration is understood *within* the context of heuristic inquiry, rather than as an expression of its result. This example also shows how Aristotle's two objectives are closely connected.

3. Definition and Demonstration

So far I have traced Aristotle's general plan of inquiry theory. Objects of inquiry extend to all the things in the world. In a sense, this is not surprising, since anything whatsoever can be examined by one of Aristotle's four questions. Even so, Aristotle's ambitious plan is surrounded by difficulties. An immediate question concerns whether his causal regimentation of *what it is* is justified. Can his understanding of the four items of inquiry by [I & IIa,b] accommodate any thing/event whatsoever? We have already been given cause for concern as to whether it will include substances amongst its objects. If it fails to do so, Aristotle's HDI will not be comprehensive and will for this reason be a failure.

Fortunately, Aristotle is fully aware of this potential difficulty. He faces up to this and other, related challenges and difficulties in *Posterior Analytics* II 3 to 7.

In these chapters, Aristotle is concerned with the relation between definition and demonstration, both of which he claims are vehicles for strict knowledge. His

HDI, based on the identity between *what S is* and the *why SP is*—that is what some subject is and why some subject has some certain feature—has to unify these items within the methods of either definition or demonstration. Aristotle tackles some difficulties concerning [A] definition and [B] demonstration in II 3, by raising difficulties about (1) their objects and items, (2) the forms of predication they employ, and (3) their methods.

With respect to (1), Aristotle maintains that while [A] definition is concerned with (1a1) 'what it is and substance (*tou ti esti kai ousias*)', [B] syllogism or demonstration is concerned with (1b1) '*per se* attributes and accidental attributes'. Further, while definition (1a2) 'proves the *what it is*', demonstration (1b2) 'proves *that it is*'. Finally, demonstrations (1b3) 'presuppose and assume the *what it is*'.

With respect to (2), Aristotle contends that while [A] definition is formed by (2a1) the universal and affirmative proposition in which (2a2) 'no other thing is predicated of other thing', [B] demonstration contains (2b1) a negative proposition due to the constraint of its underlying logic and (2b2) 'proves something of something'. All cases of 'the *what it is* (*to ti esti*)' at the linguistic level are constituted by (2a3) 'universal and affirmative' predications. With respect to (3), while [A] definition gains knowledge with 'enough confidence based on induction',[9] [B] demonstration requires the use of deductive syllogism. Unless difficulties attendant to all these contentions are overcome, Aristotle's project of unifying inquiry into 'what?' and 'why?' will fail.

In this regard, it is essential for Aristotle to investigate the possibility of having a syllogism or demonstration of *what it is* or of substance. If he is successful in this investigation, demonstration and definition will be compatible. Accordingly, Aristotle asks a series of related questions:

- How does one prove the *what it is*? (90a36)
- How does the definer prove the substance or the *what it is* (*tên ousian ê to ti estin*)? (92a34)
- Is there a syllogism and a demonstration of the *what it is* or not? (91a13)
- Is there a demonstration of the *what it is* according to a substance (*to ti esti kat' ousian*')?'(92a6)

He poses similar questions altogether nine times in between II 3 and 10 (cf. 90b19, 92b4, 93a2, 15, 94a15).

I shall investigate what Aristotle seeks to achieve when he treats both 'substance' and '*what it is*' or 'the *what it was to be*' (*to ti ên einai*; often translated as *essence*)' (91a25, 91b9, 92a6). Why does he use these terms in his HDI? The answer returns us to Aristotle's relation to his predecessors. He implies that the Socratic 'what is S?' question has to be properly articulated if one is to avoid the difficulties that beset Socratic inquiry. One reason for supposing that this is so derives from Aristotle's practice in the *Topics*. In fact, the terminology Aristotle employs in his HDI is derived from his *theory* of dialectic in *Topics* I, in which he analyses the 'what is S?' question in terms of the theories of predicables and of categories. One of the four predicables discussed there is a kind of an account called 'defining-phrase (*horos*)' which, according to Aristotle, signifies the *what it was to be* (or essence, *to ti ên einai*). Ten categories of entities, including centrally the category of substance, are distinguished according to an analysis of the categories of predications on the basis of the theory of predicables. In my view, his distinctions between the four predicables, ten categories of predications, and ten categories of entities are all in different ways the result of Aristotle's analysis of the Socratic 'what is S?' question.[10] They are the devices for dialectical *practices* carried out using interrogatives whose answers are given by 'yes' or 'no', 'without [asking] 'what is it?' (*chôris tou ti esti*)' question (*Met.* XIII 4 1078b26, *Top.* I 4 101b28–33, VIII 2 158a14–21).

When Aristotle puts these expressions together, he has both the linguistic level and ontological level in mind, as we have seen in his distinction between [Q1] and [Q2], and aims to show the correspondence between them. The question 'what is it?' (*ti esti;*) is a linguistic one and its reply conveyed by the words 'the what it is (*to ti esti*)' will also be expressed linguistically by identifying the object (cf. 90b4). A linguistic activity of this type usually has a referential role: 'what (it) is' signifies a reality. When we find this locution, we should keep in mind that the linguistic activity of identifying S by an account points us towards finding what S is in reality. In our context, Aristotle conveys 'what substance is' by these same words (91a25, 92a6). His concern, in this context, is precisely whether there is a demonstration of what substance is.

According to Aristotle's account of the dual function of signification in *Topics* I 9, the linguistic act of signifying what Callias is also signifies a substance, namely Callias himself. He says that 'man [1] in *signifying* what it is [2] *signifies* sometimes substance, sometimes quality (*ho to ti esti sêmainôn hote men ousian sêmainei*)...when a man [Callias] is set before him and he says what is set there is a man or an animal, he [1] *states* what it [Callias] is and [2] *signifies* a substance' (103b27–31). In my view, the semantic notion 'signify' is employed in this passage, once to convey the linguistic act of stating 'what it is' and once to refer to the substance signified by that act.[11] This dual function is no doubt at work in the *Metaphysics*. He says, for instance, "being'...signifies [1] what it is and [2] some this (*tode ti*)' (VII 1 1028b12).

When 'what it was to be' is put together with both 'what it is' and 'substance', the former qualifies the latter two more strictly (91a25, b9, 26). In *Topics* I 4–9, Aristotle has established that what is sought by the 'what is S?' question is to be investigated in terms of the theories of predicables and of predications developed in connection with the method of division in the Academy. His theory of predicables is constituted by four possible answers to the Socratic 'what is S?' question. He mentions the four possible replies to this question as the four types of identity between a relevant thing S and the sorts of things able to be predicated of S: 'accident', 'property', 'genus', and finally 'defining-phrase (*horos*)' which alone signifies *the what it was to be* (the essence). These four possible answers, all of which are called 'definitory (*horika*)', are supposed to exhaust all possible replies to the Socratic 'what is S?' question and thus to offer an exhaustive and mutually exclusive classification of the answers available to this question (102a9). For instance, Laches answers the question 'what is courage?' by proposing that courage is 'not to retreat at the front of battle field'

(*Laches* 190e). However, since a failure to retreat may be caused by being frozen in place due to cowardice, this phrase signifies a merely accidental feature of courage. The expression of 'essence (*to ti ên einai S*)' is, in my view, formulated from Socrates' second attempt to ask the 'what is *S*?' question in a situation when Socrates, who is not satisfied by the interlocutor's first answer, poses the question again, seeking to determine what *S* is in itself, essentially and not accidentally. This is what is conveyed by the Greek locution using the imperfect tense, literally 'what was then it for *S* to be *S*?'[12] This formulation gives way to Aristotle's own more abbreviated locution, 'the what it was to be'—that is, then, what it was for *S* to be *S*, for example, what it was, all along, for a man to be a man, or for courage to be courage, not accidentally, but essentially (103a25–27, cf. 1041a28). Among the four predicables, only the defining-phrase provides this sort of answer. In this sense, essence is introduced as the formal notion of a definable entity.

In I 9, Aristotle enumerates ten categories (genera) of entities such as substance and quality on the basis of the ten categories of predications which are classified according to the relevant kinds of interrogatives such as 'what is it?' and 'what is it like?' The identity question: 'what is it?' can be raised to each category of entities. A substance-term is defined by a substance-term. Likewise a quality-term 'white' is defined by a quality-term 'colour'. Among these ten genera of entities, 'what is it?' is primarily addressed to substance. While other entities accept 'of-other (*peri heterou*) predication', where one thing is predicated of another underlying thing, such as 'man is white', substance alone does not accept anything but 'of-itself (*peri hautou*) predication' (103b35–39). This is because, for instance, in a predication 'white is man', since 'man' does not signify what white is, nor how white is nor any other genus of predication, this kind of *of-other* predication does not produce any significant predication. Thus, this kind of predication does not signify one of ten genera of entities either. We are now in a better position to understand passages such as those in the *Metaphysics* which say that 'the essence [thing itself] will primarily and simply belong to substance' (VII 4 1030a29f.). As we shall confirm later, this derives from the causal treatment of explanation developed in the *Posterior Analytics*.

There is already an indication of causal treatment of the essence in the *Topics*, although the issue of identifying a thing remains a *topos* (a point of examination). In *Topics* VI 13, the essence is presented and examined as a possibility among three candidates. He says, 'See whether in defining anything, a man has defined it as [a] these things, or as [b] made from these things or as [c] this together with this' (150a1–3). While [a] is made of simple addition of its elements such as 'justice' to be 'temperance and courage', an example of [c] is 'honey water'. But [b] opens the possibility for a causally unified entity, of a sort leading to the matter-form composite in the *Metaphysics*. Aristotle sets out a *topos* concerning [b]: 'See if he has failed to state the manner of their composition; for saying that it is made from these things is not enough to make the thing intelligible. For the substance of each of the compounds is not merely that it is made from these things, but that it is made from them *in this way*, as in the case of a house' (150b22–27).

In the *Posterior Analytics*, which in general presupposes the *Topics*, Aristotle is engaged in developing a causal interpretation of *what it is* and substance based on the direction proposed under [b] in the *Topics*. If there is a causally basic unifying feature which is in itself a part of all elements of what S is, it can be counted as what unifies all other elements.[13] That is why, for instance, a name 'Socrates' doubly signifies (*ditton sêmainein*) both the composite Socrates, which is the shape involving the relevant matter, and his soul as his form (*Met.* VII 6 1031b23, VIII 3 1043a29-b4). Aristotle says that 'some *this* is said according to the shape and the form' (*DA* II 1 412a8).

In his HDI, 'substance' is expressed in two ways, one of which is, as it was qualified by [Q2], its simple use standing for [S1] an independent underlying entity, the other of which is accompanied by a thing expressed in genitive case such as [S2] 'substance of something' or 'substance of each thing' ([S1]: e.g., 90a10, b30, 91b9, 92a6, b13, 29, 93b26; [S2]: 83b26, 90b16, 96a34, b12). I take it that by [S2], if I may borrow the locutions of the vocabulary passage of 'substance' in *Metaphysics* V 8, Aristotle means either [Sb] 'immanent constituent(s)' as 'the cause of being in the things which are not said of underlying' or [Sc] 'the *what it was to be*' (1017b15–23). ([Sa] in *Metaphysics* V 8 is the same as [S1] (1017b13)). [Sc] is introduced in the same way as [S2], such that 'this [the *what it was to be*] is said to be substance of each thing (*ousia hekastou*) whose account is a definition' (1017b21).

In his HDI, when Aristotle refers to 'the cause of being...substance' (90a9f), the cause of substance must itself be substance, in a manner corresponding to both [Sb] and [Sc], provided that [Sc] is interpreted causally. This is possible and does not violate the independence criterion of substance, insofar as the substance and its *cause* as substance cannot be separated in reality. While Aristotle holds that 'the number of causes is...the same as that of the things understood under the "why?" question', 'essence' is mentioned as one of four causes 'as the *what it was to be*, the whole, the synthesis and the form', although strictly speaking the form is 'the account of essence' (*Phys.* II 7 198a14f., *Met.* V 2 1013b22, a27). In fact, when Aristotle refers to [S2], he seems to have [Sb] and/or [Sc] in mind (83a24, a39, 90b16, 93a12f, 96a34f., cf. 1017b21f., 983a27). In a passage exploring 'how one should hunt the predicates in *what it is*', Aristotle says that 'this synthesis must be the substance of the thing (*ousia tou pragmatos*)' (96a22, 34). For example, every triad possesses the elements number, odd, and prime in both senses (i.e., not divided, not added). The defining-phrase of 'triad' is 'prime odd number' which signifies the *what it was to be* a triad (96a35f). I take it that because of the totality of elements of what S is, 'the substance of each thing S' is nothing but 'each thing S', which is to say, then, the substance itself.

This correspondence explains why 'substance *simpliciter*' as a subject and the defining-phrase as a predicate, can signify the same entity, namely a substance. Granted that a strict identity predication is given by 'man is rational animal', [S1] 'man' and [S2] 'rational animal' signify a substance. One support for this claim is the phrase 'the elements in the substance of each thing (*hosa en tê(i) ousia(i) hekastou*)' (83b26–27). [S2] is here signified by the predicate of *what each thing is*. The reason why he employs [S1] and [S2] is that 'substance' in these two expressions signifies the same entity (substance), because these state inter-substitutable sub-jects and predicates. If this is correct, we can understand why [Sa] substance, as the independent underlying S, can be an entity identical with [Sc], the *what it was to be S*. Also, because of the immanent totality of [Sc], it opens the possibility of understanding the essence as [Sb] 'the cause of being'.

As we have seen in the aporematic chapters II 3–7, if [A] definition and [B] demonstration were irrelevant with respect to (1), (2), and (3), there would not be a way to have a demonstration of *what it is* and of substance. Its function and scope would be limited. Indeed, any inquiry theory which fails to provide some way to come to know substance will be a failure. The remaining question is whether it is possible for Aristotle to provide some such way.

4. Logical and Ontological Conditions for Demonstration of *What It Is*

In *Posterior Analytics* II 8–10, Aristotle develops his general plan of HDI by over-coming the suggestion that definition and demonstration are irrelevant to each other. He develops a causal turn of *what it is* and in the process creates a new theory of definition. In this connection, he concentrates on making clear how demonstra-tion contributes to grasping the *what it is* in the sense of the *what it was to be* (93a19, 91a25, cf. *DA* III 6 430b27 *tou ti esti kata to ti ên einai*). In II 8 Aristotle sets out the logical and ontological conditions for demonstrating *what S is* on the basis of his causal way of interpreting the Socratic 'what is S?' question. He proceeds by treating this question as an attempt 'to know the cause of the what S is'. He says that:

> We must consider again...what the definition is and whether there is *in some way* demonstration and definition of what it [S] is, or in no way at all. As we said [in II 2], (P) since it is the same thing to know [IIb] 'what S is (*eidenai ti esti*)' and to know [I & IIb] 'the cause [M] of the what S is (*eidenai to aition tou ti esti*)', [(Q)]...(P') the account of this is that there is some cause [M] and this [M] is the same as the thing S or another, but if it is another, the thing S is either demonstrable or indemonstrable, then, (R) if the cause is another and it is possible to demonstrate [what S is], (S) it is necessary for the cause to be a middle term [M] and [for what S is] to be proved in the first figure. For what is proved is both universal and affirmative (93a3–9).

This line of reasoning might be interpreted in several different ways. For instance, in the chain of inference ((P)-(S)), Philoponus and Barnes insert (Q) as the con-sequent of (P), i.e., 'Since (P) and (P'), then (Q): 'there is in some way demonstra-tion of what it is'.[14] By taking the argument this way, they imply that Aristotle has already established the existence of a demonstration of *what it is* by deducing (Q).

Then the reasoning as a whole will be something like $((P \land P') \to Q) \land (R \to S)$; but in this reconstruction, the argument does not flow at all smoothly. In fact, (R) states the same content as (Q) in the mode of a hypothetical possibility.

Still, this same chain of inference may be understood in another way. As Zabarella construes it, 'nothing should be added and Aristotle's sentence is perfect (*perfectam*)' as written.[15] What Aristotle does in this passage is to set out the logical and ontological *conditions* for demonstrating *what it is*. (P) describes a cognitive state on the basis of his causal regimentation of what S is, such that to know the cause which makes S *what it is*, in the sense of the essence of S, is the same as to know what S is. (P) is grounded by (P'). Because (P') states a general analysis of the relations between the thing and its cause on demonstrability in which one combination serves for (P'). It states that there is a distinct cause M of S, so that S can be demonstrated by M. Thus, to know M is the same as to know what S is.

On the basis of this causal regimentation of *what it is*, Aristotle draws (R): '*then, if (ei toinun)* the cause is another and it is possible to demonstrate [what S is at all] ...'. Importantly, (R) states that the relevant possibility is hypothetically. It is in fact the antecedent of a conditional sentence, which implies that Aristotle is not committed to (Q) as yet, but is instead here in the process of establishing the ontological and logical condition of the demonstrability of *what it is*. *Provided* (R), then, Aristotle makes clear the conclusion (S): (1) the cause must be placed as the middle term M, (2) the cause, i.e., M must be something other than S, and (3) the proof must be carried out by the first figure *Barbara* such that the universal affirmation is secured. Then the whole argument will be like $((P' \to P) \land ((P \land R) \to S))$. This interpretation improved upon that favoured by Philoponus and Barnes, at least as regards the flow of argument. In terms of content, too, this interpretation has the benefit of making Aristotle consistent in such a way that he raises the general conditions of demonstrating *what it is* without introducing the unwarranted claim (Q). So far, in fact, he is merely interested in establishing his results *given* a specified assumption. That is why he says a few lines later, after introducing Xenocrates' ill-fated method for proving the essence, that 'we say in which way it is *permitted*, speaking again from the beginning' (93a15f.). So far, Aristotle has shown only that demonstration of an essence is possible; he has yet to show that such demonstrations are actual.

On this reconstruction, Aristotle's conclusion (S) is ultimately justified by (P). (P) is grounded by the causal regimentation of *what it is*. Concerning (P), however, we confront a textual problem. Bekker's reading: 'to aition tou ti esti' (93a4: *BnAn^c*) must be correct rather than Ross's reading: 'to aition tou ei esti' (*AB²dE^cP*, Zabarella, Waitz) according to the context of the paragraph.[16] At issue is the matter of specifying the formal conditions for demonstrating *what it is*. Since the demonstration of 'if it is (*ei esti*)' in the sense of 'the cause of its being' (Charles, Zabarella) has been already established in II 1–7, there is no need to state (R) as a conditional.[17] The basic assumption is that under the rubric of the Socratic 'what is S?' question, an inquirer in fact seeks 'the cause of *what S is*' rather than 'the cause of *if S is*'. Aristotle in II 2 has established that what is sought by [IIb], that is, by a 'what is S?' question, is nothing other than [I & IIb], that is, the middle term [M] of 'what S is'.

He identifies there seeking [IIb] 'what is harmony?' with seeking [I&IIb] 'what is the numerical ratio?' (II 2 90a18–23). Thus, for instance, to know what an eclipse is is the same as to know the cause which makes an eclipse what an eclipse is.

The Socratic 'what is S?' question can thus be understood causally. (P') provides the reason why: the M is either identical with S or another, and if it is another, S is either demonstrable or indemonstrable. If it is demonstrable, the identity of S as *what S is* is fixed by demonstrating this by means of the middle term M. Accordingly, *what S is* must be able to be articulated in terms which are mediated by M. Thus, (S): It must be carried out by a syllogism in the first figure in those cases whose cause M is distinct from S. In this passage, in sum, Aristotle specifies the formal constraints on the scope of heuristic inquiry in order to show that his general plan of HDI is a viable one.

5. *LOGIKOS* SYLLOGISM

Aristotle investigates the topic of how demonstrations regarding substances are to proceed by first examining an attempt to demonstrate a claim about the substantial soul, as proposed by his colleague Xenocrates. He says:

> Indeed, the one just being examined [in II 4]: to prove *the what it [S] is (to ti esti)* through another [what S is] may be one method. For among the terms of what S is, it is necessary for the middle term to be what S is, and among the terms of properties (*idiôn*) it must be proper (*idion*). Hence, among the terms of the *what it was to be* the same thing (*tôn ti ên einai tô (i) autô (i) pragmati*), one proves but the other does not. Thus it has been said earlier that this way would not be a demonstration, but a formal syllogism (*logikos sullogismos*) of what S is (93a9–15).

The type of syllogism is called a 'formal syllogism' because it appeals to a notion of 'sameness' which is a general and formal characteristic of being. The principle of non-contradiction, to which such general notions as 'sameness' and 'otherness' belong, is the basic device of every *logikos* (formal and general) analysis of being. The *logikos* argument as a 'philosophical investigation according to the truth (*pros philosophian kat' aletheian*)' is carried out attending to 'how one should speak (*pôs dei legein*)' on the basis of the principle of non-contradiction (*Top.* I 14 105b19–37, *Met.* VII 4 1030a27). As we have seen, Aristotle's theories of the predicables and categories are themselves an outcome of a *logikos* analysis of being. One way to prove *what S is* is to deduce it through a distinct account of the same S. This is also the case for properties as well. But the *what it was to be S* is constituted by both *what S is* and what is *proper* to S. 'Hence (*hôste*)', Aristotle infers, the same situation applies to the essence as well.

In II 6, Aristotle reminds us of the formal and thus non-causal constitution of essence in *Topics* I 4–5, that 'the *what it was to be S* is the *property* composed from the things in *what S is*, and that these *alone* are in what S is, and that the *whole* is proper to *S'* (92a7f.). By introducing the notion of essence whose account is the defining-phrase, Aristotle expresses the strict identity between what is signified by a name and what is signified by its defining-phrase. Among the relevant terms, one account proves while another account of the same thing does not. If one tries to prove the *what it is* in the sense of the *what it was to be* (essence) as the conclusion, one has to assume the account which signifies the same essence in a premise. A premise can only convey to its conclusion those characteristics which the premise already implies in itself. Now, there is, according to Aristotle, only one essence for each thing. Consequently, unless there is a single essence in a relevant thing, there is no single entity either (cf. *Top.* VI 4 141a24). This, then, shows where the *logikos* syllogism of Xenocrates goes away. Since it 'assumes what one must prove', this type of syllogism commits the logical fallacy of *petitio principii* (cf. *APr* II 16). It follows as a general consequence, then, that one cannot prove an essence in the conclusion of a demonstration.

The particular example of the formal syllogism ascribed to Xenocrates is about soul and is constituted by 'the cause of its own being alive': *A*, 'just what is a number that moves itself': *B*, and 'soul': *C* (91a37-b1). In this syllogism, which is non-causal, *what the soul is* is assumed in a premise 'in the sense of its being the same (*hôs to auto on*)' (91b1). In speaking in this way, Aristotle means that the defining-phrases in the premise and the conclusion are the same insofar as they signify the same entity. When Aristotle says 'being the same', he refers to the strict identity between a thing and its essence. But, insofar as these items or terms are labelled by different letters such as '*A*', '*B*', and '*C*', this alleged formal syllogism is valid and indeed an example of *Barbara* at the formal level. If there were no other way of demonstrating the essence than the formal syllogism, Aristotle's inquiry theory would stall and grind to a halt: to move his theory forward, Aristotle needs to make a causal turn, one involving the essence.

6. Degrees of Information in Syllogistic Formation

After having examined a *logikos* syllogism, Aristotle embarks 'from the beginning' on a new way to search for the demonstration of *what it is* (93a15f). In this project his aim is to unify heuristic inquiry and demonstration so as to make heuristic knowledge scientific even while making demonstration a viable method of scientific investigation. In this combination, the possibility of demonstration of *what it is* is a key issue.

In this new start, Aristotle pursues his programme of HDI at its most vigorous. The goal of heuristic inquiry is still to grasp *what it is* in the sense of 'the what it was to be (essence)' or 'thing itself' of, for instance, 'thunder', 'man', and 'soul' (93a19–24). He says that:

We seek [Ib] the reason why by grasping [Ia] the fact, although sometimes it becomes evident simultaneously; yet it is not possible to know [Ib] the reason why before [Ia] the fact, and clearly in just the same way without grasping [IIa] that it exists, it is not possible to know [IIb] the *what it was to be (to ti ên einai)*. For it is impossible to know [IIb] *what it is*, without knowing [IIa] *if it is*. As to [IIa], the *if it is*, sometimes we grasp this accidentally and sometimes when grasping *something of the thing itself (ti autou tou pragmatos)*, e.g., of thunder as *a sort of* sound of clouds, and of eclipse as *a sort of* loss of light, and of man as *a sort of* animal, and of soul as a thing moving itself. In the case where we know accidentally that it exists *(hoti estin)*, we are in a hopeless position as regards finding out [IIb] *what it is*. For we do not even know [IIa] that it exists. And to seek *what something is* when one does not know *that it is* is to seek nothing. But when one possesses something [of the *what it is*], it is easier to seek. Hence, to the degree that we grasp [IIa] *that it exists*, to that extent we are also in a position to find out [IIb] the *what it is*. Therefore, of things which we grasp *something* of the *what it is (ti tou ti estin)*, let it be (1) *at first* this way. [Consider, for instance] 'eclipse' A, 'moon' C, 'screening by the earth' B....When we find it [B], we know the fact and the reason why at once, if it is through immediate premises. *However*, (2) if this is not the case, we know the fact but not the reason why. 'Moon' C, 'eclipse' A, 'not being able to cast shadow at full moon nothing evident between us' B.... (3) What is thunder? Extinction of fire in cloud. Why does it thunder? Because *the* fire in *the* cloud belongs to *the* to be extinguished. 'Cloud' C, 'thunder' A, 'extinction of fire' B....The A 'sound' belongs to the B. At least the B is an account of the first extreme term, the A. But if there may be another middle term again of this [A], it will be from the remaining accounts (93a16–35).

In this passage, we first have to confirm that the phrase 'the thing itself' is introduced to govern the whole process of inquiry from [IIa] to [IIb]. This is so because this phrase stands for the *what it was to be* (essence), which shows the ultimate goal of inquiry into 'what is it?' (93a19, 22). The reason why 'soul' does not admit of the qualification 'a sort of', but rather signifies the thing itself, is that since the soul is identical with its essence, there is no room for dividing one part of *what the soul is* from another part of *what the soul is*. This kind of indemonstrable thing, signified by an immediate term, cannot be articulated into terms mediated by a middle term. Nevertheless, Aristotle mentions this case in order to show the comprehensiveness of heuristic inquiry. As it is developed in *De Anima* I 1, it is useful for an inquiry into what soul is to investigate its various attributes, even if the soul itself may only be grasped by a method other than a demonstration (402b18–25, *DA* III 6 430b27f.).

Aristotle's new procedure is to formulate the relevant knowledge-producing syllogism in the context of inquiry, in which an inquirer grasps *'something* of the what it is' or *'something* of the thing itself'. The terms in question vary according to the degrees of finding 'something' (93a22, 29). What is common to the three examples he introduces is that one should put 'something' of what it is in a middle term. Depending on the appropriateness of the middle term grasped, the proposed syllogism is judged as part of a successful (or unsuccessful) inquiry. If the syllogism involves an immediate premise with a major term, it is part of a successful inquiry.

In the case of (1), since this is constituted through the immediate premises, both [Ib] and [IIb] in the sense of essence are grasped. In the case of (2), only [Ia] and [IIa] are grasped. That is why an inquiry still goes on 'to seek what *B* is, whether it is screening or rotation of moon or extinction' (93b5). In the case of (3), there may be another middle term which is the account of *A* 'thunder' or 'sound'. The content of the *A* term can either be the object investigated (e.g., thunder) or its genus (e.g., sound) at this stage of inquiry. This is because an inquirer has already grasped 'thunder' at this stage as 'a sort of sound of clouds' (93a22). Unless we attend to the actual context of inquiry, we will not understand Aristotle's discussion of the exchange of terms. As B. Landor says when speaking of these terms, 'they thus (as we would say) can be substituted one for another in all referentially transparent contexts'.[18] By using this substitution, an inquirer can find another term which explains the *A* term more properly. In the cases like (2) and perhaps (3), Aristotle shows an on-going investigation in the search of a proper demonstration of *what it is.*

Distinguishing elements of *what it is* explains how demonstration can be part of a search and also shows how heuristic inquiry can be guided by the constraints of demonstrations. As these examples make clear, Aristotle pays attention to the degrees of information contained in the discovery of the [a] stage of route [II]. The information gained in finding the [a] stage enables one to reach the [b] stage of grasping *what it is.* In other words, Aristotle aims to refer to '*something (ti)* of the *what it is*' and then to formulate the middle term so as to complete his search by finding an immediate premise which accounts for the *A* term (93a22, 28, 29, 35). Since 'something' is specified by the concrete 'cause' in 'the cause of the *what it is*' (93a4), this is an example of successful inquiry. Demonstration of *what it is* is gained through the complementarity of demonstration and heuristic inquiry.

7. Demonstrable and Indemonstrable Entities

We can now confirm which entities are objects of demonstration and which are not. Within the formal constraints of demonstrating *what it is*, entities can be divided initially into two groups. As to the things identical with their causes, Aristotle says in II 9 that 'Hence, it is obvious that among the things of *what it is (tôn ti esti)*, some are immediate and principles, which must be assumed or revealed by another method with respect both to their being and what it is' (93b21–23). Immediate terms and principles such as 'unit' in 'arithmetic' are identical with their causes (93b24). Even if one tries to demonstrate what these entities are, one is able to offer at best only a *logikos* syllogism.

We might yet seek another method to grasp what such entities are. In II 10, Aristotle mentions as another kind of definition: 'The definition of immedite things is an indemonstrable *posit (thesis)* of *what it is*' (94a9f). A *posit* is an immediate syllogistic principle which cannot be proved (72a15–24). Nonetheless, Aristotle claims that we are able to gain indemonstrable knowledge of a thing which is initially presented as a *posit*. By occurring within a deductive system of a science, indemonstrable primaries of that science, such as 'magnitude' in geometry, can be grasped through a sort of feedback mechanism, because they do admit of demonstrations with respect to their primary features. An inquirer gains indemonstrable knowledge of primary and immediate things by grasping that the whole system of a science depends on them. Aristotle says that 'We claim that not every instance of knowledge is demonstrative, but in the case of immediate things there is indemonstrable knowledge' (72b18f.). In this way, the *what it is* of an immediate principle presented as a *posit* can be known on the basis of its existence, which is indirectly warranted on the basis of a demonstration of the existence of its attributes, whose *what it is* can, by contrast, also be known *via* demonstration. For instance, without referring to the *unit*, one cannot ultimately establish the knowledge of even basic attributes of being a unit, but these include the numbers and the rules of arithmetic governing them.

Among the objects whose causes are distinct, some are demonstrable and others are indemonstrable (93a6). As to the indemonstrable, Aristotle focuses on their 'accidental attributes' (90a11), although even in this case one may structure a syllogism, but only insofar as there is a cause pertinent to them. As to the demonstrable, Aristotle says in II 9 that 'of things having a middle term and things of which there is some other cause of substance, as we said, one makes clear *what it is* through demonstration without demonstrating *what it is*' (93b25–28). 'Substance' here does not mean [S2] 'essence' but rather [S1] an independent 'underlying' entity, because every attempt to deduce an essence is only *logikos*, as we have already seen (Section 5). 'Substance' must mean [S1] an independent underlying entity whose cause is distinct, but may not be separated in terms of being. According to the examples in II 8, as we saw, 'man' is such a substance but 'soul' is not (93a23f). As Aristotle makes clear in *Metaphysics* VIII 2, '[S1] 'soul' and [M] 'to be soul' are the same, but [M] 'to be man' and [S1] 'man' are not the same, unless even the bare soul is to be called 'man''(1043b2–4). Thus we have to seek a middle term in the case of that kind of substance which is not separated in fact, but is separated in account. This is a welcome result, since if substances such as man were excluded from the scope of inquiry due to purely logical constraints, Aristotle's HDI would cease to be an attractive project.

8. *WHAT IT WAS TO BE* (ESSENCE) AS A CAUSALLY BASIC UNIFYING FEATURE

It is generally agreed that insofar as a proper efficient cause occupies the middle term, an inquirer can discover a successful demonstration. For example, being screened by the earth explains why the moon suffers an eclipse, and the sap's being solidified explains why broad-leaved trees shed leaves and so on (II 8,16). In these cases, 'the universal comes to be known to us' (90a28). In such cases of successful demonstration, three terms are commensurate in extension and reciprocally predicable. Importantly, however, Aristotle argues in a passage of the *Metaphysics* that the efficient cause and the final cause can be regarded as essence. He says: 'Why are these bricks and stones a house? Thus it is evident that an inquirer seeks the cause. But this is, to speak formally (*hôs logikôs eipein*), the *what it was to be*, which in some cases is the for the sake of something…and in some cases is the what moved first' (1041a28–30). Discussions at the *logikos* level can be complementary to the *phusikos* (physical) level.

In *Posterior Analytics* II 11, Aristotle argues that the *what it was to be* (essence) can be taken to be a cause. Aristotle offers a demonstration by taking an essence as a middle term involving two kinds of *per se* predications. He regards a mathematical proof of the right angle in a semicircle as admitting of scientific knowledge. He says that 'we think that we know something scientifically when we know its cause; and, these are four kinds, one of which is 'the *what it was to be*', the other is '*given so and so, it is necessary that this is so*'' (94a20–22). I shall call the first cause 'the synthetic cause' and the second 'the necessitating cause'. Aristotle offers a mathematical proof whose middle term satisfies both these two causes.

In this connection, he inquires into [Ib] 'Why is the angle in the semicircle a right angle? And from what entity being given, does it follow that it is a right angle?' (94a28). Its demonstration is constituted by 'half of two rights': B, 'right angle': A, 'the angle in a semicircle': C, where C in fact stands for an angle of a triangle drawn in a semicircle. The demonstration is: A φaB [*per se* 2], BφaC [*per se*1], then A φaC [*per se* 2 via the major and minor] (where 'φa' stands for 'belong to all').

He offers a proof in which the three terms are in fact identical but do not constitute a *logikos* syllogism. This is because Aristotle does not deduce one account of the essence from another account of same essence. The subjects to which the identical angle belong are different. While the conclusion: 'a right angle belongs to the angle [of a triangle drawn] in a semicircle' exhibits a *property* of the triangle drawn in a semicircle, the necessitating cause, the B term, is taken to be the *essence* of the angle in the semicircle. The necessitating cause B, which is gained from drawing the two isosceles triangles, constitutes the relevant angle in a semicircle.[19] In this example, a peculiar property is deduced from the synthetic cause (that is, the essence). What is made clear in this proof is that the necessitating cause B, which is expressed by an infinitive verb, is the essence too. Aristotle says that 'Thus it is in virtue of being B: half of two rights, that A belongs to C. But this [B] was the *being right* in the semicircle (*to en hêmikukuliô (i) orthên einai*). But this [B] is identical with the *what it was to be* [of A in C], since it is what the account [of A in C] signifies. Furthermore, it has been proved that the *what it was to be* is a cause by being the middle term' (94a32–36). The nominative use of infinitive 'to be *F*' (which serves as an abbreviation of 'the what it was to be *F*', that is, the locution which signifies a synthetic cause B), has the role of making the question [Ib] 'Why is the angle in the semicircle a right angle?' and the question [IIb] 'What was it then for the angle in the semicircle to be a right angle?' the same. The answer to [Ib] is given by 'because of the half of two rights' and the one to [IIb] is given by 'being the half of two rights'. The latter answer directly exhibits the essence of the right angle in a semicircle.

The essence is, however, not merely captured by the *logikos* (formal) fashion, but is introduced by establishing a necessitating cause. Thus, Aristotle expresses the identity between these causes by saying that 'this ($B =$ the necessitating cause) is identical with the *what it was to be*'. He uses the word 'identical' to emphasize the actual identity between them, knowledge of which is gained through the process of proof. Aristotle makes explicit his causal interpretation of the *what it was to be* by concluding that 'it was proved that the *what it was to be* is a cause by being the middle term' (94a35). This sentence shows that the essence is the cause referred to by the middle term, and so is to be understood in terms of being a necessitating cause within this particular causal account. Once again, Aristotle expresses much the same view in the *Metaphysics*, when he introduces the essence as a causally basic unifying feature for substance. He says: 'Causes are spoken of in four senses, whose one cause we say the substance and the *what it was to be*. Because *why it is* is led to the ultimate account, but the first *reason why* is a cause and a principle' (*Met.* I 3 983a26–29, cf. 988b28, 1040b24).

Since the essence is causally basic, it is in effect the whole which is ideally being predicated reciprocally among three terms (cf. 99a16–29). When 'the cause': B and 'the item of which it is the cause': A and 'the item for which it is the cause': C 'follow one another' in the sense of being reciprocally predicable, an inquirer gains proper scientific knowledge (99a16f). This is because the B term, which gives an account of the A term, is an ingredient in an immediate proposition, that is, one for which there is no other middle term (72a7f, 99a21f.). This demonstration begs no questions: the *property* of C, i.e., A (A φα C) is deduced from the *essence* of A in C, i.e., B. The essence discovered unifies all the relevant elements present in the object in such a way that A φα C because of B.

9. CONCLUSION: A NEW THEORY OF DEFINITION BASED ON THE THEORY OF DEMONSTRATION

We have traced the way in which Aristotle carries out his plan of developing HDI. The causal regimentation of what it is (as the *what it was to be*, or essence) opens the way to grasp *what something is* on the basis of a knowledge-producing syllogism. We are now in a better position to understand Aristotle's conclusion in *Posterior Analytics* II 8:

> We have stated how the *what it is* is grasped and becomes known such that neither a syllogism nor a demonstration of the *what it is* comes about, yet it is made plain *through* a syllogism and *through* a demonstration. Therefore, it is not possible to know the *what it is* without a demonstration of a thing whose cause is another, nor is there a demonstration of it, just as we said in the aporematic chapters (93b15–20).

Aristotle reaches this conclusion only after having considered 'in which way it [demonstrating *what it is*] is permitted (*endechetai*), from the beginning' (93a16). His view is that '*what it [S] is*' should be *causally* understood, as the cause which makes S what S is. Insofar as the cause is distinct in account from the thing whose cause it is, grasping the essence is made possible on the basis of a knowledge-producing syllogism. An inquirer cannot demonstrate *what it is* by producing a conclusion which reveals the essence, but must instead locate the essence among the premises as the causally basic unifying feature of the item in question. The indispensability of demonstration is shown in three distinct ways in *Posterior Analytics* II 8, where it becomes clear that the process of formulating a demonstrative syllogism closely parallels the path of heuristic inquiry (Section 6). Thus, Aristotle establishes the necessity of having a demonstration if one is to grasp the essence of a thing whose cause is distinct, even though there is no demonstration of its essence.

In II 10 Aristotle develops his new theory of definition by addressing the question of 'how the *what it is* is articulated into the defining-phrases' (II 13 96a20). Aristotle introduces three types of defining-phrase (*horos*), each of which *will be* (*estai*) constituents of the three types of definition (93b30, 94a1).[20] (His use of the future indicates that the definitional account is yet to be discovered.) He introduces explicitly the causal definition whose defining-phrase (b') is said to be an 'account exhibiting why it is' (93b38). Then he says:

> Thus, while (a') the first defining-phrase signifies but does not prove, it is evident that (b') the latter type *will be* like a demonstration of the *what it is*, differing from a demonstration in the arrangement of terms. For, there is a difference between saying why there is thunder and what thunder is. For one will say that 'it is in this way (*houtôs*) because *the* fire is extinguished in *the* clouds'. But 'what is thunder?' [B] 'It is a sound of fire being extinguished in clouds'. Thus, the same account is said in another way, first as a continuous demonstration (*apodeixsis sunechês*) and second as a definition (93b38–94a7).

The (b') defining-phrase constitutes a type of definition, namely [B], which exhibits the totality of *what it is* by specifying the 'something' of 'something of the *what it is*' as 'the cause of the *what it is*'. Since saying *why thunder is* and saying *what thunder is* differ in respect of the arrangement of terms, the type [B] definition based on (b') is said to be only '*like* a demonstration of the what it is'. In II 8 Aristotle rejects the possibility of a demonstration of *what it is* in the sense of demonstrating the essence as the conclusion. However, in II 10, Aristotle holds that it is permitted (*endechetai*) as the *continuous* (*sunechês*) demonstration of the *what it is*, which is effected through pointing to 'the same account' as implicit in both definition and demonstration. This type of continuous demonstration is in effect identical with the account of his type [B] definition (cf.75b30f.). The type [B] definition is also called 'a syllogism of the *what it is*, differing in aspect from the demonstration', in which 'syllogism' is a combination of accounts of the *what it is* (94a11). In this way, Aristotle specifies 'in what sense (*pôs*) there is a demonstration of the *what it is*' (94a14).

There is also (c') a third defining-phrase which articulates the *what it is*. Aristotle says that 'A defining-phrase (*horos*) of thunder is 'sound in clouds'. But this is a conclusion of the demonstration of the *what it is*' (94a7f.). He refers to 'the demonstration of the *what it is*' in this passage in order to show that this type of defining-phrase (c') constitutes a part of the *continuous* demonstration of the *what it is*. This is not a *logikos* syllogism because what is deduced from the synthetic cause as the essence is a part of *what it is*. As we have seen in Section 8, which investigated II 11, 'the synthetic cause' as the essence can occupy the place of the middle term. Consequently, one can deduce either a property or a part of *what it is*, insofar as the synthetic cause unifies all elements of *what it is* and the properties of the thing whose cause it is. Insofar as (c') is involved in a continuous demonstration, it constitutes a part of the *what it is* which can be explained by the causally basic unifying feature, i.e., the essence.

The relevant part is referred to by the phrase 'in this way', by which Aristotle indicates that he is here speaking of the actual point of a heuristic inquiry. It is possible to have a continuous demonstration in the context of actual inquiry. In this context, Aristotle counts 'the conclusion of demonstration of the *what it is*' (94a13) as a type [C] definition, because this type of account is constituted by a genus (sound) and a differentia (in clouds) according to his theory of division. When Aristotle says at the beginning of II 10 that 'Since a definition *is said* (*legetai*) to be an account of the *what it is*', he reminds us that the Academic tradition of definition is the starting-point of his new theory of definition (93b29). In this sense, the defining-phrase (c') satisfies the basic requirement for definition as laid down in the Academy.

Aristotle characterizes [A] as one type of definition that 'the definition of the immediate terms is an indemonstrable posit of the *what it is*' (94a9) and also characterizes [A] in a succinct way as 'an indemonstrable account of the *what it is*' (94a11). Its defining-phrase is (a') *some* account (*logos tis*) of what a name or name-like account signifies, although (a') can signify both (b') *why it is* and (c') *what is demonstrated* (93b30, 39). (Empty names such as 'goatstag' are excluded from (a') by its being limited with a qualification 'some' such that empty entities signified by the relevant names cannot be defined.) [21] While the signification of a name is 'assumed' in a demonstrative science investigating its 'primaries and their theorems' with respect to their being and what they are, what is signified by (a'), i.e., some account of what a name signifies, can be known through a demonstration leading to [B] or [C], as well as by other methods leading to [A] (76a31–36, 100b5–17). Since [B] and [C] are realized by gaining a continuous demonstration, (a') is assigned only for [A] the definition of the immediate terms of a science such as 'the unit' in the arithmetic (93b22–24). When we are considering the kind of thing whose cause is identical with the very thing under investigation, this type of definition [A] is gained through the activities of a demonstrative science as a whole. In this way, the *what it is* is set out in three types of definition, based on three types of defining-phrase, and allocated its proper position in a demonstrative science. This is how Aristotle succeeds in developing his combined heuristic demonstrative inquiry theory HDI.

Acknowledgements

I thank David Bronstein and Kyuichiro Takahashi for their helpful comments. I thank David Charles for his guidance on this treatise for more than 25 years. And I thank Christopher Shields for his detailed editorial comments and corrections.

Notes

1. By appealing to the ambiguity of the word '*epistêmê*', meaning either 'the cognitive activity of a knowing person' or 'a body of knowledge, a science—a system of propositions', M. Burnyeat claims that Aristotle did not distinguish philosophy of science from epistemology. (M. Burnyeat, 'Aristotle on Understanding Knowledge', *Aristotle on Science: The Posterior Analytics*, p. 97–99, 109–115, 138f (Padua 1981)). It is not the case, however, that Aristotle has left undiscussed the ambiguity of '*epistêmê*' among a cognitive state, a propositional object, and a science. When it is required to distinguish one of these possible meanings, he does so by employing non-ambiguous expressions.

   Aristotle describes '*epistêmê*' from two perspectives, either of the system of producing a propositional object or of grasping it. While the productive aspect is developed by employing the preposition '*ek* (from, based on)' accompanied by 'principles', the epistemic aspect is developed by employing the preposition '*dia* (through)' accompanied by 'demonstration', through which one grasps a cognitive state. 'The scientific preposition': '*ek*' is contrasted with 'the epistemic preposition': '*dia*'. When Aristotle employs '*ek*' with 'principles' or 'premises', he always uses it with a verb denoting inference such as 'to demonstrate' or 'deduce'. For instance, Aristotle says that '*from* truths (*eks alêthôn*) one can *deduce* (*sullogisasthai*) without demonstrating, but *from* necessities one cannot *deduce* without demonstrating' (74b15–17, e.g., 75a30, 76a14, 77b4f., 78a5). What is deduced is not immediately a cognitive state but a propositional object.

   On the other hand, '*epistêmê*' as a cognitive state is always accompanied not by '*ek*', but by '*dia*'. (While '*dia*' could be accompanied by the proof verbs, '*ek*' is never accompanied by the epistemic verbs (92b12,93a10)). For instance, Aristotle says 'anyone who is going to have knowledge *through* demonstration (*tên epistêmên di'apodeikseôs*) must not only be more familiar with the principles and better convinced because of them than of what is being proved' (72a37–39, e.g.,71b17, 83b38, 84a5, 87b19, 88a11, 99b20, cf. 79a25, 83b36, 86a36, 88b31). Aristotle did not think that one *knows* 'from principles' but *knows* 'through demonstration'.

   We should understand 'the demonstrative science' (e.g.,76a37, 84a10) primarily as the system or the method of generating knowledge *simpliciter* rather than a sequence of propositions or 'a system of propositions' as the result of scientific activity (M. Burnyeat). A system which makes '*epistêmê*' possible is itself called '*epistêmê*', too. In fact Aristotle says, by personifying it, 'Every demonstrative science (*pâsa apodeiktikê epistêmê*) demonstrates (*apodeiknusi*) from the primaries'(76b11–15).

   Thus his project for the ideal structure of yielding strict knowledge primarily results in the system of demonstrative science at the structural level, not at the cognitive level. Structure of science is conceptually distinguished from epistemology, i.e., how do we have knowledge, although both can be complementary in creating a unified theory of demonstration.

2. J. Barnes, in his second edition of *Aristotle Posterior Analytics* (Oxford 1993), recollected various responses to his idea in 1969 based on his sharp awareness of discrepancy between a full-fledged philosophical theory of axiomatized science and actual scientific practices. There he says 'I argued (in 1969) that in *APst* "Aristotle was not telling the scientist how to conduct his research: he was giving the pedagogue advice on the most efficient and economic method of bettering his charges. The theory of demonstration offers a formal account of how an achieved body of knowledge should be presented and taught". The negative side of this thesis—that *APst* does not present a theory of scientific method—is, I still think, certainly true; and it has been widely accepted.... *APst* is primarily concerned to investigate how the various facts and theories which practicing scientists discover or construct should be systematically organized and intelligibly presented' (xviii f.). In what follows, I shall argue that the theory of demonstration contains far more rich philosophical ideas and contents than Barnes claims.

3. D. Charles, *Aristotle on Meaning and Essence*, p. 70 (Oxford 2000).

4. Charles, *ibid.*, p. 71.

5. Since W. D. Ross and J. Barnes confused the linguistic qualification [Q1] how to express the items of inquiry with the ontological qualification [Q2] how to express the objects of inquiry, they were puzzled by the text that 'night' or 'eclipse' which 'is surely attribute' is dealt with by the route [II]. While Ross accuses Aristotle that 'he is making his vocabulary as he goes, and has not succeeded in making it as clear-cut as might be wished', Barnes falsely claims that 'Thus [Ia] and [IIa] are to be distinguished by the content and not the form of their interrogations' (W. D. Ross, *Aristotle's Prior and Posterior Analytics*, p. 610 (Oxford 1949), J. Barnes, *ibid.*, p. 203). Philoponus did not distinguish [Q1] from [Q2] by taking both at the ontological level. Neither J. Zabarella nor T. Waitz distinguished [Q1] from [Q2]. I. Philoponus, *Analytica Posteriora*, p. 338, ed. M.Wallies (Berlin 1909), J. Zabarella, *Opera Logica*, p. 1050 (Frankfurt 1608, 1966), T. Waitz, *Aristotelis Organon II*, p. 380 (Lipsiae 1844).

6. W. D. Ross, who failed to separate [Q1] from [Q2], says that '[II] the questions *ei esti* and *ti esti*, which in B.1 referred to substances, have in B.2 come to refer so much more to attributes and events that the former reference has almost receded from Aristotle's mind, although traces of it still remain'. J. Barnes even deletes the word (So) 'ousia' (90a10) in II 2 W. D. Ross, *ibid.*, p. 612, J. Barnes, *ibid.*, p. 48, 204.

7. Barnes, *ibid.*, p. 204.

8. Commentators take it that the last two *per se* predications are irrelevant to the demonstrative science (e.g. Philoponus, *ibid.*, p. 64, Zabarella, *ibid.*, p. 708, Ross, *ibid.*, p. 60, Barnes, *ibid.*, p. 114). In my view, the *per se* predication 3: 'what is not said of some other underlying belong to itself' characterizes the underlying subjects like unit or magnitude, i.e., primary terms of a science (73b5–8). The *per se* predication 4: 'what belongs to something because of itself (*di' hauto*) belongs to it in itself' characterizes the causal necessity through empirical investigation, by grasping 'no longer because of another thing (*ouketi di' allo*)' through the process of 'by other thing' (73b10f., 48a35, 85b30–86a3).

9. In 90b12–17, 'induction' which brings enough confidence is mentioned as a method of gaining knowledge of 'substance of something' by definition. This reading is contrasted with Barnes; *ibid.*, p. 50.

10. As to the theories of predicables and predications, see Chiba, 'Aristotle on Essence and Defining-phrase in his Dialectic', *Definition in Greek Philosophy*, ed., D. Charles (Oxford 2010), pp. 220–45.

11. On the dual function of signification, see K. Chiba, *ibid*, pp. 239–245. C. Shields discusses the dual function of signification in detail. C. Shields, *Order in Multiplicity: Homonymy in the Philosophy of Aristotle*, ch. 3 pp. 75ff (Oxford 1999).

12. W. Goodwin comments on the imperfect 'was' (*ên*) which usually accompanies the particles 'then (*pote* or *ara*) as follows; 'The imperfect 'was' (*ên*) (generally with '*ara*') may express a fact which is just recognized as such by the speaker or writer, having previously been denied, overlooked, or not understood'. I call this use of the imperfect the 'dialectical imperfect'. W. Goodwin, *Syntax of the Moods and Tenses of the Greek Verb*, p. 13 (London 1929).

13. There is an analogical case of this. When Aristotle faces a *theologia* (*metaphysica particularis*)-*ontologia* (*metaphysica generalis*) *aporia* concerning the first philosophy, he describes 'immovable substance' as 'being *universal* in this way, because it is *first*'(1026a30). The essence which is a causally basic unifying feature seems to universally permeate all elements unified by it. As to the Aristotelian explanatory approach which specifies the causally basic unifying feature, see in detail D. Charles, *ibid.*, ch. 8, pp. 197ff.

14. Barnes, *ibid.*, p. 207, Philoponus, *ibid.*, p. 365.

15. J. Zabarella, *ibid.*, p. 1110.

16. Ross, *ibid.*, 93a4: *ad loc.*, I. Bekker, *Aristotelis Opera Tomus I, ad loc.*(Oxonii 1837), Philoponus, *ibid.*, *ad loc.* In his discussion of MSS traditions, Ross himself admits in general that '*B* and *n*, then are the most important MSS' (*ibid.*, p. 89). This locution is also employed when Aristotle regards Platonic Ideas to be the causes for other things of their identities: 'while the Ideas are the causes of the *what it is* for other things (*tou ti estin aitia tois allois*), the unity is the one for ideas'(*Met*. I 6 988a10).

17. Charles, *ibid.*, p. 180. Zabarella, *ibid.*, p. 1110.

18. B. Landor, 'Aristotle on Demonstrating Essence', *Apeiron*, Vol. XIX. No. 2 , p. 130 (1985). In this paper, Landor sharply points out internal inconsistencies involved in the interpretations of such commentators as Philoponus, Le Blond, S. Mansion, J. Barnes on II 8–10. But he himself does not resolve them because he does not commit to the interpretation of essence as the causally basic unifying feature nor take the Bekker reading of the 93a4 '*aition tou ti esti*'.

19. As to the process of proof, see T. Heath, *Mathematics in Aristotle*, p. 37f (Oxford 1949).

20. As to the distinction of *horos* and *horismos*, see Chiba, *ibid.*, pp. 217–20. As to the theory of definition in II 10, see K. Chiba, 'Aristotle's Theory of Definition in *Posterior Analytics* B.10', *Journal of the Graduate School of Letters*, pp. 1–17 Vol. 3 2008. http://hdl.handle.net/2115/32407.

21. I read the first lines of II 10 as follows: 'Since a definition is said to be an account of the *what it is*, it is obvious (*phaneron*) that some account (*tis logos*) of what a name or name-like expression signifies will be it. For instance, the what 'triangle' signifies is what triangle is insofar as it is triangle. Grasping that the very thing [which is signified by 'triangle'] exists, we seek why it is. As to the things whose existence we do not know, however, it is difficult to assume [what the relevant name signifies] in this way (*houtôs labein*) [as the account of what it is]. The reason of the difficulty has been stated already [92b19–25] that we do not know whether it exists or not except accidentally'(93b29–35). (I read 93b31: '*to ti sêmainei, ti esti hê trigônon*' by following not Ross' but Bekker's text. As to the reading of 'to assume (*labein*)'(b32), see 92b15–17: 'While the geometer *assumed* (*elaben*) what 'triangle' signifies, he proves that it exists'(cf.76a33,76b7, 71a12)).

   When Aristotle makes an 'obviousness' claim on the relation between (a') some account of what a name signifies and a kind of definition, he has the four formal combinations between them in mind: (1)S^+E^+, (2)S^+E^-, (3)S^-E^+, (4)S^-E^-, where S^+ stands for grasping an account of what a name signifies and E^+ stands for grasping an account of *what it is*. Since (3) and (4) are excluded from the outset because of definition's linguistic characteristic (the dual function of signification) and (2) was already denied in II 7 92b26–34 because of definition's ontological characteristic, (1) alone among the signifying accounts (1) and (2) will *obviously* constitute a definition. This triangle example raises a case in which an account of what a name signifies is the account of *what it is*. 'Some account (phrase)' of signification will constitute a type of definition. See a parallel passage with 'some account (*tis logos*)' in *Topics* I 5 101b38–102a5: see in detail K. Chiba (2008).

BIBLIOGRAPHY

Barnes, J. (1993) *Aristotle Posterior Analytics* (Oxford).

Bekker, I. (1837) *Aristotelis Opera, Tomus I* (Oxford).

Burnyeat, M. (1981) 'Aristotle on Understanding Knowledge', in *Aristotle on Science: The Posterior Analytics* (Padua), 97–139.

Charles, D. (2000) *Aristotle on Meaning and Essence* (Oxford).

Chiba, K. (2008) 'Aristotle's Theory of Definition in *Posterior Analytics* B.10', *Journal of the Graduate School of Letters* 3 (Hokkaido), 1–17.

Chiba, K. (2010) 'Aristotle on Essence and Defining-phrase in his Dialectic', in D. Charles, ed. *Definition in Greek Philosophy* (Oxford), 203-251.

Goodwin,W. (1929) *Syntax of the Moods and Tenses of the Greek Verb* (London).

Heath,T. (1949) *Mathematics in Aristotle* (Oxford), 203-251.

Landor, B. (1985) 'Aristotle on Demonstrating Essence', *Apeiron* 19 (2), 116–132.

Philoponus, I. (1909) *In Aristotelis Analytica priora commentaria*, ed. M. Wallies (Berlin).

Ross, W.D. (1949) *Aristotle's Prior and Posterior Analytics* (Oxford).

Shields, C. (1999) *Order in Multiplicity: Homonymy in the Philosophy of Aristotle* (Oxford).

Waitz, W. (1844) *Aristotelis Organon II* (Leipzig).

Zabarella, J. (1966) *Opera Logica* (Frankfurt).

PART III

EXPLANATION AND NATURE

ALTERATION AND PERSISTENCE: FORM AND MATTER IN THE *PHYSICS* AND *DE GENERATIONE ET CORRUPTIONE*

S. MARC COHEN

I. *PHYSICS*

ARISTOTLE's *Physics* is a study of nature (*phusis*) and of natural objects (*ta phusei*). These objects, he says (*Phys.* I 2 185a12–13)—either all of them or at least some of them—are in motion. That is, they are *kinoumena*, things that are subject to change. He does not argue in support of this proposition; he simply lays it down without argument (*hupokeisthô*), for it is not the job of a philosophical study of nature to prove that there are things that can undergo change.

Parmenides had argued that change was altogether impossible, and Aristotle quite correctly notes that this position rules out the possibility of an account of nature. But even if Parmenides is wrong (and in *Physics* I 3 Aristotle exposes what he takes to be the fallacies in Parmenides' arguments), it is still incumbent upon a study of nature to provide an account of how change is possible. The first book of the *Physics* is largely devoted to this task.

Aristotle characterizes his project somewhat differently, however. First, his description of the phenomenon he wishes to explicate is not *change* but rather *coming-to-be* or *becoming* (*genesis*). And second, he says that he is attempting to provide the *first principles* (*archai*) of becoming. Nevertheless, our characterisation seems appropriate. For (1) the becoming or coming-to-be that Aristotle is discussing is what happens when something grows (becomes larger), or changes temperature (becomes hotter), or moves (comes to be in a different place), or comes into existence (comes to be, *simpliciter*). Coming-to-be, that is to say, is just changing in one way or another. And (2) the first principles of a given phenomenon are just the more basic concepts to which we must appeal in stating how that phenomenon occurs. So if we wish to understand what change is and how it occurs, we must provide its first principles.

In reviewing the history of his subject (as he so often does in introducing a topic for discussion) Aristotle points out that all his predecessors who recognize the reality of change 'identify the contraries with the principles' (188a27). That is, the Pre-socratic philosophers who (unlike Parmenides and Melissus) thought that change really occurs think that the notion of contrariety must be appealed to in accounting for change. Aristotle readily concurs, but he is not content merely to signal agreement. For, he insists, 'we must see how this can be arrived at as a reasoned result' (188a32).

Suppose we have a case in which 'white comes to be'[1] (188a35) and we try to account for it without the notion of contrariety. Perhaps a musician returns well tanned from a Caribbean vacation and stays indoors for a month at his piano, thereby losing his tan and becoming pale. What has happened? Well, he has acquired a new attribute—being pale. And what was he before being pale? To say 'he was musical' would be true, but irrelevant (188a35-b2):

> For how could white come from musical, unless musical happened to be an attribute of the not-white or of the black? No, white comes from not-white...Similarly, musical comes to be from non-musical.

So 'becomes white from being musical' is not the correct way to describe this case of becoming (even if it was the musician's devotion to his craft that led him to stay out of the sun and sit all day at his piano). The correct description brings out that there are not just a pair of attributes involved, but a pair of *contrary* attributes.[2]

One might well complain that there is no need to make explicit an attribute that antedates the change—to say 'becomes white *from being black*'—since 'becomes white' by itself entails that there was a change. After all, a thing that was already white cannot *become* white. But this misses the point of Aristotle's analysis. For he is trying to provide the first principles of becoming, and so cannot allow any of the implications of the term 'becomes' to creep into his account without explicit acknowledgement.

An easy way to do this (although it is not Aristotle's way) is to leave 'becomes' out of the account altogether and make do with attributes and tenses of the verb 'to be'. Instead of saying 'from being musical it becomes white' we would have to say 'first (at t_1) it was musical, and later (at t_2) it was white'. And the inadequacy of this formulation is immediately apparent, for it is does not entail that there was any coming-to-be at all. Even if our musician was pale all along, it would still be true that at t_1 he was musical and at t_2 he was white. What is missing, of course, is anything that entails that he *became* white, viz., that at t_1 he was not-white. So we need more than time and attributes in our account, but time and *contrary* attributes.

Aristotle thus concludes, at the end of *Physics* I 5, that the principles will be at least two—a *pair* of contraries for each case of coming-to-be. But that will not be enough, as he argues in the next chapter (189a22–26):

> For it is difficult to see how either density should be of such a nature as to act in any way on rarity or rarity on density. The same is true of any other pair of contraries...both act on a third thing different from both.

This third principle Aristotle dubs the *underlying thing* (*hupokeimenon*), a term often translated as *subject* or *substratum*. In most cases the underlying thing is what persists through the change. For example, in Aristotle's case of the pale musician, the subject is the man who once was dark and became pale. And, in general, in any change there is something, x, such that x was F at t_1 and x was G at t_2, where t_1 and t_2 are different times and F and G are contraries.[3] This is a rough, preliminary, characterisation of the tripartite analysis of becoming that Aristotle settles on in *Physics* I 7.

But when he takes up the topic of change again in *Physics* V,[4] Aristotle uses slightly different terminology for the ingredients of his analysis. He points out that 'every change is *from* something and *to* something' (225a1), and these two 'somethings' are traditionally called the *termini* of change: (1) the *terminus a quo* (the 'from which'—an attribute[5] possessed by the subject at the start of the change that is no longer present after the change) and (2) the *terminus ad quem* (the 'to which'—an opposed attribute possessed by the subject at the completion of the change but not present at the start). Curiously, however, Aristotle goes on to describe these *termini* as 'subject' (*hupokeimenon*) and 'non-subject' (*mê hupokeimenon*), according as the terms used are positive (e.g., 'musical') or negative ('non-musical'). It is possible that he is using *hupokeimenon* here in an entirely different sense, but it is more likely that he thinks that there is more than one thing that can correctly be considered the *hupokeimenon* of change.

This suspicion is borne out by an examination of Aristotle's discussion of the example with which he begins *Physics* I 7: the case of the man who becomes musical. Aristotle focuses on 'that which becomes' (*to gignomenon*) and 'what it becomes' (*ho gignetai*)—clearly the *termini* of the change—and he says (190a15) that the *gignomenon* is what 'underlies' (*hupokeisthai*), i.e., is the subject of the change. And at 190a2–5, Aristotle applies the terms *gignomenon* and *ho gignetai* to any of the following: the man, the musical, the not-musical, the musical man, and the not-musical man. Only one of these items (the man) persists through the change, so it is clear that the subject (*hupokeimenon*) of change is not always the persisting item, but may be one of the *termini*.

I have claimed that either of the *termini* might be considered the subject of the change, but it might be objected that Aristotle has made room only for the *terminus a quo*. For 190a15 explicitly recognizes *to gignomenon* as *a hupokeimenon*, but says nothing about *ho gignetai*, which we have taken to be the *terminus ad quem*. But in fact he uses the term *gignomenon* more loosely, sometimes applying it to the *terminus ad quem*. For example, at 190b11, he says:

> ...there is, on the one hand, something which comes to be (*ti gignomenon*), and, on the other, the thing which comes to be that (*ho touto gignetai*).

Here the *gignomenon* must be the *terminus ad quem*—the object that results at the end of the change—since it is being contrasted with *ho touto gignetai* ('the thing which comes to be that'), which is either the *terminus a quo* or the persisting element. The importance of keeping the *terminus ad quem* in the running as a possible subject of change will emerge as we proceed.

Still, it is not immediately apparent why Aristotle should say that a non-persisting *terminus* may be the subject of the change, since in the example that he discusses at such length in *Physics* I 7 it seems so clear that it is the man—i.e., the persisting item—that is the subject. It is the man, after all, who is first unmusical and later becomes musical. In what sort of case might the subject be a non-persisting item?

We get our answer at 190a31–33, where Aristotle distinguishes between simple and qualified coming-to-be:

> Things are said to come to be in many ways, and some things are said, not to come to be, but to come to be something, while only substances are said to come to be without qualification (*haplôs*[6]).

Qualified coming-to-be, or becoming *something*, is expressed by the use of a complement with the verb 'becomes' (*gignetai*)—'becomes pale' or 'becomes musical'. The use of the complement indicates that the becoming is not the coming into existence of a new subject, but the alteration of an already existing one. In qualified coming-to-be, the man does not come to be, full-stop, but comes to be pale or musical. A case of coming-to-be without qualification, by contrast, occurs when the subject comes into, or goes out of, existence. In such a case, of course, the subject of the change cannot be the persisting item. For the persisting item in a given change does not come into or go out of existence in that change.

One might well complain that it is entirely arbitrary whether one characterizes a becoming as qualified or unqualified. Take the case of the man who becomes musical. If one takes the subject of the change to be the man, we have qualified coming-to-be, for the man does not come into existence; rather, he comes to be *something*, that is, he becomes musical. But suppose we take the *terminus ad quem*—the musical—to be the subject; then we would seem to have a case of unqualified coming-to-be. For something new has come into existence; after the change there was one more musician in the world than there had been before. So one and the same case of becoming can be described either as qualified becoming (a man's becoming musical) or as unqualified becoming (a musician's coming into being).

Aristotle, however, resists this temptation. At 190a33 he tells us that 'only substances are said to come to be without qualification'. (Hence unqualified coming-to-be is sometimes called 'substantial change'—change that involves the generation or destruction of a substance.) And at *Gen. et Corr.* I 4 (319b25–31) he discusses this very example, pointing out that the reason we do not have here a case of unqualified coming-to-be is that the persisting subject of the change is a man, a substance.

The coming-to-be of a musician is therefore *not* an unqualified coming-to-be, but merely an alteration in the 'underlying' man who becomes musical. This result fits in well with Aristotle's theory of categories, according to which *musician* (as opposed to *man* or *tiger*) would not be considered a term for a substance, but rather a term for a compound of a substance and a quality. And the coming-to-be of such a compound is not an unqualified coming-to-be, but merely an alteration of its underlying substance. (Hence qualified coming-to-be is sometimes called 'accidental change'—a change through which a substance[7] persists as its subject.)

The change in the case of the musical man, that is to say, is a change in *quality*—what Aristotle elsewhere describes as alteration, *alloiôsis*. In alteration, the persisting subject of the change is a substance (e.g., a man) and the contraries are a pair of incompatible qualities. Similarly, there are changes in which the persisting subject is a substance and the two *termini* are drawn from other categories. In *Physics* V 1, Aristotle adds quantity and place as categories in which substances can undergo *kinêsis*, for clearly substances grow and move about.

Most of the examples Aristotle discusses in *Physics* I are of accidental change. But it is clear that he thinks that his tripartite analysis of coming-to-be in *Physics* I 7 accommodates substantial change, as well. As we will see, however, such an accommodation introduces some new complexities.

Aristotle raises the issue at 190b1–10:

> But that substances too . . . come to be from some underlying thing, will appear on examination. For we find in every case something that underlies from which that which comes to be proceeds; for instance, animals and plants from seed. Things which come to be without qualification, come to be in different ways: by change of shape, as a statue; by addition, as things which grow; by taking away, as the Hermes from the stone; by putting together, as a house; by alteration, as things which turn in respect of their matter. It is plain that these are all cases of coming to be from some underlying thing.

We have been presented with a variety of cases in which a substance comes to be 'from some underlying thing' (*ex hupokeimenou tinos*), but it is clear that not all of these underlying things are on the same footing. In the first case, we get the result we would expect. An animal or plant is generated out of a seed (*sperma*). The seed is the *terminus a quo* of the change, and so does not persist in the result. But, of course, we view the change as the generation of a plant or animal, not the destruction of a seed, so from that perspective the subject of the change is the *terminus ad quem*—the plant or animal that comes into existence.[8]

But the situation is different in the other cases Aristotle cites. In the case of the statue, the underlying thing would appear to be the bronze from which (and of which) the statue is made. Once the bronze has been appropriately shaped, we no longer simply have some bronze, but a statue made of bronze. The bronze, however, was present both before and after the change, so if this is to be a case of substantial change, the bronze cannot be its *hupokeimenon* in the sense required for a substantial change. The case of a statue made of stone ('Hermes from the stone') is different in one respect—we have *taking away*, not *change of shape*, as the relevant operation—but it is the same in other respects. For the stone, like the bronze, is a persisting item—the stone is still there in the resulting statue. Similarly, the generation of a house occurs when the bricks, boards, nails, etc., of which it is to be constructed get put together in the appropriate way (i.e., in accordance with the plans drawn up by the architect). Once again, the *hupokeimenon* that Aristotle has identified seems to be something that persists in the *terminus ad quem*, which would disqualify the example as a case of substantial change.

It seems clear that Aristotle has been using *hupokeimenon* in two different ways in this passage, sometimes to pick out the persisting element and sometimes to pick out one of the *termini*. I surmise that at this stage in his discussion of the topic of becoming, he has not yet fully disentangled these two different senses of *hupokeimenon*. It is apparent that he needs a special term for the persisting element in a change, which will be the subject, in that sense, of substantial as well as accidental changes. And a brief survey of his examples in 190b1–10 makes it clear what we should expect that to be. For in all the examples in which the *hupokeimenon* is a persisting item (bricks and boards in the case of a house, bronze in the case of a statue, stone in the case of Hermes), the persisting *hupokeimenon* is what Aristotle would describe as matter (*hulê*). The one example of a non-persisting *hupokeimenon* is the seed, which clearly is not the matter of the resulting plant or animal.

That the persisting item—whatever it might be—can be called the matter of the change is immediately suggested at 190b25, where Aristotle lists *man* alongside *gold* as an example of matter. From the point of view of an ontological classification, of course, *man* is not matter, but substance. But when a man is the persisting element in a change (e.g., when he becomes musical), the man is the matter of the change. The point is finally stated explicitly in *Physics* I 9 (192a32–33):

> For my definition of matter is just this—the primary *hupokeimenon* of each thing,
> from which it comes to be, and *which persists in the result* ....

Aristotle now has the ingredients in place to provide a single analysis that covers all cases of coming-to-be and still permits a distinction between accidental and substantial change. Just as a substance is the persisting element (the 'matter') that is present in both of the *termini* of accidental change, so too there is matter that persists (and so, in a sense 'underlies') in cases of substantial change, where the substance that is generated or destroyed is not available to be the persisting item.

Incorporating substantial change into his tripartite analysis, however, requires Aristotle to modify it. For although he will insist that every change has a persisting element, he can no longer maintain that the *termini* will always be a pair of contraries or even a pair of intermediates on a scale whose end points are contraries. The reason is simple: substances do not have contraries (*Cat.* 3b24). So the generation of a horse or a statue cannot have as its *terminus a quo* the contrary of a horse or of a statue, for there are no such things.

Aristotle addresses the issue at 190b11:

> Thus, from what has been said, whatever comes to be is always complex. There is, on the one hand, something which comes to be [the *terminus ad quem*], and, on the other, the thing which comes to be that—the latter in two senses, either the subject [*hupokeimenon*] or the opposite [*terminus a quo*]. By the opposite I mean the unmusical, by the subject, man; and similarly I call the *absence of shape or form or order* the opposite, and the bronze or stone or gold the subject.

Notice that 'contrary' (*enantion*) has now been replaced by 'opposite' (*antikeimenon*), a more generic term (see *Cat.* 10 and *Met.* V 10) covering more cases of opposition than strict contrariety. In the case of the generation of a substance, the *terminus a quo* is simply the lack or privation (*sterêsis*) of the form of that substance in the matter underlying the change. A statue comes to be when bronze or stone acquires a certain form or shape. In general, the generation of a substance consists of the appropriate matter taking on the appropriate form. Whereas the three ingredients of accidental change are a substance and a pair of contraries, the three ingredients of substantial change are matter, form, and privation.

At this stage, it would appear that the underlying matter in a given substantial change is some specific kind of stuff, the kind in question dependent on the type of substance being generated. Thus, statues are made of bronze or stone, houses of bricks and boards, animals of flesh, etc. Each kind of change has some specific kind of matter as its persisting ingredient. But what Aristotle says at 190a9–12 is often taken to suggest quite a different idea:

> The *hupokeimenon* can be known by analogy. For as the bronze is to the statue, the wood to the bed, or the matter and the formless before receiving form to any thing which has form, so is the *hupokeimenon* to substance, i.e., the 'this' or existent.

Bronze and wood seem to be presented here as analogues rather than as examples of the persisting element in substantial change: what persists in a substantial change stands to the substance that is generated as bronze stands to the statue that is made of it. After all, bronze and wood can be known by perception, and so can be known more directly than merely by analogy. But if bronze cannot serve as the persisting element in substantial change, one might well wonder what kind of matter Aristotle has in mind. A common answer is *prime* matter—a kind of matter that (unlike bronze or stone) has no form or nature of its own, and so can serve as a subject for more determinate kinds of matter such as bronze and stone and hence as the ultimate subject of the substances composed of those kinds of matter. Such matter is not perceptible, and hence its existence must be hypothesized; it is known only by analogy to the more determinate kinds of matter that we can perceive.

Whether in this passage Aristotle is alluding to prime matter, and even whether he endorses the concept of prime matter anywhere in his works, are issues that have long been in dispute. We will defer discussion of the second issue until section

II. As for the first, we can safely note that the account that he gives in the *Physics* of the generation and destruction of substances does not explicitly endorse or by itself logically commit him to the employment of such a concept. First, the claim that the *hupokeimenon* can be known by analogy does not entail that the stuff that serves as the persisting element is not perceptible. What we know by analogy is not the nature of the persisting element in a given substantial change but the role that it plays in the generation of a substance—a role analogous to that of bronze in the generation of a statue, or wood in the generation of a bed. Any such analogue of bronze or stone may, for all this passage requires, be determinate and perceptible. Second, although Aristotle's tripartite analysis of becoming maintains that for every change there is a persisting element, it does not require that there be a single element so basic that it persists through every change. The account of substantial change in the *Physics* is devoid of any commitment to prime matter.[9]

II. *De Generatione et Corruptione*

Aristotle takes up the topics of alteration and coming-to-be again in *Gen. et Corr.*, announcing near the beginning of the work (314a5–7) that we must inquire:

> whether we are to suppose that the nature of alteration and generation is the same or different, as they are certainly distinguished in name.

The inquiry begins in *Gen. et Corr.* I 3. The conclusions Aristotle would like to reach are that there is a viable distinction between generation and alteration, that both occur, and that neither can be reduced to the other. We recall that his position in the *Physics* is that the difference between alteration and generation is that the former is qualified coming-to-be (coming to be *something*) whose persisting element is a substance, while the latter is unqualified coming-to-be (coming-to-be *simpliciter*) in which a substance is generated or destroyed. Not surprisingly, Aristotle refers (317b14) to his solution in the *Physics*, but also announces—with uncommon candor—that even granted the distinctions on which that solution is based:

> there remains a question of remarkable difficulty, which we must take up once again, namely, how is coming to be simpliciter possible.... (317b17–19)

The reason for his continued puzzlement is not hard to discern. The solution he offered in the *Physics* treated generation (which is one kind of substantial change) as a change whose *terminus ad quem* is a substance that is the subject of the change, but it still allowed there to be a *hupokeimenon* in another sense—the matter that persists through the change. But given that even in generation we have something that persists, it would seem reasonable to insist that here too we have a case in which the subject (the matter) becomes *something* (i.e., takes on a form that it lacked before the change). Viewed in this way, our alleged case of generation seems to be a kind of alteration (or qualified coming-to-be) after all. From this perspective, the (alleged) coming-to-be of a substance turns out to be merely an alteration of its underlying matter.[10] So how, after all, is coming-to-be *simpliciter* possible?

It might be tempting to suppose that we could distinguish coming-to-be *simpliciter* from alteration by claiming that in the former there is nothing that persists through the change. For there can be no alteration if there is no subject that persists through it. But, not surprisingly, Aristotle resists this temptation, for it would involve abandoning what he takes to be his distinctive and novel contribution to the solution of the problem of change. An alternative that he does consider is that in coming-to-be *simpliciter* the *terminus a quo* is 'not being *simpliciter*' (317b11). But he quickly abandons this alternative, for it threatens to reintroduce the Parmenidean puzzles that he was trying to solve in the first place (317b29–31):

> the principal and perpetual fear of the early philosophers will be realized, namely, the coming to be of something from nothing previously existing.

Aristotle begins his assault on this problem by addressing a seemingly different question, but one that he thinks will help point the way to a solution to the main problem: how is it that generation and destruction continue to occur, again and again (318a16–20)?

> If some one of the things which exist is always disappearing, why has not the universe been entirely spent and taken its departure long ago, if, that is, there was only a limited quantity of matter for the generation of each of the things coming into being? For it is certainly not because the matter of generation is infinite that it does not give out. That is impossible....

His solution is to adopt a kind of conservation principle (318a24–25): 'the corruption of one thing is the generation of another, and vice versa'. Notice that this principle is stronger than what is needed merely to avoid the result that it would take only a finite series of corruptions to culminate in the disappearance of all material objects. The problem of disappearance could be solved by a weaker principle: that the corruption of one thing is always accompanied by the generation of another.[11] But the weaker principle does not foreclose the familiar Parmenidean worry, for it leaves open the possibility that the corruption of any object x (*in nihil*) is always accompanied by the generation of some other object y (*ex nihilo*). The stronger principle, however, denies that the generation and corruption in question are two distinct changes. It does not claim merely that the corruption of x is simultaneous with the generation of y, but that the corruption of x and the generation of y are one and the same event. So x is not corrupted into nothingness, but into y, and y is not generated *ex nihilo*, but *ex x*.

But the conservation principle raises questions of its own. Aristotle puts it this way (318a28–30):

> Why are some things said to come to be and to cease to be *simpliciter* and others not *simpliciter*,...if one and the same thing is both the generation of A and the perishing of B, and vice versa? (*Dia ti de pote ta men haplôs ginesthai legesthai kai*

phtheiresthai to d' oukh haplôs,...eiper to auto esti genesis men toudi phthora de toudi, kai phthora men toudi genesis de toudi).

This appears to be a question about the distinction (D_1) between substantial and accidental change, and it is not immediately apparent why the conservation principle should raise this question. The conservation principle seems to entail that no substantial change is exclusively a generation, rather than a corruption, or vice versa; it does not seem on its face to threaten D_1. It is rather the distinction (D_2) between generation and corruption that seems threatened: if every generation is also a corruption, and vice versa, why are some substantial changes considered simply[12] generations (rather than corruptions), and others simply corruptions (rather than generations)?

Aristotle's answer makes it clear that, at least initially, it is D_2 that he has in mind. At 318b19 he gives the view of 'most people' (*tois pollois*) concerning the distinction he is discussing:

> ...when the change is to perceptible matter, they say that generation occurs, when to matter that is not apparent, corruption. They distinguish what is and what is not by their perceiving or not perceiving it....

Clearly, this is a theory about D_2, the distinction between generation and corruption: where the *terminus ad quem* is perceptible (and the *terminus a quo* is not), people call the change a generation; where the *terminus a quo* is perceptible (and the *terminus ad quem* is not), they call the change a corruption. Presumably, if this theory about D_2 were to be extended to D_1, it would hold that whereas substantial change involves imperceptible matter as one of the *termini*, alteration would be a change from perceptible matter to perceptible matter.[13] Yet Aristotle never puts forward any such view as one that the many might hold about D_1.

At any rate, they are wrong about D_2, Aristotle says (318b27–32), for on their account something's turning into wind or air would be a corruption, and something's turning into earth would be a generation, whereas 'in truth wind and air are more *some this* and form (*tode ti kai eidos*) than earth is'. So the view of the many doesn't get the distinction between generation and corruption right in all cases. The correct view, Aristotle thinks (318b1ff.), is that it depends on which of the *termini* is an individual substance (*tode ti*), for it is only substances that can be said to be *simpliciter*. So, presumably, when a tree is burned into ashes—a change that the conservation principle counts as both the corruption of the tree and the generation of the ashes—we have a case of corruption *simpliciter*, since the *terminus a quo* is a substance. On the other hand, when a seed grows into a tree, the *terminus ad quem* is a substance, and so we have a case of generation *simpliciter*. So much for D_2.

By 319a5, Aristotle has finally made the distinction between D_1 and D_2 explicit, and points out that although he has dealt adequately with D_2, he has not yet addressed D_1:

> ...all that has so far been determined is why, when every instance of corruption is the generation of something else, we do not attribute 'coming to be' and 'ceasing to be' impartially to the things which change into one another; but the problem

that was mentioned later was not this, but why that which learns is not said to come to be *simpliciter* but to come to be knowledgeable, whereas that which is born *is* said to come to be.

But the conservation principle still seems to pose a threat even to D_1. Take the case of the generation of a statue. It comes to be not *ex nihilo* but out of an unformed piece of bronze—out of matter and privation, as the account in the *Physics* puts it. The generation of the statue, according to the conservation principle, is the destruction of something, but of what? The only plausible candidate[14] seems to be the privation of form in the bronze, for that is what is 'destroyed' when the bronze is formed into a statue. But once put that way it becomes obvious that there still seems to be alteration, or qualified coming-to-be, here: the bronze was unformed, and comes to be something (*gignetai ti*), viz., a statue. Even if the coming-to-be of the statue is the corruption of the unformed state of the bronze, it still turns out to be an alteration in the piece of bronze that persists through the change.

Aristotle's solution is that 'this distinction (i.e., D_1) is made in terms of the categories' (319a12–13):

> For some things signify an individual (*tode ti*), some a quality, some a quantity. So those which do not signify substance (*ousia*) are not said to come to be *simpliciter* but to come to be something.

'That which learns' (*to manthanon*) is not a substance, and so does not come to be *simpliciter*. The coming to be of that which learns is in fact an alteration of an underlying substance—a man comes to be knowledgeable. The coming to be of the statue (a case which Aristotle does not actually discuss here) would presumably be regarded as a generation, since the statue that comes to be is a substance.[15] If this were an alteration, its persisting subject would be the piece of bronze. But since that does not count as a substance,[16] the subject of this change is not the matter that persists through it but its *terminus ad quem*.

Although the defense of D_1 might seem to be complete, Aristotle takes up the topic once again and devotes all of the brief chapter 4 to it. It is important to understand why he believes that D_1 is still in need of examination. In the cases of substantial change that he has discussed so far (e.g., the ones catalogued at *Physics* 190b1–10), it is clear that even when a substance is generated or destroyed, there is some matter that persists through the change—bronze in the case of a statue, or wood in the case of a house. But in *Gen. et Corr.* he is going to move on to cases of elemental transformation (e.g., air into water), and in these it is less obvious what, if anything, persists. So the problem will be to show that a tripartite account of change in general (along the lines of *Physics* I 7) that applies to both generation and alteration still allows for a viable distinction between them. To put the point another way: if there are substantial changes through which nothing persists, how can any change through which something does persist, such as the non-elemental ones catalogued in the *Physics*, be considered genuine coming-to-be *simpliciter*?

Any account of Aristotle's treatment of this topic is bound to be controversial, for it hinges (as noted in section I) on the much-disputed issue of his commitment to prime matter. On the traditional account, Aristotle posits (although perhaps only implicitly) an imperceptible prime matter as the thing that persists in cases of elemental transformation; according to many recent commentators, however, his account of such transformations does not include or require prime matter.[17] The interpretation presented here falls into the traditional camp, but the reader is advised to consult the copious literature on this topic for alternative readings on points of detail.

Aristotle begins *Gen. et Corr.* I 4 by pointing out (319b8–10) that all changes involve both a subject (*hupokeimenon*) and an attribute (*pathos*) of a sort that can be predicated of the subject, and says that either one of these is capable of 'change' (*metabolê*). Clearly he does not mean that either can *undergo* change, since a *pathos* is not capable of change in that sense—it cannot undergo change. Rather, he means that either is capable of being *replaced*.[18] The difference between alteration and generation depends on which of these gets replaced.

Aristotle begins with alteration (319b10–12):

> It is alteration when the *hupokeimenon* remains, being something perceptible, but change occurs (*metaballei*) in the *pathê* which belong to it, whether these are contraries or intermediates.

This characterisation of accidental change accords with our expectations. For the subject is a persisting substance, and the *termini* are a pair of opposed attributes, one of which 'replaces' the other. Since Aristotle says that either *hupokeimenon* or *pathos* can be replaced, one might assume that he is also suggesting that either can persist. If so, substantial change would occur when a *pathos* remains but the *hupokeimenon* of which it is a pathos gets replaced by another *hupokeimenon*.[19] But this reading is problematic.

First, how can a pathos remain if the *hupokeimenon* of which it is a pathos gets replaced? Aristotle's usual doctrine is that *pathê* are ontologically dependent items that depend for their existence on the subjects in which they inhere. Second, since there are cases in which one element is transformed into another with which it shares no *pathos* (e.g., fire into water, as Aristotle explicitly recognizes at *Gen. et Corr.* II 4 331b6 and II 5 332b24), there are substantial changes in which no *pathos* can be the persisting item. So it is not likely that he is claiming in *Gen. et Corr.* I 4 that in substantial change the *pathos* persists after the *hupokeimenon* of which it was an attribute has ceased to exist.

We had better examine Aristotle's text more closely. As we will see, he does not in fact assert that in substantial change a *pathos* is the persisting item, but strongly suggests that an imperceptible *hupokeimenon* does persist. In contrast to alteration, in which a perceptible *hupokeimenon* remains (319b10), Aristotle says this about substantial change (319b14–17):

> When, however, the whole thing changes without anything perceptible remaining as the same *hupokeimenon*, but the way the seed changes entirely into blood, water into air, or air entirely into water, then . . . it is a case of generation (and corruption of something else) . . . .

There is no mention here of a *pathos* persisting. Indeed, the passage does not strictly assert that *anything* persists, and Aristotle's claim that there is 'nothing perceptible remaining as the same *hupokeimenon*' (*mê hupomenontos aisthêtou tinos hôs hupokeimenou tou autou*) has been taken to mean that there is nothing at all that persists as *hupokeimenon* (i.e., no underlying matter persists) and hence that the only thing left that could persist is a *pathos* of the *terminus a quo*. But the claim that nothing perceptible persists *as subject* (*hôs hupokeimenou*) does not entail that nothing persists.[20] Nor does it entail that something does persist, of course, but at the very least it invites the question: And what if something imperceptible persists as subject?[21] This question seems even more appropriate given that Aristotle has characterized alteration as a change in which a *perceptible* subject persists. If he thought that *nothing* persisted as subject in substantial change, there would have been no point in saying that something *perceptible* persists in alteration. It would have been more to the point to say simply that in alteration the subject persists, and in substantial change it does not.

It is true, of course, that in one sense the *hupokeimenon* of a substantial change does not persist (the subject in that sense is the substance generated or destroyed). But that leaves room, as we have seen, for a subject in another sense that does persist—something that stands to the substance as bronze does to the statue, the matter that persists through the change (as Aristotle has told us in *Physics* I 9, there must be in every change). Since the changes under consideration are at the elemental level, the persisting *hupokeimenon* will be imperceptible.

It is true that in the next (unfortunately convoluted) paragraph (319b20–23), Aristotle does discuss cases in which a *pathos* persists through a change, but this can hardly be a basis for saying that in substantial change the persisting item must be a *pathos*. For although his precise point here is somewhat obscure, it is clear that he takes the possibility of a *pathos* persisting to threaten the substantiality of the change and to make it count, instead, as an alteration. There is no suggestion that substantial changes are ones in which a *pathos* is the persisting item. Nor is there any suggestion that in substantial changes *nothing* persists. The point, rather, is that nothing *perceptible* persists.

Gen. et Corr. I 4 thus seems to support the following interpretation: (1) although in substantial change a *terminus* as *hupokeimenon* is generated or destroyed, a *hupokeimenon* in another sense persists through the change, and (2) in the case of elemental transformation, what persists is imperceptible prime matter. It is now time to see whether this interpretation is supported by Aristotle's discussion of elemental transformation in *Gen. et Corr.* II.

In *Gen. et Corr.* II 1–5, Aristotle lays out his theory of 'the so-called elements (*stoicheia*)' (328b31) and how they are generated and destroyed. He has in mind the four elements of the sublunary realm first hypothesized by Empedocles—earth, air, fire, and water—and he uses the term 'so-called' (*kaloumena*) advisedly, since on his theory they are not really elemental in the sense of being basic, ungenerable, and indestructible principles (*archai*). He prefers to call them 'primary bodies' (*sômata prôta*) or 'simple bodies' (*hapla sômata*), typically reserving the term *stoicheia* for the differentiae (essential properties) of these bodies.[22] The reason the primary bodies are not truly elements, on his view, is that they can be generated and destroyed, in that they are capable of being transformed into one another. It is the burden of these chapters to give an account of such transformations.

Gen. et Corr. II 1 announces that the generation of the primary bodies involves both matter and 'contrarieties', i.e., pairs of contrary properties such as wet-dry and hot-cold (329a24–26):

> Our view is that there is a matter of the perceptible bodies, but that this is not separable but is always together with a contrariety, from which the so-called 'elements' come to be.

The wording is ambiguous: the grammatical antecedent of the word 'which' (*hês*) in 'from which' might be 'matter' (*hulên*) or 'contrariety' (*enantiôseôs*).[23] But although both readings are grammatically possible, better sense is made of the passage if we take 'matter' to be the antecedent.[24] For although the thing 'from which' a primary body comes to be might be in one sense the persisting matter and in another the *terminus a quo*, that *terminus* would always be a contrary (e.g., wet) not a contrariety (e.g., the pair wet-dry).

So there is matter underlying the primary bodies, and this matter is involved in their generation. But is it prime matter, i.e., matter that is devoid of perceptible essential properties? We are told that this matter is 'not separable' (*ou chôristên*) and 'always together with a contrariety'. And this might suggest that the matter in question is ordinary empirical matter, the kind which is 'inseparable' and 'together with a contrariety' in the sense that it cannot exist without the perceptible characteristics which make up its essential properties. Thus, for example, air is not separable from its essential properties of wetness and hotness, for air just is the primary body that is defined by this pair of characteristics. But this cannot be what Aristotle means here. For air cannot be an example of the matter underlying the primary bodies since air is one of the primary bodies.

So it must be prime matter that Aristotle here has in mind. In what sense, then, can *it* be said to be 'not separable'? The point cannot be that the matter in question is inseparable from (i.e., cannot be devoid of) its perceptible essential properties, for it has no such properties. Rather, the point is that it can never be found 'neat', that is, without being the matter of one of the primary bodies and hence underlying the essential properties of whatever primary body it is the matter of at a given point in time. 'Separate' here does not mean 'without its essential properties' but 'on its own, without underlying something or other'.

Aristotle goes on (329a29) to describe the matter thus identified as 'a principle that is really first' (*archên men kai prôtên*); he gives a secondary status to the contrarieties that it underlies, and 'only thirdly are fire and water and the like' (329a35). Elemental transformation will thus be accounted for in terms of the basic contrarieties and the matter that underlies them. The next chapter, *Gen. et Corr.* II 2, investigates these contrarieties.

The basic contrarieties provide the 'forms and principles' (*eidê kai archas*, 329b9) of the primary bodies, but not all contrarieties do so. Whiteness and blackness, for example, or sweetness and bitterness, do not 'make an element' (*ouden poiei stoi-cheion*, 329b14). This means that such properties are not differentiae of any of the primary bodies. In order to be a differentia of a primary body, a property has to be tangible, i.e., perceptible by the sense of touch. This narrows down the candidate contrarieties to the following: hot-cold, dry-wet, heavy-light, hard-soft, viscous-brittle, rough-smooth, and coarse-fine (329b18). Of these it is the first two (hot-cold and dry-wet) that are basic, and it is the burden of the rest of the chapter to show that the remaining ones are reducible to these two. Aristotle concludes that there are really only four tangible properties that serve as the differentiae for all four of the primary bodies (330a24–25):

> ...all the other differentiae are reducible to these four primary ones [heat, cold, wetness, dryness], whereas these cannot further be reduced to any smaller number.

Gen. et Corr. II 3 shows how the four primary bodies—fire, air, water, and earth—can be accounted for in terms of combinations of these four basic tangible properties. Abstractly, Aristotle notes, four properties can combine pair-wise in six different ways, but of the four properties we are dealing with (HCWD) there are only four possible combinations: HD, HW, CD, CW. 'It is impossible,' Aristotle notes, 'for one and the same thing to be both hot and cold, or, again, wet and dry' (330a32). So each of the four primary bodies has as its differentiae one of these four logically consistent pairs of elemental properties: fire is dry and hot, air is hot and wet, water is wet and cold, earth is cold and dry. Note that so arranged, the four primary bodies form a cyclical order in which each has exactly one elementary property in common with each of its neighbors.

In *Gen. et Corr.* II 4, Aristotle turns to the topic of the reciprocal transformation of the primary bodies. His aim is to describe how the transformations occur, and to determine whether 'every one can come to be from every other one' (331a11). The last question is important for our purposes, since it bears on the issue of whether a *pathos* might be the persisting ingredient in an elemental transformation. If a persisting *pathos* were required, only some such transformations could occur. Fire could turn into air (since both are hot), but not into water (since they have no differentia in common that might persist through the transformation); likewise, air could turn into water (since both are wet), but not into earth. But in fact, Aristotle asserts, 'all are by nature able to change into each other' (331a13; cf. also 332b27). He notes that when two primary bodies do not have a differentia in common—are not 'consecutive' (*ephexês*) in the cycle,[25] he says—the transformation is 'more difficult' (331b7) and 'takes longer' (331b12).

Aristotle describes the primary bodies (such as fire and water) that do not have a differentia in common as 'contraries' (331a2). It is possible that he thinks that the transformation of a body into its contrary takes longer because the transformation would have to be indirect. Fire would not transform directly into water, but would first have to transform into one of the two, air or earth, that are next to it in the cyclical order.[26] For example, if the dryness of fire is replaced by wetness, it would transform into air, which could in turn transform into water when its warmth is replaced by coldness. But even if Aristotle thinks that this is the only way the reciprocal transformation of contraries can take place, it does not support the 'persisting *pathos*' interpretation. For even if Aristotle thinks that fire transforms into water only by becoming air or earth first, he explicitly states, as we have seen above, both that fire can transform into water and that no *pathos* of fire persists in the water it turns into. The only thing that can persist in the transformation of non-neighbors in the cycle is their common matter.

Finally, Aristotle argues in *Gen. et Corr.* II 5 that no one of the four primary bodies is more basic than any of the others, and that therefore none of them is the fundamental material principle of all things. For our purposes, it is important only to note that it is precisely the reciprocal transformation of the primary bodies that ensures this result. Aristotle's argument for this conclusion (332a4–17) is less than pellucid, but the idea seems to be this. Suppose one of the four primary bodies were the single basic element. For example, Aristotle says, 'if it were air, given that it persisted, what there would be would be alteration not generation' (332a8). Each primary body would be, fundamentally, a kind of air. So when air transforms into fire, what it becomes is hot, dry, air. But this is just alteration of the underlying air, and not generation at all. What is worse, if air were to change into water, the result of the transformation would be cold (since it is water), but also hot (since it is air). But this is impossible, 'because the same thing would then be simultaneously hot and cold' (332a17). We may safely infer, I think, that the matter underlying elemental transformations cannot have any member of the basic contrarieties as an essential property. So none of the four primary bodies is the 'first element'. And this is because if there were a first element, it would have to persist through substantial changes.

It thus appears that the place of prime matter in Aristotle's account of substantial change as the thing that persists through elemental transformation is secure.[27] What remains at issue, however, is precisely what it is for prime matter to underlie such changes. The topic is too large and difficult for us to take up here, but we can at least note some of the contenders.

On the traditional interpretation, prime matter is imperceptible stuff that is devoid of essential properties—it is matter without form. 'It is nothing in actuality, whereas it is everything in potentiality.'[28] In spite of the fact that it has no essential properties, it can be the bearer of accidental properties. It persists when the substance it is the matter of goes out of existence. For example, when air is transformed into water, the air goes out of existence by losing the heat that is essential to it, but the prime matter underlying the air persists. It ceases to be (accidentally) hot, but remains (accidentally) wet. When it becomes cold, water (which is essentially wet and cold) comes into existence. The reason why this is a case in which air *turns into* water—rather than simply vanishing and being replaced by water that is created *ex nihilo*—is that the prime matter which was formerly hot and wet becomes cold and wet.

Such a conception of prime matter is difficult, to say the least. Even some of those who attribute it to Aristotle concede that it is inconsistent with other views that he holds,[29] or even simply incoherent on its own.[30] Still, the textual evidence for prime matter is strong, and there have been some recent efforts to reconstruct on Aristotle's behalf a conception of prime matter that is more palatable than the traditional notion of a physically indeterminate stuff. Dorothea Frede (2004: 304) suggests that '"prime matter" is nothing but the *potential* of the simple bodies to engage in different basic combinations', but this seems to be an endorsement of prime matter in name only. For Frede also says that 'the simple bodies are...strange entities: they consist of two *differentiae* with no underlying matter' (p. 304) and 'there is no further substrate (*hupokeimenon*) that underlies the elementary compound' (p. 305).

Sheldon Cohen (1984) argues that although for Aristotle there is a common matter underlying the four elements, it is not the characterless prime matter as traditionally conceived. He takes Aristotle's insistence (329a26) that the underlying matter is 'always with contrariety' to mean precisely that this matter is *not* bare. ('Why accuse Aristotle of holding to a bare stuff if he insists that it is always clothed?' p. 176.) Of course, even if prime matter is not bare, it may still be insisted that it is at any rate devoid of essential properties. But Cohen replies that Aristotle does not require this. All he needs is a basic matter that does not have any of the differentiae of the four primary bodies as an essential property. It is thus free to have other essential properties, and Cohen offers as candidates: spatial extension, the potentiality for rectilinear motion, and the inability to underlie transformations into *aithêr*.[31] Finally, even apart from the considerations above, a common matter for elemental transformation need not be the basic matter underlying all change, for it does not underlie the generation of 'flesh and bones, milk and blood, houses and bricks, bronze and pitch, and many, many, other things' (p. 179). Cohen's reason for this last claim is that he thinks that Aristotle denies that the *is potentially* relation is transitive (p. 183). Prime matter, so construed, is not an unintelligible part of an incoherent metaphysical theory, but merely an intelligible part of a false physical theory.

It is clear that prime matter on Cohen's scaled-back conception of it is immune to many of the problems that plague it on the traditional conception. The question is whether Aristotle's text can sustain the reading Cohen gives it. The reader will note several points (the transitivity of *is potentially*, the reading of 329a26) on which Cohen's interpretation is at odds with the one presented here.

David Charles (2004) offers a non-traditional account of prime matter as a logical entity, not a material one. He notes that Aristotle's language in describing the matter underlying earth and fire is very much like the language he uses in the *Physics* to describe the *now*. The matter of the elements is 'the same, in so far as it is that thing, whatever it is, that underlies' (319b5); similarly, the *now* is 'the same [sc. from one occasion to another] in so far as it is that thing, whatever it is, that is the *now*' (219b12–13). What is the same, from one occasion to another, is the role that numerically distinct moments play in dividing time into before and after. Similarly, what is the same in the case of the matter of the elements is the role that these matters play in underlying basic elemental change. Just as we do not need to suppose that there is a special kind of *now* over and above such ordinary *nows* as 1:01 or 1:02, in order to hold that the *now* is what divides time into before and after, so too 'there is no need to postulate an imperceptible material underlier to account for elemental change' (Charles, 2004: 161). Charles agrees that prime matter is the 'one thing in virtue of being which all matters, involved in basic elemental change, are the same' (p. 155) but claims that prime matter is a logical (or abstract) object,[32] not a material object (pp. 162–3):

> In one case [prime matter] will be the matter of fire and in another the matter of earth. Prime matter, so understood, will be a distinctive logical (or abstract) object....In the case of elemental change, there need...be no single material substratum which persists throughout the elemental change from earth to fire via air.

Charles's resourceful deflation of Aristotelian prime matter is perhaps the most detailed and sophisticated such effort to date. Yet it leaves some nagging questions behind. Here are two. (1) As Charles himself admits, his account of prime matter requires him to read Aristotle as engaged in 'a systematic attempt to modify his *Physics*-style view that a material substratum must persist throughout any case of change' (p. 165). Yet there is no word in *Gen. et Corr.* that any such abandonment of a fundamental principle of the *Physics* is taking place. (2) Charles frequently tells us that the specific kinds of matter that play the role of the abstract object prime matter are, e.g., 'the matter of earth' and 'the matter of air.' But what are these kinds of matter? On Charles' view, there have to be some specific kinds of matter—some kinds of material object—that play the role of the (abstract object) prime matter. But what kinds of matter are these? Charles never tells us. And there is no indication in *Gen. et Corr.* that Aristotle had any such kinds of matter in mind. Nowhere does he tell us that he thinks that the matter of air is a different kind of matter from the matter of earth, even though both can play the role of prime matter. Nor does Aristotle's physical theory make room for the properties that might distinguish these specifically different kinds of matter. So even if Charles has carved out a logical space in which a theory of prime matter as an abstract object might be made to fit, it seems doubtful that Aristotle's is such a theory.

NOTES

1. The Greek for 'white comes to be' (*leukon gignetai*) could equally well be translated 'comes to be white'. Since it is clear that Aristotle does not mean to be discussing the coming into existence of the attribute of whiteness, the second translation might seem preferable. But there is still an ambiguity in his account that the first translation preserves, between a thing's becoming white and a white thing's coming into existence.
2. Notice that, technically speaking, Aristotle does not restrict himself to contraries (e.g., white/black) as principles of coming-to-be but also includes contradictories (e.g., white/not-white, musical/non-musical). At this stage the distinction is unimportant, but it comes into play in *Physics* V, where he wishes to distinguish change in the broadest sense

(*metabolê*) from the more specific kind of change (*kinêsis*) that involves the passage from one contrary to another (or to or from an intermediate between a pair of contraries).

3. Again, to capture Aristotle's idea adequately this schema should be a bit more complicated. *F* and *G* need not be contraries, but might be contradictories (musical/non-musical) or intermediates between a pair of contraries (light gray/dark gray).

4. Here Aristotle is discussing change in the broadest sense (*metabolê*), not just the passage between contraries (*kinêsis*).

5. It is sometimes more appropriate to take a *terminus* to be an individual as *characterized* by an attribute (e.g., the musical thing), rather than as an attribute (e.g., musicality) of that individual. The issue is complicated by the fact that Aristotle often picks out the *terminus* with an expression, such as *to mousikon* (literally, 'the musical'), which is ambiguous between these two possibilities.

6. *Haplôs*, 'simply,' or 'without qualification,' is often translated by the Latin *simpliciter*, as I will do occasionally in the remainder of this chapter.

7. Typically, the persisting item in an accidental change will be a substance. But in some cases the same matter that can underlie a substantial change (e.g., bronze) can be altered in ways that do not involve the generation or destruction of a substance. For example, a quantity of bronze may be moved or heated; or a heap of bricks and boards may be rearranged into a slightly differently shaped heap. In neither case do we have substantial change, since no new substance has been created. Aristotle can mark such cases off from substantial changes by appealing to the fact that their *termini* are accidental characteristics rather than the forms that embody the essential characteristics of a substance.

8. In *Gen. et Corr.* I 3 (318a24–25), Aristotle explicitly claims that the generation of one thing is the destruction of another. We will examine this claim in section II below.

9. Note, however, that in *Physics* I 7 Aristotle does not consider cases of elemental transformation (e.g., water into fire). A case can be made that the account in *Physics* I 7 together with *De Generatione et Corruptione's* doctrine of elemental transformation does commit Aristotle to prime matter. Cf. Bostock (2006: 19) and Waterlow (1982: 46). We will consider this in section II below.

10. Cf. Charlton (1970: 75–76).

11. Cf. Williams (1982: 88).

12. Williams (1982: 89) thinks that Aristotle here uses *haplôs* in a new way that he does not clearly distinguish from the old one. Algra (2004: 98) disagrees.

13. A change from imperceptible matter to imperceptible matter would presumably not be noticed, and so the possibility of such a change would not be taken into account by the view of the many.

14. *Pace* Jones (1974), who thinks that the matter is the material individual that is the *terminus a quo* of the change, which is 'used up' and hence no longer exists after the change. Jones's interpretation is adequately rebutted by Code (1976).

15. I assume that the statue would count as a substance. Aristotle is not consistent on this point.

16. The argument that the matter of which an individual is composed is not its substance is long and complex, and is not given in the physical works but in the *Metaphysics*—see esp. VII 3. How matter fits into the categorial scheme to which Aristotle appeals is also obscure.

17. The dispute is far too complex for detailed treatment here. The traditional account goes back to Philoponus (in *Gen. et Corr.*: 44, 18–24; 45, 11–22; 48, 6–9; 145, 27–146, 5) and became entrenched in the scholastic notion of *materia prima*. It is endorsed by Solmsen

(1958), Robinson (1974), Dancy (1978), Williams (1982), and Bostock (2006), among others. Opponents of prime matter include King (1956), Charlton (1970), Jones (1974), Furth (1988), Gill (1989), and Broadie (2004) (reversing the position she took in Waterlow (1982: 46)). The trend among recent scholars is to reject the traditional interpretation. Cf. Algra (2004: 91): '... today the politically correct view appears to be that there is no such thing as prime matter in Aristotle at all, and that this is in fact how it *should* be, the notion itself being basically un-Aristotelian, or even intrinsically incoherent.'

18. Cf. Gill (1989: 53–57), Broadie (2004: 124).

19. Thus King (1956: 376ff.), Furth (1988: 221–227), Broadie (2004: 124).

20. Cf. Code (1976: 365).

21. Brunschwig (2004: 41). It seems scarcely credible that Aristotle might have in mind the (irrelevant) possibility of something perceptible persisting, but not as subject.

22. At 330a30b1 Aristotle uses the term *stoicheia* to refer to the basic properties *hot, cold, wet,* and *dry.* At 331a15–16 he calls these properties differentiae of the primary bodies.

23. *Pace* Broadie (2004: 140), who says that there is 'no doubt' that it refers grammatically to *enantiôseôs.*

24. Williams (1982: 155–156) provides an excellent detailed discussion of this passage. See also Broadie (2004: 140–142), who comes to a different conclusion about it.

25. The cycle of elements is: fire, air, water, earth, fire, etc.... Thus, fire and air are consecutive, as are fire and earth; water and air are consecutive, as are water and earth. The non-consecutive elements (fire and water, air and earth) are 'contraries'.

26. At issue here is whether the *changes into* relation is transitive. The transformation of fire into water described above would presuppose transitivity if it depends on the presence of an intermediate (either air or earth) into which fire would change directly. Although *Met.* IX 7 1049a17–18 is often taken to deny transitivity ('earth is not yet potentially a statue, for it must first change into bronze'), I think this is a mistake. The point of this passage, rather, is that a thing that is made of *x* can be described as '*x*-en' only if *x* is its *proximate* matter. Thus, Aristotle allows (1049a20) that a chest made of wood is wooden, and that wood (which is made of earth) is earthen, but denies that the chest is correctly described as 'earthen'. (To be earthen a chest would have to be made of *earth*, i.e., have earth as its proximate matter.) This does not imply that the earth cannot be transformed, albeit indirectly, into a chest made of wood, and hence does not rule out the transitivity of the *changes into* relation. Further evidence of transitivity can be found at 1044a20–22: 'There come to be several matters for the same thing, when the one matter is matter for the other; e.g., phlegm comes from the fat and [hence also] from the sweet, if the fat comes from the sweet....' On the issue of transitivity, see also Cohen (1984: 183–184) and Bostock (2006: 17).

27. Aristotle makes this explicit at *De Caelo* IV 5 312a31–32: 'There must be a common matter of all four [primary bodies]—especially if they come to be out of one another....'. Although this seems to clinch the case for Aristotle's commitment to prime matter, opponents have been resourceful in trying to avoid it. Broadie (2004), for example, who thinks that the matter underlying a substantial change is not something that persists but rather is the pre-existing thing that undergoes the change, suggests that any one of the four primary bodies can be the common matter for all elemental transformations if it is the one from which the cyclical process of transformations begins. There are a number of problems with this interpretation: (1) it denies that there is anything that persists in elemental transformation; (2) as Charles (2004: 168) points out, it does not explain why there is just *one* common matter, since a cycle of elemental transformations can begin with any of the four primary bodies, and Aristotle never

gives any indication that he thinks there is a single favoured primary body (e.g., fire) from which all cyclical transformations begin; (3) it conflicts with the conclusion of *Gen. et Corr.* II 5 that none of the primary bodies is a fundamental material principle; (4) it requires a tortuous reinterpretation of the account of the principles of substantial change in *Gen. et Corr.* II 1 (329a33–35). Aristotle there claims that there are three principles: first, 'potentially perceptible body'; second, the contrarieties; and third, 'fire and water and such'. Broadie must construe 'potentially perceptible body' to refer not to prime matter but to the very same simple bodies—fire, water, etc.—that are explicitly identified as the third principle. Her reasoning is that 'the simple bodies play two roles in this scheme' and that an actually perceptible body such as water may be picked out as only 'potentially perceptible' because 'its potential for such change is not something about it that is perceptible' (p. 142). One might just as well describe a magician whose sleight of hand is so good that one cannot see him palm a card as an 'imperceptible magician'.

28. Brunschwig (2004: 40).
29. Loux (1991: 239–252) claims that it is inconsistent with the essentialism of *Met.* VII and VIII, but that Aristotle is nevertheless committed to it.
30. Williams (1982: 219): '... there is...a real confusion in Aristotle's thinking, a notion of prime matter which is internally incoherent...but it is nevertheless there in much of what Aristotle wrote.'
31. *Aithêr* is the matter of the non-terrestrial realm that includes the moon, sun, and stars. Its natural movement is circular, unlike the four simple bodies of the sublunary realm, whose natural movement is rectilinear. *Aithêr* is ungenerated and indestructible, which means that it cannot reciprocally transform into earth, water, air, or fire. Cf. *DC* I 2–3.
32. Charles likens his 'logical objects' to Kit Fine's 'arbitrary objects'; cf. Fine (1985).

BIBLIOGRAPHY

Algra, K. (2004) 'On *Generation and Corruption* I. 3: substantial change and the problem of non-being', in F. De Haas and J. Mansfeld, eds., *Aristotle: On Generation and Corruption, Book I: Symposium Aristotelicum* (Oxford: Clarendon Press), 91–121.

Bostock, D. (2006) *Space, Time, Matter, and Form: Essays on Aristotle's Physics* (Oxford: Clarendon Press).

Broadie, S. (2004) 'On *Generation and Corruption* I. 4: distinguishing alteration—substantial change, elemental change, and first matter in GC', in F. De Haas and J. Mansfeld, eds., *Aristotle: On Generation and Corruption, Book I: Symposium Aristotelicum* (Oxford: Clarendon Press), 123–50.

Brunschwig, J. (2004) 'On *Generation and Corruption* I. 1: a false start?', in F. De Haas and J. Mansfeld, eds., *Aristotle: On Generation and Corruption, Book I: Symposium Aristotelicum* (Oxford: Clarendon Press), 25–63.

Charles, D. (2004) 'Simple genesis and prime matter', in F. De Haas and J. Mansfeld, eds., *Aristotle: On Generation and Corruption, Book I: Symposium Aristotelicum* (Oxford: Clarendon Press), 151–69.

Charlton, W. (1970) *Aristotle's Physics: Books I and II* (Oxford: Clarendon Press).

Code, A. (1976) 'The persistence of Aristotelian matter', *Philosophical Studies* 29, 357–67.

Cohen, S. (1984) 'Aristotle's doctrine of the material substrate', *Philosophical Review* 93, 171–94.

Dancy, R.M. (1978) 'On some of Aristotle's second thoughts about substances: matter',
    Philosophical Review 87, 372–413.
De Haas, F. and J. Mansfeld, eds. (2004) *Aristotle: On Generation and Corruption, Book I:
    Symposium Aristotelicum* (Oxford: Clarendon Press).
Fine, K. (1985) *Reasoning with Arbitrary Objects* (Oxford: Blackwell).
Frede, D. (2004) '*On Generation and Corruption* I. 4: on mixture and mixables', in F.
    De Haas and J. Mansfeld, eds., *Aristotle: On Generation and Corruption, Book I:
    Symposium Aristotelicum* (Oxford: Clarendon Press), 289–314.
Furth, M. (1988) *Substance, Form, and Psyche: An Aristotelian Metaphysics* (Cambridge:
    Cambridge Univ. Press).
Gill, M.L. (1989) *Aristotle on Substance* (Princeton: Princeton Univ. Press).
Jones, B. (1974) 'Aristotle's introduction of matter', *Philosophical Review* 83, 474–500.
King, H.R. (1956) 'Aristotle without *materia prima*', *Journal of the History of Ideas*, 17,
    370–87.
Loux, M. (1991) *Primary Ousia: an Essay on Aristotle's Metaphysics Z and H* (Ithaca, N.Y.:
    Cornell Univ. Press).
Robinson, H.M. (1974) 'Prime matter in Aristotle', *Phronesis* 19, 168–88.
Solmsen, F. (1958) 'Aristotle and prime matter', *Journal of the History of Ideas* 19, 243–52.
Waterlow, S. (1982) *Nature, Change, and Agency in Aristotle's Physics* (Oxford: Clarendon
    Press).
Williams, C.J.F. (1982) *Aristotle's De Generatione et Corruptione* (Oxford: Clarendon Press).

CHAPTER 10

....

TELEOLOGICAL
CAUSATION

....

DAVID CHARLES

1. INTRODUCTION

....

ARISTOTLE introduces the fourth cause, the teleological cause, in *Physics* II 3 as follows:

> Again a mode of cause is the goal. This is that for the sake of which - as health is for walking. We answer the question 'Why does he walk?' by saying 'to be healthy', thinking that in saying this we have stated the cause. The same is true also of what happens or is present as an intermediary as a result of someone else's action on the way to the goal: slimming, purging, drugs or surgical instruments. All these are for the sake of the goal, even though they differ as some are activities, others instruments (194b32–195a3).

Later in the same chapter he comments:

> '... the others are causes as the goal, that is the good of the other things involved; for that for the sake of which is, by nature, the best, that is the goal of the things that lead up to it' (195a23–5).

In these passages, the teleological cause is introduced on the basis of the idea of something's being for the sake of a goal: the good to be achieved. The goal causes an activity to occur or an instrument to exist. They happen or exist because of some good that results from them. While Aristotle, as we shall see, discerns teleological causation in a wide range of cases, these passages contain his key thought. Some things happen or exist because of some further good they help to produce.

Aristotle gave the teleological cause a major role in his discussions of physics, metaphysics, biology, psychology, and ethics. In his view, his predecessors erred in ignoring or in failing to give a proper account of it. Aristotle's use of the teleological cause constitutes one of the most distinctive aspects of his philosophy. It is also one of the most controversial. For while he used it widely and with considerable confidence, many later critics have regarded it as mysterious and fundamentally flawed. How, they reasonably ask, can things be caused to happen because of some good they help to produce? How does goodness cause things to happen?

In this essay, my aim is to address three introductory, but basic, questions about Aristotle's account:

[1] How did he characterize teleological causation?
[2] What, in his view, is its basis? How did he see it working as a cause?
[3] What, in his view, is its range? Where is it applicable and where not?

I shall focus initially on questions [1] and [2] as these need to be answered before one can seriously address question [3]. My primary goal is to understand what, in Aristotle's view, teleological causation is. Without this, our discussion of issues concerning the range and defensibility of his account must remain hopelessly superficial.

2. Aristotle's General Characterisation of Teleological Causation

(a) What is the teleological cause? Goals and the good

Aristotle, as we have seen, takes as his starting point the idea of the goal, that for the sake of which. He uses the idea of *that for the sake of which* in two ways, distinguishing between that which benefits (*tini*) from (e.g.) an action and that for whom the action is done (*hou heneka*: DA 415b21ff., *Met.* 1072b3ff.). We might describe his distinction as one between that for whom the action is good (*tini*) and that for whose sake it is done (*hou heneka*). In *Physics* 194a35 he draws a similar distinction in the case of the goal (*telos*), separating the beneficiary of an action from what was aimed at when the action was done. Armed with this distinction, Aristotle can distinguish three types of case:

[1] actions which occur for the sake of someone (or something) who is benefitted by what occurs;
[2] actions which occur for the sake of someone (or something) who is not benefitted by what occurs;
[3] actions which benefit someone but do not occur for the sake of the beneficiary.[1]

In some cases of type [1], the agent may act for his (or her) own sake with the aim of benefitting himself. But there may also be type [1] cases where the beneficiary is someone else for whose benefit the agent acts. For example, someone might act altruistically for the sake of his friend or, in the upper reaches of the cosmos, a star or planet might act for the sake of the object whose position it stabilizes.[2] In some type [2] cases, by contrast, that for whose sake the action is done may not be the kind of object which can be benefitted by the actions in question. Thus, in even higher parts of the cosmos, some beings may act for the sake of the Unmoved Mover even though the latter is not (and cannot be) benefitted by their action. Similarly, a religious person might act for the sake of God while believing that He cannot be benefitted by any action of ours. In type [3] cases, something may result which benefits A even though the action is not done for this reason. Thus, in one of Aristotle's examples, I may gain some benefit from going to the well even though I do not go there for that reason. The resulting gain is a side effect of what was done without itself being sought by the agent.[3] It is only type [1] and [2] cases that are instances of teleological causation: here what occurs does so *because* it leads to the goal, the good in question (*hou heneka*). In type [3] cases, by contrast, although A (or B) may be benefitted, what occurs does not do so *because* it leads to the resulting benefit.[4]

What is it to be goal in the way required in cases [1] and [2]? In *Physics* 198b8, Aristotle characterizes the teleological cause as what 'is better, not simply but with regard to the nature of each thing'. The goal is something which it is good for the agent to bring about (given his or her nature). It is not a goal for the agent simply in virtue of its being good. It has to be something which it is better for the agent to bring about than not bring about. (Agents, in this formulation, include plants, animals, and humans.) It is good from the agent's standpoint.

What is it for something to be good for the agent (given its nature) to bring about? In some type (1) cases, what is aimed at is something which benefits the agent. In these cases, what is aimed at is something which is good for the agent himself. The agent (A) has a self-directed desire or need to bring it about. His (or her) life will go better if this goal is achieved. He has an interest in achieving the goal. In other type (1) cases, the agent aims to bring about something which is good for someone or something else. In these cases, the agent will have a desire to bring about something which is good for the patient (P). P's life will go better if the goal is achieved, and A has a desire to contribute to P's doing well. In all type (1) cases, someone's life (whether A's or P's) will go better if the goal is achieved. In type (2) cases, the agent will act because he (or she) has a desire or need to act for the sake of P (even though P is not benefitted by the action). What is done will be a good thing for A to do, given its nature, since he (or she) has desires or needs which are (in some way) directed towards P. An agent may, for example, desire to do a noble action for God's sake, inspired by God's goodness. While type (1) and (2) cases are importantly different, in all of them the goal is something which is desired or needed by an agent. This is not to say that something is a goal for A simply in virtue of being desired or needed by A. It is only to claim that something would not be a goal for A unless it was something which was (in one of the differing ways mentioned) desired or needed by A.[5]

In the *Physics,* Aristotle gives several examples of teleological causation. One group includes actions, such as walking for health, and natural processes (such as a plant's roots pushing down for nutrition (199a29) or its leaves emerging to protect its fruit (199a28)). In these cases, the actions or processes are ways of achieving an end state desired or needed by the agent, animal, or plant. Aristotle characterizes all these as alive (see *DA* 410b23f., 413a22; *PA* 681a12ff.) and as such they have the goal of living or living well (*DA* 415b14, 435b21f.). The actions or processes described contribute to the goal of the agent's or plant's living or living well. Their life is sustained or goes better if the goal is achieved. Another group of examples includes artifacts (such as medical instruments or axes: 200b5) and parts of animals (such as teeth: 198b29 or the organs of the body).[6] Artifacts are required for the goals of the designer or user of the object (such as cutting in the case of the axe). The goal is what the user aims to achieve by using the axe. Parts of the body, analogously, are required for the goals of the animal whose parts they are (as the eye is required for seeing, an ingredient in living well for the animal in question). Both artifacts and parts of organisms are present because they are required for or contribute towards some relevant goal, which is desired or needed by either the agent, animal, or plant which has them. In all these examples the goal is something needed or desired by the agent or organism in question. Given these needs or desires, it is better that the artifacts or parts are present than that they are not.

(b) What is caused by the teleological cause?

When Aristotle first introduces the teleological cause, what is caused is someone's walking. The teleological cause, health (194b32ff.), causes an agent to walk in a way (or at a time) which is useful (or good) for him (or her). It does not make her walk all the time or when it is bad for her health to do so. It will, rather, cause her to walk *in just those ways* and *at just those times* which are good for her health. In another of Aristotle's examples, the teleological cause (cutting) causes a saw to have sharp teeth (*Phys.* 200b5f.). This cause is responsible for the presence of such teeth, located where they are, in the saw. They are present, situated in just the way which is useful or good for cutting, because their presence, so located, is good (or useful) for the goal of cutting. In this case, the teleological cause makes the saw have teeth where (and only where) caused they should be (given the goal).

It is important to note that, in these cases, what is caused teleologically is not simply a person's walking at a given time or a saw's having sharp teeth. It is rather their walking or having sharp teeth *in just those ways (or at times or locations) which are (in the relevant way) good or useful.* What is teleologically is not simply someone's walking at times when it is (as it happens) beneficial for them to do so but rather their walking *at just those times when it is beneficial for them to do so.*

This is why the relevant goal causes the agent to walk or the saw to have teeth *in just those ways and places that are beneficial or useful to achieve the relevant goal.*[7]

In the *Physics*, Aristotle considers in some detail the concurrent development of 'sharp teeth, useful for cutting, and flat teeth, useful for grinding' in certain animals (198b25ff.). The teleological cause will (if it follows the pattern of the previous examples) cause such teeth to emerge *in just those ways and at just those locations and times which are useful for the organism's eating and digestion.* Its teeth will co-develop in just these ways and these places because co-developing in just these ways and places is good for its eating. Sharp and flat teeth co-develop in an organism which needs such teeth positioned in the way they are because it is good for it to have such teeth so located. What is teleologically caused is *the development of teeth in ways, times, and places which are beneficial for the organism in question.*[8]

In the case just described, one may explain, without a teleological cause, in terms of efficient and material causes why sharp teeth come to be (at a given time) and why flat teeth come to be in certain animals (at the same time) and then observe that such teeth are indeed useful to those animals in achieving their aims. But one will lack a cause of their coming to be in just those ways, times, and positions that are useful for the animal. For there will be nothing to connect their co-occurring in just those places and times with the usefulness they have for the organism in question. It will be an accident that the sharp and flat teeth come to be in ways, times, and places which are useful for the organism. The teleological cause fills this explanatory gap by accounting for the occurrence of sharp and flat teeth in A at just those times and places where it is useful for them to occur in terms of their usefulness for A's goals. Understood teleologically, these teeth come to be present in just the manner and at just the times and positions which are good for A because their coming to be present together in these ways, places, and times is good for A.

This point sheds light on Aristotle's criticism of a proposal to account in efficient (or material) causal terms for the coming to be of sharp teeth and of flat teeth in animals of a given type.[9] While the co-emergence of such teeth is (it will be accepted) good for the organism in question, this proposal offers no causal account of why both sets of teeth emerge *together in just those ways and at just those times and locations which are good for the organism.* Indeed, from the standpoint criticized, it is a matter of chance that they emerge together in precisely those ways, times, and places that benefit the organism (198b29).[10] So understood, Aristotle's opponent will agree with the suggestion that, in the case of natural parts, they come to be either

[P] . . . . . . by chance or for the sake of a goal. (199a3f.).

In his view, they emerge together in places, times, and ways which are beneficial to the organism by chance. There is, for him, no causal explanation of why they *emerge together in just the ways, times, and places that are beneficial to the organism.*[11]

It may be helpful to follow Aristotle's discussion of this view a stage further. Aristotle assumes that his opponent will concede that the type of natural parts under discussion always or for the most part co-emerge in places, times, and ways that are beneficial for the animal (198b35–6, 199a6ff.). However, once he has made this further concession, he is (in Aristotle's view) in serious difficulties—at least if he also accepts the earlier claim that things that happen by chance do not happen 'always or for the most part.' (198b32ff). If natural parts develop in ways, places, and times that regularly benefit the organism that possesses them, this cannot be so 'by chance'. If so, Aristotle's opponent must conclude, given his agreement to [P], that natural parts come to be in ways which benefit S for the sake of a goal.[12]

Aristotle's criticism of his opponent's view, so understood, is best seen as an argument against a specific opponent who does away with teleological causation while, at the same time, accepting (i) that the alternatives mentioned in [P] apply to the relevant subject matter (formation of animal parts in ways, times, and places which benefit the organism) and (ii) Aristotle's account of chance. At this point in *Physics* II, Aristotle takes as his default position the existence of genuine examples of teleological causation (in the cases of agency and natural processes) and seeks to undermine a specific type of argument against this view. He is not (at this point) trying to establish the legitimacy of teleological causation from a neutral starting point or considering whether it can withstand all possible criticisms.[13]

To summarize: we have seen that Aristotle's basic account of teleological causation has two distinctive features:

(A) The cause is a goal which it is good for the agent (given its nature) to bring about (or possess). This is only possible if it is better for the agent (given its desires or needs) that the goal in question comes to be (or exists). Their life will be sustained or go better if the goal is achieved.
(B) What is caused is the coming to be (or being) of certain features in ways (places, times etc.) which are good or useful ways to achieve the goal in question.

Both points are important. Given (A), not any natural end point of a process will be a goal (in the relevant sense). Death, for example, is not a goal when it is not tied to the interests, desires, or needs of the organism in question.[14] Death is not, in these cases, something which is good for the organism to bring about. Similarly, the end points of natural processes (such as a stone rolling down a hill to stop at the bottom) will not be goals if the stone has no desire or need to stop there. It is not good *for the stone* (given its nature) that it stops where it does. Its life (or existence) does not go better because it stops at this point rather than any other. Given (B), it is not enough for teleological explanation to account for the coming to be of something which is, in fact, useful for the goal to be achieved (or in ways which are in fact useful for that goal). What is teleologically caused is the coming to be (or being) of something *in a manner and at a place and time which are good for that goal*.[15] For example, what occurs happens in a good way or good place or good time (to achieve the goal) because this is how it should happen to achieve that goal.

Aristotle develops (B) further in *Physics* II 8. First he emphasizes that in cases of coming to be, each stage of what occurs happens as and where it does (first, second, third) because of the goal (199a8–10). One teleological cause accounts not simply for the occurrence of each stage in a process but also for its occurrence where and when it occurs. More fully, each stage occurs at a given place (and in a given manner) because its presence at that point is the best way to achieve the goal (or, at least, a good way to do so). Second, he notes that mistakes can occur in cases of teleological causation (199a33-b7). This happens when a stage in a process is not completed in the way required to reach the goal. Here stages do not occur in the ways or at the places they should if the goal is to be achieved. These are mistakes precisely because they do not occur in the good manner or good location required by the goal. Mistakes arise because what occurs is not controlled in the way it should be by the teleological cause.

In cases where what is caused is coming to be, each stage of what occurs will be controlled by the good to be achieved. There can, of course, be processes which regularly arrive at given end points without being teleologically caused. When stones roll down a hill, the way in which they do so is controlled solely by their weight and the slope of the hill, not by any good to be achieved. A stone does not make mistakes when it rolls down a hill because what occurs is not the type of process whose stages occur as they do because they are good (or the best) ways to arrive at the valley below. Indeed, without teleology there can be no talk of mistakes.

If processes are to be teleologically caused, they must not only result in the coming to be of certain features in ways (places, times, etc.) which are good or useful for the agent or organism in question but must also happen by routes each stage of which occurs in given ways (places, times, etc.) because these are good ones to bring such features about.[16]

(c) The logical form of teleological causal statements: hypothetical necessity

Aristotle considers the best way to characterize teleological causal claims in *Physics* II 9 and suggests the following:

> if the goal is to be or is, what occurs before it will be or is. (*Physics* 200a20).

Since this is a case of hypothetical necessity, this claim is shorthand for

> if the goal G is to be or is and $A_1....A_n$ are required for G, necessarily $A_1....A_n$ will come to be or is.

He illustrates his claim with one of his favourite examples: house-building.

> if the house is to be, and bricks and stones are required for the house, necessarily bricks and stones will come to be or be present. (200a21ff.)

This is hypothetical in that it begins from the hypothesis that the house is to be. It says, in effect,

> Hypothesize [or assume] that G is to be: $A_1....A_n$ will necessarily come to be [or are].[17]

This form of statement does not allow one to deduce that $A_1 \ldots A_n$ necessarily will come to be. One could only infer this if G itself in fact comes to be. Further, one could only infer that $A_1 \ldots A_n$ were themselves necessary if G was also necessary.

Aristotle describes the goal as 'the starting point' (*arche*) in this case and understands this as claiming more than is sufficient for the coming to be of $A_1 \ldots A_n$ (200a22ff.). His idea is that the goal is that because of which $A_1 \ldots A_n$ come to be or are. This characterisation fits the remarks in the last section. The goal causes what occurs for its sake to occur in the way and at the place they do. Their occurrence in this way is caused and controlled by their goal. One might express this idea as follows:

> (C) if the goal G is to be or is and $A_1 \ldots A_n$ are required for G, necessarily as a causal result $A_1 \ldots A_n$ will come to be (or are) in the way they do (or are).

Hypothetical necessity is appropriate in characterising teleological causation. First, since the cause is not itself necessary, the most that can be inferred is that the effect is necessary if the cause exists. One cannot deduce the simple necessity of the effect.[18] Second, in this case the cause does not have to exist, let alone exist before the effect, if it is to be a cause. The most that is required is that one hypothesizes the future existence of a cause of a given type. It follows that since the teleological cause need not be an actual particular future event, it cannot involve particular events (mysteriously) pulling the present towards them.[19] While the first feature may be shared with non-necessary efficient causes in the natural world, the second is a distinctive feature of teleological causes.

In sum: Aristotle's account of teleological causation needs to meet the three conditions (A), (B), and (C) set out in this section. He has to show how things happen (or are present) because they are good in cases where

> (A) The cause is a goal which it is good for the agent (or organism) to bring about (or possess). This is only possible if the goal is connected in one of the ways mentioned above with the desires or needs of an agent or organism (where these include plants, animals, and humans). Their life will be sustained or go better if the goal is achieved.
> (B) What is caused is (i) the coming to be (or being) of certain features at places and times which are good or useful for the goal to be achieved (ii) by routes each stage of which occurs in ways which are good ones for the goal to be achieved.
> (C) if the goal G is to be or is and $A_1 \ldots A_n$ are required for G, necessarily as a causal result $A_1 \ldots A_n$ will come to be (or are) in the way they do (or are).

In order to meet these three requirements, Aristotle needs to show how the goodness of goals leads to and controls what occurs in the cases he has considered. He has to provide some basis for the claim that (in these ways) things happen (or are present) because they are good. There is, it seems, no way for him to evade this fundamental challenge.

3. What Is the Basis of Aristotle's Account?

In Aristotle's account, certain processes occur for the sake of a goal. Indeed, they are caused to occur in the way they do because of that goal. To his critics, these claims appear wholly mysterious. How, they ask, can anything be caused to occur by a goal? Perhaps we can make what occurs intelligible (or even re-assuring) by thinking of it *as if* it were goal-directed. But that is quite different from claiming that what occurs is caused to occur by that goal. For in the latter case, the goal must make some difference to what actually occurs, not just to our way of thinking about it. In this section, I shall consider two ways to make sense of Aristotle's account.

Model I: goal-directed efficient causes

The first interpretation runs as follows: in all cases of teleological causation there is a distinctive type of efficient cause, one directed towards the good of the organism or the agent. In the case of natural processes, the capacity may be a capacity for Form. In the case of intentional action, the capacity may be a desire for certain goods. Things happen for the sake of a goal because there is a goal-directed efficient cause in the agent or the organism involved.[20]

This interpretation has several attractive features. It apparently satisfies the three requirements set out in the previous section. The goal to be achieved is connected with the desires or needs of an agent or organism. There will only be goals when the agent has a desire for certain goods or the organism has a need of certain goods. Second, what is caused is not simply the occurrence of certain phenomena but rather their occurrence as something useful for the agent or organism. This is because the desires or capacities are directed at some good and so what occurs (if all goes well) will be beneficial to the agent or organism in question. Third, there can be a teleological cause even when the goal is not reached. In such cases, the goal-directed efficient cause will be prevented from reaching its goal by external circumstances.

The great merit of this interpretation is that it offers a clear account of Aristotle's view of the teleological cause. It is a distinctive type of efficient cause: one which is, in its nature, goal directed. Armed with this account, he can easily distinguish cases of genuine teleological causation from ones in which accidental benefit results. For the latter will not be caused by a goal-directed efficient cause of the appropriate type. However, while this interpretation can be developed further in a number of different ways, there are concerns about its adequacy.[21] Or so I shall argue.

Concern (i): This interpretation takes as its starting point the idea of a goal-directed capacity which functions as an efficient cause of processes or actions.

While this model may be adequate to account for Aristotle's discussions in *Physics* II, it cannot do justice to all the cases of teleological causation he considers. In the *Parts of Animals,* he develops his account further, setting out a complex teleological order:

[1] Activities of the organism: walking, seeing.
[2] Parts of animals: legs [with capacities for walking] eyes [with capacities for seeing].
[3] Natural processes which lead to the formation of those parts [generation of animals].
[4] Capacities which lead to the generation of those processes [capacities for generation of animals].[22]

In this order, [1] is the teleological cause of [2], [2] of [3], and [3] of [4]. To give an example: the capacity for walking is present for the sake of walking and the capacity to act in ways required to form parts of animals which can walk is also present for the sake of walking. There is a teleological cause of the presence of the capacities mentioned at lines [2] and [4]. If this is correct, the basis for teleological causation cannot be the existence of goal-directed capacities, whether at line [2] or line [4] since their existence is itself teleologically explained.

Nor is this pattern confined to the biological works. In the *Metaphysics,* he considers a similar account for artifacts such as houses or axes:

[1] Activities: saving possessions/cutting
[2] Artifacts which are present for the sake of these activities: houses/axes
[3] Processes of constructing these artifacts; house-building/making the axe
[4] Capacities for constructing these artifacts: skills.

As before, [1] is the teleological cause of [2], [2] of [3], and [3] of [4]. In this order, the lowest level can be described as being for the sake of the highest level and for the sake of other stages above in the hierarchy. If so, the activities at line [1] are the teleological causes for the artifacts with their distinctive capacities at line [2] and for the capacities to construct those artifacts at line [4]. If this is correct, the basis for teleological causation cannot be the existence of goal-directed capacities (whether at line [2] or [4]) since their existence is itself teleologically caused.[23]

Aristotle frequently distinguishes the order of efficient and teleological causation, noting that they proceed in different directions and from different starting points.[24] In many cases when there is a teleological causal story there is also an efficient causal one involving a goal-directed capacity. However, since he points only to a teleological cause to account for the presence of the relevant efficient cause (the goal-directed capacity), teleological causation cannot itself be a species of efficient causation with goal-directed efficient causes. Indeed, he conspicuously fails to offer an efficient causal account (as a modern 'adaptationist' biologist might) of why the animals in question have developed this type of goal-directed capacity.[25]

In response to this concern, it may be suggested that even if the capacity which serves as an efficient cause is defined as goal-directed, it is not itself teleologically caused by the goal. The goal, that is, may be part of the formal cause of the capacity but does not teleologically cause its presence. However, this suggestion suffers two major disadvantages. The texts certainly suggest that the capacity's being present for the sake of the goal is a case of teleological causation in line with other such cases.[26] The efficient causal interpretation fails to capture the way in which the final cause explains the directedness of the relevant capacity. This crucial connection, characteristic of teleological explanation, is (it seems) left unexplained in the purely efficient causal model. Nor can one say the goal in question is simply the formal cause of the relevant capacity. For Aristotle often insists that the formal and final causes are the same, suggesting that one feature (here the goal) is both the formal and final cause of the relevant phenomenon.[27] Indeed, in *Metaphysics* IX 8 it appears that something is the formal cause of the relevant capacity because it is its final cause.[28]

Concern (ii): In the *Physics*, Aristotle focuses on the processes of animal formation and on actions that bring things (such as health) into existence. In these contexts, he concentrates on lines [3] and [4] in the teleological chains set out above and says little about lines [1] and [2]. This focus might encourage a proponent of the efficient causal model to take the capacity *to become* an F (mentioned at line [4]) as the starting point of the relevant teleological sequence and to seek to explain the capacities *to be* an F (mentioned at line [2]) in terms of capacities *to become* an F. On this view, something existing for the sake of a goal G is to be explained in terms of its coming to be for the sake of that goal. Further, its coming to be for the sake of that goal is itself to be explained in terms of a capacity to become an organism with that goal. Indeed, this will be the natural order of explanation if one adopts the causal model just introduced.[29]

Aristotle, however, does not proceed in this direction but takes the capacity *to be* an F as teleologically prior to the capacity *to become* an F (as in the order set out above). He makes no attempt to carry through the ambitious task of explaining capacities *to be* an F in terms of the capacity *to become* an F by taking as basic (e.g.) the capacity successfully to produce (or reproduce) F's or suggesting that our present capacities are to be explained in terms of past adaptations or successfully inherited characteristics. Indeed, in *Parts of Animals*, the order of explanation runs in the opposite direction. It is because we have the capacities *to be* F's that we have the capacities *to become* F's.[30]

Concern (iii): In the efficient causal interpretation, the cause explains not simply the occurrence of certain phenomena but rather the occurrence of something useful for the agent or organism. This is because the desires or capacities of the agent (or nature) are aimed at some good. The organism is naturally inclined to achieve something that is good for it. However, in this interpretation, values (such as being good) are not the type of thing that can cause the agent or organism to have these goals. Indeed, one motivation for the causal interpretation is to avoid treating goodness as itself a cause. Rather, it presents the organism as beginning with certain good goals, not themselves selected because they are good, and adopting means which will achieve those goals. The means too will not be selected because they are good but simply because they are necessary or sufficient to achieve the goal in question. (I assume here that the efficient causal model is not underwritten by an evolutionary account of why the organism has certain goals and adopts certain means.)

Aristotle, however, does not see the situation in this way but talks of nature 'using' certain means, like a craftsman, because they are the best means available (see *De Incessu Animalium*: 704b11–17). Elsewhere, he speaks of nature 'correctly using' material in the hoofs of solid hoofed animals, taking it from their upper parts and giving them one horn only (*PA* 663a31ff.).[31] While in the *Physics* his view may be consistent with the purely efficient causal model, elsewhere he insists on means being selected because they are good (just as an agent might select means to his end because they are good).[32] In both cases, the selection of means will be sensitive to (and dependent on) the goodness of the means selected. Their selection itself is teleologically explained: certain means are selected because they are good.

If this is correct, there will be a good-based explanation of why the organism has certain capacities and goals, and of why it selects one means rather than another to achieve them. The efficient causal interpretation fails to make room for Aristotle's teleological (good-based) explanations of why the organism or agent has certain capacities and goals and of why it selects certain means to realize them.

While there may be ways to reply to these objections, I shall (for present purposes) regard them as sufficient to motivate the search for an alternative. This task is particularly pressing since we seem to have reached an impasse. The causal efficient interpretation, although readily comprehensible, seems not to do justice to Aristotle's account. In particular, it fails to accommodate the fact that (in his view) capacities, goals, and means are selected because they are good. However, the alternative, good-based interpretation leaves it wholly mysterious how things happen (or come to be present) simply because they are good. We are confronted, at last, with the basic question: how can goodness cause things to happen?[33]

Model II: sensitivity to goodness

In the *Physics* Aristotle compares craft and nature as teleological causes. While he is not seeking to analyse natural teleology as an instance of craft teleology, his discussion of the case of craft may be helpful in showing how goals, means, and capacities are present for the sake of some good. His discussion of craft can be generalized to the other key examples. Indeed, there is some evidence for thinking that this is how he conceived of the matter.

The craftsman's actions are guided by the goodness of certain goals and of certain ways to achieve them. As a craftsman, he knows how to achieve good goals by good means. If he is a master craftsman, he will achieve good goals by good means because he himself knows that they are good goals and good means.[34] To be a craftsman of this type is to be sensitive to and guided by the goodness of his goals and of the means he selects to achieve them. He acts in the way he does because of the goodness of these goals and these means. It is not (as in the purely causal efficient model) that he happens to have certain goals and reliably selects means which will achieve them. Rather, he has these goals and selects these means because he knows that they are good. Indeed, his craft is designed to achieve good goals by good means because they are good. It exists because it is a way to achieve what is good because it is good. In internalizing this craft the master craftsman comes to be guided in his actions by the goodness of its goals and means because he knows that they are good. This is what it is to be a craftsman of this type.

In this case, the goal (let us say a fine house) is connected with the desires or aims of the master builder. Second, given this goal, he will act in ways which are useful in achieving it. This is why, for example, bricks and stones are positioned in places which are good ones if he is to achieve his goal. Third, he will do what is required to achieve his goal because he is guided by the goodness of that goal and of the means required to achieve it. Given the goodness of the goal, the craftsman will act in the ways required to achieve it. This might be expressed as follows:

> Since G is good for S to achieve & $A_1 ... A_n$ are required for G, necessarily because of G, S will do $A_1 ... A_n$

The basis for this claim is the fact that the craftsman, as one who has internalized his skill, is guided in his actions by the goodness of certain goals and of certain means to achieve them. The craftsman may, of course, fail to achieve his goal if circumstances are adverse. Hence a more accurate statement of the view would be

> There are some circumstances such that if G is good for S to achieve & $A_1 ... A_n$ are required for G, necessarily because of G, S will (in those circumstances) do $A_1 ... A_n$

This captures the idea that when S is a craftsman what he does (in certain unspecified favourable circumstances) will be determined by the goodness of certain goals and of the means required to achieve them. His actions will, in those conditions, be necessitated by the goodness of the goals and of the means required to achieve them. The craftsman must, of course, have the skill required to build well. Indeed, his skill may be the efficient cause of his actions. However, since his skill is guided by the goodness of certain goals and means, what he does is fundamentally caused (in the way just described) by their goodness.

This model applies to the rational, or better, knowledgeable, agent quite generally. In Aristotle's example, a person walks for health because she knows that health is a good thing for her to achieve and is guided by that perception. Indeed, to be a rational (or knowledgeable) agent is to be sensitive to and guided by the goodness of certain goals and certain means to achieve them. She acts in the way she does because of the goodness of these goals and of these means. It is not just that knowledgeable agents happen to have good goals and work out reliable means to achieve them. Rather they have these goals and select these means because they know that these goals and means are good ones. Further, they know that they are good ones because they are good. If S is a rational (or knowledgeable) agent, she will act in given ways because so acting is a good way to achieve a good goal. Where S is a rational agent, the following will be true:

> There are some circumstances such that if G is good for S to achieve & $A_1....A_n$ are required for G, necessarily because of G, S will (in those circumstances) do $A_1....A_n$

Rational agents must, of course, have the desires and understanding required to act well. Indeed, these desires or this understanding will be the efficient causes of his action. However, since their desires and understanding are guided by the goodness of certain goals and means, what they do will be fundamentally caused by their goodness.

Did Aristotle apply this model to natural organisms such as plants and animals? Consider one of his examples: plants push their roots down in order to reach their goal, water, required for their nutrition. According to the present suggestion, to be a natural organism is to be organized so as to achieve goals which are good for that organism by means which are good means to do so. It is not simply that natural organisms happen to have good goals and select good means to achieve them. Rather they have these goals and act in the way they do because having these goals and acting this way are good for them. Indeed, to be an organism is to be guided in one's movements by the goodness (for oneself) of certain goals and means. They move in the way they do because so moving is a good way for them to achieve a good goal (such as remaining alive or living well). In the case of natural organisms, as in that of rational agents and the craftsman, it will be true that:

> There are some circumstances such that if G is good for S (the natural organism) to achieve & $A_1....A_n$ are required for G, then necessarily because of G, S will (in those circumstances) do $A_1....A_n$.

There will, no doubt, be goal-directed capacities in natural organisms which are the efficient causes of its moving as it does. But these goal-directed capacities are present in natural organisms because such organisms are (in some way) sensitive to and guided by the goodness of certain goals and of the means required to achieve them. Indeed this is what it is to be an organism of this type.

Consider next the parts of plants: their roots are organized in the way they are so as to contribute to the organism's goals in the best way possible, and they are so organized because this is the best way to contribute to those goals. Indeed, this is what it is to be a part of an organism. If to be an organism is to be determined in one's organization by the goodness (for the organism in question) of certain goals and of the means to achieve them, to be part of an organism is to be organized in a way that is determined by the goodness of those goals. Here, too, given the goodness of the goal for the natural organism, it will (as a natural organism) have (in favourable conditions) those parts that are required for those goals. So understood, to be a natural organism is to be determined in its movements and internal parts by the goodness of certain goals and means. Its actions and organization are sensitive to and guided by what is good for it. Its life requires or goes better if it achieves these goals. To use a modern metaphor, a natural organism is 'programmed' to be and act in ways which are good for it because being and acting in these ways is good for it. (I shall consider these claims in the final section of this essay in asking whether Aristotle's account, so understood, withstands philosophical scrutiny.)

Aristotle seems drawn towards this viewpoint when in the *Physics* he describes *what something is* and *what it is for* as the same (198a25) and states that *what something is* is its goal (198b3ff.). On this understanding to be a plant is to be so organized as to achieve a given goal and its natural movements are those which are directed towards achieving this goal. Aristotle, as we have noted, discerns teleological causation in both nature and craft (see *Phys.* II 8 199a10ff.). We can now see why. In both, good means are selected to achieve their distinctive goals because they are good means to goals which are good for them (*qua* craftsman or organism). Indeed, what it is to be a nature (or a craftsman) is to be such as to seek what is good for each to do (or possess) *because* it is good for each to do (or possess). Since, in his account, plants and their natural processes are defined in terms of their goals, Aristotle is justified in commenting:

> ...one who talks of chance [in the way Empedokles does in rejecting talk of teleology] destroys what happens by nature and nature itself. For things that happen by nature proceed continuously from a definite starting point in these things towards a goal unless something obstructs (199b16ff.).

Since natures and natural processes are defined in terms of the relevant nature's goals, one who, like Empedokles, rejects talk of teleological causes, gives up talk of natures and natural processes. In Aristotle's view, one cannot achieve a proper account of what plants are (their natures) without invoking their teleological cause.

While this important remark is introduced without much support in the *Physics*, Aristotle develops his position more fully in the *Metaphysics* and his biological writings. In *Metaphysics* VII 17, he connects the basic essence (what it is to be something) in the case of substances with their final cause, invoking his *Analytics*-style account in which the basic essence explains a kind's other features (1041a29ff.). Against this background, a kind's properties, organization, and characteristic movements will be the ones required to achieve its distinctive goods. Indeed, it will have these properties, organization, and characteristic movements because they are the ones required to achieve those goals. They will contribute well towards achieving its distinctive goods. In the theoretical sections of *Parts of Animals* he develops a similar line, taking the goal as that for the sake of which everything in nature comes to be and is what it is (639b33ff.) and identifying nature with the goal (642a17ff.), which is the starting point in the causal account of why things are the way they are (642a22ff.). In this context, as in the *Metaphysics*, an organism's properties, movements, and organisation will be caused to be the way they are by its distinctive goal (what is good for it: living in a given way).

In Aristotle's account of teleological causation, what occurs is controlled by a goal (as its *archê*) where (i) the goal in question is tied (directly or indirectly) to an agent's (or organism's) desires or needs and (ii) the agents or organisms are essentially organized to achieve such goals by good (or the best) means. At this point, one reaches bedrock in Aristotle's account: there are agents and organisms essentially organized to achieve certain distinctive goals: the ones which it is good for those agents and organisms to bring about. There is a deep interdependency between certain natures (or organisms) and certain goods: there are natures which are organized to bring about certain goods, those which are good for those natures to bring about (or possess). These are organisms whose life will go better for them (or continue) if they achieve these goals. Their actions and organization are sensitive to and guided by what is good for them (given their natures).

This model distinguishes between cases of genuine teleological causation and those where a result is beneficial but not teleologically caused. In the latter, what occurs is not controlled by a good needed or desired by an agent essentially organized to achieve that goal by the best means. Heavy snowfalls in winter, no doubt, benefit Alpine skiers, hoteliers, and sky instructors. But it does not fall for their sake if (i) neither it (nor the water that constitutes it) has desires or needs, still less desires or needs directed towards successful skiing holidays and (ii) neither it (nor the water) is organized to achieve such goals in ways sensitive to what is the best means to do it (e.g., by falling in just those places and times where snow is beneficial for skiing). If snow and water are not sensitive to the goodness of these goals (for humans) or of the required means, the beneficial results of Alpine snowfall will not be teleologically caused. Snow, when it falls in winter on the high passes of France and Switzerland, does not do so (in Aristotle's account) for the sake of the tourist or the tourist trade.

It is important to note that one could not vindicate the claim that winter snowfall is a case of teleological causation (in Aristotle's account) simply by attributing to snow (or water) the (amazing!) need or desire to benefit Alpine skiers (or humans more generally). First, to be a teleological cause, such an aim would have to play a causal role in accounting for snow's falling *where* and *when* it does. However, as things are, the material nature of water and surrounding atmospheric conditions are by themselves sufficient to account for Alpine winter snow. Second, snow would have to have this aim (or desire) because it is a kind of nature that is (in some way) sensitive to the benefits that result from Alpine winter tourism. Otherwise falling from the sky over ski resorts would not be something which is good for snow to do. Its life (or existence) will not go better for it because it falls where it does. Finally, snow's desire to benefit Alpine skiers and hoteliers would have to be connected with its specific material constituents in such a way as to form one unified nature. More specifically, snow's matter would have had to be organized in such a way that had the interests of the Alpine tourist trade been different, snow would have fallen in different places and times. If snow's matter is not organized in this way, it will not be integrated with the relevant desire (or goal) in the way required to form a unified nature. However, if matter and the hypothesized goal-directed capacity are not so connected, the latter will not be a teleological cause. For snow will not be a unified nature organized to produce the relevant benefit for skiers, etc. In sum, to establish the presence of a teleological cause, it is not enough merely to posit the existence of a goal-directed capacity. One needs to show (i) that it plays a genuine causal role, (ii) is present because it is good for the organism (given its nature), and (iii) is part of an appropriately organized (and unified) nature.

Consider the Aristotelian example of the ox neck joined (by chance) to a human head which works for the benefit of the new compound organism (e.g., by keeping the human head in position).[35] Here, too, the resulting benefit for the new organism will not be teleologically explained since the ox neck is not in the position it is in order to contribute to the good of the new organism. It may indeed be good for the new organism that it is present. But it is not present where it is because it is good for the new organism that it is there. Rather, the ox neck has the capacities it does because they are needed by an ox, with its distinctive nature and needs. Since the ox neck is not organized to support a human head in the new hybrid organism, the benefit it brings for that organism (in the case envisaged) will not be teleologically explained. Nor will the new organism itself constitute the relevant type of appropriately organized nature.

Aristotle's account of teleological causation, so understood, is substantive and controversial. It requires (or so I have argued) the presence of (i) goals, tied to the desires and needs of an agent or organism which are required if it is to live (or live well); (ii) agents and organisms essentially defined in terms of sensitivity to such goals; and (iii) capacities present (in appropriately unified natures) for the sake of actions directed towards such goals. While in many cases teleological causation co-exists with efficient causation, the two forms of causation are distinct. Even where they co-exist, teleological causal claims are not true simply in virtue of efficient causal ones.

I shall consider some of the philosophical problems in Aristotle's account in the final section of this essay. However, before doing so, there is a prior question: what is the range of cases to which Aristotle wishes to apply his account? In addressing this issue, it is important to keep firmly in mind his preferred view of teleological causation. In it, as we have seen, it is a non-trivial task to establish the presence of teleological causes. In the next section, I shall examine four controversial cases and argue that only one of them meets the three substantial conditions (i)-(iii) just isolated. Indeed, Aristotle, I shall argue, does not intend the others to be taken as genuine cases of teleological causation. We can see these discussions in a proper focus only if we approach them with a clear view of his account of the teleological cause. Those who wish to interpret these cases differently owe us an alternative account of Aristotle's view of teleological causation. (Nearly always they proceed without one to hand.)

4. The Range of Aristotle's Account

[1] Sharks

Aristotle comments that the location of the mouth in sharks and dolphins gives a benefit to other animals which can escape more easily. He writes:

> Nature appears to do this not only for the sake of the preservation of other animals (for during the turn other animals escape because of the delay...). PA 696b23ff.

Although the location of the shark's mouth benefits the other fish, their being benefitted is not, it seems, teleologically caused by that benefit. For if it were, the sharks would have as their goal their contribution to the life of other species. Making this contribution would be part of living well (or living) for the shark. They would have to desire the welfare of the other fish or be governed by a need to protect them. Further, sharks would have their distinctive types of mouth because it was a good way for them to achieve this other-directed goal. Since none of these claims is plausible (and Aristotle makes no attempt to defend them), the benefit that results to other species will not itself be teleologically explained in his account.[36] These are cases, discussed in Section 2(a) above, where a benefit accrues (*tini*) which is not a teleological cause (*hou heneka*).

Aristotle mentions other cases that should be treated in the same way. Thus, when he says that nature makes animals for the sake of humans (*Pol.* 1256b15–22), this need (and should) mean only that other animals benefit humans, not that so benefitting them is one of their goals. It is, after all, not part of what living or living well is for a sheep that it ends up on your dinner table, still less something that it desires or needs!

[2] Rainfall in the Mediterranean Winter

Aristotle notes, in his discussion in the *Physics*, that rainfall occurs frequently during the Mediterranean winter (*Phys.* 199a1–2) and suggests that winter rainfall happens in that region 'always or for most part' (*Phys.* 198b35) and occurs 'by nature'. He also thinks that it does not occur by chance (*Phys.*199a1f.). From these considerations, some have concluded that if he thinks that everything comes to be either by chance or for a goal, he must accept that winter rainfall is teleologically caused.[37]

I suggested above that Aristotle's premise:

> [P] If it is thought that anything comes to be by chance or for a goal.... (199a3ff.)

should be interpreted as applying only to any natural phenomena for which the alternatives are 'by chance or the sake of a goal'. Such cases will include the formation of natural parts in ways that are beneficial for the animals in question: the cases marked out as 'these things' in 198b35 which refer back to the cases under discussion in 198b25ff. It is important to note that [P], so interpreted, is acceptable to Empedokles, who holds that the coming to be of animals happens by chance (198b27, 196a23f.). However, he would not have accepted that all natural phenomena happen either by chance or for a goal since, in his view, many of these happen by necessity without the involvement of either chance or final causation (see 196a17ff.). Indeed, he only talks of chance in some parts of his theory, as when accounting for the origin of parts of animals. Elsewhere he detects the operation of non-chance (and non-teleological) efficient causes, such as fire and strife: see 196a15–18, 23–24. Against this background, Aristotle could not simply take it as established (or as generally agreed) that every natural process happens either by chance or for the sake of the goal. Since he is aiming to show that Empedokles himself (and those who think like him) will be forced to accept that the formation of animal parts happens for the sake of a goal (199a5-7), he cannot (justifiably) rely on an unrestricted version of [P] which (he knows) Empedokles would reject.

The interpretation of [P], offered above, is in line with Aristotle's discussion earlier in *Physics* II. Some things are said to happen by nature without reference to a goal: those which have their own source of movement in the way fire does when it is carried downwards (192b14). Many, not just Empedokles, believe that fire and water operate in just this way without a goal (193a22ff., 29ff.).[38] Elsewhere, Aristotle himself describes fire as rising and water falling, once drawn up by heat, because of their material properties (*Meteor.* 339a30, 390a39). Indeed, in the immediate context of *Physics* II 8, Aristotle had focused on just this eventuality in talking of the necessary (non-chance) movements of the hot and the cold without invoking any teleological notions (198b19–20: see 198b12–15). In the *Physics*, he uses 'shape' (*morphê*) to designate a goal (199a31ff.) and connects it with the use of 'nature' which refers to what grows (see 193b16ff.): animals, plants, human agents. In *Phys.* 199a20–34, Aristotle is explicitly employing this narrower notion of nature, not the broader one introduced at the outset, of something which has within it its own source of change and rest. In effect, he is distinguishing (as *Physics* II progresses) a wider use of 'nature', which applies *inter alia* to earth, air, and fire, from the more restricted one which does not. So far from preparing his readers for the unrestricted claim that everything in the natural world happens either by chance or for a goal, he has encouraged them to think that many things happen by necessity (without chance) as a result of efficient causation alone. Against this background, it is most unlikely that in 199a3-4 he simply takes for granted an unrestricted version of [P] which applies to all natural phenomena. It is not, given his earlier remarks, something which seems to be the case. It was certainly not something which was widely held to be true.

The interpretation offered of [P] above is, of course, what is required by Aristotle's discussion of teleological causation (when understood as above). Rain, even in winter, does not have the goal of falling to the earth as it has no need or desire to be there. It does not fall because it is good for it to do so. Things are not better for it if it falls there. (It has no life!) Nor is its movement controlled by this goal. Had things been different and it had been better for it to fall elsewhere, it would not have done so. It does not have capacities of a type which are sensitive to the goal of aiding the agricultural community.[39] Rain falls because its matter is the way it is (see *Meteor.* 346b26ff.). Indeed, rain and water are not the types of thing they are because they have the goal of falling in winter (let alone in the Mediterranean!). In these respects, the case of winter rainfall resembles the example of Alpine snowfall discussed above. While both may benefit some people, they are not caused to occur in the way they do for the sake of the benefit that results. Neither has goal-directed capacities (i) that play a genuine causal role (ii) are present because it is good for the organism (given its nature) and (iii) are part of an appropriately organized (and unified) nature.

In Aristotle's account, many things happen by nature because of the matter of the substances involved and not because of any goal. Water and fire, for example, moves towards their natural places in the cosmos because of their matter. Indeed, were they (*per impossibile*) to have a need to survive, they would not, in Aristotle's cosmos, go to their natural place. Their continued existence is better ensured by their reciprocal movements. (Aristotle does not consider the question of whether earth and fire would survive were the cosmos destroyed.) The best way for them to continue to exist is for them to be disposed to take part in this cyclical pattern. While Aristotle talks of earth and water as going towards their form (*eidos*)[40] when they move to their natural position, he never says that they do so *for the sake of* (*hou heneka*) being there. Nor does he anywhere suggest that it is good for water or earth to move towards that place. Had this been his view, he would have needed to show how these cases can satisfy the requirements on teleological causation noted at the end of the previous section (Section 3). Since he makes no attempt to do so, the movements of water or fire towards their natural place should be distinguished from ones in which there is a goal (as in the case of animal development) which causes the movement to happen in the way it does because it is good that it should happen in this way.

[3] Eternity: Elemental Cycles v. Reproduction of Plants and Animals

In Aristotle's account, as we have noted, water is transformed into air, air into fire, and back again into water. There is an eternal cyclical movement (*Gen. et Corr.* 337a3ff.) of the material elements which collectively 'imitate' the circular movement of the stars (*Met.* 1050b28ff.).[41] Aristotle provides an efficient causal account of their movement (*Gen. et Corr.* 337a7–15, 17–33, *Meteor.* 346b26ff.) and also suggests elsewhere that their eternal cyclical generation is necessary if there is to be an eternal heaven and an eternal movement of the outer sphere (*DC* II 3 286a13-b2). But does he see their cyclical movement as teleologically caused? What does his talk of 'imitation' require?

While Aristotle argues in *De Caelo* II 3 that the cyclical eternal generation of elements is necessary if there is to be an immortal heaven and outer sphere, this does not by itself show that the cyclical movement of the elements is teleologically caused. Aristotle could be merely noting that their eternal movement is a necessary condition of the eternity of the heavens. There must always be a cyclical generation of elements if the heaven and outer sphere are to persist for ever. As we noted in Section 2(a) more than this is required for teleological causation: what occurs must happen as a causal result of the goal, not merely a necessary condition of its occurrence. Further, if their cyclical movement is to be teleologically explained, the elements themselves would have to have their eternity or that of the heavens as their goal. Otherwise, what occurs will not satisfy the conditions for teleological causation set out above. It will not be controlled by, or sensitive to, the goals in question.

It is difficult to see how water or air can have goals (in Aristotle's account) if this requires them to have needs or desires. It makes no sense to talk of their existence (or life) being better *for them* because they move in certain ways. Further, their movements appear to be controlled by their matter (and the efficient causal impact of the upper cosmos) not by a goal (see *Meteor.* 346b26ff.). Against this background, it is significant that when, at *Meteor.* 346b36f., Aristotle speaks of the seasonal cycle of the elements as 'imitating' the annual movement of the sun ('the moisture rises and falls as the sun moves in the ecliptic'), he claims only that the cycle (not the elements themselves) 'imitates' the movement of the sun. Since cycles are not the types of thing to have desires or needs, his claim can only mean that the cycle 'is like' or 'reflects' the movement of the sun.[42] As we would have predicted, he is carefully avoiding attributing the desire or need to imitate to the basic material elements.

However, elsewhere, in *Gen. et Corr.* 336b25ff., Aristotle does note that 'we say that everything aims at what is better and that being is better than not being' and adds that God 'filled up the universe' by making generation continual (in cases where the individual substances themselves cannot last for ever). This is why there is cyclical generation in the case of simple bodies. The first remark suggests that since being is better than not being, the elements themselves will aim at keeping going for ever (or the closest they can get to it). The second is of a piece with the global teleological speculation pursued further by Aristotle's reference to the Creator God with the plan of making generation continual. In the present case, he introduces talk of such a God with no supporting evidence (or context) apart (possibly) from a considerably earlier reference to Empedokles' Gods a few pages earlier in 333b21ff. But what do these passages show? In assessing them, it is important to consider Aristotle's goal in talking in this way in *Gen. et Corr.* and elsewhere.

In *De Caelo* 284b44ff. Aristotle notes that it is good to believe old stories about the gods, and speaks, in the same spirit, of heaven as 'ensouled' (285a27ff.). Indeed, in *De Caelo* he sometimes identifies God with nature as doing nothing in vain in language which recalls the *Timaeus* (271a33ff.). Later, he suggests that we should think of heavenly bodies as partaking of life and action (292a22ff.) as, if we do so, 'what happens will not appear unbelievable (*paradoxon*)'. In the same spirit, he suggests that we should think of their movements as governed by teleological principles (292a23–8) and compare them with the actions of animals and plants (292b1–3). We should think in this way because if we do, what occurs, albeit in far away regions where we have little to go on, will not seem unexpected or improbable (292a17–18). We will have a reasonable account of what occurs, which solves problems, is supported by popular opinions and by analogies with other cases, and is preferable to other accounts which result in absurdities or serious difficulties.[43] In the language of the *Timaeus*, we will have a plausible (or reasonable) account (*eikos logos*) of what occurs.

Against this background, when in *Gen. et Corr.* 336b25ff. Aristotle talks of the Creator God as 'filling up the universe' so as to make generation continual, his remarks can (and I think should) be interpreted as using teleological and theological language in an attempt to make what occurs seem intelligible (or non paradoxical) to us. He will be aiming at providing a *Timaeus*-style reasonable account of what occurs and permitting himself to use mythological stories for this purpose. His way of talking in no way commits him to accepting that there are in reality teleological causes at work in these cases. While what he says leaves open the possibility that there are causes of this type, he has not attempted to show that this is the case (or what they are).[44] Indeed, he allows that we cannot (whether as humans or at present) establish the existence of such teleological causes. In his project of providing a plausible account of reality, Aristotle can use theological terms (taken from earlier writers of traditions) and rely (in some measure) on what we are naturally inclined to say. Thus when Aristotle remarks in *Gen. et Corr.* 336b25ff. that 'we say that everything aims at what is better and that existence is better than non-existence' he is pointing to material which supports a 'reasonable account' of the subject matter. He need not be endorsing this as his account of what actually is the case. Indeed, in his view, our epistemic limitations prevent us from establishing the existence of teleological causes in this area.[45]

Had Aristotle wished to establish that there were genuine teleological causes of the cyclical movements of earth or water, he would have needed to show how these basic material elements could be governed by goals in the way required. To do this, he would have to show how they can (i) have desires or needs to live for ever and (ii) be defined as the substances they are in terms of their sensitivity to this goal and (iii) have capacities which are present because they are directed towards this goal. It would have taken a great deal of work (which Aristotle nowhere attempts) to show how such capacities and desires or needs can be generated from the material nature of earth or water or integrated with it to form one unified substance. He would have needed to make sense of the idea of their continual existence being good for them. Without this supporting background, the best he can offer is a 'reasonable account' in teleological terms aimed at making their characteristic movements intelligible (or even only 'non-paradoxical') to us.

The situation is different when Aristotle considers animal and plant reproduction, claiming that each aims to produce another like itself (*DA* 415a28ff., 416b23ff.) and adding that they do so 'in order to share in the eternal and the divine as far as possible. For they all desire this, the final cause of their natural activity' (415a29ff.). In this case, each animal and plant has a goal-directed capacity for reproduction. Perhaps even plants have a need to produce 'another like itself'. Animals may well desire to do so. Both are organized to achieve this goal. In their case, there is the foothold required to specify (in some detail) the relevant teleological cause. Aristotle is not merely using teleological vocabulary, as in the case of the elements, to make what happens seem non-paradoxical to us. He is connecting reproduction with the needs, desires, and capacities of the unified organisms in question. Given their natures, it is good for them to reproduce in the way they do.

There is, however, a difficulty. It is by no mean obvious that individual animals, let alone plants, have a desire (or need) for the eternal and the divine (or even for being part of a species which is eternal). Did Aristotle think that, appearances notwithstanding, they literally did, perhaps following Diotima's 'prophetic' remarks in the *Symposium* that all mortal nature seeks as far as it can to be immortal (207D2)? Had he done so, their situation would still have been unlike that of the elements since their need for (or desire for) immortality is grounded in their need or desire to produce another like itself. However, in *DA* 415b4ff., Aristotle may simply mean that the individual plant or animal aims at the eternal *only to the extent* of aiming at producing another like itself. There may be nothing more to their desire for the eternal than this. Elsewhere Aristotle speaks of the goal of the animal *as a genus* as being to share in the eternal as far as possible through the eternal persistence of its form (*GA* 731b32ff.). But this generalizing reference to the eternal may serve only to describe (in an abstracted way) what is common to the goals of each species of animal. While one aims to survive as a man, another as a horse, their goals (properly speaking) are the eternity of their species, not eternity itself. In the case of individual men or horses, their specific goal may simply be to reproduce something like itself. Neither their actions nor those of their species are teleologically governed by the goal of eternity itself. If we choose to follow Diotima in representing each animal's goal (whether individual or species) as manifesting a desire for eternity, we are speaking in an abstracted way about a variety of distinct, and more specific, teleological goals. Diotima herself, no doubt, was merely offering a plausible account (or myth), designed to make the activities of many species intelligible (or non-paradoxical).

While Aristotle's remarks on the divine and the eternal in the context of reproduction are telegrammatic and elusive, they rest on the presence of a genuine capacity in an organism (whether plant or animal) which is explained by its goal: producing 'another like oneself.' Further, this goal may plausibly be connected with the desires or needs of the organism in question: reproducing may indeed be part of their life. In these respects, his discussion of reproduction differs from that of the elements. In the biological domain, we know that there are genuine teleological causes at work, even if these can sometimes be characterized in terms which recall Diotima's religious perspective. In the case of the cyclical movement of the elements, by contrast, the 'reasonable account' offered lacks a secure basis in genuine teleological causes of which we have knowledge.

[4] Global Teleology

In *De Caelo* Aristotle is content, as we have just noted, to use teleological language to make the heavens and their movements seem 'non- paradoxical' or 'reasonable' to us. As part of this project, he can describe heavenly bodies as partaking in life and action (292a22ff.) and think of their movements as being like those of animals (292b1–3). Further, he can present each of them as making a contribution to a single good (such as survival or movement) even though the value of their contribution varies. Indeed, in some contexts he goes so far as to personify 'nature' as a distinctive agent which 'balances things and produces a certain order' (293a2–4) and 'gives many bodies a single locomotion and many locomotions to a single body.' These latter descriptions should not be taken as his literally positing a cosmic nature with its own goals. For, as we have seen, since they form part of a discussion aimed at making some distant phenomena seem 'non-paradoxical', Aristotle is not committed to their literal truth. Indeed, his personification of nature may serve simply to summarize what he had previously said about individual stars and heavenly bodies, described in his own 'reasonable account' as individually aiming, in their differing ways, at a shared goal (such as survival or locomotion). In these ways, his talk of cosmic nature as a guiding agent is at two removes from establishing it as a genuine teleological cause. It offers a striking way to summarize the role of other features whose individual activity is part of his 'reasonable account'. Had he wanted to establish that there is a cosmic nature which is a genuine teleological cause, he would have needed to show that there was such a nature with its own life and goals which controlled the movement of the other astral phenomena he describes.[46]

Aristotle's discussion in *Metaphysics* XII 7–10 resembles that in *De Caelo* in several ways. He defends the first stage of his account by saying that it offers a possible way out of an *aporia* and points to many difficulties that will arise if it is not true (1072a18–20: for the difficulties, see 1071b22ff.). Later, in XII 10 (1075a25ff.), he notes that alternative accounts of the role of good in the cosmos have 'impossible' or 'strange' (*atopa*) consequences. Here, too, he advances mythological support in its favour (1074b1–14), relies on what we are inclined to say about the divine (1072b27), and, at a crucial point, simply assumes (without any supporting argument) that spheres are moved by unmoved movers because they are intelligent beings with desires of a certain type (1072a27ff.). In *De Caelo* he is more explicit about the status of the latter assumed point, noting that 'it is generally taken to be the case' (*dokei*) that stars are moved because they are intelligent beings, which share in life and action (*DC* 292a22ff.).[47] If so, we can see his aim in XII 10, more fully realized in *De Caelo*, as being to offer a reasonable account in teleological terms which makes the relevant phenomena intelligible or non-surprising, not to establish that teleological causes are actually at work in reality. In both works, he often speaks of his claims as 'reasonable' (*eulogon*: 1074a16, 24, b28), suggesting that he is offering a plausible account (*eikos logos*) of the subject matter, uncommitted to the literal truth of what he says. Were he to wish to establish his account as literally true, he would need to spell out a genuine teleological causal account of (e.g.) the movement of the stars or of the secondary unmoved movers (1072b14ff.).[48] Since he makes no attempt to do so, regarding the task as beyond what we can know, it is best to see him as giving a reasonable account of this subject matter. For, if his aim is only to make it intelligible that nature can depend on a first unmoved mover, he does not have to specify the teleological causes in the way required for this to be the case.[49]

Aristotle suggests in XII 10 that everything (including the sublunary world) is 'ordered together in a way'.[50] Although they are not all ordered in the same way, they are 'not unconnected' in that everything is directed to one thing (1075a16–18). Since he does not specify further what the one thing in question is, it might be (i) the survival of life (or animate locomotion) or (ii) the survival of the whole cosmos. In either case the ways things act to pursue this goal will differ as will the value of their contribution.[51] Aristotle comments as follows:

> For this kind of starting point in each is their nature (1075a22ff.)

In the immediate context this remark need only mean (i) that everything in the sublunary world manifests in its own different way a type of activity which is directed towards one thing (such as (e.g.) survival of life or the survival of the whole cosmos) and (ii) the varying starting points from which each acts (in their different ways for the sake of this goal) constitute their distinctive natures.[52] So understood, the differing ways in which men and fish act so as 'to do their bit' to ensure the survival of life indicate their distinctive natures. Aristotle supports this claim by noting that each thing is dissolved (and so provides material for rebirth) and also shares in other (unspecified) activities directed towards the common goal (1075a23–4). If so, all will be 'in a way' connected because each plays its own role in ensuring (e.g.) the survival of life or the cosmos (or the continuation of locomotion). In some cases, as noted in the earlier discussion of reproduction, they can do so simply by aiming at creating another animal (or plant) like themselves. If we are inclined to see all animals as aiming at the survival of life (or the whole cosmos) in this way (and by passing on their matter 'as significant soil' to others on their death), we may generalize from individual cases (with more limited goals) to truths about the genus: animal (compare GA 731b32ff.). This would constitute our way of describing the activities of individual organisms (or types of organism) so as to portray them all as having (in their different ways) a goal in common. There is certainly no need to invoke a further, shared, cosmic nature to tell this story, still less to attribute to it the desires, needs, or capacities needed to underwrite a genuine cosmic teleology. All that is offered is a generalization designed to depict, in an abstracted way, the differing activities of differing animal or plant natures in a common light.

Some scholars, however, have taken Aristotle to introduce (in these lines) a single cosmic nature, literally understood, as the organizational principle which makes each individual (or individual species) what it is. In their view, a cosmic nature of this type is required to explain why everything shares in the common activity of maintaining the survival of life (or the survival of the whole). They translate 1075a22 as follows:

> For this kind of principle in each of them is nature[53]

and understand 'nature' to refer not to the nature of the species (understood dis-
tributively as 'the nature of each of them') but rather to one single cosmic nature,
construed literally as the organizational principle that belongs to each thing. On
their interpretation, all individual natures are in different ways grounded in one
cosmic nature (as all individuals are, in Schopenhauer's much later suggestion, the
expression of one cosmic will). So understood, in this one line Aristotle finally
'comes clean', momentarily revealing himself as literally committed to one explanatorily basic unitary cosmic nature, going far beyond his more cautious claims
earlier in *Metaphysics* XII or *De Caelo*.[54]

It would be most surprising had Aristotle chosen to take the huge step of
expressing unqualified (and literal) attachment to the reality of a cosmic nature
of the type required in an ambiguous 'one liner', introduced without further argumentative support. To sustain such a move, he would have needed, given his views
on teleological causation, (i) to establish it as a nature with its own goals, desires,
and needs, and as living a life (compare his discussion of stars in 1074b22ff.), (ii) to
show that (and how) it has certain goals because they are good, and (iii) to establish
that (and how) it is a properly organized and unified nature. All three claims would
have needed defence had he intended his talk of 'cosmic nature' literally to indicate
a genuine teleological cause, distinguishing his present approach from the far more
cautious one adopted in *De Caelo*. Since Aristotle makes no attempt to meet any of
these three conditions, we should seek alternative ways to understand his remark
in 1075a22.

While the interpretation I sketched above avoids all reference to one cosmic nature,
the passages we have considered in *De Caelo* suggest an alternative, more concessive,
strategy.[55] Even if Aristotle does introduce talk of cosmic nature in this passage, his
remark may, as in *De Caelo* 292b2–4, merely serve to describe in 'personifying' terms
what had previously been said about individual natures. It would not refer literally to
a distinctive type of cosmic organism (or agent) whose capacities and desires explain
how individual natures act. In the 'reasonable account' he is offering, he is able to use
personifying (or even theological) forms of description to make what occurs seem
intelligible to us, without any commitment to their literal truth. Understood in this
way, Aristotle need not be seen as taking (in this one line) the major and philosophically undefended step on which the literalist interpreter insists. He is rather advancing
(in an admittedly sketchy way) the type of plausible (or reasonable) account he develops in more detail when personifying 'nature' in *De Caelo*.

Aristotle's telegrammatic remark about the role of nature in *Metaphysics*
1075a22ff. stands in need of further explication using materials he develops elsewhere in *De Anima* or *De Caelo*. Either it is a form of abstracted generalization or
part of a plausible 'personifying' account. However, whichever alternative is preferred, this one line does not commit him to the literal truth of claims about a
cosmic nature. Nor should this surprise us given what he would have had to do to
establish the truth of a teleological causal account involving a cosmic nature.

In sum: only one of the cases discussed in this section (that of animal and plant reproduction) meets Aristotle's own conditions for teleological causation (as set out in the previous sections). The others are not examples where what occurs (or is present) is controlled by a good tied (directly or indirectly) to the desires or needs of an agent or a nature, essentially organized to achieve such goals by the best means. It is, I have argued, a mistake to understand any mention of (i) benefit (as in the case of the shark) or of (ii) regularity (as in the case of winter rainfall) or of (iii) teleologically inspired ways of giving a plausible (*eikos logos*) or 'non-paradoxical' view of the phenomena as requiring the presence of genuine Aristotelian teleological causes. Indeed, in my view, one will only be tempted to understand these cases in this way if one is operating without a clear or explicit account of what is required in a genuine case of Aristotelian teleological causation.

5. SOME QUESTIONS AVOIDED: TWO UNAVOIDABLE ISSUES

In Aristotle's account (as set out in Section 2), teleological causation is not a species of efficient causation. There are, it seems, teleological causes of the presence of efficient causes and of why those causes operate as they do (via the best means and towards good goals). Aristotle seems to assume that this is a valid form of causal explanation which can stand alongside efficient and material causation, without being reduced to either. A complete story couched in terms of efficient and material causation (were one to be possible) would not capture the explanatory work by teleological causation. This would be true even if the relevant capacities invoked in efficient causation were good-directed ones: for one would still fail to account for *their presence* in terms of the good they bring about. *A fortiori*, it would be true if the relevant efficient (and material) causal story did not invoke goodness at all.

The account so far sketched has several important gaps:

(1) I have not discussed (in any detail) the question of whether Aristotle's opponents who objected to teleological causation were reductionists, eliminativists, or neither. My only claim is that, according to Aristotle, they did not offer an explanation of why certain things happen for the good of the agent or organism but regarded the resulting benefit as a matter of chance.[56]

(2) I have not discussed the question of whether Aristotle was justified in his criticisms of those of his predecessors, especially Anaxagoras and Plato, who had invoked the teleological cause. While he describes them (somewhat dismissively) in *Met.* II 7 988b8–15 as 'both saying and not saying that the good is a cause', we have not examined how his account is meant to be superior to those he criticizes.[57]

(3) I have not discussed the ways in which Aristotle sought to intertwine his teleological, efficient, and material causal stories in his own positive account of the subject matter.[58]

(4) I have not considered in any detail what arguments (if any) Aristotle adduces in favour of the causal role of goals in the cases where he claims to detect it.

While some of these issues have been extensively discussed in recent years, my focus has been on the simpler, more basic, question: what is Aristotle's account of teleological causation? While the answer to this question has important implications for the four questions just noted, I shall not pursue them here.

It may, nonetheless, be helpful to conclude by noting two areas in which Aristotle's account (as I have presented it) is philosophically controversial. My aim is only to show that it should not be rejected out of hand.

[A] Agency

Many philosophers will not accept that the actions of the rational agent or the craftsman are teleologically caused. They reject Aristotle's account of rational agents as acting on the basis of their sensitivity to what is in fact good for them. Some do not accept the idea that there are objective goods in the worlds which guide our actions. Others prefer to see the relevant actions as (efficiently) caused by our beliefs and desires without reference to further factors in the world. For the latter group, even if there were objective goods in the world, they play no causal role in the explanation of action.

It should be noted, however, that Aristotle's approach has its current defenders who begin (as he did) by crediting wise people with knowledge of what is good, which guides their subsequent actions. In this view, their knowledge is based on what is good for them to do, and they act as they do because it is good for them to do so.[59] This remains an intuitive and well defended view, as defensible today as it was in Aristotle's own day.

[B] Natural Organisms

Many more will not accept Aristotle's account of teleological causation as applied to natures and organisms. Certainly, it must be conceded that it is more open to criticism than his views about agency. For, while he characterized organisms as essentially designed to achieve certain goals because they are good for them, he gave no account of the way in which such organisms are sensitive to their goals. While the rational agent or craftsman may see certain goals as good and select them because they are good, plants (at least) cannot be sensitive in this way to what is good for them.[60] It does not seem sufficient to say: they are organized (or 'programmed') in a certain way *because* being so organized is good for them without offering any further account of how they are sensitive to the goodness of their organization. Indeed, many believe that today we have a better account of why plants and animals came to be organized in the way that is beneficial for them (in terms of the theory of adaptation), which does not involve attributing to them any form of sensitivity to goodness. Aristotle's account of teleology will be rejected because it does not offer the best explanation of why plants and animals are organized in ways that are beneficial to them.

It is worth noting, in considering this objection, that defenders of the central claims of Aristotelian teleology (as set out here) need not reject the facts (whatever they may be) of evolutionary history. What is at issue is whether the *theory* of adaptation (as developed by Darwin and his successors) provides the best possible explanation of why animals (and plants) have come to have the features they do. If it does, Aristotle's account will not give the best explanation of these phenomena and should be rejected.

Can Aristotle's viewpoint be defended? One attempt runs as follows: while adaptation, no doubt, plays an important role in accounting for the survival of animals with certain features, it may turn out not to give the complete explanation of why they have developed in the way they have. Features of the specific physical contexts in which animals find themselves and of their specific genetic codes (with their distinctive features and limitations) may also play an important role. Indeed, it may not prove possible to develop a general, unitary, context-free, account of why species of animals which survive have the features they do. If particular explanations are context-specific and fail to generalize in the way the theory of adaptation requires, we will lack a satisfying general account of why plants and animals have the features they do.[61] In such an eventuality, the only defensible explanation of why the species are as they are may simply be that they have (by some route or other) developed a 'programme' which is governed by what is good for them. If no general account can be given (along adaptationist lines) of why animals have the 'programmes' they do, one response would be to suggest (along Aristotelian lines) that they simply have them *because* it is good for them to do so. Even if there can be no general theory linking their 'programme' and what is good for them, they will still have it (in some way or other) because it is good for them to do so. No better explanation than this relatively modest (and undemanding) one may be available.

These are, of course, controversial and unresolved questions whose discussion would take us far afield. My aim in this brief final section has been a limited one: to note that Aristotle's account of teleological causation does not stand or fall with his remarks on natural organisms. For even if the latter are rejected, human actions may still happen because it is good (for us) that they do.[62]

NOTES

1. This distinction is clearly drawn by W. Kullmann in his 'Different Conceptions of the final cause in Aristotle', in *Aristotle on Nature and Living Things* (ed.) A. Gotthelf, (Bristol 1985), pp. 169–174. The three cases can all be described in terms of 'that for the sake of which' (*hou heneka*) and 'goal' (*telos*). However, in the light of the distinction Kullmann notes, we cannot conclude that all three are cases of teleological (or final) causes since some may not be causes at all. Aristotle, I shall argue, points to this ambiguity in order to distinguish cases where the goal (*telos*) is a cause from those where it is simply a result.

2. See for example *Met.* 1074a25ff. I shall return to this example below.

3. See *Phys.* 196b32ff. In some cases, actions done for the sake of A (where A is also benefitted by what is done) will also result in some benefit for B. But the benefit to B, *ex hypothesi*, will not be that for which the action is done (even if it is a necessary consequence of the action). So understood, B's benefit will not be a final cause (in the sense relevant for teleological causation).

4. I return to this distinction in considering Aristotle's comments on teleological causation in *Physics* II 8 below.

5. In some type (1) cases, what is desired by S need not actually be good for S. Here something can still be a goal for S provided that S aims at it and takes it as an apparent good (*Phys.* 195a25–6, *Met.* 1013b28, *Top.* 146b36, *DA* 433a29ff.). Aristotle's discussion allows apparent goods as well as actual goods to be goals. Aristotle talks of the object of desire as either the good or the apparent good. Is this an exclusive or an inclusive disjunction? It might be an exclusive disjunction: in one case the object desired is an external object which is good, in the latter an internal object of the imagination. Alternatively, the apparent good may be an external object imagined to be good. Either way, there would be a causal route beginning with an external object which is grasped by the thinker which leads him to desire to act (431b11ff.). These important but controversial issues need further discussion.

6. Aristotle gives many examples of the latter in *De Partibus Animalium*. For a general statement of his view, see 645b14: 'every part of the body, like every other instrument, is for the sake of a goal'. For a fine discussion of specific examples, see James Lennox's 'Material and Formal Natures in Aristotle's *De Partibus Animalium*', *Aristotelische Biologie*, (ed). W. Kullmann and S. Föllinger (Stuttgart 1997), pp. 163–181.

7. It is important to note that Aristotle is not explaining why sharp teeth are useful to the animal in question but why they actually come to be (or are present) in just those ways and at locations which are useful to that animal. That is, he is addressing the question:

   [1] 'Why do sharp teeth emerge (or are present) at just those places and in just those ways which are good for the organism?' and not

   [2] 'Why are sharp teeth (situated where they are) good for the organism?'
   To answer question [2] one does not need to say anything about what caused the emergence (or presence) of such teeth. It may well be that if one does not address question [2] one will exclude too much from one's account of the animal in question, leaving it unacceptably impoverished. However, [1] is the claim relevant to the causal role of the teleological cause.

8. It is important to note that what has to be explained in Aristotle's example in 198b25–32, 199a3ff. is not (i) simply *the co-occurrence of flat and sharp teeth* (which are

beneficial to the organism) nor (ii) *how such teeth cause benefit to the organism* nor (iii) a combination of (i) and (ii) (the co-occurrence of flat and sharp teeth, which are beneficial, and how they benefit the organism). What has to be explained is rather *the co-occurrence of sharp and flat teeth in ways and places which are beneficial to the organism.* While in an earlier paper ('Teleological Causation in the Physics' in *Physics*, Lindsay Judson (ed.), (Oxford 1991) I understood the *explanandum* to be simply the fact of co-occurrence, I have been persuaded by Lindsay Judson ('Aristotelian Teleology', *Oxford Studies in Ancient Philosophy* 2005, pp. 352–3) of the importance of taking *benefit to the organism* as part of the *explanandum.* In this essay, I attempt to develop this idea in two ways (which Judson may find congenial):

(i) by connecting it with Aristotle's examples of human actions and artefacts in *Physics* II (such as walking and axes) and
(ii) by suggesting that in these cases Aristotle focuses on the question ('why do useful sharp teeth (or walks) come to be in ways which are beneficial to the organism?') and not on the (distinct) question of why (or how) sharp teeth, (walks, etc.) are useful or beneficial for the animals that have them.

In my view, in his discussion of animal parts, Aristotle attempts to explain not simply (a) the co-occurrence of teeth that are beneficial to the organism and (b) the benefit accrues to the organism as a result but rather (c) the co-occurrence of two sets of teeth *in ways and places which are beneficial to the organism.* In (c), the *explananda* are not the co-occurrence of teeth and the benefit that results from their co-occurrence but rather the co-occurrence of these teeth *in just those ways and places which benefit the organism.*

9. It is not clear whether Aristotle envisaged his opponent as thinking that (i) there was (or could be) one efficient cause of an animal's coming to have both sharp and flat teeth at the same time or (ii) there were two (completely) independent efficient causes at work, one producing sharp teeth at t_i, one producing flat teeth at t_i and no cause of their co-occurrence. If the opponent took the latter option, he would focus on questions such as:
[A] 'Why do sharp teeth emerge at t_i, in certain places (physically specified) in this organism? Why do flat teeth emerge at t_i, in certain places (physically specified) in this organism?'
and not on the question:
[B] 'Why do sharp and flat teeth *co-emerge* in this organism?'
Either way, the opponent will not seek to answer
[C] Why do sharp and flat teeth *co-emerge in ways and places that are beneficial to this organism?*
Nor will his conception of the type of organism in question be one in which such teeth are co-located where they are for the organism's benefit. However, even if he only addresses [A], he will be able to define (non-teleologically) the type of organism in question as the one present on those occasions when sharp and flat teeth emerge (as it happens) at the same time in certain physically specified positions. If he considers [B], he can define the type of organism as one in which flat and sharp teeth regularly co-occur in physically specified positions. For a somewhat contrasting account, which represents Aristotle's Empedoklean opponent as a committed 'eliminativist' about kinds, see Susan Sauvé Meyer's 'Aristotle, Teleology and Reduction', *Philosophical Review* 101, (1992), 791–821.

10. The proposal which Aristotle considers in these lines seems to result from his own thought experiment and not to correspond to any specific proposal of Empedokles. For discussion of this issue, see Oliver Primavesi's essay 'Aristoteles oder Empedokles? Charles Darwin und Eduard Zeller über einen antiken Ansatz zur Evolutionstheorie', in *Eduard Zeller: Philosophie und Wissenschaftgeschichte im 19 Jahrhundert'*, G. Hartung (ed.), (Berlin 2010), pp. 25–65. For the reasons set out by Primavesi, I refer to Aristotle's interlocutor in this passage as 'his opponent' and not as 'Empedokles'.

11. On this understanding, neither Aristotle nor his opponent is committing himself in these lines to the dialectically highly controversial view that *all* natural phenomena (including winter rainfall) occur either by chance or for a goal. Some may, they may agree, happen by necessity, neither by chance nor for a goal. (There is, one should note, no use of 'all' or 'these cases' in the first clause of 199a3–4 to steer us back either to *all* natural occurrences or to the last mentioned cases of heat and rainfall.) The only assumption at issue is that there is a subset of cases (such as those involved in the co-formation of natural parts *in ways etc. beneficial to the organism*) which happen (i) not by necessity but (ii) either by chance or for a goal. There are two ways to translate 199a3ff. so as to sustain this interpretation.
[A] 'If it is also accepted that anything is either from chance or for the sake of a goal, and that these cases cannot be by chance, they are for the sake of the goal'.
On this interpretation, Aristotle considers (in the first clause) only cases where the (exhaustive) alternatives are: they occur by chance or for the sake of the goal. He is talking *only* of a subset of cases (within the class of natural phenomena) which occur either by chance or for a goal. Such cases will include the formation of natural parts in ways beneficial to the organism on which he currently focuses. They will be the ones referred to by 'these things' in 199a4 (mentioned in 198b34) and 'such things' in 199a6. An alternative runs as follows:
[B] 'If it is also accepted that these things are either from chance or for the sake of a goal, and that they cannot be by chance, they are for the sake of the goal'.
On this interpretation, 'these things' in 199a4 (i.e., the formation of natural parts in ways which benefit the organism) is the implied subject both of 'they occur either by chance or for a goal' in 199a3–4 and of 'they cannot be by chance.' [For a similar use in English, consider the sentences: (i) 'If he is not in London, then if John is in Cardiff, he will be at the match' (where 'John' is the implied subject of the first 'he') and the more colloquial (ii) 'If not in London, then if John is in Cardiff, he will be at the match.'] Both [A] and [B] are as acceptable grammatically and considerably preferable interpretatively to the suggestion that Aristotle and his opponent introduce and accept (in these two lines) the highly contentious assumption that
[C] '... everything (in nature) is either from chance or for the sake of a goal ....'
I am indebted to Jonathan Barnes and Bruno Currie for detailed discussion on this passage.

12. To block this argument, Aristotle's opponent would need to give an efficient (non-teleological) causal account of why natural parts come about together regularly in ways which benefit the organism. If he had such account, he could either claim that natural parts come to be regularly and by chance (rejecting Aristotle's account of chance) or withdraw his agreement to the claim that such things happen by chance, suggesting that they come to be neither from chance nor for a goal but as the result of a regular efficient causal sequence. What he cannot do is stand by the following three inconsistent premises:

1. These things (natural parts which come to be in ways which are useful) and everything which happens by nature (*ta phusei*) come to be always and for the most

part. (Examples of things that happen by nature will include winter rainfall: a non-teleological case: 198b34–199a3.)

2. These things (natural parts which are useful) come to be by chance in ways which are useful: 198b27, 29.

3. Things that happen by chance do not happen always or for the most part (198b36–199a2).

13. J.M. Cooper took a different view in his 'Aristotle on Natural Teleology', *Language and Logos*, eds. M. Schofield and M. Nussbaum, (Cambridge 1982), pp. 187–222. For a similar view of Aristotle's aim in this passage, see Margaret Scharle's 'Elemental Teleology in Aristotle's *Physics* 2.8', *Oxford Studies in Ancient Philosophy* xxxiv, 2008, pp. 150–54. For further discussion of this issue, see my 'Teleological Causation in the Physics' in *Aristotle's Physics,* L. Judson (ed.), (Oxford 1991), pp. 101–28.

14. See *Physics* 194a31ff: Aristotle cites a poet saying in jest 'he has reached his end (death) for which he was born', noting that the joke indicates that not every last stage is a goal.

15. Although rainfall in the Mediterranean winter may result in the growth of the crops, rain does not fall where and when it does because those places and times are useful for the crops (or for the farmers who grow them). So understood, benefit to the crops (even if it reliably results) is not the teleological cause of the rain falling when and where it does. Of course, the farmers plant their crops to use this rainfall but that is a wholly different issue! I return to this example, discussed by Aristotle in *Physics* 198b17ff., in Section 4.

16. (B) clearly distinguishes between cases of genuine teleological causation and those where although what occurs benefits someone (or something) what occurs does not happen *for the sake of* that benefit (or beneficiary). See note 1 above. Given this important distinction, one cannot justifiably lump all such cases together as instances (in Aristotle's account) of teleological (or final) causation.

17. I defend this view of hypothetical necessity in more detail in my 'Aristotle on Hypothetical Necessity and Irreducibility', *Pacific Philosophical Quarterly* 69, (1988), 3–20. For a somewhat contrasting view, see J.M. Cooper's 'Hypothetical Necessity', *Aristotle on Nature and Living Things*, A. Gotthelf (ed.), (Pittsburgh 1986), pp. 151–67.

18. There are, I have argued, cases of efficient causation which Aristotle counts as instances of hypothetical necessity. I defend this liberal account of hypothetical necessity in 'Aristotle on Hypothetical Necessity and Irreducibility', pp. 8–18. In the present essay, my focus is mainly on the form of such claims.

19. The agent or organism is better seen as responding to general features of the goal (such as the goodness of health or wealth). (C) is best read as follows: if a certain type of goal is to be (or is), and $A_1...A_n$ are required for a goal of that type, necessarily as a causal result $A_1...A_n$ will come to be (or are).

20. The most systematic modern proponent of this view is Allan Gotthelf in his 'Aristotle's Conception of Final Causality', *Review of Metaphysics* 30, (1976/7), 26–254. Others who have written in a somewhat similar vein include Martha Nussbaum, *Aristotle's De Motu Animalium,* Princeton, 1978, p. 84, Susan Sauvé Meyer, 'Aristotle, Teleology and Reduction', *Philosophical Review* 101, (1992), 809 (when referring to 'thought' and 'nature' as the relevant efficient causes) and David Furley, 'What Kind is Aristotle's Final Cause?', *Rationality in Greek Thought*, eds. M. Frede and G. Striker, Oxford, 1996, pp. 59–79. Sauvé Meyer later suggests ('Aristotle, Teleology and Reduction', *Philosophical Review* 101, (1992), p. 811) that Aristotle may have accounted for the continued existence of animal offspring with certain parts in terms of what was

required for their parents successfully to reproduce. But this latter 'adaptationist' suggestion (for which there is no direct textual evidence in Aristotle's writings) seems difficult (i) to generalize to the case of the origin of the species he considers, (ii) to be made consistent with his insistence that teleological causation begins with what is (or will be) good for the organism, not with what was good (for its parents).

21. One account seeks to reduce talk of goodness to non-valuational terms (such as actuality), another takes as basic 'good-directed capacities'. The former view, developed by Allan Gotthelf, is thoroughly 'naturalistic' in outlook, aiming to account for teleological causation in terms of non-valuational efficient causes. For this account, see his 'The Place of Good in Aristotle's Natural Teleology', *Proceedings of the Boston Area Colloquium in Ancient Philosophy*, iv, 1988.

22. For the causal priority of line 1 over line 2, see for example *PA* 645b14 (and the other examples usefully collected by J. G. Lennox in his 'Material and Formal Natures in Aristotle's *De Partibus Animalium*'). For the priority of lines 1 and 2 over 3 (and 4), see (for example) *PA* 640a19–25 (which is helpfully discussed by Alan Code in his 'The Priority of Final Causes Over Efficient Causes in Aristotle's *PA*' in *Aristotelische Biologie*, W. Kullmann and S. Föllinger (eds.), (Stuttgart 1997), pp. 128–143).

23. See, for example, *Met.* 1050a25ff., where Aristotle, having previously claimed that housebuilding is the teleological cause of the capacity to build (1050a11ff.), suggests that the house is a prior teleological cause. (I discuss this passage in more detail in my 'Θ 7 and 8: some issues concerning potentiality and actuality' in *Essays in Honour of Allan Gotthelf*, eds. J. Lennox and R. Bolton, (Cambridge 2010). Houses, themselves, have a teleological cause (*Met.* 1041a29f.): they are present for the safety of the belongings and people they contain (1043a16ff.).

24. See for example, *APo* II 10 94b21ff.

25. Comparable issues arise in the case of intentional action. It is not enough, by Aristotle's lights, to invoke a good-directed efficient cause, a desire directed to an end state which it is, for example, in fact good for the organism to achieve. For there is a further question: why is this desire directed towards this goal? And why does the desirer seek to achieve this goal by means which are good? The answer in both cases is: because these goals (and these means) are good. To omit this answer is to miss the idea of the process being controlled by the goodness of the end state and the goodness of the means to that end state. See, for example, *De Anima* 433b12ff., where the starting point of the relevant explanation is the good to be achieved. (Hume, by contrast, was willing to begin his account with desires as basic, independent existents, whose presence is not explained by antecedent values.)

26. See, for example, *Met.* 1050a8–10.

27. See, for example, *Phys.* 198b2–4.

28. See, for example, 1050a15–25. For further discussion, see my 'Θ 7 and 8: some issues concerning potentiality and actuality' in *Essays in Honour of Allan Gotthelf*, eds. R. Bolton and J. G. Lennox, (Cambridge 2010).

29. Allan Gotthelf suggests this line of thought in his 'Aristotle's Conception of Final Causality', *Review of Metaphysics* 30, (1976/7), n. 19.

30. See, for example, Alan Code's 'The Priority of Final Causes Over Efficient Causes in Aristotle's *PA*', pp. 136–43.

31. For a range of such examples, see J. G. Lennox, Material and Formal Natures in Aristotle's *De Partibus Animalium*, pp. 170–1.

32. I argue for the neutrality of the *Physics* on this issue in my 'Teleological Causation in the Physics' in *Aristotle's Physics* L. Judson (ed.), (Oxford 1991), pp. 101–28.

33. For a very clear and influential statement of this problem, see David Furley's 'What Kind is Aristotle's Final Cause?', *Rationality in Greek Thought*, p. 67ff. Although J. M. Cooper, 'Aristotle on Natural Teleology', *Language and Logos*, M. Schofield and M. Nussbaum (eds.), (Cambridge 1982), p. 215 is correct to emphasize that, for Aristotle, the existence of goals 'controls and directs' certain aspects of processes, he does not spell out how they do so.

34. Aristotle discusses the master craftsman in *Metaphysics* I 1 981a30ff.

35. This example is based on Aristotle's discussion of 'man-faced oxprogeny' in *Physics* 198b32.

36. The shape of the shark's mouth may, of course, be teleologically explained, and its shape (thus explained) may indeed (efficiently) causally result in benefit to other fish. But that does not mean that the resulting benefit to other fish is itself teleologically explained. For a somewhat different view of this case, see Lindsay Judson's 'Aristotelian Teleology', *Oxford Studies in Ancient Philosophy* (2005), pp. 36–4, esp. n. 70.

37. This line of argument was first set out, with great clarity, by David Furley in his 'The Rainfall Example in *Physics* ii.8' in *Aristotle on Nature and Living Things*, ed. A. Gotthelf, (Bristol 1985), pp. 177–182. For a helpful overview of the subsequent development of Furley's interpretation, see Margaret Scharle's 'Elemental Teleology in Aristotle's *Physics* 2.8', *Oxford Studies in Ancient Philosophy* xxxiv, 2008, pp. 150–4. I have offered an alternative understanding of the scope of Aristotle's claim in *Physics* 199a3–4 in note 11 above.

38. These cases will be instances of 'things that happens by nature' (198b35) to be distinguished from the subclass of natural occurrences Aristotle is focusing on: those involved in the formation of natural parts (referred to by 'these' in 198b35). He illustrates the general claim that natural phenomena happen always or for the most part by referring to the case of winter rainfall (198b35–199a3) before returning to consider the relevant subclass involving natural parts (perhaps indicated by 'these' in 199a4).

39. While winter rain fall may benefit humans or seeds, it is not caused to fall in order to produce this benefit. In this respect, it resembles Aristotle's favoured examples of non-teleological (efficiently caused) processes in the *Analytics*: eclipses and thunder (*APo* 93a30ff., 94a5ff. where he dismisses the Pythagorean account of the purpose of thunder (94b32ff.). He is clearly aware of many non-purposive regularities in the natural world (see, for example, *PA* 676b16–677b10, *GA* 778a29–b6). For an opposing view, see Diana Quarantotto's 'Ontologia della causa finale aristotelica', Elenchos 2001, pp. 329–65.

40. See *DC* 310a34ff.

41. Aristotle is clear that earth and fire 'imitate' the 'indestructible movers' in being always in movement (*Met.* 1050b28f.). But his remark may merely point to a way in which earth and fire are *like* the indestructible movers and need not suggest that they intentionally imitate them.

42. He adds that we should think of the seasonal cycle of the elements as being like a river with a circular course, 'which rises and falls…when the sun is near it rises, when it recedes it falls again. This [seasonal process] is naturally disposed (*ethelei*) to come to be [or occur] indefinitely at least with regard to its ordering.' The term '*ethelei*', which means 'wants' when applied to agents, can mean 'tends to…' or 'is naturally disposed to…'(LSJ) when applied to processes or inanimate bodies. There is no reason to suggest that the elements have wishes or desires to be eternal, let alone to hunt for some mysterious type of desire which can be present without the presence of a faculty of desire.

43. For example, in *De Caelo* II 5 288a1ff. Aristotle argues that if one assumes that nature always follows the best course, the relevant difficulty will be resolved. We will have something which may stand as the reason sought, even if we have not demonstrated that this is the case. Similarly, in II 11 291b12ff. he suggests that the most reasonable view is that stars are spherical on the assumption that 'nature does nothing in vain'. In both cases, adopting the teleological viewpoint allows us to put forward a reasonable account of phenomena for which we cannot demonstrate the relevant explanations (288a28ff.). Aristotle's consistent use of the term 'reasonable' (*eikos*) in *De Caelo* II recalls the type of 'likely' account (*eikos logos*) developed by Plato in the *Timaeus*. For further details on the latter see T. K. Johansen, *Plato's Natural Philosophy* (Cambridge 2004), pp. 51ff.

44. Even if teleological causation is invoked in the best explanation available to Aristotle, it does not follow that he thought that it would be employed in the best explanation (*tout court*). He could be agnostic on this point, waiting for the evidence to come in. Similarly, it does not follow from the fact that he describes the heaven and heavenly bodies as alive (in, e.g., *De Caelo* 285a277ff.) that this is his actual view (or part of what he took to be the best explanation *tout court*). For a somewhat contrasting view, see A. Falcon, *Aristotle and the Science of Nature, Unity without Uniformity* (Cambridge 2005), pp. 19, 74 and M. R. Johnson, *Aristotle on Teleology* (Oxford 2005), pp. 136–40.

45. This is not, of course, to say that Aristotle regarded such explanations as literally false, only to be entertained by us 'as if' they were true. In this respect, his approach is different from Kant who in his *Critique of Teleological Judgement* understood teleological maxims as 'subjective' and 'principles of reflection'. (See, for example, his 'Dialectic of Teleological Judgement', II, 10.).

46. I am much indebted to Mariska Leunissen's helpful discussion of teleology in *De Caelo* in her 'Explanation and Teleology in Aristotle's Cosmology', *New Perspectives on Aristotle's De Caelo,* A. C. Bowen and C. Wildberg (eds.), (Leiden 2009), pp. 215–238. She argues convincingly that the teleological arguments deployed in *De Caelo* II are not exclusively (or mainly) 'dialectical' (pp. 216–7). Many are aimed to cohere not with widely held opinions but with what is independently plausible or with results which Aristotle takes himself to have established about (e.g.) the explanation of animal behaviour.

47. Since some heavenly bodies are conceived of as sharing in life and *praxis*, they may be thought of acting for the sake of something else. Their actions may spring from their love of some higher being. See also *Met.* 1074a25–27, 1072b27–30.

48. Several such gaps are noted by Michael Frede in his Introduction to *Aristotle's Metaphysics Lambda*, Oxford 2000, M. Frede and D. Charles, eds., pp. 37–8. To establish a teleological causal account, Aristotle would have needed to connect the relevant desires of the heavenly bodies with their material natures and show how they come to have goal-directed capacities of the relevant type. If he had done this, his account might have offered the best (and not just a possible) explanation of the phenomena under discussion.

49. It is not my suggestion that *all* claims in *Lambda* 6–10 are put forward only as 'reasonable'. Aristotle may well have taken some of them to be established as true by his own argumentation (here or elsewhere). My suggestion is only that his use of teleology to make intelligible the eternity and dependence of the cosmos on the prime mover are best seen as ingredients in a 'reasonable account' (which builds on and goes beyond what he has 'proved' to be the case). If this is correct, it is important to consider which other claims in *Lambda* 6–10 (if any) are put forward only as 'reasonable'.

50. This passage is discussed by M.R. Johnson, *Aristotle on Teleology*, Oxford 2005, pp. 280–6, I. Bodnar in 'Teleology across Natures', *Rhizai* 2 (2005), 9–29, and Lindsay Judson in an unpublished paper 'Teleology and Goodness in *Metaphysics Lambda*'. While Judson and I both reject the literalist 'cosmic nature' interpretation of *Lambda* 10, we do so in somewhat different ways.

51. Aristotle illustrates this latter point by an analogy: in a household some do a great deal of the good activity [good *praxis*] characteristic of the household; others, like animals or slaves, do little of it (and most of what they do is not part of the household's good activity). While they may prepare the way for others to do good *praxis* (*Pol.* 1254a8), they do not much good *praxis* themselves. Indeed, most of what they do makes no difference to whether there is good *praxis* in the household. They could, after all, be working equally hard and there would be no good *praxis* at all!

52 Grammatically, one can achieve this result by

(i) taking *hekastou* and *autôn* as a unit with *archê* and understanding them both also with *phusis*,

or (possibly)

(ii) taking *hekastou* with *archê* and *autôn* with *phusis*.

There is no need to alter the text to support this interpretation. I have been helped in thinking about this passage by M.R. Johnson, *Aristotle on Teleology* (Oxford 2005), pp. 280–6 and an unpublished paper by Lindsay Judson.

53. In effect, they take 'nature' and 'not their nature' as the predicate. For a view of this kind, see Charles Kahn, 'On the Place of the Prime Mover in Aristotle's Teleology' in *Aristotle on the Nature of Living Things*, A. Gotthelf (ed.), (Cambridge 1985), pp. 183–205 and David Sedley, '*Metaphysics* Λ.10' in *Aristotle's Metaphysics Lambda* (Oxford 2000), M. Frede and D. Charles (eds)., pp. 327–36.

54. To sustain this alternative, one would need to think of Aristotle as generalizing his earlier account of the household to permit talk of the nature of the household as an organizational principle and teleological cause. This is permissible, it is claimed, as Aristotle talks of the nature of the city in the required way. However, on the one occasion he uses that phrase, it signifies the end point achieved when each individual in the city achieves their goals (see 1252b30ff.) and thus makes an appropriate contribution to good of the whole (*Pol.* 1278b15ff.). In this context, talk of the nature of the city simply describes the end point of natural changes when all goes well (see *Phys.* 193b12) and does not play the role of a teleological explanatory principle. For an excellent discussion of Aristotle's views on the city, see Robert Wardy, 'Aristotelian Rainfall and the Lore of Averages', *Phronesis* 38 (1993), pp. 18–30.

55. In *De Caelo* 293a3–4 Aristotle uses personifying talk of nature to make it intelligible how different divine bodies co-exist in an ordered way, some having many activities, others only a few. It might be thought that Aristotle needs to employ a similar idea in *Metaphysics* XII 10 to explain how individual species, pursuing their own survival in differing ways, all survive together in one relatively harmonious world order. Since their survival in such an order cannot be an accident, Aristotle (it will be said) needs to use talk of a cosmic nature if he is to offer a 'reasonable account' of the inter-species order he finds in the world. While this line of thought is attractive, it is not mandatory. Nor is it clear that Aristotle pursued it in XII 10. He may have thought that the good order of the whole is achieved when each individual species reproduces (or moves) as is good for it and believed that, if this is achieved, each species will continue to survive in the way appropriate for it. (This way of thinking, of course, rests on the assumption

that there are no species which will, when all goes well for them, destroy (for example, by hunting or competing for food) the other species around them. But Aristotle, if he considered this possibility, might have taken it as a background datum, supported by the evidence of which he was aware and not in need of teleological explanation, that the continued reproduction and movement of one species will not (in favourable conditions) lead to the extinction of any other species, let alone the world as a whole).

56. This issue is interestingly discussed in Susan Sauvé Meyer's 'Aristotle, Teleology and Reduction', *Philosophical Review* 101 (1992), 791–821.

57. For a helpful discussion of Plato's views in the *Timaeus*, see T. K. Johansen, *Plato's Natural Philosophy, A Study of the Timaeus-Critias,* Cambridge 2004.

58. I sketch one view of this in my 'Aristotle on Hypothetical Necessity and Irreducibility', *Pacific Philosophical Quarterly* 69 (1988), 21ff. For an alternative account, see A. Gotthelf, 'Aristotle's Conception of Final Causality', *Review of Metaphysics* 30 (1976/7), and G. Freudenthal, *Aristotle's Theory of Material Substance* (Oxford 1995). These issues remain moot.

59. See, for example, Rowland Stout's *Things That Happen Because They Should* (Oxford 1996). Stout develops a line of approach which is congenial to externalism about value.

60. Plants are, of course, an extreme case. In considering animals, Aristotle regularly suggests that they are sensitive to what is good for them because what is good is pleasant for them (see, for example, *DA* 413b23, 414b3ff., 431a10ff.). Further, they may well be organized so that (i) what is good for them is pleasant to them and (ii) they are guided in their actions by what is pleasant for them. If so, in their case, there is a connection, albeit indirect, between the goodness of their goal and their actions (via their response to pleasure). They are sensitive to the goodness of a given goal because they are sensitive to the pleasure it gives them. Such animals may be defined as ones which are pleasure-sensitive to their distinctive goals and the means to achieve them (as the craftsman is knowledge-sensitive to his goals).

61. For a recent statement of this concern, see Jerry Fodor's 'Against Darwinism', *Mind and Language* 23 (1), (2008), 1–24. For further discussion, see J. Fodor and M. Piattelli-Palmarini, *What Darwin Got Wrong* (New York 2010).

62. I am indebted to Allan Gotthelf for many discussions of these issues over many years and for his advice on the present essay. I have also gained from comments on an earlier draft of this paper from Jonathan Barnes, Kei Chiba, Ursula Coope, Bruno Currie, Andrea Falcon, Thomas Johansen, Lindsay Judson, James Lennox, Mariska Leunissen, Jessica Moss, Takashi Ochi, Oliver Primavesi, Diana Quarantotto, Christopher Shields, Jennifer Whiting and members of the 'pro-seminar' in the University of Toronto.

BIBLIOGRAPHY

Bodnar, I. (2005) 'Teleology across Natures', *Rhizai* 2, 9–29.

Charles, D. (1991) 'Teleological Causation in the Physics' in *Physics*, L. Judson, ed. (Oxford: Oxford Univ. Press), 101–28.

_____ (1988) 'Aristotle on Hypothetical Necessity and Irreducibility', *Pacific Philosophical Quarterly* 69, 1–53.

_____ (2010) 'Θ 7 and 8: Some Issues Concerning Potentiality and Actuality' in *Being, Nature, and Life in Aristotle*, J. Lennox and R. Bolton, eds. (Cambridge: Cambridge Univ. Press), 168–197.

Code, A. (1997) 'The Priority of Final Causes Over Efficient Causes in Aristotle's *PA*' in *Aristotelische Biologie*, W. Kullmann and S. Föllinger, eds. (Stuttgart: F. Steiner Verlag), 128–143.

Cooper, J. M. (1985) 'Hypothetical Necessity', in *Aristotle on Nature and Living Things*, A. Gotthelf, ed. (Cambridge: Cambridge Univ. Press), 150–167.

———— (1986) 'Aristotle on Natural Teleology', in *Language and Logos*, M. Schofield and M. Nussbaum, eds. (Cambridge: Cambridge Univ. Press), 187–222.

Falcon, A. (2005) *Aristotle and the Science of Nature, Unity without Uniformity* (Cambridge: Cambridge Univ. Press).

Fodor, J. (2008) 'Against Darwinism', *Mind and Language* 23, 1–24.

Fodor, J. and Piattelli-Palmarini, M. (2010) *What Darwin Got Wrong* (New York: Farrar, Strauss, and Giroux).

Frede, M. and Charles, D., eds. (2000) *Aristotle's Metaphysics Lambda* (Oxford: Oxford Univ. Press).

Freudenthal, G. (1995) *Aristotle's Theory of Material Substance* (Oxford: Oxford Univ. Press).

Furley, D. (1985) 'The Rainfall Example in *Physics* ii.8' in *Aristotle on Nature and Living Things*, A. Gotthelf, ed. (Cambridge: Cambridge Univ. Press), 177–182.

———— (1996) 'What Kind of Cause is Aristotle's Final Cause?', *Rationality in Greek Thought*, M. Frede and G. Striker, eds. (Oxford Univ. Press), 59–79.

Gotthelf, A. (1976/1977) 'Aristotle's Conception of Final Causality', *Review of Metaphysics*, 30: 226–254; reprinted with additional notes and a Postscript in *Philosophical Issues in Aristotle's Biology*, A. Gotthelf and J. G. Lennox, eds. (Cambridge: Cambridge Univ. Press, 1987), 204–242.

———— (1988) 'The Place of the Good in Aristotle's Teleology', in *Proceedings of the Boston Colloquium in Ancient Philosophy* 4, J. Cleary and D.C. Shartin, eds. (Lanham, Md.: Univ. Press of America), 13–39.

———— (1997) 'Understanding Aristotle's Teleology', in *Final Causality in Nature and Human Affairs*, R. Hassing, ed. (Washington DC: Catholic Univ. Press), 71–82.

Johansen, T.K. (2004), *Plato's Natural Philosophy A Study of the Timaeus-Critias* (Cambridge: Cambridge Univ. Press).

Johnson, M.R. (2005) *Aristotle on Teleology* (Oxford: Oxford Univ. Press).

Judson, L. (2005) 'Aristotelian Teleology', *Oxford Studies in Ancient Philosophy*, 29, 341–365.

———— (unpublished) 'Teleology and Goodness in *Metaphysics Lambda*'.

Kahn, C. (1985) 'On the Place of the Prime Mover in Aristotle's Teleology' in *Aristotle on the Nature of Living Things*, A. Gotthelf , ed. (Cambridge: Cambridge Univ. Press), 183–205.

Kullmann, W. (1985), 'Different Conceptions of the Final Cause in Aristotle', in *Aristotle on Nature and Living Things*, A. Gotthelf, ed. (Cambridge: Cambridge Univ. Press), 169–174.

Lennox, J. (1977) 'Material and Formal Natures in Aristotle's *De Partibus Animalium*', *Aristotelische Biologie*, W. Kullmann and S. Föllinger, eds. (Stuttgart: F. Steiner Verlag), 163–181.

Leunissen, M. (2009) 'Explanation and Teleology in Aristotle's Cosmology', in *New Perspectives on Aristotle's De Caelo*, A.C. Bowen and C. Wildberg, eds. (Leiden: Brill), 215–238.

———— (2010) *Explanation and Teleology in Aristotle's Science of Nature* (Cambridge: Cambridge Univ. Press).

Meyer, S.S. (1992) 'Aristotle, Teleology and Reduction', *Philosophical Review* 101, 791–821.

Nussbaum, M. (1978) *Aristotle's De Motu Animalium* (Princeton: Princeton Univ. Press).

Primavesi, O. (2010) 'Aristoteles oder Empedokles? Charles Darwin und Eduard Zeller über einen antiken Ansatz zur Evolutionstheorie', in *Eduard Zeller: Philosophie und Wissenschaftgeschichte im 19 Jahrhundert'*, G. Hartung, ed. (Berlin: de Gruyter), 25–65.

Quarantotto, D. (2005) *Causa finale, sostanza, essenza in Aristotele, Saggi sulla struttura dei processi teleologici naturali e sulla funzione dei telos* (Napoli: Bibliopolis).

Sharle, M. (2005) 'Elemental Teleology in Aristotle's *Physics* II 8', *Oxford Studies in Ancient Philosophy* 29, 341–365.

Sedley, D. (2000) '*Metaphysics* Λ.10' in *Aristotle's Metaphysics Lambda*, M. Frede and D. Charles, eds. (Oxford: Oxford Univ. Press), 327–36.

Stout, R. (1996) *Things That Happen Because They Should* (Oxford: Oxford Univ. Press).

Wardy, R. (1993) 'Aristotelian Rainfall and the Lore of Averages', *Phronesis*, 18–30.

Wieland, W. (1975) 'The Problem of Teleology', in *Articles on Aristotle,* J. Barnes, M. Schofield, R. Sorabji , eds. (London: Duckworth), 141–160; originally published as chapter 16, "Zum Teleologieproblem", of *Die aristotelische Physik* (Göttingen: Vandenhoeck und Ruprecht), 1962.

CHAPTER 11

ARISTOTLE ON THE INFINITE

URSULA COOPE

1. THE PROBLEM

ARISTOTLE starts his positive account of the infinite by raising a problem: 'if one supposes it not to exist, many impossible things result, and equally if one supposes it to exist' (*Phys.* 203b31ff.). On the one hand, his views on time, extended magnitudes, and number imply that there must be some sense in which the infinite exists, for he holds that time has no beginning or end, magnitudes are infinitely divisible, and there is no highest number (206a9ff.). On the other hand, he claims that 'impossible things result' from supposing that there is an infinite.

His arguments against the possibility of an infinite focus on two types of case. He argues, first, that there cannot be something, separable from the objects of sense perception, that is essentially 'just infinite'. Such a thing (he claims) would either have no parts (and hence not be a quantity at all), or it would have parts that were themselves infinite (with, what he takes to be, the obviously absurd consequence that there would be many infinites within the infinite) (204a20ff.). Second, he claims that there cannot be an infinitely extended perceptible body. Many of his arguments for this second claim rely on his other physical views. For instance, he holds that if some one type of stuff were infinitely extended, its powers would swamp those of everything else (if there were an infinite sea of water, everything would be wet) (204b24ff.). Moreover, he claims that if there were an infinite body, there could be no natural places. An infinite body could not be structured in the way the Aristotelian universe is: it could not have extremes and a centre (*Phys.* III 5 205a8ff.).

So far, it is not clear that there is any real problem here. Aristotle has argued that there can be no infinite perceptible body and that there can be no separable substance whose essence is simply to be infinite. *Prima facie*, neither claim casts doubt on the possibility of the kinds of infinite he wants to admit: infinite time or motion, infinitely divisible magnitudes, and infinitely many numbers.[1] However, he clearly takes himself to have raised a general problem about how anything can be infinite: to have shown that 'impossible things result' from supposing the infinite to exist. What is this general problem?

To be infinite (*apeiron*) is to be without a limit or a boundary. Aristotle describes the infinite as 'that of which there is always something outside' (207a2), and he contrasts this with a whole: something 'from which no part is absent'. There is, then, a peculiar sense in which anything infinite is 'incomplete': nothing would count as its completion.[2] If something is infinite, there is no such thing as 'all' of it.[3] Any boundary that we attempt to draw round it must always leave something out.

How can there be such a thing? Aristotle holds that nothing that exists all at once can be incomplete (and hence infinite) in the relevant sense. He does not really explain why this is so. He may be influenced by the simple thought that there is no such thing as *all* of an infinite, and hence it cannot all be at once. Or he may think that the impossibility of a contemporaneous infinite follows from the spatial finitude of the universe. He has argued (on physical grounds) that the universe must be finite in extent. It seems to follow that spatially located things, if they exist simultaneously, must all fall within certain boundaries (at the very least, they must be within the boundaries of the universe). If there were an infinite plurality of such things (for example, infinitely many points on a finite line), this would be an infinite plurality that could be confined between bounds. This, Aristotle thinks, is impossible.

On Aristotle's view, a plurality cannot escape having bounds if all of its members exist at once. There remains, however, the possibility that a plurality of successively existing things could be infinite. Aristotle tells us that 'in general, the infinite is in virtue of one thing's constantly being taken after another—what is taken is always finite, but always one followed by another' (206a25–9). This explains how certain *successive* infinites can be possible. For example, every man has a father, who also has a father, and so on. To suppose that this series goes on forever is not to suppose that there is a bounded infinite. The series is not bounded in time (as an infinite plurality of events occurring between T1 and T2 would be); neither is it bounded in space (as an infinite plurality of simultaneously existing men would be). When Aristotle says that the infinite is in virtue of one thing's constantly being taken after another, he is *not* allowing that it is possible for there to be a whole infinite series provided that the series is spread out over time. His view, rather, is that a series of successively existing things need not constitute a whole.

However, there remains a problem about infinite divisibility. If a finite thing is infinitely divisible, this might seem to imply that it has infinitely many parts, with the consequence that these parts constitute a bounded infinite plurality. On Aristotle's view, this is impossible. For instance, a finite period of time cannot be made up of infinitely many sub-periods.[4] Moreover, in the case of a *spatial* magnitude, infinite divisibility seems to have a further impossible consequence. When a spatial magnitude is divided, 'what is taken persists' (206b1). Because of this, if such a magnitude were to be divided into infinitely many parts, these parts would not only form a bounded infinite plurality, they would also exist *all at once*. In his account of the infinite, Aristotle focuses on this difficult case. We can now begin to understand the problem he is addressing: given that a spatial magnitude cannot contain infinitely many parts, in what sense can such a magnitude be infinitely divisible?

It might seem that there is a fairly quick and straightforward answer to this. Aristotle could simply maintain that between any two divisions we make in a magnitude, it will always be possible to make another one. This, in itself, need not imply that there are ever infinitely many of anything. Why, then, does Aristotle think he has identified a puzzle about the infinite? The answer, I think, is that he is assuming that facts of this sort cannot simply be brutely true. The fact that between any two divisions in a magnitude it is always possible to make another one is a fact that must be grounded in some capacity of the magnitude. It must hold *in virtue of* some capacity the magnitude has for being divided. The question then arises how this capacity should be characterized. It can't be a capacity for *being in a state of infinite dividedness*. At least, this seems to be ruled out by the claim that it is impossible for infinitely many things to exist simultaneously. If a magnitude cannot be in infinitely many parts, then presumably it cannot have the capacity to be in infinitely many parts.

At this point, someone might object that even if facts about the ways in which it is possible to divide a magnitude must be grounded in facts about the capacities of the magnitude, there needn't be some *one* capacity in virtue of which a magnitude is infinitely divisible. Instead, it might be suggested, what grounds the fact that we can always make another division in the magnitude is the magnitude's possession of infinitely many potentials for division. The magnitude has a potential to be divided here, and a potential to be divided here, and a potential to be divided here, and so on. Any one of these potentials can be fulfilled, though they cannot all be fulfilled at once. But Aristotle does not consider this solution here. The reason, I conjecture, is that to admit that a magnitude had infinitely many potentials for division would be to admit that there could, after all, be a simultaneous infinite plurality: a plurality of potential dividing-points (here and here and here...).[5]

Alternatively, it might be suggested that the magnitude has *one* potential and this potential is a potential to be divided *anywhere* (though not everywhere). In a sense, this is the answer that Aristotle gives. However, there are (on his view) difficulties involved in spelling out exactly what such a potential might be. We have already seen that this potential should not be reduced to an infinite plurality of potentials (a potential to be divided here, another potential to be divided here, etc.). If instead we think that a magnitude has a single potential that is a potential to be divided anywhere, the question arises: what counts as the fulfilment of this potential? One possible answer is that this potential is fulfilled by any division in the magnitude. In a sense, this is obviously right. However, for Aristotle, it cannot be the full story.

To understand why, we need to think a little more about the relation between a potential and its fulfilment. Suppose I have the potential to jump four feet. In one sense, I exercise this potential whenever I jump less than four feet. I am using my potential to jump four feet when I jump three feet. The potential is *defined*, however, by the fulfilment that is its maximal exercise: it is a potential to jump four feet.[6] Aristotle explains this in *De Caelo* I 11 281a13–5: 'If something can lift a hundred talents, it can also lift two, and if it can walk a hundred stades, then also two. But the capacity is for the maximum'. We need to distinguish, then, between the fulfilment that defines a potential and other ways of fulfilling that potential. The fulfilment that defines a potential is its maximal fulfilment. My suggestion is that *being divided here* stands to *the potential to be divided anywhere* as *jumping three feet* stands to *the potential to jump four feet*: it is a fulfilment of the potential but it is not the kind of fulfilment that defines the potential. What, then, is the fulfilment that *defines* a potential to be divided anywhere? It is this question that poses a problem for Aristotle, for it is hard to see what could count as the maximal exercise of this potential.

The challenge Aristotle faces, then, is to explain what potential we are attributing to a magnitude when we say that it is infinitely divisible. Can he explain what this potential is without committing himself to the possibility of a bounded infinite plurality (either of divisions or of potential divisions)?

2. ARISTOTLE'S ANSWER: POTENTIALITY AND THE COMPARISON WITH A DAY OR CONTEST

Aristotle begins his solution by claiming that there is a sense in which the infinite is, and a sense in which it is not. The way he spells this out seems deliberately paradoxical. He first says that the infinite is potentially, but is not actually. He then goes on to add that there is, in fact, a sense in which the infinite is actual: it is actual in the sense in which a day or a contest is actual. It will be helpful to look at each of these two claims in turn.

'The infinite is in no other way than this: potentially' (206b12)

Aristotle seems to hold that though nothing can be actually infinite, certain things can be potentially infinite. He explains:

> That magnitude is not infinite in actuality has already been said, but it is infinite by division (for it is not difficult to refute indivisible lines) so that it remains for the infinite to be potentially (206a16–18).

His reasoning here is very condensed. It relies on two contrasts: first, between being infinite in actuality and being infinite in potentiality; second, between being infinite in size and being infinite 'by division'. When Aristotle says that magnitude is not infinite in actuality, part of what he means is that no magnitude can be infinite *in size*. It is misleading to put this as a claim about how the infinite can be 'in actuality', since he holds that a magnitude cannot even be *potentially* infinitely big. Though nothing can be infinitely big, Aristotle maintains that there is *a* sense in which the infinite is associated with magnitude: magnitudes are infinitely divisible. (This is guaranteed, he thinks, by the impossibility of there being indivisible lines.) When he goes on to say that 'it remains for the infinite to be potentially', he is drawing a contrast with *another* way in which the infinite might be supposed to be actual. His point is that since it is impossible for there to be a bounded infinite plurality, no magnitude can be in a state of *actual infinite dividedness*. A magnitude has a *potential* in virtue of which it is infinitely divisible, but it cannot in fact be in a state of infinite dividedness.

Aristotle now goes on to explain that 'potential' is used here in a special sense. When we say that a magnitude is potentially infinite by division, we are attributing to it a potential that could not be completely fulfilled. He makes this clear when he contrasts this with the usual sense of 'potentially':

> 'Being potentially' should not be understood in such a way that (just as if it is possible for this to be a statue, it will be a statue) so also there is an infinite that will be actually (206a18–21).

If a lump of bronze is potentially a statue, something could be done to the bronze that would result in its being a statue. Aristotle wants to stress, this is not the sense in which the line has a potential for being divided ad infinitum. It is not the case that something could be done to the line that would result in its being in a state of actual infinite dividedness.[7]

What does Aristotle mean by this claim that there is some sense in which the infinite is potentially but not actually? This is puzzling both in itself and in the light of other things that he says. It is puzzling in itself because is hard to see what can be meant by saying that something is potentially F, if this does not imply that that thing *could* be actually F. For instance, if a magnitude has the potential to be in a state of infinite dividedness, surely this implies that that magnitude could actually be in a state of infinite dividedness. But Aristotle is committed to denying that a magnitude could be in such a state. He is *not* saying that though magnitudes have the potential to be infinitely divided, *as it happens* none of them will fulfill this potential. His view is that there *cannot* be a bounded infinite plurality, not just that there *will not* be one.

Another reason for being puzzled about this claim that the infinite is potentially but not actually lies in Aristotle's own views elsewhere.[8] Aristotle argues, in *Metaphysics* IX, that actuality is prior to potentiality. This means, among other things, that a potentiality must be understood in terms of some corresponding actuality (*Met.*IX 8 1049b12–17). But in the case of the potential infinite, there seems to be no corresponding actuality that can be prior. For there can be no such thing as the actual infinite. When we say that a magnitude is infinitely divisible, we are ascribing to it a certain potential. We are left with the question: what is the actuality in terms of which this potential is defined (or, in other words, what is it a potential *for*)? If there is no answer to this question, then it isn't clear in what sense we have specified a potential at all.

A final puzzle is that within this discussion of the infinite itself, Aristotle seems to contradict this claim that there can be no actual infinite. After saying that the infinite is 'in no other way than this: potentially', he adds 'and it is actually too, in the way that we say that the day and the contest are' (206b12–14). However we understand this, we seem to be left with a puzzle. How can it *both* be true that the infinite is 'in no other way than' potentially *and* be true that there is a way in which it is 'actually too'? Doesn't the second of these claims simply contradict the first?

The infinite is 'actually too, in the way in which we say the day or the contest is' (206b13–14)

What exactly is meant by this comparison between the way in which the infinite is and the way in which the day or the contest is? Aristotle spells it out as follows:

> But since being is in many ways, just as the day or the contest is by the constant occurring of other and other, in this way too the infinite is. (For in these cases also there is 'potentially' and 'actually'. The Olympic games *are* both in virtue of the contest's being able to occur and in virtue of the contest's occurring) (206a21–5).

There are two things that might be meant by this claim that the day or contest is 'by the constant occurring of other and other'. Aristotle could be comparing the way in which the infinite is actual to the way in which the universal, *day* or, *Olympics* is actual. The universal, *day*, is actual in virtue of the fact that there is one day after another; similarly, *the Olympics* is actual in virtue of the fact that there is one series of games after another (for example, in virtue of the fact that the 2012 games is, the 2008 games is, and so on). On this reading, 'the contest', at 206a24, refers to one or other set of Olympics (e.g., the 2008 games or the 2012 games), and Aristotle is saying that the universal, *the Olympics*, is actual both because there is the potential for a future set of Olympic games to occur, and also because one particular set of Olympic games is currently occurring.

Alternatively, Aristotle's thought might be that the infinite is actual in the way in which a *particular* day or contest is actual. For a day or a contest to be actual is for it to be *going on*. The day is not all there at once; while it is going on, it is always 'other and other'. If this is Aristotle's point, then 'the Olympic games' probably refers to a particular set of Olympics (e.g., the 2012 Olympics), and 'the contest' (206a24) to one or other of the contests that makes up a particular Olympics. For the 2012 Olympics to be occurring is for some contest, e.g., sprinting, to be occurring and some other contest, e.g., swimming, to be potentially occurring.[9] When we say that the 2012 Olympics is going on, we don't mean that all the contests are currently going on. The 2012 Olympics occurs by one contest's occurring after another.

There are, I think, grounds for preferring the second interpretation. Aristotle uses the expression 'always other and other' elsewhere in the *Physics* (in his account of time): 'just as the change is always other and other, so also is the time' (219b9–10). In this context, his point seems quite clearly to be that, while it is going on, any particular change (and hence any period of time) is always other and other.

Further evidence for this second interpretation can be found in a later passage in the discussion of the infinite. This passage (206a29–33) is bracketed by Ross, who surmises that it was 'an alternative version [of 206a18–29] which occurred in the margin of the original and was at an early date incorporated into the text in most of the manuscripts'.[10] However, provided that these lines were written by Aristotle, they can still help us to understand what he means when he compares the infinite to a day or a contest. In these lines he draws a contrast between the being of a day or contest and the being of a substance (a 'this'):

> Further being is said in several ways, so that one should not take the infinite as a this (*tode ti*), such as a man or a house, but should take it in the sense in which we speak of a day and a contest, which have their being not in the sense that some substance has come to be, but [have being] always in coming to be and passing away, finite, but always different and different (206a29–33).

The point Aristotle is making here is not about the universal *day* or *contest*. After all, he could claim with equal justification that the universal, *man,* is actual in virtue of one man coming to be after another. His point is rather to draw attention to a difference between the way in which a particular substance (such as a man) is and the way in which a particular day or contest is. The difference is that, unlike a substance, a day or a contest has its 'being in coming to be'.[11]

If this interpretation is right, it leaves us facing a double challenge. We need to understand in what way the being of the infinite is like the being of a day or a contest. In what sense does the infinite have its 'being in coming to be'? But we also need to understand the respect in which the infinite differs from the day and the contest. A particular day or contest is a finite thing, the whole of which is spread over a certain definite period of time. As we have seen, Aristotle thinks that an infinite cannot be a whole. How can an infinite, though actual in the way that a day or a contest is, nevertheless be something that is always incomplete?

In this section, I have outlined some puzzling features of Aristotle's account of the infinite. If we are to understand this account we need to explain *both* the remark that the infinite is actually *and* the claim that it is, in a sense, only potentially. Moreover, we need to spell out the way in which the being of the infinite is like the being of a day or a contest, without losing sight of the way in which any infinite must differ from these finite occurrences.

Two interesting, and contrasting, interpretations of Aristotle's account can be found in the work of Jaako Hintikka and of Jonathan Lear.[12] As we shall see, each provides insights into some of Aristotle's puzzling remarks. Hintikka tries to explain the sense in which the infinite is actually, and the sense in which its being is like the being of a day or a contest. Lear focuses on the sense in which the infinite is only potential, and emphasizes that an infinite, unlike a day or a contest, is always incomplete. Neither of these interpretations, however, can explain what is most puzzling about Aristotle's account: the fact that he says *all* of these things together.

3. Two contrasting interpretations: Hintikka and Lear

Hintikka denies that Aristotle is committed to the view that there is a sense in which the infinite is potentially but not actually. He thinks we can avoid attributing this view to him if we make proper use of the distinction he draws between two senses of 'is': a sense that attaches to processes (or more generally, things that have their being in becoming[13]) and a sense that attaches to substances. There is, he says, one sense of 'is' in which the infinite can be both potentially and actually and there is another sense of 'is' in which there cannot be either a potential or an actual infinite. The sense of 'is' in which the infinite can be both potentially and actually is the sense that attaches to processes: the infinite 'is' in the sense that a process is: by one finite part of it occurring after another. The sense of 'is' in which the infinite cannot be either potentially or actually is the sense of 'is' that attaches to a substance such as a man. If a man is, then all of him is at once. But it is impossible for an infinite to be in this sense.

If we apply this to the case of infinite divisibility, we get the following claims. A line cannot be in a state of having been divided into infinitely many parts. But then also, a line cannot even be potentially in such a state. However, the process of dividing the line into infinitely many parts can be going on: one part of it after another. There can, for instance, be a process of dividing the line in half, the halves into quarters, the quarters into eighths, and so on. The line has the potential to be undergoing this process. In that sense, when the line is not undergoing this process, the process is potential. But this process can also be actual, in the sense that it could be actually occurring. Hintikka concludes: 'In the *precise* sense…in which the infinite…[exists] potentially, for Aristotle, it also exists actually.'[14]

For Hintikka, this interpretation is part of a more general attempt to argue that Aristotle was committed to the principle of plenitude (the principle that any potential must at some point be actualized), but one does not have to accept this further claim about the principle of plenitude to find Hintikka's interpretation attractive.[15] On this interpretation, we avoid having to attribute to Aristotle the view that there is some potential that by its nature could not possibly be fulfilled, a view that is problematic whether or not one accepts the principle of plenitude. Instead, Aristotle's account turns out to be unproblematic: there is a potential for undergoing a process (a process of being infinitely divided) and this potential can be fulfilled; but there is no potential for being in an infinitely divided state and, unsurprisingly, there is no possibility of something's actually being in such a state.

Moreover, this interpretation can make sense of Aristotle's claim that the infinite is actual in the way in which a day or a contest is, but is not actual in the way in which a man or a house is. According to Hintikka, the sense in which the infinite is actual is that it is *going on*. Just as a day or a contest is 'by always one thing and another occurring' (206a22), so also a magnitude's potential for being divided is actualized in the process of one division after another occurring. When a man or a house is, all its parts exist at once. The infinite cannot be actual (or even potential) in this sense: a magnitude cannot be, either potentially or actually, in a state of infinite dividedness.

However, in spite of these advantages, there are two respects in which this interpretation is unsatisfactory. First, though it explains the way in which the being of the infinite is like the being of a day or contest, it does not account for the way in which it is fundamentally unlike them: there is such a thing as a whole day or contest, but there is no such thing as a whole infinite. Second, however strange we may find this, Aristotle does seem to imply that there is a certain sense in which the infinite is only potentially. As we have seen, even the remark that favours Hintikka's interpretation—the remark that the infinite 'is actually too, in the way in which a day or a contest is'—is preceded by the claim that the infinite is 'in no other way but potentially' (206b12).[16] Bostock (who follows Hintikka's interpretation) notices this second problem. He asks: 'what, then, has become of the claim that the infinite is potential but *not* actual?' He answers that Aristotle's point is 'just that the process of dividing a line into infinitely many parts is one that cannot be *completed*.'[17] But this answer, by itself, is inadequate. What is needed is an explanation of the connection between the uncompleteability of this process and the existence of an unfulfillable potential. If Aristotle simply meant that the process of dividing a line into infinitely many parts could not be completed, why did he express himself, in what seems a perversely paradoxical way, by saying that the infinite is potentially in a way that it is not actually?

Aristotle is, then, unlikely to have had the simple view that Hintikka attributes to him. But this still leaves the question: why didn't he have this view? After all, it would be a way of solving the puzzle we started with: it would explain the sense in which a magnitude is infinitely divisible without committing Aristotle to the view that an infinite plurality of divisions (or of potential divisions) is possible. Does Aristotle have some good reason for maintaining that the potential in virtue of which something is infinitely divisible is a potential that cannot be fully realized? Or is his account simply confused, so that Hintikka could at least claim to tell us what Aristotle should have said?

Jonathan Lear argues that Aristotle would reject the view that Hintikka attributes to him, and that he would be right to do so. Hintikka thinks that the actuality of the infinite consists in the actuality of an infinite process of division. Lear's objection to this is simple. No infinite process of division ever in fact occurs: 'there is no process which could correctly be considered the actualization of an infinite division of a line'. Lear defends this claim by pointing out that 'any such process will terminate after finitely many divisions.' A physical process of cutting the magnitude will terminate after finitely many divisions, because any physical cut we make in the magnitude 'will have finite size and thus the magnitude will be completely destroyed after only finitely many cuts'.[18] On the other hand, if I instead attempt to divide the line 'in thought', this process will also eventually come to an end, for the simple reason that 'no mortal could carry out more than a finite number of theoretical divisions.'[19]

According to Lear, then, any process of dividing the magnitude will be finite. Lear argues that these finite processes of division 'bear witness to' the infinite divisibility of the magnitude. This is because, though there could not in fact be a process of infinitely dividing the magnitude in thought, the reason why such a process is impossible has nothing to do with the structure of the magnitude. When my activity of dividing the magnitude is brought to the end by my death, there will always remain further divisions that I could have made had I lived longer. A finite process of division 'bears witness to' the infinite divisibility of the magnitude because such a process of division does not exhaust the magnitude's potential for being divided.

One great advantage of Lear's account is that it makes sense of Aristotle's claim that the infinite is potentially in a way that it is not actually. For a magnitude to be infinitely divisible is for it to have potentials that could never be fully actualized by any process of dividing. However, Lear's interpretation leaves it mysterious how Aristotle can claim that the infinite is actually 'in the way that a day or a contest is'. Lear is right to emphasize that the way in which a day or a contest is cannot be just the same as the way in which a process of division ad infinitum is. As we saw earlier, there is a certain point at which a day or a contest is over, but this could not be true of a process of division ad infinitum. Nevertheless, Aristotle clearly means to say that there is a way in which the potential infinite is actual, and he tells us that the way in which the potential infinite is actual is *like* the way in which a day or a contest is actual. Lear's interpretation, on which a process of division merely 'bears witness' to the infinite divisibility of a magnitude, cannot account for this.

4. CAN A PROCESS OF DIVISION AD INFINITUM BE OCCURRING?

I have argued that Hintikka's interpretation cannot do justice to Aristotle's claim that the infinite is only potentially, while Lear cannot make sense of his claim that the infinite is actually too, in the way that a day or a contest is. Is there any way to make sense of both of these claims at once?

As a first step, we should ask whether Lear has really shown that it is impossible for there to be an infinite process of division. There are, in fact, two things Lear might mean by this: (i) a process of division ad infinitum cannot *occur*, (ii) a process of division ad infinitum cannot *be occurring*. I shall argue that we should accept (i) and reject (ii). The sense in which it is impossible for there to be an infinite process of division is that it is impossible for such a process to occur. This still leaves it open that such a process might be occurring.

In arguing that it is impossible for a process of infinite division to occur, Lear appeals to considerations about human mortality and the size of physical cuts. Such a process would, he says, inevitably be interrupted after finitely many steps. However, on Aristotle's view, there is a deeper reason why such a process could not occur. Even if, *per impossibile*, such a process were to continue without interruption, it could not be said to *occur*. Aristotle holds that there are some processes that will go on forever without interruption (for example, he thinks that the revolutions of the heavenly spheres will go on forever), but I want to suggest that he would deny that any of these processes occurs. They are processes that *are occurring*, but never *occur*. The reason is that a process *occurs* only if the whole of it occurs, but in the case of an infinite process there is no such thing as the whole of it. A finite process, such as a contest, occurs over a certain length of time; what this means is that the whole process is spread out over a certain length of time. But this is not true of an infinite process. On Aristotle's view, the whole of such a process could not occur even over infinitely much time, for as we have seen, he holds that being infinite implies not being whole (206b33ff.).[20]

None of these considerations, however, shows that it is impossible for a process of division ad infinitum to *be occurring*. And in fact, though Lear insists that 'an actual process of division, which terminates after finitely many divisions, having failed to carry out all possible divisions, is all that a witness to the existence of the potential infinite could consist in,' he then goes on to add, 'while such a process is occurring one can say that the infinite is actually coming to be, one division after another'.[21] If it is true to say that the infinite 'is actually coming to be' while the process is going on, this is surely just because the magnitude is *being divided* ad infinitum. Moreover, if he admitted this possibility, Lear would be in a better position to defend his claim that a finite process of division 'bears witness' to the infinite divisibility of a magnitude. After all, how can the fact that a magnitude undergoes a *finite* process of division show that that magnitude is infinitely divisible? In a world in which magnitudes weren't infinitely divisible, there could also be finite processes of division (and indeed, there could be finite processes of division that stopped before all possible divisions had been made). On the other hand, a process of *dividing a magnitude ad infinitum* could bear witness to the infinite divisibility of the magnitude—and could do so even if the process were interrupted after finitely many steps. For only a magnitude that was infinitely divisible could *be undergoing* such a process.

Let us allow, then, that a magnitude can *be undergoing* a process of division ad infinitum, even though it cannot *undergo* such a process. This might seem to open up a way of defending Hintikka against Lear's criticism. Hintikka should say that infinite divisibility is the potential for a certain process to be occurring. This potential is completely fulfilled when a magnitude is *being divided* ad infinitum. Of course, the whole of such a process can never occur, but that (he might say) does not imply that the magnitude has some potential that cannot be fulfilled. The magnitude cannot undergo a whole process of division ad infinitum, but then it does not have the potential to undergo such a process; on the other hand, the magnitude does have the potential to be undergoing a process of division ad infinitum, and this potential can be fulfilled.

This would allow Hintikka to explain both the way in which a process of division ad infinitum is like a day or a game, and the way in which it is not like them. Like them, a process of division ad infinitum is something that can be occurring; unlike them, it cannot occur. However, this view still fails to make sense of Aristotle's claim that the infinite is potentially in a way in which it is not actually. To understand why Aristotle says this, we need to think more carefully about the way in which a process is the fulfilment of a potential.

5. PROCESS, POTENTIAL, AND FULFILMENT

Hintikka's view (or at least, the modified version of it that I have described) depends upon a certain assumption about the kind of potential that is fulfilled when a process is occurring. It assumes that (in cases where *phi-ing* is a process) *phi-ing* is the fulfilment of a potential to *be phi-ing*. This, I shall argue, is an assumption that Aristotle would reject. He would reject it because of his views about the nature of a process.

In *Metaphysics* IX 6 1048b18–35, Aristotle draws a distinction between an activity (*energeia*) and a process (*kinêsis*).[22] Examples of activities are: seeing, exercising one's understanding. Examples of processes are: becoming an oak tree, going for a run.[23] The difference Aristotle highlights in *Metaphysics* IX is this. In the case of an activity, while one is *phi-ing* one is in a state of having *phi-ed* and conversely, when one is in a state of having *phi-ed*, one is *phi-ing*. For example, while one is seeing one is in a state of having seen, and vice versa. In the case of a process, the relation between *phi-ing* and having *phi-ed* is different: while one is *phi-ing* one has not *phi-ed*, and when one has *phi-ed* one is no longer *phi-ing*. For example, while an acorn is becoming an oak, it has not yet become an oak, and when it has become an oak it is no longer becoming one.

To understand this distinction (and to defend it against what would otherwise be obvious counterexamples), it is necessary to take the perfect here as a marker of aspect, rather than tense. 'X has phi-ed' indicates that X's *phi-ing* is now complete and successful, rather than that there is some *phi-ing* (even some complete and successful *phi-ing*) in X's past. This explains why Aristotle can claim that one is seeing when one is in a state of having seen, and vice versa. The point is that one's seeing is fully complete at all and only those times at which it is going on. The fact that the perfect is being used here as a marker of aspect also explains why *going for a run* can be an example of a process. Of course, while I am running, it will be true of me that there is some running in my past (both because I have been running on earlier occasions and because I have already done some running on this one). Nevertheless, while I am running, I have not yet completed the run that I am now doing; and when I have completed my run, I am no longer doing that run. This is the sense in which, for Aristotle, 'I am running' is not compatible with 'I have run'.[24] A sign of this difference between *seeing* and *going for a run* is that it makes sense to say 'I have not yet finished my run', but it does not make sense to say 'I have not yet finished my seeing'.[25]

I want to argue that this distinction marks a difference between the way in which a process (on the one hand) and an activity (on the other) is the fulfilment of a potential. Undergoing a process essentially involves having some potential that is not fully realized, whereas engaging in an activity does not essentially involve having an unrealized potential. Of course, when I am engaged in an activity (such as seeing), I will have all sorts of unrealized potentials. (Perhaps I am not using my sense of smell.) The point is that having such unrealized potentials is not essential to what it is to be engaged in the activity of seeing, whereas there will always be a certain unrealized potential that is essential to the undergoing of a process.

What does this tell us about the way in which an activity or a process is the fulfilment of a potential? Consider first an activity. To be seeing is to be completely fulfilling a potential to see. (A potential to see just is a potential to be engaged in seeing.) In contrast, to be engaged in a process is not to be completely fulfilling some potential. The potential in terms of which a process is defined is a potential that is *not* completely fulfilled while the process is going on. To suppose otherwise would be to mistakenly assimilate a process to an activity.

Becoming an oak tree, then, is not the fulfilment of a potential *to be becoming an oak tree*. For that would be a potential that was completely fulfilled at any moment at which the process was going on. Similarly, *running round the block* is not the fulfilment of a potential *to be running round the block*. Such a potential would be completely fulfilled as soon as I was engaged in running round the block.

For a process to be going on is for some potential to be *incompletely* fulfilled. What, then, are the relevant potentials in our two examples? In becoming an oak tree, an acorn is progressing towards some definite end state: the state of being an oak tree. This makes it natural to suppose that the relevant potential is a potential to be in this end state. To be becoming an oak tree is to be incompletely fulfilling a potential to be an oak tree. This is a potential that is completely fulfilled only when the process is over.

Our other example, *running round the block,* is rather different. This is not a progression towards some end state. After all, to run around something is to end up where one began. I want to suggest that the relevant potential in this case is a potential that is completely fulfilled by the occurrence of the whole run. Once this potential has been completely fulfilled, it will be true to say, 'I ran round the block' (as opposed to, merely, 'I was running round the block'). While I am still running, the potential has not yet been completely fulfilled. (Indeed, if my run is interrupted, it may never be.) It is a potential that is completely fulfilled over a period of time (the period of time occupied by my run) rather than at an instant. This, then, is the potential that I am incompletely fulfilling while I am running round the block. We could call it a potential *to run round the block*.[26]

What is the relevance of all this to our discussion of Hintikka? According to Hintikka, Aristotle's account of infinite divisibility does not imply that there are unfulfillable potentialities: a magnitude has the potential to be undergoing the process of being infinitely divided (and this, Hintikka thinks, is a potential that can be fulfilled); on the other hand, a magnitude cannot be in a state of infinite dividedness, and it does not have the potential to be in such a state. My objection to this is that it depends upon a mistaken view of what it is for something to be undergoing a process. Suppose that it is true that a magnitude can be undergoing a process of being divided ad infinitum. I have argued that in undergoing a process, a thing must be *incompletely* fulfilling some potential. It follows that the potential in virtue of which a magnitude is *being divided* ad infinitum must be a potential that is only incompletely fulfilled while the magnitude is undergoing this process. The relevant potential, then, cannot be a potential 'to be undergoing the process of being infinitely divided', for that would be a potential that was completely fulfilled at any moment when the magnitude was undergoing such a process.[27]

6. WHAT POTENTIAL DO WE ASCRIBE TO A MAGNITUDE WHEN WE SAY THAT IT IS INFINITELY DIVISIBLE?

This brings us back to our original question. What potential do we ascribe to a magnitude when we say that it is infinitely divisible? I have suggested that the potential in question is *incompletely* fulfilled when the magnitude is undergoing a process of being divided ad infinitum. But what is this potential? In particular, what would be its complete fulfilment?

It is not a potential for *being in a state of infinite dividedness*: on Aristotle's view, nothing has the potential to be in such a state. Is it, then, a potential that is completely fulfilled by the occurrence of the whole process of division (as the potential to run a race is completely fulfilled by the occurrence of the whole run)? This too is impossible. As we have seen, there is no such thing as a *whole* process of getting divided ad infinitum. What, then, is this potential that we are trying to describe? I shall argue that it is a potential that *has* no complete fulfilment.

But how can there be a potential that has no complete fulfilment? Usually, we define a potential by saying what would count as completely fulfilling that potential (a potential to jump three feet is a potential that is completely fulfilled by a three-foot jump).[28] If a potential has no complete fulfilment, then how can we specify what potential it is? The answer is that we have to define this potential in a non-standard way: we have to specify what would count as fulfilling it *as completely as possible*. When we say that a magnitude is infinitely divisible, the potential we attribute to it should be defined as follows. It is a potential that *has no complete fulfilment* but that is fulfilled *as completely as it can be* in the process by which the line is *being divided* ad infinitum. There is thus a sense in which it, like other potentials, is defined by its maximal fulfilment, but the maximal fulfilment that defines it is not a complete fulfilment, merely a fulfilment that is *as complete as possible*.

Here an obvious objection presents itself. What does it mean to say that a certain potential is fulfilled as completely as possible, but is not fulfilled completely? Normally, our understanding of the notion of a potential's being *incompletely* fulfilled depends upon an implied contrast with its being completely fulfilled (for example, in running round the block one is *incompletely* fulfilling a certain potential—a potential that would be completely fulfilled by the occurrence of the whole run). I have claimed that when it is undergoing a process of division ad infinitum, a magnitude is incompletely fulfilling a certain potential. But in this case there is no implied contrast with a possible complete fulfilment: in undergoing that process, the magnitude's potential is as completely fulfilled as possible. Why, then, insist that the potential is only incompletely fulfilled?

The answer lies in the difference between process and activity. For a magnitude to be getting divided ad infinitum is for it to be undergoing a process, not engaging in an activity. *Getting divided ad infinitum* meets Aristotle's tests for being a process. When the magnitude is *getting divided ad infinitum*, it has not *been divided ad infinitum*. Moreover, *getting divided ad infinitum* can be interrupted: it makes sense to say that the magnitude was being divided ad infinitum but that the process was interrupted after only a few divisions. According to Aristotle, if something is undergoing a process, it must be incompletely fulfilling some potential. As we have seen, that is what it is to be undergoing a process. A process is something that is by its very nature incomplete while it is going on. To be undergoing a process is always to be doing something that, in a certain sense, points beyond itself. This is why Aristotle holds that when a magnitude is being divided ad infinitum, its potential for division is only being incompletely fulfilled, even though this potential is being fulfilled as completely as possible.

7. Aristotle's Puzzling Remarks Explained

We can now understand Aristotle's puzzling remarks about the infinite. The sense in which the infinite is 'in no other way than' potentially is this: the potential that we ascribe to something when we say that it is infinitely divisible is a potential that *cannot* be completely fulfilled. This need not commit Aristotle to the strange view that something is at one and the same time potentially F and incapable of being F. The potential in question (since it has no complete fulfilment) cannot be described as a potential to be F. It is, rather, the potential that is fulfilled as completely as possible in the undergoing of a process of division ad infinitum.

Moreover, we can now see why Aristotle wants to say *both* that the infinite is in no other way than potentially *and* that it is actually too in the way that the day and the games are. The potential that we ascribe to something when we say that it is infinitely divisible is a potential that can be fulfilled in a way: it can be *incompletely* fulfilled. It is incompletely fulfilled while the magnitude is being divided ad infinitum, just as the potential for a day to occur is incompletely fulfilled while the day is going on, or the potential for a game to occur is incompletely fulfilled while the game is taking place. The difference is that in the case of these potentials (for the day or the game to occur), there is a corresponding complete fulfilment (the occurrence of the day or of the game), whereas the potential we ascribe to something when we say it is infinitely divisible is a potential that has no complete fulfilment. It is thus 'only potential', in that it has no complete fulfilment, but also 'actual' in a way, in that it does (like the potential involved in the day or the games) have an incomplete fulfilment.

I have argued that Aristotle's puzzle about the infinite stems from a worry about how there can be something that is essentially incomplete: something that *cannot* be a whole. Aristotle thinks that there is a sense in which matter is essentially incomplete (and for this reason, he compares the way in which the infinite is to the way in which matter is).[29] But matter never exists by itself. It is always completed by something else: form. So we are still left asking how there could be something that exists *only* in an incomplete way: something that is neither a whole in and of itself nor is completed by anything external to it. Aristotle's answer is to appeal to the incomplete way in which a process is, while it is occurring. Most processes, of course, *also* exist as a whole: they occur over a certain length of time. But an infinite process is only ever underway. It *only* has the incomplete kind of being that we ascribe to a process when we say that it is occurring. This is why Aristotle says that the infinite 'has its being in becoming' (206a32). It is by reflecting on the nature of processes that he is able to make sense of the kind of incompleteness that he ascribes to the infinite.[30]

Notes

1. Interestingly, Aristotle's argument that there cannot be anything that is 'just infinite' relies on the assumption that an infinite cannot have as a part another infinite. This

might seem to cast doubt on the possibility of infinite time. If time is infinite, surely the past and future are parts of time that are infinite. It is unclear to me whether Aristotle himself saw this difficulty or how he would resolve it.

2. Commentators sometimes question how Aristotle can say that the past is infinite, given that the past is over and in that sense, completed. But the past is not 'complete' in the sense that I mean here, for it is not encompassed within bounds. Though bounded on one side by the now, it has (on Aristotle's view) no other boundary: there is no beginning of time.

3. Aristotle *may* be making this point in 207a12 ('that from which there is something absent outside is not all, whatever may be absent'), but see Hussey (1993) *ad loc.* for an alternative translation and interpretation. Hussey takes Aristotle to be saying that if there is void (absence) outside something, then that thing is not all there is (since void is something that is).

4. This, I take it, is implied by Aristotle's response to Zeno in *Physics* VIII 8. He asks whether it is possible to traverse infinitely many parts *either in time or space*. His reply is that this is not possible if they are in actuality but is possible if they are in potentiality (263b3–6).

5. It is sometimes claimed that Aristotle allows that there can be an infinite plurality of potential things at *Physics* VIII 8 263a28-b6. I disagree: for my interpretation of these lines, see Coope, 2005, p.10, n. 22.

6. *A three feet jump* could be the fulfilment of any number of different potentials (a potential to jump three feet, a potential to jump four feet, a potential to jump five feet and so on), but it can only be the *maximal* fulfilment of a potential to jump three feet. That is why it is possible to define a potential with reference to its maximal fulfilment, but not with reference to just any fulfilment.

7. In his brief remarks about the infinite in *Metaphysics* IX, he makes the same point by saying that the sense in which the infinite is potentially is not that it will be 'actually separate' (1048b14–15).

8. See Stephen Makin '*Energeia* and *Dunamis*', in this volume, Chapter 16, for a discussion of Aristotle's views elsewhere on the relation between actuality and potentiality.

9. Terry Irwin suggested to me this interpretation of the sentence about the Olympics. Another possibility is that Aristotle's point is simply that we say of a particular set of Olympics (or a particular day) both that it actually is (when it is going on) and that it potentially is (when it is about to occur). This way of taking the sentence is consistent with the second interpretation above, but has Aristotle making a less interesting point.

10. Ross (pp. 555–6, 1936) argues that a29–33 interrupts the flow of the surrounding argument. But he also cites evidence from the Greek commentators. Themistius seems to have had a conflation of both passages before him. Philoponous says (468.9) that a29–33 was omitted in the more accurate manuscripts. Simplicius (495.8) says that it was omitted in many of the manuscripts and that Alexander knew this.

11. Myles Burnyeat has suggested an emendation to Aristotle's discussion of the infinite in *Metaphysics* IX (1048b14–17), which (if right) would have him making the same point there. Instead of '*gnôsei*' (line b15), he reads '*genesei*'. See Makin (2006), who adopts this emendation, and translates: 'The infinite is not potentially in this way, namely that it will be actually separate, but by coming into being. For it is the division's not coming to an end which makes it the case that this actuality is potentially, and not the infinite being separated'.

12. Hintikka, J. 'Aristotelian infinity' *Philosophical Review*, v. 75, n. 2., 1966, pp.197–218, (and in *Time and Necessity*, 1973). Lear, J. 'Aristotelian infinity' *Proceedings of the Aristotelian Society* 80, 1979, 187–210.

13. A period of time has its being in becoming, in the relevant sense, but is not itself a process.
14. Hintikka (1966) p. 200.
15. And indeed, this interpretation is adopted, without the assumption about the principle of plenitude, by Bostock (1972) 'Zeno and the potential infinite', *Proceedings of the Aristotelian Society* 73, 37–51.
16. Though note that one manuscript (E) omits the phrase 'it is in no other way' (206b12).
17. Bostock (1972) p. 39.
18. Lear, (1979) p. 190. Strictly speaking, the fact that physical cuts are all of finite size does not show that the magnitude will be destroyed after finitely many cuts. The second cut could be half the size of the first, the third cut half the size of the second, and so on ad infinitum. However, Lear's main point here is surely right. Any physical magnitude will disintegrate after finitely many cuts. Actual physical cuts cannot be made smaller and smaller ad infinitum.
19. As Lear acknowledges, Aristotle thinks that species are permanent, so he might suppose that we could pass on the work of division from one generation to the other. Lear responds that, if the division is division in thought, then this idea of 'passing it on' does not make sense: 'there is no way in which a theoretical divider of the present generation could pass on his work to a divider of the next generation' (1979, p. 190).
20. For this reason too, Aristotle would claim that it is impossible for there to be a process in which the first division is made in a minute, the second in half a minute, the third in a quarter of a minute...and so on. (Bostock discusses processes of this kind in his 'Zeno and the potential infinite', 1972.) There can't be a whole process of infinitely dividing a magnitude—either in infinitely much time or in a finite period of time.
21. Lear (1979) p. 191.
22. For a useful discussion of this see Makin, 2006, pp. 141–50 and Burnyeat, 2008.
23. A contest (e.g., running a race) is an example of a process, but a day is not. However, a day is like a process, in that the day is not complete until it is over. It makes sense, for instance, to say that the day is not yet finished. Why does Aristotle pick as his examples *the day* and *the Olympic games*, neither of which are Aristotelian processes? The answer, I think, is that a paradigmatic Aristotelian process is a progression towards some particular end state. The *day* and *the Olympic games* share important features of Aristotelian processes (e.g., when the day is occurring it has not occurred), but they are not progressions towards some end state. This makes them suitable for comparing with the odd kind of process under consideration here: a process of getting divided ad infinitum. The example I consider below of *running round the block* is in this respect like the day or the Olympic games.
24. To spell this out fully needs some care. (i) 'Successful' here must mean: successful relative to a goal internal to the process. My reason for going for a run might be that I want to feel the wind in my hair, and I may have achieved this goal as soon as I am running. But this goal is not the internal goal of running. (ii) Aimlessly running about (as opposed to going for a run) is a more problematic example, as it is unclear what would count as its being complete; aimlessly running about doesn't fit very well into Aristotle's distinction between process and activity.
25. Of course, if someone said this, we would probably do our best to make sense of it. We might take it to mean: 'I want to spend some more time looking at this.'
26. Perhaps Aristotle would have said, even in this case, that the relevant potential is completely fulfilled only at the final instant of the run. If so, then he could have argued straightforwardly that in the case of infinite processes with no final instant, the relevant

potential is one that has no complete fulfillment. This would follow simply from the fact that such processes have no final instant. However, in a sense this conclusion would be reached too easily: someone might object that it was simply a consequence of the mistaken attempt to treat all processes as progressions towards some end state. I want to argue that Aristotle could draw his conclusion (that the relevant potential, in the case of infinite processes, is one that has no complete fulfilment) even if he had the view I suggest here, that the potential that is incompletely fulfilled in a process like *running round the block* is a potential that is completely fulfilled over the period of time occupied by the whole run. The fact that his own examples here are of *the day* and *the Olympic games* (certainly not paradigmatic Aristotelian processes) suggests that he wanted to compare the process of division ad infinitum with something that, though process-like, was not a progression towards an end. My example of *running round the block* is meant to be an example of a process of this sort. My thought is that, in the context of discussing infinite processes, Aristotle wanted to emphasize the difference between this kind of example and the kind of process that is a progression towards an end state.

27. Someone might make the following objection to my argument in this section. Suppose we grant that *running round the block* is not *defined* as the complete fulfilment of a potential to be running round the block (but rather as the incomplete fulfilment of some other potential). It could nevertheless be *true* that in running round the block I am completely fulfilling a potential to be running round the block. We can accept the point about definition without denying that in running round the block I am completely fulfilling some potential. In reply, I would say two things. First, once we admit that running round the block is the incomplete fulfilment of a potential to run round the block, there is no need to introduce a further potential: a potential to *be running round the block*. I doubt whether Aristotle would recognize the existence of a potential that, in this sense, did no work. Second, even if Aristotle were to admit the existence of such a potential, the important point would stand: when a thing is undergoing a process, there is some potential that it is *incompletely* fulfilling. (It will turn out that, for a process of division ad infinitum to be going on, there must be some potential that is being incompletely fulfilled, and this must be a potential that *cannot* be completely fulfilled.)

28. See my remarks in Section 1 on *De Caelo* I 11.

29. Like matter, the infinite is potentially, and like matter the infinite is not a whole (207a15ff.). The infinite is also closely connected to matter because matter, as such, is infinitely divisible. I take it that Aristotle is talking about *matter* (this thing that is infinite, in the sense of being infinitely divisible) in the difficult lines 207a21ff., when he says that it is 'surrounded' (a25) and is 'whole and finite not in itself but in respect of something else' (a23–24). The point is that the thing that is infinite (i.e., infinitely divisible) is matter and it (matter) is, *qua* infinitely divisible, surrounded and that it (matter) is whole and finite in respect of something else (its form).

30. Thanks to Stephen Makin, Adrian Moore, and audiences at Cambridge, Oxford, Berlin, and Cornell for comments on earlier versions of this paper.

Bibliography

Bostock, D. (1972) 'Zeno and the potential infinite', *Proceedings of the Aristotelian Society* 73, 37–51.

Burnyeat, M.F. (2008) '*Kinêsis* vs. *Energeia*: A much-read passage in (but not of) Aristotle's *Metaphysics*', in *Oxford Studies in Ancient Philosophy*, 34, 219–92.

Coope, U. (2005) *Time for Aristotle: Physics IV.10–14* (Oxford: Oxford Univ. Press).

Hintikka, J. (1996) 'Aristotelian infinity', *Philosophical Review* 75, n.2, 197–18; (and in *Time and Necessity*, 1973).

Hussey, E. (1993) *Aristotle Physics Books III and IV* (Oxford: Oxford Univ. Press).

Lear, J. (1979) 'Aristotelian infinity' *Proceedings of the Aristotelian Society* 80, 187–210.

Makin, S. (2006) *Aristotle Metaphysics Book Theta* (Oxford: Oxford Univ. Press).

Ross, W. (1936) *Aristotle Physics* (Oxford: Oxford Univ. Press).

CHAPTER 12

THE COMPLEXITY OF ARISTOTLE'S STUDY OF ANIMALS

JAMES G. LENNOX

I. INTRODUCTION

THIS chapter will discuss the puzzling complexity of Aristotle's investigations of animals. I am going to go into their complexity in some detail; and I hope to motivate the reader to follow by pointing out that these investigations are complex in ways that can help us to explore issues central to understanding Aristotle's metaphysics and epistemology.

The place to begin is with a brief reminder of the *range* of Aristotle's writings related to animals: *Historia animalium* (*HA*, 10 books), *Dissections* (an uncertain number, all lost),[1] *De partibus animalium* (*PA*, 4 books), *De generatione animalium* (*GA*, 5 books), *De motu animalium* (*MA*, 1 book), *De incessu animalium* (*IA*, 1 book), *Parva naturalia* (*PN* = *De sensu et sensibilibus, De memoria et reminiscentia, De somno et vigilia, De insomniis, De divinatione per somnum, De longitudine et brevitate vitae, De juventute et senectute, De vita et morte, De respiratione*).[2] There are, in addition to this long list of works, at least two others that are so intimately tied to this animal project that, however one sees the relationship, they need to be mentioned: *De Anima* (*DA*), and *Meteorologica* IV (Meteor. IV).

Putting aside questions about how editors at various stages of textual editing and transmission decided to package these works, there are many different, somewhat self-contained and somewhat inter-dependent studies here. This in itself is puzzling, and if it does not seem so to the modern reader, that is likely because we have come to expect a science constituted of highly specialized sub-disciplines rather loosely connected to each other. But an investigation of the natural world so organized was unprecedented in Ancient Greece. By the beginning of the fourth century BC mathematics was *beginning* to take on an articulated structure,[3] but those who wrote on nature did precisely that: they wrote all-encompassing works *On Nature*.[4] Perhaps because most of them saw their goal as finding one or a few unchanging starting points that would explain *all* natural phenomena, the *physiologoi* before Aristotle tended to write narrative cosmogonies about nature in general.[5] Aristotle is the first person in the history of science to see the study of nature as an articulated complex of interrelated, yet somewhat autonomous, investigations. Understanding why goes to the heart of what is philosophically distinctive about him.

Even within the Aristotelian framework of an articulated series of natural investigations, his investigation of animals is idiosyncratic. It is the only one of his investigations of nature that has a rich and self-conscious *internal* articulation of its own, reflected in the many independent treatises catalogued above. Why did he not write, as the medieval philosophers apparently thought he should have, one work *De animalibus*?[6] To give this question reality, consider a single work and its independence: Why does Aristotle present the investigation of 'the common cause of animal motion' (as Aristotle characterizes the subject of *De motu animalium*) as distinct and independent from a study of the causes of the different *forms* of animal locomotion, the announced project of *De incessu animalium*? And, since *De incessu* is a study of the causes of the different organs of locomotion in different animals, why is it not simply included as part of the study of the limbs of animals in *De partibus animalium* IV? Neither question can be answered by appeal to accidents of textual transmission: each of the three works just mentioned opens with its own justification for its independence. In fact those very 'openings' are among the details that can provide answers to some of the above questions.

II. *HISTORIA*, EXPERIENCE, AND THE SEARCH FOR CAUSES

Let us begin with the largest and in certain ways the most mysterious work in the collection, *Historia animalium*. It consists of nine books, organized more or less according to the plan outlined in its first six chapters, and a tenth, apparently an exploration of the female contribution to generation that, on grounds of methodology and doctrine, is likely misplaced.[7] In the other animal studies, *HA* is referenced a number of times, often in conjunction with what were likely collections of anatomical drawings or diagrams, the *Anatomai* or *Dissections*.[8] Studies of this

work in recent decades, following the lead of David Balme,[9] have stressed that there
is an overall plan of organization to the work. Its overarching goal appears to be
to provide a record of universal correlations among *differences* found throughout
the animal kingdom, differences that fall under four broad headings: differences
in parts, in activities, in ways of life, and in habits or characters. The first four
books, for example, are more or less restricted to identifying, and finding universal
correlations among, the different *parts* of animals: for example, identifying lungs
and differentiations among lungs; and noting that all animals with lungs also have
windpipes and an esophagus (*HA* II 15). But the organization is more systematic
and complicated than this suggests: there are separate sections devoted to the parts
of the blooded and the bloodless animals; and within these broad categories, discussions of the *external* and *internal* parts, and the *uniform* and *non-uniform* parts,
are also distinguished. Finally, Aristotle takes some pains to identify a number
of major groups of animals, which he refers to as *megista genê* (very large kinds)
within the blooded and bloodless groups. These kinds (among the blooded, birds,
fish, four-legged live bearing, four-legged egg laying land animals, and cetaceans[10];
among the bloodless, insects, hard-shelled, soft-shelled, and soft-bodied animals[11])
are not exhaustive (among species not captured, for example, are human beings),
nor do they play a central role in the organization of *HA*. But within the discussion
of the various kinds of differences in the blooded or bloodless animals, Aristotle
will often review those differences 'kind by kind.'[12]

From the way this information is presented, it is clear that a complicated method
of differential division was used in the process of organizing the data, broadly in
line with the norms for the use of such a method laid out in *PA* I 2–4. Aristotle concludes a lengthy introduction outlining the ways in which animals are alike and
different with respect to their parts, activities, ways of life, and character by distinguishing the work to be done (I 6 490a7–14) from the ultimate goal, demonstrative
knowledge of animals.[13] The immediate task, he explains, is a *historia* of animals
by means of which we grasp their attributes and differences. This is 'pre-causal'
and 'pre-demonstrative', but on its basis we will be able to distinguish the starting
points of demonstration from the facts to be demonstrated. And in line with this
characterisation, and in stark contrast to *PA*, *HA* is almost entirely devoid of the
network of concepts Aristotle uses when definition and causal demonstration are
being sought or provided—none of the many universal correlations identified is
said to be necessary; no causal explanations for correlations are provided; no part
is given a functional definition; and nothing is ever said about what a part exists for
the sake of, or about its essence. Indeed, even the distinction between matter and
form is generally ignored; 'form' is used often, but always to refer to a sub-division
of a wider 'kind'. Moreover, as Aristotle is concluding his introductory 'sketch' of
the methods to be used in his history of animals, he says that this is the *natural*
way to proceed:

> These things have been said in this way now as an outline, to provide a taste of
> the things, however many they may be, about which we must study, in order that
> we may first grasp their differences and attributes in every case. (We will speak in

greater detail in what follows.) After this is done, we must attempt to discover the causes of these differences and attributes. For to pursue the inquiry (*poieisthai tên methodên*) in this way is natural (*kata phusin*), once there is an investigation (*historia*) about each kind; since it becomes apparent from these investigations both about which things and from which things the demonstration (*hê apodeixis*) ought to be carried out (*HA* I 6 491a7-14).

In this passage one hears echoes of passages in the *Analytics* about a 'factual' (*hoti*) stage of inquiry based on experience that will serve as the basis for a 'reasoned fact' (*dioti*) stage, in which one searches for and finds causes that are used to explain the information gathered in that previous stage (*APr* I 30, 46a20-24; *APo* II 1, 89b29-35; compare *PA* I 1 639b7-10, *PA* II 1 646a8-12; *IA* 1 704b8-10).[14]

These closing remarks of its introduction urge us to consider *HA* as a work that self-consciously conforms to Aristotle's explicit norms about inquiry aimed at demonstrative knowledge in the *Posterior Analytics*—in particular, it appears to be a presentation of information organized according to the norms of 'pre-demonstrative' or 'pre-causal' inquiry. But there are a number of mysteries that emerge once one considers *HA* from this perspective. First, in no other investigation of nature does Aristotle devote a distinct treatise to a self-consciously pre-demonstrative presentation of data; that he believes knowledge of causes and essences of the objects in any domain somehow arises out of a systematic empirical investigation of that domain is not in question. But neither in his cosmology nor his meteorology, to take two obvious comparisons, is there a distinct treatise, to which *De Caelo* or *Meteorology* might regularly refer, laying out the attributes and differences in an overtly non-demonstrative form. Inductivism requires that scientific investigation of a subject begin with an empirical investigation of its objects and their attributes; it does *not* require a separate treatise presenting the results of that preliminary stage of investigation composed along the lines of *HA*.

Beyond that, a number of scholars have put forward claims about *HA* that, if true, make its existence and pre-demonstrative character yet more mysterious. David Balme, the twentieth century's foremost scholar of this work, in the process of preparing a new text, translation, and commentary, became convinced that it began as a redaction of factual material already presented in the treatises devoted to a causal understanding of animals, to which new material was continually added, by Aristotle and perhaps others. Part of his argument was philological in nature, having to do with a comparison of the descriptions of identical facts in *HA* and the works that refer to it; part of it rested on details about the contents of *HA*. For example, the material in *HA* that is *not* found in the other treatises is often more detailed and sometimes disagrees with them; while some of this unique material seems to have been left at a preliminary stage of organization. Balme also had philosophical questions about the coherence of the idea that a work such as *HA* could be composed in the absence of views about the causal structure of the domain.

This is not the place to provide a detailed presentation and assessment of Balme's views on the relative dating of the various biological treatises;[15] but if they have any merit at all, it deepens the mystery of why such a work was composed in the first place, since one plausible answer is ruled out—it was *not* composed as the presentation of data at a preliminary, 'fact organizing' stage of zoological inquiry, an Aristotelian equivalent of laboratory or field notebooks, let us say.

From a very different perspective, but reaching conclusions that are in partial agreement with Balme's, David Charles has claimed that something like the theory of the soul in the *De Anima* lies behind the way the information in *HA* is organized, and thus that the narrative I presented at the outset over-emphasizes the pre-theoretical character of *HA*. That *HA* is, *in some sense*, self-consciously theoretical is common ground; disagreement arises over which theoretical commitments are in play. Research conducted over the last 40 years presents a compelling case for the claim that when *HA* was composed, Aristotle had a clear view of what a causal, demonstrative science of animals, as part of a science of nature, ought to look like.[16] Paradoxically, I think the strongest evidence for that is what *HA avoids* saying. There is an almost ritualistic formula in the work for identifying universal and co-extensive relationships among differentiae, without ever claiming that the correlations identified are necessary. The refrain, so pervasive in *PA*, that a part or behaviour is present in a certain kind of animal because nature has acted 'for the sake of something' or 'because it is better' is, therefore, also missing. In short, and as already noted, the machinery of definition and causal explanation that pervades the other studies of animals is almost entirely absent, and to such an extent that this cannot be an accident: as the closing section of *HA* I 6 reveals, it is written by an author with a clear view of what a demonstrative science of animal nature should look like, and with a theoretical perspective on the epistemology of empirical science. That epistemological perspective holds that at any stage in a scientific investigation of a subject, advances at the level of causal understanding depend on an inductive method that aids and abets the search for causes. If we keep that thought in mind and think of the written treatises we have as organized for teaching purposes, a solution to the puzzling features of *HA* emerges.

From the standpoint of the subject matter of these studies, animals, Aristotle would surely have been aware that, unlike stars and planets, there will be a never-ending influx of new information both by way of new animals that will be discovered and by way of new discoveries that dissection and careful field observation of behaviour and habits will provide. Having a work that serves as an on-going 'repository' for that information—a sort of filing system, as it were—would be critical in this investigation in a way that he might well think it would not be in others.[17]

And from the standpoint of teaching and learning, such a document, organized as it is, would serve the purpose of instruction in inductive methodology, provided Aristotle is serious about his oft-repeated claim that it is properly organized experience of and inquiry into a subject that allows us to discover the causally structured definitions that are the goals of inquiry (*APo* II 2 90a1-15).

III. 'GENERATION IS FOR THE SAKE OF BEING...'

An oddity about Aristotle's 'animal books' that likely *is* due to a later editor's decision is that what is now the first of four books *On the Parts of Animals* clearly was intended as a philosophical introduction, not just to the study of the parts of animals, but to the investigation of animals *in general*. That first book introduces itself by distinguishing between two distinct kinds of cognitive capacities that can be found in *every study and systematic inquiry (Peri pasan theôrian te kai methodon...*—a capacity properly referred to as scientific knowledge (*epistêmê*) of the subject of investigation; and a certain sort of learned skill (*hoion paideian tina*) to discriminate between well-presented and poorly presented reports of the results of an investigation (*PA* I 1 639a1-4). Among people who have this latter capacity, Aristotle introduces a further distinction, between those who are able to make such discriminations across a wide range of subjects, and those who can do so 'about something of a delimited nature'. He later claims that by using a certain set of standards, researchers with this capacity can discriminate well-formed and ill-formed claims in their discipline independently of knowing whether the claim is true or false.

This introduction leads directly into a series of questions, worded as apparent alternatives, about how a study of nature *should* be investigated. It is the subject for a book to discuss all of these questions and their relations to one another. Here I want merely to discuss one of them, selected in order to provide the reader with a general idea of the nature of the intellectual enterprise that is *PA* I, and to highlight some of its more puzzling features. But it is also a question the answer to which helps us to understand another distinctive—and puzzling—aspect of Aristotle's zoological investigation: his decision to treat the *generation* of animals as the subject for a distinct study, and the *parts* of fully developed animals as the subject for another, quite different, sort of study.

It is a question about whether the *phusikos*, in studying animals, should follow a path traveled successfully by the astronomer.

> ...whether, just as the mathematicians explain the phenomena in the case of astronomy, so the natural scientist too, having first studied the phenomena regarding the animals and the parts of each, should then state the reason why and the causes, or whether he should proceed in some other way (639b8–11).

Now that this is the way Aristotle thinks that mathematical astronomy has progressed is well known, perhaps the most commonly cited text on the subject being one we have already had occasion to consider in regard to *HA*'s stated purpose, in *Prior Analytics* I 30.

> Thus the principles are provided by experience in each case. I mean for example, astronomical experience provides the principles of astronomical knowledge; for when the appearances had been grasped sufficiently, astronomical demonstrations were easily discovered. And it is likewise with any other art or science. So that if

the predicates about each thing have been grasped, we will be well prepared to exhibit their demonstrations (46a20–24).

But while it may be 'likewise with any other art or science', the above passage does not imply that the way one proceeds from observational experience to the principles will be the same in every case—nor that the principles arrived at will be of the same character.[18] Indeed, it implies the opposite—for help in arriving at the principles of astronomy, we need *astronomical* experience. In the case of a scientific investigation of animals, we are discussing a special class of natural substances that have a vast range of diverse appearances to be grasped and that come to be by means of a complex, co-ordinated, apparently goal-oriented, process. Thus, while the way of proceeding from phenomena to causes in this passage may be relatively unproblematic as a claim about mathematical astronomy, it is genuinely unclear what the implications of the general claim are for the investigation of animals.

It is thus no mistake, but a critical part of the way in which Aristotle presents his case, that, rather than answering this question immediately, he moves on to another question about causal inquiry, one that *cannot* arise in mathematical astronomy.

> …since we see more than one cause of natural generation, e.g., both the cause 'for the sake of which' and the cause 'whence comes the origin of motion', we need also to determine, about these causes, which is naturally first and which second (639b11–14).

Mathematical astronomy will not concern itself with questions of the relative priority of two of the causes operative in nature—but it certainly is at issue in the study of animal generation. In fact, one of the most complex and methodologically important passages in Aristotle's *Generation of Animals* (II 6 742a17ff.) opens, as we will see momentarily, with a critical consideration of what his predecessors have said about the order in which animal parts develop; in that passage, Aristotle is at pains to indicate that without a proper understanding of the hierarchy of functions among the parts, and of the relationship between the efficient cause and the final cause, you will completely fail to understand the order of efficient causation in the process.

In a biological context, then, the question of whether one should first study the phenomena and then their causes is, to say the least, underspecified—since there are a number of causes operative in biological development, *which* cause should be taken up first, after a study of *which* phenomena? Given that 'the phenomena' consist of complex, temporally unfolding processes that vary remarkably from one kind to the next, is it even clear what it means to recommend studying the phenomena before one searches for their causes? It seems clear that this question can only be dealt with adequately once one takes seriously the differences between studying eternal, unchanging objects travelling in eternal and unchanging orbits and complex organisms subject to natural generation and destruction.

The argument that runs from 639b15–21, therefore, defends the causal priority of the 'cause for the sake of which' to the motive cause in 'things composed by nature and by art', and ends by asserting, though not arguing, that 'the cause for the sake of which and the noble' (*to kalon*) are present *more* in the works of nature than in those of art. Following directly after that, from 639b21 to 640a1, Aristotle argues that necessity is not present alike in all natural things, and notes that previous investigators of nature refer all explanations to necessity without acknowledging this fact. He thereby introduces a distinction between *unqualified* necessity and *conditional* necessity, the former present in eternal things, the latter present in all things that partake in generation. This distinction is thus required by the preceding argument for the priority of the final cause that is not always noticed. Aristotle's argument for the priority of the final cause depends on the thought that, in the realm of craftsmanship, in giving the *account* of a thing that comes to be, the craftsman will specify the form of the end product of his craft—a doctor will specify the state of health, and a builder the form of the house to be built. Medical or building practice, that is, will be characterized by reference to the goals they aim to achieve. He then depends on this account of the teleological nature of craftsmanship in his explication of conditional necessity:

> It is necessary that a certain sort of matter be present if there is to be a house or any other end, and this must come to be and be changed first, then that, and so on continuously up to the end and that for the sake of which each comes to be and is. And it is the same way too with things that come to be by nature (639b26–30).

The final section of this passage then builds on the two previous conclusions: 640a1–9 argues for a distinct manner of demonstration for contexts in which conditional necessity is operative, and where the starting points and definitions identify goals toward which change proceeds, provided nothing interferes.

> But the manner (*tropos*) of demonstration and of necessity are different in the natural and the theoretical sciences (639b30–640a2).

This is a very puzzling remark, of course.[19] But one plausible reading of it fits well with the interpretation I have been providing for Aristotle's concerns about causation and necessity in the argument so far. The claim that there is need for a different manner of demonstration and necessity suggests that the study of animals and plants is not to be pursued according to the methods appropriate for the heavenly bodies, for it follows immediately after Aristotle introduces the distinction between *eternal* natural beings governed by *unqualified* necessity alone and *generated* natural beings, where definitions specify goals and where *conditional* necessity specifies the relationship of matter and motive causes to such goals. This distinction is stressed in the justly well-known summative chapter of *PA* I 5, which opens by contrasting the *eternal* natural substances with those that come to be and pass away, twice acknowledging that, while the former are more divine, the latter 'take the prize with respect to scientific knowledge' (645a1–4; cf. 644b28–31). He then says:

> Since we have completed stating the way things appear to us about the divine things, it remains to speak about animal nature (*peri tês zôikês phuseôs...*) (645a4–6).

Aristotle is, then, acutely aware of a fundamental demarcation in the natural world that brings with it the question of whether the study of animal nature is simply another part of the same *methodos* as the study of the eternal natural substances or whether the differences are sufficient to consider it a distinct investigation with quite different methods of investigation and modes of demonstration.[20]

With the machinery of teleology integrated with conditional necessity in place, and a sketch of teleological demonstration governed by conditional necessity outlined, Aristotle apparently revisits his unanswered question and begins to develop an answer at 640a9–14. There will not be space here to explore it fully,[21] but there is an otherwise curious feature of his answer that is illuminated by recognizing that it is shaped by the teleological framework that is now in place.

The passage begins as if it will provide a positive response to the question about whether one is first to study the observable phenomena about animals before attempting to search for their causal explanations. But it appears to morph rather quickly into answering a slightly different question: Should one try to understand the *being* of an animal as the necessary product of its coming to be, or rather try to understand its coming to be as conditionally necessary for the being toward which it proceeds. Of course, he endorses the latter position—in words that are surely intended to remind his readers of the *Philebus*.

> For even with house building, it is rather that these things happen because the form of the house is such as it is, than that the house is such as it is because it comes to be in this way. For generation is for the sake of being; being is not for the sake of generation (640a15–19).[22]

We are now in a position to see that these two questions are more intimately related than they might first appear to be. For suppose the 'phenomena' you are concerned to study include both the anatomy and physiology—the parts and activities—of fully developed animals *and* the coming to be of those parts and activities. And suppose the causes include both the antecedent materials and moving causes out of which and by which development proceeds *and* the form and goal at the end of the process—i.e., the parts and activities of fully developed animals. The apparently straightforward suggestion that one should study the phenomena first, and then their causes, on grounds that knowledge of causal principles arises out of experience of the subject matter, now becomes quite complicated. For the processes and materials involved in an animal's coming to be can, from one perspective, be viewed as phenomena to be explained teleologically, but from another perspective can be viewed as the productive causes of the animal that comes to be. Indeed, Aristotle takes unspecified predecessors to task in the *Generation of Animals* for not recognizing such distinctions:

> Some of the early natural philosophers attempted to say which of the parts comes to be after which, being insufficiently experienced (*ou lian empeirikôs echontes*) with the facts. For among the parts, as in other things, one is by nature prior to another. But clearly 'prior' is said in many ways. For that-for-the-sake-of-which and that which is for the sake of it are different, and one of these is prior

in generation, but the other is prior in being. And that which is for the sake of something else is found in two different forms: for one is the motive source, the other is what is made use of by that for the sake of which (II 6 742a17–24).

Whoever they may be, these students of nature were inexperienced with the facts, but it looks as if the message of this passage is that, absent the proper teleological framework for looking at the facts, further experience may well have been in vain. And indeed, we know this is Aristotle's view from another passage critical of his predecessors, in this case from *On respiration*, the last of the treatises grouped together under the title *Parva naturalia*.

> One reason why most of them did not speak well about these things is both a lack of experience with the internal parts (*to te tôn moriôn apeirous einai tôn entos*) and a failure to grasp what nature produces them all for; for were they seeking that for which respiration belongs to the animals, and pursuing this while inspecting the parts, such as gills and lung, the cause would be quickly discovered (*Resp.* 3 471b23–29).

It is experience guided by a search for the part's function that will reward the investigator with a discovery of the cause. All the experience in the world, guided by an inappropriate method, will be in vain. In support of this strongly normative way of reading these passages, we may return to the passage in *GA* II 6 and follow it out a bit further.[23] After reiterating the threefold distinction among kinds of priority (742a25–36), he goes on:

> So, if there is such a part, which must be present in animals, one which has the origin and end of the entire nature, this must come to be first—as motive capacity, first, while as a part of the end it must come to be along with the whole. Thus, as many of the instrumental parts as are generative in nature must be present first (for it is for the sake of another as the origin), while as many as are among things that are for the sake of another but *not* generative in nature must be later. For which reason it is not easy to distinguish which, among the parts that are for the sake of another, is prior, or what it is these parts are for the sake of. The motive parts, being prior to the end in generation, intervene, and distinguishing between the motive and the instrumental parts is not easy. And yet, it is necessary to inquire what comes to be after what according to this method; for the end is posterior to some things, but prior to others (*GA* II 6 742a37-b12).

The method that is referred to here is that which seeks to distinguish among various senses of priority, and which orders parts, at any stage of development, between those which are constitutive of the end for the sake of which development is taking place and parts that are related to that end in two quite different senses: those which originate the change towards the end, and those which are used as instruments in achieving that end.

This might all seem like pretty heavy metaphysical artillery to wheel in for the purpose of introducing an account of embryological development, but the next few lines confirm that it does actually frame his approach to the investigation.

> And on account of this, the part having the origin comes to be first, and then, following it, the upper trunk. It is for this reason that the parts around the

head and the eyes appear largest in embryos at the start, while those below the umbilicus, such as the legs, are small. For the lower parts are for the sake of the upper and are neither part of the end nor generative of it (742b12–17).

An unusual feature of the early stages of embryonic development in all vertebrates is that the upper region, which will eventually differentiate into the various features of the head, develops first and is disproportionately large, and the eye discs are large and obvious at a very early stage. Moreover, of the internal organs, the heart appears very early, at first so small that in its systolic contraction it disappears entirely. Famously, Aristotle originated an experimental means of studying the embryonic development of a chick by taking many incubating eggs hatched on the same day and carefully opening one each day until hatching, observing the differences from one day to the next. Here is his description at day four, in which it is clear that he has taken care to observe the developing embryo in its living state.

> During this time the yolk has already migrated toward the pointed end of the egg, wherein lies the source of the egg and whence the egg hatches; and the heart is a mere blood-spot in the white. This point of blood beats and moves as if ensouled; and growing from it two blood vessels wind their way toward each of the surrounding tunics. At this time a membrane with blood-like fibers coming from the blood vessels already surrounds the white. A little later the body can be distinguished, at first small and entirely white. The head is visible, and its eyes in an extremely developed state; this persists for a long time, though eventually the eyes become small and contract (*HA* VI 3 561a4–21).[24]

IV. Delimiting Teleology

That Aristotle's understanding of biological development is teleological is well-known, though the complexity of that understanding is rarely appreciated. What is even less appreciated is that Aristotle provides us with the first discussion in the history of philosophy of the limits of teleological thinking in biology. Based on passages like the following, during a discussion of bile in the early chapters of *PA* IV, one might have inferred that he'd given the topic some thought. He reviews various theories of why animals have bile, patiently indicating that the evidence refutes all of them. He then goes on:

> Rather, just as bile, when it arises throughout the rest of the body, seems to be a residue or colliquescence, so also the bile near the liver seems to be a residue and not to be for the sake of something, as does the sediment in the stomach and intestines as well. Now sometimes nature even makes use of residues for some benefit, yet it is not on this account necessary to seek what something is for in every case; on the contrary, when certain things are such as they are, many other things happen of necessity (*PA* IV 2 677a12–18).

Now it may look, from this passage, that Aristotle's primary evidence for the absence of teleology in the case of bile is that it is a residue with no evident purpose. But his criticisms of earlier theories (the views of the *Timaeus* and of 'those around Anaxagoras' are mentioned explicitly) show a different form of reasoning in play. The theories he reviews all have implications about which animals should and should not have bile. One view links it directly to perception, and Aristotle reviews a number of animals which perceive but have no bile; another links it to acute diseases, and Aristotle shows that many animals that suffer from these diseases have no bile. He also reviews evidence that bile is not universally present in animals of the same kind. This kind of inductive reasoning is relevant to his conclusions about whether teleological explanation is appropriate, the topic with which he begins Book V of *On the Generation of Animals*. To situate that discussion, it is worth reviewing the structure of this work as a whole.

GA I is devoted primarily to a discussion of the parts related to reproduction: the first thirteen chapters discuss the reproductive organs of males and females in blooded animals (these parts were purposefully excluded from discussion in *PA*[25]); the next three to those of bloodless animals; and the remainder to the *uniform* part contributed by male and female in reproduction.[26] In *GA* II and III, after a philosophically rich introduction discussing why there is reproduction at all, and why the male and female principle are typically separate in animals, there ensues a long discussion of the causal origins of development, first in the live-bearing animals, then in the egg-laying animals, concluding with those animals that appear to be generated asexually or 'spontaneously'. *GA* IV 1–3 takes up the question of what causes this virtually universal differentiation between male and female, and includes a well-known explanation of the inheritance of sub-specific differences. Since it turns out that the same causes that lead to these two classes of difference also lead to the production of various forms of deformity (*terata*), the causes of deformity are taken up in book IV as well, as are the causes of variation in the number of offspring that are produced. Two phenomena restricted to certain females, the *mola uteri* and the production of milk around the time of birth, are next discussed, and the book concludes with a discussion of differences in gestation periods.   •

GA V announces that '[i]t is now time to study the affections by which the parts of animals differ' (778a16–17). As examples he mentions variations in eye colour, pitch of voice, hair and feather colour, some of which belong to the whole kind, some of which appear to be randomly distributed, and some of which change as the organism ages. He concludes the introduction with a caution:

> Concerning these and all such things it is no longer necessary to believe there to be the same manner of cause.[27] For as many as are not works of nature in common nor distinctive of each kind, none of these either are or come to be for the sake of something. For while an eye [is and comes to be] for the sake of something, [its being and coming to be] blue is not for the sake of something—unless this affection is distinctive of the kind. Nor in some cases does it extend to the account of the being [of the kind], but because they come to be out of necessity one ought to take the causes back to the matter and the moving source (778a29-b2).

He then refers back to what was said 'in the primary arguments' (*en tois prôtois logois*),[28] that generation follows and is for the sake of being, not the other way round (778b5–6), and reiterates that teleology will be in place in generation whenever a feature is present in the definition, is for the sake of something, or is what others are for the sake of. Reverting to his previous example, he notes that an animal will have eyes of necessity given the sort of animal it is, but it will have a certain colour of eye due to a different sort of necessity—'because it is by nature such as to act and be acted upon in this way or that' (778b16–19).

To fully understand this passage, one must study the actual explanations that Aristotle offers in the remainder of the book of variations in sleeping habits, eye colour, perceptual acuity, hair texture and colour, and so on. But even without doing so, there are important lessons to be learned here relevant to Aristotle's place in the history of philosophy. The first is that, even in the investigation of life, Aristotle does not think science extends only as far as we have access to teleological explanation—in this chapter he chastises certain of his predecessors for failing to recognize the plurality of causes that there are. This is a point we have seen him make repeatedly against those who ignore goal-causation. But here he is pointing out that the mere fact that a feature appears neither to be part of the end for the sake of which others are present, nor a feature that is present for the sake of some other feature, does *not* imply that causal understanding of its presence when and where it is present is impossible. These variations are still present of necessity—just a different sort of necessity.[29]

A second lesson of these passages that is relevant to evaluating Aristotle's place in the history of philosophy has to do with his method for making a determination about which causes are available for explanation. For, like so much of Aristotle's biological writing, these passages show a sophisticated sense of how to reason inductively. He is constantly after the actual extension of a part, behaviour, or attribute, which in practice typically leads him to search for other parts, behaviours or attributes that are co-extensive with the feature in view. The reason this is so important to him is constantly in focus: he is seeking causal explanation, and the cause of a feature must be found among those other features that are co-extensive with it.[30] If someone claims bile plays a key role in perception or acute diseases, but dissection reveals that bile is absent in many animals with sense organs or acute diseases, then we can rule those theories out. On the other hand, if bile is by chance present or absent in members of the same species, and at a higher level of generality present in some animals but absent in others, Aristotle is willing to bet against a teleological explanation for it. That does not rule it out as a subject of causal investigation, however. Notice the following reasoning about bile following the passage we quoted earlier in *PA* IV 2:

> So it is apparent that bile is not for the sake of anything, but is a by-product. For this reason those ancients speak most cleverly when, looking to the solid-hoofed animals and the deer, they say that the absence of bile is a cause of living longer; indeed, these animals are without bile and are long-lived. And in addition there are animals, not observed by those ancients, that have no bile, such as the

and the camel, and these turn out to be long-lived. In fact it is reasonable that, since the nature of the liver is vital and necessary to all blooded animals, its being of a certain character is a cause of living a shorter or longer time. And that the residue of *this* visceral organ and none of the others is of this sort is in accord with our account (677a30-b1).

A number of features of this passage are of methodological importance. First, the fact that bile is not present for the sake of anything and is a by-product does not imply that it has no causal importance. Aristotle takes up a 'clever' suggestion of unnamed ancients that he indicates he thinks is based on a quite limited amount of evidence, and adds further evidence in its favour—there is a correlation between the absence of bile and long life, which suggests that its presence might explain why certain animals, otherwise similar, are short-lived. To strengthen that hypothesis, he notes that the liver, of which bile is a by-product, is among the most vitally important viscera. He doesn't give the details of his thinking here—earlier he has argued that livers with a healthy composition either have no bile or only have it in bile ducts—but it is the form of this conjecture that is the second methodological move worthy of note. It appeals to what is *eulogon* (a36) and *kata logon* (b3).[31] Aristotle has reached a point on this issue where he thinks the inductive evidence supports a correlation between longevity and the presence or absence of bile, and he supports it by noting that bile is a by-product of one of the most vital organs to blooded animals. This passage stops short of specifying an efficient causal link between bile and length of life; and indeed, in Aristotle's small work in the *Parva naturalia*, *On Length and Shortness of Life*, he does not consider bile or the health of the liver as causes.[32] But it beautifully captures Aristotle reasoning inductively under conditions of uncertainty.

V. SOME UNEXPLORED PUZZLES

Much of my previous work on Aristotle's zoological project has explored *On the Parts of Animals* II-IV in connection with three other areas of the Aristotelian Corpus: *PA* I, Aristotle's philosophical introduction to the study of animals; *HA*, with which we began; and the *Posterior Analytics*. That research represents an attempt to deal with the issue of the extent to which Aristotle's natural science is in the spirit of his theory of scientific knowledge in his *Analytics*, works that seamlessly treat as a unity topics that in the twentieth century were rent asunder and treated as either logic, philosophy of science, or epistemology.[33] In recent years I have become more and more interested in understanding how Aristotle's investigation of animal nature is related to other aspects of his investigation of nature, and in exploring these and the other works that report on his study of nature from the standpoint of what they can tell us about the specific norms or standards that guide his *inquiries* into nature. For it now appears to me that the written works of Aristotle that have come down to us do have an important pedagogical purpose— they provide us with object lessons in how to inquire successfully into the different subjects they explore. If the reader now returns to the discussion in Sections III and IV of this chapter with that thought in mind, I hope he or she will see that investigating Aristotle's many investigations of animals has much to teach us about his views on investigation.

Notes

1. That there actually were such works is assured not only by the references found in the ancient lists (DL V. 25 lists eight books of *Dissections* and one of *Selections from the Dissections*) but by Aristotle's own references to them: eight in *HA* (497a22–24, 510a29–35, 511a13, 525a9, 529b19–20, 530a31, 565a13, 566a14), six in *GA* (719a10, 740a23–4, 746a14, 746a22, 764a35, 779a8–9), eight in *PA* (650a30, 666a9, 668b30, 674b16–17, 680a1, 684b5, 689a15, 696b15), and three in *PN* (456b2, 474b9, 478b1–2).

2. Two other works related to these studies and now lost are a work *On nutrition* and another *On plants*. The authorship of this last is never stated, and references to it in Aristotle might well be to the writings of Aristotle's younger colleague Theophrastus. (The medieval work of this name is spurious.) A work that is typically considered spurious is *On breath*, usually the last work in manuscripts of the *Parva naturalia*.

3. See *Republic* VII, 524b-531d.

4. *Peri phuseôs*. This generalization includes the *Timaeus*, as the reference in Diogenes Laertius' *Lives* (III 60: *Timaios ê peri phuseôs*) reminds us.

5. And were occasionally censored for doing so, as by the author of the Hippocratic treatise *On Ancient Medicine*—Empedocles is specifically mentioned in ch. 20, but simply as one among a number of 'doctors and sophists' who 'have written *peri phuseos*.

6. In the Latin translation made by Michael Scot from Arabic in the 13th century, the four books of our *PA* are books XI-XIV of *De animalibus, Historia animalium* I-X being treated as earlier books in a single work.

7. For details of the transmission and content of book X, see D.M. Balme, 'Aristotle *Historia Animalium* Book X' in *Aristoteles—Werk und Wirkung* (essays presented to P. Moraux). Berlin: 1985, Vol. I, 191–206.

8. For references to the *Dissections*, see note 1. Many of the references to *HA* are conjoined with references to *Dissections* (*GA* 719a10, 740a23–4, 746a14; *PA* 650a30, 666a9, 668b30, 674b16–7, 680a1, 684b5, 689a15, 696b15; *PN* 478b1–2), but occasionally it alone is referred to (*PA* 646a5, 660b1; *IA* 704b10; *PN* 477a4). It is likely significant that with all these references to *HA* in the other works, there are no references in *HA* to them. I can imagine a number of explanations for this, but have been unable to imagine a test that would differentially support one more strongly than the others.

9. See especially Balme 1987a, 1987b; 1991, Introduction; 2002, Introduction; and Gotthelf 2012c.

10. These last three answer roughly to our land mammals, reptiles, amphibians, and our aquatic mammals (whales, dolphins, porpoises, and so on). For a careful analysis of Aristotle's initial discussion of *megista genê* in *HA* I 6, see Gotthelf 2012d.

11. These last three answer roughly to our testaceous mollusks, crustaceans, and cephalopods.

12. Good examples of this technique can be seen in chapters II 12–14 and IV 1–4. However, the organization of the books of *HA* into chapters, which began in the Renaissance, can lure the modern reader into imagining a much greater role for these kinds than they actually play, since the chapter divisions were created under the illusion that these kinds were the principal organizational units. These lead to puzzling 'chapters' one or two sentences long and others that appear to begin mid-sentence.

13. For more detail on the method and structure of *HA*, see Gotthelf 1988, revised in Gotthelf 2012a, 307–343.

14. This is the thrust of Lennox 1987a, 1991, 1994 (reprinted in Lennox 2001b, chs. 1–3).

15. Lennox 1996 is an attempt to present and evaluate Balme's case for a 'late' relative date for *HA*.

16. Kullmann 1974, 2007; the work published in Gotthelf and Lennox 1987; Devereux and Pellegrin 1990; Kullmann and Föllinger 1997; Balme 1992; Charles, 2000; Balme 2002; Lennox 2001b.

17. This is not mere speculation. Note his comments about kinds of fish that apparently lack males (*GA* II 5, 741a32-b2) and about the tentative nature of his conclusions about the reproductive system of bees (*GA* III 10, 760b28–32).

18. Consider Aristotle's many remarks about how the principles of one science will differ from another with respect to precision (*APo* I 27; *Met.* I 2 982a25ff.; VI 1 1025b1–18; XIII 3 1078a9–13; *Top.* VIII 1 157a8; *EN* I 3 1094b13–14; 7 1098a25–27).

19. For a summary and discussion of various interpretations, cf. Lennox 2001a, 128–131.

20. This is a central theme of Falcon 2005 (cf. ch. 1, and ch. 4, 100–101). Falcon also has an interesting discussion (88–9) of the way in which the categorization of substance in *Met.* XII serves as the metaphysical framework for this fundamental division of *natural* substance. For how this theme determines how one reads *Meteor.* I 1, see Lennox 2010 and Burnyeat 2004, 13, n. 16.

21. For an overview of some of the key issues involved in Aristotle's defense and use of teleological explanation in a biological context, see Gotthelf 1997, revised and reprinted in Gotthelf 2012a, 67–89. Recent monographs on the subject include Johnson 2005, Leunissen 2010, and Quarantotto, 2005.

22. *Philebus* 54a8, c4; this remark in *PA* I 1 is clearly referred to as well at *GA* V 1, 778b5–6.

23. For a detailed analysis of the latter half of this long chapter embedded within a discussion of the place of teleological explanation in the overall program of *GA*, see Gotthelf 2012b.

24. In his *Exercitationes de Generatione Animalium*, William Harvey quotes Aristotle's discussion with great admiration, and gives his own account of the first appearance of the heart—although he (mistakenly) argues that it is not the heart but the blood that is pulsing, and which later forms the heart. 'At that time, the fetus in the egg passes from the life of a plant to that of an animal. Then already the limbus or hem of the colliquament begins to turn purple and is outlined with a tiny line of blood, and almost in its centre there leaps a capering bloody point which is yet so exceedingly small that in its diastole it flashes like the smallest spark of fire, and immediately upon its systole it quite escapes the eye and disappears.' (Harvey [1651] 1981, Ex. 17, 96); cf. Harvey [1628] 1976, ch. 17, 106.

25. 'Both how the parts concerned with the seed and embryo are arranged internally, and in what manner they differ are apparent with the help of the inquiry into animals

and the dissections, and will be stated later in the works on generation. But that the configuration of these parts is necessarily for their operation is not hard to see.' (*PA* IV 10 689a16–21)

26. Seed in the case of the male, menses in the case of blooded females, but the nature of the female contribution is complicated. There are a number of illuminating discussions of these chapters. See Bolton 1987; Balme 1992, 140–154; Mayhew 2004, ch. 3.

27. Peck, by translating 'the same sort of cause is operative as before' indicates that he thinks there is a contrast between a sort of cause used previously in the work and that to be used now. But the *hosa gar* that opens the next sentence strongly suggests that Aristotle is arguing that the same cause won't always be operative for the affections by which animals differ, and that he is about to explain what he means by that.

28. Pretty clearly the reference is to the passage in *PA* I 1 that was discussed on p. 295, above. The addition here of the verb 'to follow' (*akolouthein*), is interesting, however. Though its literal meaning is 'following after', in Aristotle it almost always refers to what occurs as a consequence of something else. What is (perhaps intentionally) striking about its use here is that what 'follows' comes into being *before* that which it follows.

29. Since this chapter was submitted for publication, Mariska Leunissen and Allan Gotthelf have published a very important reevaluation of *GA* V that presents a compelling case for its integral importance to the overall project of *GA* (Leunissen and Gotthelf 2010; reprinted in Gotthelf 2012a, ch. 5, 117–141). What I have written here is in the spirit of their paper, but their paper should be consulted for a detailed analysis of this book's aims and methods.

30. The issue is discussed at a very abstract level in *APo* II 16–17, and indeed ch. 17 concludes with a now familiar problem: 'Thus it is possible for there to be several causes of the same feature—but not for items of the same form. E.g., the cause of longevity for quadrupeds is their not having bile, while for birds it is their being dry (or something else).' (99b4–6)

31. On the connection between these two expressions when used in the same context, see Bolton 2009.

32. Among the puzzles I won't have space to consider here are those associated with the *Parva naturalia*, the 'little natural studies'. While some of them (*On sense perception and its objects, On memory and recollection*) appear to be closely associated with the project of the *De Anima*, and others (*On length and shortness of life, On respiration*) seem more closely associated with the zoological studies, *De sensu* opens with an overview that, allowing for a couple of oddities, introduces the work as a unit. Similar puzzles arise about *De motu animalium*, a work that introduces itself as closely related to *De incessu animalium* (*On animal locomotion*), but which also has close ties to the last five chapters of *De Anima*. Moreover, in one family of manuscripts it is placed in the *Parva naturalia*, after works associated with *De Anima* and before those with a more biological orientation. All these puzzles are subjects for another occasion, though some have at least been touched on in Lennox 2005.

33. My work on these topics can be seen in the essays that have been collected and reprinted in Lennox, *Aristotle's Philosophy of Biology*, 2001, and in the commentary to my translation of *On the Parts of Animals* (2001). Over the same period a series of papers by Allan Gotthelf has deepened our understanding of Aristotle's investigations of animals in distinctive but complementary ways. These papers, along with some being published for the first time, are now collected in Gotthelf 2012a.

BIBLIOGRAPHY

Balme, D.M. (1985) 'Aristotle's *Historia Animalium* Book X', in J. Wiesner, ed., *Aristoteles—Werk und Wirkung, Band 1* (Berlin: Walter de Gruyter), 191–206.

—— (1987a) 'The place of biology in Aristotle's philosophy', in A. Gotthelf and J.G. Lennox, eds., *Philosophical Issues in Aristotle's Biology* (Cambridge: Cambridge Univ. Press), 9–21.

—— (1987b) 'Aristotle's use of division and differentiae', in A. Gotthelf and J.G. Lennox, eds, *Philosophical Issues in Aristotle's Biology* (Cambridge: Cambridge Univ. Press), 69–90.

—— (1991) 'Introduction', in Aristotle, *History of Animals, Books VII-X*, ed. and trans. D.M. Balme, preparation A. Gotthelf (Cambridge: Harvard Univ. Press), 1–50.

—— (1992) *Aristotle: De Partibus Animalium I and De Generatione Animalium I* (Oxford: Oxford Univ. Press).

—— (2002) 'Introduction', in *Aristotle: Historia Animalium, Volume I, Books I-X: Text*, ed. and trans. D.M. Balme, Preparation A. Gotthelf (Cambridge: Cambridge Univ. Press), 1–48.

Bolton, R. (1987) 'Definition and Scientific Method in Aristotle's *Posterior Analytics* and *Generation of Animals*', in A. Gotthelf and J.G. Lennox, eds., *Philosophical Issues in Aristotle's Biology* (Cambridge: Cambridge Univ. Press), 120–66.

—— (2009) 'Two Standards for Enquiry in Aristotle's *De Caelo*', in A.C. Bowen and C. Wildberg, eds., *New Perspectives on Aristotle's* De caelo (*Philosophia antiqua* vol. 117) (Leiden/Boston: Brill), 51–82.

Burnyeat, M.F. (2004) 'Aristotle on the Foundations of Sublunary Physics', in F. de Haas and J. Mansfeld, eds., *Aristotle: On Generation and Corruption, Book I. Symposium Aristotelicum*, (Oxford: Oxford Univ. Press), 7–24.

Charles, D. (2000) *Aristotle on Meaning and Essence* (Oxford: Oxford Univ. Press).

Devereux, D. and P. Pellegrin, eds. (1990) *Biologie, Logique et Métaphysique chez Aristote* (Paris: Éditions du CNRS).

Falcon, A. (2005) *Aristotle and the Science of Nature: Unity without Uniformity* (Cambridge: Cambridge Univ. Press).

Gotthelf, A. (1988) '*Historiae* I: Plantarum et Animalium', in W.W. Fortenbaugh and R.W. Sharples, eds., *Theophrastean Studies: On Natural Science, Physics and Metaphysics, Ethics, Religion and Rhetoric* (Piscataway: Transaction Books), 100–35. Reprinted in A. Gotthelf (2012a) *Teleology, First Principles, and Scientific Method in Aristotle's Biology*, Chapter 14 (Oxford: Oxford Univ. Press).

——(1997) 'Understanding Aristotle's Teleology', in R.F. Hassing, ed., *Final Causality in Nature and Human Affairs* (Washington, D.C.), 71–82. Reprinted in A. Gotthelf (2012a) *Teleology, First Principles, and Scientific Method in Aristotle's Biology*, Chapter 3 (Oxford: Oxford Univ. Press), 67–89.

—— (2012a) *Teleology, First Principles, and Scientific Method in Aristotle's Biology* (Oxford: Oxford Univ. Press).

—— (2012b) 'Teleology and Embryogenesis in Aristotle's *Generation of Animals* II. 6', in A. Gotthelf (2012a) *Teleology, First Principles, and Scientific Method in Aristotle's Biology* (Oxford: Oxford Univ. Press), 90–116.

—— (2012c), 'Data-Organization, Classification, and Kinds: The Place of the *History of Animals* in Aristotle's Biological Enterprise', in A. Gotthelf (2012a) *Teleology, First Principles, and Scientific Method in Aristotle's Biology* (Oxford: Oxford Univ. Press), 261–292.

———— (2012d), 'History of Animals I. 6 490b7–491a6: Aristotle's megista genê', in A. Gotthelf (2012a) Teleology, First Principles, and Scientific Method in Aristotle's Biology (Oxford: Oxford Univ. Press), 293–306.

Gotthelf, A., and J.G. Lennox, eds. (1987) Philosophical Issues in Aristotle's Biology (Cambridge: Cambridge Univ. Press).

Harvey, W. [1628], An anatomical disputation concerning The Movement of the Heart and Blood in living creatures (trans. with Introduction and Notes by Gweneth Whitteridge) (London: Blackwell, 1976).

———— [1651], Disputations touching The Generation of Animals (trans. with Introduction and Notes by Gweneth Whitteridge) (London: Blackwell, 1981).

Johnson, M. (2005) Aristotle on Teleology (Oxford: Clarendon Press).

Kullmann, W. (1974) Wissenschaft und Methode (Berlin: Walter de Gruyter).

Kullmann, W. (2007) Aristoteles: Über die Teile der Lebewesen (Aristoteles Werke in Deutscher Übersetzung, Band 16: Zoologische Schriften II, Teil I) (Berlin: Akademie Verlag).

Kullmann, W. and S. Föllinger, eds. (1997) Aristotelische Biologie (Stuttgart: Franz Steiner).

Lennox, J.G. (1987a) 'Divide and Explain: The Posterior Analytics in Practice', in A. Gotthelf and J.G. Lennox, eds., Philosophical Issues in Aristotle's Biology (Cambridge: Cambridge Univ. Press), 90–120. Reprinted in J.G. Lennox (2001b), Aristotle's Philosophy of Biology, Chapter 1, (Cambridge: Cambridge Univ. Press, 2001), 7–38.

———— (1991) 'Between Data and Demonstration: The Analytics and the Historia Animalium', in Alan Bowen, ed., Science and Philosophy in Classical Greece (New York: Garland Publishing), 261–95. Reprinted in J.G. Lennox (2001b) Aristotle's Philosophy of Biology, Chapter 2 (Cambridge: Cambridge Univ. Press), 39–71.

———— (1994) 'Aristotelian Problems', Ancient Philosophy, 14, 53–77. Reprinted in J.G. Lennox (2001b), Aristotle's Philosophy of Biology, Chapter 3 (Cambridge: Cambridge Univ. Press), 72–97.

———— (1996) 'Aristotle's Biological Development: the Balme Hypothesis', in W. Wians, ed., Aristotle's Philosophical Development (Lanham, Md.: Rowman and Littlefield Publishers), 229–49.

———— (2001a) Aristotle: On the Parts of Animals, translation with introduction and commentary (Oxford: Oxford Univ. Press).

———— (2001b) Aristotle's Philosophy of Biology: Studies in the Origins of Life Science (Cambridge: Cambridge Univ. Press).

———— (2005) 'The Place of Zoology in Aristotle's Natural Philosophy', in R.W. Sharples, ed., Philosophy and the Sciences in Antiquity (Keeling Series in Ancient Philosophy), (Aldershot: Ashgate Publishing), 55–71.

———— (2010) 'Aristotle's Natural Science: the Many and the One' in J. Lesher, ed., From Inquiry to Demonstrative Knowledge: New Essays on Aristotle's Posterior Analytics (Kelowna: Academic Printing & Publishing) [Apeiron 43, nos. 2–3], 1–23.

Leunissen, M. (2010) Explanation and Teleology in Aristotle's Science of Nature (Cambridge: Cambridge Univ. Press).

Leunissen, M., and A. Gotthelf (2010) 'What's Teleology got to do with it? A Reinterpretation of Aristotle's Generation of Animals V', Phronesis 55.4, 325–356. (Reprinted in A. Gotthelf (2012a) Teleology, First Principles, and Scientific Method in Aristotle's Biology, Chapter 5 (Oxford: Oxford Univ. Press), 108–130.

Mayhew, R. (2004) The Female in Aristotle's Biology: Reason or Rationalization (Chicago: University of Chicago Press).

Quarantotto, D. (2005) Causa Finale, Sostanza, Essenza in Aristotele (Napoli: Bibliopolis).

CHAPTER 13

ARISTOTLE ON THE SEPARABILITY OF MIND

FRED D. MILLER, JR.

1. THE PROBLEM OF SEPARABILITY

THE problem of whether the mind (*nous*) is separable from the body looms over Aristotle's *De Anima*.[1] In book I, he broaches the broader question whether the affections of the soul, including emotion, desire, and perception, are separable from the body; and he concludes in a qualified way that they are not separable, although he considers thinking briefly and inconclusively as a possible exception (1 403a3–b19). In book II he follows his explication of the general definition of soul with the remark that 'neither the soul nor certain parts of it, if it naturally has parts, are separable from the body. Yet nothing prevents some [parts from being separable], because they are not the actualizations of any body' (1 413a3–7). By 'parts' (*merê*) he means separable faculties or powers, including nutrition, perception, mind, and desire (see 2 413b14–15). Later he suggests that of these faculties, mind 'alone can be separated, just as the eternal is from the mortal' (413b24–7). The issue of separability is signalled at the beginning of the treatment of mind in book III: 'Concerning the part of the soul with which the soul knows and understands—whether it is separable or not separable in magnitude but [only] in account—it is necessary to inquire what differentiates this part, and how thinking occurs' (4 429a10–13). Finally, Aristotle claims that the mind, in contrast with the perceptive faculty, is separable, (429b4–5) and subsequently that the mind more narrowly in its productive capacity is separable (5 430a17, 22–3).

The question whether the mind is separable is also relevant to the status of psychology as a science. For physics (construed broadly as natural science) considers the properties of bodies insofar as they are inseparable from matter, while first philosophy considers objects which are separable (*DA* I 1 403b9–16, cf. *Met.* VI 1 1026a5–6). If mind alone turned out to be separable from the body, the study of the soul would not belong exclusively to physics but would spill over into first philosophy. This would imply either that psychology consists of two separate sciences, or else that first philosophy and physics are not mutually exclusive.[2]

Many modern commentators are nonplussed by Aristotle's preoccupation with separability, which might be viewed as a vestige of his early infatuation with Plato's conception of death as the separation (*chôrismos*) of the soul from the body (*Phaedo* 67d4), echoed in Aristotle's own lost dialogues. His *Protrepticus* contends that among our possessions the mind and understanding (*phronêsis*) alone seem to be immortal and divine. In the *Eudemus*, according to Themistius, Aristotle argues for the immortality of the soul. Pseudo-Plutarch quotes from the *Eudemus* that 'the dead are blessed and happy' and that 'time spent dead is better than time spent alive'. Proclus also implies that Aristotle holds that souls exist before birth as well as after death; he reasons that life without the body is natural but life in the body is unnatural, 'so that it not unreasonably results that souls that pass thence forget the things there, while souls that pass hence thither continue to remember the things here'. Elias reports, 'In his dialogues [Aristotle] says that the soul is immortal because all we men instinctively make libations to the departed and swear by them, but no-one ever makes a libation to or swears by that which is completely non-existent.'[3] Many scholars view these as youthful speculations, which Aristotle put behind him after his discovery of hylomorphism.[4] The definition in *De Anima* of the soul as substantial form (*ousia hôs eidos*) or first actualization (*entelecheia*) of a natural body which potentially possesses life (II 1 412a19–28) seems to exclude the possibility of incorporeal souls. Indeed, Aristotle follows this definition with the remark that 'there is no need to inquire whether the soul and the body are one, just as there is no need either to inquire whether the wax and the shape are one, or generally the matter of each thing and that of which it is the matter' (II 2 412b6–8). Although this suggests that the soul is inseparable from the body, Aristotle adds the surprising qualification that 'nothing prevents some [parts from being separable]' and allows that the soul may be an actualization of the body like a sailor of a ship (413a4–7). Why does Aristotle leave open these possibilities? And what is his own considered view on whether any part of the soul is separable from the body?

Although separability of mind is discussed mainly in *De Anima*, Aristotle hints at the issue in the *Metaphysics*: 'We must inquire whether any [form] survives afterward. For in some cases nothing prevents this, for example if the soul is of this sort—not all soul but mind, for perhaps it is impossible for all soul to survive' (XII 3 1070a24–6). There is also a suggestive comment about the origin of the mind in *Generation of Animals*: 'It remains then for the mind alone to enter [the human embryo] from outside (*thurathen*) and for it alone to be divine. For bodily actuality has no association with its actuality' (*GA* II 3 736b24–9).[5]

Since antiquity Aristotle's enigmatic remarks on immortality have inspired legions of contending commentators.[6] Montaigne complained that 'no one knows what Aristotle has decided on this matter.... He hid behind a cloud of difficult and unintelligible words and meanings, and left his adherents as much room for debate about his judgement as about the matter itself.'[7] Despite his undeniable obscurity Aristotle leaves no doubt as to the importance of this issue, and a satisfactory interpretation of his psychology cannot neglect his pronouncements on separability. Several questions need to be addressed: What does Aristotle mean when he discusses whether or not the parts of the soul are 'separable' (or 'separate')? What specific claims does he make concerning the separability of these parts and of mind in particular? How does he support these claims? How plausible are his arguments? What do they reveal about how he understands the workings of the mind? First, however, it is necessary to consider the different senses of *chôristos*.

2. ARISTOTLE'S USES OF 'SEPARABLE' AND 'SEPARATE'

The word *chôristos* (negative, *achôristos*) is related to *chôris* (separate), which is opposed to *hama* (together). The verb *chôrizein* means to separate a thing (e.g., a plant or animal) into parts, which are described as *chôrizomena* (undergoing separation) and *kechôrismena* (separated) (*DA* II 2 413b16). Aristotle also uses *kechôrismena* (passive perfect participle) for things which are always separate, for example, the objects of first philosophy (I 1 403b15–16).[8] The verbal adjective *chôristos* is commonly translated either as 'separable' or 'separate'. When Aristotle uses these terms in connection with the soul and its parts, questions arise: Does *chôristos* mean 'separable' or 'separate'? *From what* are they alleged to be (or not to be) separable or separate? *In what respect* are they alleged to be (or not to be) separable or separate?

Chôristos: separable or separate? The *-tos* ending of Greek verbal adjectives (like '-able' in English) can connote possibility. For example, *adiairetos*, as Aristotle remarks (*DA* III 6 430b6–7), is used in two senses—in potentiality or in actuality—and thus may be translated as 'indivisible' or 'undivided' depending on context. Presumably the same is true of *chôristos*. It may well mean 'separate' when it replaces *kechôrismenos* in parallel constructions.[9] However, 'separable' is more appropriate in the following passage: 'If any act or affection is proper to the soul, it could be separated (*endechoit' an...chôrizesthai*); but if none is proper to it, it would not be separable (*chôristê*)'. (*DA* I 1 403a10–12) In general, *chôristos* may mean 'separable' when the issue is whether a part can be separated from another part or from the whole.[10] In some cases, however, which translation is correct is a matter of interpretation. For example, when Aristotle says that the mind is *chôristos*, does he mean that it is *actually* separate from the body (even when one is alive) or that it *can* be separated (from the body at death)?

Separable (or separate) from what? Aristotle sometimes asks whether items of the same type are separable from each other (for example, bodies, bodily parts, attributes, or faculties). He also asks whether an item of one type (for example, a soul, part of the soul, attribute, or faculty) is separable from an item of another type (for example, matter or body). Unfortunately, at crucial junctures he does not specify what the item is separable *from*. Often this is clear from the context, but sometimes it is controversial.

Separable (or separate) in what respect? For the purposes of this discussion, *De Anima* speaks of items as separable or separate in four different respects: spatial, definitional, ontological, taxonomical. Aristotle does not always specify the respect in which something is separable, which gives rise to a problem of interpretation.[11] The four different respects of separability are as follows.

Spatial separability Things are said to be separable (or separate) in place (*topôi*) or in magnitude (*megethei*). This is literal separation, because *chôristos* and its cognates are related to the noun *chôra*, 'space.' Bodies are spatially separate from each other when they occupy different places that do not overlap, and conjoined bodies are spatially separable when they can move to different places that do not overlap (cf. *Phys.* VI 1 231b4-6). Things are also said to be inseparable or indivisible in place and number (*topôi kai arithmôi*) (III 2 427a2, 5). The idea seems to be that tokens of the same type can be distinguished and counted if they are spatially separate, which requires that they have distinct perceptible matter.

Definitional separability Items are separate in account (*logos*) when they have different definitions, neither of which makes reference to the other.[12] Things may be separable in definition even though they are not spatially separable. For example, an arc of a circle is both concave (from the inside) and convex (from the outside). Although concave and convex have different definitions which do not refer to each other (respectively, 'bending up' and 'bending down'), they are spatially inseparable because any arc which is concave is also convex and vice versa (see *EN* I 13 1102a26–32; cf. *Phys.* IV 13 222b3, *DA* III 10 433b23).

Definitional separability is not mere difference in definition, for the latter is a symmetrical relation, while the former is asymmetric. Supposing *X* and *Y* have different definitions, if the definition of *Y* makes reference to *X* but not vice versa, then *X* is separable in definition but *Y* is not; for example, if *X* is nose and *Y* is snub (defined as 'concave nose'). Thus difference in definition is a necessary, but not sufficient, condition for definitional separability.[13]

Ontological separability When Aristotle says that only substances are separable (*Met.* VII 1 1028a33-4, *Phys.* I 2 185a31), this includes matter-form compounds; but he cannot mean that they are merely *spatially* separable. For the unmoved mover, which is a substance separate (*kechôrismenê*) from perceptible objects, can have no magnitude (cf. *Met.* XII 7 1073a3–7). Aristotle evidently has in mind *ontological* separability: that is, *X* is separable (*chôriston*) from *Y*, in the sense that *X* is able to exist without *Y*; hence, *X* could exist even if *Y* was destroyed (see *DA* I 1 403a5–12 and *Met.* VII 10

1035b23–4).[14] Aristotle designates this as 'separable without qualification' (*chôristos haplôs*), which applies to a matter-form compound (*Met.* VIII 1 1042a31–2). Although Aristotle also recognizes imperceptible separable substances (e.g., unmoved movers), he argues that universals, Platonic Forms, and mathematical objects (e.g., geometrical figures) are not ontologically separable and therefore are not substances.[15]

Although two items are ontologically separable only if they are separable in definition, the converse does not hold. For example, from the fact that the convex and the concave are separable in definition, it does not follow that they are ontologically separable, because a line is concave if, and only if, it is convex. While it is debatable whether Aristotle thinks that spatial separability entails ontological separability, he clearly does not regard spatial separability as a necessary condition for ontological separability. For, according to Aristotle, an immaterial substance such as a god is ontologically separate and yet it has no magnitude and occupies no space. (*Met.* XII 7 1073a3–12) These points will be important for the following discussion.

The distinction between ontological separability and actual separateness is relevant to parts, which can be separated only if they are not essentially dependent on the whole to which they belong. For example, a part of an animal, e.g., an arm or a foot, is essentially dependent on the whole body, in that it perishes if the whole body dies (*Met.* VII 10 1035b23–4; *Pol.* I 2 1253a18–33). Hence, 'none of them is separate [sc. ontologically], but if they are separated (*chôristhêi*), they all exist [merely] as matter' (*Met.* VII 16 1040b6–7). Such parts are as such inseparable. In some cases, however, the part can exist without the whole, for example a half-line exists in actuality when the whole line has been bisected (V 11 1019a12–14, cf. 8–10). The latter sort of part is ontologically separable as defined above.[16]

Taxonomical separability Aristotle sometimes speaks of capacities as separable in a special way. For example, the sense of touch can be separated from the other four senses because many animals possess touch but not the others (*DA* II 2 413b5–6, 415a2–6). Here Aristotle seems to mean *taxonomical* separability: *F* is separable from *G* if, and only if, something can be *F* without also being *G*.[17] This is not the same as ontological separability: The claim that some animals have only the sense of touch does not entail that an animal with all five senses would still have the sense of touch if it lost all the others.

Based on this brief survey of Aristotle's uses of *chôristos* and related terms, let us consider his claims about whether various faculties or attributes of the soul are separable or inseparable.

3. Separability Claims in *De Anima*

Aristotle's first claim about separability occurs in his discussion of the problem whether all the acts and affections of the soul (for instance, being angry, desiring,

and perceiving) are shared with the body, or whether the soul has any act or affection of its own, such as thinking. Aristotle adds, if thinking could not exist without
imagination it could not exist without the body either, tacitly assuming that imagination requires the body (I 1 403a8–10). The first claim follows:

> (A) If, then, any act or affection of the soul is proper to it, [the soul] could be
> separated (chôrizesthai); but if nothing is proper to it, it will not be separable
> (chôristê), but it will be like the straight, to which many things belong in so far
> as it is straight, for example, touching a bronze sphere at a point, although the
> straight will not touch in this way if it has been separated (chôristhen); for it is
> inseparable (achôriston), since it always exists with some body (I 1 403a10–16).

(A) evidently concerns *ontological* separability, since the soul is separable from the
body only if some act of the soul such as thinking can exist without the body.
Hence, (A) implies a criterion of *ontological separability*:

> X is ontologically separable from Y if, and only if, some act or affection of X does
> not require Y.

The straight fails to satisfy this criterion, because it must be the form of a matter-
form compound (e.g., a straight stick) in order to touch a bronze sphere at a point;
but if it is abstracted or separated in thought (as a unidimensional geometrical
line), it cannot touch the bronze sphere.[18] If even thinking depends on the body
in order to produce and retain images, then the soul will also fail the criterion.[19]
Whether or not it does is, so far, not determined.

> (B) [T]he affections of soul, in so far as they are such as passion and fear, are
> inseparable (achôrista) from the natural matter of animals in this way and not in
> the same way as a line or surface (I 1 403b17–19).

Affections of the soul, such as anger or fear, fail the criterion of ontological
separability. Aristotle has previously characterized these affections as 'enmattered
accounts' (logoi enhuloi); for example, 'anger is a certain movement of such and
such a body (or part or faculty of a body) by this or that thing and for the sake of
this or that'. A complete definition of anger would include a specification of the
bodily state (e.g., a boiling of the blood or warm substance surrounding the heart)
together with a description of its formal and final cause (e.g., a desire to return pain
for pain) (403a25-b9). Moreover, if anger is inseparable in definition from a bodily
state, it must be ontologically inseparable as well.

> (C) The mind seems likely to come to be present in us, being a sort of substance,
> and not to perish (I 4 408b18–19).

Does this imply that the mind is separable from the body? It is instructive to
consider how Aristotle deals here with the problem that elderly people may no
longer perform activities such as remembering facts or acquiring new knowledge as
well as when they were younger. Although this suggests that their soul (i.e., mind)
is affected, Aristotle remarks that 'it is perhaps better not to say that the soul is
pitying or learning or thinking discursively, but that the human being does it with
his soul' (408b13–15).[20] Using this distinction he solves the problem as follows:

Senility does not occur because the soul has been affected, but because what contains it has been affected, as also occurs in drunkenness or disease. And thinking (*to noein*) and contemplating (*to theôrein*) waste away when something else inside perishes, but it (*auto*) is unaffected (*apathes*). Discursive thinking (*to dianoeisthai*) and loving and hating are not affections (*pathê*) of this, but of that which possesses it, in so far as it possesses this. That is why when this [i.e., the possessor] perishes, [one] neither remembers nor loves; for these do not belong to this [i.e., the soul], but to the common thing, which is destroyed; and the mind is surely something more divine and unaffected (408b22–9).

Likewise, old people see poorly not because they lose the sense of sight but because their eyes wear out, 'for an old person would see like a young person if he received the same sort of eye' (408b19–22). And analogously, we might add, an archer does not lose the skill of shooting a bow merely because his arm is broken. One does not lose a capacity merely because one is unable to exercise it due to a physical impairment. Likewise, one does not lose a mental capacity even when one is impaired due to drunkenness, sickness, or senility. Even granting this, however, it does not show that the mind is ontologically separable, that is, that one could perform mental acts without a body. At most it shows that the mind is separable in definition from the body.[21]

> (D) It is not unclear then that neither the soul nor certain parts of it, if it naturally has parts, is separable from the body; for the actualization of some of them is the actualization of the parts. Yet nothing prevents some [parts from being separable], because they are not the actualizations of any body. Further, it is unclear whether the soul as actualization of the body is like a sailor of a ship (II 1 413a4–9).

This conclusion strikes many readers as incongruous, following as it does the explication of the soul as the actualization of the body and the remark that there is no need to inquire whether the soul and body are one (412b4–8). The implication is that the soul is inseparable both in definition and ontologically from the body. Why does Aristotle add the surprising qualification that some part of the soul might be separable after all?[22] As for the cryptic simile of the sailor, commentators disagree over how the sailor is supposed to correspond to the soul (or to a part of it) and whether the simile implies separability or not.[23]

Aristotle also makes the following three claims about whether the different faculties of the soul are in a way separable from each other:

> (E) This [i.e., the nutritive faculty] can be separated (*chôrizesthai*) from the other [faculties], but the others cannot be [separated] from this in mortal beings. It is obvious in plants; for they do not possess any other power of the soul....And just as the nutritive faculty can be separated (*chôrizesthai*) from touch and all the senses, so touch [can be separated] from the other senses. We call nutritive that part of the soul in which plants also share; but all animals evidently share in the sense of touch (II 2 413a31–2, b5–9).

This claim evidently involves taxonomical separability: the nutritive faculty is separable in kind from other faculties because only it belongs to plants; the sense of touch is taxonomically separable from the other senses because only it belongs to worms and such (*DA* I 5 411b29–30, II 3 415a2–3; *Somn.* 1 454a11–14). The qualification that the other faculties are taxonomically inseparable from the nutritive 'in mortal beings' may leave a loophole for the divine mind, which has no other faculty.

Aristotle then asks whether each part of the soul is 'separable (*chôriston*) in account only or also in place', which he says is easy to answer in some cases but hard in others (413b14–16).

> (F) Just as in the case of plants some plainly live when divided and separated (*chôrizomena*) from each other, since the soul in them is in actuality one in each plant, but they are potentially many, so we also see it happen in other varieties of soul in the case of insects cut in two; for each of the parts has perception and locomotion, and if perception, then also imagination and desire; for where there is perception, there is also pain and pleasure, and where these, necessarily also appetite (413b16–24).

It is noteworthy that these insects are not merely taxonomically separated (unfortunately for them). The issue is whether the psychic faculties are separated spatially and ontologically when an insect is cut in two. The answer is that the insect's faculties of perception, locomotion, imagination, and desire are spatially and ontological inseparable. Aristotle next turns to the mind:

> (G) Concerning the mind and the contemplative power it is not yet obvious, but it seems likely to be a different kind (*genos*) of soul, and it alone can be separated (*endechetai chôrizesthai*), just as the eternal from the perishable.[24] It is obvious from the foregoing that the other parts of soul are not separable (*chôrista*), as some say; it is obvious however that they are different in account. If perceiving is different from believing, the faculty of perceiving and the faculty of believing must also be different, and likewise for each of the aforementioned powers (II 2 413b24–32).

This passage suggests that the mind is separable in a stronger sense than the other faculties which differ merely in definition. *From* what the mind is separable is not stated, though the context suggests that it is separable from the other psychic faculties.[25] It is also debatable *how* it is separable: Is the point that an individual's mind may be separated from the other faculties without perishing (ontological separability) or that an imperishable being (e.g., god) may have a mind without the other faculties (taxonomical separability)? As noted in connection with (F), Aristotle has just been discussing whether the psychological faculties of insects are ontologically separable, which suggests that the issue here is the ontological separability of the mind.

Finally, in *De Anima* III Aristotle makes four controversial claims concerning the mind. The first two concern the mind (*nous*) generally:

> (H) The perceptive faculty is not without a body, but the mind is separable (*chôristos*) (4 429b4–5).

> (I) Generally, as objects [sc. of thought] are separable (*chôrista*) from matter, so also are the things pertaining to the mind (429b21–2).

These claims imply that the mind or its attributes are separable from the body. Aristotle evidently proceeds to distinguish the productive mind (*poiêtikos nous*) and passive mind (*pathêtikos nous*),[26] and it will be provisionally assumed that the following two claims apply to the productive mind (although this is controversial):

> (J) This is separable (*chôristos*) and unaffected and unmixed, since it is essentially in actuality. 5 430a17–18

> (K) Having been separated (*chôristheis*) this alone is what it is, and this alone is immortal and eternal... (430a22–3).

These four claims present several interpretive questions: (Q1) Should *chôristos* be translated 'separable' (as translated above) or 'actually separate'? In the preceding claims (A), (E), and (G) the question whether a part of the soul is *chôristos* is equivalent to 'can be separated'. 'Separable' seems appropriate if applied to a part of the soul, and Aristotle says that claim (H) holds for 'what is called the mind of the soul' (cf. 4 429a22). The same would hold for (J) and (K) if the productive mind is also part of the soul, but this is controversial (see Section 5). (Q2) From what is mind separable (or separate)? (H) indicates that the mind is separable (*chôristos*) from the body, and earlier Aristotle says that it is 'unmixed (*amigês*) with the body' (429a24–5, a18). (I) also describes the productive mind as 'unmixed' (*amigês*, 5 430a18), so assuming 'unmixed' means the same in both passages, it is reasonable to infer that the productive mind is also devoid of corporeal attributes. (Q3) In what respect is the mind separable (or separate)? Aristotle does not say,[27] but he does indicate with (H) that the mind is separable in contrast to the perceptive faculty and with (G) that the perceptive faculty is not separable but different only in definition from the other faculties. This suggests that the mind is separable in a stronger sense, that is, ontologically.[28] (Q4) In what sense is the productive mind separable (or separate)? (H) claims that the mind is *chôristos*, while (J) restricts this to the *productive* mind. Are these two claims compatible? If so, how? These difficult questions of interpretation are explored in the following two sections.

4. The Argument That Mind is Separable (*De Anima* III 4)

4.1 The argument from mind's unlimited scope

Aristotle's main argument for (H), that the mind is separable from the body, may be reconstructed as follows:

(1.1) The mind, like the perceptive faculty, knows by becoming like its objects.

(1.2) The mind can know all things.

(1.3) A cognitive faculty is limited in its ability to become like its objects if it requires the body in order to be exercised.

(1.4) A faculty is separable from the body if it does not require the body in order to be exercised.

(1.5) Therefore, the mind is separable from the body.

The premises will be discussed in turn.

Premise (1.1): The mind, like the perceptive faculty, knows by becoming like its objects. 'The Mind,' declaims Andrew Marvell, is 'that Ocean where each kind/Does streight its own resemblance find.' Along similar lines, Aristotle treats thinking as analogous to perceiving: What sees is 'coloured in a way', because 'the sense-organ is capable of receiving the perceptible object [i.e., the perceptible form] without its matter'. (II 2 425b22–4) Further, 'the activity of the perceptible object and that of the sense is one and the same, although their being (*einai*) is not the same'. (425b26–7) For example, one actually hears, if, and only if, some object is actually sounding. (Thus a tree which falls potentially makes a sound; it actually makes a sound only if there is someone to hear it.) The being or essence of sounding and hearing is different, in that sounding is a way of producing and hearing is a way of being affected. Moreover, the activity, which is both a sounding and a hearing, occurs in the perceptive faculty (426a2–4). This account may be explained in terms of another thesis: that the perceptible object and the perceptual act both consist in a certain proportion (*logos*) of opposite qualities, e.g., of sharp and flat in the case of hearing (426a27–30). The perceptible subject becomes *isomorphic* with its object and thus receives the form without the matter. Because perception involves, in some sense, the replication of the proportion of the object within the subject, the activity of the object (e.g., sounding) and of the subject (e.g., hearing) is the same thing viewed from different standpoints. Perception requires that the subject (not the object) acquire the proportion, so that the activity occurs in the subject.[29]

Aristotle supports premise (1.1) as follows:

> If thinking (*to noein*) is like perceiving it must be either a case of being affected in a way by what is thinkable, or something else of this sort. Therefore, it must be unaffected but capable of receiving the form [of its object] and potentially such as [its object] but not [identical with] this [object]. The mind must be related to thinkable objects as the perceptive faculty is to perceptible objects (III 4 429a13–18).

This passage makes two main points. The first is that the mind is unaffected or impassible, although thinking involves being affected in a way or in some other process like this. This presupposes a distinction in II 5 417b2–16 between different senses in which a thing can be 'affected' (*paschein*) or 'altered' (*alloiousthai*). In one (negative) sense a thing is affected when one of its properties is destroyed and replaced by another: for example, hot water becomes cold (cf. *Met.* V 21 1022b19–20). In another (positive) sense, a potential state becomes an actual state: for example, a potential builder becomes an actual builder, or a potential knower becomes an actual knower.[30] This distinction seems to be presupposed at III 4 429a13–18: When the mind knows an object, it actualizes its natural capacity without losing it. Hence, although the mind is affected in the positive sense, it is unaffected in the negative sense.

The second point is that the mind, like the perceptive faculty, becomes aware of an object by being assimilated to it. The above translation (with bracketed additions) implies that the mind becomes isomorphic (same in form) with its object rather than numerically identical with it. When Aristotle elsewhere says that the mind 'is in a way' the thinkable object (III 8 431b21–2), he is again speaking of *isomorphic* identity.[31] Aristotle also speaks of the mind as if it has contents. He agrees that the mind is the 'place of forms', albeit in the qualified sense that the forms are only potentially in the mind before it discovers them (cf. 4 429a27–8). Although it resembles the perceptive faculty in being a 'form of forms' (8 432a2), the mind contains objects in a different way. In the case of perception, 'the things that produce the actualities are external, the visible and the audible, and likewise for the other perceptible objects. The reason is that the actual perception is of particulars, while knowledge is of universals; and these are in a way (*pôs*) in the soul. That is why thinking is up to oneself, whenever one wishes, but perceiving is not up to oneself; for the perceptible object must be present' (II 5 417b20–6; cf. 417a27–8 and III 4 429b7). Instead of universals, Aristotle also speaks of forms: 'the stone does not exist in the soul but its form' (III 8 431b29–432a1). He means that the form is in the mind, but the use of 'in' is puzzling. If two different minds at the same time grasp the form of stone, is the same stony form present simultaneously in the two minds? It may be to avoid such worries that Aristotle also speaks of a thought or concept (*noêma*) as being in the soul just as an image is (III 7 431b6–7). A thought is a mind's way of grasping an object. If two minds think of the same thinkable object, each mind has a distinct thought. Aristotle also speaks of thoughts as combined in true or false judgements (III 6 430a27–8). But for Aristotle combining (or dividing) thoughts is the mind's way of combining or dividing objects of thought.

A few lines later, Aristotle implies that the mind becomes an object as soon as it acquires an epistemic ability: 'When it has become each thing in the way that one who knows is said [to do so] in actuality (and this occurs when he is able to exercise [his knowledge] by himself), it is then still in a potential condition, but not in the same way as before learning or discovering; and it is then able to think of itself' (III 4 429b5–9). Aristotle elsewhere (II 5 417a22–b2) distinguishes two levels of potential knowledge: being capable of acquiring knowledge, e.g., of grammar (call this *first-level potentiality*); and possessing such knowledge and being able to use it whenever one wishes if nothing prevents (call this *second-level potentiality*). Alternatively (at II 1 412a22–7) he distinguishes two levels of actualization: possessing knowledge, e.g., of a grammatical rule (call this *first-level actualization*) and exercising the knowledge, e.g., recognizing that a sentence is ungrammatical (call this *second-level actualization*). When Aristotle says (III 4 429b5–9) that the mind becomes its object when one is able to exercise one's knowledge by himself, he evidently means a second-level potentiality, which corresponds to a first-level actualization. That is, the mind is identical with its object even if it is not actually contemplating the object.[32]

Premises (1.2) and (1.3) emerge from the following passage:

> Since [the mind] thinks all things, therefore, it must be unmixed (*amigê*), as Anaxagoras says, in order to control, that is, to know. For anything alien appearing alongside it hinders and impedes it. So it can have no nature of its own except for being capable [of thinking]. Therefore, what is called the mind of the soul (and I call mind that by which the soul thinks discursively and judges) is none of the beings in actuality before it thinks (III 4 429a18–24).

Aristotle here makes an analogy between the cosmic mind, as understood by Anaxagoras,[33] and the human mind (i.e., 'what is called the mind of the soul').

Premise (1.2): The mind can know all things. When Aristotle understands Anaxagoras as claiming that the cosmic mind knows all things, he presumably means everything in the universe.[34] He makes a parallel claim about the human soul later on: through perceiving or thinking, 'the soul is in a way all things which exist, for these are either perceptible or thinkable' (III 8 431b21–2). Note that, unlike Anaxagoras' cosmic mind, the human mind is only *capable* of perceiving or knowing all things. Even so, Aristotle implicitly rejects scepticism. Although he criticizes an extreme version of scepticism which holds that 'there is no knowledge' on the grounds that we do not know the first principles from which it is deduced (*APo* I 3 72b5–6), he does not take up the view that certain kinds of objects are unknowable. One can only conjecture how he would have replied to the sceptical arguments of Pyrrho of Elis (c. 360–270 BC), Arcesilaus of Pitane (c. 316–c. 241 BC), and Sextus Empiricus (second to third century AD).[35]

Premise (1.3): A cognitive faculty is limited in its ability to become like its objects if it requires the body in order to be exercised. The Aristotelian mind might be compared to a mirror, which must lack any colour of its own if it is to reflect perfectly the colour of a mirrored object; and, likewise, the mind could not reproduce its object perfectly if it had a character of its own.[36] The power of sight itself is limited by the very fact that it must be exercised by means of eyeballs. This results in blind spots and in similar gaps for the other senses. But the mind is not limited in this way regarding possible objects of thought. The mind is like a diaphanous medium through which objects are revealed. This is why Aristotle denies that the mind is 'mixed with the body' (429a24–7, cf. 18). He maintains that the mind itself does not acquire perceptible qualities such as hot or cold or use a bodily instrument (*organon*) as does the perceptive faculty (429a24–7). It might be objected that human beings could not think if they did not have brains. Aristotle would agree because such an organ is needed for imagination—although he thinks the organ is the heart (cf. I 4 408b8; *De Iuv.* 3 469a4–24; *PA* II 1 647a25). But he would contend that there can be no thought-organ corresponding to the sense-organ—the word for thought-organ (*noêtêrion*) is not in his vocabulary.

Aristotle derives a corollary that the thinking faculty is unaffected in a different manner from the perceptive faculty (429a29-b5). The sense of hearing or sight or smell can be overloaded by an object that is too loud or too bright or pungent, so that we are less able to exercise it afterward; but after the mind thinks of a very thinkable object, the mind is more (not less) able to think of less thinkable objects.[37] In explanation of this phenomenon there follows claim (H): 'For the perceptive faculty cannot be without a body, but the mind is separable' (*chôristos*) (III 4 429b4–5). This presupposes *Premise (1.4): A faculty is separable from the body if it does not require the body in order to be exercised.* This calls to mind the criterion deployed at I 1 403a10–16:

> *X* is ontologically separable from *Y* if, and only if, some act or affection of *X* does not require *Y*.

As remarked in Section 3, (H) does not make explicit whether the mind is separable in the stronger ontological sense or in the weaker definitional sense. Aristotle does, however, argue for a further claim, (I) that what pertains to the mind is separable, which may shed light.

4.2 The argument from correlative objects

The argument at 429b10–22 may be reconstructed as follows:

(2.1) The mind is isomorphic with thinkable objects.

(2.2) Thinkable objects are separable from matter.

(2.3) If *X* and *Y* are isomorphic and *X* has attributes separable from *Z*, then *Y* also has attributes separable from *Z*.

(2.4) Therefore, 'generally, as the objects [sc. of thought] are separable (*chôrista*) from matter, so also are the things pertaining to the mind'.

Premise (2.1) is implied by premise (1.1) discussed earlier. Premise (2.2) tacitly assumes that the mind's thinkable objects are (or include) essences. In the case of material substances, the essence of *X* is different from *X*; for example, flesh is a particular hylomorphic substance with perceptible qualities, but its essence (called 'the being of flesh') is a certain proportion (*logos*) of perceptible qualities.[38] We can discriminate flesh from other objects (e.g., bone) because it has perceptible qualities like hot and cold, and we do so by means of our perceptive faculty. However, *X*'s essence differs from *X* itself in such a way that a different faculty from the perceptive is required in order to discriminate the essence of flesh, i.e., a specific proportion of elements. This other (i.e., thinking) faculty is, according to Aristotle, either a separable faculty or the same faculty in a different condition. He tries to elucidate this with an analogy: the thinking faculty is 'either separable [from the perceptive faculty] or related [to it] as a bent line is related to itself when it is straightened out' (429b16–17). He also considers the case of abstract mathematical objects such as a straight line. A geometer can discriminate between straight lines because they have 'thinkable [or intelligible] matter' (cf. *Met*.VII 10 1036a9–12). Once again the straight is different from the essence of straight (which might be identified with twoness, since a straight line is determined by two points). As with the essence of flesh, we discriminate the essence of the straight (for example, from the essence of the curved) 'by means of a different [faculty] or [by the same faculty] in another condition'. (429b20–1) Although the precise meaning of the line analogy (at b16–17) is controversial,[39] the main point is that the mind and the perceptive faculty stand in an analogous relationship with their respective objects. The essence of flesh is separable in definition but not in place from perceptible flesh (likewise for the essence of straight). 'Generally, as things [i.e., objects of thought] are separable (*chôrista*) from matter, so also are the things pertaining to the mind' (III 4 429b21–2). This needs to be qualified however. Since the essence of flesh is not ontologically separable from perceptible flesh, but only separable in definition, the most that this argument establishes is that the mind is separable in definition from the perceptive faculty and hence from the body.[40]

4.3 Puzzles concerning the mind

Aristotle next considers a couple of puzzles. First, 'if the mind is simple and unaffected and has nothing in common with anything, as Anaxagoras says, how will it think? For one thing can act on another only if they have something in common'. (429b22–6) Second, how will mind itself be an object of thought? For if mind is thinkable on account of itself and there is only one kind of thinkable object, 'either mind will belong to other things or it will have some component which makes it, like other things, thinkable' (429b26–9).

The first puzzle is solved by recalling the earlier statement that 'the mind is potentially in a way the thinkable objects, but nothing in actuality, before it thinks; and [its objects] must be present in it just as on a writing-tablet on which nothing is written in actuality; and this is what happens in the case of the mind' (429b29–430a2, cf. 429a22–9). The mind is like an empty, purely receptive container which has no actual contents until and unless it has gone through a process of learning or discovering in order to acquire contents (429b8–9).[41] The claim that the mind is devoid of actual contents before it knows its objects is explained by the aforementioned thesis that the mind is 'unmixed' with and separable from the body.

The second puzzle, whether the mind is itself an object of thought, is solved along similar lines (430a3–9). It is necessary to distinguish material objects of thought from immaterial objects. Although we can think of a material object such as a geranium, its mere existence does not entail the presence of thought. For a geranium is only potentially an object of thought, because the mind can become or contain such an object only after it has separated the essence of a geranium from the matter of the perceptible geranium (cf. 429b10–22, discussed above). The mind is an object of thought as well, 'for in the case of things without matter what thinks and what is thought are the same; for contemplative knowledge and the corresponding knowable object are the same' (430a3–5). The point of this compressed argument seems to be as follows: Since immaterial objects are identical with their own essences (cf. 329b12), they do not have to be separated from matter in order to be objects of thought; they are already directly accessible to the mind. But the mind itself is immaterial if it is separable from the body. Hence, when the mind thinks of the essence of a geranium, the mind does not have to do anything else in order to think of itself. A mind is thus *conscious* or self-aware in a way that a geranium is not: although both are possible objects of thought, a geranium has no mind and cannot think of itself. Aristotle hints here at why the mind is conscious: 'contemplative knowledge and the corresponding knowable object are the same' (403a4–5). This implies that the mind is aware of itself whenever it thinks of an object.[42] Along similar lines *Metaphysics* XII 9 1074b35–6 remarks, 'It appears that knowledge, perception, belief, and discursive thought (*dianoia*) are always of something else, and of themselves as a by-product (*en parergôi*)'.[43]

In passing, Aristotle mentions a third puzzle: 'The reason why [mind] does not always think must be considered' (430a5–6). If thought is essentially separable from the body, why do we not think all the time? For, as Aristotle has argued, thinking is unlike perceiving because it can occur even when external objects are not acting on our bodily organs. Why then does the mind go from potentiality to actuality? Perhaps Aristotle has this puzzle in mind when he distinguishes between the productive mind and the passive mind.[44]

5. THE ARGUMENT THAT THE PRODUCTIVE MIND ALONE IS SEPARABLE (*DE ANIMA* III 5)

Aristotle's brief and thorny discussion[45] should be quoted in full:

> Since just as in all nature something is matter for each genus (this is what is all those things potentially) and something else is the cause and is productive by producing all things (just as an art stands to matter), these differences must also exist in the soul. And one sort of mind exists by becoming all things, while another exists by making all things, as a sort of disposition like light. For in a way light makes potential colours into actual colours. And this mind is separable (*chôristos*), unaffected, and unmixed, since it is essentially in actuality. For the producer is always more honourable than the patient, and the principle is more honourable than the matter. Actual knowledge is the same as the object; but potential knowledge is prior in time in the individual, but on the whole it is not prior even in time. But it is not the case that it sometimes thinks and sometimes does not think. Having been separated (*chôristheis*) this is alone what it is, and this alone is immortal and eternal—but we do not remember because, while this is unaffected, the passive mind is perishable—and without this, nothing thinks (III 5 430a10–25).[46]

Since antiquity most commentators have concurred that Aristotle here distinguishes between a passive (or possible) mind and a productive mind, but even then there was radical disagreement as to what this distinction amounts to. The fundamental dispute is over how the the productive and passive minds are related to the individual soul. The argument of *De Anima* III 4 relies on an analogy between Anaxagoras' cosmic mind and the human mind. This suggests two very different lines of interpretation. On the *internalist* interpretation the productive mind is a part of the individual soul, while on the *externalist* interpretation it is a divine mind existing outside of the individual soul. The internalist interpretation has three main variants:

PMO   The part of the human mind which is productive is ontologically separable from the rest of the soul and from the body.

PMD   The part of the human mind which is productive is separable only in definition from the body.

WMO   The whole human mind, both productive and passive, is ontologically separable from the body.

The externalist interpretation has two main variants:

DMO   The divine mind (i.e., God), which is identical with the productive mind for human beings, is ontologically separate from individual human bodies and souls.

CMO   A common mind, which is the productive mind for all human beings but is distinct from the divine mind (i.e., God), is ontologically separate from individual human bodies and souls.

Although each of these interpretations has found formidable advocates,[47] the two main contenders presently are the internalist PMO and the externalist DMO. Let us briefly consider the case for each in turn beginning with PMO: the productive part of the human mind is ontologically separable. (i) The statement that the distinction between the passive and productive is 'in the soul' implies that they are parts of the individual soul. For the primary sense of 'in' is to be a part of a whole, as a part in a whole (cf. *Phys.* IV 3 210a15–16). (ii) The claim that the productive mind is separable (*chôristos*) combined with the statement, 'Having been separated (*chôristheis*) it is alone what it is...' implies that the separation occurs at some time, and only then is the productive mind's true nature revealed.[48] (iii) The intriguing aside that 'we do not remember' assumes that the productive mind is a human's true or essential self, which after separation will no longer recall the memories experienced in its previous corporeal existence, because these require the passive mind which will have perished with the body.[49] (iv) The final words, 'without this, nothing thinks,' mean that everyone needs a separable productive mind in order to think.[50] Further, PMO has firmer support than the two internalist alternatives: against WMO (the whole human mind is ontologically separable), when the text states that '*this* mind is separable, unaffected, and unmixed' (5 430a17), it refers back to the sort of mind which 'exists by making all things', in distinction from the sort of mind which 'becomes all things' (430a14–15).[51] Against PMD (the productive mind is separable only in definition), the text declares that this (i.e., the productive mind) 'is alone immortal and eternal' (430a23), which would be misleading (to say the least) if the productive mind has been merely separated in thought or definition.[52] This concludes the case for PMO.

As a philosophical thesis, however, PMO faces serious theoretical challenges: On what grounds would Aristotle have distinguished between the productive and passive minds?[53] This distinction does not appear elsewhere in his extant works. If these minds are distinct, they must have different jobs. What might these be? And even if the human mind has a productive component, why suppose that it is ontologically separable from the rest of the mind? To be sure, few philosophers today are persuaded by any traditional proofs of immortality. But do Aristotle's remarks in *De Anima* III 5 suggest an even remotely plausible argument?

In the face of such difficulties, a growing number of commentators have turned to DMO, which identifies the productive mind with the divine mind. With some ingenuity this interpretation can be reconciled with the evidence mentioned earlier. (i) When Aristotle says that the productive mind is 'in' the soul he means that it acts on it from the outside (like light shining into a window), or that it is 'in' it taxonomically as a species in a genus.[54] (ii) For DMO the productive mind is *chôristos* in the sense of being always separate from the body.[55] A greater difficulty is posed, however, by the aorist passive, *chôristheis*, 'having been separated', which seemingly implies that the productive mind is separated at some time. In defense of DMO, it has been suggested that Aristotle is here using language imprecisely, or else that he uses the participle here in a merely aspectual sense, for example, 'since it occurs separately'.[56] (iii) The clause 'we do not remember because (*hoti*) it is unaffected while the passive mind is perishable' is also vexing for DMO. It has been proposed that it be translated instead as 'we do not remember that (*hoti*) this is unaffected while the passive mind is perishable'.[57] But, then, *why* we do not remember this fact is mysterious. (iv) The final words, 'without this, nothing thinks', is consistent with DMO provided 'this' refers to the productive mind.[58] A similar defense can be mounted for CMO, which identifies the productive mind with a transcendent mind other than the divine mind (i.e., God), for example, which is in some sense common to all individuals. This interpretation appeals to commentators who find in *Metaphysics* XII the doctrine that God has only self-knowledge and no knowledge of the cosmos. Assuming this doctrine can be avoided, however, there is no other evidence for such a common mind in Aristotle. This concludes then the case for DMO: the divine mind is the ontologically separate productive mind.

However, DMO itself raises hard theoretical questions: What contribution could a divine mind make to human knowledge? Does the divine mind already know the intelligible forms of the natural universe, knowledge which is subsequently imparted to human minds when they learn?[59] But how is it possible for an eternal, disembodied, immovable mind to possess knowledge of the forms of perishable, material, mutable substances? And even if the disembodied divine mind had such knowledge, how could it communicate it to embodied human minds?[60] Finally, DMO implies that *De Anima* III 5 is an abrupt detour from what otherwise appears to be a continuous discussion of the human soul. In view of these worries, it is advisable to take more seriously the opposing internalist view (PMO) that the human mind has an ontologically separable productive component.

First it is necessary to consider how Aristotle might have argued in support of PMO. Such an argument might proceed as follows:

(3.1) When the mind thinks, it both becomes and makes all things.

(3.2) In so far as the mind becomes its object, it has a passive and potential part; and insofar as it produces its object, it has a productive and actual part.

(3.3) [What is productive and actual is (or ought to be) ontologically separable from what is essentially passive and potential.] (Tacit premise)

(3.4) Therefore, the productive mind is ontologically separable from the passive mind.

Premise (3.1) is implicit in the argument of *De Anima* III 4, discussed in the previous section. Aristotle has already established that 'the mind is potentially in a way the thinkable objects, but nothing in actuality, before it thinks' (III 4 429b29–31). There must be some explanation of how it becomes those objects. Unlike the perceptive faculty, the mind is able to think 'by itself'; because it involves universals rather than external objects, 'thinking is up to one, whenever one wishes' (429b7, cf. II 5 417b23–6).

Premise (3.2) presupposes Aristotle's theory of causation: 'Everything is affected and moved by that which is productive and in actuality' (*DA* II 5 417a17–18). Again, 'From the potential the actual always comes to be by what exists in actuality, for example a man by a man, a musician by a musician' (*Met.* IX 8 1049b24–6). This principle implies that the mind is analogous to a self-mover, as described in Aristotle's *Physics* VIII 4. A self-mover cannot move itself as a whole because it would be simultaneously potential and actual. One part of it must be moved and another unmoved.[61] Nor can the parts move each other reciprocally, because this would lead to an infinite regress and no ultimate explanation of how the potentiality is actualized. Hence the self-mover must have one part which is capable of being moved and another which is an unmoved mover, and these must be in some sense in contact with each other (*Phys.* VIII 5 258a18–21). In so far as the mind is analogous to a self-mover, one part of the mind is passive and potential, and the other is productive and actual like an unmoved mover.[62]

There is phenomenological evidence that the mind is partly productive (or active) and partly passive (or reactive). On the one hand, knowledge is something we bring about by thinking about a subject matter. Whether we maintain our mental focus or 'tune out' seems to be subject to our voluntary control. On the other hand, even when we make an effort to concentrate, we may encounter resistance as a result of fatigue, disease, senility, intoxication, or emotional arousal.[63] This is presumably because our capacity to acquire and use knowledge depends upon our capacity to construct, retrieve, and manipulate images, which in turn depends upon our perceptive faculty, which depends ultimately upon our sense-organs (*De Iuv.* 1 467b28). The complex makeup of the mind explains how we can fail to follow a proof, be stumped by a puzzle, not get a joke, overlook a clue, or miss a reply to an objection.[64]

Granting that Aristotle can distinguish between productive and passive parts of the mind, how can he establish that these parts are *ontologically* separable? Aristotle clearly needs something like tacit premise (3.3): What is productive and actual is (or ought to be) ontologically separable from what is essentially passive and potential. It is noteworthy, then, that he states this premise explicitly in *Generation of Animals*, when he tries to explain why there are two different sexes:

> The primary moving cause, to which the account and matter belong, is better and more divine in its nature than the matter, and it is better that the superior factor be separated (*kekôristhai*) from the inferior one. For this reason wherever it is possible and as far as possible, the male is separated (*kekôristai*) from the female. For the source of movement, by which what comes into being is male, is better and more divine, and the female is the matter. The male however comes together and mingles with the female for the work of reproduction; for this is common to both (*GA* II 1 732a3–11).

According to Aristotelian teleology, 'nature makes everything either because it is necessary or because it is better so' (I 3 717a15–16), and although the separation of the sexes is not necessary for reproduction (for example, plants can reproduce asexually), it is better because it is a more efficient and reliable way of producing more fully developed offspring. The argument of *De Anima* III 5 is arguably based on the same principle that it is better if the productive cause is separate from the material cause (cf. *Phys.* VIII 4 255a14–18). In the case of sexual reproduction, Aristotle offers a relatively clear and detailed (albeit mistaken) account of the distinct roles of the male and female factors and of how 'the male comes together and mingles with the female' to produce an offspring.[65]

If we grant that the productive mind stands in an analogous relation to the passive mind, how do these two minds 'come together and mingle'? Here the main clue is Aristotle's description of the productive mind 'as a sort of condition like light. For in a way light makes potential colours into actual colours' (430a15). Aristotle earlier defines light as 'the actuality of the transparent [medium, e.g., air or water] in so far as it is transparent; but potentially, where this exists, there is also darkness' (II 7 418b9–11). Though somewhat illuminating this analogy is doubly ambiguous. The first problem is whether light is actual all the time or only intermittently. The problem arises because light has different sources according to Aristotle: namely fire (a terrestrial element) or 'the body above', that is, the sun. (II 7 418b12–13) Hence there are two possible analogues: lamplight or sunlight.[66] If the productive mind is like lamplight, alternately kindled or extinguished, then it may be intermittently active, initiating acts of thinking episodically. If the productive mind is like sunlight, it is perpetually active like Plato's sun (*Rep.* VI 507d-e), and choosing to think on this view will be like throwing open the shutters to let in light that is always available. The sunlight analogy is congenial to the externalist interpretation that the productive mind is the divine mind, though it also permits an internalist interpretation on which each human mind possesses its own perpetual flame. The lamplight analogy however favors an internalist interpretation because it implies that individual productive minds could initiate cognitive acts

independently of each other. The lamplight analogy faces a textual difficulty however with the clause, 'but it is not the case that [it] sometimes thinks and sometime
does not think' (430a22). This suggests that the productive mind does not engage
in intermittent activity but is always in an actual state.[67]

The second ambiguity concerns what Aristotle means when he says that 'in
a way light makes potential colours into actual colours'. (430a16–17) This can be
understood in two different ways, depending on whether the product is actualized
on the first or the second level (as discussed in the previous section). When something is made actual on the first level, this may be called *first-level production*;
and when the product is actual on the second level, *second-level production*. On
which level is light—and its analogue, the productive mind—'productive'? If light
makes colours visible it produces on the first level; if it makes them actually seen,
it produces on the second level. Likewise if the productive mind makes objects
thinkable, it produces them on the first level; if it makes them actually thought it
produces on the second level. Which is it? [68]

Aristotle's remarks about light and vision can be used to support both interpretations. Some texts indicate that light makes colours actual on the *first* level: for
example, 'every colour is capable of moving the transparent [medium] which is in
actuality, and this is its nature'. Hence, a colour 'is not visible (*horaton*) without light,
but in every case the colour of each thing is seen (*horatai*) in light' (II 7 418a31-b3).
Even in the dark a colour has a first-level potentiality to be seen in that it has the
power to move the transparent medium which is illuminated. When light is present this becomes a second-level potentiality, corresponding to a first-level actuality:
the colour becomes actually visible. This suggests that light makes colours actual
(i.e., visible) on the first level.[69] So understood the analogy implies that the productive mind operates on the first level as well: that is, it makes potentially thinkable
objects actually thinkable, or in modern parlance it explains how the mind acquires
universal concepts and forms judgements.[70] However, some texts suggest that light
makes colours actual on the *second* level: for example, in contrast to phosphorescent
objects which are seen only in the dark, 'what is seen (*horômenon*) in the light is
colour; that is why it is not seen (*horatai*) without light'. (419a7–9) This states that a
colour is not *seen* without light and not merely that it is not visible, which suggests
that the role of light is to make a colour actually seen.[71] Perhaps the overall point of
the light analogy is that the productive mind makes potentially thinkable objects
actually thinkable (first-level production) and thereby explains why the mind is able
to actually think about such objects at will (second-level production).

Although Aristotle does not provide a single integrated discussion of mental activity, he offers suggestive remarks about how the mind uses images (*phan-
tasmata*) which are present to it like percepts (*aisthêmata*) (III 7 431a14–17, cf.
417a14–16 and *Mem* 1 449b31). He says that 'the thinking faculty thinks the forms
in the images' (III 7 431b1) and that 'the thinkable objects (*noêta*) are in the perceptible forms'. (432a4–5) However, the thinkable objects are not 'out there' in the way
that perceptible objects are. Instead, 'each of the thinkable objects is *potentially* in
the things possessing matter'. (4 430a6–7, emphasis added) The mind itself (*qua*
productive) must *make* an object actually thinkable, just as light makes potentially

visible objects actually visible. In *On Memory* Aristotle compares mental images to visible diagrams:

> For in the latter case, though we do not make any use of the fact that the quantity of the triangle is determinate, we none the less draw it with a determinate quantity. And similarly one who thinks—even if he is not thinking of something with a quantity—puts something with a quantity before his eyes, but he does not think of it as having a quantity. But if the nature [of the object] is that of things which have a quantity, but not a determinate one, he puts a determinate quantity [before his eyes], but thinks of it only as having quantity (*Mem* 1 450a2–7).

The mind uses an image to produce a thinkable object by disregarding certain of its features such as perceptible magnitude. In the case of a triangle the mind can disregard its specific size and use it to represent spatially extended triangular shapes, or it can disregard its size altogether and use it to represent a geometrical triangle. In this way the mind acquires thoughts which can represent an indefinite domain of geometrical or physical triangles; in effect, it forms universal concepts. The thinkable object is 'potentially in' the image in the sense that an image of a triangle has the potential to represent a universal domain of triangles. But this potential must be actualized through the mind's own cognitive activity as it discerns thinkable objects, as Aristotle emphasizes in the *Metaphysics*: 'So it is obvious that potential beings are discovered by being brought to actuality; and the reason is that thinking is the actuality [of the mind]; so that the potentiality comes from actuality, and by making this [distinction] people know, though the single actuality is later in generation' (*Met.* IX 9 1051a21–33).[72] These passages suggest that the mind (*qua* productive) must play an active role in acquiring as well as using knowledge.

6. CONCLUDING ASSESSMENT—MIND THE GAP

Granting that the foregoing provides some basis for the thesis that the human mind contains the productive mind as a separable part, why conclude that it is *ontologically* separable?

Crucial for Aristotle's argument is the assumption that thinking, like perceiving, is receiving a form (*DA* III 4 429a15–16, b30–1; 5 430a14–15; 7 431b17; 8 431b26–8). However, there are two different ways of receiving the form of cold. One is receiving the cold literally or physically and becoming cold. The other way is receiving it 'objectively', that is, having had it become the object of one's awareness. The latter is clearly what Aristotle means, at least when the mind thinks of an object.[73] Thinking of an object is like perceiving an object in that both are ways of representing an object; to this extent they are analogous. There are different ways of representing an object, however. One way is to simply copy or imitate the object, as when someone mimics a bon mot or malapropism uttered in the past. But it is not necessary to exemplify a characteristic directly or literally in order to represent it.

Encoding a characteristic is a way of representing an object without exemplifying it, for example, the formula H_2O encodes water without exemplifying water or even exemplifying the structure of water.[74] If it were assumed that when it perceives an object the perceptive faculty in some way exemplifies it—for example, it becomes cold when it perceives a cold object—and it is assumed that thinking resembles perceiving in this way, then Aristotle's first premise seems plausible: the mind is potentially the object which it becomes by receiving its form. These assumptions are, however, extremely controversial.[75] Why suppose that the concept of water exemplifies aqueousness in even an attenuated way, any more than the formula H_2O exemplifies aqueousness?

But there seems to be a deeper problem with PMO. Although the mind grasps the essence of flesh, which is different in definition from perceptible flesh, the essence of flesh is not ontologically separable from flesh.[76] Nor are mathematical objects ontologically separable from perceptible objects. Thus, even if it is granted that the mind becomes assimilated to its object, it does not follow that any part of the mind is ontologically separable from perceptible substance and hence from the body. Other worries arise: What intellectual activity could the productive mind carry out if it *were* separate from the body? It might be suggested that the role of the productive mind is to 'divine' thinkable forms which are never present in sense-experience, while the passive mind has the job of recognizing universals in perceptible particulars.[77] But this would imply that the productive and passive mind do not cooperate in knowing the same objects. Alternatively, it might be suggested that the productive mind already possesses all the universal knowledge which is acquired by the whole human mind when it learns. But how is it possible for it to possess such prior knowledge independently of sense-experience?

If Aristotle thought that he could establish that part of the mind was ontologically separable, he would not be the only philosopher whose reach exceeded his grasp. Still, we might wonder whether a stronger conclusion would result if the human mind could know immaterial objects such as the prime mover. In this case, it might be argued from Aristotelian premises that if an object is ontologically separable from matter it can only be known by an ontologically separable faculty. Provocatively, Aristotle asks whether the embodied mind can have incorporeal objects: 'Whether it is possible for it [i.e., the mind], while it is not separated in magnitude, to think of anything that is separated or not, must be considered later'. (III 7 431b17–19) Unfortunately he does not pursue this provocative question in any extant text—though *Metaphysics* XII may indicate his final answer.

NOTES

1. In this essay *nous* is translated as 'mind' when it refers to the cognitive faculty, although it may also be rendered as 'intellect', 'reason', or 'thought'. *Nous* has other senses: e.g., in *Posterior Analytics* it denotes the inerrant mode of judgement concerning first

principles, and in *Nicomachean Ethics* book VI it denotes an intellectual virtue. Related terms include *noein* (to think), *noêma* (a thought), *noêsis* (act of thinking), *noêtikon* (thinking faculty), *noêton* (thinkable object), *nooumenon* (object of actual thinking), and so forth.

This chapter is primarily concerned with what can be elicited from a careful reading of Aristotle's *De Anima* concerning the separability of mind. References to the prodigious secondary literature are perforce highly selective and confined to footnotes. However, my substantial debt to preceding scholars should be obvious throughout. I thank Myrna Gabbe, Eugene T. Gendlin, Lawrence Jost, David Keyt, John Lewis, Pamela Phillips, and the editor for helpful suggestions. I also received valuable feedback on earlier versions at meetings of the American Catholic Philosophical Association at Denison University (October 2006) and the Society for Ancient Greek Philosophy at Fordham University (October 2009).

2. The two sciences will not be mutually exclusive if the separable mind is a principle or cause of some of the capacities, acts, and affections of the soul that are inseparable from the body. For in this case these same inseparable psychological states will be explained by both sciences: the part of psychology belonging to physics and the part belonging to first philosophy. See also note 40 below.

3. Frag. 61 Rose; Iamblichus, *Protrepticus* B 108 Düring. Frag. 38 Rose; Themistius, *Paraph. de an.* 106.29–107.4. Frag. 44 Rose; Ps.-Plutarch, *Consolatio ad Apollonium* 115BE. Frag. 41 Rose; Proclus, *In rem. pub.* II.349.13–26. Frag. 39 Rose; Elias, *In cat.* 114.25–115.3. All translations are from Barnes 1984.

4. Jaeger (1948), Nuyens (1948), and Dancy (1996) view the dualism of Aristotle's dialogues as inconsistent with his mature hylomorphic psychology. In contrast, Gerson (2005: ch. 2 and 5) and Bos (2003: ch. 17) follow the ancient commentators who regard *De Anima* as in fundamental agreement with the *Eudemus* and even with Platonic dualism.

5. Aristotle also says that the principle of the soul in the body of the semen is 'partly separable (*chôriston*) from body and belonging to those in which something divine is included (and what is called mind is of this sort), and partly inseparable (*achôrista*)'. (*GA* II 3 737a8–11, deleting *to sperma*) He also seems to suggest that a faculty which comes from outside can exist previously (*prohuparchein*) (736b21–9). This suggestion (which recalls the report of Proclus mentioned above) prompted a controversy between Eduard Zeller and Franz Brentano over the pre-existence of the mind (see Novak 1995). These texts present difficulties, however, which are discussed in Charlton 1987.

6. Historical overviews of interpretations include Brentano 1977, Kurfess 1911, Hamelin 1953, and Blumenthal 1996. Huby 1991 discusses the usage of *nous* in Aristotle and his ancient commentators. For further references see Caston 1999: 199 n. 1 and Wedin 1988: 160–1 nn. 1–4.

7. Michel de Montaigne, *Essays* II.12, trans. Donald Frame.

8. Aristotle speaks of things as *kechôrismena* even when there is no (obvious) separator: e.g., *DA* II 2 413b5–7. Here nature (*phusis*) is presumably understood as doing the separating, e.g., Aristotle speaks of nature as mixing the male and female in plants but separating the two sexes in most animals (cf. *GA* I 23 711a28). This is another way of saying that there is a teleological explanation for why the sexes are separated or not, not to imply that nature literally acts like a craftsman.

9. Compare *DA* I 1 403b9–16 and cf. *Met.* VI 1 1026a5–6 which make basically the same distinction, but the former uses *kechôrismenos* while the latter uses *chôristos* (cf. *Met.* VII 141039a31–2). Also, *achôristos* is opposed to *kechôrismenos* at *GA* IV 1 763b24–5 (cf. *DA* III 2 427a1–2). The latter contrast also occurs at Plato *Rep.* VII 524c, although

the positive *chôristos* does not appear in Plato. Vlastos (1987:195) plausibly conjectures, however, that *chôristos* would have been accessible to Plato.

10. Morrison (1985a and 1985b) provides an informative overview of Aristotle's usage of *chôristos*, but he is not persuasive in arguing that the term always means 'separate' rather than 'separable'. In particular, he does not convincingly support his claim that *chôristos* means 'separate' at I 1 403a10–12 (quoted in the main text), and he also has difficulty with II 2 418b26–8, which treats *endechetai chôrizesthai* and *chôrista* as parallel.

11. Only the spatial and definitional senses are explicitly distinguished. See II 2 413b14, 2 413b28–9; III 4 429a11–12, 9 432a20, 10 433b24–5; cf. also *GC* I 5 320b25 and *Met.* X 1 1052b17. Corcilius and Gregoric (2010:90) assert that when Aristotle does not specify the respect in which a thing is separable, he always means the ontological sense. Although the interpretation of Aristotle would be easier if this were true, they offer no argument for it.

12. A definition (*horismos*) is an account (*logos*) that reveals the essence (*ousia* or *to ti ên einai*) of an entity. It differs from a mere description of its attributes (*sumbebêkota*) but enables us to know those attributes. See *DA* I 1 402b16–403a2 and *Met.* V 6 1016a32-b3.

13. See Whiting 2002: 144–5; cf. Corcilius and Gregoric 2010.

14. Fine (1984) gives a clear exposition of a generally accepted interpretation of ontological separability. She translates *chôristos* as 'separate', but gives it a modal sense: *able* to exist independently. Morrison (1985a and 1985b) offers an alternative account: X is separate from Y if, and only if, they are 'outside each other's ontological boundaries'. Morrison's discussion is informative, but his interpretation relies upon a metaphor of 'ontological boundaries' which is not explicit in Aristotle's text, and it omits the modal feature. It also implies that separability is a symmetrical relation, although Aristotle indicates that substances are separable from items in other categories but not vice-versa (see *Met.* VII 1 1028a31-b2). Corkum (2008) interprets *chôristos* as ontologically independent: 'A admits of the ontological status of a being independently standing in some tie to any B whatsoever' (2008:7–8). This relies on the notion of a non-relational 'tie' not explicit in Aristotle, and also apparently omits the modal feature. Therefore, this essay will follow Fine's interpretation (see also Fine 2005).

15. Aristotle criticizes Plato for ontologically separating the Forms from perceptible particulars (*Met.* XIII 9 1086a33; cf. Vlastos 1987). He contends that the Forms are even less separable than mathematical objects, which are separable 'in thought' (*noêsei*) from perceptible substances, because one can think of mathematical objects as if they existed separately although they cannot (*Phys.* II 2 193b34–194a1). For example, concavity (i.e., flatness) is separable in thought from a nose, but snubness is not (cf. *DA* III 4 429b13–14). Abstraction (*aphairesis*) is the process by which one thinks of an object separately from the matter in which it is embodied. 'When one thinks the objects of mathematics he thinks of them as separate (*kechôrismena*) though they are not separate (*kechôrismena*)'. (*DA* III 7 431b12–17). We can distinguish particular geometrical figures if we regard them as having thinkable or intelligible matter (*noêtikê hulê*) rather than perceptible matter (*Met.* VII 10 1036a10).

16. Aristotle uses the half-line to illustrate ontological priority: one thing is naturally prior to another if the former can exist without the latter but the latter cannot exist without the former (*Met.* V 11 1019a1–4, *EE* I 8 1218a1–9, *Pol.* I 2 1253a18–38). If X is ontologically prior to Y, X is also separable from Y, though the converse does not hold.

17. See Caston 1999: 209 for a useful discussion with other references; see also Broadie 1996: 164.

18. The text is confusing because it distinguishes the straight that is separated from the straight in so far as it is straight and states that only the latter touches a bronze sphere at a point. However, it may be that Aristotle is speaking in an analogical way: just as a geometrical straight line touches a sphere at a point, similarly a straight bronze rod touches a bronze sphere at a physical point (see Sophonias *Paraphr. de an.* 7, 24–7 and Aquinas *In de an.* I.2, 82–101). If the passage is understood this way, it is not necessary to delete *chalkês* (bronze) at 403a13–14 with Ross 1961.

19. This dependence of imagination on the body is implied in *De Anima* III 3 and *De Insomniis* 2.

20. This does not necessarily imply that the soul (or mind) is never the subject of activity given the context; see the following note.

21. Aristotle's argument has a limited objective: to argue in effect that it is a category mistake to describe a form as perishing rather than the physical system to which it belongs (see Wedin 1988: 213). His language is imprecise, shifting from 'soul' to 'it' to 'mind' (cf. 408b18, 23, 24, 29); but this does not vitiate the argument, as interpreted here. In fact, mind is not sharply distinguished from soul until claim (G) below. Here Aristotle does not clearly identify what does perish, alluding only vaguely to a 'common thing' (*tou koinou*) at 408b28–9. Aristotle's earlier remark that discursive thinking (*to dianoeisthai*), along with emotions and desires, is literally a sort of movement in the heart or some other organ, occurs in an 'if' clause, and may be a concession for the sake of argument (408b5–11).

22. It might be objected that each part of the soul must depend on the body, granted that the soul as a whole is inseparable. But would not such an objection commit the fallacy of division? Perhaps some part of the soul is separable even if the whole is not.

23. The sailor analogy has perplexed many commentators. Themistius understands the sailor to be 'an actualization, but a separate one' (*Paraph. de an.* 43.27), which may also be Porphyry's interpretation (cf. Karamanolis 2006: 295). Ross (1961: 214) complains that the analogy 'flatly contradicts' Aristotle's main thesis and emends the text, inserting *ê* (or) before 'like a sailor'. Tracy (1982) contends that the issue is not whether the soul is separable but whether the soul, conceived as actualization of the body, is also an efficient cause like a helmsman. On the contrary, Bos (2003: ch. 6) argues that the issue is whether the soul, though 'user' of the 'instrumental body', does not require it for intellectual activities.

24. *Genos* with the genitive may be translated alternatively, '…it seems to be a *different kind from* soul'. (413b26) However rendered, the point may be that this kind cannot be defined hylomorphically (cf. Kahn 1992: 361). Ross reads *endechetai* at 413b26 following most manuscripts. Alexander (ap. Philoponus *In de an.* 242.6–7) reads *endechesthai* governed by *eoike*, 'seems likely', which would indicate a weaker claim.

25. Cf. Barnes 1971–2: 109 n. 4; Broadie 1996: 163 n. 2; and Whiting 2002: 150–1. Hicks overtranslates *chôrista* at II 2 413b26–7 as capable of separation 'from the body'.

26. 'Productive' (*poiêtikos*) means 'able to produce or make (*poiein*) something'; 'passive' (*pathêtikos*) means 'able to be affected or acted on (*paschein*, aor. *pathein*)'. *Pathêtikos* could also be translated 'passible'. It is opposed to *apathês* 'unaffected' or 'impassible' (unable to be affected or acted on). Alternatives to 'productive mind' and 'passive mind' used here are the familiar scholastic translations 'agent intellect' and 'patient intellect'. Note that translations such as 'active mind' versus 'passive mind' misleadingly suggest that the passive mind is inactive.

27. This is surprising, since, as noted above, the treatment of mind commences with the question: 'whether it is separable with respect to magnitude or not separable in this way too but [only] with respect to account' (III 4 429a11–12). Similarly, however, Aristotle asks at III 9 432a20 whether the part of the soul that originates movement is 'separable (*chôriston*) either in magnitude or in account', but never answers the question, although he does remark later that the bodily instrument of motion is 'different in account but inseparable (*achôriston*) in magnitude' (10 433b24–5).

28. As remarked above (G) immediately follows the discussion in (F) of whether the non-mental faculties can be actually separated by cutting up insects. However, as remarked in note 24 above, if *endechesthai* is read at 413b26, then claim (G) may be the weaker claim that the mind *seems likely* to be separated.

29. The details of Aristotle's theory of perception are controversial: in perception does the sense-organ *literally* acquire the form of its object (e.g., the eye jelly turning red)? Or does becoming like an object consist merely in the perceiver becoming aware of the object? Commentators even disagree over whether Aristotle holds that perceiving requires any physiological change in the sense-organ. Seminal discussions are Sorabji 1974 (literal interpretation, defended in Everson 1997) and Burnyeat 1992 (anti-literal interpretation, defended in Johansen 1998). For further discussion and references, see Price 1998 and Miller 2000.

30. Scholars disagree over whether a positive or 'refined' alteration can be an alteration in the ordinary sense (namely, when an object loses one quality and gains another). Burnyeat (2002) contends that perception is an alteration in the special positive sense and *not* an ordinary alteration, whereas Heinaman (2007) argues that positive alterations *can* be ordinary alterations. Heinaman appeals to the fact that although Aristotle uses learning as an example of a positive alteration (*DA* II 5 417a31), he elsewhere uses it repeatedly as an example of ordinary alteration (*Phys.* V 1 224b11–13, 2 225b31–3, 226a15 and other passages cited in Heinaman 2007:141 n. 5). The main issue here is whether subjects undergo any real alteration in the ordinary sense when they perceive or know. As Burnyeat (1995) puts it, 'How much happens when Aristotle sees red and hears middle C?'

31. See Shields 1997 who attributes a 'weak isomorphism' to Aristotle. This anticipates the idea of intentionality or 'intentional inexistence' developed by Brentano (1973 and 1977). On the relation of Brentano to Aristotle, see George 1978, Sorabji 1991, and Caston 1998. See Section 6 for further discussion.

32. See Polansky 2007: 444 n. 13 and Burnyeat 2008: 23. However, later at 430a4–5 Aristotle says, 'contemplative knowledge and the corresponding knowable object are the same', which may mean that the identification occurs with actual contemplation, i.e., at the second level of actualization. If so, Aristotle may think that the mind is identical with its object on both levels but in different ways. This passage is discussed in Section 4.3 below.

33. Anaxagoras distinguishes mind from the other elements of which things are composed: 'The other things have a share in everything, but mind is unlimited and self-controlled and has been mixed with nothing, but is alone itself by itself'. (DK59B12; Simplicius *In phys.* 156.13)

34. This is probably an allusion to Anaxagoras: 'It is the finest and purest of all things and has all knowledge about everything'. (DK59B12).

35. Some scholars regard Aristotle's epistemology as vulnerable to sceptical attack, whereas others maintain that he has resources to ward off scepticism. See Long 1981, Barnes 1987, and Vasiliou 1996.

36. Cf. Ross 1924, cxli.

37. Sisko (1999) distinguishes three ways in which perception is limited according to Aristotle: *Intrinsic quality limitations*: A sense organ cannot perceive intrinsic quality Q if it is already Q itself. For example, flesh can detect hot and cold but not a mean temperature the same as itself. Thus the special senses have 'blind spots' corresponding to their own mean states. (II 11 423b30–424a10) *Scope limitations*: Each sense is confined by its organ to a particular spectrum of qualities: e.g., eyes cannot see sounds, and ears cannot hear colours. (II 6 418a11–12) *Range limitations*: An organ cannot perceive qualities if they are too intense or too faint. (III 4 429a31–b3).

38. Cf. *Gen. et Corr.* II 7 28–30: 'The dry and wet and the others [viz. hot and cold] produce flesh and bone and the other [compounds] due to [being in] a mean state'. The dry, wet, cold, and hot are essential qualities of the elements (earth, air, fire, water) out of which all material compounds are formed. Aristotle (*DA* III 4 429b12) notes, however, that in some cases (i.e., of immaterial substances) a thing is the same as its essence (cf. 430a3–4 and *Met.* VII 1 1037a33–b4).

39. Different interpretations are discussed in Rodier 1900: 445, Hicks 1907: 489–91, Theiler 1983: 141, Modrak 1986: 214, Kahn 1992: 370–2, and Polansky 2007: 445–51. It has been disputed whether the straight line represents the mind and the bent line perception, or the straight line stands for perception and the bent line the mind. Kahn favors another interpretation along lines suggested by Themistius (*Paraph. de an.* 96.21–30): the mind resembles a straight line when it thinks of an essence and a bent line when it thinks of a hylomorphic compound.

40. The idea that the mind and its correlative objects are isomorphic also seems to underlie the argument in *Parts of Animals* that natural science would encompass all of philosophy if it treated the whole soul, including the mind: 'For the mind is of thinkable objects (*noêta*). Hence, natural science will be knowledge of all things. For it belongs to the same science to contemplate mind and thinkable objects, since these are correlatives and all correlatives belong to the same science, e.g., perception and perceptible objects' (*PA* I 1 641a32–b4). Broadie (1996: 168–9) calls this the 'Correlatives Argument'.

41. Imagination is supposed to serve as the bridge between perception and thought: 'No one can learn or understand anything without perceiving; and when one contemplates one necessarily at the same time contemplates with an image; for the images are like percepts, except they are without matter'. (*DA* III 8 432a7–10) Hence, 'without an image thinking is impossible'. (*Mem* 1 450a1) As Wedin (1988: 116) remarks, 'an image is a vehicle for thought without being identical with the thought'. (This interpretation is developed more fully in Wedin 1989.) Imagination is however closely linked to perception: 'The faculty of imagination is the same as the faculty of perception, but their being is different, and imagination is the movement which comes to be due to the perception when it is actual'. (*Insomn* 1 459a15–18, cf. *DA* III 3 429a1–2, 4–5; *Mem* 1 450a10–11) The universals come to be in our minds through a complicated process beginning with perception and mediated by memory, experience, and induction (see *APo* II 19 and *Met.* I 1). See the following section on how this might bear on the argument of *De Anima* III 5.

42. Ross, following Bywater, reads *di' hautou* at 429b7 requiring the translation, 'it is then able to think by itself'. All the manuscripts read *de hauton*, however, which makes good sense and anticipates the discussion at 430a3–9; cf. Owens 1976.

43. The implications for divine mind are controversial. According to some commentators, divine mind is an exception because it knows itself only and not as by-product (e.g., Ross 1924: II.397–8). According to others divine mind knows itself by cognizing the

forms of the universe (e.g., Kahn 1985 and De Koninck 1994). See also Caston 2002 on this passage in connection with Aristotle's views on consciousness.

44. Gill (1991) and Kosman (1992) contend that this puzzle is addressed in *De Anima* III 5, against commentators who complain that Aristotle never tries to solve it (e.g., Ross 1961: 295).

45. Theiler 1983: 142: 'There is no passage of ancient philosophy that has provoked such a multitude of interpretations as this half-page chapter. Its obscurity and extreme brevity are notorious'. Rist 1966:8: 'Interpretations of this chapter have been almost as numerous as interpreters'.

46. The translation follows the text of Ross 1956 except for retaining manuscript readings of *hôsper* ('just as') at 430a10 and *energeiai* 'in actuality' instead of *energeia* at 430a18. Where the translation is unavoidably controversial, this is discussed below.

47. There are subtle variations on these interpretations, and sometimes the boundaries between them are blurry. Moreover, commentators sometimes combine interpretations or change their minds. With these caveats, advocates of these interpretations include the following: (PMO) Pseudo-Simplicius *In de an.* 240.1–248.18; Rodier 1900: 2.465; Ross 1961: 47–8; Rist 1966; Cassirer 1968: ch. 4; Ando 1971: ch. 1; Robinson 1983; Sisko 2000. (PMD) Hicks 1907, 505–6; Wedin 1988: ch. 5; Caston 1999; Shields 1997. (WMO) Theophrastus ap. Themistius *Paraph. de an.* 107.30–108.35; Plutarch ap. Pseudo-Philoponus *In de an.* 535.13–16; Philoponus *De intell.* 57.70–4; Aquinas *In de an.* 742–3; Brentano 1977: 106–61; Gerson 2005: ch. 5. (DMO) Alexander of Aphrodisias *De An.* 88.10–16 and Alexander ap. Pseudo-Philoponus *In de an.* 535.20; Avicenna *De An.* 221; Averroes *Long Comm. on De An.* III.18–20; Barnes 1971–2:113; Clark 1975: ch. 3; Guthrie 1981: 322–4; Rist 1989: 182; Pichter 1992: 391; Frede 1996; Caston 1999; Burnyeat 2008. (CMO) Marinus ap. Pseudo-Philoponus *In de an.* 535.32–536.2; Hamlyn 1968: 140; Ross 1924: 1.cxlvi. This list is perforce selective with apologies to any commentators who have been passed over or improperly pigeonholed.

48. This assumes that *chôristheis* is an ingressive aorist participle, expressing the entrance into a state or beginning of a state that is denoted by the present tense verb, *chôrizesthai* (cf. Smyth 1956: secs. 1872, 1924).

49. Compare Themistius *Paraph. de an.* 100.37: 'So we are the productive mind'. Similarly Ross (1961: 47–8): 'after separation from the passive reason, at death, the active reason is just its true self'. However, 'we do not...after death remember our life on earth, because the active reason is not affected by events, while the passive reason, which *is* affected by them, is perishable'. In contrast, in support of PMD Wedin (1988: 179–81) glosses the memory claim: 'we are not mindful of productive mind, or more precisely episodes of productive mind, while the passive mind, or more precisely what occurs in the passive mind, is perishable'. This implies that we are not aware of the mind's productive activity.

50. The Greek clause—*aneu toutou outhen noei*—can be read in four different ways: without the productive mind, nothing thinks; without the productive mind, the passive mind thinks nothing; without the passive mind, nothing thinks; without the passive mind, the productive mind thinks nothing. The main text assumes the first reading, based on Ross's punctuation. Hicks (1907: 509–10) favours the second reading after summarising the controversy. It should be noted that the first two readings both seem consistent with all the interpretations canvassed at the beginning of this section.

51. In support of WMO, Gerson (2005: 154 n. 99) following Hicks (1907: 500) translates the clause at 430a14–15 'the mind is one sort of thing by becoming all things, and another

by making all things'. This requires taking *toioutos* as predicative. However, it is in attributive position in *ho men toioutos nous*, which favours the translation in the main text. Another reason for WMO is the unqualified claim (H) that the mind is separable in *De Anima* III 4. However, the claim (J) that the productive mind is separable in *De Anima* III 5 may be a more exact restatement of claim (H). Likewise, in the earlier claim (A) it is the *soul* whose separability is in question (I 1 403a10–11), and the issue becomes more precise as *De Anima* proceeds.

52. In support of PMD see Hicks 1907: 505–6 and Wedin 1988: 190–2. Wedin appeals to the parallel with I 1 403a14–15 where a straight geometrical line has been separated (*chôristhen*) in thought. Modrak (1986: 225) understands 'alone immortal and eternal' as 'a description of what active *nous* would be like were it separated', but this counterfactual reading is hard to square with the use of the indicative mood in the main clause, 'it is (*esti*) alone what it is etc.'. Contrast the counterfactual construction at II 1 412b13–14.

53. Cf. Caston 1999: 202: 'Why on earth should Aristotle have thought there were *two* intellects?'

54. Guthrie (1981: 324) offers the former interpretation following Alexander of Aphrodisias (ap. Simplicius *In phys.* 964–5), and Caston (1999: 206) defends the latter. Burnyeat (2008: 52 n. 48) argues that 'in *all* nature' at 430a10 requires that 'in the soul' at 430a13 must be general as well, so that it cannot refer to the individual soul. This is inconclusive: Aristotle elsewhere draws parallels between individuals and collectives, e.g., *Pol.* VII 3 1325b30–2. A similar interpretative controversy concerns *EE* VIII 2 1248a26–7: 'as a god moves all in the whole universe, so it is in the soul; for in a way the divine in us moves all things'. Does 'the divine in us' refer to a god-like part of ourselves or to an external divinity at work in us?

55. Caston (1999: 208–10) interprets *chôristos* in claim (J) as that the productive mind is taxonomically separable, but (2000: 172) in claim (H) as that the human mind is separable in account (*kata logon*) from the body. This discrepancy seems problematic since Aristotle in both cases argues that the mind in question is *chôristos* because it is unmixed. It should be noted that Caston (1999) deviates from most proponents of DMO by denying the divine mind an influence on human causation.

56. Philoponus (*De intell.* 60.55) objects that the aorist *chôristheis* applied to the divine mind would imply that it was sometimes separate and sometimes not (cf. n. 48 above). Instead Aristotle applies *kechôrismenos* (perfect participle with present sense) to the divine mind in the *Metaphysics*, e.g., XII 7 1073a4, 11. Concessively Guthrie (1981: 327) suggests Aristotle speaks loosely, 'at the risk of seeming to take the easy way out'. Barnes (1971–2: 113) mentions the aorist participle used in connection with god at *EN* VIII 9 1159a5. However, here the issue is whether friendship would endure if a friend became 'separated greatly' like a god, i.e., if there occurred a disparity in certain attributes (cf. 1158b23). Caston (1999: 208) translates *chôristheis* as 'when it occurs separately', i.e., in the taxonomical sense.

57. Caston (1999: 214) argues that this translation is possible if one translates *hoti* as 'that' and deletes the preceding comma. According to Caston, the use of 'we do not remember' is merely 'philosophical and urbane' and without doctrinal significance.

58. As mentioned in note 50 the Greek clause—*aneu toutou outhen noei*—can be read in four different ways: without the productive mind, nothing thinks; without the productive mind, the passive mind thinks nothing; without the passive mind, nothing thinks; without the passive mind, the productive mind thinks nothing. The last two readings seem problematic for externalist interpretations that identify the productive mind with a transcendent mind. It is noteworthy that the fourth reading is assumed by the ancient commentators Themistus (*In de an.* 101.27), Pseudo-Simplicius (*In*

de an. 248.11), and Philoponus (*In de an.* 62.1), who all understand the clause as a continuation of the 'we do not remember' claim.

59. Kahn (1981: 413–14) conjectures that 'there must be a strict isomorphism, a kind of pre-established harmony, between the structure of the Agent Intellect and the formal, rational structure of the natural world....Even if we do not follow Alexander in assuming that the Active Intellect...is numerically identical with the divine Intellect..., they are certainly alike in kind' Kahn (1992: 374) reiterates, 'the noetic structure that is known in physics and biology—the formal structure of the natural world—will be identical with, and can be fully realized only in, the actual thought of a scientific mind', and 'the direct object of divine *noêsis* is the *noêta*, the intelligible forms of the universe'. Norman (1969) offers a similar interpretation. This interpretation is criticized by Wedin (1988: 227–45).

60. Frede (1996) and Côté (2005) defend opposing views on whether Aristotle thinks that a transcendent immaterial substance could exert immanent efficient causation within the soul.

61. Theophrastus (ap. Themistius *Paraph. de an.* 108.25) calls the productive mind 'the mover' (*ho kinôn*). Aristotle does not regard the mind as a literal self-mover however, because he denies that it is literally 'moved' when it goes from potential knowledge to actual knowledge (*Phys.* VII 3 247b4–13). The following discussion is indebted to Cassirer 1968, Shields 1994, and Wedin 1994.

62. The productive mind is essentially *energeiai* (in actuality) at III 5 430a18, according to the manuscripts. Instead, most modern editors (except Bekker) read *energeia* (an actuality) following Pseudo-Simplicius. The manuscript reading suggests that the cause is what it is in actuality, although, as Hicks (1907: 502) notes, Aristotle often seems to use both expressions equivalently.

63. See *DA* I 408b22–4 and *Phys.* VII 3 247b13–18.

64. Theophrastus (ap. Themistius *Paraph. de an.* 108.18–27) understands Aristotle this way: 'The mind is in a way mixed out of the productive and potential [minds]....Why are there forgetting and deception and falsehood? It may be because of the mixture'. See Devereux 1992: 41. See also Wians 2008 on why, according to Aristotle, it is difficult for human beings to know the highest things.

65. Male and female are defined functionally: 'By definition the male is that which is able to generate in another, and the female is that which is able to generate in itself and out of which comes to be the offspring previously existing in the generator' (*GA* I 2 716a20–3). The formal principle derives from the father alone via the semen; the mother provides only matter.

66. Wedin (1994: 83–4) distinguishes these two views under the rubrics 'spring theory' and 'surge theory'.

67. Wedin (1988: 189) who favours the lamplight or 'spring' version, translates the clause, 'it is not the case that there is something that at one time thinks and at another time does not think'; but nothing corresponds to 'there is something' in the Greek. Alternatively it would seem a stretch to suggest that Aristotle's point is that the productive mind does not think at all. Ancient commentators found this clause puzzling. Philoponus (*De intell.* 60.31) reports that some commentators proposed to delete the 'it is not the case that' (*ouch*), and it is in fact missing from Pseudo-Simplicius (*In de an.* 245.5). Philoponus himself (60.39–43) conjectures implausibly that the clause means that human minds (collectively) are always thinking.

68. This issue is well stated by Kosman (1992: 346–7), who calls the first-level interpretation 'the Standard View' because it is favoured by most commentators,

including Alexander of Aphrodisias and Aquinas. Kosman himself instead defends the second-level interpretation, as do Wedin (1989: 176; 1989:77) and Corkum (2004).

69. Compare Alexander: 'For as light is the cause of colours that are potentially visible becoming actually visible, so this third [i.e., productive] mind makes potential, that is, material mind, into actual mind by producing within it the intellectual disposition' (*De Anima* 107 31, quoted by Kosman 1992: 346).

70. This interpretation is succinctly stated by Aquinas (*In de an.* 730): 'The agent intellect…actualizes the intelligible notions themselves, abstracting them from matter, i.e., bringing them from potential to actual intelligibility'. Kahn (1981) offers a similar interpretation, although he advisedly eschews language of 'abstraction'. Cf. n. 15 above.

71. Kosman (1992: 348–9) argues that Aristotle views light as a third causal factor of perception 'on a par with' the pre-existing perceptive capacity and perceptible object. Kosman also cites *Sens* 7 447a11, 'light produces seeing'. By analogy, he argues, productive mind 'brings about the realization of second-actuality thought' (350).

72. This may shed light on the enigmatic statement that 'potential knowledge is prior in time in the individual, but on the whole it is not prior even in time'. (*DA* III 5 430a20–1, 7 431a2–3) Hicks (1907: 504), who notes the parallel with *Metaphysics*, remarks that for Aristotle, 'the potentiality is preceded by actuality, and we get knowledge by the active exercise of thought, for it is only in each individual person that the actuality, the exercise of power, is later to arise'.

73. The distinction was popularized by Brentano, who found it in Aristotle. As Brentano remarks, medieval scholastics spoke of the 'intentional inexistence' of an object in the mind (Brentano 1973: 88 and Brentano 1977: 77–80). Cf. Barnes 1971–2: 109–10 and the references in n. 31 above.

74. For the distinction between exemplifying and encoding see Shields 1997: 319–20.

75. Sisko (2000: 184) contends that Aristotle's entire argument for separability hinges largely on this tendentious first premise.

76. This underlies Aristotle's denial of the separability of Platonic Forms; cf. note 15 above.

77. See Ross 1961: 46–7.

BIBLIOGRAPHY

Ando, T. (1971) *Aristotle's Theory of Practical Cognition*, 3rd ed. (The Hague: Martinus Nijhoff).

Barnes, J. (1971–2) 'Aristotle's Concept of Mind', *Proceedings of the Aristotelian Society* 72, 101–14. Reprinted in *Articles on Aristotle*, v. 4 *Psychology & Aesthetics*, eds. J. Barnes, M. Schofield, and R. Sorabji (London: Duckworth, 1979), 32–41.

—— (1984) *The Complete Works of Aristotle: The Revised Oxford Translation* (Princeton: Princeton Univ. Press).

—— (1987) 'An Aristotelian Way with Scepticism', in *Aristotle Today*, ed. M. Matthen, (Edmonton, Alberta: Academic Publishing), 51–76.

Blumenthal, H.J. (1996) *Aristotle and Neoplatonism in Late Antiquity: Interpretations of the De Anima* (Ithaca, N.Y.: Cornell Univ. Press).

Bos, A.P. (2003) *The Soul and Its Instrumental Body: A Reinterpretation of Aristotle's Philosophy of Living Nature* (Leiden: Brill).

Brentano, F. (1973) *Psychology from an Empirical Standpoint* (London: Routledge). [Orig. *Psychologie vom empirischen Standpunkte*. Leipzig: Duncker & Humblot, 1874.]

———— (1977) *The Psychology of Aristotle, in Particular His Doctrine of the Active Intellect.* Trans. R. George (Berkeley: University of California Press, 1977). [Orig. *Die Psychologie des Aristoteles, insbesondere seine Lehre vom NOUS POIÊTIKOS.* Mainz: Franz Kirchheim, 1867.]

Broadie, S. (1996) '*Nous* and Nature in *De Anima* III', *Proceedings of the Boston Area Colloquium in Ancient Philosophy* 12, 163–92.

Burnyeat, M.F. (1992) 'Is an Aristotelian Philosophy of Mind Still Credible?' in *Essays on Aristotle's De Anima*, M.C. Nussbaum and A.O. Rorty, eds. (Oxford: Clarendon Press), 15–26.

———— (1995) 'How Much Happens When Aristotle Sees Red and Hears Middle C?' in *Essays on Aristotle's De Anima*, rev. edition, M.C. Nussbaum and A.O. Rorty, eds. (Oxford: Clarendon Press), 421–34.

———— (2002) '*De Anima* II 5', *Phronesis* 47, 29–90.

———— (2008) *Aristotle's Divine Intellect* (Milwaukee, Wisc.: Marquette Univ. Press).

Cassirer, H. (1968) *Aristotles' Schrift "Von der Seele" und ihre Stellung inerhalb der aristotelischen Philosophie* (Darmstadt: Wissenschaftliche Buchgesellschaft).

Caston, V. (1998) 'Aristotle and the Problem of Intentionality', *Philosophy and Phenomenological Research* 58, 249–98.

———— (1999) 'Aristotle's Two Intellects: A Modest Proposal', *Phronesis* 44, 199–227.

———— (2000) 'Aristotle on Understanding and the Body', *Proceedings of the Boston Area Colloquium in Ancient Philosophy* 16, 135–75.

———— (2002) 'Aristotle on Consciousness', *Mind* 111, 751–815.

Charlton, W. (1987) 'Aristotle on the Place of Mind in Nature', in *Philosophical Issues in Aristotle's Biology*, A. Gotthelf and J.G. Lennox, eds. (Cambridge: Cambridge Univ. Press), 408–23.

Clark, S. R.L. (1975) *Aristotle's Man: Speculations upon Aristotelian Anthropology* (Oxford: Oxford Univ. Press).

Corcilius, K. and Pavel Gregoric (2010) 'Separability vs. Difference: Parts and Capacities of the Soul in Aristotle'. *Oxford Studies in Ancient Philosophy* 34, 81–119.

Corkum, Ph. (2004) 'Aristotle on Consciousness', *Newsletter of the Society for Ancient Greek Philosophy* 5.1, 1–14.

———— (2008) 'Aristotle on Ontological Dependence', *Phronesis* 53, 65–92.

Côté, A. (2005) 'Intellection and Divine Causation in Aristotle', *Southern Journal of Philosophy* 43, 25–39.

Dancy, R.M. (1996) 'Keeping Body and Soul Together: On Aristotle's Theory of Forms', in *Aristotle's Philosophical Development*, W.R. Wians, ed. (Lanham, Md.: Rowman and Littlefield), 249–87.

De Koninck, Th. (1994) 'Aristotle on God as Thought Thinking Itself', *Review of Metaphysics* 47, 471–515.

Devereux, D. (1992) 'Theophrastus on the Intellect', in *Theophrastus: His Psychological, Doxographical, and Scientific Writings*, W.W. Fortenbaugh and D. Gutas, eds. (New Brunswick, N.J.: Transaction), 32–43.

Everson, S. (1997) *Aristotle on Perception* (Oxford: Clarendon Press).

Fine, G. (1984) 'Separation', *Oxford Studies in Ancient Philosophy* 2, 31–86.

———— (1985) 'Separation: A Reply to Morrison', *Oxford Studies in Ancient Philosophy* 3, 159–65. Fine (1984 and 1985) repr. in *Plato on Knowledge and Form*, Gail Fine, ed., (Oxford: Clarendon Press), 252–300.

Frede, M. (1996) 'La théorie aristotélicienne d'intellect agent', in *Corps et Âme: Sur De Anime d'Aristote*, C. Viano, ed. (Paris: Vrin), 376–90.

George, R. (1978) 'Brentano's Relation to Aristotle', in *Die Philosophie Franz Brentanos*, R.M. Chisholm and R. Haller, eds., *Grazer Philosophische Studien* 5 (Amsterdam: [Rodopi]) 249–66.

Gerson, L.P. (2005) *Aristotle and Other Platonists* (Ithaca, N.Y.: Cornell Univ. Press).

Gill, M.L. (1991) 'Aristotle on Self-Motion' in *Aristotle's Physics: A Collection of Essays*, L. Judson, ed., (Oxford: Clarendon Press), 243–65. Repr. in *Self-Motion from Aristotle to Newton*, M.L. Gill and J.G. Lennox, eds. (Princeton: Princeton Univ. Press, 1994), 15–34.

Guthrie, W.K.C. (1981) *Aristotle: An encounter* (vol. 6 *A History of Greek Philosophy*) (Cambridge: Cambridge Univ. Press).

Hamelin, O. (1953) *La théorie de l'intellect d'après Aristote et ses commentateurs* (Paris: J. Vrin).

Hamlyn, D.W. (1968) *Aristotle De Anima Books II and III* (with passages from Book I), Clarendon Aristotle Series (Oxford: Clarendon Press). Reissued with a new introduction by C. Shields, 1993.

Heinaman, R. (2007) 'Actuality, Potentiality, and *De Anima* II.5', *Phronesis* 52, 139–87.

Hicks, R.D. (1907) *Aristotle De Anima*. With translation, introduction, and notes (Cambridge: Cambridge Univ. Press).

Huby, P. (1991) 'Studies in the Development of Language about Aristotle's *Nous*', *Oxford Studies in Ancient Philosophy* supp. vol., 129–43.

Jaeger, W. (1948) *Aristotle: Fundamentals of the History of His Development*, 2nd ed., trans. R. Robinson (Oxford: Oxford Univ. Press).

Johansen, T.K. (1998) *Aristotle on the Sense-organs* (Cambridge: Cambridge Univ. Press).

Kahn, C.H. (1981) 'The Role of *Nous* in the Cognition of First Principles in *Posterior Analytics* II.19', in *Aristotle on Science: The Posterior Analytics* (Proceedings of the Eighth Symposium Aristotelicum), E. Berti, ed. (Padua: Editrice Antenore), 385–414.

——— (1985) 'The Place of the Prime Mover in Aristotle's Teleology', in *Aristotle on Nature and Living Things*, Allan Gotthelf, ed. (Pittsburgh: Mathesis Publications), 183–205.

——— (1992) 'Aristotle on Thinking', in *Essays on Aristotle's De Anima*, M.C. Nussbaum and A.O. Rorty, eds. (Oxford: Clarendon Press), 359–79.

Karamanolis, G.E. (2006) *Plato and Aristotle in Agreement? Platonists on Aristotle from Antiochus to Porphyry* (Oxford: Clarendon Press).

Kosman, L.A. (1992) 'What Does the Maker Mind Make?' in *Essays on Aristotle's De Anima*, M.C. Nussbaum and A.O. Rorty, eds. (Oxford: Clarendon Press), 343–58.

Kurfess, H. (1911) *Zur Geschichte der Erklärung der aristotelischen Lehre vom sog. NOUS POIÊTIKOS und PATHÊTIKOS* (Tübingen: G. Schnürlen); repr. (New York: Garland, 1987).

Long, A.A. (1981) 'Aristotle and the History of Greek Scepticism', in *Studies in Aristotle*, D.J. O'Meara, ed. (Washington, DC: Catholic Univ. Press), 79–106.

Miller, F.D. (2000) 'Aristotle's Philosophy of Perception', *Proceedings of the Boston Area Colloquium in Ancient Philosophy* 15, 177–213.

Modrak, D.K. (1986) 'Aristotle on Thinking', *Proceedings of the Boston Area Colloquium in Ancient Philosophy* 2, 209–36.

Morrison, D. (1985a) '*Chôristos* in Aristotle', *Harvard Studies in Classical Philology* 89, 89–105.

——— (1985b) 'Separation in Aristotle's Metaphysics', *Oxford Studies in Ancient Philosophy* 3, 125–57 and 167–73.

Norman, R. (1969) 'Aristotle's Philosopher-God', *Phronesis* 14, 63–74.

Novak, J.A. (1995) 'The Zeller-Brentano Debate on the Origin of Mind', *The Journal of Neoplatonic Studies* 3, 123–52.

Nuyens, F. (1948) *L'évolution de la psychologie d'Aristote* (Louvain: Institut supérieur de philosophie).

Owens, J. (1976) 'A Note on Aristotle, *de Anima* 3.4, 429b9', *Phoenix* 30, 107–18.

Pichter, G. (1992) *Aristoteles' 'De Anima'* (Stuttgart: Klett-Cotta).

Polansky, R. (2007) *Aristotle's De Anima* (Cambridge: Cambridge Univ. Press).

Price, A.W. (1998) 'Aristotelian Perceptions', *Proceedings of the Boston Area Colloquium in Ancient Philosophy* 12, 285–309.

Rist, J.M. (1966) 'Notes on Aristotle *De anima* 3.5', *Classical Philology* 61, 8–20.

——— (1989) *The Mind of Aristotle: A Study in Philosophical Growth* (Toronto: University of Toronto Press).

Robinson, H. (1983) 'Aristotelian Dualism', *Oxford Studies in Ancient Philosophy* 1, 123–44.

Rodier, G. (1900) *Aristote Traité de l'Ame* (Paris: Ernest Leroux).

Ross, W.D. (1924) *Aristotle, Metaphysics*, Rev. text with introduction and commentary (Oxford: Clarendon Press).

——— (1956) *Aristotelis De Anima*, Oxford Classical Texts (Oxford: Clarendon Press).

——— (1961) *Aristotle, De Anima*, Edited with introduction and commentary (Oxford: Clarendon Press).

Shields, C. (1994) 'Mind and Motion in Aristotle', in *Self-Motion from Aristotle to Newton*, M.L. Gill and J.G. Lennox, eds. (Princeton: Princeton Univ. Press), 117–33.

——— (1997) 'Intentionality and Isomorphism in Aristotle', *Proceedings of the Boston Area Colloquium in Ancient Philosophy* 11, 307–30.

Sisko, J. (1999) 'On Separating the Intellect from the Body: Aristotle's *De Anima* iii.4, 429a20-b5', *Archiv für Geschichte der Philosophie* 81, 249–67.

——— (2000) 'Aristotle's *Nous* and the Modern Mind', *Proceedings of the Boston Area Colloquium in Ancient Philosophy* 16, 177–98.

Smyth, H.W. (1956) *Greek Grammar,* rev. G.M. Messing (Cambridge: Mass.: Harvard Univ. Press).

Sorabji, R. (1974) 'Body and Soul in Aristotle', *Philosophy* 70, 470–84. Repr. in *Articles on Aristotle*, v. 4 *Psychology & Aesthetics*, J. Barnes, M. Schofield, and R. Sorabji, eds. (London: Duckworth, 1979), 42–64.

——— (1991) 'From Aristotle to Brentano: The Development of the Concept of Intentionality', *Oxford Studies in Ancient Philosophy* supp. 1, 227–59.

Theiler, W. (1983) *Über die Seele*. Aristoteles Werke in deutscher Übersetzung, v. 13, 2nd edition, (Darmstadt: Wissenschaftliche Buchgesellschaft).

Tracy, Th. (1982) 'The Soul/Boatman Analogy in Aristotle's *De Anima*', *Classical Philology* 77, 97–112.

Vasiliou, I. (1996) 'Perception, Knowledge, and the Sceptic in Aristotle', *Oxford Studies in Ancient Philosophy* 14, 83–131.

Vlastos, G. (1987) 'Separation' in Plato', *Oxford Studies in Ancient Philosophy* 5, 187–96.

Wedin, M.V. (1988) *Mind and Imagination in Aristotle* (New Haven, Conn.: Yale Univ. Press).

——— (1989) 'Aristotle on the Mechanics of Thought', *Ancient Philosophy* 9, 69–86.

——— (1994) 'Aristotle on the Mind's Self-Motion', in *Self-Motion from Aristotle to Newton*, M.L. Gill and J.G. Lennox, eds. (Princeton: Princeton Univ. Press), 81–116.

Whiting, J. (2002) 'Locomotive Soul: The Parts of Soul in Aristotle's Scientific Works', *Oxford Studies in Ancient Philosophy* 22, 141–200.

Wians, W. (2008) 'Aristotle and the Problem of Human Knowledge', *The International Journal of the Platonic Tradition* 2, 41–64.

PART IV

BEING AND BEINGS

CHAPTER 14

BEING *QUA* BEING

CHRISTOPHER SHIELDS

I. THREE PROBLEMS ABOUT THE SCIENCE OF BEING *QUA* BEING

'THERE is a science (*epistêmê*),' says Aristotle, 'which studies being *qua* being (*to on hê(i) on*), and the attributes belonging to it in its own right' (*Met.* 1003a21–22). This claim, which opens *Metaphysics* IV 1, is both surprising and unsettling—surprising because Aristotle seems elsewhere to deny the existence of any such science and unsettling because his denial seems very plausibly grounded. He claims that each science (*epistêmê*) studies a unified genus (*APo* 87a39-b1), but he denies that there is a single genus for all beings (*APo* 92b14; *Top.* 121a16, b7–9; cf. *Met.* 998b22). Evidently, his two claims conspire against the science he announces: if there is no genus of being and every science requires its own genus, then there is no science of being. This seems, moreover, to be precisely the conclusion drawn by Aristotle in his *Eudemian Ethics*, where he maintains that we should no more look for a general science of being than we should look for a general science of goodness: 'Just as being is not something single for the things mentioned [viz. items across the categories], neither is the good; nor is there a single science of being or of the good' (*EE* 1217b33–35).

How, then, does Aristotle come to speak of a science of being *qua* being? What is its defining genus? Or, to put the question more prosaically, just what does the science of being *qua* being study?

It is important to appreciate from the outset that these questions, however simple and straightforward, already mask considerable complexity, because they themselves admit of a variety of different understandings. Scholars see that there is a problem about the science of being in Aristotle, but when we examine carefully the problem they report seeing, we discover a family of discrete problems rather than a single, shared problem serving as the locus of all their concerns.[1] It accordingly behoves us to make some effort to bring the problems of the science of being *qua* being into sharper relief before proceeding. This is only to say, however, that we should apply to Aristotle an adage of his own making: those wishing to make progress in philosophy, he says, should take care to state their problems well (*Met.* 995a27). In one sense, as we shall find, stating well and clearly the problems pertaining to the science of being *qua* being proves to be at least half the battle. Fortunately, the effort is not wasted, since, as Aristotle also implies, solutions to our problems often lie latent in their most precise formulations.

That said, the first problem about the science of being *qua* being, already mooted, seems reasonably straightforward, at least in its initial formulation: every science is arrayed over a single genus; there is no genus of being; hence there is no science of being (*APo* 87a9-b31, 92b14; *Top.* 121a16, b7–9; *EE* cf. *Met.* 998b22). Let us call this the *Possibility Problem*. How, given Aristotle's strictures on science (*epistêmê*), can there be a science of being *qua* being?

There is an immediate and rather easy, if unduly deflationary response to this first problem, thus formulated: Aristotle never says that there is a science of being (*to on*).[2] What he says, rather, is that there is a science of being *qua* being (*to on hê(i) on*). So, there is no contradiction introduced by the announcement of *Metaphysics* IV—at least not on the plausible assumption that a science of being need not be the same as a science of being *qua* being. So far, then, Aristotle is not immediately subject to the Possibility Problem.

That allowed, this easy response mainly serves only to focus our attention on a series of less easily addressed questions. How exactly might a science of being *qua* being differ from a science of being? How, if such a science is permissible, does the qualifier '*qua* being' circumvent the problem about there being no genus of being? Is the suggestion, then, that there is a genus of being *qua* being? What genus might that be? At first pass, any considerations militating against a genus of being tell equally against a genus of being *qua* being.[3]

When we explore questions of this sort, our first problem, the Possibility Problem, gives way to a second, namely the *Extension Problem*. What, precisely, does the science of being *qua* being take as its object of study? Immediately after introducing the science of being *qua* being, Aristotle highlights its complete generality:

> This science is not the same as any of those called partial sciences; for none of those investigate universally concerning being *qua* being, but cut off some part of being and consider what coincides with it, as for instance the mathematical sciences do. (*Met.* 1003a23–25).

The science of being *qua* being thus contrasts with the special sciences precisely in *not* cutting off any part of being; it considers not living beings, or mathematical beings, or beings subject to motion, but rather *all* beings, in so far as they are beings and not in so far as they move or live or exhibit quantitative features. Evidently, then, the science of being *qua* being examines everything there is. So, here too there seems an easy, deflationary answer, something in the manner of Quine:

> A curious thing about the ontological problem is its simplicity. It can be put in three Anglo-Saxon monosyllables: 'What is there?' It can be answered, moreover, in a word—'Everything'—and everyone will accept this answer as true.[4]

So we might address our Extension Problem. Question: Precisely which beings does the science of being *qua* being study? Answer: All of them.

Here again, however, the deflationary answer is immediately unsatisfactory, in two distinct ways. The first is a point of language. Aristotle's locution 'being *qua* being' (*to on hê(i) on*) might be taken in various different ways. In Aristotle's Greek, the word *being* (*to on*) is a neuter participle, formed off the verb *einai*, to be. Like its English counterpart, being, *to on* may be used as a substantive, in a count-nounish sort of way ('If there are a butcher, a baker, and a candle-stick maker in the room, then there are at least three beings in the room, unless, of course, one of them has more than one job'). Or it may be used non-substantively, as an abstract participle, which beings in the substantive sense might be said to *have* or share ('Everything which has being exists in space and time, and nothing lacking being exists; so, there are no abstract objects.') This second notion of being treats being as a sort of property or at least as property-like. Here any question of how many beings there are seems ill-formed, on par with asking how many airs there are. Given this linguistic distinction, one must ask whether, when Aristotle insists that the science of being *qua* being does not cut off any part of being, he is thinking of being abstractly or substantively. That is, does the science of being *qua* being study being, that feature all and only beings have in common, or does it study, rather, all the beings there are, considered as beings, but in no other way?[5]

Secondly, and more importantly, Aristotle's actual procedure in the chapters following his introduction of a science of being *qua* being undercuts any easy suggestion that this science must be straightforwardly universal in scope. For, strikingly, his procedure in these chapters undermines any confidence we might have in the suggestion that the science of being *qua* being takes as its object *all of being* or even *all beings*. In these chapters, Aristotle focuses relentlessly on what seems to be but one kind of being, namely substantial being (*ousia*), and, ultimately, on just one substantial being, namely the unmoved mover of *Metaphysics* XII. Patzig has presented the problem trenchantly:

> One of the most difficult problems of interpretation set by the *Metaphysics* lies in the fact that in book IV the 'sought-for science' is characterised very precisely as the science of 'being qua being'...Unlike the particular sciences, it does not deal with a particular area of being, but rather investigates everything that is, in its most general structural elements and principles....But, on the other hand, and startlingly, we also discover that in *Metaphysics* VI 1...Aristotle seems first to accept this opinion and then, immediately afterwards, to embrace its exact opposite. For in VI 1 we again find an analysis of the sciences designed to establish the proper place of 'first philosophy'. Here, however, Aristotle does not, as he did in book IV, distinguish the 'sought-for science' from all other sciences by its greater

generality. First he divides philosophy into three parts: theoretical, practical, and productive; and then he splits theoretical philosophy into three disciplines. To each of these disciplines he entrusts well-defined areas as objects of research. The 'sought-for science', referred to in IV as the 'science of being qua being', he now calls 'first philosophy', and defines it as the science of what is 'changeless and self-subsistent (*akinêton kai chôriston*)'. He explicitly gives it the title of 'theology'. Physics and mathematics stand beside it as the two neighbouring disciplines in the field of theoretical philosophy.[6]

In brief, if being *qua* being studies all beings, then it is perfectly general and does not take as its object one kind of being (*ousia*, substance), or, worse, one entity within that kind, the unmoved mover; if, by contrast, it studies just one kind of being, substance, or even one substance in particular, then the science of being *qua* being is not general, but rather a special science, alongside other theoretical sciences like physics and mathematics.

So, we have a serious Extension Problem. Aristotle announces a perfectly general science, but then evidently proceeds to conduct a special science, an inquiry into one kind of being among others, namely substance—and at its extreme, one substance among others, namely the unmoved mover. In fact, Aristotle seems almost blithe on this point:

> Indeed, what was sought of old and is sought at present and always, and what is always a matter of difficulty, namely *what is being*? (*ti to on*) is this: *what is substance*? (*tis hê ousia*) (*Met.* 1028b2–4).

In this single sentence, Aristotle seems to supplant his universal science of being with a special science of substance. Hence, the Extension Problem: what, precisely, does the science of being *qua* being study, everything or only some things?

The Extension Problem is well recognized and widely addressed; indeed, it is often treated as the defining problem of the science of being *qua* being. This is unfortunate, since another, less well recognized problem is in several ways more consequential than the Extension Problem.

This is the *Intension Problem*. If it is more consequential than the Extension Problem, the Intension Problem is also slightly harder to motivate. We can approach it by returning to the language of Aristotle's introduction of the science of being *qua* being. Four terms command our immediate attention: *science (epistêmê)*; *being (to on)*; *qua (hê(i))*; and *in its own right (kath' hauto)*. We have already briefly considered the first two. The Intension Problem arises in reference to the remaining two, and especially to the last.

Typically when Aristotle uses what we will call the *qua-locution*, that is, the dative relative pronoun (*hê(i)*), which is traditionally rendered into Latin *qua*, after a substantive, he does so in order to qualify the term preceding it so as to direct attention to a subset of an entity's properties. For instance, when we say that we are considering surfaces *qua* coloured, we are focusing on the colour-features of a surface only, and ignoring, for instance, the question of whether the surface is smooth or rough, and also, indeed, any features which may be necessarily co-extensive with the surface's colour features, such as its being extended.

One immediate question concerns why Aristotle so often finds it instructive to use this device. It will prove noteworthy that very often he uses the *qua*-locution as an analytical device in sophistic contexts, when he wishes to combat seductive but fallacious inferences by focusing on those properties relevant to an inference structure while setting aside those which are not. So, for example, consider the spurious inference from:

(1) Socrates and Socrates seated are one and the same.
(2) When seated-Socrates stands, seated-Socrates goes out of existence.

to

(3) So, when seated-Socrates stands, Socrates goes out of existence.[7]

Of course, (3) does not follow from (1) and (2). What is relevant in the present context is Aristotle's diagnosis of what has gone wrong. He thinks that Socrates and Socrates-seated are indeed one and the same, but only co-incidentally (*kata sumbebêkos*). That is, seated-Socrates and Socrates are one in the sense that they coincide. Socrates is not, then, seated *per se*, in his own right (*kath' hauto*); what he is in his own right includes what he is essentially, namely a human being, a rational animal. So, since he does not go out of existence in so far as he is a human being when he rises, Socrates persists when seated-Socrates rises.

Aristotle's habit of deploying the *qua*-locution in this context suggests that, in the case of being, he means to study beings precisely in so far as they are beings, and in no other way. If this is so, then when speaking of being *qua* being, Aristotle signals that he means to refrain from studying beings in so far as they are any particular kinds of beings. Even if it is true that every being is a being of some kind or other, a metaphysician will wish to reflect upon what it is for a being to be a being *before*, so to speak, it is this or that kind of being. Looked at this way, the *qua*-locution is a sort of a filter.[8] In the phrase 'Socrates *qua* human being does not perish when Socrates *qua* seated does' the *qua*-locution filters so as to focus on one feature in the first occurrence while filtering to focus on a second, distinct feature in the second occurrence. So, by parity of reasoning, in the phrase 'being *qua* being' Aristotle means to filter out *all* features of beings beyond the bare fact of their being beings.

In focusing on beings just as beings, and in no other way, Aristotle seeks to study beings as they are in themselves, in their own right (*kath' hauto*). In this respect, his science of being proves to be like other sciences; for studying the *per se* features of things is the business of science (*epistêmê*) in general, whatever the domain in question. A science seeks to capture the nature or essence of its object of study:

> We think we understand a thing without qualification, and not in the sophistic, accidental way, whenever we think we know the cause in virtue of which something is—that it is the cause of that very thing—and also know that this cannot be otherwise. Clearly, science (*epistêmê*) is something of this sort. After all, both those in possession of science and those without it suppose that this is so—although only those in possession of science are actually in this condition. Hence, whatever is known without qualification cannot be otherwise (*APo* 71b9–16; cf. *APo* 71b33–72a5; *Top.* 141b3–14, *Phys.* 184a10–23; *Met.* 1029b3–13).

Accordingly, assuming that the science of being *qua* being meets the requisites of science in general, we should expect it to exhibit the following three features: (i) it should take as its object being *qua* being (*to on hê(i) to on*); (ii) it should state the features belonging *per se* (*kath' hauto*) to being *qua* being; and (iii) it should state the causes (*aitia*) of being *qua* being.

This last requirement Aristotle fully appreciates and acknowledges. Indeed, it seems prominent in his mind when he introduces the science in *Metaphysics* IV: 'Hence, it is also necessary for us to find the first causes (*aitia*) of being *qua* being' (*Met.* 1003a31–2). This suggests, then, that when he introduces the science of being *qua* being, Aristotle expects it to conform to the strictures on science set forth in the *Posterior Analytics*.

With this in mind, we can understand the Problem of Intension more readily. This is because the Problem of Intension pertains to the second criterion of *epistêmê*, namely that the *epistêmê* of a given domain **D** must state those features belonging to the members of **D** *per se* (*kath' hauta*). As a first approximation, we might expect these features to be those belonging *essentially* to the members of **D**. Thus, for instance, a science of human beings will capture and exhibit the *nature* of human beings, which will involve capturing and stating the essence shared by all and only members of the species *human being*. Let us suppose, in line with Aristotle's suggestion in *Nicomachean Ethics* I 5, that the nature of human beings is *to be rational*. (One might dispute this claim in more or less radical ways—by contending that essentialism is false or by contending that this misidentifies the essence of humanity—but that is not our present concern. Let essentialism of an Aristotelian variety be accepted; then the science of human beings will focus on humans *qua* rational beings.) In general, if Φ is the essence of the members of some domain **D**, the science of **D** focuses on the members of **D** *qua* Φ.

With that accepted, we can put the Problem of Intension succinctly: what might Φ be for **D** when the domain is all beings? What is it, precisely, to study beings in so far as they are beings? Are beings essentially anything at all, as beings?

We immediately run up against the worry that beings have no essence in so far as they are beings. To begin, to state the essence of some **D** seems to involve *defining* that domain, which normally proceeds by distinguishing those features which are essential to members of **D** from those which are not; this activity, however, presupposes minimal complexity for those members. Thus, human beings all have skin, and this trait, according to Aristotle's approach, is universal without being essential; other traits are accidental, manifested by some humans at some times, and these too will trivially be discounted as contenders for Φ, precisely because 'whatever is known without qualification cannot be otherwise' (*APo* 71b16). Being *qua* being, however, does not manifest any immediately discernible complexity. As Aquinas has noted in a parallel context, when speaking of actuality: 'Simple notions cannot be defined, since an infinite regress in definitions is impossible. But actuality is one of those simple notions. Hence, it cannot be defined' (Aquinas, *Comm. in Aris. Meta.* IX. 5. 1826). One might well think the same of being, in which case there would no more be a science of being *qua* being than there would be a science of actuality.

Further, recalling that Aristotle often deploys the *qua*-locution in anti-sophistic contexts, we can also raise the Problem of Intension from another angle. Both being-seated and being-human appear to be intrinsic features of Socrates. We can filter the intrinsic features of entities in various different ways by means of the *qua*-locution, and one way, especially prevalent in anti-sophistic contexts concerned with change and generation, is to filter them along the divide of what an entity is in its own right *versus* what it is co-incidentally. In this sense, the phrase *per se (kath' hauto)* is implicitly *contrastive*, selecting between different sets of an entity's intrinsic features. One is inclined to ask, then: which of being's intrinsic features belong to it merely co-incidentally (*kata sumbebêkos*)? What exact contrast does Aristotle take himself to be making in the case of being?

The Problem of Intension is thus continuous with but also crucially distinct from the other problems already introduced, the Extension Problem and the Possibility Problem. In brief, then, these three problems are:

1. The Possibility Problem: Given Aristotle's express requirements for *epistêmê*, how is a science of being *qua* being possible?
2. The Extension Problem: Presuming that it is possible, what precisely does the science of being *qua* being study?
3. The Intension Problem: If a science seeks to state the essence Φ of its domain **D**, what might Φ be when **D** is the domain of all beings?

Though clearly distinct, these problems are also importantly related. In what follows, I urge the following crucial connection: by refining and answering the Intension Problem, we are afforded answers to both the Extension and Possibility Problems.

II. Addressing the Extension Problem First

Partly because they have paid little attention to the Intension Problem, commentators have often focused first on the Extension Problem, hoping thereby also to solve the Possibility Problem. This approach merits consideration, both because it is rooted in authentically Aristotelian doctrine and because it has dominated discussion of the science of being *qua* being over much of the latter half of the twentieth century. The most influential statement owes to Patzig,[9] perhaps unsurprisingly since, as we have seen, so too does the clearest formulation of the Extension Problem in modern times.

The Extension Problem begins with a legitimate worry born of the observation that Aristotle first speaks of the science of being *qua* being quite generally, in universal terms, but then proceeds to execute it by concentrating on but one category of being, substance (*ousia*), and then ultimately on one substance, the divine substance. It would be wrong to proceed as if Aristotle himself were unaware of this concern, since he himself gives voice to what seems a nascent version of the Extension Problem in *Metaphysics* VI 1:

> Someone might raise a problem as to whether first philosophy is universal and deals with a particular genus and one particular nature…If there is no other substance apart from those constituted by nature, then physics would be the first science. But if there is some changeless substance, this is prior and philosophy is the first science, and it would be universal in this way, because it is first; and it would fall to it to investigate concerning being *qua* being, both what it is and that which belongs to it *qua* being (*Met.* 1026a23–32).

Aristotle's remark, brief though it is, seems to imply that one studies being *qua* being *by* studying the changeless prime mover, and that by engaging in the study of this object, first philosophy qualifies as universal.

This suggestion, left undeveloped by Aristotle, has recommended a promising approach to the Extension Problem, especially when it is recalled that in the beginning of *Metaphysics* IV, Aristotle calls attention to his apparatus of *core-dependent homonymy* not long after introducing the science of being *qua* being.[10] He says:

> It falls to one science to study not only things that are spoken of in virtue of one thing, but also things that are called what they are relative to one nature (*Met.* 1003b12–14; cf. *Met.* 1004a24–15).

One might study being in general, then, by studying the nature of being, and this study it will undertake by turning to its primary instance. The primary kind of being is substance (*ousia*), and the primary substance is the unmoved mover. Hence, the primary focus of being *qua* being might well be this, the most exemplary being.

More precisely, one might suggest, following Patzig,[11] that all beings in non-substance categories depend upon substance for their existence. As Aristotle himself contends, 'if there were no primary substance, nothing else could exist' (*Cat.* 2a34). So, the suggestion runs, any account of a being in a non-substance category, say quality or relation, will ultimately require some appeal to substance. Hence, the study of being ultimately leads back to substance (*ousia*). Further, even within the category of substance, there is a still more ultimate priority, in that all substances, along with all other beings, finally depend upon the unmoved mover, which Aristotle identifies as the final cause of all existence (*Met.* 1071b1–3). This, then, would give some content to Aristotle's brief suggestion that the prime mover is 'universal because it is first' (*Met.* 1026a30–31): it is the core instance of being, and because *all* being ultimately depends upon it, the prime mover attains a kind of universality in its primacy. So, the science of being *qua* being, in the end, studies the primary being, as most fundamental.

If we are prepared to grant that much, we can see both promise and problem associated with the apparatus of core-dependent homonymy as regards the Extension Problem. The promise is plain: core-dependent homonymy offers a framework within which claims about dependence can be rendered precise. More exactly, it offers a framework within which claims about dependence can be made precise without adverting to external considerations of an efficient causal sort. This is desirable because mere efficient causal dependence does not bring with it the sort of unity needed for *epistêmê*. A ship might depend upon a group of men, some ship builders, in the sense that they are its efficient cause, but Aristotle rightly shows no tendency to suggest that this suffices for there to be an *epistêmê* of man-and-ship. Rather, there is a branch of natural science which studies humans and a branch of productive science which studies shipbuilding.

This approach is promising in yet another way: if it successfully solves the Extension Problem, then it simultaneously solves the Possibility Problem. This is because it in effect proceeds by relaxing Aristotle's condition on domain specification. When Aristotle says that a single science may study 'not only things that are spoken of in virtue of one thing, but also things that are called what they are relative to one nature' (*Met.* 1003b12–14; cf. *Met.* 1004a22–25), he seems to be allowing that core-dependent homonymy, though insufficient for sameness of genus, is none the less sufficient for the sort of unity required for *epistêmê*. If that is so, and if being is itself a core-dependent homonym, then the *epistêmê* of being *qua* being is at once possible and has a subject matter.

On this approach, Aristotle can, so to speak, have it both ways about the extension of the *epistêmê* of being *qua* being. He can think of the domain of the *epistêmê* of being *qua* being as all of being, cutting off no part of it, even though its execution ultimately focuses on just one being, the primary being. So, although one is forced by Aristotle's procedure in the *Metaphysics* to ask whether the *epistêmê* of being *qua* being studies all beings insofar as they are beings, or merely one category of being, substance, or even finally, just one member of that category, the divine being, according to the current approach to the Extension Problem, this question presents a false dichotomy. The science of being *qua* being studies all beings *by* studying substance, and studies substance, finally, *by* studying the divine being.

How, precisely, though, is this study, with this focus, to be effected? In addressing this question, we encounter our first serious problem with this initially promising approach to the Extension Problem. This emerges quite clearly when we attempt to explicate the precise sense in which all beings *depend* upon substance and so ultimately upon the prime mover. In Aristotle's preferred illustrations of core-dependent homonymy, the kind of dependence envisaged is reasonably easy to state. It is *account-dependence*.[12] That is, any account of a non-core-dependent instance of Φ must appeal ineliminably and in an asymmetric way to the account of Φ as it occurs in the core instance. To illustrate, using Aristotle's own preferred illustration (*Met.* 1003a34-b6):

1. Socrates *is healthy.*
2. Socrates' diet *is healthy.*
3. Socrates' complexion *is healthy.*

We are meant to grasp three points directly, which may be most readily appreciated when stated in a semantic idiom (though, in the end, they concern essence-specifying rather than lexical definitions). First, the predicate 'is healthy' means different things in these instances. In (1), it means, let us say, 'flourishing physically'. But this could not be what it means in (2) or (3). That would yield nonsense, such as 'Socrates' diet is flourishing physically.' This lack of intersubstitutability is, Aristotle contends (*Top.* I 15), a clear indication that their meanings diverge. So, we have non-univocity across these instances. Second, we are meant to appreciate that, even so, these applications are related, and related in an intimate sort of way. They are not what Aristotle calls 'chance homonyms' (*EN* 1096b26–7), the sort we encounter in English in the case of '…is a bank', as it is applied to sides of rivers and to monetary institutions. Still, third, and most crucially, the predicates in (2) and (3) are crucially related to the predicate in (1): they depend for their explications on the predicate in (1), though the converse does not hold. To explicate the predicate '…is healthy' in (3), for instance, would be to say that Socrates' complexion 'indicates that he is *flourishing physically*' where the italicized bit is just the account of '…is healthy' in (1). By contrast, that account, which explicates the predicate as it occurs in (1), makes no reference to the accounts of the occurrences in (2) or (3). Thus, the non-core instances are account-dependent on the core instance in an asymmetrical way.

Strictly, then, we should expect the accounts of being in non-substance categories to depend in an asymmetrical way on the account of being as it is applied to substance. Here some precision is required. The suggestion is not the various non-substantial categories themselves—*being a quality* or *being a quantity* or *being a location*—do not admit of different accounts; for plainly they do. Being a quantity is not the same thing as being a quality, and neither is the same thing as being a substance. Yet that is not what is at issue. What is needed to make good on the initial promise of this approach to the Extension Problem is rather the more extreme and difficult claim that *the being* of quantities and qualities and locations and substances all differ. Moreover, again on the current approach, the problem is not just inter-categorial but also intra-categorial, because we must explain not only how the being of substances is prior to the being of non-substances but also how the being of one substance, the divine substance, is distinct from and prior to the being of other substances.

One can see the great difficulty in this suggestion by substituting *being* for *is healthy* in Aristotle's preferred illustration of the philosophical phenomenon he is seeking to capture:

1. Socrates is.
2. Socrates' being in the agora is.
3. Socrates' weighing 14 stone is.
4. The unmoved mover is.

If the predicate '…is healthy' is to be our guide, then we should expect a three-stage process in establishing that being is a core-dependent homonym. First, each of these predicates should admit of an account. Second, the accounts should prove to be non-univocal, for otherwise, we would have univocity and not homonymy, core-dependent or otherwise. Third, having proceeded that far, the accounts of (2) and (3) would need to be shown to exhibit asymmetrical, core-dependence on the account of (1), which would then in its turn need to be shown to exhibit the same form of asymmetrical core-dependence on the account of the predicate as it occurs in (4). The current approach to the Extension Problem founders at every stage. No account of this predicate has been offered; no attempt at establishing non-univocity for this predicate has been undertaken; and no ordering of these proscriptively distinct accounts in terms of core-dependence has been effected. This is perhaps unsurprising, because we are not given much to work with when we have only the predicate '...is'.

To be clear, one does not succeed in this endeavour, as many commentators seem to have supposed,[13] merely by showing (if indeed it can be shown) that items in non-substance categories depend for their existence on substances. For, let that be so. This would do nothing to show that the predicate '...is', as it applies to these members of these various categories of being is anything but univocal. Nor does it suffice to appeal in a vague way to *ways of being* in this connection. Thus, for example, in an effort to explicate and expand the governing insight of Patzig's approach to the Extension Problem, Frede contends:

> [L]et us try to understand how it is that theology is not concerned only with a particular kind of beings, but with a particular way of being, peculiar to its objects, and how it addresses itself to this way of being. By distinguishing a kind of beings and a way of being I mean to make a distinction of the following sort. Horses are a kind of beings, and camels are a different kind of beings, but neither horses nor camels have a distinctive way of being, peculiar to them; they both have the way of natural substances, as opposed to, e.g., numbers which have the way of magnitudes, or qualities which have yet a different way of being. The way magnitudes can be said to be is different from the way qualities or natural substances can be said to be. The claim, then, is that the way separate substances can be said to be is peculiar to separate substances.[14]

How many ways of being are there? It is noteworthy in this passage that we are told that there are not only distinct inter-categorial ways of being—the way of being of quantities differs from the way of being of qualities and these differ again from the way of being of substances—but also distinct intra-categorial ways of being—the way of being of natural substances differs from the way of being of separated substances. So, there are, then, at least eleven ways of being, one for each of the non-substance categories and two for the category of substance, depending on whether the substances in question are natural or separated. That there are 'at least' eleven ways of being marks the concern that we have not been given any indication how ways of being are to be generated or delimited. Do the ways of being of discrete and continuous quantities come to the same, or do they differ? The ways of being of colours and sounds? Of thoughts and perceptions? Aristotle marks many different sorts of intra-categorial divisions in his *Categories*. Should we suppose, then, that the intra-categorial divisions regarding ways of being extend beyond the category of substance, that they range across all categories for which Aristotle marks intra-categorial divisions? If limited to substance, is there some principled reason why this should be so? What of actual versus potential being, a distinction Aristotle marks as fundamental but also as fundamentally distinct from his theory of categories (*Met.* 1045b26–1046a2)? Are these again still further and discrete ways of being? Because we are not yet in a position to answer these questions, we cannot say with assurance how many ways of being there are meant to be, or even if they are to be limited or rather open-ended in number. So, we have no ready way even to begin evaluating the proposal under consideration.

Be that as it may, we are meant according to the current proposal to agree that there are several *ways of being*, and that these ways of being are to be distinguished from *kinds of beings*, and that it is the divergence in ways of being rather than in kinds of beings that grounds a solution to the Extension Problem. To make good on this suggestion, then, we would expect the proponents of this approach to the Extension Problem to: (i) provide accounts of (at least) these eleven ways of being; (ii) to show that they are non-univocal; and (iii) to exhibit the core-dependencies obtaining between them. Unfortunately, a vague gesture in the direction of putatively distinct ways of being does not suffice in this regard. Nor indeed does this gesture resonate with any explicit or implicit distinction made anywhere in the Aristotelian corpus. Although he certainly thinks that being is a core-dependent homonym, Aristotle never says that he thinks this is due to the fact that different kinds of beings—or different kinds of the same kind of being in the case of substance—exhibit different ways of being.

So, we should not be sanguine that there is a defensible approach to the Extension Problem to be developed along these lines. That said, and to be clear, in raising this problem we do not establish that this approach to the Extension Problem has nothing to commend it. On the contrary, except for the foray into (putative) ways of being, it seems initially promising, not least because the basic suggestion that being is a core-dependent homonym is plainly connected in Aristotle's text to his introduction of an *epistêmê* of being *qua* being (*Met.* 1003a33-b12). That allowed, so far at least, this approach to the Extension Problem fails to deliver on its initial promise. The best that can be said at this juncture is that this approach is unfinished. There is, unfortunately, it must also be said, reason to doubt that this circumstance will be rectified.

III. Approaching the Intension Problem

If this initially promising approach to the Extension Problem stalls, that may seem especially unwelcome. The problem, as Patzig rightly observed, has been to show how Aristotle can first trumpet the generality, the universality, of an *epistêmê* of being *qua* being only to focus narrowly on just one category of being and then on just one being within that category. So far, the apparatus of core-dependent homonymy has not been deployed to good effect in addressing this problem.

This result recommends that we step back from the problem as we have been considering it, and that we take Aristotle's own advice and set out our problems well in order to approach the issue afresh. One point of entry, less explored than the Possibility and Extension Problems, is the Intension Problem. That problem, as we have characterized it, takes as its focal point Aristotle's contention that the *epistêmê* in question studies being *qua* being and 'the attributes belonging to it *in its own right (kath' hauto)*' (*Met.* 1003a21–22). As we have seen, it is not entirely clear which features belong to being *per se*.

We can see that there is some difficulty about this matter if we pause to consider the various ways in which Aristotle's translators have rendered this phrase into English, and, more importantly, how they have glossed their translations. A non-exhaustive list already contains the following:

- Owens: 'There is a science which considers Being *qua* Being, and what belongs to it *per se*'.[15]
- 'This science treats universally of Being as Being'[16] . . . 'The short opening of Book IV is quite succinct. It must have required considerable amplification for the "hearers" during an ensuing discussion in the Lyceum'.[17]

Owens's translation is duly cautious, and his remarks fair-minded and understated; but they do not specify which features belong to being *per se*.

- Ross: 'There is a science which investigates being as being and the attributes which belong to this in virtue of its own nature'.
- 'This description of metaphysics distinguishes it from other sciences not by its method but by its subject'.[18]

Ross's translation is surprising. In what follows, however, I shall suggest that it is essentially correct—if not as a translation, then as an appropriate paraphrase of what Aristotle intends by the language of this passage. Note, however, that his gloss does not specify precisely what the subject matter of metaphysics might be and so does not address the Extension Problem. Note also that his translation raises, in an especially pressing manner, the Intension Problem: What is the nature of being as being? How, indeed, is it to be conceived as having a nature?

- Irwin: 'There is a science which studies being *qua* being and its intrinsic properties'.
- 'The science of being studies not primarily a distinct class of objects, but a distinct property of objects'.[19]

Like Ross, Irwin offers an expansive translation, and, again, like Ross, his translation captures something important but also raises a question: which property is the property studied by the science of being *qua* being?

- Apostle: 'There is a science which investigates being *qua* being and what belongs essentially to it'.
- 'The contrast between "accidentally" and "qua" seems to be that between an accidental cause and an essential cause'.[20]

Apostle, like Ross and Irwin, offers a translation which represents a decision about how best to understand the science of being *qua* being. Apostle ties Aristotle's remark to his theory of causation in his gloss. Again, this seems a reasonable suggestion, but it points to a direction of explication distinct from what either Ross or Irwin suggests.

- Kirwan: 'There is a discipline which studies that which is *qua* thing-that-is and those things that hold good of this in its own right'.
- '"In its own right" is opposed to "coincidentally"'.[21]

Finally, Kirwan offers a translation which takes a definite stand on the question mooted earlier regarding how to understand the neuter participle *to on*: he treats it as a substantive. His gloss, like Apostle's, ties Aristotle's remark to his theory of predication, again reasonably, though also again pointing towards an avenue of explication distinct from Aristotle's other expositors.

We review these various translations not to suggest that some one of them is clearly superior to the others, or still less that one of them gets Aristotle uniquely right while the others miss the mark. On the contrary, as a purely linguistic matter, none is to be wholly faulted; each is, in its own way, a fair representation of Aristotle's Greek, which, just as Owens says, requires 'considerable amplification'. Rather, the sheer number of acceptable translations, together with their various glosses, only serves to underscore the difficult urgency of the Intension Problem. The *epistêmê* announced studies being *qua* being and 'the attributes belonging to it *in its own right* (*kath' hauto*)' (*Met.* 1003a21–22). What might these be?

The glosses canvassed variously seek to illuminate Aristotle's point by way of contrast. As they note, his *epistêmê* does not concern itself with the attributes belonging to being in some way other than *in its own right* (*kath' hauto*). Yet they do not agree about the same contrast implied by his locution. According to these various renderings, the implied contrast might be a causal contrast, or a predictive contrast of one sort or another, a contrast between essence and accident, a contrast between that which does and does not pertain to something's nature, or it might, more generically, contrast the co-incidental and the non-co-incidental.

One way to approach Aristotle's probable meaning is to begin with an examination of his terminology. This is especially important because *in its own right* (*kath' hauto*), or, to use Owens's neutral Latin rendering, *per se*, is plainly a technical term for Aristotle.

In fact, the term is used widely by Aristotle, but, significantly for the current context, it features crucially in his theory of demonstration and science in the *Prior* and *Posterior Analytics*. At *Posterior Analytics* 73a34-b5, Aristotle distinguishes four different notions of *per se* predication, the second two of which cast some light on his procedure in the middle books of the *Metaphysics*. He distinguishes the following:

- Φ is predicated *kath' hauto* of x if (a) Φ is predicated of x; and (b) Φ must be mentioned in an (essence-specifying) account of x.

Thus, animal is predicated *kath' hauto* of Alcibiades, since any essence-specifying account of him will be at best incomplete for failing to mention this property.

- Φ is predicated *kath' hauto* of x if (a) Φ is predicated of x; and (b) x must be mentioned in an (essence-specifying) account of Φ.

Thus, oddness is predicated of a given number; but any account of what oddness is will perforce advert to *number* in its *definiens*. In saying that oddness is predicated of number *kath' hauto* we are highlighting, then, a metaphysically binding reciprocity between subject and predicate, though we are not thereby indicating something *essential* to the subject.

This last point merits a brief explication, because it bears on the concern already mooted about how one might conceive the essence of *being*, as opposed, for instance, to the essence of *human beings*. Aristotle's theory of essence must be distinguished from those contemporary theories of essence which are *merely modal*. Merely modal essentialism holds:

- Φ is an essential property of x *iff* if x loses Φ, then x ceases to exist.

Aristotle regards this as incorrect because insufficient: some properties are such that the entity which possesses them goes out of existence with their loss even though they are inessential. These are *idia* (*Cat.* 3a21, 4a10; *Top.* 102a18–30, 134a5–135b6), including such properties as *being grammatical* for human beings. Aristotle thinks of *idia* as follows:

> An *idion* is a property that does not reveal the essence (*to ti ên einai*), though it belongs only to that subject and is convertibly predicated of it. It is an *idion* of humans, for example, to be capable of grammatical knowledge; for if someone is a human, he is capable of knowledge, and if someone is capable of grammatical knowledge, he is a human. For no one counts something as an *idion* if it can belong to something else. For example, no one counts being asleep as an *idion* of humans, not even if at some time it should happen to belong only to humans (*Top.* 102a18–28).

Here Aristotle distinguishes two types of universally held properties which do not count as essential: those which are invariably predicated of a kind at a time, even though they need not have been (all humans at present have the property of living in a world where some humans have been to the moon), and those which are predicated of necessity, even though they are inessential, like being grammatical. This second type constitutes the class of *idia*. Thus, the Aristotelian essentialist holds:

- Φ is an essential property of x *iff* (i) if x loses Φ, then x ceases to exist; and (ii) Φ is in an objective sense an explanatorily basic feature of x.

A property Φ qualifies as explanatorily basic in an objective sense when it asymmetrically explains other features of its bearer, including even those whose loss entails the non-existence of that bearer.

With that notion of essence in hand, we can see that Aristotle means to distinguish two importantly distinct kinds of *per se* predication, the second of which has direct application to his science of being *qua* being. According to the second notion of *per se* predication adumbrated, a given whole number has the property *being even* predicated of it. As Aristotle says, *being even* is predicated of this number *per se*, but that is because in order to explicate what it is for something to be even, it will be necessary along the way to specify that it is a number. To be even is simply to be a number divisible by two without remainder. Similarly, if one predicates grammaticality of a rational being, then, in order to provide an account of grammaticality, it will be necessary to specify that grammaticality is the ability to master and manipulate syntax in a rationally constrained manner. Similarly, in line with this same form of *per se* prediction, if Φ belongs to any random being of necessity, such that in order to explicate what Φ is we must acknowledge that it pertains to all beings just because they are beings, then we have identified a feature holding universally of beings simply because they are beings—that is, a feature of beings *qua* beings.

Given his distinction between types of *per se* predication, Aristotle is in a position to characterize all beings insofar as they are beings, by focusing on just those features beings manifest *per se*; and he may do so without thereby being constrained to treat being *qua* being as having an essence to be uncovered and displayed in the way, for instance, a science of human beings would display the essence of humanity, rationality let us say. Of every being, one must say that it is a being, of course. More importantly, of every being, one must say what features it manifests just as a being, and in virtue of no other feature it has. A human being is *per se* rational, according to Aristotle, that is, insofar as it is a human being. What, if anything, might a human being be not insofar as it is a human being, but merely insofar as it is a being? In order to answer this question, we will need to point to those features a human being has in common with all other beings, no matter what sort of beings they are and merely insofar as they are beings. These are the features that belong *per se* to human beings in common with all other beings simply as beings. These are, accordingly, the attributes considered by the *epistêmê* of being *qua* being.

IV. The *Per Se* Features of Being

Aristotle's actual practice in the *Metaphysics* makes good sense if we are expecting him to assay the features of being *qua* being by focusing on just those features of beings manifested *per se* but not essentially—not essentially, that is, in the Aristotelian and not merely modal sense of essentialism. This is why we should resist Apostle's otherwise understandable periphrastic translation, that 'There is a science which investigates being *qua* being and what belongs essentially to it.' This gives a misleading impression if we are thinking strictly of Aristotelian and not merely modal essentialism. The features Aristotle in fact discusses in the *Metaphysics* hold of being not essentially in his sense, but hold rather *per se* in the sense just explicated. They are not essential in the sense of being the intrinsic, explanatorily basic features of some internally complex sort of entity like a human being. Nor are they the sorts of features which hold universally but in a contingent manner, of the sort Aristotle identifies in the *Topics*, when he rightly observes that some features may simply happen to hold of all instances of a kind without their needing to do so (*Top.* 102a18–28). The *per se* features of beings are more than universal, belonging necessarily but not essentially.

What might these features be? In executing his science of being *qua* being, Aristotle focuses on three sets of *per se* features above all others:

- Beings are as beings *logically circumscribed.*
- Beings are as beings *categorially delineated.*
- Beings are as beings *modally enmeshed.*

Let us review each of these features in turn.

One of the first orders of business for Aristotle's *epistêmê* of being *qua* being is initially somewhat perplexing: he sets out to offer an indirect defense of the principle of non-contradiction. He contends in both *Metaphysics* IV 1 and 2 that the science of being *qua* being appropriately concerns itself with substance, but he does not investigate substance immediately. This is because, as he contends, any science which considers substance will clearly need to address itself to general axioms such as the principle of non-contradiction (*Met.* 1005a19-b12). He then offers an elenchtic defense of this principle, that is, a defense which does not undertake to prove the principle of non-contradiction directly, but instead purports to show that anyone engaged in even the most rudimentary activity presupposed by science— signifying individual things—implicitly commits himself to that principle (*Met.* 1005b35–1007a20).

The precise character of Aristotle's elenchtic defense of the principle of non-contradiction does not concern us at present; still less does its ultimate defensibility.[22] Rather, in the present context, we need only appreciate why this discussion should occur where it does in Aristotle's program of scientific inquiry into being. It is not that according to Aristotle such a defense must be mounted as an indispensible preliminary to rational inquiry, although he does believe that is so. It is, rather, that a defense of the principle of non-contradiction *constitutes* the first activity of the science of being *qua* being. It belongs to all beings insofar as they are beings, he contends, to be subject to the principle of non-contradiction. The attribute *being subject to the principle of non-contradiction* belongs *per se* to all beings insofar as they are beings, and not insofar as they are this or that kind of being. It holds of human substances, of quantities of matter, of locations, and indeed all entities belonging in any arbitrarily chosen category of being. All beings, as beings, are *per se logically circumscribed.*

If the principle of non-contradiction applies to any arbitrarily selected being belonging to any category whatsoever, then this is not because it is arbitrary that every being in fact belongs to some category or other; on the contrary, according to Aristotle, every being belongs to precisely the category it does given the kind of being it is. It is not arbitrary, but rather necessary, then, that every being belong to some category or other; consequently, this feature too belongs to all beings just insofar as they are beings, that every being be *categorially delineated*. Aristotle makes this point clearly, and in connection with the final *per se* attribute he investigates with great industry in the middle books of his *Metaphysics*, namely that all beings, as beings, are either in actuality or in potentiality. They must be in this way *modally enmeshed*:

> Since being (*to on*) is said in one way with reference to what something is, or some quality or quantity, and in another way with respect to potentiality and actuality (*entelecheia*) and with respect to function, let us make determinations about potentiality and actuality—first about potentiality most properly so called, even though this is not the most useful for what we want now (*Met.* 1045b32–1046a1).

This passage, which introduces the subject matter of *Metaphysics* IX, yokes together two fundamental *per se* attributes of being, that all beings, as beings, answer first to the theory of categories and then also to the paired features of potentiality (being in *dunamei*) and actuality (being in *entelecheia(i)*).[23] His point here, as well as in the case of the principle of non-contradiction, is that it falls to the metaphysician to investigate these modalities not as propaideutic to the *epistêmê* of being *qua* being, but rather as constituting the very activity of this science. This is because every being—because it is a being and not because it is a being belonging to this or that category or because within a given category it belongs to this or that species or genus, but simply because it is a being—is something actual or potential. *Being modally enmeshed* belongs *per se* to every being, just as a being.

We can now appreciate how Ross's translation, if unduly periphrastic, is basically apt as a rudimentary interpretation of Aristotle's intended meaning: 'There is a science which investigates being as being and the attributes which belong to this in virtue of its own nature.'[24] The *epistêmê* which studies being *qua* being considers not the essence of being, in the Aristotelian sense of essence, because beings as beings have no internal logical complexity. Rather this *epistêmê* explicates the nature of beings as beings, by charting what pertains of necessity to all beings precisely and only as beings. What it uncovers is this: all beings, insofar as they are beings, are logically circumscribed, categorially delineated, and modally enmeshed. Explaining what each of these features is falls to the metaphysician, and this is why Aristotle engages in just this sort of explanatory activity in the middle books of his *Metaphysics*. In explicating each feature, it inescapably emerges that each of these features is itself a being—which is to say that each fits perfectly the paradigm of the second form of *per se* predication identified by Aristotle in the *Posterior Analytics*.

This, then, provides our approach to the Problem of Intension. One ancillary benefit of this approach is that it helps pave the way to a solution to the Possibility and Extension Problems as well. To begin, it recommends a useful articulation of the Possibility Problem along the following lines:

1. Every science is individuated by a domain unified by a property which is essential, invariant, and explanatorily basic.
2. A property Φ is essential, invariant, and explanatorily basic only if Φ is predicated *kath' hauto* of the members of some domain.
3. A property Φ is predicated *kath' hauto* of some domain only if Φ is or is subordinate to a generic property.
4. Being (*to on*) is not a genus; so, being is not a generic property.
5. Being (*to on*) is subordinate to nothing; so, being is not subordinate to a generic property.
6. Hence, there is no science whose domain is all beings with being (*to on*) as its unifying essential, invariant, and explanatorily basic property.

Hence, according to this line of thought, no science is a science of being. Nor is there a science of being *qua* being (*to on hê(i) on*): the same argument may be formulated, with the same result, by substituting being *qua* being (*to on hê(i) on*) for being (*to on*).

By assessing in some depth how Aristotle conceives *per se* predication, we see that he rejects both (1) and (3), and with good reason. A feature may well be predicated of some domain necessarily and invariantly without its being essential—in Aristotle's enhanced, non-modal sense of essence—to the members of that domain.

V. A SCIENCE OF CAUSES

If we are prepared to understand Aristotle's attitude towards the Problem of Intension along these lines, then we can understand a fair bit of his actual procedure when he turns to execute his science of being *qua* being in the *Metaphysics*. Even granting that, one important matter remains crucially unexplained, namely his investigation into substance. This is to say, then, that even if we are prepared to go along with the suggested approach to the Intension and Possibility problems, so far there is no direct application to the Extension Problem. If we allow that the *per se* features of being involve being *logically circumscribed, categorially delineated*, and *modally enmeshed*, this by itself gives us no reason to expect an intensive investigation into the nature of substance; yet this is precisely what Aristotle says his science requires (*Met.* 1028b2–7). This requires some explication and defence, since it does not seem to be the case that *being a substance* or even *being suitably related to a substance* qualifies as a *per se* feature of being. What, then, does our approach to the Intension Problem recommend as regards the Extension Problem?

The most promising avenue of investigation begins once again in a reconsideration of our statement of the problem, one directly commended by our approach to the Intension Problem. Once suitably reframed in light of that approach, the Extension Problem finds a promising resolution in one traditional treatment. Accordingly, this treatment, which takes seriously Aristotle's contention that *epistêmê* investigates the causes (*aitia*) of its special domain of inquiry, merits renewed and reinvigorated support.

Recall, then, that in contrasting genuine scientific knowledge with sophistic, Aristotle stressed awareness of causes as crucial: 'We think we understand a thing without qualification, and not in the sophistic, accidental way, whenever we think we know the cause in virtue of which something is—that it is the cause of that very thing' (*APo* 71b9–12; cf. *APo* 71b33–72a5; *Top.* 141b3–14; *Phys.* 184a10–23; *Met.* 1029b3–13). Accordingly, we should have some knowledge of being *qua* being just when, according to Aristotle, we can specify the causes of being *qua* being. So, if we find him studying the cause of being *qua* being in an effort to execute this science, we should find this unsurprising, as conforming to this scientific method, rather than as a problem about the domain of being *qua* being.

Let us, then, look afresh at the Extension Problem, in light of what we have seen about the Intension Problem. As formulated, the Extension Problem was to be a problem, effectively, about special *versus* general metaphysics: if perfectly general, then the science of being *qua* being would need to investigate all of being, and not just some part of being, or some particular beings to the exclusion of other beings; if specific, then this same science would need to focus exclusively on just certain privileged beings rather than being in its totality. In that case, however, it would be hard to appreciate how Aristotle could possibly characterize it as he does in the opening of *Metaphysics* IV 1, where he insists that his *epistêmê* is perfectly general, that it refrains from cutting off some part of being as do all other, more narrowly focused sciences. Then, in *Metaphysics* VI 1, Aristotle seems to startle his readers, just as Patzig indicates, by calling the science of being *qua* being 'first philosophy', before—again according to Patzig—he 'defines it as the science of what is "changeless and self-subsistent".' This science, named 'theology' by Aristotle, can hardly be co-extensive with the science of being *qua* being: one studies just *one* being while the other studies *all* of being.

One can thus helpfully formulate the Problem of Extension as an inconsistent triad of propositions: (i) the *epistêmê* of being *qua* being takes as its extension all beings; (ii) first philosophy, or theology, has as its extension just one being; (iii) the *epistêmê* of being *qua* being and first philosophy, or theology, are the same science.[25] In effect, the approach to the Extension problem advocated by Patzig and again, somewhat differently by Owen,[26] denies (ii): they in their different ways suppose that since (iii) is correct, then if (i) is correct, (ii) must be denied. On the approach urged, since theology *is* the *epistêmê* of being *qua* being, and that *epistêmê* studies all beings, so too must theology. It is just that the study of all beings leads us, in the normal way of core-dependent homonyms, to the core of being, divine being. We have seen, however, that this promising approach runs afoul of the clear need to specify the non-univocity of being required of all cases of core-dependent homonymy.

Even so, the general strategy embraced by this approach may yet prove fruitful, though from an altogether different angle. In particular, the suggestion that one should maintain both (i) and (iii) while jettisoning (ii) is right-minded. The first clue as to why this is so, however, tells against the particular implementation of this general strategy embraced by Patzig. This comes to the fore when we consider more minutely his contention that in *Metaphysics* VII 1 Aristotle introduces first philosophy, or theology, and then '*defines* it as the science of what is "changeless and self-subsistent"' (my emphasis). For Aristotle does no such thing. What Aristotle actually says is this:

> If there is no substance other than those which are constituted by nature, physics would be the first science (*protê epistêmê*); but if there is some other, immovable substance, the science of this will be prior and will be first philosophy—and universal in this way, because it is first. And it would belong to it to study being *qua* being—both what it is (*ti esti*) and the attributes belonging to it *qua* being (*Met.* 1026a27–33).

Aristotle does not in this passage *define* first philosophy as the subject which studies the unmovable substance; for indeed he does not define first philosophy at all, either here or elsewhere. Moreover, there is no claim even implicit in this passage to the effect that first philosophy studies *only* the divine being. Rather, Aristotle says merely that if there exists anything beyond substances constituted by nature—if there is some immovable substance (*ousia akinêtos*; *Met.* 1026a29), then its study will belong to first science, but that it will also 'belong to it [viz. this same first science] to study being *qua* being' (*peri tou ontos hê(i) on tautês an eiê theôrêsai*; *Met.* 1026a31).

Aristotle's phrasing here is a matter of some consequence. When he contends that the first philosophy is to study what is changeless and separate (as I would prefer to render *chôriston*), Aristotle does not thereby imply that this science studies *only* that being, or even that it takes it as its individuating object—as opposed to contending merely that the immovable substance is simply one particular object in its domain. Indeed, so far, at least, there is no reason to suppose that Aristotle thinks that being *qua* being must study this object insofar as it is any particular sort of being. That is, Aristotle gives in this passage no reason to conclude that being *qua* being studies the separate and unmovable substance insofar as it is a substance, or insofar as it is separate, or insofar as it is anything whatsoever other than a being. As a being, of course, the divine substance is an object of first philosophy along with every other being, insofar as it is a being and in no other way. Consequently, there is no reason to conclude that first philosophy studies this being exclusively. Still less, then, is there reason to suppose that first philosophy is defined as the study which considers this one being to the exclusion of all others.

This is fortunate, since Aristotle is adamant in the *Metaphysics* that being *qua* being is general rather than specific. Its being especially concerned with the features of some class of beings is, however, perfectly consonant with this generality—so long as Aristotle does not suggest that it studies these beings to the exclusion of other beings. He may yet draw special attention to some sub-class of beings if they are somehow primary as causes or principles of all beings. His doing so would be, in fact, in accord with his normal scientific procedure. So much, in fact, seems to be a consequence he envisages and hopes to implement successfully. That being *qua* being conforms to this general pattern of scientific inquiry Aristotle makes plain already in the first book of the *Metaphysics*:

> It is evident that this (*sophia*) is a science (*epistêmê*) of certain principles and causes (*archai* and *aitiai*). But since this is the science we are seeking, this is what we must consider: of what sorts of principles and causes is wisdom (*sophia*) a science (*epistêmê*)? (*Met.* 982a1–6)

Thus, being *qua* being, like other sciences, pursues an explanation of the items in its domain by investigating their principles and causes (cf. *Met.* 983a29, 990a2, 1013a17, 1025b4, 1042a5, 1069a26). We should thus expect this most general science to focus on those principles and causes which are the principles and causes of all beings. We should, in fact, expect this science, if it is first philosophy, the first and most primary of the theoretical sciences, to focus on the *first* principles and causes of being *qua* being.

The point I am advancing just now is hardly original with me, but was widely and thoroughly appreciated by many of Aristotle's earlier commentators. It bears renewing, however, since it seems to have receded into the background of more recent scholarship on Aristotle.[27] Versions of it were expressed by Albertus Magnus[28] and Duns Scotus,[29] and also in a characteristically clear and compelling manner by Thomas Aquinas:

> Although this science studies the three things mentioned earlier [*scil.*, first causes, maximally universal principles, and separate substances], it does not study any of them as its subject, but only being in general. For the subject of a science is the thing whose causes and attributes are studied; and it is not the very causes of the genus which are themselves under investigation. For cognition of the cause of some genus is the end which investigation in a science attains.[30]

This is just so: Aristotle does not maintain that the science of being *qua* being studies the divine substance as its sole or exclusive object. Instead, the sole and exclusive object of inquiry for the science of first philosophy is being *qua* being. Even so, first philosophy might yet investigate the divine substance as a principle (*archê*) or cause (*aition*) of all beings in so far as they are beings—if, that is, the divine being is such a principle or cause.

So far, then, we have a sort of unfinished resolution to the Problem of Extension: (ii) is false, since first philosophy, or theology, does not have as its extension just one being. So, there is no inconsistent triad and so no Problem of Extension. Significantly, this solution makes no appeal to the homonymy of being, and so finds itself unsaddled with the difficulties attendant to that approach. Just as significantly, however, this resolution remains unfinished. This is because so far it leaves two crucial questions unanswered. First, *how* is the divine being a principle or cause of all beings just insofar as they are beings? Second, *how* is substance in general a principle or cause of all beings in non-substantial categories?

It is in response to these crucial questions that our resolution of the comparatively abstract and nebulous Problem of Intension provides some especially useful direction. All beings, just insofar as they are beings, are categorially delineated and modally enmeshed. Every being is a being in some category or other (or, in the case of certain kinds of complex cases, is a being analysable into beings situated in some category or other); and every being is a being in actuality or in potentiality. Notably, when Aristotle turns to consider these latter *per se* attributes of being, that is, potentiality and actuality, he makes a connection to their being principles and causes:

> We have shown elsewhere that potentiality and being potential are spoken of in many ways (*legetai pollochôs*). Of these, those that are called in potentiality homonymously should be set aside (for some are so called because of some similarity, as in geometry and we speak of what is possible and impossible because things are or are not in a certain way); but those that relate to the same form (*to auto eidos*) are all sources (*archai*) and are spoken of with reference to the primary one [viz. the primary source (*archê*)], which is the source (*archê*) of change in something other than itself or in itself *qua* other (*Met.* 1046a4–11).

The passage presents some difficulties,[31] but in the present context one feature is both reasonably clear and clearly relevant: the *per se* feature of being modally enmeshed pertains to beings which move because motion itself requires an explanation given in terms of suitable principles, where the relevant sense of principle (*archê*) plainly includes the sense in which a principle is a cause (*aition*) (cf. *Met.* 983a29, 990a2, 1013a17, 1025b4, 1042a5, 1069a26). This is a point emphasized in Aristotle's definition of motion in the *Physics* as 'actuality of what is in potentiality *qua* such' (*Phys.* 201a10–11; *hê tou dunamei ontos entelecheia hê(i) toiouton*). So, when we think of beings which move, we must seek their principles in part in the *per se* attributes of beings in potentiality and actuality.

Not all beings move, of course. So, no account of beings *qua* beings should focus on motion as a feature of all beings. On the contrary, motion is, instead, just as Aristotle suggests, the delimiting feature of those beings studied by *Physics*. At the same time, as Aristotle goes on to make clear in his account of the *per se* feature of being modally enmeshed, *all* beings, those which move, and those which do not, manifest a dependence on what is purely actual: 'For in some cases we have change (*kinêsis*) related to potentiality (*dunamis*), and in other cases substance (*ousia*) related to some matter' (*Met.* 1048a25-b9). It is the latter sort of case, where substance (*ousia*) is related to matter which makes explicit the connection between the *per se* feature of being modally enmeshed and the theory of categories, and so to the *per se* feature of being categorially delineated, and so, finally, to the category of substance (*ousia*). For every substance (*ousia*) is, as Aristotle repeatedly emphasizes, an actuality (*Met.* 1042b11, 1043a24–35, 1044a7, 1050b2). This is because 'among all the other categories, nothing is separate (*chôriston*), but rather substance *alone*' (*Met.* 1028a33–34). If substance alone is separate, or self-subsistent, then every being is either a substance or requires the being of substance to underpin its own being. In this sense, contends Aristotle, the being of substance is a principle (*archê*) and cause (*aition*) of the being of all other beings. Inescapably, then, a science studying being as being will, in looking to its sources and causes, focus on substance (*ousia*). Far from studying substance to the exclusion of other categories of beings, according to Aristotle, the *episetêmê* of being *qua* being studies substance (*ousia*) *because* it is engaged in the activity of studying all beings as beings. Substance is a principle and cause of all other beings.

Since something may be a principle (*archê*) or cause (*aition*) of something else without its being the core of a core-dependent homonym, Aristotle need not appeal to the (putative) core homonymy of being in order to solve the Extension Problem. It is solved, rather, by the connection he draws between two *per se* features of beings insofar as they are beings, being modally enmeshed and being categorially delineated. All categorially delineated beings depend upon one category, substance (*ousia*), as their principle (*archê*) and cause (*aition*). The subject matter of first philosophy is, just as Aristotle says in introducing his science, being *qua* being. Still, because all beings, as beings and in no other way, have as a principle (*archê*) and cause (*aition*) substance (*ousia*), it falls to this same science to investigate substance [if possible] —not as an object but as a cause.

Consequently, we may revisit afresh Aristotle's alignment of the science of being *qua* being with an investigation into *ousia*: 'Indeed, what was sought of old and is sought at present and always, and what is always a matter of difficulty, namely *what is being?* (*ti to on*) is this: *what is substance?* (*tis hê ousia*)' (*Met.* 1028b2–4). He does not here *supplant* general ontology with special ontology, but announces that he intends to pursue general ontology by conducting special ontology. If our resolution of the Problem of Intension points us in the right direction, his direction of inquiry here is non-negotiable and so, ultimately, unavoidable for the metaphysician. In order to investigate being *qua* being, the metaphysician *must* investigate its principles and causes (its *archai* and *aitia*), and so must follow the road to substance (*ousia*) (*Met.* 1003b6–7). When he does so, the metaphysician does not abandon all of being as an object of study, but instead offers a suitably scientific explanation of being *qua* being by investigating its primary causes and principles.

This direction of study Aristotle articulates rather plainly already in the first book of his *Metaphysics*: 'It (*sophia*) must be a science (*epistêmê*) of first principles and causes (*prôtai archai* and *aitiai*)' (*Met.* 982b9–10; cf. *Met.* 1003a31–2).

VI. Conclusion

The *Metaphysics* announces Aristotle's *epistêmê* of being *qua* being in a self-conscious sort of way. Perhaps this science is not quite 'triumphantly affirmed and re-affirmed in the *Metaphysics*',[32] but there certainly is an air of deliberate decision about Aristotle's introduction of it, as if he thought first philosophy required a justification, perhaps because it lacks the clear purposes and agenda we identify so readily in the other theoretical sciences, mathematics and physics. Indeed, Aristotle even speaks frequently of being *qua* being as a science *which must be sought out* (*Met.* 982a1–6, 1028b2–4), as if the business of first philosophy were somehow obscured from the honest inquirer's view, whereas the puzzles of natural philosophy need no seeking but simply thrust themselves upon us. If his concern is that first philosophy, because so highly abstract, has an elusive subject matter as its quarry, then Aristotle's concern is entirely well-placed: the science of being *qua* being does need some special pleading—especially from Aristotle, who at some points in his career indicates grave reservations about the prospects of any such perfectly general science. Aristotle is, of course, hardly alone in voicing such concerns, which are commonplace even among the friends of metaphysics. As we are aware from our own current remove, worries about the provenance and point of metaphysics have plagued philosophers from Aristotle right down to the present day.[33]

From this perspective, Aristotle's self-consciousness is entirely apposite: what is it, precisely, that the first philosopher undertakes to do? Aristotle asks a question of his own in response: 'If not the philosopher, then who will ask whether Socrates and Socrates seated are one and the same' (*Met.* 1004b1–3)? The person asking such a question may at first seem charmingly *dégagé*;[34] in fact, though, this is for Aristotle an entirely earnest question whose point is grasped when we appreciate that its answer implicates us in determining what it is *in general*, and not only for Socrates, for a being to be one and the same thing, what it is, then, for a being, simply insofar as it is a being, to be something definite and determinate, for it to be one kind of thing rather than some other kind of thing, and for it to be something real and actual as opposed to something merely potential. This is just to ask, in our terminology, then, what it is for a being to be logically circumscribed, categorially delineated, and modally enmeshed. These are the sorts of questions the first philosopher addresses, as we glean from Aristotle's practice in the *Metaphysics*, and this is why the science of being *qua* being is not only possible, but also universal in extension and focused in intension. This is why, in short, Aristotle regards himself as not merely at liberty but in fact compelled to assert that 'There is a science (*epistêmê*) which studies being *qua* being, and the attributes belonging to this in its own right (*kath' hauto*)' (*Met.* 1003a21–2).[35]

Notes

1. The large modern literature on this topic reflects the lively diversity in Aristotelian philosophical scholarship. Some especially noteworthy contributions: Brentano (1962/1975), Jaeger (1923/1948), Owens (1978), Leszl (1975), Ross (1924), Aubenque (1962), and Mansion (1976).

2. This is a point clearly made by Guthrie (1981, 206–207) in passing, and developed to good effect by Code (1996). As Guthrie suggests: 'The existence of a science of being *qua* being, or ontology, so triumphantly affirmed and re-affirmed in the *Metaphysics*, appears at first sight to be contradicted by a passage from the *Eudemian Ethics* [scilicet 1217b33ff.]....It may be significant that he says only that there is no single science of being (*to on*) not of being qua being (*to on hê(i) on*).'

3. Scholars have motivated Aristotle's reservations about there being a genus of being differently. One especially rich suggestion finds a full and philosophically adroit development in Loux (1973). See Shields (1999, Ch. Nine) for a different, more critical account of Aristotle's motivations.

4. Quine (1948, 21).

5. One might have thought the answer given in the fact that *to on* is singular, so that Aristotle is thinking of being, in general, and not of beings, however many they may be. In fact, however, the linguistic data is not decisive, since *to on*, again like *being* might be a singular distributive term (like 'trout' in 'The trout is a wily fish.'), so that Aristotle is suggesting that the science of being *qua* being studies what it is for any random being to be a being, as opposed to some particular kind of being, perhaps a mathematical or a physical or a living being. Heading in the opposite direction, however, we find Aristotle willing to speak of beings *qua* beings (*onta hê(i) onta*; *Met.* 1003b15–16), where, obviously, the clear suggestion seems to be that he is treating the term substantively, and so as a sort of count-noun. So, even at the linguistic level we are left unsure which object or objects Aristotle takes the science of being *qua* being to study.

6. Patzig (1960).

7. This inference is reconstructed from *Sophistical Refutations* 5 (*SE* 5 24 179a26-b6; cf. *Met.* 1015b17, 1017b31; *Top.* 103a30; *Phys.* 190a19–21; *EE* 1240b25–260.

8. Lear (1982, 168) puts the matter clearly, though I would myself dispense with his epistemic emphasis: 'Thus to use the *qua*-operator is to place ourselves behind a veil of ignorance: we allow ourselves to know only that *b* is *F* and then determine on the basis of that knowledge alone what other properties must hold of it. If, for example, *b* is a bronze isosceles triangle—*Br(b)* & *Is(b)* & *Tr(b)*—then to consider *b* as a triangle—*b qua Tr*—is to apply a predicate filter: it filters out the predicates like Br and Is that happen to be true of *b*, but are irrelevant to our current concern.'

9. Patzig (1960). See also Wedin (2009, 139–141) and Shields (1999, Ch. Nine).

10. The phrase 'core-dependent' derives from Shields (1999), which prefers this locution to other similar terms, including Owen's (1960) 'focal meaning' and Irwin's (1998) 'focal connexion'. These are all representations of Aristotle's device of *pros hen* homonymy. On the relative merits of these terms, see Shields (1999) and Ward (2007).

11. Patzig (1960). Patzig's view was developed and defended by Frede (1987).

12. On account dependence, see Shields (2009, Chs. One and Four).

13. For a critical discussion, see Shields (1999, Ch. Nine).

14. Frede (1987, 87).

15. Owens (1978, 259).

16. Owens (1978, 259).

17. Owens (1978, 262).
18. Ross (1924 vol. i, 251).
19. Irwin (1988, 169).
20. Apostle (1966, 282).
21. Kirwan (1971, 76).
22. For an informative discussion, see Wedin (2009).
23. For an approach to this complex distinction as it features in Aristotle's discussion of substance, see Shields (2009).
24. Ross (1924 vol. i, 251).
25. Aristotle also refers to this science as wisdom (*sophia*), for example at *Met.* 982a16–19, 982b9, 996b9, 1059a18–34, 1060a10, though he also uses this same term, *sophia*, more widely to include all theoretical sciences, so that it refers not only to first philosophy but also physics and mathematics (*Met.* 981a27, 1005b1; *EN* 1141b1).
26. Owen (1960).
27. It has not disappeared altogether, however. Some scholars who adopt this general orientation include Décarie (1961), Follon (1992), and Duarte (2007).
28. Albertus Magnus, *Comm. in Met.* lib. 4, cap. 3.
29. Duns Scotus, *Exposito in Duodecim Libros Metaphysicorum Aristotelis*, lib. 4 summa prima, cap. 1.
30. Aquinas, *Comm. in Meta*, prol.
31. See Shields (2009).
32. See note 2 above.
33. The discipline as it has developed today finds ample space for volumes treating topics in *meta*-metaphysics, volumes dedicated, that is, to questions about the possibility and point of the set of inquiries descended from the science Aristotle called first philosophy. See, e.g., the engaging volume of papers edited by Chalmers *et al.* (2009).
34. See Shields (forthcoming) for an exploration of the force of this question. It may seem as if Aristotle is asking a rhetorical question ('Who will ask this question if not the philosopher?') with the obvious answer: 'Nobody'. In fact, his worry is that someone other than the philosopher stands perfectly ready to answer it, and to deleterious consequences, namely *the sophist*.
35. The topics of this chapter formed the basis of two overlapping graduate seminars at the University of Oxford. I am grateful to the students on both occasions for their beneficial participation. I especially thank one member of those seminars, Thomas Ainsworth, who additionally read a draft of this chapter and offered numerous incisive criticisms and corrections. An earlier draft was presented to the Society for Ancient Greek Philosophy in New York in 2009; the current version benefits from the instructive reactions of members of that audience. Finally, I presented the main claims contained in this chapter to the Oxford Ancient Philosophy Workshop in 2008, where probing questions and criticisms were advanced by Lesley Brown, David Charles, and Terence Irwin. I thank them all for their astute assistance.

Bibliography

Apostle, H. (1966) *Aristotle's Metaphysics: Translation and Commentary* (London: Indiana Univ. Press).

Aubenque, P. (1962) *Le problème de l'être chez Aristote* (Paris: Presses universitaires de France).

Brentano, F. (1975) *On the Several Senses of Being in Aristotle*, ed. and trans. R. George (Berkeley: Univ. of California Press). Orignially: *Von der mannigfachen Bedeutung des Seienden nach Aristoteles* (Freiburg i.B.: Herder, 1862).

Chalmers, D., D. Manley, and R. Wasserman, eds. (2009) *Metametaphysics: New Essays on the Foundations of Ontology* (Oxford: Oxford Univ. Press).

Code, A. (1996) 'Owen on the Development of Aristotle's Metaphysics', in *Aristotle's Philosophical Development: Problems and Prospects,* W. Wians, ed. (London: Rowman & Littlefield), 303–325.

—— (1997) 'Aristotle's Metaphysics as a Science of Principles,' *Revue Internationale de Philosophie* 51, 357–378.

Décarie, V. (1971) *L'objet de la métaphysique selon Aristote* (Paris: Vrin).

Defilippo, J. (1998) 'First Philosophy and the Kinds of Substance,' *Journal of the History of Philosophy* 36, 1–28.

Duarte, S. (2007) 'Aristotle's Theology and Its Relation to the Science of Being *qua* Being,' *Apeiron* 40 (3), 267–318.

Ferejohn, M. (1980) 'Aristotle on Focal Meaning and the Unity of Science', *Phronesis* 25, 117–128.

Follon, J. (1992) 'Le concept de philosophie première dans la *Métaphysique* d'Aristote,' *Revue Philosophique de Louvain*, 90, S. 387–421.

Frede, M. (1987) 'The Unity of General and Special Metaphysics: Aristotle's Conception of Metaphysics,' *Essays in Ancient Philosophy* (Oxford: Clarendon Press), 81–95.

Gerson, L. (1991) 'Causality, Univocity, and First Philosophy in *Metaphysics* ii', *Ancient Philosophy* 11, 331–348.

Gill, M.L, (2006) 'First Philosophy in Aristotle', in *A Companion to Ancient Philosophy: Blackwell Companions to Philosophy*, M. Gill, ed. (Oxford: Blackwell Publishing), 347–373.

Guthrie, W.K.C. (1981) *A History of Greek Philosophy vol VI: Aristotle: An Encounter* (Cambridge: Cambridge Univ. Press).

Jaeger, W. (1948) *Aristotle: Fundamentals of the History of his Development*, trans. R. Robinson, 2nd ed. (Oxford: Clarendon Press). Originally: *Aristoteles: Grundlegung einer Geschichte seiner Entwicklung* (Berlin: Weidmann, 1923).

Kirwan, C. (1971) *Aristotle Metaphysics Books Γ, Δ, and E* (Oxford: Clarendon Press).

Lear, J. (1982) 'Aristotle's Philosophy of Mathematics,' *The Philosophical Review* 91, 161–192.

Leszl, W. (1975) *Aristotle's Conception of Ontology* (Padua: Antore).

Loux, M. (1973) 'Aristotle on the Transcendentals,' *Phronesis* 18, 225–239.

Mansion, A. (1958) 'Philosophie première, philosophie seconde et métaphysique chez Aristote', *Revue philosophique de Louvain* 56, 165–221.

Mansion, S. (1976) *Le jugement d'existence chez Aristote,* 2nd ed. (Louvain: Éditions de l'Institut supérieur de philosophie).

Merlan, P. (1968) 'On the Terms 'Metaphysics' and 'Being-qua-Being'', *Monist* 52, 174–194.

Moreau, J. (1977) 'Remarques sur l'ontologie aristotelicienne,' *Revue Philosophique de Louvain* 75, 577–611.

Owen, G.E.L., 'Logic and Metaphysics in Some Early Works of Aristotle', in I. Düring and G.E.L. Owen, eds., *Aristotle and Plato in the Mid-Fourth Century*, 163–190; reprinted in M. Nussbaum, ed., *Logic, Science, and Dialectic* (London: Duckworth, 1986).

Owens, J. (1978) *The Doctrine of Being in Aristotle's Metaphysics*, 3rd ed. (Toronto: Pontifical Institute of Medieval Studies).

—— (1992) 'The Keystone of the Aristotelian 'Metaphysics', *Journal of Neoplatonic Studies* 1, 125–131.

Patzig, G. (1962) Theologie und ontology in der 'Metaphysik' des Aristoteles', *Kant-Studien* 52, 185–205; trans. by J. Barnes as 'Theology and Ontology in Aristotle's Metaphysics', in J. Barnes, M. Schofield, and R. Sorabji, eds., *Articles on Aristotle* vol. 3 (London: Duckworth: 1979), 33–49.

Quine, W.V.O. (1948) 'On What There Is', *Review of Metaphysics* 2, 21–38.

Reiner, H. (1955) 'Die Entstehung der Lehre vom bibliothekarischen Ursprung des Namens Metaphysik', *Zeitschrift für philosophische Forschung*, 77–79.

Ross, W.D. (1924) *Aristotle: Metaphyics* vols. I and II (Oxford: Clarendon Press).

—— (1957) 'The Development of Aristotle's Thought', *Proceedings of the British Academy* 43, 63–78; reprinted in J. Barnes, M. Schofield, and R. Sorabji, eds., *Articles on Aristotle*, 4 vols. (London: Duckworth: 1975–9), 1–13.

Shields, C. (1999) *Order in Multiplicity: Homonymy in the Philosophy of Aristotle* (Oxford: Clarendon Press).

—— (2009) 'An Approach to Aristotelian Actuality', in P. Hacker and J. Cottingham, eds., *Mind, Method and Morality: Essays in Honour of Anthony Kenny* (Oxford: Oxford Univ. Press), 68–93.

—— (forthcoming) 'First Philosophy First: Aristotle and the Practice of Metaphysics', in R. Wardy and P. Sheffield, eds., *The Routledge Companion to Ancient Philosophy* (Cambridge: Cambridge Univ. Press).

Ward, J. (2007) *Aristotle on Homonymy: Dialectic and Science* (Cambridge Univ. Press).

Wedin, M. (2009) 'The Science and Axioms of Being', in G. Anagnostopoulos, ed., *A Companion to Aristotle* (Malden, MA: Wiley-Blackwell), 125–143.

CHAPTER 15

SUBSTANCES, COINCIDENTALS, AND ARISTOTLE'S CONSTITUENT ONTOLOGY

MICHAEL J. LOUX

I

As Aristotle sees it, familiar sensible particulars give rise to a certain philosophical project, a project common to his materialist predecessors, Parmenides, Plato, and Aristotle himself. The project gets variously labeled: we are to identify the 'elements and principles of beings', (*Met.* 983b10–11), the 'elements of beings' (989b9, 992b18) and 'the principles of beings' (985b25, 998b22).[1] What Aristotle is calling elements and principles are obviously explanatory items, but the project is not concerned with just any explanatory items—only those explanatory of the being of familiar sensibles. This idea comes out in another of Aristotle's characterisations of the project. He speaks of identifying the substance of a familiar particular (996a7, 1001a6, 1001a29, 1002a28), and he tells us that the substance of a thing is the cause of its being (1017b14–16). This talk of the cause of a thing's being is meant to exclude one of the items we typically characterize as a thing's cause. Aristotle distinguishes between the items causally responsible for the coming to be of a thing and those responsible for its being once it has come to be; and while an object's efficient cause is included among the former, it is not a candidate for status as the substance of the thing (1041a27–32).

So the project is one of identifying the principles and causes of the being of familiar objects. The project obviously falls under the purview of what (in *Metaphysics* I) Aristotle calls the science of first principles and causes or wisdom (981b28–29) and (in *Metaphysics* IV) the science that investigates being *qua* being (1003a21–2); but as the later text insists, the first philosopher is concerned not merely with the being of a thing, but with its being one as well (1003b23–1004a9). Not surprisingly, in the various texts where Aristotle tries to characterize our project, talk of the being of things goes hand in hand with talk about their unity (996a4–10, 998b22–28, 1001a4–1001b1). In tying the investigations of being and unity together, Aristotle is, of course, following a tradition stemming from Parmenides. According to that tradition, the connection between the notions of being and unity is so tight that any satisfactory account of the one cannot fail to be an account of the other; but while Aristotle agrees that the account of a thing's being and the account of its being one make up a single explanatory project, he departs from the tradition in his understanding of that project. The tradition took talk about being and unity at face value. For philosophers like Parmenides and Plato, 'being' and 'one' signify substantive contents—universals whose application to objects just is the sort of fact that calls for a philosophical explanation. Aristotle, by contrast, denies that 'being' and 'one', taken by themselves, are semantically complete expressions (see 1042b25–31, 1053b16–1054a19, and 1087b33–1088a14). As he sees it, they get a complete sense only when coupled with terms that express kinds, universals that enable us to answer the 'What is it?' question for the things to which they apply and that (typically, at least) provide principles for counting those things.[2] So there is no such thing as just plain being. There is rather being a petunia, being a horse, and being a human being; and there is no such thing as just plain being one. Instead, there is being one petunia, being one horse, and being one human being.

But if this is how we are to understand talk about being and unity, then questions about the substance of a familiar sensible particular require parsing. As Aristotle tells us in *Metaphysics* VII 17, to provide an account of the substance of a thing is not to seek an explanation for the truth of a bald existential of the form '*x* exists' or for the truth of an identity claim of the form '*x* is one with itself' (1041a6–15). Questions about the substance of a thing, he insists, are questions about the predication of a kind: we are seeking the cause or causes of a thing's being an instance of its proper kind and its being one instance of that kind (1041a20–1041b8 and 1041b11–33).[3]

So a familiar particular's being the kind of thing it is and its being one instance of that kind are not stand-alone facts. An ordinary sensible individual depends on something else for its being and unity. It derives its essential character from another thing—what we have been calling its substance; and presumably that on which it depends for its essential character will be something that has its own essential character non-derivatively. It will be a thing that has its own characteristic form of being and unity, as Aristotle puts it, in its own right.[4] The core idea, then, is that there are things that have underived essential character, and familiar particulars somehow derive their character from these privileged entities. The philosophical project concerned with the elements, principles, and substance of familiar objects is just that of telling the proper story about this derivation.

But what strategies are open to us in carrying out this project? In a number of places, Aristotle points to two such strategies. In providing our account of character derivation, we can make the substances of familiar sensibles either things that exist apart from those sensibles or things that are immanent in them (996a15–16 and 1080b4).[5] Plato and Speusippus are Aristotle's standard examples of practitioners of the first strategy. Both make non-spatiotemporal items the underived sources of character, and they tell us that it is in virtue of some sort of tie or connection to them that familiar sensibles have the character they do. There are, of course, defenders of this sort of ontological strategy in our own day.[6] Where Plato spoke of ordinary objects participating in Forms, contemporary proponents of the strategy tell us that concrete particulars exemplify or instantiate universals; but the overall strategy is the same. Nicholas Wolterstorff calls the approach the relational style of ontology.[7] Although the label 'relational' is not without its problems in this context,[8] I shall follow Wolterstorff in calling practitioners of the first of Aristotle's two approaches relational ontologists.

The opposing pattern of explanation has the underived sources of character immanent in familiar particulars. But what is the force of this talk of immanence? The use of the term 'immanent' (enuparchon) is likely meant, in part at least, to serve the essentially negative purpose of distancing this account of character derivation from that at work in the received Platonic account. On this account, the substances of familiar particulars are *not* transcendent entities like the Forms that exist in splendid isolation from sensible particulars. As a contemporary philosopher might put it, this account locates the ultimate sources of character firmly within the spatiotemporal world.

But Aristotle makes it clear that the central theme at work in this talk of immanence is a positive idea, the idea that on this ontological strategy the underived sources of character are something like parts, ingredients, or components of the things whose character they underwrite. As Aristotle puts it, on this strategy, the things that count as the substance of a familiar particular are in it in the sense that the particular is composed or made out of them (1080b1–4). The core idea, then, is that for proponents of this ontological strategy, sensible particulars have something like a mereological structure: they are wholes, complexes, or compounds made up of more finely grained objects. Contemporary defenders of this style of ontological explanation typically speak of familiar objects as wholes made up of constituents,[9] and that leads Wolterstorff to contrast relational ontologies with what he calls constituent ontologies.[10]

Now, it is, I think, clear that Aristotle himself endorses the immanentist or constituent approach to questions of character derivation.[11] He tells us, first, that individual living beings (the things that in the *Categories* he calls primary substances) have a hylomorphic structure and, second, that it is in virtue of having the matter and, especially, the form it does that an individual living being falls under the biological species that is its essence. So their matter and, especially, their form account for the essential character of individual organisms; but Aristotle invariably uses mereological language in characterising an individual and its matter and form. In identifying the contents of the category Aristotle regularly tells us that substance is threefold, that it includes 'matter, form, and that out of both' or 'matter, form, and that out of these'. (See, for example, 1029a3,5,6, and 30; 1035a1 and 2; 1042a30, 1043a19; 1070a9–13; 1070b13; 1071a9.) In both cases the third item on the list—the familiar concrete particular—is identified by way of a label that can only be understood to mean that it is something composed or made out of the first two items on the list. The same idea gets expressed in Aristotle's favourite term for the concrete individual—*sunolon*. He also calls sensible particulars *suneilemena*, *suntheta*, and *sunkeimena*. All these terms express compositional complexity; they all express the idea that familiar particulars are things that result from the combination of several other things. Again, the mereological structure of familiar particulars gets expressed in the various pronominal labels we meet in *Metaphysics* VII and elsewhere. He tells us that the familiar particular is a 'this in a this' (1036b23). The idea is that a concrete individual is nothing more than a complex or whole made up of the matter and form that get picked out by the two occurrences of the demonstrative. In a similar vein, he tells us that a sensible particular is 'these things having themselves thus' (1036b24); and using different demonstratives for the matter and form, he calls the particular a 'this such' (1033b23–24). In both cases, the suggestion is that all there is to a concrete particular is the relevant matter and form arranged in the appropriate configuration.

Individual living beings are, however, just one kind of complex, whole, or compound. Aristotle recognizes another kind—what he calls a coincidental (73b6–9).[12] Just as matter and form can combine to make up one of the things the *Categories* calls a primary substance, an individual living being can combine with an item from one of the accidental categories to constitute something like a sun-tanned human being or a wet rhinoceros. No less than individual substances these things are compounds or complexes with the relevant substance and accident their constituents.[13]

But how are we to understand this talk of constituents and wholes? Pretty clearly, the defender of the immanentist strategy, whether Aristotle or the contemporary theorist, means us to understand these notions by analogy with the commonsense notions of part and whole. There is an obvious parallel between the two pairs of concept. In both cases, we have a plurality of entities making up or composing a single object. Nonetheless, we have nothing more than analogy here. What we have been calling the constituents of a familiar object are not its commonsense parts; the former are metaphysically prior to the latter. A thing's constituents are responsible for every aspect of its character, and the thing's commonsense mereological structure is just another aspect of that character.

The contrast between constituent and commonsense part is usually left implicit in contemporary immanentists, but Aristotle makes it explicit. In *Metaphysics* VII 10 he contrasts the non-philosophical use of 'part' (the use in which a finger, say, is called a part of a human being) with the philosophical use of that term (the use in which matter and form are called parts of an individual living being). A part is somehow less than the whole into which it enters. What we pre-philosophically call a part, Aristotle wants to say, is spatially less than the thing whose part it is;[14] its primary place is a proper part of the primary place of the whole. The philosopher's parts, by contrast, are not spatial parts of a thing. They are rather parts 'out of which the substance' of the thing is composed (1034b34). Aristotle's talk of substance here is talk about what a thing is, talk about its essential character. The idea is that while all the constituents of a thing taken together yield the characteristic kind of being that counts as the essence of their whole, each of the constituents gives rise to a character that falls short of the full essential character of the composite object. The constituents or philosophical parts of a thing, then, are essentially or substantially less rather than spatially less than the thing.

So although it is compositional, the relation of constituent to whole that we meet in an immanentist ontology like Aristotle's is not the relation of commonsense part to commonsense whole. Neither is it the more general relation of part to sum or fusion at work in what is strictly called mereology, the formal theory of parts and wholes. Nor can it be assimilated to either of two other familiar compositional relations—that tying the members of a set to the set or that tying the various conjuncts of a conjunctive property to that property. Each of these assimilations has its own problems: a familiar object is neither a set nor a property; but there is a more general problem with both these assimilations, a problem they share with that involving the relation of part to sum/fusion. In all three cases, we are confronted with a relation which is necessarily such that if it is possible for a plurality of objects to compose the relevant whole (whether mereological sum, set, or fusion), then the plurality does compose it. Where we have constitution, however, the objects that together make up a composite do so only contingently: it is possible for all those objects to exist without constituting the whole. The contingency we meet here is a feature common to all immanentist or constituent ontologies, and Aristotle's is no exception. He thinks that the constituents making up a compound object are tied together by the relation or nexus of predication: one constituent is predicated of the other. Thus, a substantial form is predicated of a parcel of matter to yield an individual member of a substance kind; and an accident is predicated of an individual substance to yield what Aristotle calls a coincidental; and in both cases, he tells us, the predication holds only accidentally. Speaking about both forms of predication, he tells us that the subject of predication is always something whose 'to be is different from that of the thing predicated of it' (1029a21–24). So the predication is not an essential predication, one in which the predicate marks out its subject as what it is. What functions as a subject of either type of compound-constituting predication is something whose essential identity is independent of that predication. Accordingly, Aristotle is committed to the claim that all cases of primitive or underived predication hold only accidentally.[15] All cases where one thing is predicated essentially of another thing are cases of derived predication. Thus, a substance-kind is predicated essentially of each of the concrete particulars that are its members. In each case, however, the predication obtains only in virtue of a prior predication—one in which the associated substantial form is predicated of the appropriate parcel of matter, and that predication is merely accidental.

So in a constituent ontology like Aristotle's, a plurality of objects only contingently constitutes a familiar particular. Nonetheless, it is something like a framework principle of this style of ontology that it is essential to a concrete particular that it have precisely the constituents it does. Since a familiar particular is nothing more than its constituents arranged or configured as they are, it has its constituents necessarily. Call his claim Constituent Essentialism. The view should not be confused with what is called Mereological Essentialism. The latter tells us that its commonsense parts are essential to a concrete particular; but, as we have noted, the constituents of a thing are not its commonsense parts. Provided it is possible to lose or gain a commonsense part without undergoing a change in constituents, one can consistently be a constituent essentialist without being a mereological essentialist. No one, I suspect, would want to suggest that Aristotle is a mereological essentialist; but as a constituent ontologist he is committed to constituent essentialism, and in *De Generatione et Corruptione* I 2 he is fairly explicit about this commitment. He is distinguishing substantial change (coming to be/passing away) from one type of accidental change (alteration), and he tells us that we have an instance of the former just in case we have a change in constituents—either the matter or the form (317a23–26).

Notice that in endorsing constituent essentialism while rejecting mereological essentialism, Aristotle is committed to the idea that a thing can lose or gain a commonsense part while maintaining numerically the same matter. Again, he is fully aware of this commitment (321a22–25; 317a32ff; 319a11ff.). What he wants to claim is that when a thing gains/loses a part or grows/diminishes, the thing's matter undergoes a merely accidental change. It is numerically the same matter; it is just larger or smaller than it was.

For most constituent ontologists, however, it is not merely change in parts that is problematic. Their adherence to constituent essentialism forces them to deny the possibility of strict numerical identity through any kind of change.[16] Change always involves a thing's having new and different properties; but since they construe the properties of a thing as its constituents, they have to deny that it is numerically the same thing that enters and exits a change. Aristotle, by contrast, distinguishes between the properties constitutive of a substance and those that are predicated of it. The latter include items from the various accidental categories. Those items are, of course, not constitutive of the substance of which they are predicated; only the substance's matter and form are. Accordingly, a substance can change with respect to features from the accidental categories without jeopardy to its identity. In the case of the kind of composite Aristotle calls a coincidental, however, things are quite different. Aristotle explicitly denies that a coincidental can be a subject for the predication of any accidents (1007a2–18).[17] Only substances are subjects for accidents (1029a21–24, 1038b3–6, 1049a27–36). But clearly no coincidental can survive the loss of its constituting universal; the doctrine of constituent essentialism prohibits that. In the case of the coincidental that is the white man, that universal is the colour white, so the white man cannot survive a change in color. For the coincidental that is the wet rhinoceros, the constituting universal is the quality of being wet. Accordingly, the wet rhinoceros cannot survive a thorough drying off. In either case, the loss of the relevant accident would result in the coincidental's ceasing to exist.

So we have two principles governing the constituent-whole relation. First, it is always a contingent fact that the objects constituting a given whole actually do constitute it. Second, a complex object has its constituents essentially. A third principle is that a complex object has its constituents uniquely; or, more precisely, it has uniquely those constituents in the configuration or arrangement characteristic of the complex. I call this claim the Principle of Constituent Identity.[18] It agrees with the earlier two principles in being something like a framework constraint on constituent ontology. On that view, a concrete particular is nothing more than its constituents configured in a certain way. Accordingly, anyone who endorses that account of character derivation is committed to holding that necessarily if a thing, x, and a thing, y, have all and only the same constituents arranged in the same way, x and y are numerically identical. Pretty clearly, Aristotle endorses this principle. In the famous passage at the end of VII 8 (1034a5–8), we meet Socrates and Callias. Since they belong to the same substance kind, they have numerically one and the same substantial form; but, then, they must differ in their matter. Why? Because they are numerically different composites, and the Principle of Constituent Identity tells us that numerically different objects have numerically different constituents.

II

There are, of course, different forms the constituent strategy can take, but what we have said gives a good sense of what is common to the different forms. The strategy is opposed to what, following Wolterstorff, we have called the relational strategy. On that strategy, familiar sensibles derive their character from standing in some non-mereological relation or tie to a transcendent source of character. It is important to see that a metaphysical framework can be an instance of neither style of ontology. The frameworks of philosophers like Quine and David Lewis who want to take the phenomenon of character as a philosophical primitive are cases in point.[19] However, if one takes the fact that this or that concrete particular displays a given form of character to be a phenomenon that calls out for a substantive explanation, then those two strategies look like the only theoretical options, and Aristotle is surely right that they are opposed. But we must be careful in our formulation of the opposition; for it is possible for a given theory to invoke both strategies. Thus, one could hold that sensible particulars derive their character from immanent tropes while claiming that the tropes have their character in virtue of being instantiations of what are taken to be the ultimate sources of character, trope-types. The theory manages to instantiate both ontological strategies, however, only because it is a two-step theory. At each stage of explanation, the ontologist must choose between the two explanatory strategies.

So the theorist intent on providing a genuinely substantive explanation of a given instance of character seems forced to choose between the immanentist or constituent strategy and the relational strategy, and Aristotle chooses the former. Why does be do so? We might think we can find the philosophical motivation for Aristotle's use of the constituent strategy by examining his criticisms of Plato in places like *Metaphysics* I 9 and XIII 4–5. The difficulty, however, is that many of those criticisms are directed less at the relational strategy itself and more at Plato's own implementation of that strategy, in particular his suggestion that the principles of character convey character by functioning as paradigms; and when, in these texts, Aristotle does focus on the relational strategy itself, his criticisms can strike us as nothing more than question begging. Thus, he is not very convincing when he tells us that what we have been calling the relational strategy fails to explain the being of familiar sensibles since it refuses to locate the principles of character in the sensibles (991a13–14, 991b1–2).

In these texts we do find a pair of very general claims that might contain the seeds of more interesting arguments against the relational strategy and, therefore, in favour of the constituent strategy. Neither is well developed. One is the suggestion that a relational account has difficulty squaring with the pre-philosophical datum that familiar objects come to have the character they do only in virtue of the operation of efficient causes that are themselves just further sensible particulars.[20] The other is the suggestion that a relational account faces epistemological problems, presumably problems explaining not just our knowledge of the allegedly transcendent sources of character but also our knowledge of the fact that a given sensible particular has this or that form of character (991a12–13 and 1079b15–17). The difficulty is that if we try to work out the arguments implicit in these very general suggestions, we find that the formulation of genuinely Aristotelian arguments on either of these two fronts presupposes the appeal to themes at work in a completely independent line of argument for the idea that familiar particulars are composites of metaphysically prior entities that furnish those particulars with their character, a line of argument that is not even implicitly found in the anti-Platonism of *Metaphysics* I 9 and XIII 4–5. This line of argument is one we meet way back in *Physics* I, where Aristotle discusses the phenomena of coming to be and passing away. The central theme in that argument is that necessarily things that come to be and pass away exhibit complexity of structure. If we are to understand why Aristotle insists on the constituent strategy, we need to examine in detail both this theme and the role it plays in Aristotle's account of the coming to be and being of familiar sensible particulars.

That there is such a thing as coming to be is a pre-philosophical fact, and it is likewise a pre-philosophical fact that the phenomenon of coming to be is intimately related to the phenomenon of character. Character is, so to speak, the product of coming to be. An instance of coming to be terminates in a thing with one of the distinctive forms of character. What comes to be is a human being, a dog, or a magnolia, a grey-haired human, an arthritic dog, or a flowering magnolia. There is, however, a philosophical problem lurking in these pre-philosophical data; for there are philosophical reasons to doubt that it is so much as possible for a thing to come to be. The reasons have their roots in Parmenides' famous argument. Aristotle nicely summarizes the argument:

> None of the things that are comes to be...because what comes to be must do so either from what is or from what is not, both of which are impossible. For what is cannot come to be (because it is already), and from what is not nothing could have come to be...(191a27–30).

There is a parallel argument to show the impossibility of passing away; and since every change can be understood to be a case of coming to be and/or a case of passing away, coupling the two Parmenidean arguments turns out to yield an argument for the impossibility of change of any sort.

As Aristotle formulates it, Parmenides' argument has the structure of a dilemma. Presumably we will all agree that a thing that comes to be cannot have existed prior to its coming to be, so the only option is to embrace the opposing horn of the dilemma and to claim that what comes to be comes to be from that which is not or from nonbeing. But, then, Parmenides has us where he wants us; for clearly it is impossible for things to just 'pop' into existence. We may not buy the details of Parmenides' semantics for the term 'nothing' or 'nonbeing', but we will agree that there can be no radical emergence *ex nihilo*. At any rate, Parmenides' successors all did. Indeed, it is difficult to overestimate the impact of this argument on post-Parmenidean Greek metaphysicians. Aristotle is no exception here. In virtually every context where he approaches the phenomenon of coming to be, Aristotle reminds us that a non-negotiable constraint on our analysis is that it avoid commitment to the possibility of genuine or full-blooded emergence *ex nihilo*.[21]

The difficulty is that language conspires against us here; for sentences like

(1) The musical man comes to be

and

(2) The geranium comes to be

are vehicles for reporting truly the occurrence of the relevant changes. Those sentences, however, seem to entail precisely what the Parmenidean constraint prohibits; for both sentences suggest that what happens in each of the changes they report is that something, as we put it earlier, just 'pops' into existence. They suggest that coming to be is a radical emergence *ex nihilo*. So if we believe that there is a coming to be of things like the musical man of (1) and the geranium of (2), we need to show that, despite appearances, sentences like (1) and (2) do not entail emergence *ex nihilo*. We need to show that while they are true, such sentences admit of a paraphrase that displays them as innocent of any violation of the Parmenidean constraint.

Toward executing this strategy, Aristotle focuses on (1). What makes (1) appear problematic is that it characterizes its change by way of what we might call the complete use of the verb 'comes to be' (*gignesthai*). In that use, the verb takes no predicate complement. Aristotle, however, reminds us that we can truly characterize the same change using that verb in what we can call its incomplete use, the use in which it demands a predicate complement.[22] Indeed, he points to three different sentences that incorporate that use of the verb and enable us to characterize our change truly:

(3) The man comes to be musical.
(4) The unmusical comes to be musical.
(5) The unmusical man comes to be a musical man.

Unlike (1), each of (3), (4), and (5) suggests that our change is rooted in something that exists before the coming to be. Each has the form

_____ comes to be _____ ,

where the first blank is filled by an expression that picks out some antecedently existing thing that comes to be something and the second blank, by a predicate complement that identifies just what it is that our antecedently existing thing comes to be. If, for simplicity's sake, we take the predicate complement in all three cases to be 'musical', then we can say that each of (3)—(5) gives us a different answer to the question 'What is it that comes to be musical?'[23]

The central claim of *Physics* I is that one of our three answers to that question is superior to the other two. Throughout chapters 7–9, Aristotle contrasts perspicuous ways of characterising a change with representations of the change that, while true, are less than fully perspicuous. He suggests that we can characterize a change not only by saying what *kath' hauto* (in its own right) comes to be something, but also by saying what only *kata sumbebêkos* (by way of coincidence) comes to be that.[24] Likewise, he tells us that we can identify the change by picking out the thing that comes to be something *haplôs* (in an unqualified way) as well as by picking out what comes to be that only *pôs* (in a way) (191b14). Again, he tells us that we can identify a change by picking out that thing, *x*, such that it is *qua x* that whatever comes to be something does so; and when we do, we are characterising the change *kuriôs* (most properly); but we can identify the same change less properly, but still truly, by picking out the thing that comes to something in other less revealing ways (191a35–191b9).

So amongst the true characterisations of a change, there are better and worse characterisations. *Physics* I 7 wants to claim that when we use (3) to characterize our change, we are speaking *kuriôs*. Using (3), we report our change by identifying that thing—the man—that *kath' hauto* (rather than *kata sumbebêkos*) or *haplôs* (rather than merely *pôs*) comes to be musical. Aristotle's preference for (3) over (4) and (5) comes out in *Physics* I 7 when he tells us that

> Plainly, then, if there are causes and principles which constitute natural objects and from which they primarily are or have come to be—have come to be, I mean, what each is said to be in its substance, not what each is accidentally—plainly, I say, everything comes to be from both subject and form (190b17–20).

As we will see, 'man' expresses the subject and 'musical' the form of our change. 'Unmusical', by contrast, expresses the privation of the form; and the privation, Aristotle tells us, is merely accidental (190b27). Accordingly, the two sentences ((4) and (5)) that identify the thing that comes to be musical by way of its privation fail to provide us with fully perspicuous representations of the change, so that (3), the sentence that identifies the change by picking out its subject and form, is the characterisation that expresses our change *kuriôs*.

Why, however, should we think that (3) is a better, more perspicuous characterisation of the change than either (4) or (5)? Aristotle gives his answer earlier in chapter 7 when he tells us that of our three things—the man, the unmusical, and the unmusical man—only one survives the change (190a9–21). Prior to the change, we have both the unmusical and the unmusical man; but once the change has occurred, neither of these things exists. The upshot of the change is just that there is no longer anything answering to the labels 'the unmusical' and 'the unmusical man'. What (3) picks out as the thing that comes to be musical, however, does survive the change. The man persists; he exists before, during, and after the change.

But why should that be a reason for thinking that (3) is a more perspicuous representation of the change than (4) or (5)? Aristotle never tells us explicitly, but I think that we can see why the survival of the man is grounds for preferring (3) if we reflect on (4). Although (4) manages to be true, the thing it tells us comes to be musical is not something that properly speaking can be said to come to be musical. A thing cannot properly be said to come to be musical if it is something that never is musical, and what (4) picks out as the thing that comes to be musical is something that never is musical; that is,

(6) The unmusical is musical

is never true. By the time we have the product of our change—the musical individual, the unmusical no longer exists. The man of (3), however, does persist, and the upshot of our change is that *he* is musical, so the man of (3) is something that properly speaking, in his own right, or in an unqualified way comes to be musical. The unmusical, by contrast is something that comes to be musical only *kata sumbebêkos* (by way of an accident). It is only because it is, prior to the change, accidentally one with what in the proper sense comes to be musical that the unmusical can be said to come to be musical.

The same holds for what (5) tells us comes to be musical. (5) is true, but what it picks out as the thing that comes to be musical is not something that, properly speaking, can be said to come to be musical; for it never is musical; that is

(7)   The unmusical man is musical

is never true; but, again, because, prior to our change, the unmusical man is accidentally one with the thing that in its own right comes to be musical, we can say that it comes to be musical *kata sumbebêkos*.

This is one way to explain Aristotle's preference for (3). Another is to reflect on the fact that unless we understand them in the light of (3), it is not clear that either (4) or (5) conforms to the demands of the Parmenidean Constraint. Taken by itself, (4) suggests that our change involves two things—the unmusical and the musical and that what happens in the change is merely that the latter replaces the former. Unless we see the man as a persisting thing that is first unmusical and later musical, we have to read (4) as implying that in our change one thing—the unmusical—ceases to exist and another thing—the musical—just 'pops' into existence and takes its place. One might suppose that on this score, (5) is superior to (4). The idea would be that (5) has a single thing—the man—existing at both ends of the change and that what it tells us is that before the change that thing is unmusical and after, musical. But (5) can be understood to tell us these things only if it is read in the light of (3). Unless we read it that way, we have no right to see the labels 'unmusical man' and 'musical man' as anything but fused contexts, unanalysable expressions which, by a kind of orthographic accident, end in the same three letters. So again, we have the result that in our change one thing ceases to exist and another emerges out of nothing to take its place.

So (3) is preferable to both (4) and (5).[25] It picks out the thing that *kath' hauto* comes to be musical, the thing that properly speaking or with no qualification whatsoever can be said to come to be musical. (4) and (5) are, of course, both true, but their truth is parasitic on the truth of (3). As we said, it is only because they are accidentally one with what properly speaking can be said to come to be musical that either the unmusical or the unmusical man can be said to come to be musical. It should be obvious that the underlying idea here is that coming to be is to be understood in terms of predication. A coming to be culminates in a predication. The coming to be is directed to that predication. It gets its identity from that predication, and the thing that *kath' hauto* or properly speaking comes to be something else in a coming to be is just that antecedently existing thing that is the subject of the coming to be's culminating predication.

Here, it is important to see that in its incomplete use the verb 'comes to be' is a member of the predication family of verbs. No less than the copula 'is', that verb expresses predication. Both

(8)   The man is musical

and our (3) express a predication, the same predication. The difference is that the use of the copula in (8) enables us to display the relevant predication as one that actually obtains, as one that is an accomplished fact. (3), by contrast, expresses the predication as something in the making, as something on the road to obtaining.

So (3) displays our change as a predication in the making, a predication whose subject is an antecedently existing thing; and in so doing, (3) shows the change to be metaphysically nonproblematic. (3) shows us that there is nothing anomalous or mysterious going on: there is no emergence *ex nihilo*. What happens is merely that some antecedently existing thing comes to have something predicated of it that was not previously so predicated. Accordingly, (3) is a metaphysically innocent characterisation of our change; and what Aristotle wants to claim is that the apparently problematic

> (1)   The musical man comes to be

is to be analysed by way of (3). (1), he wants to say, is true; but its truth has none of the consequences the Parmenidean reads into it. The truth of (1) does not presuppose any kind of radical emergence of something from nothing; it does not presuppose that anything just 'pops' into existence. What it is for the musical man to come to be is for the man to come to be musical. For (1) to be true is just for (3) to be true; and the truth of (3), we have seen, has no untoward metaphysical consequences. And, of course, Aristotle wants to generalize here. He wants to claim that every sentence which, like (1), characterizes a change by way of the verb 'comes to be' in its complete use can be analysed in terms of a sentence that, like (3), characterizes the same change by way of that verb in its incomplete use.[26]

In generalizing here, Aristotle tells us that there are two cases to consider; first, the case of qualified coming to be, where the product of the coming to be is what, following Aristotle himself, we have called a coincidental and, second, the case of unqualified coming to be, where the product is one of the things the Aristotle of the *Categories* calls a primary substance (2a11–14). Aristotle is confident that the general pattern of dependency tying accidents to substances provides justification for thinking that the strategy will be successful for all instances of qualified coming to be:

> Now in all cases other than substance it is plain that there must be something underlying, namely, that which comes to be. For when a thing comes to be of such a quantity, quality or in such a relation, time, or place, a subject is always presupposed, since substance alone is not predicated of another substance, but everything else of substance (190a33–190b1).

So for the case where a coincidental comes to be, we can be sure that there is some antecedently existing thing, x, and some predicable, F, such that the coincidental's coming to be just is x's coming to be F. That this generalization of the strategy applied to (1) works so smoothly is hardly surprising, since what gets expressed by (1) is a case of qualified coming to be. Now, for any case of qualified coming to be, the surface grammar of the standard term for picking out the coincidental that comes to be in the change points us directly to the pattern of analysis that Aristotle recommends. Take the case Aristotle actually considers. The term 'musical man' is a composite expression built out of (i) a term ('man') that picks out the antecedently existing thing and (ii) a term ('musical') that signifies the accident that comes to be predicated of that thing. Accordingly, we know precisely how to move from the characterisation of the change by way of the complete use of 'comes to be' to the characterisation of the change that incorporates the incomplete use of the verb.

But in the case of unqualified coming to be, things are different. Here, the standard term for picking out the product of the coming to be is a simple expression from the category of substance (a term like 'geranium', 'cat', or 'dog'). Accordingly, we are deprived of verbal cues of the sort we met in the case of 'the musical man' for implementing the general strategy Aristotle recommends. Indeed, the fact that these terms are all syntactically incomplex suggests that the strategy will not work here at all. But, of course, if we assume that the syntax conceals a complexity mirroring that of 'the musical man', then we have grounds for thinking that the strategy can be applied to the case of substantial change. Implicitly at least, Aristotle recommends that we make this assumption. He tells us that we are to understand the case of unqualified coming to be by analogy with that of qualified coming to be (191a7–12). Accordingly, we are to suppose that a substance-term like 'geranium' has a depth structure of the form 'F-ish x', where for the coming to be of any given geranium, 'x' picks out some thing that exists before that coming to be and 'F-ish' signifies some pattern of structural and functional organization such that the geranium's coming to be can be understood to be x's coming to be F-ish. Armed with that supposition, we could go on to claim that

(2)   The geranium comes to be

is to be analysed as

(9)   The x comes to be F-ish,

so that the overall pattern of analysis could be applied to the case of unqualified no less than qualified coming to be.

Aristotle tells us that we have strong empirical support for understanding the case of substantial change in this way:

> But that substance and whatever other things are in an unqualified way come to be from some subject will be clear to one who examines; for there is always something that functions as subject from which the thing comes to be; for example, animals and plants from seeds (190b1–4).

The central case of unqualified coming to be is the case where a biological organism is generated; and Aristotle is claiming that observation confirms the hypothesis that for every instance of that case, there is some antecedently existing thing, x, such that the relevant coming to be can be understood to be x's coming to be something else. Plants and animals come to be from seeds, and observation tells us that there is a continuity of stuff that takes us from the seed to the individual organism that is the product of the change. But, then, we have empirical support for generalizing the pattern of analysis accorded the musical man to the case of individual substances. So we have the general claim that every case of coming to be is a case of some antecedently existing thing's coming to have some universal predicated of it, and the upshot is that all forms of coming to be are immune to Parmenidean attacks.

Every coming to be, then, involves some antecedently existing thing and some universal that gets predicated of it. Aristotle calls the former the subject of the change and the latter its form, and he introduces the term 'matter' as a variant for 'subject'. In later works he regiments the terminology, so that, in the case of unqualified coming to be, matter comes to have a form predicated of it; whereas, in the case of qualified or accidental change, an accident gets predicated of a substance; but here in *Physics* I 7, he summarizes his analysis by telling us that its subject/matter and form are the principles of the coming to be of a thing (190a17–23).

But they are also the principles of its being once it has come to be. In the text just mentioned, he tells us that subject/matter and form are not only the causes and principles of the coming to be of things, but also the causes and principles of their being. He speaks of 'causes and principles of natural beings from which they primarily *are* and have come to be....' (190b17–18). Accordingly, just as our (1) is to be analysed by way of (3) and (2), by way of (9), so

(10) The musical man exists

is to be analysed as

(8) The man is musical,

and

(11) The geranium exists

as

(12) The x is F-ish.

The idea that the same things that function as the principles of a thing's coming to be function as the principles of its being once it has come to be is both natural and plausible.[27] If the coming to be of an object is the coming to obtain of a certain state of affairs, then one would expect the continued being of that object to consist in the continued obtaining of that same state of affairs; but the coming to be of a familiar object is the coming to obtain of a predicative state of affairs, so it is reasonable to think that the continued existence of the thing is the continued obtaining of that same predicative state of affairs. Furthermore, this intuitively plausible idea gets reinforced by the consideration that the things that come to be also pass away; and, again, it is reasonable to suppose that one and the same state of affairs is involved in their coming to be and their passing away. In the former case, we have the coming to obtain of the state of affairs and in the later, its ceasing to obtain; but that suggests that the existence of the thing in between the two events just is the obtaining of the relevant state of affairs—a predicative state of affairs if we can trust Aristotle's account.

In any case, we have the idea that not only are subject/matter and form the principles of the coming to be of things; they are also, as our earlier texts put it, the 'elements and principles' (983b10–11) of the being of familiar particulars. So we have an account of the essential character of sensible individuals. Living beings fall under the biological kinds that make up their essences in virtue of the fact that the associated substantial form is predicated of their matter; and coincidentals are things like the white man and the wet rhinoceros in virtue of the fact that there is a substance of the appropriate kind that serves as subject for the predication of the appropriate accidental form. We have, then, the hylomorphic account and Aristotle's case for it. But is this a case for the hylomorphic account when this is understood as a claim of constituent ontology telling us that familiar particulars are complexes or wholes whose constituents are their subjects and predicated universals? Aristotle thinks so. In *Metaphysics* VII 7, he tells us that everything that comes to be has both a matter and form (1032a11–25) and then goes on both in that and succeeding chapters to tell us that everything that can be characterized in hylomorphic terms is a structured complex whose nonspatial parts or constituents are the relevant parcel of matter and the relevant form (1032b30–1033a5; 1033b11–19; 1034a26; 1034b34–1035a5). In *Metaphysics* IX 8, Aristotle seems to be proposing the stronger modal claim that necessarily for any object, x, if it is possible for x to come to be (or pass away), then there are numerically distinct items, $a \ldots n$, such that x is a composite whose constituents are $a \ldots n$ (1050b17–19; see also 1088b25–28). And in *Physics* I 7 itself, Aristotle seems to be telling us that in establishing that the subject/matter and the form are the principles of the coming to be and being of a familiar particular, he has established that the particular is a composite structure whose proper constituents are the relevant subject/matter and form (190b20–23).

But why does Aristotle think this? Why does he think that his argument for the hylomorphic analysis of familiar particulars is an argument for a constituent-whole analysis of those particulars? Unfortunately, Aristotle never tells us explicitly. Nonetheless, I think we can make out an interesting case for this claim if we reflect on the point of the account of coming to be we meet in both *Physics* I 7 and *Metaphysics* VII 7–9.[28] The point, recall, is to provide an account of coming to be that is immune from Parmenidean criticism. The basic strategy for realizing this aim is to claim that when a thing, y, comes to be, there is some antecedently existing thing, x, and some predicable, F, such that y's coming to be consists in x's coming to be F. Thus, the musical man's coming to be is the man's coming to be musical, and the geranium's coming to be is the appropriate parcel of stuff's coming to have the structural and functional organization characteristic of geraniums. It is, however, essential to the success of this analysis that the product of a coming to be (what we have been calling y) be nonidentical with the subject of that coming to be (what we have been calling x). If the thing that is x and the thing that is y are identical, then we have one of two results: either (1) y pre-exists the change along with x or (2) y does not pre-exist. However, if (1) is the case, then y cannot be said to come to be; it will have existed beforehand; and if (2) is the case, then x will come to be along with y, with x/y coming to be from nonbeing or that which is not. But these two results just are the two horns of the Parmenidean dilemma. So we need x and y to be nonidentical; and on the constituent interpretation of hylomorphic structure, that is how things turn out. On that reading, the product of a coming to be is a composite thing whose proper constituents are the antecedently existing x, and the relevant predicable F; but clearly a composite is nonidentical with each of its proper constituents. Accordingly, we can have x existing before y comes to be, so that (1) does not obtain; and since the antecedently existing x turns out to be a proper constituent of y (the F-ish x), (2) does not obtain: y can come to be without any radical emergence *ex nihilo*.

But couldn't a philosopher who rejects the constituent ontologist's account of character derivation accept the *Physics* I 7 characterisation of coming to be? Couldn't a relational ontologist who understands the being of our y (the product of the change) in relational terms as a matter of our antecedently existing x's standing in some non-mereological relation to the appropriate transcendent bearer of character accept that characterisation? Indeed, could not the austere nominalist who construes predicate-terms syncategorematically endorse that characterisation? Aristotle, I think, would say that neither philosopher could endorse the account of *Physics* I 7, at least not if the aim is to provide a consistent characterisation of coming to be that steers clear of both horns of the Parmenidean dilemma.

The point is easier to see in the case of the austere nominalist. The austere nominalist wants to deny that predicate-terms carry any ontological force. They are true of familiar objects, but they signify or express no additional entities whether immanent in or separated from the familiar objects of which they are true. But, then, the austere nominalist has to claim that the object that exists before a coming to be is numerically identical with the object that exists after. In the case of our change, we have x and nothing else. To be sure, a new predicate-expression—'F'—is true of x after the change; but the austere nominalist insists that that term is syncategorematic; and if it is, then there is no entity corresponding to it. But if that is so, then its application to x does nothing to alter the ontological landscape. What we have after the change is precisely what we had before—x and nothing else. But, then, we are confronted with the two horns of the dilemma. Either (1) we have no coming to be or (2) our coming to be is an unintelligible emergence *ex nihilo*.

But, Aristotle would claim, we have precisely the same result on a relational account of character. Before the change, we have x, but that's all we have after as well. It is true that after the change, x stands in a new non-mereological relation to an underived source of character. That source of character, however, is a transcendent entity, one that is not a part of the spatiotemporal world. Accordingly, the fact that x now stands in this new relation does nothing to add to the ontological landscape. The object expressed by the predicate-term 'F' is a separated entity, so that there is nothing there—no new entity—in x's environment that corresponds to the predicate. All that's there where x is is x itself. So, again, we have the result that the thing that is supposed to be the subject of the change is precisely the thing that emerges from the change, and we find ourselves confronting the two horns of the dilemma: either (1) there is no coming to be or (2) there is, but it is a coming to be out of that which is not.

Aristotle, however, can expect the same reply from the relationist and the austere nominalist. Both will insist that their respective accounts do, in fact, give the result that x (the subject of the change) and y (its product) are nonidentical; for both will say that for y to exist just is for x to be F. Before the change, however, x is not F, so while x exists before the change, y does not. After the change, x is F; but since that is what it is for y to exist, y does come to be. Its doing so, however, is anchored in the nonidentical x, so its coming to be is not a case of emergence *ex nihilo*.

Aristotle, however, will find this reply unsatisfactory. He will say that if the claim that y's existence is just x's being F is not a claim made within the context of a constituent ontology, then what it amounts to is nothing more than a verbal stipulation. Now, Aristotle will certainly agree that such a stipulation might have important implications for our verbal behaviour, but he will insist that if our definitory formula (y exists just in case x is F) expresses nothing but the decision to use words in a certain way, then it can carry no metaphysical or ontological force. How, Aristotle will ask, can a mere verbal stipulation on our part bring it about that there is a genuinely new entity on the scene? What we have here, he will say, is nothing more than a convention permitting us to abbreviate a phrase of the form 'Fish x' by an expression of the form 'y'; and a convention of that sort neither adds to nor subtracts from the population of the nonlinguistic world. So whatever linguistic conventions we invoke, however we decide to talk about our change, on neither the relational nor the syncategorematic approach do we have nonidentical objects before and after the change. On both accounts, we have x and nothing else. So on neither account are we able to avoid confronting the two horns of the Parmenidean dilemma.

And Aristotle will round off this reply by reminding us just how a constituent ontologist is able to keep coming to be safe from the Parmenidean challenge. On a constituent reading, y is indeed the F-ish x; but on that reading, this claim is not merely a matter of verbal stipulation. It is a genuinely ontological claim. On the constituent analysis, y is a structured whole whose numerically distinct proper constituents are the subject/matter, x, and the accident/form, F. But, then, on that analysis, x and y really are nonidentical: x is a proper constituent of y, and no composite entity is identical with any of its proper constituents. Accordingly, Aristotle can conclude that if his case for the hylomorphic characterisation of things that come to be succeeds, the case for a constituent analysis of those same things succeeds as well.

And there may be an important message for some contemporary metaphysicians in Aristotle's reminder. I am thinking of those metaphysicians who hold that genuine coming to be and passing away actually occur. It is not implausible to think that they are committed to something like the constituent characterisation of these changes found in Aristotle. When I say that genuine coming to be and passing away actually occur, what I mean is that, in the one case, we have a change whose upshot is that there now exists a thing that in no way whatsoever formerly existed and, in the other, that we have a change in which something really ceases to exist, a change, that is, whose upshot is that there formerly existed a thing that in no way whatsoever now exists. The use of tenses is crucial here. As I am understanding these phenomena, no one who defends a tenseless or B-Theory of time (whether in the 'old' or 'new' version) can consistently endorse the reality of either coming to be or passing away.[29] Defenders of that theory of time take reality to be an eternally fixed four-dimensional spread, where what exists at one time is every bit as real as what exists at any other time. Accordingly, they must deny that what I am calling genuine coming to be and passing away really occur. Theirs is a conception of reality that is essentially Parmenidean; in the strict sense, there is no change; reality is through and through static; and, of course, defenders of the B-Theory implicitly concede this; for they repeatedly charge the A-Theorist with incoherence in thinking that pure or absolute coming to be or becoming is possible, and they feel obliged to provide B-theoretic paraphrases of sentences that seem to imply the existence of real coming to be or passing away.

So only the A-Theorist can consistently endorse the reality of both genuine coming to be and genuine passing away; and not just any A-Theorist can embrace both of these kinds of change. One must be, like Aristotle, a presentist and hold that only what currently exists or what now exists is real.[30] That view of time makes possible the current existence of things that in no way formerly existed; and it makes it possible for it to be the case that there now no longer exist things that formerly did exist.

But those who, like Aristotle, endorse the kind of coming to be and passing away that presentism makes possible find themselves confronted with Parmenides' dilemma; and if we focus merely on the case of coming to be, we find a constituent analysis of the product of a coming to be a natural way to respond to Parmenides. On that approach what comes to be is a composite of a plurality of pre-existing constituents; and for that composite to come to be is for its proper constituents to come to be combined in some way. Accordingly, while the thing that comes to be is rooted or anchored in something pre-existing, it does not itself pre-exist the change. But it is plausible to claim that not just any constituents will do here. The constituents composing the product of a coming to be have to be categorially the right sorts of things. Now, what comes to be is something whose existence involves a distinctive form of character, and character hinges on the predication of a universal. This, of course, is reflected in the fact that it is things like a wet rhinoceros, a sun-burnt hyena, or a musical man as well as a geranium, a paramecium, or a human being that come to be. But, then, Aristotle's proposal that we understand the coming to be of the musical man, say, in terms of *Physics* I 7's

(3) The man comes to be musical

should prove doubly attractive to the contemporary defender of coming to be and passing away. First, it expresses our pre-philosophical thought and talk about coming to be: we typically record the coming to be of a thing by way of a sentence like

(3) that highlights the predicative role character plays in a coming to be. Second, it provides the materials for instantiating the constituent ontologist's general strategy for answering Parmenides.

III

But however things may be for the contemporary theorist, it should be clear that the roots of Aristotle's constituent approach to questions of character are to be found in his attempt to provide an analysis of coming to be that is immune to Parmenidean criticism. Familiar sublunary particulars are one and all things that come to be, and every object that comes to be is composite, a compound entity made up or composed of distinct constituents. As we have seen, there are two cases here. We have, first, the coming to be of a composite with the character associated with a substance kind; the change is a case of unqualified coming to be, and it involves a pre-existing parcel of matter of the appropriate kind coming to have the appropriate substantial form predicated of it. But, second, there is the case of qualified coming to be where the product is a coincidental; and in that case, we have a pre-existing substance coming to have an accident predicated of it.

But not only can we find in Aristotle's account of coming to be the roots of the very general idea that familiar particulars are composites; we can as well find in that account the roots of more particular features of the constituent approach. We have already noted that for constituent ontologists the various items constituting a familiar particular do so only contingently; and we have seen that Aristotle agrees. He tells us that the predicative link tying the constituents making up a composite holds only accidentally. That we have accidental predication here is no merely superficial feature of Aristotle's account. Whether our composite is a substance or a coincidental, its subject/matter is something that exists prior to the coming to be of the composite and, hence, prior to the predication of the associated universal. And our composite is not just something that comes to be; it is as well something that can and will pass away, so the predicative structure that constitutes its existence has to be one that can and will cease to obtain.

We also noted that, on a constituent approach, while the items constituting a complex do so only contingently, the whole they constitute has those constituents essentially. This idea is what we called Constituent Essentialism. Furthermore, we noted that a composite has its constituents uniquely. That idea, we said, is encapsulated in what we called the Principle of Constituent Identity. As we noted, Aristotle endorses both ideas; and each can be seen to flow naturally from Aristotle's account of the coming to be and being of familiar particulars. Just as the coming to be of the musical man is the man's coming to be musical, so the being of the musical man consists in the man's being musical; and just as the coming to be of the geranium is the appropriate parcel of matter's coming to be organized in the way characteristic of geraniums, to be for the geranium is for that parcel of matter to be organized in that way. But if these recipes give the existence conditions for the relevant composites, then surely those composites have the constituents mentioned in their respective recipes essentially or necessarily. Furthermore, if each of the composites is nothing more than those constituents arranged or configured as they are, then it is difficult to see how any other object could have precisely those same constituents configured in precisely the same way. And, of course, these are perfectly general arguments, so that we have both Mereological Essentialism and the Principle of Constituent Identity in their full generality.

Now, where a constituent ontologist makes universals constituents of familiar composites, we typically find that ontologist embracing some version of the Principle of Instantiation, the claim that necessarily each universal is instantiated. Although it is possible for a constituent ontologist to reject the principle, almost all immanentists make the instantiation of a universal a condition of its existence. Aristotle is no exception (*Cat.* 14a8–14), and the account of universals that has its roots in his account of coming to be meshes nicely with that principle. On that account, the fundamental or basic first order universals are the substantial forms and accidents that are constitutive of the two types of composites in Aristotle's theory. As they are introduced in the account of coming to be, forms and accidents are the sorts of things the subjects of change come to be; and once we have a composite, form and accident are the sorts of things the associated matter or substance is. As Aristotle puts it, they are 'suches' rather than 'thises' (*Met.* 1033b21–25). They are, so to speak, adjectival on the 'thises' of which they are predicated, and the resulting complexes are 'this suches'—predicative structures. So the fundamental universals are the ways their subjects come to be and subsequently are; they are how these subjects come to be and subsequently are. This sort of conception of universals goes hand in hand with the Principle of Instantiation; for a 'such' requires a 'this'. It is difficult to see how what is just a way a subject is could exist without some subject to be that way.

We can get at a further feature of Aristotle's constituent ontology if we press questions about the relationship between the subject entity (whether matter or substance) in a composite and the composite itself. Take the musical man. It is difficult to suppress doubts about Aristotle's claim that this is a composite of which the man is a proper constituent. As we have noted, a composite is nonidentical with each of its proper constituents. But do we not have just one entity here? The musical man, after all, just is the man who happens to musical. Yet, Aristotle insists that they are nonidentical. Indeed, as we have seen, it is essential to the success of his overall strategy for answering Parmenides that this be so. The doubts here likely go back to our discussion of *Physics* I 7's three characterisations of the sample coming to be—our (3), (4), and (5). Central to that discussion is the claim that the man, the unmusical, and the unmusical man are all nonidentical, so that (3), (4), and (5) give us three different, nonequivalent answers to the question 'What is it that comes to be musical?' But, again, don't we have just one thing here? So how do we get three nonequivalent answers to our question?

In resolving those issues, Aristotle invokes a theme that is central to his constituent ontology. In our discussion of *Physics* I 7, we mentioned the theme in passing. As we noted, Aristotle concedes that prior to our change, the man and the unmusical are one thing and that after our change, the man and the musical man are one thing. He denies, however, that we have what we nowadays call numerical identity in either case. Aristotle distinguishes between two types of unity/sameness—accidental unity/sameness and unity/sameness in being or substance. Only the latter notion, he tells us, is governed by what we call the Indiscernibility of Identicals (*Phys.* 202b15–16), and it corresponds to our notion of numerical identity.[31] So a complex is not one in being/substance with the subject entity (whether matter or substance) that is one of its proper constituents. As we would put it, they are not numerically identical. They have different life histories; one is a proper constituent of the other; and they have different properties. Nonetheless, they coincide for a time; throughout that time to point to one is to point to the other; and whatever we do to the one, we do to the other. But all these facts are accidental. While one, a composite and its constituting subject can come apart. Accordingly while nonidentical or distinct in being, a subject and its complex are accidentally one or the same.

IV

So the roots of Aristotle's constituent approach to questions of character are to be found in his account of the coming to be of familiar sensible particulars. What grounds his construal of ordinary objects as complexes composed of a plurality of nonidentical proper constituents arranged in a predicative configuration is the intuition that familiar particulars are things that come to be and pass away. It turns out that it is only if we construe them as the sorts of composites Aristotle says they are that we can show how their generation and corruption are possible. Furthermore, many of the categorial principles at work in Aristotle's constituent ontology can be seen to flow naturally out of his account of the coming to be of familiar particulars and the associated account of their being. But if this is so, what are we to make of the two claims he seems to present in *Metaphysics* I 9 and XIII 4–5 in support of his constituent or immanentist approach? These are the claims we mentioned at the beginning of Section II: the claim, first, that only an immanentist can do justice to the role of efficient causes in the natural world and the claim, second, that only an immanentist can give a satisfactory account of our knowledge both of the underived sources of character and of the familiar particulars that derive their character from them. The answer, I think, is that while these claims certainly register the belief that it is a strength of the constituent approach that it can provide a clear and compelling account of efficient causality as well as a thoroughly naturalistic account of our knowledge about character, they do not abbreviate any kind of transcendental argument designed to take us from pre-philosophical facts about causation or knowledge to the conclusion that familiar particulars are the sort of structured composites Aristotle's account takes them to be.

There is no question that the claim about causation expresses Aristotle's doubts that a relationist like Plato can succeed in accommodating the role efficient causes play in nature. As Aristotle sees it, no story about character derivation can be complete that does not do justice to the fact that concrete sensible particulars acquire their character by way of the causal activity of other concrete sensible particulars, and he surely thinks that on a view that makes the ultimate or underived sources of character things that exist apart from the spatiotemporal world, it is mysterious that the activity of finite spatiotemporal beings can play any role at all in the phenomenon of character acquisition. But when Aristotle himself attempts to show just how efficient causes operate, his account presupposes both the account of coming to be we meet in *Physics* I 7 and the constituent account of character derivation that follows from it. We do not find him arguing from the phenomenon of efficient causality to the need for a constituent ontology. The constituent framework is already in place when he tells us how efficient causes do their job.

A persistent theme in Aristotle's treatment of efficient causality is the idea that the efficient cause of a coming to be has and transmits to the subject of the change the form/accident whose predication of that subject is the culmination of the coming to be. So efficient causes are constituent contributors; they contribute one of the constituents that together make up or compose the product of their respective comings to be. In *Metaphysics* VII 7–9, this theme gets presented against the backdrop of the account of coming to be we first meet in *Physics* I 7. The claim is that whatever comes to be is a composite of nonidentical constituents, so that for a thing to come to be is for its various constituents to be put together, and for it to pass away is for those same constituents to come apart. The implicit justification for this claim is just the familiar idea that only a constituent/whole analysis of familiar particulars yields an account immune to Parmenidean criticism. It is, however, essential to success on this score that our account not have the constituents making up the product of a coming to be themselves come to be in the coming to be of the whole they constitute. Otherwise, the very result our account was seeking to avoid for the product of the coming to be will confront us in the case of the things that are its constituents. So the constituents of the product must all pre-exist the coming to be. The matter or subject, of course, pre-exists in an obvious way; but what about the predicated form or accident? Aristotle's answer is that it too pre-exists; it pre-exists in the efficient cause. There are, to be sure, different ways it can be found there. The efficient cause might have the form/accident in the standard way, the way in which the poker that warms the water has the heat; or it might have the form/accident immaterially or intentionally as the sculptor has the shape he imparts to the bronze. But in either case the agent has the form/accident and imparts it to the subject/matter to yield the composite. So what makes something an efficient cause is that it has and contributes the constituting form/accident. As Aristotle puts it in *Metaphysics* VII 9, '…that which is the primary cause in its own right of the making is a part' (1034a25–26).[32]

Pretty clearly, this account of efficient causality presupposes rather than underwrites the constituent framework that emerges from Aristotle's account of coming to be. The concept of agency developed in VII 7–9 is intelligible only against the backdrop of that framework. But what about the other theme we meet in *Metaphysics* I 9 and XIII 4–5, the idea that only a constituent ontologist can provide us with a serious account of our knowledge about character? The problem with the suggestion that this theme abbreviates a genuinely independent argument for the constituent approach is just that, as Aristotle actually develops it, his account of our acquisition of knowledge has familiar particulars as the efficient causes of both our perceptual and more strictly intellectual apprehension of the world. Accordingly, if the account of agency presupposes the constituent framework, then it is difficult to see how a theory of knowledge acquisition could provide us with an independent argument for a constituent analysis. The idea is that we come to have knowledge by way of causal interaction with things that have as their constituents the relevant sensible and intelligible forms/accidents.[33] What transpires in this interaction in the perceptual case, at least when we have epistemically favourable conditions, is that the object that has the relevant sensible qualities transmits them to an animal organism whose perceptual organs are in proper working order; and the upshot is that the organism receives the sensible qualities, not in the way the efficient cause has them, but immaterially or intentionally, so that the animal is perceptually aware of the sensible object. And something analogous happens in the noetic case. A human being whose perceptual and intellectual faculties are functioning properly in an epistemically favourable environment immaterially receives an intelligible form that is materially possessed by some object in the environment, and the human being is intellectually aware of that object.

So again, while it is certainly true that Aristotle believes a relationist like Plato will encounter difficulties providing a serious, non-metaphorical account of our knowledge of the underived sources of character as well as the things they characterize, his own account of that knowledge presupposes rather than underwrites the constituent framework. That framework has its roots, not in any independent analysis of efficient causation or any independent theory of knowledge acquisition. It has its roots rather in the prior insight that it is possible for familiar particulars to come to be and pass away only if they are structured wholes constituted by a plurality of antecedently existing items.

NOTES

1. For more detailed discussions of the themes of section I of this chapter, see Loux (2005) and Loux (2006).

2. The exception is, of course, the case of a stuff-kind.

3. For a detailed defense of this reading of *Met.* VII 17, see Loux (1991), Chapter 5.

4. Or, at least, it will ultimately involve something that has its own distinctive character in its own right.

5. See also *Metaphysics* III. The two alternatives delineated at 998a21–23 may be the pair mentioned at 996a15–16 and 1080a37–1080b4. Aristotle may be introducing the two alternatives indirectly by reference to the kinds of entities their most celebrated practitioners took to be the substance of familiar objects. Thus, we have Plato's *genê* and the material principles of a pluralist like Empedocles. See 999a17–19 for support for this reading of III 3.

6. See, for example, Plantinga (1974) and Strawson (1959).

7. See Wolterstorff (1991), 540–541 and 547–548.

8. For one thing, proponents of the opposing strategy (the immanentist strategy discussed just below in the body of the paper) make use of relations between the various items immanent in a familiar particular to explain the structure, unity, and character of the particular. For another, proponents of what Wolterstorff calls the relational strategy frequently want to deny that familiar particulars derive their character from relations to the underived sources of character. Relations, they think, represent just another form of character, and, so, they see the appeal to relations in this context to be regressive. They prefer to speak of nonrelational ties or nexus between familiar particulars and the transcendent sources of character. See, for example, Chapter 5 of Strawson (1959) and Bergmann (1967), 24ff.

9. See, for example, Bergmann (1967); Armstrong (1989), 94–95, and Armstrong (1997), 183–190.

10. See Wolterstorff (1970), 111ff. and Wolsterstorff (1991), 540–541 and 547–548.

11. I argue for this reading in Loux (1995a) and (2005). The constituent reading is the standard or traditional interpretation of the hylomorphic theory. In recent years a growing number of scholars has challenged the constituent reading. For nontraditional interpretations of the hylomorphic theory, see Sellars (1967b), Wiggins (1967), Charlton (1970), Rorty (1973), Kosman (1987), Halper (1985), Gill (1989), Scaltsas (1994a), Scaltsas (1994b), and Wedin (2000). I discuss these alternative readings in both Loux (1995a) and Loux (2005a). For another attempt at defending the traditional reading, see Lewis (1994). See also Fine (1992), Haslanger (1994), and Burnyeat (2001) for traditional readings of the hylomorphic theory.

12. See also 83a1–35, 1007b3–16, 1015b16–34, 1017a7–22, and 1029a21–23.

13. For discussions of Aristotle's theory of coincidentals, see Lewis (1982) and Lewis (1991).

14. I take it that this is what 1034b30's '*to metroun kata poson*' (that which measures according to quantity) comes to. The idea is that a commonsense part is spatially smaller than its whole and, accordingly, its dimensions can be used to provide a quantitative measure of the dimensions of the whole, so that we can say that the whole is so many feet tall or so many hands high.

15. I am thinking, of course, only of cases where the subject of predication is not a universal, but a contingent object. In the middle books of the *Metaphysics* Aristotle typically restricts talk of a universal being predicated of a subject in just this way. Accordingly, we get the result that there are just two cases of primitive or underived predication—those catalogued at 1029b21–24, 1038b4–6, and 1049a27–30.

16. See Bergmann (1967), 34; Armstrong (1997), 148–159; and Casullo (1985).

17. But Aristotle will concede that 'The white man is musical' can be used to express a truth. What the sentence expresses, however, is not a proposition to the effect that

a certain accident is predicated of a certain coincidental. It is rather the proposition that the relevant coincidental is accidentally one with/the same as something—the appropriate substance—of which the relevant accident is predicated. See 83a1–21.

18. Loux (1978), 131 and Loux (2002), 113.

19. See Quine (1954), 10ff and Lewis (1983), 349ff.

20. I take it that this is the complaint expressed at 991a8–11, 20–25, and 991b4–8 (in the M doublet, 1079b12–15, 23–30, and 1080a2–8).

21. Aristotle will, of course, allow that there is a sense in which it can be said that a thing comes to be from that which is not since a thing can be said to 'come to be from the privation which in its own nature is something which is not' (191b15–16). Using language introduced a bit later in the body of the text, we can express the non-negotiable constraint by saying that it is impossible for a thing to come to be *kath' hauto* or *haplôs* from that which is not (191b13–14). For other texts where we meet the constraint, see 187a27–29, 317b28–30, 999b30, and 1032b30–31.

22. I first presented this reading of *Physics* I 7 as the introduction to a series of lectures on Aristotle's psychology given at the Sculoa Normale Superiore in Pisa during the spring of 2001. Those lectures were published for limited distribution as *Nature, Norm, and Psyche* (Loux (2004)) in the Scuola's monograph series. For the discussion of *Physics* I 7, see Chapter 1 of that monograph. For alternative readings of *Physics* I 7, see Charlton (1970) and Scaltsas (1994b).

23. I do not discuss *Physics* I 7's comments (at 190a5–8 and 21–31) about the use of the 'from' locution to report that from which a thing comes to be. Aristotle has little to say about the philosophical implications of our use of this locution in *Physics* I 7. He has a good bit to say about it in *Metaphysics* VII 7 (1033a6–23). That discussion of the 'from' locution occurs in the midst of a long chunk of text beginning early in VII 7 and ending in VII 9, whose point is to show that, for any case of coming to be, the constituents making up the product of the coming to be pre-exist the coming to be. The point of 1033a6–23 is to show that, despite a linguistic practice that might suggest otherwise, the pre-existing matter continues to exist as a constituent in the product of the changes in question. Aristotle discusses the linguistic practice again in *Metaphysics* IX 7 (1049a18ff). Gill (1989), Chapters 5 and 7, sees this text as evidence that the mature Aristotle comes to reject the constituent reading of the hylomorphic theory in favour of a new and different model. For my reactions to Gill's reading, see Loux (1995a), Loux (1995b), and Loux (2005).

24. Although he repeatedly uses the expression '_____ comes to be _____ kata sumbebêkos', Aristotle never explicitly uses the expression '_____ comes to be _____ kath' hauto' in *Physics* I 7–9. However, at 190b18–9, he speaks of the items from which a thing comes to be *primarily*, not *kata sumbebêkos*, but *kata tên ousian* (according to its substance). Together, these three conditions give us the concept of a thing's coming to be this or that *kath' hauto*. The text in question gets discussed a paragraph down in the main body of this chapter.

25. The idea that a sentence like (3) represents the paradigmatic expression of a coming to be gets expressed in texts outside *Physics* I 7. See, for example, *Posterior Analytics* I 22, esp. 83a5–14 and *Physics* V 1 224a21–26/*Metaphysics* XI 11 1067b1–4.

26. Aristotle provides a more technical response to Parmenides in *Physics* I 8 (191a34–191b26), and he mentions still another possible response (191b27–29). Both of I 8's responses attempt to accommodate the fact (mentioned in note 15 above) that there is a sense in which it can be said that a thing comes to be from that which is not—*pôs* or *kata sumbebêkos*. The extended response of 191a34–191b26 presupposes that it is

sentences of the form of our (3) that *kuriôs* report a coming to be. For an extended discussion of *Physics* I 8's response, see Loux (1992).

27. In *Metaphysics* XIV 2, we find a nice expression of this intuition. Aristotle says, 'Since, then, a thing must have come into being out of that of which it consists...' (1088b16).

28. A first, much briefer attempt at making this point can be found in Loux (2005), Section V.

29. For the contrast here, see my 'Time' in Loux (2001), 251–259.

30. I am assuming that neither a 'growing block' theory of time (which makes what now exists and what existed in the past real) nor a 'shrinking block' theory (which makes what now exists and what will exist in the future real) nor the 'bullseye' theory (which makes the present a kind of spotlight on one part of a reality that includes both past and future) can consistently claim that both genuine coming to be and genuine passing away occur.

31. For Aristotle's account of the distinction, see *Top.* I 7. For detailed discussions of the distinction, see Lewis (1982) and Lewis (1991), Chapter 3.

32. See also *Physics* III 1–2, esp. 200b20–27, 202a3–11, and all of *Physics* III 3 as well as *De Generatione et Corruptione* I 6–8 for other discussions of efficient causality.

33. The central texts here are *De Anima* II 5, II 12, III 4, III 7, and III 8. I discuss these issues in Chapters 4–6 of Loux (2004).

Bibliography

Armstrong, D. (1989) *Universals* (Boulder, Colo.: Westview Press).

——— (1997) *A World of States of Affairs* (Cambridge: Cambridge University Press).

Barnes, J. (1984) *The Complete Works of Aristotle*, 2 vols. (Princeton, N.J.: Princeton Univ. Press).

Bergmann, G. (1967) *Realism* (Madison: University of Wisconsin Press).

Burnyeat, M. (2001) *A Map of Metaphysics Zeta* (Pittsburgh: Mathesis).

Casullo, A. (1985) 'A Fourth Version of the Bundle Theory', *Philosophical Studies* 47, 95–107.

Charlton, W. (1970) *Aristotle's Physics I, II* (Oxford: Oxford Univ. Press).

Fine, K. (1992) 'Aristotle on Matter', *Mind* 101, 35–57.

Gill, M.L. (1989) *Aristotle on Substance* (Princeton, N.J.: Princeton Univ. Press).

Gotthelf, A., and J. Lennox (1987) *Philosophical Issues in Aristotle's Biology* (Cambridge: Cambridge Univ. Press).

Halper, E. (1985) 'Metaphysics Z.12 and H.6: The Unity of Form and Composite', *Ancient Philosophy* 4, 146–59.

Haslanger, S. (1994) 'Parts, Compounds, and Substantial Unity' in *Unity, Identity and Explanation in Aristotle's Metaphysics*, T. Scaltsas, D. Charles, and M.L. Gill, eds. (Oxford: Clarendon Press), 129–70.

Kosman, L.A. (1987) 'Animals and Other Beings in Aristotle', in *Philosophical Issues in Aristotle's Biology*, A. Gotthelf and J. Lennox, eds. (Cambridge: Cambridge Univ. Press), 360–91.

Lee, E., A. Mourelatos, and R. Rorty (1973), *Exegesis and Argument* (Assen: van Gorcum).

Lewis, D. (1983) 'New Work for a Theory of Universals', *Australasian Journal of Philosophy*, 343–77.

Lewis, F. (1982) 'Accidental Sameness in Aristotle', *Philosophical Studies* 42, 1–36.

——— (1991) *Substance and Predication in Aristotle* (Cambridge: Cambridge Univ. Press).

—— (1994) 'Aristotle on the Relation between a Thing and Its Matter', in *Unity, Identity and Explanation in Aristotle's Metaphysics*, T. Scaltsas, D. Charles, and M.L. Gill, eds. (Oxford: Clarendon Press), 247–77.

Loux, M. (1978) *Substance and Attribute* (Dordrecht: Reidel).

—— (1991) *Primary Ousia* (Ithaca, N.Y.: Cornell Univ. Press).

—— (1992) 'Aristotle and Parmenides: An Interpretation of *Physics* A.8', *Proceedings of the Boston Area Colloquium in Ancient Philosophy* 8, 281–19.

—— (1995a) 'Composition and Unity', in *The Crossroads of Norm and Nature*, M. Sim, ed. (Lanham, Md.: Rowman & Littlefield), 247–79.

—— (1995b) 'APA Symposium on Aristotle's *Metaphysics*', *Ancient Philosophy* 15, 495–510.

—— (2001) *Metaphysics: Contemporary Readings* (London: Routledge).

—— (2002) *Metaphysics*, 2nd ed. (London: Routledge).

—— (2004) *Nature, Norm, and Psyche* (Pisa: Scuola Normale Superiore's monograph series).

—— (2005) 'Aristotle on Matter, Form, and Ontological Strategy', *Oxford Studies in Ancient Philosophy* XXV (1), 81–123.

—— (2006) 'Aristotle's Constituent Ontology', *Oxford Studies in Metaphysics*, vol. 2, 207–250.

Plantinga, A. (1974) *The Nature of Necessity* (Oxford: Clarendon Press).

Quine, W.V.O. (1948) 'On What There Is', *Review of Metaphysics* 2, 21–38.

Rorty, R. (1973) 'Genus as Matter: A Reading of *Metaphysics* Z-H', in *Exegesis and Argument*, E. Lee, A. Mourelatos, and R. Rorty, eds. (Assen: van Gorcum), 393–420.

Ross, W.D. (1924) *Aristotle's Metaphysics*, 2 vols. (Oxford: Clarendon Press).

—— (1936) *Aristotle's Physics* (Oxford: Clarendon Press).

—— (1949) *Aristotle's Prior and Posterior Analytics* (Oxford: Clarendon Press).

Scaltsas, T. (1994a) 'Substantial Holism' in *Unity, Identity and Explanation in Aristotle's Metaphysics*, T. Scaltsas, D. Charles, and M.L. Gill, eds. (Oxford: Clarendon Press), 107–28.

—— (1994b) *Substances and Universals in Aristotle's Metaphysics* (Ithaca, N.Y.: Cornell Univ. Press).

Scaltsas, T., D. Charles, and M. L. Gill, eds. (1994) *Unity, Identity and Explanation in Aristotle's Metaphysics*, (Oxford: Clarendon Press).

Sellars, W. (1967a) *Philosophical Perspectives*, (Springfield, Ill.: Charles Thomas).

—— (1967b) 'Raw Materials, Subjects, and Substrata', in W. Sellars (1967a), 137–52.

Sim, M. (1995) *The Crossroads of Norm and Nature* (Lanham, Md.: Rowman and Littlefield).

Strawson, P.F. (1959) *Individuals* (London: Methuen).

Wedin, M. (2000) *Aristotle's Theory of Substance* (Oxford: Oxford Univ. Press).

Wiggins, D. (1967) *Identity and Spatio-Temporal Continuity* (Oxford: Blackwell).

Wolterstorff, N. (1970) 'Bergmann's Constituent Ontology', *Nous* 4, 109–34.

—— (1991) 'Divine Simplicity', *Philosophical Perspectives* 5, 531–52.

CHAPTER 16

ENERGEIA AND *DUNAMIS*

STEPHEN MAKIN

MODAL distinctions seem very familiar to us. Modalities enter into practically every area of contemporary philosophy. Great progress has been made in understanding the variety of differences between what is possible, what is actual, and what is necessary. But things were not always so clear. We owe a great debt in this area, as in so many others, to Aristotle. Not much had been said about modal differences before Aristotle.[1] By contrast Aristotle had a lot to say on the topic, part of which comprises his discussion and use of the actuality/potentiality distinction. One important task in understanding Aristotle's discussion of actuality and potentiality is locating the distinction within the wider area of modality in general. A second is seeing how the actuality/potentiality contrast sits relative to other major Aristotelian distinctions, in particular that between the different categories. And a third is to come to a proper appreciation of how Aristotle reaches the right level of generality for his purposes in discussing the actuality/potentiality contrast, given that his most extended treatment in *Metaphysics* IX focuses on specific and different instances of the contrast. For it seems that we can approach the actuality/potentiality distinction from two different directions, as it were: from the general 'downwards', identifying the distinction against the background of broader modal notions; and from the particular 'upwards', starting with more specific instances and then widening our perspective to attain as abstract a view as required of the distinction. I will say something briefly about the 'downwards' approach in Sections I and II and then concentrate on the 'upwards' approach subsequently.[2]

I: A DISTINCTION FOR LOGIC

One very general area in which modalities are significant is the assessment of arguments. Aristotle provides us with the basics of a modal logic.[3] This ends up being less successful than its non-modal counterpart, partly because Aristotle chooses to concentrate upon a notion of possibility inconsistent with necessity, presumably being swayed by the intuition that if something *has* to be the case then it is misleading to say that it *may* or *could* be the case.[4] However the actuality/potentiality distinction is not to be located in this treatment of arguments with modalised premises and conclusions. Aristotle makes this point in a rather clear way in *Metaphysics* V 12, where he treats the family of modal notions expressed by the Greek noun *dunamis* (for present convenience read as any of the following: 'possibility', 'capacity', or 'potentiality') and its cognates (the adjective *dunaton* 'possible', 'capable'; the negative noun *adunamia* 'impossibility', 'incapacity'; the negative adjective *adunaton* 'impossible', 'incapable'). Some (im)possibilities involve no reference to a *dunamis* possessed by some bearer or other. It is possible that no-one attends my party, it is possible that there be a sea battle tomorrow, it is impossible now that I died in childhood. We are not drawn in this sort of case to seek some capacities or abilities possessed by various objects in virtue of which the (im)possibilities obtain. In other cases (im)possibilities *do* involve something possessing a relevant (in)capacity. It is impossible to dissolve gold in water because *gold* is *insoluble*. It is possible for a human to detect colours because *humans* have *visual capacities*. The distinction between actuality and potentiality is to be found among this latter type of possibility. For Aristotle's most thorough discussion of actuality and potentiality, in *Metaphysics* IX, crucially involves the notion of a *dunamis*, and assigns a privileged conceptual role to the notion of an active *dunamis*, characterized as what it is about one thing in virtue of which it can produce changes in another.

There is another difference between Aristotle's treatment of the modalities in his logic and the actuality/potentiality distinction. Aristotle's modal logic works with three modal notions: 'what belongs' (what is the case), 'what necessarily belongs' (what must be the case) and 'what may belong' (what can be the case).[5] The distinction between actuality and potentiality is focused on just these two notions, however. *Metaphysics* V contains chapters both on necessity (V 5) and on possibility (V 12); but while there are passing references in V 5 to possibility and impossibility, these do not connect in any systematic way with the discussion of *dunamis* in V 12 which is most relevant to his actuality/potentiality distinction. Again, while *Metaphysics* IX 5 argues that *necessarily* capacities are exercised in the right conditions, and while *Metaphysics* IX 8 has something to say about what is eternal, imperishable, and necessary, the fundamental notion being elucidated in IX is a dichotomy: the actual and the potential.

II: A DISTINCTION CONCERNING BEING

It seems then that the distinction between the actual and the potential is not going to be elucidated via the pioneering modal logic of the *Prior Analytics*. Rather than emerging from modal logic, the actuality/potentiality distinction has its home in Aristotelian physics and metaphysics. It is natural to ask, then, how the distinction is co-ordinated with some of the other major distinctions round which these disciplines turn.[6] *Metaphysics* V 7 is a brief account of the various ways in which *being* is spoken of. The difficulties of Aristotle's extended investigations into being are notorious.[7] So it is unsurprising that *Metaphysics* V 7 does not make much headway with the perennial problems of Aristotelian metaphysics. But the chapter does offer different sets of distinctions in terms of which we could analyse the notion of being: first accidental being; second beings in their own right, which can be analysed in terms of the categories (substance, quality, quantity, etc.); third being as truth; fourth being as distinguished between being-potentially and being-actually. This scheme, which is also found elsewhere in the *Metaphysics*, presents the actual/potential distinction as a way of structuring being alternate to, compatible with, and on the same level as that in terms of the categories.[8]

Let us think about these alternates a little further. The different categories are not all on a par. One—substance—is primary (*Met.* VII 1 1028a10-b2). The primacy of substance is what enables Aristotle to pursue a study of being as such, while respecting the fact that there is no single way in which everything that is *is* (*Met.* IV 2 1003a33-b19). Precisely what all this comes to is a matter of considerable scholarly controversy. But there is at least one clear parallel with the case of actuality and potentiality. They are not on a par either. *Metaphysics* IX 8 argues at length that actuality is primary: prior to potentiality in account and in being, and in one way temporally prior while in another temporally posterior. Indeed the priority of actuality over potentiality is the single most important result to emerge from *Metaphysics* IX, and we can best appreciate how the various discussions in *Metaphysics* IX—of capacities, change, matter, changeable substance, eternal substance, etc.—fit together by thinking about how each contributes to that climactic result.[9]

Now Aristotle does not use the same conceptual apparatus for explaining the priority of actuality over potentiality as he does for explaining that of substance over the other categories. The latter case is explicated in terms of the notion of focal meaning: explaining what it is to be a quality, or a quantity, or an item in any other non-substance category always involves reference to the central case of substance; for a quality to exist is for some substance to be qualified in a certain way.[10] As regards the priority of actuality over potentiality, the position is different. The priority of actuality *in account* consists in the fact that a potentiality is identified by reference to the correlative actuality (the capacity of sight is the capacity *to see*; to be fragile is to be liable *to shatter*), rather than vice versa (it would be odd to explain shattering as *fragility-in-action*). Quite what the priority of actuality *in being* amounts to is much more contentious, but it looks as if it concerns the (difficult) idea that an actuality can be (exist?) without a potentiality whereas a potentiality cannot be (exist?) without an actuality.[11] In fact the focal structure used to explain the inter-relation of the different categories enters Aristotle's discussion of actuality and potentiality at quite a different place, in the course of explaining in *Metaphysics* IX 1 how various types of *dunamis* relate to one another.

III: How does *Metaphysics* IX elucidate the distinction?

So much for the 'downward' approach to the potentiality/actuality distinction. It is a distinction co-ordinate with the distinction between the categories. But so far this does not tell us much about actuality and potentiality, whereas Aristotle has a lot to say about the different categories. The detail is provided by Aristotle's treatment of actuality and potentiality in *Metaphysics* IX.

In broad outline the strategy of *Metaphysics* IX looks clear enough. We have an 'upward' approach to the actual/potential distinction. Aristotle starts (chapters 1–5) by talking about one sort of potentiality: 'a potentiality for change'. These are cases in which what stands to a potentiality (such as fire's capacity to heat, or someone's capacity to play the flute) as actuality is a *change* (such as heating, or flute-playing). Later on (chapters 6 and 7) we are provided with another sort of case, in which some matter (e.g., some bricks and wood, or some flesh and bone) stands to a substance (e.g., a house, or a human being) as potentiality to actuality. Other cases are indicated as well: IX 8 considers the relation of eternal to changeable things, and IX 9 mentions the relation of geometrical figures to the constructions by which geometers present their proofs. There is significant disagreement among commentators about how to understand the apparent switch of topic at IX 6, about how we should fit together the different cases of actuality/potentiality which Aristotle considers, about the extent to which IX has a single subject matter, and about the level of generality at which Aristotle will pursue his investigation. Some see IX 1–5 and IX 6–7 as having different subject matters; they then need to explain why so much of IX should be concerned with a topic which, according to Aristotle himself, is not the 'most useful' for 'what we want now'. Others take IX 1–5 and IX 6–7 as investigating different instances of a more abstract distinction between actuality and potentiality.[12]

Whichever position one takes on these questions, however, one point about chapters 1–5 on which all can agree is the following. It is clear that Aristotle sets off at the beginning of *Metaphysics* IX to elucidate the actuality-potentiality distinction by starting from the potentiality side. But that may seem an odd way to proceed.

For, as noted already, one of the general morals of *Metaphysics* IX is that actuality is prior to potentiality: why not, then, concentrate on that side of the distinction which is primary (as the investigation of categorial being concentrates on the primary category of substance)? Further, Aristotle argues at IX 8, 1050b6–28 that there are eternal actualities which involve no corresponding potentiality.[13] How could starting from the potentiality side of the distinction cast light on *those* actualities?

One very good reason for Aristotle to start with potentiality is that there is at least a natural (Greek) language vocabulary for that side of the distinction: *dunamis* and the cognate terms mentioned earlier. By contrast, Aristotle is driven to two neologisms for the other side. The first, which occurs from the early (but fragmentary) *Protrepticus* onwards is the term *energeia*, which means 'use', 'practice', 'exercise', or 'activity'. Aristotle uses this term to talk about the difference between the inactive possession of a capacity, ability, or skill and its active use. A paradigm instance of that difference is the contrast between those asleep and those awake (a doctor does not lose, but plainly does not use, her medical skills while she sleeps). In that case, we might suspect that something more is required to express a general notion of actuality than the vocabulary of *energeia*-as-activity. For we suppose that the actual is ontologically privileged: that there is a significant ontological difference between the actual on the one hand, and the merely potential on the other. It is natural to think that when Socrates dies, when he is no longer actually alive, then something has gone out of existence. By contrast, it would be very implausible to think that something new comes into existence when Socrates awakens, which goes out of existence once he falls asleep again. Lots of people pass away in their sleep, but the significant ontological shift comes not when they fall asleep for the final time, but when they die. So it may not be surprising that Aristotle coins another new term, *entelecheia*, and that this term appears in his discussion of the soul. For the notion of being alive (being ensouled) does carry ontological weight: Socrates comes into being when he is born, and ceases to be when he ceases to be alive. And so Aristotle describes the soul as 'an actuality (*entelecheia*) of the first kind of a natural body having life potentially in it',[14] while recognizing that someone actually alive may nevertheless be asleep and inactive. There is dispute over the etymology of *entelecheia*. But most agree that this term, unlike the original *energeia*, means *actuality* from the start. However, *entelecheia* never really catches on with Aristotle at all, and it is all but abandoned in *Metaphysics* IX in favour of *energeia*.[15] In that case, whatever conclusion we draw from this tale of two neologisms, at the very least the difficulties with those terms—as opaque to an ancient Greek as they are to us—make good sense of the strategy of analysing the *potentiality* side of the distinction in order to clarify the *actuality* side. So Aristotle proceeds in *Metaphysics* IX by investigating a particular instance of the potentiality/actuality distinction—capacities and change—and he investigates that instance by analysing the notion of a capacity:

> ...let us make determinations about potentiality (*dunamis*) and fulfilment (*entelecheia*) as well—and first about potentiality most properly so called, though it is not the most useful for what we want now. For potentiality (*dunamis*) and actuality (*energeia*) extend more widely than those cases which are so called

only in respect of change. But when we have spoken about this, we shall in the distinctions about actuality (*energeia*) clarify the others as well.

(*Met.* IX 1 1045b34–1046a4)

IV: Different types of capacity

How does Aristotle 'make determinations' concerning capacities for change? He identifies one type of capacity—an active capacity—as the central case. An active capacity is defined as 'an origin of change in something else or in itself *qua* something else'.[16] Examples would be the heat of a fire (a fire cannot make *itself* any hotter), or the medical skill of a doctor (a doctor can heal herself, but only by following exactly the same procedures that she would follow if she were healing someone else). Notice that defining active capacities in these terms makes them a sort of dual to an Aristotelian nature, which is defined as 'a principle of movement, not, however, in something else but in the thing itself *qua* itself'.[17] Both active capacities and natures are origins of change. They differ as regards the location of the changes which they originate, and in other ways too—for example, natures are innate while (at least some) capacities can be acquired and lost.[18] But they are both alike 'drivers' of change in the world, and as we shall see, that similarity is significant as regards the priority of actuality over potentiality in the case of capacities. Indeed Aristotle emphasizes its significance by reminding us, at the beginning and end of *Metaphysics* IX 8 (1049a5–10 and 1051a2–3), that the conclusions established in that chapter about the priority of actuality over potentiality apply to *all* origins of change, be they capacities or natures. Once active capacities are identified as the central type of potentiality for change, other types of capacity can be defined: for example, the passive capacity of glass to be melted, or the capacity of this detergent (not merely) to cut through grease (but to do so) *well*. Aristotle's thought is that, just in the case of substance vis-à-vis the other categories, explaining the secondary cases will involve reference to (the account of) the central case.[19]

Since an active capacity is 'an origin of change in something else or in itself *qua* something else', it follows that capacities for change must be actualized in pairs. When a fire's (active) capacity to heat results in an increase in temperature, there must be something which has been made hotter, and that patient must be something with the passive capacity to be heated (no amount of heating a colour or a sheet of asbestos will produce any increase in temperature). Now Aristotle argues in *Physics* III 3 that when an agent does something to a patient, there is a *single* resultant change which is located in the patient. This view of agency is well illustrated by Aristotle's own example of teaching and learning. Given that I know about horses I have the capacity to teach you; given that you understand English and can follow well structured explanations you have the capacity to be taught by me. If my lecture to you on equine anatomy is a successful episode of teaching/ learning, then there is just one change which is *guaranteed* to have taken place: first of all you didn't know about equine anatomy and now you do. No doubt lots of other changes have taken place too, but we cannot specify what they are just on the basis of the fact that a successful episode of teaching/learning has taken place. Then, as Aristotle says, the change that is *guaranteed* to have occurred if my teaching and your learning capacities have been exercised takes place in *you* (the learner); and no change *of that type* will take place in me (the teacher)—my knowledge of equine anatomy is just the same after the lecture as before it.

So in the first part of *Metaphysics* IX Aristotle investigates in detail the way in which correlative active and passive capacities are related to the single change that is their joint exercise. His investigation of capacities for change is aimed at establishing something important for the project of *Metaphysics* IX as a whole: the principle that *of necessity* appropriate pairs of active and passive capacities in the right relation issue in a change. Once that principle is established to his satisfaction in IX 5 Aristotle will immediately move on in IX 6 from capacities for change to another case of the potentiality/actuality distinction. Why is that principle, about the necessary exercise of appropriate pairs of active and passive capacities in the right relation, important enough to bring the IX 1–5 discussion of capacities for change to an end? The answer is that *that* is the result required to explicate the priority of actuality over potentiality in the case of capacities for change. Once we have got that far with the capacity/change case, it is time to move on to another.

V: DIFFERENT TYPES OF *ACTIVE* CAPACITY

However, Aristotle has to take some care in stating that result precisely, since there are two further differences among active capacities which Aristotle thinks map onto one another, and which have to be taken into account. First, in *Metaphysics* IX 2 Aristotle distinguishes rational from non-rational capacities. The former can be possessed only by rational agents, *qua* rational, since such capacities involve knowledge and understanding, and therefore require rationality. An example would be medical skill, which is essentially an understanding of what health is and a consequent ability to work out the steps required in various situations to attain it.[20] Non-rational capacities, by contrast, are all those that are not rational.[21] Second, in the same chapter he distinguishes one-way and two-way capacities: 'for example, heat [is a capacity] only for heating, while the medical craft [is a capacity] for both disease and health'.[22] This second distinction, more subtle than it might at first sight appear, comes to the following. A *one*-way capacity is such that there is some *one* description such that any exercise of that capacity in normal conditions (i.e., in the absence of interference) is guaranteed to satisfy that description, however many other descriptions it might also satisfy as well. Fire has the capacity to *heat*. It could be that lighting a fire brings about a drop in temperature (for example by triggering a thermostat, which starts an electric fan, which lowers the temperature), but this would be a situation in which the exercise of fire's capacity is interfered with by the thermostat-fan apparatus. But if the situation is normal and nothing interferes, then any exercise of the capacity will be an instance of *heating*, no matter what other type that instance of heating might also fall under (it might be a charring, burning, browning, melting, solidifying or …). A two-way capacity, on the other hand, may result in either of a pair of opposed changes, without there being any interference involved. An expert doctor might exercise her skill either in curing or in killing. Which she opts for will depend on what she wants. Usually she wants to heal her patients, but now she is faced with the fiend who ruined her life. If she does choose expertly to kill that bitter enemy, we should not think of her hatred for that person as interfering with her medical knowledge, but rather as giving her a reason to use that knowledge in one way rather than another (by contrast the death would be due to interference if the patient died due to the failure of vital equipment, or an unforeseen infection). Aristotle then argues in IX 2 that while these are different distinctions, they are not independent: any rational capacity is a two-way capacity, and any non-rational capacity a one-way capacity.

With all this in place Aristotle can argue in IX 5 that as regards one-way capacities, it is necessary that, if an agent with a one-way active capacity is in the right relation to a patient with the appropriate passive capacity then the two capacities are exercised and a change occurs. Take as an example the (one way) capacity to heat. The view is that *of necessity* if there is something hot (e.g., a fire) in the right relation (i.e., physical contact) with something heatable (e.g., a pan of milk) then heating occurs (the water gets hotter). And a related, though importantly different, claim also holds concerning two-way capacities and the changes that are *their* exercise: in that case it is necessary that if an agent has a two-way capacity, and is in the right relation to a patient with the appropriate passive capacity, and the agent chooses to exercise the capacity in *this* way, then the capacities are exercised, and *this* change occurs.

VI: FURTHER COMPLEXITY

In order to appreciate what all this shows about the priority of actuality in the case of capacities for change, and its significance for the overall discussion in *Metaphysics* 1–5 IX, it is best to simplify for the while, and focus just on one-way capacities. For Aristotle thinks that there is further complexity to be accommodated, even when the one-way/two-way and non-rational/rational distinctions have been taken into account, if we are to properly appreciate the way in which a change is prior to the capacities from which it originates.

In the course of *Metaphysics* IX 5 we read the following:

> For it is not necessary to specify in addition that nothing external prevent it; for it has the capacity in so far as it is a capacity for acting, and that is not in any and every condition, but just in some circumstances, in which external things preventing will be ruled out as well; for these are set aside by some of the things present in the specification of the capacity.
>
> (Met. IX 5 1048a16–21)

This is extremely opaque, even by Aristotle's standards. But there must be something very important here, since otherwise it will be mysterious why Aristotle should find it necessary to comment in this way on his principles about the exercise of capacities. It seems that Aristotle is insisting that what he has already said is fine as it stands: as regards one-way capacities, it is necessary that, if an agent with a one-way active capacity is in the right relation to a patient with the appropriate passive capacity, then the two capacities are exercised, and a change occurs. We do not need to protect the principle against counter-example by adding some saving clause along the lines 'and if nothing external prevents it' (1048a16). One can imagine the sort of counter-example which might look threatening. I put my cool milk (something with the capacity to be heated) on top of (in the right relation to) the hot fire (something with the capacity to heat), but nothing happened *because the back door was wide open and the cooling draft interfered.*

Armed with that sort of example, someone might allege first that Aristotle's principle is false as it stands, and second that the way to secure its truth is to add the saving clause 'so long as nothing interferes and stops/prevents the capacities being exercised'. Aristotle's response above is extremely bold. We do not need to add any reference to the absence of external hindrances, he seems to be saying, since all such conditions are already included in the proper specification of the active capacity in question. In other words, once we specify correctly what it is that the agent has the capacity to *do*, the issues about external hindrance are taken care of. It is very difficult to see exactly what Aristotle means by this; it is even more difficult to see why he should think it a plausible claim to make.[23] But one thing we can see with a fair degree of clarity is that Aristotle has a strong motivation for wanting to make (and defend) that opaque move. For the crucial point Aristotle wants from the first part of *Metaphysics* IX is that the single change (e.g., a heating), which of necessity occurs when (objects possessing) the right capacities are in the right relation, stands as something actual to *those two capacities.* That single change *is actually* what the active and passive capacities *are potentially.* And that would not be at all plausible if the relation of agent and patient to the change were on all fours with that of any old object which might be a relevant feature of the background conditions. It may well be plausible to see heating as the (joint) actuality of the capacities to heat and be heated. But it would be very *im*plausible to think that the change similarly stands as an actuality relative to all those capacities connected in one way or another with hindrances which must be absent (e.g., the capacity of draughts to cool), and background conditions which must be present (e.g., the capacity of oxygen to sustain the fire), if heating is to occur.

VII: CAPACITIES AND ANOTHER TYPE OF MODALITY

Now consider Aristotle's principle once again. If factors external to agent and patient do not need to be mentioned, then what sort of thing *would* get in the way of a change occurring? It would appear that all that's relevant, according to Aristotle, are the agent's (precisely specified) active capacity, the patient's (precisely specified) passive capacity, and the appropriate relation of agent to patient. Consider the sort of case in which one of these relevant factors goes wrong. For example, the fire is capable of burning the wood, but the wood hasn't been placed on the fire (it's in the wrong relation); the blacksmith is capable of forging horseshoes, but the iron hasn't yet cooled sufficiently to be hammered (it doesn't have the right passive capacity). Obviously, the expected change will not occur: the fire won't burn the wood which is in the other room, and the blacksmith won't do anything with overly hot metal. Is that all there is to it? It is tempting to think there's more to say: that in those circumstances it's not just that there won't be any burning or smithying going on, but that there *can't* be. A comment at *Metaphysics* IX 5 1048a15–16 suggests that Aristotle recognizes this point.[24] But it is a a difficult one to manage, and the more difficult the more one is working with a limited modal vocabulary (as Aristotle is with *dunamis* and its cognates). One wants to say that if there's no wood in the workshop, then it's not merely that no woodwork *will* occur, but that it's not *possible* for woodwork to occur. After all, it might be that no carpentry *does* occur while the works manager is away on his lunch break, but that would be due to the carpenter's indolence: he could have been doing some woodwork, but he was lazy. By contrast, if the wood isn't there then he *couldn't* be carving.

Now this last modality appears to be something distinct from the capacities Aristotle has been examining in IX 1–5, and which stand to changes as potential to actual. When we say that the woodless carpenter *couldn't* be carving, we don't mean that he lacks the capacity that is skill in carpentry, for craftsmen do not lose and gain their skills over and again as the appropriate materials are removed or replaced. They gain them by instruction, and might lose them through old age. Indeed, in *Metaphysics* IX 3 Aristotle lambasts those whose refusal to admit any modal distinctions forces them to such ludicrous admissions as that we go blind every time we close our eyes; and the idea that someone should lose and regain their skill in carpentry as wood is removed from and returned to the workshop is equally fantastic. So does *Metaphysics* IX have anything to say about the sort of modality at play when we say, for example, that in the absence of wood [i.e., no (object with) passive capacity] it's *not possible* for the skilled carpenter [i.e., (object with) active capacity] to carve [i.e., change which stands as joint actuality to those capacities]?

It is not at all clear how to answer this. One option would be to say that it is precisely this sort of modality which is picked up by a test Aristotle provides in *Metaphysics* IX 3, following on his criticisms of those who deny there are unexercised capacities:[25]

> And this is what is *dunaton* [possible]—that for which, if the actuality (*energeia*) of which it is said to have the *dunamis* [possibility? capacity? potentiality?] obtains, there will be nothing impossible.
>
> (*Met.* IX 3 1047a24–26)

This is similar to the definition provided in Aristotle's development of modal logic,[26] although significantly the *Metaphysics* IX 3 version omits the 'not necessary' clause of *Prior Analytics* I 13 which corresponds to Aristotle's focus there on two-way possibility. The IX 3 test does not seem to characterize the idea of a capacity for change (the subject of IX 1–2 and 5). There is nothing impossible (by which Aristotle means an outright contradiction) in someone who doesn't have any medical skill nevertheless healing someone. Education in medicine crucially requires those who don't (yet) have the medical craft to prescribe treatments, and lots of those treatments will be healings (we would hope). But if this test does characterize a modality distinct from that illustrated by the capacity-change relation, then a host of difficult questions open up. How are these distinct modalities related in *Metaphysics* IX; are they ever run together (a particular risk when different modalities are expressed by limited vocabulary); could it remain plausible to suppose that there is the dominant focus in IX 1–5 on *priority* (in this case, of change over capacities) that I have been emphasizing?[27]

VIII: Capacities, natures, and (mere) dispositions

Let us go back to Aristotle's principle. The difficult questions arose from the following line of thought. Take a (precisely specified) active capacity. Suppose it is not currently being exercised. That is either because whatever is in the right relation to the agent doesn't have the appropriate passive capacity (example: the white hot metal is in the grasp of the skilled smith but is not yet malleable), or because whatever does have the appropriate passive capacity is not in the right relation to the agent (example: the wood is combustible but is in the next room). Aristotle is at pains to say, however opaquely, that the occurrence of *external* prevention has been accommodated.

All that could get in the way of, all that is *left* to prevent, the (precisely specified) active capacity being exercised is the unavailability of the appropriate (precisely specified) passive capacity. If that is the force of Aristotle's principle, then we have the idea that of necessity if nothing prevents an active capacity being exercised (i.e., if it's not that the appropriate passive capacity is 'unavailable'), then it *is* exercised, and that if it *isn't* exercised, then something is stopping it. (And not just *something*: it will be the absence of (something with) the appropriate passive capacity.) And that, one could argue, comes to thinking of the change-capacity relation in a different light. It shifts the balance from the capacities (which are potentialities) to the change (which is the actuality corresponding to those potentialities). It is not that the change is something extra, over and above the capacities, which goes along with them in the right conditions, but otherwise not; it is rather that the capacities *are* the change, but prevented from happening or 'held back'. This shift from the capacity to the change is what the priority (in account and in being) of actuality over potentiality comes to in the case of change and capacities.

The idea that active capacities which aren't being exercised are being 'held back', that capacities are 'striving' for exercise should be less surprising in view of the fact noted earlier, that active capacities for change are significantly like Aristotelian natures: the first a source of change in things other than the bearer, the second a source of change in the bearer itself. Aristotle explicitly describes a nature as a 'striving', an 'impulse', a 'drive' (a *hormê*). Doing so gets at the difference between a nature and a mere disposition. To say that something has a (mere) disposition is to say that *if* it is put in such and such conditions, *then* it will exhibit such and such behaviour. A rubber band has the disposition to stretch *if* a force is applied, but does not in itself have any impulse or drive to increase its length. Its increases in length are due to other agents, and a passive response to their input. But it cannot really be that *every* change and activity in the world is the response of something to the conditions in which it is placed, since if everything were a mere *response*, nothing would be driving or originating the world's changes. So Aristotle's view emphasizes that a nature is not a mere disposition to respond, but a default activity in the absence of interference. While a rubber band will stretch *if* a force is applied, a tree will send down roots and produce leaves *unless* something stops it. And what holds of natures holds of capacities for change. An active capacity *goes off* unless it is prevented from doing so—either by the total absence of, or an inappropriate relation to, a suitable patient.

IX: PRIORITY

We are now in a better position to appreciate the significance of *Metaphysics* IX 1–5. It might have seemed surprising that so much attention was devoted by Aristotle to capacities for change. After all, the principle that of necessity appropriate pairs of

active and passive capacities are exercised when (their bearers are) in the right relation is one with which a student of Aristotle's physics would already be familiar,[28]
and the fact that it is a claim about *changes* might suggest that it is too limited in
scope for the project of *Metaphysics* IX. Indeed, as Aristotle says at the start of IX,
the discussion of potentiality for change in chapters 1–5

> is…not the most useful for what we want now. For potentiality and actuality
> extend more widely than those cases which are so called only in respect of
> change.

(Met. IX 1 1045b36–1046a2)

What Aristotle 'wants now' as he embarks on *Metaphysics* IX is to provide some
elucidation of actuality and potentiality in general, respecting the fact that that distinction is one on a level with the notion of substance and the categorial analysis of
being. For just as the metaphysician needs to understand the notion of substance
in such a way that it can be applied to both the changeable and the non-changing
worlds, so too the discussion of actuality and potentiality should not be limited
to the realm of change and the relation of change to capacities. Given that general
purpose, why should it be so important to argue for the principle that of necessity
some limited set of potentialities (i.e., capacities for change), appropriately paired
and in the right relation, are actualized (change occurs)? The reason, as suggested
earlier, is that this principle is what grounds the priority of actuality over potentiality in the case of change and capacities for change.[29] If that is the main import
of IX 1–5, then we should expect the same emphasis on priority to be central to
Aristotle's discussion of another case of the potential/actual distinction: the relation between matter and substance. Is that expectation borne out?

X: MATTER AND SUBSTANCE

Once we have been thinking about the capacity-change relation, there is a considerable intuitive appeal to viewing the relation of matter to substance from the
same potentiality/actuality perspective. For example, if someone has the potter's
craft (active capacity), and exercises it on some suitably workable clay (passive
capacity), she will end up working (change) that clay (some matter) into a pot (a
quasi-substance). This illustrates the plausible parallel connection between the
capacity-change case and some obvious examples of matter and substance. But
it must also be true that even such favourable examples of matter turned into a
(quasi)-substance require a broader perspective on the potentiality-actuality distinction *Metaphysics* IX 1–5 provided. For even in these favourable cases the relation of capacity to change (e.g., of potter's skill to pot-turning) is quite a different

relation from that of clay to pot. And there will be further cases to consider, as when matter composes rather than being turned into a substance, which do not have even this connection with capacities and change. So with the relation of matter and substance we have a new case of the potentiality-actuality relation.

One might reasonably suspect that Aristotle's discussion of matter and substance will involve greater difficulties than his treatment of capacities for change. *Metaphysics* IX 7 includes arguments intended to show that the matter of an F is potentially F so long as that matter is suitable for turning into an F just by an exercise of the appropriate F-directed capacity: some wood is potentially a table so long as it can be turned into a table simply and solely by the exercise of a carpenter's skill.[30] It is harder, though, to appreciate the way in which the matter of a living organism stands to that organism as potential to actual, since flesh and bone, for example, are never 'turned into' a living organism. Yet it is precisely this type of matter-substance relation that we would have to be thinking about in order to make headway with Aristotle's suggestion in *Metaphysics* VIII 6 as to how to solve a problem concerning the unity of form and matter in a compound substance:[31]

> The reason is that people look for a unifying formula (*logos henopoios*) and a difference (*diaphora*) between potentiality (*dunamis*) and actuality (*entelecheia*). But, as has been said, the proximate matter and the form are one and the same thing, the one potentially (*dunamei*), the other actually (*energeiai*). Therefore to ask the cause of their being one is like asking the cause of unity in general; for each thing is a unity, and the potential (*to dunamei*) and the actual (*to energeiai*) are somehow one.

> (*Met.* VIII 6 1045b16–21)

How far would failure in making sense of all of Aristotle's claims about matter and substance be failure in the project of *Metaphysics* IX as a whole? This depends on how far one thinks the purpose of the discussion in IX is to accommodate problems arising from Aristotle's hylomorphic metaphysics of substance in *Metaphysics* VII-VIII.[32] But one cannot really come to a decision on that issue without providing a full account of the place of IX within the *Metaphysics*, which would in its turn require progress on thorny questions concerning the internal structure of the *Metaphysics* as a whole.

I will put the difficulties of Aristotle's account of matter and substance aside, and close with some general comments on the 'upwards' approach of IX to the actuality/potentiality distinction—the strategy of elucidating that distinction by examining specific and different cases which fall under it. When the only case on the table was that of capacities for change, the only question about priority that one could reasonably ask was: is a change prior to the pair of capacities of which it is the joint exercise? But once the case of matter and substance is introduced, logical room opens up for asking questions not specifically about capacities for change, nor specifically about the matter of substances, but at a more abstract level about potentiality and actuality in general. With the case of matter and substance in view we can ask *two* questions about priority. *First* is substance prior to matter?

And *second* is actuality generally prior to potentiality? A positive answer to the first of those questions is what is required for *Metaphysics* VIII 6's resolution of problems concerning hylomorphism (though, as noted, the prospects for success may seem poor). But it is the second question that is of greater significance for the project of first philosophy, and the general 'science of being'. For one main purpose of *Metaphysics* IX is to assure us that actuality remains prior to potentiality once we move outside the realm of changing beings and consider the scale of unchanging and immaterial substances introduced in *Metaphysics* XII.[33] Aristotle's talk in IX 6 of an *analogy* between capacities and changes, and matter and substance is, I think, intended to direct our attention to this second more abstract level. On the one hand, the argument in *Metaphysics* IX 8 has to proceed case by case for the different instances of potentiality-actuality, since the abstract actuality-potentiality relation always has to be manifest in some specific type of instance or other. But on the other hand, there is a general pattern about which *something* can be said on the basis of grasping the analogies between different cases, so that it turns out that in a way the whole of *Theta* has a single subject matter: that analogical relation.

Notes

1. It would be wrong to think that nothing had been said. For example, Parmenides' statements of the ways of inquiry have modal content, and modal notions turn up elsewhere in the poem (DK 28 B2.3–6 = Kirk, Raven, Schofield (*The Presocratic Philosophers* 2nd edition Cambridge University Press, 1983; abbreviated to KRS for this note), §291'The one, that [it] is and that it is impossible for [it] not to be, is the path of Persuasion (for she attends upon Truth); the other, that [it] is not and that it is needful that [it] not be, that I declare to you is an altogether indiscernible track'; B8.30–32 = KRS §298 'For strong Necessity holds it within the bonds of a limit, which keeps it in on every side'. The sole remaining fragment of Leucippus contains the word *necessity* (DK 67 B 2 = KRS §569 'Nothing occurs at random, but everything for a reason and by necessity'). If we are to believe Furth's reconstruction of Anaxagoras, that philosopher's murky remarks are an attempt to get at the distinction between what is manifest (actual) and what is latent (potential): Montgomery Furth, 'A Philosophical Hero: Anaxagoras and the Eleatics', *Oxford Studies in Ancient Philosophy* 9 (1991), 95–129. Plato distinguishes between possession and use of knowledge (*Theaetetus* 197b-d). The materialist Giants in the *Sophist* are offered the idea that the mark of what is real is the capacity to affect or be affected (*Sophist* 247d-e).

2. In what follows quotations from Aristotle will generally follow the Revised Oxford Translation (*The Complete Works of Aristotle* (Princeton University Press, 1984: two volumes) edited bu Jonathan Barnes). In the case of *Metaphysics* IX, however, I will use my own translation from the Clarendon Aristotle series *Aristotle: Metaphysics Book Θ* translated with Introduction and Commentary by Stephen Makin (Clarendon Press, Oxford, 2006).

3. See *Prior Analytics* I 3 and I 8–22. Aristotle sketches the modal differences which his logic aims to accommodate at the opening of *APo* I 8 (29b29–32: 'Since there is a difference according as something belongs [*huparchein*], necessarily belongs [*ex anankês huparchein*] or may belong [*endechesthai huparchein*] (for many things

belong, but not necessarily [*ouk ex anankês*], others neither necessarily nor indeed at all, but it is possible for them to belong [*ta d'out ex anankês outh' huparchei holôs, endechetai d'huparchein* ...]'). See also note 5 below.

4. Aristotle is sensitive to competing intuitions in this area. At *De Interpretatione* 12–13, the smoothest account of the logical relations between different modalities is obtained by reliance on a notion of possibility according to which what is possible follows from what is necessary (see *DI* 13 22b11 'for the necessary to be is possible to be', with comments at Ackrill (*Aristotle's Categories and De Interpretatione* (Oxford University Press, 1963), 151–152). At *APo* I 13 32a17–21 by contrast possibility is defined as inconsistent with necessity (32a18–19 'I use the terms 'to be possible' [*endechesthai*] and 'the possible' [*to endechomenon*] of that which is not necessary...'); the notion of possibility as following from necessity is there given as a secondary case (32a20–21 'We say indeed, homonymously, of the necessary that it is possible'. I will say something later about the related test for possibility given at *Metaphysics* IX 3 1047a24–26. On Aristotle's modal logic see McCall, *Aristotle's Modal Syllogistic* (North-Holland, Amsterdam, 1963); van Rijen, *Aspects of Aristotle's Logic of Modalities* (D. Reidel, Dordrecht, 1989); Patterson, *Aristotle's Modal Logic: Essence and Entailment in the Organon* (Cambridge University Press, 1995); Thom, *The Logic of Essentialism: An Interpretation of Aristotle's Modal Syllogistic* (Kluwer, Dirdrecht, 1996).

5. See *APo* I 8 29b29–32, quoted in note 3 above.

6. In what follows I concentrate on the relation of the actuality/potentiality distinction, to the categories. It is also related to a fundamental distinction of Aristotle's physics, that between form and matter. For more on the form/matter distinction, see S. Marc Cohen's 'Alteration and Persistence: Form and Matter in the *Physics* and *de Generatione et Corruptione*', Chapter 9 in this volume. On the parallel with actuality/potentiality see *DA* II 1 412a9–11 and at greater length 412a19–26; *Met.* VIII 1 1042a26–27; 2 1042b8–10, and 1043a14–21; 6 1045b18–21. The form/matter distinction appears (first?) in *Physics* I 7–9, where Aristotle relies on it to give an account of change which is resistant to the arguments mounted by Parmenides and his followers against the existence of change; Aristotle says at 191b27–28 that the actuality/potentiality distinction could have been used to reply to those arguments in place of that between form and matter.

There is room for disagreement as to whether the actuality/potentiality and form/matter parallel obtains trivially and definitionally, or whether its doing so is a substantive result to be established by argument.

The following (non-Aristotelian) argument would make the parallel attractive. Start from the form/matter (hylomorphic) analysis of change. If some matter comes to compose something (e.g., this lump of clay is turned into a statue), then a change occurs: the clay initially lacks the statue-form, and then possesses it. Change is a transition between *contrary* properties (e.g. *Phys.* V 1 224b28–35). But explaining what it is for two properties to be *contraries* requires reference to some single item which *can be* each of the contrary properties. For it is not sufficient for F and G to be contraries, just that there be *some* object A such that A cannot be F and G at the same time; if it were then, if it is impossible that A be F then F would be contrary to any property you like (it is not possible that this apple be prime; so it is not possible that it be prime and G at the same time, for any G you like). Nor is it sufficient for F and G to be contraries that *all* objects are such that it is impossible that they be F and G at the same time; if it were then, if it is impossible for *any* object to be F, then

F would be contrary to any property you like (it is not possible for *any* object to be the largest prime; so it is not possible for any object to be the largest prime and G for any G you like). What is required for F and G to be contraries is (a) that something can be F, (b) that anything that can be F can be G and *vice versa*, and (c) that nothing can be F and G at the same time. (a) is required because (b) alone does not rule out cases in which both F and G are properties which nothing can possess (in the absence of (a) the properties of being-the-largest-prime and being-a-male-ewe would count as contraries, which looks implausible). Since (a)-(c) together explicate what it is for properties being contraries, and since (a) and (b) together direct our attention to something which can be both F and G (i.e., the contrary termini of a change), then we have the connection Aristotle wants between the *matter* underlying change and what has the *potentiality* for each of the contrary termini of a change.

7. See elsewhere in this volume Chapter 14, Shields, 'Being *qua* Being'; Chapter 15, Loux, 'Substances, Coincidentals, and Aristotle's Constituent Ontology'; and Chapter 17, Menn, 'Aristotle's Theology'.

8. See the start of *Met.* VI 2 (1026a33–1026b2). A more detailed investigation of each of these divisions of being follows: VI 2–3 on accidental being, VII-VIII on being as divided among the categories and concentrating on the privileged case of substance; VI 4 and IX 10 on being as truth; IX 1–9 on being as actuality and potentiality.

9. Aristotle's view, it should be noted, is that actuality is prior to the potentiality to which it stands as actuality. This is quite different from the view that if something possesses a potentiality (capacity) then that potentiality is derived from some actual features of its possessor. In fact, the modern inclination to suppose that potentialities must be grounded in some material basis of their bearers is rather at odds with Aristotle's understanding of the priority of actuality.

10. See for example *Met.* IV 2 1003a33–34 and 1003b1–10. The term 'focal meaning' is due to Owen, 'Logic and Metaphysics in Some Earlier Works of Aristotle', in I. Düring and G.E.L. Owen, eds., *Aristotle and Plato in the Mid-Fourth Century* (Göteborg: Elanders Boktryckeri Aktiebolag, 1960), 180–199; (reprinted as Owen, *Logic, Science and Dialectic*, ed., M. Nussbaum (Duckworth, London, 1986), chapter 10. Others prefer different terminology. For a full discussion of these issues see Shields, *Order in Multiplicity: Homonymy in the Philosophy of Aristotle* (Oxford University Press, 1999) and Ward, *Aristotle on Homonymy: Dialectic and Science* (Cambridge University Press, 2007).

11. See *Met.* V 11 1019a1–4. For a discussion of this notion of priority, see Dancy, 'Aristotle and the Priority of Actuality', in S. Knuuttila, ed., *Reforging the Great Chain of Being* (D. Reidel, Dordrecht, 1981), 73–115; Cleary, *Aristotle on the Many Senses of Priority* (*Journal of the History of Philosophy*, Monograph Series: Southern Illinois University Press, Carbondale, Ill., 1988); Witt, 'The Priority of Actuality in Aristotle' in Scaltsas, Charles, Gill, eds., *Unity, Identity and Explanation in Aristotle's Metaphysics* (Clarendon Press, Oxford, 1994), 215–228; Panayides, 'Aristotle on the Priority of Actuality in Substance', *Ancient Philosophy* 19 (1999), 327–344; Makin, 'What Does Aristotle Mean by Priority in Substance', *Oxford Studies in Ancient Philosophy* 24 (2003) 209–238; Peramatzis, 'Aristotle's Notion of Priority in Nature and Substance', *Oxford Studies in Ancient Philosophy* 35 (2008), 187–247; Peramatzis, *Priority in Aristotle's Metaphysics* (Oxford University Press, 2011).

12. See Ross, *Aristotle's Metaphysics: Revised Text with Introduction and Commentary* cxxiv-cxxv (Clarendon Press, Oxford, 1924: two volumes); Frede, 'Aristotle's Notion of Potentiality in *Metaphysics* Θ' Scaltsas, Charles, Gill, eds., *Unity, Identity and*

Explanation in Aristotle's Metaphysics (Clarendon Press, Oxford, 1994), 173–193; Makin, *Theta* (Clarendon Press, Oxford, 2006), 18–21;, Shields, 'An Approach to Aristotelian Actuality' in *Mind, Method and Morality: Essays in Honour of Anthony Kenny*, eds., P. Hacker and J. Cottingham (Oxford University Press: 2009), 68–93; Anagnostopoulos, 'Senses of *Dunamis* and the Structure of Aristotle's *Metaphysics* Θ', *Phronesis* 56 (2011) 388-425

13. See also *Met.* XII 6–7, especially 1071b17–20 and 1072a24–26. What about the other way round: could there be potentialities with no corresponding actuality? *DI* 13 23a23–26 suggests there could: 'some things are actualities without capabilities [*ta aneu dunameôs enegeiai*] (like the primary substances), others with capability [*ta meta dunameôs*] (and these are prior by nature but posterior in time to the capability), and others are never actualities but only capabilities [*ta oudepote energeiai eisin alla dunameis monon*]'. Perhaps the potentiality of earth to move to the centre of the cosmos would be an example. This potentiality explains a good deal about the movement of lumps of earth. But nothing could ever arrive at the centre of the cosmos, because there is always something else already there. This is a difficult area, however. Some take Aristotle to understand modality in temporal terms, which would perhaps rule out *eternally* unactualized potentialities: see Hintikka, *Time and Necessity: Studies in Aristotle's Theory of Modality* (Clarendon Press, Oxford, 1973); Waterlow, *Passage and Possibility: A Study of Aristotle's Modal Concepts* (Clarendon Press, Oxford, 1982); Judson, 'Eternity and Necessity in *De Caelo* I.12', *Oxford Studies in Ancient Philosophy* 1 (1983), 217–55. See also in this volume Coope, Chapter 11, 'Aristotle on the Infinite', who discusses the intriguing case of the infinite divisibility of continuous magnitudes: it might seem that a continuous magnitude has some sort of potentiality for infinite division, although no magnitude can ever have been infinitely divided (see *Phys.* III 6, and in particular 206b12–16, and *Met.* IX 6, 1048b9–17).

14. *DA* 2 1 412a27–28.

15. For more on these neologisms see Chen C-H, 'Different Meanings of the Term Energeia in the Philosophy of Aristotle', *Philosophy and Phenomenological Research* 17 (1956), 56–65; Blair, 'The Meaning of "Energeia" and "Entelecheia" in Aristotle', *International Philosophical Quarterly* 7 (1967), 101–117; Graham, 'The Etymology of Entelecheia', *American Journal of Philology* 110 (1989), 73–80; Blair, *Energeia and Entelecheia: 'Act' in Aristotle* (University of Ottawa Press, Ottawa, 1992); Blair, 'Aristotle on *Entelecheia*: A Reply to Daniel Graham' *American Journal of Philology* 114 (1993), 91–97; Menn, 'The Origins of Aristotle's Concept of Energeia: Energeia and Dunamis', *Ancient Philosophy* 14 (1994), 73–114; Graham, 'The Development of Aristotle's Concept of Actuality: Comments on a Reconstruction by Stephen Menn' *Ancient Philosophy* 15 (1995), 551–564; Blair, 'Unfortunately, It Is A Bit More Complex: Reflections on *Energeia*', *Ancient Philosophy* 15 (1995), 565–580. See also Jonathan Beere, *Doing and Being: An Interpretation of Aristotle's* Metaphysics *Theta* (Oxford University Press, 2009), in particular chapter 8, for some pessimistic reflections on whether there is a single unambiguous translation which would fit all Aristotelian usages of the neologisms *energeia* and *entelecheia*.

16. *Met.* IX 1 1046a10–11.

17. *Met.* IX 8 1049b9–10. The canonical text concerning natures is *Phys.* II 1. There is a considerable literature on this notion. Some excellent pieces are Waterlow, *Nature, Change and Agency* (Clarendon Press, Oxford, 1982); Kelsey, 'Aristotle's Definition of Nature', *OSAP* 25 (2003), 59–87; and Wardy, 'The Mysterious Aristotelian Olive', *Science in Context* 18 (2005), 69–91.

18. *Phys.* II 1 192b18–19: a nature is 'an innate impulse for change' (*hormê metabolês emphuton*). On the acquisition and loss of capacities, see *Met.* IX 3 1047a1–2; IX 5 1047b31–35; and IX 8 1049b29–1050a3.

19. Compare *Met.* IX 1 1045b29–32 on the priority of substance ('the others are called beings in accordance with the account of substance, i.e., quantity, quality, and the others which are so called: for they will involve the account of substance, as we said in the earlier discussions') with 1046a15–16 on the priority of active capacity ('for there is in all these definitions [of types of capacity] the account of the primary capacity').

20. See *Met.*VII 7 1032b6–9, 17–21 for the structure of the skilled deliberations and decisions guided by such rational capacities.

21. *Met.* IX 2 1046a36–1046b4. Rational capacities are possessed by rational agents *qua rational*. So rational agents will possess lots of non-rational capacities: for example, human beings have the capacity to digest, to see, to produce heat, but could retain these even if, due to major physical trauma, they lost their rational powers.

22. *Met.* IX 2 1046b6–7.

23. I tried to make headway on these two points at Makin, *Theta* (Clarendon Press, Oxford, 2006), 118–124. I am less confident now that I was entirely successful. See also Moline, 'Provided Nothing External Interferes' *Mind* 84 (1975), 244–254.

24. '*Met.* IX 5 1048b15–16: And it has [the capacity] when the patient is present and has [its capacity] in this way; and if not it will not be capable of acting' (*echei de parontos tou pathêtikou kai hôdi echontos*). This opaque sentence immediately precedes the passage quoted in the preceding section, in which Aristotle says that we do not need to include a saving clause about the absence of external prevention. For discussion and a defence of my interpretation of 1048a15–16 see Makin, *Aristotle: Metaphysics Book Θ* (Clarendon Press, Oxford, 2006), 112–118.

25. Because the discussion in Section VII concerns the thought that there are two types of modality at play in *Metaphysics* IX 1–5 (a capacity, skill, or ability; and another type), I have given alternate translations of the modal terms in citing 1047a24–26, so as not to beg any questions.

26. See *APo* I 13 32a18–20: 'I use the terms 'to be possible' (*endechesthai*) and 'the possible' (*to endechomenon*) of that which is not necessary but, being assumed, results in nothing impossible'.

27. I have been selective in appealing to chapters 1, 2, and 5 of *Metaphysics* IX. There is material in the first five chapters which appears to have little to do with capacities for change (for example IX 4 1047b14–30, which appears to be an argument for a pair of modal theses).

28. For appeal to and use of this principle in natural science, see, e.g., *Phys.* VIII 1 251b1–5, 8 4 255a34–255b1; *MA* 8 702a12–15; *GA* II 4 740b21–24.

29. A question. If a change is prior to a capacity—if the capacity just *is* the change *in potentiality*—then how can citation of a capacity be explanatory, as the characterisation of a capacity as an *origin* (*archê*) of change suggests it is. The answer is that Aristotle's principle leaves a great deal open. It doesn't say anything about what happens when an active capacity is interfered with. It doesn't say everything that there is to say about what occurs when an active capacity is exercised: it says, for example, that a fire's active capacity to heat will produce heating so long as nothing prevents it, but it doesn't say anything about how the heating is manifest in different circumstances (sometimes as liquifying, e.g., of ice; sometimes as solidifying, e.g., of clay). And it doesn't say anything about the interactions between the simultaneous exercises of different active capacities, as happens commonly in a complex world such as ours. There will be lots of cases where it is no trivial matter to trace some outcome back to a particular pair of active and passive capacities. Citing the

dormitive power of opium may not be much of an explanation of someone's falling asleep. But consider instead someone who has been administered a cocktail of inter-acting drugs, and whose blood pressure suddenly and mysteriously drops. It might well be very explanatory to track that critical drop down to the dormitive power of the opiates he was given, rather than, e.g., the anti-inflammatory powers of the steroids he also took.

30. See *Metaphysics* IX 7 1048b37–1049a18, and Frede, 'Aristotle's Notion of Potentiality in *Metaphysics* Θ' in Scaltsas, Charles, Gill, eds., *Unity, Identity and Explanation in Aristotle's Metaphysics* (Clarendon Press, Oxford, 1994), 173–193.

31. There is disagreement about the precise problem under consideration in *Metaphysics* VIII 6, and about the relation of the material in that chapter to the discussion in VII 12 of the unity of definition (how is it that rational animal succeeds in defining a substantial kind while heavy animal does not?). On VIII 6 in particular, see Halper, 'Metaphysics Z 12 and H 6: The Unity of Form and Composite' *Ancient Philosophy* 4 (1984), 146–159; Gill, 'Aristotle on Substance' (Princeton University Press, Princeton, N.J., 1989) especially chapters 4 and 5; Loux, 'An Examination of *Metaphysics* H6', in *The Crossroads of Norm and Nature*, ed. May Sim (Rowman and Littlefield, Lanham Md., 1995), 247–279; Harte, 'Aristotle *Metaphysics* H6: A Dialogue with Platonism' *Phronesis* 41 (1996) 276–304; Kim, '*Metaphysics* H6 and the Problem of Unity', *Journal of the History of Philosophy* 46 (2008), 25–42.

32. I now think there was an over-concentration in Makin, *Aristotle: Metaphysics Book* Θ (Clarendon Press, Oxford, 2006) on this purpose for IX. The treatise also contributes to the project of *Metaphysics* XII, and is relevant to the *aporia* at III 6 1002b32–1003a5 (1002b32–34 'Closely connected with this is the question whether the elements exist potentially (*dunamei*) or in some other way (*ê tin' heteron tropon*)'.

33. Notice how Aristotle closes the IX 8 discussion of priority: 1051a2–3: 'Therefore, that actuality is prior both to potentiality and to every origin of change is evident'. I take this as an entirely general conclusion. 'Every origin of change' (*pasa archê metablêtikês*) refers to *both* origins in one thing of change in another (i.e., capacities for change) *and* origins in one thing of change in that thing (i.e., natures); 'potentiality' (*dunamis*) refers to the other cases which can be brought under the potentiality-actuality relation (matter-substance, temporary-eternal things). IX 9 comments briefly on the relative values of potentialities and actualities (1051a4–21), and on the actualizing of potential constructions in geometrical proofs (1051a21–33). In both cases, Aristotle's interest predominantly concerns the priority—evaluative and epistemic—of actuality over potentiality (1051a4–5 'the actuality is also better and more valuable than the good potentiality'; 1051a15–16 'it is necessary also in the case of bad things for the end and the actuality to be worse than the potentiality'; 1051a17–19 'so it is clear that the bad is not in addition to the things; for the bad is posterior in nature (*husteron têi phusei*) to the potentiality'; 1051a29–30 'so that it is evident that the things which are potentially (*ta dunamei*) are discovered when they are drawn out into actuality (*eis energeian*)'.

BIBLIOGRAPHY

Anagnostopoulos, A. (2011) 'Senses of *Dunamis* and the Structure of Aristotle's *Metaphysics* Θ' *Phronesis* 56, 388–425.

Aristotle (1984) *The Complete Works of Aristotle: The Revised Oxford Translation*, edited by J. Barnes (Princeton: Princeton Univ. Press).

Aristotle (2006) *Metaphysics Book Θ*, translated with Introduction and commentary by Stephen Makin (Oxford: Clarendon Press).

Beere, J. (2009) *Doing and Being: An Interpretation of Aristotle's* Metaphysics *Theta* (Oxford: Oxford Univ. Press).

Blair, G.A. (1967) 'The Meaning of "Energeia" and "Entelecheia" in Aristotle', *International Philosophical Quarterly* 7, 101–117.

——— (1992) *Energeia and Entelecheia: 'Act' in Aristotle* (Ottawa: University of Ottawa Press).

——— (1993) 'Aristotle on *Entelecheia*: a Reply to Daniel Graham', *American Journal of Philology* 114, 91–97.

——— (1995) 'Unfortunately, It Is a Bit More Complex: Reflections on *Energeia*', *Ancient Philosophy* 15, 565–580.

Chen, C.-H. (1956) 'Different Meanings of the Term Energeia in the Philosophy of Aristotle', *Philosophy and Phenomenological Research* 17, 56–65.

Cleary, J.J. (1988) *Aristotle on the Many Senses of Priority*, Journal of the History of Philosophy Monograph Series (Carbondale: Southern Illinois Univ. Press).

Dancy, R.M. (1981) 'Aristotle and the Priority of Actuality' in S. Knuuttila, ed., *Reforging the Great Chain of Being* (Dordrecht: D. Reidel), 73–115.

Frede, M. (1994) 'Aristotle's Notion of Potentiality in *Metaphysics* Θ', in T. Scaltsas, D. Charles, and M.L. Gill, eds., *Unity, Identity and Explanation in Aristotle's Metaphysics* (Oxford: Clarendon Press), 173–193.

Furth, M. (1991) 'A Philosophical Hero: Anaxagoras and the Eleatics', *Oxford Studies in Ancient Philosophy* 9, 95–129.

Gill, M.L. (1989) *Aristotle on Substance* (Princeton: Princeton Univ. Press).

Graham, D.W. (1989) 'The Etymology of Entelecheia', *American Journal of Philology* 110, 73–80.

Graham, D.W. (1995) 'The Development of Aristotle's Concept of Actuality: Comments on a Reconstruction by Stephen Menn', *Ancient Philosophy* 15, 551–564.

Halper, E. (1984) '*Metaphysics* Z12 and H6: The Unity of Form and Composite', *Ancient Philosophy* 4, 146–159.

Harte, V. (1996) 'Aristotle *Metaphysics* H6: A Dialogue with Platonism', *Phronesis* 41, 276–304.

Hintikka, J. (1973) *Time and Necessity: Studies in Aristotle's Theory of Modality* (Oxford: Clarendon Press).

Judson, L. (1983) 'Eternity and Necessity in *De Caelo* I.12', *Oxford Studies in Ancient Philosophy* 1, 217–55.

Kelsey, S. (2003) 'Aristotle's Definition of Nature', *Oxford Studies in Ancient Philosophy* 25, 59–87.

Kim, H.-K. (2008)'*Metaphysics* H6 and the Problem of Unity', *Journal of the History of Philosophy* 46, 25–42.

Loux, M. (1995) 'An Examination of *Metaphysics* H6', in *The Crossroads of Norm and Nature,* ed., May Sim (Lanham Md.: Rowman and Littlefield), 247–279.

Makin, S. (2003) 'What Does Aristotle Mean by Priority in Substance', *Oxford Studies in Ancient Philosophy* 24, 209–238.

McCall, S. (1963) *Aristotle's Modal Syllogistic* (Amsterdam: North-Holland).

Menn, S. (1994) 'The Origins of Aristotle's Concept of Energeia: Energeia and Dunamis', *Ancient Philosophy* 14, 73–114.

Moline, J. (1975) 'Provided Nothing External Interferes', *Mind* 84, 244–254.

Owen, G.E.L. (1960) 'Logic and Metaphysics in Some Earlier Works of Aristotle', in I. Düring and G.E.L. Owen, eds., *Aristotle and Plato in the Mid-Fourth Century* (Göteborg: Elanders Boktryckeri Aktiebolag), 180–199.

—— (1986) *Logic, Science and Dialectic,* M. Nussbaum, ed. (London: Duckworth).

Panayides, C.Y. (1999) 'Aristotle on the Priority of Actuality in Substance', *Ancient Philosophy* 19, 327–344.

Patterson, R. (1995) *Aristotle's Modal Logic: Essence and Entailment in the Organon* (Cambridge: Cambridge Univ. Press).

Peramatzis, M.M. (2008) 'Aristotle's Notion of Priority in Nature and Substance', *Oxford Studies in Ancient Philosophy* 35, 187–247.

—— (2011) *Priority in Aristotle's Metaphysics* (Oxford: Oxford Univ. Press).

Ross, W.D. (1924) *Aristotle's Metaphysics: Revised Text with Introduction and Commentary* (Oxford: Clarendon Press), cxxiv–cxxv.

Shields, C. (1999) *Order in Multiplicity: Homonymy in the Philosophy of Aristotle* (Oxford: Oxford Univ. Press).

—— (2009) 'An Approach to Aristotelian Actuality', in *Mind, Method and Morality: Essays in Honour of Anthony Kenny,* P. Hacker and J. Cottingham, eds. (Oxford: Oxford Univ. Press), 68–93.

Thom, P. (1996) *The Logic of Essentialism: An Interpretation of Aristotle's Modal Syllogistic* (Dirdrecht: Kluwer).

van Rijen, J. (1989) *Aspects of Aristotle's Logic of Modalities* (Dordrecht: D. Reidel).

Ward, J. (2007) *Aristotle on Homonymy: Dialectic and Science* (Cambridge: Cambridge Univ. Press).

Wardy, R. (2005) 'The Mysterious Aristotelian Olive', *Science in Context* 18, 69–91.

Waterlow (Broadie), S. (1982a) *Passage and Possibility: A Study of Aristotle's Modal Concepts* (Oxford: Clarendon Press).

—— (1982b) *Nature, Change and Agency* (Oxford: Clarendon Press).

Witt, C. (1994) 'The Priority of Actuality in Aristotle', in T. Scaltsas, D. Charles, M.L. Gill, eds., *Unity, Identity and Explanation in Aristotle's Metaphysics* (Oxford: Clarendon Press), 215–228.

CHAPTER 17

ARISTOTLE'S THEOLOGY

STEPHEN MENN[1]

A standard way of thinking about Aristotle's theology goes roughly as follows. Aristotle's God, or his substitute for the gods, is the unmoved mover. This is a form which governs the motion of the heavens in something like the way that our soul governs our body; but because of the greater perfection of the heavenly bodies, which do not need nutritive or sensory functions, in the case of the heavens the form is not ontologically dependent on its body and has its activity separate from the body, and so remains entirely unchanged. The explanatory gap that Aristotle fills with this mover is a by-product of archaic celestial physics, and even within that physics its causality is so slight that we might suspect Aristotle of inventing make-work for it to do; it does not seem to act on the world, or even to know the world, and if it is supposed to satisfy any religious aspirations, it does so badly. So we have little impulse to believe that such a thing actually exists. But if we treat it as a thought-experiment, it may satisfy metaphysical aspirations: *if* such a thing exists, it will be a paradigm of what a form, a substance, a being should be when entirely independent of matter and other things; and, because the only activity remaining for it is pure contemplation detached from sensation and practical needs, it may also be a paradigm of the metaphysician.

This way of thinking about Aristotle's theology is not entirely false, but it is badly misleading. First, Aristotle has no word like 'God' with a capital 'G': he believes in many gods and divine things, and they are not all unmoved movers. When Aristotle speaks of '*theologikē*', and when I following him will speak of 'theology', he means not the study of a single God, but the study of gods and divine things in general. (He often uses 'god' as a collective singular, like 'man'.) Second, he believes in many unmoved movers, and they are not all gods:

besides the many unmoved movers of the heavens, each human or animal soul is an unmoved mover (see discussion below). Aristotle never uses the phrase 'the unmoved mover' to pick out just one being (or even to pick out the many movers of the heavenly spheres), and that phrase would not express the essence of the beings it applies to. When he wants to express more adequately the essence of his single first principle, he calls it not 'god' or 'unmoved mover', but '*nous*' [Reason or intellect] or '*noêsis*' [thinking or intellectual apprehension], or the Good. He never says that it is a form, and it does not seem to be a substance or a being in any stronger sense than other substances are, but its activity is needed for the actual existence of an ordered world.[2] And our knowledge of its existence and activity does seem to be a way of satisfying a religious aspiration.

To see what sort of religious interest there might be in such a being, and how the words 'god' and 'divine' enter into Aristotle's philosophy, it is best to start with what he says about gods and divine things in moral and political contexts.[3] In the *Metaphysics* Aristotle cites a definition of god as 'best eternal living thing' (XII 7 1072b28–9), which is close to the formula of the pseudo-Platonic *Definitions*, 'immortal living thing self-sufficient with regard to happiness' (411a3).[4] The gods, and the inhabitants of the Isles of the Blessed (likewise supposed immortal), thus serve as limiting cases for happiness, free from the limitations of human life. Their happiness, like ours, must consist in an activity exercising virtue; and reflecting on the kind of virtue that someone freed from mortal limitations would exercise helps us to isolate the constituents of a good life that have their goodness purely in themselves, not conditioned by the existence of evils. If one must defend oneself and one's city in battle, courageous action is better than cowardly action, but it would be better not to have occasions that call for courage; but if the bad background conditions were removed, what sort of good activities would remain?

> We have supposed that the gods are most of all blessed and happy; so what kind of practical action is it fitting to attribute to them? *Just* actions? They would seem ridiculous, making contracts and returning deposits and the like. *Brave* actions, submitting to fearful things and accepting danger because it is noble? *Generous* actions? To whom will they give? It is absurd if they too are to have money or something of the kind. And *temperate* actions, what would they be? The praise is vulgar, for they do not have base appetites. If we examine, all these things seem to be about actions which are petty and unworthy of the gods. Yet everyone has supposed that they *live*, and so that they *act*: surely they are not asleep like Endymion. But if someone is alive and practical action is taken away, and still more productive action, what is left to him except contemplation? So the activity of god, excelling in blessedness, would be contemplative activity (*EN* X 8 1178b8–22).

The consequence is not only that the gods do not have the moral virtues (against Plato's insistence that the gods are just), but also that they do not have practical intellectual virtue or *phronêsis* ['prudence' or practical wisdom], the disposition to deliberate well about one's own or collective action (against Plato's insistence that the gods plan providentially for humans and the cosmos). And thus, as Aristotle infers at the end of the *Eudemian Ethics*, a god will not rule by giving commands, e.g., to be worshipped in a certain way:[5] Aristotle assumes that a god would do so only if he had some need of us or would be somehow benefitted by our action, and a god is (as the pseudo-Platonic *Definition* puts it) 'self-sufficient with regard to happiness'.

We humans, unlike the gods, need *phronêsis* to plan our lives, and moral virtues to regulate our irrational appetites, and we must be concerned with securing necessary things, and with things that are good only presupposing evils. But *phronêsis* should take as its highest aim some pure good, and the only one we have found is contemplation. Contemplating what? Aristotle says that theoretical or contemplative wisdom, *sophia*, is 'intellectual perception [*nous*] and scientific knowledge [*epistêmê*] of the things that are most honourable by nature' (*EE* V 7 = *EN* VI 7 1141b2–3); and in the same passage Aristotle casually substitutes 'divine things' or 'daemonic things' as if equivalent to 'honourable things'. *Phronêsis*, unlike *sophia*, is relative to the species of the reasoner, and for a human being involves knowledge of human things; 'and if [it is said] that man is the best of the animals, this makes no difference, for there are things much more divine by nature than man is, of which the most manifest are those out of which the cosmos is composed [i.e., the heavenly bodies]' (1141a33–b2). And this distinction between *phronêsis* and the higher *sophia* it aims to secure arises not only in individual life-planning, but also for the whole city. Thus Aristotle stresses that the statesman should aim chiefly not at war or acquiring possessions for the city and citizens, or even at fostering political or moral virtue, but rather at the right use of peaceful leisure, in activities that would be valuable even if there were no threat of foreign or civil war, no injustices to correct, and no shortages to fill; and these activities, to the extent that the whole city can take part in them and the statesman can plan for them, will be *theôria* ['contemplation'] as achieved at festivals of the gods.

Indeed, the primary sense of *theôria* and the cognate verb *theôrein* in Greek is attending and looking on at religious festivals, understood broadly to include athletic and musical and poetic and theatrical competitions; this is a paradigm case of a seeing value purely for its own sake. The philosophers extend the term metaphorically first to contemplation of the cosmos and then to contemplation of causes prior to the cosmos, and the concern of the statesman and citizenry for religious performances gives them a model for thinking about these extended kinds of *theôria*. Thus *EE* V 13 (= *EN* VI 13) says that *phronêsis* 'is not master of *sophia*...just as [the art of] medicine is not master of health: for it does not *use* it but provides for it to come about; so it gives commands *for the sake of* it, not *to* it. It would be like saying that politics rules over the gods, because it gives commands about everything in the city [sc. including public worship]' (1145a6–11, compare 1143b33–5). This comparison is taken up at the end of the *Eudemian Ethics*: 'god does not rule by giving commands, but is that for the sake of which *phronêsis* gives commands... So whatever choice and acquisition of naturally good things—whether goods of the body, or wealth, or friends, or other goods—will most produce the contemplation [*theôria*] of god, that is the best, and this is the finest standard. And if anything, through defect or excess, prevents us from serving [*therapeuein*] and contemplating [*theôrein*] god, that is bad' (*EE* VIII 3 1249b13–20).[6] '*Therapeuein* and *theôrein* god,' taken literally, would mean participating in and observing religious performances; where, since Aristotle insists that a god cannot be benefitted, the value of the serving seems to reduce to the value of the contemplating. (Aristotle distinguishes two senses of 'for the sake of', and says that the god is that 'for the sake of which' *phronêsis* gives commands, not as 'to benefit whom [*to hô(i)*] but as 'to attain which' [*to hou*]—as, when you do something for the sake of health or of money, you are not trying to benefit the health or the money, but to possess them. To 'possess' something is to be in whatever relation to it allows you to exercise the appropriate activity involving it, so presumably to possess a god is to be able to contemplate the god.)[7] But while the right use of leisure at festivals is certainly a legitimate aim of politics, Aristotle does not literally mean that this is the highest aim of *phronêsis*. The same value that is secured for the whole city by *theôria* at festivals can be better achieved, at least for some individuals, by contemplating other things:

> As we travel to Olympia for the sake of the spectacle itself, even if nothing more were to follow from it (for the spectacle itself is worth more than much money), and as we view the Dionysia not in order to gain anything from the actors (indeed we spend money on them), and as there are many other spectacles we should prefer to much money, so too the contemplation of the universe is to be honoured above all the things that are thought useful. For surely it cannot be right that we should take great pains to go to see men imitating women and slaves, and not think it right to view without payment the nature and reality of things (*Protrepticus* B44 Düring, tr. Düring).[8]

The *Protrepticus* and the ethical treatises thus motivate the pursuit of *sophia*, a knowledge enabling specifically philosophical contemplation. Perhaps this will be contemplation of the cosmos and of the heavenly bodies (not just staring at them, but astronomical study), a view Aristotle attributes to Anaxagoras (*EE* I 5 1216a11–16); or perhaps we can come to know causes beyond the cosmos which are even more worth contemplating, a claim that Plato makes for the Forms and especially for the Form of the Good. *Metaphysics* I takes up this pursuit of *sophia* through the investigation of the first causes and principles of the manifest things (described in I 1–2, with close echoes of the ethical treatises and *Protrepticus*), and I 2 says that this knowledge will be 'divine' in two senses, both by being the kind of knowledge that the gods would have, and by being knowledge about divine things or about gods, since 'everyone thinks that god is a cause and a principle' (983a5–10). This leaves open the possibility that wisdom will be knowledge of the heavens, since the heavenly bodies are certainly divine. But in *Metaphysics* VI 1 Aristotle raises the question of whether there are eternally unchanging substances, beyond the substances constituted by nature (which are all changeable, even the eternal heavenly ones), and proposes that, if so, they will be the objects of a theoretical science other than physics, which he calls *theologikê* ['theological (science)', i.e., 'science which speaks about the gods, or about divine things', 1026a18–22], and he argues that, if so, this *theologikê* will best meet the aspirations to wisdom described in I 1–2. The claim is not so surprising (Plato too thinks that there are eternally unchanging substances, the Forms, which he also calls divine, and that they are more worth contemplating than natural things), but the term 'theologikê' is. The theologoi ['speakers about the gods'] in Aristotle are poets like Homer and Hesiod and Orpheus, whom Aristotle refuses to consider as philosophers; the phusikoi ['physicists' or natural philosophers] beginning with Thales at least tried to reason systematically about the nature of things, and can be taken seriously as philosophers (on the occasions when Aristotle assimilates the two groups it is to undermine the phusikoi, not to praise the theologoi). Aristotle carefully avoids describing his wisdom as theologia (which is always what the poets do), but still he is claiming that philosophy can achieve the poets' aspiration to know and describe divine things beyond the domain of physics. Plato too claims that, in grasping the Forms through dialectical practice as described in Republic VII, he can achieve this aspiration, succeeding where the poets (sharply criticized for their anthropomorphic and otherwise unworthy descriptions of the gods) have failed. But Aristotle is not convinced that Plato has succeeded any better than the poets:

> Although [the doctrine of Forms] involves difficulty in many places, what is most absurd is to say that there are natures beyond those which are within the heaven, but to say that these are the same as the sensibles, except that the former are eternal and the latter are corruptible. For they say that there is a man-himself and horse-itself and health-itself, and nothing else, doing something close to those who said that there were gods, but in human form: for neither did those people [the poets] make [the gods] anything other than eternal men, nor do these people [the Platonists] make the Forms anything other than eternal sensibles (Met. III 2 997b5–12).

Here Aristotle is taking up the criticism that philosophers from Xenophanes through Plato had directed against the anthropomorphic gods of Homer and Hesiod, and turns it against Plato. When the poets claim to have knowledge of the gods, this is exciting; but when they actually describe the gods, it is disappointingly obvious that they have no special knowledge of a domain beyond the human, and are merely projecting the familiar mortal things onto an eternal realm; and, Aristotle says, Plato is doing the same. 'Those who speak of Forms in one way speak rightly by separating them, if indeed these are substances; but in another way not rightly, because they say that the one-over-many is a Form. And the reason is that they cannot tell what the substances of this kind are, the incorruptible ones beyond the individuals and sensibles: so they make these the same in species [or form, eidos] with the corruptibles (for these we know), man-himself and horse-itself, adding to the sensibles the word 'itself'. But even if we had never seen the stars, nonetheless (I deem) there would still be eternal substances beyond those we knew; so also in the present case, even if we cannot tell what they are, it is still doubtless necessary that there should be some' (Met. VII 16 1040b27–1041a3). Here 'even if we had never seen the stars' means 'even if we had never emerged from the cave':9 the Platonists have recognized that we are living in a cave in the sensible world, but have fooled themselves into thinking they have found a passageway out, when in fact they 'have never seen the stars' and are acquainted only with the familiar things down here. In these passages Aristotle does not make explicit why there could not be an incorruptible or even unchangeable horse, the same in species with horses down here; but the reason would be that (as we learn from *Parts of Animals* I) a scientific definition of horse has to mention the organic parts of a horse, that these parts are not these parts unless they are organs of these vital activities, and that activities of eating, reproducing, or running away from predators make no sense for a necessarily immortal being (and moving at all is impossible for an unchangeable being).

Aristotle's criticism here of the poets and of Plato on the Forms closely resembles his criticism in EN X 8 of attributing moral (as opposed to intellectual) virtue to the gods: in both cases he intends to eliminate any predicates of divine things that would in fact apply only to some lower kind of thing, and in both cases he intends to emerge with a positive account of divine things, better grounded than what his predecessors have said and stripped of the improper assimilation of divine to lower things. There is no very short way to describe this procedure in English, or in Greek, but some Arabic terminology may help. In Muslim theological discussions, and in discussions in other religious communities within the Muslim world, there is a wide consensus that *tashbîh* should be avoided, where '*tashbîh*' means literally 'assimilation' (making or declaring something to be like something else) but in this context means specifically describing God in ways that assimilate him to things other than God, often but not necessarily human beings. The opposite of *tashbîh* is *tanzîh*, literally 'purification' but in this context specifically purifying God from descriptions inappropriate to him, either by denying these descriptions or by reinterpreting them so as to make clear the meanings in which they are appropriate to God and to distinguish them from the meanings in which they are not appropriate. Everyone agrees that *tanzîh* is a good thing, but the problem is to find a principled criterion for which descriptions of God are appropriate and which are improper *tashbîh*, and to do this in a way that does not lead to the extreme of *ta'tîl*, literally 'nullification'—having nothing left to assert about God, about what he is in himself or how he acts on other things, or how he knows or is known, because all the available descriptions have been either denied or reinterpreted in such a way as to have no content left. One reason that many Muslim thinkers were interested in Aristotle, and in the Greek commentators through whom they read Aristotle, was precisely that they saw them as trying to avoid (by denial or reinterpretation) the *tashbîh* that seems to occur in the poets and in Plato; and while certainly not all of Aristotle's criticisms of Plato fall under this heading, this does capture one thing that Aristotle is doing accurately enough that it is reasonable to adopt the Arabic terminology.[10]

There is, however, an important difference. For Muslim monotheists, every being is either God or something created by God, and *tashbîh* is assimilating God to anything created by God, whereas for Aristotle there are gods or divine things at many levels, and the error that we can call *tashbîh* consists in assimilating any such divine being to anything lower than it—attributing to divine things beyond the physical world predicates proper to physical things, attributing to heavenly things predicates proper to sublunar things, attributing to souls predicates proper to bodies. In the texts we have seen from *Metaphysics* III 2 997b5–12 and VII 16 1040b27–1041a3, Aristotle is concerned mainly with substances existing beyond the physical world, and assumed to be immaterial and unchanging (so too *De Caelo* I 9 278b21–279b3, about the things existing 'beyond the heaven', and free from time and change): these things might not be gods, since they might not be alive, but they are certainly 'divine things', meaning at least that they share traditional attributes of the gods such as eternal existence and freedom from all deficiency. (In this sense Plato contrasts a 'divine' circle and sphere with 'human' ones, *Philebus* 62a7-b2, and cf. *Parmenides* 134c10-e8.) In *De Caelo* I 2–3, however, Aristotle is arguing that the *heavenly bodies*, because they move naturally around the centre of the universe rather than towards it or away from it, must not be made of the same elements as sublunar things, must be free from the natural contrarieties of sublunar things, and must therefore be free from generation, corruption, growth or diminution, and alteration. In this way Aristotle claims to give a foundation in argument for the opinion that the heavenly bodies are 'divine', which is implicitly presupposed by everyone who represents the gods as dwelling in the heavens (*DC* I 3 270b4–11).[11] In other texts Aristotle argues against people, including Plato, who attribute to the *soul* predicates appropriate only to bodies. In particular, Aristotle thinks that motion (*kinêsis*, either locomotion or change of quantity or quality) can properly be attributed only to bodies (the soul can be said to be moved only *per accidens*, inasmuch as the living body is moved), and so he argues against people who think that the soul is moved either in thinking or in sensing or in moving the body. This involves a critique, not only of pre-Socratics like Democritus who think the soul actually is a body, but also of Plato, who in the *Timaeus* seems to describe souls both of humans and of the cosmos as three-dimensionally co-extended with their bodies, as being in motion and communicating motion to their bodies in voluntary locomotion, as picking up motion from their bodies in sensation, and as moving themselves in perfect circles in rational thinking or in distorted patterns when their rationality is disrupted.[12] Plato also argues in *Phaedrus* 245c5–246a2 that since it is distinctive of living as opposed to non-living bodies that they are self-moving, and since souls are the distinctive principles of living things, souls must be self-moving, and make the living composite self-moving by communicating their motion to the body. Whether Aristotle is talking about entirely immaterial and unchanging things, about the heavenly bodies, or about souls, the problem is to make it intelligible what these things are like in themselves, and how they can be causes to sublunar bodies (for instance, how souls can move their bodies), without sharing the characteristics of these bodies.

Concentrating on the case of entirely immaterial and unchanging things: Aristotle thinks that Plato's inappropriate descriptions of these things (as a man-himself, horse-itself, and so on) result from his positing the wrong sort of causal connections, namely, making these things the *formal* causes of the familiar sensible things; and since, as Aristotle thinks, it is nonsense for the formal cause of something to exist separately from it, Plato winds up positing new substances with only a fictitious causal connection to the sensible things he claims to be explaining (*Met.* I 9 991b1–3, 992a26–9). Aristotle wants instead to reach immaterial substances as a different kind of cause of sensible things, through a kind of causality which will lead us to understand how different these immaterial substances are from the sensible things that they cause.

*****

Aristotle's disagreement with Plato is not just about how to infer to unchanging substances, but also about how to infer to the first principle or first cause of all, and about how it should be described. Plato calls this first principle the good-itself; he also describes it in *Republic* VI-VII as the 'idea of the good', and thus a separate formal cause of goodness to all good things; and apparently in his Lecture on the Good he identified it with the one-itself, a cause (apparently a formal cause) in the first instance to numbers, and only indirectly to other things. Aristotle agrees with Plato that wisdom will be knowledge of 'the good, and the best in all nature' (*Met.* I 2 982b4–10, esp. b6–7), and he is willing to describe the first cause as a 'good-itself' (the good exists 'separated and itself-by-itself', *Met.* XII 10 1075a11–15; the 'good-itself' is 'that to which it belongs both to be first among goods, and to be by its presence the cause to the others of their being good', *EE* I 8 1217b3–5, and this will be a final cause, 1218b7–12). But Aristotle does not think of the search for a good-itself as peculiar to Plato (he calls Empedocles' Love a good-itself, *Metaphysics* I 4 985a4–10, and would probably apply the same description to Anaxagoras' *nous* or Reason, see XII 10 1075b8), and he can endorse a good-itself while rejecting Plato's description of the good-itself as an 'idea of the good' and formal cause of goodness: indeed, Aristotle says that *even if there were* a separate formal cause of goodness (and, in fact, there are no separate formal causes), it would be no better than other good things, and so would not be a good-itself (*EE* I 8 1218a8–15). Aristotle also rejects Plato's identification of the good-itself with the one-itself, the formal cause of unity to the numbers (and to the Forms if they are identified with numbers).[13] More generally, Aristotle thinks that the reduction of Forms to numbers and of philosophy to mathematics, while perhaps a plausible way to avoid *tashbîh*, means that our explanations in fact have nothing to do with goodness, even if we *say* that the first principle of numbers is also the good (*Met.* I 9 992a29-b1, III 2 996a22-b1, XIV 4 1091a29-XIV 5 1092a11; *EE* I 8 1218a15–32).[14]

In *Metaphysics* I Aristotle formulates this criticism of Plato as an extension of Plato's criticism of Anaxagoras in the *Phaedo*. When Anaxagoras says that '*nous* ordered all things,' he is (Plato and Aristotle think) implicitly claiming to explain the world through the good, but his actual explanations use *nous* only as a 'source of motion' or efficient cause, stirring up the cosmogonic vortex: even if *nous* is in fact good, these explanations don't use it as a cause *qua* good, and inferring to *nous* as this kind of cause doesn't give us knowledge of its goodness. Plato's alternative, in the Lecture on the Good, is to look for the good first principle as a one-itself and formal cause of unity, but here too, even if the one is in fact good, these explanations are not using it as a cause *qua* good: only a *final* cause or 'for the sake of which' is a cause by being good, and a cause of its effects' being good in their lesser degrees, and only things which are capable of change are for the sake of something.[15] For this reason, in trying to infer causally to a good first principle, Aristotle will start not from mathematically described objects but from physical things, looking for their causes of motion and order; so he will be doing something more like what Anaxagoras did, or what Plato did in the *Timaeus* in talking about the demiurge, than like what Plato did in the Lecture on the Good. In looking for causes of motion, Aristotle is in the first instance (like Anaxagoras) looking for efficient causes; but he claims that when we do this in the right way, it will ultimately lead us to something that is also a final cause. And he claims that this will also lead us to a cause that is eternally unchanging, and that pursuing formal causes will not.

This is not the most obvious way to look for eternally unchanging causes: we might more naturally have hoped to find eternally unchanging causes by starting from eternally unchanging mathematical things, and we might think that causes of change would themselves be changing things. However, Aristotle is looking above all for causes of the stable order of the cosmos, including the stable pattern of motions in the cosmos (the motions of the heavenly bodies, the cycle of the seasons, the life-cycles of plant and animal species), and he is hardly the first to think that this order, and these motions, depend on causes beyond the visible bodies of the cosmos: Anaxagoras' *nous*, Empedocles' Love, and the demiurge of the *Timaeus* (who is probably to be identified with the *nous* of *Philebus* 28c6–30e3) are all such causes of motion and order, and Aristotle will place himself in the line of Anaxagoras and Plato in describing his moving and ordering principle as *nous*.[16] But Anaxagoras and Empedocles and Plato had not represented these causes as entirely unchanging. Anaxagoras' *nous* and Empedocles' Love and Strife seem to be three-dimensionally extended things, present within as well as outside the cosmos, and moved in moving the cosmos; also *nous* changes from inactivity (rest?) to activity (motion?) when it begins to stir up the cosmogonic vortex, and Love and Strife take turns in dominating the cosmos. Even the demiurge of the *Timaeus*, although he is separate and non-spatial and ought to be immune to change, seems to change from inactivity (not intervening in the chaotic Receptacle) to activity (producing the ordered world). Aristotle, however, thinks that nothing that undergoes change, including the change from inactivity to activity, can be strictly a principle, i.e., be prior to everything else: whatever passes from being potentially F to being actually F must be actualized by something that is already in some way actually F, and in particular whatever passes from being inactive to being active, must be caused to act by something that is already acting. A world-history such as Anaxagoras describes, where everything had been quiescent from eternity, and then *nous* began to stir up the vortex, is impossible, since there could be no sufficient reason for *nous* to act now that would not also have been a sufficient reason for it to act previously; a world-history such as Empedocles describes, in which Love and Strife alternate in dominating the cosmos, is possible, but there would have to

be some prior cause, always uniformly acting, which would explain why Love and
Strife are successively active and inactive, and why they dominate for equal time-
periods (e.g., you could imagine something causing the uniform rotation of a circle
on which both Love and Strife are carried, moving each of them successively away
from the cosmos and back toward it again).[17] Aristotle's project of reasoning from
physical things to a first principle which will be just as unchangingly eternal as
Plato's Forms and numbers and Good will depend on finding a causal chain connecting orderly motion in the cosmos with a cause that is pure actuality with no
unactualized potentialities, and which is therefore eternally acting, and eternally
acting in the same way. This will involve a *tanzîh* of the first principle, a purification of what people ordinarily say about it, since most descriptions of it, and in
particular most descriptions of how it could cause motion in something else, will
at least implicitly involve attributing motion or potentiality to the cause. Indeed,
we might suspect either that the idea of such a principle is self-contradictory, or at
least that it will lead to *ta'tîl*, to having nothing left to say about what it is in itself
or how it acts and causes.

The fact is that until the post-Hellenistic revival of Aristotelianism (perhaps
until the second century AD), Aristotle and his immediate students Theophrastus
and Eudemus were the only philosophers to maintain that an unmoved thing can
cause motion to something else.[18] Thus in *Laws* X, building on the *Phaedrus'* argument that the essence of soul is self-motion (soul is the cause of life and thus of self-
motion to animal bodies, therefore soul is primarily self-moved and by moving
the body makes the soul-body complex self-moved, *Phaedrus* 245c5–246a2, cited
above), Plato argues that soul is prior to body in the cosmos: everything that is
moved by another is moved either by something self-moved or by something that is
moved by another, and so if an infinite regress can be excluded, the first principle of
motion will be self-moved, and will therefore be a soul. There is a logical gap in this
argument, because what moves something might be neither self-moved nor moved
by another, since it might not be moved at all. But either Plato has never considered
the possibility that something itself unmoved could set something else in motion,
or he regards it as too absurd to need refutation. And there are at least two reasons
why he, and Greek philosophers in general, would be reluctant to admit that an
unmoved thing could cause motion. First, if X moves Y, and X is itself unchanging, then it seems that X cannot *start* to move Y, since there could be no sufficient
reason for X to move Y now that would not also have been a sufficient reason for
it to move Y previously. This is basically correct, and it shows (as above against
Anaxagoras) that an initial unmoving configuration cannot generate motion, but
it does not exclude the possibility that X may have been moving Y, perhaps in a circle, from eternity (it might also be that, while X has always been acting in the same
way, Y starts moving only now, because some other circumstance has changed,
e.g., some obstacle has been removed). A second objection, however, is that for X
to move Y is for X to *do* something. As Sextus Empiricus will put the argument,
'what moves [something else] is *acting* in some way [*energei ti*], but what acts is in
motion, therefore what moves [something else] is in motion' (*Against the Physicists*

II, 76), and apparently all Hellenistic philosophers would accept this. They might posit unmovable objects, such as the void or numbers or *lekta* ['sayables' or Stoic thought-contents], but these objects do not act, and so do not move anything; and perhaps Plato's Forms, which are also immovable, do not act either. (Plato might be committed to saying that the demiurge is an unmoved mover, and *Sophist* 248c4-e4 might imply that Forms in being known can act on the soul without being moved; but if so Plato seems to have forgotten this possibility in the *Laws*.)

Aristotle's answer to this argument, and to Plato's argument in *Laws* X that the first mover is self-moving, depends on his conceptual distinction between activity [*energeia*] and motion [*kinêsis*], and his claim that there are some *energeiai* which are not *kinêseis* (that is, activities which are not changes in the thing which is acting, although they may involve change in some object or instrument of the action): thus an art, as a disposition in the soul, 'acts' when it is exercised, without any alteration in the art itself, and a colour 'acts' on the eye in causing vision, with neither qualitative nor local change in the colour. This gives Aristotle an alternative possibility to Plato's description of the soul as a self-moving source of motion: Aristotle agrees with Plato that the soul is the cause of the fact that the animal moves itself, but he rejects the inference that the *soul* moves itself.[19] Aristotle's alternative is that the soul is an *unmoved* mover of the animal body, and that the soul-body composite is self-moving in virtue of having two components, one of which moves the other, and neither of which moves itself. (If a soul were *absolutely* unmoved, then it would always act in the same way, and would be necessarily immortal; but because the soul is moved *per accidens* when the body is locally moved or alters or grows, the soul will produce different kinds of action, and may cease altogether to act and to exist if the body no longer supplies the organs it needs for its action.) So on this alternative the soul's action on the body would be an *energeia* that is not a *kinêsis*; but, since all of the familiar ways for one body to act on another body involve the first body being moved (either moved *in order* to move the second body, as when the first body pushes the second, or moved *as a result* of moving the second body, as when the first body heats the second body and is itself cooled in the process), our ignorance of soul's distinctive mode of action tempts us to *tashbîh*, to the assumption that the soul moves the body in the same way that a body moves a body. And Aristotle thinks the *Timaeus* falls into *tashbîh* as much as the pre-Socratics who actually make the soul a body: 'Democritus ... says that the indivisible spheres are moved, since it is their nature never to rest, and that they move the whole body and drag it along with them ... but the soul does not seem to move the body in *that* way, but by choosing and thinking. And Timaeus too physicizes [*phusiologei*] that the soul moves the body in this same way, namely that by being moved itself it also moves the body, since it is interwoven with it' (*DA* I 3 406b20–28). It is likewise *tashbîh* when Plato says that the soul's rational cognitions are circular motions, and its irrational cognitions are rectilinear motions disturbing these cognitions, and Aristotle duly compiles arguments that intellection cannot be a rotation (407a2–34). And the issues about how the soul thinks and how it moves the body combine, since Plato's evidence that the world-soul is moved in circles, and therefore rationally, is the fact that it moves the heavenly bodies in circles: he identifies the soul's movement around the celestial poles, carrying the whole heaven, with its activity of intellectual knowing, and the soul's movement around the poles of the ecliptic, carrying the seven planets at different speeds, with its stable true opining about the sensibles (*Timaeus* 37b3-c5). Plato is thus directly copying the structure of the heavenly motions onto the structure of soul, as Aristotle contemptuously puts it 'as if the locomotions of the heavens were the motions of soul' (*DA* I 3 407a1–2). When Aristotle says that 'the soul does not seem to move the body in *that* way, but by choosing and thinking,' his point is that the causality of choosing is *teleological*, doing something because the result is or appears to be good: to explain voluntary motion by psychic pushing is as inappropriate as explaining why Socrates has chosen to remain sitting on this prison bench by citing his bones and sinews.

So far we have just seen Aristotle arguing that the soul *need* not be moved in acting, and that representations of it as moving come from an inappropriate extension of the kinds of activities we perceive in bodies. He tries in various ways (in *DA* I 3 and *Phys.* VIII 5) to develop these thoughts into rather technical arguments that the soul *cannot* be moved; a common theme underlying many of the arguments is that for the soul to preserve a constant pattern of motion in the body, the soul must itself be immune to the body's changes. So, for instance, it is wrong to attribute the growth of living things to fire, on the ground that 'this alone of bodies is seen to be nourished and to grow' (*DA* II 4 416a10–12), since 'the growth of fire [tends] to infinity, as long as fuel is present, but all things constituted by nature have a limit and a *logos* of size and growth; and these belong to soul, not to fire, and to *logos* rather than to matter' (a13–14); and the advantage of positing soul rather than fire as the cause of growth would be lost if the soul itself grew along with the body instead of remaining constant. Again, Aristotle argues that if the soul moved itself, it would be 'displaced' in whatever respect it was moved in (e.g., its location or its size); and if, as Plato says in the *Phaedrus*, the soul's self-motion does not merely affect its accidental attributes but constitutes the soul's essence, then 'the soul would be displaced out of its essence' (*DA* I 3 406b11–15). Plato says that only what moves itself, and does so by its essence, 'does not depart from itself' (*Phaedrus* 245c7–8), and so will always remain moved in the same way and able to move other things in the same way, but Aristotle replies that the continuity and inexhaustibility of motion depend on an *unchanging* cause. Perhaps Plato recognizes this point, and tries to specify an unchanging essence of the soul, namely motion (or self-motion) itself, since he seems to say at *Laws* X 895a5–896b3 that the soul is the 'self-moving motion' itself rather than an underlying moved subject; Aristotle will reject a self-subsistent motion as absurd, but Plato is responding to some of the same pressures that will lead Aristotle too to describe the divine Reason as a self-subsisting activity. So too in the *Timaeus*, where the soul's motion is a rotation around its own axis, thus the mutual displacement of indistinguishable parts of a continuous substance: Aristotle ridicules this description, but it is as perhaps as close as Plato can come to describing an activity without any change of state in the acting subject and yet sufficient to cause motion in other things.

*****

Guided by his criticisms of Plato on the soul's self-motion, Aristotle sets out, in *Physics* VIII, to give a revised version of Plato's cosmotheological argument in *Laws* X.[20] As we saw, Plato there uses the conception of soul as a self-moving source of motion to argue that all motion in the cosmos proceeds from souls, which (because their motion proceeds from themselves and so will never fail) must be immortal; thus the motions of the heavenly bodies, in particular, will proceed from one or more immortal celestial souls; and since the motions of the heavenly bodies are the resultant of some number of simple circular motions, the heavenly souls, moving themselves (and therefore the bodies) in these simple circular motions, must be perfectly rational and good, and deserving of being called gods. At the most basic level, Aristotle's plan is to argue from the fact of motion to a first mover; to argue that this first mover cannot be self-moved but must rather be unmoved (if a chain of moving causes leads us up to a self-moved mover, such as an animal, then he will argue that that mover decomposes into an unmoved mover and what it moves, such as the soul and its body); and then to conclude that this first mover, or these first movers, since they are unmoved, must be eternal. Aristotle does not say anything in *Physics* VIII about the movers being alive or being good or being gods, but he does describe them as movers of eternal uniform circular motions, and he gives the physical foundations for *Metaphysics* XII to draw the more specifically theological conclusions.

However, for several reasons, Aristotle's argument is in fact much more complicated than this. First, while Plato seems not to worry about the possibility of infinite regresses of moving causes, Aristotle does try to argue that the kind of infinite regress that would threaten his argument is impossible. Second, even if there is no infinite regress and we reach a first moving cause in a given series, and even if this must be unmoved, on Aristotle's grounds this cannot be enough to infer that the cause is eternal: the soul of any individual animal, for Aristotle, is an unmoved mover sufficient to start a chain of movers, but it is moved *per accidens* by the animal's body, its activity and existence depend on the body's being in an appropriate condition, and so when the animal comes-to-be and passes away, the soul too (without arising from or passing back into any soul-matter) *per accidens* comes-to-be and passes away.[21] This makes it more difficult to conclude that the fact of motion requires an *eternal* unmoved mover. Aristotle might overcome this difficulty by reasoning back, not just to the first cause of any given motion, but to the first cause or causes of the heavenly motions, which must be as eternal as these motions themselves are. This would be following the model of *Laws* X, and indeed Aristotle winds up doing something like this. But there is something remarkable about his argument-strategy in *Physics* VIII which this description fails to capture. What Aristotle calls his 'physics' or 'on nature' in the broad sense includes the *De Caelo*, *Generation and Corruption*, and *Meteorology*, and perhaps also the biological and psychological treatises: so in particular it includes his account of the five simple bodies with their different natural motions (toward the center or away from the center or around the center) and the structure of the cosmos they compose. But the eight books which we call the *Physics* in the narrower sense, a kind of extended prolegomenon to the physical treatises, are devoted to a general analysis of motion and its preconditions (place, time, continuity, infinity …) and causes, without systematic reliance on the notion of the cosmos or the particular kinds of natural bodies and their motions, although Aristotle does not rigorously exclude all such considerations. *Physics* VIII is the concluding flourish of the *Physics* in this sense, trying to show that the analyses of previous books, without empirical support from cosmology, are sufficient to infer to a cause beyond the physical world, and so to give the physical foundations for *theologikê*. He does not try to conceal that he is talking about the heavenly bodies and inferring to their unmoved movers. But he does this in abstract and general terms, arguing that something like the eternal motion of the heavens is presupposed by the existence of any motion, and not relying, as *Laws* X does, on empirical astronomical theory to show that the motions of the heavens can be decomposed into uniform circular motions.

The plan of argument goes broadly like this. In *Physics* VIII 1–2, beginning from the fact that there is motion now, Aristotle argues that there must always have been motion (since, if there was previously not motion, there could be no sufficient reason for motion to begin now rather than earlier or later), and a symmetrical argument is supposed to show that there also always *will be* motion. This is supposed to show that motion is eternal only in a weak sense, i.e., in the sense that there is always some motion or other, not in the strong sense that there is some one motion that always exists. (Aristotle has discussed the identity-conditions of motions in *Physics* V 4: a motion is numerically one through time if it is continuous, which requires that it be the motion of a single persisting subject, in a continuous time, and toward the same final state or in the same spatial direction; it should preferably also be uniform in speed.) In fact Aristotle thinks that the objects we ordinarily perceive are not always in motion, but alternate between motion and rest; but he sets out to infer from these motions, first to at least one eternal thing eternally moved in a single continuous motion, and then to at least one eternally unmoved thing (this plan described *Physics* VIII 3). He argues in VIII 4 that anything that is moved is moved *by* something, either by itself (or some part of itself) or by another. This is not obvious in the case of the natural upward and downward motions of the four simple bodies (they do not move themselves, which is distinctive of living things—'they have a principle of motion, not of *moving* [transitive] or acting, but of being acted on', 255b30–31), but Aristotle argues (255b13–256a3) that when this drop of water (say) moves downward to its natural place, the *per se* mover is whatever originally generated this water above the natural place of water.[22] Next, in VIII 5, he argues against the possibility of an infinite regress of *per se* moving causes: if X is moved by Y, and if Y is moved by Z *per se* (i.e., inasmuch as Y is the mover of X, not in some other respect), then Z is the real mover of X, and Y is merely transmitting the motion as an instrument of

Z's causality; if there is no non-instrumental mover at the head of the series, X will not be moved at all (256a4-b3, with further arguments through 257a27). While Aristotle says that such a first mover must be either self-moved or unmoved, and that if it is self-moved it must contain an unmoved component which will be the truly *first* mover (257a27–258b9),[23] he cannot and does not infer that this first mover will be *absolutely* unmoved, or that it is eternal. It must be able to initiate a genuinely new chain of moving causes (so not just transmitting a motion), but it can be affected, at least in the way that a soul is moved *per accidens* when its body is moved; and some unmoved movers, rather than being eternal, may exist at one time and not exist at an earlier or later time, although they do not *per se* come-to-be or perish, because the self-moved movers of which they are constituents come-to-be and perish.

Then, however, the argument takes a new turn:

> But the cause of the fact that some things [i.e., some self-movers] come-to-be and others perish, and that this happens continuously, is not any of the things that are unmoved but do not always exist; nor are *these* the causes of *these*, and something else of *those*. For neither each of them, nor all of them together, is the cause of [this happening] always and continuously: for this fact is eternal and necessary; and all [the non-eternal unmoved things together] are infinite, and do not all exist together. So it is clear that, even if thousands of unmoved movers and many self-movers pass away and others come-to-be to replace them, and *this* is an unmoved mover of *this*, and something else is an unmoved mover of *that*, nonetheless there is something which surrounds [them all], and this is over and above each of them, and is a cause of the fact that some of them are and others are not and of continuous change [i.e., of the fact that the self-movers, and thereby their unmoved moving constituents, continuously come-to-be and pass away]: this is a cause of motion to these [self-moved movers, or their unmoved moving constituents], and they to other things (*Phys.* VIII 6 258b26–259a6).

Here, empirically, the self-movers are animals (or plants), and the unmoved movers which do not always exist are their unmoved components, namely their souls. Aristotle is saying that these non-eternal unmoved movers, the souls, are not sufficient to explain the eternal generation and perishing of the animals (and thus incidentally of their souls). The soul of Peleus does explain the coming-to-be of Achilles (and of his soul), and so we might think that souls-in-general explain coming-to-be-in-general, with the coming-to-be of each animal (and its soul) explained by the soul of its father. But, Aristotle is now saying, there is also a further *explanandum*, namely that this process of generation and replenishment of the species happens 'always and continuously'. That effect certainly is not caused by the soul of Peleus, since the effect is eternal and the soul of Peleus is not, but Aristotle also claims that this effect cannot be adequately explained by 'all of them together', since they 'do not all exist together' and (apparently for this reason) cannot cooperate to produce a single effect; if the effect, the eternity of the species, were just the by-product of infinitely many uncoordinated acts of infinitely many temporal causes, it would not be 'necessary', which it must be, if the species is an object of Aristotelian science.

This turn of argument is crucial to the plan of *Physics* VIII. Aristotle is claiming that an eternal unmoved mover is needed, not to account for the fact of motion as such, but to account for the inexhaustibility of generation and thus for the fact that at every time there are *some* unmoved movers, i.e., some souls, which in turn initiate chains of moving causes and so account for the fact of motion. To see better why he thinks that there is a further *explanandum* here, and why the many souls 'all together' could not explain it, it may help to see how the continuous replenishment of the species could fail. When Aristotle says that there is 'something which surrounds [them all] ... and is a cause of the fact that some of them are and others are not and of continuous change' he is empirically thinking of the heavenly bodies, and especially of the yearly circuit of the sun around the zodiac, which he describes notably in *Generation and Corruption* II 10 as the cause of the cycle of the seasons and of the cyclical generation and corruption of the simple bodies and their compounds and of plant and animal species. As Aristotle says in that chapter and in *Generation of Animals* IV 10, all sublunar species have natural periods which they 'aim' at (*boulontai, Generation of Animals* IV 10 777b18), a natural lifespan and also natural periods of gestation and maturation, and these periods are determined as multiples of periods of the heavenly bodies. Thus the heavenly bodies and especially the sun, by one mechanism or another, act as a metronome, setting the periods of things down here, which without the motions of the heavenly bodies, without anything to measure objectively equal periods of time, would have no natural periods to aim at. So, if we imagine that there were no motion in the heavens giving rise to the period of a year, there would be no more reason why a given species should grow and reproduce and perish so that the average interval between the birth of a parent and the birth of its offspring is N years, than that the interval should be N years in this generation, N/2 years in the next generation, N/4 years in the next, and so on, so that infinitely many generations would have exhausted themselves after 2N years; or, equally, biological processes might slow down so that I proceed halfway toward death (or my child in the womb proceeds halfway toward full formation) in a year, half the remaining process is completed in the next year, half the remainder in the next year, and so on, so that no one ever finishes dying or being born. (You might think of the myth in Plato's *Statesman* 269a1–271c2, where the reversal of the cosmic rotation leads to a reversal of all biological processes: this is probably not meant quite seriously, but it depends on the serious idea that the speed—if not the direction—of the cosmic rotation determines the speed of biological processes.)

Now in *Physics* VIII Aristotle insists on speaking in the abstract, so he does not say in VIII 6 that the motions of the heavenly bodies are needed to produce the regularity and inexhaustibility of generation; he just says that there is *some* numerically single motion which co-exists with the whole eternal succession of non-eternal unmoved movers, and which must therefore itself be eternal and continuous, and clearly also uniform. He then argues in VIII 7–9 that an eternally continuous motion must be a locomotion, and specifically a rotation, since a qualitative alteration, or growth and diminution, or rectilinear locomotion, would have to reach a limit, rest at that limit, and then begin a new motion in the opposite direction: so such a motion could not be eternally continuous, and would need some prior continuous motion as the cause of its eternal alternation, as we saw above in Aristotle's argument against Empedocles. (Aristotle's paradigm for explaining eternally alternating motions through eternally continuous circular motions comes from mathematical astronomy. The regular yearly alternation between the qualitative motion of heating, from winter solstice to summer solstice, and the motion of cooling, from summer solstice to winter solstice, is explained by the alternation between the rectilinear motion of the sun northward from winter solstice to summer solstice—so that it comes closer to us in the northern hemisphere, reaching a greater height above our horizon and staying above the horizon for longer—and then southward again from summer solstice to winter solstice. But this in turn is explained by the single continuous rotation of the sun around the circle of the zodiac, which brings it from its southern limit in Capricorn at winter solstice to its northern limit in Cancer at summer solstice and back again.)[24] Of course, by itself this argument does not get us from the non-eternal unmoved movers to an eternal unmoved mover, but only to an eternal continuous motion, and thus also to an eternally persisting subject of motion. But if we now apply to this eternal motion the argument that every motion is caused by a first unmoved mover, then, since a single continuous motion must be caused by a single eternally acting mover and not by a succession of movers, we will reach an *eternal* unmoved mover. Aristotle also says that in this way we will reach an unmoved mover which is not moved even *per accidens*, and which therefore cannot come-to-be or perish even *per accidens*, and is therefore eternal (259b20–28); but, as we will see, 'eternal unmoved mover' and 'unmoved mover not moved even *per accidens*' are not quite equivalent.

In the last chapter of the *Physics* (VIII 10), Aristotle tries to infer a series of negative attributes of the first mover of an eternally continuous motion, reserving the positive attributes for *Metaphysics* XII. First, of course, it must be unmoved. Aristotle also tries to show that it cannot be a body, or a power (like heat or weight) extended across a body. His argument is that since it produces an infinite motion (a uniform motion for an infinite time), the mover's power must be infinite; but an infinite power cannot be extended across a finite magnitude (because it would be divided into infinite part-powers present in the finite parts of the magnitude, and paradoxes result if an infinite whole has infinite parts), nor can it be extended across an infinite magnitude, since Aristotle has argued in *Physics* III 5 that there are no actually infinite magnitudes; consequently, the mover's power is not present in any magnitude or any divisible subject at all. This argument would imply (even without the VIII 5 argument that self-movers are decomposable) that the heavenly bodies cannot be self-moving, and also that they cannot be moved by a self-moving soul co-extended with the heaven. But, although Aristotle is clearly proud of the argument—which brings together premises from different parts of the *Physics* into a concluding flourish—it can be challenged in a number of ways on Aristotelian grounds, and in particular it is not clear that it succeeds in excluding self-moving bodies or souls. In *De Caelo* I 2–3 Aristotle argues that the heavenly spheres are made of a substance which naturally rotates around the centre of the universe, and he seems there to think that this is a sufficient explanation for their motion, without invoking any further moving cause: we might put this by saying that when a body has its natural motion it does not need anything to move it, or we might put it by saying that the heavenly spheres are self-moving (if, as Aristotle says, self-motion is distinctive of living things, then let them be living). If Aristotle now claims that the sphere to move itself would require infinite power (perhaps something analogous to an infinite weight), and that this infinite power could not be distributed across a finite sphere, we might reply that a finite power would suffice; that the power will be proportional to the speed at which it moves the body rather than to the time for which it moves the body; and that a naturally rotating body, unlike a heavy body, has no natural place at which to rest and therefore will have no reason to stop at any particular time, and therefore will continue forever with whatever motion it has. (Aristotle claims in *Physics* VIII 10 that a projectile does not stay in motion of itself when it has left the thrower's hand, being rather moved by the air between the hand and the projectile, but even in antiquity there were readers who found this explanation incredible; and even if sublunar bodies tended to stop when left to themselves, surely a naturally rotating body would not?)[25] If Aristotle claims that, because the motion produced is constant, the mover too must be constant and unmoved, we might reply that the minimal change undergone by a self-turning sphere (the mutual displacement of indiscernible parts of a plenum) will not make any difference to the motive power it exerts, and will not stop it from eternally producing the same motion in itself.

However, Aristotle has some reasonable points to make in response. First and most obviously, the nature of the heavenly bodies, without any further mover, might be sufficient to explain why they rotate around the center of the universe, but surely not to explain why they rotate around the particular axes they do, with the particular velocities they do; a star near the pole of a rotating sphere will move with a much slower absolute velocity than a star on the equator, and it will not even move around the center of the universe, but around a point near the pole on the axis, and it is hopeless to try to explain this difference by the nature of the aether. (Even in the *De Caelo*, Aristotle is well aware that the different heavenly spheres move around different axes and with different periods, and he thinks that this achieves some good—the cycles of the seasons and of sublunar animal species depend on the inclination of the zodiac to the celestial equator—and so whatever determines their particular circular motions is acting for some good [see *DC* II 2–3 and II 12]. In *Generation and Corruption* II 10 he says that 'the god' [336b31–2] arranged the circular motions of the heavens to secure the continuity of sublunar generation, but it is hard to understand what this god's activity would be.)[26] Beyond this, one of Aristotle's technical arguments in *Physics* VIII 5 against a self-moving first source of motion, if we think it through, can help to bring out his underlying reasons for rejecting either self-moving heavens or self-moving souls as a sufficient explanation for the rotation of the heavens. If a self-moved mover has parts, each of which moves the other (or each of which moves the next in a circular succession), then, Aristotle says, there will be no necessity for part A, when it moves part B, to be moved in return; so either A necessarily produces eternal motion as an unmoved mover is supposed to (whether or not it is, contingently, also moved), or it is not in fact necessary that the composite AB be eternally moved (this *seems* to be the thought at 257b20–25).

We can better appreciate the force of this argument if we see who would have held the view Aristotle criticizes. An obvious target is Democritus: he explains the motion of the heavens by a vortex, like Anaxagoras, but he does not posit a further moving cause like Anaxagoras' *nous*; rather, it happens by chance that these bodies are moved and are constrained by the membrane that surrounds the cosmos, so that each body bumps into and moves the body next ahead of it in the direction of the cosmic rotation, and so the motion is sustained (so esp. Diogenes Laertius IX, 31–2, attributed to Leucippus, and included in Leucippus A1 in Diels-Kranz). It seems right to say that this will not explain the necessity of continuous circular motion (let alone of the complex superposition of circular motions of different axes and periods), and indeed Democritus will agree that the motion was begun and sustained by chance constraints. The uniform rotation of a sphere on its axis seems like an activity that would persist without change, without needing any cause for its persistence, but Aristotle thinks the plausibility breaks down when we analyse the sphere into its many parts: none of them is determined to move by its own nature (anyway not determined to rotate around *this* axis at *this* speed), rather each moves because it is bumped by the one behind it, there is only the illusion of a single necessary eternal motion, and Democritus is unusually frank in admitting it. (This is why Aristotle raised the problem of projectile motion in *Physics* VIII 10, to say that the projectile moves only as long as it is moved by something in contact with it, by a chain of movers each imparting to the next the power to move its successor, and that there is only the illusion of a single continuous motion of the projectile: unless we are willing to say that the motions of the heavens are like this, it is not sufficient to say that the motion of the heaven is sustained by the heaven.) Plato, of course, fully agrees with Aristotle that the eternal and mathematically precise (and good-directed) motions of the heavens cannot be explained by a vortex, and this is why he introduces self-moving souls to move them instead. But if souls are extended, then the soul will move itself because each soul-part is bumped by the part behind it, and the same difficulty will recur. Perhaps Plato's talk of the soul being co-extended with the body was just a poetic image, and the soul is not really extended. But then it will not rotate; and Aristotle thinks he can show that 'indivisible' or non-extended things cannot move at all (because S can be in motion—which is *continuous* change—from not-F to F only if, while the motion is underway, part of S is in not-F and part of S is in F);[27] and so if we refine Plato in this way, his moving soul will no longer be a self-moved mover, but an unmoved mover without magnitude, which is what Aristotle wants to establish.

So Aristotle reaches eternally unmoved movers by refining Plato as Plato refined Democritus; and it seems that Aristotle was not the first person to do this. The end of *Metaphysics* XII 7 sums up the lessons of *Physics* VIII as follows: 'it is clear from what has been said that there is some substance which is eternal and unmoved and separated from the sensibles, and it has also been shown that this substance can have no magnitude, but is partless and indivisible ... [for the *Phys.* VIII 10 reason that neither a finite nor an infinite magnitude can contain an infinite power]...but also that it is unaffected and unaltered, for the other motions are posterior to motion in place' (1073a3–12). It is striking that all of these negative attributes (except perhaps 'separated') are satisfied by the theory that Aristotle attributes in *On the Motion of Animals* 3 to an unknown Academic (the usual guess is Speusippus), that the movers of each heavenly sphere are its *poles*.[28] The poles are indivisible points, and if they spin and move the whole sphere around them by the force of their spinning, they will not be moved—the sphere is moved because all of its parts are moved, but the pole is not a *part* of the sphere, and its spinning around the axis is no change whatever. The force that Plato had spread out in a soul co-extensive with the sphere is now infinitely concentrated in an indivisible point, whose activity explains the axis and speed of the sphere's motion. Whoever invented this theory seems to have been the pioneer of unmoved movers, and Aristotle would have developed his own theory by building on and criticizing this one, as he does in *On the Motion of Animals*: he objects there that the *two* poles cannot produce a single motion (true, but reformulate to say that the mover is the *axis* joining the two poles),[29] and more seriously that points are abstractions from the bodies they limit and not substances in themselves, and therefore not bearers of forces (699a20–24). Aristotle's alternative is, as he says here, that the unmoved movers of the heavenly spheres are *outside* them, so 'separate' in a stronger sense (699b32–5; compare the divine things outside the heavens in *DC* I 9 278b21–279b3). But *Physics* VIII in itself seems consistent with the movers being the poles (it is deliberately abstaining from determining the positive nature of the movers). And *Physics* VIII has a further connection with the pole theory. Aristotle insists there that every unmoved mover which is not moved even *per accidens* is eternal, but not conversely that every eternal unmoved mover is not moved even *per accidens*. 'It is not the same thing to be moved *per accidens* by oneself and by another: [being moved *per accidens*] by another belongs also to some of the principles of the things in the heavens, [namely the movers of those heavenly bodies] which are moved with several motions, whereas [being moved *per accidens* by oneself] belongs only to corruptible things [i.e., to souls which move themselves *per accidens* when they move their bodies]' (*Phys.* VIII 6 259b28–31). On the pole theory, the poles of a sphere would not be moved even *per accidens* by the motion they themselves produce, but the poles of a lower sphere would be moved *per accidens* when the higher sphere in which they are embedded, in a Eudoxus-style astronomical model, is moved. If the movers of the sphere were not moved even *per accidens*, then they would always produce absolutely the same motion, i.e., rotation around the same axis, whereas in fact they produce rotation around an axis that is itself changing in accord with the motion of the higher sphere; only the motion of the outermost sphere is rotation around an unchanging axis, and so only the movers of the outermost sphere are unmoved even *per accidens*. And these considerations will hold even if the movers of the spheres are not the poles: the movers of the spheres other than the outermost will still somehow have to be moved *per accidens* with the motion of the higher sphere, and so Aristotle says in *Metaphysics* XII 8 only of 'the principle and the first of beings' that it 'is unmoved both *per se* and *per accidens*, producing the first eternal and single motion' (1073a23–5), while he says of the motions proper to the planets only that they 'must be moved by a substance that is unmoved *per se* and eternal' (1073a32–4, cp. a26–7), conspicuously failing to say that these movers are not moved even *per accidens*.

*****

Physics VIII is not *theologikê* or scientific wisdom, but only the physical foundation for *theologikê*. In *Metaphysics* XII, Aristotle tries to go further to give a positive description of the nature and causality of the movers of the heavens, in such a way as to satisfy the descriptions of wisdom that we have seen from *Metaphysics* I and *Eudemian Ethics* V = *Nicomachean Ethics* VI.[30] *Physics* VIII, and its summary at *Metaphysics* XII 7 1073a3–12, say negatively that the movers of the heavens are unmoved (and separate and unextended). As we saw above, the reason why it seems paradoxical for X to move Y while remaining itself unmoved is that for X to move Y is for X to *act* [*energein*], and the activities [*energeiai*] that we are ordinarily familiar with involve change or motion [*kinêsis*] on the part of the acting subject; and so a main task of *Metaphysics* XII will be to describe this *energeia* in a way that does not entail *kinêsis*. As we also saw above, Aristotle argues that the first principle must be pure actuality, with no non-actualized potentialities, and this gives a criterion for *tanzîh*: no state or activity should be attributed to the first principle which would imply change or potentiality. The question is whether this allows us to give any positive description of the principle and its causality. XII 7 says, 'the object of desire [*orekton*] and object of thought [*noêton*] move in this way: they move without being moved' (1072a26–7). This picks up one of Aristotle's basic models for an unmoved mover: against the 'Heracliteans' of the *Theaetetus* who think that both percipient and perceived are altered in sense-perception, Aristotle insists that (say) a colour, as a persisting disposition, acts on the eye (and on the transparent medium between itself and the eye) without itself being changed.[31] (Nowadays we would say that although the colour or the coloured object is not changed *by being seen*, *in order to be seen* it must reflect photons, which involves a very slight change in the object's momentum and perhaps also in its energy level.) The movers of the heavens are not bodies or qualities of bodies, so they are not grasped by sensation: if the heavens cognize the movers at all, it must be by some direct intellectual perception, but however that may work, the object will be just as unchanged as an object of vision. An object of vision or thought will not, *qua* object of vision or thought, produce any motion in the perceiver beyond the act of vision or thought itself, and this is why Aristotle adds 'the object of desire.' But the object of desire can produce a motion only by first producing an act of cognition: for example, a piece of fruit might produce in an animal a cognition of itself as *red* and *round*, and thus (by the workings of the animal's imagination) produce a cognition of itself as *ripe fruit*, and thus produce a cognition of itself as *desirable*, and thus produce a motion of the animal toward the fruit. (See Aristotle's analysis in *DA* III 10 and *MA* 6, passages echoed in *Metaphysics* XII 7.) So Aristotle is not saying that this kind of unmoved mover is only a final cause: it must first produce motion (at least, produce a cognition of itself as good and desirable) as an efficient cause, and only thereby can it act as a final cause.

There are a number of puzzles connected with Aristotle's description of the movers in XII 7, of which I'll mention two now. One puzzle is that Aristotle seems to assume that the mover *is* an object of cognition and desire, as if these were the *only* examples of unmoved movers, although he elsewhere gives another example, an art in the soul, which is exercised and acts on its object without being qualitatively changed: as noted above, Aristotle uses the art model in trying to understand how the soul itself can be an unmoved mover of the body.[32] Another puzzle is that, while Aristotle starts the chapter by positing that the mover is an *object* of thought and desire for the heavens, by the end of the chapter he is speaking of the mover as *nous* or Reason, thus as itself thinking, and as itself living and happy (these descriptions slip in somewhere between 1072b13 and b30): how did he get from the one description to the other? Of course, Aristotle's description of *nous* as producing a circular motion in the heavens is a critically revised version of the descriptions in Anaxagoras and the *Timaeus*, and Aristotle may have strategies for getting a reader who comes in as an Anaxagorean or Platonist to accept his revised version instead, but at the beginning of XII 7 he did not seem to be supposing that his readers had any such commitments: so why should they agree that the mover is not only *noêton* but itself *nous*?

The solution to both puzzles is a premise that Aristotle is assuming from the *De Anima*, that the knowledge of an object X is the form of the object X, present in the soul without its matter (so, for sensation, *DA* II 12 424a17–24, and for intellectual cognition *DA* III 4 429a13–18). But what if the object X has no matter to begin with—if it is a separate immaterial substance like the movers of the heavens? In this case the knowledge of X cannot be the form of X without its matter, but must be simply identical to X. Aristotle says in *De Anima* III 4 that

> in the case of things without matter the knower [*nooun*] and the thing known [*nooumenon*] are the same: for theoretical knowledge [*epistêmê*] and what is known [*epistêton*] in this way are the same...whereas in the case of things that have matter [the knowledge] is *potentially* each of the things known [*noêta*] [sc. as the art of housebuilding is the potentiality for each house it could build] (430a3–7: the last clause is often translated differently, but the difference will not have much bearing on the case of immaterial objects).

and, relying on the *De Anima*, he repeats much the same in *Metaphysics* XII 9:

> in some cases the knowledge [*epistêmê*] *is* the object: in the productive [sciences, the knowledge is] the substance and essence without the matter, but in the theoretical [sciences] the formula [*logos*] is [simultaneously] the object and the knowledge [*noêsis*]. So the thing known [*nooumenon*] and the knowledge [*nous*]

will not be different, in things which do not have matter; they will be the same, and the knowledge [*noêsis*] will be one with the thing known [*nooumenon*] (1074b38–1075a5).

In both of these texts Aristotle contrasts theoretical knowledge with knowledge of things that have matter, apparently counting all sciences of enmattered things, not just carpentry but also physics, as 'productive' knowledge:[33] the strictly theoretical sciences, the sciences of unchanging immaterial things, are simply identical with their objects, or to put it the other way around, their objects are themselves sciences. Since you and I can know the same immaterial object X, the science of X—which is just X itself—must be 'in' my soul in such a way that it can also be in your soul, without being divided up. So such knowledge is not in the usual sense an *accident* of me: the only sense in which we can say that it is *in* me, or that I *have* [*echein*] it as a *hexis* [habit or disposition, but literally 'having'], is that it is capable of acting in me, i.e., of being exercised in my acts of contemplating it.[34] And this explains why Aristotle did not consider two different possible models for the unmoved movers of the heavens, namely things that move as objects of cognition and things that move as arts: the two models come to the same thing, since the heavens' immaterial objects of cognition *are* also the arts or sciences that move the heavens.

Aristotle thus combines premises from the *Physics* and the *De Anima* to show that, as Anaxagoras and Plato say, the heavens are moved by *nous*. As a corollary, he infers that the movers of the heavens are gods: 'life also belongs to it, for the *energeia* of *nous* is a life [sc. this and the *energeia* of sensation being the two kinds of lives], and it is the *energeia* and its *per se energeia* is [a] best and eternal life, and we say that god is [a] best eternal living thing', so that this *nous* falls under something like the pseudo-Platonic *Definition* of a god which I cited at the beginning of this chapter (so XII 7 1072b26–9, compare *Definitions* 411a3). This allows Aristotle to deliver on the promise made in *Metaphysics* I 2 that wisdom would be knowledge of god, since 'everyone thinks that god is a cause and a principle' (983a8–9, cited above). And since the god has, and is, the knowledge that the heaven has, that is, the knowledge of the god, which we also acquire in wisdom, Aristotle can also redeem the other half of I 2's promise, that wisdom will be the kind of knowledge that a god would have (983a5–10).

Aristotle can then turn to a critical purification of Anaxagoras' and Plato's descriptions of what *nous* is in itself, what it knows, and how it is a cause of the motion of the heavens and of cosmic order, rejecting in particular any description that would imply change or potentiality in *nous*. Of course Plato had already begun the process of purifying Anaxagoras' descriptions, which he had criticized in the *Phaedo* and tries to improve on in the *Timaeus*. The *Phaedo* criticizes those, including Anaxagoras, who explain the stability of the earth by positing a vortex, as if looking for 'a stronger and more immortal Atlas', and do not believe in the 'power of these things' being arranged in the best possible way' (99b6–c6): in the *Timaeus*, Plato tries both to explain each action of the demiurge by saying that the world would be best so (best given the constraints which the demiurge's matter imposes on him), and also to show the demiurge bringing about this best outcome, not by imposing it violently, but by 'persuasion'. Plato also says that what the demiurge makes cannot be dissolved except by the demiurge's will, and that the demiurge would not will to dissolve what he had once made (41a7-b6): therefore the demiurge himself makes only things that will be immortal, namely the world as a whole and the heavenly bodies and cosmic and celestial souls and the rational parts of human souls, while sublunar living things and the irrational parts of human and animal souls are produced by the 'young gods', i.e., the ensouled heavenly bodies (see the programmatic 41a7-d3, and, for the young gods' work, the sequel through 44c4 and 69a6–72b5). This might be taken to mean that the causality *nous* is always mediated through the heavens, whose eternal rotation imitates the eternally constant activity of *nous*, and through rational souls, which have knowledge, and move in rational patterns, to the extent that they participate in Reason-itself; and this too is a way of eliminating both violence and changeability from *nous*'s causality. Aristotle accepts these improvements on Anaxagoras, but he thinks Plato does not live up to his own program for how to describe *nous*'s causality. Most obviously, Plato describes the demiurge as beginning to act in time, although the reasons against his ceasing to act and letting his creatures be dissolved should equally be reasons against his having previously not yet acted to create them. Plato once explicitly describes the demiurge as doing something 'by violence' (35a6–8, of fitting the nature of the Different in with the nature of the Same in constructing the world-soul), and he describes the demiurge as imposing polyhedral shapes on earth, water, air, and fire, which it does not seem that he could do without violence (and how does he do it without hands or other movable parts?), and which is not mediated by the heavens or by rational souls. The demiurge also imposes circular motion (directly or via the world-soul) on the heavenly bodies, which are made of fire, and Aristotle, implicitly using his own premise that fire naturally moves away from the centre, infers that this would be a violent imposition of a motion unnatural to them (*DC* II 1 284a27–35). Aristotle eliminates all this by making the heavens out of aether, existing and rotating from eternity; the heavenly spheres, or perhaps instead the stars, may still be alive and have souls, but if so their souls are not constraining them against their nature, but at most determining the axis and speed of their rotation.

Plato also tries to give content to Anaxagoras' description of the world-ordering cause as *nous* by supplying an eternal unchanging object for its thinking, a perfect living-thing-itself to be a model for an ensouled physical world (*Timaeus* 30c2–31b3). Aristotle, like Plato, thinks that *nous* is thinking an eternal unchanging object; because it is unchanging, the knowledge of it must be theoretical, and yet, for Aristotle as for Plato, the world's order must ultimately arise from this theoretical knowledge rather than from practical or productive knowledge directed toward the physical world itself. In *Metaphysics* XII 9, Aristotle raises, and tries to resolve, problems about the object of *nous*'s knowledge. These are in part problems of *tanzîh*, problems of adequately representing the divine: 'the discussion of *nous* involves some problems: for it seems to be the most divine of the things that are apparent to us, but how it must be in order to be such [sc. most divine] involves some difficulties. For if it thinks [*noei*] nothing, what would be worthy of reverence [*semnon*] about it? It would be like one who sleeps' (1074b15–18)—like Endymion in *Nicomachean Ethics* X 8, discussed above as a counter-model to the gods. Now if the divine *nous* were simply a *power* of intellectual cognition, there might be no determinate answer to the question of what it knows: one and the same power might be able to know many different things. But since it is not merely a *power* of knowledge (or a substance which is a bearer of such a power) but a separately existing *act* of knowledge, it must be knowledge *of* something in particular, and eternally and essentially knowledge of the same thing. (We might contrast it with a Platonic Form of Knowledge, which, Aristotle argues at *Metaphysics* IX 8 1050b34–1051a2, would be only a power—presumably because it must apply equally to all knowledge and so cannot itself be knowledge of anything in particular—and so would be less knowing than the activities that it is the power for.) Aristotle had argued in XII 6 that the first principle must be active from all eternity and by its essence, on the ground that otherwise there would be a regress to a prior active cause to awaken it from potentiality to activity; here in XII 9 he makes a similar argument that it is eternally and essentially actually *knowing*, not from the premise that it is causally first, but from the premise that it is best or most 'worthy of reverence': 'if it thinks [*noei*] but something else is in control [*kurion*] of this, since what its substance is is not [the act of] thinking [*noêsis*] but a power, it would not be the best substance: for what is worthy of honour [*timion*] belongs to it through its [act of] thinking [*noein*]' (1074b18–21). Both arguments turn on a regress: what actualizes S's power would be prior to S, both causally and in value. But what actualizes S's knowledge of X, at least in theoretical knowledge of immaterial things, is the object X itself, which, as we have seen, Aristotle identifies with the knowledge of X, subsisting by itself but 'present' in S in the sense that it is capable of acting on S and producing S's activity of contemplating X. So if S is a theoretical *nous* which is not identical with the object it knows, S will be of itself only potentially knowing, needing to be actualized by a prior theoretical *nous* which *is* identical with the object it knows, and this prior *nous* is the principle which Aristotle intends to describe.

We can thus say that for Aristotle, by contrast with the *Timaeus*, the demiurge does not look to a living-thing-itself outside him, so that he would be dependent on it in order to actualize his knowledge and thus to attain perfection; rather, the living-thing-itself just is the demiurgic *nous*. And it is paradigmatically living, not as in Plato by being most universal, containing fish and bird and land-animal and (celestial) god, but rather by being the best kind of life, which is as we have seen the activity of *nous*. Aristotle also argues that this object of the divine thought is not, as in the *Timaeus*, composite, containing a plurality of parts or forms (the premise that the living-thing-itself is the same as the demiurge does not automatically imply this, since the demiurge himself might contain such a plurality): he claims (XII 9 1075a5–10) that any such composition would entail potentiality, and a transition from contemplating one object to contemplating another. His point is in part that the divine knowledge cannot be a demonstrative knowledge, in which conclusions are deduced by putting two or more premises together, since (he thinks) this would entail that the conclusion was first known only potentially, and then acquires actuality from the actual knowledge of the premises: whatever the divine knowledge is *of*, it must be *of* all simultaneously. But he also thinks that it cannot be even a *simultaneous* grasp of many separate objects, since one act of knowledge must be *of* one thing, nor of a single composite object, since he thinks that any composition involves potentiality. While the argument for this is not clearly spelled out in XII 9, the underlying thought seems to be that if something is a whole of parts, it is both one and many, and being one and being many are (as Plato also thinks) contraries; and the only way that a single subject can have contrary attributes is if it has one of them in actuality and the other in potentiality. So a whole of parts must be actually one whole, and potentially many parts, since it *can* be divided: but in eternal unchangeable things, there is no potentiality and no way that anything can be divided, and so if an object is one it cannot also be many, and cannot have any distinguishable parts.[35]

Aristotle thus collapses the distinction between the demiurge and the living-thing-itself; and by eliminating all plurality from within the living-thing-itself, he also collapses the distinction between the living-thing-itself and the first principle, the good-itself, which is the highest object of the deimurge's (or of anyone's) contemplation. Recall that in *Metaphysics* I Aristotle had inquired into the different principles that earlier philosophers had posited as a good-itself (Anaxagoras' *nous*, Empedocles' Love, Plato's One) and the different ways that these principles were supposed to be causes. *Nous*, for Anaxagoras (and for Plato, who thinks that it is inferior to the first principle), would be an efficient cause of motion and order, whereas the object of *nous*'s thought would presumably be a formal cause (like the living-thing-itself or the One) or a final cause (like the good-itself if we could elaborate a teleological account of how *nous* acts for the sake of this good). Aristotle takes up all of these issues from *Metaphysics* I in XII 10 1075a25-b11, with a view to showing that he has satisfied the desiderata of wisdom that Anaxagoras and Empedocles and Plato had failed to achieve.[36] He has refined Anaxagoras' and Plato's accounts of the causality of *nous*—it is an efficient cause, but a very 'refined' efficient cause, presenting itself to the heavens and perhaps to other rational beings as an object of knowledge and desire, and so causing them to move for its sake. But, by identifying *nous* with its highest object the good-itself, he has also explained what this good is and how it is a cause: it is not the one-itself and formal cause to numbers, but *nous*—a 'refined' *nous* that is pure actuality, with all that implies—and a final cause, and 'refined' efficient cause, to physical things, in the first instance to the heavenly bodies and thus also to the sublunar world that they move and order. Because it is always acting, and always acting in the same way, and always producing cosmic order, it is not a 'principle' of the world by being temporally prior to it, but by a causal and axiological and perhaps some kind of ontological priority. It has no contrary principle like Empedocles' Strife, since that would imply that both principles had potentiality, competing to exercise their power on the material substratum and perhaps alternating in governing it (cf. 1075b20–24); such alternation is possible only if there is a prior principle which is pure actuality, always acting uniformly to secure the regular alternation of the two competing lower principles.

*****

Puzzles and difficulties remain, and have been raised at least since the *Metaphysics* of Aristotle's student Theophrastus: it is hard to believe that they were not discussed in Aristotle's circle within his lifetime.[37] The most obvious difficulty is why, when the heavens, or the individual stars, contemplate their movers (the first good-itself, or the subordinate unmoved movers, whatever these are exactly), this should inspire them to move in circles. If this is supposed to be like the way that a red round fruit causes an animal to move toward the fruit, there is an obvious difference, in that moving toward the fruit gets the animal closer to the fruit, and will in most cases lead to the animal actually eating the fruit, whereas rotating does not bring the sphere or the star any closer to its mover, and does not seem to lead to any further activity beyond itself. If the star is led to move in circles forever like a greyhound following a mechanical rabbit around a track, this involves deception and frustration, and seems inappropriate to the causality of *nous* and of the good.[38] Now perhaps Aristotle would say that he cannot be expected to know exactly how causality works in the heavens, and that he does not need to: he begins from the effect, the eternal motions of the heavens, and he infers that they can only be caused by an eternally unmoved object of thought and desire, even if he does not know exactly why this cause should produce the observed effects. But we would like to have at least some comparison or model for understanding how this causality might work. The idea that *nous* will produce a circular motion in the heavens is of course there both in Anaxagoras and in Plato. Aristotle has rejected Plato's claim that rational cognition just *is* circular motion, if not of a body then of an extended soul. But he might still say, as Plato also does (*Timaeus* 34a1–5), that the uniform circular motion of a body is the best *likeness* of *nous* of which bodies are capable. This might be spelled out using Aristotle's claim that the divine *nous* is activity without change: bodies, due to their inferior status, cannot have activity without change, and it is better to imitate the divine changeless activity by acting and changing than by not changing and not acting; and the kind of activity-through-change that best imitates the divine changeless activity is a motion that is itself eternally uniform and changeless, the rotation of a sphere around an axis through its centre.[39] We might also say that if the heavens' cognition somehow causes motion, then since the cognition is constant it will always produce the *same* motion, so if it produces any motion at all it will necessarily be an eternal circular motion.

These explanations are, however, particularly unenlightening on why the heavens respond by moving in a *plurality* of circular motions, with different periods and around different axes: and it is not just that different heavenly spheres have each their own circular motion, rather each of the lower spheres is itself moved by a plurality of motions, the motion peculiar to it and motions it shares with the higher spheres, including the daily rotation which all the spheres share with the sphere of the fixed stars. (It is unclear whether they are moved *by* the sphere of the fixed stars, or simply by the same mover that moves it too.) Perhaps, as *Generation and Corruption* II 10 suggests, they do it in order to bring out the continuous generation of plant and animal species on earth; but it is mysterious how either the heavens or their movers could be aware of anything sublunar. The texts of Aristotle do not clear this up, but they do make an interesting suggestion. *Metaphysics* XII 8 says that each locomotion in the heavens is 'for the sake of the stars' (1074a25–31), i.e., that if Jupiter is carried by four compounded circular motions, each of which is originally the motion of one first sphere and then of other spheres carried inside it, including the innermost sphere of the complex, which carries Jupiter, then these four motions are all for the sake of Jupiter, and there are no superfluous motions and superfluous spheres which do not contribute to bringing about the characteristic complex movement of some star. This seems surprising, because Aristotle has insisted in the previous chapter that the heavenly motions are for the sake of their incorporeal *movers*. The solution must be that, as we saw in discussing the *Eudemian Ethics*, there are two senses of 'for the sake of which,' namely 'to benefit whom' and 'to attain which'. As Aristotle says about the god of *Eudemian Ethics* VIII 3, the movers of the heavens cannot be benefitted, so they must be the final cause as to-attain-which, and the stars—not the spheres—must be the final cause as to-benefit-whom. (Aristotle apparently also draws this distinction, apparently with this intention, at *Metaphysics* XII 7 1072b1–3, but the text is disputed.)⁴⁰

Aristotle has a peculiar and interesting development of this idea in *De Caelo* II 12, where he is asking why some stars perform one single rotation, others a smaller or larger number, and in particular why, although the fixed stars, which are furthest from us, have only a single motion, the planets which are closest to the fixed stars have more motions and the sun and the moon, which are closer to the earth, have fewer.⁴¹ His proposed answer is that 'it is likely that the good [*to eu*] should belong without action [*praxis*] to what is in the best condition; to what is closest to it, through a single small [action]; to what is further, through more [actions]—just as, in the body, one is in a good condition even without exercising, another after walking around a little, another also requires running and wrestling and getting covered in dust, and to yet another, however much it laboured, the good would not belong, but only something else [i.e., some imitation or substitute for the desired good]' (292a22–8). The first case, the thing that has no need of action to achieve the good, is itself the good, the end which the others are striving to attain—'what is in the best condition has no need of action [praxis] for it is itself that for the sake of which, and action always involves two things, when there is both the for-the-sake-of-which and what is for its sake' (292b4–7)—and this will not be a star but the unmoved good-itself. (He is not denying that it has any activity, *energeia*, but only that it has a practical activity, *praxis*, aiming at achieving some end beyond the activity itself, which is what he denies to the gods in *Nicomachean Ethics* X 8; *praxis* requires motion, while *energeia* need not.) The second case will be that of the fixed stars, and the third that of the planets close to the fixed stars, which

Aristotle compares to humans who do X in order to attain health, who must do Y in order to do X, and so on. The fourth case is also real: 'for another person it is impossible to proceed toward becoming healthy, but only toward running or losing weight, and one of these is the end for such people. For it would be the best for everyone to attain *that* end, but if they can't, it is better in proportion as it is closer to the best [end]. And for this reason the earth does not move at all, and the things close to it move with few motions, for they do not arrive at the ultimate [end], but only however far they are able to achieve [*tunchanein*] the most divine principle; whereas the first heaven achieves it straightaway by a single motion, and the things in between the first thing and the last things do achieve it, but achieve it through more motions' (292b15–15). In the context of Aristotle's argument, the 'things close to the earth' which move with few motions must be the sun and moon, and Aristotle must be saying—bizarre as it sounds—that they, like the earth, do not achieve the good at which all things aim, but only some imitation or approximation of it. But the first god is the for-the-sake-of-which, as to-attain-which, for all the stars including the sun and moon, even if they do not in fact attain it, just as the god is the to-attain-which for all human beings in *Eudemian Ethics* VIII 3, discussed above. And while humans best 'attain' the god by contemplating him, we cannot achieve this end directly, ignoring practical action, but must have a set of personal habits, or of laws for the whole city, which are conducive to this end; achieving this end will be easier for some, harder for others, and others will have to settle for an imitation of philosophical contemplation of the god.[42] We have seen some guesses as to why the fixed stars must rotate in order to 'attain' the first god, but it is hard to guess why Saturn cannot 'attain' the same god by a single rotation, but requires four different rotations, enabled by four different spheres, as means to that end. But we can observe that Saturn does in fact move in this way, and we can infer that Saturn, because of some weakness of its nature, must require this extra discipline in order to be benefitted: its complex movements might be compared to those of a choral dance at a festival (for the comparison see *Timaeus* 40c3-d3 and especially ps.-Plato [Philip of Opus] *Epinomis* 982d7-e6). And sublunar things, and even apparently the lower reaches of the heavens, are so badly off that there is no point in our following this complicated discipline.

To return, finally, to *Metaphysics* XII, Aristotle develops a similar idea in XII 10, when he describes how all things in the cosmos are 'ordered' toward the first good-itself, as the different members of a household or a city or an army are ordered toward some one good; 'they are all ordered together toward one [end], but, as in a household the free [family members] have the least license to act at random, but all or most [of their activities] are ordered, whereas the slaves and the beasts have little that is [directed] to the common [end], and much that is at random' (1075a18–22). Of course the slaves are required to act in the interests of the free family members or citizens, but (in Aristotle's ideal) the free family members or citizens have their lives regulated in the way that is most conducive to virtue, whereas with the slaves the ruler gives up on this goal, and is content if they will provide the external necessities for the free persons; the slaves can live with their morals unregulated in such spare time as they may have. Or perhaps the slaves too can achieve some imitation of virtue, since Aristotle thinks that sublunar things, which correspond to the slaves in the analogy, can imitate the activities of the heavenly bodies by going through the cycles of elemental transformations and of the reproduction of plant and animal species (cf. here 1075a22–5). We can hope that human beings have some higher destiny than the rest of the sublunar world, that we, like the stars, can actually 'attain' the highest god, by contemplating him, and carrying out some complicated series of practical activities to dispose ourselves, individually and collectively, for this end; or that, even if we fall short of this contemplation, we can achieve some higher perfection than simply reproducing the species. Plato in the *Timaeus* stresses just this exceptional status of human rational souls within the sublunar world.[43] Given what Aristotle says in the ethical treatises, and given the whole project of the *Metaphysics*, directed toward a contemplation of the divine first cause, we can assume that Aristotle agrees with Plato on this, despite the pessimism of *De Caelo* II 12 even about the sun and moon (and presumably *a fortiori* about humans). But here he is concentrated enough on the orderliness of the stars, who contemplate the god far better than humans can, and who in Plato's image 'dance' for the god (or for the many higher and lower gods) far better than humans can, that he does not even bother to say where humans fit into the scheme.

NOTES

1. I would like to thank Andrea Falcon, Silvia Fazzo, Carlos Fraenkel, and Christopher Shields for comments on various stages and sections of this paper.
2. Eugene Ryan, 'Pure Form in Aristotle', *Phronesis* 18 (1973), 209–24, helped bring to scholars' attention the fact that Aristotle never refers to separate immaterial substances as forms, except when he is talking about things that Plato mistakenly believed in. While many interpreters have attributed to Aristotle the view that being (and/or substance) is said by 'focal meaning', primarily of divine immaterial substances and derivatively of material substances (notably Joseph Owens, *The Doctrine of Being in the Aristotelian Metaphysics* (Toronto, 1951); Günther Patzig, 'Theology and Ontology in Aristotle's Metaphysics', in Jonathan Barnes, Malcolm Schofield, and Richard Sorabji, *Articles on Aristotle* (London, 1979), v.3, 33–49; Michael Frede, 'The Unity of General and Special Metaphysics: Aristotle's Conception of Metaphysics', in his *Essays in Ancient Philosophy* (Minneapolis, Minn., 1987), 81–95), there is no textual support for this idea. Pierre Aubenque in *Le problème de l'être chez Aristote* (Paris, 1962) maintains that being is said *equivocally*, rather than by focal meaning, of God and other things; there is no evidence for this either, except that *Metaphysics* X 10 says that what is imperishable and what is perishable are 'different in genus'.
3. There is a full discussion of all of Aristotle's assertions about gods in Richard Bodéüs, *Aristotle and the Theology of Living Immortals*, trans. Jan Garrett (Albany, N.Y., 2000), including many passages which modern readers tend to dismiss as non-serious. I think Bodéüs goes too far, but his book is a very useful corrective to the prevailing tendency to shrink Aristotle's account of God or gods to *Metaphysics* XII and a few related passages.

4. These *Definitions*, although not really by Plato, are attributed to him in the
   manuscripts, and are printed at the end of the OCT Plato, and translated in J.M.
   Cooper and D.S. Hutchinson, eds., *Plato: Complete Works* (Indianapolis, Ind., 1997).
   They seem to come from the early Academy. It is not out of the question that they
   might be influenced by Aristotle as well as by other sources, but there is no clear case of
   this, and they seem to be independent of him. Often several alternative definitions are
   given for a single term, and while these might be compatible, they might also represent
   different opinions within the Academy.

5. '[A] god does not rule by giving commands, but is that for the sake of which *phronêsis*
   commands—for the for-the-sake-of-which is twofold: they have been distinguished
   elsewhere—since he himself is in need of nothing' (*EE* VIII 3 1249b13–16): on the two
   senses of 'for-the-sake-of-which', see notes 7 and 40 below. Note that some editors,
   including Jonathan Barnes in the Revised Oxford Translation of the *Complete Works
   of Aristotle* (2 vols., Princeton, N.J., 1984), print what I am calling *EE* VIII as part of
   EE VII, so that *EE* VIII 3 will be *EE* VII 15. Also note that the *EE* and *EN* share three
   books, *EE* IV-VI = *EN* V-VII: these are usually printed with the *EN*, but most scholars
   think that they were originally intended as part of the *EE*, and we can trace lines of
   argument beginning in these books and extending to *EE* VIII 3.

6. Rejecting the bizarre emendation in the OCT, which for no reason turns the
   transmitted *ton theon therapeuein kai theôrein* ('serving and contemplating god') into *to
   en hêmin theion therapeuein kai theôrein* ('serving and contemplating the divine in us'),
   and similarly turns the earlier *tên tou theou theôrian* ('the contemplation of god') into
   tên tou theiou theôrian ('the contemplation of the divine').

7. This passage says 'the for-the-sake-of-which is twofold: they have been distinguished
   elsewhere' (1249b15). It does not actually say what the two senses of 'for-the-sake-
   of-which' are, but we can supply 'to-benefit-whom' [*to hô(i)*] and 'to-attain-which'
   [*to hou*] from two passages in *DA* II 4 415b2–3 and 415b20–21, both of which say, in
   almost but not quite identical wording, 'the for-the-sake-of-which is twofold, the
   to-attain-which and the to-benefit-whom'. (*Met.* XII 7 1072b2–3 probably draws the
   same distinction in slightly different terminology, but the text is disputed, see note 40
   below.) The same distinction is also referred to in *Physics* II 2, where we use things as
   if they existed for our sake, 'for we are ourselves an end: for the for-the-sake-of-which
   is twofold, as has been said in *On Philosophy*' (194a35–6), the point being that we are
   an end as to-benefit-whom rather than (the more usual sense) to-attain-which. In the
   De Anima passages, one time he has just said that animals and plants reproduce their
   kind 'in order that they may participate in the eternal and the divine so far as they are
   able: for they all [or: for all things] strive after it, and for its sake they do what they do
   by nature' (415a29-b2), and the other time he has just said that the bodies of animals
   and plants are 'instruments of the soul' or 'for the sake of the soul' (416a18–20). To
   explain how the same things can be both for the sake of the soul and for the sake
   of the eternal and the divine, he distinguishes senses of 'for the sake of': the point
   is evidently that they are for the sake of the soul as to-benefit-whom and for the
   sake of the eternal and the divine as to-attain-which or to-participate-in-which. See
   Ross' commentary on the *De Anima* (Aristotle, *De anima*, edited with introduction
   and commentary by Sir David Ross, Oxford, 1961) for this explanation. Thus the
   genitive in *to hou* is what Smyth calls a 'genitive of the end desired,' 'used with
   verbs signifying *to aim at, strive after, desire*' (H.W. Smyth, *Greek Grammar*, revised
   edition, Cambridge, Mass., 1956, p. 321). It should be noted that many continental
   interpreters do not take the genitive this way, but merely as repeating the *hou* in *hou*

heneka: sometimes it is said that the genitive signifies what is objectively valuable, the dative what is valuable from some individual point of view, or that the genitive signifies an immanent end, the dative a transcendent end (so that in *De Anima* II 4 the divine would be the *hô(i)* and the soul the *hou*), but they have no plausible syntactic explanation for the contrast of genitive and dative. See, for instance, Konrad Gaiser, 'Das zweifache Telos bei Aristoteles,' in Ingemar Düring, ed., *Naturphilosophie bei Aristoteles und Theophrast* (Heidelberg, 1969), 97–113.

8. I am taking this from Ingemar Düring, *Aristotle's Protrepticus: an Attempt at Reconstruction* (Göteborg, 1961). Barnes in the *Complete Works of Aristotle* reprints Düring's translation (in this case it's on p. 2409, unchanged), but Düring provides much more information which is useful for evaluating the text. For the most recent judgement on Düring's reconstruction of the *Protrepticus*, see D.S. Hutchinson and M.R. Johnson, 'Authenticating Aristotle's *Protrepticus*,' *Oxford Studies in Ancient Philosophy* 29 (Winter 2005), 193–294.

9. Compare Aristotle's version of the cave story, Cicero *De natura deorum* II 27, 95, where the stars are the supreme object of contemplation the cave-dwellers are cut off from (by contrast with Plato's emphasis on the sun). But here he is interested in, literally, the stars, in themselves and as evidence for further divine causes, while in *Metaphysics* VII 16 the stars are being cited merely as a comparison for what Aristotle is really concerned with, the existence of *unmoved* or *non-bodily* eternal substances.

10. The terminology and issues of *tashbîh* and *tanzîh* begin in *kalâm* (Islamic theology) but are taken up by the *falâsifa* (Greek-style philosophers); a starting point is Josef van Ess's article 'Tashbîh wa-Tanzîh' in the *Encyclopedia of Islam*, 2nd edition. Al-Fârâbî, in his *Harmony of Plato and Aristotle*, attributes to Aristotle a concern to avoid *tashbîh* particularly in what he says about a divine efficient cause of the world (where Aristotle is trying to avoid implying production out of a pre-existing matter or in a stage-by-stage temporal process) and about divine paradigms of sensible things (where he is trying to avoid implying that there are further worlds similar to this sensible one). The Fârâbî treatise has been translated in *Alfarabi: The Political Writings: 'Selected Aphorisms' and Other Texts*, translated and annotated by Charles Butterworth (Ithaca, N.Y., 2001), pp. 115–67. (The attribution to Fârâbî has been challenged by Marwan Rashed, 'On the Authorship of the Treatise *On the Harmonization of the Opinions of the Two Sages* attributed to Al-Fârâbî,' *Arabic Sciences and Philosophy* 19 (2009), 43–82, with discussion of views and arguments on both sides, but my point here will not be affected.) Note that while the standard view both in *kalâm* and in *falsafa* (Greek-style philosophy) is that *tashbîh* should be avoided and *tanzîh* practiced, Ibn 'Arabî idiosyncratically claims that both *tashbîh* and *tanzîh* are necessary, corresponding to different aspects of God: much of what one can find in popular sources, especially on the Internet, propagates Ibn 'Arabî's idiosyncrasies as though they were the standard Muslim way of thinking.

11. Aristotle is not himself saying that the gods dwell in the heavens, but rather endorsing the serious opinion which underlies this poetic representation, namely that the heavenly bodies are perfect and eternal—thus 'divine' or akin to the nature of the gods—and would therefore be appropriate places to imagine the gods as dwelling.

12. For the world's soul as co-extended with its body, see *Timaeus* 36d8–37a2; the motions of the world-soul described at 36b6-d7 also carry the heavenly bodies with them, 38c7–39b2; 42e5–44c4 gives a vivid description of how the rational circular motions in the human soul are blocked or distorted by the rectilinear motions of nutrition and sensation spilling over to the soul from the body.

13. For Aristotle's attribution of this view to Plato, see *Metaphysics* I 6; for his rejection of the view, see esp. *Metaphysics* XIV 4 1091a29–XIV 5 1092a11.

14. On Aristotle's acceptance of a good-itself, and on his criticism of Plato's candidates for a good-itself (the idea of the good, and—what Aristotle apparently regards as Plato's more serious candidate—the One), see my 'Aristotle and Plato on God as Nous and as the Good', *Review of Metaphysics* 45 (1992), 543–73, and 'La sagesse comme science des quatre causes?' (forthcoming in Maddalena Bonelli, ed., *Aristote: physique et métaphysique*, Paris, 2012).

15. Aristotle's introduction of Anaxagoras on *nous* at *Metaphysics* I 3 984b15–19 echoes *Phaedo* 97b8-d4, and even more clearly Aristotle's criticism of Anaxagoras' insufficient use of *nous* as a cause at I 4 985a16–21 echoes *Phaedo* 98b7-c2. But, Aristotle says in I 7 that Plato is himself in much the same state as Anaxagoras: 'those who speak of *nous* or love posit these causes as good, but they do not speak as if anything is or comes to be *for the sake of* these things, but rather as if motions arise from them [i.e., as if they are efficient rather than final causes]; *and in the same way* also those who say that the one or being exists say that such a nature is a cause of *ousia* [i.e., a formal cause], but not that [anything] is or comes to be *for its sake*. The result is that in one way they do, and in another way do not, say that the good is a cause: they do not say so unqualifiedly, but only *per accidens*' (I 7 988b8–16). For the objections against seeking final causes of unchanging (esp. mathematical) things, see *Metaphysics* III 2 996a22-b1 and *Eudemian Ethics* I 8 1218a15–32; on which passage, and on Plato's Lecture on the Good, see the important article of Jacques Brunschwig, 'EE I,8 1218a15–32 et le ΠΕΡΙ ΤΑΓΑΘΟΥ', in Paul Moraux and Dieter Harlfinger, eds., *Untersuchungen zur Eudemischen Ethik* (Berlin, 1971), 197–222.

16. For arguments that the demiurge of the *Timaeus* is identical with the *nous* of the *Philebus* (and of *Laws* X and XII), and discussion of how this *nous* is to be understood, see my *Plato on God as Nous* (Carbondale, Ill., 1995). My main thesis was that '*nous*,' in this context, means not 'mind' or 'intellect' but something like 'Reason' or 'rationality': it is not a rational soul, or the rational power or activity of such a soul, but rather an intellectual virtue which souls can participate in, to greater or lesser degrees as their cognition and action are more or less rational; and, like other virtues according to Plato, it exists in itself, independently of any souls that participate in it. I also argue that Anaxagoras too thinks of the world-governing *nous*, not as a single mind, but as Reason or rationality, an independently existing *bodily* substance that living things can participate in by having some portion of it present in their bodies. The texts in Plato that have sometimes been taken as saying that *nous* cannot exist except in soul are really saying that only souls (and not, as Anaxagoras thinks, bodies) can participate in *nous*, or that only souls can do so directly, and bodies only by means of souls. For other views, see F.M. Cornford, *Plato's Cosmology* (London, 1937), esp. pp. 38–9 and p.197; Harold Cherniss, *Aristotle's Criticism of Plato and the Academy*, v.1 (Baltimore, Md., 1944), esp. p. 425; Reginald Hackforth, 'Plato's Theism', in R.E. Allen, ed., *Studies in Plato's Metaphysics* (London, 1965), 439–47; and Richard Mohr, *The Platonic Cosmology* (Leiden, 1985). There is a survey of the debate (in German) in Michael Bordt, *Platons Theologie* (Freiburg, 2006).

17. See *Physics* VIII 1 for why Empedocles' world-history is preferable to Anaxagoras', and why it would still need to be supplemented by a further cause. But if there is a period of complete rest when love or strife has triumphed, Empedocles will be just as unable as Anaxagoras to explain why motion will start again.

18. For Theophrastus on the possibility of an unmoved mover and of something acting [*energein*] without being in motion, see his *Metaphysics* 7b9–15 and Fr. 307D in William Fortenbaugh, Pamela Huby, Robert Sharples, and Dimitri Gutas, eds., *Theophrastus*

of Eresus: Sources for His Life, Thought, Writings and Influence (2 vols., Leiden, 1992).
Eudemus in his *Physics*, following Aristotle's *Physics*, argues that the first mover is
unmoved, see his Frr. 120, 121, and 123b in Fritz Wehrli, *Die Schule des Aristoteles* (2nd
ed., 10 vols., Basel, 1967), v. 8, but seems not to speak of 'activity' in this context. The
first writer I know of who revives the ideas of an unmoved mover and of acting without
being in motion is the Platonist Alcinous (second century AD?), *Didaskalikos* 10,2
(available in English translation, Alcinous, *The Handbook of Platonism*, tr. John Dillon,
Oxford, 1993); they are then taken up by Alexander of Aphrodisias.

19. The art is an efficient cause of the artifact, indeed more strictly an efficient cause than
    the artisan is, *Physics* II 3 esp. 195b21–5; the art acts without itself being affected, or is
    an unmoved mover, *On Generation and Corruption* I 7 324a24-b13. Aristotle sometimes
    compares the relation between a soul and its body to the relation between an artisan
    and his tools (so *Eudemian Ethics* VII 9 1241b17–19), but elsewhere, when he is being
    more precise (as at *De Anima* I 3 407b20–26), to the relation between an *art* and its
    tools. Thus the way that the art moves its tools, without being itself affected, gives him a
    model for the soul's action on the body, although, since the living body is a *natural* tool
    (an 'organic natural body', *De Anima* II 1 412a27-b6), the soul is an *internal* source of
    motion, whereas an art moves its tools from outside. For full discussion and citations
    of all the relevant texts, see my 'Aristotle's Definition of Soul and the Programme of the
    De Anima,' *Oxford Studies in Ancient Philosophy* 22 (Summer 2002), 83–139.

20. Aristotle says different things about the divine principle or principles of motion,
    and their relations to the heaven, in different places; there may be tensions or even
    inconsistencies, which may indicate that he changed his mind about some of the issues.
    Besides *Physics* VIII and *Metaphysics* XII, and various discussions in the *De Caelo* and
    briefly in other physical works (mainly the *On Generation and Corruption*), there are
    also the fragments of the *De Philosophia*. Werner Jaeger in *Aristotle: Fundamentals
    of the History of his Development* (tr. Richard Robinson, Oxford, 1934, 2nd ed. 1948)
    tries to give a history of Aristotle's development on this and other issues; Hans von
    Arnim, *Die Entstehung der Gotteslehre des Aristoteles* (Vienna, 1931), makes a more
    serious attempt to survey all the evidence, and gives a rather different developmental
    scheme; W.K.C. Guthrie, 'The Development of Aristotle's Theology', *Classical Quarterly*
    27 (1933), 162–71 and 28 (1934), 90–98, gives essentially an English summary of von
    Arnim. These writers are often rather obsessed with—and sometimes outraged at—the
    plurality of unmoved movers in *Metaphysics* XII 8, and have often tried to show
    that it was only at a very late stage in his career that Aristotle accepted this, but it is
    attested for *Physics* VIII 6 (see my discussion further on) and also apparently for the
    De Philosophia, Cicero *De natura deorum* I,13,33, since the *mens = nous* there seems
    to be different from what moves the world by *replicatio*, which apparently means a
    reverse rotation. In any case, given Aristotle's commitments, there is no way to explain
    the plurality of rotations of the heavenly bodies without such a plurality of movers.
    (Jaeger pointed to stylistic differences between *Metaphysics* XII 8 and the rest of
    XII, by which he claimed to show that XII 8 was a later addition by Aristotle to the
    'monotheistic' main body of XII, but it is at least as likely, as argued by Friedrich Blass,
    'Aristotelisches,' *Rheinisches Museum* 30 (1875), 481–505, that Aristotle in writing XII
    incorporated [much of] XII 8 from an *earlier* text, perhaps the *De Philosophia*.) Also
    von Arnim and some others are convinced that at an early stage, represented notably
    by the *De Philosophia*, Aristotle did not believe in an incorporeal divine mover, but
    rather in something like a divine self-moving aether as the highest principle; this
    seems to me to be plainly contradicted by the *De Philosophia* fragment cited, and the
    difference between the two senses of 'for the sake of which', cited by *Physics* II from the

De Philosophia, is very likely to have been used to explain how an eternally unmoved substance, although it cannot be benefitted or otherwise affected, can be a final cause of the motion of the heavens.

21. For the distinction between souls as things moved not *per se* but *per accidens* and things that are not moved even *per accidens*, see especially *Physics* VIII 6, discussed below. On souls and other forms incidentally coming to exist and ceasing to exist when the composites they are in are generated and corrupted, see notably *Physics* VIII 6 258b16–22 and *Metaphysics* VII 15 1039b20–27 and VIII 3 1043b13–21; Ross gives a list (not complete) of passages where Aristotle refers to something 'existing at one time and not existing at another time without process of coming-to-be and passing-away' in his *Aristotle's Metaphysics* (2 vols., Oxford, 1924), v. 1, p. 360, on *Metaphysics* VI 2 1026b23.

22. Aristotle also says (255b24–9) that the *per accidens* mover of a heavy or light body's natural motion is the obstacle-remover, e.g., the person who lets go of a stone or tilts a bucket so that the water can run out; but fundamentally the reason why the water falls is that there was water above the natural place of water, and the *per se* mover will be whatever brought this about. Presumably if, instead of something generating water above the natural place of water (say by condensing air in the clouds into water), something takes water that was in its natural place and lifts it above its natural place, this lifter will be the *per se* mover of the water's eventual fall.

23. See the discussion above on the *De Anima* on why the soul is not self-moved but unmoved; on Aristotle on self-motion generally see the articles collected in Mary Louise Gill and James Lennox, *Self-Motion* (Princeton, N.J., 1994).

24. The conception of the sun as moving in the circle or band of the zodiac, against the background of the sphere of fixed stars, seems to have been introduced into Greece from Babylonia in the fifth century: it is first attested in Oenopides and Philolaus. But many Greek writers even afterwards instead think of the sun as having two separate motions, a motion every day from east to west, and also a motion northward from winter to summer solstice and southward from summer to winter solstice; Aristotle at *Metaphysics* I 2 983a15 mentions the solstices, literally the 'turnings' of the sun at its northern and southern limits, as a typical source of wonder requiring explanation. Typical explanations offered are either that the sun encounters seasonal winds or patches of compressed air which blow it back when it reaches these limits, or that it travels in search of nourishment from exhalations from the sea, which cannot be found north or south of a certain range; these explanations would not posit eternal constantly acting causes, but rather contrary causes of the sun's northward and southward motions. Aristotle deliberately rejects these explanations, which continue to be offered by Stoics (e.g., Cleanthes at Cicero *De natura deorum* III, 14, 37) and Epicureans (e.g., Lucretius V, 517–25 and 637–49), and substitutes the explanations of mathematical astronomy. Assuming that the sun moves uniformly in the circle of the ecliptic (the circle in the middle of the zodiac band), its motion can be modelled by assuming that it rides on the equator of a sphere, rotating uniformly with a period of one year, whose pole is imbedded in a larger sphere which carries the fixed stars and which rotates uniformly around its own poles with a period of one sidereal day (roughly 23 hours 56 minutes). Eudoxus' models for the sun, moon, and planets, and their later modifications by Callippus and by Aristotle himself, which model more complicated movements with more complicated arrangements of uniformly rotating spheres with their poles embedded in larger spheres, are known to us chiefly from *Metaphysics* XII 8 and from Simplicius' commentary on *De Caelo* II 12. These sources are not fully transparent. The standard reconstruction, due to the nineteenth-century astronomer

Giovanni Schiaparelli, is presented in T.L. Heath, *Aristarchus of Samos* (Oxford, 1913), 28–33; and G.E.R. Lloyd, *Early Greek Science: Thales to Aristotle* (London, 1970), chapter 7. Revisionist proposals have been made by Henry Mendell, 'Reflections on Eudoxus, Callippus, and Their Curves: Hippopedes and Callippopedes', *Centaurus* 40 (1998), 77–275 and 'The Trouble with Eudoxus', in P. Suppes, J.M. Moravscik, and H. Mendell, eds., *Ancient and Medieval Traditions in the Exact Sciences* (Stanford, Calif., 2000), 59–138; by Ido Yavetz, 'On the Homocentric Spheres of Eudoxus', *Archive for the History of Exact Sciences* 51 (1998), 221–78; and 'On Simplicius' Testimony Regarding Eudoxan Lunar Theory', *Science in Context* 16 (2003), 319–29; and by Alan Bowen, 'Simplicius and the Early History of Greek Planetary Theory', *Perspectives on Science* 10 (2002), 155–67.

25. An entry-point for the complex history of objections and alternatives to Aristotle's account of projectile motion is Richard Sorabji, *Matter, Space and Motion* (Ithaca, N.Y., 1988), chapter 14, mainly on John Philoponus.

26. David Sedley, in his article 'Is Aristotle's Teleology Anthropocentric?', *Phronesis* 36 (1991), 179–96, in his chapter on *Metaphysics* XII 10 in Michael Frede and David Charles, eds., *Aristotle's Metaphysics Lambda: Symposium Aristotelicum* (Oxford, 2000), and in the Aristotle chapter in his *Creationism and its Critics in Antiquity* (Berkeley, Calif., 2007), has given the best modern defense of an overall cosmic teleology in Aristotle, which the natures of individual things or even of species would be insufficient to explain. (He does not especially concentrate on the structure and motions of the heavens.) Sedley agrees that Aristotle does not believe in any divine providential action intentionally directed toward the universe, and that passages such as *Gen. et Corr.* II 10 336b31–2 are merely figurative (so *Creationism* p. 168).

27. So *Phys.* VI 4 234b10–20, taken up in *Phys.* VIII 5 257a33-b1 and used in the following argument.

28. Leonardo Tarán prints *On the Motion of Animals* 3 699a12–24 as Fr. 62 in his *Speusippus of Athens: A Critical Study with a Collection of the Related Texts and Commentary* (Leiden, 1981); as Tarán makes clear in his commentary, pp. 386–8, he is following arguments of Cherniss in attributing this theory to Speusippus. The basic reason is that Aristotle attributes to Speusippus the view that points are real substances (and principles of geometrical magnitudes), whereas he attributes to Plato and Xenocrates the theory of indivisible lines, and the view that points are a geometrical fiction. This is true, and *On the Motion of Animals* 3 cannot be referring to Plato or Xenocrates, but other Academics are possible: in particular, it might be Eudoxus. (People sometimes say that Eudoxus as a mathematician would not be interested in these philosophical issues, but we know he had views about pleasure and about participation in the forms.) However, since Speusippus thought that the one was the principle of numbers and the point of geometricals, it would not be surprising if he thought that a *rotating* point was the principle of astronomicals.

29. But such a reformulation—the mover is the axis—might leave the opponent open to Aristotle's argument at *On the Motion of Animals* 3 699a27-b11, that the heavens cannot be moved by something *inside* them, since it would not have something unmoved to rest against (just as, in the example of *MA* 2, a boat cannot be moved by someone inside it, unless he can rest his oar or stick against something resisting outside the boat). Aristotle considers here the possibility that the earth might not count as properly part of the heavens, since it is not moved along with their motions, so perhaps the axis might support itself against the earth; but, since the earth surely has lesser power of resistance than the heavens, the torque-force that the axis is trying to exert on the heavens would more easily set the earth rotating instead.

30. For *Metaphysics* I and *EE* V = *EN* VI, see pp. 424–5 above. On *Metaphysics* XII, see the commentaries on individual chapters in Frede and Charles, op. cit.

31. On the activity of colours, see *De Anima* II 7. It is clear enough that the colour is a second potentiality in the sense of *DA* II 5 and is not changed when the potentiality is exercised; Aristotle apparently says that explicitly at *DA* III 7 431a4–7, although this passage is often translated differently. On the 'Heracliteans', see *Theaetetus* 156a2–157c1 and 159c15-d6: in their view wine is not sweet in itself and does not persistently remain sweet (nor does it have any other persistent character), rather the sweetness generated in the encounter with the tongue renders the wine sweet at this moment and in this relation. In *DA* III 10 433b10–18, the object of desire [*orekton*] moves without being moved, by causing the animal first to perceive and then to desire it.

32. On arts as unmoved movers, see above p.432 and note 19 and my article there cited. While Aristotle says that 'the object of desire and object of thought move in this way, they move without being moved' (XII 7 1072a26–7, quoted above), and that 'it moves as an object of love [*hôs erômenon*] (1072b3), strictly speaking he does not say that it *is* a final cause or an object of desire, and this has been denied by Sarah Broadie (in 'Que fait le premier moteur d'Aristote?', *Revue Philosophique de la France et de l'étranger* 183 (1993), 375–411) and by Enrico Berti (notably in his chapter on XII 6 in Frede and Charles, op. cit.), who maintain that the unmoved movers of the heavens are exclusively efficient causes; and indeed there are difficulties (of which more below) in understanding how these eternally separated substances can be final causes. (It should also be noted that one manuscript, codex T, has not *hôs erômenon* but *hôs horômenon*, 'as an object of sight.') But, if XII 7 is not clear enough, XII 10 1075a36-b10 (to be read in conjunction with I 7 988b8–16, cited in note 15 above) shows that Aristotle thinks a major advantage of his account of the causality of the good first principle, in comparison with the accounts of Anaxagoras, Empedocles, and Plato, is that it makes the good principle a final cause and thus a cause *qua* good, although it is *also* an efficient cause: 'Anaxagoras [makes] the good a principle as a mover [i.e., an efficient cause]: for *nous* moves. But it moves for the sake of something, so that [it and what it moves for the sake of] will be different, except as *we* say: for [the art of] medicine [analogous to *nous*] and health [analogous to the good] are in a way the same thing' (XII 10 1075b8–10). Indeed, the good as the principle for-the-sake-of-which and *nous* as the moving principle will be *absolutely* identical, since the separate good-itself (1075a11–15) will not be distinguished from *nous* as health is from medicine, by being present in some matter.

33. This is also the classification implied at *Parts of Animals* I 1 639b30–640a9, where physics is contrasted with the theoretical sciences, but goes contrary to the more famous *Metaphysics* VI 1 1025b18–1026a22. The idea in *PA* I 1 is not that physics will help us actually produce something, but rather that our knowledge will trace the same steps that nature goes through in producing natural things, just as to have scientific knowledge of houses I must trace the same steps that the housebuilder goes through in his productive knowledge: this is why physics, like knowledge of houses and unlike 'the theoretical sciences', starts with final causes and derives the means and parts and processes which lead to these results.

34. In *DA* III 5, speaking of a self-subsisting knowledge (which 'when it has been separated, is just what it [essentially] is' rather than an attribute of some other underlying subject, 430a22–3), he says that 'actual knowledge [*epistêmê*] is identical with its object' (430a19–20): this object, or this self-subsisting knowledge, must be not a matter-form composite or the form of such a composite, nor an accident of some

underlying subject, but rather a separate immaterial substance. 'Potential [knowledge] is prior in time in the individual [knower], but overall it is not prior even in time; and it is not the case that it [= the actual knowledge] knows [*noei* = exercises its knowledge in contemplation] at one time and does not know at another time' (430a20–22): so in such cases the actual knowledge of X, that is, X itself, has existed from eternity, but it is not always *my* knowledge, and it is not always acting on *me* in such a way that I will be contemplating it. It is clear that the self-subsisting knowledge (*epistêmê* or *nous*) described in *Metaphysics* XII 9 falls under the account Aristotle is giving here in *De Anima* III 5: whether *DA* III 5 is talking *about* (say) the mover of the daily motion of the heavens, or merely about something analogous to it, is disputed, as its causal role in the individual soul's knowing, and indeed everything else about this chapter. For the complex history of disputes about *DA* III 5 and connected texts, entry ways are provided by H.A. Davidson, *Alfarabi, Avicenna and Averroes on Intellect* (Oxford, 1992) and F.M. Schroeder and R.B. Todd, *Two Greek Aristotelian Commentators on Intellect* [annotated translations of Alexander and Themistius] (Toronto, 1990). An entry into the more recent debate is Victor Caston, 'Aristotle's Two Intellects: A Modest Proposal', *Phronesis* 44 (1999), 199–227; I discuss the issues at length in an unpublished paper, 'From *De anima* III,4 to *De anima* III,5.'

35. On the impossibility of part-whole structure without potentiality, presupposed at XII 9 1075a5–10, see *Metaphysics* XIV 2 1088b14–28 and VII 13 1039a3–14 (and compare *Physics* I 2 185b25–186a3). Despite XII 9, there have been perennial attempts (going back at least to Themistius' paraphrase of XII) to find some scope for Aristotle's first *nous* to know individual sensible things, or at least the universal forms of sensible things, so as to have some plurality in its knowledge-contents. This might be supported by 'providential' passages such as *Gen. et Corr.* II 10 336b31–2 (cited above), and by Aristotle's criticism of Empedocles' implication that his Sphairos cannot have knowledge of Strife (*Met.* III 4 1000b3–6), but it is not compatible with XII 9 or with the principles that underlie it, namely that the purely actual *nous* is identical with its knowledge, that the knowledge of X is identical with X or with X stripped of its matter, and there is no composition in a purely actual being. For the perennial discomfort with XII 9 and proposals for how to relieve it, see most recently the chapters by Jacques Brunschwig and Aryeh Kosman in Frede and Charles, op. cit.

36. Aristotle begins XII 10, in a passage already noted, by asking 'in which way the nature of the whole possesses the good and the best, whether as something separated and itself-by-itself, or as the order', concluding that it is both, as the army has both its immanent order and the separate general as its good, but primarily the separate general, corresponding to *nous* identified with the good-itself, since the order exists (or is good) on account of the general (1075a11–15). Later in the chapter he contrasts his account with other accounts which (he says) are not able to solve the difficulties about the first principles. Some—he means especially Speusippus— 'don't even make the good and the bad [to be] principles, although the good is in all things most of all a principle', while 'the others do rightly in saying that it is a principle, but they do not say *how* the good is a principle, whether as end or as mover or as form' (1075a36–b1). He then gives criticisms of Anaxagoras' and Empedocles' descriptions of the good principle as an efficient cause (b1–11), as he had already given criticisms of Plato's description of the good principle as the One and as a formal cause opposed to a bad material principle (a32–36). Aristotle tries to show that by positing the good as an efficient cause which is also a final cause (so that it acts for its own sake, not for the sake of anything else—see 1075b8–10, cited in note 32 above), which is not a constituent

of things as form or matter, and which does not have a contrary bad principle (either as matter or as something with which it competes to inform some matter or act on some patient), he can avoid all of the difficulties that he has raised for earlier philosophers. Note that while Aristotle assumes that Plato's first principle, the good-itself, is not *nous* but the One, some ancient Platonists (notably Alcinous, *Didaskalikos* chapter 10) identify it rather with *nous*. This seems unlikely, since the good-itself is supposed to be a principle *of the forms themselves*, while *nous* (or the demiurge) is cited rather as a cause of matter's participating in form, and does not seem to be responsible for the forms themselves; or, if it is, not as an efficient-moving cause, which is the causal role that Aristotle and Plato (*Philebus* 26e1–27c1, 28c1–30e3) assign to *nous*.

37. Theophrastus' *Metaphysics* has been translated by W.D. Ross and F.H. Fobes (Oxford, 1929) and by Marlein van Raalte (Leiden, 1993a), and into French (Théophraste, *Métaphysique*) by André Laks and Glenn Most (Paris, 1993b). Laks and Most provide a very helpful introduction and notes, van Raalte a philological commentary; both give references to the literature and controversies about this text (e.g., its title, whether it was written in Aristotle's lifetime, whether it is complete or a fragment, why it is written in *aporiai*, whether Theophrastus had intended answers to the *aporiai* and if so what they were). Theophrastus' *Metaphysics* remains the most stimulating critical discussion of the issues of Aristotle's *Metaphysics*, especially the more 'theological' issues. Many modern writers (including Ross) dislike the text because it seems to be concentrating on Aristotle's theology at the expense of his more fundamental ontology; but Theophrastus is likely to have understood Aristotle better than Ross did.

38. Although Pierre Aubenque did argue that Aristotle saw the life of the heavens as a life of eternal frustration, *Le problème de l'être chez Aristote* (Paris, 1962), esp. pp. 367–8 (God is 'the goal, always deferred, of a search and an effort') and pp. 386–90. Even Aubenque tried to show that a positive good resulted, an imitation of God, although this imitation is not, as in Plato, God's acting on the world to produce an image of himself, but the world's trying, in its imperfect way, to make up for the fact that God is *not* present in it and does *not* act upon it.

39. The idea that the rotation of the heavens imitates the activity of their movers is very widespread, going back apparently to Theophrastus, *Metaphysics* 5a23–8 and taken up by late ancient and medieval commentators, but it has no direct textual support in Aristotle, and it has been challenged by Berti and Broadie in the papers cited above. Aristotle does say that the cycle of the sublunar elements 'imitates' the motion of the heavens (*Met.* IX 8 1050b28–30, *Gen. et Corr.* II 10 336b26-a7, *Meteor.* I 9 346b35–347a1). See also *EE* VI 14 = *EN* VII 14 1154b20–31, discussing pleasure. '[A] god eternally enjoys a single simple pleasure, for there is an activity not only of motion but also of non-motion, and pleasure is [present] more in rest than in motion' (b26–8): *we*, however, cannot pleasantly persist in performing a single simple activity, and can only enjoy more complex and intrinsically less pleasant and less valuable activities, due to a deficiency in our nature which Aristotle compares to the condition of the sick (or Fury-troubled) Orestes in Euripides' *Orestes*, who cannot rest comfortably in any one position, and for whom 'change in all things is sweet…for it contains a seeming of health, and seeming prevails, even if it is far from truth' (*Orestes* 234–6, partly quoted by Aristotle 1154b28–9).

40. On *EE* VIII 3 and the two senses of 'for the sake of which', see pp. 424–5 and notes 5 and 7 above. *Metaphysics* XII 7 1072b1–3, as printed both by Ross and by Jaeger, says 'that the for-the-sake-of-which exists in unmoved things, [the] division [or distinction, *diairesis*] makes clear: for the for-the-sake-of-which is both *tini* [= for something?] and *tinos* [= of something?], of which the one is [sc. among unmoved things?] and the

other is not.' This seems to be drawing the same distinction, using the dative *tini* and the genitive *tinos*, that is drawn in *De Anima* II 4 (cited above) using the dative *hô(i)* and the genitive *hou*. Aristotle would then be saying that final causes to-benefit-whom cannot exist among eternally unchangeable things (which cannot be affected and thus cannot be benefitted), but that final causes to-attain-which can—which is very close to the point he is making at least in *EE* VIII 3 and perhaps in the other texts where he draws this distinction. However, XII 7 1072b1–3 does not actually say this in any of the manuscripts that have been used as the basis for modern editions. In the crucial clause, as Ross and Jaeger print it *esti gar tini to hou heneka kai tinos,* manuscripts E and J have simply *esti gar tini to hou heneka,* while A^b has *esti gar tini to hou heneka tinos.* The text of E and J is not perfectly grammatical but can be understood: it would mean 'the for-the-sake-of-which belongs to something [i.e., there is something that is for the sake of it], of which the one [sc. the for-the-sake-of-which] exists [among unmoved things] and the other [sc. what is for the sake of it] does not', in other words that while there is a legitimate objection against eternally unchangeable things *having* final causes (for which see III 2 996a21–9), it does not tell against their *being* final causes to the heavens. (But it might be a stretch to call this a *diairesis*.) See Silvia Fazzo, 'Lambda 7 1072b2–3,' *Elenchos* 23 (2002), 357–76 [in Italian], for a defence of the reading of E and J and of this interpretation of the text. But this text has not been accepted by any of the editors after Bekker. Schwegler, followed by Bonitz, had conjectured *esti gar ditton to hou eneka* 'for the for-the-sake-of-which is twofold,' which would bring it very close to the passages in *EE* VIII 3 and *DA* II 4 and also *Phys.* II 2. Christ instead took the text of A^b and inserted an 'and,' *esti gar tini to hou heneka kai tinos,* 'the for-the-sake-of-which is both *tini* [= to benefit someone] and *tinos* [= to attain something],' which Ross and Jaeger accept, especially because Christ's conjecture was confirmed by the Arabic translation '*wa-dhâlika anna mâ min ajlihi yûjadu li-shay'in wa-li-dhâ shay'un, wa-dhâlika minhumâ mawjûdun, wa-ammâ hâdhâ fa-laysa bi-mawjûdin*' transmitted in Averroes' commentary, where '*li-shay'in wa-li-dhâ shay'un*' seems to be translating '*tini kai tinos*', probably without fully understanding what the distinction between the dative and the genitive is supposed to convey. (Averroes takes them to be a final cause which is a substance and a final cause which is an accident, so that in that sense the former 'is' and the latter 'is not'.) This reconstruction of the Greek behind the Arabic has been challenged in different ways by Fazzo in the article cited and by Cecilia Martini Bonadeo, '*Hôs erômenon*: alcune interpretazioni di *Metaph.* Λ 7' in Vincenza Celluprica and Cristina D'Ancona, eds., *Aristotele e i suoi esegeti neoplatonici* (Rome, 2004), 211–43, but I think that it is correct. This reconstruction from the Arabic also corresponds to a reading attested twice in the Greek manuscript tradition. A scholium in codex E, curiously not cited by Christ or Ross or Jaeger, confirms that some manuscripts had what these modern editors print: *proskeitai en tisi to kai tinos*—i.e., some manuscripts add *kai tinos,* presumably after *esti gar tini to hou heneka,* or conceivably after *esti gar tini* and before *to hou heneka.* (Silvia Fazzo called attention to this scholium in her *Il libro Lambda della Metafisica di Aristotele: Introduzione, edizione critica, studio, commento, appendici,* dissertation Lille/Trento, 2009, in the 'Note sulla costituzione del testo,' *ad locum.*) And codex V^d, which no editor has yet collated, writes *esti gar tini to hou heneka kai tinos,* with the '*kai tinos*' added above the line by a later hand. However, what is 'to benefit someone' or 'to attain something' would not be the for-the-sake-of-which but rather what is for its sake. So Aristotle's pronouns here should be read not (with Christ and Ross and Jaeger) as *tini* and *tinos* indefinite, without accents or with grave accents on the first syllable, 'to benefit someone' and 'to attain something', but as *tini* and *tinos* interrogative, with acute accents on the final syllable, 'to-benefit-what' and 'to-attain-what', like *to dia ti* with an acute accent on *ti*, 'the on-account-of-what', i.e., the 'why' or the cause.

41. This is true on Eudoxus' system, which Aristotle initially followed, and which he describes at *Metaphysics* XII 8 1073b17–32, but not on Callippus' system, which he later adopted with his own modifications, and which he briefly describes at 1073b32–8 (his own modifications and conclusions 1073b38–1074a14).

42. On 'attaining' or 'possessing' a god, see above, p.425. When someone imitates philosophical contemplation, say by attendance at religious ceremonies or musical or athletic competitions, or by practical reasoning and action, this need not mean that he is consciously aiming at philosophical contemplation and deciding to settle for second-best. It means that, whether he knows it or not, the objective end [*telos*] of his actions is philosophical contemplation, and that a scientific observer would explain what he in fact does by noting that it was as close as he could come to this end, as an animal or plant perpetuates its species because this comes as close as it can to individual immortality (see *DA* II 4 415a26–b7). On Aristotle on imitation, and on second-best lives as imitations of the contemplative life, see Gabriel Richardson Lear, *Happy Lives and the Highest Good* (Princeton, N.J., 2004).

43. As we saw above, the demiurge directly produces the rational parts of human souls, as he had produced the world-soul and the overall structure of the world and each of the heavenly bodies, which are all immortal and all are governed by reason (and therefore have uniform circular motion), whereas the 'young gods' (the heavenly bodies) produce both the human body and the irrational parts of the human soul, which are not directly governed by reason (and therefore have irregular motions and are mortal). Presumably human beings attain their end, not simply by contemplating the heavenly bodies (although this is a useful means), but by being rational in the same way that heavenly souls are rational, and contemplating the same things that the heavenly souls contemplate.

BIBLIOGRAPHY

Alcinous (1993) *The Handbook of Platonism*, tr. John Dillon (Oxford).

Aubenque, Pierre (1962) *Le problème de l'être chez Aristote* (Paris).

Barnes, Jonathan, ed. (1984) *The Complete Works of Aristotle* (2 vols., Princeton, N.J.).

Blass, Friedrich (1875) 'Aristotelisches', *Rheinisches Museum* 30, 481–505.

Bodéüs, Richard (2000) *Aristotle and the Theology of Living Immortals*, tr. Jan Garrett (Albany, N.Y.).

Bordt, Michael (2006) *Platons Theologie* (Freiburg).

Bowen, Alan C. (2002) 'Simplicius and the Early History of Greek Planetary Theory', *Perspectives on Science* 10, 155–67.

Broadie, Sarah (1993) 'Que fait le premier moteur d'Aristote?', *Revue Philosophique de la France et de l'étranger* 183, 375–411.

Brunschwig, Jacques (1971) 'EE I,8 1218a15–32 et le ΠΕΡΙ ΤΑΓΑΘΟΥ', in Paul Moraux and Dieter Harlfinger, eds., *Untersuchungen zur Eudemischen Ethik* (Berlin), 197–222.

Butterworth, Charles, tr. (2001) *Alfarabi: The Political Writings: 'Selected Aphorisms' and Other Texts* (Ithaca, N.Y.).

Caston, Victor (1999) 'Aristotle's Two Intellects: A Modest Proposal', *Phronesis* 44, 199–227.

Cherniss, Harold F. (1944) *Aristotle's Criticism of Plato and the Academy*, v.1 (Baltimore, Md.).

Cooper, J.M., and D.S. Hutchinson, eds. (1997) *Plato: Complete Works* (Indianapolis, Ind.).

Cornford, F.M. (1937) *Plato's Cosmology* (London).

Davidson, H.A. (1992) *Alfarabi, Avicenna and Averroes on Intellect* (Oxford).

Düring, Ingemar (1961) *Aristotle's Protrepticus: an Attempt at Reconstruction* (Göteborg).

Fazzo, Silvia (2002) 'Lambda 7 1072b2–3', *Elenchos* 23, 357–76.

Fazzo, Silvia (2009) *Il libro Lambda della Metafisica di Aristotele: Introduzione, edizione critica, studio, commento, appendici*, dissertation Lille/Trento.

Fortenbaugh, William, Pamela Huby, Robert Sharples, and Dimitri Gutas, eds. (1992) *Theophrastus of Eresus: Sources for His Life, Thought, Writings and Influence,* 2 vols. (Leiden).

Frede, Michael (1987) 'The Unity of General and Special Metaphysics: Aristotle's Conception of Metaphysics', in his *Essays in Ancient Philosophy* (Minneapolis, Minn.), 81–95.

Frede, Michael, and David Charles, eds. (2000) *Aristotle's Metaphysics Lambda: Symposium Aristotelicum* (Oxford).

Gaiser, Konrad (1969) 'Das zweifache Telos bei Aristoteles', in Ingemar Düring, ed., *Naturphilosophie bei Aristoteles und Theophrast* (Heidelberg), 97–113.

Gill, Mary Louise, and James Lennox, eds. (1994) *Self-Motion* (Princeton, N.J).

Guthrie, W.K.C. 'The Development of Aristotle's Theology', *Classical Quarterly* 27 (1933), 162–71 and *Classical Quarterly* 28 (1934), 90–98.

Hackforth, Reginald (1965) 'Plato's Theism', in R. E. Allen, ed., *Studies in Plato's Metaphysics* (London), 439–47.

Heath, Thomas L. (1913) *Aristarchus of Samos* (Oxford).

Hutchinson, D.S., and M.R. Johnson (2005) 'Authenticating Aristotle's Protrepticus', *Oxford Studies in Ancient Philosophy* 29 (Winter), 193–294.

Jaeger, Werner (1948) *Aristotle: Fundamentals of the History of his Development,* tr. Richard Robinson, 2nd ed. (Oxford).

Lear, Gabriel Richardson (2004) *Happy Lives and the Highest Good* (Princeton, N.J.).

Lloyd, G.E.R. (1970) *Early Greek Science: Thales to Aristotle* (London).

Martini Bonadeo, Cecilia (2004) '*Hôs erômenon*: alcune interpretazioni di *Metaph.* L 7', in Vincenza Celluprica and Cristina D'Ancona, eds., *Aristotele e i suoi esegeti neoplatonici* (Rome), 211–43.

Mendell, Henry (1998) 'Reflections on Eudoxus, Callippus, and Their Curves: Hippopedes and Callippopedes', *Centaurus* 40, 77–275.

——— (2000) 'The Trouble with Eudoxus', in P. Suppes, J.M. Moravscik, and H. Mendell, eds., *Ancient and Medieval Traditions in the Exact Sciences* (Stanford, Calif.), 59–138.

Menn, Stephen (1992) 'Aristotle and Plato on God as Nous and as the Good', *Review of Metaphysics* 45, 543–73.

——— (1995) *Plato on God as Nous* (Carbondale, Ill.).

——— (2002) 'Aristotle's Definition of Soul and the Programme of the *De Anima*', *Oxford Studies in Ancient Philosophy* 22 (Summer), 83–139.

——— (forthcoming) 'La sagesse comme science des quatre causes?', in Maddalena Bonelli, ed., *Aristote: physique et métaphysique* (Paris).

——— (unpublished) 'From *De anima* III,4 to *De anima* III,5'.

Mohr, Richard (1985) *The Platonic Cosmology* (Leiden).

Owens, Joseph (1951) *The Doctrine of Being in the Aristotelian Metaphysics* (Toronto).

Patzig, Günther (1979) 'Theology and Ontology in Aristotle's Metaphysics', in Jonathan Barnes, Malcolm Schofield, and Richard Sorabji, eds., *Articles on Aristotle* (London), v.3, 33–49.

Rashed, Marwan (2009) 'On the Authorship of the Treatise *On the Harmonization of the Opinions of the Two Sages* attributed to Al-Fârâbî', *Arabic Sciences and Philosophy* 19, 43–82.

Ross, W.D. ed., (1924) *Aristotle's Metaphysics* (2 vols., Oxford).

——— (1961) *Aristotle De Anima*, edited with introduction and commentary (Oxford).

Ryan, Eugene E. (1973) 'Pure Form in Aristotle', *Phronesis* 18, 209–24.

Schroeder, Frederic M., and Robert B. Todd (1990) *Two Greek Aristotelian Commentators on Intellect* (Toronto).

Sedley, David (1991) 'Is Aristotle's Teleology Anthropocentric?', *Phronesis* 36, 179–96.

——— (2007) *Creationism and its Critics in Antiquity* (Berkeley, Calif.).

Smyth, Herbert W. (1956) *Greek Grammar*, revised edition (Cambridge, Mass.).

Sorabji, Richard (1988) *Matter, Space and Motion* (Ithaca, N.Y.).

Tarán, Leonardo (1981) *Speusippus of Athens: A Critical Study with a Collection of the Related Texts and Commentary* (Leiden).

Theophrastus (1929) *Metaphysics*, ed. and tr. W.D. Ross and Francis H. Fobes (Oxford).

Theophrastus (1993a) *Metaphysics*, ed. and tr. and comm. Marlein van Raalte (Leiden).

Théophraste (1993b) *Métaphysique*, ed. and tr. André Laks and Glenn Most (Paris).

van Ess, Josef, 'Tashbîh wa-Tanzîh', *Encyclopedia of Islam*, 2nd ed.

von Arnim, Hans (1931) *Die Entstehung der Gotteslehre des Aristoteles* (Vienna).

Wehrli, Fritz (1967) *Die Schule des Aristoteles*, 10 vols., 2nd ed. (Basel).

Yavetz, Ido (1998) 'On the Homocentric Spheres of Eudoxus', *Archive for the History of Exact Sciences* 51, 221–78.

——— (2003) 'On Simplicius' Testimony Regarding Eudoxan Lunar Theory', *Science in Context* 16, 319–29.

CHAPTER 18

ARISTOTLE'S PHILOSOPHY OF MATHEMATICS

DAVID BOSTOCK

MUCH of Aristotle's thought developed in reaction to Plato's views, and this is certainly true of his philosophy of mathematics. So I begin with a quick sketch of Plato's position.

1. THE PLATONIC BACKGROUND

To judge from his dialogue, the *Meno*, the first thing that struck Plato as an interesting and important feature of mathematics was its epistemology: in this subject we can apparently just 'draw knowledge out of ourselves'. In the *Meno* this leads Plato to suppose that the knowledge must already be somehow within us, and he offers the explanation that we are 'recollecting' it from a previous existence (*Meno* 82b-86b). This somewhat fanciful theory of 'recollection' seems to have been abandoned in Plato's later thought.[1] (That would explain why Aristotle never mentions it in any of his numerous criticisms of the Platonic theory.[2]) But in any case Plato never did abandon the thought behind it, namely that our knowledge of mathematics does *not* depend upon our observation and experience of this world. In modern terminology, it is a priori.

From this initial thought about how our mathematical knowledge is obtained nothing strictly follows about what that knowledge is knowledge of. But it does *suggest* the further view that it is not knowledge of what we observe and experience in this world, and Plato very soon came to add that claim, even if it had not been there initially. (The *Meno* is somewhat evasive on this point.) His main argument is that the objects which mathematics is about are *ideal*, or *perfect*, in a way which distinguishes them from anything to be found in this world. The argument most obviously applies to geometry, for geometry concerns perfect squares, perfect circles, and the like, whereas no material object ever is perfect in this way. Of course geometers do in practice draw perceptible diagrams to illustrate their reasoning, but the diagrams are only a rough guide to what they are actually thinking of, and they will always be more or less inaccurate (*Republic* 510d-511a). The real objects of geometry are not visible objects at all, and are available only to thought and not to perception.

Plato supposes that the same applies to arithmetic, since it is the study of what may be called 'perfect' numbers. It was usual in his day to explain a number as 'a plurality of units',[3] and he supposes that these should be 'perfect' units, meaning by this that they are not divisible in any way and are in all respects perfectly equal to one another. (An underlying thought here is that in the equation '3 = 1+1+1' the 'ones' are exactly the same as one another.) Once more, no such units are to be found in this world that we experience (*Phaedo* 72e-77a, *Republic* 525d-526a, *Philebus* 56d-57a). He also has this further thought: anything in this world that is an example of one number will also be an example of another, as, e.g., what we count as one thing (one finger) we may also count as three things (three finger-joints) or as an indefinite plurality (e.g., of atoms) (*Republic*, 524d-525a, *Parmenides* 129c-d, *Philebus* 14c-e). By contrast, the number one which figures in arithmetic is quite distinct from the number three, which again goes to show that the objects that arithmetic is about are available to thought, but not to perception.

This is the basic Platonic position. Plato himself soon came to introduce a hesitation over the epistemology. He noted that the contemporary geometer starts from 'hypotheses' (i.e., axioms, or definitions, or both) which he does not justify, and he came to think that this meant that geometers now do not have what is properly counted as *knowledge*. But at the same time he seems to have thought that this defect could in principle be remedied (*Republic* 509d-511e). It appears that he also introduced a complication into the ontology, for Aristotle tells us that he made a distinction between the *forms* of those things that mathematics studies (e.g., in his language 'the square itself' and 'the one itself') and *examples* of them that are 'intermediate' between forms and perceptible things. These 'intermediates' resemble all of Plato's forms in being eternal, unchangeable, and objects of thought rather than perception. But they also resemble the perceptible instances in that there are many of each kind, whereas there is only one unique form for each kind (*Metaphysics* I 987b14–18). It is disputed whether this doctrine is to be found in Plato's dialogues,[4] but in any case there is no doubt that Aristotle ascribes it to Plato, and his criticisms of Plato's views on mathematics are very often focused upon it. He does not give us Plato's reasons for the doctrine, but the usual explanation is that geometers often prove theorems which concern several squares (e.g., Pythagoras' theorem), and again that in arithmetic one assumes the existence of many units. So the entities of which mathematical theorems are true must be these 'intermediate' entities, and cannot be the unique forms which Plato also posited (not only in these cases but in many others too, which have no connection with mathematics).

My discussion will rely on this distinction. For there are very many places where Aristotle criticizes Plato's general theory of forms, and I shall simply set these on one side. Even if Plato is wrong about forms in general, still there is the different question of whether he might be right about these so-called 'intermediates' that he takes to be the objects which mathematics is about. So I now turn to Aristotle's rejection of this idea.

2. Aristotle's Objections to Plato

Aristotle certainly thinks that Plato was wrong to 'separate' the objects of mathematics from the familiar objects that we experience in this world. His main arguments on this point are in chapter 2 of Book XIII of the *Metaphysics*, which I now consider. In broad outline there are three distinct lines of argument, at 1076b11–39, 1076b39–1077a14, and 1077a14-b11. I take them in turn.[5]

1076b11–39. The bulk of this argument concerns the objects of geometry, i.e., points, lines, planes, and solids. Aristotle begins with the idea that if we assume the existence of separate and ideal geometrical solids, over and above the perceptible solids of this world, then we must do the same for planes and lines and points too. So far, so good. But then he goes on to claim that there will therefore have to be *both* the ideal planes that are the surfaces of these posited ideal solids *and* the ideal planes that are separately posited, thus making two different kinds of ideal plane.[6] Similarly there will be three kinds of ideal line—i.e., those separately posited, those that are the boundaries of the planes separately posited, and those that are the boundaries of the planes which are the surfaces of the solids separately posited. And by the same reasoning there will be four kinds of ideal points. This, he very reasonably claims, is an absurd proliferation. But why should we suppose that the Platonist is committed to it?

The reason Aristotle gives is that planes considered on their own are 'prior' to planes considered as the surfaces of solids, because planes are simpler (less compounded) than solids. In the same way lines are simpler than planes, and hence prior to them, and points are simpler than lines. He evidently supposes that the Platonist would be bound to accept this claim of 'priority', and his reason appears to be that the Platonist *does* count the separated objects of mathematics as 'prior' to the objects in this world. His suggestion seems to be that this latter 'priority' is taken to arise because the separated objects are simpler than the familiar perceptible ones, presumably on the ground that the latter do have (perceptible) matter while the former do not. So the Platonist, in order to be consistent, must suppose that in *all* cases what is simpler is 'prior' to what is more complex, and so will exist separately from it. (This reconstruction of Aristotle's argument builds rather a lot into the very brief explanation that he gives at 1076b18–21, namely: 'The uncompounded is prior to the compounded; and if imperceptible bodies are prior to perceptible ones then by the same reasoning planes on their own are prior to the planes in the unchanging solids'. But I see no better way of spelling out what the argument is supposed to be.)

It is clear that no Platonist need be disturbed by this reasoning. He could simply refrain from the initial claim that the imperceptible objects of mathematics are 'prior' to the perceptible objects of this world. After all, what he mainly wishes to insist upon is that both exist, and for this he does not need to claim that either is 'prior' to the other. Moreover, if (like Plato himself) he does wish to claim that the imperceptible is in some way 'prior', this need not be for the reason that Aristotle gives, namely that it is less compounded. He is more likely to say that it is because it is more intelligible, and he can then go on to add that mathematical points, lines, planes, and solids are all *equally* intelligible. This would again put a stop to Aristotle's argument. More pertinently, he might employ a tactic which Aristotle himself very often employs, and insist that there are different kinds of priority.[7] So he could accept that points are prior to lines, lines to planes, and planes to solids in *one* way (e.g., in simplicity) without accepting the consequence that Aristotle draws, namely that they are also prior in another way, in that points must be able to exist separately from lines, and so on. Indeed, this is almost what Aristotle says himself at the end of this chapter, where he notes that what is prior 'in definition' need not also be prior 'in substance', i.e., need not be capable of a separate existence. The objects with which geometry is concerned (which he describes as those obtained 'by abstraction') may perhaps be prior in the first way without being prior in the second (1077b1–11). It is clear that the Platonist could say the same about points and lines, lines and planes, planes and solids.

One could suggest some other considerations that may have influenced Aristotle in this argument. For example, it might be said that since plane geometry can be (and usually is) studied without any consideration of solid geometry, the objects of plane geometry must be capable of existing without the objects of solid geometry. But I see no reason why the Platonist should be committed to that principle. Again, Annas (1976, p.141) proposes the idea that mathematical objects introduced in two quite distinct ways, i.e., as the ideals to which physical planes approximate, and as the surfaces of ideals to which physical solids approximate, must be assumed to be different objects. But it is clear that a Platonist need not be committed to this principle either. I conclude that this first argument of Aristotle's is quite easily resisted.

As a coda to his argument Aristotle adds that the same point will apply to the numbers studied in arithmetic, because numbers are 'prior' to points, which in turn are 'prior' to all other geometrical entities. The 'priority' that he has in mind seems to be that a number may be explained simply as a plurality of units, without mentioning position, whereas a point is sometimes explained as 'a unit with a position' (e.g., *APo* I 27 87a36–8). So points are defined by *adding* something to the (simpler) notion of an arithmetical unit. From this he infers that the Platonist is committed to saying that there must be even more kinds of number than there are kinds of point. But it is again quite clear that this does not follow. From the Platonist point of view the same number may perfectly well apply to collections of different kinds of things. So I now leave this first stretch of argument and pass on to the next.

1076b39–1077a14. Here Aristotle's objection is that the Platonist principles which are applied to arithmetic and geometry should also apply equally well to other areas of human knowledge, once more leading to a needless reduplication of reality. He first instances astronomy, optics, and harmonics (1076b39–1077a9), and then switches to a rather different kind of example, namely the recently discovered general theory of proportion, which applies simultaneously to all quantities whatever (1077a9–14).

The point that he makes about astronomy, optics, and harmonics would surely not disturb Plato in the least. For Plato himself did claim that there was a kind of 'ideal' astronomy, which studied 'ideal' heavenly motion, without paying attention to the vagaries in the perceptible motions of perceptible heavenly bodies (*Republic* 528e-530c). He made a similar claim about harmonics, taking it to be essentially a study of numerical relationships, and independent of the rough and ready concords and discords that we are aware of in perceptible sounds (*Republic* 530d-531c). He did not actually say anything similar about optics, but he surely could have done so: a suitable 'idealized' optics would study the behaviour of an 'ideal' light, e.g., light which really does travel in 'ideally' straight lines and is not subject to the distortions that are brought about by atmospheric refraction, and the like. It is true that Plato does not seem to suppose that these 'idealized' sciences would require any further 'ideal objects' than are already postulated for ordinary arithmetic and geometry. (For example, in astronomy all that we would need would be perfect spheres rotating with a perfectly uniform angular velocity.[8]) If we had found Aristotle's first line of argument compelling, we might think that that was not enough. But in any case Plato might have been entirely ready to accept the conclusion that Aristotle is aiming for. He was not shy of accepting 'intelligible objects' distinct from the perceptible ones. (Aristotle's concluding remark is that an idealized optics and harmonics presupposes an idealized vision and hearing, and hence some idealized animals to possess them (1077a5–9). But there is obviously no reason to accept this, for Plato's idea was to mathematicise these sciences in a way which cut them free from *any* connection with perception.)

I think that *we* may be sympathetic to what seems to be Aristotle's main line of thought in this argument, namely that sciences may 'idealize' without our having to suppose that the objects which they treat of do really exist in their ideal form, not in this world but in another. I shall come back to this thought later. But here I should say that this talk of 'idealization' is *my* way of making sense of what Aristotle says in this context, and the text that we actually have does not introduce this idea at all. All that it says is that if there are 'intermediates' for geometry then there ought to be similar 'intermediates' for other sciences too, but it does not even hint at why such 'intermediates' might be thought to be required in either case.[9]

At 1077a9–14 we find a different line of argument. A recent innovation in mathematics was the introduction of a *general* theory of proportion, i.e., of the conditions under which one can truly say such things as '*x* bears to *y* the same ratio as *z* bears to *w*'. This theory applies without alteration to all quantities whatever, i.e., to all respects in which bodies may be quantifiable, such as plurality, length, time, weight, and so on. (The important mathematical innovation is that it shows for the first time how proportions may be applied to incommensurable quantities.)[10] Aristotle is impressed by this theory, as an excellent example of the kind of generalisation that one seeks in mathematics (and other sciences), and he quite often refers to it.[11] He seems to have no single word for all those different quantities to which the theory applies—a natural suggestion might be *megethos*, which is Euclid's terminology but not Aristotle's—but let us just call them 'quantities'. Then his argument is that since this is a reputable branch of mathematics, the Platonist should posit 'separable' items which it studies, items that are 'intermediate' between the general form of a quantity, and the various particular quantities which are also supposed to exist separately, e.g., numbers and lengths and times.

It is difficult to assess this argument because we do not know why Plato (or one who was attracted to his position) wanted to posit these 'intermediates' in the first place. But if the idea was as I have suggested, namely that many perfect examples are needed because it is perfect examples that mathematics is about, then one must say that the argument has no force at all. Certainly, the Platonist will want a general form of quantity, and he will want a number of perfect examples of quantities. But he already *has* these, insofar as he has already assumed the existence of perfect numbers, perfect lengths, perfect areas, and so on. Why should he need anything more? Why would he have to suppose that there must *also* be perfect instances of quantity, which are, as it were 'neutral between' all the particular kinds of quantity? (They would be, as Locke might somewhat carelessly have said, 'all and none of these at once'.) Well, perhaps there is a reason, but if so Aristotle certainly has not told us what it is.

As with the first argument that he offers in this discussion, Aristotle's general point is that the Platonic theory leads to a useless proliferation of entities. The first argument relies upon a general principle about priority which the Platonist could very fairly reject, and the second functions by attempting to press certain analogies, though the underlying principles have not been stated at all. Moreover, in neither case would the argument show that this proliferation of entities was impossible, and one can see how a committed Platonist might be ready to accept the enlarged universe. More importantly, Aristotle's arguments do not show that such a proliferation is useless, because it simply does not address the question of what *use* the Platonist thinks that it has. This is a point that I shall come back to. Meanwhile, let us pass on to the final stretch of argument.

1077a14-b11. These final arguments seem largely to miss the point. In Aristotle's own preferred scheme of things, if we set aside God and the heavenly bodies, the entities which most deserve the title of 'substance', i.e., the things that exist in the fullest way, are living things, especially animals, and perhaps man in particular. He sometimes seems to say that, since these things have the highest value, everything else which exists must be regarded as existing only for their sake.[12] Obviously Plato would not agree with this, but for the sake of argument he could do so. After all, Aristotle is not claiming that other things do not exist at all. For example, he would not say that his basic physical elements, such as air and water, have *no* existence, even if he wishes to add that they have 'less actuality' and are 'less complete' and 'less of a whole [i.e., a unity]' than are living things (1077a26–31; cf. 1040b5–16). The Platonist could similarly claim that what he regards as the objects of mathematics *do* exist, even if Aristotle does wish to count them as *less* 'actual', 'complete', and 'whole' than are his own favoured kind of substances. For the Platonist thinks that he has good reason to suppose that they must exist, but that reason presumably does not require us to set any particular value upon them. (No doubt Plato does in fact value a priori knowledge above empirical knowledge, and this is taken to carry with it corresponding valuations for their respective objects. But Plato's ontology is independent of this, and anyway Aristotle is here paying no attention to epistemology.) So far, then, there is no serious case for the Platonist to answer.

Indeed, in this passage Aristotle himself apparently accepts that the Platonist's mathematical objects do exist, since he seems to admit that they are 'prior in generation' (1077a17–20). He is apparently relying on the idea that a line is 'generated' from a point, i.e., by the movement of that point, and similarly a plane from a line and a solid from a plane (1077a24–6). This is evidently not a central part of a Platonist position, though apparently it was adopted by Platonists whom Aristotle knew. But in any case the Platonist would presumably be thinking of the 'generation' of *mathematical* lines, planes, and solids, not of physical bodies. Apparently Aristotle is thinking differently, because he goes on to say that a solid can be further improved to become a living thing (1077a26–31), and presumably that could not be said of the Platonist's mathematical solids. Perhaps the theory that he is speaking of holds that physical solid bodies are somehow 'generated from' mathematical solids, but that is an idea which one cannot easily understand.

A different point that is raised at 1077a20–4 is the question of what it is that makes a mathematical entity a 'unity' (or, more literally, 'one thing'). Aristotle claims that a thing's 'soul' (*psuchê*) is a comprehensible cause of its 'unity', and observes that Plato's mathematical entities do not have souls. But one cannot see any worthwhile argument here, for it is obvious that souls cannot be the *only* causes of 'unity'. For example, even Aristotle will surely accept that such a thing as a stone is, in its own way, a 'unity' (i.e., is 'one thing'). He does not have much to say about the 'cause' of this. He can tell us that a stone is a 'continuous' object (*suneches*), with all its parts 'held together' (*sunechomena*), but he has no explanation of what it is that holds them together.[13] The Platonist can similarly say that his geometrical objects are 'one thing' by being continuous, but he need not suppose that there is anything which literally 'holds together' their various parts. There is a genuine question of why it is that many physical objects cohere, so that their parts cannot be separated from one another by a mere touch, but no such question arises for purely geometrical objects.[14]

In any case, Aristotle's objections in this final stretch of argument are weak, both because they presuppose his own favoured view of reality, and because they do not really address the basic point at issue. The fundamental question is whether Plato is right in supposing that there must *exist* some intelligible but non-perceptible objects for mathematics to be about; what kind of *value* these objects have (if they do exist) is altogether a secondary matter. Besides this, the chapter as a whole would surely not convince any Platonist opponent, because it never asks what *reasons* Plato might have had for positing such objects, and so it offers no response to these reasons. As I see it, Plato's basic argument is very simple: mathematics concerns objects that are perfect or ideal in a way that no perceptible object is; but the statements of mathematics are true; therefore such objects must exist. What is wrong with this reasoning? Aristotle *never* explicitly addresses this question, though surely he should have done.

A surprising feature of his discussion is that it does not even tell us whether he accepts the Platonic premise, i.e., whether he too thinks that the objects of mathematics are perfect or ideal in a way that no ordinary perceptible object is. The claim that they are occurs only once, in the preliminary discussion of problems in *Metaphysics* III, and in that context it gives no reason to suppose that Aristotle himself accepts it; we may easily regard it just as a line of thought that he puts into the mouth of his Platonist opponent. (See note 9.) On the other side, there is one stray passage which apparently claims that ordinary perceptible objects *are* perfect examples of the geometer's claims; at any rate it appears to say that a material straight edge really does touch a material sphere at just one point (*De Anima* I 1 403a12–16). But I think one should be very suspicious of this passage. As the text stands its claim is quite unexpected, without parallel elsewhere, *and* it makes no sensible contribution to its context.[15] If we set this odd and isolated passage on one side, there is nowhere where Aristotle directly asserts, or directly denies, that the objects of mathematics have a kind of perfection that is not found in perceptible things. This silence is both surprising and very vexing, for it must make a difference to our interpretation of his positive views.

The most likely explanation for his silence is that he did not think that he had anything new to say on this topic but was ready to subscribe to the view that was generally accepted at the time, which was Plato's. It is true that Aristotle does not have the theoretical reason that Plato and other atomists had for saying that at least some familiar geometrical figures must be physically impossible. Plato is committed to this, for it is impossible to put together a perfect sphere from atoms of the shapes that Plato allows in his *Timaeus* (i.e., cube, tetrahedron, octahedron,

icosahedron).[16] But Aristotle is not an atomist, and he believes in the strict continuity of matter, so that line of thought would not apply to him. On the other hand
he *also* believed that material objects are in fact very much as they appear to be to
the naked eye, and surely a material sphere resting on a material flat surface does
not even *appear* to touch the surface at just one point. So I think it most likely that
he did accept the Platonic premise, that material objects do not *perfectly* exemplify
the properties which the geometer speaks of. If so, then I fear that he probably took
the same view of the arithmetician's 'pluralities of units', though he surely should
not have done. Let us take these in turn.

Arithmetic. We, who have been taught by Frege, can clearly see that Plato
was mistaken when he claimed that this subject introduces idealizations. The
source of his error is that he takes it for granted that, when numbers are applied
to ordinary perceptible objects, they are applied 'directly'; i.e., that it is the object
itself that is said to have this or that number. But Frege made it quite clear that
this is not so. In his language, a 'statement of number' makes an assertion about
a *concept*, not an object, i.e., it says how many objects fall under that concept.
(An alternative view, which for present purposes we need not distinguish, is that
numbers apply not to physical objects but to sets of those objects, and they tell us
how many members the set has.) To illustrate, one may ask (say) how many cows
there are in this field, and then one is asking of the *concept* 'a cow in this field'
how many objects fall under it. The answer will (in most cases) be entirely unambiguous, say sixteen. There is nothing 'imperfect' in this application of the number. One may say that here we take as our 'units' the cows in the field, but there is
no implication that a cow is an indivisible object, or that the cows are 'equal' to
one another in any respect beyond all being cows in this field. Nor is it implied
that the matter in question could not be counted under some other concept—i.e.,
taking something else as the 'unit'—say pairs of cows or kilograms of cow.

Aristotle has grasped this point. He frequently compares counting to measuring, with the idea that in each case one *chooses* something as the 'unit', which is then
treated for that purpose as indivisible. (E.g.: 'The measure must always be something that is the same for all [the things measured], for example if the measure is a
horse then horses [are being measured], and if a man then men' (*Metaphysics* XIV 1
1088a8–9).[17] Notice that my supplement 'measured' would in each case be very naturally replaced by 'counted'.) What is somewhat surprising is that he never presents
this as a criticism of Plato. He certainly argues against the conclusions that Plato was
led to, and he points to a number of difficulties in the view that a number is 'really'
a plurality of 'perfect units' which enjoy a 'separate' existence. (This is the theme
of most of chapters 6–8 of Book XIII, to 1083b23. The arguments are often cogent,
but I shall not discuss them here.[18]) But he does not seem to have asked just what it
was that led Plato astray, so we get no diagnosis of the opponent's errors. Worse, the
positive account that we do get—and which I come to shortly—leaves us very much
at a loss as to just what Aristotle wants to put in place of Plato's picture.

Geometry. It is fair to say that geometry 'idealizes', in that it concerns what
has to be true of *perfect* squares, circles, and so on. But the first thing to say is

that what geometry claims about perfect circles may very well be true even if there are no perfect circles at all, for the claims may be construed hypothetically: *if* there are any perfect circles, then such-&-such will be true of them (e.g., they can touch a perfectly straight line at just one point and no more). One might ask how geometry can be so useful in practice if there are no such entities as it speaks of, but (*a*) this is a question for the Platonist too (since 'in practice' means 'in this perceptible world'), and anyway (*b*) the question is quite easy to answer.

We are nowadays familiar with a wide range of scientific theories which may be said to 'idealize'. Consider, for example, the theory of how an 'ideal gas' would behave—e.g., it would obey Boyle's law precisely—and this theory of 'ideal' gases is extremely helpful in understanding the behaviour of actual gases, even though no actual gas is an ideal gas. This is because the ideal theory simplifies the actual situation by ignoring certain features which make only a small difference in practice. (In this case the ideal theory ignores the actual size of the molecules of the gas, and any attractive or repulsive force that those molecules exert upon one another.) But no one nowadays could suppose that because this theory is helpful in practice there must really *be* 'ideal gases' somewhere, if not in this world then in another; that reaction would plainly be absurd. Something similar may be said of the idealizations in geometry. For example, a carpenter who wishes to make a square table will use the geometric theory of perfect squares in order to work out how to proceed. He will know that in practice he cannot actually produce a *perfectly* straight edge, but he can produce one that is very nearly straight, and that is good enough. It obviously explains why the geometric theory of perfect squares is in practice a very effective guide for him. We may infer that geometry may perfectly well be viewed as a study of the spatial features—shape, size, relative position, and so on—of ordinary perceptible things. As ordinarily pursued, especially at an elementary level, it does no doubt involve some idealization of these features, but that is no good reason for saying that it is not really concerned with this kind of thing at all, but with some other 'ideal objects' that are not even in principle accessible to perception. All this, however, is on the assumption that geometry may be construed hypothetically: it tells us that *if* there are perfect squares, perfect circles, and so on, then they must have such-&-such properties. That is helpful, because it implies that the approximate squares and circles which we perceive will have those properties approximately. But, one may ask, does not geometry (as ordinarily pursued) assert outright that *there are* perfect circles? That is a question which I must come back to.

Let us now move on to what Aristotle gives us by way of a positive account of what actually does happen in mathematics. The main source here is chapter 3 of Book XIII of the *Metaphysics*, but it is a standard complaint that this is really only an outline sketch of his position, which leaves many gaps. There are similar outlines elsewhere, principally in *Physics* II 2 193b22–194a12, *De Anima* III 7 431b12–17, and *Metaphysics* XI 3 1061a28-b4. But even if we put all such passages together, we still get only a broad outline, with many gaps.

3. ARISTOTLE'S POSITIVE ACCOUNT

The discussion in XIII 3 is mostly about geometry, so let us start with that. For the most part this discussion seems to claim that there are no special objects which deserve to be called 'the objects of geometry', for geometry is a theory of perfectly ordinary perceptible objects. It may *look* as if it concerns objects of a special kind—points, lines, planes, and so on—but that is an illusion due to the fact that it treats of perceptible objects in a highly general and abstract way. For lines and planes, squares and circles, *are* perceptible features of perceptible objects, and what is special to geometry is that it prescinds from all *other* features of these objects. As Aristotle often says elsewhere (though not as it happens in XIII 3), geometry proceeds by 'abstraction' (*aphairesis*), which simply ignores, discounts, or 'subtracts' all features of perceptible objects other than their purely geometrical features.[19] As he says here in XIII 3, it considers these objects only *qua* (*hê(i)*) having geometrical features (1077b17–34), or regarding their other features as merely *accidental* (*kata sumbebêkos*) to its concerns (1077b34–1078a9). On this view, geometrical claims about triangles or squares or circles are not claims about special 'intelligible but imperceptible objects', but simply highly general claims about all ordinary objects that are triangular or square or circular.

I think that this *is* Aristotle's real view, but even in XIII 3 there are two brief remarks which apparently introduce a different theme. At 1078a2–5 he says, somewhat unexpectedly, that mathematics is not a study of what is perceptible, even if what it studies does happen to be perceptible. More important is 1078a17–25 which says that the mathematician *posits* (*tithetai*) something as separate, though it is not really separate. He adds that this leads to no falsehood, apparently because the mathematician does not take the separateness as one of his premises. A similar theme is elaborated at greater length in *Physics* II 2, which is also intended as a general description of the nature of mathematics. At 193b31–5 we hear that the mathematician, since he is not concerned with features accidental to his study, does *separate* what he is concerned with, for it can be separated 'in thought', even if not in fact. And again we are told that this leads to no falsehood.[20] On the contrary, Aristotle seems to hold that such a fictional 'separation' is distinctly helpful, both in mathematics and in other subjects too (1078a21–31).

A question which our texts do not resolve is this: just what kind of thing is a mathematical object conceived as being, when it is conceived as 'separate'? I think myself that the most likely answer is that it is conceived as the Platonist would conceive it, i.e., as existing in its own separate 'world', intelligible and not perceptible. Further, if—as seems probable—Aristotle concedes that perceptible objects do not *perfectly* exemplify the properties treated in elementary geometry, then it will presumably be this mental 'separation' that smooths out the actual imperfections. But it must be admitted that this is pure speculation, and cannot be supported from anything in our texts.

One thing that we can plausibly suppose is that Aristotle means to be speaking of the nature of these objects-conceived-as-separate when he implies that they are made of a kind of stuff which he calls 'intelligible matter'. (This is mentioned by name only at *Metaphysics* VII 10 1036a1–12; VII 11 1036b32–1037a5; and VIII 6 1045a33–6. In the first two places it is explicitly said to be the matter of the objects of mathematics, and I believe that the same applies to the third, though this interpretation is disputed.[21] We may also note XI 1 1059b14–16, which mentions the matter of mathematical objects as a topic for discussion) The role of this 'intelligible matter' must surely be to allow there to be many mathematical objects of each type—e.g., many circles exactly similar to one another—differentiated from one another by their different matter. That is, it answers the need which (as we conjecture) led Plato to posit mathematical objects as 'intermediates', rather than forms proper. (From our own point of view we might prefer to say that geometrical objects are thought of as being in an 'intelligible space', and differentiated from one another by their different positions in that space. That would make almost no difference to the overall picture.[22]) I add that, just as Aristotle does not think that geometrical entities do *really* exist separately, so he also does not think that there is *really* this imperceptible quasi-stuff that he calls 'intelligible matter'. For in VII 10 1036a9–12, he describes it as 'that which is present in perceptible things, but not *qua* perceptible'. This means, I presume, that it is thought of by abstraction, paying no attention to the particular *kinds* of matter that perceptible things are actually made of, but retaining enough in thought to provide a way of distinguishing one from another. One can at least say that this invocation of 'intelligible matter' makes it clear that the objects of mathematics, when conceived as separate, are still conceived as particulars rather than universals. But it still leaves many questions open.

One further, and rather puzzling, piece of evidence is this. At the end of XIII 2 Aristotle has concluded his negative discussion with 'it is clear that [the objects of mathematics] either do not exist at all, or exist only in a way; and hence that they do not exist *haplôs* [i.e., as substances do?]. For we speak of existence in many ways' (1077b15–17). (At the start of his discussion he has said: 'our debate will be not whether they exist but in what way they exist', 1076a35–6.) But in the middle of his positive account in XIII 3 he has said: 'it is *haplôs* true to say that the objects of mathematics exist, and are as they are said to be' (1077b32–4). And he adds at the end, apparently in elucidation of these remarks: 'the geometers speak truly, and they speak of things that do exist; for existence is twofold, either in actuality (*entelecheia(i)*) or in the way of matter (*hulikôs*) (1078a28–31). The implication must surely be that the objects of geometry 'exist in the way of matter', and it is plausible to suppose that this concerns those objects conceived as separate. But what does it mean? There are, broadly speaking, two kinds of answer.

One of them supposes that Aristotle does seriously mean to liken geometrical objects to matter. Then, since Aristotle standardly thinks of matter as 'what underlies', the idea is that Aristotle's geometrical objects are to be thought of as 'underlying' the ordinary perceptible objects. This view is advocated by Mueller [1970] and Modrak [1989]. Given this approach, it may at first sight be tempting to identify 'intelligible matter' with what is usually called 'prime matter' (though 'ultimate matter' would be a better name), for in Aristotle's view this is a stuff that underlies all material objects. But, on reflection, the temptation must be resisted. Mueller does resist it, but I think for the wrong reason. Relying on the controversial passage at *Metaphysics* VII 3 1029a12–18, he thinks that Aristotle there says that if one strips away all the properties of a body one is left just with length, breadth, and depth, and then if one takes away these too what is left is just (prime) matter. Equating intelligible matter with extension, he takes it that this is what is here referred to as 'length, breadth, and depth', and that prime matter is not reached until this too is taken away. On his account, 'Pure extension does not seem to be sensible in the way that triangularity is, nor is it completely undifferentiated or purely potential in the way that prime matter seems to be' (p.105). But I think that this misunderstands the concept of prime matter, which is to be construed as a genuine material stuff out of which material things are made, and always found with one of the attributes hot or cold, wet or dry, heavy or light, and occupying a definite region of physical space.[23] But the intelligible matter which differentiates geometrical objects is surely not conceived as capable of possessing any such attributes. Prime matter is what material things are (ultimately) *made of*, but intelligible matter cannot underlie them in *that* sense, and I do not see any other sense that might be appropriate. Moreover if, as Mueller and Modrak both assume, it is intelligible matter that is supposed to be *perfectly* square, spherical, and so on, how can it be regarded as 'underlying' the material objects that are only *imperfect* examples of these properties? I do not see any answer to that question.

The alternative view is that when Aristotle speaks of geometrical objects as existing 'in the way that matter does' his words are not to be taken too literally. He constantly associates matter with potentiality, and all that he is really meaning to assert here is that geometrical objects have a potential existence, presumably because it is *possible* that they should be physically exemplified.[24] The consequence will be that—at least in most cases—the perfect geometrical objects have *no* actual existence. But there is a line of interpretation, favoured by Lear [1982] and Hussey [1983] which takes Aristotle's view to be that mathematical objects may also exist actually in another way, if not in the physical world then in thought. There is some evidence for this. At *Metaphysics* IX 9 1051a21–33 Aristotle notes that geometers will (often) prove things by 'constructing' lines additional to those originally given. He comments that this construction makes actual what was previously only potential, 'and the explanation is that thinking is actuality' (a30–1). This must imply that merely thinking of a line thereby actualizes it, which is no doubt connected with his well-known view that in thought the mind *becomes* those objects which it is thinking of (*De Anima* III 4–8). Of course it will still be the case that almost all geometrically possible configurations exist only potentially, but perhaps they can be actualized not only by being physically embodied but also by being thought of. This question of what can be actualized simply by thought is one that we shall have to come back to, when considering Aristotle's views on infinity. Meanwhile, let us sum up the position so far.

In *Metaphysics* XIII 3, and for the most part in his programmatic discussions elsewhere, Aristotle is mainly concerned with geometry. It seems probable— though there is no compelling evidence—that he accepts the Platonic premise that (elementary) geometry idealizes, insofar as it treats of perfect examples of the shapes which actual physical objects exemplify only imperfectly. But he evidently does not accept the Platonic conclusion that these perfect examples must therefore exist in some 'other world', separated from the things in this world that (imperfectly) resemble them. He admits that geometers speak and think *as if* their objects are so separated, but he regards that as a mere fiction (though a useful one). Such geometrical objects may be said to exist 'potentially', but they do not exist actually unless either they are physically embodied or at least are thought of (i.e., imagined as physically embodied?).

These discussions do not have much to say about the objects of arithmetic, i.e., the numbers, but they do fairly clearly assume that much the same account applies in this case too. So numbers actually exist only when there are actual collections of physical objects that have that number, or (perhaps) when they are actively thought of. Again, the arithmetician will *conceive* of the numbers as separate entities, though they are not really. I *suspect* that, in Aristotle's view, this again is conceiving of them in the Platonic way, i.e., as made up of 'perfect units', but one cannot be at all sure about this. As I have mentioned, much of XIII 6–8 argues (very successfully) that numbers cannot *really* be like this, so it is not clear whether Aristotle means to concede that this is how they are in practice thought of. But he offers no other account of how a mathematician might 'picture' the numbers.[25]

This account of arithmetic leaves many questions unanswered, and one can only guess at the answers that Aristotle might have given. For example, I would *expect* him to say that a simple statement of pure arithmetic, such as '7 + 5 = 12', should not be interpreted as referring to some puzzling entities called 'the numbers themselves', but as generalizing over ordinary things in some such way as this: if there are 7 cows in one field, and 5 in another, then there are 12 in both fields taken together; and the same holds not only for cows and fields but also for everything else too. In fact he does not actually say this, or anything like it; he is completely silent on the meaning of arithmetical equations. Again, I would *expect* him to say that we find out that 7 + 5 = 12 by the ordinary procedure of counting cows in fields, and other such familiar objects. But in fact he never does explicitly address the question of how we come to know such truths of simple arithmetic, and he never does respond to the Platonic claim that the knowledge must be a priori.

Here too all that we have are some very general and programmatic pronouncements. In the well-known final chapter of the *Posterior Analytics* (i.e., II 19) he claims that *all* knowledge stems from experience. Perception is of particulars, but memory allows one to retain many particular cases in one's mind, and this gives one understanding of universals. This is put forward as an account of how one grasps 'by induction' the first principles of any science, and the similar account in *Metaphysics* I 1 makes it clear that mathematics is not an exception (981a1–3, b20–5), but it is quite clear that this says far too little. Indeed, Aristotle claims that we must somehow come to see that these first principles are *necessary* truths, but has no explanation of how we could ever do this. Elsewhere we find the different idea that what Aristotle calls 'dialectic' also has a part to play in the discovery of first principles, but again the discussion stays at a very superficial level, and Aristotle really has nothing useful to say about how it could do so.[26] One can only conclude that he must think that our knowledge of mathematics (like our knowledge of everything else) is empirical and not a priori, but he has not addressed the problem in any detail.

It is obvious that there are many objections to this general position. I here just mention two that are pressed by Frege in his well-known criticism of Mill's empiricism. (i) Surely we do not discover by experimental counting that 70,000 + 50,000 = 120,000? We are confident that we know things about large numbers, which one could not claim to have experienced. This is evidently because we are applying general laws, which we take to hold of absolutely all numbers without exception. But it is not at all clear how our knowledge of these laws could come from experience. (ii) We take it for granted that numbers apply in the same way to things of all types, and not only to objects that could be perceived (e.g., to gods, thoughts, propositions, and—to take an incestuous example—to numbers themselves). But how could that be reasonable if our arithmetical knowledge is all based upon what we do perceive?

Well, I cannot here offer responses on Aristotle's behalf, partly because it cannot be done in just a few words, and partly because his own position is given so sketchily that it is not clear how it should be elaborated.[27] Instead, I turn to a line of objection which he himself did notice as a problem, and did respond to, namely the use that is made in mathematics of the notion of infinity. Even the elementary arithmetic and geometry that Aristotle was familiar with do often invoke infinities. But how could this be, if they are based upon perception? For surely we do not perceive infinities?

4. Aristotle on Infinity

Aristotle's treatment of infinity is in chapters 4–8 of *Physics* III. After introducing the subject in chapter 4, the first positive claim for which he argues (in chapter 5) is that there is not and cannot be any body that is infinitely large. This is because he actually believes something stronger, namely that the universe is a finite sphere, which (he assumes) cannot either expand or contract over time, so the size of the universe is a maximum size that cannot ever be exceeded. In his view, there is absolutely nothing outside this universe, not even empty space, so there is a definite limit even to the possible sizes of things. I shall not rehearse his arguments, which—unsurprisingly—carry no conviction for one who has been brought up to believe in the Newtonian infinity of space. I merely note that this is his view.

In consequence he must deny one of the usual postulates of ordinary Euclidean geometry, namely that a straight line can be extended in either direction to any desired distance (Euclid, postulate 2). For in his view there could not be any straight line that is longer than the diameter of the universe. It follows that he cannot accept the Euclidean definition of parallel lines (Euclid, definition 23), as lines in the same plane which will never meet, however far extended. Consequently he must deny Euclid's well-known postulate of parallels (postulate 5), at least in Euclid's formulation. This has led Hintikka to conclude that his geometry must be non-Euclidean,[28] but that is so only in a quite trivial sense. For parallelism can easily be defined in other ways, and of course one can apply Euclidean geometry to a finite space, as in effect Aristotle says himself. At 207b27–34 he claims that his position 'does not deprive the mathematicians of their study', since they do not really need an infinite length, nor even the permission always to extend a finite length. His idea is that whatever may be proved on this assumption could instead be proved by considering a smaller but similar figure, and then arguing that what holds for the smaller figure (which *is* small enough to be extended as desired) must also hold for the larger original, if the two are exactly similar.[29] So his denial of an infinite length is indeed harmless from the mathematician's point of view, but his other claims are less straightforward.

Early in his discussion Aristotle has mentioned five reasons which lead people to believe in the infinite (203b15–25). These include the claims that time must be infinite, since it has no beginning and no end, and that magnitudes must be infinitely divisible, and finally:

> Above all, and most decisively, the argument that makes a common difficulty for all thinkers: because they do not give out in thought, number and mathematical magnitudes and what is outside the heavens are all thought to be infinite (203b22–5, tr. Hussey).

The other considerations that he notes in this introductory passage are clearly ones that he does not accept, and indeed they have no force. Moreover, we have noted that in chapter 5 he simply denies the claimed infinity for mathematical magnitudes, and for what is outside the heavens. But the other problems are mentioned once more when he begins his positive account of infinity at the start of chapter 6:

> If there is, unqualifiedly, no infinite, it is clear that many impossible things result. For there will be a beginning and an end of time, and magnitudes will not be divisible into magnitudes, and number will not be infinite (206a9–12, tr. Hussey).

His position is that there must be *some* sense in which these things can be said to be infinite, even if it is not 'unqualifiedly' (*haplôs*). I must here set aside his position on time, with the excuse that this is a question in physics or metaphysics, but not in mathematics.[30] But the infinite divisibility of geometrical magnitudes, and the infinity of the numbers, are central topics.

I am in agreement with Hintikka [1966] that Aristotle tends to mis-describe his position on infinity by saying that infinity is always potential, and apparently implying that it cannot be actual. (This *must* be wrong, for to say that something is potential just *is* to say that it is possible that it should be actual.) His real position is better put in this way. He assumes (without evident warrant) that an infinite totality could exist only as the result of an infinite process being completed, and he (understandably) believes that an infinite process—i.e., a process that has no end—cannot ever be completed. So the main claim is that what is infinite can only be a process, and not a (completed) totality. (That the infinite exists only in the way that a process does is clearly implied by *Physics* III 6 206a18-b3. That there may perfectly well be a process that is actually infinite is implied by 206b13–14; I presume that—in Aristotle's view—the succession of days from today onwards is an example.[31]) All genuine occurrences of infinity must therefore be construed as (unending) processes, and not as (completed) totalities.

He applies this view to the supposed infinite divisibility of a geometrical object, such as a line. There could (in theory) be an unending process of dividing a finite line into parts. To cite Zeno's well-known example, one may take half of a line, and then half of what remains, and then half of what still remains, and so on forever (*Phys.* VI 2 233a13–31 and VI 9 239b9–14). But Aristotle holds that these parts, and the points that would divide them from one another, do not *actually* exist until the divisions are actually made. This is because, if they do exist, then one who moves over a finite distance must have *completed* an infinite series of smaller movements, each half as long as its predecessor, which he regards as impossible. So his idea is that one who simply moves in a continuous way over a certain distance does not count as 'actualising' any point on that distance. To do so he would have to pause at the point, or stick in a marker, or just count the point as he passes it. The general idea, I think, is that to 'actualize' a point one must *do* something, at or to that point, which singles it out from all neighbouring points. And the (rather plausible) thought is that no infinite series of such *doings* could be completed in a finite time.[32] Consequently a finite line will never contain infinitely many actual points (or actual parts), but we can still say that its divisibility is 'potentially infinite', on the ground that, however many divisions have been made so far, another is always possible.

This position is compatible with the basic assumptions of Greek geometry. It would not be compatible with today's geometry, which treats *all* geometrical entities simply as sets of points, so that the subject would collapse if we do not admit that there are infinitely many points. But in any case Aristotle could not have accepted the contemporary approach, for at *Physics* VI 1 231a21-b18, he argues with some cogency that a line *cannot* be regarded as made up of nothing but points, and his argument (if it were valid) would show that a line cannot simply be just a set of points.[33] Obviously he would say the same of planes and of solids. This contradicts nothing that Greek geometry assumed, for in geometrical practice points, lines, planes, and solids were all taken as equally basic entities. Besides, a common view was that the most basic kind of entity is the solid, since planes may be regarded as the surfaces of solids, lines as the boundaries of planes, and points as the limits of lines. On this view points are the *least* basic of geometrical entities.

Where one might expect a tension is over the existential postulates of geometry, for do not these assume that *there are* points, lines, planes, and so on, even when there is nothing that has marked them out? But, on reflection, this is not obvious. As Heath has remarked (1921, p. 336), Aristotle shows no knowledge of what we think of as Euclid's existential postulates, and he plausibly infers from this that the postulates were not known in Aristotle's day. It is true that no one could suppose that geometry, as actually practised, is entirely without existential assumptions, but Aristotle's own pronouncements on this topic are few and extremely imprecise,[34] so let us turn to Euclid's. As it happens, Euclid makes no explicit claim about the existence of points (though he should have done so), but he is quite definite about lines. His first three postulates are

Let the following be postulated:

(1)   to draw a straight line from any point to any point,
(2)   to produce a finite straight line continuously in a straight line,
(3)   to describe a circle with any centre and distance.

(I quote Heath's translation, [1925, pp. 195–9].)

I say no more about the second, for I have earlier remarked that it is not essential, but what of the first and third?

We are inclined to say that they postulate the existence of certain lines, but that is not quite what Euclid actually says. He may readily be interpreted as claiming not that these lines do (already) exist, but that they can (if we wish) be brought into existence by being drawn. (His proofs often require them to *be* drawn.) It is often said of Greek geometry that it is 'constructive' in the sense that it does not assume the existence of any figure that cannot be constructed (with ruler and compasses). In that case Aristotle need have no quarrel with it. For such a construction must be describable, and Aristotle is perhaps entitled to assume that it does not exist until it has been described (or, anyway, imagined). On that view, there will never be a time when there are more than finitely many geometrical figures in existence, so his account of infinity may still stand. But although it is commonly held that Greek geometry was 'constructive', in the sense roughly indicated here, I do not think that the same is ever said about arithmetic. This is a more serious problem for him.

As I have already noted, he has earlier acknowledged that everyone believes that there are infinitely many numbers. He has suggested that this is because the numbers do not give out 'in our thought' (203b22–5), but apparently he is committed to saying that they do give out in fact. For if a number exists only when there is a collection of physical objects that has that number, then there cannot (according to him) be infinitely many of them. This is because he holds that the universe is finite in extent, and that physical objects never are infinitely divided, from which it must follow that every actual collection is finite. The same conclusion holds if we add, as Aristotle *might* desire, that simply thinking of a particular number is enough to 'actualize' it. For still at any one time there will be only finitely many numbers that have actually been thought of. Does Aristotle mean to accept this conclusion? I believe so. Indeed, I think that he does not even wish to allow that merely thinking of a number is enough to 'actualize' it. At any rate, he has introduced the problem by noting that numbers do not give out 'in our thought', and he apparently ends his discussion by saying that this is irrelevant. He ends in chapter 8 by briefly reviewing the opening considerations, and on this one he comments that

> It is absurd to rely on thought: the excess and the deficiency are not in the actual thing but in thought. Thus, one might think of each of us as being many times as large as himself, increasing each of us ad infinitum; but it is not for *this* reason, because someone thinks it is so, that anyone exceeds this particular size that we have, but because it is the case; and *that* [someone's thinking it] just happens to be true [when it is true] (208a14–19, tr. Hussey).

The illustration, in terms of an imagined increase in size, *could* be taken to indicate that this response is meant only to rebut the idea that 'mathematical magnitudes, and what is outside the heavens' must be infinite for the reason that 'they do not give out in our thought'. One might suggest that the case of the numbers is not meant to be included here. But then one has to admit that he nowhere does address this case. His general doctrine is that there may be processes that are actually infinite, but no totality can be more than potentially infinite, so one must conclude that—in his view—this applies to the numbers too: they also are only *potentially* infinite.

There is some support for this from elsewhere. It is true that at *De Caelo* I 5 272a1–3, he remarks as an aside that since there is no greatest number the numbers are infinite. But it seems to me very likely that most of the *De Caelo* was written before Aristotle had worked out the theory of infinity that we find in *Physics* III. On the other side, in *Physics* III 5 another casual aside goes in the opposite direction:

> Nor, for that matter, can there be a separated infinite number: for number, or what has number, is countable, and so, if it is possible to count what is countable, it would then be possible to traverse the infinite (204b7–10, tr. Hussey).

We may put together with this a more considered remark from *Metaphysics* XIII 8, which is not a mere aside but part of a serious criticism of the Platonic theory:

> Besides, number must be either infinite or finite, since they make number separate, so one of the two must be the case. Clearly, it cannot be infinite. Infinite number is neither odd nor even, but generation of numbers is always of an odd number or an even one (1083b37–1084a4, tr. Annas).

In each of these passages the argument is this. If Plato is right, and the numbers do have a separate existence, then there must be such a thing as the number of all the numbers. This would have to be an infinite number. But there cannot be an infinite number, (a) because—since number is countable—that would mean that one could count to infinity, and (b) because every number must be either odd or even, but an infinite number could not be either.

Naturally, these arguments cut no ice with us. We need not admit that there has to be such a thing as the number of all the finite numbers, but we are now quite familiar with the idea that there is, namely $\aleph_0$. This is unlike the finite numbers in both the ways that Aristotle mentions, i.e., one cannot count up to it and it is neither odd nor even, but still there is good reason to count it as a number. Unsurprisingly, Aristotle has failed to see this possibility. But a question which arises is whether these objections that he raises are supposed to apply only to the Platonic conception of numbers as separately existing, or whether they would also apply to numbers existing only in Aristotle's way, i.e., as existing *in* (collections of) independently existing items. So far as one can see, the points made would apply equally in either case. If so, then numbers are no exception to his overall position. The series of numbers is *potentially* infinite, but only potentially. That is to say that at no time will there *actually* be more than finitely many of them.

I regard this conclusion as clearly absurd. One asks, for example, how many numbers there are *today*, and surely no answer is possible. The conception is that more may be realized tomorrow, but that there must be some definite (and finite) answer to how many there are now, and every such answer is ridiculous. It is of course true that the numbers do not give out 'in our thought', but it is very difficult to take seriously the idea that they do give out 'in fact'.

Could Aristotle evade this criticism? Well, I believe he could, but only by applying to arithmetic a line of thought that he must accept for geometry, although he never candidly admits it. Geometry is an idealising subject. It *assumes* the existence of all kinds of perfect figures, and surely most of them are not actually exemplified in the physical world, and do not exist in any other way either. In that way it is a fiction. But obviously it is a very useful fiction, and its practical applications are immensely valuable. I think that Aristotle should say the same about arithmetic. It too 'idealizes' by assuming that every number really does have a successor, although (in Aristotle's view) this is not actually true. That is its way of 'smoothing out' the imperfections of the world that we actually inhabit. But at the same time it is supremely obvious that this 'fictional', 'idealized', 'smoothed out' theory is something which, in practice, we cannot do without.

Is that a defensible position?

APPENDIX: *DE ANIMA* I 1 403a12–16

In the first chapter of the *De Anima* Aristotle is setting out various questions concerning the soul which will need to be considered. One of these is whether a soul can exist in separation from a body, and his outline answer is that this will be possible if there is something that it does (or undergoes) that does not involve the body, but not otherwise. Our text then runs:

> But if there is nothing peculiar to it, it will not be separable, but it will be like the straight, to which, *qua* straight, many properties belong, e.g., it will touch a bronze sphere at a point, although the straight if separated will not so touch; for it is inseparable, if it is always found with some body (tr. Hamlyn, 1968).[35]

This says something quite unexpected, namely that enmattered straight edges do ('*qua* straight') touch enmattered spheres at just one point, though a separated straight <line> will not do this, because—the text surely implies—there is no such thing as a separated straight line. This is in itself a strange thing to say, and it is very difficult to believe that it is what Aristotle really intended.

First, the final sentence of this same chapter (403b17–19), which apparently refers back to our passage, surely implies that *there are* separable (geometrical) lines:

> We were saying that the affections of the soul are, at any rate in so far as they are such <as> passion and fear, inseparable in this way from the natural matter of the animals in which they occur, and not in the same way as a line or a surface (tr. Hamlyn, 1968).[36]

As we know, Aristotle's overall position on the philosophy of mathematics is that one can 'separate' geometrical entities 'in thought', even though they do not actually enjoy a separate existence; and this contrasts with such things as a snub nose, which cannot be separated even in thought (*Phys.* II 2 193b31–194a7). Hence in the present context, in which geometry is mentioned only in order to clarify the points being made about the soul, it would not be surprising if Aristotle consistently took either view, i.e., either that geometrical lines can be separated from physical matter (sc. in thought) or that they cannot be so separated (sc. in fact). But it really is surprising if, in the course of the same discussion, he switches without warning from the one view to the other. So I am sure that our text must have gone wrong somewhere. (The emendations incorporated by Ross are of little significance here, for one would surely interpret the text in the same way with or without them.)

Second, it is surely the first passage that is more likely to be wrong. For the second passage, which is presumably intended just to remind us of the first, makes a perfectly straightforward and relevant contrast: lines and surfaces *can* be considered in abstraction from the material bodies in which they are found, whereas souls cannot, at least insofar as they are subjects of such things as anger and fear. This is because lines have properties which do not involve the bodies they are found in, whereas souls (as so far considered) do. By contrast, the first passage (as our text has it) is odd in itself and makes no sensible contribution to its context. As I have said, there is nowhere else in Aristotle's discussion of geometry, apart perhaps from this passage, that unambiguously says either that physical objects do, or that they do not, perfectly exemplify the properties that geometers consider. As I have also said, the natural explanation for this silence is that Aristotle says nothing on this topic because he thinks of himself as merely accepting the usual view. Since the usual view at the time was surely the one shared by Plato and Protagoras, namely that physical spheres and physical straight edges never do meet at just one point (998a2–4), that is the view which most modern interpreters attribute to him (though with one prominent exception).[37] Certainly it is a view which ordinary observation cannot refute, and would appear to confirm, and so it seems best to assume that he did indeed hold it. But then he cannot have meant to say that an enmattered line touches an enmattered sphere at just one point.

In that case what should we say of the sentence with which we began? It appears that the general sense required will be the opposite of what our text appears to say. For what is needed is the thought that, if the soul is as envisaged, then it will be like a physically embodied straight edge, which—because it is *not* perfectly straight— will not actually touch a bronze sphere at just one point. It is only the straight line that is separated (sc. in thought) that can do that, but the soul (as we are here envisaging it) cannot be so separated. Here is one way of changing the text, so as to make it mean something like this

(i)   *alla kathaper* needs to be changed to something like *ou gar kathaper*, for the reprise at 403b17–19 makes it clear that Aristotle's point is that the soul is *not* like the line.

(ii) We can perhaps interpret *to euthu, hê(i) euthu* to mean 'the straight considered as *perfectly* straight, i.e., as separate'. (This is certainly not the usual way of construing Aristotle's *qua*-locution, but in the present context it is perhaps possible.)

(iii) For Ross's *houtô chôristhen* , which emends the *toutou chôristhen* of all mss., read, e.g., *houtô ou chôristhen*.

(iv) For *achôriston gar either* read *chôriston gar*, and understand the text to mean 'for it (i.e., the straight) *is* separable <sc. in thought> even if <in fact> it exists always in some body'; *or* possibly understand this clause as referring back to the main subject of discussion, i.e., the soul, and saying that it (i.e., the soul) is not a separable thing if it is always found with some body. (However, this latter reading would not explain the contrast between souls and lines that is presumably intended.)

I cannot pretend that this set of emendations looks very plausible, from a palaeographic point of view, but I do think that something along these lines is needed. The passage must be altered somehow.

For what is the alternative? If the present text is kept, it is saying that the (enmattered) straight edge *does* have a certain property, namely of touching the (enmattered) sphere at just one point, which the separated straight edge does not have, simply because there is no such thing as a separated straight edge. That is in itself a very odd way of putting things, and besides it is entirely irrelevant to its context. It clearly does *not* illustrate the point that the soul may exist in separation from the body if and only if there is something that it does (or undergoes) which does not involve the body. There is simply no connection between the two claims.

Lear [1982] holds that Aristotle believes that physical objects do *perfectly* exemplify the properties that the geometer speaks of, and his argument relies strongly on our passage from the *De Anima* (pp. 175–82). The other points that he makes on this issue are of no significance, for of course it is usual practice to talk of bronze spheres, or round tables, without meaning to imply that these things are *perfectly* round or spherical. But I aim to have shown that this one passage is not trustworthy. There *must* be *something* wrong with it. Perhaps a better palaeographer than I am could make a more plausible suggestion as to just how the error has arisen.

NOTES

1. The theory is found principally at *Meno* 82b-86b and *Phaedo* 72e-77a. It recurs at *Phaedrus* 249b-c, and *Timaeus* 41d-e may possibly be intended to hint at it. But the hint is doubtful, and one could discount the *Phaedrus* passage as merely one of the 'poetical embellishments' that Socrates later apologises for (*Phaedrus* 257a). The more important point is that the theory is not implied anywhere in the discussions of the nature of knowledge in the *Republic*, or later in the *Theaetetus*.

2. There is what may be a veiled allusion to this theory at *APo* II 19 99b25-7.

3. Aristotle endorses, or anyway reports, this characterisation of a number on many occasions, e.g., *Phys.* 207b5–10, *Met.* 1039a11–14, 1053a24–30, 1057a2–5. It is also Euclid's definition (*Elements*, Book VII, def 2). (It implies that neither zero nor one is a number, but in practice the number series was usually counted as beginning with one. Zero was not recognized as a number until many centuries later.)

4. Some interpreters have thought that this doctrine is needed to explain what Plato says about mathematics in the Simile of the Divided Line at *Republic* 509d-511e. (I mention Wedberg [1955] and more recently Burnyeat [2000].) The majority (including myself) think that he could not have intended to introduce it here without a single word of explanation, and that it must be one of his later 'unwritten' doctrines.

5. I leave aside the opening paragraph at 1076a38-b11, which argues against the view that the objects of mathematics exist (as independent substances?) *in* perceptible things, and not separated from them. The argument here resembles a line of thought presented in Aristotle's preliminary discussion of problems, at *Metaphysics* III 2 998a7–19. As Ross observes (1924, *ad* 998a7) we do not know of anyone who held this view. Aristotle's main objection is that in that case mathematical objects would undergo the kind of changes that perceptible objects do, e.g., motion (998a14–15) and division (1076b3–11), which he regards as absurd. There is a full discussion of this paragraph in White (1993, pp.168–77).

6. Aristotle unexpectedly says not 'two' but 'three', apparently supposing that there will have to be yet a third kind of ideal plane, i.e., those 'over and above' the planes that are the surfaces of the separately existing solids (1076b29–32). (Consequently he finds four kinds of line, and five kinds of point.) I shall simply ignore this complication to his argument, which seems poorly motivated and is anyway of no importance.

7. I have reviewed Aristotle's use of this idea in my *Aristotle's Metaphysics, books Z and H* (Oxford, 1994), pp. 63–4.

8. I am thinking, of course, of the ingenious theory of planetary motion proposed by Eudoxus. Unfortunately this thought is anachronistic, for it seems very probable that Plato's *Republic* precedes this theory. We do not know quite what Plato thought would figure in an 'idealized' astronomy.

9. Our text at 1076b39–1077a9 is a recapitulation of a line of argument given at greater length in chapter 2 of Book III of the *Metaphysics* at 997b12–34. (The longer text

elucidates our mutilated sentence at 1077a3–4, making it clear that Aristotle finds something absurd in the idea that the supposed intermediate objects of astronomy should be in any way in motion (997b19–20), but still it gives no reason.) Even this longer version fails to say *why* someone might think that intermediates are required at all. It is *followed* (at 997b35–998a6) by a passage claiming that perceptible lines are never perfectly straight or perfectly circular, but no connection between these two ideas is made explicit. (The summary version in *Met.* VI 1, at 1059b3–12, does more strongly suggest a connection, but this may be due not to Aristotle himself but to a pupil.)

10. The theory is due to Eudoxus. The classical exposition is in Euclid, *Elements*, Book V, but this exposition is of course later than Aristotle.

11. E.g., *APo* 74a17–25, 85a37-b1, 99a8–11, *Met.* VI 1 1026a23–7.

12. Whether these remarks should be taken as expressing his sincere and considered opinion is debatable. I have discussed the issue in my *Space, Time, Matter, and Form: Essays on Aristotle's Physics* (Oxford, 2006) Essay 4.

13. The point is noted by Gill (1989, ch.7) and by Freudenthal (1995, ch.1). (Freudenthal supposes that Aristotle wishes to invoke *pneuma* as the solution, but this would not apply to non-living things.)

14. Here Aristotle appears to be asking about the cause of the 'unity' of a geometrical figure, such as a circle. Elsewhere he asks about the cause of the 'unity' of a number, once more implying that he does have an answer to this question while the Platonist does not (e.g., *Met.* VIII 1044a2–9 and 1045a7–12). But it is not at all clear what his answer is. (I have offered a suggestion in my *Aristotle's Metaphysics*, 1994, pp. 268–9.)

15. Since the passage needs an extended discussion, I have postponed it to an appendix.

16. The same thought is attributed to Democritus at D/K 68B155a.

17. I translate the mss. reading. Ross prefers to emend to '… if horses [are being measured] then the measure is a horse, and if men then a man'. But in either case the main idea is the same. Other passages of the *Metaphysics* which clearly show a good understanding of how numbers are applied in practice are: V 6 1016b17–24; X 1, 1052b15–17, 1053a24–30, 1054a4–9; XIII 7 1082b16–19; XIV 1 1087b33–1088a14. Cf. also 1052b31–1053a2; 1092b19–20; *Phys.* IV 12, 220a19–22.

18. I shall also leave undiscussed Aristotle's arguments, which occupy most of Book XIV, against the Platonic idea that the numbers (and other things) are somehow 'generated' from 'the one' and 'the indefinite dyad'.

19. 'Abstraction' is the usual translation, so I retain it. But Cleary [1985] has very reasonably suggested that 'subtraction' would be preferable, as better preserving the contrast that Aristotle sometimes draws between *aphairesis* and *prosthesis*, i.e., subtraction and addition.

20. The account in *De Anima* III 7 431b12–17, is similar.

21. I have discussed the passage in my *Aristotle's Metaphysics*, 1994, 280–3.

22. For matter, rather than position, as what distinguishes different objects of the same form, see, e.g., *Metaphysics* VII 8 1034a5–8.

23. I have discussed Aristotle's concept of prime matter in my 'Aristotle's Theory of Matter', in D. Sfendoni-Mentzou, J. Hattiangadi, and D. Johnson, eds., *Aristotle and Contemporary Science* (New York, 2001).

24. Similarly, Aristotle's main claim about the infinite (which I shall discuss shortly) is that it is potential and never actual, and this leads him to assimilate it to matter (*Phys.* III 206b14–16, 207a21–2, 207b34–208a4), though really the two have nothing in common.

25. The Pythagoreans used to picture the numbers as dots arranged in certain patterns, which led them to speak of triangular numbers, square numbers, oblong numbers, and so on. But Aristotle regularly describes the 'units' that numbers are (supposed to be) made of as 'without position', so he probably did not subscribe to this picture.

26. My *Aristotle's Ethics,* pp. 219–26 (Oxford, 2000) offers something by way of a general discussion of how Aristotle thinks that first principles are reached. I do not repeat it here.

27. I have given a general discussion of empiricism as a philosophy of mathematics in 'Empiricism in the Philosophy of Mathematics', in A. Irvine, *Philosophy of Mathematics* (2009).

28. Hintikka (1966, pp. 128–30).

29. As was in effect discovered by the English mathematician John Wallis (1616–1703), and known to Gerolamo Saccheri in his book *Euclides ab omni naevo vindicatus* (1733), the assumption that, for any figure, there is a similar but smaller figure of any size you please, is characteristic of a Euclidean space, and could replace Euclid's parallel postulate. So as it happens Aristotle's response is relying on Euclidean geometry. (I take the information from Heath, 1925, pp. 210–12.)

30. On the account that I shall give, the forwards infinity of time is not a problem, but the backwards infinity would certainly seem to be. It is strange that Aristotle never seems to notice this problem, though it is the backwards infinity for which he genuinely has a strong argument (i.e., at *Physics* VIII 1 251a11-b10). (I have made a brief remark on this problem in my *Space, Time, Matter, and Form: Essays on Aristotle's Physics* (2006), 126–7.)

31. I have tried to argue this in more detail in my 'Aristotle, Zeno, and the Potential Infinite' (1972/3). I note here that Lear [1979/80] thinks that Aristotle must mean what he says when he apparently claims that even a process can only be potentially infinite, and must therefore hold that every process does in fact stop at some time. I see no good reason to agree.

32. I have argued in 'Aristotle, Zeno, and the Potential Infinite' that although this thought is 'plausible' still it is false. My argument relied on some such general account of what it is to 'actualize' a point as is indicated here, but Charlton (1991) has responded that Aristotle recognizes only one way of 'actualizing' a point, namely by pausing at it. If that were so, his doctrine could evidently be rejected as far too narrow. But it is not so: the example of simply counting a point (e.g., as one passes it) is taken from Aristotle himself (*Phys.* VIII 8 263a4–11, 15–18, 25–6).

33. I have discussed this argument in 'Aristotle on Continuity in *Physics* VI', in L. Judson, ed., *Aristotle's Physics: a Collection of Essays* (Oxford, 1991).

34. At *Posterior Analytics* I 10 he says that a science must start by assuming about its basic entities—e.g., units for arithmetic, points and lines for geometry—not only what they are but also that they are. In other cases it can only assume what a thing is (i.e., its definition), but must prove that it is (76a31–6, b3–11). Should we take this as implying that a geometer must *prove* that some lines are straight, and some circular?

35. *ei de mêthen estin idion autês, ouk an eiê chôristê, alla kathaper tô(i) euthei, hê(i) euthu, polla sumbainei, hoion haptesthai tês chalkês sphairas kata stigmên, ou mentoi g' hapsetai houtô chôristhen to euthu. achôriston gar, eiper aei meta sômatos tinos estin.* This is the text that Ross prints in his (1956). Later in his (1961) he brackets *chalkês*—thinking that Aristotle cannot have meant material spheres—and reads *ti euthu* in place of *to euthu.* Neither of these emendations has any mss. authority. (He also changes *houtô* to *houtôs.*)

36. *elegomen dê hoti ta pathê tês psuchês houtôs achôrista tês phusikês hulês tôn zô(i)ôn, hê(i) ge toiauth' huparchei <hoia> thumos kai phobos, kai ouch hôsper grammê kai epipedon..* This is Ross's text both in his (1956) and in his (1961). His *houtôs achôrista* emends the reading of almost all mss, which is either *ou chôrista* or *achôrista*.

37. The exception is Lear (1982), who relies heavily on our passage from the *De Anima*, though even he does not go so far as to claim that *every* geometrically possible shape has some perfect physical embodiment. (So one asks: which of them do; and how could the answer to this question be important for understanding Aristotle's overall position?) On the other side I mention Mueller (1970), Annas (1976, p. 29), Hussey (1983, Appx A) and (1991), Modrak (1989).

BIBLIOGRAPHY

Annas, J. (1976) *Aristotle's Metaphysics, Books M and N* (Oxford: Clarendon Press).

Bostock D. (1972/3) 'Aristotle, Zeno, and the Potential Infinite', *Proceedings of the Aristotelian Society* 73, 37–51. Repr. in Bostock [2006].

———— (1991) 'Aristotle on Continuity in *Physics* VI', in L. Judson, ed., *Aristotle's Physics: A Collection of Essays,* (Oxford: Clarendon Press), 179–212. Repr. in Bostock [2006].

———— (1994) *Aristotle's Metaphysics, books Z and H,* (Oxford: Clarendon Press).

———— (2000) *Aristotle's Ethics,* (Oxford: Oxford Univ. Press).

———— (2001) 'Aristotle's Theory of Matter', in D. Sfendoni-Mentzou, J. Hattiangadi, and D. Johnson, eds., *Aristotle and Contemporary Science,* vol. 2 (New York: Peter Lang), 3–22. Repr. in Bostock [2006].

———— (2006) *Space, Time, Matter, and Form: Essays on Aristotle's Physics* (Oxford: Clarendon Press).

———— (2009) 'Empiricism in the Philosophy of Mathematics', in A. Irvine, ed., *Philosophy of Mathematics* (North Holland, Elsevir).

Burnyeat, M. (2000) 'Plato on Why Mathematics is good for the Soul', *Proceedings of the British Academy* 103, 1–81.

Charlton W. (1991) 'Aristotle's Potential Infinities', in L. Judson, ed., *Aristotle's Physics: A Collection of Essays* (Oxford: Clarendon Press), 129–49.

Cleary, J.J. (1985) 'On the terminology of 'Abstraction' in Aristotle', *Phronesis* 30, 13–45.

Diels, H., rev. W. Kranz (= D/K) (1961) *Die Fragmente der Vorsokratiker,* 10th ed. (Berlin, Weidmannsche Verlagsbuchhandlung).

Freudenthal, G. (1995) *Aristotle's Theory of Material Substance* (Oxford: Oxford Univ. Press).

Gill, M.L. (1989) *Aristotle on Substance* (Princeton: Princeton Univ. Press).

Hamlyn, D.W. (1968) *Aristotle's De Anima, books II and III* (Oxford: Clarendon Press).

Heath, Sir T.L. (1921) *A History of Greek Mathematics,* vol. 1 (Oxford: Clarendon Press).

———— (1925) *The Thirteen Books of Euclid's Elements.* Repr. New York: Dover Books, 1956.

Hintikka, J. (1966) 'Aristotelian Infinity', *Philosophical Review* 75, 197–212. Repr. in J. Barnes, M. Schofield, and R. Sorabji, eds., *Articles on Aristotle,* vol. 3 (London: Duckworth, 1979).

Hussey E. (1983) *Aristotle's Physics, books III and IV* (Oxford: Clarendon Press).

———— (1991) 'Aristotle on Mathematical Objects', *Apeiron* 24, 105–33.

Lear J. (1979/80) 'Aristotelian Infinity', *Proceedings of the Aristotelian Society* 80, 187–210.

———— (1982) 'Aristotle's Philosophy of Mathematics', *Philosophical Review* 91, 161–92.

Modrak, D.K.W. (1989) 'Aristotle on the difference between Mathematics and Physics and First Philosophy', *Apeiron* 22, 121–39.

Mueller, I. (1970) 'Aristotle on Geometrical Objects', *Archiv für Geschichte der Philosophie* 52, 156–71. Repr. in J. Barnes, M. Schofield, R. Sorabji, eds., *Articles on Aristotle*, vol. 3 (London: Duckworth, 1979).

Ross, Sir W.D. (1924) *Aristotle's Metaphysics*, 2 vols. (Oxford: Clarendon Press).

———— (1956) *Aristotelis De Anima* (Oxford: Clarendon Press).

———— (1961) *Aristotle, De Anima* (Oxford: Clarendon Press).

Wedberg, A. (1955) *Plato's Philosophy of Mathematics* (Stockholm: Almqvist & Wiksell).

White, M.J. (1993) 'The metaphysical location of Aristotle's *mathematika*', *Phronesis* 38, 166–82.

PART V

ETHICS AND POLITICS

CHAPTER 19

....

CONCEPTIONS OF HAPPINESS IN THE *NICOMACHEAN ETHICS*

....

T. H. IRWIN

1. A DEBATE ABOUT HAPPINESS

....

ARISTOTLE begins the *Nicomachean Ethics*[1] by asking what the final good for human beings is. He identifies this final good with happiness, and in the rest of Book I he asks what happiness is.[2] In I 7 he reaches an 'outline' of an answer, claiming that the human good, i.e., happiness, is activity of the soul in accordance with the best and most perfect (or complete) virtue in a perfect life. But he does not say what the best and most perfect virtue is. Towards the end of the last book of the *Ethics*, he seems to answer this question by arguing that the best and most perfect virtue is theoretical wisdom (*sophia*) exercised in theoretical study or contemplation (*theôria*) of universal and necessary truths about the universe.

Readers have found this answer unsatisfactory, for two main reasons:

1. This purely intellectualist conception of the human good seems too narrow. If we identify the human good, as Aristotle does, with the realization of human nature and the human soul, his conception of the good seems to omit many aspects of human nature that we might take to be important. We seem to be more than purely intellectual beings; we have non-rational aspects that seem to have some claim, according to Aristotle's appeal to nature, to satisfaction and fulfilment. Moreover, even if we think of ourselves as rational beings, Aristotle seems to leave out too much; for we are rational agents, not simply pure theorists.

2. The intellectualist view seems inconsistent with the rest of the *Ethics*, for Books II-IX give an account of the virtues of character and intellect, and of their interaction in the virtue of prudence (*phronêsis*). Aristotle discusses the virtues of human beings as rational agents who also have non-rational desires connected to their bodily nature. The virtues of character harmonize the rational with the non-rational aspects of human nature.[3] Aristotle takes these conditions to be elements of the human good. Hence he should not hold a purely intellectualist view that identifies the human good exclusively with theoretical activity. He should hold a pluralist view that recognizes the virtues of character among the elements of the human good.

The second of these objections to a purely intellectualist conception of happiness is the more important for the interpreter of the *Ethics*. If we could defend the first objection but could not find any support for it in Aristotle, we would simply dissent from Aristotle's conception of happiness. Our dissent might be correct, but it would not necessarily help us to understand Aristotle better. But if the second objection is correct, it shows us that Aristotle agrees with the ethical views that conflict with a purely intellectualist conception. In that case, it is worth our while to reconsider whether he holds this conception.

This dispute about the interpretation of the *Ethics* has been pursued at some length in modern discussions.[4] The debate has now advanced far enough to make some of the main arguments on each side fairly familiar, but it has not produced a consensus. I will try to set out some of the reasons that make each interpretation plausible. I cannot reasonably aim at completeness (or perfection), and I am certainly not aiming at originality.

This may appear to be a rather narrow exegetical dispute that is both well worn and of limited interest. It might seem more reasonable to discuss some aspects of Aristotle's conception of the good that we might be inclined to take seriously, instead of discussing an intellectualist doctrine that we are disposed to reject. But this appearance is misleading; if we pursue these exegetical questions about happiness, we will find that they lead us into some basic questions about Aristotle's ethical doctrine. I will point out these questions as we come to them.

In Sections 4–10 I set out the case for an intellectualist conception by examining some of the main points in Books I and X. In these sections I try to do the best I can for the intellectualist conception, and I do not pause to criticize this case. In Sections 12–17 I discuss some aspects of Book I that do not seem to me to fit the intellectualist conception, and I put forward a more plausible account of Book I. In Sections 19–20 I consider how well this account fits Book X.

2. A CONSISTENT ACCOUNT?

Should we look for an interpretation that gives Aristotle a consistent position? If we read a modern book on the human good that seemed to offer blatantly inconsistent answers to the basic questions it raised, but did not point out the inconsistency, we would wonder whether we had understood the author, or else we might suppose it was a rather defective book. But ought we to be surprised by a sharp conflict within the *Ethics*?

The debate about the nature of happiness is not the only prolonged and recalcitrant dispute about the interpretation of Aristotle. Another long-standing dispute concerns his doctrine of substance in the *Metaphysics*. Disputed points here involve (1) the claim of particulars and universals to be substances, and (2) the claim of material and non-material beings to be substances. The second dispute raises some of the questions about human and divine reality that also arise in the *Ethics*.

Why are these disputes about the interpretation of Aristotle so difficult to settle? Some possible answers are: (1) We are too dense to grasp Aristotle's plain meaning. (2) Our philosophical biases and presuppositions make it difficult for us to grasp Aristotle's position. (3) Aristotle expresses himself obscurely. (4) Aristotle is inconsistent, so that each interpretation fits some of what he says. (5) His remarks are too vague to settle the question. (As the modern euphemism puts it, his text 'under-deteremines' our interpretations.) (6) Aristotle finds himself attracted to both of the positions that cause the disputes among interpreters.

A case could be made for each explanation of the dispute about happiness (and the list does not exhaust the possibilities). The sixth especially deserves consideration. Aristotle begins the *Ethics* by saying that he will not examine all the beliefs about the good, but only those that seem to be especially current, or that seem to have some argument in their favour (1095a28–30). If two conflicting views are current or defensible enough to deserve examination, we should not be surprised if Aristotle seems to make a good case for them. If he believes it is a good case, we should not be surprised if we find it difficult to decide which view he accepts. It does not follow that he has no definite belief, or that we cannot discover it. If we think we have discovered it, we should not be put off by the fact that he makes a strong case on the other side.

Why might Aristotle not declare his choice between the two positions that he defends? Most of the evidence for a pluralist account comes from Book I, and most of the evidence for a monist account comes from Book X. If we had Book I without Book X, many readers would hesitate to ascribe monism to Aristotle, and if we had Book X without Book I, many would find it difficult to ascribe pluralism to him. Might Aristotle have come to the last book of the *EN* without a vivid memory of what he said in the first book, and might that be why the two accounts of happiness conflict?

We do not know how the *EN* came into being, or how long the process took. Some signs of non-consecutive and possibly interrupted composition are these: (1) Probably Books V-VII were originally meant to be *EE* IV-VI. We do not know whether, or how much, they were revised for the *EN* (if the *EN* is the later treatise). (2) The two books on friendship (VIII-IX) may appear to be disproportionately long for the *EN*; perhaps they were originally an independent essay. (3) The discussion of pleasure in *EN* X does not fit perfectly into the present *EN*. It follows a discussion of pleasure in *EN* VII (= *EE* VI), but does not mention it.

In the light of this evidence might we not take the discussion of happiness in *EN* X to be imperfectly fused with the rest of the *EN*? An extreme view might take all of Books V-X to have been compiled from odds and ends. Perhaps an essay (or lecture) on happiness (our Book X, 6–8) was among the papers that were taken out of Aristotle's filing cabinets and were stitched together (by Aristotle or Nicomachus?) to make our *EN*. We are not surprised to find that a modern author expresses different views in the course of a collection of essays written over many years. Perhaps the *EN* is a collection of Aristotle's papers rather than a continuous treatise.[5]

It is worth mentioning these possibilities to prevent ourselves from assuming that we know more than we in fact know about the origins and character of the *EN*. Nonetheless, we have some reason to suppose that Aristotle intends Book X to fit what he has said in Book I. After he gives an initial series of arguments for the identification of happiness with theoretical study (in X 6), he remarks that 'this would seem to agree both with the previous things and with the truth' (1177a18–19). What are 'the previous things'? He mentions 'the self-sufficiency that is spoken of' (1177a27), and he has spoken of it in I 7. The other features that he ascribes to happiness appear to fit what he has said in Book I.[6]

This is not a proof that Aristotle has Book I in mind, as it appears in our text. He may refer to an earlier lecture that only partly resembles our present text of Book I. Further study of X 7 is needed to decide about the apparent backward references. But at least we have a possible basis for claiming that Aristotle intends his remarks about happiness in the *EN* to form a single statement of his views, rather than offering two unconnected statements. After these cautions about the character, or possible character, of the *EN*, we may turn to more specific reasons for ascribing one or another view of happiness to Aristotle.

3. CRITERIA FOR HAPPINESS

Before we consider the contribution of Book I to the argument, we need to define some of the questions more precisely.

'Happiness is theoretical study' and 'Happiness is theoretical study and moral virtue' are two answers to the question 'What is happiness?' But they are not the most basic answers to this question. They presuppose some more abstract answers. Each of these specifications of happiness can be defended by appeal to some more general description of happiness. We need to see what the right general description is. Let us consider an analogy. Suppose I maintain that Candidate A should be offered an academic position over Candidate B because A has published a good book and B has published nothing. I assume that the most important qualification for the position is good publications. If you maintain that B should be offered the position over A, because B is an excellent teacher and A is a soporific teacher, you assume that good teaching is the most important qualification. We do not disagree about the comparative merits of A and B as writers and teachers; we disagree about which qualifications are most important.

Similarly, then, we can decide whether happiness is theoretical study or something more only if we can appraise the qualifications of each candidate for happiness, and see whether these are the most important qualifications. Until we face these questions we do not know whether we disagree about how far the different candidates meet a single standard, or about what the relevant standard is. Hence we need to try to decide what the appropriate standard is. We need to answer the question 'What is happiness?' in such a way that we find some standard that we can use to decide between different candidates and different qualifications.

4. THE FINALITY OF HAPPINESS

What, then, does Aristotle tell us about the standards for happiness? He begins the *Ethics* with a puzzling claim about the good:

> If there is some end of the things achievable by action that we wish for because of itself, and the other things because of it,... it is clear that this would be the good and the best (1094b18–22).

This claim is puzzling because 'the good and the best' seems to suggest that we are speaking of one good, but the description Aristotle has offered seems to apply to many goods. For there seem to be many things that we wish for because of themselves; there seem to be many non-instrumental goods, and not just one.

Fortunately, we need not linger on this passage, because Aristotle explains his point better when he returns to a discussion of 'the good and the best' in Chapter 7. He confronts the objection we have raised by recognizing that there seem to be many different ends – health for medicine, victory for generalship, and so on. He continues:

> And so, if there is some end of all the things achievable in action, this would be the good achievable in action; but if more, these (1097a22–4).

After mentioning the ends of various pursuits, Aristotle now introduces the possibility of one end for all pursuits, but he does not affirm that there is any such end. Let us call this a *universal* end.

Aristotle now explains the character of a universal end:

> Since the ends appear more than one, and we choose some of them (for instance, wealth, flutes, and, in general, instruments) because of something else, it is clear that not all are *teleia*. But the best appears something *teleion*. And so, if only

some one is *teleion*, the good we seek would be this; if more, the most *teleion* (1095a25–30).

The end we are looking for is the best good, and therefore has to be a *teleion* end, indeed the most *teleion* of all the *teleion* ends.

What, then, does it mean to say that an end is *teleion*? Aristotle now explains:

> We say that an object of pursuit in its own right is more *teleion* than an object of pursuit because of something else, and that what is never an object of choice because of something else is more *teleion* than things that are objects of choice in their own right and because of this, and hence what is always an object of choice in its own right and never because of something else is *teleion* without qualification (1097a30–4).

Aristotle seems to offer a straightforward explanation of '*teleion*'. He seems to rely on the connexion between '*teleion*' and '*telos*' (end, goal), and to affirm that something is *teleion* to the extent that it is an end and not a means to an end. We may represent this connexion in English by rendering '*teleion*' by 'final'. Something that is only an end and never a means is the most final end and final without qualification.

We have now found one criterion for the good; it has to be final without qualification, and therefore cannot be a means to any end. Aristotle now applies this criterion in order to identify happiness as the good:

> Now happiness most of all seems to be such [sc., final without qualification]; for we choose it always because of itself and never because of something else, but honour, pleasure, understanding, and every virtue we choose also because of themselves (for we would choose each of them nothing coming from it), but we also choose them for the sake of happiness, supposing that through them we shall be happy. But no one ever chooses happiness for their sake, or, quite generally, for the sake of anything else (1097a34-b6).

He recognizes honour and so on as non-instrumental goods, because we would choose them even if they had no further result, but he argues that they are not final without qualification, whereas happiness is final without qualification.

We might infer that since happiness is final without qualification, it cannot contain anything that is not final without qualification; for if it did, it would be partly pursued for the sake of something else. If this is correct, nothing that can be chosen for the sake of happiness can be an element of happiness, because it would be a non-final element of something that is final without qualification.

Once he has introduced happiness, Aristotle speaks as though there is only one unqualifiedly final end. He has anticipated this claim about uniqueness in Chapter 2. He suggests that if there is such a thing as 'the good and the best', it will give us a target to aim at in planning our lives (1094a18–24). This good is the end that political science aims at, subordinating every other good to it (1094a26-b7). These claims are considerably exaggerated if we have to refer to more than one unqualifiedly final end. But Aristotle's claims about finality do not show that there is only one unqualifiedly final end. His argument seems to allow two unqualifiedly final goods neither of which is to be chosen for the sake of anything else. If, for instance, we pursue Y and Z for the sake of A and pursue W and X for the sake of B, neither A nor B will be wholly ultimate. But it does not follow that some end beyond A and B is more ultimate; for we might pursue all of W, X, Y, and Z for the sake of both A and B. (If, for instance, we spend a fortnight climbing in the Rockies, we might do all we do during this fortnight for the sake of our health and for the sake of seeing spectacular views. Perhaps neither of these ends is any more final than the other two.) It is not clear, therefore, why Aristotle assumes that happiness is the unique unqualifiedly final end.

5. HAPPINESS AND SELF-SUFFICIENCY

Once he has argued that happiness is the good because it is unqualifiedly final, Aristotle draws a further conclusion from unqualified finality.

> The same [sc., that happiness is final? that happiness is the good?] also appears to follow from self-sufficiency; for the final good seems to be self-sufficient. … We take the self-sufficient <to be> what alone makes a life an object of choice[7] and lacking nothing; and we think happiness is such. (1097b6–16)

If, therefore, a good is unqualifiedly final, it must by itself (or 'alone') make one's life lack nothing (or 'need (*endees*) nothing') (1097b14–16) and thereby an appropriate object of choice. Why does Aristotle believe that self-sufficiency, so understood, follows from finality?

Perhaps he means that an end that does not make life worth choosing would only be worth pursuing for the sake of an end that makes life worth choosing. Similarly (he might argue) an end that leaves life lacking something would only be worth pursuing for an end that makes life lack nothing. Hence an unqualifiedly final end – one that is chosen for its own sake and not for the sake of something else – must be self-sufficient.

The cogency of this argument depends on how we understand 'an object of choice' (or 'worth choosing', *haireton*) and 'lacking nothing'. We might understand 'worth choosing' in two ways: (a) As far as it goes, it makes life worth choosing, because it is one non-instrumental good. (b) It makes life worth choosing all things considered, because it is a large enough good to outweigh any evils in life. Any sort of final good, even if it is not unqualifiedly final, meets the minimal condition in (a). But even an unqualifiedly final good does not seem to meet the more stringent condition in (b). The mere fact that a life contains some non-instrumental good that is not chosen for the sake of anything else does not seem to imply anything about the comparative weight of this good in comparison with the evils that are present in a life that contains this good.

We might hope for some clarification from 'lacking nothing'. But this condition itself needs to be clarified. We might say that a life lacks something if (1) we can think of adding something to it that would make it a better life, or if (2) it needs something else added to make it choiceworthy. If we favour (2), we might prefer to render '*endees*' by 'needing' rather than 'lacking' (an equally permissible translation). Neither explanation of 'lacking nothing' makes it evident why an unqualifiedly final good should make life lacking in nothing. The mere fact of unqualified finality does not satisfy the stringent condition in (1), and the less stringent condition in (2) raises the questions we have already raised about finality and choiceworthiness.

6. Happiness and other goods: counting together

After these remarks on self-sufficiency, Aristotle adds a further claim about happiness:

> Moreover, <we think happiness is> most choiceworthy[8] of all, not being counted together. But being counted together, clearly, <we think it> more choiceworthy with the smallest of goods; for what is added becomes an extra quantity of goods, and the greater of <two> goods is always more choiceworthy. Happiness, then, appears something final and self-sufficient, being <the> end of the things achievable in action (1097b16–20).

This 'counting' condition is apparently important, but also obscure. It is not clear whether this is (a) a further aspect of self-sufficiency, or (b) a further aspect of the perfection of happiness. We might expect (a), given that Aristotle concludes this passage by saying: 'Happiness, then, appears as something complete and self-sufficient, being the end of things achievable in action'. But the grammar may support (b); Aristotle does not say that the self-sufficient is most choiceworthy, but that happiness is.[9]

A more important question concerns the meaning of the counting condition. What is happiness counted or not counted together with? The second sentence suggests that 'being counted together' means 'being counted together with goods that lie outside it'. In that case we might take Aristotle to contrast two situations: (1) Happiness is not counted together with the goods that lie outside it. In that case, it is the most choiceworthy good. (2) It is counted together with them. In that case the additional goods that are outside happiness make a good (i.e., happiness plus these further goods) that is greater than happiness alone.

If this is what Aristotle means, the counting condition helpfully clarifies what he means by saying that happiness is the greatest good, or the most choiceworthy good. He means that it is the greatest single good if it is compared to each of the other goods taken individually; it is greater than pleasure, greater than honour, and so on. But he does not mean that it is as great a good as the totality formed from happiness and these other goods; on the contrary, since these are non-instrumental goods, their combination with happiness makes a greater good than happiness alone. Happiness, therefore, is a final but non-comprehensive end. The counting condition affirms that the addition of non-instrumental goods to happiness produces a greater good than happiness alone.

7. Happiness as fulfilment of the human function

To reach a more definite conception of happiness Aristotle introduces the human function, which he has already introduced implicitly in his objections to the life of pleasure (1095b19–20). He argues that the human function must consist in an activity that is distinctive of human beings, in contrast to activities that human beings share with plants and animals. This is an activity of the rational part of the soul. Hence the human good consists in activity of the soul in accord with reason, and, since it is good activity, in accord with virtue (1097b22–1098a18).

Aristotle appeals again to finality. He explains 'in accord with virtue' by adding that the relevant activity must be in accord with final virtue, and that if there are more final virtues than one, it must be in accord with the most final of these. The most final end, as he explained earlier (1097a30–5), is unqualifiedly final, and so never to be chosen for the sake of some other end. The most final virtue, then, should be the one whose activity is an unqualifiedly final end.

This passage supports the conclusion we drew from the counting condition, since it gives us a further reason for denying that Aristotle treats happiness as a comprehensive end. For the best and most final virtue is the one virtue whose activity is an unqualifiedly final end. But Aristotle has allowed that there are virtues whose activities are non-instrumental goods but not unqualifiedly final ends. These are activities that we choose both for their own sakes and for the sake of happiness. They are goods that—according to the counting condition—we can add to happiness to produce a greater good than happiness.

According to this argument, therefore, Book I does not treat happiness as a comprehensive end that includes all non-instrumental goods; for some of these goods are not unqualifiedly final. If Aristotle had maintained that the unqualifiedly final good is the only non-instrumental good, he would have maintained a comprehensive and monist conception of happiness. But, given his recognition of non-instrumental goods that are not unqualifiedly final, he maintains a monist non-comprehensive conception. He does not reduce the moral virtues and their expressions in action to a purely instrumental role. In relation to happiness they are purely instrumental goods; but their relation to happiness does not wholly determine their role in our choices and actions. We may also choose them for their own sakes without reference to happiness.

8. Some difficulties in Book I

We have now seen why a non-comprehensive monist conception of happiness can be defended from Book I. Its main supports are these: (1) The unqualified finality of happiness. (2) The recognition of non-instrumental goods that are not unqualifiedly final. (3) The counting condition. (4) The identification of happiness with the activity of the best and most final virtue among the final virtues.

Before we turn to Book X, however, we may usefully remind ourselves of some unanswered questions that we have raised in our discussion of the main argument in Book I.

1. If happiness is an unqualifiedly final and non-comprehensive end, how far should we accept Aristotle's initial claim that the discovery of the good for human beings will make a difference to our lives by giving us a target to aim at? His claim is correct; insofar as happiness is unqualifiedly final, we cannot find any end beyond it. But it is not clear what difference the discovery of such an end should make to our lives. An unqualifiedly final end does not seem to be necessarily more choice-worthy than any other end or combination of ends. If happiness is an unqualifiedly final and non-comprehensive end, it seems to have a rather restricted role in choice and action.

2. Aristotle has not explained why only one end can be unqualifiedly final, and hence he has not explained why he speaks of the best and most final of the virtues in the singular. It is still not clear why a monist conception of happiness should be preferred over a conception that allows two or more unqualifiedly final goods.

3. We have not seen why an unqualifiedly final end has to be self-sufficient, given Aristotle's conception of self-sufficiency.

These unanswered questions do not show that we have misunderstood Aristotle. They may show that his argument fails at these points, or that we have overlooked reasons that can be given in its support. But they deserve to be borne in mind when we try to complete our account of happiness from Book X.

9. THEORETICAL STUDY AS A CANDIDATE
FOR HAPPINESS

Book I has set out the criteria for happiness: it is an unqualifiedly final and non-comprehensive end that consists in the exercise of the human function in the activity of the best and most final virtue. It has not said what sort of activity meets these criteria. Book X argues that the relevant activity is theoretical study. Aristotle resumes the discussion of happiness by reminding us that we take it to be 'the (or 'an'?) end of human things' (1176a31–2). He reminds us of different features of happiness that he mentioned in Book I, and now argues that theoretical study has these features.

He appeals to the claim that happiness is activity in accordance with virtue. In Book I he spoke of the best and most final virtue. But now he speaks of the 'supreme' (*kratistê*) virtue, which is the virtue of the best thing; this virtue is the most divine element in us, and its activity is final (*teleia*) happiness (1177a12–17). The function argument picks out theoretical study because it is the virtue of the best element in us, and hence it implies that happiness consists in theoretical study. We should actualize the virtue of the best part of us, and so we should realize the divine element in us as far as we can. This advice to actualize the divine does not conflict with the appeal to the human function, because the best virtue of a human being is the virtue of the best part of a human being, which is divine.

The different features of happiness mentioned in Book I support the claims of theoretical study. It is more self-sufficient than any of the activities of the moral virtues, because they depend on external resources, other people, and so on, whereas it does not depend on these external conditions (1177a27-b1). It is also more final than the activities of the moral virtues.

> Besides, it would seem to be liked alone because of itself (*monê di' hautên*);[10] for nothing comes about from it beyond having studied, but from the virtues concerned with action we try to a greater or lesser extent to gain something beyond the action (1177b1–4).

Aristotle seems to recall his claim that the moral virtues are chosen both for their own sake and for the sake of happiness, and to maintain that this is not true of theoretical study.

In this defence of the claims of theoretical study Aristotle seems to recognize the implications of the counting condition. For he does not argue that we cannot add other goods to theoretical study in order to produce a better good. Nor does he claim that we do or should choose moral virtues and virtuous actions only for the sake of theoretical study. He maintains, therefore, that theoretical study is most choiceworthy, not counted together with these other goods. It is a non-comprehensive end.

Once he has argued that theoretical study meets the criteria for happiness, Aristotle turns to a comparison with other virtues, and defends his previous point that theoretical study is more independent of external conditions than the moral virtues are (1178a9-b7). It is not completely independent, since we still need to live a human life, but it is maximally independent and hence maximally self-sufficient. Moreover, the gods do not exercise moral virtues, but they lack no essential element of happiness. Since they engage in pure intellectual activity, this activity is sufficient for perfect happiness (1178b7–23). We engage in morally virtuous activity because we are imperfect, compared with the gods, but it is no part of the perfect happiness that we enjoy in so far as we realize the divine element in us.

10. Implications of a monist conception of happiness

When Aristotle claims that perfect happiness consists in theoretical study, he seems to affirm a monist conception of happiness. He has not shown that only one activity could meet his conditions for being wholly ultimate, but his survey of theoretical study in comparison with the activities of other virtues persuades him that in fact it is the only wholly ultimate activity.

He has also said something to explain why we should guide our lives by appeal to happiness, as he understands it. For theoretical study is not only wholly ultimate, but also best, by being the activity of the best part of us. Since we achieve the human good by realizing the best and most perfect virtue, we achieve it by theoretical study; for it is both best (by realizing the divine part) and most perfect (by being wholly ultimate).

None of this argument requires a comprehensive conception of happiness. Aristotle does not affirm that theoretical study is the only non-instrumental good.[11] The value of theoretical study gives us a reason to practise the moral virtues for the sake of maintaining a life devoted to theoretical study, but Aristotle does not say that this is the only reason for those who are capable of theoretical study to practise these virtues. He does not even say that this is an end of moral virtue. He remarks that we need to practise the moral virtues for the sake of living a human life (*anthrôpeuesthai*, 1178b7). If we were right in our account of finality and of the counting condition, Aristotle accepts a non-comprehensive conception of happiness.

This point casts doubt on some of the most frequent ethical objections to a monist and intellectualist conception of happiness. If we reject a comprehensive conception, happiness need not absorb all our reasons for action; a non-comprehensive conception leaves us with goods lying outside happiness, and these goods seem to give us reasons for action. Aristotle does not consider the objection that his conception of happiness leaves us with no reason to practise the moral virtues for their own sakes. If we are right, that objection does not arise.

Still, his monist conception may be open to objections. For though theoretical study is not the only source of reasons (given a monist conception), it is the only source of reasons based on happiness, human nature, and the human function. If we begin by considering the nature of human beings as rational agents who have both rational and non-rational aspects, but we end by considering only the divine and purely theoretical aspects of human beings, we seem to have revised our conception of human nature rather sharply, and with inadequate reason.[12] Aristotle supports the revision by claiming that theoretical study realizes the best part of us. But it is not clear why we should agree that we have realized human nature if we have only realized the best part of it, to the exclusion of the rest. If Aristotle's naturalism is fundamental in his ethical argument, his monist conception of happiness seems to cast some doubt on the foundations of his theory. Either naturalism is less important than we might have thought (since human nature is replaced by the best part of human nature) or else we have reason to doubt his exclusive concentration on the divine aspect of humanity.

11. REMAINING QUESTIONS ABOUT BOOKS I AND X

The connexions between this argument in Book X and the account of happiness in Book I suggest that Aristotle intends both books to be part of a single discussion of happiness. The correspondences are close enough to show that these two books of the *Ethics* are not just two papers pulled out of Aristotle's files. But how close are the connexions between the two books, as we have understood them?

Book X has more to say about the self-sufficiency of happiness, and so it might seem to offer some clarification of the claims that we found puzzling in Book I. But in fact it raises a further difficulty. Book I introduced self-sufficiency because it was supposed to be an implication of finality; but we found it difficult to understand how it could be. Book X does not resolve this difficulty, because it does not try to show that the sort of self-sufficiency it describes follows from finality, or even from unqualified finality.

It was difficult to say in Book I whether Aristotle supposed that the finality or self-sufficiency of happiness implied, or followed from, its being the non-comprehensive best and most choiceworthy good. The argument to show that theoretical study is the best good does not depend on the finality or self-sufficiency of study, but on the claim that it is the actualization of the best part of human nature.

If, then, we read Book X without Book I, we would gather that the finality, the self-sufficiency, and the non-comprehensive supreme choiceworthiness of happiness are three independent criteria, each of which is satisfied, for independent reasons, by theoretical study. This is not, however, the way in which Book I presents these criteria. Hence Book X does not fit perfectly with Book I if we take both of them to present a non-comprehensive monist conception of happiness.

These apparent differences between the two books do not show that we must have misunderstood them. We may simply have discovered that Aristotle does not completely execute the aims that he sets himself in Book I. Still, we should consider these difficulties of interpretation together with those we have already found. They are serious enough to justify a review of Book I, to see whether it really supports the account we have offered.

Our non-comprehensive account of happiness relied heavily on the claim that happiness is unqualifiedly final, chosen only for its own sake and never for the sake of anything else. This claim seems to be solidly based in Aristotle's remark that x is more *teleion* than y if x is pursued only for its own sake, but y is pursued for the sake of something else (1097a30–2). We supposed that Aristotle here explains what he means by '*teleion*', and for this reason we translated '*teleion*' by 'final'. But was our supposition justified? To answer this question, we should examine the context of the crucial argument in I 7. First I will discuss a remark at the end of Chapter 7. Then I will consider the significance of Chapter 2. These passages from before and after the main passage in Chapter 7 will help us to decide about the interpretation of the main passage.

12. HAPPINESS AND A COMPLETE LIFE

A non-comprehensive account runs into a difficulty when we try to make it fit a clause in the definition of happiness that we have not yet considered. Aristotle defines happiness as activity of the soul in accordance with the most *teleion* virtue (if there are *teleion* virtues than one) in a *teleion* life. He glosses '*teleion* life' by remarking that one swallow does not make a spring, and neither does one day or a short time make a person happy. Some translators who use 'final' or 'perfect' earlier in the chapter change horses in mid-stream and render *teleion* by 'complete' in this sentence. They are surely right. 'Final life' is difficult to understand. 'Perfect life' is more intelligible, but still not clear. What kind of perfection might Aristotle have in mind?

Perfection may be treated as equivalent to completeness; we achieve a perfect score on a test if we get all the answers right. But it may not imply completeness. If I am setting out to paint a room, I may paint one wall with exquisite care, so that no one could improve on the work I have done. In this respect my work of painting the room is perfect, but it is certainly not complete. Alternatively, I might complete the work because I have painted the whole room adequately, even if I have not painted it all perfectly (I may have left a few minor streaks that will not bother anyone). It is worth asking, then, whether Aristotle's claim that happiness requires a *teleion* life refers to a perfect life (in the sense that does not imply completeness) or to a complete life.[13]

Fortunately, Aristotle helps us to answer this question. In the present passage he connects being *teleion* with an appropriate length of time (1097b18–20), and he marks the same connexion in Book X (1177b24–6), where he speaks of a *teleion* length of life. He takes a *teleion* length of life to be a long time that allows great and fine achievements (1101a22–3). This may not be a perfect length of life; as Aristotle recognizes, it may have some ups and downs (1100b22–5), but it is complete in so far as it lacks nothing that we need for the actions that constitute happiness. Hence the best rendering for '*teleion*' in the remarks on the *teleion* life is 'complete'. The introduction of a complete life is an important stage in the argument about happiness, because it introduces the lengthy discussion of happiness and external circumstances that follows in Chapters 9–11.

Given the importance of this remark on the complete life, it is difficult not to render '*teleion*' by 'complete' in the earlier part of Chapter 7. If we use 'final' until we come to the *teleion* life, and then abruptly change to 'complete', we suggest that Aristotle has shifted from one sense of '*teleion*' to another at an important stage in his argument. This shift – without warning or justification – wrecks his argument to show that happiness requires a *teleion* life. Before we conclude that Aristotle has wrecked his argument, we should see whether we might plausibly render '*teleion*' by 'complete' throughout Chapter 7. If this is the right rendering, Aristotle affirms that happiness is in some way comprehensive. And so we ought to reconsider Book I to see whether Aristotle seems to accept a comprehensive conception.

13. Happiness and the Comprehensive Science

Before we reconsider Chapter 7, it is helpful to go back to the beginning of Chapter 2, which we passed over briefly earlier. Some of Aristotle's initial remarks seem to treat the ultimate good as a comprehensive end. We noticed that he thinks the discovery of a single good for the sake of which we pursue everything else will provide a target for us to aim at in our lives. The science of this single good is political science, because this is the most 'architectonic' science. The various disciplines are subordinate to it, because its end includes the ends of the other sciences, and so turns out to be the human good (1094a26-b7). This description of the end suggests a comprehensive and pluralist conception; the ends of the different subordinate sciences seem to be parts of the ultimate end that includes them.

We might reject this suggestion, and argue that inclusion may be explained consistently with a monist conception of the end.[14] Perhaps inclusion allows a purely instrumental relation between the end of political science and the ends of subordinate sciences. The end of bridle-making is included in the end of horse-riding, because there is no aspect of the end of bridle-making that falls outside riding a horse; that is the only end that determines the end of bridle-making.

This instrumental explanation of inclusion, however, does not seem to allow a non-comprehensive conception of happiness. For if we pursue virtue partly for the sake of happiness and partly for its own sake, its end does not seem to fall wholly within happiness. But if we are to combine a monist conception of happiness with Aristotle's recognition of non-instrumental goods other than happiness, we need a non-comprehensive conception. According to such a conception, the end of virtue is not wholly subordinate to happiness, because the effect of virtue on happiness gives us only one of our reasons to pursue it. But the instrumental account of inclusion does not allow these ends that lie outside happiness. An instrumental account of inclusion allows only a comprehensive monist conception that makes happiness the only non-instrumental good. But this conception conflicts with Aristotle's recognition of non-ultimate non-instrumental goods.

Even if an instrumental account of inclusion did not raise this difficulty for a monist conception, it would not fit Aristotle's views on subordinate ends. Among the sciences subordinate to political science he mentions 'practical' as well as 'productive' sciences.[15] These sciences are concerned with 'action' (*praxis*) in Aristotle's technical use, and not simply with production (*poiêsis*). According to this use, action differs from production because action has some end that does not lie beyond it; 'good action itself is the end' (1140b6–7). If Aristotle is considering action as well as production, he refers to more than purely instrumental subordination. For practical sciences achieve an end that is not simply an instrumental good. In that case, the ultimate good includes subordinate goods by being more comprehensive; it includes them as parts, not simply as instrumental means. This conception of the practical sciences introduces the possibility of a comprehensive conception of happiness.

How can the end of a practical science be both a non-instrumental good and a part of the human good? One end is subordinate to a second end in so far as it is chosen for the sake of the second end. But if it is a means to the second end, is it not instrumental to it? To answer this question many students of Aristotle have distinguished two ways in which one thing can be chosen for the sake of or as a means to another: an instrumental means is separate from the end, and causally contributes to it, so that the end is its effect, whereas a component means is a part of the end and not separate from it.[16] Hence components of an end are means to it and are chosen for its sake, but are parts and not merely instrumental means.

The division between two types of means has not been invented simply to make the notion of a comprehensive end seem more plausible. We need this division if we are to understand other central elements of the *Ethics*. These elements include Aristotle's claims about moral virtue and decision (*prohairesis*). Aristotle affirms: (1) The virtuous person decides on the virtuous action for its own sake. (2) Decision is the outcome of deliberation, and both deliberation and decision are about means to ends, not about ends in themselves. These two claims seem to force him into a contradiction; for the first claim implies that we can decide on things non-instrumentally, as goods in their own right, whereas the second seems to deny this. We remove the contradiction if we allow deliberation and decision to be about components, not only about instrumental means. Once we allow that, we can say that the virtuous person decides on virtuous action as a part of happiness, not as purely instrumental to it. If we are warranted in applying the division of means to Aristotle's doctrine of virtue and decision, we can usefully apply it to his doctrine of happiness as well.[17]

Aristotle's claim about the comprehensive character of political science supports a comprehensive conception of happiness as a complete good. We have some reason, therefore, when we confront the argument of Chapter 7, to suppose that he takes happiness to be complete, and that therefore 'teleion' is appropriately rendered by 'complete'. Having found some support for this rendering both from Chapter 2 and from the end of Chapter 7, we can now return to the passage that seemed to support a non-comprehensive conception of happiness.

14. HAPPINESS V. SUBORDINATE ENDS

Aristotle claims that an end chosen only for its own sake is more *teleion* than an end chosen both for its own sake and for the sake of something else (1097a30–4). On this point he contrasts happiness with virtue and other non-instrumental goods; since we choose these both for their own sakes and for the sake of happiness, they are less *teleion* than happiness. Previously we took this passage to explain the meaning of '*teleion*', and so we rendered it by 'final'. But if we take '*teleion*' to mean 'complete', this passage expresses a synthetic and non-obvious claim that what is chosen only for its own sake is unqualifiedly complete, and more complete than things that are chosen both for their own sake and for the sake of something else.

Our previous discussion of choosing one thing 'as a means to' or 'for the sake of' another suggests two ways of understanding this remark about choosing virtue for the sake of happiness:

(1) We choose virtue both for its own sake and because of some further causal and instrumental effects, whereas we do not choose happiness because of any further causal and instrumental effects. We might choose to walk four miles a day both because we enjoy walking in itself and because walking has further instrumental effects on our heart, muscles, lungs, and so on, that make it good for our

health. Similarly, if we identify happiness with theoretical study, we may say that moral virtue is to be chosen both for its own sake and for its causal contribution to theoretical study (e.g., by maintaining the society in which we are free to engage in theoretical study, or by ordering our impulses and desires so that we can concentrate without distraction).

(2) We choose virtue both for its own sake and because it is a part of happiness. In this case 'for the sake of' marks the relation of part to whole, not the relation of instrumental means to external end. We might choose one element in a meal both for itself and for its place in the meal; hence mashed potatoes might be good both in themselves and as accompanying bangers. Similarly, bravery may be good (a) because it is the rational control of fear and daring, (b) because it is one of the virtues that together achieve the mean, (c) because it secures the life of a community, and (d) because it promotes theoretical study. In this case the first feature makes bravery choiceworthy in itself, the second makes it a part that is choiceworthy for the sake of the whole it belongs to, and the third and fourth make it choiceworthy for its results.

Which of these relations does Aristotle have in mind when he says that we choose virtue for the sake of happiness? To explain his claim that we choose things because of themselves, he adds: 'for we would choose each of them, nothing coming from it' (*apobainontos*, 1097b3–4). 'Coming from' does not imply a purely instrumental relation. Similarly, when Aristotle says we also choose them for the sake of happiness, supposing that through them we will be happy, he picks terms ('for the sake of', 'through') that may refer equally to instrumental and to constitutive relations.

Moreover, one of his examples suggests that he has non-instrumental relations in mind. His examples of non-ultimate non-instrumental goods are pleasure, understanding (*nous*), and every virtue. He might have in mind the instrumental relation of understanding (other than theoretical study, as he conceives it) and moral virtue to happiness, but it is less plausible to suppose that he has this in mind for pleasure. Admittedly, some pleasures contribute instrumentally to theoretical study; they offer us relaxation that makes it easier for us to concentrate again (1177a32-b1); but it would be strange to describe this aspect of pleasure by saying that we suppose we will be happy through pleasure. In the case of pleasure, 'through' seems to fit a constitutive relation. We may infer that in this passage Aristotle refers primarily to the constitutive relation of non-ultimate non-instrumental goods to happiness.

It is enough for present purposes, however, if this passage does not prevent non-ultimate non-instrumental goods from constituting happiness. If that is so, the passage casts doubt on a monist conception of happiness. A comprehensive monist conception affirms that happiness includes all non-instrumental goods, and that it includes only theoretical contemplation; hence it recognizes only one non-instrumental good, and so conflicts with Aristotle's recognition of a plurality of non-instrumental goods. A non-comprehensive monist conception affirms that happiness is unqualifiedly final because it contains nothing that is less than unqualifiedly final; but if happiness contains non-final non-instrumental goods, it contains elements that are not unqualifiedly final. Hence, if this passage allows non-ultimate constituents of an ultimate good, it does not fit either version of a monist conception of happiness.

Defenders of a monist conception may answer that this passage does not express Aristotle's considered view. He says that 'we choose' the virtues and so on for these two reasons. Perhaps the 'we' who choose them are the people beginning the inquiry, and the 'we' who complete the inquiry in Book X will no longer take these non-ultimate goods to be non-instrumentally choiceworthy.[18] But if we do not think the passage represents Aristotle's considered view, we cannot use it as part of his formal account of happiness. Given that he probably does not mean to rule out non-final goods as constituents of happiness, he probably does not affirm in this passage that happiness has no parts that are not unqualifiedly final.

What, then, does the passage affirm about happiness? If we recall the reasons we have found (the comprehensive character of the end of political science, and the probable sense of '*teleion*') for supposing that Aristotle has in mind a complete and composite good, we can readily understand the passage. Aristotle claims that an ultimate end must be complete, and that in this respect it differs from the non-instrumental goods that are non-ultimate ends. He is not saying that the ultimate (i.e., last) end must be the most final (i.e., last), which would be close to a tautology. He is saying that the ultimate end must be complete, because it must include all non-ultimate non-instrumental goods. And so he affirms more fully and explicitly what he has already suggested about the end of political science.

If this is the right way to understand the relation of happiness to non-final goods, we can resolve a difficulty that we noticed earlier, and explain why Aristotle supposes that there is only one ultimate end. We noticed that he seemed to have no reason to believe that there could be only one unqualifiedly final end. But it is clear why he believes there is only one complete end. If all non-instrumental goods other than happiness are pursued for the sake of happiness, insofar as they are parts of it, happiness is the single end that includes them all.

15. Completeness and self-sufficiency

We can now consider how well this interpretation of Aristotle's remarks fits his claim that the *teleion* is self-sufficient, and to his explanation of self-sufficiency. We found it difficult to explain why he might believe that the unqualifiedly final is self-sufficient, but his argument is easier to explain if he means that the complete is self-sufficient.

He clarifies his conception of self-sufficiency in a comment that we ignored when we set out the case for a monist conception.

> What we call self-sufficient is not <what is sufficient> for a solitary person by himself, living an isolated life, but also for parents, children, wife and in general for friends and fellow-citizens, since a human being is a naturally political <animal>. But of these we must impose some limit; for if we extend it to parents' parents and children's children and to friends of friends, we shall go on without limit; but we must examine this another time (1097b8–14).

A self-sufficient good for one person must include not only the good of that person but the good of other people as well. The clause 'since a human being ...' gives a reason for this expanded scope of an individual person's good. Since a human being's nature requires living in an appropriate society, a human being's good includes the good of an appropriate society as well.

This gloss makes it clear that self-sufficiency is not the same as independence of anything outside oneself. A good that extends to other people is more dependent on circumstances external to oneself than a less extended good would be. If I have friends, the death of one of them is bad for me, and if I am a member of a community, the collapse of the community is bad for me. Aristotle's gloss favours an expansive conception of self-sufficiency.

The passage on self-sufficiency is easy to understand if it explains the claim that happiness is complete. When Aristotle says that the self-sufficient is whatever all by itself (*monoumenon*) makes a life choiceworthy and lacking in nothing, we should understand 'all by itself' in accord with the previous remark about self-sufficiency. If he were relying on a non-comprehensive conception of happiness, he might mean that happiness, excluding all non-ultimate non-instrumental goods, makes life choiceworthy and lacking in nothing. But this would say the opposite of what he has implied in the remark about other people's happiness, which is a non-ultimate good in relation to one's own happiness. More probably, then, he means that happiness by itself includes all the component non-ultimate goods that are needed to make life lacking in nothing (and hence complete). And so the whole passage on self-sufficiency supports a comprehensive and pluralist conception.

We might object that Aristotle can hardly have a comprehensive pluralist conception in mind because it would be too demanding. What does it mean to say that a life lacks nothing or needs nothing? Do we lack something if we can think of something that would improve our life? Or do we just say that it comprehends all we need, or comprehends enough? But how do we fix 'all we need' or 'enough'? Where do we draw this line?

Fortunately, Aristotle recognizes that his claims about happiness raise this question about where we are to draw the relevant line. For after he insists that the self-sufficient good has to include the good of members of different societies, he comments that this expansion has to stop somewhere; if we extend it temporally and spatially to parents' parents, children's children, and friends of friends, we will have nowhere to stop (1097b11–13). If he were setting out a non-comprehensive or comprehensive monist view, the problem about drawing a line would not arise. He says this is a problem to be discussed another time (1097b13–14). We need not consider how, or even whether, he deals with the problem; his acknowledgement supports a comprehensive and pluralist conception of happiness.

16. THE COUNTING CONDITION RECONSIDERED

The counting condition, interpreted as we interpreted it earlier, supports a non-comprehensive conception of happiness. But that is not the only possible interpretation. According to a comprehensive conception, happiness is the most choiceworthy good because it is not counted together with other goods, as one single good among many. If it were counted in this way, we could produce a greater good than happiness by adding the smallest good external to it; but in fact we cannot produce a greater good than happiness. Since virtue, e.g., is already included in happiness, we cannot really add virtue to happiness. If we were to count the goodness of happiness and the goodness of virtue, we would be counting the goodness of virtue twice; for we would already have counted it in the goodness of happiness. It would be like asking whether there are more people in California and San Francisco than in California. That question is misconceived because the people in California already include the people in San Francisco.[19]

It is difficult to decide whether the comprehensive or the non-comprehensive interpretation of the counting condition is to be preferred if we look just at this passage in isolation.[20] But in the light of the most plausible interpretation of the argument so far, a decision is easier. Since Chapter 7 so far, and especially the section on self-sufficiency, has affirmed that happiness is complete, we should prefer the comprehensive interpretation of the counting condition. The non-comprehensive interpretation would contradict the point of the previous argument.

We might wonder whether the comprehensive interpretation commits Aristotle to an unreasonably strong claim about the impossibility of improving happiness. Does he really mean that if we form a conception of happiness, but we can think of some way of making happiness, as we conceive it, better, our conception must have been mistaken? Such a conception seems to make happiness an unattainable ideal. Perhaps that does not show that it could not be Aristotle's conception. But it also seems to conflict with his views on the role of fortune. He acknowledges that if happy people are also especially fortunate, this good fortune makes them more blessed, because it adds adornment to their lives and they use it finely (1100b25–8). Does he not admit that we can count happiness together with other goods (the goods resulting from good fortune) to make a greater good? If he admits that, and he also accepts the form of the counting condition that denies the possibility of counting together, he contradicts himself.

This objection sets out from the aspect of self-sufficiency that requires a self-sufficient good to make life lacking in nothing. But we saw that Aristotle acknowledges that his requirement raises a question about where we are to draw the line. His acknowledgement suggests that he accepts the comprehensive conception. Moreover, the objection derived from happiness and good fortune misconceives Aristotle's claims. His claim about good fortune does not affirm what the counting condition denies. He would contradict the counting condition (as we have understood it) if he affirmed that good fortune added to happiness creates a greater good than happiness alone; but he does not affirm this. He affirms only that good fortune allows a higher degree of happiness; the fortunate happy person enjoys not a greater good than happiness, but a higher degree of the same good.[21]

But does this explanation rely on a tenable distinction? How are we to distinguish a higher degree of the same good from a greater good? Aristotle might answer that the account of happiness includes some features that admit of degrees, and so these allow for degrees of happiness. He alludes to such features when he explains completeness. A complete life requires a suitable length of time and suitable circumstances that allow significant achievements (cf. 1101a11–13), and the happy person has to be 'sufficiently' (hikanôs) supplied with external goods (1101a15). Happiness, then, may be complete in so far as it fulfils all reasonable expectations far enough; if we over-fulfil them, we do not go beyond happiness to a greater good, but we are happier. Aristotle's claims about happiness, so understood, support a comprehensive conception of happiness.

17. THE HUMAN FUNCTION AND
THE RATIONAL LIFE

Perhaps we have found some good reasons to favour a comprehensive and pluralist conception of happiness. Still, defenders of a monist view might reply that Aristotle may not take the first part of Chapter 7 very seriously. He remarks that we might find the conclusion that happiness is the best thing rather a commonplace, and still look for a clearer account of what the good is (1097b22–4). He therefore offers an account of the human function to support an account of the good in outline.[22] If, then, the function argument tells strongly in favour of a non-comprehensive conception, or of a comprehensive monist conception, we might fairly attribute such a conception to him, despite the doubts that we have raised in examining the first part of Chapter 7.

The conclusions we draw from the function argument will partly depend on what we say about the claim that the distinctively human function is 'some sort of life of action of the having reason; of this one as obedient to reason, the other as having reason and thinking' (1098a3–5). I have translated the passage literally and awkwardly, because the supplements that clarify its sense may be controversial.

Questions about this passage are complicated by the fact that some editors reject the second clause ('of this…thinking') as a later addition.[23] Since the presence or absence of the clause may be quite significant for evaluating a monist conception, we need to see whether the clause deserves its place in the text.

The clause anticipates Aristotle's comments in Chapter 13 about the two ways in which we can speak of a 'rational' part. Two reasons for suspicion of the clause have been given: (1) The reference to non-rational desires is out of place in the context. (2) The Greek rendered by 'obedient' (*epipeithes*) occurs only here in Aristotle; apart from this passage it is not attested until the first century AD, in Aspasius' commentary on the passage. Editors suggest, therefore, that the passage is a marginal gloss by a reader who wanted to draw attention to the treatment of the rational part in Chapter 13, and that the gloss was mistakenly inserted in the text.

The first of these reasons can be dismissed for the moment. A reference to non-rational desires is out of place if Aristotle identifies happiness exclusively with theoretical reason and he affirms or anticipates that identification in the function argument. But if we are not already convinced on these points, the clause seems quite relevant. The reference to the part that is obedient to (or 'open to persuasion by') reason is relevant to the distinctively human function, since this is the difference between human passions and the wholly non-rational desires of other animals.[24] Aristotle points out that distinctively human and rational activities include the persuasive influence of reason on passions and the response of passions to that influence. If Aristotle expounds a pluralist view, this reminder of the extent of rational action is appropriate.

The linguistic argument is also weak. If all the Greek literary texts with psychological or philosophical content written up to 100 AD had survived, we might reasonably take an anomalously early occurrence of a word to cast doubt on a passage. But since most of them have not survived, we cannot rest much weight on such arguments. Moreover, the verb *epipeithesthai* (from which *epipeithes* is derived) is quite common in Homer (whose use of it may have been in Aristotle's mind). The word is not a good enough reason to condemn the passage.

We could be more confident about the passage if we could show that it is not merely appropriate to the context, but actually required by it. Some points in its favour are these: (1) The next clause begins: 'This also being spoken of in two ways' (1098a5). 'This' refers back to 'life', but the 'also' (*kai*) implies that something else has already been said to be spoken of in two ways. The only possible reference is to 'the having reason', i.e., the rational part of the soul, which, according to the suspected passage, includes both the inherently rational part and the part obedient to reason. If we delete the suspected passage on the two ways of being rational, the 'also' makes no sense.[25] (2) Aristotle infers that the human function is activity of the soul 'in accord with reason or not without reason' (1098a7–8). This disjunction is relevant if it refers to the inherently rational part (in 'in accord with reason') and the obedient part (in 'not without reason'). But if we delete the suspected clause, it is not clear why the disjunction is needed. (3) When Aristotle restates this point, he says that the human function is 'activity and actions with reason' (1098a14).[26] The phrase 'with reason' recalls 'not without reason', and secures a role for the obedient part. Though he also refers to the human function as 'activity in accord with reason' without any qualification, the occurrences of 'not without' and 'with' indicate that he includes the obedient part.

The function argument, therefore, includes the disputed clause. The human good cannot consist exclusively in the inherently rational activity either of theoretical study or of practical reason; it also consists in the virtuous activity that harmonizes the obedient part with practical reason. And so the function argument supports a pluralist conception of happiness. Editors who have deleted the suspected clause because it does not fit a monist conception have implicitly conceded that a monist conception does not explain the text.

Aristotle now states his account of the good by saying that it is activity in accord with virtue, and, if there are more virtues than one, in accord with the best and most complete virtue, in a complete life (1098a16–18). This passage raises a difficulty similar to the one that arose in a previous remark on plurality. Earlier, Aristotle said that if there are more complete ends than one, the human good will be the most complete of these (1097a28–30). Later he identifies happiness with the best activities 'or one of them, the best one' (1099a29–31). Does a pluralist conception of happiness fit these remarks that seem to pick one activity out of a plurality and identify just this one with happiness?

But if we understand completeness by reference to the relation between a whole and its parts, Aristotle's claims about the most complete end and the most complete virtue are reasonable. His preference for the singular ('complete virtue') over the plural ('all the virtues') is reasonable in the light of his conception of wholes. Even if happiness includes all virtuous activities, acting for the sake of happiness is different from acting for the sake of all virtuous activities, because happiness is an integrated activity that combines virtuous activities in an organized way of life. The complete virtue that we actualize in happiness is not simply a collection of goods; for the different goods are adjusted to one another. In speaking of complete virtue Aristotle emphasizes the organic character of happiness and of the virtuous activity that achieves it. His remark about complete virtue in the singular allows a pluralist conception of happiness.

Our further study of Book I, therefore, suggests that Aristotle neither asserts nor anticipates a non-comprehensive or monist conception of happiness. Moreover, it gives us strong reasons to attribute a comprehensive and pluralist conception to him. The discussion of completeness and self-sufficiency, and the account of the human function, exclude a monist view that confines happiness to the realization of the inherently rational part. A comprehensive conception explains Aristotle's argument at the points where a non-comprehensive conception could not explain it. If, then, we consider Book I without reference to the rest of the *Ethics*, we ought not to attribute a monist and intellectualist conception to Aristotle.

But we have already rejected this approach to Book I. We should take account of what comes later to see whether we can resolve ambiguities in Book I. Conversely, remarks that seem unambiguous in the context of Book I may allow other possibilities of interpretation if we reflect on the whole treatise. We need to return to Book X, therefore, to see whether we were right to believe that it supports a monist conception. But before we turn back to Book X, we should consider Books II-IX, to see whether they tell us anything relevant to our questions about happiness. If it is legitimate to interpret one part of the *Ethics* in the light of another, we should attend to any evidence offered by these books. To answer this question completely, we would need to discuss the whole moral theory set out in the *Ethics*. Since we cannot do that, we can confine ourselves to some possibly significant passages.

18. MORAL VIRTUE AND HAPPINESS

A bare list of some salient passages in Books II-IX might include these:

1. The function argument is relevant to the discussion of moral virtue (1106a15–24). Aristotle affirms that we realize the human function in prudence and moral virtue, not only in theoretical wisdom (1144a6–11). He confirms the claim in I 7 that happiness has to include the harmony of the non-rational but obedient part with the inherently rational part.

2. He relies on a holist conception of happiness when he speaks of general justice achieving 'happiness and its parts' for the political community (1129b17–19). This role for general justice fits the architectonic role that he ascribes to political science in I 2. Since the end of political science includes the ends of practical sciences, it is a whole that includes non-instrumental goods as its parts.

3. The deliberation of the prudent person supports a comprehensive conception of happiness. If we supposed that happiness is just one good, and that the good pursued by the moral virtues is a non-instrumental good external to happiness, we would not expect prudence to confine its deliberation to happiness. But it seems to confine its deliberation in exactly this way. According to Aristotle, prudent people do not confine themselves to specific non-ultimate goods, such as health or strength, but deliberate with reference to 'living well as a whole' (1140a25–8).[27]

4. Aristotle reinforces this point in his description of practical reasoning. He says that it begins with 'Since this is the end and the best', which is apparent only to the good person (1144a29–36). He does not suggest that prudence confines itself to some restricted or second-best end that is the focus of the moral virtues. He claims that prudence deliberates in the light of a correct conception of happiness and that it correctly concludes that morally virtuous action is to be preferred.

5. He does not believe, however, that prudence takes the morally virtuous life to be the whole of happiness. The architectonic and superordinate roles of prudence do not make prudence the best form of knowledge. The best form is theoretical wisdom, and prudence provides for the exercise of theoretical wisdom (1145a6–11).

6. In the defence of friendship Aristotle appeals both to the political nature of human beings (1169b16–19) and to the self-sufficiency of happiness (1170b17–19), arguing that without friendship our life will be lacking something. His use of this argument implies an expanded conception of self-sufficiency. At this important point in the argument, he shows that he still has in mind his initial discussion of happiness, and that he takes it to support the inclusion of friendship in the happy person's life.

Among these passages (2)-(5) raise a special question. For they are taken from the 'Common Books' (V-VII) that were probably written as parts of the *EE*.[28] We might argue that, though these books maintain a pluralist conception of happiness, this is the conception accepted in the *EE*, not in the *EN*, and so they do not throw any light on Aristotle's views in the *EN*.

But even if we accepted this objection, we would not remove all the evidence for the continued acceptance of a pluralist conception; passages (1) and (6) come from undoubted books of the *EN*. But we ought not to accept the objection in any case. For even if the three Common Books were originally written for the *EE*, Aristotle may have decided to include them in the *EN*. If he was satisfied with these earlier books, he can hardly have supposed that they disagreed fundamentally with his current conception of happiness. If, then, the Common Books maintain a pluralist conception, and Aristotle put them in the *EN*, he probably accepted a pluralist conception when he put them there. If it was not Aristotle but an early editor who put these books in the *EN*, this editor probably saw no conflict between their pluralist conception of happiness and the rest of the *EN*. The editor may have been wrong, but his judgment should not be dismissed without consideration.

We have good reason to maintain, therefore, that *EN* II-IX both maintain a pluralist conception of happiness and recognize the supreme value of theoretical study. Book VI shows that Aristotle is not trying to describe a second-best life for someone who is incapable of theoretical study, and that he is not ignoring the superior goodness of theoretical study. Keeping its superior goodness in mind, he nonetheless asserts that the deliberation of the prudent person about 'the best and the end' will result in a decision to act virtuously for its own sake. If this deliberation results from reflexion on happiness, it requires us to pursue virtuous action as a part of happiness. Aristotle reminds us of his reason for this claim; it depends on the function argument, understood so as to require the life of moral virtue. This is how we understood the function argument in discussing I 7.

19. HAPPINESS AND FUNCTION IN BOOK X

Since we have reason to find a comprehensive pluralist conception in Books I-IX, and since Book X seems to refer back to Book I, we need to reconsider Book X. Three possibilities are open: (1) Book I and Book X are inconsistent. (2) Book X

allows the pluralist conception we have favoured for Book I. (3) On further reflexion Book I turns out to allow the monist conception that we find in Book X. Our
discussion of Book I should dispose us against the third option. If Book X clearly
rules out a pluralist conception, the first option is preferable to the third, in the
light of what we have said about the function argument.

It would not be difficult to reconcile Book X with Book I if Book X said no
more than that theoretical study is the greatest single good. The difficulty arises
from the passages that seem to identify happiness with theoretical study. What do
they actually say or imply?

Book X does not directly answer the questions that the formal account in Book
I has raised. Book I defines the human good as activity in accord with the best and
most complete virtue. Book X, however, claims that since happiness is activity in
accord with virtue, it is reasonable for it to be in accord with the supreme (*kratistê*)
virtue, which will be the virtue of the best part (1177a12–14). We would have had a
straight answer to the question raised by Book I if Aristotle had said, 'Since happiness is activity in accord with the most complete virtue, and since the most complete virtue is the virtue of the best part of us, happiness is activity in accord with
that virtue.' This, however, is not what he says. We might think that the 'supreme
virtue' (*kratistê aretê*) is the same as the best (*aristê*) virtue mentioned in Book I;
but Book X does not mention the most complete virtue mentioned in Book I. And
so it is not clear that theoretical study is intended to be activity in accord with the
best and most complete virtue.

Book X becomes still more puzzling because it introduces completeness at a
point where Book I did not introduce it. Instead of identifying theoretical study
with happiness, Aristotle claims that it is *teleion* happiness (1177a17, b24).[29] The
most plausible account of Book I requires us to render '*teleion*' by 'complete' here.
How should we understand complete happiness in the light of Book I? At first
sight, the addition of 'complete' may seem superfluous, since happiness has been
defined as being the most complete end. If Aristotle speaks of complete happiness,
he seems to allow the possibility of incomplete happiness. If some form of happiness is incomplete, it is in some way a complete good (since happiness is complete),
but is still incomplete in some other respect.

The comparisons between theoretical study and the activities of the moral virtues may be taken to explain the ways in which theoretical study is more complete
than these other activities are. Theoretical study is (1) supreme, because it realizes
the best element in us and because it has the best objects; (2) most continuous; (3)
pleasantest, because it has the purest and most stable pleasures; (4) most self-sufficient, because it does not depend on other people as the moral virtues do; (5) pursued
because of itself alone; (6) found in leisure rather than in the laborious activities of
the moral virtues (1177a19-b26). The aims of theoretical study can be fulfilled with
less co-operation from external conditions than we require for the aims of the other
virtues. In this respect, it is the virtuous activity that is the most complete in itself.

We might object, on behalf of the pluralist conception, that these desirable
features of theoretical study do not make it identical to happiness. For happiness

has to realize human nature and the human function, but theoretical study cannot do that. In reply Aristotle seems to say three different things: (1) At first he seems to dismiss any appeal to the human function, by arguing that we ought to realize the best part of ourselves, since that allows us to live a divine life as far as we can (1177b26–1178a2). (2) But then he tries to fit his claims with the function argument, by claiming that a person seems to be his intellect (*nous*), and hence he lives his own life by living the life that realizes his intellect (1178a2–4). (3) He reasserts this claim with a possible qualification, suggesting that intellect is 'most of all' (*malista*) the human being (1178a6–8).

This last remark may be Aristotle's considered view on the relation of theoretical study to the human function. He argues that theoretical study is the best realization of the human function, not that it completely realizes the human function. The passage in which he claims that a human being is intellect most of all seems to echo a passage in Book IX. In the earlier passage, he also claims that a human being is most of all his most controlling part, which is his intellect; that is why the continent person does what he himself wants, and that is why we do what we ourselves want insofar as we act voluntarily on our rational choices (1168b27–1169a3). Hence Book X seems to appeal to an earlier claim about a person and his intellect.

But the earlier claim raises a question about Book X. In Book IX, Aristotle argues for the identification of the intellect with the self by a comparison with the identification of a city with its ruling element. We may say that the state does what the governing element does insofar as the governing element has a representative role; it is entitled to act on behalf of the citizens insofar as it properly speaks for them. The intellect that has a similar controlling role in the person should also, therefore, have a representative role that entitles it to speak for the whole person. It is the best part insofar as it is best qualified to choose on behalf of the whole person. Book X repeats the claim that intellect is the controlling element (1178a3),[30] but Aristotle now emphasizes the superiority of its activity, not its representative character.

This comparison between Book IX and Book X might cast doubt on Aristotle's argument for the identification of happiness with theoretical study in Book X. For we might object that he overlooks the point that the function argument affirms, and that the passage in Book IX reaffirms, that the complete good is the good for human nature as a whole, embracing theoretical intellect, practical reason, and non-rational desires insofar as they are harmonized with practical reason. It would be strange, however, if Aristotle overlooked this point entirely; for he recalls the passage in Book IX that recognizes precisely the role of intellect that his argument in Book X seems to leave out.

This apparently strange result might lead us in different directions: (1) We might revive the suggestion that Book X is independent of the rest of the *Ethics*, despite appearances. (2) We might reconsider our account of Book I. (3) We might decide that Aristotle has contradicted himself. (4) We might look for evidence to show that he has taken proper account of the function argument. Since the comparison between Book IX and Book X has made the first three options less attractive, we should ask whether the fourth is viable.

20. PLURALISM IN BOOK X?

After repeating his comparison between the relative independence of theoretical study from external conditions and the dependence of the other virtues on such conditions, Aristotle adds a new point. Though the externals that are needed for other virtues are even a hindrance to theoretical study, we need them none the less, insofar as we are human beings and live with others; for in living a human life (*anthrôpeuesthai*) we choose to do the actions that accord with virtue (1178b3–7).

We might understand this passage in two ways: (1) Since we are not pure intellects, but we have material bodies, we find human society useful to supply us with the resources we need to allow theoretical study; hence virtuous actions are useful to us. (2) Since we are not pure intellects, but human beings, our good consists partly in the possession and actualization of the social virtues.

The instrumental argument in (1) fits Aristotle's later remark that we need health, food, and other services because our nature is not self-sufficient for study (1178b33–5). But it does not do justice to 'insofar as he [sc., the one engaged in theoretical study] is a human being'. Here Aristotle seems to introduce a remark about essence; in saying that a human being 'lives with others', he recalls his claim that a human being is essentially social. His next phrase supports this interpretation as well. In choosing 'to do the actions that accord with virtue' (*ta kata tên aretên prattein*) we do not simply choose to do virtuous actions; we also choose to do them in accord with virtue. Acting in accord with virtue is a mark of the virtuous person; when we act in accord with virtue, we act in accord with correct reason, and that is what the virtuous and prudent person does (1144a13–20). If Aristotle is speaking exactly in saying that we choose the actions in accord with virtue rather than simply saying that we choose virtuous actions, he implies that happiness includes morally virtuous action as a non-instrumental good, and hence as a part.

The question about happiness and external goods returns a little later, when Aristotle maintains that we do not need a high level of external goods. Does he mean that theoretical study needs only modest external resources? Or does he mean that we can also act virtuously with modest resources? He begins by referring only to the demands of theoretical study. But he continues by going further. He reminds us that even with moderate resources we can act 'in accord with virtue' and do 'fine' (*kala*) and 'decent' (*epieikê*) actions. In his support he points to the actions of private citizens without large resources (1179a5–9). He does not seem to refer to private citizens who have engaged exclusively in theoretical study; when he compares them with the actions of rich and powerful people, he is thinking of how they have manifested moral virtue.

To support his claim that we need only moderate resources, Aristotle appeals to the view of Solon that happy people who were moderately supplied with external goods did the finest actions, and lived their lives temperately (1179a9–13). Solon was not thinking of people who chose virtuous actions only because of instrumental calculation about what they needed for theoretical study; he was counting as happy those who had exercised the moral virtues. Aristotle introduces the virtues rather than simply virtuous action, by saying that such people had lived 'temperately'. According to his normal use of adverbs referring to the virtues, these people had not simply done what a temperate person would do, but had done it in the right way, as a result of being temperate, and hence caring about temperate action for its own sake (1105a28-b9).

In these remarks on the moral virtues Aristotle has not even said (though no doubt he believes) that they are useful for supplying the external goods needed for theoretical study. He assumes that happy people will cultivate the moral virtues and act on them, and hence he implies that they will value the moral virtues non-instrumentally. Since their valuation is correct, moral virtues and virtuous actions are parts of happiness.

These passages do not suggest that morally virtuous action is part of happiness only for people who are incapable of theoretical study, or lack the leisure for it. Aristotle has said that the life according to the moral virtues is second best to the life of theoretical study (1178a9–10), because these virtues are human rather than divine. But he does not say that a life including both theoretical study and the moral virtues is only second best. We might think that he implies this, on the ground that the more inclusive life would waste time on second-best activities instead of concentrating, as it should, on the best activities as far as it can. But Aristotle does not endorse this conclusion. On the contrary, since the human good realizes human nature as a whole, it is better than a life that ignores the moral virtues, even though these virtues in themselves are inferior to theoretical wisdom.

Even if we have found evidence in Book X to support a pluralist conception of happiness, we may be unsatisfied. If this is Aristotle's view, why, we may ask, is it so difficult to find? Why does he lay such emphasis on the supreme value of theoretical study, and say so little about the fulfilment of other aspects of human nature? If he had clearly intended to state a pluralist view, could he not have stated it more clearly and unambiguously?

These are reasonable questions, but they should not be allowed to distract us from the cogent reasons for ascribing a pluralist conception to Aristotle throughout the *Ethics*. Aristotle's emphasis in Book X is intelligible if we suppose that he rejects an excessively moralistic conception of happiness. In the bulk of the *Ethics* he denies that the moral virtues are purely instrumental – either as supports for a social order that allows the secure pursuit of private pleasures or as supports for a purely intellectual life. At the end of the *Ethics* he corrects any impression he might have given that he simply identifies the human good with the practice of the moral virtues. Though he takes these virtues to be important elements of the human good, he does not believe they should be the exclusive focus of our attention. We ought not to ignore or conceal his belief in the secondary status of the moral virtues. Nor, however, ought we to allow this belief to distort our interpretation of the *Ethics* as a whole.

NOTES

1. I will use '*Ethics*' hereinafter for the *Nicomachean Ethics (EN)*, since the problem I discuss arises primarily about this work. I will refer only occasionally to the two other ethical works in the Corpus, the *Eudemian Ethics* and the *Magna Moralia*. Though they have quite a bit to say on the components of happiness, the question of internal consistency is peculiar to the *EN*. I use the Oxford Classical Text of Bywater. He supports some of his textual decisions in Bywater (1892).

2. I will not pause to discuss the important questions about the relation between the human good and happiness. I will use 'happiness' to render 'eudaimonia' with the usual cautions directed at readers who interpret the English word (questionably) in a hedonist or subjectivist sense. See Irwin (2007) §13, 836.

3. I will speak rather loosely of the *êthikai aretai* as 'moral virtues', to suggest that they cover the area of morality. Even if this suggestion is mistaken, these virtues include social virtues, including justice and bravery, that involve one's relations to the needs and expectations of other individuals and of one's community.

4. The contours of recent discussion were partly formed by Austin (1979, but originally composed in the 1930s and 1940s), Hardie (1980, including a revision of an earlier essay), and Ackrill (1974), who gradually formulated a clear statement of the main questions. Ackrill's sketch of a comprehensive and pluralist interpretation of the *Ethics* has attracted considerable support, but also considerable opposition; Kenny (1992) and Kraut (1989), among others, have offered powerful defences of a monist view. The most recent full defence of a monist view is Lear (2004). I will not try to discuss the contributions to this discussion point by point, or even to list them all. Some of them are cited in the bibliography to Lear (2004).

5. See, esp., Kenny (1978).

6. See §9 below.

7. Some manuscripts have either *arkion* ('sufficient') *kai haireton* or *haireton kai arkion* instead of *haireton* alone. Bywater presumably thinks the extra words are a gloss, but they may be worth considering.

8. The superlative of '*haireton*', rendered 'object of choice' above.

9. This is settled by the feminine *hairetôtatên*, agreeing with *eudaimonian*.

10. For this sense of the phrase (i.e., 'by itself', 'in isolation') cf. *PA* 643a24–6. An alternative translation would be 'would seem to be the only <activity?> liked because of itself' (see, e.g., Ross, Rowe). This has the unwelcome result that Aristotle affirms that theoretical study is the only non-instrumental good, so that he affirms comprehensive monism, contrary to the rest of his argument.

11. This point turns on the interpretation of 1177b1. See the previous note.

12. This question is discussed by Scott (1999) and Charles (1999).

13. The interpretation of *teleios bios* is discussed by Stewart (1892) (who refers to Rassow's view) and by Gauthier.

14. Kraut (1989) tries to explain this passage so as to allow a non-comprehensive conception.

15. All the manuscripts read *praktikais* in 1094b4. Bywater deletes it in the OCT and defends the deletion in (1892).

16. For discussion and some references, see Irwin (2007), §96.

17. Lear (2004) argues that these two types of means do not exhaust the relevant uses of 'for the sake of' in the *Ethics*. She points out correctly that we might choose x for the sake of y in cases where we know we cannot get y, but x is the closest we can come to y. In such cases y guides and explains our choice of x even though x is neither a means to nor a part of y. This use of 'for the sake of' is certainly relevant to the *Ethics*; it explains, for instance, how we can still act for the sake of happiness even if external circumstances rule out our achieving happiness (if, for instance, we suffer some of the ill fortune mentioned in I 9–11, or if we have to face death as the only alternative to cowardly action). In Lear's view, we choose virtuous action because it is the closest we can come to theoretical study, and in this respect we choose it for the sake of happiness. This may be explained as a constitutive use of 'for the sake of' (virtuous action constitutes what I can do to achieve happiness, in cases where I cannot achieve happiness itself). It is difficult to see, on this account, why we should pursue morally virtuous activity for the sake of happiness, in circumstances where it is open to us to pursue theoretical study.

18. The interpretation of 1177b1 (see note 10 above) is relevant again here.

19. The comprehensive interpretation is clearly set out by Stewart (1892) ad loc., who refers to ancient commentators who favour the comprehensive and the non-comprehensive interpretation.

20. It is difficult to explain *MM* 1194a15–38 unless we take it to accept a comprehensive interpretation of the counting condition. But it does not follow that we should take the same view of the *EN*.

21. I say this on the assumption that Aristotle does not use 'blessedness' (*makariotês*) to indicate a greater good than happiness. On this question see Irwin (1985); Broadie and Rowe (2002), ad 1101a16–21; White (1992), 100.

22. On the function argument: Whiting (1988); Irwin (2007), §74.

23. Rassow (1874), 72–3, Stewart (1892), and Gauthier (1970), believe that the clause in 1098a3-4 is spurious.

24. See Aspasius ad loc. Rassow objects that the clause is 'entirely incomprehensible' to a reader who has not yet read I 13. He is right to say that Aristotle relies on some understanding of his views about parts of the soul. But he equally relies on some understanding of these views in 1097b33–1098a3.

25. Rassow admits that *kai* in 1098a5 refers to the suspected clause, and so he argues that *kai* is also spurious, an insertion designed to take account of the previous insertion of the suspected clause.

26. Bywater (1892) 23–4, brackets 1098a12–16 as a duplicate passage that interrupts Aristotle's argument. Gauthier agrees.

27. On this type of deliberation, see Broadie (1991), 198–202; Kraut (1993).

28. See §2 above.

29. The translation of *teleion* by 'complete' in this context is supported by the reference to a *teleion* length of life in 1177b25. As in I 7, this is best translated by 'complete'.

30. We might translate *kurion* by 'important'. But if we do, we lose the connexion with Book IX, where the comparison with the city suggests that *kurion* means 'controlling'.

BIBLIOGRAPHY

Ackrill, J.L. (1974) 'Aristotle on *eudaimonia*', *Proceedings of the British Academy* 60, 339–59. Reprinted in , A.O. Rorty, ed. (1980) *Essays on Aristotle's Ethics* (Berkeley), 15–34.

Aspasius (1889) in *Ethica Nicomachea quae supersunt commentaria*, ed. G. Heylbut, CAG vol. 19 (Berlin: Reimer).

Austin, J.L. (1979) '*Agathon* and *eudaimonia* in the *Ethics* of Aristotle' *Collected Papers*, J.O. Urmson and G.J. Warnock, eds., (Oxford: Oxford Univ. Press).

Broadie, S.W. (1991) *Ethics with Aristotle* (Oxford: Oxford Univ. Press).

Broadie, S.W. and C.J. Rowe, ed. and tr. (2002) *Aristotle: The Nicomachean Ethics*, translation and commentary (Oxford: Oxford Univ. Press).

Bywater, I. (1892) *Contributions to the Textual Criticism of Aristotle's Nicomachean Ethics* (Oxford: Oxford Univ. Press).

Bywater, I. (1894), ed., *Aristotelis Ethica Nicomachea* (Oxford: Oxford Univ. Press).

Charles, D. (1999) 'Aristotle on well-being and intellectual contemplation', *Supplementary Proceedings of the Aristotelian Society* 73, 205–23.

Cooper, J.M. (1987) 'Contemplation and happiness', *Synthese* 72 , 187–216. Reprinted in J. Cooper, *Reason and Emotion* (Princeton: Princeton Univ. Press).

——— (1975) *Reason and Human Good in Aristotle* (Cambridge: Harvard Univ. Press).

Crisp, R.C. (1994) 'Aristotle's inclusivism', *OSAP* 12, 111–36.

Devereux, D.T. (1981) 'Aristotle on the essence of happiness', in D.J. O'Meara, ed., *Studies in Aristotle* (Washington: Catholic Univ. of America Press), 247–260.

Engberg-Pederson, T. (1983) *Aristotle's Theory of Moral Insight* (Oxford: Oxford Univ. Press).

Gauthier, R.A. and J.Y. Jolif (1970) *Aristote: L'Ethique à Nicomaque*, 2nd edition, 4 vols., (Louvain: Publications universitaires).

Hardie, W.F.R. (1980) *Aristotle's Ethical Theory*, 2nd ed (Oxford: Oxford Univ. Press).

Heinaman, R.E. (1986) 'Eudaimonia and self-sufficiency', *Phronesis* 33, 31–53.

Irwin, T.H. (2007) *The Development of Ethics*, vol. 1., (Oxford: Oxford Univ. Press).

——— (1985) 'Permanent happiness', *OSAP* 3, 89–124.

Kenny, A.J.P. (1992) *Aristotle on the Perfect Life* (Oxford: Oxford Univ. Press).

——— (1978) *The Aristotelian Ethics* (Oxford: Oxford Univ. Press).

Keyt, D. (1983) 'Intellectualism in Aristotle', in J.P. Anton and A. Preus, eds., *Essays in Ancient Greek Philosophy*, vol. 2. (Albany: SUNY Press).

Kraut, R. (1993) 'In defence of the grand end', *Ethics* 103, 361–74.

——— (1989) *Aristotle on the Human Good* (Princeton: Princeton Univ. Press).

Lawrence, G.L. (1993) 'Aristotle on the ideal life', *Philosophical Review* 102, 1–34.

Lear , G.R. (2004) *Happy Lives and the Highest Good* (Princeton: Princeton Univ. Press).

O'Meara, D.J., ed. (1981) *Studies in Aristotle* (Washington: Catholic Univ. of America Press).

Price, A.W. (1980) 'Aristotle's ethical holism', *Mind* 89, 338–52.

Rassow, H. (1874) *Forschungen über die Nikomachische Ethik* (Weimar: H. Böhlau).

Ross, W.D. (1980) *Nicomachean Ethics*, tr. W.D. Ross, revised by J.L. Ackrill and J.O. Urmson (Oxford: Oxford Univ. Press).

Scott, D.J. (1999) 'Primary and secondary *eudaimonia*', *Supplementary Proceedings of the Aristotelian Society* 73, 225–42.

Stewart, J.A. (1892) *Notes on the Nicomachean Ethics*, 2 vols., (Oxford: Oxford Univ.Press).

White, N.P. (1981) 'Goodness and human aims in Aristotle's ethics', in D.J. O'Meara, ed., *Studies in Aristotle* (Washington: Catholic Univ. of America Press).

White, S.A. (1992) *Sovereign Virtue* (Stanford: Stanford Univ. Press).

Whiting, J.E. (1986) 'Human nature and intellectualism in Aristotle', *Archiv für Geschichte der Philosophie* 68, 70–95.

—— (1988) 'Aristotle's function argument: a defence', *Ancient Philosophy* 8, 33–48.

CHAPTER 20

ARISTOTLE ON BECOMING GOOD: HABITUATION, REFLECTION, AND PERCEPTION

RICHARD KRAUT

1. VIRTUE: SOME BACKGROUND COMMONPLACES

THE Greek noun for which 'virtue' and 'excellence' are often used as translations—*aretê* (plural: *aretai*)—is cognate to the name of the god of war, Ares (called 'Mars' in Latin) and, centuries prior to Aristotle, designated the manliness or valor of a warrior. But by the fifth and fourth centuries BC it had acquired a much wider connotation and extension. When, for example, Socrates asks Meno (in the Platonic dialogue named after him) whether he can define what *aretê* is, the reply Meno gives (71e) mentions not only the virtues of a man (amongst other things, to manage public affairs) but those of women (to oversee the household), as well as those of children, old men, and slaves. The conversation between Socrates and Meno reveals several of the commonplaces about virtue that any philosophical examination of them would have to treat seriously: virtues are related to tasks (*erga*: for example, running a city or a household) and require performing them well; typical human virtues include justice and moderation (*sophrosunê*) and not just courage; when someone is called good—that is, a good man or a good woman—that is because they have certain virtues (72a-73c). We can see, furthermore, from *Republic* Book I (352d-353d), that it is not only human beings who can be said to possess *aretai*: the same is true of animals, artifacts (knives), and organs (eyes).

These commonplaces remain in place in Aristotle's ethical writings, and from time to time he appeals to them. The function (*ergon*) of a good thing of a kind (for example, a good harpist) is to do something well, that is, in accordance with the excellence or excellences of anything of that kind. If, as Aristotle proposes (and in doing so, goes far beyond commonplaces), human beings have a distinctive function or task (*ergon*), and their good lies in a good performance of that function, then what is good for human beings consists in excellent or virtuous activity (*EN* I 7 1097b22–1098a20; cf. II 6 1105a15–19). That abstract sketch of what is good for human beings is then made more concrete throughout the rest of the *Ethics* by an analysis of what a virtue is (Book II) and a specification of the qualities that count as virtues (Books III through VI). The *Nicomachean Ethics* might have been aptly named 'The Book of Virtues', but since it examines the various vices of human beings no less than their virtues, it is designated by the broader term that encompasses all traits of character, both good and bad. Aristotle himself, in the *Politics*, refers back to his writings on *êthika*, and in doing so, emphasizes the fact that the central topic of these writings are *êthê* (plural of *êthos*), that is, traits of character. The *Nicomachean Ethics*, in other words, is the Nicomachean Character Traits.[1]

2. VIRTUES OF CHARACTER AND VIRTUES OF THOUGHT

Although the virtues of character dominate Aristotle's discussion (they are his topic in Books II through V), he insists that they are not the only kind of human virtue: there are, as well, virtues of thought (I 13 1103a1–10), and these are discussed in Book VI. The distinction between the two kinds of virtue is based on Aristotle's division between the part of the soul that enables us to engage in reasoning and the part that enables us to be responsive to reasoning (I 7 1098a4–5). At a certain stage in our development, we are able to make inferences, to guide our inferences by standards of reasoning, to respond to criticism of the conclusions we draw, to change our minds on the basis of reflection, and so on. To say that a part of our soul is the rational or reasoning part is simply a way of saying that we have these capacities and engage in these activities. Other parts of the soul are not responsive to reason at all: a child's growth, for example, is governed, Aristotle believes, by the nutritive part of the soul, but he cannot affect his rate of growth simply as a result of a process of reasoning (I 13 1102a32-b12).

Between our inferential activities and reason-indifferent processes there are kinds of activities that are not merely physical processes, and are capable of being affected by reason. Certain things in us can be described as 'listening' to reason—or (as so often happens) declining to listen, even though they could have done so (I 13 1102b25–1103a1). One can, for example, tell oneself that one's anger is fully justified, and as a result the anger might increase; conversely, if one realizes that one's anger is based on false assumptions, that should by itself bring about the dissipation of anger, and often it does. To become angry, or fearful, or to crave a certain dish is not to be engaged in a process of guiding ourselves from premises to conclusions; but if we are led to the conclusion that someone did us no injury, or is no threat, or that a certain kind of food is filled with poison, we will—if this part of the soul is in good order—lose our anger, fear, or desire to eat that item.

So we can assess the quality of someone's mental life in two rather different ways: we can ask whether someone is in good condition with respect to his inference-making skills, and we can also ask whether those parts of him that can respond to reason (his desires and emotions) are responding well. If one is in good condition in the first way, one has the virtues of thought; if one is in good condition in the second way, one has the virtues of character. The fact that Aristotle makes this distinction does not commit him to saying that one can have some or all of the ethical virtues without having any of the intellectual virtues. In fact, he insists, on the contrary, that there is one virtue of thought—the one he calls *phronêsis* (often translated 'practical wisdom')—that is intimately tied to the virtues of character: one cannot have any of those ethical virtues (justice, courage, moderation) without having *phronêsis*; and one cannot have *phronêsis* unless one also has those ethical virtues (VI 13 aa44b30–32). To be in all respects a good person consists in being in good condition with respect to one's affective responsiveness and also to be in good condition with respect to the inferences by which one is led to act in certain ways. And each of these two kinds of good condition depends on the other.

3. SOCRATIC INTELLECTUALISM

Aristotle is aware of the possibility of taking a more intellectual approach to the question of what it is to be a good person. Some of the short works of Plato that focus on the virtues—for example, *Euthyphro*, *Laches*, *Charmides*—rely on the idea that having such virtues as piety, courage, and moderation is a matter of being skilled in a certain branch of thought. In these and similar works (other examples would be *Lysis*, *Meno*, *Protagoras*, and *Republic* Book I), Socrates relentlessly compares a good person to someone who has developed expertise in some practical sphere of thinking and doing. A doctor, for example, has his peculiar area of expertise: he is knowledgeable about health. That is a subject he has studied, and since he has given considerable thought to this topic, he can explain why he prescribes this treatment rather than that. Socrates assumes that the virtues that make someone a good human being will be intellectual skills in precisely the same way: there must be a topic about which a good person is knowledgeable, and acquiring a virtue will simply be a process of becoming an expert about that topic.

Aristotle agrees with Socrates that being a good human being consists in being good at thinking about a certain topic. That is, it *partly* consists in thinking well about what is good for human beings in general (*EN* VI 5 1140a25–8). Being a good person is not simply a matter of having one's behaviour conform to some appropriate standard. It consists in *acting* well. But to act (*prattein*) is not merely to move one's body in a way that brings about certain results. When we act, what we do is the outcome of a process of reasoning, and that chain of events can be assessed as a whole. In making that assessment, we ask whether what we did was done for the right reason. We consider the whole process of reasoning that led a person to move as he did (or refrain from moving). If someone brought about good results but was trying to achieve different results, or was merely following someone else's orders, or was merely trying to impress onlookers, that makes a difference to our assessment of whether he is a good human being. So, in at least these ways, being a good person consists in measuring up to a standard of good reasoning.

But Aristotle also disagrees with Socrates in a fundamental way. People who are trained in the specialized crafts—medicine, architecture, cooking, making shoes—acquire knowledge of facts and practical know-how that they might or might not decide to put into practice. A doctor learns how to heal, but what he learns about the way the body functions also equips him to make people less fit and healthy. His study of the effects of various elements on the body could lead him to concoct poisons no less than remedies for poisons (*Met.* IX 2 1046b5–24). That is because his training as a doctor is not at the same time a training of his desires and emotions. Rather, his education is simply a tool that he may use or decline to use as it was intended. Aristotle sees, however, that this is not the way we think of the qualities that make someone a good human being. To become a just person involves not only the acquisition of a certain way of thinking, but also the development of certain kinds of desires and feelings, and it is precisely because it involves a training of the affective (but reason-responsive) side of human nature that those who have the virtues can be relied on to act in characteristic ways. A just person will act justly, when it is possible to do so, because his justice is not something that he can set aside whenever he chooses. He has become the sort of person who aims, with every part of the soul that can be summoned, at acting justly.

That is why he says: 'the inquiries Socrates used to undertake were in one way correct and in another way in error. For insofar as he thought all the virtues are practical wisdom, he was in error, but insofar as he thought they all require practical wisdom, what he used to say was right' (VI 13 1144b18–21). To hold that all of the virtues are practical wisdom is to hold that there is nothing to being a good person but having in good condition the part of the soul with which one makes practical inferences. Aristotle rejects that Socratic thesis because he thinks this is only one of the standards that it is appropriate to expect a good person to meet.

4. 'THOUGHT ITSELF MOVES NOTHING ...'

Aristotle holds that the mere acquisition of craft knowledge or any other knowledge that is not at the same time a training of our affective and conative side does not by itself lead to action. His thoughts along these lines are most clearly expressed in the last book of the *De Anima*. There he points out that the acquisition of medical knowledge does not by itself cause someone to act; even though medical knowledge is pertinent to action, by itself it does not produce motion (*DA* III 9 433a4–7). What must be true of a person who possesses knowledge of medicine, if it is to be the case that such knowledge results in action? Aristotle's answer is: he must have a *desire*—more precisely, a desire to use that knowledge (for good or ill). 'That which moves is a single thing: that which desires' (*to orektikon*, III 10 433a22). He adds: 'it seems that thought (*nous*) does not move in the absence of desire' (a22–23).

What Aristotle says here does not decisively rule out the possibility that the acquisition of medical knowledge might by itself produce a desire to heal. It would, in other words, be consistent with what he says to suppose that inquiries into what health is, and how it can be fostered, regularly lead to the creation of a desire to heal. To put this idea in a more general form: acquiring knowledge about how to do something might always lead to a desire to do it, or might tend to create such a desire. But that idea is utterly implausible, and Aristotle is justified in tacitly rejecting it. He rightly insists, as we have seen, that craft knowledge can be used to bring about opposite conditions (*Met.* IX 2 1046b5–24). And he is no doubt thinking of craft knowledge when he claims that it is desire, not bare intellection devoid of desire, that moves us to act (*DA* III 10 433a22–23). If the mere understanding of how something can be done were enough to produce a desire to do it, that desire would merely be an intermediate stage in the production of action, and the deeper cause of action would lie in the thinking that lies behind a desire.[2]

The impotence of thought that is isolated from desire is affirmed again in the *Nicomachean Ethics*: 'Thought (*dianoia*) itself moves nothing, but thought that is for the sake of something and practical does' (VI 2 1139a32–3). Aristotle's compressed statement can be more fully expressed in this way: thought that is undertaken for the sake of achieving some goal that is desired is the kind of thought that moves us. For Aristotle says, in the portion of VI 2 that leads to this statement, that it is desire and thought working and fused together that leads to action. He is thinking here of actions that are undertaken because they are decided upon: they are selected on the basis of a deliberative process as the things that are to be done in this particular situation. To ascribe to someone a virtue is not merely to say how he acts, but also to say something about what underlies those acts: it is to characterize him as someone who *decides* well in a certain range of situations. The just person, for example, does not merely produce results that happen to be just; he is good at deciding about how to deal with situations that call for justice. And the psychological condition that consists in the decision (*prohairesis*) that has been reached—not the content of the decision (to do such and such), but the attitude taken towards that content—is a desire, or more fully, a 'deliberative desire' (1139a23, *orexis bouleutikê*). What it is for someone to be a good person, then, is for both aspects of *prohairesis* to be doing their jobs well: one must have the right sorts of desires, and one must be good at the form of reasoning that Aristotle characterizes as deliberative (1139a23–6).

These ideas are more fully developed in the chapters of *Nicomachean Ethics* Book III that are devoted to decision, deliberation, and wish. The state of mind that one is in, when one has made a decision, must be distinguished from a belief (III 2 1111b32–1112a13). To have resolved to do V must be distinguished from having some belief about V—for example, the belief that it would be good for one to do V. Beliefs are not by their very nature infused with desire and motive force, but a different category of psychological states—the ones that we call 'intentions', 'plans', 'resolutions' and the like—are so infused, and the state of mind that Aristotle calls a *prohairesis* falls into this category. What leads to a decision is a conative state that Aristotle calls *boulêsis* (normally translated 'wish')—something that takes some end or goal (*telos*) for its object. To get from a wish to a decision, we deliberate.

This is a process of going from the general to the concrete. A doctor, for example, has a standing goal of healing his patients, but that by itself is not a *prohairesis* to do anything, because it lacks the concrete particularity of a decision. Merely having the general plan of healing people cannot by itself result in the performance of a particular action. What must intervene is a thinking process that reveals the best way to achieve the goal from which deliberation starts. This is not necessarily a process of finding instrumental means to an end. If one's goal is write a poem about a certain subject, for example, finding the material wherewithal to bring this about is only a small part of the problem; one must also find the right words, and these are not a means to the production of the poem, but rather constitute its production. Similarly, if one's goal is to be a good father to one's child, or a good friend to a certain person, or a good citizen of a certain community, one's deliberation about how to bring this about will only partly be devoted to the question of finding instrumental means. Much of the hard work that must be done will be devoted to answering the question: what would be good for one's child, one's friends, and one's political community? But no amount of thinking about these problems will lead to action, unless what lies behind such thinking is the desire to help these individuals.

5. CLEVERNESS

Of course, one virtue of thought that everyone needs is the ability to work out the best instrumental means for the accomplishment of one's goals. That is the intellectual skill that Aristotle calls cleverness (*deinotês*, VI 12 1144a26–9). It is a skill of the thinking part of the soul that can be possessed by those who have bad ends, no less than by those whose ends are good. It is an intellectual quality that anyone who aspires to *phronêsis* must acquire, for one will be of little use to anyone if one lacks the know-how and the mental ability to acquire the information that is needed to achieve what one sets out to do. The formation of good intentions does not make one a good human being; nor is it sufficient to be resolute in carrying out those intentions. For if one is not good at working out means to one's ends—if one is content to remain incompetent as an effective agent in the world—one can reasonably be blamed for not having taken the steps that could and should have been taken to do some good for others and oneself.[3]

Even so, that sort of know-how and competence is not all there is to the virtue of *phronêsis*. For, as we have seen (section 4), not everything that needs to be done in order to bring about the realization of a general goal can be described as a problem of finding the material resources or tools that one needs.

6. 'VIRTUE MAKES THE GOAL CORRECT ...'

Aristotle says several times that there is a division of labor between the virtues of character on the one hand and *phronêsis* on the other. The former kind of virtue 'makes the goal (*skopon*) correct, whereas *phronêsis* makes the things done for the goal correct' (VI 12 1144a7–9; cf. VI 12 1144a20–22). Similarly, he says that virtue 'makes one attain the end (*telos*)' whereas *phronêsis* makes one attain the things that are done for the end (VI 13 1145a5–6). A similar idea is put forward in VII 8: neither in mathematics nor in practical matters does reason (*logos*) 'teach the starting points' (*archai*); rather, virtue, either natural or habituated teaches the right opinion about the starting point' (1151a17–19). In this last passage, Aristotle implies that there is a limitation in the competence of *phronêsis* for the same reason that there is a limitation in any intellectual skill that takes one justifiably from one premise to another, but does not tell one which premises are the best or right ones to start from. We do not reason our way toward having the goal from which deliberation begins. It matters a great deal what the starting point of practical and theoretical thinking is, but skill in reasoning from starting points cannot be the skill that enables us to start with the right material upon which reasoning does its work.

What kind of competencies will do that job—the job of insuring that the start-ing points of practical reasoning are the right starting points? Aristotle assumes that they must be the competencies of some part of the soul other than the one that engages in reasoning. That of course must be the part of the soul that feels and desires. It is because of the good condition of that conative and affective compo-nent of the psyche that thinking about what to do starts in the right place.

There is a serious difficulty in making sense of this aspect of Aristotle's moral psychology. For when he introduces the idea that we must distinguish the virtues of practical thinking from the virtues of character, he portrays the reasoning part as the superior partner. The non-inferential and affective part of the soul does well or goes astray depending on whether it plays its subordinate role well—that is, depending on whether or not it listens to reason, or pulls us towards some alter-native that reason has decided against (I 13 1102b31–1103a3). But in Books VI and VII, as we have seen, it looks as though reason must take its cue from conation and affect. It is confined to the job of making concrete the general goals that we desire. Those desires must be directed at appropriate objects; otherwise, although we will get what we want, what we achieve will do no good. But it might now seem as though one must be lucky enough to have desires that happen to be directed at what is genuinely worthwhile, and that it is beyond our powers of reasoning to make the most important decisions about how we should live our lives. Apparently, we simply have to hope that the things we want are the goals that are the proper starting points for practical thinking.

Yet that cannot be what Aristotle really believes. For the *Nicomachean Ethics* begins with the thought that we students of the subject are about to take control of our lives by figuring out what is the highest end for human beings. The study of this subject (politics), we are assured, will make a great difference to the course of our lives (I 2 1094a22–4). By framing his ethical inquiry in this way, Aristotle implies that the kind of lives we live depends on the reasoned choices we make about what our ultimate ends should be.

7. THE STAGES OF ETHICAL DEVELOPMENT

To see our way through this difficulty, it will be helpful to review some of the statements that Aristotle makes about the various stages human beings go through as they develop an outlook on how to live their lives.[4] A normal human being is born with the capacity to reason, but that capacity, unlike our capacities for per-ception (*EN* II 1 1103a28–31), cannot be exercised immediately (*Pol.* I 13 1260a13). It takes many years for the various skills of practical reasoning—to compare the merits of alternative courses of action, to foresee future opportunities or hazards, to plan for the long term, and so on—to be put into operation. Whether we acquire defects or excellences of character depends partly on those with whom we come into contact—on our families and on the customs of the wider political community (*EN* X 9 1179b31–5). We are beings who naturally delight in the pleasures of imitation and representation (*Poet.* 4 1448b4–9), and are therefore apt to reproduce the behaviour and adopt the attitudes of people for whom we develop some trust, or admiration, or love. But Aristotle does not think that the whole of childhood is a condition of passivity; rather, he suggests that, at a certain point in our development, we begin to be responsible for the way in which our character takes shape (*EN* III 5 1114b22–3).

Even before we arrive at that period of active control, we can be said to display the primitive beginning of character traits—the qualities that Aristotle calls 'natural virtues' (VI 13 1144b36). He says that there is a way in which even a child can be called just, or moderate, or brave (1144b4–6). Although he does not say more precisely what he has in mind, we can reasonably suppose that he is thinking of the way in which a young child can be induced to behave well in ordinary ways—for example, to share with others, or to cope with pain, or to postpone gratification.

Furthermore, Aristotle frequently calls attention to the fact that human beings have an innate suitability for social and civic life. Part of what it is for human beings to be naturally political animals is for them to be disposed to enter into cooperative arrangements even with individuals who are not members of their families.[5] That aspect of sociability is widespread and begins at an early age. Being disposed to share with others and to help them with small favours are characteristics that might plausibly be called natural. Under a wide range of favourable circumstances, these are more likely to be the responses of small children to others than sheer indifference or hostility.

'Some think it is nature that makes people good; some think it is habit; some that it is teaching. The natural element clearly does not depend on us, but belongs by divine causes of some kind to the truly fortunate; while discussion (*logos*) and teaching do not have force in all cases, but the soul of the student must have been prepared beforehand, through its habits, to be fine in what it likes and disdains, like earth that is going to nourish seed' (X 9 1179b20–26). Here Aristotle implies that some outstandingly fortunate individuals are blessed with a great natural headstart in the acquisition of virtue. Although the stages of habituation and reflection presumably cannot be bypassed, a lucky few are propelled through them by the great natural advantages with which they begin. But Aristotle must be assuming that such cases are rare. In the normal case, as we have seen, he assumes that human beings begin with some tendency—it need not be particularly strong—to move forward along the path of good development. Normal children, in other words (those who are neither defective nor extraordinarily gifted in affect and thought), have a natural tendency to act in ways that show the initial traces of more mature forms of acting well. To arrive at full maturity and genuine excellence of character, we must all go through a process of habituation.

In another passage, Aristotle notes that the Greek word for habit (*ethos*) by itself suggests that the traits of character (*êthê*) are formed by a process of habituation (II 1 1103a17–18). It can be called habituation because there is an element of repetition in it. As Aristotle says, we become just by performing just acts, courageous by performing courageous acts, and so on (II 1 1103a34–1103b2). But it would be a mistake to think that he takes this to be a mindless and routine process (although that is how some very simple habits are formed). If one repeatedly makes a conscious effort to brush one's teeth after every meal, one will eventually find oneself reaching for one's toothbrush after a meal, even without conscious effort. But that process of thoughtless routinization cannot be what Aristotle has in mind when he says that we become just by doing just acts. Like every virtue of character, justice in its full form is suffused with practical wisdom; a just person is good at thinking about problems that call for a just response. That kind of thoughtfulness cannot be acquired by automatically and mindlessly repeating some single type of action like brushing one's teeth. Sometimes, for example, a child who is learning how to be just will recognize that an equal division is what a situation calls for; at other times, he will see that some deserve more, or need more, than others; and that these are appropriate reasons for deviation from an allocation in which each gets the same share. To become just by repeatedly doing what is just is to encounter many situations in which one must come to a decision about what is just, and in this way to develop sufficient experience and insight regarding such matters.[6]

As we have seen, Aristotle emphasizes that a child who is learning how to be virtuous must *also* develop the proper affective responses. As he says, a child must be 'fine in what he likes and disdains' (X 9 1179b25–6). Presumably this means that a child must (for example) come to enjoy treating other people justly, and seeing them treated justly by others; he must also come to be repelled by injustice—not merely when he is at the receiving end, but also whenever anyone suffers an injustice. But the fact that the acquisition of good habits in childhood involves an education of the affective side of the soul does not mean that this is *all* that is involved—that the child's capacity for active thought is entirely dormant. The child's mind, after all, does not suddenly and magically spring into action at a single moment at the end of childhood. It grows, and does so gradually. That means that it is somehow learning as the early years go by. Aristotle, we can safely assume, realizes that children think in increasingly sophisticated ways about justice, as they learn to love it and are repelled by its opposite. He offers no theory about what takes place in a child's rational soul, as he encounters more and more situations that call for justice, moderation, courage, and the like. He simply notes that a child becomes just, courageous, and so on by gaining experience, that is, by encountering situations that call for a just and courageous response. What he must be assuming is that such situations call for not only an affective response but also for the development of problem-solving skills, and that it is only in this way that the not-yet-mature rational faculty of a child blossoms into its mature state.

Aristotle is not committed to the absurd idea that there is a bright line that marks the point at which a maturing individual can be said to have completed his acquisition of the virtues of character—to have reached the point at which he has progressed so far beyond the natural virtues from which he began that he can be said to have these virtues in the strict sense (VI 13 1144b4–6). One tries to be good by acting well in all kinds of situations that call for thoughtful actions and emotionally appropriate responses; one keeps on trying; and at some point, one has developed these skills fully enough to qualify as a good human being.

Nonetheless, Aristotle does indicate that, if one is to become fully virtuous, the period of habituation that takes place during childhood must be followed by a further stage of growth that is marked by reasoning rather than habituation. After all, when he talks about habituation, he describes it as preparation for something further: 'the soul of the student must have been prepared beforehand, like earth that is going to nourish seed' (X 9 1179b24–26). That further stage is one in which there is discussion (*logos*) and teaching (*didachê*, b23–4). The child is no longer a child; reason has now become sophisticated enough to be exposed to the full range of considerations that can be brought to bear on practical problem-solving. It is at this point that practical wisdom (*phronêsis*) must be acquired.

How is that to be done? The answer Aristotle gives, in this passage, is: through teaching and discussion (1179b23). That is how *any* intellectual virtue is acquired (II 1 1103a15). When a student of a subject is ready for this stage of rationality, he no longer needs further experience (a16); experience is the prerequisite of this stage, but not its content. One needs to become a student of practical matters; one needs teachers, and one needs discussion. Evidently, Aristotle holds that to become a completely good person—to acquire practical wisdom—one must go through a period of reflection in which one talks with others (whom one regards as teachers) about the subjects in which one has already developed, through the acquisition of appropriate habits, considerable skill. He is assuming, then, that the discussions he is having with the students for whom the *Nicomachean Ethics* was written are precisely what they need, in order to complete their moral education.

He tells them that they are not yet completely good: 'The present study is not for the sake of knowledge (*theôria*), as others are, for we are investigating what virtue is not in order to know it, but in order to become good; for otherwise it would be of no use' (II 2 1103b26–9). Those who study with him must have been 'brought up well in their habits' (I 4 1095b4), but that does not mean that they already have the virtues in the strict and fullest sense. After all, to be completely good requires *phronêsis* (VI 13 1144b30–31), and that intellectual virtue involves an understanding of what is good for human beings in general (VI 5 1140b4–6). That is not something that the students who arrive at Aristotle's door already know, or have thought very much about—otherwise they would not have to investigate these matters with him. What the ethical education of a child is missing is a philosophical component, and that must now be added, before he can be called practically wise. However much he learned about justice and the other virtues through experience, he must now reflect upon that experience in a systematic way, by making use of whatever earlier thinkers have written about the subject, and whatever is widely assumed to be correct by sensible people.[7] He must develop a conception of what is good, what virtue is, and so on; because only in that way he will be able to become more articulate and knowledgeable about the highest object of deliberation, and more able to hit the target at which he is aiming (I 2 1094a22–24).

Aristotle is, in this respect, a follower of Socrates. Socrates insists that a good human being must excel as a thinker. He must lead an examined life (Plato's *Apology* 38a), and that is a life in which one skillfully addresses such questions as 'What is good?', 'What is justice?', and 'What is friendship?' Socrates' mistake, according to Aristotle, is to have entirely neglected the preparatory training, which is to a large extent affective, that precedes the philosophical examination of justice and other such matters. He overlooked the vital point that a good person is not only someone who is in good condition as regards the thinking part of the soul, but also as regards the affective part of the soul. Nonetheless, Socratic intellectualism is not entirely abandoned. Aristotle accepts Socrates' radical thesis that philosophy plays an essential role in the acquisition of the virtues. One becomes wise in practical matters only by asking and systematically answering the very questions Socrates posed.[8]

Even if someone has acquired good habits, and then becomes reflective about practical matters, there is no guarantee that he will, as a result of that reflection, become a better person. In fact, it is possible that he will become worse, if he reasons badly about goodness, justice, friendship, and so on. Aristotle makes this observation in his brief discussion of moral education in Book VII of the *Politics*. He notes, as he does in *EN* X 9, that three factors are involved in the process of becoming good: nature, habit, and reason. One must have a soul that has a certain nature; then those natural qualities must be taken in the right direction by a process of habituation; and then those good habits must come under the guidance of reason. But, he notes, reason can undo all of the good work accomplished by the two earlier factors. 'People do many things contrary to their habits and their nature, because of reason, if they are persuaded that it is better to do otherwise' (*Pol.* VII 13 1332b6–8). That is certainly a sound observation. Most habits are not unbreakable, even when they build upon natural dispositions. Nature may incline us in one direction rather than another, and habituation may reinforce those tendencies. But we can stand back from the tendencies that we have acquired in this way, and decide that we should re-shape ourselves. The power of reasoning is sufficient to bring about this transformation.

It might be thought that this remark about the power of reason is contradicted by Aristotle's thesis that thought by itself does not move us. If the whole force of our early education can be overturned because we are persuaded to chart a different course, does that not show that reason can, in isolation from every other element of the soul, affect our behaviour? Or, at any rate, cannot reasoning arrive at the conclusion that we should want to change our lives? And can it not thereby bring about such a desire?

8. The pitfalls of practical reflection

There is no contradiction. But before we see why, we should ask ourselves what Aristotle has in mind when he says that reason can undo the good work of nature and habit. What he must mean is that when a person who has been brought up in good habits begins to reflect on such questions as 'What is good?' and 'What is just?', there is no guarantee that he will arrive at the right answers. The conception of well-being (*eudaimonia*, often translated 'happiness') that he reasons his way towards, as a result of his studies, may be one that denies the value of the very qualities he has acquired. He wants what is good for himself and for others, but he might accept arguments that purport to show that in nearly all cases the course of action that is in his interest is one that requires him to injure other people—to treat them unjustly, to save his skin when he is in danger, to choose the pleasant alternative even when his fellow citizens will thereby suffer, and so on. Aristotle can hold that those conclusions might be arrived at through a genuine process of reasoning, but of course he will insist that entirely *good* reasoning cannot have these results (because the conclusions are false). Unfortunately, he offers no suggestions about why it is that some people are led astray by bad arguments, even when those arguments do not correspond with what they might be inclined to suppose because of their earlier education. Perhaps he assumes that some people are not highly competent when they reflect philosophically upon questions that cannot be answered simply on the basis of beliefs they acquired at an early point in their lives. Perhaps he also supposes that some people are more susceptible than they should be to the persuasive force with which arguments can be invested by skilled and unscrupulous practitioners of the oratorical art.

Those who are led astray by their reflections surely have powerful desires for objects that they take to be good—good for themselves and for others. Those desires are what lead them to investigate, in a reflective and systematic way, general questions about what is good. It would be completely unrealistic to suppose that anyone might undertake a serious study of well-being if he did not already have a desire that he and presumably some others (his family, or friends, or fellow citizens) do well. When thinking about well-being leads someone astray, that is not a counter-example to Aristotle's thesis that thought by itself does not move us, because thinking about well-being is always in service to a desire for well-being (one's own, or that of others, or both). Aristotle's observation that reason can undermine the combined force of nature and habit must be taken to mean, not that reason in isolation from desire can have this effect, but that our desire for what is good, backed by a bad theory about what is good, can be so powerful that it leads us to break even those habits that came naturally to us and gathered strength over the course of our childhood.

But the possibility that Aristotle mentions in *Politics* VII 13—that someone may start off well in life, and then be ruined by bad reasoning—is not something he takes to be the typical course of human development. When things go amiss in the ethical development of a normal human being, they typically do so during that early period when a person is forming the affective and cognitive habits that will guide him over the course of the rest of his life. Before a person gets to the point at which he has the experience and skills of reasoning that make him capable of arriving at a true and philosophical outlook on well-being, he has already developed tendencies to care more about certain things than others. If the habits a person forms are particularly defective, it is very likely, when he reaches the point in life when he can form a general outlook on what is worthwhile, that he will assume that his best policy is to pursue, as much as he can, such goals as physical pleasures, luxuries and comforts, power over others, public honors and so on—even when doing so causes harm to others. Such a person pursues to excess various things that it would be perfectly reasonable to pursue to a moderate degree, but he would not agree with anyone who suggested to him that his pursuit of them is excessive, and it would be rather difficult to persuade him that his way of life is misguided, that he is being led astray by a systematically defective way of making decisions.

Aristotle describes the situation of such a person by saying (VII 8 1151a15–26) that he is mistaken in his starting point (archê, sometimes translated 'principle'). A self-indulgent person, for example, is utterly convinced that well-being consists in pleasure, and it is that assumption that lies behind his plans and undertakings. When he pursues pleasures, nothing within him causes him to doubt that this is the standard he should use to evaluate his options. Furthermore, if someone were to try to prove to him that his equation of well-being with physical pleasure is mistaken, it would be difficult to persuade him that this is the case (X 9 1179b4–18). To begin with, it is likely that he is not the sort of person who will take seriously the possibility that philosophical reflection about practical matters has any value. If one can manage to engage him in conversation, it is not likely that he will enter the discussion with an open mind. And even if he makes a sincere effort to step back and examine his way of life, he is quite limited in what he can bring to this inquiry, because the habits he has formed have closed down his receptivity to certain experiences and their pleasures (b15–16). He may never have developed any enjoyment of treating others justly, for example. And so if we suggest to him that well-being might consist in such acts as these, our proposal will not correspond to anything in his experience. The chances are small, then, that such a person will be able to bring about a change in his fundamental orientation.

If human beings were so constituted that they are always convinced by good arguments about how to get what they most want, we could persuade this person to alter his ways. For he wants, above all, what is best (for himself and presumably at least some others); and good reasoning shows that he is not achieving what is best (for any of them). Unfortunately, human beings are not constructed in this way. In order for us to recognize the cogency of certain arguments about practical matters, we must be a certain kind of person: someone who has formed good habits of feeling. Having a desire for what is good is not enough, even if this desire organizes our practical thinking.

9. 'VIRTUE PRESERVES THE STARTING POINT ...'

This is what Aristotle has in mind when he says that 'virtue preserves the starting point (*archê*), whereas vice destroys it' (VII 8 1151a15–16). What he means, as the rest of this passage shows, is that it is the condition of the affective and reason-responsive part of someone's soul that determines whether 'the starting point' is preserved in him or destroyed. By someone's 'starting point' he means, as he says (a16), the end for the sake of which he acts. We act for the sake of ends even when we are children, and have not yet fully developed our capacity to reflect on them and to ask whether they can be validated. When children have the natural virtues (as they do in normal cases), that affective gift—not their reasoning capacity (which, is after all, extremely rudimentary)—explains why they so often go aright in the ends they set themselves. And then eventually, as they develop, a decisive turning point is reached. In many cases, a maturing person misshapes his character by adopting bad habits of feeling and action. In doing so, he corrupts or destroys the starting point. He still sets ends, of course, but more and more, the ends he sets himself are misguided. There is no way for others to appeal to his reason to set things back on course, because at this point his capacity to reason is not sufficiently mature to make so great a difference in his life. So the starting points he uses to guide himself are not the ones he should have.

But in other cases, a different course of life is selected—again not because people reason their way towards it (their reasoning capacity is still under-developed), but because they have chosen to continue developing the natural virtues with which they started. Their starting points are preserved; that is, the ends they set themselves continue to be good, at least for the most part. What is it that teaches them to have right opinions about the goals they pursue? That is, why is their opinion that *this* (their goal here and now) is the best end so often right? Their capacity to engage in reasoning about ends is still not mature enough to be the dominant factor in their lives. Rather, the reason they so often go aright is that the affective aspect of their souls warms to good goals and is repelled by bad ones.

None of this means that when the capacity to reason about the overall shape of our lives is fully developed, we are locked into a way of thinking from which there is no escape, and so we must simply endorse all the goals we have come to like, on the grounds that we are accustomed to them and find them appealing. The passage we noted in *Politics* VII 13 is by itself enough evidence to show that Aristotle does not have so limited a conception of the power of reason. Even when all goes well in the earlier part of one's life, one might decide to make radical changes, when one comes to reflect on the shape one wants one's life to have over the long term. If one has become the sort of person who is willing to follow arguments wherever they lead, there is nothing that guarantees that one will arrive at the conclusion that well-being consists in virtuous activity, and that the traits one has long assumed are virtues—justice, courage, and the like—really are excellent qualities.

When we engage in philosophical reflection about the ends we should pursue, as Aristotle's students do, and we come to the right conclusion about what well-being is, it might be said that it is *reason* that teaches us the right opinion about the starting points. At any rate, it is by virtue of our using our capacity to reason that we successfully work through the philosophical arguments about well-being. But there would be something quite misleading about saying that we have the right starting points because of our capacity to reason. After all, our capacity to reason is no greater than that of many people who lead unethical lives. It is not as though the arguments philosophers present about the nature of well-being are so complex and difficult that it requires extraordinary intellectual ability to follow them. When we ask, 'Why is it that some adults live their lives well, and pursue worthwhile ends, whereas others do not?', it would be a distortion, Aristotle thinks, to reply that those who are living as they should, do so because they are better able to reason than others. But if we merely say, instead, that, as it happens, some people have in fact reasoned well about these matters (as some no doubt have), and others poorly or not at all (surely there are such people), that statement only pushes our question back one stage: we will then want to know *why* there is this difference amongst people. The answer will be that before the capacity to reason was fully activated, differences amongst these two groups were already at work, and these differences explain why some reasoned well about well-being and others poorly or not at all. Some of them shaped their character in one way, others in another. Those who turned themselves into people with good habits thereby put themselves into an excellent position to understand what is ultimately good; those who did not created a severe handicap for themselves.

But why, it might be asked, did some choose, at an early point in their lives, to acquire good habits, and others did not? To that question, Aristotle offers no answer, and perhaps none is possible. Of course, one can say that some people were fortunate enough to have good parents or good friends or a good community; and others did not. Aristotle is fully aware that these factors make a great difference, but he also insists that we are not entirely passive in our development. In any case, if we point to the influence of these individuals (family, friends, community members) in a person's early life, and appeal to that influence in our explanation of why some have good ends and others do not, we are not disagreeing with Aristotle's claim that it is not reason that makes the difference between these two groups.

When Aristotle says that 'virtue makes the goal (*skopon*) correct (VI 12 1144a7–9; cf. VI 12 1144a20–22) or 'makes one attain the end (*telos*)' (VI 13 1145a5–6), he is presumably making a point identical or quite similar to the one made in the passage we have been examining, in which he claims that natural or habituated virtue is the teacher of right opinion about the starting point (VII 8 1151a17–19). What he means is that the reason why one person starts from the right place in his deliberations, and another from the wrong place, lies in the differences in the conditions of the affective parts of their souls. Deliberation at least occasionally starts from a desire to achieve the good or goods that one equates with well-being.

Some have a correct understanding of what well-being is, whereas others do not. The reason why there is this difference lies in the fact that some have developed good affective habits and others have not.

10. Deliberation about mid-level goals

But the remarks Aristotle makes in VI 12, just cited, may also be intended to have a broader application. For it need not always be the case that the starting point of deliberation is one's conception of well-being. In fact, quite often, a process of practical reasoning is initiated by a desire for a goal that is far more concrete than the one that forms one's conception of *eudaimonia* (happiness).

Obviously, it is not built into the nature of deliberation that it begins from a goal that the deliberator equates with the highest good. If one is trained as a doctor, for example, then on those occasions that call upon one's skills as a doctor, one begins to deliberate by taking as one's end the health of this or that patient. That need not mean that one takes health to be the highest good a human being can attain. And there are presumably many other cases in which one is confronted with a situation that calls for deliberation, and in which one does not reach all the way back to a conception of well-being and take that to be the starting point of one's practical thinking.[9] In certain situations, for example, if one is a good human being, one will immediately want to help someone in need of assistance. But other people who are in precisely those circumstances will have no such desire. (Conversely, a good person will at times want to prevent someone from getting what he seeks, whereas a bad person will lend him a hand.) The series of mental events that is included in any particular process of deliberation is initiated not by a process of reasoning, but by a desire for a certain goal. In some cases, it is precisely the goal that someone should be trying to achieve in the circumstances; in other cases, it is the wrong goal. Are those who go aright in their deliberations about these concrete ends merely lucky, in that they happen to start at the right place? Not at all: they start at the right place because of the good condition of the affective element of their souls. They are the sort of people who love to help their friends, and that is why they immediately feel a desire to give them assistance, and to find a way to do so, whenever they recognize that their friends need them.

But Aristotle does not believe that this is the whole story. For if someone has thought about what well-being is—and a practically wise person is someone who has done this—then he has asked himself whether it is good to have friends, and good (for himself and others) to cultivate and act on a desire to help them, and what it is that helping another human being consists in. In a fully virtuous person, the deliberative process that begins with a desire to help a friend is not an episode that is unconnected to other events in his mental history, nor is it unrelated to any other component of his psychology. Even though this particular bout of deliberative thinking did not start with a conscious rehearsal of thoughts about what well-being consists in, a good person's conception of well-being informs all of his deliberations. For whenever he aims at a goal, he aims at something that he takes to be good, and he must take it to be good because it has a place in his general understanding of what *eudaimonia* or well-being is. If he is deliberating about a good that he takes to play a subordinate role amongst a hierarchy of ends—if, for example, he is trying to restore his friend to health, not because he takes health to be the good itself, but rather because he considers it an essential condition of well-being—then he will be able to give a justification for wanting to restore his friend to health, even though the process of deliberation he actually went through did not include that justification. (Presumably, he wanted to help immediately after he saw that he was needed, without consciously thinking about how to justify that desire, and without rehearsing in his mind his ideas about what well-being is.)

We may ask why he deliberated about *that* concrete and correct goal (his friend's health). The answer is: because he had a desire to secure it. Why did he have that desire? Because the affective part of his soul is disposed in a certain way—a good way. How did it come to be disposed in that way? Because a complex process of training produced it—a process that included both excellent reflection about the ends a person should pursue because they are best, and excellent habituation of the emotions. Why did he develop in these good ways, whereas others have not? The single most important explanatory difference, as we have seen, lies in feeling rather than reason: for the most part, the reason why some develop practical wisdom and complete ethical virtue, whereas others do not, consists in the difference between the ways they were habituated before they achieved full rationality. That is why Aristotle thinks that, on the one hand, the possession of practical wisdom should be invoked as the explanation of why someone does well in the way he proceeds from the ends he sets; and why, on the other hand, it is not practical wisdom but virtue of character (natural or habituated) that explains why someone starts thinking about what to do here rather than there—proceeding from a desire for this worthwhile goal rather than some misguided end he might have pursued instead.

11. EXCEPTIONS TO RULES AND THE PERCEPTION OF PARTICULARS

Let us look more closely now, not at the developmental process that leads to full virtue, but to its final result. What is a good person like, according to Aristotle? He is someone whose reason and emotions are so well-trained and harmonious that he can determine what the best action is, in any situation he encounters, and is glad to perform such actions precisely because they fit their occasion.[10] What makes a good person stand out, according to this picture, is not his understanding of or adherence to a list of rules or any other body of propositions, but a problem-solving cognitive and affective skill. Aristotle's conception of a good human being, so described, seems to be a very different person from the paragon of moral goodness who inhabits the pages of a great deal of modern moral philosophy, especially that portion of it that has been influenced by Kant.

Kant's ideal agent is a follower of universal moral laws—exceptionless principles that any rational being is capable of formulating, and the application of which to particular circumstances rarely requires extraordinary efforts or unusual insight. Everyone, Kant assumes, knows that it is morally wrong to make false promises, to tell lies, to take one's life merely to relieve one's unhappiness, to be indifferent to the happiness of others, and so on. It might be thought that Aristotle's good person, by contrast, excels in each situation not because he has in his head a rule book (not, at any rate, a book of exceptionless rules), but rather because he has developed a sharp eye for detail that the recognition of general principles cannot by itself impart.

We have already begun to see why this contrast between the Aristotelian and the Kantian portraits of a good person cannot be quite right, as it stands. At any rate, I have presented (in sections 3 and 7) the fully virtuous agent, as Aristotle conceives him, as someone who has engaged in ethical reflection of a very high order. He has employed a philosophical methodology to arrive at a conception of human well-being, and this is what guides him in all that he does. He excels at determining what should be done in each situation because he recognizes that certain goods (namely, the excellent activities of the rational soul), being precisely what *eudaimonia* is, take priority over all others. He knows how to deal with the particulars of each situation because he has learned how to classify those particulars—to see that they should be grouped together, and in that sense are instances of a universal rule.

Nonetheless, Aristotle emphasizes, almost from the start of the *Nicomachean Ethics*, that because there is considerable variation in the subject of his investigation, we must be satisfied with truths that hold only for the most part, and not universally (I 3 1094b14–22). It is likely that he expects his audience to be familiar with this point, since he says so little to support it. Presumably he takes them to be familiar with the passage in Plato's *Republic* in which Socrates reminds Polemarchus that one must not give a weapon back to its owner if he has gone mad (331e-332a). Socrates is not denying that in general it is right to return what one owes; he is merely pointing out that we must make an exception when giving back what one owes is likely to cause great damage. No one in this dialogue suggests that we might be able to formulate an exceptionless principle complex enough to cover all circumstances in which one should pay what one owes. Justice is understood as a harmony of the soul, rather than adherence to a list of complex and exceptionless rules.

It might similarly be supposed that, according to Aristotle, a good person cannot be defined as someone who abides by such and such exceptionless universal statements. At any rate, when he discusses the individual virtues—courage, moderation, generosity, and so on—he shows no interest in formulating a list of rules to which a person who has these virtues adheres. The courageous person, for example, is described as someone who will have the right degree of fear and confidence—the degree, in other words, that is suitable to the circumstances he confronts. Will such a person always stand his ground, and never retreat? Of course not. Similarly, the person who excels with respect to anger may sometimes strike out in anger—but only when such an action is called for by the circumstances. What is true of him without exception is that he has and expresses the amount of anger that is appropriate to the occasion.

It might be suggested that for Aristotle it is nonetheless important that an ethical agent have in his head a large stock of generalizations that hold for the most part. For example, being courageous might consist partly in knowing that as a general rule a courageous person stands his ground. Similarly, having excellent control over anger might consist partly in knowing that for the most part one should not express one's anger violently. But Aristotle seems uninterested in the project of formulating generally but not universally valid practical rules. At any rate, even if he tacitly assumes that there are many such propositions, that still leaves the ethical agent with the ongoing burden of deciding, case by case, whether he is now confronted with circumstances in which a rule that is true in many cases is also true in this one. Even if one should, for the most part, restrain the expression of anger, that would give one no reason to hold back in *this* instance, if every aspect of the current situation indicates that here and now the expression of anger is the only satisfactory response.

Other passages also point to the conclusion that for Aristotle practical generalizations, even those that admit of exceptions, are peripheral to ethical life. We get an unmistakable hint of this at the end of his criticism of the Platonic conception of the good (I 6). He points out that doctors, so far from needing knowledge of the form of the good, do not need even an understanding of *health*. What they must study, he says, is not health, period, but *human* health. And even that, Aristotle immediately adds, is not quite so: what a doctor examines is the health of *this* human being, 'for he heals individual by individual' (1097a14). A doctor, in other words, must be attentive to the ways in which the particular patient he is healing differs from all others. Medication that works for the most part must not be used in any individual case if, in the particular instance, it will be harmless or worse.

That point about health is one that Aristotle expects his readers to apply to the kinds of goods with which the ethical agent deals. But it remains submerged in the *Nicomachean Ethics* until he makes it explicit in his treatment of the virtues as intermediate states (II 6). In that discussion, he insists that just as a doctor will prescribe a diet that is peculiarly appropriate to an athlete in training, and not some amount of food that is halfway between what is generally excessive and generally deficient, so too the ethical agent will aim at a relative, not an absolute, mean. He will, in other words, look for what is neither excessive nor deficient with respect to the individuals who will be affected by what he does (1106a25–b5). Even if it is true for the most part that human beings need only a moderate level of external resources to live well (X 8 1179a12–13), a particular person in certain circumstances may need more (or less) than that. That generalization about the adequacy of moderate resources is salient only as a guideline, and has no force as a justification in unusual circumstances. And whether the present circumstances are usual or unusual is a matter that requires constant attention.

Aristotle calls practical wisdom (*phronêsis*: the virtue by which we excel as practical reasoners) the 'eye of the soul' (VI 12 1144a29–30), and notes that those who have a great deal of experience can often use that experience to 'see correctly' (VI 11 1143b13–14). Those perceptual expressions suggest that over time some people develop the ability to size up the situations they encounter and to sense immediately what their alternatives are, which reasons favour or disfavour alternative courses of action, and what, all things considered, should be done. They know what to do in each situation because they have become discerning people. They might be able to formulate reliable generalizations or even exceptionless rules, but whether they can articulate such propositions or not, what accounts for their going right is their case-by-case perceptiveness. The rules that they might formulate would be mere summaries of what they have learned by their familiarity with many cases. Clearly, if that is the status of ethical generalizations, they are, at most, secondary elements of ethical life.

In several passages, Aristotle speaks of the virtuous person as a standard (*kanôn*) or measure (*metron*) of ethical truths (III 5 1113a33, X 5 1176a17–19). [11] What appears to be the case to an ordinary or corrupt person—what he takes to be pleasant, or fine, or advantageous—may not be such. But what appears to a good person to be pleasant, fine, or advantageous must really be so; that is what permits Aristotle to call him a standard or measure. We should not take this to mean that ethical truths are made true by their appearing to be the case to a good person. The order of explanation goes the other way: what makes someone a good person is the ability to discern ethical truth. In calling good human beings a standard or measure, Aristotle is asking his readers to conceive of them not as flesh and blood people whom they have occasionally encountered (for all of these real people may occasionally err), but as perfect models or paradigms to which we can only aspire.

We might find in the paradigmatic status of the good person another indication that universal generalizations play no important role in Aristotle's ethical theory. A follower of Kant would never say that the good person is the measure or standard of moral rightness. For a Kantian, what makes an action right, rather, is its conformity to the moral law: that universal principle is the standard or measure to which we should look, as we act. But we might conjecture that Aristotle does not explain rightness in this way because he does not believe that there is any moral principle that provides the measure of the rightness of an act. A conclusion about what is to be done in any particular case is something that results from premises about the circumstances of that particular case, not from the fact that the selected act falls under a general rule. A good person is an ideal discerner of such circumstances.

12. MURDER, THEFT, AND ADULTERY

But now we must turn to a passage that seems to cast doubt on the accuracy of the picture we have been drawing. Aristotle says at one point that certain actions and emotions are 'named in such a way that directly connects them with badness'" (*phaulotês*) (II 6 1107a9–10), and as examples of such actions he mentions (a11–12) *moicheia* ('adultery', 'fornication'), *klopê* (theft), and *androphonia* (murder). We cannot take him to mean that for the most part such actions should be avoided, for he says explicitly that when any of these terms applies to an action, that settles the matter: the agent has gone wrong (*hamartanein*, a17).

The Greek word *androphonia* (literally: 'man killing') had a special legal sense, and was used in the courtroom to designate the sorts of crimes that would now be called homicide, manslaughter, murder, and so on. It is reasonable to assume that this is the way in which Aristotle is using the word here, since he certainly does not mean to say that killing a human being is always wrong. Presumably his idea is that if someone has committed the sort of crime that is properly classified as *androphonia*, then he has, in all cases, done what he ought not (whether or not he has been indicted or convicted). That leaves room for the possibility that even when a killing falls within the category of legally prohibited acts, the law cited by the prosecutor might be too general, and the killer might in fact be blameless. Should that be the case, any equitable juror will realize that the killer is to be acquitted and the defect in the law corrected (V 10). So, although *androphonia* is always blameworthy, what counts as *androphonia* is not a matter that is entirely settled solely by the law; in order to justify applying the word *androphonia* to someone's action, one must show that he deserves to be blamed for what he did.

It would be a mistake to infer that it is empty or trivial to claim that *androphonia* is always wrong. If someone has violated the law of *androphonia*, he has done something whose justification can always be appropriately questioned by other members of his community. Unless it can be shown that there is a defect in the law that was violated, and that the sort of killing that took place is not one that the legislator could have meant to ban, he has, in all such cases, gone seriously wrong. So, at any rate, says Aristotle.

Like the word *androphonia*, *moicheia* (adultery) and *klopê* (theft) were legal terms, and we can assume that Aristotle is using them in that sense. Although it should not be taken for granted that *moicheia* was applied to all and only the sorts of acts that are typically classified as adultery in modern societies, it is certainly a term that would apply to sexual intercourse between a man and a woman who is legally recognized as the wife of another (living) man. In subscribing to the view, commonplace in his time and place, that no one should ever engage in adultery, Aristotle is being more strict than some readers may expect him to be, in light of the opening pronouncement of the *Ethics* that in this subject we are discussing what holds true only for the most part and not universally.

His unconditional condemnation of theft also shows a surprising strictness. In fact, it is reasonable to suppose that Aristotle is being *too* strict about this matter. Why, for example, should one not take away one's friend's weapon even without his permission, if he has become dangerous to himself or others? That would normally be described as justified theft. Could it be that Aristotle disagrees, and would withhold the term *klopê* when taking someone's possessions is the best thing to do? Perhaps. But in any case it is far-fetched to make the same supposition about *moicheia*. It is doubtful that, according to Aristotle, sexual intercourse with the wife of another (living) man can ever be justified.

Nonetheless, we should be careful not to make too much of the fact that Aristotle recognizes a few exceptionless principles. When he says, for example, that adultery is always wrong, he need not be taken to mean that each particular act of adultery is to be avoided because it would violate a general principle for the regulation of human behaviour. For the direction of explanation may go from the particular cases to the general rule, rather than the other way round. In other words, the universal generalization that all adultery is wrong may rest on the fact that, without exception, each particular act of adultery has brought about so much harm. This particular act of adultery should be avoided because it does great harm to A and B; that one because it does great harm to C and D; and so on. Noticing how destructive each act of infidelity is, we generalize, and say that this sort of behaviour is always to be avoided. It is not because there is a rule against adultery that it is wrong whenever it occurs; rather, it does great harm whenever it occurs, and that is why we can correctly formulate an exceptionless generalization about its wrongness. So, at any rate, Aristotle might suppose.

Our passage in *EN* II 6 does not tell us which is the correct order of explanation—from each particular instance to a universal generalization, or the other way round—but it would fit well with Aristotle's general approach to practical matters to make the exceptionless universal rule rest on all of its instances. For he emphasizes the importance of experience in practical matters, and can reasonably be taken to mean that in order to recognize the truth of practical principles that hold for the most part, one must have considerable experience of the areas of human life governed by those principles (VI 8 1142a11–15, VI 11 1143b11–14). To realize, for example, that generally repaying a creditor takes priority over lending money to a friend (IX 2 1164b31–3), one must know, from first-hand experience, something about friendship, economic transactions, and the like. Someone might come to *believe* this generalization because he has read it in a book, but in any case, we can take Aristotle to mean that it cannot be *known* by someone unless he has acquired considerable familiarity with particular facts, and uses those facts to support the generalization. It is reasonable to make the same point about the hand-ful of exceptionless rules that Aristotle endorses. If adultery, for example, is always to be avoided, that is because in each and every case it does great harm. Presumably knowledge of that universal truth rests on long familiarity with the way in which adultery affects the lives of husbands, wives, children, and other members of the community.

13. JUSTICE AND LAW

But universal truths about practical matters have a far more important role to play in Aristotle's conception of practical thinking than we have recognized so far. That gap in our understanding must now be filled.

To begin with, we must keep in mind that Aristotle characterizes the person who has the general virtue of justice as *nomimos* (*EN* V 1 1129a33). (The term can be translated 'lawful' or 'law-abiding'.) It is clear from his political writings that it is one mark of a well-governed city that its rulers and citizens hold the *nomoi* (laws, whether written or unwritten) of the community in high regard, and generally abide by them (*Pol.* III 16 1287a28–32, IV 4 1292a1–6, IV 5 1292b4–7). Laws by their very nature are general (*EN* V 10 1137b13). Aristotle distinguishes them from decrees (*psêphismata*), which are directives meant to apply only to the situation at hand; and he warns against excessive reliance on these short-term and highly specific rules or commands (*Pol.* IV 4 1292a4–37, IV 6 1293a30–34). It is precisely because laws are by their nature applicable to a wide variety of circumstances that Aristotle thinks they are, from time to time, in need of judicial correction. Generalizations about practical matters always run the risk of overlooking the complexity of their subject.

We should also remind ourselves that Aristotle conceives of the work we call the *Nicomachean Ethics* as a contribution to political philosophy. He notes in I 2 that the subject being investigated is one that belongs to political science to study. As he proceeds, he reminds the reader several times that his topics are those that a good legislator must understand,[12] and he closes (X 9) with arguments for the importance of carrying forward his results to the study of constitutional design. Making, applying, and abiding by the laws of the community are not peripheral activities of the audience for whom this treatise is intended. The virtuous indi-viduals who are Aristotle's audience are therefore, in a certain sense, people who are pre-occupied with rules—or rather, with certain kinds of rules, namely *nomoi*. (These are the social norms of existing political communities. By contrast, Kant conceives of the good person as someone who abides by the ideal legislation of a notional realm—the kingdom of ends.) That does not mean that *every* act they undertake is chosen because it falls under a rule. Nor does it mean that they always abide by or enforce the rules of their community—for sometimes laws are overly general and are not to be strictly applied or enforced. But even though Aristotle never holds that all right action is obedience to some law or other, he assumes that it is the very nature of a good human being that he tends to be a good citizen, that good citizenship involves taking an active part in civic affairs, and that this consists in deliberating with others in the assembly, serving on juries, doing one's share in ruling and being ruled, and abiding by the community's written rules and unwritten norms, all of which are general in scope (*Pol.* I 1 1275a22–3, III 4 1277b13–16).

14. THE PRACTICAL VALUE OF ETHICAL REFLECTION

To return now to a theme of sections 3 and 7: it must be emphasized that, according to Aristotle, certain additional universal truths—beyond those that affirm the wrongness of murder, theft, and adultery—are of great practical value. Any human being who fails to recognize them will go seriously astray. These universal practical truths are the ones that constitute his ethical theory. They are not generalizations that most speakers of English would call 'moral principles' or even 'moral generalizations'. Nonetheless, one cannot be the sort of individual Aristotle would count as a good human being unless one recognizes the truths of these exceptionless generalizations, and puts them into practice.

Consider, for example, the generalization with which the *Nicomachean Ethics* opens: 'every craft and every inquiry, and likewise every action and decision, seems to aim at some good ...' (I 1 1094a1–2). That can reasonably be taken to mean that whenever we act for a reason, the reason that we propose to ourselves adverts to something good that our action does for someone. We can also safely take Aristotle to be assuming that this is as it should be: all rational action *ought* to be an attempt to do something good for someone.

The statement that we ought always to do some good might not be labeled a 'moral principle', or for that matter, any sort of 'principle'. Nonetheless, it is an exceptionless generalization to which Aristotle subscribes. And it would be a mistake to suppose that it has little or no practical import. Of course, the statement that one must do good does not, on its own, tell one which particular actions one must perform, because it does not say anything about what is good. But that does not show that the command to do only what is good is insignificant. One need only remind oneself that it rules out returning harm for harm, which is one common conception of justice. Returning harm for harm does no good: its point is to make someone worse off, not better off.

Aristotle's statement that we always aim at something good leads him to notice that goods differ in importance, and this sends him searching for an account of which goods are highest. He realizes that this is a contested question. Although he does not expect anyone to question the assumption that we rightly aim at good, he knows that people differ about what is good and also about which goods are most desirable. His claim that the highest good consists in the excellent exercise of the reasoning and reason-responsive parts of the soul (*EN* I 7 1098a16–18) is not meant to express a point that all human beings already believe. He knows that it is a thesis that some will reject, and that he will be unable to persuade everyone that it is true. Furthermore, he presents it as a truth of considerable practical value. Just as an archer will better be able to hit his target if he knows something about what he is aiming at, so we will better be able to achieve the highest good if we develop a theory about what it is (*EN* I 2 1094a22–6).

We might say, then, that in a way Aristotle is trying to give his students the propositional knowledge of practical truths that Socrates sought from his interlocutors. Recall what Socrates seeks in the *Euthyphro*, for example: he wants to know whether what his interlocutor is about to do—prosecute his father—is pious; and of course he wants to know whether the charges against him—that he has been guilty of impiety in the conduct of his life—are correct. And to do that, he is looking for a criterion by which he can determine which acts are pious, and an explanation for their piety or impiety. He is searching for a theory—a body of propositions—that will help him make decisions. He will not be satisfied with the response that when it comes to decision-making, we need know-how, and not propositional knowledge. Socrates' outlook is also Aristotle's. He takes it to be obvious that if you cannot say what the highest good is, you are rather unlikely to achieve it.

Aristotle does not suffer from the illusion that ethical theory can eliminate or diminish the difficulty we so often have when we make decisions about everyday matters. It cannot provide what we would call a 'mechanical' decision procedure: an 'algorithm' for sizing up each particular situation and deciding which of the alternatives that face us is the best choice. Deliberation, as Aristotle conceives of it, is necessarily a process that resists routinization (III 1112a34-b9). To deliberate well, one needs not only a general picture of what living well consists in; one also needs to become astute at foreseeing consequences, at imagining alternatives, at finding the right means to one's ends, at perceiving telling details, and so on. But in addition to these skills, one must also bring to one's decision-making the general framework that only a philosophical training can provide—a framework in which one seeks something good in every situation, recognizes that some goods are worth choosing over others, that some goods are not to be sought without limit, and that some are to be welcomed only when they are combined with others. Without that general framework, one will not be able to excel as a friend, or a parent, or a citizen, because one will not understand what it is that one should be trying to help one's friends, children, and fellow citizens achieve.

This way of reading Aristotle places him firmly in the camp of Socrates and Plato. Each finds a way of saying that in order to excel as a human being—in order to be a completely just, wise, good person—one must use a distinctively philosophical methodology to construct a normative theory. One cannot rest content with the skills, concepts, and commonsense outlook that one receives when one goes through the normal developmental processes of childhood. For Aristotle, that childhood training is a prerequisite for the further intellectual explorations one must undertake as an adult, if one wants to complete one's moral education and become a genuinely good human being.

Notes

1. He refers to his *êthika* or *êthikoi logoi* (ethical discourses) at *Politics* II 2 1261a31, III 9 1280a18, III 12 1282b20, IV 11 1295a36, VII 13 1332a8, and VII 13 1332a22. I assume that these are references to the *Eudemian Ethics*, but that leaves intact the point that he would not object to calling what we know as the *Nicomachean Ethics* an *êthikos logos*. On the compositional order of these works, see Kraut, *Aristotle: Political Philosophy*, Oxford: Oxford University Press, 2002, pp. 16–19.

2. For a recent theory of action that provides a striking alternative to Aristotle's, by giving the recognition of reasons a far larger role to play in human motivation, see T.M. Scanlon, *What We Owe to Each Other*, Cambridge, Mass.: Belknap Press, 1998, pp. 33–55.

3. I set aside a merely verbal question: does cleverness take us from a *prohairesis* to some mental state whose content is more concrete than that of a *prohairesis*? Or is the content of a *prohairesis* precisely whichever concrete type of action that cleverness has settled upon?

4. Readers should also consult T.H. Irwin, 'Aristotle on Reason, Desire and Virtue', *Journal of Philosophy* 72 (1975), 567–78; and M.F. Burnyeat, 'Aristotle on Learning to be Good', in Amélie Oksenberg Rorty, *Essays on Aristotle's Ethics*, Berkeley: University of California Press, 1980, pp. 69–92.

5. Aristotle calls human beings naturally political in seven passages: *HA* I 1 487b33–488a14; *EN* I 7 1097b11, VIII 12 1162a17–18, IX 9 1169b18–19; *EE* VII 10 1242a22–3; *Pol.* I 2 1253a7–8, III 6 1278b19. In some of these passages (e.g., *EN* IX 9) he is alluding to our aversion to complete isolation, but in others (e.g., *Pol.* III 6)) he posits a tendency to enter into cooperative relations beyond those of the family, and without regard to the instrumental value of such relations. For discussion, see Kraut, *Aristotle: Political Philosophy*, pp. 247–53. I elaborate more fully on these ideas in 'Nature in Aristotle's Ethics and Politics', in David Keyt and Fred Miller Jr., eds., *Ancient Greek Political Theory* (2007), Cambridge: Cambridge University Press.

6. For a helpful discussion, which I follow here, see Richard Sorabji, 'Aristotle on the Role of Intellect in Virtue', in Rorty, ed., *Essays on Aristotle's Ethics* (1980), pp. 201–220.

7. On Aristotle's method for arriving at a full understanding of ethics, see Richard Kraut, 'How to Justify Ethical Propositions: Aristotle's Method', in Richard Kraut, ed., *The Blackwell Guide to Aristotle's Nicomachean Ethics*, Malden, Mass: Blackwell, 2006, pp. 76–95.

8. For a different way of reading Aristotle, see Sarah Broadie, *Ethics with Aristotle*, New York: Oxford University Press, 1991, pp. 198–202. My view is further developed in Richard Kraut, 'In Defense of the Grand End', *Ethics* 103 (1993), pp. 361–74.

9. See III 1 1110a13–15, where Aristotle speaks of an end (*telos*) not as something that is a standing goal over a long stretch of one's life, but something that is sought when the right time for it occurs. At III 3 1112b15–26, he notes that we sometimes conclude that we should not pursue an end after discovering that it cannot be achieved. That is the sort of thing that happens often enough in our pursuit of short-term and highly concrete goals, but rarely in our pursuit of the aims that remain in place and guide us over the course of a lifetime.

10. On the good person's internal harmony, see I 13 1102b26–8 and IX 4 1166a13–29; his unerring ability to determine how to act, II 6 1106b21–3 and III 4 1113a32–3; his enjoyment of exercising the virtues, I 8 1099a7–15 and II 3 1104b3–8.

11. For further discussion, see Timothy Chappell, '"The Good Man is the Measure of All Things": Objectivity without World-Centeredness in Aristotle's Moral Epistemology', in Christopher Gill, ed., *Virtue, Norms, and Objectivity: Issues in Ancient and Modern Ethics*, Oxford: Clarendon Press, 2005, pp. 233–56.

12. See *EN* I 3 1095a2–3, I 4 1095a14–17, I 4 1095b4–6, I 9 1099b29–32, I 13 1102a7–9, I 13 1102a18–21, II 3 1105a10–12, and VII 11 1152b1–2.

BIBLIOGRAPHY

Broadie, Sarah (1991) *Ethics with Aristotle* (New York: Oxford Univ. Press).

Brown, Lesley (1997) 'What Is the Mean Relative to Us in Aristotle's Ethics?' *Phronesis* 42, 77–93.

Burnyeat, Myles F. (1980) 'Aristotle on Learning to Be Good', in Amélie Oksenberg Rorty, ed., *Essays on Aristotle's Ethics* (Berkeley: University of California Press), 69–92.

Chappell, Timothy (2005) "The Good Man Is the Measure of All Things": Objectivity without World-Centeredness in Aristotle's Moral Epistemology', in Christopher Gill, ed., *Virtue, Norms, and Objectivity: Issues in Ancient and Modern Ethics* (Oxford: Clarendon Press), 233–56.

Cooper, John M. (1999) *Reason and Emotion: Essays on Ancient Moral Psychology and Ethical Theory* (Princeton: Princeton Univ. Press).

Engberg-Pedersen, Troels (1983) *Aristotle's Theory of Moral Insight* (Oxford: Clarendon Press).

Gottlieb, Paula (2009) *The Virtue of Aristotle's Ethics* (Cambridge: Cambridge Univ. Press).

Hardie, William F. R. (1980) *Aristotle's Ethical Theory*, 2nd ed. (Oxford: Clarendon Press).

Hutchinson, D.S. (1986) *The Virtues of Aristotle* (London: Routledge & Kegan Paul).

Irwin, Terence (1975) 'Aristotle on Reason, Desire and Virtue', *Journal of Philosophy* 72, 567–78.

——— (1988) *Aristotle's First Principles* (Oxford: Clarendon Press).

Kraut, Richard (1993) 'In Defense of the Grand End', *Ethics* 103, 361–74.

——— (2002) *Aristotle: Political Philosophy* (Oxford: Oxford Univ. Press).

——— (2006) 'How to Justify Ethical Propositions: Aristotle's Method', in Richard Kraut, ed., *The Blackwell Guide to Aristotle's Nicomachean Ethics* (Malden, Mass: Blackwell).

——— (2007) 'Nature in Aristotle's Ethics and Politics', in David Keyt and Fred D. Miller, Jr., eds., *Freedom, Reason, and the Polis: Essays in Ancient Greek Political Philosophy* (Cambridge: Cambridge Univ. Press), 199–219.

Lorenz, Hendrik (2006) *The Brute Within: Appetitive Desire in Plato and Aristotle* (Oxford: Clarendon Press).

―――― (2009) 'Virtue of Character in Aristotle's Nicomachean Ethics', *Oxford Studies in Ancient Philosophy* 37, 177–212.

McDowell, John (2009) 'Deliberation and Moral Development in Aristotle's Ethics', in J. McDowell, *The Engaged Intellect: Philosophical Essays* (Cambridge: Harvard Univ. Press), 41–58.

Moss, Jessica (forthcoming) *Aristotle on the Apparent Good* (Oxford: Oxford Univ. Press).

Nussbaum, Martha C. (1986) *The Fragility of Goodness* (Cambridge: Cambridge Univ. Press).

Pearson, Giles (2011) 'Non-rational desire and Aristotle's moral psychology', in Jon Miller, ed., *Aristotle's Nicomachean Ethics: A Critical Guide* (Cambridge: Cambridge Univ. Press), 144–169.

Reeve, C.D.C. (1992) *Practices of Reason* (Oxford: Oxford Univ. Press).

Scanlon, Thomas M. (1998) *What We Owe to Each Other* (Cambridge, Mass.: Belknap Press).

Sorabji, Richard (1980) 'Aristotle on the Role of Intellect in Virtue', in Amélie Oksenberg Rorty, ed., *Essays on Aristotle's Ethics* (Berkeley: University of California Press), 201–220.

Vasiliou, Iakovos (2011) 'Aristotle, agents, and actions', in Jon Miller, ed., *Aristotle's Nicomachean Ethics: A Critical Guide* (Cambridge: Cambridge Univ. Press), 170–190.

Wiggins, David (1975) 'Deliberation and Practical Reason', in Amélie Oksenberg Rorty, ed., *Essays on Aristotle's Ethics* (Berkeley: University of California Press), 221–240.

CHAPTER 21

ARISTOTLE'S *POLITICS*

PIERRE PELLEGRIN

I. The Position of Politics in Aristotle's Thought

Is there something like an Aristotelian political thought or philosophy? Apparently so: we have a special treatise by Aristotle which takes as its object the consideration of the city (*polis*)—its components, its functioning, and, most of all, the different possible forms of constitution it may have. This treatise was probably given its title, *Politics*, by Aristotle himself,[1] though it has come down to us in what seems an unfinished or amputated form. We also have the *Constitution of the Athenians*, which preserves a trace of the 'political' documents gathered by Aristotle and his colleagues and students in the Lyceum. Ancient sources report that they had compiled 158 constitutions of different cities and peoples. But it is important to avoid anachronism, and so to be aware of the position Aristotle attributes to his political research. As we shall see, his political philosophy, if any, is based upon an analysis, objective as well as prescriptive, of the political reality of his day. But such an analysis is affected by at least two factors: first, Aristotle's own conception of knowledge and philosophy, and, second, the specific characteristics of the crucial historical period Aristotle was living in.

The first of these factors is particularly obvious if one compares, as has been often done, Aristotle's texts on the city to those by Plato. Here, though, caution will be required. As we shall come to appreciate, one idea commonly sounded among historians of political doctrines is wholly false. This is the idea that Aristotle was a realist who intended to correct Plato's utopian excesses. Rather, the main difference between Plato and Aristotle is probably in the kind of autonomy each offers 'political science'. According to Plato, at least in the *Republic*, there is no real political science, because there is only one science, which he calls 'dialectic', which encompasses everything. The dialectician alone, because he masters the general principles of knowledge, is truly a geometer, an astronomer...and also the legislator and the ruler of a good city. The only king that such a city deserves is the philosopher. Aristotle, by contrast, has an approach that divides knowledge into theoretical and practical domains, and attributes different aspects of the theoretical domain, together with what he calls 'human affairs', to different sciences.[2] What Aristotle refers to as the 'practical sciences', which deal with contingent objects depending on human will, exhibit a rationality of their own. The clearest evidence for this is perhaps the difference between virtue as applied to the theoretical and practical domains. It is not the same virtue which makes people excellent in both. Aristotle is probably the first thinker who has made explicit the distinction between the excellent theoretician, who possesses 'wisdom' (*sophia*), and the excellent practitioner, who possesses 'prudence' (*phronêsis*): Thales and Anaxagoras, Aristotle says, are wise, but not prudent.[3]

But in the practical domain, i.e., the domain of human actions, Aristotle does not restrict politics to what we call, and what ancient Greeks probably also called, 'politics', that is, to the administration of the city. What we call—and what the very titles of some Aristotelian treatises seem to induce us to call—'ethics' and 'politics' are not properly speaking different disciplines, but aspects, or moments, of one and the same research programme, the object of which is a specific rational knowledge aiming at reaching the 'human good', both individual (which is the object of ethics), and collective (which is the object of politics). Now, it is noteworthy that when he wants to label the knowledge sought in this research programme Aristotle calls it 'politics'. It is therefore not entirely surprising that it is in the *Nicomachean Ethics* that we find Aristotle offering his most complete definition of the term 'politics'. Properly speaking, politics and prudence are one and the same state,[4] though one can speak of 'politics' at different levels: 'of the disposition as it relates to the city, the architectonic form of wisdom is legislative expertise, while the form of wisdom at the level of particulars is known by the generic name "politics", and this is concerned with action and deliberation, since a decree is something to be acted upon, as what comes last in the process' (*EN* 1141b24–28, Rowe mod.). The eminent form of political wisdom is that of the legislator, whereas what is usually, and, according to Aristotle, rightly, called 'politics' is restricted to the sphere of the particular. At least three meanings of the term 'politics' are therefore available: it may refer to the whole sphere of the human good, and in this sense it includes ethics; it may also refer to the wisdom of the politician par excellence, viz. the legislator; and, finally, it may indicate the specific skill of one who partakes in the administration of the city.

In the practical area, the 'architectonic' science is politics, because, according to the very definition of 'architectonic', it uses the other sciences, while they do not use it, just as the 'architect', in the etymological sense, uses workers who do not use him in return. But there is a more specific reason to offer so dominant a position to politics. 'The true politician', Aristotle says, 'will have worked at virtue more than anything; for what he wants is to make the members of the citizen-body good, and obedient to the laws' (*EN* 1102a8). Now, since Aristotle thinks that virtue is the end product of repeated good actions, and that what is good and bad is, in the last resort, determined by laws, one can understand why the existence and the enforcement of good laws are the basic conditions for virtue among individuals.

'Political science' is then not under the tutelage of theoretical sciences. This does not mean, however, that it is an empirical discipline. This is clear from what has been said already. To describe the domain of politics as that of 'prudence' (*phronêsis*) is to warn against two possible deviations: (i) against any kind of intellectualism, since theoretical knowledge concerns the universal, and, as Aristotle often reminds us, the prudential person is someone who has knowledge of the particular;[5] and (ii) against a kind of narrowly empiricist orientation, which Aristotle's prudent person needs to avoid when referring to both the particular and the universal. Actually, the relationship between politics and theory needs to be considered more closely.

II. POLITICS AND THEORY

In the *Nicomachean Ethics*, Aristotle wonders to whom the ethical treatises written by the philosopher should be addressed. For such treatises do not share the status of the treatises aimed at pure speculation, but have instead a practical goal. Aristotle speaks ironically of those who replace medical treatments with the reading of medical books. In politics too, the goal is to realize the conditions for virtue in the citizen's life, which is the main condition for happiness. That acknowledged, practice does not preclude theory. Although no one is cured by reading a medical book, this fact hardly rules out out the study of medicine; in the same way, the legislator cannot ignore the theoretical disciplines which concern his domain of action. Here we find what is probably the main reason for the composite character of Aristotle's *Politics*. It contains 'prescriptive' texts, which indicate what to do in order to help the city to reach its goal, and also 'objective' texts, which analyse historical and social reality. Of course, this does not rule out the idea, supported by many commentators, that these texts might derive from different periods in Aristotle's career, and that they may have been put together either by Aristotle himself or by some editor. Even so, it is unnecessary, and indeed unwarranted, to explain the difference in perspective of these passages primarily by presumed differences in the dates of their composition. In fact, Aristotle never saw any reason to depart from his prescriptive point of view. On the contrary, this is part of what his programme of politics requires of him.

In Aristotle's *Politics* one can see a reordering of the roles of political actors, when compared to what they were among Aristotle's predecessors. For, if the legislator becomes the central character of politics, the question of the formation of such a legislator will necessarily be brought forward. It is precisely at this point, rather than in the ruling of the city, that the philosopher becomes concerned. Indeed, the *Politics* can be considered to be mainly a work the philosopher addresses to the legislator;[6] for this purpose the *Politics* calls upon the philosopher to exhibit an amazing amount of knowledge and to adopt various points of view. For a modern reader, this makes the *Politics* a treatise which is both unclassifiable and fascinating: Aristotle in turns makes use of history, sociology, anthropology, economy, psychology, politology, constitutional science, urbanism, but also mathematics, biology, etc. It is hard to resist the idea that this new task ascribed to the philosopher has to be related to the new historical conditions which prevailed in Aristotle's time. This is the second factor mentioned above. When the legitimacy of power is to be found in a dynasty, and no longer in the body of the citizens of a city, the political reformer can at best be the prince's advisor or educator, and that is what Aristotle actually was, at least for a short period.

III. THE FAMILY AND THE CITY

There are two immediately striking things for one who takes a look at the *Politics*, so to speak, from the outside. The first is that among all the ancient texts which have come down to us, it is in the *Politics*, and the *Politics* alone, in which one can find a tentative conceptual analysis of a reality which is properly Greek, namely the city (*polis*). In the other Greek writers, the *polis* is present, even omnipresent. In the case of political speeches of the orators, for instance, one finds constant reference to the *polis*, but there is nothing like an analysis of it. The same is true for another salient trait of the Greek social landscape, but a trait which, far from being proper to the Greek cultural milieu, is common to almost every ancient society, namely slavery. Slaves are everywhere in Greek literature, as they were in Greek reality, but the *Politics* alone intends to cast some light on the very concepts of slave and slavery. The second striking thing is the place devoted by Aristotle to the city as the most developed form of social life, and indeed as providing the unextendable horizon of the perfect human life. This focus Aristotle offers the city even at the precise moment as it is witnessing its historical fate, its end as institution, due largely to Aristotle's own 'master' and friend, the king of Macedon.

In Book I of the *Politics*, one can find the most precise argument in all surviving ancient literature for the natural, and non-conventional, nature of human society. The basic 'social actors' are in need of one another, and this is the reason why they engage in hierarchical mutual relationships. There are two major relations of this kind. The first is that of man and woman for the sake of procreation. There is actually a natural striving, which can be found in all living beings including plants, to 'leave behind another that is like oneself' (*Pol.* 1252a30). When Aristotle says that 'they do not do so from deliberate choice' (*Pol.* 1252a28), this does not mean that human beings cannot deliberate about whether they should have children or not, but rather that this striving itself is not an object of choice. The second basic relationship is between ruler and ruled. Crucially, the relationship of ruler and ruled of interest to Aristotle is one which holds 'by nature', for it is equally true that there are many relations of domination which are against nature.

These two major kinds of relationship are not on the same level, since the first one is a species of the second one, man being superior to woman by nature. The very notion of domination, or power, is analysed by Aristotle in a very subtle way, such an analysis being the ultimate basis for his political philosophy. In the very first chapter of the *Politics*, Aristotle criticizes the Platonists, without explicitly naming them, because they think that power is of one and the same species, its varieties differing only in quantity. A king, for instance, has power over more people than a father does. Aristotle, by contrast, distinguishes between *different species* of power—of the husband over his wife, of the father over his children, of the master over his slave, of the king over his subjects, of the magistrate over his fellow citizens. These different species of power have different criteria and must be exercised in different ways. Consequently, there is some confusion concerning which relationships generate situations that turn out to be against nature and therefore damaging to the well-being of the city and its citizens.

The two basic hierarchical relationships, that of the male and the female and that of the master and the slave by nature, make up what Aristotle calls the 'first family' (*Pol.* 1252b10), which is called 'first' presumably because in more developed forms the family will equally include other relationships, like the parent-child relationship. That a man should not treat his wife as a slave is explained through a teleological argument. Unlike the Delphian smiths who make knives for two purposes—killing the victim of a sacrifice and cutting it—nature 'does nothing skimpily' (*Pol.* 1252b1), assigning one function to one instrument. Thus women, having to perform a reproductive function, should not be used for another function. Of course, one individual may have several functions, but under different qualifications: a man may be involved in a marital relationship and in fatherhood, but *qua* husband and *qua* father. 'The barbarians, on the other hand, give the same position to woman and slave. The reason for this is that they have no naturally ruling element; with them, the partnership of man and woman is that of female slave and male slave' (*Pol.* 1252b7). This is a particularly striking example: the universal slavery which, so to speak, infects all social relations within the great oriental kingdoms in Asia or Egypt—which will be called later 'oriental despotism'—leaves room for no other relationship of power beyond despotism. In the very next sentence Aristotle, relying on a quotation from Euripides, contends that this fact provides the basis of the right of the Greeks to rule, and more precisely to enslave the barbarians.

Such a right is, according to Aristotle, a natural one. Before we come back to slavery, then, we have to shed some light on the cardinal notions of 'nature' and 'natural', without which Aristotle's political philosophy cannot be understood. In opposition to the Sophists' conventionalism, Aristotle affirms the natural character of some human associations, in particular the family (*oikia*)[7] and the city (*polis*). The natural end of a family is to satisfy the 'needs of daily life'. When several families unite 'for the sake of non-daily needs' (*Pol.* 1252b15), they make a village, which is a natural association too. Villages can also gather into a larger society. The city, finally, is the next and ultimate stage of human natural development. At this point we have to avoid an almost universal misreading: when Aristotle writes that 'that is why every city exists by nature, since the first communities do' (*Pol.* 1252b30), he does not mean that the naturalness of the villages constituting the city is the cause of the naturalness of the city, as it is generally said.[8] Just a few lines before Aristotle had written that 'a complete community composed of several villages, once it reaches the limit of full self-sufficiency, is a city' (*Pol.* 125b27). This means that it is not just any gathering of villages which makes a city, but a gathering which makes the new society a fully self-sufficient one. Then the fact that villages are natural associations is a necessary condition for the naturalness of the city, not the cause of it. As evidence for the naturalness of the city, Aristotle offers the fact the city is the end of the communities coming before it. For a city is a community which is able to provide its citizens not only with the means for 'living', that is to say the satisfaction of their needs, including quite developed and sophisticated ones, but also with what Aristotle calls 'living well', an expression which he considers to be a synonym with 'happiness' (*eudaimonia*). This is because, due to their own nature, human beings, and more precisely men, are not only endowed with the kinds of needs satisfied by the communities existing prior to the city, but are also destined for happiness, that is for the full accomplishment of their humanity.

It is only within a collective life regulated by the laws of a good constitution, the citizens of which are both the subjects and the makers, that men fully realize their humanity. Thus it is within a city that men can reach what Aristotle had laid down as the goal of ethics, namely happiness. This gives one more reason, perhaps the main reason, for which politics is 'architectonic' relative to ethics. One cannot find the requisites for happiness within a family, a village, or an association of villages, even if they can offer a quite refined form of life. The coming to be of the city is the effect of what Hegel would call a 'ruse of reason', because the city is not the conscious goal at which the people who established it were aiming. For it is for the sake of *living* that people gather, and they do their best to live better and better (*Pol.* 1252b29), but the city offered them, in addition, access to 'living well'—though they had neither looked for nor anticipated that end. The main cause of such a development is human nature itself, because 'man is by nature a political animal' (*Pol.* 1253a2–7). But a moving cause is also needed if this nature is to be actualized (*Pol.* 1253a30); this cause is the founder of the city, quite a significant character in the Greek collective imagination (cf. *Pol.* 1253a30). This political nature of man is also expressed by Aristotle in another way, when he describes the city as defining the boundaries of the human sphere: 'One who is incapable of participating or who is in need of nothing through being self-sufficient is no part of a city, and so is either a beast or a god' (1253a27). Aristotle makes a further step. Of course, it is because of the needs they have that human beings form families and villages; but it is due to the political nature of men that 'even when they do not need one another's help, people nonetheless desire to live together' (*Pol.* 1278b20).

Human beings, on the other hand, are not the only animals labelled as 'political'. A passage from the *History of Animals* (487b33ff.) offers a double division of animals into solitary and gregarious, and of the gregarious into political and dispersed. The political animals are those having an activity (*ergon*) in common. Aristotle gives as examples: human beings, bees, wasps, ants, and cranes. Another passage, in the *Politics* 1253a7ff., one of the most famous and the most commented upon of the Aristotelian corpus, says: 'that man is more[9] a political animal than any kind of bee or any herd animal is clear. For, as we assert, nature does nothing in vain; and man alone among the animals has speech (*logos*)'. Now, speech 'serves to reveal the advantageous and the harmful, and hence the just and the unjust. For it is proper to man as compared to the other animals that he alone perceives the good and the bad and the just and the unjust and other things of this kind. And it is community in these that makes a family and a city'. Here again the argument is a teleological one, and it relies on some understood premises. If nature does nothing in vain, it must be for some purpose that it provided human beings with speech. But speech is the appropriate instrument to signify to other people what is good and bad, just and unjust. Sharing those values, on the other hand, 'makes' (*poiei*) natural societies like the family and the city. Therefore, if they did not live in families or cities, human beings would possess the faculty of speech in vain. Now we have seen that the city is the end of the family. Therefore, it is in cities that speech will fully perform its function.

The doctrine according to which the city is the end of the family is endorsed by Aristotle through two strong claims. The first one is that the city, as an end for the family, is to be considered the nature of the family, just as the horse is the nature of the colt (*Pol.* 1252b31). The second one is that the city is prior to the family 'and to each of us' (*Pol.* 1253a19), in the way the whole is prior to its parts, just as, in Aristotle's example, the living body is prior to its hand or foot. If we take this analogy seriously, we have to acknowledge that, according to Aristotle, just as in the case of a dead hand or a stone hand, a man who is not part of a city should be called a man only homonymously. For when separated from the city, he would not completely fulfil the very concept of 'man'. This is the farthest point Aristotle ever reached in adopting such a Platonic posture advocating a dependency of the individual on the city.

But this picture of man as a 'member' of the city should be mitigated, for though Aristotle often parallels human societies and living organisms, the city cannot be considered to be a *substance* (*ousia*), and, in this sense, a city *does not have* a nature. It is not 'by nature' either, in the strict sense used in the *Physics*,[10] since the city is not a property of a natural substance. This is true of the family and of the village too. We have, therefore, to admit that in the *Politics*, 'by nature', when applied to the city, has a sense which differs slightly from that we find in the *Physics*. Such a sense is nonetheless not a metaphorical one, as some have said. In the same way, the claim according to which 'man is by nature a political animal' should not be taken without care. This question has been made much clearer by an article by Wolfgang Kullmann.[11] He remarks that 'it follows from the description of man as *zôon* that "political" above all describes a biological condition of a group of animals' (p. 101). 'Political' is a character of 'man', but it is neither his nature nor a part of his nature, nor even something proper to him. We therefore cannot speak of 'Aristotle's definition of man as a political animal by nature', as interpreters often do.

It is then because of what man's nature is—and he does have a nature since he is a substance—that properties like polity belong to him by nature, in the same way that his 'economic' character and his belonging to a village do as well. The city is, of course, the framework within which a man can accomplish his own nature, that is, develop his natural capacities, but the city does not make man political, even if good laws should develop the potential polity of the citizens: where there are no men *sufficiently* political, there is no city. At *Politics* 1280a32, Aristotle writes that there is no city composed of slaves or animals, even of political animals, and we know that he also denied the existence of cities composed of barbarians.

The main criterion according to which a human community has reached the stage of the city is 'self-sufficiency' (*autarkeia*), a concept all the more obscure in that it is not mainly an economic one. Or more precisely, Aristotle does acknowledge such an economic sense,[12] but makes clear that what is at stake here is 'full self-sufficiency'. A human society is self-sufficient when it does not depend on some exterior factors for its functioning or its survival. In this sense 'self-sufficient' is almost a synonym for 'perfect' or 'complete' (*teleion*). Such a true and complete self-sufficiency cannot be found but within a city. So, a city completely independent from an economic point of view would certainly not be said to be 'self-sufficient' by Aristotle if it were nonetheless under the political domination of an exterior society. Indeed, this sort of attitude helps to explain why later in the history of ancient philosophy we find that when the notion of political sufficiency has retreated, self-sufficiency retreats within the individual sage himself.

Turning to smaller natural units, we find that the family has a logic which is different from that of the city. In families, given the nature of the needs they are supposed to satisfy—reproduction and preservation, i.e., the 'daily needs'—self-sufficiency is mainly economic. This is actually a tautology, as least in Greek, since 'economy' comes from *oikia*, 'family'. The idea is that the family be able to preserve itself in relying only on its own working force. This is not to be taken too narrowly, since Aristotle considers trade to be natural under certain conditions. Swapping one useful thing for one, even if this includes money, is natural: Aristotle is the first to lay down the distinction between use value and exchange value. If, as Karl Polanyi has claimed in a remarkable article,[13] 'Aristotle discovers economy', it is among other reasons because he has been the first to see clearly the very functioning of the market economy, a form of which develops at his time, and because he desperately tries to keep the political sphere free from any contamination by the economic sphere.

From the very beginning of the cities onward, there was a sharp conflict between the familial and political spheres, which has been very well pictured in Sophocles' *Antigone*. To prevent the civic duties from being endangered by the solidarities of the blood, Plato advocated the disappearance of the family itself. Aristotle offers at the same time a deeper analysis of the ways the family endangers the city, and a less radical solution. The familial (economic) sphere, which is natural and necessary for the city to satisfy the natural needs of its members, and which is, first of all, the place where new citizens are produced, has to remain subordinated to the city. That is, the family has to serve the goals of the city. Translating this into epistemological terms, politics is architectonic in relation to economics.[14]

When, on the contrary, economy imposes its own law upon the city, the city has a deviated constitution, and is, therefore, unable to achieve the natural goal of a city, namely happiness. This deviation is of two kinds, which are quite frequent in Aristotle's time: it is either an *oligarchy*, which is, in fact, a plutocracy, or a tyranny in which the tyrant is the only rich man. Under the name of *khrêmatistikê*, Aristotle describes an art, or expertise, which makes the economic sphere autonomous, an art for which there is 'no limit to wealth and possession' (*Pol.* 1256b41). When the householder, who very quickly becomes an entrepreneur, aims at increasing his wealth without limits and organizes his life and the life of the whole family from such a perspective, he simply cannot be a citizen in the proper sense of this term. This is why Aristotle excludes craftsmen from the body of the citizens, an exclusion which has been misunderstood by modern readers. Like many people in his time, Aristotle probably despised manual labour, but not mainly because he socially despised 'base-born' people. The main reason is that in order to live life whose goal is to earn as much money as possible a person must develop certain dispositions over others and therefore also, ultimately, must develop a character incompatible with the life of a citizen

IV. THE POLITICS OF SLAVERY

In fact, the political nature and destination of man requires a kind virtue of which many are incapable. Accordingly, one of the main tasks of the legislator is to keep out of power those who are incapable of realizing their political nature, where this includes but is not limited to manual workers. Importantly, Aristotle's exclusion of many human beings from the political sphere becomes even clearer with the existence of what he calls 'slaves by nature'. According to Aristotle, nature provided some people with a faculty for foresight, and therefore of ruling, and others with the mere faculty of executing orders. He even remarks that nature has the tendency to exhibit such a difference in the bodies themselves, as she makes the body of slaves 'strong with the view to necessary use' and that of the free persons 'straight and useless for such tasks' (*Pol.* 1254b27). But Aristotle is wise enough to acknowledge that such a rule has many exceptions. Aristotle was indeed not in favour of the slavery that existed in his time; he nevertheless favours a real form of slavery, in which the terms 'slave' (*doulos*) and 'slavery' (*douleia*) are not used metaphorically. Thus, when Aristotle writes that a slave by nature 'is the man of another man, ... and a man is another's who, though a man, is an acquired possession' (*Pol.* 1254a15), one can see that even the most anti-egalitarian of our contemporaries cannot agree with all Aristotelian positions.

The ultimate basis for this natural division of human beings into ruling and ruled is a geographic one. There are, of course, individual accidents that may give a free man a degenerated child, but if one considers the entire humankind, at least the part of it known to Aristotle, it is the climate which, in the end, determines the characters, and hence the ethical dispositions, and so finally the political capacities of human beings. Neither the barbarians from cold regions, i.e., from Western Europe, nor those from warm countries, i.e., from Asia Minor, are fitted for political life, the requirements for which are intelligence and courage: the first ones because they are brave but stupid, and the second ones because they are clever but cowardly. The Greeks alone, who live in temperate regions, combine intelligence and courage.[15] With such a theory of climates, which was not an innovation on Aristotle's part, as we find versions of it in Plato's *Republic* and in the Hippocratic treatise *On Waters, Airs and Places*, Aristotle agrees with the spirit of ancient medicine. For the great majority of ancient physicians, before as well as after Aristotle, were determinists in that they regarded both normal and pathological spiritual states as the effects of the interaction between the elementary components of the body and the environment. Aristotle's theory of slavery, as dependent both on physics and ethics, is a good example of the kind of knowledge the legislator has to be taught by the philosopher.

Concerning slaves, Aristotle has recourse to a very unusual method, as Victor Goldschmidt rightly pointed out.[16] In chapter 4 of Book I of the *Politics*, he first develops the very concept of 'slave', before considering 'whether someone is like this by nature or not' (*Pol.* 1254a17). Then Aristotle feels able to answer the question about the legitimacy of slavery and to widen his research to the family in general, of which slavery forms a part. For the main aspect of Aristotle's natural slavery is that it is a slavery restricted to the family,[17] a position that has to be properly understood. In fact the purely instrumental description of the slave that can be found in the *Politics*—especially in the famous passage in which Aristotle writes that 'if the shuttles would weave themselves and picks play themselves the lyre' there would be no need of slaves (*Pol.* 1253b37)—is only superficial. In linking slaves not with production, but with action (*praxis*), that is, with life (*bios*),[18] Aristotle gets to the point of saying that 'the slave is a part of his master, namely an animate and separate part of his body' (*Pol.* 1255b11). Such a description insists on the integration of the slave into the lineage of the family, and at the same time gives quite a physical and fusional image of the family, which, again, opposes it to the political community. For in a certain way, children are also parts of their parents' body.[19]

There is a last point of Aristotle's theory of slavery to be considered with some care, because it has been misunderstood by many commentators.[20] Aristotle says that both the ruling and the ruled have the same interest in the situation of domination. Commentators consider this as meaning that since slaves are incapable of 'foreseeing with the mind' (*Pol.* 1252a32) or of deliberating, the master helps the slave out in taking over these activities for him.[21] Then, just as the child could not survive without his parents, in the same way the slave could not survive by himself without his master. His inability to foresee the future would render him incapable.

Two passages may, and should, be opposed to such a reading of the text of *Politics* I. In Book III, Aristotle makes a considerable move toward a more balanced approach by means of his distinction between the rule of the master over his slaves and that of the father over his children. In this last case, the father rules essentially for the benefit of the children. The goal is, in fact, to help the children, at least the boys, to develop their own faculties to later become good citizens. There is nothing like this in the case of slaves: 'the power of the master, though being in truth advantageous both to the slave by nature and to the master by nature, has actually in view primarily the advantage of the master, and only by accident for the advantage of the slave' (*Pol.* 1278b 32). In Book I, Aristotle compares slaves to animals,[22] a comparison which is worth considering for the present topic: 'tame animals,' Aristotle writes, 'have a better nature than wild ones, and it is better for all of them to be ruled by man, since in this way their preservation (*sôteria*) is insured' (*Pol.* 1254b10). This passage does not allude to domesticated animals alone, but to all animals. Now, Aristotle himself recognizes that no animal needs to be tamed by man to survive, including even, then, human beings: 'All the kinds of animals that are tame exist also in a wild state, for instance horses, oxen, swine, humans, sheep, goats, dogs' (*HA* 488a30).

What Aristotle means by claiming that the ruled have an interest in being ruled, in the case of slaves as well as in the case of animals, is that it is better for an inferior being to take part in the activity of a superior being, rather than to restrict himself to his own activity. Just as it is 'according to nature and advantageous that the body be governed by the soul' (*Pol.* 1254b6), because the body has to leave aside its own interest (pleasure, for instance) for the benefit of the part which is better than the body itself, in the same way the slave has a natural advantage to partake in the common activity with his master, not from the point of view of his own nature of slave, but because this common activity is 'more natural' than his own, in the sense that it is conceived of by and for the benefit of a more perfect being. The same is true for the relation of animals to human beings who are 'more natural than the other animals' (*IA* 4 706a19, cf. 5 706b10). The common activity in which the slaves take a part is the realization of the happiness of the citizens in the city.

This is, in the final analysis, Aristotle's justification for slavery. Slaves do not need masters to survive, and masters do not absolutely need slaves. More exactly the city does not need slaves *economically*: it would be possible to imagine another way of producing what the city needs, perhaps, for example, by independent small producers paying a rent. But the Aristotelian city *politically* needs slaves, because the basic structure of the city is the articulation between the familial and the political spheres, and because in the familial sphere, the productive function has to be assigned to people who are purely subordinates and who are with their masters in a quasi-biological relationship. Masters need slaves to be citizens, which they could not be without slaves to carry out various necessary tasks; such tasks would not only waste the time needed by citizens for political life, but also could turn the citizen into a *homo economicus* rather than a political animal. Aristotle is so aware of the danger of a contamination of the citizens by the economic sphere, that he recommends to the citizens that they not have a direct relationship with their slaves: 'the science of using slaves is neither great nor admirable: it consists in the slave to know how to execute, and in the master to know how to order. That is why those who are in a position to avoid this trouble leave this job to a steward, while they occupy themselves with politics or philosophy' (*Pol.* 1255b33).

V. City, Citizen, Constitution

After *Politics* II, which deals with actual constitutions imagined by other political thinkers, as a preparatory study to that of the perfect constitution, at the beginning of *Politics* III Aristotle makes a double reduction. Within a research on constitution, Aristotle writes: 'for one investigating constitutions...the first investigation is about the city: what actually is the city?' (*Pol.* 1274b32). Then he says that to illuminate what the city is, we must know what the citizen is, because the city is made of citizens, and eventually, when the crucial problem of the identity of the city is mentioned, or rather mentioned again (what makes a city to remain the same in time, and, therefore, who is responsible for the past decisions of the city?), Aristotle concludes that the constitution must be defined.

After criticizing the then usual definitions of the citizen—for example 'the one born from two citizens' or the one who actually lives within the city—Aristotle proposes a properly political definition of the citizen: a citizen is one 'sharing the function of a judge and a magistrate' (*Pol.* 1275a22). The question is, therefore, to know where the power is. In a democracy, for instance, members of the assembly are not only citizens, but should also be counted as magistrates, because, Aristotle says, 'it would be ridiculous to deprive of the title of magistrate those with the greatest power' (*Pol.* 1275a28). Thus, Aristotle concludes: 'in brief, we call a city the multitude of such people [i.e., the people sharing the function of a judge and a magistrate] when it is fitted to self-sufficiency' (*Pol.* 1275b20). In fact, then, one is or is not a citizen in a city relative to its constitution, a constitution being 'the arrangement of the city with respect to its offices, namely the one that has power over everything' (*Pol.* 1278b8). Elsewhere Aristotle says that a constitution is 'a kind of life for the city' (*Pol.* 1295a40), recognizing so far that there is no city without a constitution. Such an organisation is a guarantee for the reign of the law within the city. As a result, because citizenship varies with the nature of the regime, in some cases the city includes a very small number of citizens; this is the case in aristocracies, for instance, in which the power is concentrated in few hands. Monarchy is a border-line case, in which one individual has all, or almost all, the power. This case provides us with an essential aspect of the definition of the citizen. The difference between political kingship (i.e., monarchy as the constitution of a city) and the absolute barbarian monarchies, is that in the former the power is exerted 'according to the law' (*kata nomon*, cf. *Pol.* 1285a4). Of tyranny in its 'pure' form, where the power of one individual is wielded according to his own pleasure, Aristotle says that it is the 'farthest removed from being a constitution' (*Pol.* 1289b2). In this case, there is no longer a political power, but a despotic power, as is the case among barbarians. In the end, constitution is the main object of Aristotle's *Politics*.

Next, Aristotle deals with the subject of central concern to him in the *Politics*, namely the excellence of the constitution. The definition he has given of the citizen is adapted also to those who hold their position unjustly, as Aristotle himself acknowledges (*Pol.* 1276a5). But, from several points of view, this is not satisfactory. First, there is a practical problem Aristotle, and probably his contemporaries, were deeply concerned with, namely the question of determining the degree to which a city is constrained by the decisions its previous rulers have made if they happened to be bad people. Thus transpires, for example, in the case of a tyrant or of constitutions 'based on force and not aiming at common advantage' (*Pol.* 1276a12). But the main problem is that of the goal of the city. In an important passage in *Politics* III 9, Aristotle warns against what he regards as mere counterfeits of the city. Neither living together, nor making a military alliance, practicing endogamy, or establishing economic agreements, or even all these things all together, make a city (*Pol.* 1280b29). 'It is virtue and vice that one who is concerned by a good legislation gives a careful attention to. It is thus clear that the city which deserves such a name, and not that named just in a manner of speaking, must care about virtue, otherwise the political community would become a military alliance, differing from the others only by location...; and law becomes a mere convention' (*Pol.* 1280b5).

Here we again come upon evidence for the coexistence of prescriptive and objective sides in Aristotle's analysis. Often seen as a contradiction to be referred to Aristotle's evolution,[23] such a co-existence is rather the expression of a complementarity. Even when we feel fascinated by some descriptive analysis in the *Politics*, those which belong to history of science, such as those which fall under social anthropology, history, political anthropology,[24] we must not forget the fundamental normativity of Aristotle's text. This normativity occurs at two levels. Everybody agrees on the first one: the background of Aristotle's reflexion is the distinction between right and deviated constitutions. The second one, by contrast, has not found favour with many interpreters: in all cases the legislator has to deal with, according to Aristotle, he must aim at an *excellent* constitution.

A city cannot have the ethical destination that nature assigns to it unless it is governed by a right constitution. A constitution is right when it works according to 'common advantage' (*koinon sumpheron*), and a constitution is deviated when it works for the benefit of an individual or a group. There are three main kinds of right constitutions, according to the number of people who have the power; and to each of them there corresponds a deviated form. When one individual governs for the common advantage, there is a kingship, the deviation of which is a tyranny; when the power is in the hands of a small number of people for common advantage, there is an aristocracy, the deviation of which is an oligarchy; when the masses govern rightly, there is a constitutional regime (*polity*), the deviation of which is a democracy, a term which, in Aristotle as well as in Plato, indicates what we would call a demagogy. This 'common advantage' is a basically ethical advantage, which concerns the citizens alone, and not the other inhabitants of the city, that is, slaves, women, children, manual workers, foreigners, and the like. The starting point of Aristotle's reflexion is that 'a city is the community of families and villages having a perfect and self-sufficient life.... Therefore the political community must be regarded as being for the sake of noble actions, not for the sake of living together' (*Pol.* 1280b40). What the city aims at is not to make the citizens more wealthy, or to satisfy all their desires, but to make them virtuous in order to make them happy. Then, the general principle of any legal system is expressed in the next sentence: 'Hence those who contribute most to a community of this kind have a greater part from the city than those who are equal or greater in freedom or birth, but unequal in political virtue, or those who outdo them in wealth, but whom they outdo in virtue' (*Pol.* 1281a4).

Politics III 4, a crucial and obscure chapter, deals with the difference between the virtue (excellence) of the good man and that of the citizen. By good man we should understand the complete virtuous man, that is the 'prudent' man. This chapter is usually taken to mean that Aristotle assumes, in quite a realist way, that 'if it is impossible for a city to be constituted of excellent people, and if, nevertheless, each should perform his own task well,... there will not be a single virtue for the citizen and the good man' (*Pol.* 1276b37). To describe such a situation, Aristotle has recourse, at the beginning of the chapter, to technical comparisons, like those of navigation and choir singing: just as in the case of the excellence of a good sailor or a good chorus singer, the excellence of a good citizen consists in his ability to perform well his task in his own position for the good of the common enterprise, that is for the preservation of the constitution. It is certainly the case that Aristotle recognizes the excellence of the city as a community in which every individual performs his task well without also being necessarily a virtuous man. This is what could be called 'functional excellence'. But this is not Aristotle's last word, as can be seen in this very chapter *Politics* III 4. At 1276b35 Aristotle makes a fresh start: 'it is

surely possible to go over the same argument by another way, through a diaporematic method, in reference to the excellent constitution.' The diaporematic method
consists in considering opposite arguments on some subject. In effect, to the functional excellence picture, Aristotle opposes a second opinion according to which
there is a kind of civic excellence which is one and the same as the excellence of the
good man. Such an excellence is the excellence of the ruler. In some citizens, then,
the excellence is an ethical one, even though some others, presumably the majority
of the civic body, merely share in the excellence of the ruled. It is in the latter case
that the comparison with the sailors applies most clearly. The ruler and the ruled
are so different from each other that they should have a different kind of education.
This is especially visible in the case of cities ruled by a prince or a tyrant, such as
Jason who 'did not know how to be a private individual,' because he has been educated only to rule (*Pol.* 1277a25).

But things are different in 'the kind of rule exercised over people who are similar in kind, i.e., free, and which we call 'political rule'' (*Pol.* 1277b7). In this sort
of case a citizen should share in both excellences, that of the ruler and that of the
ruled, because he will in turn be in each of those positions. Aristotle does not
give much detail on how the good citizen in this sense will exercise his excellence
as a ruled person. When he says that 'prudence is the only excellence proper to
the ruler, for the others, it would seem, are necessarily common to both ruler and
ruled, and indeed prudence is not the excellence of the ruled, but true opinion is'
(*Pol.* 1277b25), we should probably understand that, when ruled, the citizen, though
he is a potential ruler, just relies on true opinion to wisely obey the law. True opinion is the excellence of one who adheres to good laws, decrees, and decisions that
he did not himself make. But such a problem is of almost no practical importance,
since in cities with such virtuous citizens the citizens are, so to speak, constantly in
power. This is what a right constitution should be: a regime in which only prudent
people are in power. Only these people are citizens in a full sense, even if the citizens in a functionally excellent city may also be called citizens in a weaker sense.
It must be the case that in some cities those who are citizens in their own right are
very few in number.

To the crucial question to whom the power should be attributed, Aristotle, in
the passage at *Politics* 1281a4 quoted above, answers, in a clear but general way, that
one should have power and 'political excellence' in the same proportion. To make
it more obvious, Aristotle makes an explicit allusion to the doctrine of 'distributive
justice' which he develops in the *Nicomachean Ethics* V 3. From a certain point of
view, political virtue is shared by a small group of citizens. This is the sort of excellence that helps the city to reach its goal, namely a happy life for its citizens; such
excellence directs the city in this way because a ruler who rules exhibits it and in
fact rules *qua* having it; that is, because he rules precisely in so far as he is excellent
in this respect. Those who base their conception of justice on something else are
wrong.

In *Politics* III 9, Aristotle considers the conceptions of justice the supporters of
democracy and of oligarchy have. All of them agree, and Aristotle agrees too, on

the principle according to which the city should give equally to equal people. But the oligarchs think that the equality which is to be taken into account is that of wealth, while the democrats think that it is freedom. Concerning freedom, things are clear: the very concept of 'citizen' involves freedom. For the democrats, then, all free men should be citizens, because they are equally free. Concerning wealth, Aristotle's position is that it is to some extent necessary to have some wealth to be virtuous and, therefore happy: the excellent constitution is 'established on virtue furnished with means' (*Pol.* 1289a32). But freedom and wealth must be devoted to the efficient functioning of a good constitution, keeping the democrats and the oligarchs away from their bad propensities. That there are good and bad uses of democracy and oligarchy will be seen later.

In conclusion, we grasp an essential character of the excellent constitution: in such a constitution, the power, or at least the most important offices, are distributed to those who can hold them in the best way for the common good, that is, as Aristotle says in the passages just quoted, to citizens who are 'good' and 'prudent'.

VI. The Excellent Constitution

The fact that there are several kinds of constitution was for Aristotle both an observed fact and a 'theoretical object', since his predecessors, especially Plato, intended to account for this fact. This is, for Aristotle, of special importance for at least two reasons. First, because this constitutional diversity helps him to conceive of the excellence of constitutions in a radically new way, second, because the science of constitutions is the core of the political science the philosopher should teach to the legislator.

Above all, we have, one more time, to abandon a conception shared until recently by most commentators to the effect that Aristotle in the *Politics* seeks to depart from Plato's utopia, by reverting to 'common sense' or, at least, to feasible projects. It is surely true that Aristotle intends to propose conceptual models that can be carried out in reality. But, if we read the texts carefully, we find that it is no less clear that what Aristotle intends to realize is well and truly the happy life for the citizens, in all the cases with which the legislator must deal; and this presupposes *an excellent constitution*. Because we are Cartesian, we can hardly conceive of excellence (or perfection) other than as something universal and unique.[25] The discussion Aristotle offers in the *Nicomachean Ethics* (1134b18ff.) of a conventionalist conception of the just, however, which was probably that of the Sophists, reveals what his position on this point was. Sophists say that the natural is what is universally the case, for example fire burns in Greece as well as in Persia, while all social and moral rules, they say, are variable, because conventional. Aristotle replies that there are, of course, social practices which are purely conventional and, therefore, restricted to a definite area. Political life, on the other hand, is founded on laws which are both natural and variable for the reason, which happens to be absolutely crucial in Aristotle's political philosophy, that a law cannot be said to be just or unjust except in relation to the constitution in which this law takes place. Now, 'there is only one constitution which is everywhere the best by nature' (*EN* 1135a5).

'Everywhere' has here a distributive sense:[26] in a given place at a given time, there is only one constitution which is the best by nature. In other words, the abstract universal rule according to which an excellent constitution is that in which the people who hold the power are those who deserve this power (namely the 'prudent' men who have a sufficient amount of political virtue), depends on the actual situation of the human group under consideration, and first of all on the number of prudent men contained in this group. For a given city at a given moment, though, there is but one form of constitution which happens to be natural, and to try to impose any other would be to impose a constitution which is against the nature of the city under consideration.

That is why, Aristotle says, in old times cities were almost necessarily governed by kings: when a city is constituted from a gathering of families, only one individual has enough of political virtue to be a true citizen, the others being, so to speak, 'pre-political' (*Pol.* 1252b25, 1285b6, 1286b8). Kingship will therefore be the political system best fitted to such people, and will also be in consequence just; not a kingship aiming at the satisfaction of the king's desires, but one founded on the dominance of laws. Hereditary succession to the throne, for instance, will be included in the legislation. If the king, suddenly or progressively, happens to govern to his own advantage or to that of his lineage, he will become a tyrant, and the first thing he will try to do is to free himself from the tutelage of the law. But if the king is virtuous, he will be the gravedigger of the monarchy, since he will reign by developing virtue in his subjects as far as he can. Such a development, as we have seen, is an effect of the obedience to laws. When a certain number of his subjects have acquired a sufficient amount of virtue, and particularly enough of political virtue—which means that they are no longer just householders and members of a lineage, but that they are also able to express their political nature—it would be unjust and against nature not to share the power with them. Kingship must then be replaced with an aristocracy. When virtue has spread enough throughout the social body, aristocracy should give way to a constitutional regime (*polity*). In each of these situations, there is one and only one constitution which is excellent (cf. *Pol.* 1288a8).

On the one hand, then, the unqualified question of which constitution is the best or the 'ideal' one is in Aristotle's view meaningless. For not only are all the right constitutions equally entitled to be called 'excellent', but to try to impose a *polity* on a people not suited to such a constitution would certainly not make the *polity* an 'ideal' constitution. That said, Aristotle does recognize some superiority in a constitution in which virtue is most widespread within the body of the citizens. That is why aristocracy is 'preferable' to kingship (*Pol.* 1286b5). In this respect, the constitutional regime (*polity*) is the ideal end of the history of the city, even if one has to agree that it is hardly attainable.

In striving to attain the best possible constitution in any given circumstance, the legislator, and consequently the philosopher who teaches and advises him, may have to face one of three situations. For, if a city functions well in making its citizens happy, it has no more need of a legislator than a healthy person needs a doctor. First the legislator may be asked to give laws to a city which has no laws at all, that is, a collection of people which is not yet a city. Aristotle alludes to such a man in *Politics* I, as we have already seen (1253a30), naming such a legislator 'responsible for the greatest of goods': he is the legislator in the primary sense, whom cities used to worship continually. But most of the time the legislator is faced with cities which function, but function badly. The correct procedure in this case is in accordance with an Academic practice, since Plato used to send pupils of his school as advisers to the princes. In such a 'curative' posture, the legislator may have to face two different situations, according to whether the city functions badly because it is not ruled by the laws adapted to its constitution, or because the city does not have the constitution it should have.

I still think[27] that this is exactly what Aristotle says in *Politics* IV 1. Let us consider the crucial passage at 1288b20–34. Aristotle distinguishes three cases with which political science has to deal, the best constitution absolutely speaking (*haplôs*, b25), the best constitution 'in a given situation' (*ek tôn hupokeimenôn*, b25), the best constitution in a given genus (*ex hupotheseôs*, b28, *aristên* is understood after *ex hypotheseôs*). Those three cases correspond in effect to three possible situations the legislator may have to meet: founding a city out of nothing, reforming a city by a change of its constitutional form, and reforming a city in keeping its constitutional form. We should note that the expression 'the constitution which is most fitting for all cities' (*Pol.* 1288b34) is certainly to be understood in a distributive sense. In the third case, the goal is to establish, or re-establish, a compatibility between constitution and legislation, in order to ensure, for instance, that democratic-inspired laws do not infect the elitism-inspired constitution which happens to be the constitution adapted to the people under consideration. In the second case, the legislator intends to change the very form of the constitution in the city, because the present form is not in harmony with the 'ethical substance' of this city. Such an intervention should have the effect of putting the city on the way to a right constitution.

One of the main difficulties of this crucial chapter is that *Politics* IV 1 is, so to speak, highly prescriptive and highly positive at the same time. The legislator's goal is clearly presented as being to reach the excellent constitution in every case. But to achieve such a difficult task, the legislator has to master a constitutional science which takes into account all kinds of constitutions and not only the excellent ones: just as gymnastic is the art which studies which exercise is best adapted to anyone, 'it is thus evident that it belongs to the same science to study what is the excellent constitution, that is to say what it must be like according to our wishes if there were no external obstacles, and also what is the constitution adapted to what people,

for in many cases people cannot reach the excellent constitution' (*Pol.* 1288b21).
Aristotle probably means that they cannot reach any kind of excellent constitution
by themselves. One further step should be made. When Aristotle writes in *Politics*
IV 2, as quoted above, that the legislator should determine which constitution is
the best after the excellent one—and even, if this second-best one is not attainable
by the people he is considering, to determine which is the third-best, fourth-best,
and so on (*Pol.* 1289b17)—this does not at all mean that Aristotle is ready to resign
himself to giving cities a second or third-choice constitution. In fact it is very suitable, and almost necessary, that a given body of citizens be prepared to live, at least
immediately, under some constitution other than the one which is properly excellent for it. To suppose otherwise would certainly be utopian and, in any case, would
lead to a dead-end. The second-best constitution is on its way to the excellent one,
and it is by its actual functioning that it can have a chance to improve and to spread
political virtue widely among the citizens. That is why all non-excellent constitutions need, in the first instance, time.

VII. Political Science and *Realpolitik*

That allowed, it is undeniable that Aristotle is quite aware of the fact that virtue as
he describes it is 'beyond the reach of ordinary people' (*Pol.* 1295a27). Accordingly,
he several times affirms that the legislator he is addressing—the potential reader of
the *Politics*—has to take such a weakness into account and to offer constitutional
changes that are both appropriate and feasible. This leads Aristotle to propose for
the cities a kind of constitutional excellence that I have called a 'functional' one.
In this perspective, the objective at which the legislator aims, by the means of the
reforms he proposes to the city, is to make the constitution able to last as long as
possible. We have to examine this 'realist' side of Aristotle's *Politics*, before proposing an interpretation of it.

Of course, mastering a constitutional science requires a huge body of knowledge. Without knowledge drawn from outside the confines of the field of politics, genuine progress towards excellence would not be practicable; this is why, as
I mentioned earlier, the legislator should have some skill in history, psychology,
etc. This broader knowledge is reflected in the program laid down in the *Politics*
IV 2: the first thing to be determined, Aristotle says, is how many varieties of
constitution there are; the next one, is to know which constitution, being second,
third, etc. after the excellent one, can be attained by a given people; and finally the
political philosopher should determine how to establish these constitutions and so
should know how the constitutions might be destroyed or preserved. It is clear that
a proper understanding of the diversity of constitutions is both the first element

of this programme and a prerequisite for the further ones. The basic assumption of this functional approach is that 'as long as [the parts any constitution is made of] are in a fine condition, the constitution is necessarily in a fine condition' (*Pol.* 1297b38). For a constitution is not a homogeneous reality, but is composed of parts, each of which has its own function. The city is not homogeneous either, and Aristotle reproaches Plato for having ignored that 'a city consists not only of people more numerous than in a family, but also differing in kind' (*Pol.* 1261a22). To make the diversity of constitutions intelligible, we should consider the parts making up both cities and constitutions.

One of the most theoretically exciting parts of Aristotle's political philosophy is precisely his approach to the diversity of constitutions through a consideration of their parts.[28] In *Politics* III and most of all in *Politics* IV, Aristotle offers an increasingly refined analysis of constitutional diversity. Leaving aside the genetic analysis that can be found in *Politics* I, according to which a city is composed of families and individuals, Aristotle considers a city as being composed of citizens. In a striking passage of *Politics* IV, Aristotle makes a parallel between the ways to determine how many animal species there are and how many constitutions there are. Concerning the animals, 'we should first determine the organs that are necessary to every animal, namely some sense organs, the parts which digest and collect the food…, and, finally, the organs of locomotion' (*Pol.* 1290b25).

This project of combining the parts had by each city is achieved in two different ways. First, Aristotle takes as parts of the city the various groups of citizens competing for political power. Two of these groups are of particular importance, the rich and the free, to which correspond the two main regimes Aristotle was able to see around him as well as in Greek history, namely oligarchy and democracy. But the usual classification, even in the form revised by Aristotle, which distinguishes six varieties of constitutions, three right and three deviated, is obviously insufficient for the Aristotelian legislator. This is why Aristotle takes the further step of distinguishing several kinds of democracies and oligarchies, according to which part of a people (in democracy) or which part of the rich (in oligarchy) has the power. In Politics IV 4, 5, and 6, for instance, he gives two lists of the different kinds of democracies and oligarchies: the first list is purely descriptive, whereas the second list provides the causes why things are as they are.

The second way in which Aristotle makes the diversity of constitutions intelligible, through a definition of the parts making up a constitution, can be found in the last three chapters of *Politics* IV. This is probably one of the most remarkable theoretical moves made by Aristotle in the *Politics*, but it is also one that has been completely underestimated by commentators. The basis of Aristotle's analysis is that:

> Every constitution has three parts.…As these parts differ from one another, constitutions differ. Of these parts, one deliberates about common affairs, the second one is concerned with magistracies (what they should be, over what they should exercise their authority, and what should be the mode of electing to them), the third one is the judicial part (*Pol.* 1297b37–41).

If we take the example of the deliberative part, we see that what Aristote aims at is an a priori construction of all the possible forms of the deliberative part, and, at the next stage, of all the possible forms of constitution. 'It is necessary, Aristotle writes, that all those decisions [that is the decision left to the deliberative part: war, peace, alliances, laws, great punishments, election of the magistrates, audits] be left either all to all, or all to some…, or some to some and the other to others, or some to all and the other to some' (*Pol.* 1298a7). These criteria are not induced from the observation of political reality, but they constitute an exhaustive list determined a priori. This remark is sufficient to topple all the unfair criticisms addressed to these three chapters by many commentators.

Politics IV 15, which considers the part dealing with the magistracies, is even more important. Aristotle first seems to follow the same path as he had in chapter 14, i.e., to determine how many magistracies there are, what their field is, etc. But he corrects himself, saying, first, that not any charge is a magistracy, but only those which entail political power. In this respect, priests and ambassadors are not magistrates. But Aristotle makes a second move. For it is impossible to constitute an a priori list of magistracies: the only possible list can be made from the observation of existing magistracies. But this would be contrary to Aristotle's present theoretical method. Therefore, Aristotle adopts another point of view, and makes an a priori list of all the possible ways people can be nominated to magistracies. Three points of view should be taken into account about magistracies: who appoints, who is appointed, and in what way they are appointed. The first two can be divided according to the same criteria, i.e.—by/among all, by/among some, some by/among all and some by/among some—and the third one can be divided 'by election, by lot, some by election and some by lot'. This gives at least twelve combinations. At the end, the mode of appointment to magistracies is probably the most characteristic feature of a constitution.

Such an extraordinary method provides the legislator with a quite sophisticated way of grasping the diversity of constitutions, one which leaves far behind the 'old' method based on the determination of the class which has the power. The outcome of this a priori method cannot coincide with the usual list of six constitutions:

> One should take into account the various combinations of the varieties of the parts we have considered, because their combinations make constitutions overlap one another, so that some aristocracies are oligarchical, and some polities quite democratic. I mean the combinations not yet considered, as when the deliberative part and the part concerned with magistracies are constituted oligarchically, and the courts aristocratically (*Pol.* 1316b39).

In this way, we end up with a great number of constitutions.

Now, being such a complex balance of parts, a constitution is at risk of being changed sometimes by a small alteration in one of its parts, even one that has remained unnoticed, as happened in Ambracia where the property qualification went so low that the oligarchic constitution took a democratic turn (*Pol.* 1301a20).

Politics V, which is perhaps the birth certificate of political science as well as its greatest achievement, is entirely devoted to the investigation of:

> The sources of change in constitutions, how many they are and of what kinds; what destroys each constitution; from what kind and into what kind they mainly change; also the way to preserve constitutions in general and each in particular; finally the means by which each constitution is mainly preserved (*Pol.* 1301a31).

Or, to use other terms, the practical goal of *Politics* V is to teach the legislators how to preserve constitutions, with the help of an amazingly subtle theory of political changes. Such an analysis takes for granted the combinatory analysis of the diversity of constitutions proposed at the end of *Politics* IV. The general condition which makes these changes possible is the endless fight of political factions, the most typical of which is the mass of the poor and the small number of the wealthy. Then the restlessness of factions is dangerous for cities, all the more in that 'those who would be most justified in starting factions, that is the outstandingly virtuous men, are the least to do so' (*Pol.* 1301a39).

Politics V 2 provides the general framework for the investigation of constitutional changes. We have to explain constitutional changes by referring to three factors. The first one is the state of mind the people are in, some having the impression that they have less than they should, and others trying to get more than they have. The second is that 'for the sake of which changes arise'; on this point Aristotle's answer is 'profit, honour, and their contraries' (*Pol.* 1302a32), which must be understood as the wish to share in profit, avoid dishonour, etc. The third factor is divided by Aristotle into seven main categories, which, he says, may be divided in turn: the first two are also profit and honour, but as producing jealousy because they are in other hands, the others are arrogance, terror, superiority, contempt, and disproportionate development. Aristotle adds four causes, namely electioneering, carelessness, progressive alteration, and lack of homogeneity, which operate 'in another way' (*Pol.* 1302b4), presumably because they do not cause factions properly speaking.

Legislators have therefore to work in a world that I have depicted as a 'Darwinian' one.[29] For constitutional evolution is explained by referring both to an internal tendency the constitutions have to transform themselves, and to a selection due to the requirements of the environment. Let us see examples of this. Among the causes of change listed by Aristotle, disproportionate development is quite remarkable:

> Just as a living body is composed of parts which must grow proportionally if balance is to be saved, since otherwise it would be destroyed (if, for example, the foot of an animal were four cubits [1.78 m.] long and the rest of its body two spans [0.44 m.]; the species may even change to another one if this disproportionate growth is not only quantitative but also qualitative), so a city also is composed of parts, one of which often grows without being noticed, for example the mass of the poor in democracies or polities. This may sometimes happen by chance, as in Tarentum when many notables were killed by the Iapygians (*Pol.* 1302b34).

If a constitution wants to get a 'vital advantage' upon the others, it has to take into account two factors, because:

> All constitutions are subject to change, sometimes from within, sometimes from
> the exterior when there is a constitution of a contrary kind nearby or far away
> but endowed with power. This is what happened with Athens and Sparta, for the
> Athenians threw away the oligarchies everywhere, and the Spartans the popular
> regimes (*Pol.* 1307b19; cf. 1328b7).

What a constitution should oppose to a change coming either from within itself or
from outside is its own stability.

But such stability depends heavily on both the political and the historical
environment. At *Politics* 1312b38, Aristotle says that 'kingship is destroyed least by
external causes, which is also why it is long-lasting. Its destruction comes mainly
out of itself.... Kingships no longer come into existence nowadays'. The seventeenth-century commentator Sylvester Maurus is probably right to understand
that Aristotle means that exterior enemies find little support, or no support at all,
in the subjects of the king. But nowadays, as people have left behind them the patri-
archal life, kingship can no longer exist. Since cities became larger (cf. *Pol.* 1297b26)
and people are more educated (for instance in rhetoric, cf. *Pol.* 1305a10), a popular
regime is more likely to be stable than an aristocratic or an oligarchic one (cf. *Pol.*
1307a16), because the requirements a popular regime has to meet to be stable are
met more easily. That is what Aristotle says at *Politics* 1308a3: 'some aristocracies
and oligarchies survive not because they are stable by themselves, but because their
magistrates treat well those who are excluded from political life as well as those
who are parts of the ruling group'. In order to be stable, then, an oligarchy, all other
factors being equal, has to appoint clever magistrates to counter the frustrations
of the masses deprived of power. The difference in perspective with what has been
said earlier is striking. A polity is the best possible regime, not only because it is
based on a larger body of virtuous citizens, but also because it gives the city more
stability.

We find here what has been considered a dark side of this Aristotelian realism, which gives Aristotle's position a Machiavellian touch. Aristotle, for instance,
advocates an alarmist presentation of some situations by the magistrates, because
fear is a cause of social cohesion (*Pol.* 1308a27). But the most remarkable passage in
such a vein is certainly the chapter in which Aristotle analyses the causes of sedi-
tion in tyrannies and gives advice to the tyrant as to how he might perpetuate his
power. 'Tyrannies are preserved in two ways that are completely opposite to one
another' (*Pol.* 1313a34). The first way 'that has been handed down' is to increase the
tyrannical character of the tyranny, by making oppression stronger, spying upon
the subjects, developing corruption, using tricks, rendering people more and more
vile. The second way, on the contrary, enjoins the tyrant to get nearer to kingship,
at least apparently: 'it is a way of preservation for tyranny to make it more kingly'
(*Pol.* 1314a34). By being aware, for example, how families are offended by the sexual
abuse of their members, the tyrant who wants to have sex with a boy or a girl will
do his best to convince the family that he is driven by love. So the parents will be
flattered rather than humiliated.

What makes Aristotle's position completely different from Machiavellianism is the very Aristotelian conception of virtue as a state which becomes rooted in the soul by the way of the regular practice of good deeds. In mimicking virtue, the tyrant improves himself, just as Pascal's libertine makes his way toward faith by kneeling down. In this sense, Aristotle is a true *reformist*. A revolution may, in some cases, be the only available solution to get out of helpless situations, and Aristotle shares the admiration the Greeks had for the tyrannicides. But most of the time, it is by progressively improving the constitution that it is made better. Thus, as has been convincingly shown,[30] it is not because he wishes to be a conservative that Aristotle is, generally speaking, hostile to change of the laws. But because, first, the laws must have enough time to shape the character of the citizens; and, second, given that the laws depend on the constitution and not the other way around, changing the laws would jeopardize the constitution.

The legislators, therefore, will usually advocate measures for preserving the constitution, and reinforcing its improving capacities. Aristotle is so confident in the *natural* attraction of human beings toward the good, that he sees vicious cities as capable of improving by regulating themselves to last as long as possible. Oligarchy, for instance, as *Politics* V 6 explains, is threatened by two major dangers, the lack of satisfaction of the masses on the one hand, and the demagogic tendency of some oligarchs on the other. Therefore, if it wants to last long, an oligarchy would be well advised to take into account the demands of the masses and to involve them in office-holding. So, in this way, oligarchy will improve and tend toward a right form of constitution, namely a constitutional regime. Here Aristotle develops his remarkable idea that *a certain kind* of mixture of some elements of deviated constitutions may produce a right constitution, while another kind of mixture may worsen the constitution. This is mainly true for the two major regimes available in Aristotle's time, namely oligarchy and democracy.

As we have already seen, democrats and oligarchs have divergent conceptions of equality and justice: 'for the ones think that, if they are unequal in a certain respect, in goods for example, they are wholly unequal, while the others suppose that if they are equal in a certain other respect, namely freedom, they are equal generally' (*Pol.* 1280a22). Both parties are right to some extent and to some extent wrong, since there is a political and an anti-political use of wealth and freedom. Thus, when democracy and oligarchy combine their bad sides, that is unlimited attraction for money and demagogy, the result is the worst of the constitutions, tyranny: 'Tyranny is composed of the ultimate sort of oligarchy and of democracy; hence it is the most harmful constitution to the ruled, inasmuch as it is composed of two bad constitutions and involves the deviations and the errors of both of them' (*Pol.* 1310b3). But when they combine their good sides, the just recognition of work and the taste for freedom, the result is a constitutional regime. 'The criterion of a good mixture of democracy and oligarchy is that it should be possible for the same constitution to be spoken of as either a democracy or an oligarchy' (*Pol.* 1294b14).

At the end of the day, we see that when he appears as a realist or even as a kind of cynic or Machiavellian, Aristotle still has as his goal the establishment of an excellent constitution, that is, one which will make the citizens virtuous and therefore happy. There are not two projects, different from each other, in Aristotle's *Politics*, one idealistic and the other one realistic, but two approaches which, even if they are expressed in texts that have been written at different periods in Aristotle's lifetime, are compatible with each other.

VIII. Conclusion

Aristotle's political thought had almost no posterity in antiquity. There is no Greek commentary on the *Politics* and apparently it was never translated into Arabic. The main reason for this lack of interest has possibly been given above: Aristotle's thought, centred as it is on the very notion of the *polis*, was deemed outmoded when the *polis* disappeared as a political reality. One may wonder, however, on the assumption that the division of labour between the legislator and the philosopher advocated by Aristotle is right, what kind of teaching the philosopher from the Lyceum could have provided the legislator in the late fourth and early third centuries BC. For in fact Aristotle is not, or not only, a reactionary bound to a vanished reality. On the contrary, he offered an impressively complete, highly acute analysis of the crisis of the city. And this he did in a most remarkable way. Aristotle does not take the actual historical situation of his time as a starting point in his analysis of the crisis of the city. On the Macedonians, for instance, the *Politics* says almost nothing.[31] Alexander is never named, and there is no allusion to his great project of political and biological fusion between the Greek-Macedonians and the Persians. There may be some contingent reasons for this: Aristotle, as a Macedonian subject was suspect to the Athenians to the point where he eventually had to flee Athens. Further, perhaps his relationship with Alexander deteriorated and became worse and worse as their lives progressed down very different paths; but this cannot be the main reason.

On the contrary, Aristotle is not an historian. What Karl Polanyi saw better than anyone else, in the article quoted above, is that Aristotle was the first—and for many centuries the only—thinker who analysed the threat that the development of the merchant economy posed to the political society of his time. He was the first to grasp the difference between *Gemeinschaft* and *Gesellschaft*.[32] Thus, he did not *describe*, with the help of historical examples, the end of the ancient world and the birth of the new one. But he did theorize that transformation. About tyranny, we have seen, Aristotle was able to combine in the *Politics* a 'realist' analysis of social and political reality with a reaffirmation of the ethical destination of human beings. Aristotle's position is nevertheless an enigmatic one. He seems to think that the city, especially through the education of children, can resist the very transformations his brilliant analyses tend to show as ineluctable.

Notes

1. Cf. *Rhet.* I 8 1366a21.
2. Cf. P. Pellegrin, 'The Aristotelian Way', in M.-L. Gill & P. Pellegrin, eds., *A Companion to Ancient Philosophy*, Oxford 2006.
3. *EN* V I7 1141b4.
4. *EN* V 8 1141b23.
5. *EN* VI 7 1141b8ff.
6. Cf. R. Bodéüs, *The Political Dimensions of Aristotle's Ethics*, SUNY Press 1993.
7. It must be noted that this term does not mean family in the modern sense, even when the modern family is understood to include more than two generations. The word *oikia* indicates a lineage which extends to people who are not even biologically related, including most notably servants.
8. Cf. for example P.L. Phillips Simpson, *A Philosophical Commentary on The Politics of Aristotle*, University of North Carolina Press 1998, p. 21.
9. The text could also be read as meaning: 'man is a political animal rather than any kind of bee…'. But this would go against the *History of Animals* passage.
10. Cf. *Phy.* II 1 192b33: 'things have a nature which have a principle of this kind [i.e., of change and rest in themselves]…. The term "according to nature" is applied to all these things and also to the attributes which belong to them in virtue of what they are, for instance the property of fire to be carried upwards' (trans. Hardie and Gaye).
11. 'Der Mensch als politisches Lebewesen bei Aristoteles', *Hermes*, 1980, 419–43; English tranlation in D. Keyt and F. Miller, eds., *A Companion to Aristotle's Politics*, Blackwell 1991, pp. 94–117: 'Man as a Political Animal in Aristotle'.
12. Cf. VII 4 1326b2: a city with too many people 'while it is self-sufficient with necessary things, in the way a nation is, is still no city'.
13. 'Aristotle discovers the economy', in *Trade and market in early Empires*, Glencoe, Ill. 1957.
14. The treatise entitled *Economics* is probably not by Aristotle, but is good evidence of the Peripatetic position on the administration of the household.
15. Cf.*Pol.* VII 7.
16. 'La théorie aristotélicienne de l' esclavage et sa méthode', in *Zetesis. Album Amicorum (Mélanges E. De Strycker)*, Antwerpen, 1973, pp. 147–163.
17. Such a domestic slavery existed in many stateless societies. Cf. P. Pellegrin, 'La Théorie aristotélicienne de l'esclavage: tendances actuelles de l'interprétation', *Revue Philosophique* 1982, no. 2, pp. 345–357.
18. This does not mean that slaves are restricted to household work, *pace* Jacques Brunschwig, 'L'esclavage chez Aristote', *Cahiers philosophiques* (CNDP), Sept. 1979.
19. 'The family is the partnership constituted by nature for daily needs. Charondas called its members 'peers of the mess', Epimenides of Crete 'peers of the manger'. The first partnership arising from the union of several families and for the sake of non-daily needs is the village…this is why cities were at first under kings, and some people are even now…. For those who joined together were already under a king, since every family was under the eldest as a king, and also were the unions of families constituting the village as a result of kinship' (*Pol.* 1252b12).

20. Cf. P. Pellegrin, 'Hausverwaltung und Sklaverei (I 3–13)', in O. Höffe, ed., *Aristoteles Politik*, Akademie Verlag, 2001, pp. 37–57.

21. Cf., for instance, M. Schofield: 'they [the slaves] need someone else to deliberate on their behalf if they are to survive', 'Ideology and Philosophy in Aristotle's Theory of Slavery', in G. Patzig, ed., *Aristoteles Politik. Akten des XI. Symposium Aristotelicum*, Göttingen, 1990, p. 14.

22. The passage I 5 1254b22–3 seems to deny that slaves have reason. In fact, not to mention the fact that the text is ambiguous and that it may allude not to reason as a whole but to rational knowledge originating in perception, it actually contrasts animals, which do not perceive reason and slaves who do. In any case the passage I 13 1260b5 is quite clear: 'those who deny reason to slaves...do not argue correctly'.

23. This so-called opposition is the main cause for the re-ordering of the books, which can be traced back at least to the sixteenth century.

24. Aristotle's *Physics*, on the contrary, is not to be included in the history of physics.

25. Descartes, for instance, concerning the States takes as evident that 'their imperfections, if they have some, since their diversity is enough to prove that some do ...' (*Discourse on Method* part II).

26. Even commentators as remarkable as Gauthier and Jolif ignore this.

27. Cf. P. Pellegrin, 'La *Politique* d'Aristote: Unité et fractures. Eloge de la lecture sommaire', *Revue philosophique*, 1987, no. 2, 129–159, reprinted in P. Aubenque, ed., *Aristote politique. Etudes sur la* Politique *d'Aristote*, Paris PUF 1993, pp. 3–34.

28. Cf. Pierre Pellegrin, 'Parties de la cité, parties de la constitution', in C. Natali, ed., *Aristotle: Metaphysics and Practical Philosophy. Essays in Honour of Enrico Berti*, (Louvain la Neuve, 2011), 177–200.

29. Cf. 'Naturalité, excellence, diversité. Politique et biologie chez Aristote', in *Aristoteles' 'Politik'* herausgegeben von Günther Patzig (actes du XI° *Symposium Aristotelicum*) (Göttingen) 1990, p. 132.

30. J. Brunschwig, 'Du mouvement et de l'immobilité de la loi', *Revue Internationale de Philosophie*, 133–134 (1980), pp. 512–40.

31. At V 4 1304a13 Aristotle alludes to the sacred war initiated by the Phocidians to control the sanctuary of Delphi, which gave Philip of Macedon a pretext to intervene in Greek affairs; at V 10 1310b39 he includes the kings of Macedon as people who increased their territory; at V 10 1311b1 he alludes to Pausanias' revolt againt Philip; at VII 2 1324b15 Macedonians are said to be a barbarian and warlike people.

32. Relying on the distinction proposed by Henry S. Maine between the societies founded on *contractus* and those founded on *status*, Ferdinand Tönnies made a distinction between *Gemeinschaft* (community) and *Gesellschaft* (society). The first is an auto-regulated group into which economic mechanisms are 'inserted', and the second is a group based on a contract with an 'independent' economy.

Bibliography

Bodéüs, R. (1993) *The Political Dimensions of Aristotle's Ethics* (New York: SUNY Press).

Brunschwig, J. (1979) 'L' esclavage chez Aristote', *Cahiers philosophiques*.

_____ (1980) 'Du mouvement et de l'immobilité de la loi', *Revue Internationale de Philosophie* 133–34, 512–40.

Goldschmidt, V. (1973) 'La théorie aristotélicienne de l'esclavage et sa méthode', in *Zetesis, Album Amicorum [...] E. de Strycker*, (Antwerpen: De Nederlandsche Boekhandel), 147–63.

Kullmann, W. (1991) 'Der Mensch als politisches Lebewesen bei Aristoteles', *Hermes* 1980, 419–43; English trans. in D. Keyt and F. Miller, eds., *A Companion to Aristotle's Politics* (Blackwell, 1991), 94–117: 'Man as a Political Animal in Aristotle'.

Pellegrin, P. (1982) 'La théorie aristotélicienne de l'esclavage: tendances actuelles de l'interprétation', *Revue Philosophique* 2, 345–57.

_____ (1990) 'Naturalité, excellence, diversité. Politique et biologie chez Aristote', in G. Patzig, ed., *Aristoteles Politik* (Göttingen: Vandenhoeck & Ruprecht).

_____ (1987) 'La *Politique* d'Aristote: Unité et fractures. Eloge de la lecture sommaire', *Revue philosophique*, 2, 129–59; repr. in P. Aubenque, ed., *Aristote politique. Etudes sur la Politique d' Aristote*, (Paris: PUF, 1993), 3–34.

_____ (2001) 'Hausverwaltung und Sklaverei (I 3–13)', in O. Höffe, ed., *Aristoteles, Politik*, (Berlin: Akademie Verlag), 37–57.

_____ (2006) 'The Aristotelian Way', in M.L. Gill and P. Pellegrin, eds., *A Companion to Ancient Philosophy* (Oxford : Blackwell Pub.).

_____ (2011), 'Parties de la cité, parties de la constitution', in C. Natali, ed., *Aristotle: Metaphysics and Practical Philosophy. Essays in Honour of Enrico Berti* (Louvain la Neuve: Peeters Pub.), 177–200.

Phillips Simpson, P.L. (1998) *A Philosophical Commentary on The Politics of Aristotle* (Chapel Hill, N.C.: Univ. of North Carolina Press).

Polanyi, K. (1957) 'Aristotle Discovers the Economy', in *Trade and Market in Early Empires*, (Glencoe, Ill.).

Schofield, M., (1990) 'Ideology and Philosophy in Aristotle's Theory of Slavery', in G. Patzig, ed., *Aristoteles Politik* (Göttingen: Vandenhoeck & Ruprecht).

PART VI

RHETORIC AND THE ARTS

CHAPTER 22

ARISTOTLE ON THE MORAL PSYCHOLOGY OF PERSUASION[1]

CHRISTOF RAPP

1. INTRODUCTION

THIS chapter discusses some core theorems of Aristotle's account of persuasion as it is set out in his work on rhetoric. The *Rhetoric* consists of three books, the first two of which develop a more or less coherent project, whereas the third, as I think, introduces two relatively independent and self-contained projects that deal with the topic of linguistic form or style, as well as with the division of parts of public speech. For the sake of brevity I will focus on the project of the first two books, *Rhetoric* I and II.

It is the declared ambition of *Rhetoric* I and II to develop a *technê*, or art, of rhetoric, and the central tool of this *technê* is, as it were, the introduction of three technical means of persuasion. The technical character of this art of persuasion represents, in Aristotle's view, a decisive form of progress in comparison with, and in contradistinction, to all previous manuals of rhetoric, which, as Aristotle seems to assume, for the most part offer persuasive techniques that are non-technical, i.e., are based neither on a proper *technê* nor on a proper understanding of the nature of persuasion. The disadvantage of such non-technical manuals of persuasion is twofold: First, and above all, they fail to be maximally persuasive, whereas Aristotle's art of rhetoric describes itself as the attempt to see and to analyse methodologically the persuasive potential of any given rhetorical situation (*Rhet.* I 2 1355b25ff.). Second, such non-technical manuals of persuasion are bound to deploy some persuasive tricks or tools that may seem censurable, or, as Aristotle notes, are in fact censured to the extent that their use in public speech is forbidden, especially in cities with good legislation (*Rhet.* I 1 1354a31—b11).

By highlighting the technical, *technê*-based, status of his own theory of persuasion, Aristotle implicitly suggests that his own approach to persuasion is grounded in the proper understanding of persuasion that he finds lacking in the manuals of his predecessors. And it is this very nature of persuasion or, rather, Aristotle's assumptions about the nature of persuasion, that provides the focus of the present paper. Unfortunately, due to the peculiar character of Aristotle's work on rhetoric as it has come down to us, the discussions of this work seem more directly concerned with the formulation of the rhetorical means or techniques that follow from a certain understanding of the nature of persuasion than with the elucidation of the nature of persuasion itself. Consequently, we will have to proceed by considering the techniques of persuasion that Aristotle actually suggests, those he regards as the properly technical, art-based ones, and to inquire thereby into the assumptions he makes about the anatomy of persuasion which underlie and motivate these techniques.

2. Two claims in Aristotle's *Rhetoric*

Probably the best point to start with is two claims that Aristotle eventually makes in the course of his work on rhetoric. The first claim is explicitly stated with different wording in several passages of the *Rhetoric* and is sometimes seen as implicitly playing a role in how Aristotle ranks and assigns significance to the different means of persuasion he considers. *Ceteris paribus*, this first claim consists in saying that proof and argument are central to persuasion: if you want to make someone believe what you believe or what you want him to believe, then don't employ slander, flattery, distraction, emotional appeals, or bombast; don't call your wife and kids up on to the speaker's platform, and don't count on the effect of their moaning and lamentation. On the contrary, one should refrain from all these sorts of trickery, which have given rhetoric a bad reputation; instead, one should try to speak to the point and to find arguments or proofs for whatever conviction one wishes to communicate to the audience. This first claim can be extracted from several passages, for example from the following quotations (A) and (B):

> **(A)** …for we are most convinced when we suppose something to have been proven (*Rhet.* I 1 1255a5–6).

Here Aristotle clearly states that we are *malista*, most or most easily, convinced whenever we think something has been proven or demonstrated.

> **(B)** …but they say nothing about enthymemes, which are the body of persuasion (*Rhet.* I 1 1254a14–15).

According to (B) it is the enthymeme, which is, in Aristotle's terminology, nothing but the rhetorical proof, i.e., the proof used in a rhetorical setting, that is the body of persuasion, and this again is to say that it is central to or the core of persuasion.

In a sense, one might think, this claim that arguments or proofs are central to persuasion is not overwhelmingly challenging or surprising. On the other hand, this statement has a couple of far-reaching implications. In saying this, Aristotle sets himself apart from common rhetorical practices, such as the aforementioned ones, that are vulnerable to a variety of criticism; and at the same time, he responds to those who—following the spirit of Plato's dialogue *Gorgias*—are suspicious of the very possibility of an art-based rhetoric. And what is perhaps even more important, by saying that persuasion properly understood is a matter of argument and proof, Aristotle claims the dialectician's responsibility for the development of the proper art of persuasion. And this is not a negligible step, because dialectic, as it were, is a philosophical endeavour, so that Aristotle's claim amounts to nothing less than saying that rhetoric, properly understood, is not an alternative or a competitor to philosophy, but ultimately nothing but a sub-field or a proper extension of a certain sub-field of philosophical investigation, namely of dialectic. And indeed, the famous opening sentence of Aristotle's *Rhetoric* states that rhetoric is a counterpart of dialectic (*Rhet.* I 1 1354a1). This affinity between rhetoric and dialectic again shapes major parts of the terminological inventory of the *Rhetoric*: just as does Aristotle's book on dialectic, the *Topics*, the *Rhetoric* speaks of *sullogismoi*, of *protaseis* (premises), of *topoi*, of refutations, of inductions, of *endoxa* (accepted beliefs), of conclusive and non-conclusive arguments, etc. In short, what we are aiming at is the claim that we cannot understand the undertaking of Aristotle's *Rhetoric* appropriately without acknowledging the close connection between rhetoric and dialectic, and this connection again makes sense only against the background of our first claim, the claim that argument and proof are central to persuasion or, to put it the other way around, that persuasion essentially rests on proof and argument.

However, we find a second claim in the *Rhetoric*, no less important, that might seem to create a certain tension with the first claim; this is the claim that proofs and arguments, however central and important they may be, are not sufficient to persuade, at least not in all cases, or, to look at it from a different angle, proof and argument alone do not exhaust the available sources of persuasion. This second claim is clearly stated in (C):

> (C) But since rhetoric aims at a judgement (*krisis*)…it is necessary not only to look at the argument, that it may be conclusive and convincing but also to present oneself as a certain kind of person and to prepare the audience (*Rhet.* II 1 1377b21–24).

According to (C), it seems that for those who want to effectively steer or control their audience's judgement, it is not enough to look to the argument, that it may be conclusive, demonstrative, and convincing; it is also necessary to use methods that are not argumentative, at least not in the sense of putting forward statements and trying to give reasons for holding such statements. Actually, Aristotle uses this formula, namely that we should not only look to the arguments or proofs, when he proceeds from the discussion of rhetorical arguments to the discussion of the persuasive techniques that became famous under the headings of '*êthos*' and '*pathos*', character and emotion. These are sometimes even rendered as the two non-rational means of persuasion, presupposing that nothing beside argument could ever be rational. However, I suggest that we should stick to saying that they are non-argumentative, at least not in the sense of premise-conclusion arguments.

These two claims, extracted from (A) and (B) on the one hand and from (C) on the other, lie close to the core of Aristotle's technique of persuasion. They do not contradict each other, since it is perfectly consistent to say that one thing is essential or central to another, but that it is nevertheless not exhaustive of that thing and has to be complemented by something else. However, there remains a certain tension between the two claims, since with respect to the first claim, we have to find out why proof and argument can be said to be central to the persuasive process, while with respect to the second claim, we have to inquire to what degree proof and argument must be regarded as insufficient and how they can be sensibly complemented by something else.

Now one tendency in the literature on Aristotle's *Rhetoric* is, as I see it, to exaggerate the tension between these two claims; sometimes they are even seen as representing two incompatible layers within the *Rhetoric*.[2] Another tendency is that, in accordance with certain fashionable views about the supposed weakness of arguments as such or about the need to broaden the notion of rationality, the second of the two claims is used to weaken or even to deny the first claim.[3] My view is, roughly, that there is neither a need to see these two claims as incompatible nor indeed any reason to weaken one of them at the cost of the other. I rather tend to think that a closer look at the relation between these two claims will help to elucidate certain assumptions that Aristotle seems to make concerning the moral psychology of persuasion.

3. MORAL PSYCHOLOGICAL ISSUES

What is the reason for calling this sort of inquiry a 'moral psychological' one? Moral psychology, as I understand it, is first of all dedicated to the exploration of the human soul with respect to the soul's capacity to desire and to form decisions. More precisely, there are two opposed explanatory directions in moral psychology: in some cases we start with observations about our way of deciding and of acting in order to arrive at conclusions about the soul's architecture, while in some other cases it is the other way around, namely that we use certain assumptions about the different capacities of the soul in order to account for specific phenomena in the realm of human action and conduct. Originally and typically, moral-psychological questions occur in the face of phenomena that at least seem to call for an explanation in terms of different parts or, at least, capacities of the soul. For example, in the context of possible or manifest conflicts between different sorts of desire, as given most notably in the case of *akrasia* or weakness of the will, where the actor is torn between two opposed impulses, or, to take another example, in the context of education, insofar as it seems attractive to model the different needs and requirements in the course of ontogenetic human development as the alternating predominance of different parts of the soul.

If we sketch the project of moral psychology more or less along these lines, then it is obvious that it is the moral psychologist's job, if anybody's, to deal with the question of how we can lead, guide, steer, or form the soul, or, vice versa, how and why the soul is responsive to specific persuasive, musical, or educational efforts. Now, in order to account for the relation between the two claims that I quoted in the previous section, we will obviously have to touch on certain assumptions concerning the responsiveness of our souls to various sorts of influences, both argumentative and non-argumentative. And this is why I think that a full analysis of persuasion is a matter of moral psychology—in the depicted sense.

In a way, Plato was the first to acknowledge that we need something like the project of moral psychology in order to give an art- or *technê*-based analysis of persuasion, since in his *Phaedrus* he was quite explicit about the point that the rhetorician has to be an expert in psychological matters and must even practice a sort of *psychagôgia*, the art of leading the soul:

> **(D)** Since the nature of speech is in fact to direct the soul, whoever intends to be a rhetorician must know how many kinds of soul there are. Their number is so-and-so many; each is of such-and-such a sort; hence some people have such-and-such a character and others have such-and-such. Those distinctions established, there are, in turn, so-and-so many kinds of speech, each of such and such a sort (*Phaedrus* 271c10–272b5, tr. Nehamas/Woodruff).

Unfortunately, Plato somehow obscured the significance of his discovery by requiring that the rhetorician must not only have knowledge in the field of moral psychology but also must understand the nature of the whole.

In a sense, the idea that true rhetoric has to include *psychagôgia* and that *psychagôgia* again must be based on the philosophical study of the soul was taken up by Aristotle in his work on rhetoric. Aristotle, however, did not literally carry out the hints that Plato gave in this context, namely that we have to distinguish types of soul that allegedly correspond to types of speech. That rhetoric in the Aristotelian sense nevertheless has to include moral-psychological considerations comes out most clearly when Aristotle says that rhetoric is an offshoot not only of dialectic, but also of the study of character (I 2 1356a25–27); and the concession that rhetoric is not only based on dialectic, but must also rely on what Aristotle calls the study of character, is made in the same context as that in which the two non-argumentative means of persuasion are introduced.

We can therefore say that for Aristotle the proper account of persuasion involves dialectic, (at least) insofar as persuasion has to do with arguments, and it also involves moral psychology, since it does not rely solely on arguments.

4. WHAT DOES RHETORIC AIM AT?

Before continuing and discussing the three technical means of persuasion, we should briefly pause here and address the question of what rhetoric or rhetorical persuasion ultimately aims at. At first glance, this seems to be a trivial question, since it can hardly be doubted that rhetorical persuasion aims at the persuasion of an audience. However, the very notion of being persuaded might be ambivalent. Aristotle, for example, famously depicts several kinds and degrees of being persuaded. When, for example, differentiating several kinds of knowledge in the context of *akrasia*, he seems to assume that we sometimes hold opinions in a rather superficial way, just like the drunken man who does not really grasp what he says or the way someone reciting the verses of Empedocles cannot mean what he spells out (*EN* VII 3 1147a20). In the same context, Aristotle also uses the metaphor of an opinion that has not yet grown into us or not yet pervaded us (*EN* VII 3 1147a22). This could be taken as a basis for distinguishing between weaker and stronger senses of being persuaded. Furthermore, in the context of moral education, Aristotle emphasizes the need for repetition and the need to ultimately desire what one ought to do, and this effect again could reasonably be pictured as a sort of in-depth persuasion.

Now it is tempting to think that it is the very purpose of writing a book-long treatise on persuasion to develop these stronger senses of persuasion, especially since the *Rhetoric* deals with emotion and character and Aristotle is famous for holding that it is the aim of education not only to communicate opinions, but also to shape the traits of character and the emotional reactions that correspond to certain convictions. However, I think this is an expectation that will be disappointed. Aristotle's *Rhetoric* deals exclusively with those acts of persuasion that are relevant for public speech, and the purpose of public speeches is a rather restricted one. For example, Aristotle does not seem to expect that public speeches will have a direct pedagogical effect because education is a long-term affair, involving praise and blame, personal encouragement and punishment, whereas the public orator does not have such means at his disposal and is supposed to remain within the well-defined, restrictive frame of either the judicial or the political or the ceremonial speech. At the very end of the *Nicomachean Ethics* Aristotle says:

> (E) If speeches were in themselves enough to make men good, they would justly, as Theognis says, have won very great rewards, and such rewards should have

been provided; but as things are...they are not able to encourage the many to nobility and goodness (*EN* X 9 1179b4–10, tr. Ross/Urmson, modified).

Rhetoric has to deal with existing long-term convictions, but a single speech cannot change our attitude towards the most important things, i.e., virtues and vices and everything else that makes the difference between a good and a depraved character.

The problem that is relevant in our context, however, is not only that the public speech is pedagogically inert; the point is that the rhetorical persuasion, as described in Aristotle's *Rhetoric*, aims at the listener's judgement (*krisis*) and at nothing else. And this again means, I take it, that rhetorical persuasion tries to make people accept a proposition they haven't held before, no more, no less. In particular, the public speech does not primarily try to evoke our desire to do what we have judged to be good; the orator's job is to modify our judgements about, for example, what is good and what is not. This represents an important departure from those commentators who assume that Aristotle is interested in character and emotions because he wants to bring about a practical decision (*prohairesis*),[4] for which purpose we have to address the audience's judgement as well as its desire. In my view, the introduction of character and emotions is meant, as we will see, to modify the audience's judgements and for nothing else. One preliminary argument in favour of my reading would be that in many cases, including, for example, judicial speech, where the audience has to judge (theoretically) whether someone is guilty or not, the model of the practical decision is entirely out of place. By contrast, *prohairesis* always concerns, in Aristotle's usage, ways of acting that are open to the agent at the time of his decision.

5. THREE MEANS OF PERSUASION (*PISTEIS*): *ÊTHOS/PATHOS/LOGOS*

Finally, then, we can proceed to the three means of persuasion to which I have already alluded several times. As I said in the very beginning, the three means of persuasion represent Aristotle's artistic or technical approach to rhetoric in *Rhetoric* I and II, as opposed to the supposedly non-technical, not *technê*-based, approaches of Aristotle's predecessors. The famous introduction of these three means of persuasion takes place in the section of text that is quoted in (F), which for the purpose of further reference is subdivided into four subsections:

> **(F.1)** Of the *pisteis*, some are non-technical, some *technê*-based. I call non-technical those that are not provided by us but are pre-existing, as for example, witnesses, testimony of slaves taken under torture, contracts and such like; and

technê-based whatever can be prepared by method and by us; thus, one must use the former and invent the latter. Of the *pisteis* provided through speech there are three species: for some are in the character (*êthos*) of the speaker, and some in disposing the listener in some way, and some in the argument (*logos*) itself, by showing or seeming to show something (*Rhet.* I 2 1355b35–1356a4, tr. Kennedy, modified).

Section (F.1) first refers to the difference between means of persuasion that are provided by the *technê* and the means that are not: the latter deal with pre-existing facts, e.g., witnesses, contracts, etc. (a brief discussion of these means is given in *Rhetoric* I 15), while the former have to be provided by the speech itself. Then the section introduces the famous three technical means of persuasion that are based on either *êthos* or *pathos* or *logos*. The Greek word for means of persuasion is '*pisteis*', the plural of *pistis*, which can be used to signify the quality of being persuasive, the process of persuasion, or the resulting state of being persuaded, etc. In the traditional, pre-Aristotelian rhetoric, it was meant to designate the part of the speech in which the orator was supposed to present his proofs. In the present context, I take it to mean something like 'means' or 'modes' of persuading, in the sense of bringing about a state of persuasion in the audience.

Although this threefold division *êthos, pathos, logos.* is Aristotle's main tool for conceptually analysing the process of persuasion, he never explicitly justifies either the division itself or its completeness. The best interpreters can do for the theoretical justification of this theorem is to take recourse in the triangle of object, speaker, and addressee, and to associate these three angles of the triangle with each of the three means of persuasion. The same triangle can indeed be found in Aristotle's *Rhetoric* (namely in chapter I 3), but unfortunately, in a completely different context.—In any event, instead of dwelling on the tripartition itself, Aristotle hastens to explain the three means of persuasion one by one:

> **(F.2)** Through character whenever the speech is spoken in such a way as to make the speaker trustworthy, for we believe decent people more easily and more quickly on all subjects in general and completely so in cases where there is no exact knowledge but room for differing opinions. And this should result from the speech, not from a previous opinion that the speaker is a certain kind of person … (*Rhet.* I 2, 1356a5–10, tr. Kennedy, modified).

Section (F.2) is about *êthos*, which turns out to be more or less equivalent to the credibility of the speaker. His credibility or trustworthiness is one factor in persuasion, and it is a factor, as Aristotle seems to think, that has often been underestimated. Sometimes speakers happen to be trustworthy because of the long-standing reputation they have acquired by their way of living—and such a good reputation, certainly, may be useful for someone who wants to present himself in public—but this is not exactly what Aristotle is interested in, since whether we have a good reputation or not is a matter of how we have lived so far and not a matter of rhetorical technique. The fact that we have lived a morally good life, for example, is neither necessary nor sufficient for appearing to be a trustworthy speaker. From the rhetorical point of view, the question is just how we can render ourselves trustworthy, whether we deserve to be seen as trustworthy or not.

> **(F.3)** Through the hearers when they are led to feel emotion (*pathos*) by the speech, for we do not give the same judgement when grieved and rejoicing or when being friendly and hostile. To this and only this we said contemporary technical writers try to give their attention... (*Rhet.* I 2 1356a14–17, tr. Kennedy, modified).

Section (F.3) comments on the *pistis* of *pathos*. The rhetorician has to pay attention to the emotional state of the audience, although Aristotle seems to think that his predecessors were misled when they almost exclusively dealt with the emotional aspects of persuasion (*Rhet.* I 1 1354a11–16). By emotion Aristotle means something like anger, pity, fear, and the like, which is always followed by pleasure and pain. In chapters II 2–11 of the *Rhetoric*, Aristotle offers an extended discussion of several emotions that might be useful for the rhetorician. In order to arouse emotions, Aristotle says, one must be observant of three factors, the state of mind in which people are, say, angry, the type of person at whom they are angry, and the kind of occasion or reason making them angry (*Rhet.* II 1 1378a22–26). In most of the chapters about particular emotions, Aristotle derives these three factors from an initial, supposedly arbitrary definition of each emotion. In a nutshell, I think, it is most significant with regard to Aristotle's technique of the rhetorical arousal of emotions that the three factors mentioned can be influenced by *what* the orator says. (The *way* the orator expresses himself may also make a difference regarding emotional reaction; however, this is a matter of the selection of words or style, *lexis*, which is the topic of *Rhetoric* III 1–12.) For example, in order to make the audience angry, the orator must say or prove that the specific reason for anger is given, namely an insult or humiliation done by someone who is not entitled to do so. If it is, as Aristotle thinks, e.g., a sort of insult or humiliation when we forget other people's names (*Rhet.* II 2 1379b34), then the orator can, for example, point out that someone actually forgot our names, so that we will get angry at that person. And, to take another example, if people are more vulnerable to fear when they happen to be in a state in which they expect that something painful is likely to happen to them, it might help if the orator reminds the audience of painful things or embarrassing defeats they suffered in the past (*Rhet.* II 5 1383a8–12), and so on and so forth.

> **(F.4)** Persuasion occurs through the arguments (*logoi*) when we show the truth or the apparent truth from whatever is persuasive in each case. Since persuasions come about through these three means, it is clear that to grasp an understanding of them is the function of one who can draw conclusions (*sullogisasthai*) and be observant about characters and virtues and, third, about emotions (what each of the emotions is and what its qualities are and from what it comes to be and how). The result is that rhetoric is a certain kind of offshoot of dialectic and the study of character (which is justly called *hê politikê*). (*Rhet.* I 2 1356a19–27, tr. Kennedy, modified.)

Finally, in Section (F.4) Aristotle introduces *logos*, the means of persuasion that is based on proofs or arguments. For Aristotle, there are always two species of arguments: inductions and deductions (*APo* I 1 71a5ff.). In the field of rhetoric, how-ever, the inductive argument is the example (*paradeigma*); the deductive argument in rhetoric is the enthymeme (*Rhet.* II 1 1356b4ff., 1356b16–18). Although Aristotle says that there are exactly two forms of argument, an inductive and a deductive one, the *Rhetoric* almost exclusively focuses on the deductive form of argument, the enthymeme. Traditionally, the enthymeme has been taken to be an abbrevi-ated, incomplete, or truncated syllogism. But this is not what Aristotle actually says. He calls the enthymeme the rhetorical proof, which means that it is not a sci-entific proof, but rather a sort of proof that has been adjusted to the conditions of public speech. And since every proof is a *sullogismos*,[5] the enthymeme is a kind of *sullogismos*. Hence Aristotle says that in order to formulate good enthymemes, we must have the same competence that is required for all other kinds of *sullogismoi*, and we must also have a further competence concerning the differences between regular and rhetorical *sullogismoi*. It turns out that there are exactly two factors that the dialectician has to keep in mind if he wants to become a rhetorician as well (I 1 1355a11–14; I 2 1357a1–4): first, the typical subjects of public speech—unlike the subjects of dialectic and theoretical philosophy—do not belong to the things that are necessarily the case, but are amongst those things that are the goal of practical deliberation and can also be otherwise. Second, as opposed to well-trained dia-lecticians, the audience of public speech seems to be characterized by intellectual inadequacy; above all, the members of a jury or assembly are not accustomed to following a longer chain of inferences. Therefore, enthymemes must not be as pre-cise as a scientific demonstration and should be shorter than ordinary dialectical arguments.

This, however, is not to say that the enthymeme is *defined* by incompleteness and brevity. The orator can avoid lengthy chains of arguments by selecting the right premises, i.e., premises that are not too far from the intended conclusions, or by omitting intermediate deductive steps. But even the latter case, the omission of intermediate deductive steps, does not necessarily imply logical incompleteness; the required brevity of an enthymeme can also be a matter of avoiding unneces-sary deductions by which the orator wants to introduce the premises of the main argument. Thus persuasion by argument is primarily a matter of enthymemes, and enthymemes resemble or belong to the deductive type of reasoning but are adjusted to the specific requirements of public speech, and these requirements again con-cern the subject matter of public speeches or the audience's inability to follow long chains of argument.

Aristotle concludes Section (F) by pointing out that due to the three means of persuasion, the rhetorician needs two types of competence: a logical type of com-petence in order to deal with *sullogismoi* of all kinds and to master the means of persuasion called 'logos', and also the competence in what Aristotle calls 'the study of character' in order to deal with *êthos* and *pathos*. With respect to these latter two means of persuasion, Aristotle explains that the rhetorician must be observant of three things, namely character, virtues, and emotions, and this again brings him close to what we characterized above as the agenda of moral psychology.

6. HOW *LOGOS* PERSUADES

In quotation (A), Aristotle stated that we are most convinced—most easily convinced or most strongly convinced—whenever we think that something has been proven or demonstrated. This, I think, is anything but a trivial claim. By saying this, Aristotle aligns the field of persuasion with other processes of understanding and learning. And indeed, when Aristotle speaks of evidence in the context of scientific or logical proofs, he sometimes adopts a vocabulary that is not entirely different from the rhetorical one: for example, he depicts both teaching and persuading in terms of premises the addressee is supposed to know, to understand, or to accept, and conclusions that are to be derived from those premises. Or, to take another example, primary scientific premises are said to carry their own *pistis*, i.e., credibility or evidence (*Topics* I 1 100b1f.), so that the issue of *pistis* and, in general, the issue of being persuasive, is not just a question of oratory but, to a certain extent, also belongs to epistemology and the theory of demonstration. And this supposed similarity between quite different fields of discourse seems to be one of the preconditions for Aristotle's practice of using one and the same scheme, the scheme of inductive and deductive arguments, to account for such different things as scientific demonstrations, dialectical disputations, and rhetorical persuasion.[6]

Against that background one straightforward way to construe the implications of the statement in quotation (A) would be this: if proofs or demonstrations are so central to persuasion, it might be—*ceteris paribus*—sufficient to formulate demonstrations in order to persuade an audience. However, this construal would be vulnerable to several objections, even from an Aristotelian point of view. For example, one such objection is that the subject matter of public speech concerns things about which we can deliberate and hence do not involve the kind of necessity that is required for proper demonstrations; another is the objection that in this case, we would not need the art of rhetoric, because we could use the same sort of demonstration for the purpose of persuasion that we are accustomed to using for the purpose of teaching. Aristotle, however, insists that although the general structures of learning and becoming persuaded are similar (and although, I would like to add, the successful process of learning will result in a state of persuasion, too), being persuaded in the rhetorical sense still differs from learning. Once he even says that learning is impossible for the audience of a public speech (*Rhet.* I 1 1354b26ff.), most probably because the subject matter of rhetoric cannot really be learned or because the student must grant the truth of the deployed premises, even if he does not yet understand or believe those premises, which the audience of a public speech would never do, especially since such an audience is exposed to rival speakers with possibly contradicting premises.

Therefore, rather than requiring that persuasion should consist of a series of full-blown proofs, the statement that proofs are central to persuasion seems to mean that the process of persuasion essentially consists in proving something on the basis of what the audience already believes (*Rhet.* I 2 1356b29f.). We can make people accept a certain proposition by connecting it with something they already believe, accept, or approve: in order to convince the audience of a proposition B, the dialectically instructed speaker will take up a proposition A—one already approved by the audience—from which the target proposition B deductively follows, or at least seems to follow. Given certain subsidiary conditions, whoever is convinced of proposition A will also be convinced of proposition B once he or she learns that there is an inferential connection between the two propositions.

On this account, persuasion by proof seems to be possible only if there are preexisting convictions in the audience upon which the orator can build his proofs or from which he can deduce or derive the proposition he is aiming at. This is a remarkable consequence, but it is not surprising, at least not given the similarity to the process of learning, of which Aristotle also says that it always has to start from pre-existing knowledge. In the field of rhetoric, however, the premises that the orator uses are not supposed to be principles and not even to be explanatory. If they happen to explain what the orator deduces from them, this would not be an obstacle; but rhetoric is also the field that is famous for the use of sign arguments, and in the case of sign arguments we do not attempt to explain anything, but just to indicate its existence, truth, or plausibility (as smoke indicates that there is fire, or fever that someone is ill, etc.). What matters for (rhetorical) persuasion is only the fact that the audience already believes or accepts the involved premises, and this again is the reason why, in Aristotelian terms, the rhetorician has to be an expert in *endoxa*—accepted opinions. And expertise in accepted opinions is indeed a part of the dialectician's competence. In the scholarship of recent decades it has often been said that these *endoxa* play a role in many branches of Aristotle's philosophy. However, the dialectically instructed rhetorician is not interested in all kinds of *endoxa*—not, for example, in the views that are held by a few experts—but only in the subset of *endoxa* that Aristotle sometimes calls *koina* (I 1 1355a27), the commonly accepted opinions. For the rhetorician, when confronted with a mass audience, cannot deal with individual opinions (I 2 1356b28–35) but only with average opinions.

7. WHY *LOGOS* IS, AFTER ALL, INSUFFICIENT

In the model of persuasion just sketched, persuasion comes about (a) if we already believe certain premises and (b) if we come to see that something else follows from the assumed premises, or if, even simpler, something is in itself persuasive (*Rhet.* I 2 1356b28ff.). Now, the practice of accepting B, if it follows from an already accepted

A, constitutes a very important consistency criterion, and this consistency criterion is part of what we would call 'requirements of rationality'. Hence we could say that Aristotle's model of persuasion, in the sense we have just sketched, relies on such requirements of rationality. Wherever there is a requirement, one could say, there is at least the theoretical possibility that someone could fail to meet this requirement. And, what is more, with respect to the sort of requirement we called a requirement of rationality, we all know and Aristotle often says—in many different contexts—that not everyone is always willing or able to match what rationality demands from us. Therefore the Aristotelian model of proof-based persuasion—in spite of its charming simplicity—has the disadvantage that not everyone will actually be persuaded by such a persuasion process, since probably not everyone, as we already implied, will form his or her judgements in accord with these standards of rationality.

However, Aristotle, I would like to suggest, turns this weakness of his proof-based model into a strength of his general approach, by explicitly admitting and addressing the phenomenon that the process of judgement formation is responsive or vulnerable to factors beyond the solely argumentative ones. Let us go back to the first part of quotation (C): 'But since rhetoric aims at a judgement (*krisis*)...it is necessary [for the orator] not only to look at the argument, that it may be conclusive and convincing....' Here, I take it, Aristotle clearly expresses that the actual formation of a judgement (even in the sense of *krisis*, not in the more demanding sense of *prohairesis*) is responsive to additional factors beside conclusiveness. He does not say that there are many such factors and that the argumentative aspect is only one amongst many others, but he clearly admits that, since we are speaking of judgements, we have to consider factors beyond mere argumentation.

In a sense, the situation with judgement formation seems to be similar to the antecedents of actions and the possibility of akratic actions: we start with certain premises we happen to accept and are then supposed to draw a conclusion and to act or to judge in accordance with them, and in both cases, this opens the possibility that we may fail either to act or to judge in the appropriate way although we are, in principle, rational beings and capable of acting and judging in accordance with reason. In the case of action, Aristotle notoriously oscillates between calling the action and the immediate step prior to the action the conclusion (actually, in the case of *akrasia*, Aristotle uses this ambiguity to define two types of *akrasia*, the weak and the impulsive form: the weak agent does not stick to the conclusion drawn, whereas the impulsive one jumps to an action that is not in line with what he should conclude from the given premises). Likewise in the case of judgement formation, we are not told whether people sometimes fail to draw the conclusion or whether they fail to judge in accordance with the conclusion drawn.

How far does this analogy between judgement formation and action go? On the one hand, the analogy can surely be extended. For example, readers of the Aristotelian ethical writings are acquainted with the idea that people differ with respect to their abilities to listen to what reason says and to act in accordance with it. And more or less the same seems to be true of judgement formation: people differ in their readiness to form judgements in accordance with pertinent facts and in accordance with rational standards. Furthermore, it is a well-known theorem of Aristotelian ethics that it is a matter of education and exercise to improve one's capability to act and to live in accordance with reason; in particular, young people must first get accustomed to 'listening' to what reason says. And again the same seems to hold of judgement formation, since Aristotle seems to think that it is due to their lack of exercise that ordinary people, as opposed to dialecticians, are not capable of following longer chains of arguments, and that uneducated people are prone to distraction and to the influence of non-pertinent factors.

On the other hand, the analogy must not be overstated, since in the case of action and *akrasia* everything depends on whether at the moment of action there is a consonance or dissonance of desire and judgement, whereas in the case of judgement formation no specific desire is involved, so that the failure to judge in accordance with the conclusion cannot be accounted for by reference to opposing desires.

It seems, therefore, that we should not push this analogy too far—*unless* we would like to construe the stating of the judgement as a sort of action that requires a certain amount of desire in order to physically articulate the judgement. *If*, for example, we think of the act of voting, i.e., of visibly giving one's vote or casting one's ballot, and *if* we think that this is what Aristotle refers to when speaking of the judgement, then it is trivially true that judgements are actions and that whatever holds of actions also holds of the act of judging; and then again a particular act of judgement could manifest a genuine and full-blown case of *akrasia*, namely whenever we fail to cast our ballots in accordance with what we judged to be the best option. However, it seems that there are substantial reasons for not assimilating judgements to actions. Most notably, the paradigmatic actions in Aristotle's terminology involve the movement of bodily limbs, but this is not essential in the case of judgement formation. Furthermore, we are used to saying that we act in accordance with our judgement, but if judging itself is essentially regarded as a type of action, in accordance with which judgement do we act when judging, etc.? It therefore seems that there actually is an analogy between failing to judge on the basis of conclusive arguments and failing to act in accordance with one's best judgement. Still, it is no more than an analogy.

At any rate, once it is clearly spelled out that it is not a trivial step to judge in accordance with what the orator wants us to derive from accepted premises, it is obvious that the *technê*-based rhetorician has to devise a way to secure that the audience will actually judge in accordance with the given arguments or to stabilize the step from given premises to the acceptance of the required conclusion. What Aristotle has to contribute to this sort of concern, I think, comes out in the second part of quotation (C): the orator should '... not only look at the argument, that it may be conclusive and convincing', but should also 'present himself as a certain kind of person and to prepare the audience'. And since this sentence is meant as a transition from the treatment of argumentative persuasion to the announced treatment of the two non-argumentative means of persuasion, there is no doubt that the second part of quotation (C) refers to *êthos* and *pathos*. If we take this seriously, the two non-argumentative means of persuasion come in precisely in order to secure that the target persons will actually judge in accordance with the given proofs or arguments. How *êthos* and *pathos* can do this job is far from clear at this stage of the discussion (and actually even Aristotle's explicit discussion of *êthos* and *pathos* leaves open how exactly they are meant to complement or to support the argumentative part of persuasion), but according to (C) it is clear that they are introduced just because the actual formation of judgements is not sufficiently explained by the effect of arguments. The formulation that one should look '*not only*' at the conclusiveness of the arguments provided might be read as suggesting that the use of arguments still is a basic option—although arguments do not bring about the intended judgement in each and every case. And Aristotle's tacit assumption that, in principle, *êthos* and *pathos* can fill the gap that is left behind by the mere use of arguments, seems to express confidence on Aristotle's part that there are no other factors relevant for the formation of judgements or, at least, no factors that could be provided by the art, *technê*, of rhetoric (assuming that the inquiry into style, *lexis*, in the third book belongs to an independent enterprise). Let us check this interim result with what Aristotle actually says about these two means of persuasion.

8. *ÊTHOS*

With respect to the means of persuasion labelled as *êthos*, the first difficulty consists in determining where exactly in the *Rhetoric* this topic is treated. At first glance it looks as if the topic of character is discussed in chapters 12–17 of *Rhetoric* II, since these chapters actually deal with various types of character, for example, the character of the young, the old, and the middle-aged. And since these chapters on types of character directly follow the discussion of emotions in chapters 2–11 of *Rhetoric* II, which are clearly meant to explore *pathos*, it is natural to expect that the official treatment of *êthos* would follow in the subsequent chapters. On closer examination, however, it turns out that chapters II 12–17, although they are concerned with types of character, say nothing about how the orator should present himself as a certain type of person and, hence, that they cannot be intended as the discussion of the corresponding means of persuasion (obviously these chapters are primarily interested in types of character insofar as people of different characters are disposed to different types of emotions; hence the discussion in these chapters can be understood as a useful continuation of the topic of emotions). Where else can we find Aristotle's discussion of *êthos* ? In the course of his *Rhetoric*, Aristotle tells his readers several times how they can present themselves as having a good or virtuous character, for example by quoting moral maxims or by expressing one's own moral convictions

wherever possible. This seems to be the traditional understanding of how the character of the orator can have a persuasive impact, namely by presenting himself as
a person who argues from a moral point of view. However, there is one passage in
which the strategy of moralization itself is not what Aristotle has in mind when
introducing *êthos*, but is only a part of Aristotle's full account of how the orator can
achieve the appearance of being a credible person. This full account of *êthos* can be
found in a few lines of *Rhetoric* II 1, the same chapter in which he has pointed out
that it is not enough to look at the conclusiveness of the argument:

> (G) There are three reasons why speakers themselves are credible; for there are
> three things we trust other than logical demonstrations. These are practical
> wisdom and virtue and good will; for speakers make mistakes in what they say
> or advise through [failure to exhibit] either all or one of these: for either through
> lack of practical wisdom they do not form opinions rightly; or through forming
> opinions rightly they do not say what they think because of a bad character, or
> they are prudent and fair-minded but lack good will, so that it is possible for
> people not to give the best advice although they know what it is. These are the only
> possibilities. Therefore, a person seeming to have all these qualities is necessarily
> persuasive to the hearers (*Rhet.* II 1 1378a6–15, tr. Kennedy, modified).

What Aristotle describes here is a sort of exclusion procedure by which we
exclude possible reasons for distrusting an orator. We would have reason to distrust
the orator if he has no good judgement; or if he has a good judgement, but a bad
character; or if he has good judgement and good character, but lacks benevolence.
However, when an orator displays good judgement, good character, and benevolence, there is no reason left for (rationally) doubting what he recommends. The
traditional attempt to express one's own moral convictions and to present oneself
as a person of good character is only one element within this strategy. The overall
strategy is to exclude reasons the hearer could have for doubting the speaker's credibility, so that the three elements, good judgement, good character, and benevolence, are all subordinated to the goal of appearing to be credible. It is noteworthy
that these three elements of credibility are introduced as being on a par with proofs
or demonstration, insofar as they are factors because of which we are convinced or
persuaded. Therefore the best way to construe what Aristotle has to say about the
character, it seems to me, is to assume a sort of second-order judgement, namely
the second-order judgement that propositions put forward by the credible speaker
are true or acceptable. Therefore it would also be misleading to picture persuasion
through character as something irrational. Nor is the means of persuasion called
êthos meant to address non-rational parts of our soul in particular. The effect of
persuasion through character, or so it seems, is a judgement—though not a judgement about the case in question but about the credibility of the speaker.

How does this account accord with what we said above (see Section 7) about the
role of the non-argumentative means of persuasion? Let us assume that the audience
is somehow suspicious of the speaker. Either this suspicion has a rational foundation
or not; if it has, there must be a reason for the suspicious attitude, and this reason
will be of one of the three types that were mentioned in quotation (G). As long as the

audience has reasons to distrust the speaker, it is plausible to assume that they will not form their final judgement in accordance with the arguments brought forward by the speaker, or at least that they will be reluctant to do so. One can speculate that even if the listeners are, in principle, prepared to accept the premises put forward by the speaker, they will not be willing to follow the suggested conclusions, as long as they have reason to doubt either the speaker's intellectual capability or the integrity of his character or his benevolent attitude. In this case, it may not even be irrational not to judge in accordance with the delivered arguments, as long as it is rational not to trust the speaker's judgement in general. More generally, one could even say that the less precise or cogent the given proofs or arguments are, the more rational it becomes to make the speaker's credibility a determining factor within the formation of a particular judgement. And indeed, Aristotle seems to think that the genuine subject matter of public speeches is such that it does not, or does not always, allow of exact knowledge and of demonstrations, but leaves room for disagreement and differing opinions (see above, quotation (F.2)).[7]

Taking all this into account, it seems that in some cases—whenever the audience is suspiciously minded—it is a necessary precondition of successful persuasion that the speaker allay the audience's suspicion by using *êthos*. In all other cases, persuasion will come about *mallon kai thatton* (*Rhet.* I 2 1356a7), if the orator manages to present himself as credible: '*mallon*' can mean either 'to a greater extent' or, what seems to be the better justified option in the present context, 'more easily' and 'more readily', while '*thatton*' means 'more quickly'. Saying that we are *more easily* and *more quickly* convinced if the speaker is trustworthy does not imply that the speaker's credibility alone would do the job of persuading somebody. Rather, it is compatible with the idea formulated above in Section 7, namely that *êthos* as a non-argumentative means of persuasion is introduced in order to 'secure' or to 'stabilize' the argument-based process of persuasion, for example by allaying manifest suspicions or simply by making this process smoother and quicker or, generally speaking, by making it more likely and probable that the audience will actually reach the intended conclusion, or form its judgement or cast its vote in accordance with that conclusion. Of course, the less weight the arguments themselves can bear (whether because no cogent proofs are available, or because the proofs given are feeble, or because the subject matter does not admit of cogent proof), the more weight will fall upon the credibility of the speaker—to the point where, precisely due to the absence of cogent argumentation, the audience accepts the credible speaker's contentions because his credibility lends credence to his claims.[8]

9. PATHOS

The issue of emotional persuasion is quite a controversial one. What worries commentators are the questions of whether it is legitimate at all to play upon the audience's emotional reactions and whether Aristotle himself denies the legitimacy of the use of emotions, as he seems to do in some passages of his *Rhetoric*, even while recommending it in other passages. These questions are almost always discussed in connection with the following text:

> **(H)** As things are now, those who have composed arts of speech have worked, as it were, on a small part of the subject; for only *pisteis* are technical, other things are supplementary and these writers say nothing about enthymemes, which are the body of persuasion, while they give most of their attention to matters external to the subject; for slander and pity and anger and such emotions of the soul do not relate to facts, but are appeals to the members of the jury. As a result, if all trials were conducted as they are in some present-day states and especially in those well governed, [the writers of these arts] would have nothing to say…etc. (*Rhet.* I 1 1354a11–21, tr. Kennedy, modified).

Aristotle thus reproaches his predecessors for these sorts of practices in the first chapter of the *Rhetoric* (from which quotation (H) is taken), while already in the second chapter he develops the doctrine of the three technical means of persuasion, one of which is, notably, the arousal of emotions: *pathos*. This apparent contradiction has always irritated Aristotle's interpreters. For a long time there was even the suspicion that the first chapter of the *Rhetoric* containing the critique of arousing emotions was written for a different occasion and the rest of the treatise added on to this after the fact.[9] However, in my view, this alleged inconsistency between the critique of predecessors in the first chapter and Aristotle's own technique of arousing emotions is not insoluble. At this point of the discussion, I confine myself to a quite formalistic reply to the inconsistency charge.

To begin with, Aristotle does not reproach his predecessors in (H) for using emotions at all, but for being *mostly* concerned with them and for neglecting the enthymeme, which he takes to be the body of persuasion, i.e., to be central to persuasion. It is perfectly consistent to say this and to accept at the same time a model in which argumentative persuasion—persuasion through enthymemes and examples—is fundamental, and to contend that emotions play a *certain*, but not the predominant role in persuasion. This is indeed the decisive move one needs to make against the charge of inconsistency. And it is remarkable in this context that in quotation (F.3), when introducing the technical arousal of emotion, Aristotle does so in full awareness of his former criticism of the predecessors and explicitly refers back to his point that former writers gave their attention to nothing else but emotional excitement. Had he just changed his views concerning the use of emotions he would not reasonably wish to emphasize his earlier views; on the contrary, we would expect him to shamefacedly hide or play down his change of mind.

Furthermore, what seems to matter is the *way* we arouse emotions, and in this context it is remarkable that Aristotle thought of the conventional arousing of emotions as foreign to the art (*technê*) of rhetoric, whereas he claims to teach a method based on that art. This observation should warn us against simply identifying the conventional use of emotions with what the Aristotelian rhetorician does when manipulating the emotions of the audience.

Finally, Aristotle says of the traditional arousal of emotion that it *hinders* or *obstructs* a genuine judgement (*Rhet.* I 1 1354a24–26, 1354b33–1355a1), whereas the arousal of emotion in accordance with the art as he sees it *modifies* the judgement of the listener thus affected.

This latter point is of importance for our current project. Given that it is not trivial that people actually judge in accord with what they conclude from given premises, it is natural to wonder, as we have, whether and how the orator can influence the process of judgement formation by means that go beyond argumentative persuasion. In quotation (F.3) Aristotle introduced the topic of emotions because, as he said, we differ in our judgements depending on the emotions we happen to have. And in the following quotation, Aristotle confirms that, under the influence of emotions, things do not seem the same to us, i.e., we do not perceive or judge them in the same way during an episode of emotion:

> **(I)** ... for things do not seem the same to those who are friendly and those who are hostile, nor [the same] to the angry and the calm, but either altogether different or different in importance: to one who is friendly, the person about whom he passes judgement seems not to do wrong or only in a small way; to one who is hostile, the opposite ... (*Rhet.* II 1 1377b31–1378a3, tr. Kennedy, modified).

In this passage, which, curiously enough, is the most explicit one we happen to have on the effect of emotions in a public speech, it is clear that emotions are employed in order to modify the audience's judgements; for the line of interpretation chosen in this chapter, it is important to stress that this, i.e., the assumption of possibly modifying or modulating effects on the judgement, is different from saying that we are agitated by emotions to the point that we cannot judge any longer.

But what can it reasonably mean that we do not judge any longer? Aristotle makes use of this phrase as he proceeds, without explaining it. However we can speculate as to the cases in which he would reasonably deny that the vote given relies on a proper judgement. For example, if one uses his vote just in order to flatter or to harm one of the litigants without really taking the particular facts or bits of evidence into account, this would probably fall short of what we mean by 'judging the case at hand'; and indeed this seems to be the context in which Aristotle introduces the notion of 'not (really) judging'. To a certain extent, the effect of emotions can be analogously construed: if one votes favourably for those one likes and unfavourably for those one dislikes without considering what they have actually or probably done, we would have reason not to accept this as a full-blown judgement—at least not as a judgement *about* the case at hand or *about* the given facts and evidence. Possibly there is only a graduated difference between these cases and the cases in which the emotions are said not to obstruct, but only to modify, the judgement. For the present purpose, however, it is sufficient to note that nothing in quotations (C) and (I) commits us to thinking of the former, judgement-hindering sort of impact.

However, even if that much is granted, passage (I) leaves room for speculation as to how exactly the emotions are meant to influence our judgement. It seems fair to say that, according to this passage, emotions dispose us to judge in one way rather than another, but how exactly would they do that? I do not know a particular passage in Aristotle's *Rhetoric* that would enlighten this precise point. In *De Insomniis* Aristotle informs us that strong emotions may cause perceptual delusions and that for those who already are in an emotional state, even something with a remote similarity to a typical object of emotion may suffice to make such an object appear to us (3 460b4–16). Similarly, *De Anima* I 1 (403a19–22) tells us that if the body already is in a state of, say, anger, feeble impressions or appearances are sufficient to cause a new episode of anger. The lesson we can learn from passages like these for our present purpose is a restricted one, since the case of perceptual deception is not exactly pertinent and neither of these passages addresses the questions of how the physical changes that co-occur with a state of emotion affect the process of judgement formation. What seems to be similar, however, to the description given in quotation (I) is the idea that episodes of emotion are apt to alter our scope or focus of attention: those in an anxious state of mind will focus on the intimidating features of a situation, so that a remote resemblance to typical objects of fear will be enough to make such persons think of a seriously intimidating object. More or less the same description can be applied to the situation pictured in quotation (I): things do not appear to be the same to those who are in different or even opposed emotional states. One and the same course of action, for example, may seem to be a crime to the hostile-minded observer and not a crime or only a negligible one to the friendly-minded observer. Again, we could say that the friendly-minded observer pays attention exclusively to those features of the situation that make the suspect appear in a favourable light or that are even apt to acquit him of the charge in question, while the hostile judge will tend to focus on the opposed aspects of the same situation.

If, lacking more explicit explanations, we assume that something like this is in the background of quotation (I), it would be consistent to construe the influence of emotions on the process of judgement formation as follows. In principle, people can form their judgement in accordance with one or the other set of opinions or convictions. The orator who wants the audience to reach a certain conclusion will try to refer the audience to those opinions or convictions that can serve as premises for the intended conclusion. If emotions have the power, as we said, to change the focus of attention, the presence of a particular emotion can either distract the audience from these premises (and, hence, prevent them from drawing the conclusion or from forming their judgement in accordance with the conclusion), or can support the orator in the effort of highlighting one particular set of premises and drawing the audience's attention to them. If, for example, the orator has given arguments and proofs to the effect that the defendant is guilty, the presence of unfavourable emotions regarding the defendant will focus attention on those arguments and facts that prove his guilt. If, to take another example, the orator tries to persuade the audience that an invasion of a neighbour's territory is too dangerous, the presence of fear and anxiety would focus the audience's attention on premises and arguments that suggest the high risk of such an endeavour. In this sense, one could say that people are 'more easily' or 'more quickly' persuaded, when they are under the influence of a certain emotion. And in the same sense, one could say that *pathos* is apt to 'support' or 'stabilize' the process of judgement formation.

10. Conclusion

Rhetorical persuasion aims at the audience's judgement—no more, no less. The most straightforward way to influence someone's judgement is to give proofs or arguments. In the field of rhetoric or public speech, Aristotle recommends basing proofs on premises that are already accepted by the audience. Rhetoric therefore requires a general competence in argumentation of any sort and a more specified expertise in accepted opinions. Both sorts of competence can be found in dialectic, and hence rhetoric can be based on the theoretical inventory of dialectic. However, Aristotle acknowledges a phenomenon that we tried to describe as a sort of weakness of judgement, i.e., the phenomenon that people do not always and necessarily form their judgements in accordance with proofs or in accordance with what would follow from certain premises they happen to be convinced of. This is the point, I tried to suggest, where *êthos* and *pathos* come in. With these non-argumentative means of persuasion, the orator can influence the audience's judgement, even if the audience (for one or another of the reasons we have sketched) is not willing or not able to follow the orator's argument. Therefore, *êthos* and *pathos* can be used, as I put it, to stabilize the process of judgement formation even under circumstances that do not provide the ideal background for proofs and arguments. Using these means of persuasion, the orator increases the impact he can have on the listener's judgement. However, just as the doctor cannot heal each and every patient by the use of his *technê*, the rhetorician cannot persuade each and every audience, even if he possesses the art of rhetoric in the fullest sense.

Notes

1. Earlier versions of this text were presented in Helsinki, Leiden, New York, and Oslo. I would like to thank the audiences for very valuable comments.
2. An analogous tension is observed with respect to the relation between chapters I 1 and I 2 of the *Rhetoric*, since the former chapter includes our quotations (A) and (B), whereas the latter introduces the non-argumentative means of persuasion (see below, Section 9). Hence, for example, Jonathan Barnes, *The Cambridge Companion to Aristotle*, Cambridge, 1995, p. 262, asks: 'Perhaps we should rather suppose that the two chapters are doublets, one of them originally written to supplant the other, which were unconvincingly published together by Andronicus?' A similar discussion can be found in the early twentieth century: Friedrich Marx, *Aristoteles Rhetorik* (Berichte der königlich sächsischen Gesellschaft der Wissenschaften zu Leipzig 52), Leipzig, 1900, found the tension between the two chapters so tremendous that he came to doubt the authenticity of chapter I 1, and Adolf Kantelhardt, *De Aristotelis Rhetoricis*, doctoral dissertation, Göttingen, 1911, introduced the editor hypothesis to account for the differences between these two chapters. Some authors found chapter I 1 differed from I 2 and the rest of the book by displaying a more 'Platonic' spirit; see P. Gohlke, *Aristoteles, Die Lehrschriften*, vol. III.1: Rhetorik, Paderborn, 1959, p. 242; W. Fortenbaugh, 'Aristotle's Platonic Attitude Towards Delivery', in *Philosophy*

and Rhetoric 19, 1986, pp. 242–254, 248. A more recent treatment of the supposed 'contradiction' in Aristotle's *Rhetoric* that focuses on the more specific problem of arousal of emotions is given by Jamie Dow, 'A Supposed Contradiction about Emotion-Arousal in Aristotle's *Rhetoric*', in: *Phronesis* 52, 2007, 382–402.

3. See, e.g., Eugene Garver, *Aristotle's Rhetoric. An Art of Character*, Chicago/London, 1994, who offers some quite peculiar theses about the relation between argumentative and non-argumentative means of persuasion; most peculiarly he claims that *logos* is not capable of persuading on its own. For example, see p. 147: 'Aristotle's purpose…is to show that even when rhetorical reason looks most logical and most independent of purpose, it is still persuasive only as evidence of phronêsis and character'.

4. See, for example, A.O. Rorty: 'The Directions of Aristotle's Rhetoric', in: *Review of Metaphysics* 46, 1992, 63–95, p. 73: 'But since choice requires the conjunction of thought (*dianoia*) and desire (*orexis*), the rhetorician must influence the desires as well as the beliefs of his audience'.

5. Here I am paraphrasing *Rhetoric* II 1 1378a6–15.

6. One could also invoke in this context the fact that, for Aristotle, the formation of opinion, conviction, or judgement is in general connected with inferences of a kind. In *De Anima* III 11 434a10–11, e.g., he takes for granted that *doxa* in the proper sense derives from an inference (*sullogismos*).

7. Public speeches are about actions and other human affairs. Aristotle assumes that this is a realm that does not allow of demonstrations in the strict sense. This assumption again is based on a generic statement about the instability of all moral and other human affairs. However, it does not yet mean that there are no cogent proofs or arguments in the domain of rhetoric. On the contrary, Aristotle considers certain sign arguments necessary (forensic evidence, for example, which is crucial in a judicial speech, can be construed as sign argument) and, when characterising the status of rhetorical arguments, he only says that *few* arguments are taken from necessary premises (see *Rhet.* I 2 1357a22–33). Whether cogent proofs are possible or not therefore seems to be a matter of degree; accordingly, the question of whether it is rational to base one's judgement more on the credibility of the speaker or more on the conclusiveness of the arguments he puts forward might also be regarded as a matter of degree.

8. To this latter possibility Aristotle seems to allude in quotation (F.2), when contrasting the *mallon kai thatton*-case with cases in which there is not exact knowledge and people therefore 'completely' (*pantelôs*) trust the credible person. On the impossibility of proofs also compare the previous footnote.

9. See above, note 2.

BIBLIOGRAPHY

Burnyeat, Myles (1994) 'Enthymeme: The Logic of Persuasion', in D.J. Furley and A. Nehamas, eds., *Aristotle's Rhetoric* (Princeton: Princeton Univ. Press), 3–55.

Cooper, John M. (1993) 'Rhetoric, Dialectic, and the Passions', in *Oxford Studies in Ancient Philosophy* 11, 175–198.

Cope, Edward M. (1867) *An Introduction to Aristotle's Rhetoric* (Cambridge: Cambridge Univ. Press); repr. (Hildesheim: Olms, 1970).

——— (1877) *The Rhetoric of Aristotle, with a Commentary*. Rev. and ed. by J. Sandys, 3 vols. (Cambridge: Cambridge Univ. Press); repr. (Hildesheim: Olms, 1970).

Dow, Jamie (2007) 'A Supposed Contradiction about Emotion-Arousal in Aristotle's Rhetoric', *Phronesis* 52, 382–402.

Dufour, Médéric, and André Wartelle (1960–73) *Aristote, Rhétorique*. Texte établi et traduit, 3 vols, (Paris: Les Belles Lettres).

Fortenbaugh, William W. (1970) 'Aristotle's *Rhetoric* on Emotions', *Archiv füer Geschichte der Philosophie* 52, 40–70.

——— (1986) 'Aristotle's Platonic Attitude Towards Delivery', *Philosophy and Rhetoric* 19, 242–254.

Freese, John Henry (1926) *Aristotle, The 'Art' of Rhetoric* (London/Cambridge, Mass.: Harvard Univ. Press).

Furley, David J. and Alexander Nehamas, eds. (1994) *Aristotle's Rhetoric* (Princeton: Princeton Univ. Press).

Grimaldi, William M.A. (1980/1988) *Aristotle, Rhetoric I-II. A Commentary* (New York: Fordham Univ. Press).

Kantelhardt, Adolf (1911) *De Aristotelis Rhetoricis*, Doctoral Dissertation (Göttingen: Officina Academica Dieterichiana).

Kassel, Rudolf (1976) *Aristotelis Ars Rhetorica* (Berlin/New York: De Gruyter).

Kennedy, George A. (1991) *Aristotle, On Rhetoric. A Theory of Civic Discourse*. Translated with introduction, notes, and appendices (New York/Oxford: Oxford Univ. Press).

Leighton, Stephen (1982) 'Aristotle and the Emotions', *Phronesis* 27, 144–174.

Marx, Friedrich (1900) *Aristoteles Rhetorik,* Berichte der königlich sächsischen Gesellschaft der Wissenschaften zu Leipzig 52, (Leipzig: Teubner).

Raphael, Sally (1974) 'Rhetoric, Dialectic and Syllogistic Argument: Aristotle's Position in Rhetoric I-II', *Phronesis* 19, 153–167.

Rapp, Christof (2002) *Aristoteles, Rhetorik*. Translation, introduction, and commentary, 2 vols., (Berlin: Akademie Verlag).

Rorty, Amelie O. (1992) 'The Directions of Aristotle's Rhetoric', *Review of Metaphysics* 46, 63–95.

——— ed. (1996) *Essays on Aristotle's Rhetoric* (Berkeley/Los Angeles/London: University of California Press).

Ross, William D., ed. (1959) *Aristotelis ars rhetorica* (Oxford: Clarendon Press).

Ryan, Eugene E. (1984) *Aristotle's Theory of Rhetorical Argumentation* (Montréal: Les Éditions Bellarmin).

Solmsen, Friedrich (1938) 'Aristotle and Cicero on the Orator's Playing upon the Feelings', *Classical Philology* 33, 390–404.

....

CHAPTER 23

ARISTOTLE ON
POETRY

....

ANNAMARIA SCHIAPARELLI
AND PAOLO CRIVELLI

ARISTOTLE'S *Poetics* is one of the deepest and most influential philosophical works on art, or rather on a specific art. The treatise was hardly known in antiquity, but the interest of Italian humanists in the sixteenth century gave it a central place in literary criticism, which it has retained up to the present day. It is not a polished piece, and it was not 'published': like many other works in the Aristotelian corpus, it was probably a collection of notes for (or even from) a lecture course.

The treatise pursues several aims. One of these, the most general, is to classify the works that can be labelled 'poetical composition' and their parts. Another more specific aim is to vindicate poetry in the face of the criticism levelled at it by Plato, whose views linger in the background like a ghost that cannot be easily laid to rest. Another specific aim is to explain some concepts that are fundamental for the understanding of poetry, e.g., that of imitation. Furthermore, the discussion of some forms of poetry was probably a useful way to express ideas about education and political life in the city, and to convey thoughts about the relation between people's actions and their characters.

The range of issues covered by the *Poetics* makes it reasonable to bring the topics under two headings: Aristotle's views on poetry in general and his account of tragedy (the genre that has the lion's share of the treatise).

I. POETRY

The structure of the Poetics. The treatise, in the form in which it has been handed down to us, comprises 26 chapters. It is organized in a straightforward manner: while chapters 1–5 concern poetry as a whole, the remaining chapters 6–26 focus on specific genres. In particular, chapters 6–22 (the largest portion of the treatise) are on tragedy, chapters 23–25 on epic, and the final chapter 26 attempts a comparison of tragedy and epic.

Aristotle announces (6 1449b21–2) that he intends to deal also with comedy, but nothing on this topic has reached us. Since some ancient catalogues of Aristotle's works report the existence of a *Treatise on the Art of Poetry* in two books,[1] and since what has been handed down to us of the *Poetics* constitutes only one book, it may be plausibly deduced that the treatment of comedy (and perhaps that of iambic satire) belonged to a lost second book of the *Poetics*. This is confirmed by a passage in Eustratius' *Commentary on the Nicomachean Ethics* (320, 18), which speaks of *the first book* of Aristotle's *Poetics*. Traces of the lost second book are probably preserved in a corrupt and meager summary known as the *Tractatus Coislinianus*.[2]

What is the Poetics *concerned with?* The treatise is normally referred to as *Poetics*. One should however bear in mind that 'poetics' is more a transliteration than a translation of '*poiêtikê*', the Greek word at the center of the title '*peri poiêtikês*' with which the treatise has been handed down to us. The Greek word '*poiêtikê*' is short for the phrase '*poiêtikê technê*', which could be rendered by 'poetic art' or 'art of poetry'. A less misleading translation of the title of our treatise would therefore be '*On the Art of Poetry*'. Even this rendering, however, would be inaccurate. For 'poetry' in English means something like 'art of writing poems', while for Aristotle '*poiêtikê*' has a wider meaning. To be sure, Aristotle never defines '*poiêtikê*', but some remarks at the beginning of the treatise indicate that it includes 'epic and tragic poetry and moreover comedy and dithyramb and most of the art of the aulos[3] and of the lyre' (1 1447a13–15) and 'the art of dancers' (1447a27).

It is not clear that the arts listed by Aristotle under the heading of '*poiêtikê*' form a unified kind. Taking into account the Greek practice of reading out poetry in public performances, we may note that a unifying trait is that all the products of the listed arts have a temporal dimension: they have temporal parts (one can speak of the first half of a tragedy). This trait distinguishes them from the products of painting and sculpture, which have spatial but no temporal parts (one can speak of the left part of a statue). We shall often use 'poetry' as a technical term which we stipulate to match Aristotle's '*poiêtikê*' (similarly with 'poet', 'poetic', and 'poem'). Thus, on our usage, epic, tragedy, instrumental music, dance, etc. are all forms of poetry.[4]

Despite the doubts raised in the last paragraph, we shall assume that poetry is a unified kind. Aristotle classifies all the activities of the arts with which his treatise is concerned as 'imitations' ('*mimêseis*', 1447a16).[5] He therefore seems to place poetry within imitative art as a species within its genus (cf. 9 1451b28–9). But he does not indicate the differentia that distinguishes this species from other imitative arts: had he done so, he would have offered a definition of poetry (a definition of a species is given by specifying its genus and its constitutive differentia). Instead of giving the differentia *constitutive* of the species poetry, Aristotle goes straight into presenting differentiae *divisive* of this species, namely differentiae that are constitutive of subordinate species of it, those whereby the various poetic arts differ from one another. He distinguishes three groups of such differentiae: some concern the media on which the imitating art operates, others relate to the imitated object, yet others are linked with the manner in which the imitation takes place.

As for the media, poetic arts can produce their imitations in rhythm, discourse, or melody (either on their own or in combination). For instance, the arts of the aulos and of the lyre produce their imitations in rhythm and melody; the art of dancers employs rhythm alone (for dancers imitate 'through rhythms translated into movements', 1 1447a27–8); yet other arts adopt discourse as their medium (some of them with rhythm, i.e., metrical forms, others in plain language). The possible combinations of three factors are seven (= $2^3 - 1$, the number of the non-empty subsets of a set with 3 elements). Given that melody cannot be separated from rhythm, the seven possible combinations reduce to five. Here they are with the corresponding poetic arts:[6]

Rhythm	Dance
Discourse	Prose-imitation (mimes, Socratic dialogues)
Rhythm + discourse	Elegies, epic
Rhythm + melody	Instrumental music
Rhythm + discourse + melody	Lyrics, tragedy, comedy

As for imitated objects, the arts imitate people in action which are either 'better than our normal level, or worse than it, or much the same' (2 1448a4–5). This distinction is important because Aristotle takes one of the crucial differences between tragedy and comedy to consist in the fact that the objects imitated by the former are elevated while those of the latter are focused on the base.

Finally, the difference about the manner in which the imitation takes place concerns mainly the arts whose medium is discourse. Aristotle distinguishes three cases: it is possible for the poet 'to imitate in the same media the same objects either sometimes narrating, sometimes becoming someone other than himself (as Homer does), or remaining himself without changing [*sc.* only narrating], or in such a way that all those imitating act and perform actions' (3 1448a21–4). In other words, Aristotle is distinguishing between purely dramatic, purely narrative, and partly-dramatic-partly-narrative poetry.[7]

The three parallel sets of differentiae provided by Aristotle, which generate alternative families of species, seem to yield different and reciprocally incompatible

partitions of the species poetry: while tragedy and comedy fall under different species with respect to the differentiae concerned with imitated objects (for they imitate, respectively, elevated and base characters), they fall under the same species
with respect to the differentiae concerned with the manner in which the imitation
takes place (for they are both purely dramatic). One way out of the difficulty is
to assume that the differentiae concerning the imitated objects generate parallel
subspecies of the subspecies generated by another set of differentiae: just as the
differentiae *affirmative* and *negative* give rise to parallel divisions of the species
universal proposition and *particular proposition* (so as to generate the subspecies
*universal affirmative proposition, universal negative proposition, particular affir-
mative proposition,* and *particular negative proposition*), so also the differentiae
dealing-with-better-than-average and *dealing-with-worse-than-average* generate
parallel divisions of the species *purely-dramatic-poetry, purely-narrative-poetry,*
and *partly-dramatic-partly-narrative poetry.* Another possibility is that Aristotle
accepted the existence of alternative and reciprocally incompatible partitions of
species. Yet other possibilities are that he planned to revise his account or believed
that a full technical classification could not be provided.

Imitation. Any attempt to understand what Aristotle means by '*mimêsis*' must
begin with some remarks about the translation of this Greek word. Although it is
now customary to render '*mimêsis*' with 'imitation', this choice is not uncontroversial and has been differently challenged.[8] For example, some think that '*mimêsis*'
would be best translated as 'representation', and 'indication' or 'expression' would
also be suitable in certain contexts.[9] We shall follow the tradition and accept 'imitation' since a different translation would lose the immediate reference to Plato's
use of the same word to discuss analogous topics. However, it must be said that by
'imitation' Aristotle probably means something different from what Plato is traditionally taken to associate with that word. Whereas in the Platonic understanding
'imitation' seems to stand for a mental capacity or activity deprived of any cognitive power, in Aristotle's *Poetics*, in particular in its account of tragedy, it appears
to be linked with a more positive function that contributes to the acquisition of
certain truths about people's actions and characters.

Aristotle does not say much about imitation and its role in poetry. Here are two
of the few pieces of information he provides:

> T 1 …for these too [sc. dancers] imitate characters, emotions, and actions
> through rhythms translated into movements (*Poet.* 1 1447a27–8).

> T 2 Two causes, both natural, seem to have given rise, broadly speaking, to
> poetry. For imitating is connatural to men from childhood and by it they differ
> from the other animals, because man is the most imitative animal and forms his
> first apprehensions through imitation. It is also connatural that they all enjoy
> imitations. A sign of this is what happens in practice:[10] for we enjoy looking at the
> most accurate images of things which are themselves painful to look at, e.g., the
> forms of the vilest beasts and of corpses. The cause of this too is that apprehension
> is most pleasant not only to philosophers but likewise to others too, although

they have a small share of it. For it is because of this [sc. apprehension] that they enjoy looking at images, since by looking it results that they apprehend and infer [*manthanein kai syllogizesthai*] what each thing is, e.g., that this is that. For if they happen not to have seen the thing before, it will produce pleasure not insofar as it is an image but because of its execution, or its color, or for some other such cause (*Poet.* 4 1448b4–19).

The various points made in T 2 remain for the most part underdeveloped and fail to yield a compact and complete view. The passage puts forward two theses: that imitation is connatural to human beings, and that the enjoyment of imitation is connatural to human beings. The stress on the naturalness of imitation and its enjoyment aims at answering the question of why poetry came about: it originated because imitation and its enjoyment are connatural to human beings. By answering the question about the origin of poetry Aristotle is making the first move in his account of how poetry began and grew (more on this below).

The first thesis put forward in T 2 is that imitation is connatural to human beings. This thesis, paired with the view that imitation differentiates human beings from other animals (1448b6–7), is justified by the claim that human beings are the 'most imitative' animals (1448b7) and form their 'first apprehensions through imitation' (1448b7–8). Aristotle is probably referring to the fact that human beings apprehend certain skills by imitating those who already practice them: in this way a child learns to speak a certain language and to walk, and adults as well as children learn to play the aulos. It is worth noting that the claim that human beings form their 'first apprehensions through imitation' (1448b7–8) could perhaps be interpreted differently: Aristotle could mean that knowledge is acquired from experience and ultimately perception, which he regards as an 'assimilation' of the soul to the things perceived (to be assimilated is to become similar and hence to imitate). Presenting imitation in a way that it becomes so strongly linked with the process of apprehension of a skill surely helps to redeem it from Plato's condemnation.

In what way does imitation differentiate human beings from other animals? Aristotle surely does not mean that only human beings exercise imitation: he must have been aware that other animals also do. The justification offered by Aristotle sheds some light on what he means: imitation differentiates human beings from all other animals in that human beings exercise imitation more than all other animals. One is tempted to raise the objection that some other animals (e.g., apes) are even more imitative than human beings. This objection may be answered by standing by the claim that human beings are the animals that exercise imitation to the greatest degree: other animals *seem* more imitative than human beings because in their case imitation remains in its pure state (it is merely a repetition of behaviours, and it does not give rise to more advanced mental states). In human beings, the presence of imitation is less evident because it leads to an apprehension of a higher order.

The imitation involved in the apprehension of skills has a very tenuous link with poetry: the most one can say (and even this seems far-fetched) is that by imitating characters of certain types actors somehow apprehend what it is to be a person of that sort. Furthermore, insofar as it is the capacity involved in the apprehension of skills, imitation seems to have little to do with the experience of an audience viewing or listening to a poem.

The second thesis put forward in T 2 is that the enjoyment of imitation is connatural to human beings. This second thesis is justified by appeal to the enjoyment we get by 'looking at the most precise images of things which are themselves painful to look at, e.g., the forms of the vilest beasts and of corpses' (1448b10–12). Aristotle goes on to explain why we experience such an enjoyment: it is because 'apprehension is most pleasant' (1448b13) to all human beings and we apprehend by means of images of the sort just mentioned. What sort of apprehension does Aristotle have in mind? He gives a hint near the end of T 2: the apprehension that gives us enjoyment consists in our recognizing 'what each thing is' (1448b16–17), i.e., what each element of the image represents and what the represented thing is (these are two sides of the same coin). For instance, the enjoyable apprehension Aristotle has in mind is what we experience when in looking at Raphael's painting of the School of Athens we recognize that this is Plato, this is Aristotle, etc., or (to go back to Aristotle's own example of images of the vilest things) we see a drawing of a lobster and recognize that these are the antennae, these are the chelae, this is the tail, etc. What we acquire apprehension of is the image itself (insofar as we understand what *it* and *its elements* represent) and the situation or story depicted in the image (insofar as we understand *what* it and its elements represent).[11] What painters imitate is primarily the situation or story depicted in their images (here the temptation to translate '*mimêsis*', etc. by 'representation', etc. is strong);[12] but the viewers of an image have access to the depicted situation or story only thanks to the fact that the image to some extent copies the real world, which is therefore also imitated by the painter. It cannot, however, be excluded that Aristotle intends us to grasp also another connection between images and apprehension (one that is not prominent in passage T 2 but could be taken for granted): the didactic use of images in explaining what the real world is like. In this case, Aristotle would have in mind something like the drawing of a lobster in a zoology book whereby we apprehend what lobsters are like (we learn that they have antennae, chelae, a tail, etc.). This second connection between images and apprehension may perhaps be brought under the first as the special case where what is depicted in the image is the real world.

We pointed out earlier that the imitation involved in the apprehension of skills has at best a tenuous link with poetry. The two kinds of apprehension connected with images (the second, as we said, merely understood, if at all present) have perhaps a closer tie with poetry. In the first place, by recognizing elements of the action performed on stage ('That is poison', 'That is a glass', 'He is drinking') the audience may gain an understanding both of the performance itself and of what is going on in the situation or the story staged in the performance. What the spectators understand (with enjoyment) is what each element of the performance represents and what the represented things and actions are (as we said, these are two sides of the same coin). What poets imitate is primarily the situation or story they themselves create in their poems; but, at least in the case of drama, the spectators have access to this situation or story thanks to the fact that the performance resembles the real world, which is therefore also imitated by the poet. Thus, the situations or stories created by poets and represented by their poems are not purely fictional worlds: they are limited by constraints that have to do with verisimilitude.[13] Secondly, the spectators perhaps learn something about the real world. In T 1 Aristotle had pointed out that artists 'imitate characters, emotions, and actions' (1447a28), and in his later discussion of tragedy he insists that the plot should offer a plausible succession of events, whereby they follow one another in accordance with an inner logic. In this perspective, dramas would teach the audience something about the real world: not about astronomy or zoology (armillary spheres and textbook drawings of lobsters serve such purposes), but about characters, emotions, and actions and how they follow one another. If Aristotle recognizes such a didactic role to poetry, then he is giving back to poets at least part of their eminent position as educators, a position that Plato had forcefully deprived them of.

An objection might be raised at this point: Aristotle remarks that imitation is what distinguishes poets from scientists, like Empedocles, who write in verse (cf. 2 1447b13–23). This might be taken to refute any suggestion that the imitation at stake in poetry is the imitation of the real world in some medium: for, if that were the case, Empedocles would be exercising imitation no less than Homer. In other words, Aristotle's remark might be taken to imply that the imitation he regards as central to poetry and other artistic activities is not the imitation which (one might think) is involved in trying to describe the world as it is. This objection surely carries some weight. But it can be blocked by assuming that when he speaks of imitation in connection with poetry, Aristotle means imitation of characters, emotions, and actions. His position could be that although Homer no less than Empedocles tries to describe the real world as it is, the two authors attend to different aspects of it: Empedocles is interested in chemistry and cosmology, Homer in characters, emotions, and actions.

What we have said goes some way towards explaining why Aristotle takes imitation to cover all forms of poetry. This is remarkable because it constitutes an innovation with respect to the early books of the *Republic* (e.g., III 392D–394D): while Plato there identifies imitation with purely dramatic poetry, where the poet becomes someone other than himself, i.e., 'impersonates' someone, Aristotle classifies purely dramatic poetry as a special type of imitation among others.[14] Indeed, not only all poetry is imitation, but painting and sculpture also fall under this description.

Near the end of T 2 Aristotle touches briefly upon another aspect of the enjoyment of images, and, by analogy, of poetic works: the image 'will produce pleasure…because of its execution, or its colour, or for some other such cause' (1448b18–19). This is surely an important aspect of the enjoyment of a poetic work. Insofar as this enjoyment arises from the admiration of the poet's skill, it is again tied to the cognitive sphere. It is hard to say whether by making this remark Aristotle intended the harmony of colours also to be a source of pleasure.

The poetic genres examined by Aristotle. We mentioned earlier that one of the classifications of poetry introduced by Aristotle has to do with the imitated objects:

the arts imitate people in action which are either 'better than our normal level, or worse than it, or much the same' (2 1448a4–5). This classification comes to dominate the later chapters of the *Poetics*: Aristotle discusses poetry concerned with people better than our normal level, namely tragedy and epic, and in the lost part of the work he had dealt with poetry concerned with people worse than our normal level, namely comedy. It is worth noting that by setting up his inquiry in this way, Aristotle tacitly restricts its scope: dance and instrumental music fade out with no further specific discussion in the *Poetics*.

The view that tragedy and comedy deal (respectively) with people 'better' and 'worse' than our normal level is rather crude. In point of fact, Aristotle later refines it. He observes that the base characters imitated by comedy are not wholly vicious. Comedy deals with the laughable, which is a subclass of the ugly: 'for the laughable is a fault and a disgrace involving neither pain nor destruction' (5 1449a34–5). By the same token, tragedy should be concerned with people 'not preeminent in virtue and justice' (13 1453a8): for (as we shall see) tragedy is supposed to arouse fear—and we cannot feel fear for things happening to people too different from us.

The development of poetry. After his initial classifications, Aristotle begins his study of poetry by reviewing its origins and development (4–5 1448b4–1449b20). He does this partly a priori (by considering what must have been the origins of the poetic art, given that human nature has certain characteristics), partly on an empirical basis (having gathered as many data as possible about the early stages of the discipline). Aristotle's interest in the origins and development of the discipline reflects a biological outlook he brings to it: just as the study of living beings must proceed by considering how they are born and develop until they reach the stage where they fully flourish, so also the study of poetry must proceed by considering its origins and development (the remarks on tragedy's accomplishment of its nature at 4 1449a14–15 recall what could be said about fully developed animals). The adoption of a biological outlook is distinctive of Aristotle. But one wonders whether it might be a source of mistakes: there are reasons for doubting that poetry, or any other productive discipline (e.g., carpentry or computer industry), is born and grows in the same way as a plant or an animal.[15]

Passage T 2 is the very beginning of Aristotle's 'history of poetry': the insistence on the naturalness of imitation and its enjoyment for human beings aims at providing part of an explanation of how poetry began (another component of the explanation being that melody and rhythm also come naturally to us, cf. 4 1448b20–1). Aristotle suggests that these natural human inclinations gave rise to poetic improvisations which then gradually developed into poetry as we know it. He also maintains that the characters of the earliest authors led them to produce imitations of objects of different sorts: more serious poets produced imitations of noble people and actions, which in the first instance took the form of hymns and encomia, while more vulgar poets produced imitations of base actions and people, which at the beginning were mere invectives. For both kinds of imitations, Aristotle recognizes Homer's eminent position: not only did he produce poetic masterpieces in his epic poems imitating noble objects, but he also excelled in the imitation of base objects (Aristotle mentions the *Margites*, a now lost burlesque epic which is not now, and was not always in antiquity, attributed to Homer). By praising Homer, Aristotle is probably once again distancing himself from the criticism leveled at that poet by Plato. From these initial imitations of noble and base objects later authors developed tragedy and comedy because they identified in them a greater potential. Specifically, tragedy and comedy arose from the introduction of improvised spoken parts within dithyrambs and phallic songs respectively (cf. 4 1449a9–15).

Aristotle then discusses the development of each of the major genres he is interested in: tragedy, comedy, and epic. With respect to tragedy (4 1449a15–31) he examines the various meters it adopted, the evolution of the number of actors, and the varying weight attributed to the chorus and speech. The examination of the development of comedy (5 1449a32–1449b9) is relatively scant due to the lack of sources. With respect to epic (5 1449b9–20) Aristotle gives up the attempt to trace its development and concentrates on how it resembles and differs from tragedy, with which it shares the trait of dealing with elevated objects. Apart from its having parts not only in dramatic but also in narrative mode, epic differs from tragedy in length (tragedy 'endeavors so far as possible to stay within a single revolution of the sun or close to it, while epic is unlimited in time span', 1449b12–13) and meter (epic is in a single kind of verse whereas tragedy adopts more than one).

The three 'unities'. It has been often assumed that Aristotle's *Poetics* puts forward three requirements of unity for tragedy: 'unity of time' (the time taken by the play on stage should be the same as that of the represented story), 'of place' (the place where the represented story takes place should be the same throughout the tragedy), and 'of action' (there should be a single action in the represented story). These requirements of unity played a major role in the theory and practice of classical modern tragedy.

Only some of these requirements of unity can be traced back to the *Poetics*. The evidence for crediting Aristotle with the requirement of 'unity of time' is rather slight: it is, in point of fact, nothing more than the remark mentioned in the last subsection about the limit of 'a single revolution of the sun'. The evidence for the requirement of 'unity of place' is even thinner: what we find in Aristotle is merely the platitude that tragedy cannot represent actions happening at the same time in different places. By contrast, there is substantial evidence for crediting Aristotle with the requirement of 'unity of action': a lot of what Aristotle says about tragedy's plot goes in this direction.

II. Tragedy

Aristotle's definition of tragedy. Aristotle opens his discussion of tragedy by offering a definition of its essence:

> T 3 But let us speak of tragedy, taking up the definition of its essence [*horon tês ousias*], which draws on what has been said. Tragedy, then, is an imitation of

an action that is elevated and complete and has magnitude [*praxeôs spoudaias kai teleias megethos echousês*], by discourse embellished in different forms in its different sections [*hêdusmenô(i) logô(i) chôris hekastô(i) tôn eidôn en tois moriois*], of people acting and not by narration [*drôntôn kai ou di' apaggelias*], and through pity and fear accomplishing the purification of such emotions [*di' eleou kai phobou peraisnousa tên tôn toioutôn pathêmatôn katharsin*] (*Poet.* 6 1449b22–8).

It is remarkable that Aristotle begins his discussion of tragedy by offering an essential definition of it: this is unlike his methodology in other inquiries, where an essential definition is either never offered or reached only after a painstaking discussion of the views of earlier thinkers or empirical data. Aristotle says that his definition draws on things previously said. In fact, many of the points made in this definition either had already been made earlier in the treatise or relate to issues previously raised—many, but not all.

The first point, that tragedy is an imitation of an action, harks back to T 1's claim that the imitation that constitutes an essential trait of poetry is of 'characters, emotions, and actions' (1 1447a28). But the connection of tragedy with action is prominent and emphatic. This is confirmed by Aristotle's later remark that 'tragedy is an imitation not of human beings but of action and life' (6 1450a16–17). As is well known, the relation between people's characters and their actions, in this order, was central to Aristotle's project in the *Ethics*. However, here we find a shift in perspective: in the discussion of tragedy, more emphasis is given to actions than to characters. The claim that the objects of tragic imitation are actions is therefore remarkable.

The second point, that the action imitated by tragedy is 'elevated' (1449b24), picks up the earlier thesis that the objects imitated by tragedy are 'better than our normal level' (2 1448a4). Similarly, the point that tragedy is an imitation 'of people acting and not by narration' (1449b26–7) picks up a view put forward previously: the manner in which tragedy's imitation takes place is purely dramatic. The somewhat cryptic point that tragedy's imitation is 'by discourse embellished in different forms in its different sections' (1449b25–6) is explained by Aristotle shortly afterwards: it is about the media in which tragic imitation takes place. The medium is always that of discourse in meter, but in some of the tragedy's parts it is accompanied by melody. Moreover, the visual aspect (masks and scenery) plays a role. Meter, melody, and the visual aspect are all treated as embellishments of discourse. Note that Aristotle's definition requires tragedy to be verse drama.

On the other hand, the point that the action imitated by tragedy is 'complete and has magnitude' (1449b25) corresponds to nothing that had been said earlier. Aristotle explains it later (7 1450b23–1451a15) in the context of his discussion of tragedy's plot. A tragedy is complete, or a whole, in that it has a beginning, a middle, and an end. A beginning is something that need not follow from something else but after which something else necessarily follows; an end is something that follows necessarily from something else but need not have something else following from it; and a middle is something that follows necessarily from something else and also has something else following necessarily from it. Aristotle is hinting that the starting point of a tragedy must be such that the audience should not wonder 'How did this come about?', and its end must be such as not to raise the question 'What next?'. The concept of magnitude is linked by Aristotle with two important traits of tragedy. First, Aristotle associates magnitude with beauty (the concept of beauty makes here one of its rare showings): 'beauty consists in magnitude and order' (7 1450b36–7). So, the imitated action must be as large as possible without damage to the audience's capacity to remember what went on at the beginning (there must not be more than one can take in). Secondly, Aristotle links magnitude with other important traits of the action imitated by tragedy: the imitated action must be large enough to allow a transformation to occur either from adversity to prosperity or from prosperity to adversity, in a sequence of events that is either probable or necessary. Reversal of fortune is one of the typical traits of tragedy. Moreover, the reversal must occur not in an arbitrary or far-fetched way: the action narrated must be at least probable.

Purification. The last point of Aristotle's definition is that tragedy's imitation arouses pity and fear in order to achieve 'the purification of such emotions' (1449b27–8). The idea of a purification from pity and fear corresponds to nothing that had been said earlier. The claim that tragic imitation must arouse pity and fear returns later,[16] but not in connection with purification.[17] The question of what this means has dominated Western philosophy and literary criticism since the Renaissance: commentators have interpreted this last point of Aristotle's definition in many and deeply different ways (some even despair of being able to explain it and contemplate the possibility of expunging the relevant phrase from the Greek text).[18]

Some external evidence may however be brought in. In one later passage Aristotle says that 'the poet must procure through imitation the pleasure arising from pity and fear' (14 1453b12–13). The fact that pity and fear experienced in a theatrical performance are pleasant was commonly recognized by Greek thinkers,[19] but not much of an attempt was made to explain why it occurs and to square it with the unpleasantness of the pity and fear due to 'real' reasons.[20] The link of pleasure with pity and fear provides evidence for introducing a passage from the *Politics* where Aristotle connects the purification from pity and fear with pleasure:

> T 4 We accept the division of melodies proposed by certain philosophers, by regarding some as ethical [*êthika*], others as of action [*praktika*], and others as enthusiastic [*enthoustiastika*], and the division of modes according to their nature corresponding to each of these melodies. But we maintain further that music should be studied for the sake not of one but of many benefits, that is to say, with a view to education, to purification (what we call 'purification' we state simply now, but we will say it again more clearly in the work on poetry [*ti de legomen tên katharsin, nun men haplôs, palin d' en tois peri poiêtikês eroumen saphesteron*]), and, thirdly, for amusement, for relaxation and recreation after exertion. It is clear, therefore, that all the modes must be employed by us, but not all of them in the same manner. In education the most ethical modes must be employed, but in listening to the

performances of others the modes of action and the enthusiastic ones must be employed. For feelings that exist very strongly in some souls are present in all, but differ by being less or more intense: pity and fear, for instance, and even enthusiasm. Some persons are capable of being possessed by this motion, and we see them restored as a result of the sacred melodies—when they have used the melodies that excite the soul to a frenzy—as though they had found healing and purification [*hôsper iatreias tuchontas kai katharseôs*]. Those who are influenced by pity or fear, and every emotional nature, must have a like experience, and others insofar as each is susceptible to such emotions, and all come to have a certain purification and are lightened with pleasure [*pasi gignesthai tina katharsin kai kouphizesthai meth' hêdonês*]. The melodies of purification likewise give an innocent pleasure to human beings [*ta melê ta kathartika parechei charan ablabê tois anthrôpois*]. Such are then the modes and the melodies in which those who perform music at the theatre should be invited to compete (*Pol.* VIII 7 1341b32–1342a18).

In passage T 4 Aristotle speaks of a purification of the emotions of pity and fear which is achieved by music and generates pleasure (the reference to a precise treatment of purification in the context of the discussion of poetry is often regarded as an indication that purification was discussed in the lost second book of the *Poetics*). Two main interpretations of tragic purification, or rather families of interpretations, have been offered. Both have strengths but also weaknesses.

According to the religious interpretation, tragic purification is something like the cleansing from sacral contaminations that occurs in the celebrations of mysteries. According to this exegesis, the purification of the emotions of pity and fear that tragedy brings has primarily a moral dimension: morally reproachable passions are either eliminated or transformed in such a way as to become acceptable.

According to the medical interpretation, tragic purification is something like the purging of noxious fluids. According to this exegesis, the tragic purification of the emotions of pity and fear may well bring about the complete expulsion of the emotions, although it cannot be ruled out that only part of the emotions is eliminated. The result of tragic purification is that the subject who experienced it is more able to handle emotions: he or she is a more balanced person, more specifically, he or she will not be subject to excessively strong emotions. Some commentators speak of a homeopathic therapy: experiencing emotions of a certain sort puts one in a better position with respect to emotions of that sort. Some even go so far as to assume that this homeopathic therapy does not concern only the psychological level but also the balance of the bodily humours which medicine of Aristotle's time assumed to be crucial to health (in particular, it would bring about a purgation of the black bile, whose excess brings instability, sensuality, or even madness).[21]

We cannot pursue here the arguments that tell against or in favour of either of these interpretations. Similarly, we cannot expound the many variations of these exegeses put forward by different commentators. We should only point out that no acceptable interpretation should saddle Aristotle with the view that purification will bring about the complete elimination of certain emotions: such a position would not be easy to reconcile with the position of Aristotle in the *Ethics*, where the key notion is not that of elimination but that of appropriate balance of emotions. The agents should train themselves in such a way that they do not fall into an inappropriate excess of, say, bodily desires, pity, fear, anger, or shame (to name some cases).

Tragic error. The last point of Aristotle's definition of tragedy, that concerning the purification from pity and fear, obviously requires tragedies to raise pity and fear. This circumstance provides Aristotle with an opportunity to discuss the characteristics of plots which are most apt to induce these emotions.

As we pointed out earlier, an important trait of the action imitated by tragedy is the presence of a reversal of fortune. Accordingly, in chapter 13 (1452b30–1453a17) Aristotle examines which kinds of reversals of fortune cause pity and fear. A wicked man whose fortune turns from bad to good will not induce pity or fear. Again, a wicked man who suffers the opposite reversal, from good to bad fortune, will arouse feelings of humane sympathy, but not pity or fear. A good man whose fortune suffers a reversal either from bad to good or from good to bad will again fail to be an occasion for pity or fear (reversals of the last kind are rather repugnant). Thus, reversals of fortune affecting people who are either good or wicked are not appropriate to tragedy (1452b30–1453a7). Guided by the intuition that pity is felt for an undeserving victim of adversity while fear is felt for people like ourselves (1453a4–6), Aristotle states that the action imitated by tragedy should be about 'someone not preeminent in virtue and justice, but who enjoys a high reputation and prosperity, and who falls into adversity not through vice and depravity, but through some kind of error [*hamartia*]' (1453a8–10, cf. 1453a13–17).

One of the most debated points of Aristotle's *Poetics* concerns what kind of error the tragic hero is supposed to commit. Aristotle seems to think that this error must not be such as to make the hero into an evil person and must not affect his or her being an undeserving victim of the adversity. It is therefore unlikely that the error Aristotle has in mind might be a moral fault. Some light is shed on the nature of the tragic error in chapter 14 (1453b14–1454a9), where Aristotle classifies the types of incident which may be described in a tragedy and ranks them as more or less appropriate to the tragic genre. His ranking is as follows. The kind of incident that is least suitable for tragedy is that where the hero commits a horrible deed in knowledge and cognizance of what he or she is doing (as with Medea's killing of her children). More appropriate is the case where the hero commits a horrible deed in ignorance of what he or she is doing but discovers it later (as with Oedipus' vicissitudes with his parents). The kind of incident that is most appropriate to tragedy is that where the hero is on the verge of committing some horrible deed while failing to realize what he or she is about to do, but understands what is going on and therefore refrains from committing the horrible deed (as with Iphigenia, who recognizes her brother Orestes before sacrificing him). There is some tension between the positions put forward by Aristotle in chapters 13 and 14: in chapter 13 he seems to favour plots with an unhappy ending whereas in chapter 14 he ranks most highly those with a happy ending. But let us leave this tension on one side: the crucial point is that the account of chapter 14 suggests that the error of the tragic hero mentioned in chapter 13 is a case of ignorance of the facts of the matter. This makes it tempting to assume that the error commit-ted by the tragic hero is simply a mistake due to ignorance. The case Aristotle has in mind is probably that of Oedipus, who kills his father and has sexual rela-tions with his mother, all of which comes about out of his ignorance. If this is right, the ignorance in question will have to be one for which the hero cannot be held responsible; otherwise, at least according to the position put forward in the *Nicomachean Ethics* (III 1 1110b24–30), the hero will be responsible for the horrible action he or she perpetrates and will therefore be regarded as deserving punish-ment. One may, however, well wonder whether we should agree: is Aristotle right in assuming that the tragedy would have been of lesser quality if Oedipus could have been held responsible for his ignorance?

NOTES

1. Cf. D.L. 5. 24; the 75th item in the *Vita Hesychiana*.
2. Cf. Janko (1984).
3. The aulos was a reed pipe. It was used to accompany both parts of drama and other forms of poetry, and for purely instrumental music.
4. There is also another, wider use of '*poiêtikê*' in Aristotle. In the *Metaphysics* he says that 'all thought is either practical [*praktikê*] or productive [*poiêtikê*] or theoretic [*theôrêtikê*]' (VI 1 1025b25). Every *poiêtikê* art in the sense of the *Poetics* is surely a *poiêtikê* art in the sense of the *Metaphysics*, but the converse fails (consider cobblery).
5. For the translation of '*mimêsis*' by 'imitation' cf. below, text to note 9.
6. Cf. Ross (1923), 291.
7. Aristotle is here picking up a distinction drawn by Plato in the *Republic* (III 392D–394D). But cf. below, text to note 14.
8. Cf., e.g., Donini (2008), XXI.
9. Cf. Lucas (1968), 259; Halliwell (1986), 71, 192.
10. Alternatively: '... with the works of art' (cf. 26 1462a18).
11. Cf. Kosman (1992), 56, 70.
12. Cf. above, text to note 9.
13. Commentators debate the extent to which the situations or stories created by poets are fictional (cf. Donini (2008), XXII-XXIII).
14. In one passage (24 1460a5–8) Aristotle speaks as if only purely dramatic poetry were imitation: the Platonic position resurfaces (cf. Kosman [1992], 53). In *Republic* X Plato appears to operate with a more general notion of imitation.
15. Cf. Barnes (1995a), 284.
16. Cf. 9 1452a1–3; 11 1452a38–1452b1; 13 1452b30–1453a7; 14 1453b1–7 1453b12–13; 1453b17–18; 19 1456b2–4.
17. The word 'purification' occurs only one other time in the treatise (at 17 1455b15): it refers to the ritual of purification by which Orestes is recognized by his sister Iphigenia.
18. Cf. Woodruff (2009), 622.
19. Cf. Pl. *Philebus* 47E1–48A7; Aristippus *ap.* D.L. 2.90.
20. Cf. Lucas (1968), 275.
21. Cf. Lucas (1968), 284–6.

BIBLIOGRAPHY

Anagnostopoulos, G., ed. (2009) *A Companion to Aristotle* (Chichester).

Barnes, J. (1995a) 'Rhetoric and Poetics' in J. Barnes, ed., *The Cambridge Companion to Aristotle* (1995b), 259–85.

Barnes, J., ed. (1995b) *The Cambridge Companion to Aristotle* (Cambridge).

Donini, P., trans. and comm. (2008) *Aristotele: Poetica* (Turin).

Hardy, J. (1952) *Aristote: Poétique* (Paris).

Halliwell, S. (1986) *Aristotle's Poetics* (London).

——— trans. and comm. (1995) *Aristotle: Poetics* (Cambridge, Mass./London).

Janko, R. (1984) *Aristotle on Comedy: Towards a Reconstruction of Poetics II* (London).

Kassel, R., ed. (1965) *Aristotelis de Arte Poetica Liber* (Oxford).

Kosman, A. (1992) 'Acting: *Drama* as the *Mimēsis* of *Praxis*' in A. Oksenberg Rorty, ed., *Essays on Aristotle's Poetics* (Princeton), 51–72.

Lucas, D.W., comm. (1968) *Aristotle: Poetics* (Oxford).

Montanari, F., and A. Barbino, trans. and comm. (2009) *Aristotele: Poetica* (Milan).

Oksenberg Rorty, A., ed. (1992) *Essays on Aristotle's* Poetics (Princeton).

Ross, W.D. (1995) *Aristotle*, 6th ed. (London).

Woodruff, P. (2009) 'Aristotle's *Poetics*: The Aim of Tragedy' in G. Anagnostopoulos, ed., *A Companion to Aristotle* (Malden, MA), 612–27.

PART VII

AFTER ARISTOTLE

CHAPTER 24

MEANING: ANCIENT COMMENTS ON FIVE LINES OF ARISTOTLE

RICHARD SORABJI

THE opening five lines of *On Interpretation* 1 contain Aristotle's influential account of the meaning of verbs and names, in which he describes them as signs of mental experiences which are in turn likenesses of actual things. The passage occasioned much comment from the ancient commentators, and among modern philosophers the resulting tradition has been criticized by Hilary Putnam.

> First we must lay down what a name is and what a verb, then what is negation and affirmation and statement and sentence.

> What are in vocal sounds (*phônê*) are symbols (*sumbola*) of experiences (*pathêmata*) in the soul, and written [marks] are symbols of what are in vocal sounds. And as letters are not the same for all men, so neither are vocal sounds the same. But the things of which these are in the first place signs (*sêmeia*), namely experiences (*pathêmata*) of the soul, are the same for all, and the things of which these [experiences] are likenesses (*homoiômata*), actual things, are also the same (*On Interpretation* 1, 16a3–8).

BEARING ON MODERN PHILOSOPHY

Many modern philosophers hold that thinking involves having *representations*, and there is discussion (e.g., Michael Tye) of whether these representations should be likenesses of what is thought, or rather some kind of symbols. On a view espoused by Jerry Fodor, we shall see, the symbols constituting thought form a special language of thought, *mentalese*, which is different from any natural language. On another view (Norman Malcolm, Hilary Putnam), representations are not needed for thought at all.

Where Aristotle stands on these issues depends on how the above five lines are taken. The lines treat two things as symbols and one as a likeness. What is the likeness? Is it a thought, a mental image, or what? It makes a very big difference where thoughts enter into Aristotle's story. Thoughts had better not be likenesses if they are to play the role of words in mentalese, as one ancient commentator suggested they did.

Aristotle connects his inquiry with the question of whether names and verbs are natural or conventional. He wants something to be natural and therefore the same for all people. But what is it that is the same for all? Do we all have the same thoughts or the same mental images when we think of justice or lunar eclipse?

The answers to these questions depend on a very close reading of Aristotle's five lines, and the ancient commentators gave them a very close reading, though Neoplatonists, we shall see, may have read them differently from Alexander, the last great member of Aristotle's own school. We must look at the interpretations, if we are to get nearer discovering where Aristotle stood on the philosophical questions just mentioned.

CONFINED TO NAMES AND VERBS

One of the first things noticed by the ancient commentators Ammonius, Boethius (who draws on Porphyry), and Stephanus is that this is not a general account of meaning.[1] If, as they think, it is an account of meaning, it concerns only the meaning of names and verbs, although that may not be as big a restriction as it seems, given that a name and a verb together can constitute a whole sentence. There are eight parts of speech (*lexis*) recognized by Aristotle at *Poetics* 20 1456b20: letter, syllable, conjunction, name, verb, article, case, sentence, but of these only name and verb are treated by Aristotle as parts of the sentence (*logos*), according to Ammonius, who is perhaps drawing this out of Aristotle *On Interpretation* 16b22–5. Moreover, Boethius insists, name and verb are the only parts required by the statement-making sentences in which Aristotle is interested here. Other parts of speech are dealt with by the commentators in one of two ways. Some parts of speech can play the role of a noun, as can a pronoun like 'I', some of a verb, as can a name like '[is a] substance', although Ammonius contests Alexander's view that an adverb is a name, which was presumably based on Aristotle's more cautious statement that adverbs are inflections formed from adjectival names, as 'usefully' from 'useful'.[2] In other instances, parts of speech are used, such as conjunctions, articles, prepositions, and indeed adverbs, which are no more parts of a sentence than one would count as parts of a ship bolts, sail-cloth, pitch, bonds, and nails, since they cannot be put together with each other to compose a complete sentence.

IN SPOKEN SOUNDS

On one view, it is because he is confining himself to verbs and names that Aristotle speaks not of spoken sounds generally, but of *what is in* spoken sounds. Admittedly, Alexander, Aristotle's greatest defender in the Aristotelian school, had written a different view in his commentary of around 200 AD, so Boethius tells us, namely that Aristotle meant the *thoughts* in spoken sounds to be symbols of experiences.[3] But Boethius reports Porphyry as taking the point to be that Aristotle cannot say that all spoken sounds are symbols of thoughts, since some spoken sounds ('*garalus*' in Boethius' example and the barking of an angry dog) are meaningless, so Aristotle's reference must be to some sub-class of spoken sounds, and the obvious sub-class comprises the verbs and names that have been mentioned as the first subject for study in the first sentence of the quotation. There are traces of the same interpretation in Boethius' older contemporary Ammonius.[4]

ARE EXPERIENCES IDENTICAL WITH, OR MERELY SYMBOLIZED BY, THOUGHTS?

What are the experiences? The answer was unanimous among the ancient Neoplatonist commentators whose comments on the passage are extant, in sequence Porphyry around 300 AD, and in the fifth to sixth centuries Proclus, Ammonius, Boethius writing in Latin, and Stephanus.[5] Boethius is our source for Porphyry, regarding him as pre-eminent, above even Alexander, in intellectual sharpness and ability to marshal his ideas, and following him as far as possible.[6] According to all of these, the experiences are *thoughts*, and indeed thoughts are mentioned almost immediately next in lines 16a9–11: 'Just as sometimes there is thought in the soul without truth or falsity, but sometimes there is thought to which truth or falsity must belong, so also is it in vocal sound'. In equating experiences with thoughts, the ancient commentators did not by 'thoughts' mean thinkings, but thoughts that we think. Presumably the experiences were not thoughts for Alexander, because he regards what is in spoken sounds to be thoughts, which suggests that thoughts are merely symbols of experiences, not identical with them. The idea that thoughts are symbols rather than likenesses will turn out to be significant later.

Likenesses

If experiences are thoughts, how can they for Aristotle be likenesses of things? Admittedly, the thought symbolized by a whole sentence may be considered by Aristotle to be similar in structure to reality, but how can the thoughts symbolized by separate names or verbs be likenesses? Does not a likeness have to be like? Ammonius, who regards himself as recording the views of his teacher Proclus with some additions of his own,[7] answers that Aristotle believes that in thinking we receive the intelligible form of what is being thought and this form is a likeness.[8] Putnam has described this view of Aristotle's as giving the same structure to reality as to thought.[9] But what is an intelligible form? It would be speaking very roughly to say that the intelligible form of a thing is its defining characteristics. Rather we should say that it is the less material ones, since the defining characteristics of natural objects include a reference to matter along with form. A further qualification is that we can think of individuals and of non-existent things, neither of which have proper definitions, according to Aristotle. Another is that the form received in thinking about (for example) a dog, if we are to follow Aristotle's insistence on the analogy between thought and sense perception, is received at a higher level of actuality in the thinker's mind than it has in any dog.[10] Nonetheless, the intelligible form of dog and of whiteness is the same form whether in the white dog or in the thinker's mind.

An alternative interpretation of the talk of likeness would be that Aristotle is thinking of the experiences not as thoughts but as mental images which resemble what is thought. We tend to underestimate the potential of mental images, whereas Aristotle tended, I believe, to overestimate it.[11] He says that there is no human thinking without a mental image (that is how I have elsewhere argued *phantasma* should be understood).[12] Thus in thinking of a triangle, we 'place before the [mind's] eye' an image of a triangle but ignore any features of the image that may be irrelevant such as its particular size. We can even use a mental image of a triangle to think about something unextended, in which case we will ignore the extension of the image.[13] In this case there is little likeness between the unextended thing and the image, although there may still be a likeness between it and the intelligible form which we make actual by attending to the relevant features of the image. (How we know which features to attend to is unexplained.)

There is another problem about likeness which has also been brought out by Hilary Putnam in his attack on the widespread modern idea that thinking involves a *representation* in the mind, an idea that he regards as in some sense 'Aristotelian'.[14] The problem is that people may be ignorant in various ways about the thing they are thinking of, and for that reason will not necessarily have in mind anything that is *like* what they are thinking of. If they think of going to Delhi for the first time, they may envisage it as having streets paved with gold, so that there is nothing very *like* Delhi in their minds. Of course in one sense they are representing Delhi, but only in the sense of *thinking* of it as being a certain way.

The point about ignorance was extraordinarily well made by Aristotle himself, although for different purposes. In *Posterior Analytics* II 8, Aristotle discusses not the meaning of names and verbs, but the definitions of things studied by scientists. But these scientific entities, for example eclipses or being eclipsed, are referred to by names or verbs, so the discussion of their definitions is relevant. Aristotle distinguishes the lay person who knows that lunar eclipse is some sort of loss of light by the moon from the scientist who knows that it is the moon's loss of light due to the earth's shadow and on the other side from the person who knows only an accidental feature, that the moon sometimes casts no shadow despite the absence of any solid obstruction between us and it. The person with the accidental feature does not know what lunar eclipse is, whereas the lay person grasps something of what it is. At least he knows the general type under which it falls. The idea that the lay person's talk of lunar eclipse appeals to an unspecified uniting essence anticipates the ideas of Locke, Leibniz, Putnam, and Saul Kripke, and I have extolled it elsewhere.[15]

Aristotle's lay person is not going to have a complete likeness in mind, because what he has in mind will not incorporate the idea of the earth's shadow. But we can go further. David Charles has drawn attention to the significance of two passages in the *Posterior Analytics*: II 7 92b5–7 and II 10 93b30–2.[16] Aristotle there says that one can have an account of what a name *signifies* even though no such thing exists, as with the name 'goat-stag' which *signifies* animal composed of goat and stag,[17] or even before one has discovered whether the thing exists. But Aristotle regards it as impossible for an account to tell us what something non-existent *is*. The commentary of Themistius in the fourth century AD is particularly interesting.[18] He illustrates the case of the non-existent by vacuum, whose existence Aristotle denied. The person who knows the *signification* of the name 'vacuum' will have in mind a description, e.g., the very one that Aristotle gave elsewhere: 'a place empty of body', but I am not sure that the description can provide a *likeness* of vacuum, if it does not tell us what vacuum *is*. Clearer is the next case if Themistius is right that the person who does not know whether the thing exists can be illustrated by the case of a person who thinks of lunar eclipse as the moon's not showing even though it is full. This description is intended to be the one that Aristotle regarded as giving us *no part* of what lunar eclipse is. In that case the description looks even further from providing a *likeness*.

It was, however, the intelligible form, not the description, that Aristotle's ancient commentators took to be a likeness. But there is a problem about intelligible form too. Does the lay person have in mind some formal characteristics of lunar eclipse? Unfortunately, Aristotle might think lunar loss of light to be a material rather than a formal characteristic. Worse, Aristotle would be disinclined to say that there was any form of a non-existent thing, yet one can think of vacuum or goat-stag. At best Aristotle might deal with the further case of a person with the merely accidental description of lunar eclipse as 'what makes my dog howl'. Such a thinker receives a form allright, but not the form of lunar eclipse, merely the form of something accidentally connected with lunar eclipse, a howling dog. Consequently, the experience is also a likeness only of something accidentally connected with lunar eclipse. All this creates difficulty for Aristotle's requirement of likeness.

ROLE OF IMAGES

Despite what I have said, images certainly do play an important role in Aristotle's account of meaning. Boethius rejects the interpretation of *experiences* as images on another ground, that Aristotle shows he is discussing *thoughts*, when he continues almost immediately after our quotation to discuss how truth or falsity does not arise from isolated thoughts (*noêmata*) corresponding to an isolated verb or name, but only from combined thoughts. Boethius understands this against the background of Aristotle *On the Soul* III 8 432a10–14, which says that only a combination of thoughts, not one of images, yields truth or falsity, and that images merely accompany thoughts without being identical with them.[19] Why then do the ancient commentators still give an important role to images?

The answer emerges when we ask why the thoughts are called *pathêmata*. Although I have translated the word as 'experiences', the root 'path-' carries an implication of being *passively* affected. But why should thoughts be considered passive, and where in *On the Soul* did Aristotle describe them that way, as he claims to have done in the words immediately following our quotation? The question was enough to make the Aristotelian Andronicus in the first century BC think that the entire work *On Interpretation* was non-Aristotelian.[20] The answer given by other ancient commentators accords a big role to the imagination. Boethius' reply is that the thinker receives the intelligible form into his imagination, and hence passively.[21] Ammonius draws attention to a doctrine found in his teacher Proclus. Proclus was only following earlier commentators in finding three types of intellect distinguished in Aristotle's *On the Soul* III 5, but what is not extant in earlier commentators is his claim that someone (evidently Aristotle) identifies the passive intellect with imagination.[22] This is, in fact, to go totally against Aristotle, who insisted that imagination was a perceptual faculty, not an intellectual one.[23] What has happened is that the images of imagination, instead of being a necessary accompaniment of human thinking, as with Aristotle, have been made into a kind of thinking. Boethius continues to give an enlarged role to imagination in our thought processes when he goes on to describe what happens when we have in mind an isolated concept such as human. The distinctive property of human is said to arise not, as one might expect, in intellect or thought, but in imagination.[24] Below I shall consider a description in a commentary ascribed to Ammonius' pupil Philoponus of how perception imprints in the imagination an image of someone which bears the stain both of shared and of individuating properties, that is both of mortal, rational animal, and of long-haired and pale. I have elsewhere traced an enlarged role for imagination in other interpreters of Aristotle earlier than Ammonius.[25] The fullest enlargement extant is provided by Porphyry, whose commentary on Aristotle is Boethius' main source, but it is provided in Porphyry's commentary on a different thinker, Ptolemy. For Porphyry the imagination acquires a bigger role, but one that makes it no longer merely passive as it was to be in Boethius, since it actually creates concepts (*ennoiai*) by giving exactitude to the inaccurate data of sense. It works out the exact structure of things like people filling in the details as they descry people at a distance coming in to shore.[26]

Experiences, not things

Alexander, we learn from Boethius, had asked[27] why Aristotle does not treat spoken sounds as being primarily about things, not experiences, but the answer recorded seems to say little more than that this view is right. Boethius does not offer as an answer the point he makes a little earlier that there can be thoughts of non-existent centaurs and chimaeras, but he could have said that in these cases there is no *thing* available.[28]

Mentalese

As I have elsewhere pointed out,[29] Boethius attributes to Porphyry the view that there are names and verbs in thought which differ from those that are spoken, while the spoken ones also differ from the written.[30] One wonders how the names and verbs that are thought, spoken, and written can avoid being the same. The spoken and written ones in Aristotle's case are both Greek, so it does not seem very likely that he is referring to the idea of a language of thought that is different from Greek and from any natural language, but that idea has been revived in modern times by Jerry Fodor.[31] Fodor is interested in a language of thought that corresponds to whole sentences of any level of complexity, not just to simple sentences consisting of names and verbs. Nonetheless, he and Boethius' Porphyry alike are speaking of a language of thought, and it is this language that Fodor calls mentalese. Aristotle's own point is probably merely that the names are in different media. But here is Boethius' very different account in his second commentary *On Aristotle On Interpretation* 29, 29–30, 10 (Meiser), of how Porphyry took Aristotle:

> Porphyry asks why Aristotle says 'what are in vocal sounds' and not just 'vocal sounds' and again why 'written marks' and not 'letters'. He resolves the question

as follows. It is said that for the Peripatetics there are three kinds of speech, one that is written in letters, another that is put forth in vocal sound, a third that is composed in the mind. But if there are three kinds of speech, there is no doubt that the parts of speech are also threefold. So since it is principally verb and name that are the parts of speech, there will be some verbs and names that are written, others that are spoken, and others that are exercised in the silence of the mind.

Thus verbs or names in the mind are not the same as spoken ones in a different medium, but are different verbs and names. It is this that suggests they belong to mentalese.

Boethius is writing in the wake of another Christian Latin author, Augustine, and Augustine speaks quite explicitly of a mental type of word. It is

[a word that] does not belong to any language, at any rate not to any of those which are called the languages of the nations, of which our own Latin is one.... When we say something true, that is, something we know, from the knowledge which we hold in our memory, necessarily the word is born which is entirely of the same kind as the knowledge from which it is born. The thought formed from the thing which we know is the word which we say in our heart, which is neither Greek nor Latin, nor of any other language.... The word which is sounded externally is a sign of the word that shines inside, to which the name 'word' is more applicable. [...This word] is a prerequisite of any language, but is prior to all the signs by which it is communicated

(*On the Trinity* 15.10.19–20)

This word, then, stands in need of a sign if it is to be communicated, so that soliloquy is causally prior to communication, rather than being causally derivative from it, as Wittgenstein, Paul Grice, and much modern psychology would suggest. It does not involve even silently imagined sounds. The closest analogue is the Word of God. Thomas Aquinas was to say that this constitutes the language of angels,[32] and Curzio Chiesa has in effect traced the history of mentalese, though this was not his intention, through the Middle Ages to modern times.[33] What Fodor, following Chomsky, has resuscitated is a theory with a very long history, and that is what Boethius understands Porphyry as reading into Aristotle.

DOES MENTALESE IMPLY THAT THOUGHTS ARE AFTER ALL SYMBOLS RATHER THAN LIKENESSES?

I suggested earlier that Alexander's remarks suggest a divergence from the Neoplatonist interpretation that thoughts are *likenesses* of things. Instead, thoughts are rather symbols of experiences and it is only the experiences that are likenesses of things. Chiesa traces how medieval interpretations, starting with Roger Bacon and Robert Kilwardby, also turned Aristotle's thoughts into symbols or signs rather than likenesses, though in this case into signs of things rather than of experiences. He suggests how other remarks of Boethius might have encouraged this interpretation. The idea of a mental language of thought, mentalese, encourages the idea further, because, if there are mental words, they ought to be symbols, like spoken words. By the time of Thomas Aquinas, Scotus, and Occam, Chiesa argues, concepts are mental words and hence signs or symbols of things, rather than likenesses. If both words and thoughts are symbols of things, this raises the question in Occam and Descartes of whether one needs more than words. And if there are mental signs or symbols, this raises the question for Leibniz of whether one can think exclusively with the symbols as a shorthand, and leave out the ideas which they symbolize. Frege dealt a final blow to the idea of thoughts as likenesses, Chiesa suggests, when he insisted that we must think through signs or symbols. It might be added that those who hold that our thoughts require, or are even identical with, representations in the brain nonetheless tend to regard these representations not as pictorial likenesses, but as in some way symbolic.[34]

I thus see Boethius' interpretation of Porphyry and, if it influenced Boethius, Augustine's word said in the heart that is neither Latin not Greek, as creating a distinctive departure from Neoplatonism. It means that if there are thoughts which correspond not to whole sentences but to names and verbs, then these thoughts will not be likenesses of things, but symbols, even though neither Boethius nor Porphyry seems to have drawn that conclusion. In the late nineteenth century, Sir Francis Galton claimed to discover that people not perverted by too much intellectualism, the wives of the fellows of the Royal Society though not the fellows themselves, needed pictorial mental likenesses when asked to remember their breakfasts.[35] But the more recent view among those who believe that thinking must involve representations tends to be that the representations needed are symbols, not likenesses.

SAME FOR ALL

According to our original quotation from Chapter 1 of Aristotle's *On Interpretation*, experiences and things are the same for everyone. Proclus, Ammonius, and Boethius point out that the question of what is or is not the same for everyone is connected with the question of Plato's *Cratylus*.[36] Plato's treatment there of proper and common names canvasses the idea that a correct name implies through its etymology a disguised description that reveals a thing's nature, and is therefore a natural, not a conventional, name. This is Plato's best known discussion, but we shall see that the *Theaetetus* also had an influence on the treatment of names.

Aristotle's verdict by contrast in chapter 2 of *On Interpretation* is that names are variable because imposed by convention (*kata sunthêkên*, 16a19) even though he had earlier maintained that experiences and things are the same. Aristotle explicitly contrasts convention with nature in chapter 2 at 16a26–9.

Two objections had been raised by Aristotelians earlier than Alexander to the claim that experiences and things are the same for everyone. Herminus, one of Alexander's teachers in the second century AD, had objected that there are ambiguous words and these arouse diverse experiences. Consequently, he proposed to eliminate from Aristotle's text the reference to sameness of experiences and things by substituting the word *tauta*, 'these' for *t'auta* 'the same', so as to read '*these* are experiences', '*these* are things', instead of 'experiences are the *same*', 'things are the *same*'. The spellings would not have been differentiated in the original. In reply, Boethius approves of Alexander who, followed by Porphyry, answered that an ambiguous meaning can be clarified.[37] But this seems an inadequate answer on its own. A better answer is suggested in the formulations given by Boethius, Ammonius, and Stephanus themselves, which put the point in terms of how things are conceived, not of the meanings of words. It is not the case that what is a horse for the Romans is a stone for the barbarians; it is possible for two people to think differently about horse, but the thought connected with horse is the same.[38] The case of a horse, however, will turn out not to be so safe.

Nonetheless, another commentator from the Aristotelian school, also from the second century, Aspasius, raised a harder objection against the claim of sameness. How can the experiences be the same for everyone when there are such different opinions about justice and goodness, or, Boethius adds, God? Boethius' answer does not seem to me adequate when he says that in these cases what is naturally just or good, as opposed to what is legally just or good, is the same for everyone and you either understand or fail to understand, while concerning God there is a common understanding among different cults of a certain highest nature.[39]

But elsewhere Aristotle's discussion casts doubt on the idea that experiences are the same for everyone, when he says in *Posterior Analytics* II 8, as mentioned above, that the lay person has a different conception of lunar eclipse from the expert scientist. The lay person thinks of it as *some* sort of loss of light by the moon; the scientific expert as the moon's loss of light due to the earth's shadow. A problem that arises about this is how people communicate with each other if they have different conceptions. Aristotle naturally does not see any problem about the layman and scientist communicating, because the scientist completes the conception of lunar eclipse that the lay person already has. But actually the problem is more severe because over the course of time science may change its mind about every aspect of the definition. Eclipses may turn out to involve loss of radio waves rather than of light. Gold may come to be defined not only by reference to the number of protons in the nucleus of its atoms, but also as not even a metal, if the concept of a metal turns out not to be scientifically viable. Yet despite a revision of all parts of the earlier definitions of eclipse or of gold, scientists may still want to say that they have made a discovery about eclipse or about gold, rather than merely having changed to discussing something different from eclipse or gold in the original sense. One modern way of dealing with this problem advocated by Putnam is to make continuity of meaning depend not on continuity of definition, but on continuity in agreement by and large about which samples should be counted as eclipse or as gold.[40] Aristotle does not see the need for any such manoeuvre.

But how can Aristotle's people communicate about lunar eclipse if they know only different *accidental* marks of lunar eclipse, one thinking of it as what makes my dog howl and another as what prevents the moon casting shadows despite the absence of an obstruction? In fact each party will convey something to the other by using the words 'lunar eclipse', but what will be activated in the other is only the other's *accidental* conception. If Themistius is right, what has been activated in each case is still an account of what the name 'lunar eclipse' signifies. But it is only an interpretation of Aristotle that he would include these accidental descriptions as giving the signification, and perhaps Aristotle would not have wanted this.

The Neoplatonist Porphyry, commenting on Aristotle at the end of the third century AD, goes in the opposite direction. He points out that it is the experts in science who typically have different conceptions from each other about the true nature of things, whereas ordinary speakers can share the same conception.[41] Aristotle himself unwittingly bears witness to this point, because his whole method involves starting from the diverse mistaken conceptions of preceding thinkers about each subject and correcting them.

It has been brought out by Robert van den Berg that the Neoplatonists Iamblichus and Proclus disagree with Porphyry. They put a premium on the expert's understanding of names, not the layman's, because, for example, the equal sticks and stones known to the layman are not unqualifiedly equal, so Plato had argued in *Phaedo* 74A-D. Only The Equal itself, the Platonic Form known to the expert, is unqualifiedly equal.[42] This has implications for common names like 'equal' and 'horse', and for proper names. Ordinary speakers can apply the name for horse to the right particulars by observing Greek usage, but only the philosopher can apply it as is naturally appropriate.[43] As regards proper names, Iamblichus urges us to forget all human conceptions (*epinoiai*) about the names of the gods. In divine names there is a symbolical character mark (*kharaktêr*) of divine likeness, and some special humans have been allowed to know the right name and even to learn from it the divine essence.[44] Proclus also holds that some divine names are revealed by the gods. In other cases, there are secret marks implanted by the gods in our souls, and priests (theurgists) imitate these secret marks by names, using intellect and linguistic imagination (*phantasia lektikê*) to make the names like the gods.[45] These marks had already been discussed by Iamblichus. They attract the good will of the gods and enable us to return to the gods through prayer.[46] On this theory, the signification of the right name is guaranteed independently of human convention, but the price is that only the privileged know the name or signification.

It has been pointed out to me[47] that Proclus allows multiple conceptions associated with a name, though only one correct conception, the expert's. His example of 'horse' already illustrates that.[48] The idea of Plato's *Cratylus* that etymology carries implications means that the name 'wine' carries the vulgar implication of a misguided state of mind, and the implication known to the expert of transcendent intellect. The names of the gods Dionysus and Aphrodite can refer through their etymology either to wine and to the foam of sperm, or at the expert's level to higher manifestations, e.g., in the case of Aphrodite to a cohesive force.[49] The human name 'Orestes' was used by his father as etymologically implying swiftness, but was allowed by Fate as etymologically implying the beast-like behaviour of matricide.[50]

Different connotations of proper names are allowed for in another tradition stemming from Plato, but in this case, I believe, from his *Theaetetus*. The commentary ascribed to Philoponus on Book II of Aristotle's *Posterior Analytics* discusses Aristotle's unexpected claim at II 19 100a17 that although one perceives a particular, as he always says, perception is nonetheless of the universal. 'Philoponus' understands, as mentioned above, that perception imprints in the imagination an image of someone which bears the stain both of shared and of individuating properties (*idiotêtes*), that is both of mortal, rational animal and of long-haired and pale. He adds that the individual actually consists of (*sunhistasthai*, 437, 13 and 32) these individuating properties.[51] The discussion goes back to Porphyry, who in turn, as I have argued elsewhere,[52] draws on Plato's *Theaetetus*. Porphyry says in his *Introduction* (*Isagôgê*) at 7, 16–24 that an individual (*atomon*) like Socrates is called an individual because an individual consists of individuating qualities (*ex idiotêtôn sunhistasthai*) the conglomeration (*athroisma*) of which would never come into being identically in anything else. Plato had himself offered an account of what is needed in order to think of an individual at *Theaetetus* 209C. Socrates cannot even have an opinion about Theaetetus unless the unique snub-nosedness of Theaetetus has been imprinted in Socrates along with the other characteristics of which Theaetetus consists (*ex hôn ei su*). Plato uses the word *idios* of individuating characteristics at 154A, 166C, and the word *athroisma* at 157B-C for a conglomeration of characteristics and their source to which people give the (common) name of 'man', or 'stone'. His account here of the uniquely identifying description required for thinking of an individual is much more demanding than anything in Aristotle.

I have said that Plato influenced Porphyry 650 years later around 300 AD. But before that, Plato's discussion influenced theories of proper names in Stoics and, as David Robertson has brought out, in Christians.[53] According to the Stoics, a proper name indicates an individuating (*idia*) quality.[54] The Christian Origen in the third century AD repeats that a proper name presents the individuating (*idia*) quality of what is named, and adds that there is an individuating quality for each of St Paul's body, soul, and intellect, so three altogether.[55] There is a further development, Robertson points out, in the Christian Basil of Caesarea, who is later than Porphyry in the fourth century AD.[56] On hearing the names 'Peter' or 'Paul', we think of a conglomeration (*sundromê*) of individuating properties (*idiômata*). This conglomeration is not like that cited above from Porphyry and 'Philoponus', for whom the conglomeration is *collectively* unique to the individual. It is more like the conglomeration hinted at by Plato, in that *each* of the properties listed is unique to Peter, like being the rock on which the Church is built.

Basil's treatment carries advantages and disadvantages. The big disadvantage is that for each individuating characteristic listed, Basil uses a proper name such as 'the Church' to secure uniqueness, but then he cannot give a general account of how proper names secure uniqueness in the first place. On the other hand, this method exonerates him from tackling the question parallel to one that was raised above for common names, how different speakers communicate about the same thing, if they are using different conceptions of it. For Basil each conception picks out Peter uniquely. The best known solution in modern theory as to how people communicate through a proper name to which they attach different conceptions is that devised independently by Saul Kripke and Keith Donnellan. On this theory, a name succeeds in naming not by being associated with a conception or description of what is named, but through a causal link which starts from the original application of a name and finishes by causing the present use of the name, even though the sound and shape of the name and the conceptions and descriptions associated with it may all have changed radically over the course of time.[57] I do not see anything quite of this kind in antiquity. There is a causal theory of divine names, but the causal element concerns the efficacy of non-conventional names in ritual, not their signification.[58]

The Platonist theories I have been looking at in this last section cast doubt on Aristotle's claim that experiences in meaning are the same for all.

Notes

1. Ammonius *Commentary* 12, 16–13, 9; 14, 18–15, 13; Boethius 2nd *Commentary* 14, 9–15, 31; Stephanus *Commentary* 3, 13–38. I am greatly indebted to comments by David Blank, Robert van den Berg, and David Charles, which have led to substantial improvements in the following account.
2. Ammonius *Commentary* 13, 19–14, 17; David Blank cites in his translation Aristotle *Topics* 148a10–13.
3. Alexander ap. Boethius *2nd Commentary* 35, 21–9.
4. Porphyry ap. Boethius *2nd Commentary* 29, 29–33, 6; Ammonius *Commentary* 22, 9–11; 22, 21–7; 23, 5–9.
5. Proclus *On Plato's Cratylus* 15, 27–9, Pasquali; Ammonius *On Aristotle On Interpretation* 18, 23–26, 2; Boethius *1st Commentary on Aristotle On Interpretation* 36, 22–41, 15; Boethius *2nd Commentary on Aristotle On Interpretation* 20, 9–45, 25, Meiser; Stephanus *On Aristotle On Interpretation* 4, 36–6, 21. The undated anonymous commentary and the scholia from Olympiodorus both edited by Leonardo Tarán, Meisenheim am Glan 1978, do not include comments on this question.
6. Boethius *2nd Commentary on Aristotle On Interpretation* 7, 5–9.
7. Ammonius *op. cit.* 1.6–11.
8. Ammonius *op. cit.* 20, 22–4.
9. Hilary Putnam, 'Aristotle after Wittgenstein', in R. W. Sharples, ed., *Modern Thinkers and Ancient Thinkers* (London, 1993) 117–137.

10. Aristotle applies this idea to the reception of form in perception, *DA* III 2 426a15–26; analogy with thinking esp. Book III, chs. 4, 7, and 8.

11. So the introduction to the second edition of Richard Sorabji, *Aristotle on Memory*, London 2004, Chicago 2006.

12. Aristotle *DA* III 7–8 431a16; 431b2; 432a3–14. I defend this interpretation of *phantasma* in the introduction to the 2nd edition of Richard Sorabji, *Aristotle on Memory*, London 2004, Chicago 2006.

13. Aristotle *On Memory* 1 449b30–450a7.

14. Hilary Putnam, *Representation and Reality*, Cambridge, Mass., 1988, Chs 1–3; similarly 'Aristotle after Wittgenstein', in R. W. Sharples, ed., *Modern Thinkers and Ancient Thinkers* (London 1993) esp. 129. For Norman Malcolm's quite different attack on the idea that remembering must involve representation, see Norman Malcolm, 'Memory and representation', *Nous* 4, 1970. 59–70.

15. Discussed by Richard Sorabji, 'Aristotle and Oxford philosophy', *Australasian Philosophical Quarterly* 6, 1969, 127–35; *Necessity, Cause and Blame*, London and Ithaca, N.Y., 1980, chs. 12–13. When I asked Kripke why he did not regard Aristotle as an ally, he gave me the charmingly self-deprecating answer that his teacher, Rogers Albritton, had said that Aristotle was only for the clever, so he (Kripke) had avoided Aristotle.

16. David Charles, *Aristotle on Meaning and Essence*, Oxford, 2000, Ch. 2.

17. So say the commentaries of 'Philoponus' and Eustratius *ad loc.*

18. Themistius *Commentary on Aristotle Posterior Analytics* 51, 3–10.

19. Boethius *2nd Commentary* 27, 25–28, 18.

20. Ammonius *Commentary* 5, 28–6, 4.

21. Boethius *2nd Commentary* 33, 33–34, 5.

22. Proclus *Commentary on Euclid Book 1*, 51, 20–52, 20; Ammonius *Commentary* 6, 4–14; cf. 26, 1–2. For translations of the same doctrine in Ammonius' pupils Philoponus, Simplicius, and Asclepius, see Richard Sorabji, *Philosophy of the Commentators 200–600 ad. A Sourcebook* vol. 1, 3j.

23. Aristotle *DA* III 3 428a18–24.

24. Boethius *2nd Commentary* 44, 16–18.

25. Aristotle's school according to Sextus Empiricus *Against the Mathematicians* 7. 221–2; Themistius *Commentary on Aristotle On the Soul* 98, 35–99, 10, cited in Richard Sorabji, 'The ancient commentators on concept formation', in Frans de Haas, Mariska Leunissen, Marije Martijn, eds., *Interpretations of Aristotle's Posterior Analytics*, Brill, Leiden 2011; reprinted with changes in David Charles, ed., *Definition in Greek Philosophy*, Oxford, 2010.

26. Porphyry *Commentary on Ptolemy's Harmonics* 13, 21–14, 11.

27. Alexander ap. Boethius *2nd Commentary* 40, 28–41, 13.

28. Boethius *2nd Commentary* 22, 2–6.

29. Richard Sorabji, *The Philosophy of the Commentators 200—600 ad*, vol. 3, *Logic and Metaphysics*, Ch. 7b.

30. Porphyry ap. Boethius *2nd Commentary* 29, 29–30, 10; Ammonius *Commentary* 22, 12–21.

31. Jerry Fodor, *The Language of Thought*, New York, 1975, based on the work of Noam Chomsky, and criticized by Hilary Putnam, *Representation and Reality*, Cambridge, Mass., 1988.

32. Tiziana Suarez-Nani, *Connaissance et langage des anges selon Thomas d'Aquin et Gilles de Rome*, Paris: Vrin, 2002 (*Études de philosophie médiévale* vol. LXXXV), see esp. p. 193 for the basis in Augustine.

33. Curzio Chiesa, 'Les origines de la "révolution linguistique"'. *Revue de Théologie et de Philosophie* 117, 1985, 261–84.

34. See Michael Tye, *The Imagery Debate*, Cambridge, Mass., 1991.

35. Francis Galton, *Inquiries into Human Faculties*, London 1883, 2nd edition 1907.

36. Proclus *Commentary on Plato's Cratylus* 58. 25, 17–26, 3; Boethius *2nd Commentary* 37, 20–9; Ammonius *Commentary* 19, 4–6.

37. Boethius *2nd Commentary* 39, 25–40, 28; Ammonius *Commentary* 24, 12–21 records Herminus' reading without the reason for it.

38. Boethius *1st Commentary* 37, 30–38, 5; *2nd Commentary* 38, 22–4; Ammonius *Commentary* 19, 11–12; Stephanus *Commentary on Aristotle On Interpretation* 6, 10–11.

39. Boethius *2nd Commentary* 41, 13–42, 6.

40. Hilary Putnam, e.g., 'the meaning of "meaning"', *Minnesota Studies in the Philosophy of Science* 7, ed. K. Gunderson, Minneapolis, 1975.

41. Porphyry ap. Simplicius *Commentary on Aristotle Categories* 213, 10–20.

42. Proclus *Commentary on Plato's Parmenides* 852, 27–37. The situation is made clear by Robert van den Berg, 'Proclus' criticism of Porphyry's semantic theory', in Gerd van Riel, Caroline Macé, eds, *Platonic Ideas and Concept Formation in Ancient and Medieval Thought*, Leuven, 2004, 155–169.

43. Proclus *Commentary on Plato First Alcibiades* 258, 20–259, 13.

44. Iamblichus *On the Mysteries of the Egyptians* 7.4, 255, 5–256, 9.

45. Proclus *Commentary on Plato's Cratylus* 71, 31, 24–32, 5; 51, 31, 24–32, 5.

46. Iamblichus ap. Proclus *Commentary on Plato's Timaeus* 1.209, 1–212, 6, Diehl.

47. Private communication from Robert van den Berg drawn from his *Proclus' Commentary on the Cratylus in Context*, Brill, Leiden 2008. I owe the next three references to him.

48. Proclus *Commentary on Plato First Alcibiades* 258, 20–259, 13.

49. Proclus *Commentary on Plato's Cratylus* 182–3, 108, 13–111, 20.

50. Proclus *Commentary on Plato's Cratylus* LXXXVII, 43, 22–8.

51. 'Philoponus', Commentary on Aristotle *Posterior Analytics* 437, 15–438, 2.

52. Richard Sorabji, *Philosophy of the Commentators 200–600 AD*, vol. 3, 6b (6b and 7e translate all the texts mentioned here on individuals and proper names), and *Self: Ancient and Modern Insights about Individuality, Life and Death*, Chicago and Oxford, 2006, with further material in *Matter, Space and Motion*, London and Ithaca, N.Y., 1988, Ch. 4.

53. I owe the information on Christians to David Robertson, 'Proper names' in *Grammar, Logic and Philosophy of Language in Basil of Caesarea: The Stoic Legacy in Fourth Century Patristics*, Ph.D. diss. University of London 2000, and 'A Patristic theory of proper names', *Archiv für Geschichte der Philosophie* 2002, 1–19.

54. Diogenes Laertius *Lives of Eminent Philosophers* 7.58.

55. Origen *On Prayer* Ch. 24, sec.2, *Die griechischen christlichen Schriftstellen* vol. 2, Koetschau.

56. Basil of Caesarea *Against Eunomius* 2.4.1–26, Durand-Doutreleau.

57. Saul Kripke, *Naming and Necessity*, three lectures originally published in G. Harman, D. Davidson, eds., *Semantics of Natural Languages*, Dordrecht, 1972, 253–355, with appendix 763–9; Keith Donnellan, 'Proper names and identifying descriptions'. *Synthese* 21, 1970, 335–358 and in Donald Davidson, Gilbert Harman, eds., *Semantics of Natural Language*, Dordrecht, 1972.

58. Many of the relevant texts are translated in Richard Sorabji, *Philosophy of the Commentators 220–600 ad*, vol. 3, 7c-d. See also vol. 1, 18c5.

Bibliography

Blank, David (1996) *Ammonius on Aristotle: On interpretation* 1–8, annotated translation by D. Blank (London: Duckworth).

Charles, David (2002) *Aristotle on Meaning and Essence* (Oxford: Clarendon Press).

—— ed. (2010) *Definition in Greek Philosophy* (Oxford: Oxford Univ. Press).

Chiesa, Curzio (1985) 'Les origines de la "révolution linguistique"', *Revue de Théologie et de Philosophie* 117, 261–84.

Donnellan, Keith (1970) 'Proper Names and Identifying Descriptions', *Synthese* 21, 335–358.

Duvick, Brian (2007) *Proclus on Plato's Cratylus*, annotated translation by B. Duvick (London: Duckworth).

Galton, Francis (1883) *Inquiries into Human Faculties*, 2nd ed. (London: Macmillan).

de Haas, Frans, Mariska Leunissen, Marije Martijn, eds. (2011) *Interpreting Aristotle's Posterior Analytics in Late Antiquity and Beyond* (Leiden: Brill).

Fodor, Jerry (1975) *The Language of Thought* (New York: Crowell).

Kripke, Saul (1972) *Naming and Necessity*, three lectures originally published in *Semantics of Natural Languages*, G. Harman, D. Davidson, eds. (Dordrecht: Reidel), 253–355, with appendix, 763–9.

Malcolm, Norman (1970) 'Memory and representation', *Nous* 4, 59–70.

Putnam, Hilary (1975) 'The Meaning of "Meaning"', in K. Gunderson, ed., *Language, mind, and knowledge* (Minneapolis: Univ. of Minnesota Press).

—— (1988) *Representation and Reality* (Cambridge, Mass./London: MIT Press).

—— (1993) 'Aristotle after Wittgenstein', in R.W. Sharples, ed., *Modern Thinkers and Ancient Thinkers* (London: UCL Press).

Robertson, David (2002) 'A Patristic Theory of Proper Names', *Archiv für Geschichte der Philosophie*, 1–19.

Smith, Andrew (2008) *Boethius on Aristotle: On interpretation* 1–3, annotated translation by A. Smith (London: Duckworth).

Sorabji, Richard (1969) 'Aristotle and Oxford Philosophy', *Australasian Philosophical Quarterly* 6, 127–35.

—— (2006) *Aristotle on Memory*, 2nd ed. (Chicago: Univ. of Chicago Press).

—— (2004) *The Philosophy of the Commentators, 200-600 AD: A Sourcebook* (London: Duckworth).

Tye, Michael (1991) *The Imagery Debate* (Cambridge, Mass./London: MIT Press).

van den Berg, Robbert (2004) 'Proclus' Criticism of Porphyry's Semantic Theory', in G. van Riel, C. Macé, eds., *Platonic Ideas and Concept Formation in Ancient and Medieval Thought*, (Leuven: Leuven Univ. Press), 155–169.

—— (2008) *Proclus' Commentary on the Cratylus in Context*, (Leiden: Brill).

CHAPTER 25

ARISTOTLE IN THE ARABIC COMMENTARY TRADITION

PETER ADAMSON

In late antiquity, the commentary became the most prominent genre of philosophical writing. Aristotle was the author who received the lion's share of attention, even though the commentators, beginning with Porphyry, were Platonists. They did produce commentaries on Plato as well as Aristotle,[1] but the latter's writings are the subjects of a sizeable majority of extant Greek philosophical commentaries.[2] This fact is often explained in light of the pedagogical purposes for which commentaries were written. Since Aristotle was seen not only as harmonious with Plato, but as more suitable for initial study in philosophy, commentaries for the use of students were naturally more often devoted to his works than to Plato's. A similar point applies to the proportion of extant commentaries on different parts of Aristotle's corpus.[3] Because logic was the first part of the philosophical curriculum, followed by physics and psychology, and only then finishing with metaphysics, we have many commentaries for Aristotle's *organon*, and quite a few for the physical works. By contrast, in the post-Plotinian period there are only two extant commentaries on the Metaphysics, one by Syrianus, which covers only Metaphysics III–IV and XIII–XIV, and another by Asclepius which covers Metaphysics I–VII.[4] The practice of writing commentaries on Aristotle, and the curriculum the commentaries were meant to support, cut across confessional lines. For instance Porphyry, Syrianus, the head of the Alexandrian school Ammonius, and his student Simplicius were all pagans. Indeed Porphyry and Simplicius were bitterly hostile to Christianity.[5] Yet the commentary tradition continues smoothly into Christianity with Christian members of the school of Ammonius, and also into Latin with the works of Boethius.

All of this applies, *mutatis mutandis*, to the Arabic commentary tradition. Here commentaries on Plato are even more marginal. This can be explained not only by the same issue of Aristotle's role in the philosophical curriculum, but also by the fact that the transmission of Plato into Arabic was patchy, whereas most of the works of Aristotle we know today were also available in Arabic.[6] (The latter may itself result from the former; that is, one reason Plato was not much translated is that his works were not standardly studied as part of a broad philosophical education.) Here too, commentaries focus on the earlier parts of the Aristotelian curriculum, with most emphasis on the logical and physical works. Only the greatest commentator of the Arabic tradition, Averroes, commented extensively on the *De Anima* or the *Metaphysics*.[7] As in the Greek tradition, confessional divides were no obstacle to continuous and even co-ordinated efforts to understand Aristotle.[8] This is best shown by the group of commentators known as the 'Baghdad school', who will be discussed below. For most, but not all, of the members of this 'school' were Christians, including its founder Abū Bishr Mattā.

There are at least three good reasons to study the Arabic tradition of commentary on Aristotle. First, it can enhance our understanding of the Greek tradition, not only by providing us with meticulous and insightful readings of Aristotle, as do the Greek commentaries, but also because otherwise lost Greek material is preserved in Arabic translation.[9] Second, no attempt to write the history of philosophy in the Islamic world can afford to ignore the commentators. Two of the most important Muslim philosophers, al-Fārābī and Averroes, produced numerous extant commentaries, and in the case of Averroes at least there is little doubt that he considered his commentaries on Aristotle to be the most important of his philosophical works. Third, some of the most interesting philosophical ideas produced in the medieval Arabic tradition are to be found in commentaries. Perhaps the best example is Averroes' mature position on intellect, which is presented in his *Long Commentary on the De Anima*.

Before exploring the output of the Arabic commentators themselves, a word about lost Greek material preserved in Arabic. At one time this was seen as the chief interest of the Arabic tradition for the historian of philosophy. Now this is no longer the case, given the growing interest taken in Arabic philosophy in its own right. And it is important not to overstate the extent to which lost Greek works are preserved in Arabic. But the fact remains that the Arabic tradition does preserve important works, and this is especially true for the Greek commentators. To give just a few examples, the great Aristotelian commentator Alexander of Aphrodisias wrote numerous works which are lost in Greek but extant in Arabic, such as his treatise on providence and another work on the principles of the universe.[10] Themistius' commentary on *Metaphysics* XII is preserved in Arabic, Latin, and Hebrew, but not in Greek.[11] Portions of Philoponus' commentary on the *Physics* are preserved only in Arabic,[12] in the so-called 'Baghdad *Physics*' which is further discussed below. Averroes is a major additional source for several Greek commentators, especially Alexander and Themistius.

The fact that so many Greek commentaries were translated into Arabic, and the fact that Averroes and others actually quote the Greek commentators in their own commentaries, already shows the degree of continuity that exists between the Greek and Arabic philosophical traditions.[13] In fact we can establish a more or less unbroken chain of authors who did philosophy by commenting on Aristotle, spanning from Greek through Syriac and into Arabic. The late antique philosophical tradition terminates with the Alexandrian commentators in the sixth century. Some of these commentators were Christian, as mentioned above, and their work would be taken on by two further Christian traditions. In Byzantium, commentaries on Aristotle continued to be produced in Greek. Elsewhere in the East, a monastic tradition of Syriac literature includes translations of, and commentaries on, Aristotle, though this seems to have been limited to the logical corpus.[14] When the translation of Aristotle and other Greek philosophical and scientific works began in earnest under the ʿAbbāsid caliphs, there was a direct link to this Syriac tradition.[15] This is, not least, because the translators often hailed from Syria or had a Syrian background. For instance Ibn Nāʿima al-Ḥimṣī, who wrote partial translations of the works of Plotinus and Philoponus' *Physics* commentary, was as his name indicates from Emesa (*ḥimṣ*) in Syria.[16] The great Ḥunayn Ibn Isḥāq (d. c. 873) hailed from Iraq, but he and his school translated from Greek via Syriac into Arabic. His speciality was medical literature, and he sought out and translated works of Galen. But the circle gathered around him, and especially his son Isḥāq Ibn Ḥunayn, produced many of the Arabic versions of Aristotle that would be used by subsequent philosophers. All these translators just mentioned were among the Greek-speaking Christians who were handsomely paid by the Muslim intelligentsia and political rulers to create an Arabic version of the Greek scientific corpus.

Greek commentators were, as we have seen, being translated into Arabic right along with the works of Aristotle himself. So it was natural for philosophers writing original works in Arabic to understand Aristotle in light of these commentaries, and to produce commentaries of their own. This is shown already by the output of the first man to engage with the Greek tradition by writing original philosophical works in Arabic, al-Kindī (d. c. 870).[17] Al-Kindī was deeply influenced by the Greek commentators, though it seems that he engaged more with independent treatises written by commentators like Philoponus and Alexander, rather than with their commentaries. The most prominent example is al-Kindī's proof that the world is not eternal, for which he drew on Philoponus' critique of Aristotle's *Physics* and *On the Heavens*.[18] His doctrine on divine providence is indebted to the writings of Alexander on this topic.[19] Al-Kindī also followed the example of these authors by writing commentaries of his own, but unfortunately his apparently rather extensive writings in this area are almost entirely lost. According to the list of his books provided by the *Fihrist* (or '*List*') of the tenth-century author Ibn al-Nadīm, al-Kindī was especially engaged with logic. He wrote, for instance, an account of the purpose and topic of the *Categories*,[20] a summary of Porphyry's *Isagoge*, and abridgments or paraphrases that related to other works of the *organon* like the *Sophistical Refutations*. We are also told that he wrote a work called *On the Physics* (*Sam' al-kiyān*), and this may have been a commentary.[21]

Though the works just mentioned are all lost, we get a good idea of al-Kindī's knowledge of Aristotle from his *On the Quantity of Aristotle's Books*, which itemizes each work in the corpus and briefly explains the topic of each.[22] This itemization again shows the influence of the late ancient curriculum, as al-Kindī emphasizes the need to study Aristotle's works in the correct order. He begins, as is traditional, with the logical works, and it is these works about which he is best informed. He thus devotes more discussion to the *organon* than to works on physics, psychology, or ethics (his knowledge of the ethical works and the *Politics* seems to be especially sketchy; they are mentioned at the very end almost as an afterthought). This is unsurprising given the centrality of the logical works in the Syriac tradition, which will remain a feature of the Arabic reception of Aristotle. If we go ahead a generation or two, we find that philosophers who were influenced by al-Kindī also tended to concentrate on logic.[23] His student al-Sarakhsī (d. 899) produced a voluminous corpus of philosophical works which are almost entirely lost. Again, our information shows that he wrote treatises, paraphrases, or commentaries on almost the whole *organon*.[24] A second generation student of al-Kindī, al-ʿĀmirī (991), also seems to have written commentaries on Aristotle: it is no surprise that the only one for which we (perhaps) have extant fragments is a commentary on the *Categories*.[25]

This same period was also the time of the most significant group of commentators on Aristotle to work in the heartlands of Islam: the Peripatetic 'school' founded by Abū Bishr Mattā (d. 940).[26] As mentioned above, this school was made up mostly of Christians, but its most famous representative was the Muslim al-Fārābī (d. 950). Most of the extant commentaries on Aristotle derive either from this group, which was based in Baghdad in the 10th-11th centuries, or from two commentators who lived later in Muslim Spain (Andalusia): Ibn Bājja (d. 1139), known in Latin as Avempace, and Ibn Rushd (d. 1198), known in Latin as Averroes. Averroes was certainly the most important Arabic commentator on Aristotle, and was simply called 'the Commentator' by Aquinas and other philosophers in Christian Europe, whom he deeply influenced. But it is not always realized that Ibn Bājja and Averroes were hearkening back to the project of the Baghdad school when they wrote their commentaries. In particular, they admired and followed al-Fārābī, agreeing with the assessment of Avicenna (Ibn Sīnā, d. 1037) in seeing him as the preeminent member of the Baghdad school, perhaps in part because he was a Muslim, but mostly because of his outstanding expertise in logic.

It is in these two bursts of activity, and especially in the works of al-Fārābī and Averroes, that we find the highpoints of the Arabic commentary tradition. In fact, though, it is misleading to speak only of 'commentaries'. Averroes' treatments of Aristotle were in fact written in a range of different styles, and only a few of these works can be described as commentaries in any strict sense. Traditionally, his expositions of Aristotle are divided into short, middle, and long commentaries.

But as Dimitri Gutas has pointed out, this division 'fails accurately to depict what Averroes actually did, but rather seems to reflect European perceptions of the *Latin* Averroes'.[27] What Averroes actually did was in large part to follow the lead of al-Fārābī and Ibn Bājja. All three of these authors produced independent treatises on topics drawn from Aristotle—for instance all three wrote brief works on the nature of the intellect, which are tied to Aristotle's *De Anima* thematically but are not presented as expositions of the text.[28] All three authors furthermore wrote epitomes of Aristotelian works, which summarize and even rearrange the source text. Particular energy was devoted to logic: al-Fārābī wrote epitomes of the entire *organon* (including not only Porphyry's *Isagoge* but also the *Rhetoric* and *Poetics*[29]), Ibn Bājja wrote commentaries on these epitomes,[30] and Averroes composed an 'abstract' of al-Fārābī's epitomes.[31] He wrote epitomes of his own for other Aristotelian works, such as the *Metaphysics*.[32] These epitomes need to be distinguished from longer expositions which clarify and convey the main points of an Aristotelian work. These expositions have a fairly fluid structure, and referring to them collectively as 'paraphrases' or 'middle commentaries' suggests more uniformity than is displayed by the texts themselves. Still, a good comparison here would be the so-called 'paraphrase commentaries' of Themistius. Examples of this form in the Arabic tradition include Ibn Bājja's exposition of the *Physics* and the works that go under the rubric of 'middle commentaries' in Averroes.[33]

Finally, there are the works that actually fulfill our expectations of a proper 'commentary', in which the Aristotelian work is quoted in lemmata, each lemma being discussed in detail. Like their Greek models, these commentaries are massive and extraordinarily detailed, and would be of use only to a highly specialized and well-informed reader. So it is unsurprising that these lengthy commentaries are often lost. One example is al-Fārābī's commentary *ad litteram* on the *Nicomachean Ethics*, which is no longer extant but was still known in Andalusia.[34] We do have examples from the Baghdad school, however: al-Fārābī's commentary on *On Interpretation*, the logical commentaries of Ibn al-Ṭayyib, and the Baghdad *Physics* (all discussed below). History has been rather unkind to the 'long' commentaries—i.e., lemmatized commentaries—of Averroes, which are mostly lost in their Arabic originals. We have Arabic texts for his lemmatized commentaries on the *Posterior Analytics* and *Metaphysics*,[35] but the commentaries on the *De Anima, De Caelo,* and *Physics* are extant only in Latin or in Latin and Hebrew. As we will see below, the fact that many of Averroes' treatments of Aristotle are lost in Arabic is an important clue about the way that philosophy in the Muslim world was already moving away from a focus on Aristotle in the 12th–13th centuries.

As this survey has already suggested, logic was central to the activities of both the Baghdad school and the Andalusian revival. This focus on logic can be traced back to the founder of the Baghdad Aristotelians, Abū Bishr Mattā, who is perhaps best known for being on the losing side of a debate over the relative merits of logic and grammar. This debate is an oft-cited example of early resistance to the incursion of Greek ideas into Muslim intellectual culture.[36] Abū Bishr, who also translated philosophical works from Syriac into Arabic, wrote several commentaries on

Aristotle's logical works. These are unfortunately lost, as are most of the commentaries of Yaḥyā Ibn ʿAdī (d. 974), who studied with both Abū Bishr and al-Fārābī.[37] We do have an opportunity to compare al-Fārābī and Ibn ʿAdī as commentators in the case of *On Interpretation*, because al-Fārābī's commentary and a short exposition of this text are extant,[38] and Ibn ʿAdī appends a commentary on the famous chapter 9 of the work (concerning the 'sea battle' argument for determinism) to an otherwise independent treatise on the nature of possibility.[39] The last representative of the Baghdad school, Abū l-Faraj Ibn al-Ṭayyib, produced two extensive commentaries which have come down to us, on Porphyry's *Isagoge* and the *Categories*.[40]

All these commentaries show the extensive influence of the Alexandrian commentators.[41] They are still quoted at length by Ibn al-Ṭayyib, and in a remarkable commentary on the *Physics* produced jointly by several members of the school. This 'Baghdad *Physics*', extant in only a single manuscript, includes the Arabic translation of the *Physics* by Isḥāq Ibn Ḥunayn, passages from the *Physics* commentaries of Alexander and Philoponus in Arabic translation, and collated comments by several members of the Baghdad school, including Abū Bishr, Ibn ʿAdī, the latter's student Ibn al-Samḥ, and Ibn al-Ṭayyib.[42] This manuscript is a valuable document for understanding the activities of the Baghdad school. One particularly striking feature is that the Greek commentators, especially Philoponus (called Yaḥyā in the text, creating potential confusion with Yaḥyā Ibn ʿAdī), are treated as interlocutors, fellow interpreters whose exegesis is useful though not beyond criticism. For example, both Ibn ʿAdī and Ibn al-Samḥ leap to defend Aristotle's original view against the innovations of Philoponus, respectively on the topics of place and motion.[43] The latter issue of motion is especially interesting: Philoponus had introduced the un-Aristotelian idea of 'impressed power', which has been compared to the modern theory of impetus.[44] Aristotle had argued that the speed of a moving body is inversely proportional to the density of the medium through which the body moves. Thus motion through a void would, absurdly, be infinitely fast (*Physics* IV 9). Philoponus disagrees, holding that motion through a void is possible, its speed being determined by its impressed power or impetus. Whereas Ibn al-Samḥ rejects this innovation, the later Andalusian commentator Ibn Bājja builds upon it, holding that the medium serves only to slow down the moving body.[45] The process of innovation and retrenchment to Aristotelian orthodoxy was repeated when Averroes rejected the impetus theory in the version put forward by Ibn Bājja, just as Ibn al-Samḥ had rejected the version found in Philoponus.[46]

Formal aspects of the Baghdad *Physics* and the lengthy commentaries of Ibn al-Ṭayyib also show the impact of the Greek tradition.[47] For instance, some late Greek commentaries, such as those by Olympiodorus, quote lemmata from Aristotle and then summarize the gist of each lemma (the *theôria*) before moving on to a detailed discussion, which proceeds through the text phrase by phrase (the *lexis*). This is imitated by Ibn al-Ṭayyib.[48] Another overt debt to the Alexandrian tradition is the practice of beginning commentaries with a series of standard questions about the Aristotelian text: why is it titled as it is, what is its place in the corpus, what is its subject-matter (*topos*), and so on. Ibn al-Ṭayyib again provides a good example. In his prolegomenon to the *Categories*, he not only covers these standard questions, but also follows the Alexandrian practice of devoting a special discussion, at the beginning of commentaries on the *Categories*, to certain questions regarding philosophy as a whole. For example, how many philosophical schools are there? What is the goal of philosophy? How should Aristotle's corpus be divided? And so on.⁴⁹

Another example of Alexandrian influence is the interest members of the Baghdad school take in issues of methodology and the philosophical curriculum. In several of his works, al-Fārābī emphasizes the need to study the philosophical sciences in the correct order, and shows how one science naturally leads on to another in the systematic way sketched in Aristotle's *Posterior Analytics*.⁵⁰ A striking difference between al-Kindī's aforementioned *On the Quantity of Aristotle's Books* and al-Fārābī's own summary of the Aristotelian corpus is that al-Fārābī makes a more serious effort to describe the corpus as a structured curriculum.⁵¹ Al-Kindī too says that Aristotle's works must be studied in the correct order, as we have seen. But he does not explain the links between the various works in any detail, perhaps in part because his knowledge of these works is less complete than al-Fārābī's. This question of how the branches of philosophy interrelate is not merely an abstract methodological issue. It can and does have specific consequences in deciding the meaning of Aristotle's texts. For instance, in his discussion of the deterministic argument of *On Interpretation* 9, al-Fārābī chastises Greek commentators who thought that Aristotle was trying to prove that determinism is false. This cannot be right, because determinism is not an issue that can appropriately be settled in a logical work. Logic, he says, does not tell us 'regarding the natures of things that exist, how they exist.' Rather, according to al-Fārābī, Aristotle simply assumes the falsity of determinism in order to make a properly logical point about the 'indeterminacy' of assertions about the future.⁵²

The most important such procedural question to arise in the Arabic tradition concerned the relation of physics to metaphysics. Though it was widely agreed that physics is subordinate to metaphysics—after all, metaphysics is 'first philosophy'—there was considerable disagreement about which science is responsible for proving God's existence. The central figure here, as so often in the history of philosophy in the Muslim world, was Avicenna. His self-consciously original approach to philosophy is shown by the fact that instead of writing commentaries on Aristotle, he composed self-contained works covering more or less the same ground as Aristotle's corpus (and then some, since for instance mathematics was also included).⁵³ The most voluminous of these Avicennan works is *The Healing* (*al-Shifāʾ*), a massive collection of original treatises on every area of philosophy. But he wrote others, including the enigmatic *Pointers and Reminders* (*al-Ishārāt wa-l-tanbīhāt*). If Avicenna intended these works effectively to supplant Aristotle with a new system, then his intentions were largely fulfilled. As we will see below, in the post-Avicennan tradition philosophical commentary was mostly devoted to expounding Avicenna, rather than Aristotle. Avicenna did weave Aristotelian themes into his system, so that for instance the *Metaphysics* or *Divine Science*

(*Ilāhiyyāt*) of the *Healing* is related to the *Metaphysics* of Aristotle in an articulated and coherent way.[54] But his handling and placement of these themes was, again, self-consciously innovative.

A prime example is this question I have just raised: which branch of philosophy proves God's existence, physics or metaphysics? Aristotle certainly seems to prove the existence of the First Mover in *Physics* VIII, based on the need for an eternal, immaterial mover to explain the eternal circular motion of the heavens. But Avicenna developed a famous proof for God which requires no physical premises. Rather, his proof begins from the 'immediate' notions of existence, necessity and contingency. Avicenna argues that the existence of contingent objects (things 'possible in themselves') requires a cause external to the aggregate of these objects, which will be an existent that is necessary in itself. He further argues that this Necessary Existent would have the attributes we associate with God.[55] In his commentaries, Averroes repeatedly criticizes this strategy of proving the existence of God in metaphysics, and of using a proof that supposedly proceeds from first principles. Rather, as he says in numerous contexts including his *Long Commentary on the Metaphysics*, it is physics that proves the existence of God on the basis of eternal motion.[56] Here he follows not only Aristotle but also al-Fārābī, whose *Attainment of Happiness* likewise claims that natural philosophy leads on to metaphysics by proving the existence of immaterial movers.

This methodological debate must be understood within the context of a broader problem about the subject-matter of metaphysics itself. For late ancient Platonists, metaphysics or first philosophy was the study of divine principles. Aristotle sometimes seems to support this view as well, especially in an influential passage at *Metaphysics* VI 1. Here he says that theoretical philosophy is divided into mathematics, physics, and 'first science' or 'theology (*theologikê*)', the latter dealing with things that 'exist separately and are immovable'. There is a long tradition of reading the entire *Metaphysics* in light of this passage, as devoted specifically to divine things (God and the celestial movers, and perhaps also human souls). We find this attitude in al-Kindī's *On the Quantity of Aristotle's Books* and also in Ibn 'Adī's commentary on *Metaphysics* II.[57] This would align the project of the *Metaphysics* nicely with the theological preoccupations of Neoplatonism. Such an understanding of Aristotle's project makes it easier to see how the Arabic version of Plotinus' *Enneads* could be harmonized with the Aristotelian corpus and even mistaken for a work by Aristotle himself. But al-Fārābī puts forward a more subtle view of 'first philosophy' in his short work *On the Aims of the Philosopher*, which explains the purpose of the *Metaphysics* and each of its books.[58] He claims that the subject-matter of first philosophy or metaphysics is not God and other divine entities, but being as such. This includes the study of divine principles—which are the causes of other beings—but also of material substances, as well as universal principles of reasoning (such as the principle of non-contradiction) that apply equally to all beings. Avicenna follows al-Fārābī's identification of the subject-matter of metaphysics: being as such, and not the divine.

But what does all this have to do with the question of whether physics or metaphysics proves the existence of God? The connection lies in another methodological principle taken from the *Posterior Analytics*, namely that no science proves the existence of its own subject-matter. This rule makes a certain amount of sense. After all, if a subject-matter fails to exist, then there will be no science of this subject-matter. And it seems circular that a science should prove that there is a need for itself. Aristotle puts the rule into practice elsewhere, for instance, in Book I of the *Physics* when he states that the student of physics need not prove the existence of motion. Aristotle goes on to do so anyway, but this, he says, is simply because of the philosophical interest of the question, not because the task is incumbent upon the student of physics (I 2 184b25–185a20). By denying that God is the subject-matter of metaphysics, Avicenna was able to reconcile his 'metaphysical' proof of God with Aristotle's methodological stricture. But the manoeuvre did not meet with Averroes' approval. Though he too was deeply influenced by al-Fārābī's understanding of the *Metaphysics*,[59] in at least some passages he adopted a more 'theological' reading of the work. He was no doubt at least partially motivated by the desire to retain Aristotle's proof of God as the first cause of motion in the *Physics*. For by holding that God and the other celestial movers are at least part of the subject-matter of metaphysics, Averroes could show that a properly metaphysical proof of their existence was illegitimate. Rather, God can be approached only from the lower science of physics, using a proof that moves from empirical observation of God's effects to His existence, rather than proceeding on the basis of immediately evident first principles.[60]

On this and on other topics, Averroes intended to provide an authentic reading of Aristotle shorn of Platonist and Avicennan presuppositions. This meant a meticulous reading of Aristotle's texts and an unashamed acceptance of passages where Aristotle rejects Platonist metaphysical commitments. Significantly, for Averroes the most important previous commentator on Aristotle was the Peripatetic Alexander, whereas the Baghdad school was influenced primarily by the late Alexandrian Neoplatonist school (though they too read and made use of Alexander). Averroes' reading of Aristotle is, in short, a far cry from the Platonizing and harmonizing approach of al-Kindī. In his determination to achieve fidelity to Aristotle, Averroes also departed from and indeed frequently attacked the innovations of Avicenna. More difficult is the question of the extent to which Averroes' reading is presaged by al-Fārābī. He is credited with having written *On the Harmony of the Two Sages*, which systematically undermines reasons for thinking there is any significant disagreement between Plato and Aristotle.[61] If the *Harmony* is indeed a work of al-Fārābī, it shows that he was fully committed to compatability of Plato and Aristotle, a thesis usually associated with Greek Neoplatonists (even though it was clearly accepted only with reservations, if at all, by some Neoplatonists, such as Syrianus). Furthermore, his own systematic works make extensive use of such standard Neoplatonic notions as emanation. However, in other contexts al-Fārābī has no qualms about mentioning, and agreeing with, Aristotle's hostility towards Platonic Forms. For this and other reasons it has recently been questioned whether the *Harmony* is genuinely a work of al-Fārābī. If it is not, it may nonetheless represent the attitude of other Baghdad Aristotelians. For there are reasons to think that Ibn ʿAdī adhered more closely to a Kindian understanding of Greek philosophy as a single, harmonious body of doctrine.[62]

In light of Averroes' determination to 'de-Platonise' the Aristotle handed down to him, it is often thought ironic that he developed a theory of intellect which seems to go beyond any of his predecessors in a Platonising direction. The theory, sometimes misleadingly called 'monopsychism' (misleading because *psuchê* in Greek means 'soul,' and this theory concerns not the soul but specifically the intellect), is the most notorious interpretation of Aristotle presented in any Arabic commentary. But despite its notoriety it is often misunderstood, and one misunderstanding that needs to be avoided is the notion that the theory grows out of a Platonist tradition. Rather, it grows out of Averroes' sustained engagement with Aristotle and specifically the *De Anima*. Averroes' views on the correct reading of the teaching on intellect in the *De Anima* evolved throughout his career, so that we find three different interpretations in the epitome ('short commentary'), the exposition ('middle commentary'), and the lemmatized *Long Commentary*.[63] His final position is found in the *Long Commentary*, which defends the controversial and seemingly preposterous claim that there is only one intellect for all of mankind.

The first thing that should be said here is that Averroes was far from being the first to posit a single intellect to explain all human thought. Many, indeed most, readings of Aristotle from late antiquity through the Arabic tradition suppose that there is a single intellect which is a repository of universal and intelligible forms, and which enables us to grasp these intelligibles. For such authors as al-Fārābī and Avicenna, this single intellect is to be found already in Aristotle: it is the entity discussed in the enigmatic fifth chapter of *De Anima* III. They refer to it as the 'active intellect'.[64] It has a dual role in the Farabian and Avicennan systems. On the one hand, the active intellect emanates forms into suitably prepared matter, and this accounts for the generation of material substances such as animals and individual humans. On the other hand, the intellect illuminates a suitably prepared human soul with intelligible forms. This is meant to explain how humans can achieve an adequate grasp of necessary and universal intelligibles, which might be difficult to account for by appealing to the empirical process of abstraction.[65] The theory sounds rather Platonist, and indeed there is a clear similarity between this version of Aristotelian noetics and the doctrine of Plotinus, for whom the universal intellect is just identical with the realm of Platonic Forms. But al-Fārābī and Avicenna saw their embrace of the active intellect as perfectly consistent with Aristotle's anti-Platonic strictures. For the intelligible forms in this intellect are thoughts in a mind, not separately existing paradigms.

Averroes, then, was not saying anything unusual in arguing that a single, universal intellect is involved in human thought. Where he departs from the tradition is rather in affirming that there is only one *material* or *potential* human intellect. Al-Fārābī and Avicenna, like the Greek commentators, had assumed that each human has an intellective or rational soul which is unique to him or her. It is this numerically distinct intellect which has the potential to receive intelligibles from the single active intellect. Against this, Averroes points out that there cannot be two numerically distinct potentialities for exactly the same actuality, unless this potentiality is seated in a numerically distinct body. But we know from *De Anima* III 4 that the human intellect has no bodily organ. If there is no material object to individuate the human capacity for thought, then there is no way of individuating two distinct instances of such a capacity. Rather, there is only one capacity which we all share, and it is permanently and fully actualized by the universal active intellect. This explains why two people who are thinking about the same intelligible object are quite literally having the *same* thought, and not two distinct thoughts that are very similar to one another. To put it another way, there is only one correct scientific understanding of any intelligible, as opposed to a distinct understanding for each person who comes to grasp the intelligible in question.

The extent to which this position is anti-Platonist is shown by the fact that Averroes adheres to an empiricist, 'bottom up' account of how universal intellection is generated. Individual humans have lower psychological faculties (memory, imagination, and what he refers to as 'cogitation') seated in their brains, and these serve as the basis for a universal abstractive grasp of intelligibles. The involvement of these lower faculties also explains how it can be that, if the universal intellect belongs to all of us and is always thinking about everything, each human has only intermittent experiences of intellecting certain intelligibles to the exclusion of others. It is only when *my* imagination, memory, and so on are used as the basis for universal intellection that *I* have the experience of intellecting. Thus Averroes already anticipates and answers a complaint of Thomas Aquinas, who attacks the teaching of the unity of the material intellect by saying that it cannot account for the fact that *this* man thinks.[66] While it is true that there is only one intellect for all of us, there is an explanation for why this man has the subjective experience of thinking and that man does not. It is just that this explanation is grounded in psychological faculties lower than the intellect.[67]

Averroes' theory of the material intellect sparked a great deal of controversy in Latin Christian philosophy, as did his acceptance of the world's eternity. But even those Christians who, like Aquinas, opposed his teaching on these two issues still saw him as the most reliable and important commentator on Aristotle. Similarly, in the Jewish tradition Maimonides (d. 1204) commends the use of Averroes as a guide to Aristotle, while Levi Ben Gerson (Gersonides, d. 1344) and his students composed super-commentaries, i.e., commentaries on Averroes' commentaries.[68] In both Hebrew and Latin, the translations of Averroes' commentaries were an important means of transmitting the Aristotelian text itself.[69] For when the long commentaries were translated, the lemmata of the Aristotelian text were translated along with them. All of this is in stark contrast to the fortunes of Averroes in the Arabic-speaking Muslim world. It is telling that, as mentioned above, many of his commentaries are lost in Arabic but extant in Latin, Hebrew, or both. Even his magisterial *Long Commentary on the Metaphysics* is preserved in only a single Arabic manuscript.

The reasons are not far to seek. For one thing, Averroes worked on the geographical fringes of the Muslim world, in Andalusia, and unlike his fellow Andalusians Ibn ʿArabī and Maimonides he never travelled to the East. To this one can add the technical and even forbidding nature of his commentaries. It's not surprising that the more accessible *Decisive Treatise* and *Incoherence of the Incoherence*, Averroes' response to al-Ghazālī's *Incoherence of the Philosophers*, are indeed extant in Arabic and were read to some extent in the later Muslim tradition. Yet a more fundamental reason for Averroes' lack of influence was the very nature of his commentatorial enterprise. As we have seen, Averroes rejected the innovations of Avicenna and tried to return to a more authentic and detailed reading of Aristotle. This may have been an avant garde project when al-Fārābī and his colleagues undertook it in tenth-century Baghdad, but by the late twelfth century it was decidedly old hat. The Muslim philosophical tradition had moved on to grappling with the thought of Avicenna, and although Avicenna was far from universally accepted or admired, his philosophy demanded a detailed engagement rather than the reactionary criticism he provoked from Averroes.

A dramatic illustration of this is the fact that the tradition of philosophical commentary not only continued in the eastern Islamic world, but actually blossomed; yet almost none of the commentaries expounded Aristotle. There is a vast extant corpus of commentaries that fuse philosophical discussions with discussions of the Muslim creed or themes in Islamic theology, as well as commentaries on philosophical works.[70] Within the latter category there are many commentaries devoted to Avicenna's writings, especially his *Pointers and Reminders*, whose compressed and allusive writing style invited commentators to try their hand at expounding the text.[71] The most important commentators on this text were Fakhr al-Dīn al-Rāzī (d. 1210) and Naṣīr al-Dīn al-Ṭūsī (d. 1274). Al-Rāzī, an important theologian in his own right, fashioned his commentary into a complex dialectical critique of Avicenna, which provoked a defensive and generally approving commentary from al-Ṭūsī. These two commentators are only the best-known representatives of a tendency in the Muslim philosophical tradition, from the eleventh century onwards, to engage primarily (if often critically) with Avicenna and not with Aristotle.[72] There are exceptions, notably ʿAbd al-Laṭīf al-Baghdādī (d. 1231), who wrote a paraphrase commentary of *Metaphysics* XII and whose hostility to Avicenna was easily a match for that shown by Averroes.[73] Generally speaking, though, the direct engagement with Aristotle ended rapidly in the East once Avicenna came on the scene, and the surge of interest in Andalusia with Ibn Bājja and Averroes was a short-lived exception.

Despite this, philosophy in the Islamic world continued to engage with Aristotelian ideas and themes for centuries to come. Indeed this engagement persisted for at least as long as in the West, where Aristotle continued to be a more directly dominant figure through the Renaissance. If we consider a later development like the so-called school of Isfahan, a group of thinkers who revived Neoplatonism under the Safavids in Iran during the 16–17th centuries, we do not find any commentaries on Aristotle himself.[74] Yet it has recently been argued that their most famous representative, Mullā Ṣadrā (d. 1640), structured his magnum opus *The Four Journeys* around themes drawn from Aristotle's *Metaphysics*.[75] More broadly, the terminology and problems of philosophy in this later period are often reminiscent of Avicenna, who despite all his innovations served as a conduit for Aristotelian thought. A standard question discussed in the later tradition, for instance, was 'does the Necessary Existent have knowledge of particulars?' That is, does God know about each of the things that exist in the created realm? This is a difficulty first discussed explicitly by Avicenna, posed in Avicennan language. Yet that very language preserves Aristotelian vocabulary. In our example, the Arabic word for 'particulars' would be *al-juz'iyyāt*, corresponding to *ta kath' hekasta*. Furthermore, Avicenna's reasons for denying that God knows particulars as such are rooted in Aristotle.[76] So it was Avicenna, more than any other thinker, who was responsible for putting an end to an interfaith culture of Arabic commentary on Aristotle. But it was also Avicenna, more than any other thinker, who passed on Aristotelian concepts, terms, and difficulties to the later philosophical and theological tradition in the Islamic world.[77]

Notes

1. For Porphyry as the starting-point of this tradition see G. Karamanolis, 'Porphyry: the First Platonist Commentator on Aristotle,' in P. Adamson, H. Baltussen, and M.W.F. Stone eds., *Philosophy, Science and Exegesis in Greek, Arabic and Latin Commentaries*, 2 vols (London: 2004), vol. 1, 97–120. Porphyry also commented on Plato, though these commentaries are lost (unless we ascribe to him the anonymous *Commentary on the Parmenides*). Despite the fact that all subsquent commentators on Aristotle, with the arguable exception of Themistius, were card-carrying Platonists, Olympiodorus (d. 565 AD) is the only Greek commentator for whom we have extant commentaries on both Plato and Aristotle. Of course the tradition of commentary on Plato is dominated by Proclus, from whom we have commentaries on the *Cratylus*, *First Alcibiades*, *Parmenides*, *Republic*, and *Timaeus*.

2. Indeed commentaries on Aristotle, and independent works by these same commentators, constitute approximately *half* of all directly preserved Greek philosophical works, by the reckoning of R. Goulet, 'La conservation et la transmission des textes philosophiques grecs,' in C. D'Ancona ed., *Libraries of the Neoplatonists* (Leiden: 2007), 29–61; see the remarkable pie chart at p. 60. According to this chart, works by Neoplatonists make up approximately 80 percent of all directly extant Greek philosophical literature.

3. Of course many more commentaries were produced than are extant today, both in the Greek and Arabic traditions. Thus our surviving evidence is an imperfect guide to the priorities and interests that held sway in these traditions. On the other hand, such factors as teaching needs can also help explain not only why certain commentaries were written, but also why they were, or were not, preserved down to the present day. The points that follow, regarding the dominance of logic for instance, or the dominance of Aristotle over Plato in the Arabic tradition, are largely borne out by our information about lost commentaries as well as by the extant evidence. But we know that Plato

was in fact read in Arabic, at least in paraphrase versions, more often than would be suggested by the texts we possess now.

4. For English translations, see J. Dillon and D. O'Meara (trans.), *Syrianus: On Aristotle Metaphysics 3-4* (London: 2008); and *Syrianus: On Aristotle Metaphysics 13-14* (London: 2006). There was also a commentary by Themistius, which is no longer extant in Greek; see note 11.

5. See recently M. Edwards, 'Porphyry and the Christians', in G. Karamanolis and A. Sheppard, eds., *Studies on Porphyry* (London: 2007). H. Baltussen, *Philosophy and Exegesis in Simplicius. The Methodology of a Commentator* (London: Duckworth, 2008) emphasizes the anti-Christian polemic in Simplicius' work. Anti-Christian sentiment has also been suspected in Proclus' work: see H.D. Saffrey, 'Allusions antichrétiennes chez Proclus, le diadoque platonicien', *Revue des Sciences philosophiques et théologiques* 59 (1975), 553-63.

6. See F. Rosenthal, 'On the Knowledge of Plato's Philosophy in the Islamic World', *Islamic Culture* 14 (1940), 387-422; F.E. Peters, *Aristoteles Arabus* (Leiden: 1968). The only significant extant commentary on Plato from the Arabic-speaking world is Averroes' commentary on the *Republic*. See R. Lerner, trans., *Averroes on Plato's Republic* (Ithaca, N.Y.: 1974).

7. There are, however, notes on the *De Anima* and *Metaphysics* XII by Avicenna; see note 53. We also have evidence that Ibn al-Ṭayyib, on whom see below, wrote a commentary on the *Metaphysics*. And we have an extant commentary, again on book XII, by the mathematician and philosopher Thābit Ibn Qurra. On this see now D.C. Reisman and A. Bertolacci, 'Thābit Ibn Qurra's Concise Exposition of Aristotle's *Metaphysics*: Text, Translation and Commentary', in R. Rashed and M. Rashed, eds., *Sciences and Philosophy in 9th Century Baghdad. Thābit Ibn Qurra (826-901)* (Berlin: 2009), 715-76.

8. This is one reason I speak here of an *Arabic* tradition of commentary on Aristotle, rather than an *Islamic* tradition.

9. It should also not be forgotten that Arabic translations of Aristotle and of Greek commentaries are sometimes several hundred years earlier than the earliest Greek manuscripts we have. They provide an important resource for establishing the text of even extant Greek works.

10. For the former see the translations in P. Thillet, *Alexandre d'Aphrodise: Traité de la providence* (Lagrasse: 2003); and S. Fazzo and M. Zonta, *Alessandro di Afrodisia: La Provvidenza* (Milan: 1998). For the latter, see C. Genequand, *Alexander of Aphrodisias on the Cosmos* (Leiden: 2001).

11. See the translation of R. Brague, *Themistius: Paraphrase de la métaphysique d'Aristote: Livre Lambda* (Paris: 1999).

12. For an English translation of these sections see P. Lettinck and J. O. Urmson, trans., *Philoponus: On Aristotle Physics 5-8; Simplicius: On Aristotle on the Void* (London: 1994). The Arabic tradition also provides important evidence concerning Philoponus' critique of Aristotle's position on the eternity of the world. See, for instance, S. Pines, 'An Arabic summary of a lost work of John Philoponus', *Israel Oriental Studies* 2 (1972), 320-52.

13. See the useful overviews of what was translated in C. D'Ancona, 'Greek Sources in Arabic and Islamic Philosophy', online at the Stanford Encyclopedia of Philosophy; and in D'Ancona, 'Greek into Arabic: Neoplatonism in Translation', in P. Adamson and R. C. Taylor, eds., *The Cambridge Companion to Arabic Philosophy* (Cambridge: 2005), 10-31.

14. See, e.g., H. Hugonnard-Roche, 'L'intermédiaire syriaque dans la trasmission de la philosophie grecque à l'arabe: le cas de l'Organon d'Aristote', *Arabic Sciences and Philosophy* 1 (1991), 187-209; S. Brock, 'The Syriac commentary tradition', in

C. Burnett, ed., *Glosses and Commentaries on Aristotelian Logical Texts: The Syriac, Arabic and Medieval Latin Traditions* (London: 1993). There are numerous extant Syriac commentaries on the *Isagoge, Categories, On Interpretation,* and *Prior Analytics;* see the useful list at Brock, 11–15. An issue that arises here is how much of the *organon* was studied in the Syriac tradition. On this see further D. Gutas, 'The 'Alexandria to Baghdad' complex of narratives. A contribution to the study of philosophical and medical historiography among the Arabs,' *Documenti e Studi sulla Tradizione Filosofica Medievale* 10 (1999), 155–193.

15. For the translation movement see D. Gutas, *Greek Thought, Arabic Culture: The Graeco-Arabic Translation movement in Baghdad and early society (2nd-4th/8th-10th centuries)* (London: 1998).

16. For his translation of Plotinus, part of which was mistaken for a work by Aristotle and called the *Theology of Aristotle,* see P. Adamson, *The Arabic Plotinus* (London: 2002).

17. On whom see P. Adamson, *Al-Kindī* (New York: 2007).

18. See H. A. Davidson, 'John Philoponus as a Source of Medieval Islamic and Jewish Proofs of Creation', *Journal of the American Oriental Society* 89 (1969), 357–91; and Adamson, *Al-Kindī* (see previous note), ch. 4.

19. See S. Fazzo and H. Wiesner, 'Alexander of Aphrodisias in the Kindī Circle and in al-Kindī's Cosmology', *Arabic Sciences and Philosophy* 3 (1993), 119–53; and Adamson, *Al-Kindī* (see note 17), ch. 8.

20. This is clearly related to the set of propaedeutic questions asked about each Aristotelian work by Greek commentators, which I discuss further below.

21. For a list of al-Kindī's writings see R. J. McCarthy, *al-Taṣānīf al-mansuba ilā Faylasūf al-ʿarab* (Baghdad: 1962); and for an English translation of the whole *Fihrist* see B. Dodge, *The Fihrist of al-Nadim* (New York: 1970), with the list of al-Kindī's works at 615–26.

22. See M. Guidi and R. Walzer, *Uno Scritto Introduttivo allo Studio di Aristotele* (Rome: 1940).

23. For this line of thinkers, whom I have elsewhere called the 'Kindian tradition,' see P. Adamson, 'The Kindian Tradition: the Structure of Philosophy in Arabic Neoplatonism,' in C. D'Ancona ed., *Libraries of the Neoplatonists* (Leiden: 2007), 351–70.

24. See F. Rosenthal, *Aḥmad b. aṭ-Ṭayyib* (New Haven: 1943), 54.

25. See E. Wakelnig, 'Philosophical Fragments of al-ʿĀmirī Preserved Mainly in al-Tawḥīdī, Miskawayh and in the Texts of the Ṣiwān al-ḥikma Tradition', in P. Adamson, ed., *In the Age of al-Fārābī: Arabic Philosophy in the Fourth/Tenth Century* (London: 2007), 220.

26. On whom see P. Adamson, 'Knowledge of Universals and Particulars in the Baghdad School', *Documenti e Studi sulla Tradizione Filosofica Medievale* 18 (2007), 141–64.

27. D. Gutas, 'Aspects of Literary Form and Genre in Arabic Logical Works', in Burnett, ed., *Glosses and Commentaries* (see note 14), 29–76, at 55.

28. We already find a work of this kind by al-Kindī: his *On the Intellect,* on which see J. Jolivet, *L'Intellect selon Kindī* (Leiden: 1971); P. Adamson, *Al-Kindī* (see note 17 above), 118–27. For al-Fārābī's *On the Intellect* see the English translation in J. McGinnis and D. C. Reisman, ed. and trans., *Classical Arabic Philosophy: an Anthology of Sources* (Indianapolis: 2007), 68–78. For Ibn Bājja's *On Conjunction* see M. Asín Palacios, 'Un texto de Avempace sobre la unión del intelecto con el hombre', in *Al-Andalus* 7 (1942), 1–47. Averroes wrote several epistles on the topic; see K. P. Bland, trans., *Averroes. Epistle on the Possibility of Conjunction* (New York:

1982); M. Geoffroy and C. Steel, *Averroès. La Béatitude de l'Âme. Éditions, traductions et études* (Paris: 2001).

29. On this inclusive version of the *organon* see D. L. Black, *Logic and Aristotle's Rhetoric and Poetics in Medieval Arabic Philosophy* (Leiden: 1990).

30. See M. Fakhry, *Ta'ālīq Ibn Bājja 'alā manṭiq Arisṭū* (Beirut: 1994).

31. On this see again Gutas, 'Aspects of Literary Form' (note 27 above), esp. 47–50, 54–6.

32. This work is an example of the fact that epitomes could radically rearrange the source text: see R. Arnzen, 'Ibn Rushd on the Structure of Aristotle's *Metaphysics*,' *Documenti e Studi sulla Tradizione Filosofica Medievale* 21 (2010), 375–410.

33. For Ibn Bājja on the *Physics* see P. Lettinck, *Aristotle's Physics and It's Reception in the Arabic World* (Leiden: 1994). It's worth noting that Averroes wrote 'commentaries' of this sort on Galen as well as Aristotle; we can also put his commentary on Plato's *Republic* into this category.

34. It is referred to by Ibn Bājja, Averroes, and Maimonides: see A. A. Akasoy and A. Fidora, *The Arabic Version of the Nicomachean Ethics* (Leiden: 2005), 49–52.

35. For the *Posterior Analytics* commentary see A. Badawī, ed., *Ibn Rushd. Grand commentaire et Paraphrase des Seconds Analytiques d'Aristote* (Kuwait: 1984). For the *Metaphysics* commentary see Averroès, *Tafsīr Mā Ba'd at-Ṭabī'at*, ed. M. Bouyges, 3 vols. (Beirut: 1938–52).

36. For a translation of the report of this debate, see D. S. Margoliouth, 'The Discussion Between Abu Bishr Matta and Abu Sa'id al-Sirafi on the Merits of Logic and Grammar', *Journal of the Royal Asiatic Society* (1905), 79–129.

37. See G. Endress, *The Works of Yaḥyā Ibn 'Adī. An Analytical Inventory* (Weisbaden: 1977).

38. F. W. Zimmermann, *Al-Farabi's Commentary and Short Treatise on Aristotle's De Interpretatione* (Oxford: 1981); A. Hasnawi, 'Fārābī et la pratique de l'exégèse philosophique (remarques sur son *Commentaire au De Interpretatione* d'Aristote)', *Revue de Synthese* 3rd series, 117 (1985), 27–59.

39. For which see C. Ehrig-Eggert, 'Yaḥyā ibn 'Adī: Über den Nachweis der Natur des Möglichen,' *Zeitschrift für Geschichte der arabisch-islamischen Wissenschaften* 5 (1989), 283–97 (Arabic text 63–97). Part of this work is translated in McGinnis and Reisman, *Classical Arabic Philosophy*, 128–39. (See note 28.) On the topic see further P. Adamson, 'The Arabic Sea Battle: al-Fārābī on the Problem of Future Contingents', *Archiv für Geschichte der Philosophie* 88 (2006), 163–188, and 'Freedom and Determinism,' in R. Pasnau, ed., *The Cambridge History of Medieval Philosophy*, 2 vols (Cambridge: 2010), vol.1, 399–413.

40. See K. Gyekye, ed., *Ibn al-Ṭayyib's Commentary on Porphyry's Eisagoge* (Beirut: 1975); id. (trans.), *Arabic Logic: Ibn al-Ṭayyib's Commentary on Porphyry's Eisagoge* (Albany: 1979); C. Ferrari, *Die Kategorienkommentar von Abū l-Faraj 'Abdallāh Ibn al-Ṭayyib* (Leiden: 2006).

41. Al-Fārābī's indebtedness to the Alexandrians is emphasized in P. Vallat, *Farabi et l'école d'Alexandrie* (Paris: 2004).

42. On this commentary see Lettinck, *Aristotle's Physics* (see note 33). Lettinck summarizes and discusses the comments of the Baghdad school alongside the later *Physics* commentary of Ibn Bājja. See further E. Giannakis, *Philoponus in the Arabic Tradition of Aristotle's Physics*, D. Phil. Thesis (Oxford 1992); id., 'The Structure of Abū l-Ḥusayn al-Baṣrī's Copy of Aristotle's Physics', *Zeitschrift für Geschichte der arabisch-islamischen Wissenschaften* 8 (1993), 251–58.

43. See the summary of Lettinck, *Aristotle's Physics* (see note 33), 19, 21; E. Giannakis, 'Yaḥyā ibn ʿAdī Against John Philoponus on Place and Void', in *Zeitschrift für Geschichte der arabisch-islamischen Wissenschaften* 12 (1998), 245–302.

44. On this see F. W. Zimmermann, 'Philoponus' Impetus Theory in the Arabic Tradition', in R. Sorabji, ed., *Philoponus and the Rejection of Aristotelian Science* (London: 1987), 121–9; R. Sorabji, *Matter, Space, and Motion* (London: 1988).

45. See S. Pines, 'La dynamique d'Ibn Bājja', in *Mélanges Alexandre Koyré I* (Paris: 1964), 442–68; Lettinck, *Aristotle's Physics*, 342; id., 'The Transformation of Aristotle's "Physical Philosophy" in Ibn Bājja's Commentaries', in F. J. Ragep and S. P. Ragep, eds., *Tradition, Transmission, Transformation* (Leiden: 1996), 65–70; J. Puig Montada, 'Philosophy in Andalusia: Ibn Bājja and Ibn Ṭufayl', in P. Adamson and R. C. Taylor, eds., *The Cambridge Companion to Arabic Philosophy* (Cambridge: 2005), 155–79, at 160–1.

46. See Lettinck, *Aristotle's Physics*, 343–4.

47. Ibn al-Ṭayyib wrote a very large number of commentaries on Aristotle, most of which are lost; see Ferrari, *Der Kategorienkommentar*, 30–1 (see note 40).

48. See Ferrari, *Der Kategorienkommentar*, 44; Hasnawi, 'Fārābī et la pratique', 53. I have proposed seeing this as a structuring principle of Ibn ʿAdī's commentary on *Metaphysics* α: see P. Adamson, 'Yaḥyā Ibn ʿAdī and Averroes on *Metaphysics* Alpha Elatton', *Documenti e Studi sulla Tradizione Filosofica Medievale* 21 (2010), 343–74.

49. See Ferrari, *Der Kategorienkommentar*, 95ff. Cf. L. G. Westerink, 'The Alexandrian Commentators and the Introductions to their Commentaries', in R. Sorabji, ed., *Aristotle Transformed* (London: 1990), 325–48. A similar set of opening questions was applied to the medical writings of Galen and Hippocrates. See H. Biesterfeldt, 'Palladius on the Hippocratic *Aphorisms*', in *Libraries of the Neoplatonists* (see note 2), 385–97, at 391–2.

50. A good example can be found in his *Attainment of Happiness*. See al-Fārābī, *Taḥṣīl al-saʿāda* (Hyderabad: 1346 A.H.), English version in M. Mahdi, trans., *Alfarabi: Philosophy of Plato and Aristotle* (Ithaca, N.Y.: 1962).

51. See for instance his *Philosophy of Aristotle*: al-Fārābī, *Falsafat Arisṭūṭālīs*, ed. M. Mahdi (Beirut: 1961). For an English version see again Mahdi, *Alfarabi: Philosophy of Plato and Aristotle* (see previous note).

52. See P. Adamson, 'The Arabic Sea Battle' (see note 39), 167–72. Al-Fārābī further explains that the existence of 'possibility' (i.e., contingency) is a 'first principle', whose certainty cannot be denied. Again this suggests that the rejection of determinism would belong to metaphysics, which is similarly responsible for discussing—but of course not *proving*—the principle of non-contradiction (*Metaphysics* IV). All of this contrasts interestingly to Ibn ʿAdī's handling of the same topic. Already the title of his treatise on the subject, *On Establishing the Nature of the Possible* (see note 39), shows that he is linking the argument of *On Interpretation* 9 to a more 'metaphysical' discussion. In addition, this treatise argues for, rather than merely asserting, the reality of contingency.

53. An exception was a work called *The Fair Judgement*, which contained notes on *Metaphysics* XII as well as the pseudo-Aristotelian *Theology*. There is also a series of notes on the *De Anima*: see D. Gutas, *Avicenna and the Aristotelian Tradition* (Leiden: 1988), 130–40.

54. See A. Bertolacci, *The Reception of Aristotle's Metaphysics in Avicenna's Kitāb al-Shifā'. A Milestone of Western Metaphysical Thought* (Leiden: 2006).

55. A distinctive feature of the *Healing* is that the metaphysical section does not set out this argument as it is found in other texts, including *Pointers and Reminders*. Rather the explicit proof for God in the *Healing* is based on more general causal regress arguments, inspired by *Metaphysics* II; this is part and parcel of the *Healing's* avowed dependence on the Aristotelian tradition.

56. Most of this commentary is not yet translated into English, but for the commentary on *Met.* XII see C. Genequand, trans., *Ibn Rushd's Metaphysics. A Translation with Introduction of Ibn Rushd's Commentary on Aristotle's Metaphysics, Book Lâm* (Leiden: 1984).

57. See P. Adamson, 'The Kindian Tradition' and 'Yaḥyā Ibn 'Adī and Averroes on *Metaphysics* Alpha Elatton' (see notes 23, 48).

58. On this text and its impact on Avicenna, see D. Gutas, *Avicenna and the Aristotelian Tradition* (see note 53), 238–53. See further A. Bertolacci, 'From Al-Kindī to Al-Fārābī: Avicenna's Progressive Knowledge of Aristotle's *Metaphysics* According to His Autobiography', *Arabic Sciences and Philosophy* 11 (2001), 257–95.

59. See Arnzen, 'Ibn Rushd on the Structure of Aristotle's *Metaphysics*' (note 32 above) for a reconstruction of metaphysics according to Averroes, based especially on the *Epitome*.

60. The foregoing draws heavily on A. Bertolacci, 'Avicenna and Averroes on the Proof of God's Existence and the Subject-Matter of Metaphysics', *Medioevo* 32 (2007), 61–97.

61. For a translation see C. E. Butterworth, *Alfarabi. The Political Writings: Selected Aphorisms and Other Texts* (Ithaca, N.Y.: 2001).

62. For all this see M. Rashed, 'A New List of al-Farabi's Writings and the Author of the *Harmonization of the Opinions of the Two Sages Plato and Aristotle*', *Arabic Sciences and Philosophy* 19 (2009), 43–82. For a study of the *Harmony*, including an Italian translation and a defence of its authenticity, see C. Martini Bonadeo, *Al-Farabi. L'armonia delle opinioni dei due sapienti il divino Platone e Aristotele* (Pisa: 2008).

63. For the epitome there is a Spanish translation: S. Gómez Nogales, trans., *La Psicología de Averroes. Comentario al libro sobre el alma de Aristóteles* (Madrid: 1987). For the exposition see I. Ivry, trans., *Averroes. Middle Commentary on Aristotle's De Anima* (Provo: 2002). For the *Long Commentary*, preserved only in Latin, see R. C. Taylor, trans., *Averroes. Long Commentary on the De Anima of Aristotle* (New Haven: 2009).

64. There is a precedent in the Arabic tradition in al-Kindī's *On the Intellect* (see note 28). He refers to the entity as the 'first intellect.'

65. On this topic in al-Fārābī see his *Letter on the Intellect*, translated in McGinnis and Reisman, *Classical Arabic Philosophy* (see note 28); P. Adamson, 'Knowledge of Universals and Particulars' (see note 26); D. L. Black, 'Knowledge (*'Ilm*) and Certainty (*Yaqīn*) in al-Fārābī's Epistemology', *Arabic Sciences and Philosophy* 16 (2006), 11–45; T.-A. Druart, 'Al-Farabi and Emanationism', in J. F. Wippel, ed., *Studies in Medieval Philosophy* (Washington DC: 1987), 23–43. For the topic in Avicenna see P. Adamson, 'Non-Discursive Thought in Avicenna's Commentary on the *Theology of Aristotle*', in J. McGinnis, ed., *Interpreting Avicenna: Science and Philosophy in Medieval Islam* (Leiden: 2004), 87–111; D. Gutas, 'Intuition and thinking: the Evolving Structure of Avicenna's Epistemology', and D. N. Hasse, 'Avicenna on Abstraction', both in R. Wisnovsky, ed., *Aspects of Avicenna* (Princeton: 2001), 1–38 and 39–72. More generally see also H.A. Davidson, *Alfarabi, Avicenna and Averroes on Intellect* (Oxford: 1992).

66. On the criticisms made by Aquinas see his *On the Unity of the Intellect*, trans. R. McInerny (West Lafayette: 1993). For discussion of more favourable reactions to Averroes in the Christian tradition see D. N. Hasse, 'The Attraction of Averroism in the Renaissance: Vernia, Achillini, Prassicio', in P. Adamson, H. Baltussen, M. W. F. Stone, eds., *Philosophy, Science and Exegesis in Greek, Arabic and Latin Commentaries*, 2 vols (London: 2004), vol. 2, 131–147 (see note 5); id., 'Arabic philosophy and Averroism', in J. Hankins, ed., *The Cambridge Companion to Renaissance Philosophy* (Cambridge: 2007), 113–36.

67. The literature on Averroes' position is extensive. See for instance D. L. Black, 'Conjunction and the Identity of Knower and Known in Averroes', *American Catholic Philosophical Quarterly* 73 (1999), 159–184; A. Ivry, 'Averroes on Intellection and Conjunction', *Journal of the American Oriental Society* 86 (1986), 76–85; R. C. Taylor, 'Averroes on Psychology and the Principles of Metaphysics', *Journal of the History of Philosophy* 36 (1998), 507–523; id., 'Averroes: Religious Dialectic and Aristotelian Philosophical Thought', in Adamson and Taylor, *The Cambridge Companion to Arabic Philosophy*, 180–200 (see note 45); and id., 'Separate Material Intellect in Averroes' Mature Philosophy', in *Words, Texts and Concepts Cruising the Mediterranean Sea* (Leuven: 2004), 289–309.

68. See R. Glasner, 'Levi ben Gershom and the Study of Ibn Rushd in the Fourteenth Century', *Jewish Quarterly Review* 86 (1995), 51–90.

69. S. Harvey, 'The Greek Library of the Medieval Jewish Philosophers', in *Libraries of the Neoplatonists* (see note 2), 493–506, comments: 'The Jewish Aristotelians knew Aristotle very well, but their knowledge for the most part came from Averroes' commentaries' (504).

70. On this corpus, essentially untouched by modern scholarship, see R. Wisnovsky, 'The Nature and Scope of Arabic Philosophical Commentary in Post-Classical (ca. 1100–1900 AD) Islamic Intellectual History: Some Preliminary Observations', in Adamson, Baltussen, and Stone, *Philosophy, Science and Exegesis* (see note 5), vol. 2, 149–191.

71. Wisnovsky's list (see previous note) itemises no fewer than 30 *extant* commentaries and super-commentaries on the works of Avicenna, more than half of them devoted to the *Pointers*.

72. See D. Gutas, 'The Heritage of Avicenna: The Golden Age of Arabic Philosophy, 1000-ca. 1350', in J. Janssens and D. De Smet, eds., *Avicenna and his heritage* (Leuven: 2002), 81–97; G. Endress, 'Reading Avicenna in the Madrasa. Intellectual Genealogies and Chains of Transmission of Philosophy and the Sciences in the Islamic East', in J. E. Montgomery, ed., *Arabic Theology, Arabic Philosophy. From the Many to the One: Essays in Celebration of Richard M. Frank* (Leuven: 2006), 371–423; A. Shihadeh, 'From al-Ghazālī to al-Rāzī: 6th/12th Century Developments in Muslim Philosophical Theology', *Arabic Sciences and Philosophy* 15 (2005), 141–179.

73. See A. Neuwirth, *'Abd al-Laṭīf al-Baghdādīs Bearbeitung von Buch Lambda der aristotelischen Metaphysik* (Weisbaden: 1976). On him see also D. Gutas, 'Philosophy in the Twelfth Century: One View from Baghdad, or the Repudiation of al-Ghazālī', in P. Adamson, ed., *In the Age of Averroes: Arabic Philosophy in the Sixth/Twelfth Century* (London: 2011), 9–26.

74. The exception that proves the rule is that commentaries were written on the pseudo-Aristotelian *Theology of Aristotle*: see S. Rizvi, '(Neo)Platonism Revived in the Light of the Imams: Qāḍī Saʿīd Qummī (d. AH 1107/AD 1696) and his Reception of the

Theologia Aristotelis,' in P. Adamson, ed., *Classical Arabic Philosophy: Sources and Reception* (London: 2007), 176–207.

75. R. Arnzen, 'The Structure of Mullā Ṣadrā's *al-ḥikma al-mutaʿāliya fī l-asfār al-ʿaqliyya al-arbaʿa* and his Concepts of First Philosophy and Divine Science. An Essay,' in *Medioevo* 32 (2007), 199–240.

76. Or so I have argued in P. Adamson, 'On Knowledge of Particulars', *Proceedings of the Aristotelian Society* 105 (2005), 273–94.

77. I would like to thank Amos Bertolacci for his very helpful comments on an early draft of this paper.

BIBLIOGRAPHY

Adamson, Peter (2010) 'Yaḥyā Ibn ʿAdī and Averroes on *Metaphysics* Alpha Elatton', *Documenti e Studi sulla Tradizione Filosofica Medievale* 21, 343–74.

Akasoy, Anna A., and Alexander Fidora (2005) *The Arabic Version of the Nicomachean Ethics* (Leiden: Brill), 49–52.

Bertolacci, Amos (2006) *The Reception of Aristotle's Metaphysics in Avicenna's Kitāb al-Shifāʾ. A Milestone of Western Metaphysical Thought* (Leiden: Brill).

Black, Deborah L. (1990) *Logic and Aristotle's Rhetoric and Poetics in Medieval Arabic Philosophy* (Leiden: Brill).

Burnett, Charles M., ed. (1993) *Glosses and Commentaries on Aristotelian Logical Texts: The Syriac, Arabic and Medieval Latin Traditions* (London: Warburg Institute).

Ferrari, Cleophea (2006) *Die Kategorienkommentar von Abū l-Faraj ʿAbdallāh Ibn al-Ṭayyib* (Leiden: Brill).

Genequand, Charles (1984) *Ibn Rushd's Metaphysics. A Translation with Introduction of Ibn Rushd's Commentary on Aristotle's Metaphysics, Book Lām* (Leiden: Brill).

Gutas, Dimitri (1988) *Avicenna and the Aristotelian Tradition* (Leiden: Brill).

—— (1998) *Greek Thought, Arabic Culture: The Graeco-Arabic Translation movement in Baghdad and early society (2nd-4th/8th-10th centuries)* (London: Routledge).

Gyekye, Kwame, ed. (1975) *Ibn al-Ṭayyib's Commentary on Porphyry's Eisagoge* (Beirut: Dār al-Mashriq).

—— trans. (1979) *Arabic Logic: Ibn al-Ṭayyib's Commentary on Porphyry's Eisagoge* (Albany: SUNY Press).

Hugonnard-Roche, Henri (1991) 'L'intermédiaire syriaque dans la transmission de la philosophie grecque à l'arabe: le cas de l'Organon d'Aristote', *Arabic Sciences and Philosophy* 1, 187–209.

Lettinck, Paul (1994) *Aristotle's Physics and Its Reception in the Arabic World* (Leiden: Brill).

McGinnis, Jon, and David C. Reisman, ed. and trans. (2007) *Classical Arabic Philosophy: An Anthology of Sources* (Indianapolis, Ind.: Hackett).

Peters, Francis E. (1968) *Aristoteles Arabus* (Leiden: Brill).

Reisman, David C., and Amos Bertolacci (2009) 'Thābit Ibn Qurra's Concise Exposition of Aristotle's *Metaphysics*: Text, Translation and Commentary', in *Sciences and Philosophy in 9th Century Baghdad. Thābit Ibn Qurra (826-901)*, ed. R. Rashed and M. Rashed (Berlin: de Gruyter), 715–76.

Zimmermann, Fritz W. (1981) *Al-Farabi's Commentary and Short Treatise on Aristotle's De Interpretatione* (Oxford: Oxford University Press).

CHAPTER 26

THE LATIN ARISTOTLE

ROBERT PASNAU

I. THE RISE OF SCHOLASTIC ARISTOTELIANISM

THERE is some temptation to say that the history of Aristotle in medieval Latin philosophy just is the history of medieval Latin philosophy. This would be to over-simplify matters. The fountainhead of Christian philosophy, Augustine (354–430 AD), betrays almost no familiarity with Aristotelian thought, and describes in the *Confessions* (IV.xvi.28) how he was underwhelmed by a reading of the *Categories* at the age of 20. Boethius (c. 476–c. 526) aspired to translate into Latin and comment upon the whole Aristotelian corpus, and reconcile it with Plato as well, but only a fraction of the project (the logic) was completed. It was this fragment that provided virtually the sole basis for the study of Aristotle in the Latin West until the later twelfth century, when substantially the whole Aristotelian corpus finally became available in Latin. Moreover, even once the influence of Aristotle was felt in its full force—and even more so before then—Platonism remained a strong influence on Latin philosophy. Although almost none of Plato's own works were available until the fifteenth century (almost nothing but the *Timaeus* through 53B), a version of Platonism was transmitted through the Neoplatonism infusing Augustine's thought, as well as through various Neoplatonic tracts that made their way into the Latin philosophical canon. (Of these the most notable were the *Liber de causis*, derived from Proclus, and the writings of pseudo-Dionysius. Indeed, for a time the *Liber de causis* was included among the works of Aristotle.)

There is, in short, a lot to be said about the ways in which medieval Latin philosophy is not Aristotelian. Still, it can scarcely be denied that the ideas of Aristotle are of unparalleled significance for Latin medieval thought. The most fundamental reason is that, for as long as there were schools of philosophy in the Latin Middle Ages, Aristotle's works constituted the core of the philosophical curriculum. As early as the Carolingian era, Alcuin of York (c. 735–804) built his logic textbook (*De dialectica*) on the *De interpretatione*, the *Categories*,[1] and Porphyry's introduction to Aristotelian logic, the *Isagoge*. These three works—as translated by Boethius—would become known as the *logica vetus*, and would dominate the study of logic until the twelfth century, when they were supplemented by three further Boethian translations that were recovered at this point: the *Sophistici elenchi* (*Sophistical Refutations*), the *Topics*, and the *Prior Analytics*. Although Boethius translated the *Posterior Analytics*, this work was lost, and so its influence would be felt only after the middle of the twelfth century, when it was retranslated by James of Venice.[2]

This so-called new logic, or *logica nova*, was slow to be embraced by twelfth-century philosophers. John of Salisbury (c.1115–80) famously complained of the *Posterior Analytics* that it has 'as many stumbling blocks as it has chapters'. Even so, the entire *organon* became firmly entrenched in the curriculum of the early universities. Rules set out for the University of Paris in 1215 required that lecturers in the arts be at least 21 years old, that they have attended lectures for at least six years before themselves undertaking to lecture, and that they lecture on the 'old and new dialectic' of Aristotle (as well as on the grammatical works of Priscian and Donatus).[3] Although our evidence is thin regarding the curriculum in the early medieval university, it is clear that Aristotle's logic formed the undisputed foundation of an undergraduate education.

Matters were quite different for the remainder of the Aristotelian corpus. James of Venice had in fact translated many of the most important works before 1150, including the *Physics*, *De anima*, and the first four books of the *Metaphysics*. By the end of the twelfth century, almost the entire corpus was available in Latin. Around this time, too, we begin to find newly written commentaries on the broader Aristotelian corpus, at both Paris and Oxford, but this expansion of the philosophy curriculum was problematic for two reasons. First, there was no clear place in the arts curriculum for metaphysics, ethics, and much of natural philosophy. In order for Aristotle's principal works to be studied, the traditional curriculum of the *trivium* (dialectic; grammar; rhetoric) and *quadrivium* (astronomy; arithmetic; geometry; music) needed to be radically expanded. Second, the content of these works was highly controversial. A bad-tempered decree from Paris in 1210 demanded that the body of one master be exhumed and reburied in unconsecrated ground, that the works of another be burned, and that 'neither the books of Aristotle on natural philosophy nor their commentaries be read at Paris in public or secret'—under penalty of excommunication. This prohibition was repeated in the above-quoted rules of 1215, this time with the books on metaphysics included, and it seems to have endured for decades, at least in Paris. A letter from 1229 advertising a new university in Toulouse boasted that 'those who wish to scrutinize the bosom of nature to the inmost can hear here the books of Aristotle that were forbidden at Paris'—an offer whose allure obviously depended on the continued force of the decree of 1210.

Although we have little information about how that 1210 decree was eventually overridden, a series of letters from Pope Gregory IX in 1231 suggests something of the situation. In a first letter, Gregory reaffirms the ban in Paris, 'until these books shall have been examined and purged from all suspicion of errors'. A second letter then orders that those who had violated the ban should be absolved, and a third remarks:

> But since, as we have learned, the books on nature which were prohibited at Paris in provincial council are said to contain both useful and useless matter, lest the useful be vitiated by the useless, we command your discretion...that, subtly and prudently examining the same books as is convenient, you entirely exclude what you shall find there erroneous or likely to give scandal or offense to readers, so that, what are suspect being removed, the rest may be studied without delay and without offense.

What all this suggests is that, on one hand, concern over the Aristotelian corpus was not confined to a few reactionary clerics in Paris, but extended all the way to Rome, and that on the other hand the current situation seemed untenable, inasmuch as the genie of Aristotelian metaphysics was already out of the bottle. It is not known what action, if any, was taken by the three ecclesiastical authorities to whom Gregory addressed this last letter. In any event, the curriculum was changing to such an extent that, in 1255, the full Aristotelian corpus was not only permitted to be taught in Paris, but positively required, with precise prescriptions for the minimum amount of time to be spent on each work (six weeks for *De sensu*, two for *De memoria*, and so forth).

The University of Oxford too seems to have embraced all of Aristotle's writings by the middle of the thirteenth century, although we have even less information about developments there.[4] The study of Aristotle at Oxford benefitted from the influence of Robert Grosseteste (c. 1168–1253), who taught both philosophy and theology there (before becoming bishop of Lincoln in 1235), served as chancellor, wrote seemingly the first and certainly the most influential Latin commentary on the *Posterior Analytics* (in the 1220s), and in the 1240s made the first full Latin translation of the *Nicomachean Ethics*. (His knowing Greek at all was quite remarkable in Western Europe at this time.)

Beyond Aristotle's presence in the arts faculty curriculum, there is a further question of how scholars in other faculties made use of Aristotle's work. This is a question that might be asked about the faculties of law, medicine, or theology, but it is the last of these that has been most extensively studied. The basic picture here is much the same as on the arts faculty, with the first indications of familiarity coming at the start of the thirteenth century, followed by hesitations, followed by full acceptance in the middle of the century. In Oxford, Grosseteste is the most prominent case of a theologian who studied Aristotle intensively, but this is not to say that Grosseteste's own work is predominantly Aristotelian in character. On the contrary, his work has a strong Augustinian flavour, and he cautioned against 'moderns who, with amazing blindness and presumption, try to make Aristotle the heretic into a catholic.... Let them not deceive themselves, then,... and by turning Aristotle into a catholic make themselves into heretics.'[5]

Grosseteste's counterpart at Paris was William of Auvergne (1180/90–1249), who likewise served as master of theology in the 1220s. As bishop of Paris from

1228 until his death, Auvergne exercised considerable authority over developments at the university. The first page of his *De anima* offers a clear picture of the delicate situation during these years. The preface begins with Auvergne's establishing that the study of the soul transcends natural science, given that the soul is an image of God. A few lines later he goes out of his way to note that he will later be criticizing Aristotle. Even so, he begins the first chapter by quoting Aristotle's definition of the soul. But Auvergne then feels compelled to remark, 'Let it not enter into your mind that I wish to use the words of Aristotle as if they can be relied on to prove the things I will be saying.' Instead, Auvergne stresses that in this work, as in all his others, he will be offering demonstrative proofs, not mere appeals to authority.[6]

By the middle of the century, there were far fewer hesitations about appealing to the authority of Aristotle. Albert the Great (c. 1200–1280) and Thomas Aquinas (1224/25–1274) would have applauded Auvergne's focus on proof rather than authority, but neither felt obliged to make special apologies for their use of Aristotle. On the contrary, even though they were theologians rather than philosophers, they each engaged in a massive programme to write commentaries on all of Aristotle's central philosophical texts.[7] From this time forward, although Aristotle would continually have his critics (see below), the overwhelming Aristotelian influence on scholastic thought was never in doubt.

Aquinas's philosophical writings display all the major modes of commentary on Aristotle's work. First, there is the freestanding essay form, as in his brief, early *De principiis naturae*, which seeks to summarize the fundamental doctrines of the *Physics*. Then there is the literal commentary, which is the form of all of his proper commentaries. This includes both a *divisio textus*, in which he offers an outline of the logical structure of the treatise, and what amounts to a kind of paraphrase, in which he runs through the text line by line, quoting what is clear and (usually) rephrasing what is not. (At times the paraphrase breaks into a more-or-less extended disquisition into the implications of this or that passage, and it is really only here where one is on firm ground in reading the commentaries as an expression of Aquinas's own thought.) The third main genre of commentary is the question-commentary, which amounts to a collection of disputed questions on the subject matter of a text. Aquinas' *Quaestiones de anima* are perhaps not in any sense a commentary on the *De anima*, but among later authors—with the literal commentaries of Albert and Thomas already in hand—it became very common to use the *quaestio* format of objections and replies as the vehicle for an extended study of an Aristotelian text.

The commentary project of Albert and Thomas reflects various aspects of Aristotle's influence on Latin philosophy in the mid-thirteenth century. First, it undoubtedly indicates their sense that Aristotle should be the foundation of philosophy, and that a solid understanding of philosophy should be the ground for theology. Second, it reflects the extreme obscurity of Latin translations of Aristotle. The standard translation practice of the age was literal to the extreme, so that, as much as possible, a single word in Greek was replaced by a single word in Latin, and ideally by the same word in every instance.[8] Although the fidelity of this approach has its advantages, especially for an audience that was almost universally ignorant of Greek, it obviously makes for the most appalling Latin. Hence the student—if not the teacher himself—absolutely needed a commentary of some kind. Third, it reflects their dissatisfaction with existing commentaries. The works of Aristotle did not come to the West in isolation. The same currents that brought Aristotle to Western Europe also brought Latin translations of Avicenna and Averroes. (Many other Islamic works became available at this time, too; the Greek commentaries, however, would be put into Latin only gradually as the Middle Ages progressed.) Work on Aristotle from the first half of the thirteenth century is, initially, heavily dependent on Avicenna's version of Aristotelianism. Then, beginning around 1230, the commentaries of Averroes become dominant.[9] Within a few decades, controversies arose over certain aspects of Averroes's interpretation of Aristotle—above all, over his defence of the unicity of both agent and possible intellect—controversies that continued more or less throughout the Middle Ages. But even before certain of Averroes' views became notorious, the need was plainly felt to give a Christian account of Aristotle's rich but challenging texts. This is the context for the familiar story about Albert and Thomas: each devoted a significant part of his career to showing how Aristotle could be assimilated into medieval Christianity in such a way that the faith was enriched rather than threatened.

II. The Development and Decline of Scholastic Aristotelianism

Summarising these initial stages of development, and pushing ahead into the Renaissance, one might divide the history of Aristotelianism in the Latin West as follows:

(1) Study of the logical works alone (500–1200);
(2) Expansion of the canon (1200–1255);
(3) Classical articulation (1255–1308);
(4) Innovation and experimentation (1308–....);
(5) Humanistic scholarship (1497–1637);
(6) Eclipse by the corpuscularian philosophy (1637–1700).

Any attempt at exact dates of course involves a certain amount of whimsy, but these divisions might be justified as follows. The first period begins with Boethius' translation and commentary project, and ends where the universities begin in Paris and Oxford. The second period ends where we have firm evidence that the full Aristotelian corpus was in place at Paris, which coincides with Thomas Aquinas' earliest work, bringing us into the third period. That period ends with the death of

John Duns Scotus, leading into a long period of innovation and experimentation that begins with figures like Peter Auriol (c. 1280–1322) and William Ockham (c. 1288–1347). At this point the chronology begins to run into difficulties, for whereas scholars have studied in great detail the shards of evidence from the early thirteenth century, they have largely neglected the massive amounts of material on later medieval scholasticism. It is perfectly clear that the fourteenth century witnesses a series of brilliant scholars who radically rethink the conclusions of the classical period. This list begins with Ockham, of course, and also Auriol, but should also include the Oxford Calculators (1320s–1340s), John Buridan (c. 1300–c. 1361), and also Nicole Oresme (c. 1322–1382), Marsilius of Inghen (c. 1330–1396), John Wyclif (c. 1330–1384), and Paul of Venice (c. 1369–1429)—to say nothing of controversial anti-Aristotelians like Nicholas of Autrecourt (c. 1298–1369) and John of Mirecourt (fl. c. 1345). We are only now coming to grips with the texts of all these authors,[10] but subsequent generations of medievalists are sure to regard this period as one of the highpoints of scholasticism. Beyond these figures, however, we run into some difficulty, because there has been very little work done on the first half of the fifteenth century. It takes a mix of optimism and charity, then, to see the period of innovation and experimentation as extending that far. There is, however, good reason to want to push ahead. For as the centre of philosophy gradually migrated from Paris and Oxford down to Padua, we find a kind of Aristotelianism that is, if anything, more adventuresome and lively than that of any period before it. Here too our knowledge of these texts—especially among English-language scholars—is quite limited. Still, we know enough about Italian Renaissance figures like Pietro Pomponazzi (1462–1525) and Agostino Nifo (1470–1538) to see that Aristotelianism was alive and still innovative into the turn of the sixteenth century.

So where does the fourth period stop—or is scholastic Aristotelianism perhaps *still* alive and well, somewhere in the corridors of the Vatican? One might well want to see the period extend all the way to the end of the sixteenth century, in the work of Spanish scholastics such as Domingo de Soto (1494–1560), Franciscus Toledo (1532–1596), or Francisco Suárez (1548–1617)—or the great Paduan Jacob Zabarella (1533–1589). In terms of sheer quantity, too, there continued to be massive amounts of work done along Aristotelian lines well into the seventeenth century. According to Charles Schmitt, the authoritative expert on this period, 'there are more philosophical manuscripts from the fifteenth century alone than from the previous two hundred years combined' and 'more writings devoted to his [Aristotle's] works dating from the sixteenth century than from the entire period from Boethius to Pomponazzi.'[11] Hence the usual caricature of Renaissance philosophy, that it substituted Plato for Aristotle, can scarcely be maintained.

Still, despite the quantity of Aristotelian scholarship during the Renaissance and the clear merit of some of this work, one might still want to argue that the period of innovation and experimentation begins to run out in the early sixteenth century. One familiar reason for this suggestion is the rise of humanism. We can date the beginnings of the humanistic study of Aristotle with more precision than such matters usually allow. During the last decade of the fifteenth century, Aldo Manuzio led a team of scholars in printing the first edition of Aristotle's Greek text. In 1497, as that five-volume folio *editio princeps* was nearing completion in Venice, a special chair was instituted at Padua for the study of Aristotle in Greek.[12] As these events suggest, humanism should by no means be regarded as antithetical to scholastic Aristotelianism, but instead to have shaped the character of such inquiry. Renaissance scholarship gave rise to a whole new wave of editions and translations, not just of Aristotle but of the ancient commentary tradition. Hence whereas earlier scholastics, largely ignorant of Greek, were scarcely in a position even to seek historical accuracy, scholars in the sixteenth century were increasingly expected to know both the texts and the commentaries in their original languages. This changed the way scholars thought about the study of philosophy. Whereas Aquinas could remark in passing, as if it were obvious, that 'the study of philosophy is not about knowing what individuals thought, but about the way things are,' it would seem at least to some sixteenth-century scholastics that the study of philosophy precisely is about what Aristotle and other ancients actually thought. So Zabarella, in an oration delivered on the occasion of his assuming a chair of natural philosophy at Padua in 1568, remarked that 'so long as I am an interpreter of Aristotle, I can neither follow nor defend any other opinion than that of Aristotle, although in actual fact I may think otherwise'. As for his students, they should listen to Aristotle with the thought 'not that the things they hear and are taught should absolutely be believed, but only that this is what human reason and the weakness of natural light could find and uncover'.[13]

Of course, careful textual scholarship can exist side by side—as it does today— with creative philosophical speculation. And it seems unlikely that humanistic scholarship all by itself would have managed to suppress the vitality of scholasticism if there were not a second influence at work, the Reformation. When Martin Luther was excommunicated in 1520, events were set in motion that would shape the future of Western philosophy as well as Christianity. Whereas in 1500 it seemed tolerable for Pomponazzi to articulate an Aristotelianism that cast doubt on both the soul's immortality and the occurrence of miracles, the best-known Aristotelians of the later sixteenth century adhere to a much more conservative line. This is most clearly the case for Jesuits such as Suárez and Toletus. From its foundation in 1540, the Jesuit Order expressly set itself up as a defender of the traditional theology and philosophy of the Church, against any sort of innovation. The original *Constitutions* mandate the teaching of 'those books that are found to contain more solid and safe doctrine, and those that are suspect, or whose authors are suspect, will not be taken up' (IV.14.1). Rules promulgated for the Jesuit Roman College in 1562 listed twenty-seven specific doctrines that must be held in philosophy and theology, and followed them up with these guidelines:

- New opinions, especially in weighty matters, should not be introduced without the advice and express licence of superiors.
- It is not allowed to hold views against the most received and solemn opinions and, as it were, the axioms of nearly all the philosophers and medical scholars, such as

- natural bodies consist of matter and form, and these are the principles of natural things;
- there are four elements;
- there are four primary qualities;
- there are four kinds of causes;

and others like these, although they have nothing to do with the faith. Indeed, one should teach against any common opinion rarely, and not without great cause.[14]

These four 'quasi axiomata' listed here would of course become the principal targets of the seventeenth-century movement against Aristotelianism. By this point in the history of scholasticism, one can feel the pressure of new ideas building palpably, just waiting to burst through.

The beginnings of the end of the scholastic era might be tied to the work of Descartes, whose first published work, the programmatic *Discourse on the Method of Rightly Conducting One's Reason and Seeking the Truth in the Sciences*, was published in 1637. One might prefer to focus on other works—such as Francis Bacon's *Novum Organum* (1620) or Galileo's *Dialogues Concerning the Two Chief World Systems* (1632)—but the general trend is familiar in any case: as the seventeenth century progressed, defenders of Aristotle became increasingly discredited, so that by the end of the seventeenth century only the most reactionary figures were still teaching and writing in the scholastic style. This is not to say that Aristotle himself was wholly discredited, inasmuch as authors during this period standardly distinguished between the great Aristotle and his scholastic corrupters. Thus Descartes remarks in the preface to the French edition of the *Principles of Philosophy* (1647) that whereas Aristotle (like Plato) 'had a great deal of intelligence and much wisdom ...' (CSM I 181), 'the majority of those aspiring to be philosophers in the last few centuries have blindly followed Aristotle. Indeed they have often corrupted the sense of his writings and attributed to him various opinions which he would not recognize to be his, were he now to return to this world' (CSM I 182).[15]

Harsh criticism of Aristotelianism—and indeed of Aristotle too—was hardly new in the seventeenth century. Even at the height of the classical period of scholasticism, Aristotelianism had critics who were both fierce (such as Peter John Olivi [1248–1298]) and influential (such as Bonaventure [c. 1217–1274]). Olivi ridiculed his contemporaries for following Aristotle so slavishly: 'without reason he is believed, as the god of this age'.[16] Although later Renaissance critics of Aristotelianism— such as Marsilio Ficino, Gianfrancesco Pico, and Michel de Montaigne—are perhaps better known, the truth is that Aristotle had always had his critics, in every generation of medieval scholars. What is distinctive about the seventeenth century, then, is not that Aristotelianism came under attack, but that philosophers succeeded in formulating a credible alternative. In its first incarnations—in the strictly mechanistic approach of Gassendi, Descartes, Hobbes, and others—this so-called modern philosophy often looks more like a return to the ancient teachings of Democritus or Epicurus. Such a return was not itself a particularly novel idea. Nicholas of Autrecourt and John of Mirecourt had attempted to revive atomism back in the mid-fourteenth century, but their views were quickly censured by Church authorities, effectively blocking this line of inquiry for nearly 300 years. Once these ideas were finally able to be discussed in the open, however, the dead, oppressive weight of scholasticism was cast off—not overnight, by any means, but inevitably and finally.[17] Scholastic Aristotelianism was never refuted, just abandoned by the way, leaving future generations to build on the initially crude mechanistic approach in all the brilliant variety that characterizes later seventeenth and eighteenth-century philosophy.

III. The Distinctive Character of Scholastic Aristotelianism

If I seem to have dwelled overlong on the historical trajectory of the Latin Aristotle, that is perhaps because such historical landmarks are relatively easy to set out. Much harder is to say something in general about the character of scholastic Aristotelianism. Even if one sets aside all considerations of fidelity to source, as I shall, still the range of topics is so vast that it is hard to know where to begin. Moreover, and just as significantly, although the question is often asked *What did the scholastics think about this?*—as if on a given topic there is just *a* scholastic thought—there is of course a vast and often bewildering variety of opinions on any substantive topic. Hence any adequate characterisation of Latin Aristotelianism would have to range widely not only over topics but also over authors. The task begins to look, as I remarked at the start, like nothing less than a history of the whole of medieval philosophy.

Yet even if the stress ought to remain firmly on the variety of scholastic views—and this is the topic to which I will return shortly—there are perhaps some generalizations about the period worth offering. First and foremost, medieval interpreters of Aristotle always presupposed that they were dealing with a coherent and systematic body of work. They assumed it was *coherent*, first and so they almost never took seriously the thought that Aristotle might have contradicted himself from one text to another. And since they recognized no contradictions, they had no reason to consider that Aristotle might have changed his mind, and so had no reason to postulate any sort of developmental hypothesis. Instead, they read the texts as a seamless, integrated body of work, each part of which contributed to a larger, more-or-less complete philosophical theory. In this way, too, scholastic authors read Aristotle as offering a thoroughly *systematic* philosophy, in which the logical works lay at the foundation, then the *Physics* and associated physical treatises, then the *De anima* as the foundational biological treatise, giving rise to the more specialized biological works, and so on. (One can find this ordering articulated in whole or in part in the prologues to many scholastic commentaries, and it remains with us today, preserved in the sequence of texts canonized by the 1831 Bekker edition.)

Scholastic systematizing goes beyond the natural thought that Aristotle's works can be put into some kind of coherent arrangement. What they further believed—and indeed seem to have taken much farther than Aristotle himself—was that the lessons from any one part of the corpus could be extended systematically to cover the whole. Here are two examples. First, whereas readers today tend to treat the *Categories* as a curious early work of uncertain relation to Aristotle's mature thought, the scholastics regarded it as foundational for the whole corpus (even if they disagreed about whether it should be read as mainly metaphysical or linguistic). Hence they applied the category scheme to every corner of philosophical and theological thought, so that an adequate explanation of any phenomenon would standardly begin with a discussion of what category the thing (or term) fell into. This sort of approach has as its apotheosis Suárez's long series of *Metaphysical Disputations*, more than a third of which (Questions 32–53, running to 702 pages in the standard edition) is devoted to a painstaking analysis of the ten categories.[18] Accordingly, perhaps the greatest philosophical quarrel of the later Middle Ages, the dispute over nominalism, was mainly centred not on the problem of universals, but on the reality of the various accidental categories, with the nominalists (following Ockham) endorsing the reality only of substance and quality, and realists endorsing at least quantity as well, and sometimes all nine accidental categories.[19]

Second, the account of *scientia* found in the *Posterior Analytics* was taken as definitive and binding in all areas of inquiry. Anything that would count as a science, then—including not just metaphysics and the various areas of natural philosophy, but also theology—had to satisfy the constraints Aristotle set up there. For a proposition to be the object of *scientia*, it had to be necessary and universal, known on the basis of an affirmative demonstration in the first syllogistic figure, the premises of which are necessary and explanatory of the conclusion. Hence, famously, and quite unlike Aristotle's own usual practice, scholastic philosophers actually cast their arguments in syllogistic form, quite self-consciously adhering to Aristotle's analysis of the different valid moods. They are constantly aware of whether their arguments are *propter quid* or merely *quia*, and they have a general sense of what the first principles are in any given domain. This is not to say that anyone actually succeeded in constructing a formalized derivation along Aristotelian lines in any substantive domain, but it is perhaps the most awesome feature of scholastic authors that they worked so hard, and got so far, on this project. (For a particularly vivid instance, see the first thirteen questions of Aquinas's *Summa theologiae*, where the existence and nature of God is demonstrated from first principles—or at least very nearly so.[20]) Moreover, this constant sensitivity to the formal demands of Aristotelian demonstration led them to stress the distinction between demonstrative and merely dialectical argument, and so scholastic authors were expert in the nuances of dialectical argument as set out in the *Topics*.

An important feature of scholastic epistemology that became associated with the *Posterior Analytics* framework but yet has no obvious basis there is the recurrent stress on certainty as a requirement for *scientia*. Grosseteste's commentary does not even discuss certainty, but beginning with Albert the Great this plays a central role in scholastic discussions. At the very start of Albert's commentary, he cites a comment by Ptolemy that

> a human being ought to fill his soul not with what is [merely] plausible (*probabile*) and credible (*opinabile*), because they do not yield a stable (*stantem*) disposition in the soul, but with things that are demonstrable and certain, which render the intellect certain and stable, because such things are themselves certain and eternally stable.

He then concludes that 'this is the end and the most perfect and the sole unconditionally desirable thing among the logical sciences'.[21] Subsequent discussions of *scientia* almost always give a central place to certainty, which then gets contrasted with the less-than-certain results obtainable through the merely plausible arguments of dialectic.

Ironically, this focus on certainty is one feature of scholastic thought that gets preserved—indeed, accentuated—in the iconic anti-Aristotelian texts of Descartes, and has come down to us as the dubious notion that *knowledge* requires certainty. Scholastic authors (and Descartes too, for that matter) thought no such thing. Their project was to describe a kind of epistemic ideal. They took the *Posterior Analytics* not to describe the conditions under which one would be justified in asserting a claim, but to set out a programme for obtaining the best possible understanding of any given domain. By their very nature, ideals are not usually obtainable, and one should not suppose that failure to achieve the ideal is tantamount to complete failure. Scholastic authors standardly distinguished between various grades of *scientia* that fall short of the perfect demonstrative kind, and so many forms of evidence that fail to be perfectly demonstrative might yet be perfectly adequate to ground knowledge in our sense of the term.

The foregoing remarks were an extension of the claim that scholastic philosophy can be characterized by a tendency to treat Aristotle's work as thoroughly coherent and systematic. This is surely the most striking common feature of scholastic Aristotelianism. If the scholastics share any other common tendency, it is perhaps the tendency toward reification—that is, toward understanding Aristotle's talk of form, matter, actuality, potentiality, substance, essence, and so on as picking out *res* or entities. Of course, this is also an area where scholastic authors disagreed fiercely, but even the most parsimonious of scholastics, like Ockham, seem to share a basic inclination—accepted without argument—toward treating Aristotle's conceptual framework as entailing certain ontological commitments. To again take an example from the *Posterior Analytics*, it was accepted without question by scholastic Aristotelians that the essence of a thing corresponds to some real, causally efficacious feature of that thing—either its substantial form, or its substantial form plus its common matter. *Scientia*, then, in its ideal form, requires not just the articulation of an abstract essence-specifying definition, but the grasp of a thing's substantial form. That form is a concrete thing rather than, for instance, an abstract function, inasmuch as it is causally responsible for the various intrinsic accidental features of the substance. (It should be said, too, that all the major scholastics were in agreement in treating forms as particulars rather than universals.) Suárez is simply reiterating an argument that had been made over and over by previous scholastics when he writes:

> The aggregation of multiple faculties or accidental forms in a simple substantial subject is not enough for the constitution of a natural thing.... A form is required that, as it were, rules over all those faculties and accidents, and is the source of all actions and natural motions of such a being, and in which the whole variety of accidents and powers has its root and unity.[22]

Accordingly, when seventeenth-century authors attacked the scholastic doctrine of substantial form, they were attacking not the sort of metaphysical essentialism that would be Quine's later target, but rather a chemical–biological postulate that was fundamentally opposed to any thoroughgoing mechanistic natural philosophy.

When forms are understood in this way, it immediately becomes important to understand just how many forms there are in a given substance. Hence the most contentious issues of late scholasticism revolved around questions of counting forms:

- Is the human intellect a substantial form (i.e., the rational soul), or is it a power of the rational soul, or is it a separate intelligence? (Ockham said the first; Aquinas the second; Averroists the third.)
- Do human beings have other substantial forms? (Scotus and Ockham said yes; Aquinas and Buridan said no.)
- Do the distinct parts of the body have their own distinct substantial forms? (Suárez argued yes for plants, but no for human beings.)
- Do the elemental forms of earth, air, fire, water remain when mixed? (Nearly everyone said no.)

Other sorts of questions arise for accidental forms:

- Are there distinct forms corresponding to each of the accidental categories? (Most said no.)
- Are qualities distinct forms? (Nearly everyone said yes.)
- Are quantities distinct forms? (Ockham said no; most said yes.)
- Is motion a distinct form? (Ockham said no; Buridan said yes.)

These are just some of the most prominent instances of the general scholastic tendency to conceive philosophical disputes in terms of the reality of forms. Such disputes make sense, of course, only given the shared background assumption that forms are real, irreducible entities with causal powers of their own. Hence, although some seventeenth-century authors thought Aristotelian hylomorphism was best defended by rendering it platitudinous—'who can doubt', says the *Port*

Royal Logic,[23] that everything is composed of matter and a certain form of this matter?'—the usual seventeenth-century critique of Aristotelianism was to insist that forms as conceived by the scholastics had to go.

IV. Disagreements within Scholastic Aristotelianism

The disputes over form sampled above were primarily intended to illustrate the underlying scholastic commitment to realism. But they also, of course, illustrate the extent of scholastic disagreements. And though there are things to be said about the distinctive character of scholastic Aristotelianism, those points of agreement look thin and tenuous next to the deep disagreements that divided these authors on nearly every point. As noted earlier, it is easy to overlook these differences and speak in general terms about what the scholastics thought about this or that. The reason that even specialists are sometimes tempted to talk this way is that these authors, for 400 years or more, shared the common Aristotelian vocabulary of substance, form, matter, potentiality, actuality, soul, science, demonstration, species, difference, generation, corruption, virtue, habit, substance, quality, quantity, relation, and so on. Moreover, not only did they employ a common linguistic framework, but they also endorsed a rather lengthy set of Aristotelian principles, such as these:

- A corporeal substance is a composite of form and matter
- Accidental forms inhere in their substance as in a subject
- The soul is the first actuality of a potentially living body
- The intellect begins as a blank slate
- All knowledge comes through the senses
- The generation of one thing is the corruption of another
- Matter endures through substantial change
- There are four basic elements: earth, air, fire, water

and so on.

When one sees all these authors using the same terms, and endorsing the same principles, it is natural to think that, at some level of generality, one can speak in general of *scholastic doctrines.* This is, however, simply not the case. With respect to any substantive philosophical claim, one can find the most basic sorts of disagreements even among the most important scholastic figures. The most fundamental reason this is so is that these figures, while sharing a common set of philosophical terms, did not agree on the meanings of those terms. For example, anyone who considered himself an Aristotelian agreed that matter endures through substantial change. But differences in the understanding of what matter is led to radical differences in how this claim was interpreted, with the result that two philosophers could agree on the *dictum* but yet be in complete disagreement on its actual content. Thomas Aquinas, to take one extreme, held that prime matter is pure potentiality. So while he endorses the general claim that 'it is part of the nature of change for *the same thing* to stand differently, now and earlier' (*Summa theol.* 1a 45.2 ad 2), he goes on to explain that this analysis holds for substantial change in only a qualified way: 'sometimes there is the same entity *only in potentiality*, as in substantial change, the subject of which is matter'. Although the proper understanding of Aquinas's view is subject to dispute, it is clear enough that the italicized phrase puts a rather severe qualification on the Aristotelian dictum. Others went in radically different directions. Averroists like John of Jandun (c.1285/9–1328), for instance, under the influence of Averroes' *De substantia orbis*, understood prime matter to endure through change as informed by 'indeterminate dimensions.'[24] This amounted to treating the endurance of prime matter as a thesis about the conservation of extension or body through all change, something that Aquinas denied. So although Jandun endorsed what seem to be the same *dicta* regarding prime matter, he uses them to advance claims of an entirely different kind. Others would go in still different ways, using the Aristotelian doctrine to make still other kinds of points.

It is perhaps not terribly surprising to see scholastic authors disagreeing about the nature of Aristotelian matter, since the topic remains notoriously controversial today. Similar disagreements arise, though, in every area of scholastic thought. Here are two more examples. First, consider the relationship of body and soul. What more quintessentially Aristotelian doctrine is there than that of the soul's standing as the form of the body? Scholastic authors embraced this doctrine, of course. Yet it was at the same time a notoriously difficult doctrine for Christians to embrace, since they were also committed to the idea that the human soul is a spiritual and immortal substance. Spiritual and immortal, and a substance, and at the same time the form of a body? Scholastics before Aquinas tended to insist on the spiritual substance side, at the expense of any serious attempt to embrace hylomorphism.[25] Still, it seemed to Aquinas himself, at the start of his career, that the Aristotelian approach was firmly entrenched; he refers to 'the view of Aristotle, *which all the moderns follow*, that the soul is united to body just as form to matter' (III *Sent.* 5.3.2c). Aquinas's own account of these matters is distinguished by its aggressive attempt at having the best of both worlds: a rigorously hylomorphic conception of the body as informed by the rational soul, together with an orthodox Christian account of the soul as a spiritual and immortal substance. The history of later scholastic discussions of this topic is a history of doubts about whether this could really be made to work. The range of alternatives canvassed would defy even a very prolonged summary. In broadest outlines, there was a choice between Aquinas' unitarian strategy of recognizing just a single substantial form (the rational soul) for human beings as with all substances, and the pluralists, strategy of postulating two or more forms: minimally, a bodily form for the matter (the *forma corporeitatis*) and then a rational soul to inform the body. This dispute initially pitted Aquinas (the first to maintain this position with any clarity) against Henry of Ghent (d. 1293), Scotus, and Ockham, and continued to divide scholastics into the seventeenth century.

The plurality of forms dispute is another illustration of how fundamental disagreements among 'Aristotelian' scholastics reduced the apparently common points of agreement to little more than a matter of shared catchphrases. Everyone agreed that the rational soul is the form of the body. But given their disagreements over the meaning of 'soul', 'form' and 'body', philosophers were very often just as far apart on their understanding of these matters as were philosophers in ancient Greece, or in Anglophone philosophy today. Thus, for Aquinas, the *body* that the rational soul informs is actually prime matter, whereas for pluralists it is a composite of matter and one or more prior substantial forms. For Aquinas, a *form* (that is, a substantial form) is responsible for the composite's existence in such a way that no part of that composite can exist without the form. For the pluralists, in contrast, the body might exist both before and after its union with the rational soul. Finally, a *soul*, for Aquinas, explains all of the intrinsic features of a living thing, even those not immediately associated with life (e.g., shape and size), whereas for the pluralists the soul accounts for only certain features of the living substance. Still, one might think, there is some kind of underlying agreement among all parties here, inasmuch as they all basically endorse Aristotelian hylomorphism. This is just what I am denying. The disagreements just sketched lie at the heart of what they took the doctrine of hylomorphism to be. Show me some deeper substantive theses of hylomorphism, and I will show you how they fought over those, too.

What unanimity there was among the scholastics was a product of ecclesiastical fiat. Olivi, one of Aquinas's very most sceptical critics, argued circa 1280 that the rational soul could not be the form of the body at all. He called it 'not only contrary to reason but also dangerous to the faith' to hold that 'the [soul's] intellective and free part is the form of the body per se and considered as such' (II *Sent.* q. 51; ed. Jansen, II.104).[26] At the Council of Vienne, in 1312, this was judged to go too far. Pope Clement V declared it a heresy to hold that 'the rational or intellective soul is not per se and essentially the form of the human body', and subsequent scholars were accordingly compelled—literally on pain of death—to toe the Aristotelian line in this regard. (Consider how much had changed in the century since the *anti*-Aristotelian decree of 1210.) Accordingly, one can always find the shared catchphrases mentioned earlier, catchphrases that were obligatory into the seventeenth century, at least among Catholics, in light of the Fifth Lateran Council's having expressly reaffirmed the Council of Vienne, using exactly the same words, in 1513. But though the Church could require philosophers to use certain patterns of words, it was quite unable to control how those words were understood.

My second example concerns scholastic discussions of accidents, where a strikingly similar story can be told. The catchphrase here is that accidents are things distinct from substances. This issue attracted little critical attention during the classical period—Aquinas did not even bother to write a commentary on the *Categories*, the fundamental text—but it was the defining dispute of both later scholasticism and the seventeenth century. Ockham set things in motion by arguing that only accidents in the category of quality are real, and that all other accidents can be reduced to either substance or quality.[27] A generation later, John of Mirecourt would go one step farther and propose eliminating quality as well, leaving an ontology that consisted only of substances. Again, this was judged to go too far. In 1347, the University of Paris condemned the following view:

> That it is plausible, in the natural light [of reason], that there are *no* accidents, but that *every thing* is a substance, and that if not for faith this view should be held and can plausibly be held.

As with the Council of Vienne's statement about the soul, one naturally wonders why Church authorities would feel the need to weigh in on such murky philosophical questions. In each case, the answer is that they thought these philosophical doctrines were required to support Christian doctrines—here, the Eucharistic doctrine that the qualities of the host survive transubstantiation. So whereas in the early thirteenth century it was quite unclear whether Aristotelianism could be made compatible with Church teachings, by the fourteenth century those teachings were positively thought to rest on a certain reading of Aristotle's metaphysics. In this regard, the great figures of classical scholasticism were more effective advocates of Aristotle than they could possibly have imagined.

The language of the 1347 condemnation goes a step farther than the Council of Vienne. That earlier prohibition had spoken only of what scholars must teach as true. This left it open for a careful philosopher like Buridan to distinguish between what he holds as true on the basis of faith, and what can be shown by natural reason. (To natural reason, Buridan says, the materialism of Alexander of Aphrodisias is entirely defensible.)[28] The condemnation of 1347 leaves no such room for philosophical speculation, proscribing even the claim that the rejection of real accidents is philosophically plausible. Hence, after 1347, although philosophers could go as far as Ockham and reject the accidental categories outside of quality, they could not do away with real accidents altogether. From this point until the seventeenth century, Christian authors felt obligated to postulate quality as an irreducible ontological category. This included the four primary qualities (hot, cold, wet, dry), and also the proper sensible qualities (colour, sound, taste, and odour), and perhaps various sorts of states and dispositions as well. When Francis Bacon remarks that 'ipsissimus calor, sive quid ipsum caloris, sit motus et nihil aliud' ('heat its very self, or what heat is, is motion and nothing else', *Novum organum* II.20) he was challenging the central orthodoxy of scholastic natural philosophy. And although Bacon could get away with this in protestant England in 1620, a group of three young scholars who attempted a similar attack on this and other Aristotelian dogmas four years later in Paris were expelled from the city along with a warning to all, on pain of death, against holding or teaching any maxims contrary to the ancient authors and the theologians.[29] Describing these events a generation later, Jean de Launoy described this as one of the high points in the long and ongoing *fortuna* of Aristotle at Paris.[30] From our vantage point, of course, it serves only as a peculiar coda to Aristotle's long tenure as the Philosopher.

V. Conclusion

Although scholastic philosophy is thoroughly and deeply Aristotelian, it is nevertheless a field of richly original and diverse doctrines. The tendency to treat scholasticism as if it has a core of common teachings is a natural misconception, one that will be dispelled only by further study and growing familiarity with the great philosophical landmarks of the period. Among classical scholars, it is perhaps common to think of medieval Aristotelianism as something of an embarrassment to the master himself, in the way that scholastic Latin is an embarrassment to the legacy of Cicero. To the medievalist, in contrast, the scholastic era takes on the aspect of a vast and fertile landscape for the nurture of various concepts set out in an obscure albeit provocative style by a talented forerunner.

Notes

1. Strictly speaking, Alcuin relied upon a gloss of the *Categories* written by Themistius, but ascribed (in Alcuin's day) to Augustine. This is one of many cases where misascriptions gave an initial authority to works that might otherwise have been less influential. Other examples include the *Liber de causis*, as already mentioned, and the works of pseudo-Dionysius, which were claimed to be written by a disciple of Saint Paul. For information on pseudo-Aristotle in the Middle Ages, see Steven Williams, 'Defining the Corpus Aristotelicum: Scholastic Awareness of Aristotelian Spuria in the High Middle Ages', *Journal of the Warburg and Courtauld Institutes* 58 (1995) 29–51; Charles B. Schmitt, 'Pseudo-Aristotle in the Latin Middle Ages', in J. Kraye et al., eds., *Pseudo-Aristotle in the Middle Ages: The* Theology *and Other Texts* (London: Warburg Institute, 1986), 3–14. Although Thomas Aquinas is regularly credited with discovering that the *Liber de causis* derives from Proclus, Williams shows that he was in fact not the first to recognize this.

2. For further information on the introduction of Aristotle into the Latin West, see C. H. Lohr, 'The Medieval Interpretation of Aristotle', in N. Kretzmann et al., eds., *The Cambridge History of Later Medieval Philosophy* (Cambridge: Cambridge University Press, 1982), 80–98; David Luscombe, *Medieval Thought* (Oxford: Oxford University Press, 1997). For Boethius, see James Shiel, 'Boethius' Commentaries on Aristotle', in R. Sorabji, ed., *Aristotle Transformed: The Ancient Commentators and their Influence* (Ithaca, N.Y.: Cornell University Press, 1990), 349–72; and Sten Ebbesen, 'Boethius as an Aristotelian Commentator', in *ibid.*, 373–91. For more detailed information on the earlier Middle Ages, see John Marenbon, 'Medieval Latin Commentaries and Glosses on Aristotelian Logical Texts, before ca. 1150 A.D.' in C. Burnett, ed., *Glosses and Commentaries on Aristotelian Logical Texts: The Syriac, Arabic, and Medieval Latin Traditions* (London: Warburg Institute, 1993) 77–127; and Charles Burnett, 'The Introduction of Aristotle's Natural Philosophy into Great Britain: A Preliminary Survey of the Manuscript Evidence', in J. Marenbon, ed., *Aristotle in Britain during the Middle Ages* (Brepols, 1996), 21–50. On the seemingly important role of medical scholars at Salerno in the transmission of Aristotle's text, see Danielle Jacquart, 'Aristotelian thought in Salerno', in P. Dronke, ed., *A History of Twelfth-Century Philosophy*

(Cambridge: Cambridge University Press, 1988), 407–28. For a complete guide to medieval translations of Greek philosophical texts into Latin, Arabic, and Hebrew, see Appendix B to the new *Cambridge History of Medieval Philosophy*, tr. R. Pasnau (Cambridge: Cambridge University Press, 2010).

3. This and the other documents discussed below are usefully collected and translated in Lynn Thorndike, *University Records and Life in the Middle Ages* (New York: Columbia University Press, 1944). For good overviews of the rise of Aristotelianism in the medieval university, see Luca Bianchi, *Censure et liberté intellectuelle à l'Université de Paris (XIIIᵉ-XIVᵉ siècles)* (Paris: Les Belles Lettres, 1999), 89–127; Fernand van Steenberghen, *Aristotle in the West: The Origins of Latin Aristotelianism*, tr. L. Johnston (Louvain: Nauwelaerts, 1970); Mark D. Jordan, 'Aristotelianism, Medieval', in E. Craig, ed., *Routledge Encyclopedia of Philosophy* (London: Routledge, 1998); Gordon Leff, 'The *Trivium* and the Three Philosophies', in Hilde de Ridder-Symoens, ed., *A History of the University in Europe: Volume 1, Universities in the Middle Ages* (Cambridge: Cambridge University Press, 1992), 307–36.

4. For details, see D.A. Callus, 'Introduction of Aristotelian Learning to Oxford', *Proceedings of the British Academy* 29 (1943), 229–81, and J.A. Weisheipl, 'Science in the Thirteenth Century', in *The History of the University of Oxford: Volume 1. The Early Oxford Schools*, ed. J.I. Catto (Oxford: Oxford University Press, 1984) 435–69.

5. As quoted in van Steenberghen, *Aristotle in the West*, p. 134. For Aristotle in the faculty of theology, see Monika Asztalos, 'The Faculty of Theology', in Hilde de Ridder-Symoens, ed., *A History of the University in Europe: Volume 1, Universities in the Middle Ages* (Cambridge: Cambridge University Press, 1992), 409–41.

6. William of Auvergne, *Tractatus de anima*, in *Opera Omnia* (Paris, 1674; repr. Frankfurt a.M.: Minerva, 1963); tr. R.J. Teske, *The Soul* (Milwaukee, Wisc.: Marquette University Press, 2000).

7. Most of Aquinas's commentaries have been translated into English. Almost nothing by Albert has been translated into English, however, and even the Latin texts can be difficult to obtain, since the critical edition is still largely incomplete. In discussing early Latin commentaries, one might also mention Adam of Buckfield (fl. 1238–1278), an arts master at Oxford who wrote a great many Aristotelian commentaries in the 1240s, prior to the efforts of Albert and Thomas (see Weisheipl, 'Science in the Thirteenth Century', pp. 462–63). Little of Adam's work has been edited and none translated into English (although we have many surviving manuscripts, attesting to its influence).

8. For a detailed discussion of translations and translators, including examples of Greek into Latin, see Bernard G. Dod, 'Aristoteles latinus', in Kretzmann et al., op. cit., 45–79. See also Jozef Brams, *La riscoperta di Aristotele in Occidente* (Milan: Jaca, 2003). Many of the Latin translations are available through the ongoing series *Aristoteles latinus* (1957-). The indispensable source for information on scholastic Aristotelian commentaries is Charles H. Lohr, 'Medieval Latin Aristotle Commentaries', *Traditio*, vols. 23–30 (1967–1974); *Latin Aristotle Commentaries: II, Renaissance Authors* (Florence: Olschki, 1988). The projected volume on medieval authors [up to 1500] is still available only through the installments published by *Traditio*, although an updated bibliographical guide is now available: Lohr, *Latin Aristotle Commentaries: V. Bibliography of Secondary Literature* (Florence: SISMEL, 2005).

9. For details, see R. de Vaux, *Notes et textes sur l'Avicennisme Latin aux confins des XIIe-XIIIe siècles* (Paris, 1934); R. de Vaux, 'La première entrée d'Averroës chez les Latins', *Revue des sciences philosophiques et théologiques* 22 (1933), 193–245; René Gauthier,

'Notes sur les débuts (1225–1240) du premier 'averroïsme'', in *Revue des Sciences Philosophiques et Théologiques* 66 (1982), 321–374. For an English translation of an early anonymous Latin Aristotelian treatise on the soul (c. 1225), heavily influenced by Avicenna but also with shades of Averroes, see R. Pasnau, *Cambridge Translations of Medieval Philosophical Texts. Volume 3: Mind and Knowledge* (New York: Cambridge University Press, 2002), ch. 1.

10. Brief but useful summaries of all these figures can be found in J. Gracia and T. Noone, *A Companion to Philosophy in the Middle Ages* (Oxford: Blackwell, 2003), and in Appendix C to the new *Cambridge History of Medieval Philosophy*. An indication of just how slow scholars have been to assimilate this material is that even the principal philosophical works of the brilliant Buridan—his question-commentaries on the *Physics*, *Metaphysics*, and *De anima*—are still not available in a critical edition, let alone in translation. For the Oxford Calculators, also known as the Mertonians, see J. A. Weisheipl, 'Ockham and the Mertonians', in Catto, *The History of the University of Oxford* I: 607–58, and Edith Sylla, 'The Oxford Calculators', in Kretzmann et al., *Cambridge History of Later Medieval Philosophy*, 540–63.

11. 'Towards a History of Renaissance Philosophy', in C. Webster, ed., *Reappraisals in Renaissance Thought* (London: Variorum, 1989), 9.

12. *Opera* (Venice: Aldus Manutius, 1495–1498). This was in fact the first printing of any extended prose work in the Greek alphabet. See Martin Lowry, *The World of Aldus Manutius: Business and Scholarship in Renaissance Venice* (Ithaca, N.Y.: Cornell University Press, 1979). On the earliest efforts to teach Aristotle in Greek, see Charles B. Schmitt, 'Aristotelian Textual Studies at Padua: The Case of Francesco Cavalli', *The Aristotelian Tradition and Renaissance Universities* (London: Variorum, 1984), 288–90, and also, in that same volume, 'Thomas Linacre and Italy', 54–55. These and other papers by Schmitt collected in three Variorum volumes serve as an excellent guide to Renaissance Aristotelianism. For a condensed survey, see Schmitt's *Aristotle and the Renaissance* (Cambridge, Mass.: Harvard University Press, 1983). See also Edward Mahoney and James South, 'Aristotelianism, Renaissance', in E. Craig, ed., *Routledge Encyclopedia of Philosophy* (London: Routledge, 1998), Brian Copenhaver and Charles B. Schmitt, *Renaissance Philosophy* (Oxford: Oxford University Press, 1992), ch. 2; Eckhard Kessler, 'The Transformation of Aristotelianism during the Renaissance', in J. Henry and S. Hutton, eds. *New Perspectives on Renaissance Thought: Essays in the History of Science, Education, and Philosophy in Memory of Charles B. Schmitt* (London: Duckworth, 1990), 137–47; Edward Mahoney, 'Aristotle and Late Medieval and Renaissance Philosophies', in R. Pozzo, ed., *The Impact of Aristotelianism on Modern Philosophy* (Washington, DC: Catholic University of America Press, 2004).

13. Thomas Aquinas, *In Aristotelis libros De caelo et mundo*, ed. R.M. Spiazzi (Rome: Marietti, 1952), I.22.228. For Zabarella, see Dominique Bouillon, 'Un discourse inédit de Iacopo Zabarella préliminaire à l'exposition de la 'Physique' d'Aristote (Padoue 1568)', *Atti e memorie dell'Accademia galileiana di scienze lettere ed arti in Padova* 111 (1998/99), 124. See also Antonino Poppi, 'Zabarella, or Aristotelianism as a Rigorous Science', in R. Pozzo, ed., *The Impact of Aristotelianism on Modern Philosophy* (Washington: Catholic University of America Press, 2004), 35–63.

14. *Monumenta paedagogica Societatis Iesu quae primam Rationem studiorum anno 1586 editam praecessere*, ed. C. Gomez Rodeles (Madrid: A. Avrial, 1901), 490–91; Ignatius of Loyola, *The Constitutions of the Society of Jesus*, tr. G.E. Ganss (St. Louis: Institute of Jesuit Sources, 1970). For further discussion of Jesuit attitudes, see Charles Lohr, 'Jesuit Aristotelianism and Sixteenth-Century Metaphysics', in *Paradosis: Studies in Memory of*

Edwin A. Quain (New York: Fordham University Press, 1976) 203–20; and Roger Ariew, 'Descartes and Scholasticism: The Intellectual Background to Descartes' Thought', in J. Cottingham, ed., *The Cambridge Companion to Descartes* (Cambridge: Cambridge University Press, 1992), 58–90. It should be stressed that the Jesuits were reacting not only to the threat of Protestantism, but also to the far more relaxed Aristotelianism prevalent in Italy. See, especially, J.H. Randall, *The School of Padua and the Emergence of Modern Science* (Padua: Editrice Antenore, 1961). As for Protestant philosophy, it was by no means inevitably anti-Aristotelian. See, e.g., Peter Petersen, *Geschichte der aristotelischen Philosophie im protestantischen Deutschland* (Leipzig: Meiner, 1921); Ulrich Gottfried Leinsle, *Das Ding und die Methode: methodische Konstitution und Gegenstand der frühen protestantischen Metaphysik* (Augsburg: MaroVerlag, 1985); and the work of Christia Mercer cited in the following note.

15. For the fate of Aristotle in the seventeenth century, see Tom Sorrell, ed., *The Rise of Modern Philosophy: The Tension between the New and Traditional Philosophies from Machiavelli to Leibniz* (Oxford: Clarendon Press, 1993), especially the contribution by Christia Mercer. See also Mercer's 'Mechanizing Aristotle: Leibniz and Reformed Philosophy', in M.A. Stewart, ed., *Studies in Seventeenth-Century Philosophy* (Clarendon: Oxford, 1997), 117–52, which is especially good on seventeenth-century attempts to reclaim Aristotle for the side of the mechanistic philosophy. Much of her earlier research is brought together in her wide-ranging *Leibniz's Metaphysics: Its Origins and Development* (Cambridge: Cambridge University Press, 2001).

16. Olivi, *Quaestiones in secundum librum Sententiarum* (Bibliotheca Franciscana Scholastica 4–6), ed. B. Jansen (Quaracchi: Collegium S. Bonaventurae, 1922–26) q. 58 ad 14 (II.482). See David Burr, "Peter John Olivi and the Philosophers", *Franciscan Studies* 31 (1971), 41–71; Edward Mahoney, 'Aristotle as "The Worst Natural Philosophy" (*pessimus naturalis*) and "The Worst Metaphysician" (*pessimus metaphysicus*): His Reputation among Some Franciscan Philosophers (Bonaventure, Francis of Meyronnes, Antonius Andreas, and Joannes Canonicus) and Later Reactions', in O. Pluta, ed., *Die Philosophie im 14. und 15. Jahrhundert* (Amsterdam: Gruener, 1988) 261–73.

17. It is only from our distant vantage-point that the process seems to have gone quickly and smoothly. It would not have seemed that way to figures like Giordano Bruno (1548–1600) or Tommaso Campanella (1568–1639), who struggled in vain to formulate a credible alternative to Aristotelianism, and were viciously persecuted for their efforts. The first generation of modern atomists (Nicholas Hill [c. 1570-c. 1610], David Gorlaeus [1591–1612], Daniel Sennert [1572–1637], and Sebastian Basso [c. 1580-after 1625]) managed to escape persecution, but also had relatively little influence on the course of events. Even in the later seventeenth century, when we think of philosophy as dominated by a handful of now-famous figures, much of what was published and taught continued to be Aristotelian in some broad sense. I am indebted to correspondence with Christia Mercer, for her insistence on the complexity of this story.

18. Francisco Suárez, *Disputationes metaphysicae* (Paris, 1866; repr. Hildesheim: Olms, 1965).

19. For this perspective on later medieval dispute over nominalism, see William J. Courtenay, 'The Reception of Ockham's Thought at the University of Paris', in Z. Kaluza and P. Vignaux, eds., *Preuve et raisons à l'Université de Paris: logique, ontologie et théologie au XIVe siècle* (Paris: Vrin, 1984), 43–64; Courtenay, 'The Reception of Ockham's Thought in Fourteenth-Century England', in A. Hudson and M. Wilks, eds., *From Ockham to Wyclif* (Oxford: Blackwell, 1987), 89–107. I discuss scholastic

treatments of the category scheme in some detail in *Metaphysical Themes 1274–1671* (Oxford: Oxford University Press, 2011).

20. See the analysis in Robert Pasnau and Christopher Shields, *The Philosophy of Aquinas* (Boulder: Westview, 2004), ch. 4.

21. Albert the Great, *Analytica Posteriora* Bk. I tr. I ch. 1, in P. Jammy, ed., *Opera Omnia* (Lyon, 1651), vol. 1, pp. 513–14.

22. Suárez, *Disputationes metaphysicae* XV.1.7; tr. J. Kronen and J. Reedy, *On the Formal Cause of Substance: Metaphysical Disputation XV* (Milwaukee, Wisc.: Marquette University Press, 2000). I discuss scholastic theories of substantial form in detail in Metaphysical Themes chs. 24–25.

23. Antoine Arnauld and Pierre Nicole, *Logic or the Art of Thinking*, tr. J.V. Buroker (Cambridge: Cambridge University Press, 1996), p. 19.

24. John of Jandun, *Quaestiones super De substantia orbis*, in *Ioannis de Iandvno in libros Aristotelis De coelo et mvndo quae extant qvaestiones svbtilissimae qvibvs nvper consvlto adiecimvs Averrois sermonem De substantia orbis cum eiusdem Ioannis commentario ac quaestionibus* (Venice ap. Iuntas, 1552), Q6. Compare *Averroes' De substantia orbis: Critical Edition of the Hebrew Text with English Translation and Commentary*, ed. A. Hyman (Cambridge, Mass: Medieval Academy of America, 1986), ch. 1.

25. Étienne Gilson remarks: '[T]he definition of the soul as a spiritual substance...was the unanimous opinion of all [scholastic authors prior to Aquinas]....[N]ot one of them would uphold the view that the very essence of this substance was to be the form of the body' (*A History of Christian Philosophy in the Middle Ages* [New York: Random House, 1955], 361). Still well worth reading is A.C. Pegis, *St. Thomas and the Problem of the Soul in the Thirteenth Century* (Toronto: Pontifical Institute of Mediaeval Studies, 1934). More recently, see Richard Dales, *The Problem of the Rational Soul in the Thirteenth Century* (Leiden: Brill, 1995). For Aquinas, see Pasnau, *Thomas Aquinas on Human Nature: A Philosophical Study of* ST 1a 75–89 (New York: Cambridge University Press), chs. 1–5.

26. For details see Robert Pasnau, 'Olivi on the Metaphysics of Soul', *Medieval Philosophy and Theology* 6 (1997) 109–32.

27. See Marilyn Adams, *William Ockham* (Notre Dame, Ind.: University of Notre Dame Press, 1987), chs. 5–9. Although Ockham started the controversy, Olivi deserves credit for having taken the same line some forty years earlier (see, e.g., II *Sent.* q. 28 [ed. Jansen, I.483–84]).

28. See Jack Zupko, 'On Buridan's Alleged Alexandrianism: Heterodoxy and Natural Philosophy in Fourteenth-Century Paris', *Vivarium* 42 (2004) 42–57.

29. See Daniel Garber, 'Defending Aristotle/Defending Society in the Early 17th Century Paris', in W. Detel and C. Zittel (eds.) *Wissensideale und Wissenskulturen in der freuhen Neuzeit: Ideals and Cultures of Knowledge in Early Modern Europe* (Frankfurt: Akademie Verlag, 2002), 135–60.

30. Jean de Launoy, *De varia Aristotelis in academia Parisiensi fortuna* (Paris, 1662), 3rd ed., 201.

Bibliography

Adams, M. M. (1987) *William Ockham* (Notre Dame, Ind.: Univ. of Notre Dame Press).

Albert the Great (1651) *Opera Omnia*, ed. P. Jammy (Lyon).

Ariew, R. (1992) 'Descartes and Scholasticism: The Intellectual Background to Descartes'
   Thought', in J. Cottingham, ed., *The Cambridge Companion to Descartes* (Cambridge:
   Cambridge Univ. Press), 58–90.

Aristotle (1495–1498) *Opera* (Venice: Aldus Manutius).

Arnauld, A., and Pierre Nicole (1996) *Logic or the Art of Thinking*, tr. J.V. Buroker
   (Cambridge: Cambridge Univ. Press).

Asztalos, M. (1992) 'The Faculty of Theology', in Hilde de Ridder-Symoens, ed., *A History
   of the University in Europe: Volume 1, Universities in the Middle Ages* (Cambridge:
   Cambridge Univ. Press), 409–41.

Averroes (1986) *De substantia orbis: Critical Edition of the Hebrew Text with English
   Translation and Commentary*, A. Hyman, ed., (Cambridge, Mass: Medieval Academy of
   America).

Bianchi, L. (1999) *Censure et liberté intellectuelle à l'Université de Paris (XIIIe-XIVe siècles)*
   (Paris: Les Belles Lettres).

Bouillon, D. (1998/99) 'Un discourse inédit de Iacopo Zabarella préliminaire à l'exposition
   de la "Physique" d'Aristote (Padoue 1568)', *Atti e memorie dell'Accademia galileiana di
   scienze lettere ed arti in Padova* 111, 119–27.

Brams, J. (2003) *La riscoperta di Aristotele in Occidente* (Milan: Jaca).

Burnett, C. (1996) 'The Introduction of Aristotle's Natural Philosophy into Great Britain:
   A Preliminary Survey of the Manuscript Evidence', in J. Marenbon, ed., *Aristotle in
   Britain during the Middle Ages* ([Turnhout]: Brepols), 21–50.

Burr, D. (1971) 'Peter John Olivi and the Philosophers', *Franciscan Studies* 31, 41–71.

Callus, D. A. (1943) 'Introduction of Aristotelian Learning to Oxford', *Proceedings of the
   British Academy* 29, 229–81.

Copenhaver, B., and Charles B. Schmitt (1992) *Renaissance Philosophy* (Oxford: Oxford
   Univ. Press).

Courtenay, W. J. (1984) 'The Reception of Ockham's Thought at the University of Paris', in
   Z. Kaluza and P. Vignaux, eds., *Preuve et raisons à l'Université de Paris: logique, ontologie
   et théologie au XIVe siècle* (Paris: Vrin), 43–64.

——— (1987) 'The Reception of Ockham's Thought in Fourteenth-Century England', in A.
   Hudson and M. Wilks, eds., *From Ockham to Wyclif* (Oxford: Blackwell), 89–107.

Dales, R. C. (1995) *The Problem of the Rational Soul in the Thirteenth Century*
   (Leiden: Brill).

de Launoy, Jean (1662) *De varia Aristotelis in academia Parisiensi fortuna*, 3rd edition (Paris).

de Vaux, Roland (1933) 'La première entrée d'Averroës chez les Latins', *Revue des sciences
   philosophiques et théologiques* 22, 193–245.

——— (1934) *Notes et textes sur l'Avicennisme Latin aux confins des XIIe-XIIIe siècles* (Paris:
   Vrin).

Dod, B. G. (1982) 'Aristoteles latinus', in N. Kretzmann et al., eds., *The Cambridge History of
   Later Medieval Philosophy* (Cambridge: Cambridge Univ. Press), 45–79.

Ebbesen, S. (1990) 'Boethius as an Aristotelian Commentator', in R. Sorabji, ed., *Aristotle
   Transformed: The Ancient Commentators and Their Influence* (Ithaca, N.Y.: Cornell Univ.
   Press), 373–91.

Francisco, S. (1866) *Disputationes metaphysicae* (Paris); Repr. Hildesheim: Olms, 1965).

Francisco, S. (2000) *On the Formal Cause of Substance: Metaphysical Disputation XV*, tr.
   J. Kronen and J. Reedy (Milwaukee, Wisc.: Marquette Univ. Press).

Garber, D. (2002) 'Defending Aristotle/Defending Society in the Early 17th Century
   Paris', in W. Detel and C. Zittel, eds., *Wissensideale und Wissenskulturen in der frühen*

Neuzeit: Ideals and Cultures of Knowledge in Early Modern Europe (Frankfurt: Akademie Verlag), 135–60.

Gauthier, R. (1982) 'Notes sur les débuts (1225–1240) du premier "averroïsme"', in *Revue des Sciences Philosophiques et Théologiques* 66, 321–374.

Gilson, E. (1955) *A History of Christian Philosophy in the Middle Ages* (New York: Random House).

Gómez Rodeles, Cecilio et al., eds. (1901) *Monumenta paedagogica Societatis Jesu, quae primam Rationem studiorum 1586 editam praecessere* (Madrid: A. Avrial).

Gracia, Jorge J. E., and Timothy B. Noone (2003) *A Companion to Philosophy in the Middle Ages* (Oxford: Blackwell).

Ignatius of Loyola (1970) *The Constitutions of the Society of Jesus*, tr. G.E. Ganss (St. Louis: Institute of Jesuit Sources).

Jacquart, D. (1988) 'Aristotelian thought in Salerno', in P. Dronke, ed., *A History of Twelfth-Century Philosophy* (Cambridge: Cambridge Univ. Press), 407–28.

John of Jandun (1552) *Quaestiones super De substantia orbis*, in *Ioannis de Iandvno in libros Aristotelis De coelo et mvndo quae extant qvaestiones svbtilissimae qvibvs nvper consvlto adiecimvs Averrois sermonem De substantia orbis cum eiusdem Ioannis commentario ac quaestionibus* (Venice ap. Iuntas).

Jordan, M. D. (1998) 'Aristotelianism, Medieval', in E. Craig, ed., *Routledge Encyclopedia of Philosophy* (London: Routledge).

Kessler, E. (1990) 'The Transformation of Aristotelianism during the Renaissance', in J. Henry and S. Hutton, eds., *New Perspectives on Renaissance Thought: Essays in the History of Science, Education, and Philosophy in Memory of Charles B. Schmitt* (London: Duckworth), 137–47.

Leff, G. (1992) 'The *Trivium* and the Three Philosophies', in Hilde de Ridder-Symoens, ed., *A History of the University in Europe: Volume 1, Universities in the Middle Ages* (Cambridge: Cambridge Univ. Press), 307–36.

Leinsle, U. G. (1985) *Das Ding und die Methode: methodische Konstitution und Gegenstand der frühen protestantischen Metaphysik* (Augsburg: MaroVerlag).

Lohr, C. H. (1976) 'Jesuit Aristotelianism and Sixteenth-Century Metaphysics', in *Paradosis: Studies in Memory of Edwin A. Quain* (New York: Fordham Univ. Press), 203–20.

⸻ (1967–1974) *Medieval Latin Aristotle Commentaries*, Traditio, vols. 23–30 (New York: Fordham University Press).

⸻ (1982) 'The Medieval Interpretation of Aristotle', in N. Kretzmann et al., eds., *The Cambridge History of Later Medieval Philosophy* (Cambridge: Cambridge Univ. Press), 80–98.

⸻ (1988) *Latin Aristotle Commentaries: II, Renaissance Authors* (Florence: Olschki).

⸻ (2005) *Latin Aristotle Commentaries: V. Bibliography of Secondary Literature* (Florence: SISMEL).

Lowry, M. (1979) *The World of Aldus Manutius: Business and Scholarship in Renaissance Venice* (Ithaca, N.Y.: Cornell Univ. Press).

Luscombe, D. (1997) *Medieval Thought* (Oxford: Oxford Univ. Press).

Mahoney, E. (2004) 'Aristotle and Late Medieval and Renaissance Philosophies', in R. Pozzo, ed., *The Impact of Aristotelianism on Modern Philosophy* (Washington, D.C.: Catholic Univ. of America Press).

⸻ (1988) 'Aristotle as "The Worst Natural Philosophy" (*pessimus naturalis*) and "The Worst Metaphysician" (*pessimus metaphysicus*): His Reputation among Some Franciscan Philosophers (Bonaventure, Francis of Meyronnes, Antonius Andreas, and

Joannes Canonicus) and Later Reactions', in O. Pluta,. ed., *Die Philosophie im 14. und 15. Jahrhundert* (Amsterdam: Gruener), 261–73.

Mahoney, E., and James South. (1998) 'Aristotelianism, Renaissance', in E. Craig, ed., *Routledge Encyclopedia of Philosophy* (London: Routledge).

Marenbon, J. (1993) 'Medieval Latin Commentaries and Glosses on Aristotelian Logical Texts, before ca. 1150 a.d.', in C. Burnett, ed., *Glosses and Commentaries on Aristotelian Logical Texts: The Syriac, Arabic, and Medieval Latin Traditions* (London: Warburg Institute), 77–127.

Mercer, C. (2001) *Leibniz's Metaphysics: Its Origins and Development* (Cambridge: Cambridge Univ. Press).

——(1997) 'Mechanizing Aristotle: Leibniz and Reformed Philosophy', in M.A. Stewart, ed., *Studies in Seventeenth-Century Philosophy* (Oxford: Clarendon Press), 117–52.

Pasnau, R. (1997) 'Olivi on the Metaphysics of Soul', *Medieval Philosophy and Theology* 6, 109–32.

—— (2002) *Cambridge Translations of Medieval Philosophical Texts. Volume 3: Mind and Knowledge* (New York: Cambridge Univ. Press).

—— (2005) *Thomas Aquinas on Human Nature: A Philosophical Study of* Summa theologiae *1a 75–89* (New York: Cambridge Univ. Press).

——(2010) *The Cambridge History of Medieval Philosophy* (Cambridge: Cambridge Univ. Press).

—— (2011) *Metaphysical Themes 1274–1671* (Oxford: Clarendon Press).

Olivi, P. J. (1922–26) *Quaestiones in secundum librum Sententiarum* (Bibliotheca Franciscana Scholastica 4–6), ed. by B. Jansen (Quaracchi: Collegium S. Bonaventurae).

Pasnau, R. and Christopher Shields (2004) *The Philosophy of Aquinas* (Boulder, Colo.: Westview).

Pegis, A. C. (1934) *St. Thomas and the Problem of the Soul in the Thirteenth Century* (Toronto: Pontifical Institute of Mediaeval Studies).

Petersen, P. (1921) *Geschichte der aristotelischen Philosophie im protestantischen Deutschland* (Leipzig: Meiner).

Poppi, A. (2004) 'Zabarella, or Aristotelianism as a Rigorous Science', in R. Pozzo, ed., *The Impact of Aristotelianism on Modern Philosophy* (Washington: Catholic Univ. of America Press), pp. 35–63.

Randall, J. H. (1961) *The School of Padua and the Emergence of Modern Science* (Padua: Editrice Antenore).

Schmitt, C. B. (1983) *Aristotle and the Renaissance* (Cambridge, Mass.: Harvard University Press).

——(1984) 'Aristotelian Textual Studies at Padua: The Case of Francesco Cavalli', *The Aristotelian Tradition and Renaissance Universities* (London: Variorum), 288–90.

—— (1984) 'Thomas Linacre and Italy', *The Aristotelian Tradition and Renaissance Universities* (London: Variorum), XII.

—— (1986) 'Pseudo-Aristotle in the Latin Middle Ages', in J. Kraye et al., eds., *Pseudo-Aristotle in the Middle Ages: The Theology and Other Texts* (London: Warburg Institute), 3–14.

—— (1989) 'Towards a History of Renaissance Philosophy', in C. Webster, ed., *Reappraisals in Renaissance Thought* (London: Variorum), XV.

Shiel, J. (1990) 'Boethius' Commentaries on Aristotle', in R. Sorabji, ed., *Aristotle Transformed: The Ancient Commentators and their Influence* (Ithaca, N.Y.: Cornell Univ. Press), 349–72.

Sorrell, T., ed. (1993) *The Rise of Modern Philosophy: The Tension between the New and Traditional Philosophies from Machiavelli to Leibniz* (Oxford: Clarendon Press).

Thomas A. (1952) *In Aristotelis libros De caelo et mundo*, ed., R.M. Spiazzi (Rome: Marietti).

Thorndike, L. (1944) *University Records and Life in the Middle Ages* (New York: Columbia Univ. Press).

van Steenberghen, Fernand (1970) *Aristotle in the West: The Origins of Latin Aristotelianism*, tr. L. Johnston (Louvain: Nauwelaerts).

Weisheipl, J. A. (1984) 'Science in the Thirteenth Century', in *The History of the University of Oxford: Volume 1. The Early Oxford Schools*, ed., J.I. Catto (Oxford: Oxford Univ. Press), 435–69.

William of Auvergne (2000) *The Soul*, tr. R.J. Teske (Milwaukee, Wisc.: Marquette Univ. Press).

——— (1674) *Tractatus de anima*, in *Opera Omnia* (Paris); Repr. (Frankfurt a.M.: Minerva, 1963).

Williams, S. (1995) 'Defining the Corpus Aristotelicum: Scholastic Awareness of Aristotelian Spuria in the High Middle Ages', *Journal of the Warburg and Courtauld Institutes* 58, 29–51.

Zupko, J. (2004) 'On Buridan's Alleged Alexandrianism: Heterodoxy and Natural Philosophy in Fourteenth-Century Paris', *Vivarium* 42, 42–57.

General Bibliography

....

This bibliography supplements the individual chapter bibliographies by recommending: (i) in the first instance online bibliographies; (ii) then also standard editions of Aristotle's works in English translation; (iii) translations and commentaries intended for further philosophical study, published in the Clarendon Aristotle Series; (iv) general omnibus books for those seeking to familiarize themselves with the main outlines of Aristotle's thought; (v) anthologies and guidebooks directed primarily to students; and (vi) online resources, drawn from articles in the *Stanford Encyclopedia of Philosophy*, many of which feature further bibliographies relevant to their individual topics.

(i) *Online Bibliographies*

Although they remain valuable, print bibliographies suffer from being out of date more or less from the moment they appear. Dynamic online bibliographies have the advantage of admitting augmentation as new works appear. Four on-line bibliographies will prove worth consulting, both now and especially as the publication date of this volume recedes into the past.

The first is the bibliography to Shields, 'Aristotle,' in the *Stanford Encyclopedia of Philosophy*:

- http://plato.stanford.edu/entries/aristotle/

This entry divides Aristotle's works into sections comparable to those employed in the present volume, and emphasizes especially influential publications and other works which advance the study of Aristotle in significant ways. It is updated at regular intervals.

The second recommended online bibliography, unlike the first, is not open-access and so can be accessed only by subscription, whether individual or institutional. It is, however, many times more comprehensive. Compiled by Dr. Richard Ingardia, the bibliography is published by Brill Publishers. The site is accessible under:

- http://bibliographies.brillonline.com

Dr. Ingardia's bibliography, covering over 100 years of scholarship in all major European languages, now runs to over 50, 000 entries and will continue to be updated twice per year. It is fully searchable and allows users to export and print its entries.

A third online bibliography is offered under the auspices of Oxford University Press in the Oxford Online Bibliographies series. The Aristotle bibliography, assembled by Prof. Christof Rapp, is limited in scope, because it aims to provide a guided introduction to the most significant works on Aristotle. Although the works cited are not all elementary, they have been selected with an eye on guiding students to further study. The site is accessible under:

- http://oxfordbibliographiesonline.com/

This work is available by subscription only.

An open-access bibliography, *Philosophiae ianua bibliographica*, created by Joachim Aul, which includes a full complement of works on Aristotle, not restricted to English, is available in the online German magazine, *Information Philosophie*:

- http://www.information-philosophie.de/

The extensive Aristotle bibliography available here can be accessed through the general bibliographical section, where philosophers and philosophical topics are arranged alphabetically (beginning on the homepage, under *Informationen* and then *Bibliographie*).

(ii) *Translations:*
Aristotle's collected works were translated into English by a team of translators between 1912 and 1954, and made available in twelve volumes under the title *The Oxford Translation of Aristotle*. This work was superseded in 1984 by a revised and augmented version edited by Jonathan Barnes, available in two volumes:

- J. Barnes, ed. (1984) *The Complete Works of Aristotle: the Revised Oxford Translation,* vols. 1 and 2 (Princeton: Princeton Univ. Press).

This same work is also available in a searchable format online, by subscription:

- *The Complete Works of Aristotle: Electronic Edition* (InteLex) Past Masters: http://www.nlx.com/collections/8

The electronic version permits simple and sophisticated searches of the entire Aristotelian corpus in translation.

Although not comprehensive, a full and judiciously selected presentation of Aristotle's works in English translation is provided in:

- Fine, G., and T. Irwin (1995) *Aristotle: Selections* (Indianapolis: Hackett Pubs.).

Despite its offering only selections, this work affords some advantages over the still invaluable *Revised Oxford Translation*. Although expertly revised by Barnes, the *Revised Oxford Translation* remains the work of many different hands, drawn from across the twentieth century, deploying uncoordinated diction and reflecting different translational idioms. In addition to its uniform diction, *Aristotle: Selections* offers a succinct and instructive glossary of topics and terms, an especially useful study aid to those not already familiar with Aristotle's thought.

(iii) *Translations with commentaries*:
Founded by J.L. Austen, and edited in turn by John Ackrill and its current editor Lindsay Judson, the Clarendon Aristotle Series from Oxford University Press offers the most complete and accurate set of translations, with explanatory and critical notes, of Aristotle's works in English. Those wishing to pursue individual works will find them invaluable. Currently published in the series are:

- Ackrill, J.L. (1963) *Categories and De Interpretatione,* translated with notes (Oxford: Clarendon Press).
- Annas, J. (1976) *Aristotle's Metaphysics M and N,* translated with introduction and notes (Oxford: Clarendon Press).
- Balme, D. (1992) *De Partibus Animalium I and De Generatione Animalium I* (with passages from Book II 1–3), translated with an introduction and notes (Oxford: Clarendon Press).

- Barnes, J. (1994) *Posterior Analytics,* translated with a commentary, 2nd ed. (Oxford: Clarendon Press).
- Bostock, D. (1994) Aristotle: *Metaphysics VII–VIII,* translated with commentary (Oxford: Clarendon Press).
- Charlton, W. (1970/1984) *Physics Books I and II,* translated with introduction, commentary, note on recent work, and revised bibliography (Oxford: Clarendon Press).
- Graham, D. (1999) *Aristotle, Physics Book VIII,* translated with a commentary (Oxford: Clarendon Press).
- Hamlyn, D.W. (1993) *Aristotle's De Anima Books II and III, with selections from Book I,* translated with introduction and notes, and a report on recent work and updated bibliography by C. Shields (Oxford: Clarendon Press).
- Hussey, E. (1993) *Aristotle, Physics Books III and IV,* translated with introduction and notes (Oxford: Clarendon Press).
- Keyt, D. (1999) *Politics, Books V and VI,* translated with a commentary (Oxford: Clarendon Press).
- Kirwan, C. (1993) *Aristotle: Metaphysics Γ, Δ and E,* translated with notes, 2nd ed. (Oxford: Clarendon Press).
- Kraut, R. (1998) *Politics Books VII and VIII,* translated with a commentary (Oxford: Clarendon Press).
- Lennox, J.G. (2002) *On the Parts of Animals,* translated with a commentary (Oxford: Clarendon Press).
- Madigan, A. (1999) *Aristotle: Metaphysics Books B and K 1–2,* translated with commentary (Oxford: Clarendon Press).
- Makin, S. (2006) *Metaphysics Theta,* translated with an introduction and commentary (Oxford: Clarendon Press).
- Pakaluk, M. (1998) *Aristotle: Nicomachean Ethics Books VIII and IX,* translated with a commentary (Oxford: Clarendon Press).
- Robinson, R. (1995) *Aristotle: Politics III–IV,* translated with notes, supplementary material by David Keyt (Oxford: Clarendon Press).
- Saunders, T. (1996) *Politics: Books I and II,* translated with a commentary (Oxford: Clarendon Press).
- Smith, R. (1997) *Topics Books I and VIII,* with excerpts from related texts, translated with a commentary (Oxford: Clarendon Press).
- Striker, G. (2009) *Prior Analytics Book I,* translated with an introduction and commentary (Oxford: Clarendon Press).
- Taylor, C.C.W. (2006) *Nicomachean Ethics, Books II–IV,* translated with an introduction and commentary (Oxford: Clarendon Press).
- Williams, C.J.F. (1982) *Aristotle's De Generatione et Corruptione,* translated with notes (Oxford: Clarendon Press).
- Woods, M. (1982) *Aristotle's Eudemian Ethics Books I, II, and VIII,* translated with a commentary (Oxford: Clarendon Press).

Forthcoming in this series are:

- Judson, L. (forthcoming) *Aristotle's Metaphysics Lambda,* translated with introduction and notes (Oxford: Clarendon Press).
- Shields, C. (forthcoming) *Aristotle's De Anima,* translated with introduction and notes (Oxford: Clarendon Press).

(iv) *Comprehensive Overviews of Aristotle*:

Single-volume comprehensive treatments of Aristotle's thought are perforce selective. Some seek to be purely expositional; others aim to recount Aristotle's primary arguments; and still others engage in some amount of critical appraisal. They therefore have different virtues, suited to different audiences. Some synoptic works of these different styles include:

- Ackrill, J.L. (1981) *Aristotle the Philosopher* (Oxford: Oxford Univ. Press).
- Allan, D.J. (1952) *The Philosophy of Aristotle* (Oxford: Oxford Univ. Press).
- Barnes, J. (1982) *Aristotle* (Oxford: Oxford Univ. Press).
- Grote, G. (1883) *Aristotle*, 3rd ed. (London: J. Murray).
- Guthrie, W.K.C. (1981) *A History of Greek Philosophy vol. VI: Aristotle: An Encounter* (Cambridge: Cambridge Univ. Press).
- Irwin, T. (1988) *Aristotle's First Principles* (Oxford: Oxford Univ. Press).
- Jaeger, W. (1948) *Aristotle: Fundamentals of the History of his Development*, 2nd ed., translated by Richard Robinson (Oxford: Oxford Univ. Press).
- Lear, Jonathan (1988), *Aristotle: the Desire to Understand* (Cambridge: Cambridge Univ. Press).
- Ross, W.D. (1923) *Aristotle* (London: Methuen and Co.).
- Shields, C. (2007) *Aristotle* (London: Routledge).

(v) *General Guide Books to Aristotle*

Among the proliferation of handbooks, guides, and companions dedicated to the study of Ancient Philosophy, one finds many dozens of chapters devoted to Aristotle's works. Two general guide books dedicated to Aristotle alone are:

- Anagnostopoulos, G. (2009) *A Companion to Aristotle* (Malden, MA: Wiley-Blackwell).
- Barnes, J. (1995) *The Cambridge Companion to Aristotle* (Cambridge: Cambridge Univ. Press).

Barnes's volume includes an excellent extensive bibliography presented in a discursive fashion, which has been partially derived from an earlier, excellent collection of papers on Aristotle:

- Barnes, J., M. Schofield, and R. Sorabji, eds., *Articles on Aristotle* vols 1–4:
  - Vol. 1. (1975) *Science* (London: Duckworth).
  - Vol. 2. (1977) *Ethics and Politics* (London: Duckworth).
  - Vol. 3. (1979) *Metaphysics* (London: Duckworth).
  - Vol. 4. (1979) *Psychology and Aesthetics* (London: Duckworth).

These volumes feature many articles which have proven seminal in the study of Aristotle.

(vi) *Web-based resources*

The *Stanford Encyclopedia of Aristotle* has an extensive and growing number of entries on Aristotle, each with its own bibliography. The entries are arranged in three tiers. First is a general entry on Aristotle:

- Shields, Christopher, 'Aristotle': http://plato.stanford.edu/entries/aristotle/

There follows a group of core articles covering general topics in Aristotle's philosophy:

- Cohen, S. Marc, 'Aristotle's Metaphysics': http://plato.stanford.edu/entries/aristotle-metaphysics/

- Kraut, Richard, 'Aristotle's Ethics': http://plato.stanford.edu/entries/aristotle-ethics/
- Lennox, James, 'Aristotle's Biology': http://plato.stanford.edu/entries/aristotle-biology/
- Miller, Fred D., 'Aristotle's Political Theory': http://plato.stanford.edu/entries/aristotle-politics/
- Rapp, Christof, 'Aristotle's Rhetoric': http://plato.stanford.edu/entries/aristotle-rhetoric/
- Shields, Christopher, 'Aristotle's Psychology': http://plato.stanford.edu/entries/aristotle-psychology/
- Smith, Robin, 'Aristotle's Logic': http://plato.stanford.edu/entries/aristotle-logic/
- Studtmann, Paul, 'Aristotle's Categories': http://plato.stanford.edu/entries/aristotle-categories/

Finally, there are a series of articles on special topics, which take up more detailed issues, emphasizing issues which have been of special concern to recent Aristotelian scholarship. This list of entries is growing, but at this printing includes:

- Bodnar, Istvan, 'Aristotle's Natural Philosophy': http://plato.stanford.edu/entries/aristotle-natphil/
- Falcon, Andrea, 'Aristotle on Causality': http://plato.stanford.edu/entries/aristotle-causality/
- Gottlieb, Paula, 'Aristotle on Non-contradiction': http://plato.stanford.edu/entries/aristotle-noncontradiction/
- Mendell, Henry, 'Aristotle and Mathematics': http://plato.stanford.edu/entries/aristotle-mathematics/

Index Locorum

....

Index Nominum

SUBJECT INDEX

Entries in **bold** indicate a central or extended discussion.

CPSIA information can be obtained at www.ICGtesting.com
Printed in the USA
BVOW09s0345080915

416644BV00008B/26/P